P9-DED-333

PAGE 50

ON THE ROAD

YOUR COMPLETE DESTINATION GUIDE
In-depth reviews, detailed listings
and insider tips

Directory
A–Z

THIS EDITION WRITTEN AND RESEARCHED BY

Andrea Schulte-Peevers,
Kerry Christiani, Marc Di Duca, Anthony Haywood,
Daniel Robinson, Ryan Ver Berkmoes

welcome to
Germany

Bewitching Scenery

Few countries have had as much impact on the world as Germany, which has given us the printing press, the automobile, aspirin and MP3 technology. This is the birthplace of Martin Luther, Albert Einstein and Karl Marx, of Goethe, Beethoven, the Brothers Grimm and other heavyweights who, each in their own way, have left their mark on human history. As you travel the country, you'll have plenty of brushes with genius, but Germany's storybook landscapes will likely leave an even bigger imprint on your memories. There's something undeniably artistic in the way the scenery unfolds – the corrugated, dune-fringed coasts of the north, the moody forests, romantic river valleys and vast vineyards of central Germany's backbone, and the off-the-charts splendour of the Alps, carved into rugged glory by glaciers and the elements. All are integral parts of a magical natural matrix that's bound to give your camera a workout. As much fun as it may be to rev up the engine on the autobahn, getting off the highway lets you soak up the epic scenery that makes each delicious, slow, winding kilometre so precious.

Pleasures of Civilisation

You'll encounter history in towns where streets were laid out long before Columbus set sail and in castles that loom above prim, half-timbered villages where flower

Prepare for a roller coaster of feasts, treats and temptations as you take in Germany's soul-stirring scenery, spirit-lifting culture, big-city beauties, romantic palaces and half-timbered towns.

(left) Autumn in the majestic Bavarian Alps
(below) Berlin's bars; part of Germany's cultural kaleidoscope

boxes billow with crimson geraniums. The great cities – Berlin, Munich, Hamburg and Leipzig among them – come in more flavours than a jar of jelly beans but will all wow you with a cultural kaleidoscope that spans the arc from art museums and high-brow opera to naughty cabaret and underground clubs. And wherever you go, Romanesque, Gothic and baroque classics rub rafters with architectural creations from modern masters like Daniel Libeskind, David Chipperfield and Frank Gehry.

Gastro Delights

Eating well is as important to a memorable journey as captivating scenery and great architecture. And you'll quickly discover that German food is so much more than sausages and pretzels, schnitzel and roast pork accompanied by big mugs of foamy beer. Beyond the clichés awaits a cornucopia of regional and seasonal palate teasers. Share the German people's obsession with white asparagus in spring, chanterelle mushrooms in summer and game in autumn. Indulge in black forest gateau, doner kebab, *Spätzle* or Michelin-starred haute cuisine. Sample not just famous beer but also world-class wines, most notably the noble riesling, while exploring ancient cellars. Experiencing the country through its food and drink will add a rich layer to your memories (and possibly your belly!).

› Germany

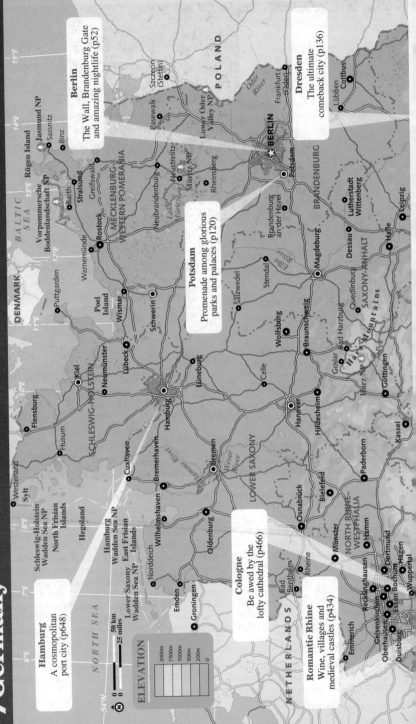

Hamburg
A cosmopolitan port city (p648)

Berlin
The Wall, Brandenburg Gate and amazing nightlife (p52)

Dresden
The ultimate comeback city (p136)

Potsdam
Promenade among glorious parks and palaces (p120)

Cologne
Be awed by the lofty cathedral (p466)

Romantic Rhine
Wine, villages and medieval castles (p434)

ELEVATION

3000m
1500m
1000m
500m
200m
0

0   50 km
0   25 miles

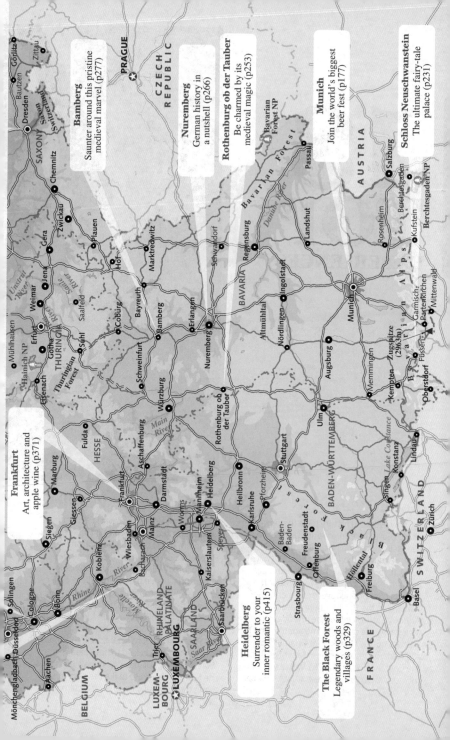

Bamberg
Saunter around this pristine medieval marvel (p277)

Nuremberg
German history in a nutshell (p266)

Rothenburg ob der Tauber
Be charmed by its medieval magic (p253)

Munich
Join the world's biggest beer fest (p177)

Schloss Neuschwanstein
The ultimate fairy-tale palace (p231)

Frankfurt
Art, architecture and apple wine (p371)

Heidelberg
Surrender to your inner romantic (p415)

The Black Forest
Legendary woods and villages (p329)

18
TOP
EXPERIENCES

Berlin Wall

1 Few events in history have the power to move the entire world. The Kennedy assassination; landing on the moon; 9/11... And, of course, the fall of the Berlin Wall in 1989. If you were alive back then and old enough, you will probably remember the crowds of euphoric revellers cheering and dancing at the Brandenburg Gate (p58). Although little is left of the physical barrier, its legacy lives on in the imagination and in places such as Checkpoint Charlie (p61), the Gedenkstätte Berliner Mauer (p68) and the East Side Gallery (p76), with its colourful murals. Berlin Wall street art at Mauerpark

Schloss Neuschwanstein

2 Commissioned by Bavaria's most celebrated (and loopiest) 19th-century monarch, King Ludwig II, Neuschwanstein Palace (p231) rises from the mysterious Alpine forests like a bedtime storybook illustration. Inside the make-believe continues, with chambers and halls reflecting Ludwig's obsession with the mythical Teutonic past and his admiration for composer Wagner, in a composition that puts even the flashiest oligarch's palazzo in the shade. This sugary folly is said to have inspired Walt's castle at Disney World; now it inspires the tourist masses to make the pilgrimage along the Romantic Road, which culminates at its gates.

Oktoberfest

3 Anyone with a taste for hop-scented froth knows that the daddy of all beer festivals, Oktoberfest (p203), takes place annually in Munich. The world's favourite sud fest actually begins mid-September and runs for 16 ethanol-fuelled days on the Theresienwiese (Theresa's Meadow), with troops of crimson-faced oompah bands entertaining revellers; armies of traditionally garbed locals and foreigners guzzling their way through seven million litres of lager; and entire farms of chickens hitting the grill. So find your favourite tent and raise your 1L stein. *'Ozapft ist!'* (It is tapped!). The Ochsenbraterei tent at Theresienwiese fairgrounds

The Black Forest

4 Mist, snow or shine, this sylvan slice of southwest Germany is just beautiful. If it's back-to-nature moments you're after, the deep, dark Black Forest (p336) is the place to linger. Every valley reveals new surprises: half-timbered villages looking every inch the fairy-tale fantasy, thunderous waterfalls and cuckoo clocks the size of houses. Breathe in the cold sappy air, drive roller-coaster roads to middle-of-nowhere lakes, have your cake, walk it off on trail after gorgeously wooded trail, then hide away in a heavy-lidded farmhouse. Hear that? Silence. What a wonderful thing.

The Romantic Rhine

5 As the mighty Rhine (p434) flows from Rüdesheim to Koblenz, the landscape's unique face-off between rock and water creates a magical mix of the wild (churning whirlpools, dramatic cliffs), the agricultural (near-vertical vineyards), the medieval (hilltop castles, half-timbered hamlets), the legendary (Loreley, p441) and the modern (in the 19th-century sense – we're talking barges, ferries, passenger steamers and trains). From every riverside village, trails take you through vineyards and forests, up to panoramic viewpoints and massive stone fortresses. Burg Katz, St Goarshausen

Dresden

6 The apocalypse came on a cold February night in 1945. Hours of carpet bombing reduced Germany's 'Florence on the Elbe' into a pile of bricks. The comeback of Dresden (p136) is nothing short of a miracle. Reconstructed architectural jewels mix with stunning art collections that justify the city's place in the pantheon of European cultural capitals. Add a contagiously energetic pub quarter (p147), Daniel Libeskind's dramatically redesigned Military History Museum (p141) and a tiara of palaces along the Elbe and you've got one enticing package. Semperoper (Opera House; p141)

Heidelberg

7 The 19th-century romantics found sublime beauty and spiritual inspiration in Germany's oldest university town (p415) and so, in his way, did Mark Twain, who was beguiled by the ruins of the hillside castle (p416). Generations of students have attended lectures, sung lustily with beer steins in hand, carved their names into tavern tables and, occasionally, been sent to the student jail. All of this has left its mark on the modern-day city, where age-old traditions endure alongside world-class research, innovative cultural events and a sometimes raucous nightlife scene.

6

MATTHIAS HAKER / GETTY IMAGES ©

7

RICHARD I'ANSON / GETTY IMAGES ©

AFP / GETTY IMAGES ©

LONELY PLANET / GETTY IMAGES ©

BRIAN T. EVANS / GETTY IMAGES ©

Schloss & Park Sanssouci

8 We can pretty much guarantee that your camera will have a love affair with Potsdam's marvellous palaces, idyllic parks, stunning views, inspired architecture and tantalising Cold War sites. Just across the Glienicke 'spy bridge' from Berlin, the state capital of Brandenburg was catapulted to greatness by King Frederick the Great. His giddily rococo Sanssouci Palace (p120) is the glorious crown of this Unesco-recognised cultural tapestry that synthesises 18th-century artistic trends from around Europe into one stupendous masterpiece. A day spent here is sure to charm and enlighten you.

Nightlife in Berlin

9 Berlin's your oyster when the moon's high in the sky. Cosy pubs, riverside beach bars, beer gardens, underground dives, DJ sets, snazzy hotel lounges, designer cocktail temples – with such variety, finding a party pen to match your mood is not exactly a tall order. If you're not into hobnobbing with hipsters at hot-stepping bars or clubs, you could always relive the Roaring Twenties in a high-kicking cabaret, indulge your ears with symphonic strains in iconic concert halls or point your highbrow compass towards the opera (see p108).

German Food & Drink

10 If you crave traditional German comfort food, you'll certainly find plenty of places to indulge in a meat, potato and cabbage diet. These days, though, 'typical' German fare is lighter, healthier, creative and prepared with seasonal and locally sourced ingredients. The cities especially brim with organic eateries, gourmet kitchens, vegan bistros and a UN-worth of ethnic restaurants. Talented chefs have been racking up the Michelin stars, especially in the Black Forest. And then there's German beer and bread. Is there any other country that does either better?

Nuremberg

11 Capital of Franconia and an independent region until 1806, Nuremberg (p266) may be synonymous with Nazi rallies and grisly war trials, but there's so much more to this energetic city. Dürer hailed from the Altstadt, his house now a museum (p269); Germany's first railway trundled from here to neighbouring Fürth, leaving a trail of choo-choo heritage; and Germany's toy capital has heaps of treasures for kids to enjoy. When you're done with sightseeing, the local beer is as dark as the coffee and best employed to chase down Nuremberg's delicious finger-sized bratwurst. Frauenkirche (p267)

Picturesque Towns & Villages

12 Germany's potpourri of villages is rich, irresistible and needs to be appreciated slowly. So take your sweet time as you come upon hushed medieval hamlets and half-timbered beauties radiant with geranium-festooned windows. Follow cobbled lanes worn smooth by centuries of horses' hooves, wagon wheels and shoe leather to bustling marketplaces serenaded by lofty church spires. Stay overnight for a hearty supper in a country inn and you've got the whole fairy-tale experience. Minus the wicked witch. Schiltach (p340), the Black Forest

Cologne Cathedral

13 At unexpected moments you see it: Kölner Dom (p466), the twin-towered icon of the city towering over an urban vista, dominating the view up a road. And why shouldn't it? This perfectly formed testament to faith and conviction was started in 1248 and consecrated a 'mere' six centuries later. You can feel the echoes of the passage of time as you sit in its cavernous, stained-glass-lit interior. Climb a tower for views of the surrounding city that are like no others.

WESTEND61 / ALAMY ©

SYLVAIN SONNET / GETTY IMAGES ©

JUERGEN SACK / GETTY IMAGES ©

Hamburg

14 Anyone who thinks Germany doesn't have round-the-clock delights hasn't been to Hamburg (p648). This ancient, wealthy city on the Elbe River traces its roots back to the Hanseatic League and beyond. By day you can tour its magnificent port, explore its history in restored quarters and discover shops selling goods you didn't think were sold. By night, some of Europe's best music clubs pull in the punters, and other diversions for virtually every taste are plentiful as well. And then, another Hamburg day begins.

Brandenburg Gate

15 Who can forget the images beamed around the world in 1989 of happy throngs perched atop the Berlin Wall against the backdrop of the stately Brandenburger Tor (p58)? Overnight, the 18th-century royal city gate went from symbol of division and oppression to symbol of a united Germany. The powerful landmark is at its most atmospheric – and photogenic – at night when light bathes its stately columns and proud Goddess of Victory sculpture in a mesmerising golden glow.

Bamberg

16 Generally regarded as one of Germany's most attractive and more architecturally trustworthy towns, Bamberg (p277) is a medieval and baroque masterwork, mercifully ignored by the destruction of WWII and chock-full with Unesco-listed townhouses. Half of the Altstadt's beauty comes from its location straddling two waterways, the River Regnitz and the Rhine-Main-Danube Canal. Away from the urban eye candy, lower-brow entertainment is laid on by Bamberg's numerous breweries that cook up the town's unique smoked beer, on tap at all of its characterful inns.

Frankfurt

17 Frankfurt am Main (p371) is respected – and in some quarters feared – for its financial muscle and sky-scraper banks, but the best way to discover the city's soul and experience its surprisingly laid-back liveability is to head out of the high-rise downtown. It's easy to join frisbee-tossing locals in the grassy parkland along Main River, grab an espresso at an old-time Nordend cafe, and sip tart *Ebbelwei* (apple wine) while dining on hearty Frankfurt-style fare in the wood-panelled wine taverns of Sachsenhausen and Bornheim. Opera Square

Rothenburg ob der Tauber

18 With its jumble of neatly restored half-timbered houses enclosed by sturdy ramparts, Rothenburg ob der Tauber (p253) lays on the medieval cuteness with a trowel. One might even say it's too cute for its own good, if the inevitable deluges of day-trippers are any indication. The trick is to experience this historic wonderland at its most magical: early or late in the day when the last coaches have hit the road and you can soak up the romance all by yourself on gentle strolls along moonlit cobbled lanes.

PETER ADAMS / GETTY IMAGES ©

BRUCE M. ESBIN / GETTY IMAGES ©

need to know

Currency
» Euro (€)

Language
» German

When to Go

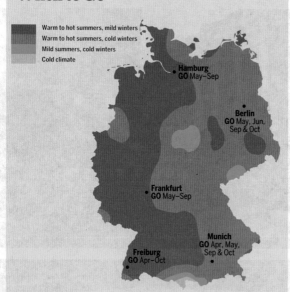

Warm to hot summers, mild winters
Warm to hot summers, cold winters
Mild summers, cold winters
Cold climate

Hamburg
GO May–Sep

Berlin
GO May, Jun, Sep & Oct

Frankfurt
GO May–Sep

Munich
GO Apr, May, Sep & Oct

Freiburg
GO Apr–Oct

High Season
(Jul & Aug)

» Busy roads and long lines at key sights

» Vacancies at a premium and higher prices in seaside and mountain resorts

» Festivals celebrate everything from music to wine, sailing to samba

Shoulder Season (Apr–Jun, Sep & Oct)

» Smaller crowds and lower prices, except public holidays

» Blooming flowers in spring; radiant foliage in autumn

» Sunny, temperate weather ideal for outdoor pursuits

Low Season
(Nov–Mar)

» No lines but shorter hours at key sights; some may close for the season

» Theatre, concert, opera season in full swing

» Ski resorts busiest in January and February

Your Daily Budget

Budget up to
€100

» Hostel, camping or private room: €12–25

» Up to €8 per meal or self-cater

» Take advantage of Happy Hours and free or low-cost museums or entertainment

Midrange
€100–200

» Private apartment or double room: €60–100

» Cafe lunch, dinner at nice restaurant: €30–40

» Couple of beers in a pub or beer garden: €8

Top End over
€200

» Fancy loft apartment or double in top-end hotel: €150

» Sit-down lunch, dinner at top-rated restaurant: €100

» Concert or opera tickets: €50

Money

» ATMs widely available in cities and towns, rarely in villages. Cash is king almost everywhere; credit cards are not widely accepted.

Visas

» Generally not required for tourist stays up to 90 days (or at all for EU nationals); some nationalities need a Schengen visa.

Mobile Phones

» Mobile phones operate on GSM900/1800. If you have a European or Australian phone, save money by slipping in a German SIM card.

Driving

» Drive on the right; the steering wheel is on the left side of the car.

Websites

» **German National Tourist Office** (www. germany-tourism.de)

» **Online German course** (www.deutsch -lernen.com)

» **About Germany** (www.tatsachen -ueber-deutschland. de) Reference tool on all aspects of German society.

» **Deutschland Online** (www.magazine -deutschland.de) Insightful features on culture, business and politics.

» **Lonely Planet** (www.lonelyplanet. com/germany) Hotel bookings, traveller forum and more.

Exchange Rates

Australia	A$1	€0.79
Canada	C$1	€0.79
Japan	¥100	€0.99
New Zealand	NZ$1	€0.63
UK	UK£1	€1.24
USA	US$1	€0.77

For current exchange rates see www.xe.com.

Important Numbers

Germany country code	49
International access code	00
Ambulance, fire brigade	112
Police	110

Arriving in Germany

» **Frankfurt Airport**
Train – S-Bahn train lines S8 and S9 link the airport with the city centre in 11 minutes several times hourly for €4.10.
Taxi – Taxis make the trip in 20 to 30 minutes and average €25.

» **Munich Airport**
Train – The S1 and S8 trains link the airport with the city centre in 45 minutes (€10.50). Bus – The Lufthansa Bus (€10.50) departs every 20 minutes and takes about the same time as the train.
Taxi – A taxi costs about €60.

Life in the Fast Lane

Driving on the autobahn can be a transporting experience, and not just in the literal sense. It's true, there really are long stretches without speed limits, so you can literally put the pedal to the metal and test your driving acumen on the smooth asphalt. If you're unaccustomed to high speeds, though, be extra careful when passing another vehicle. It takes only seconds for a car appearing far away in the rear-view mirror to close in at 200km/h. Pass as quickly as possible, then quickly return to the right lane. Don't be intimidated by aggressive speed demons who will flash their headlights or tailgate you to make you drive faster or get out of their way – it's an illegal practice, as is passing on the right. See the Transport chapter (p776) for further details.

first time

Everyone needs a helping hand when they visit a country for the first time. There are phrases to learn, customs to get used to and etiquette to understand. The following section will help demystify Germany so your first trip goes as smoothly as your fifth.

Language

It is perfectly possible to travel in Germany without speaking a word of German, but life gets easier if you master a few basic phrases. People are more likely to speak English in big cities, the western part of the country and in tourist hotspots. Things get a little trickier in rural areas, especially in the former East Germany. See the language section of this book (p789) for all the phrases you'll need to get by.

Booking Ahead

Reserving a room, even if only for the first night of your stay, is the best way to ensure a smooth start to your trip. These phrases should see you through a call if English isn't spoken.

Hello	Guten Tag
I would like to book	Ich möchte...reservieren
a single/double room	ein Einzelzimmer/Doppelzimmer
in the name of	auf den Namen
from...to...(date)	von...bis...
How much is it per night/person?	Was kostet das pro Nacht/pro Person?
Thank you very much	Vielen Dank

What to Wear

Fashion in Germany differs wildly depending on the region. Dig out your smarter threads when visiting Hamburg, Stuttgart, Frankfurt or Munich, which are considerably more fashion-conscious than say, Berlin, Cologne or Dresden. Berlin, especially, puts more emphasis on individual style than expensive labels. In general, trousers (pants) and shirts or tees for guys; dresses, skirts or trousers for women will serve you well across the country. Outside cities, shorts are fine in summer, but long sleeves are needed at night year-round. A waterproof coat and sturdy shoes are a good idea for all-weather sightseeing. For evening wear, smart casual is the norm, but upmarket places may insist on shoes (not trainers) and trousers or dresses instead of jeans. Jackets and ties are only required in casinos and by the most ostentatious establishments. Most bars and clubs have a cloakroom for bags and coats.

What to Pack

» Passport
» Credit/debit cards
» Driving licence
» Prescription medicine
» Pair of spare glasses
» Phrasebook
» Mobile (cell) phone charger
» Ebook reader
» Camera
» Travel adapter plug
» Umbrella/rain coat
» Bathing suit
» Flip-flops
» Medical kit
» Sunhat and sunglasses
» Hiking boots
» Pocket knife
» Earplugs
» Curiosity and a sense of humour

Checklist

» Make sure your passport is valid for another four months after arrival in Germany

» Make any necessary advance bookings for sights (such as the Reichstag), travel and accommodation

» Check the airline baggage restrictions

» Inform your credit-/debit-card company that you'll be travelling abroad

» Organise travel insurance (p771)

» Check if your mobile/cell phone will work in Germany (p774)

» Find out what you need to hire a car (p782)

Etiquette

Germany is a fairly formal society; the following tips will help you avoid faux pas.

» Greetings

Shake hands and say *'Guten Morgen'* (before noon), *'Guten Tag'* (between noon and 6pm) or *'Guten Abend'* (after 6pm). Use the formal *'Sie'* (you) with strangers and only switch to the informal *'du'* and first names if invited to do so. With friends and children, use first names and *'du'*.

» Asking for Help

Germans use the same word – *Entschuldigung* – to say 'excuse me' (to attract attention) and 'sorry' (to apologise).

» Eating & Drinking

If invited to dinner in a German home, always bring a small gift such as chocolates or flowers. Wait for your host to say *'Guten Appetit'* before digging in. Germans hold the fork in the left hand and the knife in the right hand. To signal that you have finished eating, lay your knife and fork parallel across your plate. Finish everything on your plate. If drinking wine, the toast is *'Zum Wohl'*, with beer it's *'Prost'*.

Tipping

» Hotels
Bellboys get about €1 to €2 per bag. Also leave a little cash for the room cleaners, €2 per day, more if you were messy.

» Restaurants
Restaurant bills always include *Bedienung* (service charge), but most people add 5% or 10% unless the service was truly abhorrent.

» Bars
Tip bartenders about 5%. For drinks brought to your table, tip as for restaurants.

» Taxis
Tip about 10%.

Money

Germany is still largely a cash-based society and credit-card use is not common. International hotel chains, high-end restaurants and car rental companies usually accept credit cards, but always make it a habit to enquire first, just to be on the safe side. Mastercard and Visa are more widely accepted, American Express and Diner's Club almost never. Avoid using your credit card for cash advances as you will be charged high fees and immediate interest. Debit cards featuring the Mastercard or Visa logos are fairly widely used. Chip-and-pin is the norm for card transactions – few places accept signatures as an alternative. ATMs are ubiquitous in towns and cities but not always in rural areas. Be wary of those not affiliated with major banks as they charge exorbitant transaction fees. ATMs do not recognise pins with more than four digits. For additional details, see p772.

what's new

For this new edition of Germany, our authors have hunted down the fresh, the revamped, the transformed, the hot and the happening. Here are a few of our favourites. For up-to-the-minute reviews and recommendations, see lonelyplanet.com/germany.

Berlin Brandenburg Airport

1 With all those well-publicised delays, we're not betting the farm but remain optimistic that planes will have started flying into Berlin's shiny new international airport before we update this book again. (p776)

Städel Museum, Frankfurt

2 Until now, the Städel was most famous for its Old Masters collection, but that may change with the opening of the spectacular new underground wing showcasing post-WWII paintings and photographs. (p380)

Militärhistorisches Museum Dresden

3 Daniel Libeskind's poignant metaphorical architecture creates a powerful setting for this revamped military history museum that's as much about peace as it is about war. (p141)

Neukölln, Berlin

4 Once a headline-making 'bad-rap ghetto', Neukölln has been catapulted to almost instant uberhipness thanks to a deluge of cash-poor but idea-rich newcomers from around the world. Great for offbeat DIY exploring. (p71)

Badeparadies, Titisee

5 In this snazzy new day spa you can relax among soaring palms, dip into an azure-blue pool, whoosh down indoor slides or sweat it out in a themed sauna. (p350)

KGB Prison, Potsdam

6 At the heart of a walled-in 'secret Soviet city' in the middle of Potsdam stood the fearsome KGB prison, whose sinister history is now commemorated with an exhibit inside the original building. (p124)

Museum Folkwang, Essen

7 Red-hot architect David Chipperfield provided the blueprint for these show-stopping new digs for this prized collection of 19th- and 20th-century masterpieces by such heavyweights as Gauguin and Van Gogh. (p505)

Luther Death House

8 This newly revamped and expanded museum in Lutherstadt Eisleben delivers an insightful journey into the last hours of the Protestant reformer's life and his thoughts about death. (p594)

Nibelungen Museum, Xanten

9 Siegfried, the hero of the medieval Nibelungen epic set to music by Richard Wagner, was born in Xanten, which now honours its famous mythological son with the engaging Museum Nibelungen(h)ort. (p502)

Leipziger Notenspur

10 Follow in the footsteps of Bach, Mendelssohn-Bartholdy, Schumann and other musical geniuses that have left their mark on Leipzig along a new interactive music trail (p159).

Stralsund

11 This postcard-pretty Baltic Sea town has truly come into its own with such developments as the Ozeaneum and the Kron-Lastadie, a cluster of casual eateries in a converted 17th-century bastion. (p706 and p708)

Schweinemuseum, Stuttgart

12 Where else but in Germany could there be a museum dedicated to the hog? Go 'oinkers' over this mindboggling pile of pig paraphernalia: from paintings to piggy banks to plush toys. (p313)

if you like...

Churches & Cathedrals

More than places of worship, churches and cathedrals are also great architectural monuments often filled with priceless treasure reflecting artistic acumen through the ages.

Cologne The riverside twin spires of the Kölner Dom, Germany's largest cathedral, dominate the city's skyline (p466)

Aachen Some 30 German kings were crowned in the Aachen Dom; where Charlemagne lies buried in an elaborate gilded shrine (p487)

Lutherstadt-Wittenberg Protestant reformer Martin Luther is buried in the Schlosskirche, the church to whose door he pinned his 95 theses in 1517 (p578)

Steingaden Rising from an Alpine meadow where a miracle-working Jesus statue was found, the Wieskirche represents the pinnacle of rococo exuberance (p235)

Dresden The harmoniously proportioned Frauenkirche rose from the ashes of WWII when its spitting-image replica reopened in 2005 (p137)

Castles & Palaces

Germany is nirvana for castle lovers, a legacy of the feudal system that saw the country divided into hundreds of fiefdoms until its 1871 unification.

Schloss Neuschwanstein Thick woods cradle Germany's most famous palace, dreamed up by a kooky king and the inspiration for Disney's Sleeping Beauty castle (p231)

Wartburg Protestant reformer Martin Luther translated the New Testament into German while in hiding at this medieval castle in Eisenach (p555)

Schloss Heidelberg Although destroyed repeatedly throughout the centuries, there's still a majesty surrounding this red-sandstone Gothic pile (p416)

Burg Hohenzollern Every bit the fairy-tale castle, the ancestral seat of the Prussian ruling family rises dramatically from an exposed crag near Tübingen (p321)

Romantic Rhine Castles More than a dozen medieval robber-baron hangouts straddle craggy hilltops along this fabled river stretch (p434)

Schloss Sanssouci Prussian king Frederick the Great sought solace amid the intimate splendour of his Potsdam summer palace (p120)

Enchanting Villages

There's no simpler pleasure than strolling around a charismatic village laced with time-worn lanes, peppered with ancient churches and anchored by a fountain-studded square.

Quedlinburg Drift around this medieval warren of cobbled lanes lined by more than 1400 half-timbered houses (p572)

Lindau Lovely Lindau has a 9th-century pedigree and a to-die-for location on an island in Lake Constance (p367)

Bacharach Plunge into the Middle Ages in this pint-sized Rhine town flanked by vineyards and lorded over by a mighty castle (p439)

Schiltach Cuddled by the Kinzig Valley, this romantic Black Forest town oozes history from every flower-festooned facade (p340)

Baden-Baden Relaxation is taken very seriously in this classy spa town in the Black Forest foothills (p329)

Görlitz Germany's easternmost town is so pristinely preserved that it's often used as a film location (p172)

Celle A radiantly old-world gem with colourfully painted and ornately carved half-timbered buildings (p610)

» Wine tasting among vineyard barrels on the German Wine Route (p431)

WWII Sites

Shudder at Nazi atrocities, then honour those who gave their lives to rid the world of the Third Reich at these original sites.

Berchtesgaden Learn how this breathtaking Alpine town became Hitler's southern head-quarters at the Dokumentation Obersalzberg, then exorcise Nazi ghosts on the trip up to the 'Eagle's Nest' (p245)

Concentration Camps The dark-est side of WWII is commemorated in camps at Bergen-Belsen (p612), Buchenwald (p551), Dachau (p223), Mittelbau Dora (p576) and Sachsenhausen (p127)

Remagen The pivotal capture of the Bridge at Remagen by American troops in March 1945 is poignantly remembered in the Friedensmuseum (p484)

Peenemünde The deadly V2 rocket was developed in a re-search facility on Usedom Island, now the Historisch-Technisches Informationszentrum (p714)

Nuremberg See the site of Nazi mass rallies at the Reichspartei-tagsgelände, then visit the courtroom where the Nuremberg Trials took place (p267)

Laboe In this town on Kiel Firth, you can clamber around WWII-era U-Boat 995, which is similar to the one featured in the 1981 movie *Das Boot* (p681)

Jewish Sites

Jewish history in Germany is often equated with the Holocaust, but even the Nazis could not wipe out 1600 years of Jewish life and cultural contributions to this country.

Holocaust Memorial Peter Eisenman poignantly captures the horror of the Holocaust with this vast undulating maze of tomblike plinths in Berlin (p58)

Jüdisches Museum Daniel Libeskind's extraordinary zinc-clad building in Berlin is a powerful metaphor for this eye-opening chronicle of Jewish life in Germany (p74)

Speyer Come to this Rhine city to see the oldest, largest and best preserved *Mikwe* (ritual bath) north of the Alps (p424)

Frankfurt am Main Two museums and a cemetery trace Jewish life, while the Wall of Names keeps alive the memory of 11,000 Frankfurt Jews mur-dered during the Holocaust (p378) (p379)

Stolpersteine The cobblestone-sized brass 'stumbling blocks' embedded in pavements throughout Germany mark the last residence of Jews deported by the Nazis (p65)

Train Journeys

Slow travel was never more fun than aboard Germany's historic trains, some of them more than 100 years old and pulled by steam locomotives.

Zugspitzbahn Have your breath quite literally taken away on this pulse-quickening journey up Germany's tallest mountain; starts in Garmisch-Partenkirchen (p237)

Molli Schmalspurbahn Since 1886 this pint-sized train has been shuttling visitors through gorgeous scenery from Bad Doberan to coastal Heiligen-damm (p702)

Harzer Schmalspurbahnen The mother lode for fans of narrow-gauge trains traverses the Harz Mountains on three scenic routes, including one up the legendary Mt Brocken (p570)

Lössnitzgrundbahn The most scenic approach to Moritzburg Castle is aboard this historic steam train chugging along between Radebeul and Radeburg, near Dresden (p150)

Thüringerwaldbahn Really more a tram than a train, this route trundles from Gotha to Tabarz, deep in the Thuringian Forest (p552)

If you like...scenic drives
Rev up your engines as you explore the Black Forest on these scenic drives (p329)

Wine Tasting

Be it at estate tastings, vineyard hikes, cellar tours or wine festivals, an immersion in German wine culture should be part of any itinerary.

Rheingau Sample renowned riesling vintages in Rüdesheim, the hub of this short east–west-flowing section of the Rhine (p436)

Kaiserstuhl Lots of sun and fertile soil create ideal growing conditions for fruity Spätburger (Pinot noir) and Grauburgunder (Pinot gris) (p349)

Deutsche Weinstrasse Winding through the Palatinate, the bucolic German Wine Route is famous for its muscular rieslings and robust Dornfelder reds (p431)

Moselle With a wine-growing tradition rooted in Roman times, this meandering region grows light-bodied whites that want to be drunk young (p446)

Historisches Museum der Pfalz Dating back 1700 years, the world's oldest wine is among the fascinating exhibits at this well-curated museum in Speyer (p424)

Great Outdoors

Germany is an all-seasons outdoor playground, so whatever your adrenaline fix, you'll find it here.

Black Forest Fir-cloaked hills, steep gorges, misty waterfalls and sweeping viewpoints await those who hit the trail in this fabled region (p329)

Spreewald Leave the crowds behind as you dip your paddles into this timeless warren of gentle waterways near Berlin (p130)

Altmühltal Radweg Pull up at a pebbled beach for a picnic after pedalling past craggy rock formations carved by this serene river in northern Bavaria (p286)

Saxon Switzerland Rock hounds can test their mettle on hundreds of climbs on soul-stirring sandstone cliffs and rockscapes (p152)

Zugspitze Only seasoned mountaineers should make the breathtaking ascent to 'the roof of Germany' (p237)

Sylt Big wind and waves translate into world-class windsurfing on this glamorous North Sea island (p688)

Oberstdorf Whether you're into downhill, cross-country or boarding, this pretty ski region has a piste with your name on it (p241)

Spa Time

Soothe achy bones or simply take a day to relax in one of Germany's many sumptuous day spas, many fed by naturally heated mineral water.

Friedrichsbad Taking the waters doesn't get more regal than at this 19th-century Roman-Irish bath in Baden-Baden (p331)

Alpamare Plunge down Germany's longest water slide at Bad Tölz' family-friendly water complex, complete with wave pool and saunas (p242)

Sole Therme For that extra glow, rub your skin with salt in this tricked-out day spa in Bad Harzburg (p569)

Meersburg Therme Relax in thermal waters, sweat it out in replica stone-age huts and take in the fabulous scenery at this waterfront spa on Lake Constance (p363)

Kaiser-Friedrich-Therme Work out the kinks in pools fed by naturally heated mineral water in this baronial spa in Wiesbaden (p403)

Carolus Thermen Bliss out in oriental pools and enjoy honey rubs and deep-tissue massages in Aachen's elegant bathing temple (p490)

If you like...industrial tourism
Find beauty and grandeur in the Unesco-honoured Völklinger Hütte near Saarbrücken (p459)

Islands

For an authentic experience off the usual tourist track, catch a boat to these off-shore escapes.

Rügen Germany's largest island has charmed visitors since the 19th century with its sandy beaches, white chalk cliffs and historic resorts (p709)

Halligen Islands There are more seals than people on these flat-as-a-pancake islets in the North Sea (p687)

Mainau If you love beautiful gardens, you'll be enchanted by the profusion of tulips, dahlias, roses and orchids in this garden island owned by a member of the Swedish royal family (p362)

Helgoland Lashed by wind and waves, there's something oddly alluring about this lone red sandstone rock in the middle of the North Sea (p691)

Hiddensee For a genuine sense of happy isolation visit this car-free Baltic island in the winter (p712)

Herreninsel This island in the Chiemsee is home to the grandest of Ludwig's II palaces, Schloss Herrenchiemsee, a tribute to French Sun King Louis XIV (p243)

German Flavours

Sure, there are pizzas and hamburgers everywhere, but for a true taste of Germany try one of these traditional dishes.

Bratwurst Nuremberg's finger-sized links, grilled and served in a bun or with sauerkraut, are top dogs in Germany (p275)

Pork knuckle A Munich beer hall like the Augustiner-Bräus-tuben is the perfect place for tackling this classic gut-buster (p213)

Doner kebab It was a Turkish immigrant in Berlin who first came up with the idea of tucking spit-roasted slivered meat into a pita bread along with salad and a garlicky sauce (p742)

Spätzle This noodle dish hails from the Stuttgart region and is often smothered in cheese or topped with lentils (p313)

Black forest gateau Enjoy a slice of this creamy liqueur-drenched sponge cake symphony at Café Schäfer in Triberg, where it was invented (p352)

Haute cuisine Baden-Württemberg has the country's greatest density of Michelin-starred restaurants, including two three-star temples in Baiersbronn (p339)

Souvenirs

Even in the age of global commerce, there are some treasures better unearthed in Germany than anywhere else.

Käthe Wohlfahrt Weihnachtsdorf In this museum-like shop in Rothenburg ob der Tauber you can stock up on Christmas angels, ornaments and nutcrackers year-round (p257)

Ampelmann The endearing fellow on East Germany's pedestrian traffic light has evolved into its own brand, with multiple stores in Berlin (p113)

Woodcarvings Carved wood sculptures are a speciality throughout the Alpine regions, but the workshops in Oberam-mergau are especially renowned (p235)

Glass Fans of the fragile can pick up exquisite hand-blown vases, glasses and bowls from traditional artisans in the Bavarian Forest (p302)

Marzipan Some of the world's best marzipan hails from Nied-eregger in the northern German town of Lübeck (p679)

Porcelain Precious porcelain is the hallmark of Meissen, the cradle of European porcelain manufacturing (p151)

month by month

January

Except in the ski resorts, the Germans have the country pretty much to themselves this month. Short and cold days make this a good time to make in-depth explorations of museums and churches.

 Mountain Madness

Grab your skis or snowboard and hit the slopes in resorts that range from glam (Garmisch-Partenkirchen, p236) to family-friendly (Bavarian Forest). No matter whether you're a black diamond daredevil or Sesame Street novice, there's a piste with your name on it.

February

It's not as sweltering as Rio, but the German Carnival is still a good excuse for a party. Ski resorts are busiest thanks to school holidays, though, so don't leave without reservations.

 Berlin Film Festival

Stars, starlets, directors and critics sashay down the red carpet for two weeks of screenings and glamour parties at the Berlinale, one of Europe's most prestigious celluloid festivals.

Karneval/ Fasching

The pre-Lenten season is celebrated with costumed street partying, parades, satirical shows and general revelry. The biggest parties are along the Rhine in Düsseldorf, Cologne and Mainz, but the Black Forest and Munich also have their own traditions.

March

Days start getting longer and the first inkling of spring is in the air. Fresh herring hits the menus, especially along the coastal regions, and dishes prepared with *Bärlauch* (wild garlic) are all the rage as well.

April

No matter if you stopped believing in the Easter Bunny long ago, there's no escaping him in Germany in April. Meanwhile, nothing epitomises the arrival of spring more than the first crop of white asparagus. Germans go nuts for it.

Walpurgisnacht

The pagan Witches' Sabbath festival (p564) on 30 April has Harz villages roaring to life as young and old dress up as witches and warlocks and parade through the streets singing and dancing.

Maifest

Villagers celebrate the end of winter on 30 April by chopping down a tree for a Maypole *(Maibaum),* painting, carving and decorating it, and staging a merry revelry with traditional costumes, singing and dancing.

May

One of the loveliest months, often surprisingly warm and sunny, perfect for ringing in beer garden season. Plenty of public holidays, which Germans turn into extended weekends or miniholidays, resulting in busy roads and lodging shortages.

Karneval der Kulturen
Hundreds of thousands of revellers celebrate Berlin's multicultural tapestry with parties, exotic nosh and a fun parade of flamboyantly dressed dancers, DJs, artists and musicians shimmying through the streets of Kreuzberg.

Labour Day
This is a public holiday in Germany, with some cities hosting political demonstrations for workers' rights. In Berlin, protests occasionally take on a violent nature, although it's now mostly a big street fair.

Muttertag
Mothers are honoured on the second Sunday of May, much to the delight of florists, sweet shops and greeting-card companies. Make restaurant reservations far in advance.

Wave-Gotik-Treffen
Thousands of Goths paint the town black as they descend upon Leipzig during the long Whitsuntide/Pentecost weekend, in what is billed as the world's largest Goth gathering.

June
Germany's festival pace quickens, while gourmets can rejoice in the bounty of fresh, local produce in the markets. Life pretty much moves outdoors as the summer solstice means the sun doesn't set until around 9.30pm.

Vatertag
Father's Day, now also known as Männertag

(Men's Day), is essentially an excuse for men to get liquored up with the blessing of the missus. It's always on Ascension Day.

Africa Festival
Europe's largest festival of African music and culture (www.africa festival.org) attracts around 100,000 people to Würzburg with concerts, foods and crafts.

Kieler Woche
More than three million salty types flock to the Baltic Sea each year, where Kiel hosts the world's biggest boat party, with hundreds of regattas, ship parades, historic vessels and nonstop partying.

Christopher Street Day
No matter your sexual persuasion, come out and paint the town pink, with more queens than at a royal wedding at major gay-pride celebrations in Berlin, Cologne and Hamburg.

July
School's out for the summer and peak travelling season starts, so you'd better be the gregarious type. Definitely prebook, whether you're headed to the mountains or the coast. It won't be the Med, but swimming is now possible in lakes, rivers, and the Baltic and North Seas.

Samba Festival
This orgy of song and dance brings around 100 bands and 3000 performers from a dozen

nations, and up to 200,000 visitors to Coburg.

Schleswig-Holstein Music Festival
Leading international musicians and promising young artists perform during this festival, in castles, churches, warehouses and animal barns throughout Germany's northernmost state. Held from mid-July until August.

August
August tends to be Germany's hottest month but days are often cooled down by afternoon thunderstorms. 'Tis the season for *Pfifferlinge* (chanterelle mushrooms) and fresh berries. Intrepid types can hunt their own in the forests.

Shooting Festivals
More than a million Germans (mostly men) belong to shooting clubs and show off their skills at marksmen's festivals. The biggest one is in Hanover; the oldest, in Düsseldorf.

Wine Festivals
With grapes ripening to a plump sweetness, the wine festival season starts, with tastings, folkloric parades, fireworks and the election of local and regional wine queens. The Dürkheimer Wurstmarkt (www.duerkheimer-wurst markt.de) is one of the biggest and most famous.

Kinderzeche
Dinkelsbühl, on the Romantic Road, hosts this 10-day festival (www.

kinderzeche.de) featuring children performing in historical re-enactments, along with a pageant and the usual merriment.

★ Wagner Festival
German high society descends upon Bayreuth (p282) to practise the art of listening at epic productions of Wagner operas staged in a custom-built festival hall. Mere mortals must hope to score tickets via a lottery system.

September

Often a great month weather-wise – not so hot, yet plenty sunny. The main travel season is over but September is still busy thanks to lots of wine and autumn festivals. Trees may start turning into a riot of colour towards the end of the month.

🏃 Berlin Marathon
Sweat it out with the other 50,000 runners or just cheer 'em on during Germany's biggest street race, which has seen nine world records set since 1977.

◉ Erntedankfest
Rural towns celebrate the harvest with decorated church altars, *Erntedankzug* (processions) and villagers dressed in folkloric garments.

★ Oktoberfest
Munich's legendary beer-swilling party (www. oktoberfest.de). Enough said.

October

Everybody's definitely back to school or business as days get shorter, colder and wetter. Trade-fair season kicks into high gear, affecting lodging prices and availability in Frankfurt, Berlin, Hamburg and other cities. Tourist offices, museums and attractions keep shorter hours. Some close down for the winter season.

◉ Frankfurt Book Fair
Bookworms invade Frankfurt for the world's largest book fair, with 7300 exhibitors from more than 100 countries.

November

If truth be told, a dreary month when people head indoors. On the plus side, queues at tourist sights are short, and theatre, concert, opera and other cultural events are plentiful. Do bring warm clothes and rain gear.

★ St Martinstag
This festival held on 10–11 November honours the 4th-century St Martin, known for his humility and generosity, with a lantern procession and a re-enactment of the famous scene where he cuts his coat in half to share with a beggar. This is followed by a big feast of stuffed roast goose.

December

Cold and sun-deprived days are brightened by Advent, the four weeks of festivities preceding Christmas that are celebrated with enchanting markets, illuminated streets, Advent calendars, candle-festooned wreaths, home-baked cookies and other rituals. The ski resorts usually get their first dusting of snow.

◉ Nikolaustag
On the eve of 5 December, German children put their boots outside the door hoping that St Nick will fill them with sweets and small toys overnight. Ill-behaved children, though, may find only a prickly rod left behind by St Nick's helper, Knecht Ruprecht.

🔒 Christmas Markets
Mulled wine, spicy gingerbread cookies, shimmering ornaments – these and lots more are typical features of German Christmas markets, held from late November until 24 December. Nuremberg's Christkindlmarkt is especially famous.

🏃 Silvester
New Year's Eve is called 'Silvester' in honour of the 4th-century pope under whom the Romans adopted Christianity as their official religion. The new year is greeted with fireworks launched by thousands of amateur pyromaniacs.

itineraries

Whether you've got five days or 50, these itineraries provide a starting point for the trip of a lifetime. Want more inspiration? Head online to lonelyplanet.com/thorntree to chat with other travellers.

Two Weeks
Top of the Pops

Bookended by great cities, this road trip lets you sample superb culture, character and architecture. Kick off with a couple of days in **Berlin** for its top-notch museums, old and bold architecture and nice-to-naughty nightlife. Next is a day in **Dresden**, in its baroque splendour on the Elbe River. Push south to **Nuremberg**, with its evocative walled medieval centre, and on to **Munich**, where an evening in a beer garden is the perfect finish to two days of palace and museum hopping. Drive to **Garmisch-Partenkirchen** to breathe the fresh Alpine air on an exhilarating train-and-cable-car trip up the **Zugspitze**, Germany's highest mountain. Spend the night here, then get up early to beat the crowds swarming 'Mad' King Ludwig II's castles in **Füssen**. In the afternoon, point the compass north for the Romantic Road, possibly overnighting in **Dinkelsbühl** or **Rothenburg ob der Tauber**. Next, cut west to historic **Heidelberg**, with its romantically ruined fortress, then north to **Worms** and **Mainz**, with their Romanesque cathedrals. After a night in enchanting Bacharach, follow the **Romantic Rhine** through fairy-tale scenery before winding up in cosmopolitan **Cologne** for a day or two of church-hopping, great art and rustic beer halls.

Two Weeks
Biggest Hits of the South

Start your driving exploration with a day in **Frankfurt**, where you can soak up culture in world-class museums, cider in traditional taverns and views of the city skyline from the river promenade. Point the compass northwest to **Koblenz**, dramatically located at the confluence of the Rhine and Moselle Rivers with the mighty Ehrenbreitstein fortress looming above. This is the gateway to the Romantic Rhine, a scene-stealing combo of steeply terraced vineyards, lordly medieval castles and higgledy-piggledy villages. Say hello to legendary Loreley rock as you follow the western river bank south, perhaps stopping in postcard-pretty **Boppard** and fairy-tale-like **Bacharach** or fancying yourself knight or damsel for a night in a luxurious castle hotel. The next morning, make a quick stop in **Mainz**, where Johannes Gutenberg ushered in the information age by inventing moveable type.

Next, follow in the footsteps of Mark Twain in bewitching **Heidelberg**, Germany's oldest university town, where you shouldn't miss a tour of the majestic and impossibly romantic castle. Take a day's break from culture in **Baden-Baden**, the legendary spa resort where royals, celebrities, politicians and mere mortals have for centuries frolicked in elegant bathing temples. From here go cuckoo for the Black Forest, a storied pastiche of forest-cloaked hills, glacial lakes, snug valleys and half-timbered villages like **Gengenbach** and **Triberg**. Build in at least half a day in student-flavoured **Freiburg**, with its imposing minster; it's the place to enjoy the crisp local wine alfresco amid tangled cobbled lanes.

From here cut east to the vast **Lake Constance** and follow its scenic northern shore, perhaps stopping in pretty Meersburg, the prehistoric Pfahlbauten (pile dwellings) or Friedrichhafen, the birthplace of the Zeppelin airship. Consider overnighting in lovely Lindau, a teensy island laced with a maze of cobbled alleys jutting into the water. You're now in Bavaria, en route to the fabled Schloss Neuschwanstein in **Füssen** and on to **Garmisch-Partenkirchen**, where a train-and-cable-car combo delivers you to the top of the Zugspitze. Come back down to earth in a beer hall in **Munich** before wrapping up your journey with a couple of days of oohing and aahing your way up the Romantic Road. Essential stops include **Rothenburg ob der Tauber** and **Würzburg**, from which it's a quick drive back to Frankfurt.

Four Weeks
Tour de Germany

This trip presents you with the mother lode of soul-stirring landscapes, villages and spirit-lifting culture in some of Germany's finest cities. Base yourself in **Berlin** for a few days, perhaps following the suggestions outlined on p59, and add a one-day excursion to park-and-palace-filled **Potsdam**. Next putter around – preferably in a kayak or canoe – one of Germany's most unusual landscapes, the canal-laced **Spreewald**, home to the Sorb ethnic minority. Make a quick detour to **Görlitz** on the Polish border, one of Germany's best-preserved small towns, then earmark two days to get properly acquainted with **Dresden's** cultural riches. Continue on to Thuringia to walk in the footsteps of Germany's greatest intellects – from Luther to Goethe to Gropius – in **Weimar** and **Erfurt**.

Spend the next three days exploring a trio of medieval gems teeming with happily restored, centuries-old buildings: compact **Bamberg** exudes romance; much bigger **Nuremberg** pegs its fame not only to its role as a medieval powerhouse but also to its less glorious Third Reich legacy; and **Regensburg** is a lively university town founded by the Romans whose many patrician towers overlook the coursing Danube. From here, wend your way towards Munich via the enchanting **Altmühltal Nature Park**. It's best savoured slowly, on foot, by bike or by boat.

Make a study of **Munich** for a couple of days, perhaps folding day trips up the **Zugspitze** or to Ludwig II's **Schloss Neuschwanstein** into your itinerary. Your route continues west to Lake Constance, where stops should include lovely **Lindau** and picture-perfect **Meersburg**. Revel in the youthful spirit of ancient **Freiburg** for a day, then point the compass north for scenic drives through the Black Forest, ending in **Baden-Baden** for the night. Relax in the town's thermal spas before ploughing on to **Heidelberg**, with its romantically ruined castle. Cut across the Rhine to **Speyer**. Take a spin around Speyer's Romanesque cathedral, then compare it to its upriver cousins in **Worms** and **Mainz**. You're in the heart of wine country now, so sample the local tipple in idyllic villages like **Bacharach** or **Boppard** as you follow the river north through the dramatic scenery of the castle-studded Romantic Rhine. The tour ends in **Cologne**, whose magnificent cathedral will come into view long before you've reached town. Great museums, Romanesque churches and Rhenish joie de vivre will easily keep you entertained for a day or two.

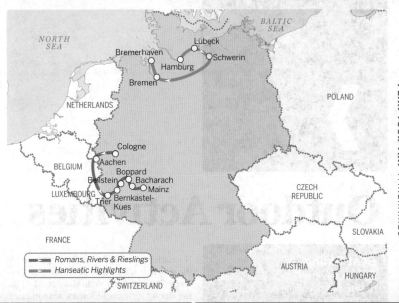

Romans, Rivers & Rieslings
Hanseatic Highlights

One Week
Romans, Rivers, Rieslings

Start in **Cologne** and let this journey of grand architecture, absorbing history, world-class art and fine wine unfurl. Stand in awe of the twin-spired Kölner Dom, explore the city's engaging museums (chocolate, contemporary art, sports – take your pick!) and indulge in a hearty supper and local *Kölsch* beer in a Rhenish tavern. Head to **Aachen** next to walk in the footsteps of Charlemagne and munch on a crunchy *Printen* cookie, then travel back in time another few centuries in storied **Trier**. More than 2000 years old, it's home to some of the finest Roman monuments north of the Alps.

The following day take your time to mosey along the serpentine Moselle River, which runs past steep vineyards to meet the Rhine at Koblenz. Swoon over crisp riesling in half-timbered **Bernkastel-Kues** or fairytale **Beilstein**, then compare it with wines produced along the Rhine. Follow that river south as it carves past picture-postcard villages like **Boppard** and **Bacharach**, and craggy cliffs crowned by medieval castles. On your last day, discover **Mainz**, with its great cathedral and fabulous museum dedicated to moveable type inventor and local boy Johannes Gutenberg.

One Week
Hanseatic Highlights

This itinerary hopscotches around northern Germany to delightful cities shaped by the sea and a long mercantile tradition rooted in the medieval Hanseatic League. You can drive it, but it's just as easily done by train. Kick-off is in cosmopolitan **Hamburg**, a city that cradles an elegant centre and an edgy new waterfront quarter, the red-brick Speicherstadt (warehouse district).

Spend a couple of days here before venturing on to **Lübeck**, an enchanting historic town, where the landmark Holsten Gate is a shutterbug favourite. Try the local marzipan and then head to pastoral **Schwerin**, a cultural hub hemmed in by crystalline lakes. Sitting pretty on an island in one of them is the much-photographed Schloss Schwerin.

Carry on to **Bremen**, the northern terminus of the 'Fairytale Road'. After greeting the statue of the Town Musicians, check out expressionist architecture, mummified corpses in the cathedral crypt, and Beck's brewery, then party till dawn in Das Viertel. Once your head's clear again, steer north to **Bremerhaven**, which was the port of dreams for millions of souls hoping for a better life in the New World. The German Emigration Centre tells their story.

Outdoor Activities

Best Skiing
Bavarian Alps A holy grail for downhill and cross-country skiers, with titanic peaks, groomed slopes and an impeccable snow record.

Best Hiking
Black Forest Mile after pine-scented mile of trails weaving through forests, mist-enshrouded valleys and half-timbered villages, freshly minted for a fairy tale.

Best Climbing
Saxon Switzerland Exhilarating 1100 peaks and scenery that moves the soul in this sandstone wonderland.

Best Canoeing
Müritz National Park A mosaic of silent lakes and reed-fringed canals, this watery wilderness is best explored by canoe.

Best Cycling
Altmühltal Radweg A 'Best of Bavaria' bike ride, taking in river bends and dense forests, ragged limestone cliffs and castle-topped villages.

No matter what kind of activity gets you off the couch, you'll be able to pursue it in Germany. There's plenty to do year-round – hiking among spring wildflowers, swimming in a lake warmed by the summer sun, biking among a kaleidoscope of autumn foliage or celebrating winter by schussing through deep powder. Wherever you go, you'll find outfitters and local operators eager to gear you up.

Hiking & Mountaineering

Wanderlust? Germans coined the word. And their passion for *Wandern* (walking) is unrivalled. High-altitude treks in the Bavarian Alps, Black Forest hikes over wooded hill and dale, Rhineland vineyard strolls – this country will soon have you itching to grab your boots and stride its 200,000km of well-signposted trails, some traversing national and nature parks or biosphere reserves.

Local tourist offices can help you find a route to match your fitness and time frame, and can supply you with maps and tips. Many offer multiday 'hiking without luggage' packages that include accommodation and luggage transfer between hotels.

The Bavarian Alps are Germany's mountaineering heartland, whether for day treks or multiday hut-to-hut clambers. Before heading out, seek local advice and instruction on routes, equipment and weather, as trails can be narrow, steep and have icy patches, even in summer.

The **Deutscher Alpenverein** (DAV; German Alpine Club; ☎089-140 030; www.alpenverein.de) is a goldmine of information and maintains hundreds of Alpine huts, where you can spend the night and get a meal. Local DAV chapters also organise courses and guided treks. Becoming a member of the organisation can yield a 30% to 50% discount on huts, and other benefits.

Rock Climbing

Clambering around steep rock faces is popular in the crag-riddled heights of central and southern Germany. Rock hounds test their mettle on limestone cliffs in Bavaria's Altmühltal Nature Park, with climbs from grades 1 to 10. Another *klettern* (climbing) hot spot, particularly among free climbers, is Saxon Switzerland, with 1100 climbing peaks, routes graded 1 to 11, and exhilarating views over bizarre sandstone rock formations. Most towns have climbing walls where you can limber up. For climbing routes, gear, walls and more, visit www.dav-felsinfo.de, www.klettern.de or www.climbing.de.

Best Walks For...

Alpine trekkers Colossal mountains and jewel-coloured lakes in the Berchtesgaden National Park (p246).

Family ramblers Partnachklamm and red squirrel-spotting on the trail shadowing Triberger Wasserfälle (p352), Germany's highest waterfall at 163m.

Beach combers Bracing sea air atop the wild limestone cliffs of Rügen's Stubbenkammer (p709) and dune walking on Sylt (p688).

Serious mountaineers Zugspitze (p237), the rooftop of Germany at 2962m. The tough ascent and phenomenal four-country views are breathtaking in every sense of the word.

Long-distance hikers Bavaria's beautiful 200km Altmühltal Panoramaweg, the wild and woody 169km Rennsteig or the 280km Westweg (p336), the ultimate Black Forest walk.

Wine lovers Vine-strewn hills in the Rhine Valley and sipping pinots along the Kaiserstuhl's 15km Winzerweg (p349).

Birdwatchers Storks, geese and cranes in the **Naturpark Elbufer-Drawehn** (www.elberadweg.de), or ospreys, white-tailed eagles and kingfishers in the Müritz National Park (p698).

Escapists The fir-cloaked hills of the Black Forest and the Bavarian Forest National Park (p303).

RESOURCES

» **German National Tourist Office** (www.germany.travel) Inspiration on walking and cycling throughout Germany.

» **Kompass** (www.kompass.de) A reliable series of 1:25,000 scale walking maps and information on trails.

» **Tourentipp** (www.tourentipp.de) Weather forecasts, hut info and walks by region.

» **Wanderbares Deutschland** (www.wanderbares-deutschland.de) Dozens of walking trails, with a handy interactive map.

» **Wandern ohne Gepäck** (www.wandern-ohne-gepaeck-deutschland.de) The 'hiking without luggage' specialists.

Rock fans The rockscapes of Saxon Switzerland and limestone cliffs in Naturpark Obere Donau (p354).

Cycling

Strap on your helmet! Germany is superb cycling territory, whether you're off on a leisurely spin along the beach, a downhill ride in the Alps or a multiday freewheeling adventure. Local tourist offices can give you advice for day trips and you can rent city, mountain and electro-bikes in most towns.

The country is also criss-crossed by more than 200 well-signposted long-distance trails covering 70,000km – ideal for *Radwandern* (bike touring). Routes combine lightly travelled back roads, forestry tracks and paved highways with dedicated bike lanes. Many traverse nature reserves, meander along rivers or venture into steep mountain terrain.

The national cycling organisation **Allgemeiner Deutscher Fahrrad Club** (ADFC; www.adfc.de) produces the best maps for on-the-road navigation. These indicate inclines, track conditions, repair shops and UTM grid coordinates for GPS users. ADFC also offers a useful directory called **Bett & Bike** (www.bettundbike.de), available online or in bookshops, that lists bicycle-friendly hotels, inns and hostels.

TED LEVINE / CORBIS ©

» (above) Hiking in the Bavarian Alps (p230)
» (left) Skiing on the slopes of Garmisch-Partenkirchen (p236)

Top Long-Distance Cycling Routes

Altmühltal Radweg (p285) Rothenburg ob der Tauber to Beilngries, following the river through the Altmühltal Nature Park; easy to moderate (160km).

Elberadweg (p585) Elbe River from Saxon Switzerland to Hamburg through wine country, heath and marshland, past Dresden, Dessau and Wittenberg (860km).

Donauradweg Neu-Ulm to Passau; delightful, easy-to-moderate riverside trip (434km).

Bodensee-Königssee Radweg Lindau to Berchtesgaden; moderate route along the foot of the Alps with lovely views (418km).

Romantische Strasse (p248) Würzburg to Füssen; easy to moderate and one of the nicest ways to explore this famous holiday route; busy during summer (359km).

Winter Sports

Modern lifts, primed ski runs from easy-peasy blues to death-wish blacks, cross-country trails through untouched nature, log huts, steaming mulled wine, hearty dinners by crackling fires – these are the hallmarks of a German skiing holiday.

The Bavarian Alps, only an hour's drive south of Munich, offer the best downhill slopes and most reliable snow conditions. The most famous and ritzy resort is Garmisch-Partenkirchen (p236), which hosted the FIS Alpine Skiing World Championship 2011 and is but a snowball's throw from Zugspitze. It has 60km of slopes, mostly geared towards intermediates. Picture-book-pretty Oberstdorf in the Allgäu Alps forms the heart of the Oberstdorf-Kleinwalsertal ski region, which has 125km of slopes. It's good for boarders, with snow parks and a half-pipe to play on, and cross-country skiers come to glide along 75km of classic and 55km of skating tracks. For low-key skiing and stunning scenery, there is Berchtesgaden and Mittenwald, presided over by the jagged Karwendel range. Can't or don't want to ski? All resorts offer snowy fun from tobogganing and ice-skating to snowshoeing and winter walking.

Elsewhere in the country, the mountains may not soar as high, but prices are cheaper and the atmosphere is less frenetic. The Bavarian Forest and the Black Forest have the most reliable snow levels, with moderate downhill action on the Grosser Arber

and Feldberg mountains, as well as abundant *Langlaufloipen* (cross-country trails).

At higher elevations, the season generally runs from late November or early December to March. Skis, boots and poles cost around €20/12 for downhill/cross-country gear hire and group lessons are between €30 and €45 per day.

Water Sports

Germany's lakes, rivers, canals and coasts offer plenty of water-based action, even if the swimming season is relatively short (June to September) since water temperatures rarely climb above 21°C.

Slip into a canoe or kayak to absorb the natural rhythm of the waterways threading through the lushly wooded Spreewald and Bavaria's Altmühltal Nature Park. Scattered with more than 100 lakes, the forested wilderness of the Müritz National Park is great for paddle-and-camp trips. Or drift across Lake Constance to Switzerland and Austria with the Alps on the horizon. The season runs from around April to October and a one-/two-person canoe or kayak will set you back around €20/30 per day.

Stiff breezes and big waves draw sailors, surfers, windsurfers and kitesurfers north. Sylt on the North Sea and Rügen on the Baltic have some of the top conditions and schools in the country for water-based activities.

RIVERBOAT ROMANCE

On a riverboat cruise, you can put your feet up and watch the outdoors drift past on some of the country's greatest rivers from Easter to October.

High on the list is the Romantic Rhine, where boats drift past vines, cliffs crowned with robber-knight castles and picturesque villages. Or combine wine tasting with a mini cruise along the Moselle between Koblenz and Trier, each bend in the river revealing vine-draped loveliness.

In Berlin you can mix sightseeing with a meander along the Spree; in Hamburg the Elbe; in Passau the Danube; in Stuttgart the Neckar. For a taste of history, hop aboard a paddle-wheel steamboat in Dresden or a punt in Tübingen.

Eat & Drink Like a Local

Best in Spring

During *Spargelzeit* Germans go wild for asparagus. *Bärlauch* (wild garlic) is bountiful and Baltic towns celebrate the humble herring. Munich throws festivals for pre-Lenten *Starkbier* (strong beer), the malty 7.5% brew monks once dubbed *flüssiges Brot* (liquid bread).

Best in Summer

Pfifferlinge (chanterelle mushrooms) and a feast of forest berries trumpet summer's arrival. Beer gardens brim with folk lapping up the warm weather, and folksy wine festivals are in full swing.

Best in Autumn

Autumn days are rich and earthy, with game, wild mushrooms and pumpkins aplenty. At Oktoberfest in September, 6.9 million partygoers wash down entire farms of pigs, oxen and chickens with *Mass* (litres) of beer.

Best in Winter

'Tis the season for gingerbread and mulled wine at Christmas.

How do the Germans eat and drink? With gusto! Germany might not have the culinary kudos of its neighbours, but its robust, fresh flavours have made it a rising star in Europe's kitchen. 'Keep it simple' and seasonal' is the ethos.

Inflected by regional tastes and what's available locally, food is bound to play a big part in your travels here. You'll never forget your first creamy forkful of real Black Forest gateau or tangy rieslings sipped in Rhineland vines, the seafood on Baltic beaches or the roast pork served with foamy *Weizen* (wheat beer) amid the thigh-slapping fun of a Bavarian beer fest. The further you venture, the more you realise how rich and varied German cuisine is. Bring an appetite and a taste for adventure and get stuck in.

Food Experiences
Cheap Eats

Some of your best German food experiences are likely to be the snack-on-the-hoof kind. Street food is a tasty way to get versed in German wurst (sausage) and chomp your way around the globe, often with change from a €5 note. In Berlin and other cities, stalls sizzle up Greek, Italian, Mexican, Middle Eastern and Chinese bites. The *Imbiss* (fast-food stall) is a ubiquitous phenomenon, allowing you to eat on the run.

Germany's Turkish population invented the modern doner kebab *(Döner)*, adding salad and garlic-yoghurt sauce to spit-roasted lamb, veal or chicken in pita bread. Most kebab joints also do vegie versions. In the briny north, snack on fish (usually herring) sandwiches.

Top Five Snacks

» Curry 36 (p102) Berlin's *Currywurst* (curried sausage) crown goes to this curb-side joint in Kreuzberg.

» Rosenthaler Grill- und Schlemmerbuffet (p98) Oscar-worthy doner kebabs and busy as a beehive.

» Bratwursthäusle (p275) Finger-sized Nuremberg bratwurst – nicely spiced and super-crisp.

» Gosch (p690) Sylt's favourite fast-fish outlet, with exceptionally fresh seafood.

» Best Worscht in Town (p393) Breathe fire with the *Schärfehölle* (hellish hotness) of these wurst.

Going Gourmet

Germany has been redeeming itself gastronomically in the past decade. Cheflebrities such as TV's Tim Mälzer and Ralf Zacherl have made cooking at home cool. In top kitchens across the country, chefs are putting a creative spin on tried-and-trusted specialities in a wave referred to as *neue Deutsche Küche* (new German cuisine).

To see Germany's meteoric rise in the Michelin world, look, for instance, to the little Black Forest town of Baiersbronn, where master chefs Harald Wohlfahrt, at Schwarzwaldstube (p339), and Peter Lumpp, at Restaurant Bareiss (p339), have both been awarded the coveted three Michelin stars. They are no exception. In 2012 Germany's Michelin skies twinkled brighter than ever before, with 208 one-star, 32 two-star and nine three-star restaurants.

Besides Michelin and Gault Millau, Germany has its own ratings and guides, including **Der Feinschmecker** (www.der-feinschmecker-club.de), **Aral's Schlemmer Atlas** (www.schlemmer-atlas.de) and **Marcellino's Restaurant Report** (www.marcellinos.de).

Meals of a Lifetime

From fine dining to hearty German grub served with a dollop of history, whet your appetite with our pick of the best.

Horváth (p99) Michelin newcomer Sebastian Frank conjures innovative Austrian flavours and textures at this canalside Berlin bistro.

Prinz Myshkin (p209) A vegetarian globetrotter dishing up palate-awakening fare in slick, vaulted surrounds.

Schwarzwaldstube (p339) Harald Wohlfahrt cooks French with precision and panache at this three Michelin-starred Black Forest hideaway.

Zur Herrenmühle (p420) Dine under 300-year-old wooden beams at this 1690 flour mill turned elegant country-style restaurant.

Altes Gasthaus Leve (p515) This golden oldie has been doing a roaring trade in Westphalian fare such as sweet-and-sour beef and lima bean stew since 1607.

Cooking Courses

Germany's fledgling cookery school scene has spread its wings of late, with a sprinkling of places where you can work your culinary magic. Reckon on paying between €140 and €240 for a day at the stove, usually including lunch and recipes to take home.

At Schwarzwaldstube, foodie classes revolve around a theme such as cooking with asparagus or making pasta. For a more traditional focus, join the kings of *Knödel* for an English-language dumpling-making workshop at Wirthaus in der Au in Munich. Search by region to find a course that suits you: check out www.kochschule.de and www.die-kochschulen.de (both in German).

Local Specialities

Drift to the Baltic and North Sea coasts for pickled herrings with oomph and sweet-and-sour specialities like *Mecklenburger Rippenbraten* (rolled pork stuffed with lemons, apples, plums and raisins). Hamburgers love their eels and *Labskaus* (minced beef, potato and beetroot, served with a fried egg and gherkins), while Bavarians match excellent beer with gut-busting platters of pork knuckles and *Klösse* (dumplings). Then there's Saxony and Thuringia for lentil and

WHAT'S HOT

» All-you-can-eat weekend brunches.

» Asian lifestyle eateries with a designer edge.

» Creative vegan and vegetarian food.

» NYC-style gourmet delis – cheesecake, bagels and cupcakes galore.

» Locavore (locally produced food).

potato soups, the Black Forest for its trout, ham and famous gateau, and rural Swabia for culinary one-offs like *Spätzle* (noodle-dumpling hybrids) and *Maultaschen* (ravioli's Teutonic relative).

Nearly every town in Germany has a weekly *Bauernmarkt* (farmers market). This is the place to bag local fruit and veg, cheese, wurst, fish, preserves, herbs and sometimes homegrown wine and schnapps. See the destination chapters for our faves. When in the countryside, keep an eye out for farms selling their own dairy goodies, sausages and honey.

Dare to Try

Feeling daring? Why not give some of Germany's more unusual dishes a whirl.

» **Sauere Kuttlen/Nierle/Lüngerl** (sour tripe/kidneys/lung) No Baden-Württemberg beer fest would be complete without these offal faves, simmered in vinegar or wine, bay, laurel, juniper and spices, and served with bread or fries.

» **Handkäs mit Musik** (hand cheese with music) Hesse's pongy sour-milk cheese, rolled by hand and marinated in oil and vinegar with onions. A sure-fire recipe for flatulence – hence the music!

» **Saumagen** Rhineland-Palatinate brings you stuffed pig stomach (reminiscent of haggis). Eat it with sauerkraut and sautéed potatoes.

» **Labskaus** Every Hamburg seafarer worth his salt adores this mishmash of corned beef, beetroot, potatoes, onions and occasionally herring, topped with a fried egg and served with gherkins.

» **Bubespitzle** Otherwise known as *Schupfnudeln*, this Swabian dish's ingredients are innocuous: potato noodles tossed in butter, served with sauerkraut and speck. But the name (literally 'little boys' penises') certainly isn't.

At the Table

Roll Out the Barrel

Up and down this hop-crazy country you will find buzzing microbreweries and brewpubs, cavernous beer halls and chestnut-shaded beer gardens that invite you to linger, quaff a cold one and raise a toast – *Prost!*

Some of the best are in Bavaria, home to Ingolstadt of 1516 Beer Purity Law fame. Munich offers a taste of Oktoberfest year-round in historic beer halls, where you can hoist a *Mass* (litre) of *Weizen* and sway to oompah bands, and leafy beer gardens for imbibing and chomping on warm pretzels *(Brez'n)* and *Weisswurst* (herb-veal-pork sausage). This festive spirit spills into other Bavarian cities such as Regensburg, Bamberg, which runs a five-brewery tour, and into villages where monks brew potent dark beers as they have for eons. Cologne is another German beer stronghold, famous for straw-gold *Kölsch* served in skinny glasses called *Stangen*.

Breweries offering a peek behind the scenes include Hamburg's **Holsten breweries** (www.holsten-pilsener.de), Beck's (p625) and Friesisches Brauhaus zu Jever (p638).

When to Eat

Though city folk might just grab a coffee en route to the office, traditionally *Frühstück* (breakfast) is a sweet and savoury smorgasbord of bread, cheese, salami, wurst, preserves, yoghurt and muesli. At weekends, it's a more leisurely, family-oriented affair. Many cafes have embraced the brunch trend, serving all-you-can-eat buffets with fresh rolls, eggs, smoked fish, fruit salad and even Prosecco.

While the older generation may still sit down for *Mittagessen* at noon sharp, the focus on lunch as the main meal of the day is waning thanks to a shift in work patterns. That said, many restaurants still tout a fixed lunch menu (*Mittagsmenü* or *Tagesmenü*), which can be an affordable way of dining at upscale restaurants.

Dinner is dished up at home around 7pm. For those who have already eaten heartily at midday, there is *Abendbrot*, bread with cold cuts. Bar the cities with their late-night dining scenes, Germans head to restaurants earlier than elsewhere in Europe, and many kitchens in rural areas stop serving at around 9pm. At home, meals are relaxed

» (above) Frothy beers aplenty at Munich's historic beer hall, the Hofbräuhaus (p213)

» (left) Cream, *Kirsch* and a whole lot of chocolatey goodness go into Germany's famed black forest gateau

PLAN YOUR TRIP EAT & DRINK LIKE A LOCAL

DOS & DON'TS

» Do say *'Guten Appetit'* (good appetite) before eating, and *'Prost!'* when drinking a toast.

» Do offer to help wash up afterwards – locals tend to be quite punctilious about housework.

» Do specify if you don't want your restaurant dishes slathered in mayonnaise, *Quark* (curd cheese) or dressing. Germans are generous in this department.

» Don't expect a glass of tap water at a restaurant or cafe; although things are changing, especially in cities, it's still an uncommon request that may not be understood or honoured.

» Don't plonk yourself down at the *Stammtisch* table. Empty or not, these are reserved for regulars only.

and require few airs and graces beyond the obligatory *'Guten Appetit'* (good appetite), exchanged before eating.

Where to Eat

Gaststätten & Gasthöfe Rural inns with a laid-back feel, local crowd and solid menu of *gutbürgerliche Küche* (home cooking).

Eiscafé Italian-style cafes where you can grab an ice cream or cappuccino and head outside.

Stehcafé A stand-up cafe for coffee and snacks at speed and on the cheap.

Cafe-Konditorei A traditional cake shop and cafe.

Ratskeller Atmospheric town-hall basement restaurant, generally more frequented by tourists than locals nowadays.

Bierkeller & Weinkeller The emphasis is on beer and wine, respectively, with a little food (sausages, pretzels, cold cuts) on the side.

Imbiss Handy speed-feed stops for savoury fodder, such as wurst-in-a-bun, kebabs or pizza.

Apfelweinwirtschaft Frankfurt's historic *Ebbelwei* (apple wine) taverns. Warm, woody and serving good honest regional fare.

Kaffee und Kuchen

Anyone who has spent any length of time in Germany knows the reverence bestowed on the three o'clock weekend ritual of *Kaffee und Kuchen* (coffee and cake). More than just a chance to devour delectable cakes and tortes, Germans see it as a social event. You'll find *Cafe-Konditoreien* (cafe-cake shops) pretty much everywhere – in castles, in the middle of the forest, even plopped on top of mountains. Track down the best by asking sweet-toothed locals where the cake is *hausgemacht* (homemade).

While coffee in Germany is not as strong as that served in France or Italy, you can expect a decent cup. All the usual varieties are on offer, including cappuccinos and lattes, although you still frequently see French-style bowls of milky coffee (*Milchkaffee*). Order a *Kanne* (pot) or *Tasse* (cup) of *Kaffee* and what you will get is filter coffee, usually with a portion of *Kaffeesahne* (condensed milk).

East Frisians in Bremen and Lower Saxony are the country's biggest consumers of tea, and have dozens of their own varieties, which they traditionally drink with cream and *Kluntje* (rock sugar). Tea frequently comes as a glass or pot of hot water, with the tea bag served to the side.

Dining Tips

One early-20th-century German book of manners that we have seen exhorts dinner guests not to use their knives to carve their initials into the table of their hosts! Things have, fortunately, moved on somewhat since those days. With good manners now automatic, there's little need to panic at the dinner table, although a few tips might come in handy for first-time visitors.

English menus are not a given, even in big cities, though the waiter or waitress will almost invariably be able to translate for you. The more rural and remote you travel, the less likely it is that the restaurant will have an English menu, or multilingual staff for that matter. It helps to learn a smattering of German.

Sometimes the person who invites will pay the bill, but generally Germans go Dutch and split it evenly. This might mean everyone chipping in at the end of a meal or asking to pay separately (*getrennte Rechnung*). Buying rounds in bars British-style is not usually the done thing, though Germans might buy each other the odd drink. In bars and beer halls, table service is still quite common and waiting staff often come around to *abkassieren* (cash up).

If you want to dine at formal or popular restaurants, it is wise to make reservations a day or two ahead. Michelin-starred restaurants are often booked up weeks in advance, especially at weekends. Most *Gasthöfe, Gaststätten*, cafes and beer halls should be able to squeeze you in at a moment's notice.

Service charge is not included in the bill. Tipping is quite an individual matter, but most Germans will tip between 5% and 10% in restaurants, and simply round to the nearest euro in cafes and bars. Do whatever you're comfortable with, given the service and setting. Give any tip directly to the server when paying your bill. Say either the amount you want to pay, or *'Stimmt so'* if you don't want change.

Travel with Children

Which Region?

Hiking & Biking
Lake Constance, Black Forest, Bavarian Forest, Harz Mountains, Elbe Bike Trail

Castles & Palaces
Romantic Rhine, Fairy-Tale Road, Schloss Neuschwanstein

City Life
Berlin, Munich, Cologne

History Lessons
Moselle, Rhine, Berlin, Munich, Bremerhaven

Watery Fun
Baltic Sea, North Sea, Chiemsee, Müritz National Park, Titisee

Travelling to Germany with tots can be child's play, especially if you keep a light schedule and involve them in trip planning. Plus, kids are a great excuse if you secretly yearn to ride roller coasters or go ape in a zoo.

Germany for Kids

If you're travelling to Germany as a family, you're sure to have a grand old time. Kids will already have seen in picture books many of the things that make the country so special: enchanting palaces and legend-shrouded castles, medieval towns and half-timbered villages, Viking ships and Roman ruins. This is the birthplace of the Brothers Grimm and their famous fairy tales. If you follow the Fairy-Tale Road (p528), you even get to see Sleeping Beauty's castle and Hamelin, the town of Pied Piper fame.

Cities too offer diversions – zoos, museums, imaginative playgrounds and outdoor pools. Tourist offices can point you to children's programs, child-care facilities and English-speaking pediatricians. If you need a babysitter, ask at your hotel for a referral.

Breastfeeding in public is practised, although most women are discreet about it. Restaurants are rarely equipped with nappy-change facilities, but some fast-food places have a fold-down change table in the women's toilet.

For an overview of kid-friendly activities in Berlin see p88, for Munich p205 and for Nuremberg p272.

Outdoor Activities

The great outdoors yields endless variety in Germany. Tourist offices can recommend walking trails suitable for families, including those pushing strollers, or can hook you up with a local guide. Also ask about kid-geared activities such as geocaching, animal-spotting safaris and nature walks.

Water rats will love frolicking on Germany's beaches, which are beautifully clean and usually devoid of big waves and dangerous undercurrents, although water temperatures rarely exceed 21°C (70°F). Lakes tend to be a bit warmer. Many have a *Strandbad* (lido) with change rooms, playgrounds, splash zones, slides, ping-pong tables, restaurants or boat rentals. Kayaking is active fun for children from the age of seven, and short excursions or multiday paddle-and-camp trips are available.

All ski resorts have ski schools with English-speaking instructors that initiate kids in the art of the snow plough in group or private lessons. Families with kids under 10 may find smaller resorts in the Bavarian Forest or Black Forest easier to navigate and better value than bigger Alpine resorts like Garmisch-Partenkirchen. All of them, of course, have plenty of off-piste fun as well: snow-shoeing, sledding, walking and ice skating.

Museums

Germany is full of kid-friendly museums that play to their imaginations or impart knowledge in interactive and engaging ways. Open-air museums like the Schwarzwälder Freilichtmuseum in the Black Forest or the Freilandmuseum Lehde in the Spreewald are fun places to learn about traditional culture. Cologne has the Schokoladen Museum (Chocolate Museum), Nuremberg the Spielzeugmuseum (Toy Museum) and Munich the Deutsches Museum (German Museum). Kid-oriented audioguides (in German and English) are becoming more widely available. Staff also run tot-geared activities, although these are usually in German.

Theme Parks

There's plenty of fun and thrills in theme parks. The country's biggest is Europa-Park near Freiburg, which has gentle rides for

TOP READS FOR KIDS

» **Look What Came from Germany** (Kevin Davis, 2000) This picture book reveals the German origins of Christmas trees, X-rays, hamburgers and more (from age seven).

» **Crusade in Jeans** (Thea Beckman, 1973) A vivid account of the Middle Ages as told by a 15-year-old time traveller (from age 11).

» **Candy Bombers** (Robert Elmer, 2006) Tale of two teenagers struggling to survive in post-WWII Berlin (from age nine).

tots, white-knuckle coasters for teens and its own mousy mascot, the Euromaus. For fishy encounters, seek out one of the country's eight SeaLife aquariums for touch tanks, fish feedings and activities. The Legoland amusement park in Ulm has shows, rides and a miniature world built from millions of Lego bricks. There's also an indoor one in Berlin. Older kids may be drawn to movie-themed parks, such as Filmpark Babelsberg in Potsdam and the Bavaria FilmStadt in Munich, for stunt shows, behind-the-scenes tours and potential actor-sightings.

See Amusements Parks on p44 for additional suggestions.

Dining Out

As long as they're not running wild, children are generally welcome in German restaurants, especially in informal cafes, bistros, pizzerias or *Gaststätten* (inns). High chairs are common and the server may even bring a damp cloth at the end of your meal to wipe sticky little fingers.

Many less-formal restaurants offer a limited *Kindermenü* (children's menu) or children's dishes (*Kinderteller*). Dishes generally loved by children include *Schnitzel mit Pommes* (schnitzel with fries), bratwurst (sausage), *Nudeln mit Tomatensosse* (pasta with tomato sauce), *Spätzle* (egg-based mini-dumpling-like noodles) or the German version of mac 'n' cheese, *Käsespätzle*. *Maultaschen*, a spin on ravioli, may also go down well. Pizzerias are cheap, ubiquitous and most will be happy to customise pizzas.

Germany is fabulous snack terrain. Larger malls have food courts, self-service cafeterias are often found in department stores and farmers markets also have food stalls. The most popular snacks on the run are bratwurst in a bun and doner kebab (sliced meat in a pita pocket with salad and sauce). And, of course, there's no shortage of international fast-food chains. Note that you have to pay extra for ketchup.

Baby food, infant formulas, soy and cow's milk, and nappies (diapers) are widely available in supermarkets and chemists (drugstores).

Drinks

Tap water is clean and fine to drink, although most cafes and restaurants are either reluctant to serve it or will refuse to. In that case, order a *Mineralwasser* (mineral water), either *mit Sprudel* (fizzy) or *ohne Sprudel* (flat). Mixing juices and fizzy mineral water (*Schorle*) is refreshing and popular, not only with kids.

Children's Discounts

Many museums, monuments and attractions are free to anyone under 18, but the cut off age varies. In general, you can assume kids under five don't pay at all. Most places also offer family tickets.

Children qualify for discounts on public transportation and tours, where they usually pay half price, sometimes less. Some hotels, including many international chains, have discounted rates for kids or don't charge extra if they're under a certain age (varying from three to 16) and stay in their parents' room without extra bedding. The *Kurtaxe* (tourist tax) you pay in most resorts gets you a *Gästekarte* (guest card) for free local transport and entry to museums, pools and attractions.

Children's Highlights

Energy Burners

» **Snow bunnies** Skiing, sledding and snow-shoeing in the Black Forest

» **Paddling** Canoeing or kayaking around spectacular scenery in the Spreewald

» **Windsurfing** Catching the wind and waves in Sylt

» **Hiking** The Black Forest is especially family friendly

» **Swimming** Head for sheltered Baltic Sea beaches

Amusement Parks

» **Märchengarten, Ludwigsburg** Low-key fairy-tale-themed park for tots

» **Steinwasen Park, near Freiburg** Forest park with rides, Alpine animals and a hanging bridge

» **Ravensburger Spieleland, Ravensburg** Board-game-inspired park with giant rubber duck races and speed cow milking

» **Feenweltchen, Saalfeld** A magical world of elves, fairies and sprites attached to a colourful grotto

» **Miniatur-Wunderland, Hamburg** One of the world's largest model railways

» **Autostadt, Wolfsburg** All things cars at the Volkswagen headquarters

Planes, Trains & Automobiles

Also see If You Like... Train Journeys (p22) for fun narrow-gauge train rides.

» **Nürburgring** Legendary car racing track

» **Technik Museum Speyer** A Boeing 747, 1960s U-boat and Soviet space shuttle await inspection

» **Deutsches Technikmuseum, Berlin** Giant shrine to technology

» **Phaeno Science Center, Wolfsburg** Exhibits and experiments in cutting-edge building by Zaha Hadid

Planning

Accommodation

Many hotels have family rooms with three or four beds, large doubles with a sofa bed or adjoining rooms with a connecting door. Practically all can provide cots, though sometimes for a small charge.

Farm stays (*Urlaub auf dem Bauernhof*) are popular with families and offer a low-key, inexpensive experience. A variation on the theme are *Heuhotels* (hay hotels), which offer the option of literally sleeping in a barn on a bed of hay. See www.heuhotels.de for details. Camping is also huge, but in summer the most popular sites book out far in advance.

Hostelling International-affiliated hostels (DJH Hostel) have family rooms and activities, but independent hostels tend to have more of a party vibe and don't always welcome children.

For details of family-friendly self-catering and home-swap options, see p768.

Getting Around

Children under 12 or smaller than 1.5m (59 inches) must ride in the back seat in cars (taxis included) and use a car seat or booster appropriate for their weight. Those older than 12 and over 1.5m tall may ride in front.

Train is a great way to get around Germany. Children under 15 travel free if accompanied by at least one parent or grandparent. The only proviso is that names of children aged between six and 14 must be registered on your ticket at the time of purchase. Children under six always travel free and without a ticket.

The superfast ICE trains have compartments for families with small children (*Kleinkindabteil*) that are equipped with tables, stroller storage, an electrical outlet (for warming bottles) and, sometimes, a change table. Book these early.

Seat reservations for families (*Familienreservierung*) cost a flat €8 for two adults and up to three children.

Useful Websites

» **Familienurlaub in Deutschland** (www.familienfreundlich.de) Hotels, tips, route planners and more.

» **German National Tourist Office** (www.germany.travel) Popular family sights and destinations.

» **Urlaub auf dem Bauernhof** (www.bauernhofurlaub.de) Over 5000 farm-stay properties throughout Germany.

regions at a glance

Berlin

Art & Culture ✓✓✓
Nightlife ✓✓✓
History ✓✓✓

Museums & Galleries
From art deco to agriculture, sex to sugar, diamonds to dinosaurs, there is hardly a theme not covered in Berlin's nearly 200 museums, most famously in the tantalising treasures of Museum Island. Artficionados can indulge their passion in countless galleries, from Old Masters to the latest art world hotshots.

Party Till You Drop
Berlin is the spiritual home of the 'lost weekend' and the living heart of the European electronic music scene. Kick off a night on the razzle in a bar or pub, catch tomorrow's headline acts in an indie music club, and then dance till dawn or beyond in clubs helmed by DJ royalty. Those who still can't get enough can choose from a slew of chilled-out after parties.

Historical Sights
In Berlin the past is always present. Strolling around boulevards and neighbourhoods, you'll pass by legendary sights that take you back to the era of Prussian glory, the dark ages of the Third Reich, the tense period of the Cold War and the euphoria of reunification. It's like a 3D textbook, only better and more fun.

p52

Around Berlin

Palaces ✓✓✓
Watery Fun ✓✓
History ✓✓

A Taste of Royalty
Schloss Sanssouci is the jewel among Potsdam's palaces, but the nearby Neues Palais, Marmorpalais and Schloss Cecilienhof – as well as Schloss Branitz near Cottbus – are other fabled and fanciful addresses.

Water World
Tour Potsdam's palaces by boat, take a punt trip to a Sorb village deep in the emerald-green Spreewald or paddle around Brandenburg an der Havel in a kayak or canoe. This region is best experienced from the water.

Momentous Moments
Visit seminal sites of the 20th century, such as Germany's first concentration camp, the palace where Allied leaders decided the country's post-WWII fate, the bridge where spies were exchanged in the Cold War, and a sinister KGB prison.

p118

Saxony

Museums ✓✓✓
Palaces ✓✓
Art & Culture ✓✓

Iconic Collections
It would take days to fully appreciate Dresden's wealth of world-class paintings, porcelain, armour, sculptures and other priceless collections. If time is tight, at least have your mind blown by the whimsical objects in the Green Vault.

Palace Envy
Style, grandeur and artistry combine in Saxony's grand palaces, such as the Elbe-fronting Schloss Pillnitz in Dresden, the moated Moritzburg and the looming Albrechtsburg in Meissen; all dream pads conceived under Saxon king August the Strong.

Artistic Legacies
Saxony's landscapes have for centuries tugged at the hearts of artists like Canaletto and Caspar David Friedrich, while musical heavyweights Bach, Schumann, Mendelssohn-Bartholdy and Wagner have shaped its musical heritage. Walk in their footsteps in Leipzig, Zwickau and Dresden.

p135

Munich

Art & Culture ✓✓✓
Beer ✓✓✓
Sports ✓✓

Classy Canvasses
Feast your eyes on a who's who of creative hotshots over the past 800 years – Dürer to Degas to Dalí – in the triumphal trio of Pinakothek museums housed in spectacular buildings that are artworks in their own right.

Bottoms Up
The Hofbräuhaus may be the world's most famous pub, but you'll find lots of cheer and beer throughout Munich. On balmy nights, there's nothing quite like clinking mugs below the ancient chestnut trees of a classic beer garden.

Sport-Seeing
The Olympiapark has hosted top athletes of the sports world, and not just since the 1972 Olympic Games. Soccer fans will want to make the pilgrimage north to the Allianz Arena, home base of Germany's most famous football team, FC Bayern München.

p177

Bavaria

Churches ✓✓✓
Villages ✓✓
Activities ✓✓✓

Baroque Beauties
If you want to 'go for baroque', you've hit the mother lode in Bavaria. Illusionary effects and contrasts between light and shadow are typical features of the style and its even more exuberant cousin, rococo. The Wieskirche in Steingaden and the Würzburg Residenz are among many resplendent examples.

Medieval Villages
Proving that good things come in small packages, Bavaria's medieval villages are endowed with timeless beauty, palpable romance and a sense of history spilling from every nook and cranny.

Outdoor Fun
Each season offers its own delights – hiking among spring wildflowers, swimming in an Alpine lake warmed by the summer sun, biking among a kaleidoscope of autumn foliage or schussing through deep powder in winter.

p226

Stuttgart & the Black Forest

Food ✓✓✓
Hiking ✓✓✓
Drives ✓✓

Gourmet Haven

Black forest gateau, brook trout, smoked ham, *Maultaschen, Spätzle* – foodies, eat your hearts out in this culinary paradise that also has the greatest density of Michelin-starred chefs in Germany.

Trail Blazing

There's something undeniably artistic in the way the Black Forest presents itself. No matter if it's a short hike to a waterfall or a multiday trek from village to village, you'll be staggering out into a wonderland of natural beauty combined with timeless traditions.

Scenic Drives

Spoiled with a pastorale of fir-cloaked hills, peaceful river valleys, crystalline lakes, dense forests and other equally lyrical landscapes, there's no better way to appreciate the Black Forest's beauty than by careening along its many scenic routes.

p305

Frankfurt & the Southern Rhineland

Wine ✓✓✓
Castles ✓✓✓
City Life ✓✓

Grape Delights

Nope, Germany is not all about beer. Hit the wine taverns or tasting rooms to put some zing in your step with crisp whites and velvety reds in some of Germany's finest growing areas hugging the Rhine and Moselle rivers.

Romantic Castles

Few buildings speak more to the imagination than hulking stone castles, sitting proudly in all their medieval splendour on craggy hilltop perches. From Heidelberg to the Romantic Rhine to the Palatinate, this region delivers them in abundance.

Frankfurt

The business of Frankfurt may be business but this 'Mainhattan' is no buttoned-up metropolis, as you'll quickly discover in its apple-wine taverns, high-class museums and by taking in the stunning skyline from its riverfront promenade.

p369

Cologne & the Northern Rhineland

History ✓✓✓
City Life ✓✓✓
Off-beat ✓✓

Historical Cities

This region is famous for its starring role in history. To appreciate its impact, visit Xanten and Cologne, both hubs of the Roman Empire; Aachen, the capital of Charlemagne's Frankish Reich; and Münster and Osnabrück where treaties ending the epic Thirty Years' War were signed.

Rhenish Style

Breaking for a glass of *Kölsch* between feeling your spirits soar at Cologne's magnificent cathedral, sampling the city's stunning portfolio of museums, checking out its edgy boutiques or taking a spin on the Rhine are all memory makers.

Industrial Inspirations

It takes ingenuity to recycle archaic industrial sites into something exciting. Follow the Ruhrgebiet's Industrial Heritage Trail to see cutting-edge art in a gas tank, rock-climb a blast furnace, sip martinis in a boiler house or listen to Mozart in a compressor hall.

p462

Central Germany

Drives ✓✓
History ✓✓✓
Outdoors ✓✓

Fairy-Tale Drive
Keep an eye out for witches, goblins, dwarfs and 'sleeping beauties' as you follow in the footsteps of the Brothers Grimm, past the misty forests, half-timbered villages and legend-shrouded castles of the Fairy-Tale Road.

Poets & Thinkers
A keystone of German culture, this region gave birth to Martin Luther and the Reformation, inspired Goethe and Schiller to pen their greatest works, launched the Bauhaus design movement and pioneered optical precision technology.

Harz Ramble
Hundreds of miles of forest trails beckon in the Harz Mountains, including the trek up myth-laden Mt Brocken. Stop also in dreamy, half-timbered Quedlinburg, explore 1000-year-old mining history in Goslar and hurtle along on a century-old narrow-gauge steam train.

p525

Lower Saxony & Bremen

Outdoors ✓✓
City Life ✓✓
Gardens ✓✓

Island Walks
Sure, you can walk around an island, but have you ever walked to an island? You can do so – with an experienced guide – across the tidal flat in the Wadden Sea National Park. Your destination? Any of the wind-swept, remote East Frisian Islands.

Hanse Meets Hi-Tech
A major trading town since the days of the Hanseatic League, Bremen now pairs a charming historic centre, dominated by a grand Gothic town hall, with a state-of-the-art container port, science centre, emigration museum and climate-change exhibit.

Glorious Gardens
A touch of Versailles in northern Germany: that's what you'll find at Hanover's Herrenhäuser Gärten, a manicured jumble of gardens accented with Europe's tallest fountain and whimsical art by late French artist Niki de Saint Phalle.

p596

Hamburg & the North

Islands ✓✓
Architecture ✓✓
City Life ✓✓✓

Remote Shores
There's almost something otherworldly about Germany's islands, from glamorous Sylt to down-to-earth Usedom. Hitting the surf, cycling the dunes, exploring windswept tracks and relaxing in a *Strandkorb* (wicker chair) on a white sandy beach are all big draws.

Hanseatic Beauties
Savour the red-brick splendour of charismatic Lübeck, Wismar, Stralsund and Greifswald, all Baltic towns with a pedigree going back to the Hanseatic League but that today are still imbued with a forward- and outward-looking spirit.

Happening Hamburg
In the 'gateway to the world' the sublime (Kunsthalle) mixes with the naughty (the Reeperbahn red-light district), the historic (St Nikolai) with the futuristic (HafenCity), the posh (Alster Lakes) with the raucous (Fischmarkt). Hamburg is sure to inspire, entertain and surprise you in myriad ways.

p644

> Every listing is recommended by our authors, and their favourite places are listed first

> Look out for these icons:

 Our author's top recommendation

 A green or sustainable option

 No payment required

See the Index for a full list of destinations covered in this book.

On the Road

Berlin

📱030 / POP 3.5 MILLION

Best Places to Eat

» Cafe Jacques (p99)
» Horváth (p99)
» Katz Orange (p96)
» Uma (p97)
» restaurant Tim Raue (p97)

Best Places to Stay

» Circus Hotel (p88)
» Michelberger Hotel (p93)
» Mandala Hotel (p92)
» EastSeven Berlin Hostel (p94)
» Motel One Berlin-Alexanderplatz (p89)

Why Go?

Berlin is a bon vivant, passionately feasting on the smorgasbord of life. It's a scene-stealing, head-turning combo of glamour and grit, teeming with top museums and galleries, grand opera and guerrilla clubs, gourmet temples and ethnic snack shacks. Over the past decade, the German capital has become a pillar of the fashion, art, design and music worlds, not just keeping with but setting new trends. A global influx of creatives has turned it into a cauldron of cultural cool on par with New York in the '80s. All this trendiness is a triumph for a city that's long been in the cross hairs of history: Berlin staged a revolution, headquartered fascists, was bombed to bits, ripped in half and finally reunited – and that was just in the 20th century! Must-sees or aimless explorations – this city delivers it all in one exciting and memorable package.

When to Go

Spring and autumn are generally best for visiting Berlin as the weather is the most stable and cultural events of all stripes are in full swing. Summers essentially bring a population exchange as locals leave town for hotter climes and tourists, especially from southern Europe, flock to Berlin to escape the heat. This is the time of outdoor anything: concerts, festivals, beer gardens, parties, beach bars, cinema. Winters are cold and dark and life moves indoors, except during Christmas market season in December.

Get Your Bearings

Key sights like the Reichstag and Brandenburger Tor, the elegant Unter den Linden boulevard and the famous Museumsinsel cluster in the historic city centre – Mitte – which is also home to the maze-like hipster quarter called Scheunenviertel. North of Mitte, charismatic Prenzlauer Berg entices with gorgeous town houses, cosy cafes and a fun flea market, while to the south loom the contemporary high-rises of Potsdamer Platz. Further south, gritty but cool Kreuzberg is party central, as is student-flavoured Friedrichshain east across the Spree River and home to the East Side Gallery stretch of the Berlin Wall. Western Berlin's hub is Charlottenburg, with great shopping and a famous royal palace.

Berlin is a sprawling city split into 12 official *Bezirke* (districts, eg Mitte, Prenzlauer Berg, Kreuzberg), which are subdivided into individual neighbourhoods called *Kieze*.

BERLIN FOR FIRST TIMERS

No one will believe you've been to Berlin if you haven't had your picture snapped against the backdrop of the Brandenburger Tor and taken in the stellar views from the top of the Reichstag dome (reserve ahead; p58). If you only have time for one museum, make it the Pergamon with its pirate's chest of ancient treasures. Pondering the Cold War on a stroll along the East Side Gallery, the longest remaining stretch of Berlin Wall, is an essential activity. Shoppers shouldn't leave without dropping in at the legendary KaDeWe department store. In summer, mingle with locals at a beach bar or in a beer garden. And don't even think about leaving without trying a *Currywurst*, the ultimate Berlin snack.

Top 5: How to Feel Like a Berliner

» Spend an afternoon wandering among the cute shops and cafes of the Bergmannkiez (p78) in Kreuzberg.

» Hire a bike and ride along the smooth tarmac of defunct Tempelhof (p74) airport.

» Get up at 6am to go clubbing at Berghain/Panorama Bar (p108).

» Have drinks or a meal at Defne (p99), Horváth (p99), Cafe Jacques (p99) or any of the other eateries along the idyllic Landwehr canal.

» See the Museumsinsel collections (p65) without the crowds on Thursday, when all five stay open as late as 10pm.

Need to Know

For security reasons, compulsory reservations for visiting the Reichstag must be made online at www.bundestag.de. Book early to secure the most convenient time slots.

Advance Planning

» **Two months** Book online tickets to the Philharmonie, Staatsoper and Sammlung Boros

» **One month** Make online reservations for the Reichstag dome, the Neues Museum and the Pergamonmuseum

» **One week** Reserve a table at trendy or Michelin-starred restaurants, especially for Friday and Saturday nights

Resources

» **Berlin tourist office** www.visitberlin.de

» **Museum guide** www.museumsportal.de

» **Club guide** www.residentadvisor.net

Berlin Highlights

1 Marvel at Nefertiti, the Pergamonaltar, the Ishtar Gate and many more ancient treasures on **Museumsinsel** (p65)

2 Let the sights drift by while sipping a cool drink on the deck of a **river boat** (p84)

3 Check out sexy bods while chilling and bronzing on the **Badeschiff** (p86), a cargo barge turned lifestyle pool

4 Put together the distinctive Berlin look by scouring the local designer boutiques of the **Scheunenviertel** (p114)

5 Get high on the knockout views from the **Reichstag** (p58) roof or the **Fernsehturm** (p67), Germany's tallest structure

6 Hobnob with **Kreuzberg** (p106) hipsters for a night of tabloid-worthy drinking and debauchery

7 Look for traces of the elusive Berlin Wall at the **Gedenkstätte Berliner Mauer** (p68)

8 Spend an afternoon treasure hunting and karaoke crooning in the **Mauerpark** (p76)

9 Get a dose of asphalt-free exercise in the vast **Tiergarten** (p70) park

10 Flash back to Roaring Twenties glamour at **Chamäleon Varieté** (p111)

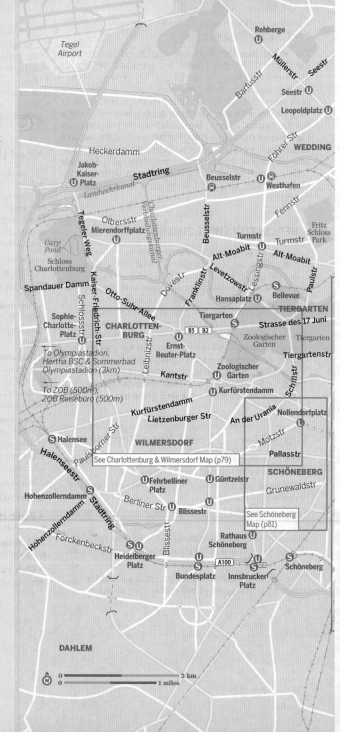

See Prenzlauer Berg Map (p77)

See Mitte Map (p60)

Markstr

Osloer Str

Koloniestr

Schulstr

Bornholmer Str

Bornholmer Str

Wisbyer Str

B109

Berliner Str

Berliner Allee

Nauener Platz

Pankstr

Gesundbrunnen

Schivelbeiner Str

Am Falkplatz

B96a

Wichertstr

Michelangelostr

Jewish cemetery Weissensee

Volkspark Humboldthain

Wedding

PRENZLAUER BERG

Brunnenstr

Schönhauser Allee

Pappelallee

Prenzlauer Allee

Greifswalder Str

Humboldthain

Mauerpark

8

Ernst-Thälmann-Park

Fennstr

Reinickendorfer Str

Husstenstr

Voltastr

Bernauer Str

Kastanienallee

Danziger Str

Greifswalder Str

Sellerstr

Heidestr

Schwartzkopffstr

Gedenkstätte Berliner Mauer

Bernauer Str

7

B2

B96a

Kniprodestr

Volkspark Prenzlauer Berg

SCHEUNENVIERTEL

Senefelderplatz

Landsberger Allee

See Mitte Map (p60)

B96

Invalidenstr

Rosenthaler Platz

Scheunenviertel

Rosa Luxemburg Platz

Torstr

Friedenstr

Volkspark Friedrichshain

Landsberger Allee

Hauptbahnhof

Chamäleon Varieté

4

Weinmeisterstr

Otto-Braun-Str

Mollstr

Petersburger Str

Thaerstr

10

River boats

Friedrichstr

Grunerstr

Schillingstr

Strausberger Platz

Frankfurter Tor

Bundestag

Reichstag

5

Museumsinsel

1

2

Fernsehturm

5

Jannowitzbrücke

Weberwiese

Frankfurter Allee

9

Tiergarten

Unter den Linden

Werderscher Markt

FRIEDRICHSHAIN

Boxhagener Str

Wühlischstr

Potsdamer Platz

Leipziger Str

B1

Spittelmarkt

Stralauer Platz

Ostbahnhof

B96a

Warschauer Str

Warschauer Str

POTSDAMER PLATZ

Kochstr

Oranienstr

Rittersr

Lindenstr

Märkisches Museum

Spree River

B96a

Mühlenstr

Stralauer Allee

Ostkreuz

Potsdamer Str

Wilhelmstr

KREUZBERG

S

B96

Gleisdreieck

Bülowstr

Kulmer Str

Mehringdamm

Moritzplatz

Prinzenstr

Böckler Park

Kreuzberg nightlife

6

B178

Skalitzerstr

Görlitzer Bahnhof

Wiener Str

Reichenberger Str

Görlitzer Park

Schlesisches Tor

Vor dem Schlesischen Tor

Badeschiff

3

Treptower Park

Treptower Park

Gneisenaustr

Yorckstr

Südstern

Urbanstr

Schönleinstr

NEUKÖLLN

Eisenstr

Kreuzbergstr

Bergmannstr

Viktoriapark

Friedhöfe an der Bergmannstrasse

Hermannplatz

Pannierstr

Kolonnenstr

Dudenstr

Platz der Luftbrücke

Columbiadamm

Volkspark Hasenheide

Sonnenallee

B96

Paradestr

Boddinstr

Rathaus Neukölln

Karl-Marx-Str

Papestr

Former Tempelhof Airport

Leinestr

See Kreuzberg & Friedrichshain Map (p72)

Tempelhofer Damm

TEMPELHOF

A100

BRITZ

History

By German standards, Berlin entered onto the stage rather late and puttered along in relative obscurity for centuries. Founded in the 13th century as a trading post, it achieved a modicum of prominence after coming under the rule of the powerful Hohenzollern clan from southern Germany in 1411. It managed to cling to power until the abolition of the monarchy in 1918.

In 1701 Elector Friedrich III was elevated to King Friedrich I, making Berlin a royal residence. The promotion significantly shaped the city, which blossomed under Friedrich I's grandson, Frederick the Great, who sought greatness as much on the battlefield as through building and embracing the ideals of the Enlightenment. The best bits of Unter den Linden date back to his reign, when Berlin blossomed into a cultural centre some even called 'Athens on the Spree'.

As throughout northern Europe, the Industrial Revolution began its march on Berlin in the 19th century, vastly expanding the city's population and spawning a new working class. Berlin boomed politically, economically and culturally, especially after becoming capital of the German Reich

Greater Berlin

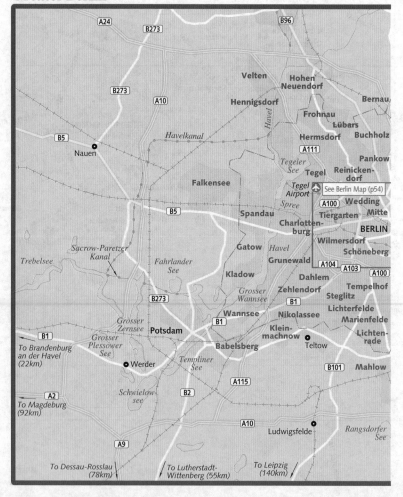

in 1871. By 1900 the population had reached two million.

World War I stifled Berlin's momentum, while the 1920s were marred by instability, corruption and inflation. Berliners responded like there was no tomorrow and made their city as much a den of decadence as a cauldron of creativity. Artists of all stripes flocked to this city of cabaret, Dada and jazz.

Hitler's rise to power put an instant damper on the fun as the dark ages of the Third Reich descended upon the world. Berlin suffered heavy bombing in WWII and a crushing invasion of 1.5 million Soviet soldiers during the final Battle of Berlin in April 1945. Few original Nazi-era sights remain, but memorials and museums keep the horror in focus.

After WWII, Germany fell into the cross hairs of the Cold War; a country divided ideologically and literally by a fortified border and the infamous Berlin Wall, whose construction began in 1961. Just how differently the two Germanys developed is still palpable in Berlin, expressed not only through Wall remnants but through vastly different urban planning and architectural styles.

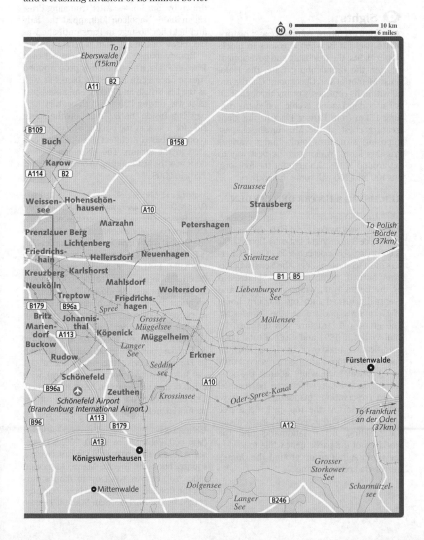

Since reunification, Berlin has again become a hotbed of creativity, with unbridled nightlife, an explosive art scene and booming fashion and design industries. Sure, problems persist – empty city coffers, high unemployment, the delayed Berlin Brandenburg Airport, to name a few – but Berlin's allure to tourists and newcomers from around the world remains unabated. It's a city that dances to its own tune, where individualism triumphs over conformity and brilliant ideas are celebrated and welcome. Few people who live here don't love it. Few people who visit will ever forget it.

Sights

A cocktail of culture, commerce and history, **Mitte** packs it in when it comes to blockbuster sights: the Reichstag and government quarter, the Brandenburg Gate, the Holocaust Memorial and Checkpoint Charlie are all within its confines. Cutting through it all is Unter den Linden, a chic boulevard running 1.5km from Pariser Platz to the giant treasure chest of the Museumsinsel, past imposing structures built under various Prussian kings. Walking is the best way to get around Mitte, although for the footsore, bus 100 and 200 will come in handy.

REICHSTAG & UNTER DEN LINDEN

[FREE] **Reichstag** HISTORIC BUILDING

(Map p60; www.bundestag.de; Platz der Republik 1; 🕐lift ride 8am-midnight, last entry 11pm; 🚌100, [S]Bundestag, [R]Brandenburger Tor) One of Berlin's most iconic buildings, the Reichstag has been burned, bombed, rebuilt, buttressed by the Berlin Wall, wrapped in fabric and eventually turned into the modern home of Germany's parliament, the Bundestag. The grand old structure was designed by Paul Wallot in 1894 and given a total post-reunification makeover by Lord Norman Foster. The famous architect preserved only its historical shell while adding the glistening glass dome, which can be reached by lift (reservations mandatory; see www.bundestag.de). At the top, pick up a free auto-activated audioguide and learn about the building, Berlin landmarks and the workings of the parliament while following the ramp spiralling up around the dome's mirror-clad central funnel.

Brandenburger Tor & Pariser Platz HISTORIC SITE

(Map p60; [S]Brandenburger Tor, [R]Brandenburger Tor) A symbol of division during the Cold War, the landmark Brandenburg Gate now epitomises German reunification and often serves as a photogenic backdrop for festivals, concerts and New Year's Eve parties. Carl Gotthard Langhans found inspiration in the Acropolis in Athens for the elegant triumphal arch, completed in 1791 as the royal city gate. It is crowned by the *Quadriga*, Johann Gottfried Schadow's sculpture of the winged goddess of victory piloting a chariot drawn by four horses. After trouncing Prussia in 1806, Napoleon kidnapped the lady and held her hostage in Paris until she was freed by a gallant Prussian general in 1815.

Brandenburger Tor stands sentinel over **Pariser Platz**, a harmoniously proportioned square once again framed by banks as well as the US, British and French embassies, just as it was during its early-19th-century heyday. Pop inside the DZ Bank on the south side for a look at the outlandish conference room US-based architect Frank Gehry created in the atrium. The US embassy next door was the last building to open on Pariser Platz in 2008.

Holocaust Memorial MEMORIAL

(Map p60; ☎2639 4336; www.stiftung-denkmal.de; Cora-Berliner-Strasse 1; admission free, audioguide €3; 🕐memorial 24hr, information centre 10am-8pm Tue-Sun, last entry 7.15pm Apr-Sep, 6.15pm Oct-Mar; [S]Brandenburger Tor, [R]Brandenburger Tor) The football-field-sized Memorial to the Murdered European Jews (colloquially known as the Holocaust Memorial) by American architect Peter Eisenman consists of 2711 sarcophagi-like concrete columns rising in sombre silence from undulating ground. You're free to access this maze at any point and make your individual journey through it. For context, visit the subterranean **Ort der Information** (information centre), with exhibits that will leave no heart untouched. The entrance is on the eastern side of the memorial, near Cora-Berliner-Strasse.

Bebelplatz MEMORIAL

(Map p60; Bebel Square; 🚌100, 200, [S]Französische Strasse, Hausvogteiplatz) On this treeless square, books by Brecht, Mann, Marx and other 'subversives' went up in flames during the first full-blown public book burning, staged by the Nazi German Student League

BERLIN IN...

One Day

Book ahead for an early time slot on the lift to the **Reichstag** dome, then snap a picture of the **Brandenburger Tor** before stumbling around the **Holocaust Memorial** and admiring the contemporary architecture of **Potsdamer Platz**. Ponder Cold War madness at **Checkpoint Charlie**, then head to **Museumsinsel** for an audience with Queen Nefertiti and the Pergamonaltar. Finish up with a night of mirth and gaiety in the Scheunenviertel.

Two Days

Kick off day two coming to grips with what life was like in divided Berlin at the **Gedenkstätte Berliner Mauer**. Intensify the experience at the **DDR Museum** and on a walk along the **East Side Gallery**. Spend the afternoon soaking up the urban spirit of Kreuzberg with its sassy shops and street art, grab dinner along the canal, drinks around Kottbusser Tor and finish up with a concert at **Lido** or **Magnet**.

Three Days

Day three starts royally at **Schloss Charlottenburg**, followed by pondering the futility of war at the **Kaiser-Wilhelm-Gedächtniskirche** and a spirit-lifting shopping spree along **Kurfürstendamm** and at the **KaDeWe**. Ride the U2 to Prenzlauer Berg and ring in the evening with a cold Pilsner at **Prater** beer garden or pub, then wrap up the day with a leisurely dinner in the neighbourhood.

in 1933. Michael Ullmann's underground installation, Empty Library, beneath a glass pane at the square's centre, poignantly commemorates the event. Surrounding the square is a trio of handsome 18th-century buildings constructed under King Frederick the Great: the Alte Königliche Bibliothek (Old Royal Library; 1780); the Staatsoper Unter den Linden (State Opera; 1743); and the copper-domed St Hedwigskirche (1783). The palatial building opposite Bebelplatz is the 1810 Humboldt Universität, where Marx and Engels studied and the Brothers Grimm and Albert Einstein taught. In 2012 it became one of Germany's 11 'elite universities'. A mighty equestrian statue of King Frederick the Great stands in the median strip of Unter den Linden.

Deutsches Historisches Museum   MUSEUM
(Map p60; ☎203 040; www.dhm.de; Unter den Linden 2; adult/concession €8/4; ⊙10am-6pm; ☺100, 200, ⓡAlexanderplatz, Hackescher Markt) This engaging museum zeroes in on two millennia of German history in all its gore and glory; not in a nutshell but on two floors of a Prussian-era armoury. Check out the Nazi globe, the pain-wracked faces of dying warrior sculptures in the courtyard, and the temporary exhibits in the boldly modern annex designed by IM Pei.

FREE Neue Wache   MEMORIAL
(Map p60; Unter den Linden 4; ⊙10am-6pm; ☺100, 200, ⓢHausvogteiplatz) This neoclassical Schinkel structure from 1818 was originally a Prussian royal guardhouse and is now an antiwar memorial with an austere interior dominated by Käthe Kollwitz's emotional sculpture of a mother cradling her dead soldier son.

FREE Friedrichswerdersche Kirche   MUSEUM
(Map p60; ☎266 424 242; www.smb.museum/fwk; Werderscher Markt; ⊙10am-6pm; ☺100, 200, ⓢHausvogteiplatz) This perkily turreted 1830 ex-church by Karl Friedrich Schinkel now shelters 19th-century German sculpture, including works by such period heavyweights as Johann Gottfried Schadow and Christian Daniel Rauch. Upstairs is an exhibit on Schinkel's life and achievements.

FREE Hitler's Bunker   HISTORIC SITE
(Map p60; cnr In den Ministergärten & Gertrud-Kolmar-Strasse; ⊙24hr; ⓢBrandenburger Tor, ⓡBrandenburger Tor) Berlin was burning and Soviet tanks were advancing relentlessly when Adolf Hitler committed suicide on 30 April 1945 alongside Eva Braun, his longtime companion, hours after their marriage.

Mitte

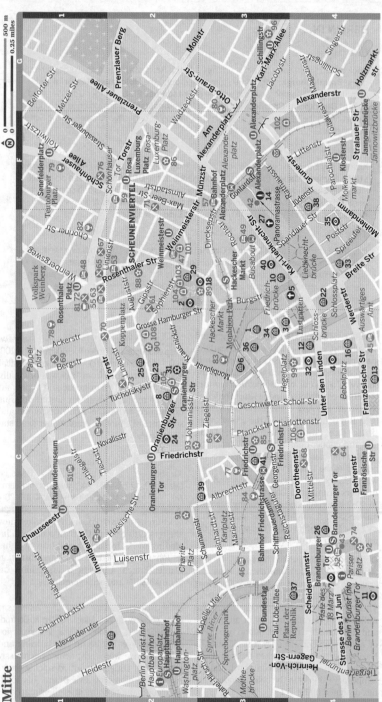

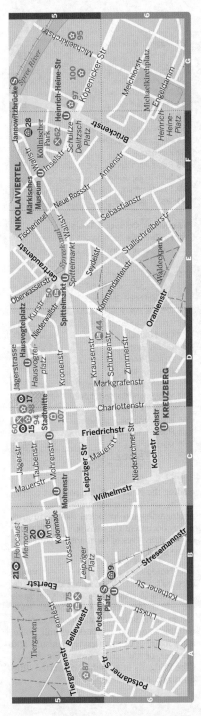

Today, a parking lot covers the site, revealing its dark history only via an information panel with a diagram of the vast bunker network, technical data on its construction and information on its post-WWII history. The interior was blown up and sealed off by the Soviets in 1947. During the construction of the adjacent apartment building in the 1980s, the remaining space was filled in with sand, gravel and detritus.

Madame Tussauds   MUSEUM
(Map p60; ☎01805-545 800; www.madame tussauds.com/berlin; Unter den Linden 74; adult/child €23/16; ☺10am-7pm, last admission 6pm; ▣100, Ⓢ Brandenburger Tor, Ⓡ Brandenburger Tor) No celebrity in town to snare your stare? Don't fret: at this legendary wax museum, Lady Gaga, Obama and Marilyn stand still – very still – for you to snap their picture. Cheesy? Yep. Fun? You bet! Best of all, you're free to touch all 82 figures, give them a kiss or whatever other silliness you can dream up. Check the website for discounts.

FRIEDRICHSTRASSE

FREE **Checkpoint Charlie**   HISTORIC SITE
(Map p72; cnr Zimmerstrasse & Friedrichstrasse; ☺24hr; Ⓢ Kochstrasse, Stadtmitte) Checkpoint Charlie was the principal gateway for foreigners and diplomats between the two Berlins from 1961 to 1990. Unfortunately, this potent symbol of the Cold War has become a tacky tourist trap. A free open-air exhibit that illustrates milestones in post-WWII history is one redeeming aspect and the Berlin Wall Panorama, a monumental 360-degree painting depicting Berlin during its division, should also have opened by the time you read this.

Gendarmenmarkt   SQUARE
(Map p60; ☺24hr; Ⓢ Französische Strasse, Stadtmitte) Berlin's most graceful square is bookended by the domed German and French cathedrals and punctuated by the grandly porticoed Konzerthaus Berlin (p111). It was named for the *Gens d'Armes*, an 18th-century Prussian regiment consisting of French Huguenot immigrants whose story is chronicled in a museum inside the French cathedral. Climb the tower here for grand views of historic Berlin.

Mauermuseum   MUSEUM
(Haus am Checkpoint Charlie; Map p72; ☎253 7250; www.mauermuseum.de; Friedrichstrasse 43-45; adult/concession €12.50/9.50; ☺9am-10pm; Ⓢ Kochstrasse, Stadtmitte) The Cold War years,

Mitte

Sights

1 Alte Nationalgalerie ... D3
2 Alter Jüdischer Friedhof ... E2
3 Altes Museum ... D3
Anne Frank Zentrum ... (see 29)
4 Bebelplatz ... D4
5 Berliner Dom ... E4
6 Bodemuseum ... D3
7 Brandenburger Tor & Pariser Platz ... B4
8 C/O Berlin ... D2
9 Dalí – Die Ausstellung ... B6
10 DDR Museum ... E3
11 Denkmal für die im Nationalsozialismus verfolgten Homosexuellen ... B4
12 Deutsches Historisches Museum ... D4
13 Emil Nolde Museum ... D4
14 Fernsehturm ... F3
15 Friedrichstadtpassagen ... C5
16 Friedrichswerdersche Kirche ... D4
Gedenkstätte Stille Helden ... (see 29)
17 Gendarmenmarkt ... D5
18 Hackesche Höfe ... E3
19 Hamburger Bahnhof – Museum für Gegenwart ... A2
20 Hitler's Bunker ... B5
21 Holocaust Memorial ... B5
22 Humboldt-Box ... E4
23 Jüdische Mädchenschule ... D2
24 Kunsthaus Tacheles ... C2
25 KW Institute for Contemporary Art ... D2
26 Madame Tussauds ... B4
27 Marienkirche ... E3
28 Märkisches Museum ... F5
29 Museum Blindenwerkstatt Otto Weidt ... E2
30 Museum für Naturkunde ... B1
31 Neue Synagoge ... D2
32 Neue Wache ... D4
33 Neuer Marstall ... E4
34 Neues Museum ... D3
35 Nikolaiviertel ... E4
36 Pergamonmuseum ... D3
37 Reichstag ... B4
38 Rotes Rathaus ... F4
39 Sammlung Boros ... C3
40 Sealife Berlin ... E3
41 Tränenpalast ... C3

Activities, Courses & Tours

42 Fat Tire Bike Tours ... F3
43 Fritz Music Tours ... B4

Sleeping

44 Adina Apartment Hotel Berlin Checkpoint Charlie ... D5
45 Arcotel John F ... D4
46 Arte Luise Kunsthotel ... B3
47 Casa Camper ... E2
48 Circus Hostel ... E1
Circus Hotel ... (see 63)
49 Citystay Hostel ... E3
50 Cosmo Hotel Berlin ... E5
51 Honigmond Garden Hotel ... C1
52 Hotel Adlon Kempinski ... B4
53 Hotel Amano ... E2
54 Hotel Honigmond ... C1
55 Mani Hotel ... E1
56 Miniloft Berlin ... B1

especially the history and horror of the Berlin Wall, are engagingly documented in this privately run tourist magnet at Checkpoint Charlie. The best bits are about ingenious escapes to the West in hot-air balloons, tunnels, concealed car compartments and even a one-man submarine.

[FREE] Tränenpalast MUSEUM

(Map p60; ☎4677 7790; www.hdg.de; Reichstagsufer 17; ⏰9am-7pm Tue-Fri, 10am-6pm Sat & Sun; [S]Friedrichstrasse, 🚌100) During the Cold War, tears flowed copiously in this glass-and-steel border-crossing pavilion where East Germans had to bid adieu to family visiting from West Germany – hence its moniker, 'Palace of Tears'. This exhibit uses original objects (including the claustrophobic passport control booths and a weapons auto-firing system), photographs and historical footage to grippingly document the division's social impact on the daily lives of Germans on both sides of the border.

Emil Nolde Museum MUSEUM

(Map p60; ☎4000 4690; www.nolde-stiftung.de; Jägerstrasse 55; adult/concession €8/3, audioguide €4; ⏰10am-7pm; [S]Französische Strasse, Hausvogteiplatz) Admire a rotating selection of paintings and watercolours by Emil Nolde, a key figure of German expressionism – and member of the artist group *Die Brücke* (The Bridge) – in a brightly converted 19th-century bank building.

57	Motel One Berlin-Alexanderplatz	F3
58	Ritz-Carlton Berlin	A5
	The Dude	(see 62)
	The Weinmeister	(see 47)
59	Wombat's City Hostel Berlin	F2

🍴 Eating

60	Augustiner am Gendarmenmarkt	C5
61	Barcomi's Deli	E2
62	Brooklyn Beef Club	F5
63	Côcô	E1
64	Cookies Cream	C4
65	Fleischerei Imbiss	E1
66	Grill Royal	C3
67	Hartweizen	E1
68	Ishin – Mittelstrasse	C4
69	Katz Orange	D1
70	Kopps	D1
71	Monsieur Vuong	F2
	Rosenburger	(see 72)
72	Rosenthaler Grill- und Schlemmerbuffet	E1
73	Schwarzwaldstuben	D2
74	Uma	B4
75	Vapiano	B5
76	White Trash Fast Food	F1

🍷 Drinking

77	Berliner Republik	C3
78	Buck and Breck	D1
79	Chantals House of Shame	F1
	Curtain Club	(see 58)
	Drayton Bar	(see 64)
80	GMF	G3
81	Mein Haus am See	E1
82	Neue Odessa Bar	E1
83	Strandbar Mitte	D3
84	Tausend	C3

✪ Entertainment

85	Admiralspalast	C3
86	Babylon	F2
87	Berliner Philharmonie	A5
88	B-Flat	E2
89	Chamäleon Varieté	E3
90	Clärchens Ballhaus	D2
	Cookies	(see 64)
91	Deutsches Theater	B2
92	Felix	B4
93	Friedrichstadtpalast	C2
94	Hochschule für Musik Hanns Eisler	C5
	Kaffee Burger	(see 59)
95	Kater Holzig	G5
96	Kino International	G3
97	KitKatClub	G5
98	Konzerthaus Berlin	C5
99	Maxim Gorki Theater	D4
100	Tresor	G5
	Weekend	(see 80)

🛍 Shopping

101	1. Absinth Depot Berlin	E2
102	Alexa	F3
103	Ampelmann Galerie	E2
104	Berlin Fashion Network	E2
105	Bonbonmacherei	D2
106	Dussmann – Das Kulturkaufhaus	C4
107	Fassbender & Rausch	C5
108	Galerie Eigen+Art	D2

[FREE] **Stasi Ausstellung** MUSEUM

(Map p72; ☎2324 7951; www.bstu.bund.de; Zimmerstrasse 90; 🕑10am-6pm; [S]Kochstrasse, Stadtmitte) How was the GDR's Ministry for State Security (Stasi) structured? How were people spied on in the GDR and by whom? How did the Stasi affect people's daily lives when it came to travel, worshipping, education or even sports? Using case studies, original objects and documents and informative panelling, this compact exhibit reveals the all-out zeal of the Stasi when it came to controlling, manipulating and repressing its own people.

SCHEUNENVIERTEL

One of Berlin's oldest urban villages, the Scheunenviertel, or Barn Quarter, packs bunches of charisma into its relatively compact frame. Its greatest charms reveal themselves in the labyrinth of quiet lanes fanning out from its main drags, Oranienburger Strasse and Rosenthaler Strasse. Embark on an aimless wander and you'll constantly stumble upon the unexpected: here, an idyllic courtyard or bleeding-edge art gallery; there, a fashion-forward boutique, shabby-chic bar or glam belle époque ballroom. Since reunification, the Scheunenviertel has also reprised its historic role as Berlin's main Jewish quarter.

DON'T MISS

TRENDY TORSTRASSE

Though loud, ho-hum and heavily trafficked, Torstrasse is booming, and not just since Brangelina were rumoured to have bought a flat nearby. With surprising speed, this main thoroughfare has turned into a funkytown strip where trendy eats pop up with the frequency of fruit-fly births, gritty-glam bars pack in night crawlers and indie boutiques lure the fashion savvy.

FREE **Hackesche Höfe**   HISTORIC SITE
(Map p60; ☎2809 8010; www.hackesche-hoefe.com; Rosenthaler Strasse 40/41, Sophienstrasse 6; ☒M1, ☒Hackescher Markt) The Hackesche Höfe is the largest and most famous of the interlinked courtyard complexes peppered throughout the Scheunenviertel. Take your sweet time pottering around this tangle of cafes, galleries, boutiques and entertainment venues. Court I, festooned with art nouveau tiles, is the prettiest.

Neue Synagoge   SYNAGOGUE
(Map p60; ☎8802 8300; www.cjudaicum.de; Oranienburger Strasse 28-30; adult/concession €3/2; ☺10am-8pm Sun & Mon, to 6pm Tue-Thu, to 5pm Fri, reduced hr Nov-Apr; ☒Oranienburger Tor, ☒Oranienburger Strasse) The sparkling gilded dome of the New Synagogue is the most visible symbol of Berlin's revitalised Jewish community. The 1866 original was Germany's largest synagogue but its modern incarnation is not so much a house of worship as a place of remembrance called Centrum

Judaicum. Climb the dome to gaze out over the Scheunenviertel's rooftops.

FREE **Jüdische Mädchenschule**   HISTORIC BUILDING
(Map p60; www.maedchenschule.org; Auguststrasse 11-13; ☺vary; ☒Oranienburger Tor, ☒M1, ☒Oranienburger Strasse) After languishing for years, the grand 1920s' former Jewish girls' school reopened in early 2012 as the new home of three renowned Berlin galleries – Eigen+Art, Camera Work and Michael Fuchs – and three eateries, including a deli, a kosher restaurant and the elegant Pauly Saal. Camera Work also operates Museum The Kennedys on the 2nd floor.

KW Institute for Contemporary Art   GALLERY
(Map p60; ☎243 4590; www.kw-berlin.de; Auguststrasse 69; adult/concession €6/4; ☺noon-7pm Tue, Wed & Fri-Sun, to 9pm Thu; ☒Oranienburger Strasse, ☒M1, ☒Oranienburger Tor) In an old margarine factory, nonprofit KW helped chart the fate of the Scheunenviertel as Berlin's original post-Wall art district and still stages shows reflecting the latest – and often radical – trends in contemporary art. Its founder, Klaus Biesenbach, was also the engine behind the **Berlin Biennale** art fair, inaugurated in 1990. The courtyard **Café Bravo** makes for a stylish coffee break.

C/O Berlin   GALLERY
(Map p60; ☎2844 4160; www.co-berlin.info; Oranienburger Strasse 35/36; ☺11am-8pm; ☒Oranienburger Tor, ☒M1, ☒Oranienburger Strasse) It's always worth checking out the latest photography exhibit at C/O, a private gal-

TICKETS TO SAVINGS

If you're on a budget, various ticket deals and passes can help you stretch your euros further. The museum clusters on Museumsinsel and the Kulturforum offer *Bereichskarten* (area tickets) that are good for same-day admission to all permanent collections in that particular area. An even better deal for the culturally obsessed, though, is the **Berlin Museum Pass** (www.visitberlin.de; adult/concession €19/9.50), which buys admission to the permanent exhibits of about 60 museums for three consecutive days, including top draws like the Pergamonmuseum. It's available at Berlin tourist offices and participating museums. The tourist offices also sell the **Berlin Welcome Card** (www.visitberlin.de; 48/72hr €17.90/23.90, 48hr incl Potsdam & up to 3 children under 15yr €19.90, 72hr incl Museuminsel €34), which entitles you to unlimited public transport and up to 50% discount to 200 sights, attractions and tours for periods of two, three or five days. It's also sold at U-Bahn and S-Bahn ticket-vending machines, BVG offices and many hotels. The **CityTourCard** (www.citytourcard.com; 48hr/72hr/5 days €16.90/22.90/29.90), which is a bit cheaper but offers fewer discounts, operates on a similar scheme.

TRACES OF JEWISH LIFE IN THE SCHEUNENVIERTEL

Jewish history is omnipresent in the Scheunenviertel, Berlin's traditional Jewish quarter. The great Enlightenment philosopher Moses Mendelssohn was among the 12,000 people buried in Alter Jüdischer Friedhof (Map p60; Grosse Hamburger Strasse; 🚊M1, 🚉Hackescher Markt), the city's oldest Jewish cemetery. The unrenovated Haus Scharzenberg, next to the Hackesche Höfe, harbours a trio of small exhibits dealing with the subject of Jewish persecution under the Nazis: the Museum Blindenwerkstatt Otto Weidt (Map p60; ☎2859 9407; www.museum-blindenwerkstatt.de; Rosenthaler Strasse 39; admission free; ⊙10am-8pm; 🚉Hackescher Markt, Weinmeisterstrasse) documents how broom and brush maker Otto Weidt saved many of his blind and deaf Jewish workers from the Nazis; the Anne Frank Zentrum (Map p60; ☎288 865 610; www.annefrank.de; Rosenthaler Strasse 39; adult/concession/child €5/2.50/free; ⊙10am-6pm Tue-Sun; 🚇Weinmeisterstrasse, 🚉Hackescher Markt) uses artefacts and photographs to tell the extraordinary story of the famous German-Jewish girl who died at Buchenwald concentration camp; and the Gedenkstätte Stille Helden (Silent Heroes Memorial Exhibit; Map p60; ☎2345 7919; www.gedenkstaette-stille-helden.de; Rosenthaler Strasse 41; ⊙10am-8pm) zeroes in on ordinary Germans who found the courage to hide and help their Jewish neighbours.

Also keep your eyes on the ground to spot small brass paving stones engraved with names in the pavement outside house entrances. Part of a nationwide project initiated by Berlin-born artist Gunter Demnig, these so-called **Stolpersteine** (stumbling blocks) are essentially mini-memorials to the people (usually Jews) who lived in the building before being killed by the Nazis.

lery that has featured such top dogs of the genre as Robert Mapplethorpe and Annie Leibovitz. After years in the palatial late-19th-century Postfuhramt (postal station) on Oranienburger Strasse, it was facing eviction by the building's latest investors at the time of writing. However, a new space may already have been found across the street in Monbijoupark. See the website for updates.

Kunsthaus Tacheles   LANDMARK
(Map p60; Oranienburger Strasse 54-56; 🚇Oranienburger Tor, 🚉Oranienburger Strasse) After the fall of the Wall, this graffiti-slathered art squat became a permanent fixture on Oranienburger Strasse, drawing locals and tourist to its galleries, cultural venues, bizarre sculptures and beer garden. Although over time it lost much of its anarchic edge, it was still one of the few bastions of alternative spirit in this heavily gentrified area. Now the Tacheles too has fallen victim to development. Things started going downhill in 1998 when the land was sold to property investors. The group went bankrupt and so the creditor bank decided to recoup its losses by auctioning off the plot. Initial attempts to evict the artists and clear the space in the summer of 2010 failed, in part because of backing by the Berlin Senate. But in mid-2012, after years of a legal tug of war, the last of the artists left the building. The structure

itself enjoys protected status, but its future and that of the empty land surrounding it remains uncertain.

MUSEUMSINSEL

At Museumsinsel (Museum Island) you can walk through ancient Babylon, meet an Egyptian queen, clamber up a Greek altar or be mesmerised by Monet's water lilies. The island is Berlin's most important treasure trove of 600,000 years of art, artefacts, sculpture and architecture spread across five museums. A Unesco World Heritage Site since 1999, the complex is undergoing a major update, masterminded by British architect David Chipperfield. It will link four of the five museums along a subterranean 'Archaeological Promenade'. At the time of writing, construction had also begun on the colonnaded James-Simon-Galerie, the future foyer and main entrance. For details, see www.museumsinsel-berlin.de.

Pergamonmuseum   MUSEUM
(Map p60; ☎266 424 242; www.smb.museum; Am Kupfergraben 5; adult/concession €8/4; ⊙10am-6pm Fri-Wed, to 8pm Thu; 🚌100; 🚉Hackescher Markt, Friedrichstrasse) Berlin's top tourist attraction, the Pergamonmuseum is an Aladdin's cave of treasures that opens a fascinating window onto the ancient world. Completed in 1920, the palatial three-wing

BERLIN SIGHTS

MUSEUM ISLAND DAY PASS

If you're going to see more than one Museumsinsel collection, it pays to get a day pass valid for one-time admission at all five for €14 (concession €7).

complex presents a rich feast of classical sculpture and monumental architecture from Greece, Rome, Babylon and the Middle East. Most of it was excavated and shipped to Berlin by German archaeologists at the turn of the 20th century. Budget at least two hours and make use of the excellent free audioguide. Also note some sections may be closed while the museum is being renovated.

The Pergamon unites three major collections, each with its own signature sights. The undisputed highlight of the Antiken-sammlung (Collection of Classical Antiquities) is the Pergamonaltar (165 BC). The pedestal of this massive marble shrine was once ringed by a sculpted frieze showing the gods locked in epic battle with the giants; remaining sections of the frieze have been reassembled on the exhibit hall's walls. The figures' anatomical detail, their emotional intensity and dramatic composition show Hellenic art at its finest. The actual sacrificial altar is at the top of the steep staircase in a colonnaded courtyard where another frieze depicts episodes from the life of Telephos, Pergamon's mythical founder.

The door to the right of the altar leads to the 17m-high Market Gate of Miletus (2nd century AD). Merchants and customers once flooded through here into the bustling market square of the wealthy Roman trading town in modern-day Turkey.

Step through the gate and travel back 800 years to yet another culture and civilisation: Babylon during the reign of King Nebuchadnezzar II. You're now in the Vorderasiatisches Museum (Museum of Near Eastern Antiquities), where it's impossible not to be awed by the reconstructed Ishtar Gate, the Processional Way leading up to it and the facade of the royal throne hall. All are sheathed in radiant blue glazed bricks and adorned with ochre reliefs of strutting lions, bulls and dragons representing Babylonian gods.

Upstairs in the Museum für Islamische Kunst (Museum of Islamic Art), top billing goes to the facade of the fortress-like,

8th-century Caliph's Palace from Mshatta in today's Jordan and to the 17th-century Aleppo Room from the house of a Christian merchant in Syria, with its richly painted, wood-panelled walls. Look closely around the central door to make out such biblical scenes as *The Last Supper* amid all the floral ornamentation.

Neues Museum   MUSEUM
(New Museum; Map p60; ✆266 424 242; www.smb. museum; Bodestrasse 1-3; adult/concession €10/5; ⏱10am-6pm Sun-Wed, to 8pm Thu-Sat; ▣100, 200, ▣Hackescher Markt) David Chipperfield's reconstruction of the bombed-out New Museum is the new home of the show-stopping Ägyptisches Museum (Egyptian Museum) and the equally enthralling Museum für Vor- und Frühgeschichtliche (Museum of Pre- and Early History). This is where you come to marvel at such unique treasures as the famous bust of 3330-year-old – yet timelessly beautiful – Queen Nefertiti; the magical Berlin Gold Hat, a tall cone elaborately swathed in bands of astrological symbols; and jewellery, weapons, and silver and gold from ancient Troy.

The building itself is a stunner in its own right. Like a giant jigsaw puzzle, Chipperfield incorporated every original shard, scrap and brick he could find into the new structure. This brilliant blend of historic and modern creates a dynamic composition of massive stairwells, intimate domed rooms, muralled halls and high-ceilinged spaces.

Because of demand, admission is by timed ticket only. To ensure admission and to cut waiting times, get advance tickets online.

Altes Museum   MUSEUM
(Old Museum; Map p60; ✆266 424 242; www.smb. museum; Am Lustgarten; adult/concession €8/4; ⏱10am-6pm Fri-Wed, to 8pm Thu; ▣100, 200, ▣Friedrichstrasse) A curtain of fluted columns gives way to the Pantheon-inspired rotunda of the grand, neoclassical Old Museum, which harbours a prized antiquities collection. In the downstairs galleries, sculptures, vases, tomb reliefs and jewellery shed light on various facets of life in ancient Greece, while upstairs the focus is on the Etruscans and Romans. Top draws include the *Praying Boy* bronze sculpture, Roman silver vessels and portraits of Caesar and Cleopatra.

Alte Nationalgalerie   MUSEUM
(Old National Gallery; Map p60; ✆266 424 242; www.smb.museum; Bodestrasse 1-3; adult/concession €8/4; ⏱10am-6pm Fri-Wed, to 10pm Thu;

100, 200, (Hackescher Markt) The Greek temple–style Old National Gallery is a three-storey showcase of top-notch 19th-century European art. To get a sense of the period's virtuosity, pay special attention to Franz Krüger and Adolf Menzel's canvases glorifying Prussia and to the moody landscapes by Romantic heart-throb, Caspar David Friedrich. There's also a sprinkling of French Impressionists in case you're keen on seeing yet another version of Monet's *Waterlilies*.

Bodemuseum
MUSEUM

(Map p60; 266 424 242; www.smb.museum; Monbijoubrücke; adult/concession €8/4; 10am-6pm Tue, Wed & Fri-Sun, to 10pm Thu; (Hackescher Markt) On the northern tip of Museumsinsel, this palatial edifice by Ernst von Ihne houses European sculpture from the Middle Ages to the 18th century, including key works by Tilmann Riemenschneider, Donatello, Giovanni Pisano and Ignaz Günther. Other rooms harbour a huge coin collection and Byzantine art, including elaborate sarcophagi, ivory carvings and mosaic icons.

Berliner Dom
CHURCH

(Berlin Cathedral; Map p60; 2026 9110; www.berlinerdom.de; Am Lustgarten; adult/concession €7/4; 9am-8pm Mon-Sat, noon-8pm Sun Apr-Sep, to 7pm Oct-Mar; 100, 200, (Hackescher Markt) Pompous yet majestic, the Italian Renaissance–style former royal court church (1905) does triple duty as house of worship, museum and concert hall. Inside, it's gilt to the hilt and outfitted with a lavish marble-and-onyx altar, a 7269-pipe Sauer organ and elaborate royal sarcophagi.

Climb the 267 steps to the gallery for glorious city views.

ALEXANDERPLATZ & AROUND
Sooner or later you will likely come through Alexanderplatz, eastern Berlin's main commercial hub. 'Alex' for short, it was named in honour of Tsar Alexander I on his 1805 visit to Berlin. Despite post-reunification attempts to temper the 1960s socialist look, Alexanderplatz remains an amorphous beast, cluttered with stores, a hotel, a fountain, a monument and a large railway station, and sliced up by roads and tram tracks. Sitting a bit off to the side is the mega-mall Alexa.

Fernsehturm
TOWER

(Map p60; ww.tv-turm.de; Panoramastrasse 1a; adult/concession €11/7, VIP €19.50/11.50; 9am-midnight Mar-Oct, from 10am Nov-Feb; 100, 200, (S)Alexanderplatz, (Alexanderplatz) Germany's tallest structure, the 368m-high TV Tower is as iconic to Berlin as the Eiffel Tower is to Paris. Come early to beat the queue for the lift to the panorama level at 203m, where views are unbeatable on clear days. Pinpoint city landmarks from here or the upstairs cafe, which makes one revolution every 30 minutes. VIP ticket holders can jump the queue. Built in 1969, the tower was supposed to demonstrate the GDR's engineering prowess but ended up being a bit of a laughing stock when it turned out that, when hit by the sun, the steel sphere below the antenna produced the reflection of a giant cross. West Berliners gleefully dubbed the phenomenon 'the Pope's revenge'.

BERLIN CITY PALACE 2.0

Starting in 2014, Germany's most ambitious, costly and controversial cultural construction project will kick off on Schlossplatz, across from Museumsinsel: the rebuilding of the Berliner Stadtschloss (Berlin City Palace; Schlossplatz) that stood in this spot for nearly 500 years. The East German government demolished the barely war-damaged structure in 1951 for ideological reasons and replaced it with an asbestos-riddled multipurpose hall called Palace of the Republic, which itself met the wrecking ball in 2008. The future doppelganger palace will have a historical facade but a modern interior that will house a cultural centre called the Humboldtforum. The oddly shaped building overlooking the site, called the Humboldt-Box (Map p60; 0180 503 0707; www.humboldt-box.com; Schlossplatz; adult/concession €4/2.50; 10am-8pm; 100, 200, (Alexanderplatz, Hackescher Markt), contains teasers from each future resident: the Ethnological Museum, the Museum of Asian Art and the Central Library, along with an amazingly detailed model of the historic city centre. Head upstairs to the cafe terrace for great views of the Berlin Dom and Altes Museum as well as the future construction site.

DDR Museum
MUSEUM

(GDR Museum; Map p60; ☑847 123 731; www.ddr -museum.de; Karl-Liebknecht-Strasse 1; adult/con-cession €6/4; ⊙10am-8pm Sun-Fri, to 10pm Sat; ☐100, 200, ☒Hackescher Markt) The touchy-feely GDR Museum does a delightful job at pulling back the iron curtain on an extinct society. You'll learn that in East Germany, kids were put through collective potty train-ing, engineers earned little more than farm-ers and everyone, it seems, went on nudist holidays. The more sinister sides of GDR life are also addressed, including the chronic supply shortages and Stasi surveillance.

Marienkirche
CHURCH

(Map p60; www.marienkirche-berlin.de; Karl-Lieb-knecht-Strasse 8; ⊙10am-6pm; ☐100,200,☒Hack-escher Markt, Alexanderplatz) This 13th-century Gothic brick gem is one of Berlin's oldest sur-viving churches. A vestibule festooned with a (badly faded) *Dance of Death* fresco cre-ated after the plague of 1486 leads to a fairly plain-Jane interior jazzed up with elaborate epitaphs and a baroque alabaster pulpit by star sculptor Andreas Schlüter. Outside, the epic Neptunbrunnen (Neptune Fountain, 1891) features frolicking buxom beauties meant to represent major rivers.

Märkisches Museum
MUSEUM

(Map p60; www.stadtmuseum.de; Am Köllnischen Park 5; adult/concession €5/3; ⊙10am-6pm Tue-Sun; ☒Märkisches Museum) Berlin's old-school history museum is a rewarding stop for any-one keen on learning how the tiny trading village of Berlin-Cölln evolved into today's metropolis. Official documents, weapons, sculptures and objects from daily life are thematically arranged, often in opulent his-toric rooms such as the Gothic chapel and the Great Hall.

Sealife Berlin
AQUARIUM

(Map p60; www.visitsealife.com; Spandauer Strasse 3; adult/child €17.50/12.50; ⊙10am-7pm, last ad-mission 6pm; ☐100, 200, ☒Hackescher Markt, Alexanderplatz) Sharks dart, moray eels lurk and spider crabs skuttle in this small but entertaining aquarium where other crowd favourites include smile-inducing seahorses, ethereal jellyfish and Ophira the Octopus. Visits conclude with a slow lift ride through the Aquadom, a 16m-tall cylindrical tropical fish tank that can be previewed for free from the lobby of the Radisson Blu Hotel.

Nikolaiviertel
NEIGHBOURHOOD

(Map p60; btwn Rathausstrasse, Breite Strasse, Spandauer Strasse & Mühlendamm; ☒Kloster-strasse) The twee Nicholas Quarter may look medieval but don't be fooled: like leg warm-ers and leotards it's a product of the 1980s, built by the GDR government to celebrate Berlin's 750th birthday. The maze of cobbled lanes, the 1230 Nikolaikirche and a handful of small museums are worth a quick look.

Rotes Rathaus
HISTORIC BUILDING

(Map p60; Rathausstrasse 15; ⊙closed to the public; ☒Alexanderplatz, Klosterstrasse, ☒Alexanderplatz) The hulking 1860 Red Town Hall is the office of Berlin's Senate and governing mayor. The moniker 'red', by the way, was inspired by the colour of its bricks and not (necessarily) the political leanings of its occupants.

HAUPTBAHNHOF TO NORDBAHNHOF

TOP CHOICE **Gedenkstätte**

Berliner Mauer
MEMORIAL

(Map p77; ☑467 986 666; www.berliner-mauer -gedenkstaette.de; Bernauer Strasse btwn Gar-tenstrasse & Brunnenstrasse; admission free; ⊙9.30am-7pm Apr-Oct, to 6pm Nov-Mar, open-air exhibit 24hr; ☒Nordbahnhof) The Berlin Wall Memorial is the central memorial site of German division. It incorporates a stretch of the original wall, along with vestiges of the border installations, escape tunnels, a chap-el and a monument. This is the only place where you can see how all the elements of the wall and the death strip fit together and how the border was enlarged and perfected over time. For a great overview of the en-tire 1km-long memorial grounds, climb the tower of the Documentation Centre near Ackerstrasse. Multimedia stations, 'archaeo-logical windows' and markers sprinkled throughout the memorial provide detailed background.

Hamburger Bahnhof – Museum für Gegenwart
GALLERY

(Map p60; ☑266 424 242; www.hamburgerbah-nhof.de; Invalidenstrasse 50-51; adult/concession €8/4; ⊙10am-6pm Tue-Fri, 11am-8pm Sat, 11am-6pm Sun; ☒Hauptbahnhof, ☒Hauptbahnhof) Berlin's main contemporary-art museum opened in 1996 in an old railway station, where the loft and grandeur are a great backdrop for the Aladdin's cave of paintings, installations, sculptures and video art. Ex-hibits span the arc of post-1950 artistic en-deavours – conceptual art, pop art, minimal art, fluxus – and include seminal works by key players like Andy Warhol, Cy Twombly, Joseph Beuys and Robert Rauschenberg.

Sammlung Boros GALLERY
(Map p60; ☎2759 4065; www.sammlung-boros.de; Reinhardtstrasse 20; adult/concession €10/6; ⏰2-6pm Fri, 10am-6pm Sat & Sun; [S]Oranienburger Tor, Friedrichstrasse, 🚋M1, 🚇Friedrichstrasse) The vibe of war still hangs over the 80 rooms of this Nazi-era bunker turned shining beacon of art thanks to Christian Boros' stellar collection of artists currently writing history – Olafur Eliasson, Damien Hirst, Sarah Lucas and Wolfgang Tilmanns among them. Entry is by guided tour (also in English) only. Book online as early as possible.

Museum für Naturkunde MUSEUM
(Museum of Natural History; Map p60; ☎2093 8591; www.naturkundemuseum-berlin.de; Invalidenstrasse 43; adult/concession €6/3.50, incl audioguide; ⏰9.30am-6pm Tue-Fri, 10am-6pm Sat & Sun; [S]Naturkundemuseum) Fossils and minerals don't quicken your pulse? Well, how about the world's largest mounted dino? The 12m-high *Brachiosaurus branchai* is joined by a dozen other Jurassic buddies, an ultrarare archaeopteryx and, soon, the world's most famous dead polar bear, Knut, ex-resident of the Berlin Zoo. Other surprises include massively magnified insect models and a spooky but artistically illuminated 'wet collection' with over a million ethanol-preserved animals.

POTSDAMER PLATZ & TIERGARTEN

Berlin's newest quarter, Potsdamer Platz was built on terrain once bifurcated by the Berlin Wall and is essentially a showcase of urban renewal. Some of the world's finest architects, including Renzo Piano, Richard Rodgers and Helmut Jahn, collaborated on this modern reinterpretation of the historic square, which had the vibrancy of New York's Times Square until WWII sucked all life out of the area.

The new Potsdamer Platz is divided into three slices: **DaimlerCity** with a large mall, public art and high-profile entertainment venues; the flashy **Sony Center** (Map p72) anchored by a plaza dramatically canopied by a tent-like glass roof; and the comparatively subdued **Beisheim Center**, which was inspired by American skyscraper design.

A visit to Potsdamer Platz is easily combined with the **Kulturforum** (Chamber Music Hall; Map p72), a cluster of world-class art museums and concert halls, including the eye-catching Berliner Philharmonie (p111), Berlin's famous classical-music venue. And if your head is spinning after all that cultural stimulus, the leafy paths of the glorious Tiergarten, one of the world's largest city parks, will likely prove a restorative antidote.

DON'T MISS

VIEW FROM THE TOP

Europe's fastest lift yo-yos up and down to the **Panoramapunkt** (Map p72; ☎2593 7080; www.panoramapunkt.de; Potsdamer Platz 1; adult/concession €5.50/4; ⏰10am-8pm, last ride 7.30pm, shorter hours in winter; 🚌M41, 200, [S]Potsdamer Platz, 🚇Potsdamer Platz) atop the red-brick Kollhoff Building. From the bi-level viewing platform at a lofty 100m, a stunning 360-degree panorama reveals the city layout and its landmarks. Study up on key moments in Potsdamer Platz history by viewing the exhibit, then finish with a java stop in the cafe.

Gemäldegalerie GALLERY
(Map p72; ☎266 424 242; www.smb.museum/gg; Matthäikirchplatz 8; adult/concession €8/4; ⏰10am-6pm Tue, Wed & Fri-Sun, to 10pm Thu; 🚌M29, M41, 200, [S]Potsdamer Platz, 🚇Potsdamer Platz) The principal Kulturforum museum boasts one of the world's finest and most comprehensive collections of European art from the 13th to the 18th centuries. Wear comfy shoes when exploring the 72 galleries: a walk past masterpieces by Rembrandt, Dürer, Hals, Vermeer, Gainsborough and many more Old Masters covers almost 2km.

Topographie des Terrors MEMORIAL
(Topography of Terror; Map p72; ☎2548 6703; www.topographie.de; Niederkirchner Strasse 8; ⏰10am-8pm May-Sep, to dusk Oct-Apr; [S]Potsdamer Platz, 🚇Potsdamer Platz) In the same spot where once stood the most feared institutions of Nazi Germany (including the Gestapo headquarters and the SS central command), this compelling exhibit dissects the anatomy of the Nazi state. By chronicling the stages of terror and persecution, it puts a face on the perpetrators and details the impact these brutal institutions had on all of Europe. A short stretch of the Berlin Wall runs along Niederkirchner Strasse.

MUSICAL LUNCHES

Give your feet a rest and your ears a workout during the free lunchtime chamber music concerts held in the foyer of the Berliner Philharmonie every Tuesday at 1pm between early September and mid-June. A cafe serves refreshments and light lunches.

Martin-Gropius-Bau GALLERY

(Map p72; ☎254 860; www.gropiusbau.de; Niederkirchner Strasse 7; admission varies; ⏲10am-7pm Wed-Mon; [S]Potsdamer Platz, 🚆Potsdamer Platz) With its mosaics, terracotta reliefs and airy atrium, the 1881 Martin-Gropius-Bau is Berlin's treasure-box showcase for travelling art shows. No matter whether it's a retrospective of Diane Arbus' iconic photographs or an ethnological exhibit on Angkor Wat, it's bound to be crème de la crème and utterly fascinating. In case you're wondering about the stately building across the street, it's the seat of the Berlin state parliament.

Neue Nationalgalerie GALLERY

(Map p72; ☎266 2951; www.neue-nationalgalerie.de; Potsdamer Strasse 50; adult/concession €10/5; ⏲10am-6pm Tue, Wed & Fri, to 10pm Thu, 11am-6pm Sat & Sun; [S]Potzdamer Platz, 🚆Potsdamer Platz) This light-flooded glass temple by Ludwig Mies van der Rohe presents international 20th-century art until 1960 in changing configurations. Expect all the usual suspects from Picasso to Dalí, plus an outstanding collection of German expressionists such as Georg Grosz and Ernst Ludwig Kirchner. The permanent collection occasionally yields to visiting blockbuster shows.

Bauhaus Archiv MUSEUM

(Map p79; ☎254 0020; www.bauhaus.de; Klingelhöferstrasse 14; adult/concession Sat-Mon €7/4, Wed-Fri €6/3; ⏲10am-5pm Wed-Mon; [S]Nollendorfplatz) At this treasure trove of all things Bauhaus, curators use study notes, workshop pieces, photographs, blueprints, models and other objects and documents to mount changing exhibits illustrating the Bauhaus theories. It's in a distinctive building designed by Bauhaus founder Walter Gropius. Great on-site cafe and shop.

Museum für Film und Fernsehen MUSEUM

(Map p72; ☎300 9030; www.deutsche-kinemathek.de; Potsdamer Strasse 2; adult/concession €6/4.50; ⏲10am-6pm Tue, Wed & Fri-Sun, to 8pm Thu; 🚌200, [S]Potsdamer Platz, 🚆Potsdamer Platz) Every February, celluloid celebs sashay down the red carpet at Potsdamer Platz venues during the Berlin International Film Festival. Germany's film history, meanwhile, gets the star treatment year-round in this engaging museum. Skip through galleries dedicated to pioneers like Fritz Lang, ground-breaking movies like Leni Riefenstahl's *Olympia* and legendary divas like Marlene Dietrich. The TV exhibit has more niche appeal but is still fun if you want to know what *Star Trek* sounds like in German.

Dalí – Die Ausstellung GALLERY

(Map p60; ☎0700-3254 237 546; www.daliberlin.de; Leipziger Platz 7; adult/concession €11/9; ⏲noon-8pm Mon-Sat, 10am-8pm Sun; 🚌200, [S]Potsdamer Platz, 🚆Potsdamer Platz) This gallery offers new perspectives on Salvador Dalí, best known for his melting watches, burning giraffes and other surreal flights of fancy. Here, the focus is primarily on his graphics, illustrations, sculptures, drawings and films. Highlights include etchings on the theme of *Tristan and Isolde*, epic sculptures like *Surrealist Angel* and the Don Quixote lithographs.

[FREE] **Gedenkstätte Deutscher Widerstand** MEMORIAL

(German Resistance Memorial Center; Map p72; ☎2699 5000; www.gdw-berlin.de; Stauffenbergstrasse 13-14; ⏲9am-6pm Mon-Wed & Fri, to 8pm Thu, 10am-6pm Sat & Sun; 🚌M29, [S]Potsdamer Platz, Kurfürstenstrasse, 🚆Potsdamer Platz) This important exhibit on German resistance to the Nazis occupies the very rooms where senior army officers, led by Claus Schenk Graf von Stauffenberg, plotted the assassination attempt on Hitler on 20 July 1944. In the yard, a memorial marks the spot where the four main conspirators were executed after the failed coup, a story poignantly retold in the 2008 blockbuster movie *Valkyrie*.

[FREE] **Tiergarten** PARK

(Map p79; 🚌200, 🚆Potsdamer Platz) Berlin's rulers used to hunt boar and pheasants in the rambling Tiergarten until Peter Lenné landscaped the grounds in the 18th century. Today, one of the world's largest urban parks is a popular place for strolling, jogging, picnicking, grill parties and, yes, gay cruising (after dark, especially around the Löwenbrücke). Walking across the entire park takes about an hour, but even a shorter stroll has its rewards. Enchanting spots include the flowery Luiseninsel and the Neuer See lake with boat rentals and the delightful Café am Neuen See (p105) beer garden and restaurant.

Tiergarten is bisected by Strasse des 17 Juni, home to a Soviet WWII memorial and a weekend flea market. Big festivals and parades are staged along here and around the landmark Siegessäule (Victory Column; Map p79; Grosser Stern; 100, 200), a paean to 19th-century Prussian military triumphs. The gilded lady on top represents the goddess of victory, but locals irreverently call her 'Gold-Else'. Views from below her skirt take in mostly Tiergarten park.

Legoland Discovery Centre AMUSEMENT PARK
(Map p72; 01805-6669 0110; www.legoland discoverycentre.de/berlin; Potsdamer Strasse 4; admission €16; ☺10am-7pm, last admission 6pm; 200, ⑤Potsdamer Platz, ⑧Potsdamer Platz) Geared towards the elementary-school set, this cute indoor amusement park features a 4D cinema, a Lego factory and a Dragon Castle 'slow-lercoaster ride'. Elsewhere, they can channel their inner ninja by battling snakes and braving a laser labyrinth at the brand new Ninjago. Grown-ups can marvel at a mini-Berlin with landmarks built entirely from those tiny plastic bricks.

Diplomatenviertel NEIGHBOURHOOD
(Diplomatic Quarter; 200, ⑤Potsdamer Platz, ⑧Potsdamer Platz) In the 19th century the quiet, villa-studded colony south of the Tiergarten was popular with Berlin intellectuals such as the Brothers Grimm and Bettina von Arnim. Embassies starting moving in during the 1920s and, a decade later, the name Diplomatenviertel (Diplomatic Quar-

ter) was coined. After WWII the obliterated area remained in a state of quiet decay while the embassies all set up in Bonn, the West German capital. After reunification, many countries rebuilt on their historic lots, which is why some of Berlin's boldest new architecture can be found on these quiet streets, which are best explored on a DIY wander.

KREUZBERG & NORTHERN NEUKÖLLN

Kreuzberg gets its street cred from being delightfully edgy, bipolar, wacky and, most of all, unpredictable. While the western half around Bergmannstrasse has an upmarket, genteel air, eastern Kreuzberg (still nicknamed SO36 after its pre-reunification postal code) is a multicultural mosaic, a bubbly hodgepodge of tousled students, aspiring creatives; shisha-smoking Turks and Arabs and international life artists. Spend a day searching for great street art, soaking up the multi-culti vibe, scarfing a shawarma, browsing vintage stores and hanging by the river or canal, then find out why Kreuzberg is also known as a night crawler's paradise.

All that hipness has spilled across the Landwehr canal to the northern reaches of Neukölln. Once making headlines for its high crime and poorly performing schools, the district has catapulted from ghetto-gritty to funkytown-hip in no time. Largely thanks to an influx of young, creative neo-Berliners (including many from Italy, Spain and England), it's engulfed in a thriving DIY ethos with new trash-trendy bars, performance spaces and galleries coming online almost daily. Explore now for an exciting offbeat experience: turbo-gentrification is just waiting in the wings.

OTHER KULTURFORUM MUSEUMS

In addition to the Gemäldegalerie and the Neue Nationalgalerie, the Kulturforum encompasses three other top-rated museums: the Kupferstichkabinett (Museum of Prints and Drawings; Map p72; 266 424 242; www.smb.museum/kk; Matthäikirchplatz; adult/concession €8/4; ☺10am-6pm Tue-Fri, 11am-6pm Sat & Sun; 200, ⑤Potsdamer Platz, ⑧Potsdamer Platz) with prints and drawings since the 14th century; the Musikinstrumenten-Museum (Musical Instruments Museum; Map p72; 254 810; www.mim-berlin.de; Tiergartenstrasse 1, enter via Ben-Gurion-Strasse; adult/concession €4/2; ☺9am-5pm Tue, Wed & Fri, to 10pm Thu, 10am-5pm Sat & Sun; 200, ⑤Potsdamer Platz, ⑧Potsdamer Platz) with rare historical instruments; and the Kunstgewerbemuseum (Museum of Decorative Arts; Map p72; 266 424 242; www.smb.museum; Matthäikirchplatz; 200, ⑤Potsdamer Platz, ⑧Potsdamer Platz), which is closed for renovation until at least mid-2014. A ticket to any Kulturforum museum entitles you to same-day admission to the permanent collections of any of the others.

Kreuzberg & Friedrichshain

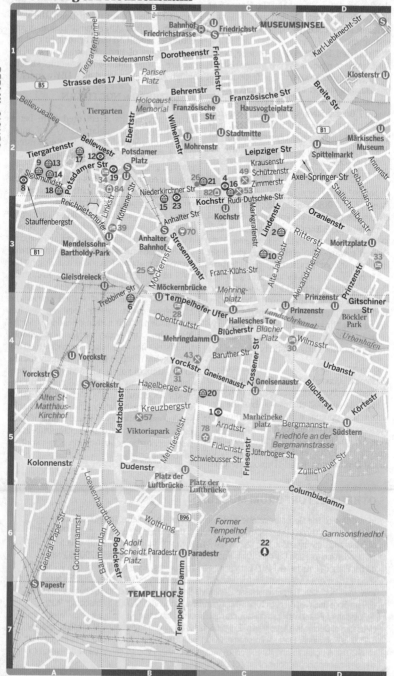

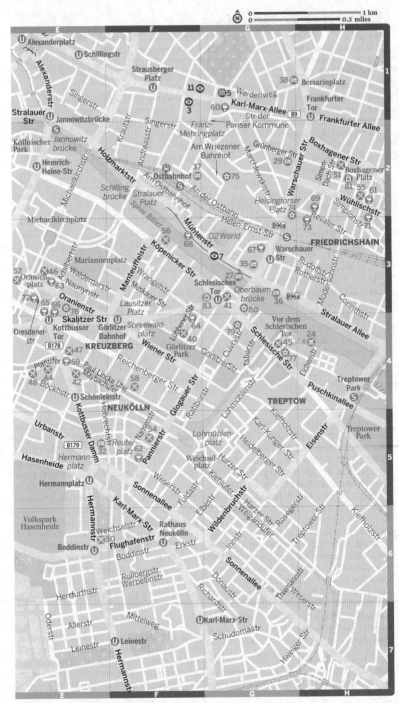

0   1 km
N
0   0.5 miles

Ⓤ Alexanderplatz
Ⓤ Schillingstr
Strausberger
Platz
Ⓤ
38 🚌 Bersarinplatz
11 ◉ 🏛5   Weidenweg
3 ◉   60   Karl-Marx-Allee
Str der
Franz-   Pariser Kommune
Mehringplatz
Frankfurter
Tor
Ⓤ Frankfurter Allee
Ⓤ Jannowitzbrücke
Stralauer
Str
Singerstr
Ⓢ
Köllnischer
Park
Jannowitz
brücke
Ⓤ
Heinrich-
Heine-Str
Michaelkirchplatz
Ostbahnhof
37 🚻
An Ostbahnhof
Am Ostbahnhof
Schilling
brücke
Stralauer
Platz
Spree River
Grünberger Str
29 🚻
Boxhagener Str
Simon-
Dach-Str
81 55 61
Boxhagener
Platz
Wühlischstr
Ⓢ
Helsingforser
Platz
75 🚻
69
Revaler Str
Simplonstr 71
73
FRIEDRICHSHAIN
Michaelkirchplatz
Mariannenplatz
56
Mühlenstr
68
Köpenicker Str
O2 World
Helen-Ernst-Str
B96a
74
◉7
67 🚻
35 Ⓤ
Warschauer
Str
Warschauer
Ⓤ Str
Rudolfstr
Rotherstr
52
Oranien-
platz
46 63
Waldemarstr
Naunynstr
Adalbertstr
Marheineke...
Wrangelstr
Muskauer Str
Schlesisches
Tor
Ⓤ
27 🚻
Oberbaum
brücke
36
B96a
Corinthstr
Stralauer Allee
72
65 66
76
Oranienstr
Skalitzer Str
Ⓤ
Görlitzer
Bahnhof
Ⓤ
Spreewald-
platz
Ⓤ
Lausitzer
Platz
Lübbener Str
83 🚻 41
80 🚻
Vor dem
Schlesischen
Tor
45 🚻
77
24
Eichenstr
Dresdener-
str
B178
47
Kottbusser
Tor
Ⓤ
KREUZBERG
Wiener Str
Görlitzer
Park
64
40
Görlitzer Str
Cuvrystr
Taborstr
Schlesische Str
Treptower
Park
Ⓢ
Puschkinallee
Planufer
59
Paul-Lincke-Ufer
Maybachufer
58
44
48
42
Böckhstr
Ⓤ Schönleinstr
Reichenberger Str
Glogauer Str
Ratiborstr
Lohmühlenstr
TREPTOW
Treptower
Park
Urbanstr
B179
Hobrechtstr
Kottbusser Damm
NEUKÖLLN
Reuter
platz
32
54
62
Nansenstr
Pannierstr
Lohmühlen-
platz
Weichsel-
platz
Karl-Kunger-Str
Kiefholzstr
Heidelberger Str
Eisenstr
Treptower
Park
Hasenheide
Hermannplatz
Ⓤ
Hermannplatz
Ⓤ
Sonnenallee
Weserstr
Fuldastr
Weichselstr
Harzer Str
Kiefufer
Elbestr
Harzer Str
Weigandufer
Rosegerstr
Kiefholzstr
Treptower Str
Volkspark
Hasenheide
Hermannstr
Weichselstr
50
Karl-Marx-Str
Rathaus
Neukölln
Ⓤ
Flughafenstr
Boddinstr
Ⓤ Erkstr
Wildenbruchstr
Innstr
Sonnenallee
Thielenstr
Weserstr
Boddinstr
Rollbergstr
Werbellinstr
Richardstr
Donaustr
Herrfurthstr
Allerstr
Mittelweg
Ⓤ Karl-Marx-Str
Oderstr
Leinestr
Ⓤ Leinestr
Schudomastr
Hertigerstr

Kreuzberg & Friedrichshain

Sights

1	Bergmannkiez	C5
2	Berlinische Galerie	C3
3	Café Sybille	F1
4	Checkpoint Charlie	C2
5	Computerspielemuseum	G1
6	Deutsches Technikmuseum	B4
7	East Side Gallery	G3
8	Gedenkstätte Deutscher Widerstand	A2
9	Gemäldegalerie	A2
10	Jüdisches Museum	C3
11	Karl-Marx-Allee	F1
12	Kulturforum	A2
13	Kunstgewerbemuseum	A2
14	Kupferstichkabinett	A2
	Legoland Discovery Centre	(see 12)
15	Martin-Gropius-Bau	B3
16	Mauermuseum	C2
	Museum für Film und Fernsehen	(see 12)
17	Musikinstrumenten-Museum	A2
18	Neue Nationalgalerie	A2
19	Panoramapunkt	B2
20	Schwules Museum	C5
	Sony Center	(see 12)
21	Stasi Ausstellung	C2
22	Tempelhofer Park	C6
23	Topographie des Terrors	B3

Activities, Courses & Tours

24	Badeschiff	H4
25	Liquidrom	B3
26	Trabi Safari	B2

Sleeping

27	Eastern Comfort Hostelboat	G3
28	Grand Hostel	B4
29	Hotel 26	G2
30	Hotel Johann	C4
31	Hotel Riehmers Hofgarten	B4
	Hotel Sarotti-Höfe	(see 20)
32	Hüttenpalast	E5
33	ÏMA Loft Apartments	D3
34	Mandala Hotel	B2
35	Michelberger Hotel	G3
36	nhow	G3
37	Ostel Hostel	F2
38	Raise a Smile Hostel	G1
39	Scandic Berlin Potsdamer Platz	B3

Eating

40	Bar Raval	F4
41	Burgermeister	G3
42	Cafe Jacques	E4
43	Curry 36	B4
44	Defne	E4
	Facil	(see 34)
45	Freischwimmer	G4
46	Henne	E3

Jüdisches Museum MUSEUM

(Jewish Museum; Map p72; ☎2599 3300; www.jmberlin.de; Lindenstrasse 9-14; adult/concession €5/2.50; ⏰10am-10pm Mon, to 8pm Tue-Sun, last admission 1hr before closing; [S]Hallesches Tor, Kochstrasse) In a landmark building by American-Polish architect Daniel Libeskind, this engaging museum offers a chronicle of the trials and triumphs in 2000 years of Jewish history in Germany. The exhibit smoothly navigates through all major periods, from the Middle Ages via the Enlightenment to the community's current renaissance. Learn about Jewish cultural contributions, holiday traditions, the difficult road to emancipation and outstanding individuals such as the philosopher Moses Mendelssohn, blue jeans inventor Levi Strauss and the painter Felix Nussbaum.

Berlinische Galerie GALLERY

(Map p72; ☎7890 2600; www.berlinischegalerie.de; Alte Jakobstrasse 124; adult/concession/child €8/5/free; ⏰10am-6pm Wed-Mon; [S]Kochstrasse, Hallesches Tor) The Berlin Gallery, in a converted glass warehouse around the corner from the Jüdisches Museum, is a superb spot for taking stock of what the local scene has been up to for, oh, the past century or so. The stark, whitewashed hall, anchored by two intersecting floating stairways, presents edgy works from major artistic periods – Berlin Secessionism (Lesser Ury, Max Liebermann) to New Objectivity (Otto Dix, George Grosz) and contemporary art by Salomé and Rainer Fetting. Jüdisches Museum ticket holders qualify for reduced admission on the same day and the following two, and vice versa.

Tempelhofer Park PARK

(Map p72; ☎2801 8162; www.tempelhoferfreiheit.de; enter via Oderstrasse, Tempelhofer Damm or Columbiadamm; ⏰sunrise-sunset; [S]Paradestrasse, Boddinstrasse, Leinestrasse) In Berlin history, the former Tempelhof airport is a site of

47 Horváth E4
48 Il Casolare E4
49 Ishin – Charlottenstrasse C2
50 Lavanderia Vecchia E6
51 Lemon Leaf H2
52 Max und Moritz E3
Qiu .... (see 34)
Restaurant Gropius .... (see 15)
53 Restaurant Tim Raue C2
54 Sauvage F5
Schwarzer Hahn .... (see 55)
55 Spätzle & Knödel H2
56 Spindler & Klatt F3
57 Tomasa B5
58 Volt F4

Drinking
59 Ankerklause E4
60 CSA G1
61 Hops & Barley H2
62 Kuschlowski F5
63 Luzia E3
64 Madame Claude F4
65 Möbel Olfe E3
66 Monarch Bar E3
67 Monster Ronson's Ichiban Karaoke G3
68 Oststrand F3
69 Place Clichy H2
Roses .... (see 76)
SchwuZ .... (see 20)
70 Solar B3
71 Süss War Gestern H3
72 Würgeengel E3
73 Zum Schmutzigen Hobby H3

Entertainment
Arsenal .... (see 12)
74 Astra Kulturhaus G2
Babylon .... (see 72)
75 Berghain/Panorama Bar G2
76 Café Fatal E3
Cinestar Original .... (see 12)
77 Club der Visionäre G4
78 English Theatre Berlin C5
Lab.oratory .... (see 75)
79 Lido G4
80 Magnet Club G3
SO36 .... (see 76)
Suicide Circus .... (see 74)
Watergate .... (see 80)

Shopping
81 Flohmarkt am Boxhagener Platz H2
82 Frau Tonis Parfum C2
Hard Wax .... (see 47)
Nowkoelln Flowmarkt .... (see 42)
83 Overkill G3
84 Potsdamer Platz Arkaden B2
Türkenmarkt .... (see 59)

legend, and not just since it so gloriously handled the Berlin Airlift of 1948–49. The last plane landed here in 2008 and a mere two years later, the airfield reopened as a public park. Now you can ponder the past while cycling, blading or strolling along the vast paths. It's a wonderfully noncommercial, creative and wide-open space dotted with barbecue lawns, dog parks, an artistic minigolf parcours, a beer garden, art installations, abandoned airplanes and urban gardening. New projects seem to go live almost overnight. Call ahead if you're interested in guided tours of the grounds.

Deutsches Technikmuseum MUSEUM
(German Museum of Technology; Map p72; ☎902 540; www.dtmb.de; Trebbiner Strasse 9; adult/concession €6/3, after 3pm if under 18 free, audioguide €2/1; 🕒9am-5.30pm Tue-Fri, 10am-6pm Sat & Sun; [S]Gleisdreieck) A roof-mounted 'candy bomber' (the plane used in the 1948 Berlin Airlift) is merely the overture to the enormous and hugely engaging German Technology Museum. Fantastic for kids, this giant shrine to technology counts the world's first computer, an entire hall of vintage locomotives and extensive exhibits on aviation and navigation among its top attractions. At the adjacent **Spectrum Science Centre**, kids can participate in around 250 experiments.

FRIEDRICHSHAIN

Rents may be rising and gentrification unstoppable, but for now, Friedrichshain, in former East Berlin, is still largely the domain of the young and free-spirited, students, artists and eccentrics. There are few standout sights, but the web of boutique- and cafe-lined streets around Boxhagener Platz will happily repay those who simply wander and soak up the district's unique character. After dark, Friedrichshain morphs into a hugely popular bar-stumbling and high-energy party zone.

DON'T MISS

BEARPIT KARAOKE

Roughly from late spring to autumn, Berlin's greatest free entertainment kicks off on Sundays around 3pm when Joe Hatchiban sets up his custom-made mobile karaoke unit in the Mauerpark's amphitheatre. As many as 2000 people cram onto the stone seats to cheer and clap for eager crooners ranging from giggling 11 year olds to Broadway-calibre belters. Give generously when Joe passes the coffee can, for this show must go on forever. See more at www.bearpitkaraoke.com or on Facebook.

East Side Gallery HISTORIC SITE
(Map p72; www.eastsidegallery-berlin.de; Mühlenstrasse btwn Oberbaumbrücke & Ostbahnhof; 🕐24hr; [S]Warschauer Strasse, 🚆Ostbahnhof, Warschauer Strasse) The year was 1989. After 28 years the Berlin Wall, that grim and grey divider of humanity, finally met its maker. Most of it was quickly dismantled, but along Mühlenstrasse, paralleling the Spree River, a 1.3km stretch became the East Side Gallery, the world's largest open-air mural collection. In more than 100 paintings, dozens of international artists translated the era's global euphoria and optimism into a mix of political statements, drug-induced musings and truly artistic visions. It was restored in 2009. In summer, beach bars like Oststrand (p107) open up along the waterfront.

Karl-Marx-Allee STREET
(Map p72; [S]Strausberger Platz, Weberwiese, Frankfurter Tor) It's easy to feel like Gulliver in the Land of Brobdingnag when walking down monumental Karl-Marx-Allee, one of Berlin's most impressive GDR-era relics. At 90m in width, it was built between 1952 and 1960 and runs for 2.3km between Alexanderplatz and Frankfurter Tor. A source of considerable East German pride, it provided modern flats for comrades and served as a backdrop for military parades. **Café Sybille** (Map p72; ☎2935 2203; www.karlmarxallee.eu; Karl-Marx-Allee 72; exhibit free, viewing platform 1-5 people €15, extra person €3; 🕐10am-8pm Mon-Fri, noon-8pm Sat & Sun; [S]Weberwiese, Strausberger Platz) has a small free exhibit about the boulevard's history and significance.

Computerspielemuseum MUSEUM
(Map p72; ☎6098 8577; www.computerspielemuseum.de; Karl-Marx-Allee 93a; adult/concession €8/5; 🕐10am-8pm Wed-Mon; [S]Weberwiese) No matter if you grew up with PacMan, World of Warcraft or nothing at all in this digital world, this delightful museum takes you on a fascinating trip down computer-game memory lane while putting the industry's evolution into historical and cultural context. Colourful and engaging, it features lots of interactive stations alongside hundreds of original exhibits, including an ultrarare 1972 Pong arcade machine and its twisted modern cousin, the 'PainStation'.

PRENZLAUER BERG

Prenzlauer Berg went from rags to riches after reunification to emerge as one of Berlin's most desirable residential neighbourhoods. Its ample charms are best experienced on a leisurely meander. Look up at gorgeously restored town houses, comb side streets for indie boutiques or carve out a spot among the yoga mamas and greying hipsters in cafes around Kollwitzplatz or Helmholtzplatz, two squares at the epicente of gentrification. Boho-bourgeois professionals, including many expats from France, Italy, the US and Britain, have displaced nearly 80% of the pre-reunification residents, who could simply no longer afford the ever-rising rents or felt no cultural affinity for fancy coffee drinks.

Thanks to these changed demographics, Prenzlauer Berg has slowly but irrevocably lost its standing as a hipster and party quarter. After coming under fire from noise-sensitive neighbours, many beloved venues have moved on to more tolerant (for now) Kreuzberg or Friedrichshain. It's quieter now, but that's just how most locals like it.

[FREE] **Mauerpark** PARK
(Map p77; www.mauerpark.info; btwn Bernauer Strasse, Schwedter Strasse & Gleimstrasse; [S]Eberswalder Strasse, 🚋M1) Long-time locals, neo-Berliners and global visitors – everyone flocks to Mauerpark, especially on Sundays. It's a wild and wacky urban tapestry where a flea market, outdoor karaoke, artists and bands provide entertainment and people gather for barbecues, basketball, badminton and boules. A graffiti-covered section of the Berlin Wall, which once bisected the park, quietly looms above it all. Views across the park from here are downright romantic at sunset, especially in late spring when purple flowers blanket the slopes.

Prenzlauer Berg

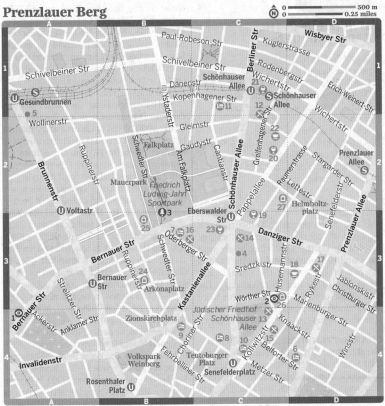

Prenzlauer Berg

LIVING IT UP IN THE BERGMANNKIEZ

One of Berlin's most charismatic neighbourhoods is the Bergmannkiez (Map p72; Bergmannstrasse & around; SMehringdamm, Gneisenaustrasse) in western Kreuzberg. It's named for its main shopping strip, Bergmannstrasse, which is chock-a-block with people-watching cafes and quirky shops. This culminates in Marheinekeplatz, punctuated by a newly renovated 19th-century gourmet market hall.

Kollwitzplatz   SQUARE

(Map p77; SSenefelderplatz) Kollwitzplatz is the heart of Prenzlauer Berg poshification. To pick up on the local vibe, linger with the macchiato mamas and media daddies in a cafe or join them at the organic farmers market (Thursday and Saturday). The park at the centre is tot haven with three playgrounds plus a bronze sculpture of the square's namesake, the artist Käthe Kollwitz.

CHARLOTTENBURG

The glittering heart of West Berlin during the Cold War, Charlottenburg has been eclipsed by historic Mitte and other eastern districts since reunification, but is now trying hard to stage a comeback with major construction and redevelopment around Zoo station. Its main artery is the 3.5km-long Kurfürstendamm (Ku'damm for short), Berlin's busiest shopping strip. Venture into the side streets for close-ups of palatial town houses, distinctive shops, ritzy restaurants and entertainment venues. Royal groupies have Schloss Charlottenburg, one of the grandest surviving Prussian palaces, to explore, and museum junkies will need at least a full day to absorb the district's cultural bounty.

TOP CHOICE Schloss Charlottenburg   PALACE

(320 911; www.spsg.de; Spandauer Damm 20-24; day pass adult/concession €15/11; 145, 309, SRichard-Wagner-Platz, Sophie-Charlotte-Platz) The grandest of Berlin's surviving nine former royal pads consists of the main palace and two outbuildings in the lovely Schlossgarten (palace park). The Schloss was built as the summer residence of Sophie Charlotte, wife of King Friedrich I. The couple's baroque living quarters in the palace's oldest section, the Altes Schloss (320 911; www.spsg.de; Spandauer Damm; adult/concession €12/8; 10am-6pm Tue-Sun Apr-Oct, to 5pm Tue-Sun Nov-Mar; 145, 309, SRichard-Wagner-Platz, Sophie-Charlotte-Platz), are an extravaganza in stucco, brocade and opulence. Highlights include the Oak Gallery, a wood-panelled festival hall draped in family portraits; the lovely Oval Hall overlooking the park; and the dazzling Porcelain Chamber, smothered in nearly 3000 pieces of Chinese and Japanese blueware. Upstairs, in the old apartments of Friedrich Wilhelm IV, you can admire the paintings, vases, tapestries, weapons and other items essential to a royal lifestyle.

The most beautiful rooms, though, are the flamboyant private chambers of Frederick the Great in the Neuer Flügel (New Wing; 320 911; www.spsg.de; Spandauer Damm 20-24; adult/concession incl audioguide €6/5; 10am-6pm Wed-Mon Apr-Oct, to 5pm Wed-Mon Nov-Mar; M45, 309, SRichard-Wagner-Platz, Sophie-Charlotte-Platz), designed by star architect *du jour* Georg Wenzeslaus von Knobelsdorff in 1746. The austere neoclassical digs of his successor, Friedrich Wilhelm II, in the same wing, pale in comparison.

Adjacent to the Neuer Flügel, the Schinkel-designed Neuer Pavillon (New Pavillon; 320 910; www.spsg.de; Spandauer Damm 20-24; adult/concession incl audioguide €4/3; 10am-6pm Tue-Sun Apr-Oct, to 5pm Nov-Mar; 309, SRichard-Wagner-Platz, Sophie-Charlotte-Platz) served as a summer retreat of Friedrich Wilhelm III and now houses paintings from the Romantic and Biedermeier periods.

In fine weather, a spin around the sprawling Schlossgarten (palace park; www.spsg.de; Spandauer Damm 20-24; SSophie-Charlotte-Platz, then 309, SRichard-Wagner-Platz, then 145) with its shady walkways, flower beds and manicured lawns is a must. In the northeast corner, you'll stumble upon the pint-size palace called Belvedere (3209 1445; www.spsg.de; Spandauer Damm 20-24; adult/concession €3/2.50; 10am-6pm Tue-Sun Apr-Oct, noon-4pm Tue-Sun Nov-Mar; SSophie-Charlotte-Platz, then 309, SRichard-Wagner-Platz, then 145), now an elegant setting for porcelain masterpieces by the royal manufacturer KPM.

Across the carp pond, the neoclassical Mausoleum (3209 1446; www.spsg.de; Spandauer Damm 20-24; 10am-6pm Tue-Sun Apr-Oct; 145, 309, SSophie-Charlotte-Platz, then 309, SRichard-Wagner-Platz, then 145) is the final home of various royals, including Emperor Wilhelm I and his wife Augusta.

Charlottenburg & Wilmersdorf

Charlottenburg & Wilmersdorf

◎ Sights

1 Bauhaus Archiv	D2
2 Berlin Aquarium	C2
3 Berlin Zoo	C2
4 Kaiser-Wilhelm-Gedächtniskirche	C2
5 Käthe-Kollwitz-Museum	B2
6 Museum für Fotografie	C2
7 Siegessäule	D1
8 Story of Berlin	B2
9 Tiergarten	D1

🛏 Sleeping

10 Hotel Art Nouveau	A2
11 Hotel Askanischer Hof	B2
12 Hotel Bogota	B2
13 Hotel Concorde Berlin	C2
14 Hotel Otto	B1
15 Louisa's Place	A3
16 Mittendrin	C2

⊗ Eating

17 Ali Baba	B2
18 Café-Restaurant Wintergarten im Literaturhaus	B2
19 Dicke Wirtin	B2
20 Good Friends	B2
21 Jules Verne	B2
22 Mr Hai Kabuki	B3
23 Osteria Centrale	B2
24 Ottenthal	B2
25 Schleusenkrug	C1

🍷 Drinking

26 Café am Neuen See	D1
27 Puro Skylounge	C2
Universum Lounge	(see 31)
Zwiebelfisch	(see 23)

🎭 Entertainment

28 A-Trane	B2
29 Bar Jeder Vernunft	C3
30 Deutsche Oper	A1
31 Schaubühne	A3
32 Staatsoper unter den Linden @ Schillertheater	B1

🛍 Shopping

33 Steiff Galerie in Berlin	B2
34 Stilwerk	B2

TOP TIPS FOR VISITING SCHLOSS CHARLOTTENBURG

» Each palace building charges separate admission, but it's best to invest in the *Tageskarte* (day pass, €15) for one-day admission to every open building.

» Visit Wednesday to Sunday, when all palace buildings are open.

» Arrive early to avoid long queues, especially on weekends and in summer.

» A palace visit is easily combined with a spin around the trio of nearby museums.

Museum Berggruen GALLERY
(☎266 424 242; www.smb.museum/mb; Schlossstrasse 1; 🚌145, 309, [S]Richard-Wagner-Platz, Sophie-Charlotte-Platz) Fans of classical modern art will be in their element at this classy museum with a special focus on Picasso, Klee, Matisse and Giacometti. It was closed for renovation at the time of writing, but a new extension should have opened by the time you read this.

Sammlung Scharf-Gerstenberg GALLERY
(☎266 424 242; www.smb.museum/ssg; Schlossstrasse 70; adult/concession €6/3; ⏲10am-6pm Tue-Sun; [S]Sophie-Charlotte-Platz, then 🚌309, [S]Richard-Wagner-Platz, then 🚌145) This stellar gallery trains the spotlight on surrealism, with large bodies of work by Magritte, Max Ernst, Dalí, Dubuffet and their 18th-century precursors such as Goya and Piranesi.

Bröhan Museum MUSEUM
(☎3269 0600; www.broehan-museum.de; Schlossstrasse 1a; adult/concession €6/4; ⏲10am-6pm Tue-Sun; [S]Sophie-Charlotte-Platz, Richard-Wagner-Platz) This fine museum displays an outstanding collection of furniture and decorative objects from the art nouveau, art deco and functionalism periods (1889–1939).

Käthe-Kollwitz-Museum MUSEUM
(Map p79; ☎882 5210; www.kaethe-kollwitz.de; Fasanenstrasse 24; adult/concession €6/3, audioguide €3; ⏲11am-6pm; [S]Uhlandstrasse) Käthe Kollwitz (1867–1945) was one of the greatest German women artists, with her social and political awareness lending a tortured power to her work. After losing both her son and grandson to the battlefields of Europe, death and motherhood became recurring themes.

Kaiser-Wilhelm-Gedächtniskirche CHURCH
(Kaiser Wilhelm Memorial Church; Map p79; ☎218 5023; www.gedaechtniskirche.com; Breitscheidplatz; ⏲9am-7pm; [S]Zoologischer Garten, Kurfürstendamm, [R]Zoologischer Garten) The bombed-out tower of this landmark church serves as an antiwar memorial, standing quiet and dignified amid the traffic. The adjacent octagonal hall of worship, added in 1961, has amazing midnight-blue glass walls and a giant Jesus 'floating' above the altar.

Museum für Fotografie MUSEUM
(Map p79; ☎3186 4825; www.smb.museum/mf; Jebensstrasse 2; adult/concession €8/4; ⏲10am-6pm Tue, Wed & Fri-Sun, to 10pm Thu; [S]Zoologischer Garten, [R]Zoologischer Garten) The artistic legacy of Helmut Newton, the Berlin-born enfant terrible of fashion and lifestyle photography, is given centre stage on two floors of Berlin's Photography Museum, located in a former Prussian officers' casino behind Bahnhof Zoo. On the top floor, the gloriously restored, barrel-vaulted **Kaisersaal** (Emperor's Hall) forms the backdrop for high-calibre changing photography exhibits drawn from the archive of the State Art Library.

Story of Berlin MUSEUM
(Map p79; ☎8872 0100; www.story-of-berlin.de; Kurfürstendamm 207-208, enter via Ku'damm Karree mall; adult/concession €10/8; ⏲10am-8pm, last admission 6pm; [S]Uhlandstrasse) This mul-

WORTH A TRIP

OLYMPIASTADION

Built for the 1936 Olympic Games, Berlin's **Olympiastadion** (☎2500 2322; www.olympiastadion-berlin.de; Olympischer Platz 3; self-guided tour adult/concession €7/5, guided general tour in German €10/8, Hertha BSC tour €11/9; ⏲9am-8pm Jun–mid-Sep, to 7pm mid-Mar–May & mid-Sep–Oct, 10am-4pm Nov–mid-Mar; [R]Olympiastadion) was completely revamped for the 2006 FIFA World Cup and now sports a spidery oval roof, snazzy VIP boxes and top-notch sound, lighting and projection systems. On non-event days (call ahead to make sure), you can tour the stadium on your own (audioguide €2.50) or join a tour for access to the changerooms, warm-up areas and VIP areas.

Schöneberg

Schöneberg

Sleeping
1 Axel Hotel A1

Eating
2 Habibi B2
3 Ousies B2

Drinking
4 Green Door B1
5 Hafen A1
6 Heile Welt B1
7 Stagger Lee B1

Entertainment
8 Connection A1

Shopping
9 KaDeWe A1
10 Markt am Winterfeldtplatz B2

timedia museum breaks down 800 years of Berlin history into bite-sized chunks that are easy to swallow but substantial enough to be satisfying. Don't miss the guided tour of a fully functional Cold War–era atomic bunker beneath the building.

Berlin Zoo ZOO

(Map p79; ☎254 010; www.zoo-berlin.de; Hardenbergplatz 8; adult/child €13/6.50, with aquarium €20/10; 🕒9am-7pm Apr–mid-Oct, 9am-5pm mid-Oct–Mar; [S]Zoologischer Garten, 🚇Zoologischer Garten) Germany's oldest animal park opened in 1844 with furry and feathered critters from the royal family's private reserve. Today some 16,000 animals from all continents, 1500 species in total, make their home here. Cheeky orang-utans, cuddly koalas, endangered rhinos, playful penguins and Bao Bao, a rare giant panda, are among the top draws.

Berlin Aquarium AQUARIUM

(Map p79; ☎254 010; www.aquarium-berlin.de; Budapester Strasse 32; adult/child €13/6.50, with zoo €20/10; 🕒9am-6pm; [S]Zoologischer Garten, 🚇Zoologischer Garten) Three floors of exotic fish, amphibians and reptiles await at this endearingly old-fashioned aquarium with its darkened halls and glowing tanks.

SCHÖNEBERG

Residential Schöneberg has a radical pedigree rooted in the squatter days of the '80s but now flaunts a mellow middle-class identity. Handsome 19th-century town houses line many of its quiet and leafy side streets, which are squeezed tight with boho cafes and indie boutiques. It's a charismatic neighbourhood perfect for exploring on foot, ideally by starting at Nollendorfplatz U-Bahn station and heading south to ethnic-flavoured Hauptstrasse, via Maassenstrasse, Goltzstrasse and Akazienstrasse (1.5km walk). On Saturday, a lively farmers' market takes over Winterfeldtplatz.

Nollendorfplatz is also the gateway to Berlin's historic gay quarter along Motzstrasse and Fuggerstrasse. One local gal who liked to party with the 'boyz' back in the 1920s was Marlene Dietrich. She's buried not far from Rathaus Schöneberg, the town hall where John F Kennedy gave his morale-boosting '*Ich bin ein Berliner!*' speech back in 1963. In the late '70s, David Bowie and Iggy Pop shared a flat at Hauptstrasse 155.

SOUTHWESTERN BERLIN

Much of Berlin's southwest is covered by forest, rivers and lakes. Besides the **Freie Universität** (☎030 8381; www.fu-berlin.de; Habelschwerdter Allee 45; [S]Thielplatz), which is one of Germany's 11 'elite' universities, and the **Botanischer Garten** (☎8385 0100; www.bgbm.org; Königin-Luise-Strasse 6-8; adult/concession €6/3, museum only €2.50/1.50; 🕒garden 9am-dusk, museum 10am-6pm; [S]Dahlem-Dorf,

ℹ BUS TOUR ON THE CHEAP

Get a crash course in 'Berlinology' by hopping on the upper deck of **bus 100 or 200** at Zoologischer Garten or Alexanderplatz and letting the landmarks whoosh by for the price of a standard bus ticket (€2.40, day pass €6.50). Bus 100 goes via the Tiergarten, 200 via Potsdamer Platz. Without traffic, trips take about 30 minutes. These buses get crowded, so watch out for pickpockets.

Botanischer Garten), you'll find several excellent museums in the district.

Museen Dahlem
MUSEUM

(266 424 242; www.smb.museum; Lansstrasse 8; adult/concession/child €6/3/free; ⏰10am-6pm Tue-Fri, 11am-6pm Sat & Sun, Junior Museum 1-6pm Tue-Fri, 11am-6pm Sat & Sun; ⓈDahlem-Dorf) Unless some mad scientist invents a magic time-travel-teleporter machine, the three collections within the Museen Dahlem are your best bet for exploring the world in a single afternoon. Highlights of the Museum of Ethnology include masks and musical instruments in the Africa exhibit and the outriggers and traditional huts in the South Seas hall. In another wing, the Museum of Asian Art displays six millennia of art. Don't miss the Japanese tearoom and a 16th-century Chinese imperial throne made of lacquered rosewood with mother-of-pearl inlay. There's also the Museum of European Cultures, with exhibits ranging from Swedish armoires to a black Venetian gondola and a giant mechanical nativity scene from Germany.

FREE AlliiertenMuseum
MUSEUM

(818 1990; www.alliiertenmuseum.de; Clayallee 135; ⏰10am-6pm Thu-Tue; ⓈOskar-Helene-Heim) The original Checkpoint Charlie guard cabin, a Berlin Airlift plane and a reconstructed spy tunnel are among the most poignant exhibits at the Allied Museum, which documents the history and challenges faced by the Western Allies during the Cold War.

Brücke Museum
GALLERY

(831 2029; www.bruecke-museum.de; Bussardsteig 9; adult/concession €5/3; ⏰11am-5pm Wed-Mon; ⓈOskar-Helene-Heim, then bus 115 to Pücklerstrasse) In 1905 Karl Schmidt-Rottluff, Erich Heckel and Ernst Ludwig Kirchner cofounded Germany's first modern-artist group, called *Die Brücke* (The Bridge). Schmitt-Rottluff's personal collection forms the core of this superb presentation of expressionist art.

FREE Haus der Wannsee-Konferenz
MEMORIAL SITE

(805 0010; www.ghwk.de; Am Grossen Wannsee 56-58; ⏰10am-6pm; Wannsee, then bus 114) In January 1942 a group of 15 high-ranking Nazi officials met in this stately villa near Lake Wannsee to hammer out the details of the 'Final Solution': the systematic deportation and murder of European Jews in Eastern Europe. Today the same building houses a memorial exhibit and an education centre about this sinister gathering and its ramifications.

Liebermann-Villa am Wannsee
MUSEUM

(8058 5900; www.max-liebermann.de; Colomierstrasse 3; adult/concession €6/4, audioguide €3; ⏰10am-6pm Wed & Fri-Mon, to 8pm Thu Apr-Sep, 11am-5pm Wed-Mon Oct-Mar; Wannsee, then bus 114) The former summer home of German Impressionist painter Max Liebermann now houses a small exhibit on the man, his family and, of course, his art. Liebermann loved the lyricism of nature and gardens in particular and often painted the scenery right outside the window of his studio. The Wannsee-facing garden cafe is a delight in fine weather.

🏃 Activities

Cycling

Berlin is flat and bike-friendly, with special bike lanes and quiet side streets for stress-free riding. There are even eye-level miniature traffic lights at intersections. Still, it pays to keep your wits about you (and preferably with a helmet on) when negotiating city streets. Getting a tyre caught in the tram tracks is particularly nasty.

Of course it's far more relaxing to pedal around leafy suburbs. The Grunewald forest, for instance, with its many lakes, is a great getaway. Or follow the course of the former Berlin Wall along the marked Berliner Mauerweg. For more ideas, consult the guide published by the bicycle club ADFC (448 4724; www.adfc-berlin.de; Brunnenstrasse 28; ⏰noon-8pm Mon-Fri, 10am-4pm Sat; ⓈBernauer Strasse, Rosenthaler Platz). It's available at its offices, bookshops and bike stores.

Bicycles *(Fahrräder)* may be taken aboard designated U-Bahn and S-Bahn cars (though not on buses) for the price of a reduced single ticket. Deutsche Bahn charges €4.50 for a bike ticket *(Fahrradkarte)* on regional RE and RB trains.

Many hostels and hotels rent bicycles to guests or can refer you to an agency. Expect to pay from €10 per day and €50 per week. A minimum cash deposit and/or ID is required. One reliable outfit with English-speaking staff and six branches throughout central Berlin is Fahrradstation (central reservations 0180-510 8000; www.fahrradstation. de). Alternatively, try Little John Bikes, with branches in Schöneberg, Mitte, Kreuzberg and Friedrichshain.

Running

Berlin offers great running terrain in its many parks. Flat and spread out, the Tiergarten (p70) is among the most popular and convenient, although the Grunewald in southwest Berlin is even prettier. The trip around the scenic Schlachtensee (in Grunewald) is 5km. The Schloss Charlottenburg (p78) park is also good for a nice, easy trot. More challenging is Volkspark Friedrichshain, which has stairs, hills and even a fitness trail.

Swimming

Berlin has lots of indoor and outdoor public pools. For the full list, see www.berliner baederbetriebe.de. Opening hours vary widely by day, time and pool, so check on-line or call ahead. Many facilities also have saunas, which generally cost between €10 and €15.

Sommerbad Olympiastadion SWIMMING (6663 1152; Osttor, Olympischer Platz 1; adult/concession €4/2.50; 7am-8pm May–mid-Sep; Olympiastadion, Olympiastadion) Do your laps in the 50m pool built for the 1936 Olympic athletes.

Strandbad Wannsee SWIMMING (www.strandbadwannsee.de; Wannseebadweg 25; adult/concession €4/2.50; Apr-Sep; Nikolassee) One of Europe's largest lakeside lidos, with 1km of sandy beach and plenty of infrastructure. Often gets packed.

Tours

Bus

You'll see them everywhere around town: colourful buses (in summer, often open-top double-deckers) that tick off all the key sights on two-hour loops with basic taped commentary in eight languages. You're free to get off and back on at any of the stops. Buses depart roughly every 15 or 30 minutes between 10am and 5pm or 6pm daily; tickets cost from €10 to €20 (half-price for teens, free for children). Traditional tours (where you stay on the bus), combination boat/bus tours as well as trips to Potsdam, Dresden and the Spreewald are also available. Look for flyers in hotel lobbies or in tourist offices.

WORTH A TRIP

FEAR & LOATHING IN EASTERN BERLIN

Anyone interested in GDR history, and the Stasi in particular, should head out to these two chilling sites.

Stasimuseum (553 6854; www.stasimuseum.de; Haus 1, Ruschestrasse 103; adult/concession €5/4; 11am-6pm Mon-Fri, noon-6pm Sat & Sun; Magdalenenstrasse) The former head office of the Ministry of State Security is now a museum, where you can marvel at cunningly low-tech surveillance devices (hidden in watering cans, rocks, even neckties), a prisoner transport van with teensy, lightless cells and the obsessively neat offices of Stasi chief Erich Mielke. Other rooms of the recently revamped three-floor presentation introduce the ideology, rituals and institutions of GDR society. Panelling is partly in English.

Stasi Prison (9860 8230; www.stiftung-hsh.de; Genslerstrasse 66; tour adult/concession €5/2.50; tours hourly 11am-3pm Mon-Fri, 10am-4pm Sat & Sun, English tour 2.30pm daily; M5 to Freienwalder Strasse, then 1km walk via Freienwalder Strasse) Victims of Stasi persecution often ended up in the grim Stasi Prison, now a memorial site officially called Gedenkstätte Hohenschönhausen. Tours reveal the full extent of the terror and cruelty perpetrated upon thousands of suspected regime opponents, many of them utterly innocent. If you've seen the Academy Award–winning movie *The Lives of Others*, you'll recognise many of the original settings.

THE BERLIN WALL

It's more than a tad ironic that Berlin's most popular tourist attraction is one that no longer exists. For 28 years the Berlin Wall, the most potent symbol of the Cold War, divided not only a city but the world.

Shortly after midnight on 13 August 1961 East German soldiers and police began rolling out miles of barbed wire that would soon be replaced with prefab concrete slabs. The wall was a desperate measure taken by the German Democratic Republic (GDR) government to stop the sustained brain and brawn drain it had experienced since its 1949 founding. Around 3.6 million people had already left for the West, putting the GDR on the verge of economic and political collapse.

Euphemistically called 'Anti-Fascist Protection Barrier', the Berlin Wall was continually reinforced and refined. In the end, it was a complex border-security system consisting of two walls hemming in a 'death strip' riddled with trenches, floodlights, patrol roads, attack dogs, electrified alarm fences and watchtowers staffed by guards with shoot-to-kill orders. Nearly 100,000 GDR citizens tried to escape, many using ingenious contraptions such as homemade hot-air balloons or U-boats. There are no exact numbers, but it is believed that hundreds died in the process.

The Wall's demise in 1989 came as unexpectedly as its construction. Once again the GDR was losing its people in droves, this time via Hungary, which had opened its borders with Austria. Major demonstrations in East Berlin culminated in early November when 500,000 people gathered on Alexanderplatz. Something had to give. It did on 9 November 1989 when a GDR spokesperson (mistakenly, it later turned out) announced during a press conference that all travel restrictions to the West would be lifted. Immediately. Amid scenes of wild partying, the two Berlins came together again. Today, only about 2km of the Berlin Wall still stand, the longest being the East Side Gallery (p76). A double row of cobblestones embedded in the pavement traces its course. For more background, swing by the Gedenkstätte Berliner Mauer (p68).

Bicycle

Companies listed here operate various English-language tours. Reservations are recommended.

Berlin on Bike BICYCLE TOUR
(Map p77; ☎4373 9999; www.berlinonbike.de; Knaackstrasse 97; tours incl bike €19, concession €17; ⏰Mar-Oct; [S]Eberswalder Strasse) Well-established company with an intriguing repertoire far beyond the blockbuster sights, with excursions heading deep behind the former Iron Curtain, along the Berlin Wall, into alt-flavoured Kreuzberg or to Berlin's hidden oases.

Fat Tire Bike Tours BICYCLE TOUR
(Map p60; ☎2404 7991; www.fattirebiketours.com/berlin; Panoramastrasse 1a; tours €24, concession €22; [S]Alexanderplatz, 🚋Alexanderplatz) Has classic Berlin, Nazi and Cold War tours as well as the fascinating Raw Tour, which gets under the urban, counter-cultural skin of the city and addresses such hot-button issues as gentrification, urban renewal and multicultural living.

Boat

A lovely way to experience Berlin on a warm day is from the deck of a boat cruising along the city's rivers, canals and lakes. Tours range from one-hour spins around the historic centre (from €11) to longer trips to Schloss Charlottenburg and beyond (from €15). Most offer live commentary in English and German. **Stern und Kreisschiffahrt** (☎536 3600; www.sternundkreis.de) is one of the main operators. The main season runs from April to mid-October, with a limited schedule in the winter months.

Walking

Several English-language walking-tour companies run introductory spins that take in both blockbuster and offbeat sights, plus themed tours (eg Third Reich, Cold War, Sachsenhausen, Potsdam). Guides are fluent English speakers, well informed, sharp witted and keen to answer your questions. Tours don't require reservations – just show up at one of the meeting points. Since these change quite frequently, keep an eye out for flyers in hotel or hostel lobbies, or at tourist offices, or contact the companies directly.

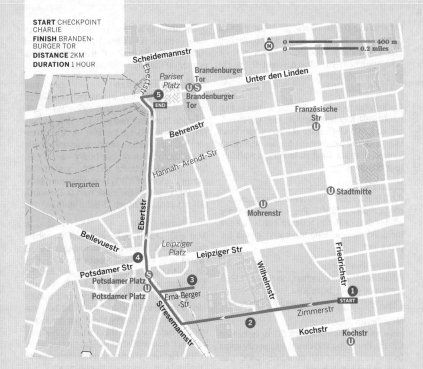

Walking Tour
Walking the Wall

For nearly three decades, the Berlin Wall divided a city and its people, becoming the most visible symbol of the Cold War. By now the two city halves have visually merged so perfectly that it takes a keen eye to tell East from West. To give you a sense of the period of division, this walk follows the most central section of the course of the Berlin Wall. For a more in-depth experience, rent the multimedia GPS-integrated WallGuide at Checkpoint Charlie. This is also where our tour kicks off.

As the third Allied checkpoint, **1 Checkpoint Charlie** got its name from the third letter in the NATO phonetic alphabet. Only weeks after the Berlin Wall was built, US and Soviet tanks faced off here in one of the tensest moments of the Cold War. Continue along **2 Niederkirchner Strasse**, past a 200m-long section of the original outer border wall. Scarred by souvenir hunters, it's now protected by a fence. The border strip was very narrow here, with the inner wall abutting such buildings as the former Nazi Air Force Ministry at the corner of Wilhelmstrasse. Turn

right on Stresemannstrasse and right again on Erna-Berger-Strasse to see one of the few remaining **3 GDR border watchtowers**. Guards had to climb up a slim round shaft via an iron ladder to reach the octagonal observation perch on top. Introduced in 1969, this cramped model was later replaced by larger square towers. Your next stop is Potsdamer Platz which, until 1990, used to be a massive no-man's land bifurcated by the wall and a death strip several hundred metres wide. Outside the northern S-Bahn station entrance, several **4 Berlin Wall segments** provide information about other wall memorial sites and future wall-related projects. Continue north to the **5 Brandenburger Tor** where construction of the wall began in the wee hours of 13 August 1961. Many statesmen exhorted against communism in front of it, including Ronald Reagan who, in 1987, uttered the famous words: 'Mr Gorbachev – tear down this wall!'. Two years later, the Berlin Wall was history.

Alternative Berlin Tours
WALKING TOUR

(☎0162-819 8264; www.alternativeberlin.com)
Free twice-daily subculture tours with a
funky-punky twist, plus a street-art workshop, the 666 Anti-Pubcrawl and a seriously
wacky Twilight Tour.

Berlin Walks
WALKING TOUR

(☎301 9194; www.berlinwalks.de; tours €12-15, concession €9-12) Get under the city's historical
skin with the local expert guides of Berlin's
longest-running English-language walking-
tour company.

Brewer's Berlin Tours
WALKING TOUR

(☎0177-388 1537; www.brewersberlintours.com;
adult/concession €15/12) Purveyors of the epic
all-day Best of Berlin tour (foot massage not
included) and a donation-based Berlin Express tour.

Insider Tour Berlin
WALKING TOUR

(☎692 3149; www.insidertour.com; tours €12-15,
concession €9-12) Insightful tours of Berlin,
plus day trips to Dresden and a pub crawl.

New Berlin Tours
WALKING TOUR

(www.newberlintours.com; adult €12-15, concession
€10-15) Energetic and entertaining city spins
by the pioneers of the donation-based 'free
tour' and the pub crawl.

Speciality Tours

Berlinagenten
CULTURAL TOUR

(☎4372 0701; www.berlinagenten.com; 3hr tour for
groups up to 10 from €350) Get a handle on Berlin's lifestyle with this clued-in company that
opens doors to hot and/or hidden bars, boutiques, restaurants, clubs, private homes and
sights. Its Gastro-Rallye delivers an insider's
primer on the city's culinary scene.

Berliner Unterwelten
GUIDED TOUR

(Map p77; ☎4991 0517; www.berliner-unterwelten.
de; Brunnenstrasse 105; adult/concession €10/8;
◷English tours 11am Wed-Mon, 1pm Mon, no tours
Wed Dec-Feb; ⑤Gesundbrunnen, ⓇGesundbrun-
nen) Explore Berlin's dark, dank underbelly
by picking your way past heavy steel doors,
hospital beds, helmets and filter systems on
a gripping tour of a WWII underground bunker. Buy tickets at the kiosk next to the south
exit of Gesundbrunnen U-Bahn station.

Fritz Music Tours
MUSIC TOURS

(Map p60; ☎3087 5633; www.musictours-berlin.
com; Unter den Linden 77; bus/walking tours €19/12,
minibus tours €45, Hansa Studios €10-20; ◷Eng-
lish bus tour 12.30pm Sun, walking tour 4pm Fri;
⑤Brandenburger Tor, ⓇBrandenburger Tor) Get the
low-down on Berlin's legendary music history
– from Bowie to U2, cult clubs to the Love Parade – along with news about who's rocking
the city right now on this dynamic 2½-hour
bus tour. Also available: walking tours, tours
of the Hansa recording studios and private
minibus tours. Reservations obligatory.

Trabi Safari
DRIVING TOUR

(Map p72; ☎2759 2273; www.trabi-safari.de; Zimmerstrasse 97; per person €30-90, Wall Ride €79-
89, prices depending on group size; ⑤Kochstrasse)
Catch the *Good Bye, Lenin!* vibe on tours of

PLAY IT COOL BY THE POOL

Viva Berlin! Take an old river barge, fill it with water, moor it in the Spree and – voila
– an urban lifestyle pool is born. In summer, a hedonistic Ibiza-vibe reigns at the artist-
designed Badeschiff (Map p72; ☎01578-591 4301; www.arena-berlin.de; Eichenstrasse 4;
summer adult/concession €4/3, winter €12; ◷8am-midnight end May-Sep/Oct; ⑤Schlesische
Strasse, ⓇTreptower Park), with bods bronzing in the sand or cooling off in the water and
a bar to fuel the fun. On scorching days, come before noon or risk a long wait. After-dark
action includes parties, bands, movies and simply chilling. In winter, an ethereally glowing plastic membrane covers the pool and a deliciously toasty chill zone with saunas
and bar. In winter (Nov-Mar) opening times range from 10am to 2pm and closing is from
10pm to 3am depending on the day of the week.

Any time of year is a fine time to feel your daily cares slip away at Liquidrom (Map
p72; ☎258 007 820; www.liquidrom-berlin.de; Möckernstrasse 10; 2hr/4hr/all day session
€19.50/24.50/29.50; ◷10am-midnight Sun-Thu, 10am-1am Fri & Sat), a stylishly minimalist
day spa that's the perfect mood enhancer on a rainy day. There are a couple of saunas,
dipping pools and lounge areas, but the star of the show is the darkened domed hall
where you float in a saltwater pool while being showered with soothing sounds and
psychedelic light projections. Pure bliss.

Berlin classic sights or the 'Wild East' with you driving or riding in a GDR-era Trabant car (Trabi) with live commentary piped into your vehicle.

✵ Festivals & Events

Berlin is very much a party town with a busy year-round calendar of concerts, street parties, mega sports events, trade shows and festivals celebrating everything from film to fetish, music to movies, travel to fashion. Berlin's tourist office (p115) website has a searchable events calendar and can also help you book tickets. To get you planning, we've listed a few highlights.

January & February

Berlinale   FILM FESTIVAL
(www.berlinale.de) Berlin's international film festival draws stars and starlets, directors and critics. The public can attend screenings, but they're often sold out quickly.

May & June

Karneval der Kulturen   STREET FAIR
(☏6097 7022; www.karneval-berlin.de) Exuberant three-day festival in the streets of Kreuzberg, culminating in a parade of costumed dancers, singers, DJs and musicians. Pentecost weekend.

Christopher Street Day   GAY, LESBIAN
(www.csd-berlin.de) People of every sexual orientation paint the town pink at one of Europe's biggest gay-pride parades and parties with more queens than you'd find at a royal wedding.

July & August

Berliner Bierfestival   BEER FESTIVAL
(www.bierfestival-berlin.de) Who needs Oktoberfest when you can have the 'world's longest beer garden'? Pick your poison from over 300 breweries from nearly 100 countries along 2km of Karl-Marx-Allee.

September & October

Berlin Music Week   MUSIC FESTIVAL
(www.berlin-music-week.de) Catch tomorrow's headliners during this week-long celebration of global music. Bring serious stamina for Clubnacht (Club Night), when one ticket buys entry to 60 clubs.

Berlin Marathon   SPORT
(www.berlin-marathon.com) Sweat it out with 50,000 other runners or just cheer 'em on during Germany's biggest street race, which has seen nine world records set since 1977.

Internationale Funkausstellung   ELECTRONICS FAIR
(www.ifa-berlin.de) Huge international consumer electronics fair showcases the latest gadgets everyone will want for Christmas.

November & December

Jazzfest Berlin   MUSIC FESTIVAL
(www.jazzfest-berlin.de) This top-rated jazz festival boogies through Berlin with dozens of performances by fresh and big-time talent.

Christmas Markets   CHRISTMAS MARKETS
Plenty of shimmering ornaments and potent mulled wine at dozens of Yuletide markets held throughout December in such locales as Breitscheidplatz and Alexanderplatz.

🛏 Sleeping

Berlin offers the gamut of places to unpack your suitcase. Just about every international chain now has a flagship in the German capital, but more interesting options that better reflect the city's verve and spirit abound. You can sleep in a former bank, boat or factory, in the home of a silent-movie diva, in a 'flying bed', or even a coffin. Standards are high but fierce competition has kept prices low compared to other capital cities. Seasonal room-rate variations are rare but prices spike during major trade shows, festivals and public holidays.

Berlin's hostel scene is as vibrant as ever and consists of both classic backie hostels and trendy flashpacker hostels. You'll find them in all districts but especially in Kreuzberg and Friedrichshain, putting you within stumbling distance of bars and clubs. Dorm beds can be had for as little as €9 but spending a little more gets you a smaller dorm or even a private room.

For style-minded wallet-watchers who've outgrown hostels, there's now an increasing number of budget designer hotels with chic interiors but small rooms and minimal amenities. Design-lovers with deeper pockets can choose from lifestyle and boutique hotels as well as *Kunsthotels* (art hotels), which are designed by artists and/or liberally sprinkled with original art. They're especially prevalent in the Mitte district.

Nostalgic types seeking Old Berlin flavour should check into a charismatic B&B, called *Hotel-Pension* or simply *Pension*. They're a dying breed, but for now there's still plenty of them, mostly in the western district of Charlottenburg, around Kurfürstendamm.

BERLIN FOR CHILDREN

Travelling to Berlin with tots can be child's play, especially if you keep a light schedule and involve the kids in the day-to-day planning. Lonely Planet's *Travel with Children* offers a wealth of tips and tricks on the subject.

Baby food, infant formula, soy and cow's milk, disposable nappies (diapers) and the like are widely available at chemists (drugstores) and in supermarkets. Breastfeeding in public is practised, although most women are discreet about it. Restaurants sometimes have a special children's menu or can prepare simple dishes, even if they're not listed. In good weather, picnics in the park or by the Spree River or Landwehr canal are a sunny option.

Lots of museums are free for children under 18, or have children's discounts, although the cut-off age varies. On public transport, children under six travel free, and those under 14 quality for the discount rate. Many stations have lifts.

As for accommodation, families should consider renting an apartment or ask for family rooms at hotels, as regular rooms tend to be rather small. Practically everyone can provide rollaway beds or cots, sometimes at a fee.

There's plenty to keep the tykes occupied, from zoos to kid-oriented museums to magic and puppet shows. Parks and imaginative playgrounds abound in all neighbourhoods. On hot summer days, a few hours spent at a public outdoor pool or a lakeside beach will go a long way towards keeping kids' tempers cool.

For wildlife observation, gravitate towards the Berlin Zoo (p81) and Aquarium (p81), which come with a petting corral and an adventure playground. Finny friends take centre stage at SeaLife Berlin (p68) – its smaller size makes it suitable for the kindergarten set, as does the affiliated Legoland Discovery Centre (p71).

Kid-friendly museums include the Museum für Naturkunde (p69), with its giant dinosaur skeletons, and the Deutsches Technikmuseum (p75), with its planes, trains and automobiles and hands-on science centre.

Older kids might get a kick out of the interactive computer games at the Computerspielemuseum (p76) or the Cold War spy and escape exhibits at the Mauermuseum (p61). Follow a visit here with a trip around Berlin's 'Wild East' in a quaint GDR-era car on a Trabi Safari (p86). And you'll score big-time with your music-loving teens if you take them on the Fritz Music Tour (p86).

Fun shops include Steiff Galerie in Berlin (p114) with its famous stuffed animals and the Ampelmann Galerie (p113).

As is the current trend, furnished flats are a popular – and economical – alternative to hotels in Berlin.

To minimise travel time, pick a place close to a U-Bahn or S-Bahn station and avoid those too far outside the S-Bahn ring.

MITTE

TOP CHOICE Circus Hotel HOTEL €€

(Map p60; ☎2000 3939; www.circus-berlin.de; Rosenthaler Strasse 1; d €80-110; @📶; SRosenthaler Platz) Our favourite budget boutique hotel. Rooms come with upbeat colours, thoughtful design details, sleek oak floors and quality beds. Unexpected perks include a well-stocked library and free iPod, netbook and DVD player rentals. Fabulous breakfast buffet to boot. Simply good value all around.

Hotel Amano HOTEL €€

(Map p60; ☎809 4150; www.amanogroup.de; Auguststrasse 43; d €80-160; P❄@📶; SRosenthaler Platz) An instant hit with style-minded wallet-watchers, Amano has inviting public areas dressed in brushed-copper walls and cocoa-hued banquettes. In rooms, white furniture teams up with oak floors and natural-toned fabrics to create crisp cosiness. The standard rooms are a case study in efficiency, so get an apartment for more elbow room. Great bar and summer rooftop terrace.

Wombat's City Hostel Berlin HOSTEL €

(Map p60; ☎8471 0820; www.wombats-hostels.com; Alte Schönhauser Strasse 2; dm/d €25/70; @📶; SRosa-Luxemburg-Platz) Wombat's has a long track record at getting hostelling right. From backpack-sized in-room lockers to individual reading lamps and a guest kitchen with dishwasher, the attention to detail here is impressive. Spacious rooms with bathrooms are as de rigueur as freebie linen and a welcome drink, best enjoyed with fellow party pilgrims in the 7th-floor Wombar. Optional breakfast is €3.80.

Motel One Berlin-Alexanderplatz HOTEL €
(Map p60; ☎2005 4080; www.motel-one.de; Dircksenstrasse 36; d from €69; [P]❄[@]📶; [S]Alexanderplatz, 🚆Alexanderplatz) If you value location over luxury, this fast-growing budget designer chain makes for an excellent crash pad. Smallish rooms come with up-to-the-minute touches (Loewe flat-screen TVs, granite counters, massage shower heads, air-con) that are normally the staple of posher players. Arne Jacobsen's turquoise egg chairs accent the hip lobby. This is the most central of seven Motel One properties around town, including one at Zoo station and another at Hauptbahnhof. See the website for details. Optional breakfast is €7.50.

Adina Apartment Hotel Berlin Checkpoint Charlie APARTMENT €€
(Map p60; ☎200 7670; www.adina.eu; Krausenstrasse 35-36; d €110-160, apt from €140; [P]❄[@]📶🏊; [S]Stadtmitte, Spittelmarkt) Adina's contemporary and roomy one- and two-bedroom apartments with full kitchens are tailor-made for cost-conscious families, anyone in need of elbow room and self-caterers (a supermarket is a minute away). Regular hotel rooms without kitchens are also available. Staff are accommodating and the pool and sauna make soothing sore muscles at the end of the day a snap. See the website for details about other Adina properties in town. Optional breakfast is €15.

The Dude BOUTIQUE HOTEL €€€
(Map p60; ☎411 988 177; www.thedudeberlin.com; Köpenicker Strasse 92; d €170-190; [P]📶; [S]Märkisches Museum, Heinrich-Heine-Platz) The Dude doesn't feel like a hotel but more like your rich grand-uncle's private mansion. Hand-picked furniture, lamps and colour schemes inspired by the proprietor's decades of travel exude an aura of timeless elegance. The most stunning element in this hushed 1822 hideaway is a Schinkel-designed spiral staircase. Breakfast (from €6) is served in the on-site deli; the **Brooklyn Beef Club** (Map p60; ☎2021 5820; www.brooklynbeefclub.com; Köpenicker Strasse 92; mains €50-100; 🕐dinner Mon-Sat; [S]Märkisches Museum) steakhouse gets top marks.

Circus Hostel HOSTEL €
(Map p60; ☎2000 3939; www.circus-hostel.de; Weinbergsweg 1a; dm €23-29, d with/without bathroom from €80/€64, 2-/4-person apt €95/150; [@]📶; [S]Rosenthaler Platz) Clean, cheerfully painted rooms, abundant showers and competent, helpful staff are among factors that keep Circus at the top of the hostel heap. Welcome tech touches include laptop and Skype phone rentals and laptop-sized in-room lockers with integrated electrical plug. To download its free self-guided MP3 city tour, go to www.circus-berlin.de/bustour.

Arte Luise Kunsthotel BOUTIQUE HOTEL €€
(Map p60; ☎284 480; www.luise-berlin.com; Luisenstrasse 19; d €100-210, without bathroom €80-110; ❄[@]📶; [S]Friedrichstrasse, 🚆Friedrichstrasse) At this 'gallery with rooms' each unit is designed by a different artist, who receives royalties whenever it's rented. Room 107, with its giant bed, and the boudoir-red 'Cabaret' (room 206) are especially memorable. Cheaper rooms are smaller and share facilities. Avoid those facing the train tracks. Optional breakfast is €11.

Cosmo Hotel Berlin HOTEL €€
(Map p60; ☎5858 2222; www.cosmo-hotel.de; Spittelmarkt 13; d €100-210; [P]❄[@]📶; [S]Spittelmarkt) Despite its ho-hum location on a busy street, this stylish hotel scores high for comfort and design. Extravagant lamps and armchairs in the lobby set the tone for rooms decked out in silver hues, even if the cheaper ones don't fit a tonne of luggage. Continental breakfast is €5, the full buffet €14.

Arcotel John F HOTEL €€
(Map p60; ☎405 0460; www.arcotelhotels.com; Werderscher Market 11; r €90-190; [P]❄[@]📶; [S]Hausvogteiplatz) This urbane lifestyle hotel pays homage to John F Kennedy with plenty of whimsical details, including hand-carved rocking chairs and curvaceous lamps inspired by Jackie's ballgowns. Rooms are smartly dressed in dark zebrano wood and a silver-white colour scheme. Optional breakfast is €18.

Mani Hotel BOUTIQUE HOTEL €
(Map p60; ☎5302 8080; www.hotel-mani.com; Torstrasse 136; d €73-174; [P]📶; [S]Rosenthaler Platz) Behind an elegant black facade on trendy Torstrasse, Mani flaunts an uncluttered urban feel and rooms that pack plenty of design cachet and creature comforts into a compact package. Optional breakfast is €15.

GAY & LESBIAN BERLIN

Berlin's legendary liberalism has spawned one of the world's biggest, most divine and most diverse GLBT playgrounds. Anything goes in 'Homopolis' (and we *do* mean anything), from the highbrow to the hands-on, the bourgeois to the bizarre, the mainstream to the flamboyant. Except for the hard-core sex places, gay spots get their share of opposite-sex and straight patrons.

The closest that Berlin comes to a 'gay village' is Schöneberg (Motzstrasse and Fuggerstrasse especially), where the rainbow flag has proudly flown since the 1920s. There's still plenty of (old-school) partying going on here, but anyone under 35 will likely feel more comfortable elsewhere. Current hipster central is Kreuzberg, which teems with party pens along Mehringdamm and Oranienstrasse. Across the river, Friedrichshain has such key clubs as Berghain/Panorama Bar (p108) and the hard-core **Lab.oratory** (Map p72; www.lab-oratory. de; Am Wriezener Bahnhof; ⏰Thu-Mon; ⑤Ostbahnhof). In Prenzlauer Berg gay-geared locales are fairly spread out, although Gleimstrasse and Greifenhagener Strasse are hubs.

Berlin's gayscape ranges from mellow cafes, campy bars and cinemas to saunas, cruising areas, clubs with dark rooms and all-out sex venues. As elsewhere, gay men have more options for having fun, but grrrls – from lipstick lesbians to hippie chicks to bad-ass dykes – won't feel left out.

Information

Mann-O-Meter (☎216 8008; www.mann-o-meter.de; Bülowstrasse 106; ⏰5-10pm Tue-Fri, 4-8pm Sat & Sun; ⑤Nollendorfplatz) One-stop information centre that also operates a hotline to report attacks on gays.

Out in Berlin This English/German booklet and website are indispensable guides to the city's queer scene.

Siegessäule Weekly freebie mag is the bible for all things gay and lesbian in Berlin.

Festivals

In mid-June, huge crowds turn out for the **Lesbisch-Schwules Strassenfest** (Lesbigay Street Festival; www.regenbogenfonds.de) in Schöneberg, which basically serves as a warm-up for Christopher Street Day (p87) later that month.

Sights

A great place to learn about Berlin's queer history is the nonprofit **Schwules Museum** (Gay Museum; Map p72; ☎6959 9050; www.schwulesmuseum.de; Mehringdamm 61; adult/concession €5/3; ⏰2-6pm Wed-Mon, to 7pm Sat; ⑤Mehringdamm), which is museum, archive and community centre all in one. Changing exhibits often focus on gay icons, artists or historical themes.

The **Denkmal für die im Nationalsozialismus verfolgten Homosexuellen** (Map p60; Ebertstrasse; ⏰2hr; ⑤Brandenburger Tor, Potsdamer Platz, Ⓡ Brandenburger Tor, Potsdamer Platz) trains the spotlight on the persecution and suffering of Europe's gay community under the Nazis. The freestanding, 4m-high, off-kilter concrete cube was designed by Danish-Norwegian artists Michael Elmgreen and Ingar Dragset. A looped video plays through a warped, narrow window.

Drinking

Heile Welt (Map p81; ☎2191 7507; Motzstrasse 5; ⏰from 6pm; ⑤Nollendorfplatz) Chic yet loungy, Schöneberg's Perfect World gets high marks for its communicative vibe, high flirt factor and handsome laddies. It's a great whistle-stop before launching into a raunchy night but gets packed in its own right as the moon rises higher in the sky.

Roses (Map p72; Oranienstrasse 187; ⏰from 9pm; ⑤Kottbusser Tor) At this Kreuzberg palace of camp and kitsch with pink furry walls Barbie would love, drinks are cheap and the bartenders pour with a generous elbow, making this a packed – and polysexual – pit stop during hard-partying nights.

Zum Schmutzigen Hobby (Map p72; www.ninaqueer.com; Revaler Strasse 99, RAW Tempel, gate 2; SWarschauer Strasse, RWarschauer Strasse) Berlin's trash-drag deity Nina Queer has flown her long-time Prenzlauer Berg coop and reopened her louche den of kitsch and glam in less hostile environs amid the Friedrichshain kool kids. Wednesday's Glamour Trivia Quiz is legendary.

Marietta (Map p77; 4372 0646; www.marietta-bar.de; Stargarder Strasse 13; from 10am; SSchönhauser Allee, M1, RSchönhauser Allee) Retro is now at this Prenzlauer Berg self-service retreat, where you can check out passing eye candy through the big window or lug your beverage to the dimly lit back room for quiet bantering. On Wednesday nights it's a launch pad for the local gay party circuit.

Hafen (Map p81; 211 4118; www.hafen-berlin.de; Motzstrasse 19; from 8pm; SNollendorfplatz) The all-comer Harbour has been a friendly stop to dock in Schöneberg for more than two decades. There are DJs, parties, drinking and flirting, plus Hendryk's hilarious Monday quiz night (in English on the first Monday of the month).

Clubbing

SchwuZ (Map p72; 693 7025; www.schwuz.de; Mehringdamm 61; from 11pm Fri & Sat; SMehringdamm) Fortify yourself upstairs at Melitta Sundström, then drop down to this queer cellar institution for some high-energy flirting and dancing at different parties nightly. Great for easing into the scene.

Connection (Map p81; www.connection-berlin.de; Fuggerstrasse 33; SWittenbergplatz) This classic men-only disco was a techno pioneer back in the '80s and still hasn't lost its grip on the scene, even though everyone's a little older now. The giant cruising labyrinth is legendary.

Berghain (p108) Take off your shirt and head to this vast post-industrial techno hellhole filled with studly queer bass junkies. With its dark and hidden corners and busy dark rooms, there's plenty of space for mischief.

Parties

Some of the best queer club nights are independent of the venues they use and may move around, although most have some temporary residency. We've given current locations, but it's best to check the websites or the listings mags for the latest scoop.

Kino International (Map p60; 2475 6011; www.yorck.de; Karl-Marx-Allee 33; SSchilling-strasse) This glamorous commie-era cinema hosts two monthly gay circuit mainstays: **Klub International**, on the first Saturday, for boys and **Girls' Town** for, well, girls on the second Saturday. On both nights, there's plenty of down-and-dirty dance music plus cocktails-with-a-view from the upstairs bar.

Chantals House of Shame (Map p60; www.siteofshame.com; Bassy Club, Schönhauser Allee 176a; from 11pm Thu; SSenefelderplatz) Trash diva Chantal's lair (currently at Bassy) is a beloved institution, as much for flirty glam factor as for the over-the-top tranny shows and the hotties who love 'em.

GMF (Map p60; www.gmf-berlin.de; Weekend, Alexanderplatz 5; 11pm Sun; SAlexanderplatz, RAlexanderplatz) At Weekend, Berlin's premier Sunday club is known for excessive SM (standing and modelling). Predominantly boyz, but girls OK.

Café Fatal (Map p72; www.cafefatal.de; SO36, Oranienstrasse 190; 7pm-2am Sun; Kottbusser Tor) All comers descend on SO36 for the ultimate rainbow tea dance that goes from 'strictly ballroom' to 'dirty dancing' in a flash. If you can't tell a waltz from a foxtrot, come at 7pm for free lessons.

Hotel Honigmond
HOTEL €€

(Map p60; ☑284 4550; www.honigmond-berlin.de; Tieckstrasse 12; d €145-235; P@🖥; ⓢOranienburger Tor) This delightful hotel scores a perfect 10 on our 'charmometer', not for being particularly lavish but for its homey yet elegant ambience. The restaurant has been a local favourite since GDR times and rooms sparkle with restored glory. The nicest among them flaunt such historic features as ornate stucco ceilings, frescoes and parquet floors.

Casa Camper
HOTEL €€€

(Map p60; ☑2000 3410; www.casacamper.com; Weinmeisterstrasse 1; r/ste from €185/325; P🖥; ⓢWeinmeisterstrasse) At this style pit for trend-conscious travellers, rooms are mod if minimalist and come with day-lit bathrooms and beds that invite hitting the snooze button. Minibars are eschewed for a top-floor lounge with stellar views, free breakfast and 24/7 snacks and drinks.

Hotel Adlon Kempinski
LUXURY HOTEL €€€

(Map p60; ☑226 10; www.kempinski.com; Pariser Platz, Unter den Linden 77; r from €250; ✳@🖥▤; ⓢBrandenburger Tor, ⓡBrandenburger Tor) Opposite Brandenburger Tor, the Adlon has been Berlin's most high-profile defender of the grand tradition since 1907. The striking lobby is a mere overture to the full symphony of luxury awaiting in spacious, amenity-laden rooms and suites where the decor is old-fashioned in a regal sort of way. A ritzy day spa, gourmet restaurants and the swank Felix (p109) nightclub add 21st-century spice.

The Weinmeister
HOTEL €€

(Map p60; ☑755 6670; www.the-weinmeister.com; Weinmeisterstrasse 2; d €140-300; P✳@🖥; ⓢWeinmeisterstrasse) Behind its shiny facade, this sassy glamour bastion unapologetically curries favour with creatives from fashion, music and film. Heck, British band Hurts and DJ Mousse T have designed their own rooms (501 and 401, respectively). You don't need to run with this crowd to appreciate the sleek rooms dressed in charcoal and chocolate, although a certain tech-savvy comes in handy when figuring out how to watch TV on the iMac.

Honigmond Garden Hotel
BOUTIQUE HOTEL €€

(Map p60; ☑284 4550; www.honigmond-berlin.de; Invalidenstrasse 122; d €125-230; P@🖥; ⓢNaturkundemuseum) Never mind the busy thoroughfare, this well-managed 20-room guesthouse is an utterly sweet retreat. Before even reaching your comfortable, antique-filled room, you'll be enchanted by the flowery garden with koi pond, fountain and old trees. The communal lounge comes with an honour bar and magazines.

POTSDAMER PLATZ & TIERGARTEN

Mandala Hotel
LUXURY HOTEL €€€

(Map p72; ☑590 050 000; www.themandala.de; Potsdamer Strasse 3; ste €145-360; P✳@🖥; ⓢPotsdamer Platz, ⓡPotsdamer Platz) How 'suite' it is to be staying at this swank cocoon of effortless sophistication and unfussy ambience. Suites come in six sizes (40 to 101 sq metres) and are equipped with a kitchenette, walk-in closets and spacious desks in case you're here to ink that deal. Wind down at the on-site spa before drinks at the stylish bar, perhaps followed by a Michelin-starred dinner at Facil (p98).

Ritz-Carlton Berlin
LUXURY HOTEL €€€

(Map p60; ☑337 777; www.ritzcarlton.com; Potsdamer Platz 3; d €176-455; P✳@🖥▤; ⓢPotsdamer Platz, ⓡPotsdamer Platz) At one of Berlin's most popular full-on luxury addresses, rooms and suites are done up in soothing natural hues and classical dark-wood furniture, enhanced by original watercolours by German contemporary artist Markus Lüpertz. Expect all the trappings of a big-league player, including a high-end restaurant, bar and spa. Optional breakfast is €38.

🌿 Scandic Berlin Potsdamer Platz
HOTEL €€

(Map p72; ☑700 7790; www.scandichotels.com; Gabriele-Tergit-Promenade 19; d €90-200, breakfast €20; P✳@🖥; ⓢMendelssohn-Bartholdy-Park) This Scandinavian import gets kudos for central location, spacious blonde-wood rooms with big bathrooms and for going the extra mile when it comes to being green. Water conservation is taking so seriously that you may see staff watering plants with a carafe from an empty restaurant table. It's a big city hotel, with all the commensurate comforts, including a restaurant, bar and gym. You can even borrow bikes or walking sticks for spins around Tiergarten. Free minibar drinks.

KREUZBERG

Hüttenpalast
HOSTEL €

(Map p72; ☑3730 5806; www.huettenpalast.de; Hobrechtstrasse 66; campervans & cabins/d without bathroom €65/85; 🖥; ⓢHermannplatz) Sure, it has regular rooms with private bathroom, but who wants those when you can sleep in a romantic wooden hut with rooftop terrace or in a quirky vintage caravan fitted with a homemade light sculpture? Welcome to Hüttenpalast, an indoor campground in an old vacuum-cleaner factory that's an unusual place to hang your hat, even by Berlin standards. Wacky and welcoming, there's also an idyllic garden and a cafe for socialising. Check-in is between 3pm and 6pm or by arrangement.

Hotel Sarotti-Höfe
HOTEL €€

(Map p72; ☑6003 1680; www.sarotti-hoefe.de; Mehringdamm 55; d €100-180; P@🕏; S Mehringdamm) You'll have sweet dreams in this 19th-century ex–chocolate factory where the courtyard-cloistered rooms are quiet despite being smack dab in the bustling quarter around Bergmannstrasse. Rooms exude elegant yesteryear flair with rich earth-toned fabrics and dark-wood furniture. Those in the deluxe category even have a small private terrace. Check-in is at the on-site cafe, where days start with an opulent breakfast (from €10).

Grand Hostel
HOSTEL €

(Map p72; ☑2009 5450; www.grandhostel-berlin. de; Tempelhofer Ufer 14; dm €12-15, d €58; @🕏; S Möckernbrücke) Afternoon tea in the library? Check. Rooms with stucco-ornamented ceilings? Got 'em. River views? Yup. OK, the Grand Hostel may be no five-star hotel, but it is one of Berlin's most comfortable and atmospheric hostels. Ensconced in a wonderful 1870s building are private rooms and dorms with quality single beds and large lockable cabinets. The Grandwich Bar serves sandwiches and weekend brunch.

Hotel Johann
HOTEL €€

(Map p72; ☑225 0740; www.hotel-johann-berlin.de; Johanniterstrasse 8; d €95-120; P@🕏; S Prinzenstrasse, Hallesches Tor) This 33-room hotel consistently tops the popularity charts, thanks to its eager-to-please service and light-flooded rooms where minimalist designer style contrasts with such historic flourishes as scalloped ceilings and brick walls. The small garden is perfect for summery breakfasts, while happening Bergmannstrasse and the Jüdisches Museum are within strolling distance.

Hotel Riehmers Hofgarten
HOTEL €€

(Map p72; ☑7809 8800; www.riehmers-hofgarten .de; Yorckstrasse 83; d €126-143; 🕏; S Mehringdamm) Take a romantic 19th-century building, add contemporary art, stir in a few zeitgeist touches such as iPod docking stations and you'll get one winning cocktail of a hotel. Riehmers' high-ceilinged rooms are modern but not stark; if you're noise-sensitive, get a courtyard-facing one. Assets include in-room tea and coffee, free laptop rentals and a popular gourmet restaurant.

FRIEDRICHSHAIN

TOP CHOICE Michelberger Hotel
HOTEL €€

(Map p72; ☑2977 8590; www.michelbergerhotel. com; Warschauer Strasse 39; d €80-180; 🕏; S Warschauer Strasse, ⓡ Warschauer Strasse) The pinnacle of creative crash pads, Michelberger perfectly encapsulates Berlin's offbeat DIY spirit. Rooms don't hide their factory pedigree but are comfortable and come in sizes suitable for lovebirds, families or rock bands. Staff are friendly and clued-in. On weekends, there's often some sort of party or concert going on in the bar-reception-lobby. Great for the young and forever young. Optional breakfast is €8.

nhow
HOTEL €€

(Map p72; ☑290 2990; www.nhow-hotels.com; Stralauer Allee 3; d €115-275; P🕏; S Warschauer Strasse, ⓡ Warschauer Strasse) nhow bills itself as a 'music and lifestyle hotel' and underscores the point by having its own on-site recording studios. The look of the place is certainly dynamic, what with a sideways tower jutting out over the Spree and Karim Rashid's vibrant digi-pop design that would make Barbie proud. Rooms are more subdued, despite the pink, blue and black colour scheme.

Ostel Hostel
HOSTEL €

(Map p72; ☑2576 8660; www.ostel.eu; Wriezener Karree 5; dm/d/apt from €15/64/80; P@🕏; S Ostbahnhof) Fancy a stay with a *Good Bye, Lenin!* vibe? Book a bed in this unusual hostel, which resuscitates socialist GDR charm with original furnishings sourced from flea markets, grannies' attics and eBay. Style police alert! With portraits of Honecker and other party apparatchiks peering down on you, you can stay in a pioneer-room dorm, a '70s holiday apartment, a prefab flat or the bugged Stasi suite. Rates include linen, towels and wi-fi.

Raise a Smile Hostel
HOSTEL €

(Map p72; ☑0172 855 6064; www.raise-a-smile -hostel-berlin.com; Weidenweg 51; dm/d from €10/40; @🕏; S Frankfurter Tor, ⓡ M10 to Bersarinplatz) This charity-run, African-themed

RENTAL APARTMENTS

For self-caterers, independent types, wallet-watchers, families and anyone in need of plenty of privacy, a short-term furnished-flat rental may well be the cat's pyjamas. Plenty of options have been popping up lately, but these are our favourites:

Brilliant Apartments (Map p77; ☎8061 4796; www.brilliant-apartments.de; Prenzlauer Berg; apt from €84; 📶; [S]Eberswalder Strasse) The name is the game in these 11 stylish and modern units with full kitchens that sleep from one to six people and are located on Oderberger Strasse and Rykestrasse, both hip drags in Prenzlauer Berg that put you close to everything.

Miniloft Berlin (Map p60; ☎847 1090; www.miniloft.com; Hessische Strasse 5, Scheunenviertel; apt from €138; 📶; [S]Naturkundemuseum) Architect-designed lofts in an energy-efficient building, some with south-facing panorama windows, others with cosy alcoves, all outfitted with modern designer furniture and kitchenettes.

T&C Apartments (Map p77; ☎405 046 612; www.tc-apartments-berlin.de; Kopenhagener Strasse 72; apt from €75; [S]Schönhauser Allee) Huge selection of stylish, hand-picked, one- to four-room apartments in Mitte, Prenzlauer Berg, Tiergarten and Schöneberg; headquarters located in Prenzlauer Berg.

ÏMA Loft Apartments (Map p72; ☎6162 8913; www.imalofts.com; Ritterstrasse 12-14; apt €55-200; 📶; [S]Moritzplatz) These uncluttered, contemporary apartments are part of the ÏMA Design Village, an old factory shared by design studios and a dance and theatre academy. They sleep one to four.

Berlin Lofts (☎0151-2121 9126; www.berlinlofts.com; Stephanstrasse 60; apt from €127; [@]📶; [S]Westhafen, Birkenstrasse, [R]Westhafen) Rents huge lofts in handsomely converted historic buildings, including an old smithy and a bi-level horse barn. The area, alas, is not nearly as hip, although public-transport connections are decent. Trivia bonus: Kommune 1, Germany's first politically motivated student commune, formed in 1967, once lived in one of the apartments.

hostel donates 100% of profits to children's projects in Zambia. Elephants, zebras, giraffes and big cats watch over guests in smallish dorms and private rooms with shared facilities. With only 18 beds, it's definitely not a party hostel, but great for banding up with fellow travellers in the lounge or the communal kitchen. Two-night minimum. Breakfast by donation.

Eastern Comfort Hostelboat HOSTEL €

(Map p72; ☎6676 3806; www.eastern-comfort.com; Mühlenstrasse 73-77; dm €16-19, d €50-78; [@]📶; [S]Warschauer Strasse, [R]Warschauer Strasse) Moored on the Spree River, right by the East Side Gallery, this floating two-boat hostel puts you within staggering distance of party-hearty Kreuzberg and Friedrichshain. Cabins are carpeted and trimmed in wood, but pretty snug (except for 'first-class'); all but the dorms have their own shower and toilet. On Wednesdays, the hostel hosts an English-language gathering of locals, expats and visitors (see p109).

🍃 **Hotel 26** HOTEL €€

(Map p72; ☎297 7780; www.hotel26-berlin.de; Grünberger Strasse 26; d from €90; [P][@]📶; [S]Warschauer Strasse, 🚋M10 to Grünberger Strasse, [R]Warschauer Strasse) Set back from the street and with a lovely garden out back, this architect-owned hotel in a revamped factory sparkles in cheery citrus colours that instantly put you in a good mood. Clear lines and blonde-wood furniture dominate both public areas and the rooms. Eco credentials include natural soaps, filtered water and an organic cafe.

PRENZLAUER BERG

[TOP CHOICE] **EastSeven Berlin Hostel** HOSTEL €

(Map p77; ☎9362 2240; www.eastseven.de; Schwedter Strasse 7; dm €17-19, d €50; [@]📶; [S]Senefelderplatz) Friendly and fun, this top-rated small hostel fires on all cylinders and is within a whisker of hip hang-outs and public transport. Cultural and language barriers melt quickly over a barbecue in the idyllic back garden, dinner in the modern kitchen (with dishwasher!) or chilling in the retro lounge. Come bedtime, retreat to comfy pine beds in brightly painted dorms with lockers, or in private rooms.

Hotel Kastanienhof
HOTEL €€

(Map p77; ☑443 050; www.kastanienhof.biz; Kastanienallee 65; d €105-140; P@🖥; SRosenthaler Platz, 🏛M1 to Zionskirchstrasse, SSenefelderplatz) This charmer puts you right onto Kastanienallee, with its many cafes and restaurants, although the hotel design itself has more of a traditional bent. Family owned and with fall-over-backwards staff, it has 35 rooms, including themed ones decorated with historical photos, paintings and information about Berlin landmarks. Bikes for hire at a small fee.

Meininger Hotel Berlin Prenzlauer Berg
HOSTEL, HOTEL €

(Map p77; ☑6663 6100; www.meininger-hotels. com; Schönhauser Allee 19; dm €15-28, d €44-100; @🖥; SSenefelderplatz) Run with panache and professionalism, this top-flight hotel-hostel combo is ideal for savvy nomads seeking plenty of comforts without dropping buckets of cash. A lift whisks you to mod rooms and dorms (all with attached bathrooms) with plenty of space, quality furnishings, flat-screen TVs and even blackout blinds to combat jetlag (or hangovers). Other assets: the all-day cafe-bar, guest kitchen and spot-on location close to sights, eats and parties. Check the website for the other five Berlin locations, including recommended ones near the Hauptbahnhof and on Oranienburger Strasse. Rates include linen.

Ackselhaus & Blue Home
BOUTIQUE HOTEL €€

(Map p77; ☑4433 7633; www.ackselhaus.de; Belforter Strasse 21; ste from €105, apt from €150; @🖥; SSenefelderplatz) At this charismatic retreat in a 19th-century building you'll sleep in large, classily decorated themed rooms (eg Africa, Rome, Maritime), each with thoughtfully picked special features, a free-standing tub perhaps, a four-poster bed or Chinese antiques. Many face the idyllic courtyard garden.

CHARLOTTENBURG & SCHÖNEBERG

TOP CHOICE Hotel Askanischer Hof
HOTEL €€

(Map p79; ☑881 8033; www.askanischer-hof.de; Kurfürstendamm 53; d €120-180; 🖥; SAdenauerplatz) If you're after character and retro flair, you'll find heaps of both at this 17-room jewel with a Roaring Twenties pedigree. An ornate oak door leads to a quiet oasis where no two rooms are alike but all are filled with antiques, lace curtains, frilly chandeliers and time-worn oriental rugs. The quaint Old Berlin charms make a popular setting for fashion shoots.

Hotel Concorde Berlin
HOTEL €€€

(Map p79; ☑800 9990; www.concorde-hotels.com/ concordeberlin; Augsburger Strasse 41; d €150-300; P✳@🖥; SKurfürstendamm) If you like edgy design combined with the amenities of a big-city property, the Concorde should fit the bill. Designed by Jan Kleihues, from the curved limestone facade to the door knobs, it channels New York efficiency, French lightness of being and Berlin-style unpretentiousness. The 311 rooms and suites are supersized, warmly furnished and accented with quality prints by contemporary German artists.

Axel Hotel
HOTEL €€

(Map p81; ☑2100 2893; www.axelhotels.com/berlin; Lietzenburger Strasse 13/15; d €130-210; P✳🖥; SWittenbergplatz) Next to Schöneberg's 'gay village', Axel cheekily bills itself as 'hetero-friendly' but is squarely aimed at the gay community. The soundproof rooms are stylish, if on the twee side, but come with king-size beds, bathrobes and above-average amenities. Follow a workout in the rooftop gym with a massage or a soak in the outdoor spa. In summer, the Sky Bar is the perfect launch pad for a night out.

Mittendrin
B&B €€

(Map p79; ☑2362 8861; www.boutique-hotel-berlin. de; Nürnberger Strasse 16; d €100-200; 🖥; SAugsburger Strasse, Wittenbergplatz) This actress-run sweet retreat close to primo shopping is a fantastic find for those who value individual service over fancy lobbies or rooftop bars. All four rooms bulge with character, hand-picked furnishings and homey extras like fresh flowers and candles. Breakfasts are gourmet affairs and, if desired, served in bed at no extra charge.

Hotel Art Nouveau
B&B €€

(Map p79; ☑327 7440; www.hotelartnouveau. de; Leibnizstrasse 59; d €96-176; P@🖥; SAdenauerplatz) A rickety birdcage lift drops you off with belle époque flourish at this fine boutique pension. Rooms skimp neither on space nor charisma, and offer a blend of youthful flair and tradition. The affable owners are fluent English speakers with a knack for colour and for sourcing fantastic pieces of art and furniture. Bonus points for the superb beds and the organic breakfast.

Hotel Otto   HOTEL €€
(Map p79; ☑5471 0080; www.hotelotto.com; Knesebeckstrasse 10; d €100-140; P🖭; SErnst-Reuter-Platz) Otto would be just another business hotel were it not for the fall-over-backwards staff and thoughtful extras such as free DVDs and a rooftop lounge with free afternoon cake and refreshments. Rooms get character from bright colour accents and warm textures, even if 'standard' ones are pretty small. Optional breakfast is €15.

Hotel Bogota   HOTEL €€
(Map p79; ☑881 5001; www.bogota.de; Schlüterstrasse 45; d €90-150, without bathroom €64-77; 🖭; SUhlandstrasse) Bogota has charmed travellers with charisma and vintage flair since 1964. Helmut Newton studied with fashion photographer Yva here in the 1930s and to this day the retro landmark hosts glam-mag photo shoots. Love those Gregorian chants in the lightcourt! Room sizes and amenities vary greatly, so ask to see a few before settling in.

Louisa's Place   BOUTIQUE HOTEL €€€
(Map p79; ☑631 030; www.louisas-place.de; Kurfürstendamm 160; ste €135-595; P@🖭🌊; SAdenauerplatz) Louisa's is the kind of place that dazzles with class not glitz, a discreet deluxe hideaway that puts great emphasis on customised guest services. Suites here are luxe and huge and have kitchens, the pool is small but refreshing and the library palatial. A high-end restaurant shares the premises. Optional breakfast is €20.

✕ Eating

If you crave traditional comfort food, you'll certainly find plenty of places to indulge in roast pork knuckles, smoked pork chops or calves liver in Berlin. These days, though, typical local fare is lighter, healthier, more creative and more likely to come from gourmet kitchens, organic eateries and a United Nations' worth of ethnic restaurants. The most exciting newcomers can usually be found in Mitte and Kreuzberg.

Eschewing tradition, a growing league of chefs has jumped on the locavore bandwagon and lets local, farm-fresh and often organic ingredients steer a seasonally calibrated menu. The Michelin testers too have confirmed that Berlin is ripe for the culinary big time by awarding their coveted stars to 13 chefs.

If there ever was a snack food with cult status, the humble *Currywurst* is it. A slivered, subtly spiced pork sausage swimming in tomato sauce and dusted with curry powder, it's as iconic as the Brandenburg Gate. A legacy of Berlin's vast Turkish community is the doner kebab, served in a pita with salad and sauce.

Berlin's multicultural tapestry has brought the world's foods to town, from Austrian schnitzel to Zambian zebra steaks. Sushi is hugely popular and Mexican and Korean restaurants have of late been proliferating. Reflecting the trend towards tasty and healthy food is the abundance of Asian eateries, especially Thai and Vietnamese.

Of late, vegan restaurants have been sprouting quicker than alfalfa, as have 'bio' cafes where dishes are prepared from organic and locally sourced ingredients. Also popular is 'guerrilla dining': secret supper parties held in private homes for short periods or at irregular intervals and often accessible by invitation only.

MITTE

TOP CHOICE Katz Orange   INTERNATIONAL €€€
(Map p60; ☑983 208 430; www.katzorange.com; Bergstrasse 22; mains €13-22; ☉dinner Tue-Sat year-round, lunch May-Sep; SRosenthaler Platz) With its gourmet organic farm-to-table menu, feel-good country styling and swift and smiling servers, the Orange Cat hits a purr-fect gastro grand slam. The setting in a historic brewery with fairy-tale flourishes is stunning, especially in summer when the patio opens. Fabulous cocktails, too.

Hartweizen   ITALIAN €€
(Map p60; ☑2849 3877; www.hartweizen.com; Torstrasse 96; mains €11-24; ☉dinner Mon-Sat; SRosenthaler Platz) With its simple wooden tables, panorama windows and bright bulbs, Hartweizen is eons away from Chianti-bottle kitsch but, quite simply, a top Italian restaurant focused on the feisty flavours of the Puglia region. The most creativity goes into the appetisers, but fish and meat are also first-rate, the pastas homemade and the wines fairly priced.

Schwarzwaldstuben   GERMAN €€
(Map p60; ☑2809 8084; Tucholskystrasse 48; dishes €7-14; ⊕Oranienburger Strasse) In the mood for a *Hansel and Gretel* moment? Then join the other 'lost kids' in this send

up of the Black Forest, complete with plastic pines and baseball-capped Bambi heads. We can't get enough of the *geschmelzte Maultaschen* (sautéed ravioli-like pasta) and the giant schnitzels, which are perfect foils for the Rothaus Tannenzäpfle beer.

TOP CHOICE **Uma** ASIAN €€€
(Map p60; ☑301 117 324; www.uma-restaurant.de; Behrenstrasse 72; mains €16-55; ☉dinner Mon-Sat; ▣100, ⑤Brandenburger Tor, ⓡBrandenburger Tor) Japanese for horse, Uma raises the bar for luxury with its exquisite decor, eye-catching artwork and Euro-inflected Asian dishes that weave flavours together like fine tapestries. Aside from sushi and sashimi, there are meaty mains from the robata (charcoal) grill and such tasty morsels as Korean fried octopus and wasabi-infused soft-shell crab meant for sharing.

Ishin – Mittelstrasse JAPANESE €€
(Map p60; www.ishin.de; Mittelstrasse 24; platter €7-18; ☉Mon-Sat; ⑤Friedrichstrasse, ⓡFriedrichstrasse) Look beyond the cafeteria-style get-up to sushi glory for minimal wallets. Combination platters are ample and affordable, especially during happy hour (all day Wednesday and Saturday, until 4pm on other days). Not in the mood for raw fish? Go for a rice bowl instead. Nice touch: the unlimited free green tea. There's another branch near **Checkpoint Charlie** (Map p72; Charlottenstrasse 16; ⑤Kochstrasse).

Monsieur Vuong ASIAN €€
(Map p60; ☑9929 6924; www.monsieurvuong.de; Alte Schönhauser Strasse 46; mains around €8; ☉noon-midnight; ⑤Weinmeisterstrasse, Rosa-Luxemburg-Platz) Berlin's godfather of upbeat Indochina nosh-stops, Monsieur has been copied many times – the concept is just that good. Pick from a compact menu of flavour-packed soups and two or three oft-changing mains, then sit back and enjoy your leftover money. Amazingly, the quality hasn't come down despite the never-ending queue. Come in the afternoon to avoid the frenzy.

Restaurant Tim Raue ASIAN €€€
(Map p72; ☑2593 7930; www.tim-raue.com; Rudi-Dutschke-Strasse 26; 2-/3-course lunch €28/38, 4-/6-course dinner €110/140; ☉Tue-Sat; ⑤Kochstrasse) Now here's a Michelin restaurant we can get our mind around. Unstuffy ambience, casually clad servers and subtly sophisticated design pair perfectly with Raue's brilliant Asian-inspired 'aroma' cuisine that

BERLIN'S BEST FOR...

» **Asian** Uma (p97)
» **Celebrity spotting** Grill Royal (p97)
» **Currywurst** Curry 36 (p102)
» **Old Berlin** Henne (p99)
» **Gourmet** restaurant Tim Raue (p97)
» **Italian** Hartweizen (p96)
» **Organic** Katz Orange (p96)
» **Neighbourhood restaurant** Cafe Jacques (p99)
» **Quirky eats** Sauvage (p102)
» **Riverside dining** Spindler & Klatt (p102)
» **Turkish** Defne (p99)
» **Vegetarian** Cookies Cream (p97)

looks like art on a plate and launches a flavour explosion in your mouth. His rave-worthy personal spin on Peking duck and creatively stuffed dim sum are perennial bestsellers.

Augustiner am Gendarmenmarkt GERMAN €€
(Map p60; ☑2045 4020; www.augustiner-braeu-berlin.de; Charlottenstrasse 55; mains €6-19; ☉10am-1am; ⑤Französische Strasse) Tourists, concert-goers and hearty food lovers rub shoulders at rustic tables in Berlin's first authentic Bavarian beer hall. Sausages, roast pork and pretzels provide rib-sticking sustenance, but there's also plenty of lighter (even meat-free) fare and great lunch specials.

Cookies Cream VEGETARIAN €€€
(Map p60; ☑2749 2940; www.cookiescream.com; Behrenstrasse 55; mains €20, 3-course menu €36; ☉dinner Tue-Sat; ☑; ⑤Französische Strasse) Kudos if you can locate this hip herbivore haven right away. Hint: the entrance is in the service alley of the Westin Grand Hotel. Ring the bell to enter an elegantly industrial loft for flesh-free, flavour-packed dishes from current-harvest ingredients. This grand culinary journey also gets you free admission into to the eponymous nightclub (p108).

Grill Royal STEAKHOUSE €€€
(Map p60; ☑2887 9288; www.grillroyal.com; Friedrichstrasse 105b; mains €16-39, steaks €18-55; ☉dinner; ⑤Friedrichstrasse, ⓡFriedrichstrasse) A platinum card is a handy accessory at this buzzy, look-at-me temple where visiting

ROSENTHALER PLATZ: SNACK CENTRAL

For feeding hunger pangs on the quick and cheap, choices could not be greater than the area around Rosenthaler Platz. Here's our personal hit list:

» **Fleischerei Imbiss** (Map p60; Torstrasse 116; snacks from €2.50; ⏲11am-2am Mon-Sat, 2pm-midnight Sun; [S]Rosenthaler Platz, [T]M1 to Rosenthaler Platz) for divine *Currywurst* with bubbly

» **Rosenthaler Grill- und Schlemmerbuffet** (Map p60; ☎283 2153; Torstrasse 125; dishes €2.50-7; ⏲24hr; [S]Rosenthaler Platz) for Oscar-worthy doner kebabs

» **Rosenburger** (Map p60; ☎2408 3037; Brunnenstrasse 196; burgers from €2.90; ⏲from 11am; [S]Rosenthaler Platz) for freshly made organic burgers

» **Côcô** (Map p60; Rosenthaler Strasse 2; sandwiches €4.20-5.50; ⏲11am-10pm Mon-Thu, 11am-midnight Fri & Sat, noon-10pm Sun; [S]Rosenthaler Platz) for bulging *bánh mì* (Vietnamese sandwiches)

A-listers, pouty models and trust-afarians slurp oysters and tuck into their prime cuts. Riverside tables beckon in fine weather.

White Trash Fast Food AMERICAN €€
(Map p60; ☎5034 8668; www.whitetrashfastfood.com; Schönhauser Allee 6-7; mains €8-20; ⏲from noon Mon-Fri, from 6pm Sat & Sun; [S]Rosa-Luxemburg-Platz) Wally Potts – city cowboy, California import and Berlin's coolest bar owner – has spun this ex-Irish pub with Chinese flourishes into a culinary punk-hole complete with in-house tattoo parlour. On some nights, DJs and bands make conversation a challenge, thus helping you focus on the manly burgers and steaks flown in straight from the US of A.

Kopps VEGAN €€
(Map p60; ☎4320 9775; www.kopps-berlin.de; Linienstrasse 94; mains €12-16; ⏲8.30am-midnight; ✎; [S]Rosenthaler Platz, [T]M1) 'German vegan' may seem like an oxymoron but not at Kopps, which dishes up delicious classics like goulash and schnitzel sans animal products. The space is sparse but stylish, with bluish-grey walls and recycled doors, and mirrors in unexpected places. Excellent breakfasts and bursting weekend brunch to boot.

Barcomi's Deli CAFE €
(Map p60; www.barcomis.de; 2nd courtyard, Sophie-Gips-Höfe, Sophienstrasse 21; dishes €2-11; ⏲9am-9pm Mon-Sat, 10am-9pm Sun; [S]Weinmeisterstrasse) Join latte-rati, families and expats at this New York-meets-Berlin deli for custom-roasted coffee, wraps, bagels with lox (smoked salmon), soups, salads and possibly the best brownies and cheesecake this side of the Hudson River. Bonus points for the charming and quiet setting in a classic Scheunenviertel courtyard.

POTSDAMER PLATZ & TIERGARTEN

Facil INTERNATIONAL €€€
(Map p72; ☎590 051 234; www.facil.de; Mandala Hotel, Potsdamer Strasse 3; 1-/2-/3-course lunch €19/29/39, dinner mains €16-55, 4-/8-course dinner €86/146; ⏲noon-3pm & 7-11pm Mon-Fri; [B]200, [S]Potsdamer Platz, [R]Potsdamer Platz) Michael Kempf's Michelin-starred fare is hugely innovative yet deliciously devoid of unnecessary flights of fancy. Enjoy it while draped into a sleek Donghia chair in the glass-enclosed dining chamber at the Mandala Hotel. Budget-savvy gourmets take advantage of the lunchtime menu.

Qiu INTERNATIONAL €€
(Map p72; ☎590 051 230; www.qiu.de; Mandala Hotel, Potsdamer Strasse 3; 2-course lunch €14; ⏲lunch Mon-Fri; [B]200, [S]Potsdamer Platz, [R]Potsdamer Platz) The two-course business lunch at this stylish lounge in the Mandala Hotel is a virtual steal, while at night the sensuous setting amid mood-lit fringe lamps and golden mosaic waterfall is great for pre-dinner or post-show cocktails.

Restaurant Gropius INTERNATIONAL €€
(Map p72; ☎2548 6406; www.mosaik-berlin.de/restaurant-gropius; Martin-Gropius-Bau, Niederkirchner Strasse 7; mains €7-18; ⏲10am-7pm Wed-Mon; [B]M41, 200, [S]Potsdamer Platz, [R]Potsdamer Platz) This restaurant inside the Martin-Gropius-Bau exhibit space presents changing smart menus inspired by an art show currently presented in the building. Enjoy it beneath crystal chandeliers in the elegant dining room or in the tree-shaded garden. Also good just for coffee and cake, or if you're visiting any exhibit.

Vapiano
ITALIAN €

(Map p60; 2300 5005; www.vapiano.de; Potsdamer Platz 5; mains €5.50-9; 11am-midnight Mon-Sat, to 11pm Sun; 200, Potsdamer Platz, Potsdamer Platz) Mix-and-match pastas, creative salads and crusty pizzas are all prepared right before your eyes amid jazzy decor by Matteo Thun at this stylish self-service canteen. Nice touch: a condiment basket with fragrant fresh basil and quality oil and balsamico. Your order is recorded on a chip card and paid for on leaving.

KREUZBERG & NORTHERN NEUKÖLLN

TOP CHOICE Cafe Jacques
INTERNATIONAL €€

(Map p72; 694 1048; Maybachufer 8; mains €12-20; dinner; Schönleinstrasse) A favourite with off-duty chefs and food-savvy locals, Jacques infallibly charms with flattering candlelight, warm decor and fantastic wine. It's the perfect date spot but, quite frankly, you only have to be in love with good food to appreciate the French- and North African–inspired blackboard menu. Charismatic owner Ahmad will happily recommend the perfect matching wine. Reservations essential.

Horváth
AUSTRIAN €€€

(Map p72; 6128 9992; www.restaurant-horvath. de; Paul-Lincke-Ufer 44a; 3-/7-course menu €40/76; dinner Tue-Sun; Kottbusser Tor) At his canalside bistro, newly minted Michelin chef Sebastian Frank performs culinary alchemy with Austrian classics, fearlessly combining textures, flavours and ingredients. To truly test his talents, order the 10-course small-plate dinner (€73). Despite the fanciful cuisine, the ambience in the elegantly rustic dining room remains relaxed.

Defne
TURKISH €€

(Map p72; 8179 7111; www.defne-restaurant. de; Planufer 92c; mains €7.50-16; dinner; Kottbusser Tor, Schönleinstrasse) If you thought Turkish cuisine stopped at the doner kebab, Defne will teach you otherwise. The appetizer platter alone elicits intense food cravings (fabulous walnut-chilli paste!), but inventive mains such as *ali nacik* (sliced lamb with pureed eggplant and yoghurt) also warrant repeat visits.

Max und Moritz
GERMAN €€

(Map p72; 6951 5911; www.maxundmoritzberlin. de; Oranienstrasse 162; mains €9-15; dinner; Moritzplatz) The patina of yesteryear hangs over this ode-to-old-school brewpub named for the cheeky Wilhelm Busch cartoon characters. Since 1902 it has lured hungry eaters with sudsy home brews and granny-style Berlin fare.

Volt
MODERN GERMAN €€€

(Map p72; 6107 4033; www.restaurant-volt.de; Paul-Lincke-Ufer 21; mains €24-32, 4-course meal €54; dinner Mon-Sat; Görlitzer Bahnhof) The theatrical setting in a 1928 transformer station would be enough to seek out the culinary outpost of Matthias Geiss, whose reputation catapulted after being named Berlin's most promising new chef in 2011. More drama awaits on the plates, where smartly combined regional meats, fish and vegetables put on an artful show in innovative yet honest-to-goodness ways.

Bar Raval
SPANISH €€

(Map p72; 8179 7111; www.barraval.de; Lübbener Strasse 1; tapas from €4; dinner; ; Görlitzer Bahnhof) Forget folklore kitsch, this tapas bar is fit for the 21st century. The delish homemade Iberian morsels pack both comfort and complexity, as do the seasonal specials and hand-picked wines. Clued-in locals invade for Monday's paella night.

Henne
GERMAN €€

(Map p72; 614 7730; www.henne-berlin.de; Leuschnerdamm 25; half chicken €7.90; dinner Tue-Sun; Moritzplatz) This Old Berlin institution operates on the KISS (keep it simple, stupid!) principle: milk-fed chicken spun on the rotisserie for moist yet crispy perfection. That's all it's been serving for over a century, alongside tangy potato and white-cabbage salads. Eat in the garden or in the woodsy dining room that's resisted the tides of time. Reservations essential.

TOP CHOICE Lavanderia Vecchia
ITALIAN €€€

(Map p72; 6272 2152; www.lavanderiavecchia.de; Flughafenstrasse 46; lunch from €4.50, 13-course dinner menu €45; lunch Tue-Fri, dinner Tue-Sat; Boddinstrasse) From the crusty bread to the digestif, the country-style dinners at the Old Laundry are truly a culinary first-class journey. Starched linens separate tables in the rustic-industrial space, where you'll be spoiled with 10 cooked-to-order antipasti courses (the octopus carpaccio is tops!), followed by pasta or risotto and a fishy or meaty main, plus dessert. Dinner starts at 7.30pm and includes a half-bottle of delicious wine, water and coffee; reservations essential.

ROBERT HARDING / GETTY IMAGES ©

3

DAVID PEEVERS / GETTY IMAGES ©

1. Schloss Charlottenburg (p78)
One of Germany's grandest surviving
Prussian palaces, Schloss Charlottenburg
oozes stucco, brocade and opulence

2. Reichstag (p58)
Lord Norman Foster's makeover of Berlin's
historic Reichstag has made a glittering
modern icon of Germany's parliament

3. Jüdisches Museum (p74)
Berlin's Jewish Museum, housed in a
landmark building by Daniel Libeskind, charts
2000 years of Jewish history in Germany

4. Holocaust Memorial (p58)
It took 2711 sarcophagi-like concrete pillars
for architects Peter Eisenman and Buro
Happold to create this haunting memorial

Tomasa INTERNATIONAL €€

(Map p72; ☎8100 9885; www.tomasa.de; Kreuzbergstrasse 62; lunch specials €5.50, mains €6-19; 🕘9am-1am Sun-Thu, to 2am Fri & Sat; 🌿👶; [S]Mehringdamm) It's not just breakfast that's a joy at this enchanting late-19th-century villa at the foot of the leafy Viktoriapark. The multitalented cooks also prepare creative salads, inspired vegetarian mains, *Flammkuchen* (Alsatian pizza) and grilled meats, often prepared with creative flourish. There's a kids' menu, plus a playroom and crayons.

Sauvage PALEOLITHIC €€

(Map p72; ☎5131 67547; www.sauvageberlin.com; Pflügerstrasse 25; mains €10-20; 🕘dinner Tue-Sun; [S]Hermannplatz) Sign up for a wild time at Berlin's first paleo restaurant, stylishly set up in a former brothel. Yup, at Sauvage you'll be eating like it's 10,000 BC: no grains, cheese or sugar but dishes featuring fish, meat, eggs, herbs, seeds, oils, fruit and wild vegetables, all organic, unprocessed and, usually, quite delicious.

Spindler & Klatt FUSION €€€

(Map p72; ☎319 881 860; www.spindlerklatt.com; Köpenicker Strasse 16-17; mains €18.50-26; 🕘8pm-1am; [S]Schlesisches Tor) It's not the hotspot it once was, but summers on the riverside terrace are still magical in this Prussian bread factory turned trendy nosh and party spot. Sit at a long table or lounge on a platform bed and tuck into fearless fusion fare. The interior is just as spectacular and morphs into a dance club after 11pm on Friday and Saturday.

Curry 36 GERMAN €

(Map p72; www.curry36.de; Mehringdamm 36; snacks €2-6; 🕘9am-4pm Mon-Sat, to 3pm Sun; [S]Mehringdamm) Top-ranked *Currywurst* purveyor that's been frying 'em up since the days when Madonna was singing about virgins.

Il Casolare ITALIAN €

(Map p72; ☎6950 6610; Grimmstrasse 30; pizza €6-9; [S]Kottbusser Tor, Schönleinstrasse) The pizzas are truly dynamite – thin, crispy, cheap and wagon-wheel-sized – and the canal-side beer garden is an idyllic spot in which to gobble them up. Staff can be frantic during busy times, so pack patience.

Burgermeister AMERICAN €

(Map p72; www.burger-meister.de; Oberbaumstrasse 8; burger €3-4; 🕘11am-2am or later; [S]Schlesisches Tor) It's green, ornate, a century old and…it used to be a toilet. Now it's a burger joint with plump all-beef patties best paired with fries and homemade dips such as peanut and mango-curry.

FRIEDRICHSHAIN

Spätzle & Knödel GERMAN €€

(Map p72; ☎2757 1151; Wühlischstrasse 20; mains €8-15; 🕘dinner; [S]Samariterstrasse) Great gastropub where you can get your southern German comfort-food fix with waist-expanding portions of roast pork, goulash and, of course, the eponymous *Spätzle* (German mac 'n' cheese) and *Knödel* (dumplings). Bonus: Augustiner, Riegele and Unertl on tap.

Lemon Leaf ASIAN €

(Map p72; ☎2900 9471; Grünberger Strasse 69; mains €5-9; 🕘noon-midnight; 🌿; [S]Frankfurter Tor) Cheap and cheerful, this place is always swarmed thanks to a light, inventive and fresh Indochinese menu that has few false notes. The homemade mango lassi is rave-worthy.

Schwarzer Hahn GERMAN €€€

(Map p72; ☎2197 0371; www.schwarzerhahn-heimatkueche.de; Seumestrasse 23; mains €14-21; 🕘lunch Mon-Fri, dinner Mon-Sat; [S]Samariterstrasse, 🚋M13, 🚆Ostkreuz, Warschauer Strasse) The select menu at this delightful slow-food bistro shines the spotlight on regionally sourced German soul food, elegantly updated for the 21st century. Service is impeccable and so are the wines. The two-course lunches are superb value at just €6.50. At dinnertime, reserve ahead for the seats at the communal wooden table.

PRENZLAUER BERG

Lucky Leek VEGAN €€

(Map p77; ☎6640 8710; www.lucky-leek.de; Kollwitzstrasse 46; mains around €12; 🕘dinner Tue & Thu-Sun; 🌿; [S]Senefelderplatz) This sprightly vegan joint crushes the competition by leagues, thanks to quality ingredients, inspired flavour combinations, creative and colourful presentation and enthusiastic staff. Creamy sweet-potato risotto, stuffed chilli tofu with orange-cinnamon glaze and white-chocolate mousse are typical menu entries.

Konnopke's Imbiss SAUSAGES €

(Map p77; Schönhauser Allee 44a; sausages €1.30-1.70; 🕘10am-8pm Mon-Fri, noon-8pm Sat; [S]Eberswalder Strasse) Brave the inevitable queue for legendary *Currywurst* from one of the city's cult sausage kitchens, now in shiny new glass digs but in the same historic spot since 1930.

Si An VIETNAMESE €€

(Map p77; ☎4050 5775; www.sian-berlin.de; Rykestrasse 36; mains €7-11; ⏰noon-midnight; [S]Eberswalder Strasse) This stylish nosh spot with Zen moss garden and handmade paper lanterns welcomes a steady stream of tousled hipsters, yoga mamas and even the occasional celeb. Whether an interpretation or a homage, dishes hum with freshness and creativity. Many are inspired by recipes from ancient Vietnamese monasteries.

A Magica ITALIAN €

(Map p77; ☎2280 8290; Greifenhagener Strasse 54; pizzas €5-10; ⏰4pm-midnight; [S]Schönhauser Allee, 🚋M1, 🚆Schönhauser Allee) Always packed, happening and noisy, this joint consistently delivers Neapolitan pizzas with pizzazz in a cosy, candlelit chamber. Luscious red house wine comes in water glasses. You should come early before local groupies invade.

Oderquelle GERMAN €€

(Map p77; ☎4400 8080; Oderberger Strasse 27; mains €8-16; ⏰dinner; [S]Eberswalder Strasse) It's always fun to pop by this woodsy resto and see what's inspired the chef this day. Most likely it'll be a delicious, well-crafted German meal, perhaps with a slight Mediterranean nuance. The generously topped and crispy *Flammkuchen* are a reliable standby.

Gugelhof FRENCH €€

(Map p77; ☎442 9229; www.gugelhof.de; Knaackstrasse 37; mains €7.50-23; ⏰4pm-midnight Mon-Fri, from 10am Sat & Sun; [S]Senefelderplatz) This country-French jewel made headlines when feeding Bill Clinton back in 2000 but thankfully hasn't coasted on its fame since. Chefs still keep things real with robust *choucroute* (a sauerkraut-based stew), cheese fondue, *Flammkuchen* and other Alsatian soul food, plus inventive daily specials. Fabulous hand-picked French and German wines.

CHARLOTTENBURG

Good Friends CHINESE €€

(Map p79; ☎313 2659; www.goodfriends-berlin.de; Kantstrasse 30; mains €10-20; ⏰noon-2am; 🚆Savignyplatz) Sinophiles tired of the Kung Pao school of Chinese cooking will appreciate the real thing at this well-established Cantonese restaurant. The ducks dangling in the window are the overture to a menu long enough to confuse Confucius. If jellyfish with eggs or fried pork belly prove too challenging, you can always fall back on, well, Kung Pao chicken.

Osteria Centrale ITALIAN €€

(Map p79; ☎3101 3263; Bleibtreustrasse 51; mains €10-20; ⏰dinner Mon-Sat; 🚆Savignyplatz) This neighbourhood Italian fits like a well-worn shoe and lets you dip into a pool of pleasurable classics from around the boot. Menu staples like octopus carpaccio, grilled calamari, truffle pasta or rosemary-scented beef stew are creatively perfected and keep regulars coming back for more.

Ottenthal AUSTRIAN €€€

(Map p79; ☎313 3162; www.ottenthal.com; Kantstrasse 153; mains €14-32; ⏰dinner; [S]Zoologischer Garten, Uhlandstrasse, 🚆Zoologischer Garten) A little shrine to Mozart is among the eye-catching elements in this neighbourhood-adored restaurant where classic Alpine cuisine gets a modern workout. The Wiener schnitzel is a dependable staple, but more innovative creations like roast pike perch with red-pepper cream are at least as convincing.

Café-Restaurant Wintergarten im Literaturhaus INTERNATIONAL €€

(Map p79; ☎882 5414; www.literaturhaus-berlin.de; Fasanenstrasse 23; mains €8-16; ⏰9.30am-1am; [S]Uhlandstrasse) The hustle and bustle of Ku'damm is only a block away from this genteel art nouveau villa with attached bookstore. Tuck into seasonal bistro cuisine amid graceful Old Berlin flair or, if weather permits, in the idyllic garden. Breakfast is served until 2pm.

Jules Verne INTERNATIONAL €€

(Map p79; ☎3180 9410; www.jules-verne-berlin.de; Schlüterstrasse 61; breakfast €4-9, 2-course lunch €5.50-7.50, dinner mains €7-17.50; ⏰9am-1am; 🍷; 🚆Savignyplatz) Jules Verne was a well-travelled man, so it's only fitting that a cafe bearing his name would feature a globetrotting menu. French oysters, Austrian schnitzel and Moroccan couscous are all perennial bestsellers. It's also a great greet-the-day spot, with substantial breakfasts served until 3pm; weekends bring a quality brunch buffet.

Mr Hai Kabuki JAPANESE €€

(Map p79; ☎8862 8136; www.mrhai.de; Olivaer Platz 10; platters €12-22; 🚌M19, 109, [S]Adenauerplatz, Uhlandstrasse) Yes, it does have classic *nigiri* and *maki* but most regulars flock to Mr Hai for more unconventional sushi morsels, composed like little works of art and featuring kimchi, pumpkin, cream or other unconventional ingredients. Sounds bizarre, but it works.

Dicke Wirtin
GERMAN €€

(Map p79; ☑312 4952; www.dicke-wirtin.de; Carmerstrasse 9; mains €6-15; ☺from noon; ☒Savignyplatz) Old Berlin charm oozes from every nook and cranny of this been-here-forever pub, which pours eight draught beers (including the superb Kloster Andechs) and nearly three dozen homemade schnapps varieties. Hearty local fare such as roast pork, fried liver or breaded schnitzel keeps brains in balance.

Schleusenkrug
GERMAN €

(Map p79; ☑313 9909; www.schleusenkrug.de; Müller-Breslau-Strasse; mains €3.50-13; ☺10am-11pm May-Sep, to 7pm Oct-Apr; ⓢZoologischer Garten, ☒Zoologischer Garten) Sitting pretty by a Landwehr canal lock, Schleusenkrug truly comes into its own in summer when the beer garden kicks into full swing. People from all walks of life hunker over mugs of foamy beer and satisfying comfort food, from grilled sausages to *Flammkuchen* and weekly changing specials. Breakfast is served until 3pm.

Ali Baba
ITALIAN €

(Map p79; ☑881 1350; www.alibaba-berlin.de; Bleibtreustrasse 45; dishes €3-9; ☺11am-2am Sun-Thu, to 3am Fri & Sat; ☒Savignyplatz) Everybody feels like family at this been-here-forever port of call, where the thin-crust pizza is delicious, the pasta piping hot and even the most expensive meat dish costs only €9. Popular with party people and posh Charlottenburgers in slumming mood.

SCHÖNEBERG

Habibi
MIDDLE EASTERN €

(Map p81; Goltzstrasse 24; snacks €2.50-5; ☺11am-3am Sun-Thu, to 5pm Fri & Sat; ⓢNollendorfplatz) *Habibi* means 'my beloved' and the object of obsession in this popular snack place is soul-sustaining felafel, best paired with a freshly pressed carrot juice. Great for restoring brain balance after a night on the razzle.

Ousies
GREEK €€

(Map p81; ☑216 7957; www.taverna-ousies.de; Grunewaldstrasse 16; small plates €4-9, mains €10-18; ☺dinner; ⓢEisenacher Strasse) You'll be as exuberant as Zorba himself at this hugely popular *ouzeria,* the Greek equivalent of a tapas bar. Order a tantalising sampling of dishes,

from *stifado* (beef stew) to *chirini tigania* (lemon-oregano-scented pork) and spinach-stuffed sardines. Reservations essential.

 ## Drinking

Berlin is a great place for boozers. From cosy pubs, riverside beach bars, chestnut-shaded beer gardens, underground dives, DJ bars, snazzy hotel lounges and designer cocktail temples, you're rarely far from a good time. Kreuzberg and Friedrichshain are currently the edgiest bar-hopping grounds, with swanky Mitte and Charlottenburg being more suited for date nights than dedicated late nights. The line between cafe and bar is often blurred, with many places changing stripes as the hands move around the clock.

MITTE

Drayton Bar
BAR

(Map p60; ☑280 8806; www.draytonberlin.com; Behrensstrasse 55; ☺Tue-Sat; ⓢFranzösische Strasse) This glamour vixen oozes 1920s sophistication from every dimly lit corner. Huge gilded peacock lamps flank the bar specialised in classic and 'cuisine style' cocktails infused with homemade syrups, herbs and spices. The entrance is via the Cookies Cream (p97) restaurant. At midnight on Tuesday, Thursday and Saturday, the bar expands into the Cookies (p108) club.

Buck and Breck
BAR

(Map p60; ☑0176-3231 5507; www.buckandbreck.com; Brunnenstrasse 177; ☺from 8pm; ⓢRosenthaler Platz) At this intimate cocktail salon behind a nameless door, Berlin barmeister Gonçalo de Sousa Monteiro treats patrons to his libational flights of fancy. Historical concoctions are his strength, including the eponymous Buck & Breck, a potent blend of cognac, bitters, absinthe and champagne. Call ahead to make sure there's an empty seat. Smoking OK.

Mein Haus am See
CAFE, BAR

(Map p60; www.mein-haus-am-see.blogspot.de; Brunnenstrasse 197/198; ☺from 9am; ⓢRosenthaler Platz, ☒M1) This 'House by the Lake' is nowhere near anything liquid, unless you count the massive amount of beverages consumed at the chill boho hang-out that multitasks as a cafe-bar, gallery, performance space and club. Separate smoking room.

Neue Odessa Bar
BAR

(Map p60; Torstrasse 89; ⓢRosenthaler Platz) Rub shoulders with a global mix of grown-ups with a hot fashion sense at this comfy-chic

PARTY MILES

» **Torstrasse, Mitte** A globe-spanning roster of shiny, happy hipsters populates the shabby-chic drinking dens lining this noisy thoroughfare.

» **Kottbusser Tor/Oranienstrasse, Kreuzberg** Grunge-tastic area best suited for dedicated drink-a-thons at Möbel Olfe (p106), Würgeengel (p106) and Monarch (p106). The closest music and dance venue is SO36 (p110).

» **Schlesische Strasse, Kreuzberg** Freestyle strip where you could kick off with cocktails at Badeschiff (p86), catch a band at Magnet Club (p110) and dance till sunrise at Watergate (p109) or Club der Visionäre (p109).

» **Revaler Strasse, Friedrichshain** The skinny-jeanster set invades the gritty clubs and bars along this 'techno strip' set up in a former train repair station.

» **Weserstrasse, Neukölln** The main party drag among many in Berlin's newest 'It Kiez' is packed with delightfully divey, improvised living-room-style bars and pubs.

» **Oranienburger Strasse, Mitte** Major tourist zone where you have to hopscotch around sex workers and pub crawlers to drown your sorrows in pricey bars.

» **Simon-Dach-Strasse, Friedrichshain** If you need a cheap buzz, head to ths well-trodden booze strip popular with field-tripping school groups and stag parties.

and always busy Torstrasse staple. The patterned wallpaper, velvet sofas and smart lamps create a cosy ambience, no matter if your taste runs towards Krusovice or cosmos. Smoking allowed.

Berliner Republik PUB
(Map p60; www.die-berliner-republik.de; Schiffbauerdamm 8; ☺10am-6am; ⑤Friedrichstrasse, ⑧Friedrichstrasse) Just as in a mini-stock exchange, the cost of drinks fluctuates with demand at this raucous riverside pub. Everyone goes Pavlovian when a heavy brass bell rings, signalling rock-bottom prices. Not too many locals, but a fun spot nonetheless.

Strandbar Mitte BAR
(Map p60; ☎2838 5588; www.strandbar-mitte.de; Monbijoustrasse 1-3; ☺from 10am May-Sep; ⑨M1, ⑧Oranienburger Strasse) With a full-on view of the Bodemuseum, palm trees and relaxed ambience, this riverside playground is great for balancing a surfeit of sightseeing stimulus with a revivifying drink. After 7pm you can tango, waltz or cha-cha under the stars.

Tausend BAR
(Map p60; www.tausendberlin.com; Schiffbauerdamm 11; ☺from 7.30pm Tue-Sat; ⑤Friedrichstrasse, ⑧Friedrichstrasse) No sign, no light, no bell, just an anonymous steel door tucked into a railway bridge leads to one of Berlin's chicest bars. Behind it, flirty frocks sip raspberry mojitos alongside vodka-mule-cradling three-day stubbles amid decor that channels '80s glam while DJs and bands fuel

the vibe. Hungry? Proceed to the Backroom Cantina behind the bar. Selective door.

POTSDAMER PLATZ & TIERGARTEN

Café am Neuen See BEER GARDEN
(Map p79; ☎254 4930; www.cafe-am-neuen-see.de; Lichtensteinallee 2; pizza €9-12.50, mains €10-26; ☺from 8am Mon-Fri, from 9am Sat & Sun; ☐100, 200) This lakeside Tiergarten restaurant serves pizza and German fare year-round, but the time to visit is during beer-garden season when long wooden tables brim with tourists and locals in search of a micro-vacation from the city bustle.

Curtain Club BAR
(Map p60; ☎337 776 196; www.ritzcarlton.de; Ritz-Carlton Berlin, Potsdamer Strasse 3; ☺from 6pm; ☐200, ⑤Potsdamer Platz, ⑧Potsdamer Platz) Every night at 6pm sharp, it's showtime inside the Ritz-Carlton: a uniformed former London Beefeater (Tower guard) ceremoniously pulls back the heavy curtains on this elegant, wood-panelled bar presided over by cocktail-meister Arnd Heissen. He'll whip up a perfect classic cocktail, but takes greatest delight in his own extravagant concoctions inspired by the world of perfumes.

Solar BAR
(Map p72; ☎0163-765 2700; www.solar-berlin.de; Stresemannstrasse 76; ☺6pm-2am Sun-Thu, to 4am Fri & Sat; ⑧Anhalter Bahnhof) Views of the skyline are truly impressive at this chic 17th-floor sky lounge with dim lighting and soft black-leather couches. Getting there aboard

an exterior glass lift is half the fun. Enter via the chunky high-rise behind the Pit Stop auto shop.

KREUZBERG & NORTHERN NEUKÖLLN

Würgeengel
BAR

(Map p72; www.wuergeengel.de; Dresdner Strasse 122; ⊙from 7pm; ⑤Kottbusser Tor) For a swish night out, point the compass to this '50s-style cocktail cave complete with glass ceiling, chandeliers and shiny black tables. It's especially busy after the final credits roll at the adjacent Babylon (Map p72; ☎6160 9693; www.yorck.de; Dresdner Strasse 126; tickets €5.50-7.50; ⑤Kottbusser Tor) cinema. The name, by the way, pays homage to the surreal 1962 Buñuel movie *Exterminating Angel*. Smoking allowed.

Ankerklause
PUB

(Map p72; ☎693 5649; www.ankerklause.de; Kottbusser Damm 104; ⊙from 4pm Mon, from 10am Tue-Sun; ⑤Kottbusser Tor) Ahoy there! This nautical kitsch tavern with an ass-kicking jukebox sets sail in an old harbour-master's shack and is great for quaffing and waving to the boats puttering along the canal. Breakfast and snacks provide sustenance.

Freischwimmer
BAR

(Map p72; ☎6107 4309; www.freischwimmer-berlin. de; Vor dem Schlesischen Tor 2a; ⊙from 4pm Tue-Fri, 10am Sat & Sun; ⑤Schlesisches Tor) In summer, few places are more idyllic than this rustic ex-boathouse turned all-day, canal-side chill zone. Come for chit-chat or postcard writing in the afternoon or a pre-clubbing warm-up. Snacks and light meals (€7 to €15) are served, but they're more of an afterthought. The entrance is to the right of Berlin's oldest petrol station. It's sometimes open in winter, but it's not the same – call ahead for hours.

Luzia
BAR

(Map p72; ☎8179 9958; Oranienstrasse 34; ⊙ noon-late; ⑤Kottbusser Tor) Tarted up nicely with vintage furniture, baroque wallpaper and whimsical wall art by Chin Chin, Luzia draws its crowd from SO36's more sophisticated urban dwellers. Some punters have derided it as Mitte-goes-Kreuzberg, but it's still a comfy spot with soft lighting that makes everyone look good. Smoker's lounge.

Monarch Bar
BAR

(Map p72; www.kottimonarch.de; Skalitzer Strasse 134; ⊙from 9pm Tue-Sat; ⑤Kottbusser Tor) Be-hind a long-steamed-up window front, eye level with the elevated U-Bahn tracks, Monarch is an ingenious blend of trashy sophistication, an international crowd and danceable tunes beyond the mainstream. Enter via the signless steel door adjacent to the doner kebab shop east of the Kaiser's supermarket. Smoking allowed.

Madame Claude
PUB

(Map p72; Lübbener Strasse 19; ⊙from 7pm; ⑤Schlesisches Tor) Gravity is literally upended at this David Lynchian booze burrow where the furniture dangles from the ceiling and the crown moulding's on the floor. Don't worry, there are still comfy sofas for entertaining your posse, plus Wednesday is music quiz night, live music or DJs and there are open-mike Sundays. Doesn't fill up until around 11pm.

Möbel Olfe
PUB

(Map p72; www.moebel-olfe.de; Reichenberger Strasse 177; ⊙Tue-Sun; ⑤Kottbusser Tor) An old furniture store has been recast as an always-busy drinking den with cheap libations and a friendly crowd that's usually mixed but goes predominantly gay on Thursdays. Enter via Dresdner Strasse.

Kuschlowski
BAR

(Map p72; ☎0176-2438 9701; www.kuschlowski.de; Weserstrasse 202; ⊙from 8pm; ⑤Hermannplatz) When fierce winter winds blow in from the east, it's the perfect time to hole up by the crackling fireplace in this ex-bordello amid retro furniture and homemade lamps. The polyethnic crowd is united by a penchant for stiff drinks, especially the many Russian vodka varieties.

FRIEDRICHSHAIN

Süss War Gestern
BAR

(Map p72; Wühlischstrasse 43; ⑤Warschauer Strasse, Samariterstrasse, ⓇWarschauer Strasse, Ostkreuz) Chilled electro and well-mixed cocktails show power in this red-tinged lounge that gives even pasty-faced hipsters a healthy glow. Only problem: once you're swallowed by the plush retro sofa, it may be hard to get up to order that next drink. Try the eponymous house cocktail, made with real root ginger, ginger ale and whisky. Smoking OK.

CSA
BAR

(Map p72; ☎2904 4741; www.csa-bar.de; Karl-Marx-Allee 96; ⊙from 7pm; ⑤Weberwiese) This chic bar right on Karl-Marx-Allee has been carved out of the eponymous Czech national airline offices and sports a wonderful 1960s vintage vibe. Dim lights and classic cocktails draw a grown-up set to the white leather bar stools.

Ostrand BEACH BAR

(Map p72; www.oststrand.de; Mühlenstrasse, Rummelsburger Platz; ⊗from 10am; ⓡOstbahnhof) Drag your flip flops to this funky beach paradise along the East Side Gallery and drink a toast to Berlin as you wiggle your toes in the sand or stretch out beneath colourful party lights on an old barge. Tanning and chilling in the daytime, partying at night.

Place Clichy BAR

(Map p72; ☑2313 8703; Simon-Dach-Strasse 22; ⊗Tue-Sat; ⓢWarschauer Strasse, ⓡWarschauer Strasse) *Chapeau!* Clichy brings a whiff of Paris to the lower end of Simon-Dach-Strasse. Candlelit, artist-designed and cosy, the postage-stamp-sized *boîte* exudes an almost existentialist vibe, so don your black turtleneck and join the chatty crowd for Bordeaux and sweaty cheeses.

Hops & Barley PUB

(Map p72; ☑2936 7534; Wühlischstrasse 40; ⓢWarschauer Strasse, ⓡWarschauer Strasse) Conversation flows as freely as the unfiltered pilsner, malty *dunkel* (dark), fruity *weizen* (wheat) and potent cider produced right at this congenial microbrewery inside a former butcher's shop. Fellow beer lovers range from skinny-jean hipsters to suits swilling post-work pints among ceramic-tiled walls and shiny copper vats. Half a litre is €3.10.

Monster Ronson's Ichiban Karaoke KARAOKE

(Map p72; ☑8975 1327; www.karaokemonster.com; Warschauer Strasse 34; ⓢWarschauer Strasse, ⓡWarschauer Strasse) Knock back a couple of brewskis if you need to loosen your nerves before belting out your best Britney or Lady Gaga at this mad, great karaoke joint. *Pop Idol* wannabes can pick from thousands of songs and hit the stage; shy types may prefer music and mischief in a private party room. Some nights are LGBT-geared, like Monday's Multisexual Box Hopping.

PRENZLAUER BERG

TOP CHOICE **Prater** BEER GARDEN

(Map p77; ☑448 5688; www.pratergarten.de; Kastanienallee 7-9; ⊗from noon Apr-Sep in good weather; ⓢEberswalder Strasse) Berlin's oldest beer garden (since 1837) has kept much of its traditional charm and is a fantastic place to hang

and guzzle a cold one beneath the ancient chestnut trees (self-service). Kids can romp around the small play area. In foul weather or winter, the adjacent woodsy restaurant is a fine place to sample classic Berlin dishes (mains €8 to €19).

Becketts Kopf BAR

(Map p77; www.becketts-kopf.de; Pappelallee 64; ⊗Tue-Sun; ⓢSchönhauser Allee, ☑12, ⓡSchönhauser Allee) Beyond Samuel Beckett's head in the window, the art of cocktail making is taken very seriously. Settle into a heavy, wine-coloured armchair in the warmly lit room and look on as the barkeeps whip high-calibre spirits, fresh juices and secret ingredients into sense-stirring classic and creative concoctions.

Deck 5 BAR

(Map p77; www.freiluftrebellen.de/deck-5; Schönhauser Allee 80; ⊗10am-midnight, in good summer weather only; ⓢSchönhauser Allee, ☑M1, ⓡSchönhauser Allee) Soak up the sunset at this beach bar in the sky while sinking your toes into tonnes of sand lugged to the top parking deck of the Schönhauser Arkaden mall. Take the lift from within the mall, or enter via a never-ending flight of stairs from Greifenhagener Strasse.

Anna Blume CAFE

(Map p77; ☑4404 8749; www.cafe-anna-blume.de; Kollwitzstrasse 83; ⊗8am-2am; ⓢEberswalder Strasse) Potent java, homemade cakes and flowers from the attached shop perfume the art nouveau interior of this corner cafe, named after a Kurt Schwitters poem. In fine weather the footpath terrace is the best people-watching perch. Great for breakfast (the tiered tray for two is tops).

August Fengler BAR

(Map p77; www.augustfengler.de; Lychener Strasse 11; ⓢEberswalder Strasse, ☑M1) With its flirty vibe, blazing dance floor and foosball in the cellar, this local institution scores a trifecta on key ingredients for a good night out. Wallet-friendly drink prices, charming bar staff and a pretense-free crowd don't hurt either. Best in the wee hours for that last guzzle. Just stay clear of those sofas or you may never leave under your own steam.

CHARLOTTENBURG & SCHÖNEBERG

Stagger Lee BAR

(Map p81; ☑2903 6158; www.staggerlee.de; Nollendorfstrasse 27; ⓢNollendorfplatz) Belly up to the polished wooden bar or plop down on chocolate-hued Chesterfield sofas at this sophisticated cocktail saloon, which pours the tried and true alongside homemade inventions like the bourbon-and-beer-sugar-based Stagger Lee Beer Old Fashioned. The name channels a famous 19th-century St Louis murderer immortalised in song by everyone from Nick Cave to The Clash.

Green Door
COCKTAIL BAR

(Map p81; ☑215 2515; www.greendoor.de; Winterfeldtstrasse 50; ☺6pm-3am; ⑤Nollendorfplatz) A long line of renowned mixologists has presided over this softly lit bar behind the eponymous green door – a nod to Prohibition-era speakeasies. Amid walls incongruously sheathed in checkered and swirling patterns, you can choose from over 500 cocktails, including some potent house concoctions. Must ring bell to enter.

Zwiebelfisch
PUB

(Map p79; ☑312 7363; www.zwiebelfisch-berlin. de; Savignyplatz 5; ☺noon-6am; ⓡSavignyplatz) With its clientele of grizzled and greying artists, actors and writers, this cosy pub has been Charlottenburg at its boho best since the patchouli-perfumed 1960s. Everyone's a little older these days, but it's still a great place for guzzling that final drink while the suits are revving up for another day in the office.

Puro Skylounge
BAR, CLUB

(Map p79; ☑2636 7875; www.puro-berlin.de; Tauentzienstrasse 11; ☺Tue-Sat; ⑤Kurfürstendamm) Puro has quite literally raised the bar in Charlottenburg – by moving it to the 20th floor of the Europa Center. Trade Berlin funky-trash for sleek decor, fabulous views and high-heeled hotties. The crowd skews young but moneyed.

Universum Lounge
BAR

(Map p79; ☑8906 4995; www.universumlounge. com; Kurfürstendamm 153; ☺6pm-3am; ⑤Adenauerplatz) The curvaceous teak bar and white leather banquettes at this spacey, retro-glam libation station fill up quickly after the curtain falls at the Schaubühne theatre, which is located in the same building, a 1920s gem by the esteemed Erich Mendelsohn.

☆ Entertainment

Sometimes it seems as though Berliners are the lotus eaters of Germany, people who love nothing better than a good time. Pack some stamina if you want to join them. With no curfew, this is a notoriously late city, where bars stay packed from dusk to dawn and beyond and some clubs don't hit their stride until 6am.

Zitty and *Tip* are the most widely read of the biweekly German-language listings magazines available at newsstands. Party-oriented *030* is a decent freezine. For up-to-the-minute happenings, also check www. sugarhigh.de and www.ronorp.net. The English-language monthly *Ex-Berliner* also has some information.

Credit-card bookings by telephone, or online through a venue's box office, are now fairly common, although many only take reservations and then make you pick up tickets in person. Ticket agencies (*Theaterkasse*) are commonly found in shopping malls and charge sometimes-steep service fees. The main online agency is www. eventim.de. Hekticket (www.hekticket.de) sells half-price tickets after 2pm for select same-day performances online and in-person at its outlets near Zoo Station and Alexanderplatz. For indie concerts and events, the best agency is Koka 36 (☑6110 1313; www. koka36.de; Oranienstrasse 29; ☺9am-7pm Mon-Fri, 10am-4pm Sat; ⑤Kottbusser Tor) in Kreuzberg.

Clubbing

Berghain/Panorama Bar
CLUB

(Map p72; www.berghain.de; Am Wriezener Bahnhof; ☺Sat; ⓡOstbahnhof) Only world-class spinmeisters heat up this hedonistic bass-junkie hellhole inside a labyrinthine former power plant. Upstairs, Panorama Bar pulsates with house and electro, while the big factory floor below is gay-leaning and hard techno. Best time: after 5am. Strict door, no cameras.

Cookies
CLUB

(Map p60; www.cookies.ch; cnr Friedrichstrasse & Unter den Linden; ☺from midnight Tue, Thu & Sat; ⑤Französische Strasse) Heinz Gindullis, aka Cookies, has done it again! For the eighth time he's reinvented his eponymous club, this time creating an indoor adult playground complete with wicked little theme rooms like a mirror cabinet, a naughty shop and even a wedding chapel. Upstairs, top electro DJs heat up the swank crowd on the mosaic dance floor that segues smoothly into the Drayton Bar (p104).

Clärchens Ballhaus
CLUB

(Map p60; ☑282 9295; www.ballhaus.de; Auguststrasse 24; ☺restaurant 12.30-11.30pm, dancing nightly; ⓖM1, ⓡOranienburger Strasse) Yesteryear is now at this late, great 19th-century dance hall where groovers and grannies hoof it across the parquet without even a touch of irony. There are different sounds nightly – salsa to swing, tango to disco – and a live band on Saturdays. The later it gets, the younger the crowd.

Club der Visionäre   CLUB
(Map p72; ☎6951 8942; www.clubdervisionaere. com; Am Flutgraben 1; ⏰from 2pm Mon-Fri, from noon Sat & Sun; ⓡTreptower Park, Schlesisches Tor) It's drinks, pizza and fine electro at this summertime chill and party playground in an old canalside boatshed. Hang out beneath the weeping willows or stake out some turf on the upstairs deck. On weekends party people invade 24/7.

Watergate   CLUB
(Map p72; ☎6128 0394; www.water-gate.de; Falckensteinstrasse 49a; ⏰from 11pm Fri & Sat; Schlesisches Tor) It's a short night's journey into day at this high-octane riverside club with two floors, panoramic windows and a floating terrace overlooking the Oberbaumbrücke and Universal Music. Top DJs keep electro-hungry hipsters hot and sweaty till way past sunrise. Long queues, tight door on weekends.

://about blank   CLUB
(http://aboutparty.net; Markgrafendamm 24c; ⏰Fri & Sat; ⓡOstkreuz) This club collective also organises cultural and political events that often segue into long, intense club nights when talented DJs feed a diverse bunch of revellers with dance-worthy electronic gruel. Drinks are fairly priced, and if you get the spirit of openness and tolerance, you'll have a grand old time here.

KitKatClub   CLUB
(Map p60; www.kitkatclub.de; Köpenicker Strasse 76, enter via Brückenstrasse; ⏰Fri-Sun; ⓢHeinrich-Heine-Strasse) This kitty is naughty, sexy and decadent, listens to techno and house, and fancies leather and lace, vinyl and whips. Berlin's most (in)famous erotic nightclub hides out at Sage Club with its multiple dance floors, themed 'play rooms' and action-packed mezzanine. The website has dress-code details.

Suicide Circus   CLUB
(Map p72; www.suicide-berlin.com; Revaler Strasse 99; ⏰usually Wed-Sun; ⓢWarschauer Strasse) Tousled hipsters in need of an eclectic electro shower invade this funkytown dancing den that at times feels like a mini-Berghain – sweaty, edgy, industrial and with a top-

BERLIN'S BOAT OF BABBLE

A fun and easy way to meet friendly locals over beer and bratwurst is at the **World Language Party**, which takes over the retro lounge of the floating Eastern Comfort Hostelboat (p94) every Wednesday from 6pm. It brings together an easy-going, all-ages international crowd, including lots of regulars, but don't be shy – people are friendly and eager to welcome newcomers. Admission is €2, which is added to your first drink. Also check MC Charles' website (www.english-events-in-berlin.de) for updates and additional goings-on.

notch sound system. In summer, watch the stars fade on the outdoor floor with chillier sounds and grilled bratwurst.

Felix   CLUB
(Map p60; www.felix-clubrestaurant.de; Behrenstrasse 72; ⏰Mon & Thu-Sat; ⓢBrandenburger Tor, ⓡBrandenburger Tor) Once past the rope of this swanky club at the Hotel Adlon, you too can shake your booty to high-octane hip hop, dance and disco beats, sip champagne cocktails and flirt up a storm. Women get free entry and a glass of prosecco on Mondays, while the worker-bee brigade kicks loose on after-work Thursdays.

Kater Holzig   CLUB
(Map p60; www.katerholzig.de; Michaelkirchstrasse 23; ⏰usually Thu-Sat; ⓢHeinrich-Heine-Strasse) 'Kater' means cat in German and this 'kitty' sits pretty in its surreal riverside playground set around a graffiti-doused old soap factory. Parties often run for 72 hours, but there's also less excessive programming such as readings, plays, concerts or films, albeit usually with David Lynchian edge. Chill al fresco in the upstairs bar, on the wooden deck or by the beach bonfire. Tough door.

Weekend   CLUB
(Map p60; www.week-end-berlin.de; Am Alexanderplatz 5; ⏰Thu-Sat; ⓢAlexanderplatz, ⓡAlexanderplatz) This house and electro den has seen hotter times, but thanks to its unbeatable location, with panoramic views of Alexanderplatz (in summer from the rooftop terrace), it's still a popular destination for an international cadre of flirty funseekers.

LOST IN THE LABYRINTH

For a spooky, mind-bender kind of experience, plunge into the **Peristal Singum** (www.karmanoia.com; Alt-Stralau 70; €10; ⊙6pm-midnight, last entry 10pm; ⧉Ostkreuz), an art installation and trippy labyrinth set up in the dark and dank bowels of Salon zur Wilden Renate (p110). Prepare to be launched on a metaphysical self-exploration in this 'landscape of wafting thoughts' that has all the warped intensity of a Dalí painting gone 3D. Definitely not for the claustrophobic!

Kaffee Burger
CLUB

(Map p60; ✆2804 6495; www.kaffeeburger.de; Torstrasse 60; ⓢRosa-Luxemburg-Platz) Nothing to do with either coffee or meat patties, this sweaty cult club with lovingly faded commie-era decor is not only the home of the famous Russendisko (Russian Disco) but a fun-for-all party pen with almost nightly concerts and dancing (indie, punk, rock, Balkan etc), plus Sunday readings.

Tresor
CLUB

(Map p60; www.tresorberlin.de; Köpenicker Strasse 70; ⊙Wed, Fri & Sat; ⓢHeinrich-Heine-Strasse) One of Berlin's longest-running techno temples, Tresor has all the right ingredients for success: the industrial maze of a derelict power station, awesome sound and a pretty consistent DJ line-up. The door is pretty loose, making this a popular destination for suburban weekend warriors.

Salon zur Wilden Renate
CLUB

(www.renate.cc; Alt Stralau 70; ⊙Fri & Sat; ⧉Ostkreuz) Yes, things can indeed get pretty wild at Renate where stellar local spinners feed self-ironic free thinkers with sweat-inducing electro in an abandoned residential building. Sofas, a fireplace room and several bars provide suitable chill zones. Crowd skews young.

Live Music
Lido
LIVE MUSIC

(Map p72; ✆6956 6840; www.lido-berlin.de; Cuvrystrasse 7; ⓢSchlesisches Tor) A 1950s cinema has been recycled into a rock-indie-electro-pop mecca with mosh-pit electricity and a crowd that cares more about the music than about looking good. Global DJs and talented

upwardly mobile live noise-makers pull in the punters. Legendary Balkan-beats parties, too.

Astra Kulturhaus
LIVE MUSIC

(Map p72; ✆2005 6767; www.astra-berlin.de; Revaler Strasse 99; ⓢWarschauer Strasse, ⧉Warschauer Strasse) With space for 1500, Astra is one of the bigger indie venues in town, yet often fills up easily, and not just for such headliners as Melissa Etheridge, Kasabian or Paul van Dyk's Vandit Records label parties. Bonus: the sweet '50s GDR decor. Beer garden in summer.

Magnet Club
LIVE MUSIC

(Map p72; www.magnet-club.de; Falckensteinstrasse 48; ⓢSchlesisches Tor) This indie and alt-sound bastion is known for bookers with an astronomer's ability to detect stars in the making. After the last riff, the mostly student-age crowd hits the dance floor to – depending on the night – Britpop, indietronics, neodisco, rock and punk.

SO36
LIVE MUSIC

(Map p72; www.so36.de; Oranienstrasse 190; ⊙most nights; ⓢKottbusser Tor) The Dead Kennedys and Die Toten Hosen played gigs at this club collective when many of today's patrons were still in nappies. The actual crowd depends on the program that night: an electro party, a punk concert, a lesbigay tea dance, a night flea market – anything goes at this long-time alt-scene epicentre.

A-Trane
JAZZ

(Map p79; ✆313 2550; www.a-trane.de; Bleibtreustrasse 1; ⊙Mon-Sat; ⧉Savignyplatz) Herbie Hancock and Diana Krall have anointed the stage of this intimate jazz club, but mostly it's emerging talent bringing their A-game to the A-Trane. Entry is free on Monday when local boy Andreas Schmidt shows off his musical skills, and after 12.30am on Saturday for the late-night jam session.

B-Flat
LIVE MUSIC

(Map p60; ✆283 3123; www.b-flat-berlin.de; Rosenthaler Strasse 13; ⊙from 8pm Sun-Thu, from 9pm Fri & Sat; ⓢWeinmeisterstrasse, Rosenthaler Platz, ⧉M1) Cool cats of all ages come to this intimate venue, where the audience sits quite literally within spitting distance of the performers. The emphasis is on acoustic music; mostly jazz, world beats, Afro-Brazilian and other soundscapes. Wednesday's free jam session often brings down the house.

Classical & Opera

Berliner Philharmonie CLASSICAL MUSIC
(Map p60; ☎2548 8999; www.berliner-philharmoniker.de; Herbert-von-Karajan-Strasse 1; 🚌200, [S]Potsdamer Platz, 🚇Potsdamer Platz) This landmark concert hall has supreme acoustics and, thanks to Hans Scharoun's clever terraced vineyard design, not a bad seat in the house. It's the home base of the world-famous Berliner Philharmoniker, currently led by Sir Simon Rattle. Concerts are also at the adjacent **Kammermusiksaal**.

Konzerthaus Berlin CLASSICAL MUSIC
(Map p60; ☎tickets 203 092 101; www.konzerthaus.de; Gendarmenmarkt 2; [S]Stadtmitte, Französische Strasse) This top-ranked concert hall – a Schinkel design from 1821 – counts the Konzerthausorchester as its 'house band' but also hosts international soloists, thematic concert cycles, children's events and other orchestras.

Staatsoper unter den Linden @ Schillertheater OPERA
(Map p79; ☎information 203 540, tickets 2035 4555; www.staatsoper-berlin.de; Bismarckstrasse 110 ; [S]Ernst-Reuter-Platz) Point your highbrow compass towards the Daniel Barenboim-led Staatsoper, Berlin's top opera company. While its historic digs on Unter den Linden are getting a facelift (probably until 2014), the high-calibre productions are staged at the Schiller Theater in Charlottenburg. All operas are sung in their original language.

Deutsche Oper OPERA
(Map p79; ☎3438 4343; www.deutscheoperberlin.de; Bismarckstrasse 35; [S]Deutsche Oper) The German Opera was founded by local citizens in 1912 as a counterpoint to the royal opera (today's Staatsoper Unter den Linden). It boasts a repertory of around 70 operas, which are all sung in their original language.

Cabaret & Varieté

[TOP CHOICE] **Bar Jeder Vernunft** CABARET
(Map p79; ☎883 1582; www.bar-jeder-vernunft.de; Schaperstrasse 24; [S]Spichernstrasse) Life's still a cabaret at this intimate 1912 art nouveau mirrored tent lined with red velvet booths. The schedule hopscotches from song-and-dance shows to comedy and chanson evenings plus, intermittently, the famous *Cabaret* cult musical itself.

Admiralspalast PERFORMING ARTS
(Map p60; ☎4799 7499; www.admiralspalast.de; Friedrichstrasse 101-102; [S]Friedrichstrasse, 🚇Friedrichstrasse) This beautifully restored 1920s party palace stages crowd-pleasing plays, concerts and musicals in its elegant historic hall, and more intimate shows – including comedy, readings, dance and theatre – on two smaller stages. Programming is international and usually of high calibre.

Chamäleon Varieté CABARET
(Map p60; ☎400 0590; www.chamaeleonberlin.com; Rosenthaler Strasse 40/41; 🚋M1, 🚇Hackescher Markt) A marriage of art nouveau charms and high-tech theatre trappings, this intimate 1920s-style cabaret in an old ballroom presents classy variety shows – comedy, juggling acts and singing – often in sassy, sexy and unconventional fashion.

Friedrichstadtpalast CABARET
(Map p60; ☎2326 2326; www.show-palace.eu; Friedrichstrasse 107; [S]Oranienburger Tor, 🚋M1) Europe's largest revue theatre has a tradition going back to the 1920s and is famous for glitzy-glam Vegas-style productions with leggy showgirls, a high-tech stage, mind-boggling special effects and plenty of artistry.

Cinemas

Venues listed below all screen English-language films. In summer, watching movies al fresco in a *Freiluftkino* (outdoor cinema) is a venerable tradition. Check the listings mags for what's on where.

Arsenal CINEMA
(Map p72; ☎2695 5100; www.arsenal-berlin.de; Sony Center, Potsdamer Strasse 21; [S]Potsdamer

[i] FREE CONCERT

The gifted students at Berlin's top-rated music academy, the **Hochschule für Musik Hanns Eisler** (Map p60; ☎688 305 700; www.hfm-berlin.de; Charlottenstrasse 55; [S]Stadtmitte, Französische Strasse), showcase their talents in several recitals weekly, most of them free or low-cost. They're held either on the main campus or nearby in the **Neuer Marstall** (Map p60; Breite Strasse; 🚌100, 200, [S]Spittelmarkt).

Platz, ⓡPotsdamer Platz) This artsy twin-screen cinema is the antithesis of popcorn culture, with a bold, daily changing global flick schedule that hopscotches from Japanese satire to Brazilian comedy and German road movies. Many films have English subtitles.

Babylon
CINEMA
(Map p60; ☎242 5969; www.babylonberlin.de; Rosa-Luxemburg-Strasse 30; ⓢRosa-Luxemburg-Platz) This top-rated indie in a 1920s cinema screens a well-curated potpourri of new German films, international art-house flicks, themed retrospectives and other stuff you'd never catch at the multiplex. For silent movies, the original theatre organ is put through its paces.

Cinestar Original
CINEMA
(Map p72; ☎2606 6400; www.cinestar.de; Sony Center, Potsdamer Strasse 4; ⓢPotsdamer Platz, ⓡPotsdamer Platz) A favourite among English-speaking expats and anglophile Germans, this state-of-the-art cinema with big screens, comfy seats and ear-popping surround sound shows the latest Hollywood blockbusters, all in English, all the time.

Theatre
Most plays are performed in German, naturally, but of late several of the major stages have started using English surtitles in some of their productions, including those listed here. Check the current schedules for specifics.

English Theatre Berlin
THEATRE
(Map p72; ☎691 1211; www.etberlin.de; Fidicinstrasse 40; ⓢPlatz der Luftbrücke) Berlin's English-language theatre has brought Pinter, Williams and Beckett to the stage for over two decades, with the occasional new play by an emerging playwright thrown into the mix. Visiting troupes provide additional impetus. All actors are native English speakers.

Deutsches Theater
THEATRE
(Map p60; ☎2844 1225; www.deutschestheater.de; Schumannstrasse 13a; ⓢOranienburger Tor) Helmed by the seminal Max Reinhardt from 1905 to 1932, the DT is still among Berlin's top stages. Its repertory includes both classical and bold new plays that often reflect the issues and big themes of today.

Schaubühne
THEATRE
(Map p79; ☎890 023; www.schaubuehne.de; Kurfürstendamm 153; ⓢAdenauerplatz) In a fabulous 1920s expressionist building by Erich Mendelsohn, this is West Berlin's main stage for experimental, contemporary theatre, of-

ten with a critical and analytical look at current social and political realities.

Maxim Gorki Theater
THEATRE
(Map p60; ☎2022 1115; www.gorki.de; Am Festungsgraben 2; ▣100, 200, ⓢFriedrichstrasse, ⓡFriedrichstrasse) The smallest of Berlin's state-funded theatres, the Gorki stages contemporary interpretations of the classics as well as plays dealing with local and regional themes.

Sport

Hertha BSC
FOOTBALL
(☎01805-189 200; www.herthabsc.de; tickets €9.50-35.50) Much to the dismay of local fans, Berlin's main football (soccer) team has been having trouble of late staying in the Bundesliga (premier league). But even when relegated to the second division, the vibe at home games in the Olympic Stadium is electric. Tickets are usually available on game day.

🔒 Shopping
Berlin's main shopping boulevard is Kurfürstendamm and its extension Tauentzienstrasse, which are chock-a-bloc with the usual-suspect high-street chains. You'll find more of the same in malls such as **Alexa** (Map p60; www.alexacentre.com; Grunerstrasse 20; ⊙10am-9pm Mon-Sat; ⓢAlexanderplatz, ⓡAlexanderplatz) near Alexanderplatz and **Potsdamer Platz Arkaden** (Map p72; ☎255 9270; www.potsdamer-platz-arkaden.de; Alte Potsdamer Strasse 7; ⊙10am-9pm Mon-Sat; ⓢPotsdamer Platz, ⓡPotsdamer Platz) at Potsdamer Platz. Indeed, getting the most out of shopping in Berlin means venturing off the high street and into the *Kieze* (neighbourhoods) for local flavour. Each comes with its own flair, identity and mix of stores calibrated to the needs, tastes and bank accounts of local residents.

Big shops in the centre are open from 10am to 8pm or 9pm. Local boutiques keep flexible hours, usually opening at 11am or noon and closing at 7pm, or even 4pm or earlier on Saturday. Many of the latter do not accept credit cards.

⌷ KaDeWe
DEPARTMENT STORE
(Map p81; www.kadewe.de; Tauentzienstrasse 21-24; ⊙10am-8pm Mon-Thu, to 9pm Fri, 9.30am-8pm Sat; ⓢWittenbergplatz) Just past the centennial mark, this venerable department store has an assortment so vast that a pirate-style campaign is the best way to plunder its

bounty. Even if you're pushed for time, don't miss the legendary 6th-floor gourmet food hall.

Dussmann – Das Kulturkaufhaus BOOKS, MUSIC

(Map p60; ☎2025 1111; www.kulturkaufhaus.de; Friedrichstrasse 90; ⏲10am-midnight Mon-Fri, to 11.30pm Sat; [S]Friedrichstrasse, 🚆Friedrichstrasse) It's easy to lose track of time in this cultural playground with wall-to-wall books, DVDs and a range of CDs that leaves no genre unaccounted. Bonus points for the reading-glass rentals, on-site cafe and a performance space used for concerts, political discussions and high-profile book readings and signings.

Fassbender & Rausch FOOD

(Map p60; ☎2045 8443; www.fassbender-rausch.com; Charlottenstrasse 60; ⏲10am-8pm Mon-Sat, 11am-8pm Sun; [S]Stadtmitte) If the Aztecs thought of chocolate as the elixir of the gods, then this emporium of truffles and pralines must be heaven. Bonus: the chocolate volcano and giant replicas of Berlin landmarks. The upstairs cafe serves sinful drinking chocolates and cakes with views of Gendarmenmarkt.

Markt am Winterfeldtplatz MARKET

(Map p81; Winterfeldtplatz; ⏲8am-2pm Wed, 8am-4pm Sat; [S]Nollendorfplatz) If it's Wednesday or Saturday morning, you're in luck because ho-hum Winterfeldtplatz erupts with farm-fresh fare. Along with seasonal produce, you'll find handmade cheeses, cured meats, tubs spilling over with olives, local honey and plenty more foodie staples and surprises. The Saturday edition also has artsy-craftsy stalls.

Kollwitzplatzmarkt MARKET

(Map p77; Kollwitzstrasse; ⏲noon-7pm Thu, 9am-4pm Sat; [S]Senefelderplatz) Berlin's poshest farmers' market has everything you need to put together a gourmet picnic or meal. Velvety Gorgonzolas, juniper-berry smoked ham, crusty sourdough bread and homemade pesto are among the exquisite (mostly organic) morsels scooped up by well-heeled health nuts and macciato mamas. Lines can be long, so pack some patience. The Saturday edition also features handicrafts.

Frau Tonis Parfum BEAUTY

(Map p72; ☎2021 5310; www.frau-tonis-parfum.com; Zimmerstrasse 13; ⏲10am-6pm Mon-Sat; [S]Kochstrasse) Follow your nose to this scent-sational made-in-Berlin perfume boutique. Try Marlene Dietrich's favourite (a bold violet) or ask for a customised fragrance.

DON'T MISS

FLEA MARKETS

» **Mauerpark** (Map p77; www.mauerparkmarkt.de; Bernauer Strasse 63-64; ⏲10am-5pm Sun; [S]Eberwalder Strasse) Crowded as hell but still urban archaeology at its finest and funnest, with lots of regular folks cleaning out their closets.

» **Arkonaplatz** (Map p77; Arkonaplatz; ⏲10am-4pm Sun; [S]Bernauer Strasse) Smallish and not so frantic, this is still an essential stop for retro fans (GDR stuff!) despite way too many pro vendors.

» **Boxhagener Platz** (Map p72; Boxhagener Platz; ⏲10am-6pm Sun; [S]Warschauer Strasse, Frankfurter Tor, 🚆Warschauer Strasse) Popular treasure-hunting grounds with plenty of entertainment, cafes and people watching.

» **Nowkoelln Flowmarkt** (Map p72; www.nowkoelln.de; Maybachufer; ⏲10am-6pm 1st & 3rd Sun of the month; [S]Kottbusser Tor, Schönleinstrasse) Idyllic canal-side location, secondhand bargains galore and handmade threads and jewellery.

Friedrichstadtpassagen SHOPPING CENTRE

(Map p60; Friedrichstrasse btwn Französische Strasse & Mohrenstrasse; ⏲10am-8pm Mon-Sat; [S]Französische Strasse, Stadtmitte) Even if you're not part of the Gucci and Prada brigade, the wow factor of this trio of shopping complexes (called *Quartiere*) linked by a subterranean passageway is undeniable. Highlights are Jean Nouvel's shimmering glass funnel inside the Galeries Lafayette, the dazzlingly patterned art-deco-style Quartier 206 and John Chamberlain's tower made from crushed automobiles in Quartier 205.

Ampelmann Galerie SOUVENIRS

(Map p60; ☎4472 6438; www.ampelmann.de; Court V, Hackesche Höfe, Rosenthaler Strasse 40-41; ⏲9.30am-10pm Mon-Sat, 10am-7pm Sun; 🚋M1, 🚆Hackescher Markt) It took a vociferous grassroots campaign to save the little Ampelmann, the endearing East German traffic-light man. Now the beloved cult figure and global brand graces an entire store's worth of T-shirts, towels, key rings, cookie cutters and other knick-knacks.

Türkenmarkt MARKET

(Turkish Market; Map p72; www.tuerkenmarkt.de; Maybachufer; 🕒11am-6.30pm Tue & Fri; [S]Schönleinstrasse, Kottbusser Tor) Berlin goes Bosporus at this lively canal-side farmers' market where headscarf-wearers mix it up with impecunious students and hobby cooks. Stock up on fragrant olives, creamy cheese spreads, crusty flatbreads and mountains of fruit and vegetables, all at bargain prices. Grab your loot and head west along the canal to find a nice picnic spot.

Overkill CLOTHING

(Map p72; ☎6107 6633; www.overkill.de; Köpenicker Strasse 195a; 🕒11am-8pm; [S]Schlesisches Tor) What started as a graffiti magazine back in 1992 has evolved into one of Germany's top spots for sneakers and streetwear. Browse an entire wall of limited editions by such cult purveyors as Onitsuka Tiger, Converse and Asics (including vegan versions), alongside import threads by hipster labels Stüssy, KidRobot, Cake and MHI.

1. Absinth Depot Berlin FOOD, DRINK

(Map p60; ☎281 6789; www.absinth-berlin.de; Weinmeisterstrasse 4; 🕒2pm-midnight Mon-Fri, 1pm-midnight Sat; [S]Weinmeisterstrasse) Van Gogh, Toulouse-Lautrec and Oscar Wilde were among the fin-de-siècle artists who drew – ahem – inspiration from the 'green fairy', as absinthe is also known. Ask this quaint shop's owner to help you pick out the perfect bottle for your own mind-altering rendezvous.

Steiff Galerie in Berlin TOYS

(Map p79; ☎8862 5006; www.steiff.de; Kurfürstendamm 38/39; [S]Uhlandstrasse) The cuddly creations of this famous stuffed-animal company, founded in 1880 by Margarete Steiff (who in 1902 invented the teddy bear – named after US president Teddy Roosevelt, whom she admired), are tailor-made for snuggles. The fluffy menagerie at this central store will have all ages feeling warm and fuzzy. Full line of Steiff kids' clothing as well.

Galerie Eigen+Art ART

(Map p60; ☎280 6605; www.eigen-art.com; Auguststrasse 26; 🕒11am-6pm Tue-Sat; [R]Oranienburger Strasse) This key gallery for all sorts of contemporary art – from painting to performance – is led by Gerd Harry Lybke, who has a knack for shepherding tomorrow's red-hot artists to international fame. Neo Rauch, Martin Eder and Carsten Nicolai have all been taken under his wing.

Stilwerk HOMEWARES

(Map p79; ☎315 150; www.stilwerk.de; Kantstrasse 17; [R]Savignyplatz) If this four-floor temple of good taste doesn't get your decorative juices flowing, nothing will. Everything for home and hearth is here – towels to mattresses – all by such top names as Bang & Olufsen, BoConcept, ligne roset et al.

Bonbonmacherei FOOD

(Map p60; ☎4405 5243; www.bonbonmacherei.de; Oranienburger Strasse 32, Heckmann Höfe; 🕒noon-8pm Wed-Sat Sep-Jun; 🚋M1, [R]Oranienburger Strasse) The aroma of peppermint and liquorice wafts through this old-fashioned basement candy kitchen, where the owners use antique equipment and time-tested recipes to churn out such tasty treats as their signature leaf-shaped *Berliner Maiblätter*.

SHOPPING STRIPS

» **Scheunenviertel** (eg Alte and Neue Schönhauser Strasse, Mulackstrasse, Auguststrasse, Münzstrasse, Torstrasse) Hipster central with local fashions hot off the sewing machine, up-to-the-minute concept stores and edgy galleries.

» **Friedrichstrasse/Gendarmenmarkt** Material-girl heaven with lots of hip big-ticket designer labels and exclusive concept stores.

» **Prenzlauer Berg** (eg Kastanienallee, Stargarder Strasse) Neat knick-knacks, buzzing boutiques, local designers, streetwear.

» **Charlottenburg** Mainstream chains to high-end spends along Kurfürstendamm and Tauentzienstrasse, speciality boutiques and galleries in side streets, and furniture and homewares on Kantstrasse.

» **Kreuzberg** Fashion-forward streetwear, vintage and home accessories along Oranienstrasse and Bergmannstrasse.

» **Schöneberg** Well-edited lifestyle boutiques for grown-up good-life lovers.

» **Friedrichshain** Wühlischstrasse and around for sassy fashions by small local labels.

Berlin Fashion Network — FASHION

(Map p60; www.berlinfashionnetwork.com; Court III, Hackesche Höfe; ⏱11am-8pm Mon-Sat; 🚌M1, 🚉Hackescher Markt) Keen on impressing your friends back home with the latest Berlin brands? At the city's most stylish concept store, you can browse two floors of home-grown his-and-her fashions, accessories, music and more with that urban, cheeky and fresh capital twist. Both new and established designers get rack space, including German Garment, ichJane, N.I.X. and Mio Animo.

Hard Wax — MUSIC

(Map p72; ☎6113 0111; www.hardwax.com; 2nd courtyard, Paul-Lincke-Ufer 44a, 3rd fl, door A; ⏱noon-8pm Mon-Sat; 🚉Kottbusser Tor) This well-hidden outpost has been on the cutting edge of electronic music for about two decades and is a must-stop for fans of techno, house, minimal and dubstep.

Ta(u)sche — ACCESSORIES

(Map p77; ☎4030 1770; www.tausche.de; Raumerstrasse 8; ⏱11am-8pm Mon-Fri, to 6pm Sat; 🚉Eberswalder Strasse) Heike Braun and Antje Strubels, both landscape architects by training, are the masterminds behind these ingenious messenger-style bags kitted out with exchangeable flaps that zip off and on in seconds. Bags come in 11 sizes with two flaps included.

ℹ Information

Emergency & Medical Services

In an emergency call 110 for the police and 112 for the fire brigade or an ambulance.

The US and UK consulates can provide lists of English-speaking doctors. The most central hospital with a 24-hour emergency room is the renowned **Charité Mitte** (☎450 50; www. charite.de; Charitéplatz 1; ⏱24hr; 🚌147, 🚉Oranienburger Tor).

Call-a-Doc (☎01805-321 303; www.calladoc. com; ⏱24hr) is a free non-emergency physician referral in your mother tongue.

Post

Post offices abound throughout Berlin. Central branches with late hours include **Charlottenburg** (Europa Presse Center, Tauentzienstrasse 9; ⏱8am-10.30pm Mon-Fri, to 10pm Sat, 11am-8pm Sun; 🚉Zoologischer Garten, 🚉Zoologischer Garten) and **Mitte** (Grunerstrasse 20; ⏱8am-9pm Mon-Sat; 🚉Alexanderplatz, 🚉Alexanderplatz).

Tourist Information

The city tourist board, **Visit Berlin** (☎2500 2333; www.visitberlin.de), operates four walk-in offices and a call centre with multilingual staff who field general questions and can make hotel and ticket bookings.

Brandenburger Tor (Brandenburger Tor, Pariser Platz; ⏱9.30am-7pm daily; 🚉Brandenburger Tor, 🚉Brandenburger Tor) Extended hours April to October.

Hauptbahnhof (⏱8am-10pm; 🚉Hauptbahnhof, 🚉Hauptbahnhof) Inside the train station, on the ground floor. Use the Europaplatz (north) entrance.

Neues Kranzler Eck (Neues Kranzler Eck, Kurfürstendamm 22; ⏱9.30am-8pm Mon-Sat, to 6pm Sun; 🚉Kurfürstendamm) Extended hours April to October.

ℹ Getting There & Away

Air

Berlin's brand-new **Berlin Brandenburg Airport** (BBI; www.berlin-airport.de) has been taking shape next to Schönefeld Airport, about 24km southeast of the city centre, since 2006. At the time of writing, construction problems and safety concerns had delayed the original June 2012 opening to autumn 2013, although further delays are possible. In the meantime, most major international airlines, as well as many discount carriers, including Ryanair, easyJet, Air Berlin and Germanwings, continue to fly into Berlin's two other airports.

Schönefeld Airport (SXF; ☎0180-5000 186; www.berlin-airport.de) About 24km southeast. Is being expanded into Berlin Brandenburg Airport.

Tegel Airport (TXL; ☎0180-5000 186; www. berlin-airport.de) About 22km northwest of the city centre.

Bus

BerlinLinienBus (☎861 9331; www. berlinlinienbus.de) The main operator; buy tickets online or at the **ZOB Reisebüro** (☎301 0380; www.zob-reisebuero.de; Masurenallee 4-6; ⏱6am-9pm Mon-Fri, 6am-8pm Sat & Sun; 🚉Kaiserdamm, 🚉Messe Nord/ICC) ticket office at the ZOB bus station.

Busabout (www.busabout.com) Backpacker-oriented hop-on, hop-off service stops at the **Citystay Hostel** (Map p60; ☎2362 4031; www. citystay.de; Rosenstrasse 16) in Mitte.

Deutsche Touring/Eurolines (☎069 790 3501; www.touring.de) Also has many domestic and international departures.

ZOB (☎3010 0175; www.iob-berlin.de; Masurenallee 4-6; 🚉Kaiserdamm, 🚉Messe Nord/ICC) Berlin's 'central' bus station is in deepest

TICKETS & PASSES

» One ticket is good on all forms of public transport. Most trips within Berlin require an AB ticket (€2.40), valid for two hours (interruptions and transfers allowed, round trips not). The short-trip ticket (*Kurzstreckenticket*, €1.40) is good for three stops on any U-Bahn or S-Bahn, or six on any bus or tram.

» Children aged six to 14 qualify for reduced *(ermässigt)* rates, while kids under six travel for free.

» One-day travel passes *(Tageskarte)* are valid for unlimited travel on all forms of public transport until 3am the following day. The cost for the AB zone is €6.50. Group day passes *(Kleingruppenkarte)* are valid for up to five people travelling together and cost €15.50.

» Buy tickets from vending machines in U-Bahn or S-Bahn stations and aboard trams, from bus drivers and at station offices and news kiosks sporting the yellow BVG logo. English instructions can be selected via the touch terminal. Don't buy tickets from scammers selling used ones at station exits.

» All tickets, except those bought from bus drivers and on trams, must be stamped before boarding. Anyone caught without a validated ticket escapes only with a red face and a €40 fine, payable on the spot.

western Berlin, next to the trade-fair grounds, about 4km west of Zoo Station.

Car

The A10 ring road links Berlin with other German and foreign cities, including the A11 to Szczecin (Stettin) in Poland; the A12 to Frankfurt an der Oder; the A13 to Dresden; the A9 to Leipzig, Nuremberg and Munich; the A2 to Hanover and the Ruhrgebiet cities; and the A24 to Hamburg.

Train

Berlin is well connected by train to other German cities, as well as to popular European destinations, including Prague, Warsaw and Amsterdam. While all long-distance trains converge at the Hauptbahnhof, some also stop at other stations such as Spandau, Ostbahnhof, Gesundbrunnen and Südkreuz.

North and southbound trains depart from the lowest floor of the **Hauptbahnhof** (www.berlin-hauptbahnhof.de; Europaplatz, Washingtonplatz; [S]Hauptbahnhof, 🚌Hauptbahnhof); east and westbound trains, as well as the S-Bahn, depart from the top level. Buy tickets in one of two *Reisezentrum* (travel centres) located between tracks 14 and 15 on the first upper floor (1F) and first lower floor (B1). The latter also has a Euraide desk staffed with English speakers who can assist with all train-related issues (tickets, rail passes).

The **left-luggage office** (€5 per piece per 24 hours) is behind the ReiseBank currency exchange on the first upper level, opposite the *Reisezentrum*. Self-service lockers are hidden on the lower level of the parking garage, accessible near the Kaiser's supermarket on the first lower floor. Other services include a 24-hour pharmacy, a tourist office and other stores open daily from 8am to 10pm.

SHORT CAB TRIPS

A great way to cover short distances quickly is the *Kurzstreckentarif* (short-trip rate), which lets up to four people ride a cab for up to 2km for a mere €4. This only works if you flag down a moving taxi and tell the driver you want a '*Kurzstrecke*' before he or she has activated the regular meter. If you want to continue past 2km, regular rates apply to the entire trip. Passengers love it, but cabbies don't, and there's been talk about getting rid of the tariff altogether.

Getting Around

To/From the Airports

TEGEL

The **TXL bus** connects Tegel with Alexanderplatz (40 minutes) every 10 minutes. For Kurfürstendamm and Zoo Station, take bus X9 (20 minutes). Tegel is not directly served by the U-Bahn, but both bus 109 and X9 stop at Jakob-Kaiser-Platz (U7), the station closest to the airport. Each of these trips costs €2.40.

Taxi rides cost about €20 to Zoologischer Garten and €23 to Alexanderplatz and should take between 30 and 45 minutes. There's a €0.50 surcharge for trips originating at the airport.

SCHÖNEFELD

Airport-Express trains make the 30-minute trip to central Berlin twice hourly. Note: these are regular regional trains, identified as RE7 and RB14 in timetables. The **S-Bahn S9** runs every 20 minutes and is slower but useful if you're headed to Friedrichshain or Prenzlauer Berg. For the *Messe* (trade-fair grounds), take the S45 to Südkreuz and change to the S41. Trains stop about 400m from the airport terminals. Free shuttle buses run every 10 minutes; walking takes about five minutes. You need a transport ticket covering zones ABC (€3.10).

Taxi rides average €40 and take 35 minutes to an hour.

BERLIN BRANDENBURG AIRPORT

Once the new airport is up and running, Airport-Express trains are expected to depart for central Berlin from the new airport's own station every 15 minutes. The trip will be covered by ABC tickets (€3.10).

Bicycle

Bicycles are great for exploring local neighbourhoods but – Berlin being as flat as a pancake – even cross-city trips don't take too long. Many hostels and hotels have bikes for guest use, often for free or a nominal fee.

Rental stations are practically at every corner. These range from convenience stores to clothing boutiques to petrol stations to bike shops. Keep an eye out for 'Rent-A-Bike' signs or consult www.adfc-berlin.de (link to Service, then ADFC Branchenbuch, then *Fahrradverleih*) for addresses. Deutsche Bahn's **Call a Bike** (☑07000 522 5522; www.callabike-interaktiv.de) ranks are now quite common in the city centre. The website www.bbbike.de is a handy route planner.

Bicycles may be taken aboard designated U-Bahn and S-Bahn carriages (usually the last car) as well as on trams and regional trains (RE, RB) and on night buses (Sunday to Thursday only). You need to get a separate ticket called a *Fahrradkarte* (bicycle ticket, €1.50).

Car & Motorcycle

Driving in Berlin is more hassle than it's worth, especially since parking is hard to find and expensive (about €1 to €2 per hour), so we highly recommend you make use of the excellent public-transport system instead. Central Berlin (defined as the area bounded by the S-Bahn circle line) is a restricted low-emission zone, which means all cars entering it need an *Umweltplakette* (emission sticker). See p783 for details.

Public Transport

Berlin's public-transport system is run by **BVG** (☑194 49; www.bvg.de) and consists of the U-Bahn, S-Bahn, regional trains, buses and trams. Get trip planning and general information via the BVG call centre or online.

BUS Buses are slow but useful for city sightseeing on the cheap. They run frequently between 4.30am and 12.30am. Night buses take over in the interim, running roughly every 30 minutes. MetroBuses, designated M19, M41 etc, operate 24/7. Buses 100 and 200 follow routes linking major sights.

S-BAHN The S-Bahn (suburban trains) don't run as frequently as U-Bahns but make fewer stops and thus are useful for covering longer distances. Denoted as S1, S2 etc in this book, they operate from 4am until 12.30am and all night on Friday, Saturday and public holidays. One of the most useful lines is the S41/S42 Ringbahn (Circle Line).

TRAM Trams only operate in the eastern districts. Those designated M1, M2 etc run 24/7.

U-BAHN U-Bahn lines (underground, subway) are best for getting around Berlin quickly. They are designated as U1, U2 etc in this book. Trains operate from 4am until about 12.30am and throughout the night on Friday, Saturday and public holidays (all lines except U4 and U55). From Sunday to Thursday, night buses (designated N2, N5 etc) follow the U-Bahn routes between 12.30am and 4am at 30-minute intervals.

Taxi

You can order a **taxi** (☑44 33 11, 20 20 20) by phone, flag one down or pick one up at a rank. At night, cabs often line up outside theatres, clubs and other venues. Flag fall is €3.20, then it's €1.65 per kilometre up to 7km and €1.28 for each kilometre after that. Up to four passengers travel for the price of one. Tip about 10%. There are no surcharges for night trips.

Around Berlin

Includes »

Best Places to Eat

» Maison Charlotte (p126)

» Schlossrestaurant Lübben (p129)

» Brauhaus Babben (p131)

Best Places to Stay

» Hotel Villa Monte Vino (p126)

» Schloss Lübbenau (p131)

» Pension zum Birnbaum (p132)

» Pension am Alten Bauernhafen (p130)

Why Go?

Berlin is fabulous, and you'll certainly want to spend quite a bit of time there, but don't forget to earmark a day (or two or three) for the surrounding state of Brandenburg. Headlining the list of discoveries here is the drop-dead-gorgeous park and palace of Sanssouci (the 'German Versailles') in Potsdam, a jewel box of a summer retreat built by King Frederick the Great and merely a quick train ride from central Berlin. This is a land shaped by water, and nowhere is this more evident than in the Spreewald, one of Germany's unique landscapes and home to the indigenous Sorb, who cling to their ancient customs and traditions in pretty, remote hamlets. A sobering antidote to all that cultural and natural splendour – and no less important or memorable – is Nazi Germany's first concentration camp at Sachsenhausen, north of Berlin.

When to Go

Water characterises much of the countryside around Berlin, meaning that you will want to visit between spring and autumn when you can experience the region at its best by taking a boat trip or hiring a kayak. Of course you won't be alone, especially on weekends and around holidays. Potsdam, too, is best visited midweek during summer, but its palaces and museum also make it a fine destination year-round. Sachsenhausen is, by definition, of timeless appeal.

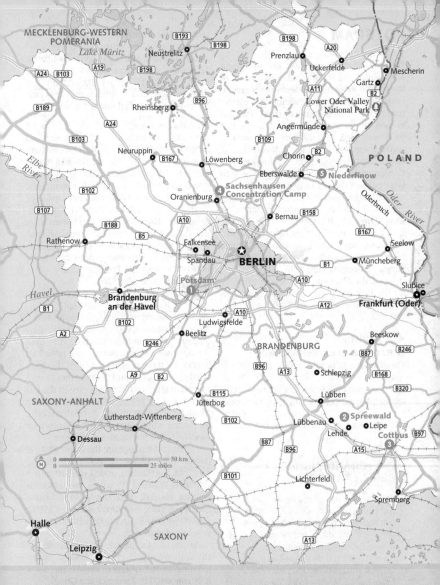

Around Berlin Highlights

1 Relive the majesty that once surrounded **Schloss Sanssouci** (p120) and other Potsdam palaces

2 Commune with nature while punting around the web of waterways in the enchanting **Spreewald** (p128)

3 Get into the mind of an eccentric aristocratic garden artist at **Schloss & Park Branitz** (p131)

4 Prepare for goosebumps as you confront the ghosts of **Sachsenhausen** (p127) concentration camp

5 Rub your eyes in disbelief at huge barges travelling in a massive **ship's lift** (p134) at Niederfinow

POTSDAM

☑0331 / POP 152,000

Potsdam, on the Havel River just southwest of Berlin, is the capital and crown jewel of the federal state of Brandenburg. Scores of visitors are drawn to the stunning architecture of this former Prussian royal seat and to soak up the air of history that hangs over its elegant parks. A visit here is essential if you're spending any time in the region at all. All this splendour didn't go unnoticed by Unesco, which gave World Heritage status to large parts of the city in 1990.

Headlining the roll call of palaces is Schloss Sanssouci, the private retreat of King Friedrich II (Frederick the Great), who was also the visionary behind many of Potsdam's other fabulous pads and parks, which miraculously survived WWII with nary a shrapnel wound. When the shooting stopped, the Allies chose Schloss Cecilienhof for the Potsdam Conference of August 1945 to lay the groundwork for Germany's postwar fate.

◉ Sights

SCHLOSS & PARK SANSSOUCI

This glorious park and palace ensemble is what happens when a king has good taste, plenty of cash and access to the finest architects and artists of the day. Park Sanssouci was dreamed up by Frederick the Great (1712–86) and is anchored by the eponymous palace, which was his favourite summer retreat, a place where he could be 'sans souci' (without cares). His grave is nearby. Frederick's great-great nephew, King Friedrich Wilhelm IV (1795–1861), added a few more palaces and buildings that reflected his intense love for all things Italian.

Schloss Sanssouci   PALACE

(Map p122; www.spsg.de; adult/concession incl audioguide Apr-Oct €12/8, Nov-Mar €8/5 ; ⊙10am-6pm Tue-Sun Apr-Oct, to 5pm Nov-Mar; ▣695, 606) The biggest stunner, and what everyone comes to see, is Schloss Sanssouci, the celebrated rococo palace designed by Georg Wenzeslaus von Knobelsdorff for King Frederick the Great in 1747. Admission is by timed ticket only; come early, preferably at opening and – if possible – avoid weekends and holidays. Otherwise, only city tours booked through the Potsdam tourist office (p127) guarantee admission.

Standouts on the audio guided tours include the Konzertsaal (concert hall), whimsically decorated with vines, grapes and even a cobweb where spiders frolic. King Frederick himself gave flute recitals here. Also note the intimate Bibliothek (library), lidded by a gilded sunburst ceiling, where the king would seek solace amid 2000 leather-bound tomes ranging from Greek poetry to the latest releases by his friend Voltaire. Another highlight is the Marmorsaal (marble room), an elegant white Carrara marble symphony modelled after the Pantheon in Rome.

Flanking the palace are the Damenflügel (Ladies' Wing; adult/concession €2/1.50; ⊙10am-6pm Sat & Sun May-Oct), added in 1840 under Friedrich Wilhelm IV, where the ladies-in-waiting resided; and the Schlossküche (palace kitchen; adult/concession €3/2.50; ⊙10am-6pm Tue-Sun Apr-Oct), with its giant wood-fired stove.

As you exit the palace, don't be fooled by the Ruinenberg, a pile of classical 'ruins' looming in the distance: they're merely a folly conceived by Frederick the Great.

Bildergalerie   GALLERY

(Map p122; Im Park Sanssouci 4; adult/concession €3/2.50; ⊙10am-6pm Tue-Sun May-Oct; ▣695, 606) The Picture Gallery is the oldest royal museum in Germany and shelters a prized collection of Old Masters, including works by Peter Paul Rubens and Caravaggio's *Doubting Thomas*.

ⓘ **BRANDENBURG-BERLIN TICKET**

The Brandenburg-Berlin Ticket (per day 1st/2nd class €48/29) entitles you and up to four accompanying passengers to one day of unlimited travel within Berlin and Brandenburg on RE, RB and S-Bahn trains as well as buses, U-Bahn and trams. Tickets are valid from 9am to 3am the following day Monday to Friday and from midnight to 3am the following day on weekends. The Brandenburg-Berlin Ticket Nacht (1st/2nd class €41/21) kicks in any day from 6pm to 6am. Children under 15 years of age travel for free if accompanied by at least one parent or grandparent. For timetable information, see www.vbb-online.de.

TIPS FOR VISITING SANSSOUCI

» Park Sanssouci is open from dawn till dusk year-round. Admission is free, but there are machines by the entrance where you can make a voluntary donation of €2.

» The palaces all have different opening hours and admission prices. Most are closed on Monday and some of the lesser ones open only at weekends and holidays in the off-season.

» A one-day pass to all Potsdam palaces is €19 (concession €14) and is sold only at Schloss Sanssouci. A day pass to all palaces *except* Schloss Sanssouci is €15 (concession €11) and sold at any of them and at the visitors centre (☎969 4200; www.spsg. de; An der Orangerie 1; ☺8.30am-6pm Apr-Oct, to 5pm Nov-Mar) at the Historic Windmill. There's also a €3 day fee for taking pictures inside the palaces.

» The palaces are fairly well spaced – it's almost 2km between the Neues Palais and Schloss Sanssouci. Take your sweet time wandering the meandering paths to discover your favourite spots.

» Cycling is officially permitted along Ökonomieweg and Maulbeerallee, which is also the route followed by bus 695, the main line to the park from the Hauptbahnhof.

» Picnicking is permitted throughout the park and there are also two restaurants: Drachenhaus (p127) and Potsdam Historische Mühle (p127).

AROUND BERLIN POTSDAM

Neue Kammern
PALACE

(Map p122; Park Sanssouci; adult/concession incl tour or audioguide €4/3; ☺10am-6pm Tue-Sun Apr-Oct, to 5pm Nov-Mar; ☒695, 606) The New Chambers were originally an orangery and later a guesthouse. The interior drips in opulence, most notably in the Ovidsaal, a grand ballroom with a gilded relief, and in the Jasper Hall, drenched in precious stones.

Historische Mühle
HISTORIC BUILDING

(Historical Mill; Map p122; adult/child incl tour €3/2, without tour €2.50/1.50; ☺10am-6pm daily Apr-Oct, 10am-4pm Sat & Sun Nov & Jan-Mar) This is a functioning replica of the palace's original 18th-century Dutch-style windmill. Admission buys access to three floors of exhibits on mill technology, a close-up of the grinding mechanism and a top-floor viewing platform.

Chinesisches Haus
HISTORIC BUILDING

(Map p122; Am Grünen Gitter; admission €2; ☺10am-6pm Tue-Sun May-Oct; ☒605 to Schloss Charlottenhof, 606 or 695 to Schloss Sanssouci, ☒91 to Schloss Charlottenhof) The 18th-century fad for the Far East is admirably reflected in the magnificent Chinese House. The cloverleaf-shaped shutterbug favourite sports an enchanting exterior of exotically garbed and gilded figures sipping tea, dancing and playing musical instruments amid palm-shaped pillars. Inside is a precious collection of Chinese and Meissen porcelain.

Neues Palais
PALACE

(New Palace; Map p122; ☎969 4200; Am Neuen Palais; adult/concession €6/5; ☺10am-6pm Wed-Mon Apr-Oct, to 5pm Nov-Mar; ☒695 or 605 to Neues Palais, ☒to Potsdam, Park Sanssouci Bahnhof) At the far western end of the park, the New Palace has made-to-impress dimensions, a central dome and a lavish exterior capped with a parade of sandstone figures. It was the final and largest palace commissioned by Frederick the Great, built in only six years, largely to demonstrate the undiminished power of the Prussian state following the bloody Seven Years War (1756–63). The king himself rarely camped out here, preferring the intimacy of Schloss Sanssouci, using it for representational purposes only. Only the last German Kaiser, Wilhelm II, used it as a residence, until 1918.

The interior attests to the high level of artistry and craftsmanship of the time. It's an opulent symphony of ceiling frescoes, gilded stucco ornamentation, ornately carved wainscoting and fanciful wall covering alongside paintings (eg by Antoine Pesne) and richly crafted furniture.

Memorable rooms include the Grottensaal (grotto hall), a rococo delight with shells, fossils and baubles set into the walls and ceilings; the Marmorsaal, a large banquet hall of Carrara marble with a wonderful ceiling fresco; and the Jagdkammer (hunting chamber), with lots of dead furry things and fine gold tracery on the walls. Frederick

Potsdam

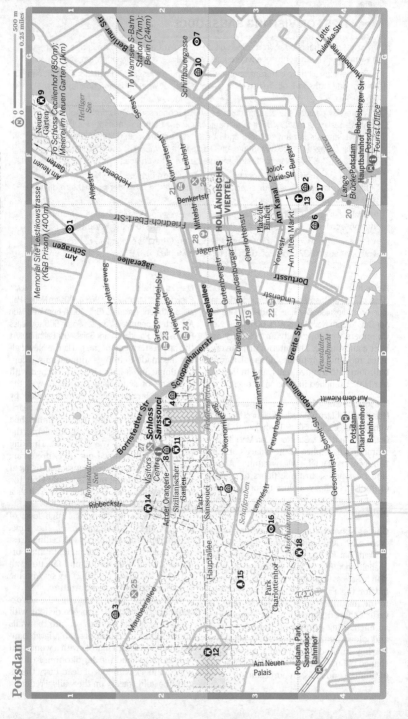

500 m
0.25 miles

To Wannsee S-Bahn
Station (7km);
Berlin (24km)

Memorial Site Leistikowstrasse
(KGB Prison) (400m)

To Schloss Cecilienhof (850m);
Meierei im Neuen Garten (1km)

Neuer
Garten

Am Neuen
Garten

Heiliger
See

Schiffbauergasse

HOLLÄNDISCHES
VIERTEL

Bornstedter
See

Ribbeckstr

Schloss
Sanssouci

Park
Sanssouci

Am Neuen
Palais

Park
Charlottenhof

Potsdam, Park
Sanssouci
Bahnhof

Potsdam

the Great's **private apartments** (Königswohnung; Map p122; adult/concession €5/4; ⊘tours 10am, noon, 2pm & 4pm Wed-Mon Apr-Oct) can only be seen on guided tours.

On weekends, admission also includes a peek inside the **Pesne-Galerie** (Map p122; adult/concession €2/1.50; ⊘10am-6pm Sat & Sun Apr-Oct), with a fine selection of works by this French painter.

The **Schlosstheater** in the south wing is only open during concerts. The pair of lavish buildings behind the palace is called the **Communs**. They originally housed the palace servants and kitchens and are now part of Potsdam University.

Orangerieschloss   PALACE

(Map p122) The dominant building in the centre of Park Sanssouci is the Orangery Palace, a 300m-long Italian Renaissance–style palace that was Friedrich Wilhelm IV's favourite building project. Tours take in the **Raphaelsaal**, with its 19th-century copies of the famous painter's masterpieces. The **tower** (€2) delivers sweeping park views. The greenhouses are still used for storing potted plants in winter.

Belvedere auf
dem Klausberg   HISTORIC BUILDING

(Map p122; ☏0331 969 4206; An der Orangerie 1; admission €2; ⊘10am-6pm Sat & Sun May-Oct) A

tree-lined path forms a visual axis from the Orangery Palace to this temple-like building, from where you can enjoy a panorama taking in the park, lakes and Potsdam itself. The upstairs hall has an impressive frescoed dome, oak parquet and fanciful stucco marble. En route, you'll pass the **Drachenhaus** (Dragon House; 1770), a fantastical Chinese palace inspired by the Ta-Ho pagoda in Canton and guarded by an entire army of dragons. It now houses a pleasant cafe-restaurant.

Park Charlottenhof   PARK

(Map p122) Laid out by Peter Lenné for Friedrich Wilhelm IV, Park Charlottenhof segues imperceptibly from Park Sanssouci but gets a lot fewer visitors. Buildings here reflect the king's passion for Italy. The small neoclassical **Schloss Charlottenhof** (Map p122; tour adult/concession €4/3; ⊘10am-6pm Tue-Sun May-Oct), for instance, was modelled after a Roman villa and features a Doric portico and bronze fountain. It was designed by Karl Friedrich Schinkel who, aided by his student Ludwig Persius, also dreamed up the nearby **Römische Bäder** (Roman Baths; Map p122; adult/concession €3/2.50; ⊘10am-6pm Tue-Sun May-Oct), a picturesque ensemble of an Italian country villa. A same-day combination ticket is €5 (concession €4).

ALTSTADT

Although Potsdam's historic town centre fell victim to WWII bombing and socialist town planning, it's still worth a leisurely stroll. Coming from Park Sanssouci, you'll pass by the baroque Brandenburger Tor (Brandenburg Gate), a triumphal arch built to commemorate Frederick the Great's 1770 victory in the Seven Years War. It's the gateway to pedestrianised Brandenburger Strasse, the main commercial drag, which takes you straight to the Holländisches Viertel (Dutch Quarter).

The southern Altstadt is anchored by the Alter Markt, where Schinkel's 1849 Nikolaikirche (Map p122; ☎270 8602; www.nikolai-potsdam.de; Am Alten Markt 1; tower €5; ☺9am-7pm Mon-Sat, 11.30am-7pm Sun), with its vast dome, cuts a commanding figure, along with the Altes Rathaus (old town hall; Map p122; Am Alten Markt), which is topped by a massive gilded figure of Atlas and is the new home of the Potsdam Museum. Taking shape on the square's south side is a replica of the Prussian Royal City Palace (Map p122; Am Alten Markt 1), which will be the future home of the Brandenburg state parliament. The original burned down to its outer walls in the final 1945 bombing raids. GDR town planners had no interest in restoring this symbol of Prussian monarchy and tore down the rest in 1960. Only the ornate Fortuna Portal was saved and it's being incorporated into the city palace 2.0. Learn more about this ambitious and controversial project at the Info-Box right on Alter Markt.

NEUER GARTEN & AROUND

North of the Potsdam old town, the winding lakeside Neuer Garten (New Garden), laid out in natural English style on the western shore of the Heiliger See, is another fine park in which to relax. A couple of palaces provide cultural diversions.

Marmorpalais   PALACE
(Map p122; ☎969 4550; www.spsg.de; Im Neuen Garten 10; tour adult/concession €5/4; ☺10am-6pm Tue-Sun May-Oct, 10am-4pm Sat & Sun Nov-Mar, 10am-6pm Sat & Sun Apr; ☐603) The neoclassical Marble Palace was built in 1792 as a summer residence for Friedrich Wilhelm II by Carl Gotthard Langhans (of Berlin's Brandenburg Gate fame) and has a stunning interior marked by a grand central staircase, marble fireplaces, stucco ceilings and lots of precious Wedgwood porcelain. The most

fanciful room is the Turkish-tent-style Orientalisches Kabinett (Oriental Cabinet).

Schloss Cecilienhof   PALACE
(☎969 4244; www.spsg.de; Im Neuen Garten 11; tours adult/concession €6/5; ☺10am-6pm Tue-Sun Apr-Oct, to 5pm Nov-Mar; ☐603) This rustic English-style country palace was completed in 1917 for crown prince Wilhelm and his wife Cecilie but is really more famous for hosting the 1945 Potsdam Conference where Stalin, Truman and Churchill hammered out Germany's postwar fate. The conference room, with its giant round table, looks as though the delegates just left.

ALEXANDROWKA & PFINGSTBERG

North of the Altstadt, Potsdam slopes up to the Pfingstberg past a Russian colony, a Russian Orthodox church and a Jewish cemetery.

Alexandrowka   NEIGHBOURHOOD
(Map p122; ☎817 0203; www.alexandrowka.de; Russische Kolonie 1; ☐92 or 96 from Hauptbahnhof) One of Potsdam's most unusual neighbourhoods, Alexandrowka is a Russian colony that was a gift from Friedrich Wilhelm III to his close friend Tsar Alexander in 1820. The first residents were the singers of a Russian military choir who had much delighted the king. Descendants of the original settlers still live in the chalet-like wooden houses surrounded by gardens and orchards. Learn more at the pretty little museum (adult/concession €3.50/3; ☺10am-6pm Tue-Sun) with nearby garden cafe. Karl Friedrich Schinkel designed the Russian Orthodox church, called Alexander-Newski-Gedächtniskirche (Russische Kolonie 14; by donation), just north of the colony.

FREE Belvedere Pfingstberg   PALACE
(☎2005 7930; www.spsg.de; ☺10am-8pm Jun-Aug, 10am-6pm Apr, May, Sep & Oct, 10am-4pm Sat & Sun Mar & Nov; ☐92 or 96 from Hauptbahnhof) For splendid views over Potsdam and surrounds, ascend the spiralling wrought-iron staircases of the twin-towered Belvedere palace commissioned by Friedrich Wilhelm IV and modelled on the Villa Medici in Rome. The 1801 Pomonatempel (☎2701972; www.spsg.de; ☺3-6pm Sat & Sun mid-Apr–Oct; ☐92 or 96 from Hauptbahnhof) just below it was Karl Friedrich Schinkel's very first architectural commission.

FREE Memorial Site
Leistikowstrasse (KGB Prison) MEMORIAL
(www.gedenkstaette-leistikowstrasse.de; Leistikowstrasse 1; ⊙2-6pm Tue-Sun) Now a memorial
site, Potsdam's central remand prison for
Soviet Counter Intelligence – colloquially
known as KGB prison – is a particularly sinister relic of the Cold War. All sorts of crimes
could land you here, including espionage,
desertion, insubordination or Nazi com-
plicity. Prisoners were often abused and
tortured until they confessed, then tried in
closed sessions without legal representa-
tion and usually sent straight to the Gulag
or the executioner. Using letters, documents,
photographs, personal items and taped
interviews, exhibits outline the fate of individuals. In the creepy basement cells you can
still see messages inmates scratched into the
walls. The building remained a prison until
1980, was then used for equipment storage
and only vacated in 1994 as one of the last
Soviet military outposts in Germany.

It was part of Military Station 7, a top-
secret walled town where ranking members
of the Soviet military lived and worked.
Locals had only a vague idea what went on
behind these walls. For a self-guided tour of
the entire compound, pick up a map at the
memorial.

SCHIFFBAUERGASSE

Ships were built, coffee was produced and
soldiers were drilled on a site that's been
reborn as a cultural hub called Schiffbauergasse (Ship Builders' Lane). On the shores
of the Tiefer See, the complex unites theatre, art and dance venues, restaurants and
high-tech businesses in new buildings and
converted industrial spaces. Stroll along the
waterfront promenade or hop on a water
taxi to explore other parts of Potsdam from
the water.

Hans-Otto-Theater THEATRE
(Map p122; ☎981 10; www.hans-otto-theater.de;
Schiffbauergasse 11; ☐93, 94 or 99 from Potsdam
Hauptbahnhof) Potsdam's main stage is the
most striking building in Schiffbauergasse.
A trio of crimson curved and floating roofs
rises above the waterfront in a paean to the
Sydney Opera House. Pritzker-Prize-winner
Gottfried Böhm incorporated an old chic-
ory mill and a former gasometer into this
extravagant design, which glows impres-
sively at night.

FREDERICK'S POSTMORTEM ODYSSEY

Frederick the Great so loved Sanssouci,
he gave specific instructions to be buried – next to his beloved dogs – on the
highest terrace of the vineyards in front
of the palace. Alas, his nephew and
successor blithely ignored his request,
putting him instead next to his father,
the 'Soldier King' Friedrich Wilhelm I, in
a nearby church. In WWII, the sarcophagi of both father and son were moved
by German soldiers for safekeeping
and, after the war, ended up in the ancestral Hohenzollern castle in southern
Germany. Only after reunification, in
1991, did Frederick the Great get his
final wish, being reburied in the exact
spot he'd personally picked out more
than 250 years before. It's marked by a
simple gravestone.

Museum Fluxus+ MUSEUM
(Map p122; ☎601 0890; www.fluxus-plus.de; Schiffbauergasse 4f; adult/concession €7.50/3; ⊙1-6pm
Wed-Sun; ☐93, 94 or 99 from Potsdam Haupbah-
nhof) This small museum specialises in art,
correspondence, objects and films related to
the 1960s avant-garde art movement called
fluxus, with an entire section dedicated to
one of its pioneers, Wolf Vostell. The '+' in
the name stands for works by contemporary
artists influenced by fluxus, such as Lutz
Friedel and Costantino Ciervo.

☞ Tours

Potsdam Sanssouci Tour GUIDED TOUR
(Map p122; tour with/without Sanssouci Palace
€27/16; ⊙Tue-Sun Apr-Oct) The local tourist
office runs the 3½-hour Potsdam Sanssouci
Tour, which checks off the highlights and
guarantees admission to Schloss Sanssouci.
Tours are in English and German and leave
at 11am from Luisenplatz and at 11.10am
from the tourist office at the Hauptbahnhof.

Schiffahrt in Potsdam BOAT
(Map p122; ☎275 9210; www.schiffahrt-in-potsdam
.de; Lange Brücke 6; ⊙departures 10am-7pm Apr-
Oct) A great way to see Potsdam is from the
deck of a cruise boat. The most popular trip
is the 90-minute *Schlösserundfahrt* palace
cruise (€13), but there's also a two-hour
'seven lake cruise' to Wannsee (€14) and a
three-hour trip around several Havel lakes

POTSDAM'S CELLULOID LEGACY

Film buffs will know that Potsdam is famous not merely for its palaces but also for being the birthplace of European film production. For it was here, in the suburb of Babelsberg, about 4km west of the city centre, where the venerable **UFA Studio** was founded in 1912. A few years later, it was already producing such seminal flicks as *Metropolis* and *Blue Angel*. Continuing as DEFA in GDR times, the dream factory was resurrected as **Studio Babelsberg** after reunification and has since produced or coproduced such international blockbusters as *Inglorious Basterds*, *Valkyrie* and *The Reader*.

There are are two ways to plug into the Potsdam film experience. In town, the handsome baroque royal stables now harbour the **Filmmuseum Potsdam** (Map p122; ☑271 810; www.filmmuseum-potsdam.de; Breite Strasse 1a; adult/concession €4.50/3.50; ☺10am-6pm Tue-Sun), which revamped its exhibit for the UFA centennial and presents an engaging romp through movie history with an emphasis on the DEFA period. In Babelsberg itself, next to the actual studios, **Filmpark Babelsberg** (☑721 2750; www.filmpark-babelsberg.de; Grossbeerenstrasse; adult/concession €21/17; ☺10am-6pm Apr-Oct; ☒601, ⓇMedienstadt Babelsberg) is a movie-themed amusement park with stunt shows, animal shows, outdoor movie sets and a studio tour with stops at the prop room, the costume department and workshops.

(€16). Boats depart from the docks near Lange Brücke.

🛏 Sleeping

Most people visit Potsdam on a day trip from Berlin, but only by spending the night can you savour the town's quiet majesty without the tour-bus crowds. The tourist office (p127) books private rooms and hotels in person, by phone or online.

TOP CHOICE **Hotel Villa Monte Vino**   HOTEL €€
(Map p122; ☑201 3339; www.hotelvillamonte vino.de; Gregor-Mendel-Strasse 27; d from €125; Ⓟ@🛜) This charming 1890 villa, complete with dreamy garden and romantic Rapunzel tower (great views!), is a superb find tucked into the leafy hillside above Schloss Sanssouci. Run by passionate owners, it harmoniously infuses historic flair with modern touches like free wi-fi throughout and a gym and sauna. Rooms don't skimp on space and are sheathed in soothing earth tones.

Hotel am Grossen Waisenhaus   HOTEL €€
(Map p122; ☑601 0780; www.hotelwaisenhaus. de; Lindenstrasse 28/29; d €80-135; Ⓟ) This minimalist but classy new entry occupies an erstwhile 18th-century barracks for married soldiers that also went through a stint as an orphanage hospital (as reflected in the name). Historical quirks combine with carefully designed contemporary features in three room categories, the nicest being the large plank-floored ones on the 1st floor.

Remise Blumberg   PENSION €€
(Map p122; ☑280 3231; www.pension-blumberg.de; Weinbergstrasse 26; d €79-92; Ⓟ🛜) In this quiet nine-room gem, run by sweet and attentive owners, you'll have plenty of space to stretch out in comfortably furnished units with full kitchens. Greet the day with an excellent breakfast (complete with sparkling wine), which, in fine weather, is served in the secluded courtyard. Other thoughtful extras include extra-thick mattresses, bike rentals and free public-transport passes.

Das Kleine Apartmenthotel im Holländerhaus   APARTMENTS €€
(Map p122; ☑279 110; www.hollaenderhaus.pots dam.de; Kurfürstenstrasse 15; apt €90-170; Ⓟ@🛜) This delightful place combines the charm of a historic Dutch Quarter building with an edgy, creative design scheme. Wood, steel and bold colour splashes give the good-sized apartments with kitchens a contemporary look. The small gym and sauna and a leafy courtyard are good unwinding spots. If you're in town for work, rent one of the temporary offices on the ground floor. Breakfast costs €8.50 to €14.

🍴 Eating & Drinking

TOP CHOICE **Maison Charlotte**   FRENCH €€€
(Map p122; ☑280 5450; www.maison-charlotte.de; Mittelstrasse 20; mains around €20, Flammkuchen €8-13; ☺noon-11pm) There's a rustic lyricism to the French country cuisine in this darling Dutch Quarter bistro, no matter whether

your appetite runs towards a simple *Flammkuchen* (Alsatian pizza), Breton fish soup or a full four-course menu (€45). Budget bon vivants come for the daily lunch special: €7.50, including a glass of wine.

Meierei im Neuen Garten   GERMAN €€
(☑704 3211; www.meierei-potsdam.de; Im Neuen Garten 10; snacks €3-7, mains €10-13; ☺11am-11pm Mon-Sat, 11am-8.30pm Sun; ☒603 to Höhenstrasse) The Berlin Wall once ran right past this brewpub that's especially lovely in summer when you can count the boats sailing on the Jungfernsee from your beer-garden table. The hearty dishes are a perfect match for the delicious Helles and seasonal suds brewed on the premises. Service can be challenged on busy days.

Drachenhaus   GERMAN €€
(Map p122; ☑505 3808; www.drachenhaus.de; Maulbeerallee 4a; mains €7.50-25; ☺11am-7pm or later Apr-Oct, 11am-6pm Tue-Sun Nov-Feb) Right in Park Sanssouci, the exotic Dragon House is a Chinese miniature palace inspired by the Ta-Ho pagoda in Canton. It now houses a pleasant cafe-restaurant serving coffee, homemade cakes and regional cuisine, in summer beneath a tree canopy.

Potsdam Historische Mühle   INTERNATIONAL €€
(Map p122; ☑281 493; www.moevenpick-restaurants.com; Zur Historischen Mühle 2; mains €10-18; ☺8am-11pm) This vast restaurant, part of the Mövenpick chain, lures punters with international favourites, a beer garden and a children's playground.

Hafthorn   PUB
(Map p122; ☑280 0820; www.hafthorn.de; Friedrich-Ebert-Strasse 90; mains €4-8; ☺from 6pm) Check your pretense at the door of this cheerily charming student pub, the home of quirky metal lamps, big burgers and delicious Bohemian beer. An all-ages crowd shares laughter inside this former bakery and, in summer, along candlelit benches in the beer garden.

ⓘ Information

Potsdam Tourist Office (☑2755 8899; www.potsdam-tourism.com; Babelsberger Strasse 16; ☺9.30am-8pm Mon-Sat May-Oct, to 6pm Mon-Sat Nov-Apr, 10am-4pm Sun year-round) inside the station, next to platform 6. There's another office at Brandenburger Tor.

ⓘ Getting There & Away

CAR Drivers coming from Berlin should take the A100 to the A115.

TRAIN Regional trains leaving from Berlin-Hauptbahnhof and Zoologischer Garten take about half an hour to reach Potsdam Hauptbahnhof; some continue on to Potsdam-Charlottenhof and Potsdam-Sanssouci, which are actually closer to Park Sanssouci . The S7 from central Berlin makes the trip in about 40 minutes. You need a ticket covering zones A, B and C (€3) for either service.

ⓘ Getting Around

BICYCLE If you want to see more of Potsdam than Sanssouci Park, a bike is ideal. You can hire one at **Potsdam per Pedales** (☑748 0057; www.potsdam-per-pedales.de; Potsdam Hauptbahnhof, platform 6/7; adult/concession per day €10.50/8; ☺9.30am-7pm Apr-Oct).

PUBLIC TRANSPORT Buses and trams operate throughout Potsdam. Bus 695 connects the Hauptbahnhof with the Altstadt and Park Sanssouci as far as the Neues Palais (single ticket €1.80, day pass €3.90).

SACHSENHAUSEN CONCENTRATION CAMP

Built by prisoners brought here from another concentration camp, Sachsenhausen opened in 1936 as a model for other camps. By 1945 about 200,000 people had passed through its gates, initially mostly political opponents but later also gypsies, gays, Jews and, after 1939, POWs from Eastern Europe, especially the Soviet Union. Tens of thousands died here from hunger, exhaustion, illness, exposure, medical experiments and executions. Thousands more succumbed during the death march of April 1945, when the Nazis evacuated the camp in advance of the Red Army. There's a memorial plaque to these victims as you approach the camp, at the corner of Strasse der Einheit and Strasse der Nationen.

After the war, the Soviets imprisoned around 60,000 German POWs in what was now Speziallager No 7 (Special Camp No 7); about 12,000 died of malnutrition and disease before it was dissolved in 1950. Soviet and GDR military continued using the grounds for another decade until the camp became a memorial site in 1961. Updated many times since, today's memorial delivers a predictably sobering experience.

◉ Sights

FREE **Gedenkstätte und Museum Sachsenhausen** MEMORIAL
(☑03301-2000; www.stiftung-bg.de; Strasse der Nationen 22; ☺8.30am-6pm mid-Mar–mid-Oct, to 4.30pm mid-Oct–mid-Mar, most exhibits closed Mon) Unless you're on a guided tour, pick up a leaflet (€0.50) or, better yet, an audio guide (€3, including leaflet) at the visitor centre to get a solid grasp of this huge site. The approach to the camp takes you past photographs taken during the death march and the camp's liberation. Just beyond the perimeter is the Neues Museum (New Museum), which has only moderately interesting exhibits on the history of the memorial site.

Proceed to Tower A, the entrance gate, cynically labelled, as at Auschwitz, *Arbeit Macht Frei* (Work Sets You Free). Beyond here is the roll-call area, with barracks and other buildings fanning out beyond. Off to the right, two restored barracks illustrate the abysmal living conditions prisoners endured. Barrack 38 has an exhibit on Jewish inmates, while Barrack 39 graphically portrays daily life at the camp. The prison, where famous inmates included Hitler's would-be assassin Georg Elser and the minister Martin Niemöller, is next door. Opposite, two original infirmary barracks have exhibits about the camp's poor medical care and on the horrid medical experiments performed on prisoners.

Further on, the Prisoners' Kitchen zeroes in on key moments in the camp's history during its various phases. Exhibits include instruments of torture, the original gallows and, in the cellar, heart-wrenching artwork scratched into the wall by prisoners.

The most sickening displays, though, deal with the extermination area called Station Z, which consisted of an execution trench, a crematorium and a gas chamber. In autumn 1941, more than 10,000 Soviet POWs were killed with a bullet to the back of the neck, shot while ostensibly being measured for uniforms. Bullets were then retrieved and reused.

In the far right corner, a new building and two original barracks house exhibits detailing what life was like when Sachsenhausen became a Soviet Special Camp.

ⓘ Getting There & Away

The S1 makes the trip thrice hourly from central Berlin (eg Friedrichstrasse station) to Oranien-burg (€3, 45 minutes). Hourly regional RE5 and RB12 trains leaving from Hauptbahnhof are faster (€3, 25 minutes). The camp is about 2km from the station in Oranienburg. Turn right onto Stralsunder Strasse, right on Bernauer Strasse, left on Strasse der Einheit and right on Strasse der Nationen. Alternatively, bus 804 makes hourly trips.

SPREEWALD

The Spreewald, a unique lacework of channels and canals hemmed in by forest, is the closest thing Berlin has to a backyard garden. Visitors come to this Unesco biosphere reserve in droves to hike, fish and punt, canoe or kayak on more than 276km of navigable waterways. The region is famous for its gherkins – over 40,000 tonnes of cucumbers are harvested here every year! Lübben and Lübbenau, the main tourist towns, often drown beneath the tides of visitors vying for rides aboard a *Kahn* (shallow punt boat), once the only way of getting around in these parts. To truly appreciate the Spreewald's unique charms, hire your own canoe or kayak or get yourself onto a walking trail.

The Spreewald is also home to members of Germany's Sorbian minority.

ⓘ Getting There & Around

Hourly RE regional trains depart central Berlin (eg Hauptbahnhof) for Lübben (€9.20, 57 minutes) and Lübbenau (€10.70, 63 minutes) en route to Cottbus (€13.40, 1½ hours). The towns are also linked by an easy 13km trail along the Spree. Cyclists can explore the region by following a section of the 260km Gurkenradweg (Cucumber Trail).

Lübben

☑03546 / POP 14,000
Tidy Lübben has a history dating back to the 12th century. Activity centres on the Schloss and the adjacent harbour area, both about 1.5km east of the train station. To get there, follow Bahnhofstrasse, turn left on Logenstrasse and continue to Ernst-von-Houwald-Damm, where you'll also find the tourist office (☑3090; www.spreewaldstadt-luebben.de; Ernst-von-Houwald-Damm 15; ☺10am-6pm Apr-Oct, 10am-4pm Mon-Fri Nov-Mar). En route, you'll pass the Paul-Gerhardt-Kirche, where 17th-century poet and hymn writer Paul

THE SORBS

The Spreewald is part of the area inhabited by the Sorbs, one of four officially recognised German national minorities (the other being Danes, Frisians and Roma/Sinti), with its own language, customs and traditions. This intriguing group, numbering around 60,000, descends from the Slavic Wends, who settled between the Elbe and Oder Rivers in the 5th century in an area called Lusatia (Luzia in Sorbian).

After Lusatia was conquered by the German king Heinrich I in 929, the Sorbs lost their political independence and, for centuries, were subjected to relentless Christianisation and Germanisation. In 1815, their land was partitioned into Lower Sorbia, centred around the Spreewald and Cottbus (Chóśebuz), which went to Prussia, while Upper Sorbia, around Bautzen (Budyšin), went to Saxony. The Upper Sorbian dialect, closely related to Czech, enjoyed a certain prestige in Saxony, but the Kingdom of Prussia tried to suppress Lower Sorbian, which is similar to Polish.

Sorbian groups banded together under a head organisation called Domowina in 1912 in order to fight for the group's rights and interests. The Nazis outlawed the organisation and banned their culture and language. In GDR times, Sorbs enjoyed protected status but were also forced to vacate large parts of their land to make room for coal-mining operations. In reunited Germany, Sorbs receive subsidies from state and federal governments (around €17 million in 2012) to keep their culture alive. Colourful Sorbian festivals such as the *Vogelhochzeit* (Birds' Wedding) on 25 January and a symbolic witch-burning on 30 April attract great media attention and huge numbers of tourists. In 2008, Stanislaw Tillich became the first Sorb to be elected governor of Saxony.

For further information, contact the **Sorbisches Institut** (Sorbian Institute; www.serbski-institut.de).

Gerhardt is buried. The Markt and Hauptstrasse are two blocks north.

⊙ Sights & Activities

Schloss PALACE
(☏187 478; www.schloss-luebben.de; Ernst-von-Houwald-Damm 14; adult/concession €4/2; ⊙10am-5pm Tue-Sun Apr-Oct, shorter hrs Nov-Mar) The prettiest building in town is the compact Schloss, which contains a fairly imaginatively presented regional-history museum; look for the interactive town model and a 2m-long medieval executioner's sword. Follow up with a (free) wander around the **Schlossinsel**, an artificial archipelago with gardens, a leafy maze, playgrounds, cafes and a harbour area where you can board punts for leisurely tours (from €8 per adult or €4 per child).

Bootsverleih Gebauer BOAT RENTAL
(☏7194; www.spreewald-bootsverleih.de; Lindenstrasse 18; single kayak 2hr/day €8/18, bicycle per day €11) Rents canoes and kayaks for one to four people as well as bicycles.

🛏 Sleeping & Eating

Hotel Lindengarten HOTEL €
(☏4172; www.spreewald-luebben.de; Treppendorfer Dorfstrasse 15; d €75; P) This family-run hotel is a class act all around and has bright and airy rooms, youthful flair and a nice restaurant serving local dishes and tapas. Free pick-ups from the station can be arranged.

DJH Hostel HOSTEL €
(☏3046; www.jh-luebben.de; Zum Wendenfürsten 8; dm €16.50-20.50, tent site €1.50; P @) This 142-bed hostel is right on the Spree, about 3km south of the train station (no bus), and also has camp sites.

TOP CHOICE **Schlossrestaurant Lübben** INTERNATIONAL €€
(☏4078; www.schlossrestaurant-luebben.de; mains €8-17; ⊙11am-11pm Tue-Sun) For a special culinary treat, book a table in the elegant palace restaurant, where classic dishes are given a local spin. Salads, for instance, might be dressed in lime-linseed vinaigrette, the pike-perch is locally caught and the crème brûlée prepared with elder flowers. In summer, you can sit in the romantic garden.

Ladencafé im Alten Gärtnerhaus MEDITERRANEAN €€
(☏186 956; www.ladencafe-luebben.de; Ernst-von-Houwald-Damm 6; mains €7-14; ⊙5-10pm Mon, noon-10pm Tue-Sun) Lovingly decorated, this little cottage with a small beer garden out back serves tasty Mediterranean fare as well

as local dishes, including fish. It's in the former palace gardener's house.

Goldener Löwe
GERMAN €€

(☎7309; www.goldenerloewe-luebben.de; Hauptstrasse 14; mains €7-11.50; ☺10am-10pm) Lübben's oldest restaurant is an ambience-laden purveyor of regional fare, including a fish platter featuring eel, perch and carp. In summer, enjoy your meal in the beer garden. It also has a few rooms for rent (doubles €65), in case you feel like dawdling.

Lübbenau

☎03542 / POP 16,800

Poet Theodor Fontane called Lübbenau the 'secret capital' of the Spreewald and, indeed, it is a pretty little town, albeit one that's often deluged by day trippers. Its entire economy seems built on tourism and no matter where you go, a forest of signs points to hotels, restaurants and other businesses, making navigating a snap. Wander away from the crowds and main street to escape the crowds. The tourist office (☎3668; www.luebbenau-spreewald.com; Ehm-Welk-Strasse 15; ☺9am-7pm Mon-Fri, 9am-4pm Sat, 10am-4pm Sun) is near the baroque Nikolaikirche church in the town centre, about 600m north of the train station.

◉ Sights & Activities

TOP CHOICE **Freilandmuseum Lehde**
MUSEUM

(☎2472; www.museum.kreis-osl.de; adult/concession €5/3.50; ☺10am-6pm Apr-Sep, to 5pm Oct) In the completely protected village of Lehde, this cluster of historic Sorb farm buildings gives you a good sense of what rural life in the Spreewald was like a century ago. Wander among the reed-covered buildings, stop at a punt-builder's workshop in use from 1884 until 1990, admire the colourful Sorb costumes or discover the secrets of the famous Spreewald gherkin. A popular two-hour boat tour (€10) goes out to Lehde from Lübbenau, but you can escape the crowds by taking a 30-minute walk instead. The route through the forest follows the Leiper Weg, which was the first road built in the Spreewald in 1935–6.

Spreewald-Museum
MUSEUM

(☎2472; www.museum.kreis-osl.de; Topfmarkt 12; adult/concession €5/3.50; ☺10am-6pm Tue-Sun Apr-Oct, noon-4pm Nov-Mar) Take a trip down the Spreewald memory lane at this imaginatively set up regional-history museum with stops at a general store, a bakery, a furrier and shoemaker and a clothing store featuring traditional Sorb garb. A sparkling new annex houses the locomotive and passenger car of the historic Spreewaldbahn, a narrow-gauge train that connected the Spreewald villages from 1898 until 1970.

FREE **Haus für Mensch und Natur**
MUSEUM

(☎892 10; Schulstrasse 9; ☺10am-5pm Tue-Sun Apr-Oct) At the main Spreewald Biosphere Reserve information centre you can learn all about the region's natural development, marvel at its incredible plant and animal diversity and test your eco-IQ at a computer game.

Punt Trips
BOAT TOURS

Several operators offer pretty much the same punting tours, from a two-hour trip to Lehde to a day-long excursion through alder forests, past old mills and historic inns, serving lunch and refreshments. If you're visiting in summer or on holiday weekends, arrive early in the day to avoid the heaviest crowds. The main embarkation points are the Kleiner Hafen (☎477 66; www.kleiner spreewaldhafen.de; Spreestrasse 10a; ☺boat tours €8-20, boat rental hour/day €2/10) and the more workmanlike Grosser Hafen (☎2225; www.grosser-kahnhafen.de; Dammstrasse 77a; boat tours €10-25). Buy tickets from the captain.

Spreewald Info
BIKE RENTAL

(☎889 977; Bahnhofstrasse 3; per day €8; ☺8am-6.30pm) Also sells train tickets and has maps and flyers.

Bootsverleih Richter
BOAT RENTAL

(☎3764; www.bootsverleih-richter.de; Dammstrasse 76a; single kayak 2hr/day €7/16; ☺9am-6pm late-Mar–mid-Oct) Active types won't have trouble hiring canoes or kayaks from several outfitters, including this dynamic operation with friendly staff and a huge fleet of well-maintained boats.

🛌 Sleeping & Eating

Check with the tourist office about private rooms (from €14) or simply walk about town and look for signs saying *Gästezimmer*. At the time of writing, Bootsverleih Richter was building a canoe-bike hostel next to its boat-rental facility, which should be ready by 2013.

PARK & SCHLOSS BRANITZ

The **Park & Schloss Branitz** (☑0355-751 50; www.pueckler-museum.de; Robinienweg 5; park free, combination ticket adult/concession €10/7; ☺10am-6pm daily Apr-Oct, 11am-5pm Tue-Sun Nov-Mar) is the highlight of a visit to Cottbus, about 35km southeast of Lübbenau. The amazing grounds result from the feverish brow of Prince Hermann von Pückler-Muskau (1785–1871) – aristocrat, writer, lady's man, eccentric and one of Germany's most formidable garden architects. From 1845 until his death, he turned his bleak ancestral family estate into an Arcadian English-style landscape park by quite literally moving earth. He shaped hills, moved trees, dug canals and lakes and built pyramid-shaped tumuli, one of which serves as his burial place alongside his wife.

For an introduction to this brilliant, if kooky, man, swing by the multimedia exhibit in the **Gutshof** (adult/concession €4.50/3.50), then see how his fascination for the exotic translated into his living space on a spin around the **Schloss** (adult/concession €5.50/4.50) itself. Highlights in this late-baroque confection by Gottfried Semper (of Dresden opera fame) include such 'souvenirs' as 3000-year-old Egyptian burial urns and rooms clad in wallpaper patterned like oriental carpets. Temporary exhibits are housed in the **Marstall** (adult/concession €3.50/2.50). Each building charges separate admission; if you're going to see all, the combination ticket represents better value.

Trains to Lübben and Lübbenau continue on to Cottbus. The park is about 4km east of the train station; bus 10 makes the trip to the park at least hourly (€1.30, 30 minutes).

Pension am Alten Bauernhafen PENSION €
(☑2930; www.am-alten-bauernhafen.de; Stottoff 5; s/d from €40/50; P) Charmingly decorated, with large rooms and a fantastic waterfront location, this big, family-run house is in a quiet side street, yet in the heart of the historic centre. Many of the breakfast items are sourced from the owner couple's own organic garden.

Hotel Nordic Spreewald HOTEL €
(☑424 41; www.hotel-nordic-spreewald.de; d €75-80; P🐾) The charming owners of this adorable oasis, about 3km outside the historic centre, often go the extra mile to make their guests happy. Feast on the bountiful breakfast buffet, then rent a bike or e-bike to explore the surrounds, surf the web while putting your feet up in the garden or retreat to squeaky-clean rooms with sitting areas and flat-screens.

Schloss Lübbenau HOTEL €€
(☑8730; www.schloss-luebbenau.de; Schlossbezirk 6; d palace/stables from €120/150; P🐾) Lübbenau's poshest digs occupy the local palace, idyllically surrounded by a tranquil park. If you need extra space, book one of the suites or apartments in the exquisitely converted 18th-century former palace stables. The prettily tiled spa in the red-brick vaulted basement is a great setting for winding down with a steam or massage.

Brauhaus & Pension Babben PENSION €
(☑2126; www.babben-bier.de; Brauhausgasse 2; d/apt from €43/55; ☺brewery from 5pm mid-Mar-Oct) Brandenburg's smallest brewery makes a mean Pilsner and seasonal beers, all of them unfiltered, unpasteurised and therefore always fresh. The menu features casual pub eats; upstairs is a handful of cosy rooms that are simply but functionally furnished and come with TV. There's also a holiday apartment across the street sleeping up to four.

BRANDENBURG AN DER HAVEL

☑03381 / POP 71,500

Brandenburg may not be Venice, but this pretty town 50km west of Berlin was definitely shaped by water. Set amid a pastoral landscape of lakes, rivers and canals, it has a historic centre with some fine examples of northern German red-brick architecture. First settled by Slavs in the 6th century, Brandenburg was a bishopric in the early Middle Ages and the capital of the margraviate (territory ruled by a margrave, a German nobleman ranking above a count) until the 15th century. Darker times arrived when the Nazis picked the town to carry out their forced euthanasia program for the mentally disabled, killing tens of thousands. Wartime bombing and GDR neglect left their scars, but these have healed nicely, making Brandenburg once again an attractive day trip from Berlin or Potsdam.

⊙ Sights & Activities

Brandenburg is split into three sections – the Neustadt, the Altstadt and the Dominsel – each on its own island in the Havel River

FREE **Dom St Peter und Paul** CHURCH
(⏸211 2223; www.dom-brandenburg.de; Burghof 10; ⏰10am-5pm Mon-Sat, 11.30am-5pm Sun, to noon Wed Jun-Sep) Treasures inside this predominanty Gothic church include a carved 14th-century Bohemian altar in the south transept, the vaulted and painted *Bunte Kapelle* (Colourful Chapel) and a fantastic baroque organ (1723). The museum has outstanding medieval vestments and a so-called *Hungertuch* (hunger blanket), with embroidered medallions depicting the life of Jesus.

Archäologisches Landesmuseum Brandenburg MUSEUM
(⏸410 4112; www.landesmuseum-brandenburg.de; Neustädtische Heidestrasse 28; adult/concession €5/3.50; ⏰10am-5pm Tue-Sun) This beautiful Gothic red-brick monastery has risen from ruins and now houses the state's archaeological collections, including rare Stone Age textiles, Bronze Age gold rings, Germanic tools and medieval coins.

Stadtmuseum im Frey-Haus MUSEUM
(⏸584 501; www.museen-brandenburg.de; Ritterstrasse 96; adult/concession €3/1; ⏰9am-5pm Tue-Fri, 10am-5pm Sat & Sun) This museum chronicles local lore from prehistory to the GDR's demise. An unexpected treat is a vast collection of locally produced mechanical toys. A more sinister object is the executioner's sword used in 1730 to behead Hans-Hermann von Katte, a close friend (and possibly lover) of the future King Frederick the Great. Accused of desertion, he was originally sentenced to life imprisonment but, wanting him dead, Frederick's father, King Friedrich Wilhelm I, had the sentence commuted and even made his son watch the execution.

Katharinenkirche CHURCH
(⏸521 162; Katharinenkirchplatz 2; ⏰10am-3pm Mon-Sat, 1-3pm Sun) This vast Gothic brick church has a lavishly detailed and decorated facade. See if you can spot your favourite biblical characters on the medieval *Meadow of Heaven* painted ceiling.

⌂ Tours

Nordstern (⏸226 960; www.nordstern-reederei .de; Neuendorfer Strasse 70; tours €8-14; ⏰Apr-Oct) and **Reederei Röding** (⏸522 331; www.fgs-hav elfee.de; Neuendorfer Strasse 82a; tours €5-12.50; ⏰Apr-Oct) operate boat tours around the Havel lakes from landing stages near the Jahrtausendbrücke.

⨭ Sleeping

Pension zum Birnbaum PENSION €
(⏸527 50; www.pension-zum-birnbaum.de; Mittel-strasse 1; d €48; P) A singing host, breakfast under a pear tree and handsomely furnished, if snug, rooms recommend this little historic inn that places you close to the train station and the Neustadt.

Sorat Hotel Brandenburg HOTEL €€
(⏸5970; www.sorat-hotels.com/brandenburg; Alt-städtischer Markt 1; d €103-146; P✳✿) You'll sleep well in bright, modern rooms (most of them facing the quiet garden) in pretty surroundings right by the Rathaus. There's a small gym and a sauna for winding down the day, and a pretty good restaurant to boot. Breakfast is €10.

✕ Eating

Cafébar Brückenhäuschen CAFE €
(⏸229 048; Ritterstrasse 76; snacks €2.50-6.50; ⏰8.30am-6.30pm Mon-Fri, from 9.30am Sat & Sun) This kiosk right by the Jahrtausendbrücke is a top address for coffee and homemade cake (try the nut tarts). In fine weather you can relax canalside in beach chairs or rent a canoe (per two hours €10, per day €28).

An der Dominsel GERMAN €€
(⏸891 807; www.restaurant-dominsel.de; Neu-städtische Fischerstrasse 14; mains €10-16; ⏰11am-10pm) The regional food, especially the fish dishes, is dependable here, but what you'll probably remember most are the fabulous Dom views across the canal. It's right by the Mühlentorturm.

Bismarck Terrassen GERMAN €€
(⏸300 939; www.bismarck-terrassen.de; Berg-strasse 20; mains €8-17; ⏰11am-10pm) Discover

your inner Prussian at this traditional restaurant, where the proprietor may greet you in Bismarck costume and seat you in a room brimming with Iron Chancellor memorabilia. The kitsch quotient is undeniable, but the Brandenburg food is authentic, delicious and plentiful. Delicious fresh and smoked fish.

Fish Shacks   SEAFOOD €
(from €1.50; ☺usually to 6pm Mon-Fri, to noon Sat) For a quick fish snack, pop into one of the little fishing shacks operated by professional fisherfolk along Mühlendamm. In summer, they set up tables on floating pontoons.

ℹ Information
Tourist Office (☎796 360; www.stg-branden burg.de; Neustädtischer Markt; ☺9am-8pm Mon-Sat year-round, 10am-3pm Sun May-Sep)

ℹ Getting There & Around
Regional trains link Brandenburg twice hourly with all major stations in central Berlin, including Hauptbahnhof (€6.40, one hour), and with Potsdam (€5.20, 30 minutes). From the station, it's about a 10-minute walk via Geschwister-Scholl-Strasse and St-Annen-Strasse to the Neustädtischer Markt. Trams 6 and 9 will get you there as well. Free parking is available at the corner of Grillendamm and Krakauer Strasse, just north of the Dom.

FRANKFURT (ODER)

☎0335 / POP 60,000
Germany's 'other' Frankfurt, on the Oder River 90km east of Berlin, was practically wiped off the map in the final days of WWII and never recovered its one-time grandeur as a medieval trading centre and university town. It didn't help that the city was split in two after the war, with the eastern suburb across the river becoming the Polish town of Słubice. The GDR era imposed a decidedly unflattering Stalinist look, but the scenic river setting, a few architectural gems and the proximity to Poland (cheaper vodka and cigarettes, for all you hedonists) make fairly compelling excuses to pop by.

◎ Sights
Marienkirche   CHURCH
(☺10am-8pm) Much of Frankfurt might be called 'aesthetically challenged', but you wouldn't know it standing on the Marktplatz, which is serenaded by the crenulated tower of the Church of St Mary, a huge red-brick Gothic hall church. Ruined by war and GDR disregard, it boasts a proud new roof and fantastic medieval stained-glass windows, which were squirrelled away as war booty in Russia until 2007.

Museum Junge Kunst   MUSEUM
(☎552 4150; www.museum-junge-kunst.de; Marktplatz 1 & Carl-Philipp-Emanuel-Bach-Strasse 11; adult/concession €4/3; ☺11am-5pm Tue-Sun) This museum has one of the most comprehensive collections of art created in the GDR and showcases the surprising diversity of artistic expression in changing exhibits. Look for paintings by Werner Tübke, sculpture by Gustav Seitz, or installations by Via Lewandowsky. Exhibits are presented in the Rathaus (note the ornate south gable) and in the riverside PackHof.

Kleist-Museum   MUSEUM
(☎531 155; www.kleist-museum.de; Faberstrasse 7; adult/concession €3/2; ☺10am-6pm Tue-Sun) Heinrich von Kleist, one of the most important poets and dramatists of the Romantic Age, was born in this town in 1777. A pilgrimage stop for literature fans, this sensitively curated exhibit in an old garrison school on the Oderpromenade river walk chronicles the life, works and importance of the man who committed suicide, along with his lover, at age 34.

🛏 Sleeping & Eating
Hotel zur Alten Oder   HOTEL €
(☎556 220; www.zuraltenoder.de; d €72; P🖥) Run with panache and attention to details, this little hotel fires on all cylinders. No two rooms are alike, sporting different colours (mostly pastels) and a vague country-style look. Breakfasts are lavish affairs that should tide you over into the early afternoon.

Turm 24   GERMAN €€
(☎504 517; www.turm24.de; Logenstrasse 8; mains €12-25; ☺11.30am-11.30pm Mon-Sat, to 10pm Sun) Some people joke that the best thing about this smart restaurant on the 24th floor of the Oderturm is that you can't see the Oderturm. Perhaps. But the views are truly fabulous and the salads, pasta and meats, while not embarking on any flights of fancy, perfectly fine.

ℹ Information

Tourist Office (☎325 216; www.tourismus-ffo. de; Karl-Marx-Strasse 189; ⏰9am-7pm Mon-Fri, 10am-2pm Sat)

ℹ Getting There & Around

Coming from Berlin, hop on the S3 at Bahnhof Ostkreuz and change to an RE train in Erkner (€9.20, 1½ hours). The central Marktplatz is about 1km northeast of the Frankfurt (Oder) train station. Follow Spiekerstrasse to Heilbronner Strasse and turn right and you'll be practically there.

CHORIN & NIEDERFINOW

About 60km northeast of Berlin, Kloster Chorin (Chorin Monastery; ☎033366-703 77; www.kloster-chorin.org; Amt Chorin 11a; adult/concession €4/2.50; ⏰9am-6pm Apr-Oct, 9am-4pm Nov-Mar) is a romantically ruined monastery near a little lake and surrounded by a lush park. Built by Cistercian monks over six decades starting in 1273, it is widely considered one of the finest red-brick Gothic structures in northern Germany. It's an enchanting setting for the Choriner Musiksommer (☎03334-818 472; www.musiksommer-chorin.de; ⏰Jun-Aug), a classical concert series featuring top talent on weekends from June to August. A shuttle bus connects Chorin train station and the Kloster before and after concerts.

About 20km southeast of Chorin, Niederfinow is famous for its spectacular Schiff-shebewerk, one of the most remarkable early-20th-century feats of engineering. It was completed in 1934 and measures 60m high, 27m wide and 94m long. Huge barges sail into a sort of giant bathtub, which is then raised or lowered 36m, water and all, between the Oder River and the Oder-Havel Canal. The lift can be viewed from the street (free), but for better views climb to the upper canal platform (adult €1, child €0.50) and view the 20-minute operation from above. Even more memorable is a trip on the lift itself aboard a little boat operated by Fahrgastschifffahrt Neumann (☎03334-244 05; www.schiffshebewerk-niederfinow.info/neumann; adult/child €7/4; ⏰11am, 1pm & 3pm late Mar-Oct). An even larger ship-lift is being planned adjacent to the existing one.

Regional trains make hourly trips to Chorin from Berlin-Hauptbahnhof (€7.70, 40 minutes) and are often met by bus 912 to the monastery. Alternatively, it's a 2.5km walk along a marked trail through the woods. There's a bike rental shop (☎033366-537 00; www.fahrradverleih-chorin.de; Bahnhofstrasse 2; per 8hr €7.50) in the train station. Seeing the monastery in the morning, then cycling over to the ship-lift and back would make a nice day trip. Alternatively, regional trains head to Niederfinow from Berlin-Hauptbahnhof with a change in Eberswalde (€6.40, 1¼ hours), or directly from S-Bahn station Lichtenberg (€6.40, one hour). The Schiffshebewerk is a scenic 2.5km walk north of the station; turn left and follow the road.

Saxony

Best Places to Eat

» Auerbachs Keller (p160)
» Filetto (p175)
» Wjelbik (p171)
» La Casina Rosa (p146)
» Restaurant Vincenz Richter (p152)

Best Places to Stay

» Hotel Börse (p174)
» Steigenberger Grandhotel Handelshof (p159)
» Schloss-Schänke (p170)
» Hotel Schloss Eckberg (p145)
» Ferdinands Homestay (p154)

Why Go?

Saxony has everything you could want in a holiday: storybook castles peering down from craggy mountaintops, cobbled marketplaces serenaded by mighty churches, exuberant palaces, nostalgic steam trains and indigenous Sorb folk traditions. And through it all courses the broad-shouldered Elbe in its steady eternal flow out to the North Sea past neatly arrayed vineyards, sculpted sandstone cliffs and villa-studded hillsides.

Many heavyweights have shaped Saxony's cultural landscape; Bach, Canaletto, Goethe and Wagner among them. Dresden's Semperoper and the Gewandhaus in Leipzig have for centuries been among the world's finest musical venues. The two cities naturally also grab top historical billing. The former became synonymous with the devastation of WWII, but has since resurrected its baroque heritage. And it was Leipzig that sparked the 'peaceful revolution' of 1989 that brought down the Berlin Wall and led to the momentous reunification of Germany.

When to Go

The cities are fun in the summer when life moves outdoors, festivals are in full swing and you can boat or cycle along the Elbe River. Thanks to lots of world-class museums and performance venues, Dresden is also a fine destination in winter, especially in December during the famous Christmas market called Striezelmarkt. Avoid Leipzig during the springtime trade-fair crunch, especially in March and April. The Bachtage in June draw scores of visitors. The trails and rock walls in Saxon Switzerland are busiest in summer and autumn.

ⓘ Getting Around

An enticement to use public transport is the **Sachsen-Ticket**, which is valid for unlimited 2nd-class travel on any regional Deutsche Bahn trains (RE, RB, S-Bahn) as well as on those operated by private companies such as ODEG from 9am until 3am the following day (from midnight on Saturday and Sunday). You can travel not only in Saxony but also in the neighbouring states of Saxony-Anhalt and Thuringia. The cost is €21 for the first person and €3 each for up to four additional people travelling together. There is no charge for bicycles. Buy tickets online or in stations from vending machines or ticket counters.

DRESDEN

♪ 0351 / POP 512,000

There are few city silhouettes more striking than Dresden's. The classic view from the Elbe's northern bank takes in spires, towers and domes belonging to palaces, churches and stately buildings. Numerous artists, most notably the Italian Canaletto, have set up their easels to capture this breathtaking panorama.

Dresden's cultural heyday came under the 18th-century reign of Augustus the Strong (August der Starke) and his son Augustus III when the Saxon capital was known as the 'Florence of the north'. Their vision produced many of Dresden's iconic buildings, including the Zwinger and the Frauenkirche. The devastating bombing raids in 1945 levelled most of these treasures. But Dresden is a survivor and many of the most important landmarks have since been rebuilt, including the elegant Frauenkirche. Today, there's a constantly evolving arts and cultural scene and zinging pub and nightlife quarters, especially in the Outer Neustadt.

So take a few days and allow yourself to be caught up in this visual and cultural feast. We promise that Dresden's world-class museums will mesmerise you, its riverside beer gardens relax you, and its light-hearted, almost Mediterranean, disposition charm you.

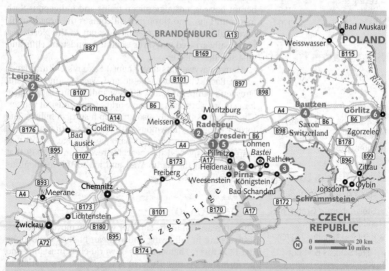

Saxony Highlights

❶ Revel in the kicking **nightlife scene** (p148) of Dresden's Neustadt, the best in the east outside of Berlin

❷ Travel back in time to the GDR at museums in **Leipzig** (p155), **Pirna** (p153) and **Radebeul** (p153)

❸ Clamber up the **Schrammsteine** (p154) for gobsmacking panoramas over the Elbe

❹ Get to know **Bautzen's Sorbs** (p170), Germany's little-known Slav minority

❺ Don sunglasses to view the dazzling treasures at Dresden's **Grünes Gewölbe** (p137)

❻ Marvel at the architecture of **Görlitz** (p172)

❼ Treat your ears to a concert at Leipzig's storied **Gewandhaus** (p163)

⊙ Sights

Key sights cluster in the compact Altstadt on the Elbe's south bank, about 1km from the Hauptbahnhof via Prager Strasse, the main pedestrianised shopping strip. From here, Augustusbrücke leads across the river to the Neustadt with its own major train station (Dresden-Neustadt) and the main pub and party quarter in the Äussere Neustadt (Outer Neustadt).

ALTSTADT

FREE Frauenkirche   CHURCH
(Map p138; www.frauenkirche-dresden.de; Neumarkt; audioguide €2.50; ⊙usually 10am-noon & 1-6pm) The domed Frauenkirche – one of Dresden's most beloved symbols – has literally risen from the city's ashes. The original graced its skyline for two centuries before collapsing two days after the devastating February 1945 bombing. The East Germans left the rubble as a war memorial but after reunification a grassroots movement helped raise funds to rebuild the landmark. It was consecrated in November 2005.

A spitting image of the original, it may not bear the gravitas of age but that only slightly detracts from its festive beauty inside and out. The altar, reassembled from nearly 2000 fragments, is especially striking. You can climb the dome (Neumarkt; adult/concession €8/5; ⊙10am-6pm Mon-Sat, 12.30-6pm Sun Mar-Oct, to 4pm Nov-Feb) for sweeping city views. The galleried interior is a wonderful place for concerts, meditations and services. Check the website for the current schedule or stop by the Frauenkirche Visitors Centre (☎6560 6701; Kulturpalast, Neumarkt; movie €2; ⊙9.30am-6pm, movie (in English) hourly 10.15am-4.15pm), which screens a movie about the church's history.

Residenzschloss   PALACE, MUSEUM
(Map p138; ☎4914 2000; www.skd.museum; Schlossplatz; adult/concession €10/7.50; ⊙10am-6pm Wed-Mon) Dresden's fortress-like Renaissance city palace was home to the Saxon rulers from 1485 to 1918 and now shelters four precious collections, including the unmissable Grünes Gewölbe (Green Vault), a real-life 'Aladdin's Cave' spilling over with precious objects wrought from gold, ivory, silver, diamonds and jewels. There's so much of it, two separate 'treasure chambers' – the Historisches Grünes Gewölbe and the Neues Grünes Gewölbe – are needed to display everything.

Another important collection is the Kupferstich-Kabinett, which counts around half a million prints and drawings by 20,000 artists (including Dürer, Rembrandt and Michelangelo) in its possession. Numismatists might want to drop by the Münzkabinett (Coin Cabinet) in the palace tower for a small array of historic coins and medals.

In 2013, the historic weapons and armour of the Rüstkammer (armoury) normally displayed in the Zwinger will also move into the Residenzschloss. Here, they will join the exotic Türckische Cammer (Turkish Chamber), one of the richest collections of Ottoman art outside Turkey. A huge three-mast tent made of gold and silk is one standout among many.

Tickets to the Residenzschloss are good for all these collections except for the Historisches Grünes Gewölbe.

TOP CHOICE Historisches Grünes Gewölbe   MUSEUM
(Map p138; ☎4914 2000; www.skd.museum; Residenzschloss, enter via Sophienstrasse or Kleiner Schlosshof; adult/under 16 incl audioguide €10/free; ⊙10am-7pm Wed-Mon) The Historical Green Vault displays some 3000 precious items in the same fashion as during the time of August der Starke, namely on shelves and tables without glass protection in a series of increasingly lavish rooms. Admission is by timed ticket only and only a limited number of visitors per hour may pass through the 'dust lock'. Get advance tickets online or by phone since only 40% are sold at the palace box office for same-day admission. If you don't have a ticket, show up before the office opens.

TOP CHOICE Neues Grünes Gewölbe   MUSEUM
(Map p138; ☎4914 2000; www.skd.museum; Residenzschloss, enter via Sophienstrasse or Kleiner Schlosshof; adult/concession incl audioguide €10/7.50; ⊙10am-6pm Wed-Mon) Also in the Residenzschloss, the New Green Vault presents some 1000 objects in 10 modern rooms. Key sights include a frigate fashioned from ivory with wafer-thin sails, a cherry pit with 185 faces carved into it and an exotic ensemble of 132 gem-studded figurines representing a royal court in India. The artistry of each item is dazzling. To avoid the worst crush of people, visit during lunchtime.

Dresden

500 m
0.25 miles

Elbe River

To Hotel Schloss
Eckberg (2km)

To Trabi
Safari (1km)

Nordstr

Forststr

Radeberger Str

Lebenerstr

18

Bischofsweg

Kamenzer Str

Priessnitzstr

14

6

Klainplatz

Bautzner Str

39

22

15

40

Görlitzer Str

Böhmische Str

Rothenburger Str

42

36

37

Hoyerswerdaer Str

32

38

5

44

45

30

48

Glacisstr

34

43

29

25

Hospitalstr

Königsbrücker Str

Jordanstr

Kunsthofpassage

52

53

Louisenstr

35

26

49

Katharinenstr

Neustadt

Wigardstr

Carolabrücke

Albertbrücke

Käthe-Ufer

Kohlwitz-Ufer

Pfefferhannsstr

Ptotenhauerstr

Elbe River

41

Holzhofgasse

Dammweg

Lössnitzstr

Erna-Berger-Str

21

47

Dr. Friedrich-Wolf-Str

Schlesischer
Platz

Dresden-
Neustadt

Antonstr

Hainstr

Albertplatz

12

Theresienstr

Nieritzstr

51

17

Königstr

Metzer Str

Rittertstr

NEUSTADT

2

Albertstr

Neustädter
Markt

Köpckestr

Haupstr

Rähnitzgasse

16

Palaisplatz

Grosse Meissner Str

Augustusbrücke

Grossenhainer Str

Gothaer Str

Leipziger Str

Marienbrücke

Devrientstr

Am
Schiesshaus

Schützengasse

Dresden
Mitte

Weisseritzstr

Ostra-Allee

9

27

23

Terrassenufer

8

Zwingerteich

Am Zwinger

Magdeburger Str

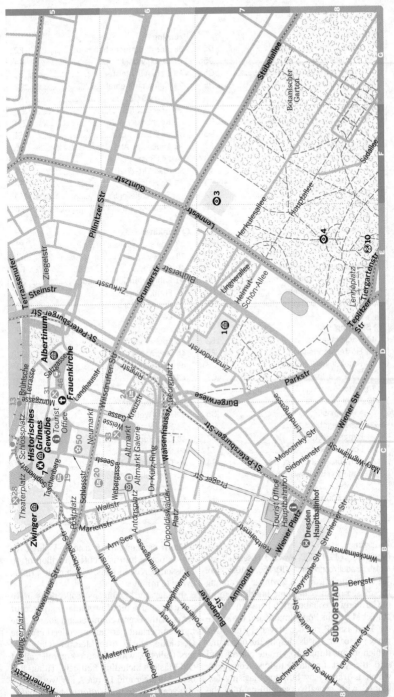

Dresden

Zwinger   MUSEUM

(Map p138; ☑4914 2000; www.skd.museum; Theaterplatz 1; adult/concession €10/7.50; ☺10am-6pm Tue-Sun) The sprawling Zwinger is among the most ravishing baroque buildings in all of Germany. A collaboration between the architect Matthäus Pöppelmann and the sculptor Balthasar Permoser, it was primarily a party palace for royals, despite the odd name (which means dungeon). Ornate portals lead into the vast fountain-studded courtyard, which is framed by buildings lavishly festooned with evocative sculpture. Atop the western pavilion stands a tense-looking Atlas. Opposite him is a cutesy carillon of 40 Meissen porcelain bells, which emit a tinkle every 15 minutes.

Inside, the Zwinger's collections have gone through a bit of a roundabout in recent years, with several comings and goings. The most important permanent collection is the **Gemäldegalerie Alte Meister** (Old Masters Gallery), which features a roll call of Old Masters including Botticelli, Titian, Rubens, Vermeer and Dürer. A key work is the 500-year-old *Sistine Madonna* by Raphael.

Admission gives you access to the **Porzellansammlung** (Porcelain Collection), a dazzling assortment of Meissen classics and East Asian treasures, and the **Mathematisch-Physikalischer Salon** whose ancient scientific instruments, globes and timepieces should again be on view following massive restoration in early 2013. A fourth exhibit, the **Rüstkammer** (Armoury) will be partly closed for refurbishment around the same time, with part of the collection moving to the Residenzschloss.

Albertinum
GALLERY

(Map p138; www.skd.museum; enter from Brühlsche Terrasse or Georg-Treu-Platz 2; adult/concession €8/6; ⊙10am-6pm; **P**) After massive renovations following severe 2002 flood damage, the Renaissance-era former arsenal is now the stunning home of the **Galerie Neue Meister** (New Masters Gallery), an ark of paintings by leading artistic lights since the Romantic period – Caspar David Friedrich to Claude Monet and Gerhard Richter – in gorgeous rooms orbiting a light-filled courtyard. One wing contains fancy sculptures from Rodin to GDR artist Wieland Förster.

Semperoper
HISTORIC BUILDING

(Map p138; ☑320 7360; www.semperoper-erleben. de; Theaterplatz 2; tour adult/concession €8/4; ⊙varies) One of Germany's most famous opera houses, the original Semperoper burned down a mere three decades after its 1841 inauguration. After reopening in 1878, the neo-Renaissance jewel entered its most dazzling period, hosting premieres of works by Richard Strauss, Carl Maria von Weber and Richard Wagner. Alas, WWII put an end to the fun and it wasn't until 1985 that music again filled the grand hall. Guided 45-minute tours operate almost daily (the 3pm tour is in English); exact times depend on the rehearsal and performance schedule. Buy advance tickets online to skip the queue.

Yenidze
ARCHITECTURE

(Map p138; ☑490 5990; www.kuppelrestaurant. de; Weisseritzstrasse 3; ⊙noon-11pm Mon-Fri, from 11am Sat & Sun) The huge mosque-like Yenidze began life in 1909 as a cigarette factory with a chimney disguised as a minaret and a stained-glass dome. Today it's home to offices and a ho-hum restaurant and beer garden beneath the dome.

DRESDEN-CARDS

The **Dresden-Card** (☑50 160 160; www.dresden.de/dresdencard) provides free public transportation as well as sweeping sightseeing discounts. Various schemes are available. The one-day **Dresden-City-Card** (single/family €10/12.50) is good for transport and discounts to 90 sights, attractions, tours and other participating venues. The two-day version (€25/46) also delivers free admission to all 13 state museums, including the Green Vaults. Regional versions (**Dresden-Regio-Card**), which include all this plus discounts to 40 additional sights, cost €48/68 for three days and €75/98 for five days.

NEUSTADT

Despite its name, Neustadt is actually an older part of Dresden that was considerably less smashed up in WWII than the Altstadt. It consists of the gentrified Innere Neustadt with Hauptstrasse as its main artery and the still delightfully wacky Äussere (Outer) Neustadt pub district north of Albertplatz.

Militärhistorisches Museum Dresden
MUSEUM

(☑823 2803; www.mhmbw.de; Olbrichtplatz 2; adult/concession €5/3; ⊙10am-6pm Tue-Sun, to 9pm Mon; ☑7 or 8 to Stauffenbergallee) Even devout pacifists will be awed by this engaging museum that reopened in 2011 in a 19th-century arsenal bisected by a bold glass-and-steel wedge designed by Daniel Libeskind. Exhibits have been updated for the 21st century, so don't expect a roll call of military victories or a parade of weapons. Instead, you'll find a progressive – and often artistic – look at the roots and ramifications of war and aggression. Exhibits in the Libeskind wedge zero in on such socio-cultural aspects as women in the war, animals in the war, war-themed toys, the economy of war and the suffering brought on by war. The historical wing presents a chronology of German wars from the Middle Ages to the 20th century. Standouts among the countless intriguing objects are a 1975 Soyuz landing capsule, a V2 rocket and personal items of concentration camp victims. Budget at least two hours to do this amazing museum justice.

FREE Kunsthofpassage ARCHITECTURE

(Map p138; www.kunsfshof-dresden.de; enter from Alaunstrasse 70 or Görlitzer Strasse 23; ⊙24hr) Take a web of grimy courtyards, a load of paint and a bunch of visionary Dresden artists and out comes the Kunsthofpassage, one of the most refreshingly artistic spaces in the Neustadt. Each one has its own charm but shutterbug favourites are the Court of the Elements, where 'music' is created by water running down interlinked rain pipes affixed to a turquoise facade, and the Court of the Animals where monkeys leap from window to window above the head of a giant giraffe.

FREE Pfunds Molkerei ARCHITECTURE

(Map p138; ☑808 080; www.pfunds.de; Bautzner Strasse 79; ⊙10am-6pm Mon-Sat, 10am-3pm Sun) The Guinness Book-certified 'world's most beautiful dairy shop' was founded in 1880 and is a riot of hand-painted tiles and enamelled sculpture, all handmade by Villeroy & Boch. The shop sells replica tiles, wines, cheeses and other milk products. Not surprisingly, the upstairs cafe-restaurant has a strong lactose theme. Slip in between coach tours for a less shuffling look round.

DRESDEN & WWII

Between 13 and 15 February 1945, British and American planes unleashed 3900 tonnes of explosives on Dresden in four huge air raids. Bombs and incendiary shells whipped up a mammoth firestorm, and ashes rained down on villages 35km away. When the blazes had died down and the dust settled, tens of thousands of Dresdners had lost their lives and 20 sq km of this once elegant baroque city lay in smouldering ruins.

Historians still argue over whether this constituted a war crime committed by the Allies on an innocent civilian population. Some claim that with the Red Army at the gates of Berlin, the war was effectively won, and the Allies gained little military advantage from the destruction of Dresden. Others have said that as the last urban centre in the east of the country left intact, Dresden could have provided shelter for German troops returning from the east and was a viable target.

Dreikönigskirche CHURCH

(Map p138; ☑812 4102; www.hdk-dkk.de; Hauptstrasse 23; tower adult/concession €1.50/1; ⊙11.30am-4pm Tue, 11am-5pm Wed-Sat, 11.30am-5pm Sun May-Oct) Designed by Zwinger-architect Pöppelmann, the most eye-catching feature of the Dreikönigskirche is the baroque altar that was ruined in 1945 and left as a memorial. Also note the 12m-long Renaissance-era Dance of Death sandstone relief opposite the altar, beneath the organ. The 88m-high tower can be scaled for some panoramic views.

GROSSER GARTEN & AROUND

Grosser Garten GARDENS

(Map p138; www.grosser-garten-dresden.de; Hauptallee 5; park admission free; ⊙24hr) The aptly named Grosser Garten (Great Garden) is a relaxing refuge during the warmer months. A visitor magnet here is the modernised Zoo Dresden (Map p138; ☑478 060; www.zoo-dresden.de; Tiergartenstrasse 1; adult/child €10/4; ⊙8.30am-6.30pm Apr-Oct, 8.30am-4.30pm Nov-Mar) in the southwest corner, where crowds gravitate towards the Africa Hall and the lion enclosure. In the northwest corner is the architecturally distinguished transparent Gläserne Manufaktur (Transparent Factory; Map p138; ☑420 4411; www.glaesernemanufaktur.de; cnr Lennéstrasse & Stübelallee; building free, tours adult/concession €5/3; ⊙11am-7pm Mon & Sun, 9am-10.30pm Wed & Thu, 9am-7pm Tue, Fri & Sat), where you can observe how the Volkswagen luxury model 'Phaeton' is being constructed. Right next to it is the free Botanischer Garten (botanical garden). From April to October, a fun way to get around the park is aboard the Dresdner Parkeisenbahn (per stop adult/concession €1/0.50; ⊙10am-6pm Tue-Sun Apr-Sep, 10am-5pm Sat & Sun Oct), a miniature train.

Deutsches Hygiene-Museum MUSEUM

(Map p138; ☑484 6400; www.dhmd.de; Lingnerplatz 1; adult/child €7/3, valid on two consecutive days; ⊙10am-6pm Tue-Sun) Not an institution dedicated to the history of cleaning products, the German Hygiene Museum is, in fact, all about human beings. The permanent exhibit uses intriguing objects, interpretive panelling, installations and interactive stations to examine the human body in its social, cultural, historical and scientific contexts. Living and dying, eating and drinking, sex and beauty are all addressed. The Children's Museum in the basement takes

A BRIDGE TOO FAR

The Saxon heartland, with Dresden at its centre, represents one of the richest cultural tapestries in Germany. This fact didn't escape the Unesco officers in charge of designating new World Heritage sites, who in 2004 welcomed a 20km section of the river valley, the Dresdner Elbtal, including Dresden's matchless baroque magnificence, into their exalted club.

But five years later, in June 2009, the Elbtal joined the most exclusive Unesco club of all. After Oman's Arabian Oryx Sanctuary, it became the second place on earth (and the first in the developed world) to have its World Cultural Heritage status revoked. The reason? The construction of the controversial four-lane Waldschlösschen Bridge across the river near the scenic spot where Canaletto once immortalised Dresden's fabulous silhouette. In a 2005 referendum, a majority of local citizens voted in favour of this bridge to alleviate the city's notoriously clogged traffic. Despite Unesco's best efforts at hammering out a compromise solution, even suggesting a tunnel as an acceptable alternative, city leaders stuck to their guns. The first vehicles may roll across the bridge in 2013.

Unesco has suggested the city may get the chance to submit a new nomination in future but with different boundaries.

four- to 12-year-olds on a interactive romp through the mysteries of the five senses.

👉 Tours

NightWalk Dresden WALKING TOUR
(Map p138; ☎01727815007; www.nightwalk-dresden. de; Albertplatz; tours €13; ☺9pm) Dresden is not all about baroque beauties, as you will discover on this intriguing 'behind the scenes' walking tour of Dresden's most interesting quarter, the Outer Neustadt. See fabulous street art, learn about what life was like in GDR times and visit fun pubs and bars. The meeting point is normally at Albertplatz but call ahead to confirm.

Sächsische Dampfschiffahrt BOAT TOUR
(☎0331-866 090; www.saechsische-dampfschif fahrt.de) Ninety-minute river tours on paddle-wheel steam boats with commentary in English and German. The company also runs scheduled service to Schloss and Park Pillnitz, Saxon Switzerland and to Meissen.

Grosse Stadtrundfahrt BUS TOUR
(Map p138; ☎899 5650; www.stadtrundfahrt.com; day pass adult/concession €20/18; ☺9.30am-5pm) This narrated hop-on, hop-off tour has 22 stops in the centre and the elegant outer villa districts along the Elbe. It includes short walking tours of the Zwinger, Fürstenzug, Frauenkirche and Pfunds Molkerei.

Trabi Safari CAR TOUR
(☎8990 0110; www.trabi-safari.de; Bremer Strasse 35; per person from €30-60) Get behind the wheel of the ultimate GDR-mobile for this 1½-hour guided drive. The price depends on the number of people in the car.

Slaughterhouse HISTORY TOUR
(☎0172 7815007) Kurt Vonnegut (1922–2007), one of America's most influential 20th-century writers, spent the end of WWII as a POW in Dresden and later based his famous 1969 novel *Slaughterhouse-Five* on his observations and experiences. Thanks to Danilo Hommel, owner of NightWalk Dresden, you can now walk in Vonnegut's footsteps while being peppered with intriguing stories about how he ended up in Dresden, how he survived the February 1945 bombing and what he saw and suffered through in the aftermath. The highlight is a visit to the slaughterhouse meat locker where Vonnegut and his fellow POWs survived the fateful bombing. Tours run for two hours and cost €12 per person. Call for times.

🎊 Festivals & Events

Internationales Dixieland Festival MUSIC FESTIVAL
(www.dixieland.de) Bands from around the world descend upon Dresden for one week in May.

Dresdener Musikfestspiele MUSIC FESTIVAL
(Music Festival; www.musikfestspiele.com) Held mid-May to June, with mostly classical music.

Bunte Republik Neustadt STREET FESTIVAL
(www.brn-dresden.de) The Outer Neustadt celebrates its alternative roots on the third June

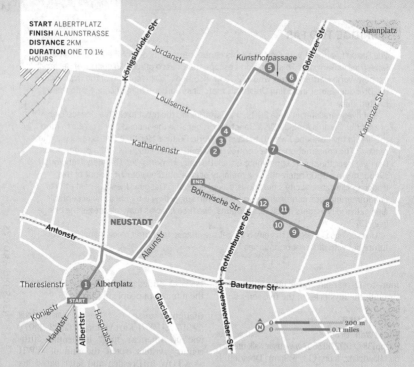

START ALBERTPLATZ
FINISH ALAUNSTRASSE
DISTANCE 2KM
DURATION ONE TO 1½ HOURS

Königsbrücker Str

Jordanstr

Louisenstr

Kunsthofpassage

Alaunplatz

Görlitzer Str

Kamenzer Str

Katharinenstr

Antonstr

NEUSTADT

Alaunstr

END
Böhmische Str

Rothenburger Str

Theresienstr   Albertplatz

START

Königstr

Hauptstr

Albertstr

Hospitalstr

Glacisstr

Hoyerswerdaer Str

Bautzner Str

N   0   200 m
     0   0.1 miles

Walking Tour
Street Art in the Outer Neustadt

❯ If you're finished feasting your eyes on Dresden's baroque beauties, it's time for a dose of real life in the colourful, alt-flavoured Äussere Neustadt (Outer Neustadt) quarter.

Start your tour on ❶ **Albertplatz**, perhaps casting a passing glance at the two fountains representing turbulent and still waters, then plunge into the depth of the Outer Neustadt via Alaunstrasse. Soon on your right is ❷ **Die Scheune**, Dresden's oldest youth club, which has been going strong since 1951. Stop to admire the latest artistic outpourings on the officially designated ❸ **Graffiti Wall** just before Katy's Garage, then rub your eyes in disbelief at the ❹ **17m-long bicycle**, an art installation by Dutch artist Wouter Mijland. Keep going on Alaunstrasse to the whimsical ❺ **Kunsthofpassage**, a cluster of five interlinked artist-designed courtyards. Give your camera a workout, then grab a yummy ice cream at ❻ **Neumanns Tiki**, family-owned since 1966, and turn right onto

Görlitzer Strasse. Make a note to come back in the evening to join the other 'lost kids' in the ❼ **'Bermuda Triangle'** of densely clustered bars and pubs around Louisenstrasse, then make your way down gritty ❽ **Martin-Luther-Strasse**, home to some especially fine street art. Next up is the Outer Neustadt's most intriguing lane, Böhmische Strasse, home to not only art squat-turned-gastropub ❾ **Raskolnikoff** but also to the intriguing ❿ **Ukdradena Galerie**, Dresden's smallest gallery. Part of an experimental street art project, it's really just a small display case affixed to a wall with a different artist installing a new exhibit every week. Across the street, you can add your own wisdom (in chalk) to a long ⓫ **blackboard** intended to combat illegal graffiti. For a time warp back to the 1960s GDR, drop by ⓬ **Hebeda's**, the oldest pub in the Neustadt. Continue one more block and you're back at Alaunstrasse.

weekend with lots of music, food and wacky merriment.

Striezelmarkt
CHRISTMAS MARKET

(www.striezel-markt.de) Sample the famous Dresdener Stollen (fruit cake) in December at one of Germany's oldest and nicest Christmas markets.

🛏 Sleeping

Dresden's hotels can be horrendously expensive, with rates among the highest in Germany. Thankfully there are plenty of cheap beds available at the city's superb hostels.

ALTSTADT

Hotel Bülow Residenz
HOTEL €€

(Map p138; ☑800 3291; www.buelow-residenz. de; Rähnitzgasse 19; d from €120, breakfast €18; P ✳ 🛜) This place occupies one of Dresden's oldest town houses and is a class act, from the welcome drink to the spacious gold-and-crimson-hued rooms baronially cloaked in antiques, paintings and porcelain. Days get off to a breezy start with a lavish breakfast in the glass-covered courtyard atrium.

Hotel Taschenbergpalais Kempinski
HOTEL €€€

(Map p138; ☑491 20; www.kempinski-dresden.de; Taschenberg 3; r €170-230; ✳ @ 🛜 ⛲) You might never get around to sightseeing when staying at this swanky 18th-century mansion where luxury is taken very seriously. Checking in here buys views over the Zwinger from rakishly handsome rooms that beautifully bridge the traditional and the contemporary with rich royal blue colour accents and marble bathrooms with Bulgari toiletries. In winter, the courtyard turns into an ice rink.

Radisson Blu Gewandhaus Hotel
HOTEL €€

(Map p138; ☑494 90; www.radissonblu.com/ gewandhaushotel-dresden; Ringstrasse 1; d from €133; P ✳ @ 🛜 ⛲) The original 18th-century trading house of tailors and fabric merchants burned down in 1945 but its modern atrium-style reincarnation smoothly hitches itself to tradition. Public areas are stunning and the Biedermeier-style rooms have marble-fitted bathrooms with whirlpool tubs. Tops for class and personal service.

Pension am Zwinger
PENSION €€

(Map p138; ☑8990 0100; www.pension-zwinger.de; Ostra-Allee 27; d €80-90; P @ 🛜) Self-caterers, families and space-cravers will appreciate these bright, functional but stylish apart-ment-style rooms with basic kitchens. It's super-central and fairly quiet, despite being on a busy street. Note that the reception is at Maxstrasse 3 about 50m away.

Ibis Budget
HOTEL €

(Map p138; ☑8339 3820; www.etaphotel.com; Wilsdruffer Strasse 25; r from €39; ✳ @ 🛜) The ship cabin-sized rooms have few frills but the key sights are just a hop, skip and jump away. With its upbeat ambience and friendly service, this is definitely a great budget base. It's part of the Altmarkt-Galerie shopping mall.

NEUSTADT

Lollis Homestay
HOSTEL €

(Map p138; ☑810 8458; www.lollishome.de; Görlitzer Strasse 34; dm €13-19, d €44-48, linen €2, breakfast €4; @ 🛜) This is a textbook backpacker hostel: friendly, communicative, casual and with neat artsy designed themed rooms (Cinema, Desert Room, Giant's Room), including a double where you live down that *Good Bye, Lenin!* vibe by bedding down in a real GDR-era Trabi car. (Old) bikes, tea and coffee are welcome freebies and the communal room and kitchen conducive to meeting fellow travellers.

Hostel Mondpalast
HOSTEL €

(Map p138; ☑563 4050; www.mondpalast.de; Louisenstrasse 77; dm €14-19.50, d €48-56, linen €2, breakfast €6.50; @) Check in at the out-of-this-world bar-cafe (with cheap drinks) before being 'beamed up' to your room in the Moon Palace – each one dedicated to a sign of the zodiac or some other spacey theme. Bike rentals and a large kitchen are also available.

TOP CHOICE Hotel Schloss Eckberg
HOTEL €€€

(☑809 90; www.schloss-eckberg.de; Bautzner Strasse 134; d from €125 in Kavaliershaus, €198 in Schloss; P ✳ @) You'll feel like royalty when arriving at this romantic estate set in its own riverside park east of the Neustadt. Rooms in the Schloss are pricier and have oodles of historic flair, but staying in the modern Kavaliershaus lets you enjoy almost as many amenities and the same dreamy setting.

Kangaroo-Stop
HOSTEL €

(Map p138; ☑314 3455; www.kangaroo-stop.de; Erna-Berger-Strasse 8-10; dm €12.50-17.50, d €40, linen €2; P @ 🛜) With an Australian theme throughout, this superb hostel is spread over two buildings: one for backies, the other for families. Some rooms have sinks, but other facilities are shared. Strike up new friendships in the kitchen-diner and communal areas, then mine the knowledgeable owner for the insider scoop on the city.

Hotel Privat
HOTEL €€

(Map p138; ☑811 770; www.das-nichtraucher-hotel.de; Forststrasse 22; s €54-69, d €69-94; P @) This small, family-run hotel in a quiet residential district has Saxon charm galore and 30 good-sized rooms, some with alcoves and balconies. Tobacco is definitely a no-no here, even in the garden.

Hotel Martha Dresden
HOTEL €€

(Map p138; ☑817 60; www.hotel-martha-hospiz.de; Nieritzstrasse 11; d €113-120; ☎) Fifty rooms with big windows, wooden floors and Biedermeier-inspired furnishings combine with an attractive winter garden, a rustic restaurant serving Saxon cooking and local wine, and a smiley welcome into a pleasant place to hang your hat. The entire hotel is wheelchair-accessible. Bike rentals are available.

Backstage
HOTEL €€

(Map p138; ☑888 7777; www.backstage-hotel.de; Priessnitzstrasse 12; r from €80; ⊙reception 7am-6pm; P☎) The production halls of the famous Pfunds Molkerei dairy shop have morphed into this jazzy sleep station where each room reflects the creative musings of a local artist. Expect four-poster beds made of bamboo, swirling Gaudí-esque bathrooms and, if you're staying on the upper floor, a breezy terrace. Optional breakfast costs €7.

Rothenburger Hof
HOTEL €€

(Map p138; ☑812 60; www.rothenburger-hof.de; Rothenburger Strasse 15-17; d €100-160, apt from €170; ☎▩) This launch pad for Dresden explorations has modernised rooms that are comfortable but in no danger of winning style awards. Let the events of the day float by while relaxing in the Moorish-style steam room or small pool. Since a tram runs along the street, quieter rooms are in the back.

✖ Eating

ALTSTADT

Ladencafé Aha
INTERNATIONAL €€

(Map p138; ☑496 0673; www.ladencafe.de; Kreuzstrasse 7; mains €4-11; ⊙10am-midnight; ☑) At this warm and cheerful smoke- and stress-free zone above a one-world store, you can sip delicious coffee, pick from the international menu or watch your kiddies play with the provided toys.

brennNessel
VEGETARIAN €€

(Map p138; ☑494 3319; www.brennnessel-dresden.de; Schützengasse 18; mains €7-13; ⊙11am-midnight) This much-beloved vegetarian gastropub with leafy cobbled courtyard beer garden is a favourite hang-out for off-duty Semperoper musicians. Choose from creative casseroles, stews, pastas and salads (great ginger-honey dressing!). Some dishes feature the namesake nettles and a separate vegan menu is available.

Cafe Alte Meister
INTERNATIONAL €€

(Map p138; ☑481 0426; www.altemeister.net; Theaterplatz 1a; mains €7-15; ⊙10am-1am) If you've worked up an appetite from museum-hopping or need a break from culture overload, retreat to this elegant filling station between the Zwinger and the Semperoper for a smoked-trout sandwich, light salad, luscious cake or energy-restoring steak. A sculpture of composer Carl Maria von Weber guards the entrance.

Sophienkeller
SAXON €€

(Map p138; ☑497 260; www.sophienkeller-dresden.de; Taschenberg 3; mains €7-14; ⊙11am-1am) The 1730s theme with waitresses trussed up in period garb may be a bit overcooked but the local specialities aren't. Most of it is rib-sticking fare, like the boneless half duck with red cabbage or the spit-roasted suckling pig. Wash it down with a mug of dark Bohemian Krušovice. Great ambience amid vaulted ceilings in the Taschenbergpalais building.

Grand Café
CAKES, SAXON €€

(Map p138; ☑496 2444; www.coselpalais-dresden.de; An der Frauenkirche 12; mains €10-15; ⊙10am-midnight) The cakes and imaginative mains are good but they almost play second fiddle to the gold-trimmed baroque Coselpalais, which makes for a stylish refuelling stop after climbing the Frauenkirche dome.

NEUSTADT

TOP CHOICE La Casina Rosa
ITALIAN €€

(Map p138; ☑801 4848; www.la-casina-rosa.de; Alaunstrasse 93; pizza & pasta €6.50-9.50; ⊙lunch Tue-Sat, dinner Mon-Sat) Everybody feels like family at this neighbourhood-adored trattoria with its warren of cosy rooms (plus idyllic summer garden) and feisty pasta and pizza, plus seasonally inspired specials. Menu stars include the richly flavoured tagliatelle with porcini, veal, cherry tomatoes and thyme, and the 'piccola Capri' pizza topped with shrimp, courgettes and rocket. Reservations are key.

PlanWirtschaft
INTERNATIONAL €€

(Map p138; ✆801 3187; Louisenstrasse 20; mains €7-14; ☺9am-1am) The winning formula at this long-time favourite: fresh ingredients sourced from local suppliers, a menu that dazzles with inventiveness and smiley staff that makes even first-timers feel at home. Sit inside the cafe, the romantic garden or the cosy brick cellar.

Lila Sosse
MODERN GERMAN €€

(Map p138; ✆803 6723; www.lilasosse.de; Alaunstrasse 70, Kunsthofpassage; appetisers €3.50-9.50, mains €13-15) This jumping joint puts a new spin on modern German cooking by serving intriguing appetisers in glass preserve jars. You're free to order just a couple (the fennel-orange salad and carp with capers are recommended) or, if your tummy needs silencing, pair them with a meaty main and dessert. Reservations essential. It's part of the charming Kunsthofpassage courtyard complex.

Cafe Continental
CAFE, INTERNATIONAL €€

(Map p138; ✆272 1722; www.cafe-continental-dresden.de; Görlitzer Strasse 1; dishes €3-13.50; ☺24hr) If the greenly lit openings behind the bar remind you of aquariums, you've hit the nail on the head, for buzzy 'Conti' was once a pet store back in GDR days. Today, it's a great place to hit no matter the hour for anything from cappuccino and cocktails to homemade cakes or a full meal. Breakfast is served until 4pm.

Stilbruch
CAFE, BAR €€

(Map p138; ✆810 8610; www.stilbruch-dresden.de; Böhmische Strasse 30; dishes €5.50-13.80; ☺from 6pm Mon-Sat) With a nod to Dalì or David Lynch, the clocks run backwards, toilets are accessed via an armoire and dishes have names like 666 or Chainsaw Massacre at this surrealist cafe-bar. It also has a great collection of board games and the world's only 'Gollard' table (a cross between golf putting and billiards).

Kochbox
SNACK BAR €

(Map p138; ✆796 7138; Görlitzer Strasse 3; dishes €3-6; ☺11am-3am) This little joint gets howling in the wee hours when starving nightowls invade in hopes of restoring balance to the brain with fist-sized burgers made from fresh (not frozen) meat.

Raskolnikoff
CAFE, BAR €€

(Map p138; ✆804 5706; www.raskolnikoff.de; Böhmische Strasse 34; mains €5-13; ☺9am-2am) An artist squat in GDR times, Raskolnikoff still brims with artsy-bohemian flair. The menu is sorted by compass direction (borscht to fish soup and steak) and in summer, the sweet little beer garden beckons. The beer comes from the Neustadt-based Schwingheuer brewery and is a steal at €2.40 per half litre. Upstairs are eight basic but handsome rooms (doubles €52 to €70).

Ararat Döner Kebab Haus
TURKISH €

(Map p138; www.ararat-dresden.de; Alaunstrasse 37; doner €3.80; ☺10am-3am Mon-Thu, to 5pm Fri & Sat, to 2am Sun) If you need to restore balance to the brain after a long night out in the Neustadt, join the flock of other party-goers descending upon this classic doner kebab joint run by an energetic team.

Curry & Co
SAUSAGES €

(Map p138; ✆209 3154; www.curryundco.com; Louisenstrasse 62; sausages €2.30-3; ☺11am-10pm Sun-Wed, to midnight Thu, to 2am Fri & Sat) This upbeat outfit has elevated the lowly *Currywurst* to an art form. Choose from smoked, all-beef, chicken or vegan varieties and pair your pick with your favourite homemade sauce, from mild curry to hot chilli-onion. Don't skip the fries.

Drinking

ALTSTADT

Twist
BAR

(Map p138; ✆795 150; Salzgasse 4; ☺from 6pm Mon-Sat) 'Twist' is indeed the name of the game at this sky bar where classic cocktails are given – often radical – new interpretations. The signature drink, Twist Innside, blends sherry with cognac, orange liqueur and sparkling wine. On the 6th floor of the Innside Hotel, you'll be at eye-level with the Frauenkirche dome.

Karl May Bar
BAR

(Map p138; ✆491 20; www.kempinski.com; Taschenberg 3; ☺6pm-2am) Cocktail connoisseurs gravitate to this sophisticated saloon inside the Taschenbergpalais hotel. Sink into a heavy burgundy-coloured leather chair to sip tried-and-true classics. Live music Friday and Saturday, happy hour 6pm to 8pm.

Fährgarten Johannstadt
BEER GARDEN

(Map p138; ✆459 6262; www.faehrgarten.de; Käthe-Kollwitz-Ufer 23b; ☺10am-1am Apr-Oct) This idyllic riverfront beer garden pulls great ales and does a mean barbecue.

NEUSTADT

If you're up for a night on the razzle, head out to the Äussere Neustadt, which is chock-a-block with cafes and bars. Alaunstrasse, Louisenstrasse and Görlitzer Strasse are where it's happening.

Lebowski Bar
BAR

(Map p138; www.dudes-bar.de; Görlitzer Strasse 5; ⊙7pm-5am Sun-Thu, to 7am Fri & Sat) When everything else is closed, 'dudes' can still toast the sunrise with a White Russian while the eponymous cult movie reels off in the background.

Lloyd's
CAFE, BAR

(Map p138; ☑501 8775; www.lloyds-cafe-bar.de; Martin-Luther-Strasse 17; mains €7.50-16.50; ⊙8am -1am) In a quiet corner of the Neustadt, Lloyd's oozes grown-up flair thanks to stylish cream-coloured leather furniture, huge mirrors and fanciful chandeliers. It's a solid pit stop from breakfast to that last expertly poured cocktail and even does a respectable afternoon tea by the fireplace.

Louisengarten
BEER GARDEN

(Map p138; www.biergarten-dresden.de; Louisen-strasse 43; ⊙4pm-1am Sun-Thu, 3pm-2am Fri & Sat) This boho-flavoured beer garden takes the 'go local' concept to the limit. Wind down the day with beer (Lenin's Hanf, aka Lenin's Hemp) supplied by the nearby Neu-städter Hausbrauerei and grilled meats courtesy of the butcher down the street.

Combo
CAFE

(Map p138; Louisenstrasse 66; ⊙9am-2am) Laid-back to the point of toppling, this '70s-retro cafe has enormous windows that fold back when the heat is on, 1960s airport furniture and great coffee served with a side of water and two gummi bears.

Cafe 100
PUB

(Map p138; ☑273 5010; www.cafe100.de; Alaun-strasse 100; ⊙8pm-open end) One of the first pubs in the Neustadt to open after the *Wende*, Cafe 100 does double duty as a studenty pub on the ground floor and a candle-lit wine bar in the cavernous cellar. Jazz fans invade during the twice-monthly jam sessions.

Frank's Bar
BAR

(Map p138; ☑6588 8380; www.franksbar.de; Alaun-strasse 80; ⊙from 7pm) Cocktails – classics to custom-made – are the poison of choice at this long-running Neustadt bar presided over by a charismatic team of mix-meisters. They also have Fosters on tap, in case you're not in a martini mood.

Neumanns Tiki
BAR

(Map p138; ☑810 3837; Görlitzer Strasse 21; ⊙11am-1am) This legendary Polynesian-style parlour has been plying locals with divine homemade ice cream since 1966 but is also a go-to place for colourful, umbrella-crowned cocktails.

☆ Entertainment

The finest all-round listings guide to Dresden is *SAX* (www.cybersax.de), sold at newsstands. Regular freebies include *Blitz* (www.blitz-world.de), *Frizz* (www.dresden-frizz.de) and *Kneipensurfer* (www.kneipensurfer.de). Each has an extensive internet presence. Print versions can be picked up at tourist offices, cafes, pubs and hostels.

Classical Music

Semperoper Dresden
OPERA

(Map p138; ☑491 1705; www.semperoper.de; Theat-erplatz 2; ⊙ticket office 10am-6pm Mon-Fri, 10am-5pm Sat & Sun) Dresden's famous opera house is the home of the Sächsische Staatsoper Dresden, which puts on brilliant performances that usually sell out. Tickets are sold by phone, in person and online.

Dresdner Philharmonie
CLASSICAL MUSIC

(Map p138; ☑486 6866; www.dresdnerphilharmonie.de) While its permanent home, the Kulturpalast, is getting a facelift, Dresden's renowned orchestra performs at venues around town. The website has all the dates and details. Buy tickets by phone or online.

Clubbing

Altes Wettbüro
CLUB

(Map p138; www.altes-wettbuero.de; Antonstrasse 8; ⊙from 8pm Tue-Sat) Dance until the stars fade at this upbeat dance temple where tousled post-college hipsters get showered by electronica, house and hip hop. Low riff-raff factor and friendly door. Occasional live bands at weekends.

Club Koralle
CLUB

(Map p138; Rothenburger Strasse 30; ⊙from 10pm Fri & Sat) Fans of cool electrobeats gravitate to this little basement club to party with established local DJs until the garbage trucks start making their rounds.

Downtown CLUB

(Map p138; ☑811 5592; http://downtown-dresden. de; Katharinenstrasse 11-13; ⊙Fri, Sat & Mon) This iconic old factory gives you Friday *and* Saturday night fever with three floors of dance action where wrinkle-free party kids shake it up till the wee hours.

Live Music

Scheune LIVE MUSIC

(Map p138; ☑3235 5640; www.scheune.org; Alaunstrasse 36-40) Generations of young folks have memories of the 'Barn', which started out as a mainstream GDR-era youth club before turning into an offbeat culture centre with almost daily concerts, cabaret, parties or performances. The cafe serves Indian food and there's a beer garden.

Blue Note JAZZ

(Map p138; ☑801 4275; www.jazzdepartment. com; Görlitzer Strasse 2b; ⊙8pm-5am) Small, smoky and smooth, this converted smithy has concerts featuring regional talent almost nightly (usually jazz, but also rock and Latin), then turns into a night-owl magnet until the wee hours. Many concerts are free. The drinks menu features beer from around the world and a mind-boggling selection of single malt whiskys.

Katy's Garage LIVE MUSIC

(Map p138; www.katysgarage.de; Alaunstrasse 48) As the name suggests, this cavernous party pit is set in a former tyre shop with matching decor and even drinks named after car parts. You know the crowd skews young if one of their theme nights is the 'Älternabend' for people over 25.

Jazzclub Neue Tonne LIVE MUSIC

(Map p138; ☑802 6017; www.jazzclubtonne.de; Königstrasse 15) Cool cats of all ages come out to this polished jazz joint for good music from local and international talent.

Gay & Lesbian Venues

Dresden doesn't have a huge lesbigay scene but what there is concentrated in the Neustadt. The magazine *GegenPol* (www. gegenpol.net) keeps tabs on the scene in print and online.

Queens & Kings GAY

(Map p138; www.queens-dresden.de; Görlitzer Strasse 2b) The 'Queens' is dead, long live the 'Queens & Kings,' across the street from the original gay fave party palace. The new version is modern, a tad chicer and dressed in flamboyant colours.

Boy's GAY

(Map p138; ☑563 3630; www.boys-dresden.de; Alaunstrasse 80; ⊙8pm-3am, to 5am Fri & Sat) This lively bar-club draws all kinds of comers with parties on Friday and Saturday, plenty of cosy corners for cuddling and fair drinks prices.

Sappho LESBIAN

(☑404 5136; www.sapphodresden.de; Hechtstrasse 23) This scene staple has been keeping lesbians happy for over a decade. On weekends the action extends to the party cellar with dance floor. Beer garden and Mediterranean menu to boot.

ⓘ Information

Krankenhaus Dresden-Friedrichstadt

(☑4800; Friedrichstrasse 41) Central hospital with 24hr emergency room.

Post offices Altmarkt-Galerie (Altmarkt-Galerie, enter from Wallstrasse; ⊙9.30am-9pm Mon-Sat); Neustadt (Königsbrücker Strasse 21-29; ⊙9am-7pm Mon-Fri, 10am-1pm Sat)

ReiseBank (☑471 2177; Wiener Platz 4, at Hauptbahnhof; ⊙8am-8pm Mon-Fri, 8am-6pm Sat, 10am-6pm Sun) Currency exchange, phone cards, money transfers

Tourist offices Frauenkirche (☑5016 0160; www.dresden-tourist.de; Schlossstrasse 23; ⊙10am-7pm Mon-Fri, 10am-6pm Sat, 10am-3pm Sun, reduced hours Jan-Mar); Hauptbahnhof (☑5016 0160; www.dresden -tourist.de; Hauptbahnhof; ⊙9am-7pm)

ⓘ Getting There & Away

AIR Dresden International (DRS; ☑881 3360; www.dresden-airport.de) has flights to many German cities and such destinations as Moscow, Vienna and Zurich.

CAR Dresden is connected to Leipzig via the A14/A4, to Berlin via the A13/A113 and to Saxon Switzerland and the Czech Republic via the B172 south. All major international car rental agencies have outlets at the airport. Europcar has a branch right by the Dresden-Neustadt train station.

TRAIN Fast trains make the trip to Dresden from Berlin-Hauptbahnhof in two hours (€38) and Leipzig in 1¼ hours (€30). The S1 local train runs half-hourly to Meissen (€5.60, 40 minutes) and Bad Schandau in Saxon Switzerland (€5.60, 45 minutes).

ⓘ Getting Around

TO/FROM THE AIRPORT Dresden airport is about 9km north of the city centre. The S2 train links the airport with the city centre several times hourly (€2). Taxis are about €20.

BICYCLE Ask at your hotel or hostel about bike rentals. **Roll On** (☎0152 2267 3460; Königsbrücker Strasse 4a/Albertplatz; bike/scooter per day from €8/21; ⊗10am-1pm Mon-Sat & 4-7pm Sat) in the Neustadt also rents scooters.

PUBLIC TRANSPORT Buses and trams are run by **Dresdner Verkehrsbetriebe** (DVB; ☎857 1011). Fares within town cost €2, a day pass €5. Buy tickets from vending machines at stops or aboard trams.

TAXI There are ranks at the Hauptbahnhof and Neustadt station, or ring ☎211 211.

AROUND DRESDEN

Dresden is surrounded by a trio of fabulous castles, all of them easily reached by public transportation, as well as the porcelain town of Meissen.

Schloss & Park Pillnitz

Baroque has gone exotic at Schloss Pillnitz (☎261 3260; www.schlosspillnitz.de; August-Böckstiegel-Strasse 2; park only €2, park, museums & greenhouses adult/concession €8/4; ⊗park 6am-dusk, museums 10am-6pm Tue-Sun May-Oct), a delightful pleasure palace festooned with fanciful Chinese flourishes. This is where the Saxon rulers once lived it up during long hot Dresden summers. Explore the wonderful gardens, then study the history of the palace and life at court in the Schlossmuseum. Two other buildings, the Wasserpalais and the Bergpalais, house the Kunstgewerbemuseum, which is filled with fancy furniture and knick-knacks from the Saxon court, including Augustus the Strong's throne. Tickets are also good for the two greenhouses (February to April only). Pillnitz is dreamily wedged in between vineyards and the Elbe, some 14km upriver from central Dresden. Drivers need to take the B6 (Bautzner Landstrasse) to Pillnitzer Landstrasse. Otherwise, take tram 6 from Dresden-Neustadt, then catch bus 63 at Schillerplatz to Pillnitzer Platz. The loveliest approach is by steamer operated by Sächsische Dampfschiffahrt (Map p138; ☎866 090; www.saechsische-dampfschiffahrt.de; one-way adult/concession €11.70/9.35) which makes the trip from Dresden's Terrassenufer in 90 minutes.

Schloss Weesenstein

A magnificent sight, on a rocky crag high above the Müglitz River, Schloss Weesenstein (☎035027-6260; www.schloss-weesenstein.de; Am Schlossberg 1, Müglitztal; adult/concession €5/2.50, audioguide €2; ⊗9am-6pm daily Apr-Oct, 10am-5pm Tue-Sun Feb, Mar, Nov & Dec, 10am-5pm Sat & Sun Jan) is an amazing alchemy of styles, blending medieval roots with Renaissance and baroque embellishments. This resulted in an architectural curiosity where the banquet halls ended up beneath the roof, the horse stables on the fifth floor and the residential quarters in the cellar.

The palace owes its distinctive looks to the noble Bünau family who dabbled with it for 12 generations from 1406 until 1772. In the 19th century, it became the private retreat of King Johann of Saxony, who distinguished himself not only as a ruler but as a philosopher and translator of Dante into German. Lavishly furnished and decorated period rooms on the ground floor contain an exhibit about the man and life at court. In keeping with the topsy-turvy architecture, the permanent exhibit takes you on a reverse journey through Saxon history, ending with the Middle Ages.

There are several restaurants, including a cafe in the former palace prison, a traditional brewpub and the upmarket Königliche Schlossküche. After filling your belly, you can take a digestive saunter in the lovely baroque park.

Schloss Weesenstein is about 16km southeast of Dresden. From Dresden Hauptbahnhof take the S1 and change to the SB72 in Heidenau (€5.60, 25 minutes). Weesenstein train station is about 500m south of the castle – follow the road up the hill. By car, take the A17 to Pirna, then head towards Glashütte and follow the signs to the Schloss.

Schloss Moritzburg

A white vision surrounded by a lake and a beautiful park, baroque Schloss Moritzburg (☎035207-8730; www.schloss-moritzburg.de; Schlossallee; adult/concession €7/3.50, audioguide €2; ⊗10am-5.30pm daily Apr-Oct, 10am-4.30pm Sat & Sun Mar) was the preferred hunting palace of the Saxon rulers and the site of some rather lavish post-hunting parties under August the Strong. No surprise then that antlers are the main decorative feature in halls sheathed in rich leather wall coverings, some painted with mythological scenes. Prized trophies include the antlers of an extinct giant stag and bizarrely misshapen ones in the Hall of Monstrosities. Considerably prettier is the legendary Federzimmer (Feather Room) downstairs whose centrepiece is a bed made from over a million colourful duck, pheasant and peacock feathers.

Moritzburg is about 14km north of Dresden. Buses 326 and 457 make regular trips from Dresden-Neustadt train station (€3.80, 30 minutes). For a more atmospheric approach, take the S1 train to Radebeul-Ost (€3.80, 15 minutes) and from there the 1884 narrow-gauge Lössnitzgrundbahn (€5.80, 30 minutes) to the palace.

Meissen

📞 03521 / POP 29,000

Straddling the Elbe around 25km upstream from Dresden, Meissen is the cradle of European porcelain manufacturing and still hitches its tourism appeal to the world-famous china first cooked up in its imposing 1710 castle. Adjacent to the soaring Gothic cathedral, it crowns a ridge above the Altstadt whose meandering cobbled lanes offer an escape from the porcelain pilgrims rolling in by tour bus.

⊙ Sights

TOP CHOICE **Erlebniswelt Haus Meissen**   MUSEUM
(📞 468 208; www.meissen.com; Talstrasse 9; adult/child €9/4.50; ⊙9am-6pm May-Oct, 9am-5pm Nov-Apr) There's no 'quiet time' to arrive at the popular and unmissable porcelain museum where you can witness the astonishing artistry and craft that makes Meissen porcelain unique. It's next to the porcelain factory, about 1km south of the Altstadt. Visits start with a 30-minute tour (with English audioguide) of the Schauwerkstätten, a series of four studios where you can observe live demonstrations of vase throwing, plate painting, figure moulding and the glazing process. This gives you a better appreciation for the thousands of pieces, displayed chronologically, at the Museum of Meissen Art inside an integrated art-nouveau villa.

Albrechtsburg   CASTLE, MUSEUM
(📞 470 70; www.albrechtsburg-meissen.de; Domplatz 1; adult/concession incl audioguide €8/4; ⊙10am-6pm Mar-Oct, 10am-5pm Nov-Feb) Lording it over Meissen, the 15th-century Albrechtsburg was the first German castle constructed for residential purposes but is more famous as the birthplace of European porcelain. It took a group of leading scientists led by Walther von Tschirnhaus and Johann Friedrich Böttger three years to discover the secret formula of the 'white gold' in 1708, a feat achieved by the Chinese thousands of years earlier. Production began in the castle in 1710 and only moved to a custom-built factory in 1863. An exhibit on the second floor chronicles how it all began; a nifty touch terminal lets you 'invent' your own porcelain. The palace is distinguished by several architectural innovations, most notably a curvilinear staircase and eye-popping cell vaulting in the Great Hall swathed in epic murals depicting scenes from the history of the palace and its builders, Elector Ernst of Saxony and his brother Albrecht.

Markt   SQUARE
The handsome Markt is flanked by colourfully painted historic town houses along with the Rathaus (1472) and the Gothic Frauenkirche (📞 453 832; Markt; tower adult/concession €2/1; ⊙usually 10am-5pm Apr-Oct). Its carillon is the world's oldest made from porcelain and chimes a different ditty six times daily. Climb the tower for fine red-roof views of the Altstadt.

Dom   CHURCH
(📞 452 490; www.dom-zu-meissen.de; Domplatz 7; adult/concession €3.50/2.50; ⊙9am-6pm, to 5pm Sat Apr-Oct, 10am-4pm Nov-Mar) Meissen's dome, a high-Gothic masterpiece begun in 1250, does not impress as much by its size as by the wealth of its interior decorations. Stained-glass windows showing scenes from the Old and New Testaments create an ethereal backdrop for the delicately carved statues in the choir, presumed to be the work of the famous Master of Naumburg. The altar triptych is attributed to Lucas Cranach the Elder. Tower tours (€2) are offered several times daily from April to October.

🛏 Sleeping

Hotel Goldener Löwe   HOTEL €€
(📞 411 10; www.welcome-hotels.com; Heinrichsplatz 6; d from €85, breakfast €11; 🅿@🛜) Everything works like a well-oiled machine behind the cheerful yellow facade of this 17th-century inn near the Markt. Rooms are a harmonious blend of antique-style furnishings and all major modcons. Wind down the day at the restaurant with a fireplace or enjoy a glass of local wine in the tavern.

Herberge Orange
HOSTEL €

(☑454 334; www.herberge-orange.de; Siebe-neichener Strasse 34; d without bathroom €35, breakfast €4; ℗) Wallet-watching nomads can shack up in this friendly riverside hostel 1.5km south of the Markt. Rates include sheets and towel; a bizarre €2 per person 'cleaning fee' will be added, though.

Hotel Burgkeller
HOTEL €€

(☑414 00; www.hotel-burgkeller-meissen.de; Domplatz 11; d €125-175; ☎) Warm reds combine with polished furniture, beamed ceilings, airy bathrooms and dreamy views at this historic hilltop charmer. Some rooms have a small balcony and there's also an apartment big enough for two couples or a family.

✕ Eating

TOP CHOICE Restaurant Vincenz

Richter
GERMAN €€€

(☑453 285; www.vincenz-richter.de; An der Frauenkirche 12; mains €10-29; ☺lunch daily, dinner Mon-Sat) Despite the historic guns and armour, the romance factor is high at this 16th-century inn, which is due to the attentive service, the classy interpretations of classic Saxon dishes and the crisp whites from the Richter's own wine estate. Terrace tables have a view of Markt.

Gasthaus zur Altstadt
GERMAN €€

(☑405 640; www.gasthaus-zur-altstadt.de; Görnische Gasse 42; mains €5-12; ☺11am-11pm) Old photographs and tchotchkes from yesteryear create cosy ambience in this unprepossessing eatery off the tourist track. The honest-to-goodness traditional German fare is delectable and portions ample. Wash it down with a local pilsner or riesling.

Domkeller
GERMAN €€

(☑457 676; www.domkeller.com; Domplatz 9; mains €9-18; ☺lunch & dinner) This atmospheric tavern has been in the hearty food and drink business since 1470. Standouts on the Saxon menu include a beer goulash served in a hollowed-out bread bowl and a meat skewer that's flambéed at the table. The terrace is tailor-made for vista junkies.

❶ Information

Tourist office (☑419 40; www.touristinfo -meissen.de; Markt 3; ☺10am-6pm Mon-Fri, 10am-4pm Sat & Sun Apr-Oct, 10am-5pm Mon-Fri, 10am-3pm Sat Nov, Dec, Feb & Mar) Also rents bicycles for €9 per day.

❶ Getting There & Around

BOAT Steam boats operated by **Sächsische Dampfschiffahrt** (☑452 139; www. saechsische-dampfschiffahrt.de; one-way/return €14/19.50) depart from the Terrassenufer in Dresden. Boats return upstream to Dresden at 2.45pm but take over three hours to make the trip. Many people opt to go one way by boat and the other by train.

BUS Stadtrundfahrt Meissen (☑741 631; www.vg-meissen.de; day pass adult/concession €5/3.50; ☺9.30am-6pm Apr-Oct)

TRAIN From Dresden, take the half-hourly S1 (€5.80, 40 minutes) to Meissen. For the porcelain factory, get off at Meissen-Triebischtal.

SAXON SWITZERLAND

About 40km south of Dresden, Saxon Switzerland (Sächsische Schweiz, aka Elbsandsteingebirge or Elbe Sandstone Mountains) embraces a unique and evocative landscape. This is wonderfully rugged country, where nature has chiselled porous rock into bizarre columns, battered cliffs, tabletop mountains and deep valleys. The Elbe courses through thick forest, past villages and mighty hilltop castles. No wonder such fabled beauty was a big hit with 19th-century Romantic artists, including the painter Caspar David Friedrich. In 1990, about a third of the area became Saxony's first and only national park. The glories continue on the Czech side of the border in the Bohemian-Switzerland National Park.

The main towns are Rathen with the famous Bastei, Königstein with its humongous fortress and Bad Schandau, the main town and commercial hub.

You could tick off the area's highlights on a long day trip from Dresden but to truly 'get' the magic of Saxon Switzerland, consider staying overnight. In addition to hiking, this is one of Germany's premier rock-climbing meccas, offering over 15,000 routes. Cyclists can follow the lovely Elberadweg. If you don't want to go it alone, hook up with **Hobbit Hikes** (☑0173 380 0675; www.hobbit-hikes.de) for guided nature walks, hikes and climbs.

❶ Getting There & Around

BOAT From April to October, steamers operated by Sächsische Dampfschiffahrt (p143) plough up the Elbe several times daily between Dresden and Bad Schandau, stopping in Rathen, Königstein and other towns. The entire trip takes 5½ hours and costs €23.90 (concession €19.10).

GDR MUSEUMS NEAR DRESDEN

Not far from Dresden, in Radebeul and Pirna, two museums offer a fascinating glimpse into an extinct society. And no, we're not talking Neanderthals or ancient Greeks. We're talking the GDR, the 'other' Germany that ceased to exist with reunification in 1990. Along with the former country's demise came the disappearance of many of its products, traditions and institutions that had shaped daily life for 40 years. A bafflingly eclectic collection of this socialist-era flotsam and jetsam – including flags and posters, typewriters and radios, uniforms and furniture, dolls and detergents – has been assembled in these two 'time capsules'.

At the **DDR Museum Pirna** (☏03501-774 842; www.ddr-museum-pirna.de; Rottwerndorferstrasse 45; adult/concession €5/4; ☺10am-6pm Tue-Sun Apr-Oct, 10am-5pm Tue-Thu, Sat & Sun Nov-Mar), in a former army barracks, you can snoop around a furnished apartment, sit in a classroom with a portrait of GDR leader Walter Ulbricht glowering down at you or find out how much a *Junge Pioniere* youth organisation uniform cost. Thousands of objects are creatively arranged and, while most are self-explanatory, others would benefit from informational text.

The **Zeitreise DDR Museum Radebeul** (☏0351-835 1780; www.ddr-museum -dresden.de; Wasastrasse 50; adult/concession €7.50/6; ☺10am-6pm Tue-Sun) is larger and better organised. Each of the four floors is dedicated to a particular theme, such as work, daily life and state institutions. This is rounded off by a fabulous collection of Trabi cars, Simson motorbikes and other vehicles. A timeline charts milestones in Cold War history and there's a restaurant serving GDR-era cuisine.

To get to the Pirna museum, take the S1 from Dresden's Hauptbahnhof to Pirna, walk five minutes to the central bus station (ZOB) and hop on local bus N for 'Geibeltbad/ Freizeitzentrum' (€3.80, 35 minutes). Pirna is on route B172.

The Zeitreise Museum is reached by taking tram 4 to Wasastrasse, eg from the Antonstrasse/Leipziger Strasse stop in Dresden-Neustadt (€3.80, 20 minutes).

You can do the entire trip or hop aboard along the way.

BUS From mid-April to October, a bus service operated by **Frank Nuhn Freizeit und Tourismus** (☏035021-99080; www.frank-nuhn -freizeit-und-tourismus.de) shuttles between Königstein, Bad Schandau and the Bastei four times daily. Buy tickets from the driver.

CAR Towns are linked to Dresden and each other by the B172; coming from Dresden, it's faster to take the A17 and pick up the B172 in Pirna. There are only three bridges across the Elbe: two in Pirna and one in Bad Schandau. Passenger ferries (bicycles allowed) cross the Elbe in Stadt Wehlen, Rathen and Königstein.

TRAIN The handy S1 connects Bad Schandau, Königstein and Rathen with Dresden, Pirna, Radebeul and Meissen every 30 minutes. Bad Schandau is also a stop on long-distance EC trains travelling between Hamburg and Vienna.

Bastei

The Bastei is a stunning rock formation nearly 200m above the Elbe and the village of **Rathen**. It's a wonderland of fluted pinnacles and offers panoramic views of the surrounding forests, cliffs and mountains. The much-photographed Basteibrücke, a sandstone bridge built in 1851, leads through the rocks to the remnants of a partly reconstructed medieval castle, the **Felsenburg Neurathen** (adult/concession €1.50/0.50; ☺9am-6pm), which is open for touring.

The Bastei is the most popular spot in the national park, so crowds are guaranteed unless you get here before 10am or after 4pm. An easy way to escape the crowd is by hitting the trail. A 5km loop leads from the car park to the Schwedenlöcher, a hideout where local troops dodged the advancing Swedes during the Thirty Years' War (1618–48).

The only sleeping option up here is the **Berghotel Bastei** (☏035024-7790; www. bastei-berghotel.de; s €49-55, d €82-122; P), a nicely spruced-up GDR-era hotel with a restaurant and terrace. Otherwise, there are more overnight options in Rathen, including the characterful **Burg Altrathen** (☏035024-7600; www.burg-altrathen.de; Am Grünbach 10-11; d €70-90; ☎) in a medieval castle. The **tourist office** (☏035024-704 22; www.kurort-rathen. de; Füllhölzelweg 1; ☺10am-noon & 1-6pm Mon-Fri,

9am-2pm Sat & Sun Eater-Oct) in Rathen can help find additional options.

ⓘ Getting There & Away

The nearest train station is in Rathen, where you need to catch the ferry across the Elbe, then follow a sweat-raising 30-minute trail to the top of the Bastei. Drivers can leave their car in the big car park near the train station. There's also a car park on the Bastei-side of the Elbe. Drive to Pirna, then follow the Basteistrasse (S167/164) to Lohmen, then catch the S165 direction Hohenstein and follow the signs. If you arrive early (before 10am) you should be able to snag a spot in the inner Bastei car park (€5.50 all day), from where it's only a 10-minute walk to the viewpoints. Otherwise, you need to park in the outer car park (€2.50 all day) about 3km away and either catch a shuttle bus (€1 each way) or walk.

Königstein

The village of Königstein would be unremarkable were it not for the massive citadel built on a tabletop mountain some 260m above the river. **Festung Königstein** (☑035021-646 07; www.festung-koenigstein.de; adult/concession €8/5 Apr-Oct, €7/5 Nov-Mar, audioguide €2.50; ⊙9am-6pm Apr-Oct, to 5pm Nov-Mar) is the largest intact fortress in the country, and so imposing and formidable that no one ever bothered to attack it. Begun in the 13th century, it was repeatedly enlarged and is now a veritable textbook in military architecture, with 30 buildings spread across 9.5 hectares. Highlights include the **Brunnenhaus**, with its seemingly bottomless well, a prickling array of German weaponry, and the **Georgenburg**, once Saxony's most feared prison, whose famous inmates included Meissen porcelain inventor Johann Friedrich Böttger. During WWII, it served as a POW camp and a refuge for art treasures from Dresden. The biggest draw, however, is the widescreen view deep into the national park and across to the Lilienstein tabletop mountain.

There are several eateries at the fortress and more in the town below. The **tourist office** (☑035021-682 61; www.koenigstein-sachsen. de; Schreiberberg 2; ⊙9am-6pm Mon-Fri, 9am-noon Sat, 10am-1pm Sun May-Oct, 9am-5.30pm Mon-Fri, 9am-10.30am Sat Nov-Apr) can help find lodgings. Pick of the litter is **Ferdinands Homestay** (☑035022-547 75; www.ferdinands homestay.de; Halbestadt 51; dm €12.50-17.50, d €30-40, tent €2.50-5.50, per camper €5, breakfast €6; ⊙Apr-Oct; **P**), a small and friendly riverside hostel and campsite combo in a secluded spot on the northern bank. Call or check the website for directions.

From April to October, the **Festungsexpress** (☑035021-99080; www.frank-nuhn -freizeit-und-tourismus.de; one-way/roundtrip €5/3; ⊙9am-4pm May-Oct, from10am Apr) tourist train makes the steep climb half-hourly from Reissiger Platz in Königstein. This drops you at the bottom of the fortress, from where you can get a lift or walk. Alternatively it's a strenuous 30- to 45-minute climb from the bottom. The nearest car park is off the B172 (exit Festung) from where it's a 10-minute walk to the fortress.

Bad Schandau

☑035022 / POP 4000

The little spa town of Bad Schandau sits right on the Elbe and is the unofficial capital of Saxon Switzerland. Most hotels, supermarkets and restaurants are here, and it's also a central base for hikes.

◉ Sights & Activities

Personenaufzug   LIFT
(adult/concession return €2.80/2.20; ⊙9am-6pm Apr & Oct, 9am-7pm May-Sep) This century-old lift whisks you up a 50m-high tower for views and access to a footbridge linking to a pretty forest path that runs into the national park.

Nationalparkzentrum   MUSEUM
(☑502 40; www.lanu.de; Dresdner Strasse 2b; adult/ concession €4/3; ⊙9am-5pm, closed Jan & Mon Nov-Mar) The National Park Centre has hohum exhibitions on flora, fauna and how the sandstone formations were shaped but the evocative visuals of the 17-minute introductory movie almost justify the admission price.

Schrammsteinaussicht   HIKING
The rugged Schrammsteine is the densest rock labyrinth in the national park and popular with rock hounds. A moderate to strenuous trail leads to a fantastic viewpoint of the rocks, the Elbe Valley and national park. There are several trailheads, including a convenient one off the B172 in Poselwitz next to a bus stop. The first 20 minutes up the steep Obrigensteig are tough but then the trail levels out and leads through fabulous rock formations. The final 'ascent' is straight up the rocks via a one-way network of steel stairs and ladders. No technical skills are required, although you should be fairly

WHAT'S IN A NAME?

With its highest peak rising to just 723m, the Saxon Switzerland ain't exactly the Alps. So how did the region get its name? Credit belongs to the Swiss. During the 18th century, the area's romantic scenery, with its needle-nose pinnacles and craggy cliffs, lured countless artists from around the world. Among them was the Swiss landscape artist Adrian Zingg and his friend, the portraitist Anton Graff, who had been hired to teach at Dresden's prestigious art academy. Both felt that the landscape very much resembled their homeland (the Swiss Jura) and voila, the phrase 'Saxon Switzerland' was born. Travel writers picked it up and so it remains to this day.

surefooted. On your descent, follow the Mittelweg to the Elbleitenweg back to the Obrigensteig.

Kirnitzschtalbahn TRAM
(www.ovps.de; Kirnitzschtalstrasse 8; adult/concession €4/2, day pass €7/3.50; ⊙9.30am-7.30pm Apr-Oct) This solar-powered tram quaintly trundles 7km northeast along the Kirnitzsch River to Beuthenfall. The Lichtenhainer waterfall is just a 500m walk away and a good spot to begin a hike among the sandstone cliffs.

🛏 Sleeping & Eating

Elbresidenz HOTEL €€€
(☑919 700; www.elbresidenz-bad-schandau.de; d €146-196; P🅿🛜) This spanking new, top-end hotel on Bad Schandau's main square will satisfy anyone's craving for luxury. Rooms are a lesson in modern elegance and there's a full range of spa cures on tap. Elbe views cost more.

Lindenhof HOTEL €€
(☑4890; www.lindenhof-bad-schandau.de; Rudolf-Sendig-Strasse 11; d €92-110; P) Smart hotel with a good traditional restaurant.

ⓘ Information

Tourist office (☑900 30; www.bad-schandau. de; Marktplatz 12; ⊙9am-9pm daily May-Sep, 9am-6pm daily Apr & Oct, 9am-6pm Mon-Fri, 9am-1pm Sat & Sun Nov-Mar, closed Wed Jan & Feb)

Leipzig

☑0341 / POP 532,000

In Goethe's *Faust,* a character named Frosch calls Leipzig 'a little Paris'. He was wrong – Leipzig is more fun and infinitely less self-important than the Gallic capital. It's an important business and transport centre, a trade-fair mecca, and – aside from Berlin – the most dynamic city in eastern Germany. Relatively low rent and throbbing nightlife are making it an attractive place for young people.

Culture has been big in Leipzig for centuries. After all, Bach's one-time backyard was also where Wagner was born and Mendelssohn-Bartholdy ran a music academy. To this day one of the world's top classical bands (the Gewandhausorchester) and oldest and finest boys choirs (the 800-year-old Thomanerchor) continue to delight audiences. Since 2012, a new tourist trail called Leipziger Notenspur links key sites in the city's musical history. When it comes to art, the neo-realistic New Leipzig School has stirred up the international art world with such protagonists as Neo Rauch and Tilo Baumgärtel for well over 10 years.

Leipzig became known as the *Stadt der Helden* (City of Heroes) for its leading role in the 1989 'Peaceful Revolution'. Its residents organised protests against the communist regime in May of that year; by October, hundreds of thousands were taking to the streets and, a few years later, the Cold War was history.

◉ Sights

FREE **Zeitgeschichtliches Forum** MUSEUM
(Forum of Contemporary History; Map p156; ☑222 00; www.hdg.de/leipzig; Grimmaische Strasse 6; ⊙9am-6pm Tue-Fri, 10am-6pm Sat & Sun) This fascinating exhibit tells the political history of the GDR from division and dictatorship to fall-of-the-Wall ecstasy and post-*Wende* blues. It's essential viewing for anyone seeking to understand the late country's political power apparatus, the systematic oppression of regime critics, milestones in inter-German and international relations and the opposition movement that led to its downfall.

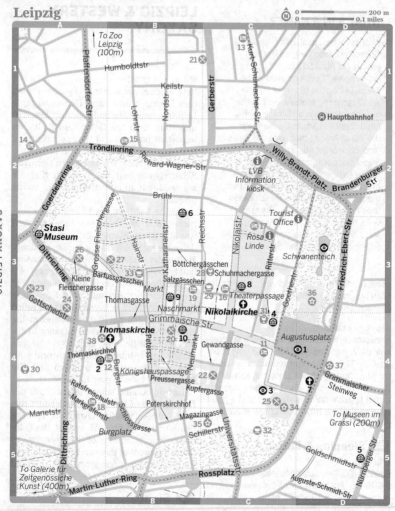

TOP CHOICE **Stasi Museum** MUSEUM

(Map p156; ☎961 2443; www.runde-ecke-leipzig. de; Dittrichring 24; ☺10am-6pm) In the GDR the walls had ears, as is chillingly documented in this exhibit in the former Leipzig headquarters of the East German secret police (the Stasi), a building known as the Runde Ecke (Round Corner). English-language audioguides aid in understanding the all-German displays on propaganda, preposterous disguises, cunning surveillance devices, recruitment (even among children), scent storage and other chilling machinations that reveal the GDR's all-out zeal when it came to controlling, manipulating and repressing its own people.

FREE **Thomaskirche** CHURCH

(Map p156; ☎222 240; www.thomaskirche.org; Thomaskirchhof 18; tower €2; ☺church 9am-6pm, tower 1pm, 2pm & 4.30pm Sat, 2pm & 3pm Sun) The composer Johann Sebastian Bach worked in the Thomaskirche as a cantor from 1723 until his death in 1750, and his remains lie buried beneath a bronze plate in front of the altar. The Thomanerchor (p164), once led by Bach, has been going strong since 1212 and

Leipzig

now includes 100 boys aged eight to 18. The church tower can be climbed.

Bach-Museum Leipzig MUSEUM
(Map p156; ☎913 7202; www.bach-leipzig.de; Thomaskirchhof 16; adult/concession €6/4, free to 16yrs; ☺10am-6pm Tue-Sun) Completely updated, this interactive museum does more than tell you about the life and accomplishments of heavyweight musician Johann Sebastian Bach. Learn how to date a Bach manuscript, listen to baroque instruments or treat your ears to any composition he ever wrote. The 'treasure room' downstairs displays original manuscripts and precious family Bibles.

Museum der Bildenden Künste MUSEUM
(Map p156; ☎216 990; www.mdbk.de; Katharinenstrasse 10; adult/concession €5/4; ☺10am-6pm Tue & Thu-Sun, noon-8pm Wed) An edgy glass cube is the home of Leipzig's fine arts museum and its well-respected collection of paintings from the 15th century to today, including works by Caspar David Friedrich, Lucas Cranach the Younger and Claude Monet. Highlights include rooms dedicated to native sons Max Beckmann, Max Klinger – whose striking Beethoven monument is a veritable symphony of marble and bronze – and Neo Rauch, a chief representative of the New Leipzig School.

Museen im Grassi MUSEUM
(www.grassimuseum.de; Johannisplatz 5-11; ☺10am-6pm Tue-Sun) The university-run Museen im Grassi harbours three fantastic collections that are often overlooked despite being a five-minute walk from Augustusplatz. At the stellar **Musikinstrumenten-Museum** (☎973 0750; adult/concession €5/3, audioguide €1) you can discover music from five centuries in rarity-filled exhibits, an interactive sound laboratory and during concerts. The **Museum für Völkerkunde** (Ethnological Museum; ☎973 1900; adult/concession €6/3) takes you on an eye-opening journey through the cultures of the world. The **Museum für Angewandte Kunst** (Museum of Applied Arts; ☎222 9100; adult/concession €5/3.50) has one of the finest collections of art-nouveau and

CHURCH OF PEACE

Leipzig's **Nikolaikirche** (Church of St Nicholas; Map p156; www.nikolaikirche-leipzig.de; Nikolaikirchhof 3; ⊙10am-6pm Mon-Sat & during services 9.30am, 11.15am & 5pm Sun) has Romanesque and Gothic roots but since 1797 has sported a striking neoclassical interior with palm-like pillars and cream-coloured pews. The design is certainly gorgeous but the church is most famous for playing a key role in the nonviolent movement that led to the downfall of the East German government. As early as 1982 it hosted 'peace prayers' on Mondays at 5pm (still held today), which over time inspired and empowered local citizens to confront the injustices plaguing their country. Starting in September 1989, the prayers were followed by candle-light demonstrations, which reached their peak on 9 October when 70,000 citizens took to the streets. The military, police and secret police stood ready to suppress the protests, as they had so violently done only two days earlier. But the order never came. The GDR leadership had capitulated. A singular palm-topped column outside the church commemorates this peaceful revolution.

art-deco furniture, porcelain, glass and ceramics in Germany.

Völkerschlachtdenkmal
MONUMENT
(☎241 6870; www.stadtgeschichtliches-museum-leipzig.de; Strasse des 18 Oktober 100; adult/child €6/4; ⊙10am-6pm Apr-Oct, to 4pm Nov-Mar; ☒2 or 15 to Völkerschlachtdenkmal) Half a million soldiers fought – and one in five died – in the epic 1813 battle that led to the decisive victory of Prussian, Austrian and Russian forces over Napoleon's army. Built a century later near the killing fields, the Monument to the Battle of the Nations is a 91m colossus, towering sombrely like something straight out of Gotham City. Views from the top are monumental. If you need to bone up on your history, swing by the integrated **Forum 1813** exhibit first.

Asisi Panometer
GALLERY
(☎355 5340; www.asisi.de; Richard-Lehmann-Strasse 114; adult/concession €10/8.50; ⊙10am-5pm Tue-Fri, 10am-6pm Sat & Sun; ☒16 to Richard-Lehmann/Zwickauer Strasse) The happy marriage of a *pano*rama (a giant 360° painting) and a gas*ometer* (a giant gas tank) is a panometer. The unusual concept is the brainchild of Berlin-based artist Yadegar Asisi, who uses paper, pencil and computer technology to create bafflingly detailed monumental scenes drawn from nature or history. A depiction of the 1813 Battle of the Nations is planned for 2013. Each work is about 100m long and 30m high.

Zoo Leipzig
ZOO
(☎593 3385; www.zoo-leipzig.de; Pfaffendorfer Strasse 29; adult/concession €17/14; ⊙9am-7pm May-Sep, 9am-6pm Apr & Oct, 9am-5pm Nov-Mar;

☒12 to Zoo) One of Germany's most progressive zoos opened its newest attraction in 2011: Gondwanaland, a jungly wonderland of 17,000 plants and 300 exotic animals. Rare and endangered species such as Komodo dragons and pigmy hippos roam around spacious enclosures in a climate-controlled hall amid fragrant tropical plants. Explore by following a jungle path, a treetop trail or by drifting along in a boat.

Stadtgeschichtliches Museum
MUSEUM
(City History Museum; Map p156; ☎965 130; www.stadtgeschichtliches-museum-leipzig.de; Markt 1; adult/concession €6/4; ⊙10am-6pm Tue-Sun) Leipzig's beautiful Renaissance town hall is an atmospheric setting to recount the twists and turns of the city's history from its roots as a key medieval trading town to the present, including stops at the Battle of the Nations and the 1989 peaceful revolution. A nearby modern extension, the **Neubau** (Böttchergässchen 3; adult/concession €3/2; ⊙10am-6pm) presents themed temporary exhibits.

Galerie für Zeitgenössische Kunst
GALLERY
(☎140 8126; www.gfzk-leipzig.de; Karl-Tauchnitz-Strasse 9-11; adult/concession per space €5/3, both spaces €8/4, free Wed; ⊙2-7pm Tue-Fri, noon-6pm Sat & Sun) Edgy contemporary art in all media is the specialty of this gallery, presented in changing exhibits in a minimalist container-like space and a late-19th-century villa.

Schumann-Haus
MUSEUM
(☎393 9620; www.schumann-verein.de; Inselstrasse 18; adult/concession €3/2; ⊙2-5pm Wed-Fri, 10am-5pm Sat & Sun) The 'Spring Symphony' is among the works Robert Schumann composed in this house where he and his wife,

pianist Clara Wieck, spent their first four years of marriage. A small exhibit provides background on the personal life and achievements of this famous musician couple.

Mendelssohn-Haus
MUSEUM

(Map p156; ☑127 0294; www.mendelssohn-stiftung.de; Goldschmidtstrasse 12; admission €4.50; ⊙10am-6pm) A key figure of the Romantic age, Felix Mendelssohn-Bartholdy was appointed music director of the Leipzig Gewandhausorchester in 1835 and held the position until shortly before his sudden death at age 38. Learn more in this intimate exhibit in the Biedermeier-furnished apartment where he lived with his family.

Augustusplatz
SQUARE

(Map p156; Augustusplatz) Massive Augustusplatz may look nondescript at best, forboding at worst, but is actually flanked by some of Leipzig's most famous buildings, including the Gewandhaus and the opera house. On its western front, the 11-storey Kroch-Haus (Map p156; Augustusplatz) was Leipzig's first high-rise and it's topped by a clock and two buff sentries. Inside is a university-run collection of Egyptian art. More eye-catching is the glass-fronted Paulinum (Map p156; Augustusplatz), the university church, which is taking shape in the same spot as the medieval Paulinerkirche that was demolished in 1968 by GDR authorities. The boldly modern structure is by Dutch architect Erick van Egeraat. For sweeping city views, ride the lift to the 29th floor of the modernist City-Hochhaus (Map p156; lift €3; ⊙terrace 9am-midnight Mon-Thu, to 1pm Fri & Sat, 11pm Sun); there's a restaurant there.

Tours

Leipzig Erleben
WALKING TOUR, BUS TOUR

(☑7104 20; www.leipzig-erleben.com; adult/concession €15/13) Runs two daily 2½-hour combination walking/bus tours in German and English departing from the tourist office. If booked separately, the walking tour is €5, the bus tour €10.

Trabi Erleben
CAR TOUR

(☑1409 0922; www.trabi-stadtrundfahrt.de; per person €28-40, depending on number of people) Explore Leipzig from behind the steering wheel or as a passenger in a GDR-built Trabi on a 90-minute self-drive put-put with live commentary piped into your vehicle. Prior reservation required.

Festivals & Events

Highlights of Leipzig's annual events calendar include the Leipziger Buchmesse (Book Fair; www.leipziger-buchmesse.de) in late March, Germany's second biggest after Frankfurt. On Whitsuntide, a black tide descends on Leipzig for the Wave-Gotik-Treffen (www.wave-gotik-treffen.de), the world's largest goth festival. The 10-day Bach Festival (www.bach-leipzig.de) takes place in late May or early June.

Sleeping

TOP CHOICE Steigenberger Grandhotel Handelshof
HOTEL €€€

(Map p156; ☑350 5810; www.steigenberger.com/Leipzig; Salzgässchen 6; r from €160; ✳@☎) Behind the imposing historic facade of a 1909 municipal trading hall, this luxe lodge outclasses most of Leipzig's hotels with its super-central location, charmingly efficient team and modern rooms dressed in crisp white-silver-purple colours. The stylish bi-level spa is the perfect bliss-out station.

Abito Suites
APARTMENT €€

(Map p156; ☑985 2788; www.abito.de; Grimmaische Strasse 16; ste €95-145) How 'suite' it is to be staying at this swank retreat atop one of Leipzig's most spectacular new buildings. Spacious and modern luxury units feature Italian designer furniture, purple and gold accents and such lifestyle essentials as illy espresso machines. Perks include sublime

LEIPZIG MUSIC TRAIL

Bach, Mendelssohn-Bartholdy, Schumann, Wagner, Mahler and Grieg are among the many world-famous musicians who've left their mark on Leipzig, a legacy that to this day is upheld by the illustrious Gewandhaus Orchestra and the St Thomas Boys' Choir. Since May 2012, you can walk in the footsteps of these greats by following the 5km Leipzig Notenspur (Leipzig Music Trail) to the places where they lived and worked. At each of the 23 stops, there are information panels in English and German and phone numbers you can call to listen to music or additional commentary. For details or to download a map, see www.notenspur-leipzig.de.

SAXONY LEIPZIG

SPOTLIGHT ON RICHARD WAGNER

Leipzig's musical legacy is also hitched to the ground-breaking – and controversial – 19th-century composer Richard Wagner, who first saw the light of day on 22 May 1813 in a Leipzig townhouse on Brühl Strasse and later hit the books at the Alte Nikolaischule (Old St Nicholas School). It was in this city where he began his musical education and wrote his first compositions. No surprise then that Leipzig will celebrate Wagner's bicentennial in 2013 with a potpourri of concerts, operas, exhibitions and tours as well as the opening of a **Richard-Wagner-Museum** (Map p156) in his old school on Nikolaikirchhof 2. The focus will be on Wagner's formative years from 1813 to 1834. For full details about the 2013 celebrations, see www.richard-wagner-leipzig.de.

views and a free minibar. There's no reception: check-in is via an automated system.

Quartier M   APARTMENT €€
(Map p156; ☏2133 8800; www.apartment-leipzig. de; Markgrafenstrasse 10; apt €75-140; ℗) The building oozes old-world flair but the roomy apartments with full kitchens above an organic supermarket are state of the art and pack plenty of modern design cachet. Some units come with balcony or terrace. Rates drop significantly for stays over seven days.

Hotel Fürstenhof   HOTEL €€€
(Map p156; ☏1400; www.hotelfuerstenhofleipzig. com; Tröndlinring 8; d from €150; ✳@⊚≋) The grande dame of the Leipzig hotel scene, with a 200-year-old pedigree, finds umpteen ways to spoil its guests. It has updated old-world flair, impeccable service, a gourmet restaurant and an oh-so-soothing grotto-style pool and spa.

arcona Living Bach 14   HOTEL, STUDIOS €€
(Map p156; ☏496 140; http://bach14.arcona.de; Thomaskirchhof 13/14; d from €90) In this new musically themed marvel, within earshot of the Thomaskirche, you'll sleep sweetly in sleek rooms decorated with sound-sculpture lamps, Bach manuscript wallpaper and colours ranging from subdued olive to perky raspberry. The quietest ones are in the new garden wing but those in the historic front

section have views of the church. Larger ones come with kitchenettes.

Motel One   HOTEL €
(Map p156; ☏337 4370; www.motel-one.de; Nikolai strasse 23; d from €69, breakfast €7.50; ℗✳⊚) The Leipzig outpost of this fast-growing budget designer chain has a five-star location opposite the Nikolaikirche and also gets most other things right, from the Zeitgeist-capturing lobby-lounge to the snug but smartly designed rooms. No surprise it's often booked out.

Pension Schlaf Gut   PENSION €
(Map p156; ☏211 0902; www.schlafgut-leipzig.de; Brühl 64-66; d €63-67, breakfast €5; ℗⊚) At this central sleep station with 24 breezy, colourful and modern digs, the base rate buys just the room, with any optional extras – like TV, kitchen use, wi-fi, daily cleaning, parking and breakfast – charged 'à la carte'. Cheaper rooms must share facilities. For longer stays, check out the company's apartment rentals (from €70). The website has details.

Hostel Sleepy Lion   HOSTEL €
(Map p156; ☏993 9480; www.hostel-leipzig.de; Jacobstrasse 1; dm/d/apt from €12.50/42/55, linen €2.50, breakfast €3.50; @⊚) This top-rated hostel gets our thumbs up with its clean and cheerfully painted en-suite rooms, a super-central location and clued-up staff. Every budget, comfort level and privacy need can be accommodated in dorms sleeping four to 10 a well as private rooms and apartments.

Central Globetrotter   HOSTEL €
(Map p156; ☏149 8960; www.globetrotter-leipzig. de; Kurt-Schumacher-Strasse 41; dm €12.50-18, d €40, linen €2.50; @⊚) This low-key, train-station-adjacent hostel has basic but clean four- to eight-bed dorms and private rooms (some with facilities) spread over three floors reached via a creaky wooden staircase. There are lockers in the corridors and gender-segregated, communal showers. Skip the anaemic breakfast buffet and whip up your own in the fully equipped kitchen.

✗ Eating

TOP CHOICE Auerbachs Keller   GERMAN €€€
(Map p156; ☏216100; www.auerbachs-keller-leipzig. de; Mädlerpassage; mains €14-22) Founded in 1525, Auerbachs Keller is one of Germany's best-known restaurants. It's cosy and touristy but the food's actually quite good and the setting memorable. In Goethe's

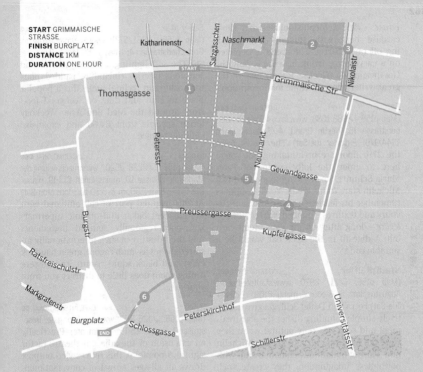

Walking Tour
Leipzig's Top Trading Palaces

> Leipzig's 500-year pedigree as a trading hub is splendidly reflected in its many historic arcades, courtyards and trade-fair palaces dotted around the city centre, each one flaunting its own character and design details. Today, the often grand buildings harbour boutiques, cafes and restaurants alongside offices and apartments on the upper floors.

The most famous arcade is the 1914 **Mädlerpassage**, a lavish mix of neo-Renaissance and art nouveau, and home to Auerbachs Keller, the restaurant featured in Goethe's *Faust*. In fact, touching the foot of the Faust statue near the Grimmaische Strasse exit is supposed to bring you good luck.

Make your way to Reichsstrasse and the gorgeously restored 1908 **Speck's Hof**, whose light-flooded atriums are decorated with murals, tiles and paintings by local artists Moritz Götze, Bruno Griesel and Johannes Grützke. Exit onto Nikolaistrasse via the attached **Hansa-Haus**, past a water-filled basin that's a copy of 3500-year-old Ming Dynasty sound bowl. Wet your hands and run them over the two pommels to make the water fizz.

Follow Nikolaistrasse down to Universitätsstrasse and the 1893 **Städtisches Kaufhaus**. It's on the site of Leipzig's first cloth exchange (Gewandhaus) and the original concert hall of the Gewandhaus Orchestra, which was torn down to make room for this neo-baroque complex.

Exit onto Neumarkt and immediately enter the **Messehofpassage**, which was the first post-WWII trade building to be completed in 1950. Remodelled a few years ago, the mushroom-shaped column near the Peterstrasse exit is the only vestige of the old arcade.

Turn left on Peterstrasse and head down to the **Petersbogen**, an elegantly curving glass-covered arcade from 2001 that replaced the Juridicum Passage, which was destroyed in WWII. Before that, Leipzig's esteemed law school stood in this place for 500 years.

Faust – Part I, Mephistopheles and Faust carouse here with students before riding off on a barrel. The scene is depicted on a carved tree trunk in what is now the Goethezimmer (Goethe Room), where the great writer allegedly came for 'inspiration'.

Falco INTERNATIONAL €€€
(Map p156; ☎988 1088; www.falco-leipzig.de; Gerberstrasse 15, Westin Grand; 4-/7-course menu €144/179; ⊙dinner Tue-Sat) The views from the 27th floor are breathtaking but you're here to enjoy the lofty cuisine of Peter Maria Schnurr, Saxony's top toque with two Michelin stars to his credit. You'll doubtless remember his fearless orchestrations of flavours and textures – dubbed *cuisine passion légère* – long after getting your credit card bill. A digestif in the sleek bar would be a suitable coda.

Stadtpfeiffer INTERNATIONAL €€€
(Map p156; ☎217 8920; www.stadtpfeiffer.de; Augustusplatz 8; 6-course menu €108; ⊙dinner Tue-Sat) Petra and Deflef Schlegel give deceptively simple sounding dishes the star treatment and so it was only natural when they were the first in Leipzig to get the Michelin nod. Pairing punctilious craftsmanship with bottomless imagination, they create such exquisitely calibrated dishes as smoked char with foie gras or warm chocolate cake with lavender ice cream. It's a relaxed spot inside the Gewandhaus concert hall.

Max Enk EUROPEAN €€€
(Map p156; ☎9999 7638; www.max-enk.de; Neumarkt 9-19; mains €18-25; ⊙noon-2pm & 6pm-1am Mon-Fri, noon-1am Sat, 11.30am-4pm Sun) People share laughs over hand-picked wines and plates of elegant comfort food kicked into high gear at this sleek new contender. The Wiener schnitzel is a reliable stand-by but you probably won't regret going out on a culinary limb with such inspired concoctions as chorizo-stuffed guinea fowl in nut butter.

Gosenschenke 'Ohne Bedenken' BREWPUB €€
(☎566 2360; www.gosenschenke.de; Menckestrasse 5; mains €11-15; ⊙from noon daily Apr-Sep, from 4pm Mon-Fri & noon Sat & Sun Oct-Mar; 🚇12 to Fritz-Seger-Strasse) This historic Leipzig institution, backed by the city's prettiest beer garden, is *the* place to sample *Gose,* a local top-fermented beer often served with a shot of liqueur. The menu requires that you surrender helplessly to your inner carnivore.

Sol y Mar MEDITERRANEAN, ASIAN €€
(Map p156; ☎961 5721; www.solymar-leipzig.de; Gottschedstrasse 4; mains €5-14; ⊙9am-late; 📶) The soft lighting, ambient sounds and sensuous interior (including padded pods for noshing in recline) make this a popular place to chill and dine on feel-good food from around the Med and Asia. Weekday lunch specials from €4.60 and expansive summer terrace.

Macis INTERNATIONAL €€€
(Map p156; ☎2228 7520; www.macis-leipzig.de; Markgrafenstrasse 10; mains lunch €13-19, dinner €18-27; ⊙8am-2.30pm & 5.30-10.30pm Mon-Sat) At this inspired port of call affiliated with the adjacent baker and organic supermarket, only regionally sourced ingredients find their destiny in such internationally inspired dishes as lamb ragout, green haddock curry and black squid risotto. The austere dining room does little to distract you from your meal.

Pilot CAFE, INTERNATIONAL €€
(Map p156; ☎126 8117; www.enk-leipzig.de; Bosestrasse 1; mains €5-15; ⊙9am-late) Practically an extension of the adjacent theatre (actor sightings possible), this retro-styled outpost draws an all-ages crowd of conversationalists with its extensive drinks selection, including rich espresso from Triest and a long tea list. The rustic menu has back-to-basic Saxon dishes along with more contemporary specials, snacks and fresh salads.

Cafe Pushkin CAFE, PUB €€
(☎392 0105; www.cafepuschkin.de; Karl-Liebknecht-Strasse 74; mains €4-10; ⊙9am-late) It's a pub, so don't expect huge flights of culinary fancy. But no matter if you just want a little sumthin' to sop up the booze or need to fill a growling tummy, the selection of grub (burgers, nachos, sausages) should do the trick. The interesting breakfasts also make it a great greet-the-day spot.

Telegraph CAFE €€
(Map p156; ☎149 4990; www.cafe-telegraph.de; Dittrichring 18-20; mains €5-11; ⊙f8am-midnight; 📶) Leipzig goes cosmopolitan at this elegantly high-ceilinged cafe with curved booths and wooden tables, a bilingual menu and a stack of international mags and dailies. It's a popular breakfast spot, available until a hangover friendly 3pm. The menu is heavy on Austrian classics.

Zum Arabischen
Coffe Baum
CAFE, GERMAN €€

(Map p156; ✍961 0060; www.coffe-baum.de; Kleine Fleischergasse 4; mains €8-16; ⊙11am-midnight) One of Europe's oldest coffeehouses, this rambling outpost has hosted poets, politicians, professors and everyone else since 1720. The warren of rooms spread over several floors is an atmospheric spot to try a Leipziger Lerche (lark), a locally famous marzipan-filled shortcrust pastry. Other cakes, light meals and alcohol are also served. The small, free 'museum' has over 500 coffee-related objects.

El-Amir
ARABIC €

(✍308 2568; Karl-Liebknecht-Strasse 59; mains €2.50-5; ⊙11am-late; ✍) No-frills landmark hole-in-the-wall doneria will help you combat beer fatigue. Finger-lickin' hummus, too.

Drinking & Entertainment

Party activity centres on four areas: the boisterous Drallewatsch pub strip, the more upmarket theatre district around Gottschedstrasse, the mix of trendy and alt-vibe joints along Karl-Liebknecht-Strasse (aka Südmeile) and pub-and-restaurant-packed Münzgasse. The best listings magazine is *Kreuzer*, although the free monthlies *Frizz* and *Blitz!* might do just fine.

Moritzbastei
CAFE, BAR

(Map p156; ✍702 590; www.moritzbastei.de; Universitätsstrasse 9; dishes €2-5; ⊙cafe & Schwalbennest from 10am Mon-Fri, noon Sat, 9am Sun, Fuchsbar from 8pm; ☏) This legendary warren of historic cellars below the old city fortifications still keeps an all-ages crowd happy with three locations in one: the sprawling **Cafe Barbarkane** for coffee, drinks or simple meals; the intimate **Schwalbennest** for wine; and the cool **Fuchsbar** for cocktails. The latter two are welcome retreats when bands or DJs take over the space after dark. Summer terrace, too.

Noels Ballroom
PUB

(✍303 2007; www.,noels-ballroom.com; Kurt-Eisner-Strasse 43; ⊙5pm-late; ☐10, 11 to Karl Liebknecht/Kurt-Eisner-Strasse) McCormacks has renamed itself but the high-octane vibe, foamy pints of Guinness and lovely flower-filled beer garden still make Noels one of the best Irish pubs in town. Great for meeting locals testing their trivia acumen on Tuesdays' quiz night (in English).

Spizz
CAFE, CLUB

(Map p156; ✍960 8043; www.spizz.org; Markt 9; ⊙cafe 9am-late, cellar varies) Tucked beneath a ho-hum all-day cafe is a low-ceilinged cellar where funky black beats, heated house, hot-stepping disco and other sounds are likely to make you want to hit the dance floor. Salsa nights, jazz concerts and piano jam sessions round off the program.

Flowerpower
PUB

(✍961 3441; Riemannstrasse 42; ⊙from 7pm) It's party time any time at this long-running super-psychedelic flashback to the '60s (cool pinball machines). Admission is always free and the music tends to be older than the crowd. If you've overdone it, you can even crash upstairs for the night for €7.50.

Café Riquet
CAFE

(Map p156; ✍961 0000; www.riquethaus.de; Schuhmachergässchen 1; ⊙9am-8pm) Two bronze elephants guard the entrance to this Viennese-style coffee house in a superb art-nouveau building topped by a Chinese-style turret. Good for a stylish coffee-and-cake break.

⌈TOP⌋ Conne Island
⌊CHOICE⌋ CLUB

(www.conne-island.de; Koburger Strasse 3; ☐9 to Koburger Brücke) Run by a collective, this cult location has defined Leipzig nightlife for ages with concerts and club nights that feed the gamut of musical appetites – punk and indie, electronica to hip-hop. It's in the southern suburb of Connewitz.

Distillery
CLUB

(✍3559 7400; www.distillery.de; Kurt-Eisner-Strasse 91; ☐9 to Kurt-Eisner/A-Hoffmann-Strasse) One of the oldest techno-house clubs in eastern Germany and still among the best. Unpretentious crowd, cool location, decent drinks prices and occasional star DJs (Ricardo Villalobos, Carl Craig, Richie Hawtin) helming the decks.

naTo
PUB

(✍391 5539; www.nato-leipzig.de; Karl-Liebknecht-Strasse 46; ☐10 or 11 to Südplatz) The mother of Leipzig's alternative-music pub-clubs, with jazz, experimental and indie sounds alongside films and theatre. Great outdoor seating in summer.

Classical Music & Opera

Gewandhausorchester
CLASSICAL MUSIC

(Map p156; ✍127 0280; www.gewandhaus.de; Augustusplatz 8; tours €4.50; ⊙tours usually 12.30pm

Thu) Led by Ricardo Chailly since 2005, the Gewandhaus is one of Europe's finest and oldest civic orchestras. With a tradition harkening back to 1743, it became an orchestra of European renown a century later under music director Felix Mendelssohn-Bartholdy. Aside from giving concerts in the Neues Gewandhaus, it also performs with the Thomaner Boys' Choir in the Thomaskirche and with the Oper Leipzig. Tickets are available by email, by phone and in person.

Thomanerchor CLASSICAL MUSIC
(Map p156; ☑984 4211; www.thomaskirche.org; Thomaskirchhof 18; tickets €2) This famous boys' choir performs Bach motets and cantatas at 6pm on Friday and 3pm on Saturday, and also sings during Sunday services at 9.30am and 6pm at the Thomaskirche. Special concerts take place throughout the year. Performances are usually filled to capacity so try to be there when doors open, 45 minutes before concerts begin.

Oper Leipzig OPERA
(Map p156; ☑126 1261; www.oper-leipzig.de; Augustusplatz 12) Leipzig's Opernhaus (opera house) has a 300-year-old tradition, though the building only went up in the 1950s. The program is an eclectic mix of classics and contemporary works; the Gewandhausorchester provides the music. Buy tickets online, by phone or in person.

LEIPZIG'S NEW CITY-TUNNEL

If all goes according to plan – and that's a big IF! – the first S-Bahn trains will finally start rumbling through the new City-Tunnel beneath Leipzig's city centre in December 2013.

Part of a masterplan to improve the efficiency of regional railway travel, the tunnel has been under construction since 2005 and will run from the Hauptbahnhof to the Bayerischer Bahnhof 2km south.

Among the six new S-Bahn lines will be a direct link between the centre, the trade-fair grounds, the airport and the city of Halle. However, construction has been delayed several times, while the cost has ballooned to just under €1 billion, causing much heated debate and criticism in these times of fiscal belt-tightening.

Theatre & Cabaret

Krystallpalast CABARET
(Map p156; ☑140 660; www.krystallpalast.de; Magazingasse 4; ☎) This company puts on glitzy variety shows where the varied line-up may include anything from snake women to jugglers and trapeze acts. Tickets are sold online, by phone and in person.

Gay & Lesbian Venues

Leipzig has only a small lesbigay scene. A good first stop is the information and advocacy centre **Rosa Linde** (☑879 6982; www.rosalinde.de; Lange Strasse 11). For low-key lounging, head to **Cafe Apart** (Map p156; ☑962 8046; www.cafe-apart.de; Reichsstrasse 16; ☑5pm-2am Mon-Sat, to midnight Sun) or **Havanna** (Map p156; www.havanna-club-leipzig. de; Goethestrasse 2; ☑5pm-late). **Cocks Bar** (Map p156; ☑2254 0306; www.cocks-bar.com; Otto-Schill-Strasse 10; ☑9am-3am Mon-Thu, to 5am Fri & Sat), as the name implies, is somewhat more hands-on with its busy cruising labyrinth and attached cinema; it draws all comers, including the gamut of fetishistas (leather, military, bears etc). The main gay party is the monthly **PonyClub** (Map p156; www.ponytanz.de; Augustusplatz 1-4; ☑last Sat of month Sep-May) where hundreds of flirty hotties sweat it up to disco-trash and electro-house amid snazzy GDR-era retro chic.

ℹ Information

The main post office, a Sparkasse ATM and a **ReiseBank** (☑980 4588; Willy-Brandt-Platz 5; ☑8am-10pm Mon-Fri, 9.30am-8pm Sat, 1-6pm Sun) branch are all in the Hauptbahnhof.

Intertel Cafe (☑462 5879; www.intertelcafe. de; Brühl 64; per hr €2; ☑10am-10pm)

Leipzig Card (www.leipzig-card.de; 1/3 days €9/18.50) Free or discounted admission to attractions, plus free travel on public transport. Available from the tourist office and most hotels.

Tourist office (☑710 4260, 710 4255 room referral; www.ltm-leipzig.de; Katharinenstrasse 8; ☑9.30am-6pm Mon-Fri Apr-Oct, 10am-6pm Mon-Fri Nov-Mar, to 4pm Sat & 3pm Sun year-round)

ℹ Getting There & Away

AIR **Leipzig-Halle Airport** (LEJ; www.leipzig -halle-airport.de) is about 21km west of Leipzig. Has domestic and international flights, including daily Ryanair service from London-Stansted, Rome, Milan and Malaga.

CAR Leipzig lies just south of the A14 Halle-Dresden autobahn and 15km east of the A9, which links Berlin to Nuremberg. **Sixt/Budget**

ESCAPE TO COLDITZ

A Renaissance castle straddling a crag above sleepy Colditz, some 46km southeast of Leipzig, **Schloss Colditz** (034381-437 77; www.schloss-colditz.com; Schlossgasse 1; museum €3, tour adult/concession €7/4; museum 10am-5pm Apr-Oct, tours 10.30am, 1pm & 3pm (confirm)) has seen stints as a hunting lodge, a poorhouse and a mental hospital. Mostly, though, it's famous as **Oflag IVC**, a WWII-era high-security prison for Allied officers, including a nephew of Winston Churchill. Most had already escaped from less secure camps and been recaptured. Some 300 made further attempts and 31 actually managed to flee. The would-be escapees were often aided by ingenious self-made gadgetry, including a glider fashioned from wood and bed sheets, and a homemade sewing machine for making bogus German uniforms. Most astounding, perhaps, is a 44m-long tunnel below the chapel that French officers dug in 1941-42, before the Germans caught them. You can see some of these contraptions, along with lots of photographs, in the small but fascinating **Fluchtmuseum** (Escape Museum) within the palace. Several inmates wrote down their experiences later, of which Pat Reid's *The Colditz Story* is the best-known account.

Colditz is at the junction of the B107 and B176 between Leipzig and Chemnitz. On weekdays bus 690 makes the trip from Leipzig Hauptbahnhof to Colditz and back several times daily (€6.30, 1½ hours). There's also a daily train service to Bad Lausick from where you hop on bus 613 (€6.30, 1¼ hours), and a weekday service via Grimma from where you need to catch bus 619 (€6.30, 1¼ hours). For specific timetables, see www.mdv.de.

(01805-252 525; www.sixt.de; Willy-Brandt-Platz, near platform 1; 7am-9.30pm Mon-Fri, 8am-5.30pm Sat, 10am-7pm Sun) and **Avis** (961 1400; www.avis.de; Willy-Brandt-Platz 5; 7am-8pm Mon-Fri, 8am-1pm Sat, 9am-noon Sun) have car rental stations at the Hauptbahnhof. All major international agencies are at the airport as well.

TRAIN Deutsche Bahn has frequent services to Frankfurt (€75, 3¾ hours), Dresden (€26, 1¼ hours) and Berlin (€45, 1¼ hours). Private Interconnex trains also go to Berlin twice daily (€19, 1¼ hours).

ⓘ Getting Around

TO/FROM THE AIRPORT The Leipzig/Halle airport is just off the A9 (Berlin–Munich) and A14 (Dresden–Hannover). RE trains leave hourly (€3.80, 15 minutes) from the Hauptbahnhof and long-distance trains also stop at the airport. Upon completion of the City-Tunnel, the S5 will be making the trip every 20 minutes. A taxi needs about 30 minutes and costs around €28.

BICYCLE Zweirad Eckhardt (961 7274; www.bikeandsport.info; Kurt-Schumacher-Strasse 4; per 24hr €8; 6am-8pm Mon-Fri, 9am-6pm Sat)

CAR Leipzig's centre is a so-called *Umweltzone* (environmental zone), meaning you need to obtain an *Umweltplakette* (emissions sticker) if you brought your own car from abroad. See p783 for details.

PUBLIC TRANSPORT Buses and trams are run by LVB (194 49; www.lvb.de), which operates an **information kiosk** (Willy-Brandt-Platz; 8am-8pm Mon-Fri, 8am-4pm Sat) outside the Hauptbahnhof. The central tram station is here as well. Single tickets cost €1.50 for up to four stops and €2.10 for longer trips; day passes are €5.

TAXI Flagfall is €2.10, each kilometre €1.90.
Funktaxi (600 500; www.funktaxi-leipzig.de)
Löwen Taxi (982 222; www.loewentaxi.de)

Chemnitz

0371 / POP 244,000

Like most of Eastern Germany's cities, Chemnitz had to reinvent itself post-*Wende*, and has done so with some measure of success. Known from 1953 to 1990 as Karl-Marx-Stadt, the GDR gave it a Stalinist makeover, and smokestack industries once earned it the nickname of 'Saxon Manchester'. Such scars don't heal easily but Chemnitz has done a remarkable job, at least in its revitalised city centre that is now a pedestrianised glass-and-steel shopping and entertainment district. Add to that a lively cultural scene, one of Europe's largest intact art-nouveau quarters and an unpretentious air, and you've got more than a few good reasons to drop by.

⊙ Sights

The central Markt is about 1km south of the Hauptbahnhof. For the scenic route, take Carolastrasse to Strasse der Nationen, turn left at the grand Theaterplatz and keep going past the Karl-Marx-Monument.

Kunstsammlungen Chemnitz   GALLERY
(Chemnitz Art Museum; ☎488 4424; www.kunst sammlungen-chemnitz.de; Theaterplatz 1; adult/concession €8/5; ⊙11am-6pm Tue-Sun) Flanking Chemnitz' most beautiful square, the historic Theaterplatz, this lovely art museum stages headline-making temporary exhibits (such as Bob Dylan's watercolours), sometimes drawn from its own collection of paintings, sculpture, graphics, textiles and crafts. Special strengths include Romantic Age painters (eg Caspar David Friedrich, Ludwig Richter) and sculptures by such hot shots as Degas, Rodin and Baselitz. The neo-baroque opera house, the St Petrikirche and a hotel complete the ensemble around Theaterplatz.

Around Markt   NEIGHBOURHOOD
Chemnitz' compact and largely pedestrianised centre is a pleasing mix of historic and modern centred on Markt. The dominant building is the stately 15th-century Altes Rathaus (Old Town Hall) whose distinctive tower sports an ornate Renaissance portal and a carillon with cute little figures reenacting town history at 11am, 4pm and 7pm. The old town hall segues into the Neues Rathaus (New Town Hall, 1911) whose imposing size is best appreciated from Neumarkt, which is also flanked by the Galerie Roter Turm. This modern shopping mall with a pleasing terracotta facade was designed by architectural top dog Hans Kollhoff. The equally esteemed Helmut Jahn dreamed up the adjacent glass-and-steel Galeria Kaufhof department store.

Karl Marx Monument   MONUMENT
(cnr Strasse der Nationen & Brückenstrasse) The 7.1m-high bronze head of Karl Marx catches the German philosopher on a very bad hair day in front of a huge frieze exhorting 'Workers of the world, unite!' in several languages. Follow Strasse der Nationen for another minute to Chemnitz' oldest building, the 12th-century Roter Turm, a former defence tower that also served stints as a courthouse and prison.

Museum Gunzenhauser   GALLERY
(☎488 7024; www.kunstsammlungen-chemnitz.de; Falkeplatz; adult/concession €7/4.50; ⊙11am-6pm Tue-Sun) A former 1930 bank building, built in austere New Objectivity style, is now a gallery of 20th-century art, most famous for its expressionist works by such key artists as Max Beckmann, Ernst Ludwig Kirchner and local boy Karl Schmidt-Rottluff. Pride of place, though, goes to a career-spanning collection of works by Otto Dix on the 3rd floor.

DAStietz   MUSEUM
(☎488 4397; ww.dastietz.de; Moritzstrasse 20) Beautifully renovated, this former 1913 department store now houses the city library as well as the Neue Sächsische Galerie (☎367 6680; www.neue-saechsische-galerie.de; adult/child €3/free; ⊙11am-5pm Thu-Mon, 11am-8pm Tue), which presents contemporary Saxon art, and the Museum für Naturkunde (Natural History Museum; ☎488 4551; www.naturkunde-chemnitz.de; adult/concession €4/2.50; ⊙10am-8pm Mon, Tue, Thu & Fri, 10am-6pm Sat & Sun), whose most interesting exhibit, the Versteinerter Wald (petrified forest), can be admired for free in the atrium; some of the stony trunks are 290 million years old.

Henry Van de Velde Museum   MUSEUM
(☎488 4424; Parkstrasse 58; adult/child €3/free; ⊙10am-6pm Wed, Fri-Sun) Around 2.5km south of the centre, this small but choice museum occupies the 1903 Villa Esche, which was Belgian artist Van de Velde's first commission in Germany. The dining room and music salon have been restored as period rooms, while upstairs you'll find a small collection of crafts and furniture. Take tram 4 to Haydnstrasse.

Kassberg   NEIGHBOURHOOD
If you enjoy architecture, a stroll around the Kassberg, one of Germany's largest art-nouveau quarters, should be rewarding. A highlight is the ornate Majolika Houses on Barbarossastrasse (near Weststrasse). The quarter starts just beyond the little Chemnitz River, about 300m west of the city centre. Bus 62 or 72 to Barbarossastrasse drops you in the thick of it.

🛏 Sleeping

Hotel an der Oper   HOTEL €€
(☎6810; www.hoteloper-chemnitz.de; Strasse der Nationen 56; d €100-135; P ❄ 🖀) With front-row views of the historic opera house, this newly renovated hotel spells comfort in

SCHLOSS AREA

About 1.3 km north of Chemnitz town centre is the Schlossteich, an idyllic park-ringed pond with a music pavilion for summer concerts. Looming above it, the **Schlosskirche** (☑369 550; http://schloss.kirche-chemnitz.info; Schlossplatz 7; ☺10am-5pm Tue-Sat, 2.30-5.30pm Sun Apr-Oct, 11am-4pm Tue-Sat Nov-Mar) is a 12th-century Benedictine monastery recast into a weighty Gothic hall church and harbouring Hans Witten's intriguing sculpture *Christ at the Column* (1515). Nearby, a late-Gothic monastery houses the **Schlossbergmuseum** (☑488 4501; www.schlossbergmuseum.de; Schlossberg 12; adult/concession €6/4; ☺11am-6pm Tue-Sun), whose vaulted interior is a rich backdrop for 15th- and 16th-century Saxon sculpture. In fine weather, wrap up with a cold one at the nearby **Miramar** (☑330 1521; www.miramar-chemnitz.de; Schlossberg 16), the nicest beer garden in town. Bus 76 makes the trip here (get off at Schlossberg).

soothing, good-sized rooms with clear, modern lines and easy-on-the-eye vanilla and chocolate hues. The chic cocktail bar has an impressive whisky selection.

Biendo Hotel HOTEL €
(☑2723 7302; www.biendo-hotel.de; Strasse der Nationen 12; d €60; P✿) Ensconced on the fifth and sixth floor of a GDR-era office building, Biendo is a brand new contender in the burgeoning budget designer hotel market. Rooms are snug but contempo-flavoured and sport sweeping city views; some have kitchenettes.

DJH Hostel HOSTEL €
(☑2780 9897; www.chemnitz-city.jugendherberge. de; Getreidemarkt 6; dm incl breakfast under/over 27 €21.50/24; ☺reception 8-11am & 4-10pm; P@) If you like your hostel with a dash of quirk and history, this new industrial-flavoured contender in a former converting station in the town centre should fit the bill. En-suite dorms sleep three to eight.

✕ Eating

Cafe Michaelis CAKES, INTERNATIONAL €€€
(☑2733 7985; www.michaelis-chemnitz.de; Am Düsseldorfer Platz 11; mains €7-20; ☺9.30am-11.30pm) A century-old Chemnitz coffeehouse tradition was revived in 2012 with the reopening of Cafe Michaelis, famous for its mindboggling selection of truly mouthwatering cakes. If you don't have a sweet tooth, opt for a crisp salad, homemade pasta or meaty main from the extensive menu. Big terrace in summer.

Kellerhaus GERMAN €€€
(☑335 1677; www.kellerhaus-chemnitz.de; Schlossberg 2; mains €10-20; ☺11am-10.30pm) For a first-rate culinary journey at moderate prices, it's well worth heading a bit away from the town

centre to this half-timbered charmer at the foot of the historic Schlossberg quarter. Carnivores especially will be in 'pig heaven'. Sit in the cosy cellar, the low-ceiling main dining room or on the terrace.

Turmbrauhaus BREWPUB
(☑909 5095; Neumarkt 2; mains €5-12.50) Watch your reflection in the polished copper brewing vats become ever mistier as you down a beer or two (half a litre for €2.60) at this upbeat brewpub.

Ratskeller GERMAN €€
(☑694 9875; www.ratskeller-chemnitz.de; Markt 1; mains €7-16; ☺11am-midnight) It probably won't be the best regional and German cuisine you'll eat on your travels, but the rustic, olde-worlde setting amid gorgeously painted vaulted ceilings may make up for any culinary shortcomings.

ℹ Information

There are several banks with ATMs around Markt.

Main post office (Strasse der Nationen 2-4; ☺9am-7pm Mon-Fri, 9am-2pm Sat)
ReiseBank (☑356 0488; Carolastrasse 2; ☺9.30am-6pm Mon-Fri)
Tourist office (☑690 680; www.chemnitz-tourismus.de; Markt 1; ☺9am-7pm Mon-Fri, 9am-4pm Sat, 11am-1pm Sun)

ℹ Getting There & Around

CAR The east–west A4 skirts Chemnitz, while the A72 heading south to the A9 (eg for Munich) originates nearby.

LOCAL TRANSPORT All trams and buses pass through the city-centre *Zentralhaltestelle* (central stop). Single tickets are €1.80, a day pass is €3.80.

TRAIN Chemnitz is linked by direct train to Dresden (€14.40, one hour), Leipzig (€16.40, one hour) and Zwickau (€5.70, 30 minutes).

Zwickau

☑ 0375 / POP 93,000

A gateway to the Erzgebirge (Iron Ore Mountains), Zwickau has written an important chapter in German automobile history. It is the birthplace of the Audi brand (in 1910) and the GDR-era Trabant, which began rolling, very slowly, off assembly lines in 1957. The town's sparkling car museum is a must for anyone even remotely interested in the subject. Production continues today courtesy of Volkswagen, which brought much-needed jobs to the area. The fairly lively centre teems with pubs and restaurants dotted around an impressive cathedral, the birth house of composer Robert Schumann and some of Germany's oldest homes.

◉ Sights

The compact and largely pedestrianised Altstadt is encircled by Dr-Friedrichs-Ring. The Hauptbahnhof is about 800m west of the ring road; simply follow Bahnhofstrasse, then Schumannstrasse.

August Horch Museum   MUSEUM
(☑2717 3812; www.horch-museum.de; Audistrasse 7; adult/concession €5.50/3.50, audioguide €2.50; ☺9.30am-5pm Tue-Sun) Zwickau's top attraction is this amazing car museum that will enlighten and entertain even non-petrol-heads. Housed within the original early-20th-century Audi factory, gleaming and imaginatively presented exhibits range from old-timer gems like the 1911 Horch Phaeton to the latest Audi R8. And, of course, there are plenty of Trabants (three million were produced in town here until 1990) and other eastern European cars. You can walk around an early gas station, inspect Audi founder August Horch's original wood-panelled office, stroll down a 1930s streetscape and even learn how Trabants were made. The museum is about 2km north of the Altstadt; take tram 4 to Kurt-Eisner-Strasse.

Dom St Marien   CHURCH
(☑274 3510; www.nicolai-kirchgemeinde.de; Domhof 10; admission €1; ☺10am-6pm Mon-Sat) This late-Gothic hall church sports intricate net vaulting and teems with art treasures, most famously the 1479 altar painting by Michael Wohlgemuth (a teacher of Albrecht Dürer) and an emotionally charged pietà (1502) by famous local sculptor Peter Breuer. There are also some ultra-rare Protestant confessionals. The facade is festooned with some 70 stone sculptures depicting the Apostles and Reformation figures. An English pamphlet has details.

Priesterhäuser Zwickau   HISTORIC BUILDING
(☑834 551; www.priesterhaeuser.de; Domhof 5-8; adult/concession €4/2; ☺1-6pm Tue-Sun) This short row of homes has origins in the 13th century and ranks among the oldest surviving residential building ensembles in Germany. Church employees lived here until the 19th century. Imagine the living conditions of the people who've come before you as you explore the restored period rooms, climb up creaky stairs, duck into small chambers or inspect the soot-stained kitchen.

Robert-Schumann-Haus   MUSEUM
(☑215 269; www.schumannzwickau.de; Hauptmarkt 5; adult/concession €4/2; ☺10am-5pm Tue-Fri, 1-5pm Sat & Sun) Romantic-era composer Robert Schumann was born and spent the first seven years of his life in this rather modest house. Exhibits trace the various life stations of the man who suffered from mental illness later in life and died in an institution at age 46. A highlight is the piano once played by Schumann's wife, Clara Wieck, herself a noted pianist. Also note the Schumann monument on nearby Hauptmarkt, which is part of the 'Schumann Trail' – ask for a pamphlet at the tourist office.

🛏 Sleeping

Brauereigasthof Zwickau   PENSION €
(☑303 2032; www.brauhaus-zwickau.de; Peter-Breuer-Strasse 12-16; d €61; P) This is an excellent bargain base. It has five simple but cosy rooms, with ancient exposed beams, above a sprawling gastropub that makes its own beer and schnapps and serves hearty meals in belt-loosening portions (€6.50 to €14).

Pension am Dom   PENSION €
(☑0177 796 7848; www.pension-zwickau.de; Marienstrasse 7; d €60) Checking into one of these six lovingly furnished rooms puts you smack dab in the centre, although not, as the name suggests, next to the Dom. Bonus points for the modern communal kitchen, a rare find outside of hostels.

LORD OF THE RINGS

More than anything else, Zwickau has been shaped by the automobile industry and by one man in particular: August Horch (1868–1951). The first Horch cars rolled onto the road in 1904 and quickly became the queen among luxury vehicles, besting even Mercedes Benz. Horch, alas, was a better engineer than a businessman and in 1909 he was fired by his investors. Not missing a step, he simply opened another factory across town, calling it Audi (Latin for *Horch*, which means 'listen' in German).

Ever wondered why the Audi symbol is four interlinking rings? They stand for Audi, Horch, DKW and Wanderer, the four Saxon car makers who merged into a single company called Auto-Union during the Great Depression. After WWII, Audi moved to Ingolstadt in Bavaria. As for Zwickau, it became the birthplace of the Trabant – the GDR's answer to the Volkswagen Beetle. The name means 'satellite' in German, and was inspired by the launch of the world's first satellite (the Soviet Sputnik) in 1957, a year before production started.

By the time it ceased, more than three million Trabis had rolled off the assembly lines here, most of them for export to other socialist countries – which is why regular GDR folks had to wait up to 13 years (!) to get one.

Because of the country's chronic steel shortage, the Trabi's body was made from reinforced plastic called Duroplast and powered by a two-stroke engine similar to that of a large lawnmower. To learn more and admire around 30 Trabis from all production phases, visit the AUTOmobile Trabantausstellung (www.intertrab.de; Uhdestrasse 12; admission €2; ⊙10am-5pm Tue & Sat May-Oct), a small museum operated by a passionate bunch of volunteers.

Aparthotel 1A
HOTEL €

(☏275 750; www.1a-aparthotel.de; Robert-Müller-Strasse 1a; d €62, breakfast €9; ⓅⓈ) No prizes for originality or flair here, just clean, comfortable and modern rooms in a fairly central location. Some rooms have been upgraded since new owners took over in 2011.

✗ Eating & Drinking

Egghead
INTERNATIONAL €€

(☏303 3386; www.egghead-restaurant.de; Peter-Breuer-Strasse 34; mains €7-12; ⊙10am-12.30am Mon-Sat; Ⓢ) Zwickau's pub row, aka Peter-Breuer-Strasse, has largely been taken over by tacky eateries, making convivial Egghead a standout. Only fresh and regional products are turned into simple yet delicious dishes in the open kitchen. Great cocktails and crêpes too.

Zur Grünhainer Kapelle
GERMAN €€

(☏536 1633; www.gruenhainer-kapelle.de; Peter-Breuer-Strasse 3; mains €8-16) Feast on Saxon dishes in this former chapel with its cross-vaulted ceilings, fabulous carved furniture and uneven art exhibits. House specialities include a rich mushroom soup and the charmingly named *besoffne Wildsau* (drunken boar)!

Wenzel's Prager Bierstuben
CZECH €€

(☏273 7542; www.wenzel-bierstuben.de; Domhof 12; mains €9-15; ⊙11am-11pm Mon-Thu, to 2am Fri & Sat, to 10pm Sun) If you've got a grumbling gut, head for this charismatic tavern for such belly-stretchers as beef goulash, mushroom-stuffed dumplings or the vampire-repellant garlic soup. Wash it down with Staropramen on tap and cap it off with a Becherovka (herbal digestif).

Da Guiseppe
ITALIAN €€

(☏786 003; www.ristorante-da-guiseppe-de; Dr-Friedrichs-Ring 20; pizza & pasta €6-12, mains €13-19; ⊙lunch Thu-Mon, dinner Wed-Mon) Heaping crisp salads, interesting pasta plates, thin-crust Neapolitan-style pizzas and creative fish and meat dishes have vaulted this convivial trattoria to the top of many a local's fave list for over 20 years.

Marktcafe
INTERNATIONAL €€

(www.marktcafe-zwickau.de; Hauptmarkt 1; mains €4-12; ⊙8am-10pm) This contempo cafe in the historic town hall has an upbeat chocolate-vanilla-cherry colour scheme and makes for a fine stop any time of day. The tiered breakfast tray for two is a winner in the morning, while the swoonworthy cake selection beckons for an afternoon coffee break.

ℹ️ Information

Post office (Hauptstrasse 18-20; ⊙9am-6.30pm Mon-Fri, 9am-1pm Sat)

Tourist office (📱271 3244; www.zwickautourist.de; Hauptstrasse 6; ⊙9am-6.30pm Mon-Fri, 10am-4pm Sat)

ℹ️ Getting There & Around

LOCAL TRANSPORT Single tickets on trams and buses are €1.80, day passes are €3.80.

TRAIN Zwickau has direct train links to Leipzig (€16.40, 1½ hours), Chemnitz (€5.70, 30 minutes) and Dresden (€23.30, 1½ hours).

EASTERN SAXONY

Bautzen

📱03591 / POP 40,500

Mustard, prisons and a German indigenous minority are the unlikely trio that come together in fascinating Bautzen. Rising high above the Spree River, no fewer than 17 towers and much of the town fortification still ring the Altstadt's labyrinth of cobbled lanes that have hardly changed for centuries. While the town is undeniably German, its heritage is also influenced by the Slavic-speaking Sorbs. Budyšin, as the Sorb language calls it, is home to several Sorb cultural institutions, and public signage is bilingual, though you'd be lucky to hear the language spoken.

⊙ Sights

TOP CHOICE **Sorbisches Museum** MUSEUM

(📱270 8700; www.museum.sorben.com; Ortenburg 3-5; adult/concession €3.50/2; ⊙10am-5pm Mon-Fri, 10am-6pm Sat & Sun Apr-Oct, closed 1hr earlier Nov-Mar) The Sorb national museum has collections and displays on absolutely every aspect of the history and culture of this intriguing – and endangered – ethnic minority. The exhibit kicks off with a general overview before documenting aspects of everyday life, such as customs and festivities, religion, architecture, music and dress. Upstairs the focus is on Sorb language and literature as well as on the emancipation movement in the 18th and 19th centuries. Perhaps the most interesting section is on the top floor, which zeros in on recent Sorb history, including the challenges the group faces to preserve its

identity in the age of globalisation. Unfortunately, there's no labelling in English.

Museum Bautzen MUSEUM

(📱498 50; www.bautzen.de/museum-bautzen; Kornmarkt 1; adult/concession €3.50/2.50; ⊙10am-6pm Tue-Sun oct-Mar, to 5pm Apr-Sep) This reinvigorated museum looks at the history of the town and region as well as local art in shiny new exhibition spaces with plenty of listening, video and interactive stations.

Reichenturm TOWER

(Reichenstrasse; adult/concession €1.40/1; ⊙10am-5pm Apr-Oct) The 1718 addition of the baroque cupola caused this 56m-high medieval structure to start tilting. Today it deviates 1.4m from the centre, making it one of the steepest leaning towers north of the Alps. Climb to the top for sweeping Altstadt views.

Dom St Petri CHURCH

(📱311 80; www.st-petri-bautzen.de; Fleischmarkt; church free, tower adult/concession €2/1; ⊙church 10am-5.30pm Mon-Sat, 1-5.30pm Sun (closes 4pm Nov-Mar), tower noon-6pm Sat, 1-6pm Sun Apr-Dec) Dominating the old meat market (Fleischmarkt), St Petri is a rare *Simultankirche*, meaning it serves both Catholics and Protestants with the former holding services in the front of the nave and the latter in the back. The waist-high iron grating separating the two was 4m high until 1952! The church tower can be climbed.

Alte Wasserkunst TOWER

(📱415 88; www.altewasserkunst.de; Wendischer Kirchhof 2; adult/concession €2.50/2; ⊙10am-5pm, to 4pm Nov-Mar) The most famous of Bautzen's many towers, the Alte Wasserkunst contains a fully functional late-medieval pumping station. Have a look at the mechanism, then make your way to the top for fabulous views, perhaps stopping to take in the regional art displayed on two floors.

🛏️ Sleeping

TOP CHOICE **Schloss-Schänke** HOTEL €€

(📱304 990; www.schloss-schaenke.net; Burgplatz 5; d from €85; 🅿️@🛜) Although a one-time Franciscan residence, rooms at this charmer are hardly monastic. For a heightened romance factor, book yourself one tucked into a nearby 17th-century defensive tower. Thoughtful attention to detail and dynamic hosts add to the appeal.

CITY OF PRISONS

It seems incongruous that the pretty, historical town of Bautzen has been known as *Gefängnisstadt* (prison town) for over a century. Its two prisons – Bautzen I and Bautzen II – were built in 1904 and 1906, respectively. Thanks to its yellow brick facade, the former earned the moniker Gelbes Elend (Yellow Misery). Life was no picnic at either facility, especially after the Nazi takeover. Scores of communists, social democrats, Sinti, Jehovas Witnesses and other 'undesirables' vanished behind the thick walls. After 1945, Bautzen I became one of 10 notorious Soviet-run 'Special Camps' where Nazis and opponents of the Stalinist system were held for years, usually without trial and under crowded, unsanitary conditions; some 3000 prisoners died before the camp closed in 1950. These days, Bautzen I has been modernised and is still used as a correctional facility.

Bautzen II, meanwhile, morphed into a notorious 'Stasi prison', controlled by the GDR Ministry of State Security. More than 2700 regime critics, would-be escapees and those who aided them, purported spies for the West and other political prisoners were incarcerated here from 1956 to 1989. Among the most famous inmates was Rudolf Bahro, who later co-founded the Green Party in West Germany. Left exactly as it was in the late 1980s, it's now a Gedenkstätte (☑404 74; www.gedenkstaette-bautzen.de; Weigangstrasse 8a; ⊙10am-4pm Tue-Sun) for the victims of political oppression. You can see prisoner transport vans, recreated prison cells from the facility's various phases, the isolation wing and historical background exhibits. Unfortunately, all interpretive signage is in German but just walking through here is still a powerful experience.

Alte Gerberei HOTEL €€
(☑272 390; www.hotel-alte-gerberei.de; Uferweg 1; d from €70; ℗) You'll find Old European charm galore in this historic eight-room pension right by the river. The flower-filled courtyard and the cosy wine restaurant are great unwinding stations after a day on the tourist track.

Pension Lausitz PENSION €
(☑378 10; www.pension-lausitz.de; Bahnhofstrasse 16; d €58) Run with charm and panache by the personable Frau Weichelt, this little pension near the train station is a comfy, squeaky clean and quiet base of operation. Bonus points for the quality mattresses and well-edited breakfast buffet.

DJH Hostel HOSTEL €
(☑403 47; www.bautzen.jugendherberge.de; Am Zwinger 1; dm incl breakfast under/over 27yr €20/23.50) The local hostel spreads over a Rapunzel-style medieval tower and two modernised town houses. Dorms sleep three to six and have a sink; toilets and showers are down the hall.

✖ Eating & Drinking

Bautzen 'restaurant row' is Schlossstrasse, although none of the eateries are truly distinguished.

TOP CHOICE Wjelbik SORBIAN €€
(☑420 60; www.wjelbik.de; Kornstrasse 7; mains €10-17; ⊙lunch & dinner Tue-Sun) At this traditional restaurant you'll be greeted Sorbian style, that is with a little bread and salt and a hearty *Witajće k nam!* (Welcome!). Enjoy the most Sorbian of dishes, 'Sorbian Wedding' (braised beef with horseradish sauce) in the dining room that manages modern and traditional in one go.

Sam's Bar CAFE, BAR €€
(☑490 964; www.sams-bar.de; Fleischmarkt 4; dishes €5-12; ⊙6pm-late Mon-Sat, from 2pm Sun) This relaxed hang-out is a fine place to get liquored up as well as for grabbing a bite. The kitchen bakes its own bread, focuses on regional and seasonal ingredients, and also likes to sneak meat-free ayurvedic dishes onto the menu. Their 'Samburger' is a local favourite.

Bautzner Senfstube GERMAN €€
(☑598 015; www.senf-stube.de; Schlossstrasse 3; mains €8-13; ⊙11am-10pm) Mustard bread, mustard salad dressing, mustard goulash, vanilla-mustard sauce, mustard potato mash – this restaurant is king when it comes to creative culinary uses of Bautzen's famous mustard. No worries if you're not a fan – there's a separate mustard-free menu as well.

ℹ Information

Post office (Postplatz 3; ⊙8.30am-6.30pm Mon-Fri, 9am-noon Sat)

Sparkasse (Kornmarkt)

Tourist office (📱420 16; www.bautzen.de; Hauptmarkt 1; ⊙9am-6pm Mon-Fri, 9am-3pm Sat & Sun Mar-Oct, shorter hours Nov-Feb)

ℹ Getting There & Away

CAR The A4 linking Dresden with Görlitz runs just south of Bautzen.

TRAIN Regional trains service Bautzen from Görlitz (€7.60, 30 minutes) and Dresden (€11.10, 45 minutes).

Görlitz

📱03581 / POP 55,400

Spared wartime destruction, Görlitz wraps fabulous architecture, an idyllic tangle of lanes and intriguing history into one magical package. Thanks to nearly 4200 heritage buildings, it's a veritable encyclopedia of European architectural styles from the Renaissance to the 19th century. The town's versatile charms have of late appeared on the radar of Hollywood location scouts: scenes from *The Reader*, *Inglorious Basterds* and

---

DON'T MISS

HEILIGES GRAB

The Heiliges Grab (📱315 864; http://kulturstiftung.kkvsol.net; Heilig-Grab-Strasse 79; admission €2; ⊙10am-6pm Mon-Sat, 11am-6pm Sun Apr-Sep, to 4pm Nov-Feb, to 5pm Mar & Oct) is a close replica of the Holy Sepulchre in Jerusalem as it looked in the Middle Ages during the time of the crusades. Among these crusaders was local boy Georg Emmerich, who made the trip primarily in atonement for knocking up the neighbour's daughter. Absolved from his sins, he returned, became the town mayor and, in 1480, instigated the construction of the Heiliges Grab. It is part of a larger ensemble that also includes a double chapel and a salvation house and marks the final stop in the *via dolorosa* (Stations of the Cross) pilgrimage path that starts at the west portal of the Peterskirche and runs via Nikolaistrasse, Bogstrasse and Steinweg.

Around the World in 80 Days were all filmed here.

Ironically, even though the Iron Curtain lifted decades ago, Görlitz is still a divided city. After WWII it was split in two when the Allies declared the Neisse River as the boundary between Germany and Poland. Görlitz' former eastern suburbs are now the Polish town of Zgorzelec, easily reached via a footbridge across the river (there are no formal border controls). There's little to see here, with savings on cigarettes and vodka being the main lure.

⊙ Sights

Görlitz' sights cluster in the Altstadt, reached from the train station via Berliner Strasse or Jakobstrasse. It is organised around several squares, most notably the Obermarkt and the Untermarkt. From the latter, Neissstrasse leads down to the river and the footbridge to Zgorzelec.

OBERMARKT & SOUTHERN ALTSTADT

Reichenbacher Turm VIEWPOINT

(www.museum-goerlitz.de; Platz des 17 Juni; adult/concession €3/2; ⊙10am-5pm Tue-Sun May-Oct) Climb the 165 steps to the top of this fortification tower that was still inhabited by a watchman until 1904. En route, exhibits on the purpose of such watchmen (eg keeping an eye out for fire or advancing marauders) provide a modest excuse to catch your breath. There's another tower a short walk south of here on Marienplatz, called Dicker Turm (Fat Tower), thanks to its 6m-thick walls.

Dreifaltigkeitskirche CHURCH

(Klosterplatz 21; audioguide €2; ⊙10am-6pm Mon-Sat, 11am-6pm Sun Apr-Oct, to 4pm Nov-Mar) Dominating Obermarkt, this 15th-century former Franciscan monastery church is packed with medieval masterpieces, most notably the baroque high altar and the late Gothic 'Golden Mary' altar.

Art Nouveau Department Store ARCHITECTURE

(Marienplatz) Until 2009 you could still buy everything from socks to clocks in this architectural stunner centred on a galleried atrium accented with wooden balustrades, floating staircases and palatial chandeliers, and lidded by an ornately patterned glass ceiling. It will remain empty (but is usually open in the daytime) until a new investor

BAD MUSKAU

Squeezed against the border with Poland, drowsy Bad Muskau is a tiny spa-village with one big attraction. Unesco-listed Muskauer Park (☑035771-631 00; www.muskauer-park. de; Neues Schloss; park free, exhibit adult/concession €6/3, tower €3/1.50; ☺exhibit 10am-6pm Apr-Oct) is the verdant masterpiece of 19th-century celebrity landscape gardener Prince Hermann von Pückler, who inherited his family estate in 1811. 'Prince Pickle', as the English dubbed him, toiled on the park for nearly 30 years but never completed his 'painting with plants' because debt forced him to sell the estate in 1844. He nevertheless set the bar high for landscapers to follow, even compiling a meticulous instruction manual on landscaping techniques. The park and town suffered enormously when the last major battle of WWII was fought on its grounds in early 1945. The same year, the park was divided between Germany and Poland when the Neisse River, which bisects Pückler's creation, became the new border.

A stroll around the landscaped park will eventually take you to its main building, the Neues Schloss, home of the tourist office (☑035771-631 00; ☺10am-6pm Apr-Oct, to 5pm Nov-Mar) in the west wing and to Pückler!, an interactive, push-button caper through the action-packed life of the park's flamboyant mastermind. Take in views of the park from the top of the palace tower.

At a whopping 560 hectares, the folly-peppered park is too large to be fully explored on foot. Bike hire (€5 per day) is available at the well-signposted Schlossvorwerk, a leafy courtyard where you'll also find a cafe, gift shops and luggage lockers.

Bad Muskau is about 55km north of Görlitz and reached by car via the B115. Coming by train, take an Ostdeutsche Eisenbahn train to Weisswasser, then change to bus 250 to Kirchplatz (€8.30, 1½ hours). The park entrance is a short signposted walk away.

If you want to find out what further shenanigans Prince Pückler was up to after leaving Bad Muskau, see p131.

can be found. Another art-nouveau delicacy is the nearby Strassburg Passage, a light-flooded shopping arcade connecting Berliner Strasse and Jacobstrasse.

UNTERMARKT & EASTERN ALTSTADT

Barockhaus   MUSEUM
(☑671 355; www.museum-goerlitz.de; Neissstrasse 30; adult/concession €5/3.50; ☺10am-5pm Tue-Sat) Johann Christian Ameiss was a wealthy merchant who translated his Midas touch into this magnificent baroque residence that later became the seat of a prestigious science society. Now a museum, its exhibits reflect both legacies. On the first floor, period-furnished family rooms (note the delicately ornamented ceilings) lead to smaller cabinets brimming with baroque porcelain, art, glass, silver and other precious objects. Exhibits on the upper floor highlight society members' diverse research interests – ranging from physics and archaeology to music – with such rare and unusual objects as a 'giraffe piano' and an electrostatic generator from 1792. Panelling is also in English.

Schlesisches Museum zu Görlitz   MUSEUM
(☑879 10; www.schlesisches-museum.de; Brüderstrasse 8; adult/concession incl audioguide €5/3; ☺10am-5pm Tue-Sun) The splendid Schönhof, a 1526 Renaissance residence, forms the atmospheric backdrop of this comprehensive exhibit on the culture and history of Silesia, a region that's often found itself in the crosshairs of political power players and repeatedly changed borders and identity over the past thousand years. The most recent change came after WWII, when most of it was incorporated into Poland, resulting in the expulsion of millions of Silesians of German ethnicity. Fine art, fabulous glass and ceramics and objects from daily life complement the historical displays spread over 17 themed rooms in the historic main building and a modern annex.

Rathaus   HISTORIC BUILDING
(Untermarkt) Görlitz' town hall takes up the entire western side of Untermarkt but the oldest and most noteworthy section is the tower building with its curving Renaissance staircase fronted by a sculpture of the goddess Justitia. Take a moment to observe the lower of the two tower clocks and you'll

WORTH A TRIP

CHOO-CHOO TRAIN TO THE MOUNTAINS

South of Zittau, the Zittauer Gebirge is the smallest low-mountain range in Europe. With its idyllic gorges, thick forests and whimsical rock formations, it's great for hiking and clearing your head. You can drive or take the bus but getting there is much more fun aboard the narrow-gauge **Zittauer Schmalspurbahn** (☎03583-540 540; www.soeg-zittau.de; round trip €12-14), which has been steaming through the trees since 1890. Historic locomotives depart year-round from an itty-bitty timber station in front of Zittau's train station up to the sleepy resort villages of Oybin and Jonsdorf, splitting at Bertsdorf. The largest and nicest town is **Oybin**, which wraps around a beehive-shaped hill topped by a romantically ruined castle and monastery. Trains also stop at the **Teufelsmühle** (Devil's Mill), built for silver miners in the 17th century, from where a trail leads up to the **Töpfer**, a photogenic 582m-high mountain whose evocative sandstone formations have been nicknamed 'tortoise' or 'breeding hen'.

notice that the helmeted soldier in the middle briefly drops his chin every minute.

Flüsterbogen   HISTORIC BUILDING
On the north side of Untermarkt, you can whisper sweet nothings to your sweetie via the reverberating stone arch in the entranceway at No 22. The Renaissance **Ratsapotheke** (pharmacy) at No 24, is easily recognised by its spidery sundial, another of Görlitz' architectural masterpieces.

Peterskirche   CHURCH
(⊙10am-6pm Mon-Sat, 11.45am-6pm Sun) Crowning Görlitz' skyline, this Gothic church is especially famous for its **Sonnenorgel** (Sun Organ), fashioned by Silesian–Italian Eugenio Casparini in 1703. It boasts 88 registers and 6095 pipes, and derives its name from the 17 circular sunshields integrated into the organ case. The church tower can be climbed (€2) but views are only so-so.

🛏 Sleeping

TOP CHOICE Hotel Börse   HOTEL €€
(☎764 20; www.boerse-goerlitz.de; Untermarkt 16; d €109-129; P@🐾) Four-poster beds, sparkling glass chandeliers, patterned parquet floors and elegant antiques are the hallmarks of this stylish yet spirited hotel in an 18th-century palace. Rooms in the affiliated **Gästehaus am Flüsterbogen** (d €95) sport a similarly subtle romantic style but are a tad bigger. For a more contemporary feel, book into the nearby **Herberge zum 6. Gebot** (d €65), which translates as 'Inn of the 6th Commandment' (that would be the one about adultery). As a sweet touch of irony, rooms are named after famous philanderers such as Henry VIII and Casanova. Check-in and breakfast are all at the Hotel Börse.

Romantik Hotel Tuchmacher   HOTEL €€€
(☎473 10; www.tuchmacher.de; Peterstrasse 8; d €132-155; P🐾) In the most coveted rooms at this posh Renaissance charmer near the Peterskirche you'll be sleeping beneath richly painted baroque ceilings, but others are just as nice with warm hues and classical furnishings. Roast in the hot tub or sauna before toasting the day over a sophisticated meal in the on-site restaurant.

Pension Goldene Feder   PENSION €
(☎400 403; www.pension-goerlitz.de; Handwerk 12; d €55-70; P) A winner for fans of such retro touches as finding writing paper, quill and ink in your room (on the flipside, don't bank on wi-fi working). Rooms harmoniously mix modern and vintage furnishings with art created by friends of the owner couple (the nicest feature thick exposed beams). Breakfast includes fruit and eggs from the family farm.

Pension Miejski   PENSION €
(☎+48 888 579 253; www.pensjonat-miejski.pl; Nowomiejjska 1, Zgorzelec; d €42; P🐾) Steps from the footbridge on the Zgorzelec side, this superb value-for-money pick delivers five impeccably maintained and good-sized rooms done up in warm browns and purple. Fast wi-fi, coffee and water are all free.

DJH Hostel   HOSTEL €
(☎649 0700; www.goerlitz-city.jugendherberge.de; Peterstrasse15;dmincl breakfast under/over27€20/23.50; ⊙check-in 4-9pm Apr-Sep, 5-8pm Oct-Mar; @) A modern hostel concealed by an historic facade, this sparkling new contender counts a

to-die-for Altstadt location and shiny en-suite rooms – sleeping four to six – with wooden bunk beds among its assets. Families can find privacy in one of five apartments.

Eating

TOP CHOICE **Filetto** ITALIAN €€
(☑421 131; Petersstrasse 1; mains €6-13.50) A Görlitz foodie fave, and for good reason. Fiery red banquettes offer a comfortable perch from which to tuck into the clever yet unfussy pastas, but it's such dishes as juicy filowrapped spinach and salmon that inspire loyalty. The French house wine is cheap and delicious. Book a table, or forget about it.

Restaurant Lucie Schulte INTERNATIONAL €€€
(☑410 260; Untermarkt 22; mains €11-18; ☉ dinner Tue-Sat) Your taste buds may well do cartwheels at this progressive venue off the romantic courtyard of the Flüsterbogen building. Creative flavour pairings like scallops with spinach and mango tartare, or potato-encrusted perch drizzled with morel sauce will have you hungering for seconds. Superb hand-picked wines to boot.

St Jonathan SAXON, MEDITERRANEAN €€€
(☑421 082; www.goerlitz-restaurant.de; Peterstrasse 16; mains €8-19) Despite its contempo furniture and stunning historic setting, this place only looks expensive. Enjoy delicious pasta, toothsome steaks or try one of the regional dishes at linen-bedecked tables beneath a painted vaulted ceiling. For a romantic tête-à-tête, book the single table inside (!) the fireplace.

ⓘ Information

Banks with ATMs are scattered throughout but especially numerous around Postplatz, which is also where you'll find the main post office.

Tourist office (☑475 70; www.goerlitz.de; Obermarkt 32; ☉9am-6pm Mon-Fri, to 5pm Sat, to 4pm Sun May-Oct, 9.30am-6pm Mon-Fri, to 2.30pm Sat & Sun Nov-Apr)

I-Vent tourist office (☑421 362; www.goerlitz-tourismus.de; Obermarkt 33; ☉9am-6pm Mon-Fri, 9.30am-5pm Sat, 9.30am-3pm Sun Apr-Oct, 9am-6pm Mon-Fri, 9.30am-3pm Sat Nov-Mar)

ⓘ Getting There & Away

CAR Görlitz is about 110km east of Dresden, just off the A4 autobahn; take exit 94 and follow the B6 to the B99 into town.

TRAIN Trains run regularly between Görlitz and Dresden (€19.80, one to 1½ hours) via Bautzen

(€7.60, 30 minutes). For Berlin (from €40.60, three hours), change in Cottbus. Trains also run to Zittau (€5.60, 40 minutes). Note that some routes are operated by the private Ostdeutsche Eisenbahn (ODEG), not Deutsche Bahn, although the tariffs are the same.

Zittau

☑03583 / POP 27,850

In the far south-east corner of Saxony, cradled by Poland and the Czech Republic, Zittau makes for an easy day trip from Dresden or Görlitz. Its largely baroque Altstadt came through WWII mostly intact, though Cold War-era neglect is still evident in places. The town is a major stop for religious pilgrims thanks to two precious late-medieval Lenten veils that are ultra-rare and stunning pieces of artistry. By contrast, the newest attraction is the bright and whimsical Pop-Art Quarter, one of the largest of its kind in Germany.

⊙ Sights

Sights cluster around the Markt, which is about 1km south of the Hauptbahnhof via Bahnhofstrasse and Bautzener Strasse. With its baroque fountain, stately town houses and imposing Italian-palazzo-style Rathaus (town hall) by Prussian master builder Karl Friedrich Schinkel, it exudes a touch of light-hearted Mediterranean flair.

**Museum Kirche zum
Heiligen Kreuz** MUSEUM
(☑500 8920; www.zittauer-fastentuecher.de; Frauenstrasse 23; adult/concession €4.50/2.50; ☉10am-6pm daily Apr-Oct, 10am-5pm Tue-Sun Nov-Mar) This former church was specifically converted to shelter Zittau's most famous attraction, the 1472 **Grosses Zittauer Fastentuch** (Large Zittau Lenten Veil). The house-sized painted linen cloth shows a complete illustrated Bible in 90-odd scenes – Genesis to the Last Judgement. Its original purpose was to conceal the altar from the congregation during Lent. Also note the morbidly charming tombstones in the church cemetery.

ⓘ TICKET TO SAVINGS

Combination tickets to see both the large and small Lenten veils are €6.50 per adult (€4.50 concession). Tickets include English-language audioguides.

Kulturhistorisches Museum Franziskanerkloster
MUSEUM

(☑554 790; www.zittauer-fastentuecher.de; Klosterstrasse 3; adult/concession €3.50/2.50; ☺10am-5pm daily Apr-Oct, closed Mon Nov-Mar) The star exhibit at this museum is the 1573 Kleines Zittauer Fastentuch (Small Zittau Lenten Veil), which depicts the crucifixion scene framed by 40 symbols of the Passion of Christ and is one of only seven such veils that have survived. The rest of the museum chronicles regional history.

Pop-Art-Viertel
NEIGHBOURHOOD

(www.mandauerglanz.de; btwn Grüne Strasse & Rosenstrasse) Zittau's newest attraction is this once drab cluster of GDR-era buildings turned colourful and fanciful living quarter dreamed up by Berlin artist Sergej Alexander Dott. It's a shutterbug's dream with giant sheep clambering around bright orange facades and centaurs and angels standing guard over a pedestrianised walkway spanned by a massive double helix.

FREE Salzhaus
HISTORIC BUILDING

(www.salzhaus-zittau.de; Neustadt; ☺8am-6.30pm) Overlooking fountain-studded Neustadt square, the weighty Salzhaus was originally a 16th-century salt storage house and now brims with market stalls, shops, restaurants and the public library.

Johanniskirche
CHURCH

(☑510 933; www.johanniskirche-zittau.de; Johannisplatz 1; tower adult/concession €1.50/1; ☺noon-6pm Mon-Fri, 10am-4pm Sat & Sun Apr-Oct, 10am-4.30pm Mon-Fri, 10am-4pm Sat & Sun Nov-Mar) Zittau's grand Church of St John has medieval roots but the current version was consecrated in 1837 and designed by Prussian starchitect Karl Friedrich Schinkel, who added the wooden coffered ceiling, the neo-Gothic north tower and the baptismal font. The south tower can be climbed for sweeping views of the mountains.

🛏 Sleeping & Eating

Hotel Dreiländereck
HOTEL €€

(☑5550; www.hotel-dle.de; Bautzener Strasse 9; d €90; P☜) This one-time brewery on Zittau's pedestrianised commercial strip is a solid pick, with warmly furnished rooms dressed in green and gold hues. The contemporary brasserie (mains €9 to €18) has vaulted ceilings, a large terrace and €5 weekday lunch specials.

Seeger Schänke
GERMAN €€

(☑510 980; www.seeger-schaenke.de; Innere Weberstrasse 38; mains €5-10; ☺11am-2pm Mon-Fri, 6-10pm daily) 'Seeger' is local dialect for 'clock', which explains the abundance of timepieces decorating this rustic pub that's often so crowded you have to shoehorn your way to a table. The secret of their success is in big portions of delicious hearty fare served by staff who are not stingy with smiles.

Savi
INTERNATIONAL €

(☑708 297; www.savi-online.de; Bautzener Strasse 10; meals €3.50-6.50) A youngish crowd pulls in at Savi around the clock for substantial breakfasts, big bowls of coffee, a light meal or a cold beer. The terrace in the pedestrian zone is a great people-watching perch. Internet access costs €2 per hour.

Dornspachhaus
GERMAN €€

(☑795 883; www.dornspachhaus.de; Bautzener Strasse 2; mains €7-16; ☺11.30am-10pm) Zittau's oldest eatery oozes history from every nook and cranny, serves delicious regional cuisine and has a lovely courtyard. A speciality is the Bohemian goulash, a creamy blend of slivered pork, pickles and mushrooms served in a bowl of bread.

❶ Information

Tourist office (☑752 200; www.zittau.eu; Markt 1; ☺9am-6pm Mon-Fri & 9am-1pm Sat year-round, 10am-noon Sun May-Oct)

❶ Getting There & Away

CAR Zittau is 36km south of Görlitz via the B99 and 48km southeast of Bautzen via the B96.

TRAIN ODEG trains run to Görlitz (€6.60, 35 minutes), while Deutsche Bahn operates a direct service to Dresden (€19.60, 1½ hours). Going to Bautzen requires a change in Görlitz (€7.60, 1½ hours).

Munich

♪089 / POP 1.38 MILLION

Best Places to Eat

» Fraunhofer (p208)
» Königsquelle (p209)
» Tantris (p209)
» Prinz Myshkin (p209)
» Marais (p211)

Best Places to Stay

» Bayerischer Hof (p203)
» La Maison (p206)
» Hotel Laimer Hof (p207)
» Anna Hotel (p205)
» Cortiina (p204)

Why Go?

The natural habitat of well-wheeled power dressers and Lederhosen-clad thigh-slappers, Mediterranean-style street cafes and Mitteleuropa beer halls, high-brow art and high-tech industry, Germany's unofficial southern capital is a flourishing success story that revels in its own contradictions. If you're looking for Alpine clichés, they're all here, but the Bavarian metropolis has many an unexpected card down its Dirndl.

But whatever else this city is, it's popular. Statistics show Munich is enticing more visitors than ever, especially in summer and during Oktoberfest when the entire planet seems to arrive to toast the town.

Munich's walkable centre retains a small-town air but holds some world-class sights, especially its art galleries and museums. Throw in royal Bavarian heritage, an entire suburb of Olympic legacy and a kitbag of dark tourism and you see why southern Germany's metropolis is such a favourite among those who seek out the past, but like to hit the town once they're done.

When to Go

Lovers of German beer will find true happiness in Munich's beer halls during Stark Bier Zeit (strong beer season). This popular beer festival takes place for three weeks in February or March and is the time to sup the strong ale monks once brewed to sustain themselves through the Lenten fast. From September to October is the best time to amble in the Englischer Garten (English Garden) as its trees fire off an autumnal salute. And in December, pretty Marienplatz at the city's heart fills with Christmassy stalls, lights and enough yuletide cheer to share among its international gaggle of shoppers.

SET YOUR BUDGET

» **Budget hotel room** €60–80

» **Two-course meal** €11–16

» **Mass of beer (1L)** €7.50

» **Zone 1 transport ticket** €2.50

» **Museum/gallery ticket** €7

Need to Know

» Many museums close on Mondays

» Booking any kind of accommodation during Oktoberfest (late Sep–early Oct) can be almost impossible, and expensive

» Most major museums charge just €1 admission on Sundays

Resources

» Munich Tourism Association www.muenchen -tourist.de

» Public Transport www.mvv.de

» Oktoberfest www.oktoberfest.de

» Munich Museums www. museen-in-muenchen.de

Art Attack

'Munich nestles between art and beer like a village between hills,' wrote 19th-century German poet Heinrich Heine, and his words ring as true today as they did back then. Visit any of Munich's galleries (especially on Sundays) and you'll find them packed to the gift shop with well-informed locals, rightly proud of their city's reputation for blockbuster art collections and leading-edge galleries. It was the Wittelbachs, Bavaria's ruling family for over 700 years, who gathered much of the city's enviable collection under several roofs. This led to the creation of the Kunstareal, an entire quarter of the city centre given over to galleries. Two 21st-century additions to the Kunstareal are the Pinakothek der Moderne and the Museum Brandhorst, and more are on their way.

CITY OF BEER

Other cities, such as Pilsen and Brussels, occasionally launch weak claims, but few can rival Munich when it comes to which city holds the title of 'beer capital of the world'. Countless beer gardens, Oktoberfest (and several other minor beer festivals), some of central Europe's best-known breweries such as Paulaner and Augustiner, myriad beers in all shades and strengths and, of course, the famous Hofbräuhaus, the mother ship of all beer halls, all form part of the hop-based culture that makes Munich to the drinker what Las Vegas is to the gambler. In fact Munich's beer halls set a high bar for all others across the world, and the unofficial franchise can be found everywhere from Tenerife to Siberia. Despite high ale consumption, public drunkenness and disorder (among locals at least) is rarely seen and most beer halls and gardens are family friendly, with kids' playgrounds and high chairs. And even if you're devoutly teetotal back home, non-alcoholic brews now enable you to relish the colour of Munich's frothy traditions minus the falling over.

Best in Munich...

» **Beer hall** Augustiner Bräustuben (p213)

» **Bavarian food** Fraunhofer (p208)

» **Vegetarian food** Prinz Myshkin (p209)

» **Partying** Kultfabrik (p214)

» **Views** Tower of St Peterskirche (p182)

» **Escape from the city** Lake Starnberg (p225)

History

It was Benedictine monks, drawn by fertile farmland and the closeness to Catholic Italy, who settled in what is now Munich. The city derives its name from the medieval *Munichen,* or monks. In 1158 the Imperial Diet in Augsburg sanctioned the rule of Heinrich der Löwe, and Munich the city was born.

In 1240 the city passed to the House of Wittelsbach, which would govern Munich (and Bavaria) until the 20th century. Munich prospered as a salt-trading centre but was hit hard by plague in 1349. The epidemic subsided only after 150 years, whereupon the relieved *Schäffler* (coopers) initiated a ritualistic dance to remind burghers of their good fortune. The *Schäfflertanz* is performed every seven years but it is reenacted daily by the little figures on the city's glockenspiel (carillon) on Marienplatz.

By the 19th century an explosion of monument building gave Munich its spectacular architecture and wide Italianate avenues. Things got out of hand after King Ludwig II ascended the throne in 1864, as spending for his grandiose projects (such as Schloss Neuschwanstein) bankrupted the royal house and threatened the government's coffers. Ironically, today they are the biggest money spinners of Bavaria's tourism industry.

Munich has seen many turbulent times but the 20th century was particularly bumpy. WWI practically starved the city to death, the Nazis first rose to prominence here and the next world war nearly wiped Munich off the map.

The 1972 Olympic Games began as a celebration of a new democratic Germany, but ended in tragedy when 17 people were killed in a terrorist hostage-taking incident. In 2006 the city won a brighter place in sporting history when it hosted the opening game of the FIFA World Cup.

Today, Munich's claim to being the 'secret capital' of Germany is alive and well. The city is recognised for its high living standards, with the most millionaires per capita in Germany after Hamburg, and for haute couture that rivals that of Paris and Milan. In 2008 the whole city took the summer off to celebrate the 850th birthday of this great metropolis.

Sights

Munich's major sights cluster around the Altstadt, with the main museum district just north of the Residenz. However, it will take another day or two to explore bohemian Schwabing, the sprawling Englischer Garten and trendy Haidhausen to the east. Northwest of the Altstadt you'll find cosmopolitan Neuhausen, the Olympiapark and another of Munich's royal highlights – Schloss Nymphenburg.

ALTSTADT

The heart and soul of the Altstadt, Marienplatz (Mary's Square) is a popular gathering spot and packs a lot of personality into its relatively small frame. It's anchored by the **Mariensäule** (Mary's Column; Map p184), built in 1638 to celebrate victory over Swedish forces during the Thirty Years' War; it's topped by a golden statue of the Virgin Mary balancing on a crescent moon. At 11am and noon (also 5pm March to October), the square jams up with tourists craning their necks to take in the animated glockenspiel in the Neues Rathaus (New Town Hall).

The bustling **Viktualienmarkt** (Map p184; 🕘Mon-Fri & Sat morning; [S]Marienplatz, [U]Marienplatz) is one of Europe's great food markets. In summer the entire place is transformed into one of the finest and most expensive beer gardens around, while in winter people huddle for warmth and schnapps in the small pubs around the square. The merchandise and food are of the finest quality, and prices tend to be high. The enormous **maypole** bears artisans' symbols and the traditional blue-and-white Bavarian stripes.

A few paces southwest of the Viktualienmarkt is the **Schrannenhalle** (Map p184; Viktualienmarkt 15; 🕘9am-8pm Mon-Sat; [S]Marienplatz, [U]Marienplatz), a 19th-century grain market hall reconstructed in 2005. The 400m-long glass-and-iron structure itself is quite impressive but shopping from the exclusive food stalls inside is expensive. One redeeming feature is that the basement holds central Munich's most accessible free toilet.

Odeonsplatz (Map p184; Odeonsplatz) marks the beginning of the Maxvorstadt, a 19th-century quarter built to link central Munich with Schwabing to the north. Leo von Klenze masterminded its overall design and several of the buildings, including the **Leuchtenberg-Palais** (Map p184; to Odeonsplatz), a stately town palace modelled after a Roman palazzo and now home of the Bavarian Finance Ministry. There are several nice, if pricey, cafes, including the plushly furnished **Cafe Tambosi** (Map p184; Odeonsplatz 18), which has a pedigree going back more

To Dachau (10km)

Am Hart Ⓤ

LERCHENAU

KOLONIE EGGARTEN

Lerchenauer Str

Milbertshofen

Frankfurter Ring Ⓤ

Ⓡ Allach

Hanauer-Str

Maosacher Str

Dachauer Str

MOOSACH

Milbertshofen Ⓤ

To Augsburg (65km)

Von-Kahr-Str

Lochha Str

A8

Menzinger Str

See Nymphenburg, Neuhausen & Olympiapark Map (p196)

Westfriedhof

BORSTEI

Baldurstr

Landshuter Allee

❹ Ⓤ

❸ **BMW Welt** Ⓤ

Olympiapark

Ackermannstr

NEULANGWIED

Verdistr

Pippinger Str

NEULUSTHEIM

Schlosspark

GERN Ⓤ

SCHWABING

Leonrodstr

Elisabethstr

Ⓡ Langwied

NEUHAUSEN

Lachnerstr

Ⓤ

Ⓤ

Holareidulijö ❻

Aubinger Str

NYMPHENBURG

Schloss Nymphenburg

Wotanstr

Arnulfstr

Ⓤ

Ⓤ **Alte Pinakothek** ❷

Ⓤ

Westkreuz Ⓡ

Laim Ⓡ

Hackerbrücke

Ⓤ

Landsberger Str

Landsberger Str

Donnersbergerbrücke

Hauptbahnhof

Ⓤ

Ⓤ

Weinbergerstr

Willbaldstr

Fürstenrieder Str

LAIM

Laimer Platz Ⓤ

WESTEND

Westendstr Ⓤ

❶ **Augustiner Bräustuben**

Klein Gärten

Blumenauer Str

Friedenheimer Str

Heimeranplatz Ⓤ

Schwanthaler Höhe Ⓤ

Ⓤ

LOCHHAM

Ammerseestr Ⓤ

Waldwiesenstr

Haderner Stern

See Westend & Theresienweise Map (p208)

Theresienwiese

A96

Westpark (Ost)

Südbahnhof Ⓡ

Planegger Str

GRÄFELFING

Grosshadern Ⓤ

Holzapfelkreuth

Westpark Ⓤ

UNTERSENDLING

Partnachplatz Ⓤ

Harras Ⓡ

Implerstr Ⓤ

Klinikum Grosshadern Ⓤ

Tischlerstr

KREUZHOF

Walfriedhofstr

Mittersendling Ⓡ

Plinganserstr

Candidstr Ⓤ

Brudermühlstr

THALKIRCHEN

PLANEGG

Münchener Str

Waldfriedhof

Forst-Kasten-Allee

Südpark

Forstenrieder Allee

Aidenbachstr Ⓤ

Obersendling Ⓤ

Thalkirchen Ⓤ

A95

Machtlfinger Str

Siemenswerke Ⓡ

Siemensallee

MARIA EINSIEDEL

Fürstenried West Ⓤ

Basler Strasse Ⓤ

FÜRSTENRIEDOST

Gautinger Str

Olympiastr

MAXHOF

FORSTENRIED

Forstenrieder Park

To Starnberg (18km);
Garmisch-Partenkirchen (80km);
Oberammergau (81km);
Füssen (95km)

Herterichstr

STADT SOLLN

HINTERBRÜHL

Geiselgasteigstr

To Bavaria Filmstadt (1km)

Munich Highlights

❶ Raising a tankard of *Weissbier* (wheat beer) at an authentic beer hall, such as the **Augustiner Bräustuben** (p213)

❷ Feeling your brow growing higher among the world-class art collections at the **Alte Pinakothek** (p189)

❸ Experiencing an incredible adrenaline rush while clambering around the roof of the Olympic Stadium, **Olympiapark** (p194)

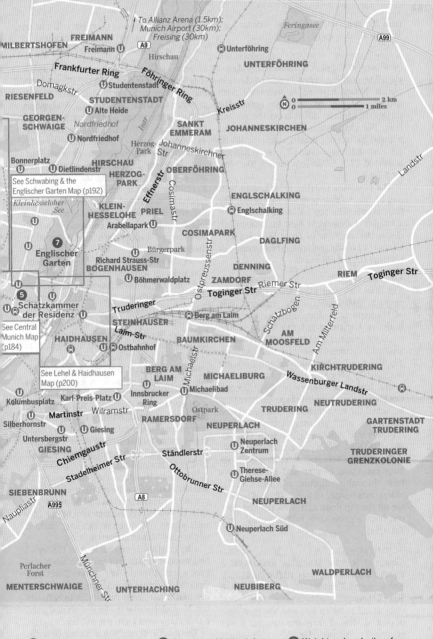

To Allianz Arena (1.5km);
Munich Airport (30km);
Freising (30km)

Feringasee

MILBERTSHOFEN

FREIMANN
Freimann Ⓤ

A9

Hirschau

Ⓤ Unterföhring

A99

UNTERFÖHRING

Frankfurter Ring

Föhringer Ring

Domagkstr

Ⓤ Studentenstadt

Kreisstr

RIESENFELD

STUDENTENSTADT

0 ————— 2 km
0 ————— 1 miles

GEORGEN-
SCHWAIGE

Ⓤ Alte Heide

Nordfriedhof

SANKT
EMMERAM

JOHANNESKIRCHEN

Isar

Ⓤ Nordfriedhof

Herzog-
Park

Johanneskirchner
Str

Bonnerplatz
Ⓤ

Ⓤ Dietlindenstr

HIRSCHAU

Herzog-
Str

OBERFÖHRING

Landstr

See Schwabing & the
Englischer Garten Map (p192)

HERZOG-
PARK

Effnerstr

Cosimastr

ENGLSCHALKING

Kleinhesseloher
See

KLEIN-
HESSELOHE

PRIEL

Ⓐ Englschalking

Ⓤ

Arabellapark Ⓤ

COSIMAPARK

DAGLFING

Ⓤ

7

Englischer
Garten

Bürgerpark

Ostpreussenstr

Ⓤ Richard Strauss-Str

BOGENHAUSEN

DENNING

RIEM

Toginger Str

Ⓤ Böhmerwaldplatz

ZAMDORF

Riemer Str

5

Schatzkammer
der Residenz

Ⓤ

Truderinger

Toginger Str

Schatzbogen

Ⓤ Berg am Laim

Am Mitterfeld

Ⓤ

Ⓤ

STEINHAUSER

Laim-Str

BAUMKIRCHEN

AM
MOOSFELD

See Central
Munich Map
(p184)

HAIDHAUSEN

Ⓐ

Ⓤ Ostbahnhof

Michaelstr

KIRCHTRUDERING

Ⓐ

See Lehel & Haidhausen
Map (p200)

BERG AM
LAIM

MICHAELIBURG

Wassenburger Landstr

NEUTRUDERING

Kolumbusplatz
Ⓤ

Karl-Preis-Platz
Ⓤ

Innsbrucker
Ring

Ⓤ Michaelibad

TRUDERING

GARTENSTADT
TRUDERING

Martinstr

Wilramstr

Ostpark

Silberhornstr
Ⓤ

Untersbergstr
Ⓤ

Ⓤ Giesing

RAMERSDORF

NEUPERLACH

TRUDERINGER
GRENZKOLONIE

GIESING

Chiemgaustr

Ständlerstr

Ⓤ Neuperlach
Zentrum

Stadelheimer Str

Ottobrunner Str

Ⓤ Therese-
Giehse-Allee

SIEBENBRUNN

A8

NEUPERLACH

Naupliastr

A995

Ⓤ Neuperlach Süd

Perlacher
Forst

Münchner
Str

WALDPERLACH

MENTERSCHWAIGE

UNTERHACHING

NEUBIBERG

❹ Getting under the high-
octane hood of the **BMW Welt**
(p195)

❺ Revelling in the blingfest
that is the **Schatzkammer der
Residenz** (p189)

❻ Squeezing Alpine-style
into lederhosen or a dirndl at a
folk costume emporium, such
as **Holareidulijö** (p217)

❼ Watching daredevil surfers
negotiate an urban wave on
the artificial stream in the
Englischer Garten (p193)

than 200 years and used to be popular with Munich's high society.

Neues Rathaus HISTORIC BUILDING

(New Town Hall; Map p184; [S]Marienplatz, [U]Marienplatz) The coal-blackened facade of the neo-Gothic Neues Rathaus is festooned with gargoyles, statues and a dragon scaling the turrets; the tourist office is on the ground floor. For pinpointing Munich's landmarks without losing your breath, catch the lift up the 85m-tall **tower** (Map p184; Neues Rathaus; adult/child €2/1; ⏰9am-7pm Mon-Fri, 10am-7pm Sat & Sun).

The **glockenspiel** (Map p184) has 43 bells and 32 figures that perform two actual historic events. The top half tells the story of a knights' tournament held in 1568 to celebrate the marriage of Duke Wilhelm V to Renata of Lothringen, while the bottom half portrays the *Schäfflertanz*.

Altes Rathaus HISTORIC BUILDING

(Old Town Hall; Map p184; Marienplatz; [S]Marienplatz, [U]Marienplatz) The eastern side of Marienplatz is dominated by the Altes Rathaus. Lightning got the better of the medieval original in 1460 and WWII bombs levelled its successor, so what you see is really the third incarnation of the building designed by Jörg von Halspach of Frauenkirche fame. On 9 November 1938, Joseph Goebbels gave a hate-filled speech here that launched the nationwide Kristallnacht (see boxed text, p727) pogroms. Today it houses the adorable **Spielzeugmuseum** (Toy Museum; Map p184; www.toymuseum.de; Marienplatz 15; adult/child €4/1; ⏰10am-5.30pm) with its huge collection of rare and precious toys from throughout Europe and the US. The oldest ones – made of paper, tin and wood – are on the top floor, and from the 3rd floor you have a great view of Marienplatz and Tal street.

St Peterskirche CHURCH

(Church of St Peter; Map p184; Rindermarkt 1; church admission free, tower adult/child €1.50/1; ⏰tower 9am-5.30pm Mon-Fri, from 10am Sat & Sun; [S]Marienplatz, [U]Marienplatz) Some 306 steps stand between you and the best view of central Munich from the 92m-tall tower of the St Peterskirche, Munich's oldest church (built in 1150). Also known as Alter Peter (Old Peter), it's a virtual textbook of art through the centuries, with its Gothic St-Martin-Altar, Johann Baptist Zimmermann baroque ceiling fresco and Ignaz Günther rococo sculptures.

Also try to find the ghoulish relics of an obscure saint named Munditia (located to the left as you look at the altar).

Münchner Stadtmuseum MUSEUM

(City Museum; Map p184; ☎2332 2370; www.stadtmuseum-online.de; St-Jakobs-Platz 1; adult/concession/child €6/3/free, audioguide €3; ⏰10am-6pm Tue-Sun; [S]Marienplatz, [U]Marienplatz) Installed for the city's 850th birthday in 2008, the **Typisch München** (Typical Munich) exhibition at this unmissable museum tells Munich's story in an imaginative, uncluttered and engaging way. Taking up the whole of a rambling building, exhibits in each section represent something quintessential about the city; a booklet/audioguide relates the tale behind them, thus condensing a long and tangled history into easily digestible themes.

Set out in chronological order, the exhibition kicks off with the founding monks and ends in the post-war boom decades. The first of five sections, 'Old Munich' contains a scale model of the city in the late 16th century (one of five commissioned by Duke Albrecht V; the Bayerisches Nationalmuseum displays the others) but the highlight here is the *The Morris Dancers*, a series of statuettes gyrating like 15th-century ravers. It's one of the most valuable works owned by the City of Munich

'New Munich' charts the Bavarian capital's 18th- and 19th-century transformation into prestigious royal capital and the making of the modern city. The *Canaletto View* gives an idea in oil paint of how Munich looked in the mid-18th century, before the Wittelsbachs launched their makeover. The section also takes a fascinating look at the origins of the Oktoberfest and Munich's cuisine, as well as the phenomenon of 'the Munich beauty' – Munich's women are regarded as Germany's most attractive.

'City of Munich' takes a look at the weird and wonderful late 19th and early 20th century, a period known for Jugendstil (art nouveau) architecture and design, Richard Wagner and avant-garde rumblings in Schwabing. Munich became the 'city of art and beer', a title many might agree it still holds today.

The fourth 'Revue' hall is a little obscure, but basically deals with the aftermath of WWI and the rise of the Nazis. The lead up to war and the city's sufferings during WWII occupy the Feuchtwangersaal, where a photo of a very determined Chamberlain stands next to the other culprits of the Munich Agreement. This is followed by a couple of fascinating rooms that paint a portrait of the modern city, including TV footage from the last 40 years.

What could not be boiled down for this exhibition is the city's role in the rise of the Nazis, and this notorious chapter has been rightly left as a powerful separate exhibition called **Nationalsozialismus in München**. This occupies an eerily windowless annex of the main building.

The Stadtmuseum's gift shop is the only one we've seen that includes a real antique/junk shop.

Jüdisches Museum MUSEUM

(Jewish Museum; Map p184; www.juedisches-museum-muenchen.de; St-Jakobs-Platz 16; adult/child €6/3; ⏲10am-6pm Tue-Sun; [S]Sendlinger Tor, 🚋Sendlinger Tor) Coming to terms with its Nazi past has not historically been a priority in Munich, which is why the opening of the Jewish Museum in 2007 was hailed as a milestone. The permanent exhibit offers an insight into Jewish history, life and culture in Munich, creatively presented over three floors. The Holocaust is dealt with, but the accent is clearly on contemporary Jewish culture.

The museum is part of the new Jewish complex on St-Jakobs-Platz that also includes a community centre with a restaurant and a bunker-like **synagogue** that's rarely open to the public. The ensemble reflects the burgeoning renaissance of Munich's Jewish population, which numbers around 9300, making it the second largest in Germany after Berlin.

Bier & Oktoberfestmuseum MUSEUM

(Map p184; www.bier-und-oktoberfestmuseum.de; Sterneckerstrasse 2; adult/concession €4/2.50; ⏲1-5pm Tue-Sat; 🚋Isartor, 🚆Isartor) Head to this popular museum to learn all about Bavarian suds and the world's most famous booze-up. The four floors heave with old brewing vats, historic photos and some of the earliest Oktoberfest regalia. The 14th-century building has some fine medieval features including painted ceilings and a kitchen with an open fire. There's an earthy pub downstairs (evenings only).

Asamkirche CHURCH

(Map p184; Sendlinger Strasse 34; [S]Sendlinger Tor, 🚋Sendlinger Tor) Though pocket-sized, the late-baroque Asamkirche, built in 1746, is as rich and epic as a giant's treasure chest. Its creators, the brothers Cosmas Damian Asam and Egid Quirin Asam, dipped deeply into their considerable talent box to swathe every inch of wall space with paintings, putti (cherubs), gold leaf and stucco flourishes.

The crowning glory is the ceiling fresco illustrating the life of St John Nepomuk to whom the church is dedicated (lie down on your back in a pew to fully appreciate the complicated perspective). The brothers lived next door and this was originally their private chapel; the main altar could be seen through a window from their home.

[FREE] **Hofbräuhaus** BEER HALL

(Map p184; www.hofbraeuhaus.de; Am Platzl 9 ; [S]Marienplatz, 🚆Marienplatz) Even teetotalling ubercool kitsch-haters will at some point gravitate, out of simple curiosity, to the Hofbräuhaus, the world's most celebrated beer hall. The writhing hordes of tourists tend to overshadow the sterling interior, where dainty twirled flowers and Bavarian flags adorn the medieval vaults.

Beer guzzling and pretzel snapping has been going on here since 1644 and the ballroom upstairs was the site of the first large meeting of the National Socialist Party on 20 February 1920.

Alter Hof PALACE

(Map p184; Burgstrasse 8; [S]Marienplatz, 🚆Marienplatz) Alter Hof was the starter home of the Wittelsbach family and has its origins in the 12th century. The Bavarian rulers moved out of this central palace as long ago as the 15th century. Visitors can only see the central courtyard where the bay window on the southern facade was nicknamed Monkey Tower in honour of a valiant ape that saved an infant Ludwig the Bavarian from the clutches of a ferocious market pig. Local lore at its most bizarre.

Münzhof HISTORIC BUILDING

(Map p184; Hofgraben 4; [S]Marienplatz, 🚆Marienplatz) The former *Münzhof* (mint) has a pretty courtyard, remarkable for its three-storey Renaissance arcades dating from 1567. An inscription on the western side of the building reads *Moneta Regis* (Money Rules), particularly apt words for this well-heeled part of Europe. The building now houses the agency charged with protecting Bavaria's many historical monuments.

Feldherrnhalle HISTORIC BUILDING

(Field Marshal's Hall; Map p184; Residenzstrasse 1; [S]Odeonsplatz) Corking up Odeonsplatz' south side

Central Munich

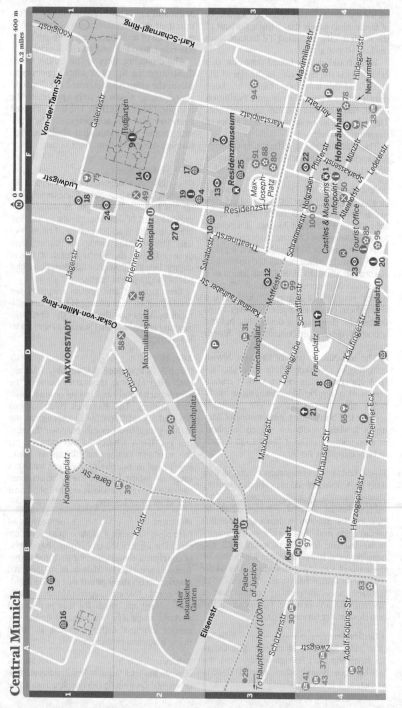

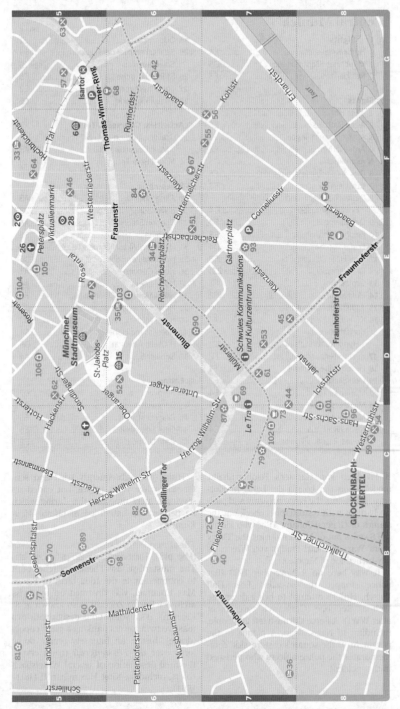

Central Munich

Top Sights

Hofbräuhaus ... F4
Münchner Stadtmuseum ... D5
Residenzmuseum ... F3

Sights

1 Alter Hof ... F4
2 Altes Rathaus ... E5
3 Antikensammlungen ... B1
4 Antiquarium ... F2
5 Asamkirche ... C5
6 Bier & Oktoberfestmuseum ... F5
7 Cuvilliés-Theater ... F3
8 Deutsches Jagd- und Fischereimuseum ... D4
9 Dianatempel ... F2
10 Feldherrnhalle ... E3
11 Frauenkirche ... D4
12 Fünf Höfe ... E3
Glockenspiel ... (see 23)
13 Grottenhof ... F3
14 Hofgarten ... F2
15 Jüdisches Museum ... D6
16 Kunstbau ... A1
Kunsthalle der Hypo-Kulturstiftung ... (see 12)
17 Kurfürstenzimmer ... F2
18 Leuchtenberg-Palais ... F1
19 Lion Statues ... F2
20 Mariensäule ... E4
21 Michaelskirche ... C4
22 Münzhof ... F4
23 Neues Rathaus ... E4
Neues Rathaus Tower ... (see 23)
24 Odeonsplatz ... E1
25 Schatzkammer der Residenz ... F3
Spielzeugmuseum ... (see 2)
26 St Peterskirche ... E5
27 Theatinerkirche ... E2
28 Viktualienmarkt ... E5

Activities, Courses & Tours

29 Grayline Hop-on-Hop-off Tours Main Departure Point ... A3
Mike's Bike Tours ... (see 2)

Sleeping

30 Anna Hotel ... A3
31 Bayerischer Hof ... D3
32 Cocoon Stachus ... A4
33 Cortiina ... F5
34 Hotel am Viktualienmarkt ... E6
35 Hotel Blauer Bock ... D6
36 Hotel Cocoon ... A7
37 Hotel Eder ... A4
38 Hotel Mandarin Oriental Munich ... F4
39 Hotel Marienbad ... C2
40 Hotel Müller ... B7
41 Hotelissimo Haberstock ... A4
42 H'Otello Advokat ... G6
43 Schiller 5 ... A4

Eating

44 Bamyan ... D7
45 Bergwolf ... D7
46 Bratwurstherzl ... F5
47 Cafe Frischhut ... E5
48 Cafe Luitpold ... E2

is Friedrich von Gärnter's Feldherrnhalle, modelled on the Loggia dei Lanzi in Florence. It honours the Bavarian army and positively drips with testosterone; check out the statues of General Johann Tilly, who kicked the Swedes out of Munich during the Thirty Years' War; and Karl Philipp von Wrede, an ally-turned-foe of Napoleon.

It was here on 9 November 1923 that police stopped the so-called Beer Hall Putsch, Hitler's attempt to bring down the Weimar Republic (Germany's government after WWI). A fierce skirmish left 20 people, including 16 Nazis, dead. A plaque in the pavement of the square's eastern side commemorates the police officers who perished in the incident.

Hitler was subsequently tried and sentenced to five years in jail, but ended up serving a mere nine months, during which he penned his hate-filled manifesto *Mein Kampf*.

Theatinerkirche CHURCH

(Map p184; Theatinerstrasse 22; [S]Odeonsplatz)

The mustard-yellow Theatinerkirche, built to commemorate the 1662 birth of Prince Max Emanuel, was dreamed up by Swiss architect Enrico Zuccalli. Also known at St Kajetan's, it's a voluptuous design with two massive twin towers flanking a giant cupola (dome). Inside, an intensely ornate dome lords over the *Fürstengruft* (royal crypt), the final destination of several Wittelsbach rulers, including King Maximilian II (1811–1864).

MUNICH SIGHTS

Fünf Höfe   ARCHITECTURE
(Map p184; www.fuenfhoefe.de; Theatinerstrasse 15; ⓈTheatinerstrasse) Munich usually feels more cosy than cosmopolitan, but one exception is the Fünf Höfe, a ritzy shopping arcade whose modernist design is as interesting as the fancy flagship and concept stores lining its passageways. The building also houses the **Kunsthalle der Hypo-Kulturstiftung** (Map p184; www.hypo-kunsthalle.de; Theatinerstrasse 8; admission varies; ⊙10am-8pm) an art space with high-calibre changing installations. Entrances to the Fünf Höfe are on Theatinerstrasse, Salvatorstrasse, Maffeistrasse and Kardinal-Faulhaber-Strasse.

Frauenkirche   CHURCH
(Church of Our Lady; Map p184; Frauenplatz 1; admission €2; ⊙7am-7pm Sat-Wed, 7am-8.30pm Thu, 7am-6pm Fri) The landmark Frauenkirche, built 1468-88, is Munich's spiritual heart and the Mt Everest among its churches. No other building in the central city may stand taller than its onion-domed twin towers, which reach a sky-scraping 99m. From April to October, you can enjoy panoramic city views from the south tower.

Bombed to bits in WWII, the reconstruction is a soaring passage of light but otherwise fairly spartan. Of note is the epic cenotaph (empty tomb) of Ludwig the Bavarian just past the entrance and the bronze plaques of Pope Benedict XVI (born in Bavaria) and his predecessor John Paul II affixed to nearby pillars.

Michaelskirche CHURCH

(Church of St Michael; Map p184; Kaufingerstrasse 52; crypt admission €2; ⏲crypt 9.30am-4.30pm Mon-Fri, 9.30am-2.30pm Sat & Sun; [S]Karlsplatz, 🚋Karlsplatz, 🚆Karlsplatz) It stands quiet and dignified amid the retail frenzy out on Kaufingerstrasse, but to fans of Ludwig II the Michaelskirche is the ultimate place of pilgrimage. Its dank crypt is the final resting place of the Mad King, whose humble tomb is usually drowned in flowers.

Completed in 1597, St Michael's was the largest Renaissance church north of the Alps when it was built. It boasts an impressive unsupported barrel-vaulted ceiling and the massive bronze statue between the two entrances shows the archangel finishing off a dragon-like creature, a classic Counter Reformation-era symbol of Catholicism triumphing over Protestantism. The building has been, and is set to be, under heavy renovation for years but you can still go inside.

Deutsches Jagd- und Fischereimuseum MUSEUM

(German Hunting & Fishing Museum; Map p184; www.jagd-fischerei-museum.de; Neuhauser Strasse 2; adult/concession €3.50/2.50; ⏲9.30am-5pm, to 9pm Thu; [S]Karlsplatz, 🚋Karlsplatz, 🚆Karlsplatz) This old-school museum occupies three floors of a former Augustinian church and contains some intriguing items to browse, such as a rococo hunting sledge and prehistoric fishing tackle as well as plenty of stuffed critters, dioramas, trophies, weapons, paintings and porcelain embellished with hunting motifs.

MUNICH'S BEST MUSEUMS

Munich has almost 50 museums, some so vast and containing so many exhibits you could spend a whole day shuffling through a single institution. Gallery fatigue strikes many a visitor and it's easy to get your *Pinakotheks* in a twist. Be selective and take your time – there's a museum to suit all interests:

» **Curious kids** KinderReich at the Deutsches Museum (p198)

» **Petrol heads** BMW Welt (p195)

» **Tech types** Deutsches Museum (p198)

» **Design devotees** Pinakothek der Moderne (p190)

» **Dino hunters** Paläontologisches Museum (p193)

» **Sovereign stalkers** Residenzmuseum (p188)

» **Art-ficionados** Alte Pinakothek (p189)

» **History groupies** Bayerisches Nationalmuseum (p194)

RESIDENZ & AROUND

The Residenz is a suitably grand palace that reflects the splendour and power of the Wittelsbach clan, the Bavarian rulers who lived here from 1385 to 1918. The edifice dwarfs Max-Joseph-Platz along with the grandiose Nationaltheater (p216), home to the Bavarian State Opera. Its museums are among the jewels in Munich's cultural crown and an unmissable part of the Bavarian experience.

Four giant bronze **lion statues** (Map p184) guard the entrance to the palace on Residenzstrasse, supported by pedestals festooned with a half-human, half-animal face. Note the creatures' remarkably shiny noses. If you wait a moment, you'll see the reason for the sheen: scores of people walk by and casually rub one or all four noses. It's supposed to bring wealth and good luck.

Tram 19 halts outside the Residenz, though the stop is called Nationaltheater.

Residenzmuseum MUSEUM

(Map p184; ☎290 671; www.residenz-muenchen.de; Marx-Joseph-Platz; adult/child €7/free, combination ticket for the museum, Schatzkammer & Cuvilliés-Theater €13/free; ⏲9am-6pm Apr–mid-Oct, 10am-5pm mid-Oct–Mar) Home to Bavaria's Wittelsbach rulers for centuries until WWI, the Residenz is Munich's number one attraction. The amazing treasures, as well as all the trappings of their lifestyles over the centuries, are on display at the Residenzmuseum, which takes up around half of the palace. Allow at least two hours to see everything at a gallop.

Tours are in the company of a rather long-winded audioguide (free) and gone are the days when the building was divided into morning and afternoon sections, all of which means a lot of ground to cover in one go. It's worth fast-forwarding to where the prescribed route splits into short and long tours and taking the long route for the most spectacular interiors.

Approximately 90 rooms are open to the public at any one time but, as renovation work is ongoing, closures are inevitable and you may not see all the highlights.

When wandering the Residenz, don't forget that only 50 sq metres of the building's roof remained intact at the end of WWII. Most of what you see today is a meticulous post-war reconstruction.

The tours kick off at the **Grottenhof** (Grotto Court), home of the wonderful *Perseusbrunnen* (Perseus Fountain), with its namesake holding the dripping head of Medusa. Next door is the famous **Antiquarium**, a barrel-vaulted hall smothered in frescoes and built to house the Wittelsbach's enormous antique collection. It's widely regarded as the finest Renaissance interior north of the Alps.

Further along the tour route, the neo-Byzantine **Hofkirche** was built for Ludwig I in 1826. After WWII only the red-brick walls were left. It reopened as an atmospheric concert venue in 2003.

Upstairs are the **Kurfürstenzimmer** (Elector's Rooms), with some stunning Italian portraits and a passage lined with two dozen views of Italy, painted by local Romantic artist Carl Rottmann. Also up here are François Cuvilliés' **Reiche Zimmer** (Rich Rooms), a six-room extravaganza of exuberant rococo carried out by the top stucco and fresco artists of the day; they're a definite highlight. More rococo magic awaits in the **Ahnengallery** (Ancestors' Gallery), with 121 portraits of the rulers of Bavaria in chronological order.

The **Hofkapelle**, reserved for the ruler and his family, fades quickly in the memory when you see the exquisite **Reichekapelle** with its blue-and-gilt ceiling, inlaid marble and 16th-century organ. Considered the finest rococo interiors in Southern Germany, the **Steinzimmer** (Stone Room) is another spot to linger longer. It was the emperor's quarters and is awash with intricately patterned and coloured marble.

Schatzkammer der Residenz   MUSEUM
(Residence Treasury; Map p184; adult/concession/under 18yr with parents €7/6/free; ☺9am-6pm Apr–mid-Oct, 10am-5pm mid-Oct–Mar) The Residenzmuseum entrance also leads to the Schatzkammer der Residenz, a veritable banker's bonus-worth of jewel-encrusted bling of yesteryear, from golden toothpicks to finely crafted swords, miniatures in ivory to gold-entombed cosmetics trunks. The 1250 incredibly intricate and attractive items on display come in every precious

material you could imagine, including lapis lazuli, crystal, coral and amber.

Definite highlights are the Bavarian crown insignia and the ruby-and-diamond-encrusted jewellery of Queen Therese (1792–1854).

Cuvilliés-Theater   HISTORIC BUILDING, THEATRE
(Map p184; adult/child €3.50/free; ☺2-6pm Mon-Sat, from 9am Sun Apr-Jul & mid-Sep–mid-Oct, 9am-6pm daily Aug–mid-Sep, shorter hours mid-Oct–Mar) Commissioned by Maximilian III in the mid-18th century, François Cuvilliés fashioned one of Europe's finest rococo theatres. Famous for hosting the premiere of Mozart's opera *Idomeneo*, restoration work in the midnoughties revived the theatre's former glory and its stage once again hosts high-brow musical and operatic performances.

Access is limited to the auditorium, where you can take a seat and admire the four tiers of loggia (galleries), dripping with rococo embellishment, at your leisure.

Hofgarten   GARDENS
(Map p184; enter from Odeonsplatz) Office workers catching some rays during their lunch break, stylish mothers pushing prams, seniors on bikes, a gaggle of chatty nuns – everybody comes to the Hofgarten. The formal court gardens with fountains, radiant flower beds, lime tree-lined gravel paths and benches galore sits just north of the Residenz. Paths converge at the **Dianatempel** (Map p184; Hofgarten), a striking octagonal pavilion honouring the Roman goddess of the hunt.

MAXVORSTADT, SCHWABING & THE ENGLISCHER GARTEN

Visitors spending even just a few hours in the city are likely to find themselves in Maxvorstadt at some point as this district is home to Munich's Kunstareal (art district), an entire neighbourhood of top-drawer museums.

Alte Pinakothek   ART MUSEUM
(Map p196; www.pinakothek.de; Barer Strasse 27; adult/child €7/5, Sun €1, audioguide €4.50; ☺10am-8pm Tue, to 6pm Wed-Sun; ☐Pinakotheken, ☐Pinakotheken) Munich's main repository of Old European Masters is crammed with all the major players that decorated canvases between the 14th and 18th centuries. This neoclassical temple was masterminded by Leo von Klenze and is a delicacy even if you can't tell your Rembrandt from your Rubens. Nearly all the paintings were collected or commissioned by Wittelsbach

rulers; it fell to Ludwig I to unite them in a single museum.

The collection is world famous for its exceptional quality and depth, especially when it comes to German masters. The oldest works are altar paintings, of which the *Four Church Fathers* (1483) by Michael Pacher, and Lucas Cranach the Elder's *Crucifixion* (1503), an emotional rendition of the suffering Jesus, stand out.

A key room is the Dürersaal upstairs. Here hangs Albrecht Dürer's famous Christlike *Self-Portrait* (1500), showing the gaze of an artist brimming with confidence. His final major work, *The Four Apostles* (1526), depicts John, Peter, Paul and Mark as rather humble men in keeping with post-Reformation ideas. Compare this to Matthias Grünewald's *Sts Erasmus and Maurice* (1523), which shows the saints dressed in rich robes like kings.

There's a choice bunch of Dutch masters, including an altarpiece by Rogier van der Weyden called *The Adoration of the Magi* (1455), plus *The Seven Joys of Mary* (1480) by Hans Memling, *Danae* (1527) by Jan Gossaert and *The Land of Cockayne* (1567) by Pieter Bruegel the Elder. Rubens fans also have reason to rejoice. At 6m in height, his epic *Last Judgment* (1617) is so big that Klenze custom-designed the hall for it. A memorable portrait is *Hélène Fourment* (1631), a youthful beauty who was the ageing Rubens' second wife.

The Italians are represented by Botticelli, Rafael, Titian and many others, while the French collection includes paintings by Nicolas Poussin, Claude Lorrain and François Boucher. The Spanish field such heavy hitters as El Greco, Murillo and Velázquez.

Budget at least two hours for a visit and, when you're finished digesting the art, take on refreshments at the wonderfully vaulted museum cafe.

Pinakothek der Moderne ART MUSEUM
(Map p196; www.pinakothek.de; Barer Strasse 40; adult/child €10/7, Sun €1; ☺10am-6pm Tue, Wed & Fri-Sun, 10am-8pm Thu; ☒Pinakotheken, ☒Pinakotheken) Germany's largest modern art museum, the Pinakothek der Moderne opened in 2002 in a blockbusting building by Stephan Braunfels that sets the perfect stage for artists and designers who dominated their respective fields throughout the last century. The spectacular four-storey interior centres on a

vast eye-like dome, which spreads soft natural light throughout blanched-white galleries.

The museum unites four significant collections under a single roof. The State Gallery of Modern Art has some exemplary modern classics by Picasso, Klee, Dalí, Kandinsky and many lesser-known works that will be new to many visitors. More recent big shots include Georg Baselitz, Andy Warhol, Cy Twombly, Dan Flavin and enfant terrible Joseph Beuys.

In a world obsessed by retro style, the New Collection is the busiest section of the museum. Housed in the basement it focuses on applied design from the Industrial Revolution via art nouveau and Bauhaus to today. VW Beetles, Eames chairs and early Apple Macs stand alongside more obscure interwar items that wouldn't be out of place in a Kraftwerk video. There's 1960s furniture, the latest spool tape recorders and an exhibition of the weirdest jewellery you'll ever witness.

The State Graphics Collection boasts some 400,000 pieces of art on paper, including drawings, prints and engravings by such craftsmen as Leonardo da Vinci and Paul Cézanne. Because of the light-sensitive nature of these works, only a tiny fraction of the collection is shown at any given time.

Finally, there's the Architecture Museum, with entire studios of drawings, blueprints, photographs and models by such top practitioners as baroque architect Balthasar Neumann, Bauhaus maven Le Corbusier and 1920s expressionist Erich Mendelsohn.

Neue Pinakothek ART MUSEUM
(Map p196; www.pinakothek.de; Barer Strasse 29; adult/child €7/5, Sun €1; ☺10am-6pm Thu-Mon, to 8pm Wed; ☒Pinakotheken, ☒Pinakotheken) Picking up where the Alte Pinakothek leaves off, the Neue Pinakothek harbours a well-respected collection of 19th- and early 20-century paintings and sculpture, from rococo to Jugendstil (art nouveau). Its imposing original structure by Friedrich von Gärtner was destroyed in WWII and not rebuilt; since 1981 works have been housed in a modernist structure by Alexander von Branca.

All the world-famous household names get wall space here, including crowd-pleasing French impressionists such as Monet, Cézanne and Degas as well as Van Gogh, whose bold pigmented *Sunflowers* (1888) radiates cheer. There are also several works by Gauguin, including *Breton Peasant Women* (1894); and by Manet, including

Breakfast in the Studio (1869). Turner gets a look-in with his dramatically sublime *Ostende* (1844).

Perhaps the most memorable canvases, though, are by Romantic painter Caspar David Friedrich, who specialised in emotionally charged, brooding landscapes such as *Riesengebirge Landscape with Rising Mist*.

Local painters represented in the exhibition include Carl Spitzweg and Wilhelm von Kobell of the so-called Dachau School; and Munich society painters such as Wilhelm von Kaulbach, Franz Lenbach and Karl von Piloty. Another focus is on the works by the Deutschrömer (German Romans), a group of neoclassicists centred around Johann Koch, who stuck mainly to Italian landscapes.

Museum Brandhorst GALLERY

(Map p196; www.museum-brandhorst.de; Theresienstrasse 35a; adult/child €7/5, Sun €1; 🕘10am-8pm Tue, to 6pm Wed-Sun; 🚌Maxvorstadt/Sammlung Brandhorst, 🚋Pinakotheken) A big, bold and aptly abstract building, clad entirely in vividly multihued ceramic tubes, the Brandhorst jostled its way into the Munich Kunstareal in a punk blaze of colour mid-2009. Its walls, floor and occasionally ceiling provide space for some of the most challenging works of art in the city, some of them instantly recognisable 20th-century images by Andy Warhol, who dominates the collection.

In fact it's Warhol who kickstarts proceedings right at the entrance with his bolshie *Hammer and Sickle* (1976). Pop art's 1960s poster boy pops up througout and even has an entire room dedicated to pieces such as his punkish *Self Portrait* (1986), *Marilyn* (1962) and *Triple Elvis* (1963).

The other prevailing artist at the Brandhorst is the lesser known Cy Twombly. His spectacular splash-and-dribble canvasses are a bit of an acquired taste, but this is the place to acquire it if ever there was one.

Elsewhere Dan Flavin floodlights various corners with his eye-watering light installations and other big names such as Mario Merz, Alex Katz and Sigmar Polke also make an appearance. Damien Hirst gets a look-in.

Städtische Galerie im Lenbachhaus GALLERY

(Municipal Gallery; Map p196; ☎2333 2000; www.lenbachhaus.de; Luisenstrasse 33; 🕘10am-6pm Tue-Sun; 🚌Königsplatz, [S]Königsplatz) Late 19th-century portraitist Franz von Lenbach used his fortune to build a fabulous Tuscan-style home, which his widow later sold to the city for a pittance on the proviso that it be used as a museum. To get things going, she also threw in a bunch of Lenbach's works. Today the gallery fills with fans of the expressionist Blauer Reiter (Blue Rider) group founded by Wassily Kandinsky and Franz Marc in 1911.

Soon joined by August Macke, Gabriele Münter, Alexej von Jawlensky and others, they rebelled against traditional academy art and instead pursued ground-breaking visions and themes. Lenbach's portraits seem comparatively staid and retro.

Contemporary art is another focal point here. The acquisition of Joseph Beuys installation *Show Your Wound* (1977) nearly caused a riot in the conservative city council, but the collection took off anyway. All the big names are here: Gerhard Richter, Sigmar Polke, Anselm Kiefer, Andy Warhol, Dan Flavin, Richard Serra and Jenny Holzer among them.

Works are also shown in the nearby **Kunstbau** (Map p184; Luisenstrasse), a 120m-long underground tunnel above the U-Bahn station Königsplatz.

The Lenbachhaus closed in 2009 for a top-to-bottom renovation directed by stellar British architect Sir Norman Foster. By the time you read this the extended and renovated building should have reopened to the public.

Glyptothek ART MUSEUM

(Map p196; www.antike-am-koenigsplatz.mwn.de; Königsplatz 3; adult/concession €3.50/2.50, Sun €1; 🕘10am-5pm Sun-Wed, to 8pm Thu, closed Mon; 🚌Königsplatz, [S]Königsplatz) If you're a fan of classical art or simply enjoy the sight of naked guys without noses (or other pertinent body parts), make a beeline to the Glyptothek. One of Munich's oldest museums, it's a feast of art and sculpture from ancient Greece and Rome amassed by Ludwig I between 1806 and 1830,

> **[i] SUNDAY BEST**
>
> Save yourself a bailout of euros by visiting the Pinakotheken, Bayerisches Nationalmuseum, Museum Brandhorst, the Glypothek, Archäologische Staatssammlung and several other less-visited museums and galleries on a Sunday when admission to each is reduced to a symbolic €1.

Schwabing & the Englischer Garten

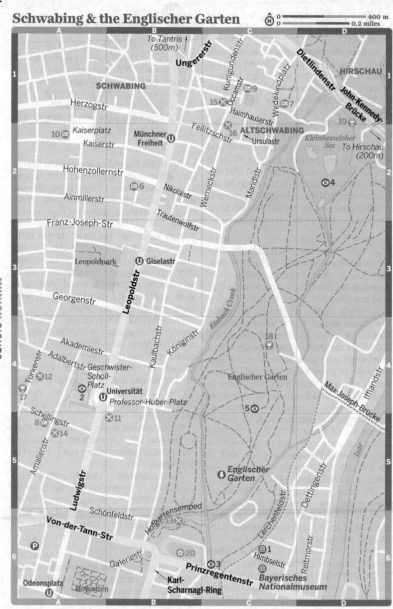

and opens a surprisingly naughty window onto the ancient world.

An undisputed highlight is the marble *Barberini Faun* (220 BC), a sleeping satyr rendered in meticulous anatomical detail and striking a pose usually assumed by centrefolds. Rooms X to XII contain superb busts, including one of a youthful Alexander the Great and several of Emperor Augustus. Also of note is the tomb relief of Mnesarete, a Greek courtesan. Don't miss the sculptures from the Aphaia Temple in Aegina

Schwabing & the Englischer Garten

Top Sights
- Bayerisches Nationalmuseum C6
- Englischer Garten C5

Sights
- 1 Archäologische Staatssammlung C6
- 2 Denk Stätte A4
- 3 Eisbach Surfers C6
- 4 Kleinhesseloher See D2
- 5 Monopteros C4

Sleeping
- 6 Cosmopolitan Hotel B2
- 7 Gästehaus Englischer Garten C1
- 8 Hotel Hauser A5
- 9 La Maison C1
- 10 Pension am Kaiserplatz A2

Eating
- 11 Café An Der Uni B5
- 12 Café Zeitgeist A4
- 13 Japanisches Teehaus B6
- 14 Pommes Boutique A5
- 15 Potting Shed C1
- 16 Tibet Kitchen C2

Drinking
- 17 Alter Simpl A4
- 18 Chinesischer Turm C4
- 19 Seehaus D1

Entertainment
- 20 P1 .... B6

with extensive supportive displays to lend context.

The inner courtyard has a calm and pleasant cafe where, in summer, classical theatre takes place under the stars.

Museum Reich der Kristalle MUSEUM
(Map p196; ☎2180 4312; Theresienstrasse 41; adult/concession €4/2; ⏲1-5pm, closed Mon; 🚋Maxvorstadt/Sammlung Brandhorst, 🚌Pinakotheken) If diamonds are your best friends, head to the Museum Reich der Kristalle, with its Fort Knox-worthy collection of gemstones and crystals, including a giant Russian emerald and meteorite fragments from Kansas.

[FREE] **Paläontologisches Museum** MUSEUM
(Palaeontological Museum; Map p196; ☎2180 6630; www.palmuc.de; Richard-Wagner-Strasse 10; admission free; ⏲8am-4pm Mon-Thu, to 2pm Fri; 🚋Königsplatz, [S]Königsplatz) The curatorial concept of the Paläontologisches Museum could use a little dusting up but otherwise this archaeological trove of prehistoric skulls and bones is anything but stuffy. The most famous resident is a fossilised archaeopteryx, the creature that forms an evolutionary link between reptile and bird.

Jurassic fans can check out the wicked horns on a triceratops skull or the delicate bone structure of a plateosaurus. What better place to bring the kids when they're passing through their 'dinosaur phase'.

Antikensammlungen MUSEUM
(Map p184; ☎5998 8830; www.antike-am-koenigsplatz.mwn.de; Königsplatz 1; adult/concession €3.50/2.50, Sun €1; ⏲10am-5pm Sun-Tue, to 8pm Wed, closed Mon; 🚋Königsplatz, [S]Königsplatz) Complementing the Glyptothek, the Antikensammlungen is an engaging showcase of exquisite Greek, Roman and Etruscan antiquities. The collection of Greek vases, each artistically decorated with gods and heroes, wars and weddings, is particularly outstanding. Other galleries present gold and silver jewellery and ornaments, figurines made from terracotta and more precious bronze, and super-fragile drinking vessels made from ancient glass.

[TOP CHOICE] **Englischer Garten** PARK
(Map p192; [S]Universität) The sprawling English Garden is among Europe's biggest city parks – it's bigger than even London's Hyde Park and New York's Central Park and is a favourite playground for locals and visitors alike. Stretching north from Prinzregentenstrasse for about 5km, it was commissioned by Elector Karl Theodor in 1789 and designed by Benjamin Thompson, an American-born scientist working as an advisor to the Bavarian government.

Paths piddle around in dark stands of mature oak and maple before emerging into sunlit meadows of lush grass. Locals are mindful of the park's popularity and tolerate the close quarters of cyclists, walkers and joggers. Street musicians dodge balls kicked by children and students sprawl on the grass to chat about missed lectures.

Sooner or later you'll find your way to the Kleinhesseloher See (Map p192), a lovely lake at the centre of the park. Work up a little sweat while taking a spin around three little islands, then quaff a well-earned foamy one at the Seehaus (Map p192; Kleinhesselohe 3; ; S Münchner Freiheit) beer garden.

Several historic follies lend the park a playful charm. The wholly unexpected Chinesischer Turm (p213) now at the heart of Munich's oldest beer garden, was built in the 18th century during a pan-European craze for all things oriental. Further south, at the top of a gentle hill, stands the heavily photographed 1838 Monopteros (Map p192), a small Greek temple whose ledges are often knee-to-knee with dangling legs belonging to people admiring the view of the Munich skyline.

Another hint of Asia awaits further south at the Japanisches Teehaus (Japanese Teahouse; Map p192; ☑224 319; ☉3pm, 4pm, 5pm Sat & Sun Apr-Oct), built for the 1972 Olympics by an idyllic duck pond. The best time to come is for an authentic tea ceremony celebrated by a Japanese tea master.

Bayerisches Nationalmuseum MUSEUM
(Map p192; www.bayerisches-nationalmuseum.de; Prinzregentenstrasse 3; adult/child €5/free, Sun €1; ☉10am-5pm Tue, Wed & Fri-Sun, to 8pm Thu; ☐Nationalmuseum/Haus Der Kunst, ☐Nationalmuseum/Haus Der Kunst) Picture the classic 19th-century museum, a palatial neo-Classical edifice overflowing with exotic treasure and thought-provoking works of art, a repository for a nation's history, a grand purpose-built display case for royal trinkets, church baubles and state-owned rarities – this is the Bavarian National Museum, a good old-fashioned museum for no-nonsense museum lovers.

Filling 40 rooms over three floors, there's a lot to get through here so be prepared for at least two hours' legwork.

Most visitors start on the first floor where hall after hall is packed with baroque, mannerist and Renaissance sculpture, ecclesiastic treasures (check out all those wobbly Gothic 'S' figures), Renaissance clothing and one-off pieces such as the 1000-year-old St Kunigunde's chest fashioned in mammoth ivory and gold. Climb to the second floor to move up in history to the rococo, Jugendstil and modern periods, represented by priceless collections of Nymphenburg and Meissen porcelain, Tiffany glass, Augsburg silver and precious items used by the Bavarian royal family. Also up here is a huge circular model of Munich in the first half of the 19th century, shortly after it was transformed into a capital fit for a kingdom.

It's easy to miss, but the building's basement also holds an evocatively displayed collection of *Krippen* (nativity scenes), some with a Cecil B DeMille-style cast of thousands. Retold in paper, wood and resin, there are Christmas story scenes here from Bohemia, Moravia and Tyrol, but the biggest contingent hails from Naples. Also here is the excellent museum shop.

Archäologische Staatssammlung MUSEUM
(State Archaeological Collection; Map p192; ☑211 2402; www.archaeologie-bayern.de; Lerchenfeldstrasse 2; adult/concession €7.50/5.50, Sun €1; ☉9.30am-5pm Tue-Sat, 10am-6pm Sun; ☐Nationalmuseum/Haus der Kunst, ☐Nationalmuseum/Haus der Kunst) It turns out Bavaria has been a popular place of residence for 120,000 years. Prehistoric Stone Age people came first, then the Romans, the Celts and finally various Germanic tribes. The Archäologische Staatssammlung opens up a window on these long-gone civilisations with cult objects, floor mosaics, jewellery, medical equipment and scores of other items.

OLYMPIAPARK & AROUND

Olympiapark OLYMPIC SITE
(Olympic Park; Map p196; www.olympiapark-muenchen.de; audio tour €7, plus €50 refundable deposit, adventure tour adult/concession €9.50/6.50, stadium tour adult/concession €7.50/5; ☉stadium tour 11am Apr-Oct; S Olympiazentrum) The area to the north of the city where soldiers once paraded and the world's first Zeppelin landed in 1909 found a new role in the 1960s as the Olympiapark. Built for the 1972 Olympic Games, it has quite a small-scale feel and some may be amazed that the games could once have been held at such a petite venue.

The complex draws people year-round with concerts, festivals and sporting events, and its swimming hall and ice-skating rink are open to the public.

A good first stop is the Info-Pavilion (☑3067 2414; ☉10am-5pm Mon-Fri, 10am-4pm Sat & Sun), which has information, maps, tour tickets and a model of the complex. Staff also rent out MP3 players for a self-guided audio tour. Tickets are also available here for the 90-minute guided Adventure

THE WHITE ROSE

Open resistance to the Nazis was rare during the Third Reich; after 1933, intimidation and the instant 'justice' of the Gestapo and SS served as powerful disincentives. One of the few groups to rebel was the ill-fated Weisse Rose (White Rose), led by Munich University students Hans and Sophie Scholl.

The nonviolent White Rose began operating in 1942, its members stealing out at night to smear 'Freedom!' and 'Down with Hitler!' on the city's walls. Soon they were printing anti-Nazi leaflets on the mass extermination of the Jews and other Nazi atrocities. One read: 'We shall not be silent – we are your guilty conscience. The White Rose will not leave you in peace.'

In February 1943, Hans and Sophie were caught distributing leaflets at the university. Together with their best friend, Christian Probst, the Scholls were arrested and charged with treason. After a summary trial, all three were found guilty and beheaded the same afternoon. Their extraordinary courage inspired the award-winning film *Sophie Scholl – Die Letzten Tage* (Sophie Scholl – The Final Days; 2005).

A memorial exhibit to the White Rose, **DenkStätte** (Map p192; Geschwister-Scholl-Platz 1; admission free; ⏲10am-4pm Mon-Fri, 11.30am-2.30pm Sat Apr-Oct) is within the Ludwig-Maximilian-Universität.

Tour, which covers the entire Olympiapark by foot and toy train.

Olympiapark has two famous eye-catchers: the 290m Olympiaturm and the warped **Olympiastadion** (Olympic Stadium; Map p196; adult/child €3/2; ⏲9am-8pm mid-May–mid-Sep, shorter hours rest of the year). Germans have a soft spot for the latter because it was on this hallowed turf in 1974 that the national soccer team – led by 'the Kaiser' Franz Beckenbauer – won the FIFA World Cup.

When the sky is clear, you'll quite literally have Munich at your feet against the breathtaking backdrop of the Alps from the top of the **Olympiaturm** (Olympic Tower; Map p196; adult/child €4.50/3; ⏲9am-midnight). Your lift ticket also buys access to the small if quirky **Rock Museum** (Map p196; ☎3067 2750; adult/concession €4/2.50; ⏲9am-midnight, last trip 11:30pm), also up on top. Ozzie Osbourne's signed guitar, a poem penned by Jim Morrison and Britney Spears' glitter jeans jostle for space with letters, photos and concert tickets, all the result of three decades of collecting by a pair of rock fans.

BMW-Welt, Museum & Plant LANDMARK, MUSEUM

(Map p196; [S]Olympiazenturm) The glass and steel double-cone tornado spiralling down from a dark cloud the size of an aircraft carrier next to the Olympiapark is the Wagnerian chunk of 21st-century architecture that holds **BMW Welt** (BMW World; ☎01802-118 822; www.bmw-welt.de; admission free, tours adult/child €7/5; ⏲9am-6pm). This is truly a petrol head's wet dream. Apart from its role as a prestigious car pick-up centre (new owners fork out €500 for the privilege), this king of car showrooms acts as a kind of shop window for BMW's latest models and a show space for the company as a whole.

Straddle a powerful motorbike, marvel at technology-packed saloons and estates (no tyre kicking please), browse the 'lifestyle' shop or take the 80-minute guided tour. On the Junior Campus, kids learn about mobility, fancy themselves car engineers and even get to design their own vehicle in workshops. Hang around long enough and you're sure to see motorbike stunts on the staircases and other petroleum-fuelled antics. The venue also hosts jazz and classical music concerts.

BMW Welt is linked via a bridge to BMW Headquarters – another stunning building of four gleaming cylinders – and to the silver bowl-shaped **BMW Museum** (Map p196; www.bmw-welt.de; adult/child €12/6; ⏲10am-6pm Tue-Sun). Redesigned from scratch and reopened in 2008, it's like no other car museum on the planet. The seven themed 'houses' examine the development of BMW's product line and include sections on motorcycles and motor racing. However, the interior design of this truly unique building, with its curvy retro feel, futuristic bridges, squares and huge backlit wall screens, almost upstages the exhibits.

With some planning, you can also tour the belly of the beast, the adjacent **BMW Plant** (☎01802-118 822; tours adult/child €8/5; ⏲Mon-Fri). Reservations are required and can be made up to six months in advance.

Nymphenburg, Neuhausen & Olympiapark

Belgrad Str

Luitpoldpark

Petuelring

Dostlerstr

Scheidplatz

Info-Pavilion

Olympiazentrum

Georg-Brauchle-Ring

Landshuter Allee

Georg-Brauchle-Ring

Westfriedhof

MOOSACH

BORSTEI

Dachauer Str

Taxistr

Waisenhaustr

Gern

GERN

Baldurstr

Hugo-Troendle-Str

Menzingerstr

Notburgastr

In den Kirschen

NEULUSTHEIM
Schlosspark

NYMPHENBURG
Nymphenburg

Nördliches
Schlossrondell

Südliches
Schlossrondell

Laimer Str

Wotanstr

To Laim S-Bahn
Station (400m)

Auffahrtsallee

Zamboninistr

Tizianstr

Prinzenstr

Romanstr

Lachnerstr

Washington-Str

Wendl-Dietrich-Str

Rotkreuzplatz
Rotkreuzplatz-Str

Königinstr

Königbauerstr

De-La-Paz-Str

To Backstage
(350m)

Wilhelm-
Hale-Str

Arnulfstr

Orffstr
Frundsbergstr

Platz der
Freiheit

Nymphenburger Str

Mailingstr

Albrechtstr

Blutenburgstr

Lazarettstr

NEUHAUSEN

Leonrodstr

Dachauer Str

Dachauer

Landshuter Allee

Ackermannstr

GEORGENSCHWAIGE

Lerchenauer Str

Olympiapark

Olympiaberg

Olympiapark

Olympic
Stadium Olympiastadion

Olympiastadion

Schwere-Reiter-Str

Hessstr

Schleissheimer Str

Herzogstr

Hohenzollernplatz

Elisabethstr

Museum
Brandhorst

Josephsplatz

Luisenstr

Theresienstr

Schellingstr

Alte
Pinakothek

Pinakothek
der Moderne

Neuherz-Str

Karlstr

Stiglmaierplatz

To Circus Krone (50m)

Georg-Brauchle-Ring

Wilhelm-

Nymphenburg, Neuhausen & Olympiapark

MUNICH SIGHTS

Tours (also in English) last 2½ hours, and children under four are not allowed.

SCHLOSS NYMPHENBURG

Schloss Nymphenburg PALACE
(Map p196; ☑179 080; www.schloss-nymphenburg.de; adult/child €6/5; ⊙9am-6pm Apr–mid-Oct, 10am-4pm mid-Oct–Mar; ⓐSchloss Nymphenburg) This commanding palace and its lavish gardens sprawl around 5km northwest of the Altstadt. Begun in 1664 as a villa for Electress Adelaide of Savoy, the stately pile was extended over the next century to create the royal family's summer residence. Franz, Duke of Bavaria, head of the once-royal Wittelsbach family, still occupies an apartment here.

The main palace building consists of a large villa and two wings of creaking parquet floors and sumptuous period rooms. Right at the beginning of the self-guided tour comes the high point of the entire Schloss, the Schönheitengalerie (Gallery of Beauties), housed in the former apartments of Queen Caroline. Some 38 portraits of attractive females chosen by an admiring King Ludwig I peer prettily from the walls. The most famous image is of Helene Sedlmayr, the daughter of a shoemaker, wearing a lavish frock the king gave her for the sitting. You'll also find Ludwig's beautiful, but notorious, lover Lola Montez, as well as 19th-century gossip-column celebrity Jane Lady Ellenborough and English beauty Lady Jane Erskin.

Further along the tour route comes the Queen's Bedroom, which still contains the sleigh bed on which Ludwig II was born, and the **King's Chamber**, resplendent with three-dimentional ceiling frescoes.

Also in the main building is the Marstall-museum (Map p196; adult/concession €4.50/3.50; ⊙9am-6pm Apr–mid-Oct, 10am-4pm mid-Oct–Mar), displaying royal coaches and riding gear. This includes Ludwig II's fairy-tale-like rococo sleigh, ingeniously fitted with oil lamps for his crazed nocturnal outings. Upstairs is the world's largest collection of old porcelain made by the famous Nymphenburger Manufaktur. Also known

THE GAMES MUST GO ON

The 1972 Summer Olympics were particularly significant for Munich as they gave the city a chance to make a historic break with the past. It was the first time the country would host the prestigious sporting event since 1936, when the games were held in Berlin under Hitler. The motto was the 'Happy Games', and the emblem was a blue sun spiral. The city built an innovative Olympic Park, which included the tent-like plexiglass canopies that were revolutionary for the times. It was the perfect opportunity to present a new, democratic Germany full of pride and optimism.

But in the final week of the games disaster struck. Members of a Palestinian terrorist group known as 'Black September' killed two Israeli athletes and took nine others hostage at the Olympic Village, demanding the release of political prisoners and an escape aircraft. During a failed rescue attempt by German security forces at Fürstenfeldbruck, a military base west of Munich, all of the hostages and most of the terrorists were killed. Competition was suspended briefly before Avery Brundage, the International Olympic Committee president, famously declared 'the Games must go on'. The bloody incident cast a pall over the entire Olympics and over sporting events in Germany for years to follow.

These tragic events are chronicled in an Oscar-winning documentary, *One Day in September* (1999) by Kevin McDonald, as well as in Steven Spielberg's historical fictional account, *Munich* (2005). The killings prompted German security to rethink its methods and create the elite counter-terrorist unit, GSG 9.

as the Sammlung Bäuml, it presents the entire product palette from the company's founding in 1747 until 1930.

The sprawling park behind Schloss Nymphenburg is a favourite spot with Münchners and visitors for strolling, jogging or whiling away a lazy afternoon. It's laid out in grand English style and accented with water features, including a large lake, a cascade and a canal, popular for feeding swans and for ice skating and ice curling when it freezes over in winter.

The park is at its most magical without the masses, early in the morning and an hour before closing. But even in the daytime you can usually commune in solitude with waterlilies and singing frogs at the Kugelweiher pond in the far northern corner.

The park's chief folly, the Amalienburg (Map p196; adult/concession €2/1), is a small hunting lodge dripping with crystal and gilt decoration; don't miss the amazing Spiegelsaal (hall of mirrors). The two-storey Pagodenburg (Map p196; adult/concession €2/1) was built in the early 18th century as a Chinese teahouse and is swathed in ceramic tiles depicting landscapes, figures and floral ornamentation. The Badenburg (Map p196; adult/concession €2/1) is a sauna and bathing house that still has its original heating system. Finally, the Magdalenenklause (adult/concession €2/1) was built as a mock hermit-age in faux ruined style. A combination ticket to all four park buildings costs €4.50/3.50 per adult/child.

HAIDHAUSEN & LEHEL

TOP CHOICE Deutsches Museum   MUSEUM

(Map p200; ☎217 91; www.deutsches-museum.de; Museumsinsel 1; adult/child €8.50/3; ◐9am-5pm; 🚇Deutsches Museum) If you're one of those people for whom science is an unfathomable turn-off, a visit to the Deutsches Museum might just show you that physics and engineering are more fun than you thought. Spending a few hours in this temple to technology is an eye-opening journey of discovery and the exhibitions and demonstrations will certainly be a hit with young, sponge-like minds.

There are tons of interactive displays (including glass blowing and paper making), live demonstrations and experiments, model coal and salt mines, and engaging sections on cave paintings, geodesy, microelectronics and astronomy. In fact, it can be pretty overwhelming after a while, so it's best to prioritise what you want to see. The place to entertain little ones is the fabulous Kinder-Reich (Childrens Kingdom; ◐9am-4.30pm) where 1000 activities, from a kid-size mouse wheel to a fully explorable fire engine and heaps of colourful blocks, await.

The Deutsches Museum's collection is so huge that some sections have been moved to separate locations. Vehicles are now in the Verkehrszentrum (p199), while aircraft are at the Flugwerft Schleissheim (p225). Combination tickets to all three museums cost €15 and may be used on separate days

WESTEND & THERESIENWIESE

Theresienwiese OKTOBERFEST GROUNDS
(Map p208; S Theresienwiese) The Theresienwiese (Theresa Meadow), better known as Wiesn, just southwest of the Altstadt is the site of the Oktoberfest. At the western end of the meadow is the Ruhmeshalle (Map p208; Hall of Fame; admission free) guarding solemn statues of Bavarian leaders, as well as the statue of Bavaria (Map p208; 290 671; adult/concession/under 18 €3.50/2.50/free; 9am-6pm Apr–mid-Oct, to 8pm during Oktoberfest), an 18m-high Amazon in the Statue of Liberty tradition, oak wreath in hand and lion at her feet.

This iron lady has a cunning design that makes her seem solid, but actually you can climb via the knee joint up to the head for a great view of the Oktoberfest. At other times, views are not particularly inspiring.

Verkehrszentrum MUSEUM
(Transport & Mobility Centre; Map p208; 500 806 762; www.deutsches-museum.de/verkehrszentrum; Theresienhöhe 14a; adult/child €6/3; 9am-5pm; S Theresienwiese) Sheltered in a historic trade-fair complex, the Verkehrszentrum features some fascinating exhibits, with hands-on displays about pioneering research and famous inventions, plus cars, boats and trains, and the history of car racing. Another section shows off the Deutsches Museum's entire vehicle collection, from the first motorcars to high-speed ICE (inter-city express) trains.

OUTER DISTRICTS

Tierpark Hellabrunn ZOO
(Hellabrunn Zoo; 625 080; www.tierpark-hellabrunn.de; Tierparkstrasse 30; adult/child €11/4.50; 9am-6pm Apr-Sep, to 5pm Oct-Mar; 52 from Marienplatz) Some 6km south of the city centre, Tierpark Hellabrunn has 5000 furry, feathered and finned friends that rarely fail to enthral the little ones. It was one of the first in the world to be set up like a geo-zoo with spacious natural habitats dividing animals by continent.

Kids can get all touchy-feely with the animals at the large petting zoo where tots get to feed deer and goats. Other crowd pleasers include the Villa Dracula (inhabited by bats, what else?), the penguins and polar bears in the Polarium, and the Orang-utan Paradise.

Allianz Arena STADIUM
(tour 01805-555 101; www.allianz-arena.de; Werner-Heisenberg-Allee 25, Fröttmaning; tour adult/child €10/6.50; tours 1pm, in English; S Fröttmaning) Sporting and architecture fans alike should take a side trip to the northern suburb of Fröttmaning, 9km north of the city centre, to see the ultraslick €340 million Allianz Arena, Munich's dramatic football stadium. The 75-minute stadium tours are hugely popular (no tours on match days); tickets are available from the 3rd-floor gift shop.

Nicknamed the life belt and rubber boat, it has walls made of inflatable cushions that can be individually lit to match the colours of the host team (red for FC Bayern, blue for TSV 1860 and white for the national side).

Activities

Boating
A lovely spot to take your sweetheart for a spin is on the Kleinhesseloher See in the English Garden. Rowing or pedal boats cost around €8 per half-hour for up to four people. Boats may also be hired at the Olympiapark.

Cycling
Munich is an excellent place for cycling, particularly along the Isar River. Some 1200km

UP ON THE ROOF

Can't make it to the Alps for a high-altitude clamber? No matter. Just head to the Olympic Stadium for a walk on the roof (adult/concessions €41/31; 2.30pm daily Apr-Oct). Yup, the roof – that famously contorted steel-and-plexiglass confection is ready for its close-up. Just like in the mountains, you'll be roped and hooked up to a steel cable as you clamber around under the eagle-eyed supervision of an experienced guide showering you with fascinating details about the stadium's architecture and construction. The minimum age is 10 and expeditions last two hours. Wear rubber-soled shoes.

Lehel & Haidhausen

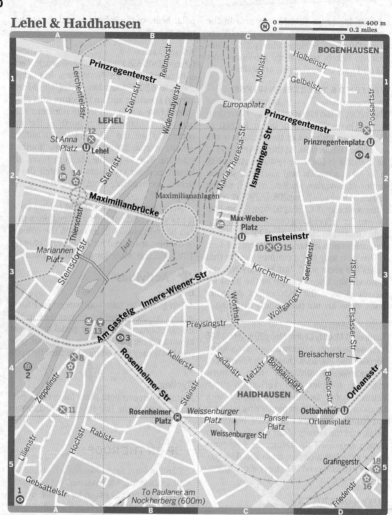

of cycle paths within the city limits make it one of Europe's friendliest places for two-wheelers.

Swimming

Bathing in the Isar River isn't advisable because of strong and unpredictable currents (especially in the English Garden).

The best public swimming pool options, both indoors, are the Olympia Schwimmhalle (Map p196; www.swm.de; Coubertinplatz 1; 3hr pass adult/concession €4.20/3.20; ⊘7am-11pm; ⓢOlympiazentrum), where Mark Spitz famously won seven gold medals in 1972;

and the spectacular Müller'sches Volksbad (Map p200; Rosenheimer Strasse 1; adult/child €4/3.10; ⊘7.30am-11pm; ⓐAm Gasteig), where you can swim in art-nouveau splendour.

Tours

For a budget tour of Munich's high-brow collections, hop aboard bus 100 Museenlinie, which runs from the Hauptbahnhof (p222) (central station) to the Ostbahnhof (east station) via 21 of the city's museums and galleries including all the big hitters. As this is an

Lehel & Haidhausen

ordinary bus route, the tour costs no more than a public transport ticket.

Radius Tours   GUIDED TOUR
(Map p208; ☑543 487 7720; www.radiustours.com; opposite track 32, Hauptbahnhof; ⊙8.30am-6pm Apr-Oct, to 2pm Nov-Mar) Entertaining and informative English-language tours include the two-hour **Priceless Munich** (⊙10am daily) walk where you pay the guide as much as you think the tour was worth; the fascinating 2.5-hour **Hitler and the Third Reich** (adult/student €12/10; ⊙3pm Apr–mid-Oct, 11.30am Fri-Tue mid-Oct–Mar) tour; and the three-hour **Prost! Beer and Food** (adult/student €22/€20; ⊙6pm selected days) tour. The company also runs popular excursions to Neuschwanstein, Salzburg and Dachau as well as a range of other themed tours.

Mike's Bike Tours   BIKE TOUR
(Map p184; ☑2554 3987; www.mikesbiketours. com; departs Altes Rathaus, Marienplatz; tours from €24) This outfit runs guided bike tours of the city from the Altes Rathaus on Marienplatz. The standard tour is around four hours long (with a one-hour beer garden break; lunch not included); the extended tour runs for seven hours and covers 15km.

New Munich   WALKING TOUR
(www.newmunich.com; ⊙10.45am & 1pm) Departing from Marienplatz, these English-language walking tours tick off all Munich's central landmarks in three hours. Guides are well informed and fun, though they are under pressure to get as much as they can in tips at the end of the tour. The company runs

a number of other tours to Dachau (€21) and Neuschwanstein (€35), as well as a four-hour pub crawl (€14) from the Hauptbahnhof.

Munich Walk Tours   WALKING TOUR
(Map p208; ☑2423 1767; www.munichwalktours. de; Arnulfstrasse 2; tours from €12) In addition to running an almost identical roster to Munich's other tour companies and acting as an agent for them (see website for times and prices), this place also rents out bicycles (€15 per 24 hours) and offers internet access (€1 per 45 minutes).

Grayline Hop-On-Hop-Off Tours   BUS TOURS
(www.grayline.com/munich; adult/child from €13/7; ⊙every 20min) This tour bus company offers a choice of three tours from one-hour highlights to 2.5-hour grand tour, as well as excursions to Ludwig II's castles, the Romantic Road, Dachau, Berchtesgaden, Zugspitze and Salzburg. All tours can be booked online and buses are of a recent vintage. The main **departure point** (Map p184) is outside the Karstadt department store opposite the Hauptbahnhof.

✪ Festivals & Events

Munich always has something to celebrate. For details check www.muenchen-tourist.de.

January–March

Fasching   CARNIVAL
A carnival beginning on 7 January and ending on Ash Wednesday involving all kinds of merriment such as costume parades and fancy-dress balls.

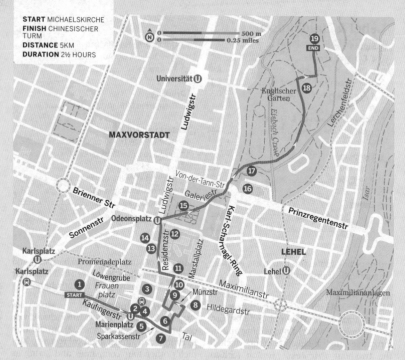

START MICHAELSKIRCHE
FINISH CHINESISCHER TURM
DISTANCE 5KM
DURATION 2½ HOURS

Walking Tour
Munich Altstadt

This Altstadt circuit takes in the key sights in Munich's historic centre and the Englischer Garten. Start at the ❶ **Michaelskirche**, a richly ornamented church and the final resting place of King Ludwig II. Proceed east along the main shopping drag until the way opens into Marienplatz, the old town square, punctuated by the ❷ **Mariensäule** in front of the neo-Gothic ❸ **Neues Rathaus**. The blue-bottomed ❹ **Fischbrunnen** gushes peacefully near the entrance. The steeple of ❺ **St Peterskirche** affords a great vista of the old town, including the ❻ **Altes Rathaus**, now home to a toy museum. To see Asam frescoes, peek inside the ❼ **Heiliggeistkirche**.

Head east on Im Tal, taking a left into Maderbräustrasse to Orlandostrasse, site of the ❽ **Hofbräuhaus**, Munich's most (in)famous beer hall. Then zigzag through the backstreets – west on Münzstrasse, left into Sparkassenstrasse and then into the alley Ledererstrasse. At Burgstrasse, turn right into the courtyard of the ❾ **Alter Hof**, the Wittelsbach's early residence in Munich. Exit north and proceed along Hofgraben, past the former ❿ **Münzhof** (mint). The street opens into Maximilian-strasse and Max-Joseph-Platz, address of the grand ⓫ **Nationaltheater** and fine opera. A treasure-filled palace and museum, the ⓬ **Residenz** was the seat of the Wittelsbach rulers for over four centuries.

Stroll north on Residenzstrasse to reach Odeonsplatz. Here looms the ⓭ **Feldherrnhalle**, a hulking shrine to war heroes. The mustard-yellow ⓮ **Theatinerkirche** contains the Wittelsbach's family crypt. Head into green territory from here, starting with the neoclassical ⓯ **Hofgarten**. Cross it diagonally and go through the underpass to enter the Englischer Garten. Proceed past the sinister-looking ⓰ **Haus der Kunst**, a gallery and one-time forum for Nazi art propaganda. The route winds past the ceremonial ⓱ **Japanisches Teehaus** and into a vast meadow popular with frisbee experts and nude sunbathers. A little hill with a classical folly, the ⓲ **Monopteros**, completes the leisurely scene. At the end, plop down in the beer garden alongside the curious, multi-tiered ⓳ **Chinesischer Turm** where an oompah band pumps out traditional tunes.

Starkbierzeit
BEER FESTIVAL

Salvator, Optimator, Unimator, Maximator and Triumphator are not the names of gladiators but in fact potent *doppelbock* brews de-kegged only between Shrovetide and Easter each year. Monks allegedly invented them to ease hunger pangs during Lent. The Paulaner am Nockherberg (☎459 9130; Hochstrasse 77) and Löwenbräukeller (Map p196; ☎526 021; Nymphenburger Strasse 2; ⊙10am-midnight; Ⓢ Stiglmaierplatz) are the places to experience festivities, though many others also serve the beer.

April–June
Frühlingsfest
BEER FESTIVAL

This mini-Oktoberfest kicks off the outdoor festival season with two weeks of beer and attractions at Theresienwiese starting around 20 April.

Maidult
MARKET

The first of three traditional dult fairs, when an open-air market takes over the Mariahilfplatz. Starts on the Saturday preceding 1 May.

Filmfest München
FILM FESTIVAL

(www.filmfest-muenchen.de) Not as glamorous as Cannes or Venice, this flick festival presents intriguing and often high-calibre fare by newbies and masters from around the world in the first week of July.

Tollwood Summer Festival
MUSIC FESTIVAL

(☎383 8500; www.tollwood.de) A world culture gala with nightly music concerts at the Olympiapark.

July–September
Christopher Street Day
GAY FESTIVAL

(www.csd-munich.de) Gay festival and parade culminating in a big street party on Marienplatz. Usually held on the second weekend in July.

Jakobidult
MARKET

The second dult (see Maidult earlier) starts on the Saturday following 25 July and continues for one week.

Opernfestspiele
MUSIC FESTIVAL

(Opera Festival; www.muenchner-opern-festspiele.de) The Bavarian State Opera brings in top-notch talent from around the world for this month-long festival, which takes place at numerous venues around the city throughout July.

NO WAVE GOODBYE

Possibly the last sport you might expect to see in Munich is surfing, but go to the southern tip of the English Garden at Prinzregentenstrasse and you'll see scores of people leaning over a bridge to cheer on wetsuit-clad daredevils as they hang on an artificially created wave in the Eisbach (Map p192). It's only a single wave, but its a damn fine one; in fact, the surfers are such an attraction, the tourist office even includes them in its brochures. A few years ago park authorities attempted to ban this watery entertainment, but a successful campaign by surfers saw plans to turn the wave off shelved. Now some of the board riders have even put in an application for their sport (river surfing) to be included in the Olympics!

To find out more about Munich's urban surfers log on to www.eisbachwelle.de.

October–December
Oktoberfest
BEER FESTIVAL

(www.oktoberfest.de) Legendary beer-swilling party running from mid-September to the first Sunday in October, held on the Theresienwiese (p204).

Munich Marathon
MARATHON

(www.muenchenmarathon.de) More than 10,000 runners from around the world take to the streets in mid-October, finishing after just over 42km at the Olympic Stadium.

Christkindlmarkt
CHRISTMAS MARKET

(Map p200; www.christkindlmarkt.de; ⊙late Nov-Christmas Eve) Traditional Christmas market on Marienplatz and a visual stunner.

🛏 Sleeping

Room rates in Munich tend to be high, and skyrocket during the Oktoberfest. Book well ahead. Budget travellers are spoilt for choice around the Hauptbahnhof, where the majority of hostels congregate, but the Altstadt has the most top-end hotels.

ALTSTADT & AROUND
TOP CHOICE Bayerischer Hof
HOTEL €€€

(Map p184; ☎212 00; www.bayerischerhof.de; Promenadeplatz 2-6; r €250-450; ❄@🛜✉;

OKTOBERFEST

It all started as an elaborate wedding toast – and turned into the world's biggest collective booze-up. In October 1810 the future king, Bavarian Crown Prince Ludwig I, married Princess Therese and the newlyweds threw an enormous party at the city gates, complete with a horse race. The next year Ludwig's fun-loving subjects came back for more. The festival was extended and, to fend off autumn, was moved forward to September. As the years rolled on, the racehorses were dropped and sometimes the party had to be cancelled, but the institution called Oktoberfest was here to stay.

Nearly two centuries later, this 16-day extravaganza draws more than six million visitors a year to celebrate a marriage of good cheer and outright debauchery. A special beer is brewed for the occasion (Wies'nbier), which is dark and strong. Müncheners spend the day at the office in lederhosen and dirndl in order to hit the festival right after work. It is Bavaria's largest tourist draw, generating about €1 billion in business. No admission is charged but most of the fun costs something.

On the meadow called Theresienwiese (Wiesn for short), a temporary city is erected, consisting of beer tents, amusements and rides – just what drinkers need after several frothy ones! The action kicks off with the Brewer's Parade at 11am on the first day of the festival. The parade begins at Sonnenstrasse and winds its way to the fairgrounds via Schwanthalerstrasse. At noon, the lord mayor stands before the thirsty crowds at Theresienwiese and, with due pomp, slams a wooden tap into a cask of beer. As the beer gushes out, the mayor exclaims, O'zapft ist's! (it's tapped!). The next day resembles the opening of the Olympics, as a young woman on horseback leads a parade of costumed participants from all over the world.

Hotels book out very quickly and prices skyrocket, so reserve accommodation as early as you can (like a year in advance). The festival is a 15-minute walk southwest of the Hauptbahnhof, and is served by its own U-Bahn station, Theresienwiese. Trams and buses have signs reading Zur Festwiese (literally 'to the Festival Meadow').

Theatinerstrasse) One of the grande dames of the Munich hotel trade, rooms at the Hof come in a number of styles, from busy Laura Ashley to minimalist cosmopolitan. The super-central location, pool and on-site cinema come in addition to impeccably behaved staff. Marble, antiques and oil paintings abound, and with ample cash you can dine till you burst at any one of the five fabulous restaurants.

Cortiina
HOTEL €€€
(Map p184; 242 2490; www.cortiina.com; Ledererstrasse 8; s €165-270, d €225-345; P✳🛜; SMarienplatz, ⓇMarienplatz) Tiptoeing between hip and haute, this hotel scores best with trendy, design-minded travellers. The street-level lounge usually buzzes with cocktail-swigging belles and beaus, but all traces of hustle evaporate the moment you step into your minimalist, feng shui-inspired room. Breakfast is an unappetising €19.50 extra.

Hotel Mandarin Oriental Munich
HOTEL €€€
(Map p184; 290 980; www.mandarinoriental.com; Neuturmstrasse 1; d €525-645; P✳@🛜🍸;

SMarienplatz, ⓇMarienplatz) These magnificent neo-Renaissance digs lure the world's glamorous, powerful and famous with opulently understated rooms and top-notch service. Paul McCartney, Bill Clinton and Prince Charles have crumpled the sheets here. Service is polite almost to a fault, but incredibly breakfast and internet access are extra.

Hotel Blauer Bock
HOTEL €€
(Map p184; 231 780; www.hotelblauerbock.de; Sebastiansplatz 9; s €55-99, d €90-153; 🛜; SMarienplatz, ⓇMarienplatz) A stuffed olive's throw away from the Viktualienmarkt, this simple hotel has successfully slipped through the net of gentrification to become the Altstadt's best deal. The cheapest, unmodernised rooms have shared facilities, the updated en-suite chambers are of a 21st-century vintage, and all are quiet, despite the location. Superb restaurant.

H'Otello Advokat
BOUTIQUE HOTEL €€
(Map p184; 4583 1200; www.hotel-advokat.de; Baaderstrasse 1; r from €135; 🛜; ⓈIsartor, ⓇIsartor) Though now not as excitingly different as it once was, Munich's first boutique hotel

is all about understated retro design and amiable service. Rooms won't fit a tonne of luggage but are nicely dressed in creamy hues, tactile fabrics and subtle lighting. Guests rave about the breakfast: a smorgasbord of fresh fruit, deli salads, smoked salmon and organic cheeses.

Hotel am Viktualienmarkt HOTEL €€
(Map p184; ☎231 1090; www.hotel-am-viktualienmarkt.de; Utzschneiderstrasse 14; d €50-120; 📶; [S]Marienplatz, [U]Marienplatz) Owners Elke and her daughter Stephanie run this good-value property with panache and a sunny attitude. The best of the 26 up-to-date rooms have wooden floors and framed poster art. All this, plus the city-centre location, makes it a superb deal.

AROUND THE HAUPTBAHNHOF

Anna Hotel DESIGN HOTEL €€€
(Map p184; ☎599 940; www.geisel-privathotels.de; Schützenstrasse 1; s €160-215, d €175-235; ❄@; [S]Karlsplatz, 🚋Karlsplatz, [U]Karlsplatz) Urban sophisticates love this designer den where you can retire to rooms dressed in sensuous Donghia furniture and regal colours, or others with a minimalist feel tempered by teakwood, marble and mosaics. The swanky restaurant-bar here is a 24/7 beehive of activity.

Hotel Cocoon DESIGN HOTEL €€
(Map p184; ☎5999 3907; www.hotel-cocoon.de; Lindwurmstrasse 35; s/d €79/99; [S]Sendlinger Tor, 🚋Sendlinger Tor) If retro design is your thing, you just struck gold. Things kick off in the reception with faux '70s veneer and suspended '60s ball chairs, and continue in

MUNICH FOR CHILDREN

(Tiny) hands down, Munich is a great city for children, with plenty of activities to please even the most attention-span-challenged tots. There are plenty of parks for romping around, swimming pools and lakes for cooling off and family-friendly beer gardens with children's playgrounds for making new friends. Many museums have special kid-oriented programs, but the highly interactive KinderReich at the Deutsches Museum (p198) specifically lures the single-digit set.

Kids love animals, of course, making the zoo Tierpark Hellabrunn (p199) a sure bet. Petting baby goats, feeding pelicans, watching falcons and hawks perform, or even riding a camel should make for some unforgettable memories. For a fishy immersion head to the new **SeaLife München** (Map p196; Willi-Daume-Platz 1; adult/child 3-14yr €15.95/10.50; ⏲10am-7pm; [S]Olympiazentrum) in the Olympic Park. Dino fans gravitate to the Paläontologisches Museum (p193), while budding scientists will find plenty to marvel at in the **Museum Mensch und Natur** (Museum of Humankind & Nature; Map p196; ☎179 5890; www.musmn.de; Schloss Nymphenburg; adult/child €3/2, Sun €1; ⏲9am-5pm Tue, Wed & Fri, to 8pm Thu, 10am-6pm Sat & Sun; 🚋Schloss Nymphenburg) in Schloss Nymphenburg. The Spielzeugmuseum (p182) is of the look-but-don't-touch variety, but kids might still get a kick out of seeing what toys grandma used to pester for.

The adorable singing and dancing marionettes performing at the **Münchner Marionettentheater** (Map p184; ☎265 712; www.muenchner-marionettentheater.de; Blumenstrasse 32; tickets €8-18; ⏲3pm Wed-Sun, 8pm Sat) have enthralled generations of wee ones. At the **Münchner Theater für Kinder** (Map p196; ☎594 545; www.muenchner-theater-fuer-kinder.de; Dachauer Strasse 46; tickets €8-11) budding thespians can enjoy fairy tales and children's classics à la *Max & Moritz* and *Pinocchio*. In winter, a show at the venerable **Circus Krone** (☎545 8000; www.circus-krone.de; Zirkus-Krone-Strasse 1-6; tickets from €15; 🚋Hackerbrücke) is a magical experience.

For hands-on fun head to the **Dschungelpalast** (☎7248 8441; www.dschungelpalast.de; Hansastrasse 41), which organises low-cost arts and crafts workshops and a Sunday family brunch.

If you happen to be in Neuhausen, near Schloss Nymphenburg, swing by **Brauseschwein** (Map p196; ☎1395 8112; Frundsbergstrasse 52; ⏲10am-1pm & 3-6.30pm Mon-Fri, 11am-2pm Sat), a wacky toy shop selling everything from penny candy to joke articles and wooden trains. Another great little shop for kids and nostalgic parents alike is **Puppenstube** (Map p196; Luisenstrasse 68), an entire emporium hung with dolls and puppets of yesteryear and today.

the rooms, which are all identical in cool oranges and greens. Every room has LCD TV, iPod dock, 'laptop cabin' and the hotel name above every bed in 1980s-style robotic lettering. The glass showers actually stand in the sleeping area, with only a kitschy Alpine meadow scene veiling life's vitals. Another branch, **Cocoon Stachus** (Map p184; Adolf-Kolping-Strasse 11), opened in 2012.

Schiller 5 HOTEL €€
(Map p184; ☎515 040; www.schiller5.com; Schillerstrasse 5; s/d from €102/144; [P]❄📶; [S]Hauptbahnhof, 🚊Hauptbahnhof, 🚆Hauptbahnhof) Not only are the pads at this semi-apartment hotel smartly trimmed, you also get a lot for your euro here in the shape of a well-equipped kitchenette, sound system, coffee machine and extra large bed in every room. Some guests complain of street noise so try to bag a room away from the hustle below.

Hotel Eder HOTEL €€
(Map p184; ☎554 660; www.hotel-eder.de; Zweigstrasse 8; s €55-140, d €65-190; 📶; [S]Hauptbahnhof, 🚊Hauptbahnhof, 🚆Hauptbahnhof) Like five storeys of small-town Bavaria teleported to the slightly seedy area south of the Hauptbahnhof, this rustic oasis has its chequered curtains, carved-wood chairs and Sisi/Ludwig II portraits firmly in place for those who didn't come all this way for the cocktails. The unevenly sized rooms are a bit vanilla, but when rates are mid to low this is a nifty deal.

Sofitel Munich Bayerpost HOTEL €€€
(Map p208; ☎599 480; www.sofitel.com; Bayerstrasse 12; s/d from €140/160; [P]❄@🏊; [S]Hauptbahnhof, 🚊Hauptbahnhof Süd, 🚆Hauptbahnhof) The restored Renaissance facade of a former post office hides this high-concept jewel, which wraps all that's great about Munich – history, innovation, elegance, the art of living – into one neat and appealing package. Be sure to make time for the luxurious spa; it's grotto-like pool juts into the atrium lobby lidded by a tinted glass roof.

Hotelissimo Haberstock HOTEL €€
(Map p184; ☎557 855; www.hotelissimo.com; Schillerstrasse 4; s/d from €74/104; 📶; [S]Hauptbahnhof, 🚊Hauptbahnhof, 🚆Hauptbahnhof) The cheery decor at this value-for-money pick reflects the vision of the owners, a husband-and-wife team with a knack for colour, fabrics and design. Easy-on-the-eye gold, brown and cream tones dominate the good-sized rooms on the lower floors, while upper rooms radiate a bolder, Mediterranean palette.

Hotel Müller HOTEL €€
(Map p184; ☎232 3860; www.hotel-mueller-muenchen.de; Fliegenstrasse 4; s/d €119/139; [P]📶; [S]Sendlinger Tor) This friendly hotel has big, bright, business-standard rooms and good price-to-quality ratio with five-star breakfasts and well-regimented staff. Despite being in the city centre, the side-street location is pretty quiet.

Wombat's Hostel HOSTEL €
(Map p208; ☎5998 9180; www.wombats-hostels.com; Senefelderstrasse 1; dm €12-24, d from €70; @📶; [S]Hauptbahnhof, 🚊Hauptbahnhof, 🚆Hauptbahnhof) Munich's top hostel is a professionally run affair with a whopping 300 dorm beds plus private rooms. Dorms are basic with no frill or theme, but with en-suite facilities, sturdy lockers and comfy pine bunks in a central location near the train station, who needs gimmicks? A free welcome drink awaits in the bar, but breakfast is €3.80 extra.

Meininger's HOSTEL, HOTEL €
(Map p208; ☎5499 8023; www.meininger-hostels.de; Landsbergerstrasse 20; dm/s/d without breakfast from €15/45/80; @📶; 🚊Holzapfelstrasse) About 800m west of the Hauptbahnhof, this energetic hostel-hotel has basic, clean and bright rooms with big dorms divided into two for a bit of privacy. Room rates vary wildly depending on date, events taking place in Munich and occupancy. Breakfast is an extra €4, bike hire €12 per day.

SCHWABING

La Maison DESIGN HOTEL €€
(Map p192; ☎3303 5550; www.hotel-la-maison.com; Occamstrasse 24; s/d from €109/119; [P]❄@; [S]Münchner Freiheit) Discerningly retro and immaculate in shades of imperial purple and uber-cool grey, this sassy number wows with its rooms flaunting heated oak floors, jet-black washbasins and starkly contrasting design throughout, though the operators still can't resist the coy pack of gummi bears on the expertly plumped pillows! Cool bar on ground level.

Gästehaus Englischer Garten GUESTHOUSE €€
(Map p192; ☎383 9410; www.hotelenglischergarten.de; Liebergesellstrasse 8; s €68-177, d €79-177; [P]@📶; [S]Münchner Freiheit) Cosily inserted into a 200-year-old ivy-clad mill, this

small guesthouse on the edge of the English Garden offers a Bavarian version of the British B&B experience. Not all rooms are en suite but the breakfast is generous and there's cycle hire (€12 per day).

Hotel Marienbad
HOTEL €€
(Map p184; ☑595 585; www.hotelmarienbad.de; Barer Strasse 11; s/d from €55/105; ☎; ⌂Otto-strasse) Back in the 19th century, Wagner, Puccini and Rilke shacked up in what once ranked among Munich's finest hotels. Still friendly and well maintained, it now flaunts an endearing alchemy of styles, from playful art nouveau to floral country Bavarian and campy 1960s utilitarian. Amenities, fortunately, are of more recent vintage.

Pension am Kaiserplatz
GUESTHOUSE €
(Map p192; ☑395 231, 349 190; www.amkaiser platz.de; Kaiserplatz 12; s €35-49, d €53-67; ☎; ⌂Kurfürstenplatz) One of the best value places to stay in the city centre, this family-run B&B in a grand Jugendstil building has generously cut, high-ceilinged rooms furnished with four decades' worth of furniture. Continental breakfast is served in your room by the always-around-to-help owners. Toilets are shared but there are in-room showers (literally). Cash only.

Hotel Hauser
HOTEL €€
(Map p192; ☑286 6750; www.hotel-hauser.de; Schellingstrasse 11; s €88-148, d €118-230; Ⓟ☎; ⓈUniversität) The ageing woody rooms here date back to the optimistic days of the economic miracle (the 1950s), but are pristinely maintained, if small. Unexpected extras include a sauna and solarium. Cash preferred.

Cosmopolitan Hotel
HOTEL €€
(Map p192; ☑383 810; www.cosmopolitan-hotel. de; Hohenzollernstrasse 5; d from €135; Ⓟ☎; ⓈMünchner Freiheit) Almost Soviet in its no-frills functionality, the decor of hollow tubing, primary colours and fake veneer here is all very '90s, but rooms are clean and well tended, and breakfasts are, by all accounts, generous. Sleep, wash, breakfast and surf, but if you want character, go elsewhere.

NYMPHENBURG, NEUHAUSEN & AROUND

🏆 TOP CHOICE Hotel Laimer Hof
HOTEL €€
(Map p196; ☑178 0380; www.laimerhof.de; Laimer Strasse 40; s/d from €65/85; Ⓟ@☎; ⌂Romanplatz) Just a five-minute amble from Schloss Nymphenburg (p197), this tranquil refuge is run by a friendly team who take

time to get to know their guests. No two of the 23 rooms are alike, but all boast antique touches, oriental carpets and golden beds. Popular with everyone from honeymooners to families, business travellers to round-the-world backpackers.

The Tent
CAMPGROUND €
(Map p196; ☑141 4300; www.the-tent.com; In den Kirschen 30; tent bunk/floor space €10.50/7.50, tent pitch from €11; ⊙Jun-Nov; ⌂Botanischer Garten) A kilometre north of Schloss Nymphenburg, this youth-oriented camping ground has classic tent pitches as well as a 160-bunk main tent with floor space and foam mats for shoestring nomads. It's the cheapest sleep in town during the Oktoberfest.

HAIDHAUSEN & LEHEL

Hotel Ritzi
HOTEL €€€
(Map p200; ☑414 240 890; www.hotel-ritzi.de; Maria-Theresia-Strasse 2a; s/d from €110/179; ☎; ⌂Maxmilianeum) At this charming art hotel next to a little park, creaky wooden stairs (no lift) lead to rooms that transport you to the Caribbean, Africa, Morocco and other exotic lands. But it's the Jugendstil features of the building that really impress, as does the much-praised restaurant downstairs.

Hotel Opéra
HOTEL €€€
(Map p200; ☑210 4940; www.hotel-opera.de; St-Anna-Strasse 10; d from €155; ⌂Maxmonument) Like the gates to heaven, a white double door opens at the touch of a tiny brass button. Beyond awaits a smart, petite cocoon of quiet sophistication, with peaches-and-cream marble floors, a chandelier scavenged from the Vatican and uniquely decorated rooms.

WESTEND & LUDWIGSVORSTADT

Hotel Mariandl
HOTEL €€
(Map p208; ☑552 9100; www.mariandl.com; Goethestrasse 51; s €65-115, d €70-165; ⓈSendlinger Tor, ⌂Sendlinger Tor) If you like your history laced with quirkiness, you'll find both aplenty in this rambling neo-Gothic mansion. It's an utterly charming place where rooms convincingly capture the Jugendstil period with hand-selected antiques and ornamented ceilings. Breakfast is served until 4pm in the Vienna-style cafe downstairs, which also has live jazz or classical music nightly.

Pension Westfalia
B&B €
(Map p208; ☑530 377; www.pension-westfalia.de; Mozartstrasse 23; s/d from €38/50; @; ⓈGoetheplatz) A stumble away from the Oktoberfest

MUNICH SLEEPING

Westend & Theresienweise

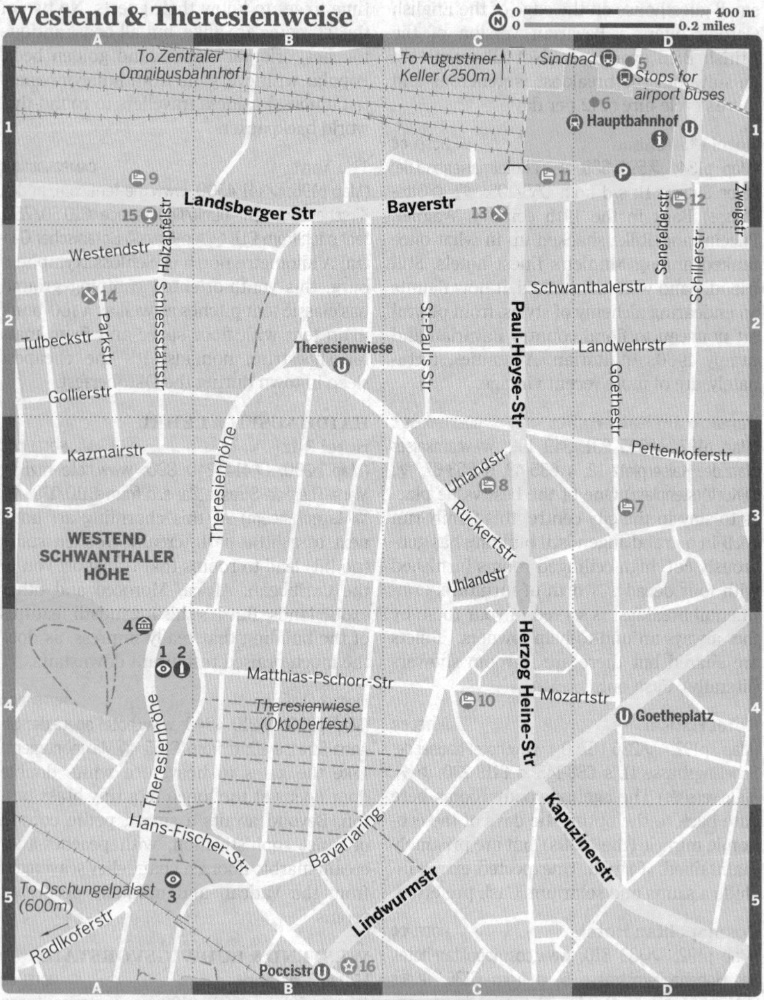

meadow, this stately four-storey villa conceals a cosy, family-run guesthouse that makes a serene base for sightseeing (outside the beer fest). Rooms are reached by lift and the cheaper ones have corridor facilities.

Hotel Uhland HOTEL €€
(Map p208; ☎543 350; www.hotel-uhland.de; Uhlandstrasse 1; s/d from €69/87; [P]📶; [S]Theresienwiese) The Uhland is an enduring favourite with regulars who expect their hotel to feel like a home away from home. Three generations of family members are constantly finding ways to improve their guests' experience, be it with wi-fi, bathroom phones, ice cubes, bike rentals or mix-your-own organic breakfast muesli.

🍴 Eating

Munich's food was once described by Viennese actor Helmut Qualtinger as 'garnish for the beer', and while that may still ring true in traditional beer halls and restaurants, where the menu rarely ventures beyond the roast pork and sausage routine, elsewhere Munich can claim to have southern Germany's most exciting cuisine scene. There's lots of exciting innovation going on in Munich's

Westend & Theresienweise

kitchens, where the best dishes make use of fresh regional, seasonal and organic ingredients. The Bavarian capital is also the best place between Vienna and Paris for a spot of internationally flavoured dining, especially when it comes to Italian and Afghan food, and even vegetarians can look forward to something other than noodles and salads.

TOP CHOICE Fraunhofer   BAVARIAN €€
(Map p184; Fraunhoferstrasse 9; mains €7-17.50; ⊙4pm-1am; ; Müllerstrasse) With its screechy parquet floors, stuccoed ceilings, wood panelling and virtually no trace that the last century even happened, this wonderfully characterful brewpub is one of the city centre's best places to explore the region with a fork. The menu is a checklist of southern German favourites, but also features at least a dozen vegetarian dishes as well as Starnberg fish.

Tantris   FINE DINING €€€
(361 9590; www.tantris.de; Johann-Fichte-Strasse 7; menu from €75; ⊙lunch & dinner Tue-Sat; Dietlindenstrasse) Tantris means 'the search for perfection' and here, at one of Germany's most famous restaurants, they're not far off it. The interior design is full-bodied '70s – all postbox reds, truffle blacks and illuminated yellows – the food gourmet sublimity and the service sometimes as unintrusive as it is efficient. The wine cellar is probably Germany's best. Reservations and a fat wallet essential.

TOP CHOICE Prinz Myshkin   VEGETARIAN €€
(Map p184; 265 596; www.prinzmyshkin.com; Hackenstrasse 2; mains €10-17; ⊙11am-12.30am;

; Marienplatz, Marienplatz) This place is proof, if any were needed, that the vegetarian experience has left the sandals, beards and lentils era. Munich's premier meat-free dining spot fills an open-plan but strangely intimate vaulted dining space, a former brewery, with health-conscious eaters, who come to savour imaginative dishes such as curry-orange-carrot soup, tofu stroganoff, 'Save the Tuna' pizza and unexpectedly good curries.

Bratwurstherzl   FRANCONIAN €
(Map p184; 295 113; Dreifaltigkeitsplatz 1; mains €6-10; ⊙10am-11pm Mon-Sat; Marienplatz, Marienplatz) Cosy panelling and an ancient vaulted brick ceiling set the tone of this Old Munich chow house with a Franconian focus. Homemade organic sausages are grilled to perfection on an open beechwood fire and served on heart-shaped pewter plates. They're best enjoyed with a cold beer straight from the wooden keg.

Daylesford Organic   ORGANIC €€
(Map p184; Ledererstrasse 3; mains €9-17; ⊙9am-8pm Mon-Sat; ; Marienplatz, Marienplatz) The Munich branch of this British organic food buffet enjoys a superb setting in the whitewashed cellars of the Zerwirk building. The fish, meat and vegetarian dishes are superb, but it's the little British elements such as curry and chutney, plus the extensive organic wine list, that make this laid-back eatery something a bit different.

Königsquelle   ALPINE €€
(Map p184; 220 071; Baaderplatz 2; mains €9-18; ⊙dinner; Isartor, Isartor) This Munich institution is well loved for its attentive

MUNICH EATING

service, expertly prepared food and dark, well-stocked hardwood bar containing what must be the Bavarian capital's best selection of malt whiskys. The hardly decipherable, handwritten menu hovers somewhere mid-Alps with anything from schnitzel to goat's cheese linguine or cannelloni to choose from.

La Baracca ITALIAN €€
(Map p184; ☎4161 7852; www.labaracca.eu; Maximiliansplatz 9; mains €5.50-14; 🕐11.30am-1am; [S]Odeonsplatz) At this great new Italian place, homely spaces such as a library and a cushion-strewn chill-out area combine effortlessly with iPad menus, an automated ordering system and a marble bar with stainless-steel stools. The ceiling is made entirely of huge lengths of driftwood, and rustic knick-knacks decorate throughout. Free wine tasting but atypically small helpings for an Italian eatery.

Vegelangelo VEGETARIAN €€
(Map p184; ☎2880 6836; www.vegelangelo.de; Thomas-Wimmer-Ring 16; mains €9-19; 🕐noon-2pm Tue-Thu, 6pm-late Mon-Sat; ✎; 🚊Isartor, 🚆Isartor) Reservations are recommended at this petite vegie spot where Indian odds and ends, a piano and a small Victorian fireplace distract little from the superb meat-free cooking, all of which can be converted to suit vegans. There's a set menu only (€24–30) policy Fridays and Saturdays. Cash only.

XII Apostel ITALIAN €€
(Map p200; Thierschplatz 6; mains €6-17; 🕐11am-1am Mon-Fri & Sun, noon-2am Sat; 🚊Lehel) Despite the expensive, exclusive feel of the dramatic dining space at this new, somewhat over-styled Italian job, resplendent in high ceiling frescoes, wood panelling and Chesterfield-style seating, the pizza-pasta menu here will not overwhelm your wallet. The triangular bar upstairs is a cool night spot in its own right. Staff speak little English.

La Bouche FRENCH €€€
(Map p184; ☎265 626; Jahnstrasse 30, enter on Westermühlstrasse; mains €13.50-19.50; 🕐noon-3pm Mon-Fri, 6pm-midnight Mon-Sat; [S]Fraunhoferstrasse) Expect good Gallic goings-on at this French-inspired port of call, where tables are squished as tight as lovers and the accent is on imaginative but gimmick-free fare, such as truffle ravioli, veal liver with caramelised apple and plenty of fish. By the way, it's much bigger than first meets the eye – there's a second room at the back.

Unionsbräu Haidhausen BREWPUB €€
(Map p200; ☎089 477 677; Einsteinstrasse 42; mains €7.50-16.50; [S]Max-Weber-Platz) This sophisticated brewpub has eight separate spaces where a mixed clientele of business types, locals and tourists slurp the house brew and feast on meat platters. There's a jazz club in the basement (Jazzclub Unterfahrt im Einstein (p216)).

Cafe Luitpold CAFE €€
(Map p184; www.cafe-luitpold.de; Briennerstrasse 11; mains €10-18; 🕐8am-7pm Mon, to 11pm Tue-Sat, 9am-7pm Sun; [S]Odeonsplatz) A cluster of pillarbox-red street-side tables and chairs announces you've arrived at this stylish but not uber-cool retreat. It offers a choice of three spaces – a lively bar, a less boisterous columned cafe and a cool palm-leaved atrium. Good for a daytime coffee-and-cake halt or a full evening blow-out with all the trimmings.

Weisses Brauhaus BAVARIAN €€
(Map p184; Tal 7; mains €8-15; [S]Marienplatz, 🚆Marienplatz) The *Weisswurst* (veal sausage) sets the standard for the rest to aspire to; sluice down a pair with the unsurpassed Schneider *Weissbier*. Of an evening the dining halls are charged with red-faced, ale-infused hilarity, with Alpine whoops accompanying the rabble-rousing oompah band.

Dreigroschenkeller THEME RESTAURANT €€
(Map p200; ☎379 558 34; Lilienstrasse 2; mains €7.50-16.50; 🕐5pm-1am Sun-Thu, to 3am Fri & Sat; 🚊Deutsches Museum) A cosy and labyrinthine brick-cellar pub with rooms based upon Bertolt Brecht's *Die Dreigroschenoper* (The Threepenny Opera), ranging from a prison cell to a red satiny salon. There are nine types of beer to choose from and an extensive menu of hearty Bavarian soak-up material.

Joe Peña's LATIN AMERICAN €€
(Map p184; Buttermelcherstrasse 17; mains €11-16; 🕐5pm-1am; 🚊Reichenbachplatz) If you came to Southern Germany to eat food from Central America, do it here. Munich's best Tex-Mex joint gets busy during happy hour (5pm to 8pm) and the nosh is tasty and as authentic as you'd expect this side of the pond.

La Vecchia Masseria ITALIAN €€
(Map p184; Mathildenstrasse 3; mains €6-15; 🕐11.30am-12.30am; [S]Sendlinger Tor, 🚊Sendlinger

Tor) One of Munich's more typically Italian *osteria*, this loud but unquestionably romantic place has earthy wooden tables, antique tin buckets, baskets and clothing irons conjuring up the ambience of an Apennine farmhouse. On occasion the chef will come out to greet you in his trademark straw hat.

Chopan AFGHAN €€
(Map p196; Elvirastrasse 18a; mains €7-17.50; ⏲6pm-midnight; [S]Maillingerstrasse) Munich has a huge Afghan community whose most respected eatery is this much-lauded restaurant done out Central Asian *caravanserai*-style with rich fabrics, multi-hued glass lanterns and geometric patterns. In this culinary Aladdin's cave you'll discover an exotic menu of lamb, lentils, rice, spinach and flatbread in various combinations, but no alcoholic beverages to see things on their way.

Potting Shed BAR, BURGERS €€
(Map p192; Occamstrasse 11; tapas €2.50-10.50, burgers €11.50-13.90; ⏲from 6pm; [S]Münchner Freiheit) This relaxed hangout serves tapas, gourmet burgers and cocktails to an easy-going evening crowd. The burger menu whisks you round the globe, but it's the house speciality, the 'Potting Shed Special' involving an organic beef burger flambéed in whisky, that catches the eye on the simple but well-concocted menu.

Schlosscafé Im Palmenhaus CAFE €€
(Map p196; mains €9-15; ⏲10am-5.30pm Tue-Sun; 🚋Schloss Nymphenburg) The glass-fronted 1820 palm house, where Ludwig II used to keep his exotic house plants warm in winter, is now a high-ceilinged and pleasantly scented cafe. It's just behind the palace.

Einstein KOSHER €€
(Map p184; St-Jakobs-Platz 18; mains €9-17; ⏲noon-3pm & 6pm-midnight Sat-Thu, noon-3pm Fri; [S]Marienplatz, 🚆Marienplatz) Reflected in the plate-glass windows of the Jewish Museum, this is the only kosher eatery in the city centre. The ID and bag search entry process is worth it for the restaurant's uncluttered lines, smartly laid tables and soothing ambience.

Tibet Kitchen TIBETAN €
(Map p192; www.tibetkitchen.de; Occamstrasse 4; mains €7.50-12.50; ⏲5-11pm Mon-Sat; [S]Münchner Freiheit) Bavaria's first and only Tibetan restaurant is an informal affair, draped in prayer flags and awash with bits of Buddhist paraphernalia. The English menu is a blessing as otherwise few would know what *momos, lugsha* and *gyathung* were. And anyone who thought Tibetans were vegetarians will be taken aback by the choice of meat dishes, though yak (sadly) makes no appearance.

Wirtshaus in der Au BAVARIAN €€
(Map p200; ☎448 1400; Lilienstrasse 51; mains €8-19; ⏲5pm-midnight Mon-Fri, from 10am Sat & Sun; 🚋Deutsches Museum) Though this traditional Bavarian restaurant has a solid 21st-century vibe, it's that time-honoured staple the dumpling that's been declared speciality here (it even runs a dumpling-making course in English). Once a brewery, the space-rich indoor dining area has chunky tiled floors, a lofty ceiling and a crackling fireplace in winter. When spring springs, the beer garden fills.

[TOP CHOICE] **Marais** CAFE €
(Map p208; Parkstrasse 2; dishes €5-12; ⏲8am-8pm Mon-Sat, 10am-6pm Sun; 🌿; 🚋Holzapfelstrasse) Is it a junk shop, a cafe or a sewing shop? Well, Westend's oddest coffeehouse is in fact all three, and everything you see in this converted haberdashery – the knick-knacks, the cakes and the antique chair you're sitting on – is for sale.

Swagat INDIAN €€
(Map p200; Prinzregentenplatz 13; mains €10-20; ⏲11.30am-2.30pm & 5.30pm-1am; 🌿; [S]Prinzregentenplatz) Though a touch shabby from the outside, inside Swagat fills every nook of an intimate cellar space with Indian fabrics, cavorting Hindu gods and snow-white tablecloths. The curry is as hot as Bavarians can take it, and there's plenty to please non-carnivores.

Götterspeise CAFE €
(Map p184; Jahnstrasse 30; snacks from €3; ⏲8am-7pm Mon-Fri, 9am-6pm Sat; 🚋Müllerstrasse) The name of this place translates as 'food of the gods' and the edible in question is that most sinful of treats, chocolate. This comes in many forms, both liquid and solid, but there are also teas, coffees and cakes, and we love the little smokers' perches outside for puffing chocoholics.

Café Zeitgeist CAFE €
(Map p192; ☎2865 9873; Türkenstrasse 74) Simply a perfect spot to pore over coffee and cake, and to watch, from a shady courtyard, the steady flow of students and trendoids pulsing along Türkenstrasse.

Café An Der Uni

CAFE €

(Map p192; Ludwigstrasse 24; snacks & mains €5-9; ⏰8am-1am Mon-Fri, from 9am Sat & Sun; 🌐📶; Ⓢ Universität) Anytime is a good time to be at charismatic CADU. Enjoy breakfast (served up until a hangover-friendly 11.30pm), a cup of Java or a Helles (light beer) in the lovely garden hidden by a wall from busy Ludwigstrasse.

Bamyan

AFGHAN €€

(Map p184; Hans-Sachs-Strasse 3; mains €8.50-17; ⏰11am-2am; 🚇 Müllerstrasse) The terms 'happy hour', 'cocktail' and 'chilled vibe' don't often go together with the word 'Afghan', but that's exactly the combination you get at this new and exotic hangout, named after the Buddha statues infamously destroyed by the Taliban in 2001. Central Asian soups, kebabs, rice and lamb dishes, and big salads are eaten at handmade tables inlaid with ornate metalwork.

Küche am Tor

GERMAN/ASIAN €

(Map p184; Lueg Ins Land 1; mains €8; ⏰noon-5pm Mon-Fri; 📶; 🚇 Isartor, 🚋 Isartor) No-nonsense, blink-and-you'd-miss-it lunch stop for local office workers with a comfortingly short menu of mostly German fare, but containing little subcontinental inflections such as red lentils, mild curry and Ayurvedic soup.

Cafe Frischhut

CAFE €

(Map p184; Prälat-Zistl-Strasse 8; pastries €1.70; ⏰7am-6pm Mon-Sat; Ⓢ Marienplatz, 🚋 Marienplatz) This incredibly popular institution serves just four traditional pastries, one of which – the *Schmalznudel* (an oily type of doughnut) – gives the place its local nickname. Every baked goodie you munch here is crisp and fragrant as they're always fresh off the hotplate out front.

MC Müller

BURGERS €

(Map p184; cnr Müllerstrasse & Fraunhoferstrasse; burgers from €5; ⏰6pm-2am Mon-Thu, to 4am Fri & Sat; 🚇 Müllerstrasse) Sixties looks and triple duty as bar, DJ lounge and burger joint until the wee hours.

Pommes Boutique

FAST FOOD €

(Map p192; Amalienstrasse 46; fries €2.50; ⏰10am-10pm Mon-Sat; Ⓢ Universität) This funkily done out lunch place serves cheap-as-chips Belgian-style fries made from organic potatoes, 30-odd dips to dunk them in and *Currywurst* to die for.

Bergwolf

FAST FOOD €

(Map p184; Fraunhoferstrasse 17; ⏰noon-2am Mon-Thu, noon-4am Fri & Sat, noon-10pm Sun, closed 3-6pm Sun-Fri; Ⓢ Fraunhoferstrasse) At this favourite pit stop for night owls, the poison of choice is *Currywurst*, a sliced spicy sausage provocatively dressed in a curried ketchup and best paired with a pile of crisp fries.

Eiscafé Sarcletti

ICE CREAM €

(Map p196; Nymphenburger Strasse 155; ⏰9am-11.30pm; 🚇 Volkartstrasse) Ice-cream addicts have been getting their gelato fix at this Munich institution since 1879. Choose from more than 50 mouth-watering flavours, from not-so-plain vanilla to honey-yoghurt or caramel.

Best Back

BAKERY €

(Map p208; Bayerstrasse 55; ⏰6.30am-midnight Mon-Fri, 7am-midnight Sat; 🚇 Holzkirchner Bahnhof) Forget the overpriced food at the train station, just a few steps from the tracks is this no-frills bakery where the same sandwiches, savouries and cakes are on sale for half the price, and coffees go for a single euro piece.

Drinking

Munich is a great place for boozers. Raucous beer halls, snazzy hotel lounges, chestnut-canopied beer gardens, hipster DJ bars, designer cocktail temples – the variety is so huge that finding a party pen to match your mood is not exactly a tall order. Generally speaking, student-flavoured places abound in Maxvorstadt and Schwabing, while traditional beer halls and taverns cluster in the Altstadt. Haidhausen attracts trendy types while the Gärtnerplatzviertel and Glockenbachviertel are a haven for gays and hipsters.

No matter where you are, you won't be far from an enticing cafe to get a Java-infused pick-me-up. Many also serve light fare and delicious cakes (often homemade) and are great places to linger, chat, write postcards or simply watch people on parade.

Bavaria's brews are best sampled in a venerable old *Bierkeller* (beer hall) or *Biergarten* (beer garden). People come here primarily to drink and, although food may be served, it is generally an afterthought. In beer gardens you are usually allowed to bring your own picnic as long as you sit at tables without tablecloths and order something to drink. Sometimes there's a resident brass band pumping oompah music. And don't even think about sitting at a *Stamm*-

tisch, a table reserved for regulars (look for a brass plaque or some other sign)!

Beer costs €6 to €7.50 per litre. A deposit of €2 or so may be charged for the glass.

Beer gardens are, for the most part, very family friendly with play areas and kiddie menus. You're also allowed to bring your own picnic if the adults are drinking. Cafes can be considered child friendly during the day.

Augustiner Bräustuben
BEER HALL

(Map p208; Landsberger Strasse 19; ⊘10am-midnight daily; ᮪Holzapfelstrasse) Depending on the wind, an aroma of hops envelops you as you approach this ultra-authentic beer hall inside the actual Augustiner brewery, popular with the brewmeisters themselves (there's an entire table reserved just for them). The Bavarian grub here is superb, especially the *Schweinshaxe* (pork knuckle).

Hofbräuhaus
BEER HALL

(Map p184; Am Platzl 9; ⊘9am-11.30pm daily; ᔡMarienplatz, ᮪Kammerspiele, ᮪Marienplatz) The mothership of all beer halls, every visitor to Munich should, at some point, make a pilgrimage to this temple of ale, if only once. The swigging hordes of tourists, swaying to the inevitable oompah band, is like something from a film set.

Alter Simpl
PUB

(Map p192; Türkenstrasse 57; ⊘11am-3am Mon-Fri, 11am-4am Sat & Sun; ᮪Schellingstrasse) Thomas Mann and Hermann Hesse used to knock 'em back at this well-scuffed and wood-panelled thirst parlour. A bookishly intellectual ambience still pervades and this is an apt spot to curl up with a weighty tome over a few Irish ales. The curious name, by the way, is an abbreviation of the satirical magazine *Simplicissimus.*

Baader Café
CAFE

(Map p184; Baaderstrasse 47; ⊘9.30am-1am daily; ᮪Fraunhoferstrasse) Around for over a quarter of a century, this literary think-and-drink place lures all sorts, from short skirts to tweed jackets, who linger over daytime coffees and night-hour cocktails. It's normally packed, even on winter Wednesday mornings, and is popular for Sunday brunch.

Salon Иркутск
BAR

(Map p196; Isabellastrasse 4; ⊘5pm-late; ᔡJosephsplatz) Escape the sugary cocktails and belly-inflating suds to one of Munich's more cultured watering holes, which touts itself as a Franco-Slavic evening bistro. You'll soon see this is no place to get slammed on Russian ethanol or cheap Gallic plonk – Monday is piano night, Wednesday French evening, and the green-painted, wood-panelled interior hosts exhibitions of local art.

Biergarten Muffatwerk
BEER GARDEN

(Map p200; Zellstrasse 4; ⊘5pm-late Mon-Thu, noon-late Fri & Sat; ᮪Am Gasteig) Think of this one as a progressive beer garden, with reggae instead of oompah, civilised imbibing instead of brainless guzzling, organic meats, fish and vegetables on the grill, and the option of chilling in lounge chairs. Plus opening hours are open-ended, meaning some very late finishes.

Hirschau
BEER GARDEN

(☑322 1080; Gysslingstrasse 15; ᔡDietlindenstrasse) This monster beer garden accommodates 1700 drinkers and puts on live jazz almost daily in summer. Dispatch the kids to the playground and adjacent minigolf course while you indulge in some tankard caressing.

Schumann's Bar
BAR

(Map p184; ☑229 060; Odeonsplatz 6-7; ⊘8am-3am Mon-Fri, 6pm-3am Sat & Sun; ᔡOdeonsplatz) Urbane and sophisticated, Schumann's has been shaking up Munich's nightlife with libational flights of fancy in an impressive range of more than 220 concoctions. It's also good for weekday breakfasts.

Braunauer Hof
BEER GARDEN

(Map p184; ☑223 613; Frauenstrasse 42; ⊘11.30am-11pm Mon-Sat; ᮪Isartor, ᮪Isartor) Near the Isartor, this pleasingly twisted beer garden is centred on a snug courtyard. There's a hedge maze, a fresco with a bizarre bunch of historical figures and a golden bull that's illuminated at night.

Chinesischer Turm
BEER GARDEN

(Chinese Tower; Map p192; ☑383 8730; Englischer Garten 3; ⊘10am-11pm daily; ᮪Chinesischer Turm, ᮪Tivolistrasse) This one's hard to ignore because of its English Garden location and pedigree as Munich's oldest beer garden (open since 1791). Camera-toting tourists and laid-back locals, picnicking families and businessmen sneaking a sly brew clomp around the wooden pagoda, showered by the strained sounds of possibly the world's drunkest oompah band.

Hirschgarten
BEER GARDEN

(Map p196; Hirschgartenallee 1; ⊘11am-11pm daily; ᮪Kriemhildenstrasse, ᮪Laim) The Everest of

MUNICH DRINKING

Munich beer gardens can accommodate up to 8000 Augustiner lovers, but still manages to feel airy and uncluttered. It's in a lovely spot in a former royal hunting preserve and rubs up against a deer enclosure and a carousel. Steer here after visiting Schloss Nymphenburg – it's only a short walk south of the palace.

Augustiner Keller BEER GARDEN
(594 393; Arnulfstrasse 52; 10am-1am Apr-Oct; ; Hopfenstrasse) Every year this leafy 5000-seat beer garden, about 500m west of the Hauptbahnhof, buzzes with fairy-lit thirst-quenching activity from the first sign that spring may have *gesprungen*. The ancient chestnuts are thick enough to seek refuge under when it rains, or else lug your mug to the actual beer cellar. Small playground.

Eat the Rich BAR
(Map p196; Hessstrasse 90; 7pm-1am Tue-Thu, to 3am Fri & Sat; Theresienstrasse) Strong cocktails served in half-litre glasses quickly loosen inhibitions at this sizzling meet market where wrinkle-free hotties mix it up with banker types halfway up the career ladder. A great spot to crash when the party's winding down everywhere else. Food is served till 2.30am.

Trachtenvogl CAFE, LOUNGE
(Map p184; Reichenbachstrasse 47; 10am-1am Sun-Thu, to 2am Fri & Sat; Fraunhoferstrasse) At night you'll have to shoehorn your way into this buzzy lair favoured by a chatty, boozy crowd of scenesters, artists and students. Daytimes are mellower, all the better to slurp its hot chocolate menu and check out the cuckoo clocks and antlers, left over from the days when this was a folkoric garment shop.

Café Cord CAFE
(Map p184; Sonnenstrasse 19; 11am-1am Mon-Sat; Karlsplatz, Karlsplatz, Karlsplatz) Set back from busy Sonnenstrasse in a modern precinct, clean-cut Cord is good stop for a light lunch or coffee or an ideal first pit stop for a long night ahead on the club circuit. In summer, the delicious global fare tastes best on the romantic, twinkle-lit courtyard.

Café am Hochhaus CAFE
(Map p184; www.cafeamhochhaus.de; Blumenstrasse 29; 8pm-3am; Müllerstrasse) Nightly DJs keep this tiny, grungey joint happy till the wee hours with standing room only and pavement spillout early doors. Decor? Think

chipped school chairs, black paint and funky photo wallpaper.

☆ Entertainment

Tickets to cultural and sporting events are available at venue box offices and official ticket outlets, such as Zentraler Kartenvorverkauf (Map p184; 292 540; www.zkv-muenchen.de), which has a handy kiosk within the Marienplatz U-Bahn station. It's also good for online bookings, as is München Ticket (Map p184; 01805 481 8181; www.muenchenticket.de; Neues Rathaus, Marienplatz), which shares premises with the tourist office.

Listings

Ezines useful for tuning into the local scene include www.munig.com, www.munichx.de, www.ganz-muenchen.de and www.muenchengehtaus.com. All are in German but are not too hard to navigate with some basic language skills.

FREE In München LISTINGS
(www.in-muenchen.de; free) This freebie mag available at bars, restaurants and shops is the most detailed print source for what's on in Munich.

Munich Found LISTINGS
(www.munichfound.de) English-language magazine geared towards expats and visitors.

Prinz München LISTINGS
(http://muenchen.prinz.de; €1) Weekly lifestyle and entertainment glossy.

Clubbing

Munich has a thriving club scene, so no matter whether your musical tastes run to disco or dancehall, house or punk, noise pop or punk-folk, you'll find some place to get those feet moving. To get the latest from the scene, peruse the listings mags or sift through the myriad flyers in shops, cafes and bars.

This being Munich, expect pretty strict doors at most venues. Dress to kill to get into the fanciest clubs. Dance floors rarely heat up before 1am, so showing up early may increase your chances of getting in without suffering the indignities of a ridiculous wait and possible rejection. If you look under 30, bring ID. Cover charges rarely exceed €15.

Kultfabrik CLUB COMPLEX
(Map p200; www.kultfabrik.de; Grafingerstrasse 6; Ostbahnhof) If you've been to Munich before,

you may remember this one-stop nightlife shop near the Ostbahnhof as Kunstpark Ost. Now the former dumpling factory has a different name but it still has more than a dozen, mostly mainstream, venues as well as numerous fast-food eateries, making it the best place in Munich to *carpe noctem*.

Electro and house beats charge up the crowd at the loungy **11er**, while hard rock hounds mash it up at **Titty Twister** and metal freaks bang on at **Refugium**. Nostalgic types can become dancing queens at such '70s and '80s emporia as **Noa**, **Rafael** and **Q Club** while central European rockabillies jive till the wee hours at **Eddy's**. For the latest line-ups, happy hours and other useful info, check the website or look around for KuFa's own listings mag, the free *Das K-Magazin*.

Harry Klein CLUB

(Map p184; www.harrykleinclub.de; Sonnenstrasse 8; ⏲from 11pm; [S]Karlsplatz, 🚋Karlsplatz, 🚆Karlsplatz) Since its move out of the Optimolwerke to the city centre, Harry Klein has come to be regarded as one of the best elektroclubs in the world. Nights here are an amazing alchemy of electro sound and visuals, with live video art projected onto the walls Kraftwerk style, blending to awe-inspiring effect with the music.

Atomic Café CLUB

(Map p184; www.atomic.de; Neuturmstrasse 5; ⏲from 10pm Tue-Sat; 🚋Kammerspiele) This bastion of indie sounds with funky '60s decor is known for bookers with a knack for catching upwardly hopeful bands before their big break. Otherwise it's party time; long-running Britwoch is the hottest Wednesday club night in town.

Optimolwerke CLUB COMPLEX

(Map p200; www.optimolwerke.de; Friedenstrasse 10; 🚆Ostbahnhof) Just behind Kultfabrik, Optimol is another clubber's paradise with about 15 different venues after dark. Latin lovers flock to **Do Brasil**, while a newcomer is **Die Burg**, which keeps the party hits and classics booming out till 6am.

P1 CLUB

(Map p192; www.p1-club.de; Prinzregentenstrasse 1; 🚋Nationalmuseum/Haus der Kunst) If you make it past the notorious face control at Munich's premier late spot, you'll encounter a crowd of Bundesliga reserve players, Q-list celebs, the odd lost piece of central European aristocracy and quite a few Russian speakers too busy seeing and being seen to actually have a good time. But it's all part of the fun, and the decor and summer terrace have their appeal.

Rote Sonne CLUB

(Map p184; www.rote-sonne.com; Maximiliansplatz 5; ⏲from 11pm Thu-Sun; 🚋Lenbachplatz) Named after a 1969 Munich cult movie starring it-girl Uschi Obermaier, the Red Sun is a fiery nirvana for fans of electronic sounds. An international roster of DJs from the US, Berlin, Paris, London and elsewhere keeps the wooden dance floor packed and sweaty until the sun rises.

Backstage CLUB

(www.backstage.eu; Reitknechtstrasse 6; ⏲from 8pm; 🚆Hirschgarten) Refreshingly nonmainstream, this groovetastic *boîte* has a chilled night beer garden and a shape-shifting line up of punk, nu metal, hip-hop, dance hall and other alternative sounds, both canned and live.

Substanz CLUB

(Map p208; Ruppertstrasse 28; [S]Poccistrasse) About as alternative as things get in Munich, this low-key, beery lair gets feet moving with house, indie or soul, tickles your funny bones during the English Comedy Club (first Sunday of the month) and brings out edgy wordsmiths for the SRO (standing-room-only) Poetry Slam (second Sunday).

Cinemas

For show information check any of the listings publications. Movies presented in their original language are denoted in listings by the acronym OF *(Originalfassung)* or OV *(Originalversion)*; those with German subtitles are marked OmU (*Original mit Untertiteln*). The following theatres all show English-language movies.

Museum-Lichtspiele CINEMA

(Map p200; ☎482 403; www.museum-lichtspiele.de; Lilienstrasse 2; 🚋Deutsches Museum) Cult cinema with wacky interior and weekly screenings of the *Rocky Horror Picture Show* (Saturday nights) and Luchino Visconti's *Death in Venice* (Sunday mornings).

Cinema CINEMA

(Map p196; ☎555 255; www.cinema-muenchen.de; Nymphenburger Strasse 31; [S]Stiglmaierplatz) Cult cinema with all films in English, all the time.

Filmtheater Sendlinger Tor   CINEMA
(Map p184; www.filmtheatersendlingertor.de; Sendlinger-Tor-Platz 11; SSendlinger Tor) This early 20th-century picture house shows more German movies than English-language pictures.

Classical & Opera

Münchner Philharmoniker   CLASSICAL MUSIC
(Map p200; 480 980; www.mphil.de; Rosenheimer Strasse 5; Am Gasteig) Munich's premier orchestra regularly performs at the Gasteig (Gasteig Culture Centre; Map p200; 480 980; www.gasteig.de; Rosenheimer Strasse 5; Am Gasteig) cultural centre. Book tickets early as performances usually sell out.

Bayerische Staatsoper   OPERA
(Bavarian State Opera; Map p184; 218 501; www.bayerische.staatsoper.de; Max-Joseph-Platz 2) Considered one of the best opera companies in the world, the Bavarian State Opera puts the emphasis on Mozart, Strauss and Wagner but doesn't shy away from early baroque pieces by Monteverdi and others of the period. In summer it hosts the prestigious Opernfestspiele (p203). Performances are at the Nationaltheater (Map p184; 218 501; www.staatstheater.bayern.de; Max-Joseph-Platz 2; Marienplatz) in the Residenz and often sell out. The opera's house band is the Bayerisches Staatsorchester, in business since 1523 and thus Munich's oldest orchestra.

BR-Symphonieorchester   CLASSICAL MUSIC
Charismatic Lithuanian maestro Mariss Jansons has rejuvenated this orchestra's play list and often performs with its choir at such venues as the Gasteig and the Prinzregententheater (Map p200; 218 502; www.prinzregententheater.de; Prinzregentenplatz 12; SPrinzregentenplatz).

Staatstheater am Gärtnerplatz   CLASSICAL MUSIC
(Map p184; 2185 1960; www.gaertnerplatz theater.de; Gärtnerplatz 3; Reichenbachplatz) The light opera and musicals normally performed at this 19th-century theatre will be farmed out to other stages between 2012 and 2015 while the building is spruced up for its 150th birthday .

Jazz

Jazzclub Unterfahrt im Einstein   BLUES, JAZZ
(Map p200; 448 2794; www.unterfahrt.de; Einsteinstrasse 42; SMax-Weber-Platz) Join a diverse crowd at this long-established, intimate club for a mixed bag of acts ranging from old bebop to edgy experimental. The Sunday open jam session is legendary.

Jazzbar Vogler   JAZZ
(Map p184; Rumfordstrasse 17; Reichenbach-platz) This intimate watering hole brings some of Munich's baddest cats to the stage. You never know who'll show up for Monday's blues-jazz-Latin jam session. Cover is added to your final bill, giving you the opportunity to listen in a bit before deciding to stay (so as not to 'buy a cat in a bag', as the Germans say).

Café am Beethovenplatz   JAZZ
(Map p208; 552 9100; Goethestrasse 51; SSendlinger Tor) Downstairs at the Hotel Mariandl (p207), this is Munich's oldest music cafe. It has an eclectic menu of sounds ranging from bossa nova to piano to Italian *canzoni* (songs). Reservations advised.

Theatre

Bayerisches Staatsschauspiel   THEATRE
(218 501) This leading ensemble has a bit of a conservative streak but still manages to find relevance for today's mad, mad world in works by Shakespeare, Schiller and other tried-and-true playwrights. Performances are in the Residenztheater (Map p184; Max-Joseph-Platz 2), the Theater im Marstall (Map p184; Marstallplatz 4) and the now fully renovated Cuvilliés-Theater (p189).

Münchener Kammerspiele   THEATRE
(Map p184; 2339 6600; www.muenchner-kammer spiele.de; Maximilianstrasse 26; Kammerspiele) Just as venerable as the Staatsschauspiel, this stage has an edgier, more populist bent and delivers provocative interpretations of the classics as well as works by contemporary playwrights. Performances are in a beautifully refurbished art-nouveau theatre at Maximilianstrasse and in the Neues Haus, a new glass cube at Falckenbergstrasse 1.

Deutsches Theater   THEATRE
(Map p184; 5523 4444; www.deutsches-theater. de; Werner-Heisenberg-Allee 11; SFröttmaning) Still occupying its impressive 'tent palace' in Fröttmaning (near the Allianz Arena), Munich's answer to London's West End hosts touring road shows, such as *Grease*, *Mamma Mia* and *Tommy*.

GOP Varieté Theater   VARIETY
(Map p200; 210 288 444; Maximilianstrasse 47; Maxmonument) Hosts a real jumble of acts

and shows, from magicians to light comedies and musicals.

Spectator Sports

FC Bayern München FOOTBALL

(☎6993 1333; www.fcbayern.de; [S]Fröttmaning) Like it or not, the Germans can play football and none do it better in the Bundesrepublik than Bayern Munich, Germany's most successful team both nationally and at a European level. Home games are played at the impressive, chameleon-like Allianz Arena (p199), built for the 2006 World Cup. Tickets can be ordered online.

Allianz Arena is also home turf for Munich's other soccer team, the perennial underdogs **TSV 1860** (www.tsv1860.de). They only play in Germany's second league but still have a passionately loyal fan base.

Shopping

Munich is a fun and sophisticated place to shop that goes far beyond chains and department stores. If you want those, head to Neuhauser Strasse and Kaufingerstrasse. Southeast of there, Sendlinger Strasse has smaller and somewhat more individualistic stores, including a few resale and vintage emporia.

To truly unchain yourself, though, you need to hit the Gärtnerplatzviertel and Glockenbachviertel, the bastion of well-edited indie stores and local designer boutiques. Hans-Sachs-Strasse and Reichenbachstrasse are especially promising. Maxvorstadt, especially Türkenstrasse, also has an interesting line-up of stores with stuff you won't find on the high street back home.

Manufactum HOMEWARES

(Map p184; Dienerstrasse 12; ⏰9.30am-7pm Mon-Sat; [S]Marienplatz, 🚇Marienplatz) Anyone with an admiration for top-quality German design classics should make a beeline for this store. Last-a-lifetime household items compete for shelf space with retro toys, Bauhaus lamps and times-gone-by stationery.

Munich Readery BOOKS

(Map p196; www.readery.de; Augustenstrasse 104; ⏰11am-8pm Mon-Fri, 10am-6pm Sat; [S]Theresienstrasse) Germany's biggest collection of secondhand English-language titles is the place to go in Bavaria for holiday reading matter. The shop holds events such as author readings and there's a monthly book club. See the website for details.

Holareidulijö CLOTHING

(Map p196; Schellingstrasse 81; ⏰noon-6.30pm Tue-Fri, 10am-1pm Sat; 🚇Schellingstrasse) Munich's only secondhand traditional clothing store is worth a look even if you don't intend buying. The shop's name is a phonetic yodel, and apparently, wearing hand-me-down lederhosen greatly reduces the risk of chaffing.

Porzellan Manufaktur Nymphenburg CERAMICS

(Map p196; ☎179 1970; Nördliches Schlossrondell 8; ⏰10am-5pm Mon-Fri; 🚇Schloss Nymphenburg) Traditional and contemporary porcelain masterpieces by the royal manufacturer. Also in the Altstadt at Odeonsplatz 1.

7 Himmel CLOTHING

(Map p184; Hans-Sachs-Strasse 17; ⏰11am-7pm Mon-Fri, 10am-6pm Sat; 🚇Müllerstrasse) Cool hunters will be in seventh heaven (a translation of the boutique's name) when browsing the assortment of fashions and accessories by hip indie labels like Pussy de Luxe, Indian Rose and Religion, all sold at surprisingly reasonable prices.

Flohmarkt Riem MARKET

(www.flohmarkt-riem.com; Willy-Brandt-Platz; ⏰6am-4pm Sat; [S]Messestadt-Ost) Play urban archaeologist and sift through heaps of junk to unearth the odd treasure at Bavaria's largest flea market. It's located outside the city centre by the trade-fair grounds in Riem.

Schuster OUTDOOR EQUIPMENT, SPORTS

(Map p184; Rosenstrasse 1-5; ⏰10am-8pm Mon-Sat; [S]Marienplatz, 🚇Marienplatz) Get tooled up for the Alps at this sports megastore boasting seven shiny floors of equipment, including cycling, skiing, travel and camping paraphernalia.

Sport Scheck OUTDOOR EQUIPMENT, SPORTS

(Map p184; Sendlinger Strasse 6 ; ⏰10am-8pm Mon-Sat; [S]Marienplatz, 🚇Marienplatz) First-rate outdoor and sports gear for flits into the Bavarian backcountry.

Loden-Frey TRADITIONAL CLOTHING

(Map p184; Maffeistrasse 5-7; ⏰10am-8pm Mon-Sat; 🚇Theatinerstrasse) Stocks a wide range of Bavarian wear. Expect to pay at least €300 for a good leather jacket, pair of lederhosen or dirndl dress.

Raritäten & Sammlungsobjekte COLLECTABLES

(Map p184; Müllerstrasse 33; ⏰10am-2pm Mon-Sat; 🚇Müllerstrasse) Rummage through heaps

WILFRIED KRECICH/WOST / GETTY IMAGES ©

1. Grand designs
Onion-domed Frauenkirche (p187) and gargoyle-festooned Neues Rathaus (p182) tower over Munich

2. Residenz (p188)
Munich's number-one attraction, the Residenz was home to Bavarian rulers for centuries

3. Asamkirche (p183)
This pocket-sized, late Baroque church is a treasure trove of gold leaf, paintings and putti (cherubs)

ALLAN BAXTER / GETTY IMAGES ©

OUT & ABOUT IN MUNICH

Munich's gay and lesbian scene is the liveliest in Bavaria but it's tame if compared to Berlin, Cologne or Amsterdam. The rainbow flag flies especially proudly along Müllerstrasse and the adjoining Glockenbachviertel and Gärtnerplatzviertel. To plug into the scene, keep an eye out for the freebie mags *Our Munich* and *Sergej*, which contain up-to-date listings and news about the community and gay-friendly establishments around town. Another source is www.gaymunich.de, which has a small section in English. For help with lodgings, check out www.gaytouristoffice.com.

Max & Milian (Map p184; Ickstattstrasse 2) a bastion for queer lit, nonfiction and mags. **Sub** ('the Sub'; ☎260 3056; www.subonline.org; Müllerstrasse 14; 🕒7-11pm Sun-Thu, 7pm-midnight Fri & Sat) is a one-stop service and information agency; lesbians can also turn to **Le Tra** (☎725 4272; www.letra.de; Angertorstrasse 3; 🕒2.30-5pm Mon & Wed, 10.30am-1pm Tue).

The festival season kicks off in April with the **Verzaubert** (www.liebefilme.com) film series featuring the best of international queer cinema at **Atelier** (Map p184; ☎591 1983; Sonnenstrasse 12; [S]Karlsplatz, 🚊Karlsplatz, 🚆Karlsplatz). The main street parties are Christopher Street Day (p203) and the **Schwules Strassenfest** (www.schwules-strassenfest.de) held in mid-August along Hans-Sachs-Strasse in the Glockenbachviertel. During Oktoberfest (p203), lesbigay folks invade the Bräurosl beer tent on the first Sunday and Fischer-Vroni on the second Monday.

Bars & Clubs

Ochsengarten (Map p184; ☎266 446; www.ochsengarten.de; Müllerstrasse 47) The first bar to open in the Bavarian capital where you have to be clad in leather, rubber, lycra, neoprene or any other kinky attire you can think of, to get in. Gay men only.

Kraftakt (Map p184; ☎2158 8881; www.kraftakt.com; Thalkirchner Strasse 4) Laid-back cafe where the only sign of gay-inclination during the day is the rainbow flag in the window. However on party nights you'll know soon enough you've come to the right/wrong address.

Nil (Map p184; www.cafenil.com; Hans-Sachs-Strasse 2; meals €3.50-8; 🕒3pm-3am) A construct in wood and marble, this chill cafe-bar is a good place to crash after the party has stopped elsewhere. If you need a reality check, a plate of its kick-ass goulash soup (€4.90) should do the trick.

Deutsche Eiche (Map p184; ☎231 1660; www.deutsche-eiche.com; Reichenbachstrasse 13) A Munich institution and gay central, this was once filmmaker Rainer Werner Fassbinder's favourite hang-out. It's still a popular spot and packs in a mixed crowd for its comfort food and fast service.

NY Club (Map p184; Sonnenstrasse 25; 🕒Fri & Sat) It had been raining men at Munich's hottest gay dance temple until a water main burst in 2012 and almost destroyed the building. But it's expected to return soon and will once again fill with Ibiza-style abandon.

Bau (Map p184; ☎269 208; www.bau-munich.de; Müllerstrasse 41) Bilevel bar that's party central for manly men with nary a twink in sight but plenty of leather, Levis and uniforms. Foam parties in the small cellar darkroom.

Prosecco (Map p184; ☎2303 2329; www.prosecco-munich.de; Theklatstrasse 1) Fun venue for dancing, cruising and drinking that attracts a mixed bunch of party people with quirky decor and a cheesy mix of music (mostly '80s and charts).

Bei Carla (Map p184; ☎4187 4168; Buttermelcherstrasse 9) This energised scene staple has been keeping lesbians happy since, well, like forever. It's a popular spot with a good mixed-age crowd, lots of regulars and snack foods if you're feeling peckish.

of glass-eyed dolls, old beer steins, 1980s toy cars and even the odd traditional glass painting at this cosy emporium, well stocked with quirky collectables gathered from Bavaria's forgotten drawers and dustiest attics. Great for sourcing unique souvenirs.

Foto-Video-Media Sauter ELECTRONICS (Map p184; Sonnenstrasse 26; ◷9.30am-8pm Mon-Fri, to 7pm Sat; [S]Sendlinger Tor) The largest camera and video shop in town.

Sebastian Wesely SOUVENIRS (Map p184; Rindermarkt 1; ◷9am-6.30pm Mon-Fri, to 6pm Sat; [S]Marienplatz, [U]Marienplatz) If you're in the market for traditional souvenirs, this little shop (in business since 1557) has floor-to-ceiling shelves of carved angels, pewter tankards, beer steins, carved figurines and handmade candles. The salespeople are quick with a smile and happy to help.

FC Bayern Fan-Shop SPORTS, SOUVENIRS (Map p184; Stachus underground mall level 1, Karlsplatz; ◷9.30am-8pm Mon-Sat; [S]Karlsplatz, [T]Karlsplatz, [U]Karlsplatz) One of seven FC Bayern outlets around the city selling shirts, scarves and myriad other types of kit belonging to southern Germany's premier soccer team.

ℹ Information

Dangers & Annoyances

During Oktoberfest crime and staggering drunks are major problems, especially around the Hauptbahnhof. It's no joke: drunks in a crowd trying to get home can get violent, and there are about 100 cases of assault every year. Leave early or stay cautious, if not sober, yourself.

Strong and unpredictable currents make cooling off in the Eisbach creek in the English Garden more dangerous than it looks. Exercise extreme caution; there have been deaths.

Even the most verdant *öko*-warrior might interrupt his/her yoghurt pot of rainwater to agree with you that fast-moving bikes in central Munich are a menace. Make sure you don't wander onto bike lanes, especially when waiting to cross the road and when alighting from buses and trams.

Emergency

Ambulance (☎192 22)

Fire (☎112)

Lost & Found (☎2339 6045; Ötztaler Strasse 17; ◷8am-noon Mon-Thu, 7am-noon Fri, 2-6pm Tue)

Police (☎110; Arnulfstrasse 1) There's a station right beside the Hauptbahnhof.

Internet Access

Most public **libraries** offer internet access to non-residents. Check www.muenchner-stadtbibliothek.de for details.

Coffee Fellows (Schützenstrasse 14; per hr €2.50; ◷7am-11.30pm) Order coffee downstairs, check emails upstairs.

Media

Abendzeitung Light broadsheet that, despite the name (meaning 'Evening News'), has a morning delivery.

Münchner Merkur The city's arch-conservative daily.

Süddeutsche Zeitung Widely read regional paper with a liberal streak. Monday's edition has a *New York Times* supplement in English.

tz Daily local tabloid.

Medical Services

The US and UK consulates can provide lists of English-speaking doctors.

Most pharmacies have employees who speak passable English, but there are several designated international pharmacies with staff fluent in English, including **Ludwigs-Apotheke** (☎550 5070; Neuhauser Strasse 11) and **Bahnhof Apotheke** (☎5998 9040; Bahnhofplatz 2).

Ärztlicher Hausbesuchdienst (☎555 566) Doctor home and hotel visits.

Bereitschaftsdienst der Münchner Ärzte (☎01805-191 212; ◷24hr) Evening and weekend nonemergency medical services with English-speaking doctors.

Chirurgische Klinik und Poliklinik (☎5160 2611; Nussbaumstrasse 20) Emergency room.

Emergency Dental Assistance (☎723 3093, 129 43)

Emergency Pharmacy (☎594 475; www.apotheken.de) Referrals to the nearest open pharmacy.

Schwabing Hospital (☎3304 0302; Kölner Platz 1) Accident and Emergency department.

ℹ CITY TOUR CARD

The Munich **City Tour Card** (www.citytourcard-muenchen.com; 1/3 days €9.90/19.90) includes all public transport in the Innenraum (Munich city: zones 1– 4 marked white on transport maps) and discounts of between 10% and 50% for more than 50 attractions, tours, eateries and theatres. These include the Residenz, the BMW Museum and the Bier und Oktoberfestmuseum. It's available at some hotels, tourist offices, Munich public transport authority (MVV) offices and U-Bahn, S-Bahn and DB vending machines.

Money

ATMs abound in the city centre, though not all take every type of card.

ReiseBank (Bahnhofplatz 2; ⊙daily 7am-10pm) Best place to change and withdraw money at the Hauptbahnhof.

Post

Post Office (Sattlerstrasse 1; ⊙9am-6pm Mon-Fri, 9am-12.30pm Sat, closed Sun) For additional branches, search www.deutschepost.de.

Tourist Information

Tourist Office (☑2339 6500; www.muenchen. de) Hauptbahnhof (Bahnhofplatz 2; ⊙9am-8pm Mon-Sat, 10am-6pm Sun) Marienplatz (Marienplatz 8, Neues Rathaus; ⊙10am-7pm Mon-Fri, to 5pm Sat, to 2pm Sun)

Castles & Museums Infopoint (☑2101 4050; www.infopoint-museen-bayern.de; Alter Hof 1; ⊙10am-6pm Mon-Sat) Central information point for museums and palaces throughout Bavaria. Has a small exhibition on the Kaiserburg.

ⓘ Getting There & Away

Air

Munich Airport (MUC; www.munich-airport.de), aka Flughafen Franz-Josef Strauss, is second in importance only to Frankfurt for international and domestic connections. The main carrier is Lufthansa (Terminal 2), but around 70 other companies operate from the airport's two runways, from major carriers such as British Airways and Emirates to minor operations such as Luxair and Carpatair.

Only one major airline from the UK doesn't use Munich's main airport – Ryanair flies into Memmingen's **Allgäu Airport** (www.allgaeu-airport. de), 125km to the west.

Bus

Europabus links Munich to the Romantic Road. For details of times and fares of this service, and all other national and international coaches, contact **Sindbad** (☑5454 8989; Arnulfstrasse 20) near the Hauptbahnhof.

The bold new Zentraler Omnibusbahnhof (ZOB) next to the Hackerbrücke S-Bahn station handles the vast majority of international and domestic coach services. There's a Eurolines/Touring office, a supermarket and various eateries on the first floor with buses departing from ground level.

BEX BerlinLinienBus (www.berlinlinienbus. de) runs daily between Berlin and Munich ZOB (one way/return €43/86, 8½ hours) via Ingolstadt, Nuremberg, Bayreuth and Leipzig.

A special **Deutsche Bahn express coach** leaves for Prague (€61, five hours, four daily) from the north side of the Hauptbahnhof.

Car & Motorcycle

Munich has autobahns radiating in all directions. Take the A9 to Nuremberg, the A8 to Salzburg, the A95 to Garmisch-Partenkirchen and the A8 to Ulm or Stuttgart.

Munich airport has branches of all major car hire companies. Book ahead for the best rates.

Train

Train connections from Munich to destinations in Bavaria are excellent and there are also numerous services to more distant cities within Germany and around Europe. All services leave from the **Hauptbahnhof** (Central Station), which is set to undergo major modernisation in coming years.

Staffed by native English speakers, **EurAide** (www.euraide.de; Desk 1, Reisezentrum, Hauptbahnhof; ⊙9.30am-8pm Mon-Fri May-Jul, 10am-7pm Mon-Fri Aug-Apr) is a friendly agency based at the Hauptbahnhof that sells all DB products, makes reservations and can create personalised rail tours of Germany and beyond. EurAide's free newsletter, *Inside Track*, is packed with practical info about the city and surroundings.

Train connections from Munich:

DESTINATION	FARE	DURATION	FREQEUNCY
Berlin	€121	6 hrs	every 2 hours
Cologne	€134	4½ hrs	hourly
Frankfurt	€95	3¼ hrs	hourly
Nuremberg	€52	1¼ hrs	twice hourly
Paris from	€143	10¾ hrs daily	(night train)
Prague	€66	5 hrs, 50 min	2 daily
Regensburg	€25.20	1½ hrs	hourly
Vienna	€85.80	4½ hours	every 2 hours
Würzburg	€67	2 hrs	twice hourly
Zürich	€75.20	4¼ hrs	3 daily

ⓘ Getting Around

Central Munich is compact enough to explore on foot. To get to the outlying suburbs, make use of the public transport network, which is extensive and efficient, if showing its age slightly.

Over the next few years, there is likely to be some disruption to Munich's public transport, especially to the S-Bahn system, as a new tunnel is burrowed beneath the city centre to relieve the pressure on the *Stammstrecke* (the trunk route via which all S-Bahn trains travel).

To/From the Airport

Munich's airport is about 30km northeast of the city and linked by S-Bahn (S1 and S8) to the Hauptbahnhof. The trip costs €10, takes about 40 minutes and runs every 20 minutes almost 24 hours a day.

The Lufthansa Airport Bus shuttles at 20-minute intervals between the airport and Arnulfstrasse at the Hauptbahnhof between 5am and 8pm. The trip takes about 45 minutes and costs €10.50 (return €17).

If you have booked a flight from Munich's 'other' airport at Memmingen (around 125km to the west) there's a special bus from the same place near the Hauptbahnhof that makes the trip up to seven times a day. The journey takes one hour and 40 minutes, and the fare is €13 (return €19.50).

A taxi from Munich Airport to the Altstadt costs in the region of €50 to €70.

Car & Motorcycle

Driving in central Munich can be a headache; many streets are one-way or pedestrian only, ticket enforcement is Orwellian and parking is a nightmare. Car parks (indicated on the tourist office map) charge about €1.50 to €2 per hour.

Public Transport

Munich's efficient public transport system is composed of buses, trams, the U-Bahn and the S-Bahn. It's operated by **MVV** (www.mvv -muenchen.de), which maintains offices in the U-Bahn stations at Marienplatz, Hauptbahnhof, Sendlinger Tor, Ostbahnhof and Poccistrasse. Staff hand out free network maps and time-tables, sell tickets and answer questions. Automated trip planning in English is best done online. The U-Bahn and S-Bahn run almost 24 hours a day, with perhaps a short gap between 2am and 4am. Night buses and trams operate in the city centre.

TICKETS & FARES The City of Munich region is divided into four zones with most places of visitor interest (except Dachau and the airport) conveniently clustering within the white *Innen-raum* (inner zone).

Short rides (*Kurzstrecke*; four bus or tram stops, or two U-Bahn or S-Bahn stops) cost €1.20, longer trips cost €2.50. Children aged between six and 14 pay a flat €1.20 regardless of the length of the trip. Day passes are €5.60 for individuals and €10.20 for up to five people travelling together. Three-day passes are €13.80/23.70 for one/five people. There's also a weekly pass called IsarCard, which costs €18.20 but is only valid from Monday to Sunday – if you buy it on Wednesday, it's still only good until Sunday.

Bikes cost €2.50 to take aboard and may only be taken on U-Bahn and S-Bahn trains, but not during the 6am to 9am and 4pm to 6pm rush hours.

Bus drivers sell single tickets and day passes but tickets for the U-/S-Bahn and other passes must be purchased from vending machines at stations or MVV offices. Tram tickets are available from vending machines aboard. Most tickets must be stamped (validated) at station platform entrances and aboard buses and trams before use. The fine for getting caught without a valid ticket is €40.

Taxi

Taxis cost €2.90 at flag fall (€3.90 if ordered by phone), plus €1.40 to €1.60 per kilometre and are not much more convenient than public transport. Luggage is charged at €0.50 per piece. Ring a taxi on ☎216 10 or ☎194 10. Taxi ranks are indicated on the city's tourist map.

AROUND MUNICH

Dachau

> 'There is a path to freedom. Its milestones are: obedience, honesty, cleanliness, sobriety, hard work, discipline, sacrifice, truthfulness and love of thy Fatherland.'

Inscription from the roof of the concentration camp at Dachau.

Dachau was the Nazis' first concentration camp, built by Heinrich Himmler in March 1933 to house political prisoners. All in all it 'processed' more than 200,000 inmates, killing between 30,000 and 43,000, and is now a haunting memorial that will stay long in the memory. Expect to spend two to three hours here to fully absorb the exhibits. Note that children under 12 may find the experience too disturbing.

Officially called the KZ-Gedenkstätte Dachau (Dachau Memorial Site; www.kz-geden kstaette-dachau.de; Alte Römerstrasse 75; admission free; ⊙9am-5pm daily), the place to start is the new visitors centre, which houses a bookshop, cafe and tour booking desk where you can pick up an audioguide (€3.50). It's on your left as you enter the main gate. Two-and-a-half-hour-long tours (€3) also run from here from Tuesday to Sunday at 11am and 1pm.

You pass into the compound itself through the Jourhaus, originally the only entrance. Set in wrought iron, the chilling slogan '*Ar-beit Macht Frei*' (Work Sets You Free) hits you at the gate.

Around Munich

0 ————— 10 km
0 ————— 5 miles

Freising
A9
Munich International Airport
A8
Dachau
A92
Schleissheim
A9
Fürstenfeldbruck
Puchheim
MUNICH
Wörthsee
A96
A95
Wesslinger See
A99
Gauting
Pilsensee
Starnberg
A8
Ammersee
Berg
Ilkahöhe
Wolfratshausen
Starnberger See
Geretsried
Weilheim
Penzberg
Bad Tölz
A95
Tegernsee

The **museum** is at the southern end of the camp. Here, a 22-minute English-language documentary runs at 10am, 11.30am, 12.30pm, 2pm and 3pm, and uses mostly post-liberation footage to outline what took place here. Either side of the small cinema extends an exhibition relating the camp's harrowing story, from a relatively orderly prison for religious inmates, leftists and criminals to an overcrowded concentration camp racked by typhus, and its eventual liberation by the US Army in April 1945.

Disturbing displays include photographs of the camp, its officers and prisoners (all male until 1944), and of horrifying 'scientific experiments' carried out by Nazi doctors. Other exhibits include a whipping block, a chart showing the system of prisoner categories (Jews, homosexuals, Jehovah's Witnesses, Poles, Roma and other 'asocial' types) and documents on the persecution of 'degenerate' authors banned by the party. There's also a lot of information on the rise of the Nazis and other concentration camps around Europe, a scale model of the camp at its greatest extent and numerous uniforms and everyday objects belonging to inmates and guards alike.

Outside, in the former roll-call square, is the **International Memorial** (1968), inscribed in English, French, Yiddish, German

and Russian, which reads 'Never Again'. Behind the exhibit building, the **bunker** was the notorious camp prison where inmates were tortured. Executions took place in the prison yard.

Inmates were housed in large barracks, now demolished, which used to line the main road north of the roll-call square. In the camp's northwestern corner is the **crematorium** and gas chamber, disguised as a shower room but never used. Several religious shrines, including a timber Russian Orthodox church, stand nearby.

Dachau is about 16km northwest of central Munich. The S2 makes the trip from Munich Hauptbahnhof to the station in Dachau in 21 minutes. You'll need a two-zone ticket (€5). Here change to bus 726 (direction Saubachsiedlung) to get to the camp. Show your stamped ticket to the driver. By car, follow Dachauer Strasse straight out to Dachau and follow the KZ-Gedenkstätte signs.

Schleissheim

When you've exhausted all possibilities in central Munich, the northern suburb of Schleissheim is well worth the short S-Bahn trip for its three regal palaces and high-flying aviation museum, a great way to entertain the kids on a rainy afternoon.

The crown jewel of the palatial trio is the **Neues Schloss Schleissheim** (New Palace; ☎ 315 8720; www.schloesser-schleissheim.de; Max-Emanuel-Platz 1; adult/concession €4.50/3.50, combination ticket for all 3 palaces €8/6; ☺ 9am-6pm Apr-Sep, 10am-4pm Oct-Mar, closed Mon year-round). This pompous pile was dreamed up by Prince-Elector Max Emanuel in 1701 in anticipation of his promotion to emperor. The promotion never came. Instead he was forced into exile for more than a decade and didn't get back to building until 1715. Cash-flow problems required the scaling back of the original plans, but given the palace's huge dimensions (the facade is 330m long) and opulent interior, it's hard to imagine where exactly the cuts fell. Some of the finest artists of the baroque era were called in to create such eye-pleasing sights as the ceremonial staircase, the Victory Hall and the Grand Gallery. There are outstanding pieces of period furniture, including the elector's four-poster bed, amazing intricately inlaid tables, and a particularly impressive ceiling fresco by Cosmas Damian Asam.

The palace is home to the Staatsgalerie (State Gallery), a selection of European baroque art drawn from the Bavarian State Collection, including works by such masters as Peter Paul Rubens, Anthony van Dyck and Carlo Saraceni. The most impressive room here is the Grand Galerie.

While construction was ongoing, the elector resided in the fanciful hunting palace of **Schloss Lustheim** (☑315 8720; adult/concession €3.50/2.50; ⊗9am-6pm Apr-Sep, 10am-4pm Oct-Mar, closed Mon year-round) on a little island in the eastern Schlosspark, providing an elegant setting for porcelain masterpieces from Meissen.

Nearby, the **Altes Schloss Schleissheim** (☑315 8720; Maximilianshof 1; adult/concession €2.50/1.50; ⊗9am-6pm Apr-Sep, 10am-4pm Oct-Mar, closed Mon year-round) is a mere shadow of its Renaissance self. It houses paintings and sculpture on religious culture and festivals from all over the world, including an impressive collection of more than 100 nativity scenes.

Only a short walk away, the **Flugwerft Schleissheim** (☑315 7140; www.deutsches-museum.de/flugwerft; Effnerstrasse 18; adult/child €6/3; ⊗9am-5pm), the aviation branch of the Deutsches Museum, makes for a nice change of pace and aesthetics. Spirits will soar at the sight of the lethal Soviet MiG-21 fighter jet, the Vietnam-era F-4E Phantom and a replica of Otto Lilienthals 1894 glider, with a revolutionary wing shaped like Batman's cape. Another highlight is the open workshop where you can observe the restoration of historical flying machines. Kids can climb into an original cockpit, land a plane and even get their pilot's licence.

To get to Schleissheim, take the S1 (direction: Freising) to Oberschleissheim (€5), then walk along Mittenheimer Strasse for about 15 minutes towards the palaces. On weekdays only, bus 292 goes to the Schloss Lustheim stop.

Starnberg

Around 25km southwest of Munich, glittering Lake Starnberg (Starnberger See) was once the haunt of Bavaria's royal family, but now provides a bit of easily accessible R&R for anyone looking to escape the hustle of the Bavarian capital.

At the northern end of the lake, the affluent, century-old town of Starnberg is the heart of the Fünf-Seen-Land (Five-Lakes-Area). Besides Lake Starnberg the area comprises the Ammersee and the much smaller Pilsensee, Wörthsee and Wesslinger See. Naturally the region attracts water-sports enthusiasts, but also has enough history to keep fans of the past happy.

The regional **Starnberger Fünf-Seen-Land tourist office** (☑08151-906 00; www.sta5.de; Wittelsbacherstrasse 2c, Starnberg; ⊗8am-6pm Mon-Fri year-round, 9am-1pm Sat May-mid-Oct) has a room-finding service.

King Ludwig II famously (and mysteriously) drowned along with his doctor in Lake Starnberg. The spot where his body was found, in the village of Berg on the eastern shore, is marked with a large cross backed by a *Votivkapelle* (Memorial Chapel). Berg is 5km from Starnberg and can be reached on foot in around an hour.

From Easter to mid-October **Bayerische-Seen-Schifffahrt** (☑08151-8061; www.seenschifffahrt.de) runs boat services from Starnberg to other lakeside towns as well as offering longer cruises. Boats dock behind the S-Bahn station in Starnberg.

If you'd rather get around the lake under your own steam, **Bike It** (☑08151-746 430; Bahnhofstrasse 1) hires out two-wheelers. **Paul Dechant** (☑08151-121 06; Hauptstrasse 20) near the S-Bahn station hires out rowing, pedal and electric-powered boats from €15 per hour.

Starnberg is a half-hour ride on S6 train from Munich Hauptbahnhof (€5).

Bavaria

Best Places to Eat

» Goldenes Posthorn (p275)

» Le Ciel (p247)

» Bürgerspital Weinstube (p252)

» Bürgerkeller (p257)

» Messerschmidt (p280)

Best Places to Stay

» Hotel Herrnschlösschen (p256)

» Hotel Elch (p272)

» Dom Hotel (p263)

» Hotel Deutscher Kaiser (p272)

» Hotel Elements (p292)

Why Go?

From the cloud-shredding Alps to the fertile Danube plain, the Free State of Bavaria is a place that keeps its clichéd promises. Story-book castles bequeathed by an oddball king poke through dark forest, cowbells tinkle in flower-filled meadows, the thwack of palm on lederhosen accompanies the clump of frothy stein on timber bench, and medieval walled towns go about their time-warped business.

But diverse Bavaria offers much more than the chocolate-box idyll. Learn about Bavaria's state-of-the-art motor industry in Ingolstadt, discover its Nazi past in Nuremberg and Berchtesgaden, sip world-class wines in Würzburg, get on the Wagner trail in Bayreuth or seek out countless kiddy attractions across the state. Destinations are often described as possessing 'something for everyone', but in Bavaria's case this is no exaggeration.

And, whatever you do in Germany's southeast, every occasion is infused with that untranslatable feel-good air of *Gemütlichkeit* (cosiness) that makes exploring the region such an easygoing experience.

When to Go

A winter journey along an off-season, tourist-free Romantic Road really sees the snow-bound route live up to its name. Come the spring, tuck into some seasonal fare as Bavaria goes crazy for asparagus during *Spargelzeit* (from late March). The summer months are all about the beer garden, and this is obviously the best time to savour the region's unsurpassed brews in the balmy, fairy-lit air. Autumn is the time to experience the dreamy haze of the Bavarian Forest and the bustle of Bavaria's cities, revived after the summer's time-out.

Fairy-Tale Castles

So just why do all those millions of visitors flock to Bavaria? If it's not for the beer then it's probably for the state's blockbuster castles and palaces. King Ludwig II's Neuschwanstein is the one everyone wants to tick off their list of '1000 things to see before I die', but did you know that Bavaria's most flamboyant monarch built two other country piles – Linderhof and Herrenchiemsee? And he was planning more when he drowned in Lake Starnberg. Away from Ludwig's marvels, others hot properties not to miss are Würzburg's Residenz, Veste Coburg and Landshut's Burg Trausnitz.

BODY & SOUL

Whether it's snowboarding in the Alps, striking a trail through the Bavarian Forest, pedalling your way through a city-centre sightseeing tour, wild swimming in Lake Starnberg, canoeing in the Altmühltal Nature Park or trying your hand at river surfing, Bavaria is definitely a place to get carbed up and kitted out for. Bavaria certainly provides ample opportunities to work off those dumplings, but if fresh-air antics seem like too much hard work, you can always retreat to a spa, water park or swimming pool.

Essential Food & Drink

» **Beer** From the proud breweries of Bamberg to tiny one-man producers in rural Franconia, from a quick summer beer-garden thirst-quencher to the millions of litres consumed at Oktoberfest, beer plays a bigger cultural role in Bavaria than almost anywhere else on earth.

» **Sausages** Almost every town in Bavaria has its own take on the banger, from the famous digit-sized bratwurst of Nuremberg to the 30cm-long Coburg whopper. Add a bun and a squirt of mustard, and a couple of these makes a respectable meal on the hop.

» **Snowballs** Unless you end up surviving in the mountains, eating snowballs is an experience you'd want to avoid, but not in Rothenburg ob der Tauber. The local sweet – strips of dough ravelled into a ball then deep fried and sprinkled with something sweet – are best eaten smashed up in their bag.

» **Wine** German wine sometimes gets bad press, but you'll forget the sceptics when you sip a glass of Franconian red or white. The main vine-cultivating areas can be found around Würzburg, with the vineyards visible from the city centre.

DISCOUNT PASSES

Staying in the Alps? Make sure your hotel or guesthouse gives you a free *Gästekarte* (guest card), which often gives you free access to public transport and discounts on sights and attractions.

Need to Know

» Many museums close on Mondays

» Travelling by train? Get yourself a Bayern-Ticket for huge savings

» Nuremberg is Bavaria's most engaging city for young children

Fast Facts

» Population: 12.6 million

» Area: 70,549 sq km

BAVARIA

Resources

» Bavarian Tourism Association (www.bayern.by)

» Castles in Bavaria (www.schloesser.bayern.de)

» State of Bavaria (www.bayern.de)

» Train and bus timetables (www.bahn.de)

Bavaria Highlights

1 Indulging your romantic fantasies at fairy-tale **Schloss Neuschwanstein** (p231)

2 Rack-and-pinioning your way to the top of the **Zugspitze** (p237), Germany's highest peak

3 Perching at the Eagle's Nest in **Berchtesgaden** (p246) to enjoy show-stopping Alpine vistas

4 Striking a trail through the tranquil wilds of the **Bavarian Forest** (p302)

5 Going full circle around the town walls of quaint **Dinkelsbühl** (p258)

6 Messing around on the waters of the achingly picturesque **Königssee** (p245)

7 Revisiting Bavaria's Nazi past in **Nuremberg** (p266)

8 Going frothy at the mouth in the hundreds of superb **beer gardens, breweries and brewpubs** across the region (p280)

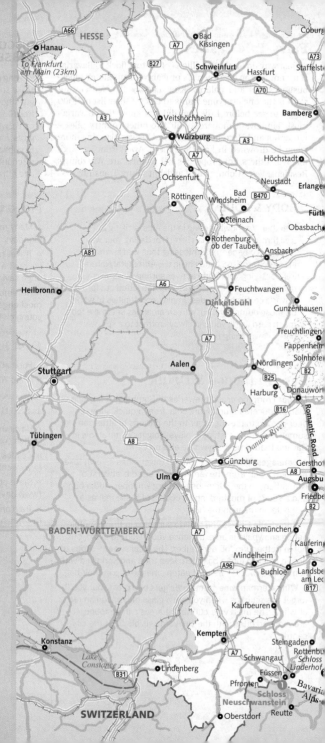

History

For centuries Bavaria was ruled as a duchy in the Holy Roman Empire, a patchwork of nations that extended from Italy to the North Sea. In the early 19th century, a conquering Napoleon annexed Bavaria, elevated it to the rank of kingdom and doubled its size. The fledgling nation became the object of power struggles between Prussia and Austria and, in 1871, was brought into the German Reich by Bismarck.

Bavaria was the only German state that refused to ratify the Basic Law (Germany's near constitution) following WWII. Instead Bavaria's leaders opted to return to its pre-war status as a 'free state', and drafted their own constitution. Almost ever since, the *Land* (state) has been ruled by the Christlich-Soziale Union (CSU), the arch-conservative party that is peculiar to Bavaria. Its dominance of the politics of a single *Land* is unique in postwar Germany, though Bavarian state elections in 2008 saw the party lose 17% of its vote, forcing it to enter a coalition with the FDP. Its sister party, the CDU, operates in the rest of the country by mutual agreement.

ⓘ Getting There & Around

Munich is Bavaria's main transport hub, second only to Frankfurt in flight and rail connections.

DON'T MISS

MUSEUM OF THE BAVARIAN KINGS

Palace-fatigued visitors to Füssen often head straight for the bus stop, coach park or nearest beer after a tour of the royal homes, most overlooking the area's third attraction, the worthwhile Museum der Bayerischen Könige (www.museumderbayerischenkoenige. de; Alpseestrasse 27; adult/concession €8.50/7; ☺8am-7pm Apr-Sep, 10am-6pm Oct-Mar), installed in a former lakeside hotel 400m from the castle ticket office (heading towards Alpsee Lake). The big-window views across the lake to the Alps are almost as stunning as the Wittelsbach bling on show, including Ludwig II's famous blue and gold robe. The architecturally stunning museum is packed with historical background on Bavaria's first family and well worth the extra legwork.

Rail is the best way to reach Munich from other parts of Germany, and the best means of getting from the Bavarian capital to other parts of Bavaria. Air links within Bavaria are much less extensive.

Without your own set of wheels in Eastern Bavaria and the Alps, you'll have to rely on bus services, which peter out in the evenings and at weekends. Trips along the Romantic Road can be done by tour bus, although again a car is a better idea. Several long-distance cycling routes cross Bavaria and the region's cities are some of the most cycle friendly in the world, so getting around on two wheels could not be easier.

If you're travelling in a group, or can assemble one (as some people do pre-departure), you can make enormous savings with the **Bayern-Ticket** (www.bahn.de; €22, plus €4 per additional passenger). This allows up to five adults unlimited travel on one weekday from 9am to 3am, or from midnight to 3am the next day on weekends. The single version, costing €22, is also a good deal and means that all fares in Bavaria are capped at that price, as long as you don't leave before 9am. Both are good for 2nd-class rail travel across Bavaria (regional trains only, no ICs or ICEs), as well as most public transport.

BAVARIAN ALPS

Stretching west from Germany's remote southeastern corner to the Allgäu region near Lake Constance, the Bavarian Alps (Bayerische Alpen) form a stunningly beautiful natural divide along the Austrian border. Ranges further south may be higher, but these mountains shoot up from the foothills so abruptly that the impact is all the more dramatic.

The region is pocked with quaint frescoed villages, spas and health retreats, and possibilities for skiing, snowboarding, hiking, canoeing and paragliding – much of it year-round. The ski season lasts from about late December until April, while summer activities stretch from late May to November.

One of the largest resorts in the area is Garmisch-Partenkirchen, one of urban Bavaria's favourite getaways. Berchtesgaden, Füssen and Oberstdorf are also sound bases.

ⓘ Getting Around

There are few direct train routes between main centres, meaning buses are the most efficient method of public transport in the Alpine area. If you're driving, sometimes a short cut via Austria works out to be quicker (such as between Garmisch-Partenkirchen and Füssen or Oberstdorf).

LUDWIG II, THE FAIRY-TALE KING

Every year on 13 June, a stirring ceremony takes place in Berg, on the eastern shore of Lake Starnberg. A small boat quietly glides towards a cross just offshore and a plain wreath is fastened to its front. The sound of a single trumpet cuts the silence as the boat returns from this solemn ritual in honour of the most beloved king ever to rule Bavaria: Ludwig II.

The cross marks the spot where Ludwig died under mysterious circumstances in 1886. His early death capped the life of a man at odds with the harsh realities of a modern world no longer in need of a romantic and idealistic monarch.

Prinz Otto Ludwig Friedrich Wilhelm was a sensitive soul, fascinated by romantic epics, architecture and music, but his parents, Maximilian II and Marie, took little interest in his musings and he suffered a lonely and joyless childhood. In 1864, at 18 years old, the prince became king. He was briefly engaged to the sister of Elisabeth (Sisi), the Austrian empress but, as a rule, he preferred the company of men. He also worshipped composer Richard Wagner, whose Bayreuth opera house was built with Ludwig's funds.

Ludwig was an enthusiastic leader initially, but Bavaria's days as a sovereign state were numbered, and he became a puppet king after the creation of the German Reich in 1871 (which had its advantages, as Bismarck gave Ludwig a hefty allowance). Ludwig withdrew completely to drink, draw up castle plans and view concerts and operas in private. His obsession with French culture and the Sun King, Louis XIV, inspired the fantastical palaces of Neuschwanstein (p231), Linderhof (p235) and Herrenchiemsee (p243) – lavish projects that spelt his undoing.

Contrary to popular belief, it was only Ludwig's purse – and not the state treasury – that was being bankrupted. However, by 1886 his ever-growing mountain of debt and erratic behaviour had put him at odds with his cabinet. The king, it seemed, needed to be 'managed'.

In January 1886, several ministers and relatives arranged a hasty psychiatric test that diagnosed Ludwig as mentally unfit to rule (this was made easier by the fact that his brother had been declared insane years earlier). That June he was removed to Schloss Berg on Lake Starnberg. A few days later the dejected bachelor and his doctor took a Sunday evening lakeside walk and were found several hours later, drowned in just a few feet of water.

No one knows with certainty what happened that night. There was no eyewitness nor any proper criminal investigation. The circumstantial evidence was conflicting and incomplete. Reports and documents were tampered with, destroyed or lost. Conspiracy theories abound. That summer the authorities opened Neuschwanstein to the public to help pay off Ludwig's huge debts. King Ludwig II was dead, but the myth, and a tourist industry, were just being born.

BAVARIA FÜSSEN

Füssen

☎ 08362 / POP 14,200

Nestled at the foot of the Alps, tourist-busy Füssen is the southern climax of the Romantic Road, with the nearby castles of Neuschwanstein and Hohenschwangau the highlight of many a southern Germany trip. But having 'done' the country's most popular tourist route and seen Ludwig II's fantasy palaces, there are other reasons to linger longer in the area. The town of Füssen is worth half a day's exploration and, from here, you can easily escape from the crowds into a landscape of gentle hiking trails and Alpine vistas.

⊙ Sights

TOP CHOICE **Schloss Neuschwanstein** CASTLE
(☎930 830; www.hohenschwangau.de; adult/concession €12/11, with Hohenschwangau €23/21; ⊙8am-5pm Apr-Sep, 9am-3pm Oct-Mar) Appearing through the mountaintops like a misty mirage is the world's most famous castle, and the model for Disney's citadel, fairy-tale Schloss Neuschwanstein.

King Ludwig II planned this castle himself, with the help of a stage designer rather than an architect, and it provides a fascinating glimpse into the king's state of mind. Built as a romantic medieval castle, work started in 1869 and, like so many of Ludwig's grand schemes, was never finished. For all the coffer-emptying sums spent on it, the king spent just over 170 days in residence.

Ludwig foresaw his showpiece palace as a giant stage on which to recreate the world of Germanic mythology in the operatic works of Richard Wagner. Its epicentre is the lavish Sängersaal (Minstrels' Hall), created to feed the king's obsession with Wagner and medieval knights. Wall frescos in the hall depict scenes from the opera *Tannhäuser*. Concerts are held here every September.

Other completed sections include Ludwig's *Tristan and Isolde*–themed bedroom, dominated by a huge Gothic-style bed crowned with intricately carved cathedral-like spires; a gaudy artificial grotto (another allusion to *Tannhäuser*); and the Byzantine Thronsaal (Throne Room) with an incredible mosaic floor containing over two million stones. The painting on the wall opposite the (throneless) throne platform depicts another castle dreamed up by Ludwig that was never built. Almost every window provides tour-halting views across the plain below.

At the end of the tour visitors are treated to a 20-minute film on the castle and its

creator, and there's a reasonably priced cafe and the inevitable gift shops.

For the postcard view of Neuschwanstein and the plains beyond, walk 10 minutes up to Marienbrücke (Mary's Bridge), which spans the spectacular Pöllat Gorge over a waterfall just above the castle. It's said Ludwig liked to come here after dark to watch the candlelight radiating from the Sängersaal.

Schloss Hohenschwangau CASTLE

(☑930 830; www.hohenschwangau.de; adult/concession €12/11, with Neuschwanstein €23/21; ☺8am-5.30pm Apr-Sep, 9am-3.30pm Oct-Mar) Ludwig spent his formative years at the sun-yellow Schloss Hohenschwangau. His father, Maximilian II, rebuilt this palace in a neo-Gothic style from 12th-century ruins left by Schwangau knights. With all this faux-medieval imagery filling his childhood, no wonder Ludwig turned out the way he did.

Far less showy than Neuschwanstein, Hohenschwangau has a distinctly lived-in feel and every piece of furniture is a used original. After his father died, Ludwig's main alteration was having stars, illuminated with hidden oil lamps, painted on the ceiling of his bedroom.

Here Ludwig first met Wagner, and the Hohenstaufensaal features a square piano where the hard-up composer would entertain Ludwig with excerpts from his latest oeuvre. Some rooms have frescos from German history and legend (including the story of the Swan Knight, *Lohengrin*). The swan theme runs throughout.

If visiting both Hohenschwangau and Neuschwanstein in the same day, timed tickets are always issued so that Hohenschwangau is first on your itinerary.

Hohes Schloss CASTLE, GALLERY

(Magnusplatz 10; adult/concession €6/4; ☺galleries 11am-5pm Tue-Sun Apr-Oct, 1-4pm Fri-Sun Nov-Mar) Füssen's compact historical centre is a tangle of lanes lorded over by the Hohes Schloss, a late-Gothic confection and one-time retreat of the bishops of Augsburg. The inner courtyard is a masterpiece of illusionary architecture dating back to 1499; you'll do a double take before realising that the gables, oriels and windows are not quite as they seem. The north wing of the palace contains the Staatsgalerie, with regional paintings and sculpture from the 15th and 16th centuries. The Städtische Gemälde-

ℹ CASTLE TICKETS & TOURS

Both castles must be seen on guided tours (in German or English), which last about 35 minutes each (Hohenschwangau is first). Timed tickets are only available from the Ticket Centre (☑930 40; www.hohenschwangau.de; Alpenseestrasse 12; ☺tickets 8am-5pm Apr-Sep, 9am-3pm Oct-Mar) at the foot of the castles. In summer, come as early as 8am to ensure you get in that day.

When visiting both castles, enough time is left between tours for the steep 30- to 40-minute walk between the castles. Alternatively, you can shell out €5 for a horse-drawn carriage ride, which is only marginally quicker.

All Munich's tour companies (p200) run day excursions out to the castles.

BAVARIA FÜSSEN

galerie (City Paintings Gallery) below is a showcase of 19th-century artists.

Museum Füssen MUSEUM
(Lechhalde 3; adult/concession €6/4; ⊙11am-5pm Tue-Sun Apr-Oct, 1-4pm Fri-Sun Nov-Mar) Below the Hohes Schloss, and integrated into the former Abbey of St Mang, this museum highlights Füssen's heyday as a 16th-century violin-making centre. You can also view the abbey's festive baroque rooms, Romanesque cloister and the St Anna Kapelle (AD 830).

Tegelbergbahn
CABLE CAR

(☎983 60; www.tegelbergbahn.de; one-way/return €11.50/18; ⊙9am-5pm) For fabulous views of the Alps and the Forggensee, take this cable car to the top of the Tegelberg (1730m), a prime launch point for hang-gliders and parasailers. From here it's a wonderful hike down to the castles (two to three hours; follow the signs to Königsschlösser). To get to the valley station, take RVO bus 73 or 78 (p234) from Füssen Bahnhof.

🛏 Sleeping

Accommodation in the area is surprisingly good value and the tourist office can help track down private rooms from as low as €25 per person.

Altstadt Hotel zum Hechten
HOTEL €€

(☎916 00; www.hotel-hechten.com; Ritterstrasse 6; s €59-65, d €90-99; 🐾) This is one of Füssen's oldest hotels and a barrel of fun. Public areas are traditional in style but the bedrooms are mostly airy, light and brightly renovated. Children are welcome and one of Füssen's better eateries awaits downstairs.

Pension Kössler
GUESTHOUSE €€

(☎4069; www.pension-koessler.de; Zalingerstrasse 1; s/d €40/80) This three-storey Alpine guesthouse with a friendly family atmosphere offers outstanding value. Rooms are simple but comfortable and all have private bathroom, TV, phone and balcony – some overlook the attractive garden. Turning up unannounced is not recommended; call ahead.

Hotel Sonne
HOTEL €€

(☎9080; www.hotel-sonne.de; Prinzregentenplatz 1; s/d from €79/109; 🅿🐾) Although traditional looking from outside, this Altstadt favourite offers an unexpected design-hotel experience within. Themed rooms feature everything from swooping bed canopies to heavy velvet drapes and antique-style furniture, all intended to make you feel as though you've bagged a royal residence for the night.

House LA
HOSTEL €

(☎evenings 607 366, mobile 0170 624 8610; www.housela.de; Welfenstrasse 39; dm from €18) A 15-minute walk west of the train station, this small, basic apartment hostel offers spacious rooms (some with balconies) and breakfast (€2 extra) on a rear patio with mountain views. Call ahead as it's unstaffed during the day.

✕ Eating

Beim Olivenbauer
ALPINE €€

(Ottostrasse 7; mains €6-16; ⊙11.30am-11.30pm) Northern Italy meets Tyrol meets the Allgäu at this fun eatery, its interior a jumble of Doric columns, mismatched tables and chairs, multi-hued paint and assorted rural knick-knackery. Treat yourself to a wheel of pizza and a glass of Austrian wine, or go local with a plate of *Maultaschen* and a mug of Paulaner. There's a kids corner in the main dining room and a sunny beer garden out front. Takeaway pizza service available.

Zum Hechten
BAVARIAN €€

(Ritterstrasse 6; mains €7-16; ⊙10am-10pm) Füssen's best hotel-restaurant keeps things regional with a menu of Allgäu staples like schnitzel and noodles, Bavarian pork-themed favourites, and local specialities such as venison goulash from the Ammertal. Post-meal, relax in the wood-panelled dining room caressing a König Ludwig Dunkel, one of Germany's best dark beers brewed by the current head of the Wittelsbach family.

Franziskaner Stüberl
BAVARIAN €€

(☎371 24; Kemptener Strasse 1; mains €5.50-15; ⊙lunch & dinner) This quaint restaurant specialises in *Schweinshaxe* (pork knuckle) and schnitzel, prepared in more varieties than you can shake a haunch at. Non-carnivores go for the scrumptious *Käsespätzle* (rolled cheese noodles) and the huge salads.

❶ Information

Füssen Tourist Office (☎938 50; www.fuessen.de; Kaiser-Maximilian-Platz 1; ⊙9am-6.30pm Mon-Fri, 10am-2pm Sat, 10am-noon Sun May-Oct, 9am-5pm Mon-Fri, 10am-2pm Sat Nov-Apr)

❶ Getting There & Away

BUS The Europabus (p248), which runs up and down the Romantic Road, leaves from stop 3 outside Füssen train station at 8am. It arrives in Füssen after 8pm.

TRAIN If you want to do the castles in a single day from Munich, you'll need to start early. The first train leaves Munich at 4.48am (€24, change in Kaufbeuren), reaching Füssen at 7.26am. Otherwise, direct trains leave Munich once every two hours throughout the day.

❶ Getting Around

BUS **RVO buses 78 and 73** (www.rvo-bus.de) serve the castles from Füssen Bahnhof (€4 return), also stopping at the Tegelbergbahn valley station.

TAXI Taxis to the castles are about €10 each way.

Wieskirche

Known as 'Wies' for short, the **Wieskirche** (☑08862-932 930; www.wieskirche.de; ⊙8am-5pm) is one of Bavaria's best-known baroque churches and a Unesco-listed heritage site. About a million visitors a year flock to see this stuccoed wonder, the monumental work of the legendary artist brothers Dominikus and Johann Baptist Zimmermann.

In 1730, a farmer in Steingaden, about 30km northeast of Füssen, witnessed the miracle of his Christ statue shedding tears. Pilgrims poured into the town in such numbers over the next decade that the local abbot commissioned a new church to house the weepy work. Inside the almost circular structure, eight snow-white pillars are topped by gold capital stones and swirling decorations. The unsupported dome must have seemed like God's work in the mid-17th century, its surface adorned with a pastel ceiling fresco celebrating Christ's resurrection.

From Füssen, regional RVO bus 73 (p234) makes the journey up to six times daily. The Europabus also stops here long enough in both directions to have a brief look round then get back on. By car, take the B17 northeast and turn right (east) at Steingaden.

Schloss Linderhof

A pocket-sized trove of weird treasures, **Schloss Linderhof** (☑08822-920 30; adult/concession €8.50/7.50; ⊙9am-6pm Apr–mid-Oct, 10am-4pm mid-Oct–Mar) was Ludwig II's smallest but most sumptuous palace, and the only one he lived to see fully completed. Finished in 1878, the palace hugs a steep hillside in a fantasy landscape of French gardens, fountains and follies. The reclusive king used the palace as a retreat and hardly ever received visitors here. Like Herrenchiemsee (p243), Linderhof was inspired by Versailles and dedicated to Louis XIV, the French Sun King.

Linderhof's myth-laden, jewel-encrusted rooms are a monument to the king's excesses that so unsettled the governors in Munich. The **private bedroom** is the largest, heavily ornamented and anchored by an enormous 108-candle crystal chandelier weighing 500kg. An artificial waterfall, built to cool the room in summer, cascades just outside the window. The **dining room** reflects the king's fetish for privacy and inventions. The

king ate from a mechanised dining board, whimsically labelled 'Table, Lay Yourself', that sank through the floor so that his servants could replenish it without being seen.

Created by the famous court gardener Carl von Effner, the gardens and outbuildings, open April to October, are as fascinating as the castle itself. The highlight is the oriental-style **Moorish Kiosk**, where Ludwig, dressed in oriental garb, would preside over nightly entertainment from a peacock throne. Underwater light dances on the stalactites in the **Venus Grotto**, an artificial cave inspired by a stage set for Wagner's *Tannhäuser*. Now sadly empty, Ludwig's fantastic conch-shaped boat is moored by the shore.

Linderhof is about 13km west of Oberammergau and 26km northwest of Garmisch-Partenkirchen. Bus 9622 travels to Linderhof from Oberammergau 10 times a day. If coming from Garmisch-Partenkirchen, change in Ettal or Oberammergau. The last service from Linderhof is just before 7pm but, if you miss it, the 13km vista-rich hike back to Oberammergau is an easygoing amble along the valley floor through shady woodland.

Oberammergau

☑08822 / POP 5230

Quietly quaint Oberammergau occupies a wide valley surrounded by the dark forests and snow-dusted peaks of the Ammergauer Alps. The centre is packed with traditional painted houses, woodcarving shops and awestruck tourists who come here to learn about the town's world-famous Passion Play. It's also a great budget base for hikes and cross-country skiing trips into easily accessible Alpine backcountry.

A blend of opera, ritual and Hollywood epic, the **Passion Play** (www.passionplay-oberammergau.com) has been performed every year ending in a zero (plus some extra years for a variety of reasons) since the late 17th century as a collective thank you from the villagers for being spared the plague. Half the village takes part, sewing amazing costumes and growing hair and beards for their roles (no wigs or false hair allowed). The next performances will take place between May and October 2020, but tours of the **Passionstheater** (📞945 8833; Passionswiese 1; theatre tour & Oberammergau Museum admission adult/child/concession €8/3/6; ⏰tours 9.30am-5pm Apr-Oct) enable you to take a peek at the costumes and sets anytime. The theatre doesn't lie dormant in the decade between Passion Plays – ask the tourist office about music, plays and opera performances that take place here over the summer.

The town's other claim to fame is **Lüftmalerei**, the eye-popping house facades painted in an illusionist style. Images usually have a religious flavour, but some also show hilarious beer-hall scenes or fairy-tale motifs, like *Little Red Riding Hood* at Ettalerstrasse 48 or *Hänsel und Gretel* at No 41 down the road. The pick of the crop is the amazing **Pilatushaus** (Ludwig-Thoma-Strasse 10; ⏰3-5pm Tue-Sat May-Oct), whose painted columns snap into 3D as you approach. It contains a gallery and several craft workshops.

Oberammergau is also celebrated for its intricate **woodcarvings**. Workshops abound around town, where skilled craftspeople can produce anything from an entire nativity scene in single walnut shell to a life-size Virgin Mary. Speciality shops and the **Oberammergau Museum** (📞941 36; www.oberammergaumuseum.de; Dorfstrasse 8; ⏰10am-5pm Tue-Sun Apr-Oct) display fine examples of the art.

Oberammergau has a **DJH hostel** (📞4114; www.oberammergau.jugendherberge.de; Malensteinweg 10; dm from €16.80) as well as several guesthouses, including the exceptionally good-value **Gästehaus Richter** (📞935 765; www.gaestehaus-richter.de; Welfengasse 2; s €28-35, d €56-70; 📶) with immaculate ensuite rooms, a guest kitchen and a filling Alpine breakfast. Recently updated **Hotel Turmwirt** (📞926 00; www.turmwirt.de; Ettalerstrasse 2; s/d from €75/99) next to the church has pristine business-standard rooms, some with Alpine views from the balconies and bits of woodcarving art throughout.

The **tourist office** (📞922 740; www.ammergauer-alpen.de; Eugen-Papst-Strasse 9a; ⏰9am-6pm Mon-Fri, 9am-1pm Sat) can help find accommodation.

Hourly trains connect Munich with Oberammergau (change at Murnau; €18.10, 1¾ hours). Hourly **RVO bus 9606** (www.rvo-bus.de) goes direct to Garmisch-Partenkirchen via Ettal; change at Echelsbacher Brücke for Füssen.

Ettal

Ettal would be just another bend in the road were it not for its famous monastery, **Kloster Ettal** (www.kloster-ettal.de; Kaiser-Ludwig-Platz 1). The highlight here is the sugary rococo basilica housing the monks' prized possession, a marble madonna brought from Rome by Ludwig der Bayer in 1330. However, some might argue that the real high point is sampling the monastically distilled Ettaler Klosterlikör, an equally sugary herbal digestif.

Ettal is 5km south of Oberammergau, an easy hike along the Ammer River. Otherwise take bus 9606 from Garmisch-Partenkirchen or Oberammergau.

Garmisch-Partenkirchen

📞08821 / POP 26,000

An incredibly popular hang-out for outdoorsy types and moneyed socialites, the double-barrelled resort of Garmisch-Partenkirchen is blessed with a fabled setting a snowball's throw from the Alps. To say you 'wintered in Garmisch' still has an aristocratic ring, and the area offers some of the best skiing in the land, including runs on Germany's highest peak, the Zugspitze (2964m).

The towns of Garmisch and Partenkirchen were merged for the 1936 Winter Olympics and, to this day, host international skiing events. Each retains its own distinct character: Garmisch has a more cosmopolitan, 21st-century feel, while Partenkirchen has retained its old-world Alpine village vibe.

Garmisch-Partenkirchen also makes a handy base for excursions to Ludwig II's palaces, including nearby Schloss Linderhof (p235) and the lesser-known Jagdschloss Schachen (p237), as well as Oberammergau (p236) and even, at a push, Neuschwanstein (p231) and Hohenschwangau (p232) castles.

Around Garmisch-Partenkirchen

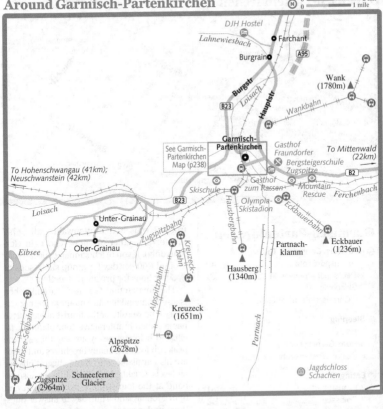

◉ Sights

Zugspitze
MOUNTAIN

(www.zugspitze.de) Views from Germany's rooftop are quite literally breathtaking and, on good days, extend into four countries. Skiing and hiking are the main activities here. The trip to the Zugspitze summit via the Zugspitzbahn is as memorable as it is popular; beat the crowds by starting early in the day and, if possible, skip weekends altogether. In Garmisch, board the **Zahnradbahn** (cogwheel train) at its own station behind the Hauptbahnhof. Trains first chug along the mountain base to the Eibsee, a forest lake, then wind their way through a mountain tunnel up to the Schneeferner Glacier (2600m). Here, you'll switch to the **Gletscherbahn** cable car for the final ascent to the summit. When you're done soaking in the panorama, board the **Eibsee-Seilbahn**, a steep cable car, that sways and swings its way back down to the Eibsee in about 10

minutes. It's not for vertigo sufferers, but the views surely are tremendous.

Most people come up on the train and take the cable car back down, but it works just as well the other way around. Either way, the entire trip costs €39/21.50 per adult/child in winter and €49.50/28 in summer. Winter rates include a day ski pass.

Partnachklamm
GORGE

(www.partnachklamm.eu; adult/child €3/1.50; ☺9am-5pm Oct-Easter, 8am-6pm Easter-Sep) One of the area's main attractions is the dramatically beautiful Partnachklamm, a narrow 700m-long gorge with walls rising up to 80m. A circular walk hewn from the rock takes you through the gorge, which is spectacular in winter when you can walk beneath curtains of icicles and frozen waterfalls.

Jagdschloss Schachen
CASTLE

(☑920 30; adult/concession €4.50/3.50; ☺Jun-Oct) A popular hiking route is to King

Garmisch-Partenkirchen

Garmisch-Partenkirchen

Ludwig II's hunting lodge, Jagdschloss Schachen, which can be reached via the Partnachklamm in about a four-hour hike. A plain wooden hut from the outside, the interior is surprisingly magnificent; the **Moorish Room** is something straight out of *Arabian Nights*.

🏃 Activities

Garmisch has two big ski fields: the Zugspitze plateau (2964m) and the Classic Ski Area (Alpspitze, 2628m; Hausberg, 1340m; Kreuzeck, 1651m; €33/18.50 day pass per adult/child). Local buses serve all the valley stations. Cross-country ski trails run along the main valleys, including a long section

from Garmisch to Mittenwald; call ☎797 979 for a weather or snow report (in German only). If you're a beginner, expect to pay around €60 per day for group ski lessons or €45 per hour for private instruction.

The area around Garmisch-Partenkirchen is also prime hiking and mountaineering territory. The website of the tourist office (p240) has a superbly interactive tour-planning facility to help you plot your way through the peaks on foot, and many brochures and maps are also available with route suggestions for all levels. Qualified Alpine guides are also on hand at the tourist office between 4pm and 6pm Monday and Thursday to answer questions and provide all kinds of information. Hiking to the Zugspitze (p237) summit is only possible in summer and is only recommended for those with experience in mountaineering.

Skischule SKIING
(☎4931; www.skischule-gap.de; Am Hausberg 8) Ski hire and courses.

Alpensport Total SKIING
(Map p238; ☎1425; www.alpensporttotal.de; Marienplatz 18) Winter ski school and hire centre that organises other outdoor activities in the warmer months.

Bergsteigerschule Zugspitze HIKING
(☎589 99; www.bergsteigerschule-zugspitze.de; Am Kreuzeckbahnhof 12a) A mountaineering school, offering guided hikes and courses.

Deutscher Alpenverein HIKING
(Map p238; ☎2701; www.alpenverein-gapa.de; Hindenburgstrasse 38) This outdoor organisation offers guided hikes and courses.

📖 Sleeping

The tourist office operates a 24-hour outdoor room-reservation noticeboard.

Hotel Garmischer Hof HOTEL €€
(Map p238; ☑9110; www.garmischer-hof.de; Chamonixstrasse 10; s €59-94, d €94-136; 🅿🖥) Property of the Seiwald family since 1928, many a climber, skier and Alpine adventurer has creased the sheets at this welcoming inn. Rooms are simply furnished but cosy, breakfast is served in the vaulted cafe-restaurant and there's a sauna providing après-ski relief.

Reindl's Partenkirchner Hof HOTEL €€€
(Map p238; ☑943 870; www.reindls.de; Bahnhofstrasse 15; s/d from €80/176; 🅿@🖥) Though Reindl's doesn't look worthy of its five stars from the outside, this elegant, tri-winged luxury hotel is stacked with perks, a wine bar and a top-notch gourmet restaurant. Rooms are studies in folk-themed elegance and some enjoy gobsmacking mountain views.

Hostel 2962 HOSTEL €
(Map p238; ☑957 50; www.hostel2962.com; Partnachauenstrasse 3; dm/d from €20/60; 🖥) Touted as a hostel, the former Hotel Schell is essentially a typical Garmisch hotel, but a good choice nonetheless. If you can get into one of the four-bed dorms, it's the cheapest sleep in town. Breakfast is an extra €6 if you stay in a dorm.

Gasthof zum Rassen HOTEL €€
(☑2089; www.gasthof-rassen.de; Ludwigstrasse 45; s €32-53, d €52-90; 🅿) This beautifully frescoed 14th-century building is home to a great budget option where the simply furnished, contemporary rooms contrast with the traditionally frilly styling of the communal areas. The cavernous event hall, formerly a brewery, houses Bavaria's oldest folk theatre.

DJH Hostel HOSTEL €
(☑967 050; www.garmisch.jugendherberge.de; Jochstrasse 10; dm €23.10; 🅿@) The standards at this smart, immaculately maintained hostel are as good as some chain hotels. Rooms have Ikea-style furnishings and fruity colour schemes, and there are indoor and outdoor climbing walls if the Alps are not enough.

🍴 Eating

Gasthof Fraundorfer BAVARIAN €€
(☑9270; Ludwigstrasse 24; mains €8-20, breakfast €9.80; ⊙7am-1am Thu-Mon, from 5pm Wed) If you came to the Alps to experience yodelling, knee slapping and red-faced locals in

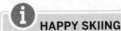

HAPPY SKIING

A **Happy Ski Card** (two days, adult/child €69/41.50) covers all the slopes, plus other ski areas around the Zugspitze, including Mittenwald and Ehrwald (an incredible 231km of pistes and 106 ski lifts).

lederhosen, you just arrived at the right address. Steins of frothing ale fuel the increasingly raucous atmosphere as the evening progresses and monster portions of plattered pig meat push belt buckles to the limit. Decor ranges from baroque cherubs to hunting trophies and the 'Sports Corner'. Unmissable.

Zum Wildschütz BAVARIAN €€
(Map p238; ☑3290; Bankgasse 9; mains €6-17; ⊙11am-10pm) The best place in town for fresh venison, rabbit, wild boar and other seasonal game dishes, this place is, not surprisingly, popular with hunters. The Tyrolean and south Bavarian takes on schnitzel aren't bad either. If you prefer your victuals critter free, look elsewhere.

Isi's Goldener Engel BAVARIAN €€
(Map p238; ☑948 757; Bankgasse 5; mains €8-15; ⊙11.30am-2.30pm & 5-10pm) The 'Golden Angel' is a rococo riot, complete with wacky frescos and gold-leaf-sheathed ceilings that wouldn't look out of place in a church. It's family run, neighbourhood adored and delivers classic Bavarian cooking, including a mean pork knuckle with the crust done just so.

Bräustüberl GERMAN €€
(Map p238; ☑2312; Fürstenstrasse 23; mains €6-17) A short walk from the centre, this quintessentially Bavarian tavern is the place to cosy up with some local nosh, served by Dirndltrussed waitresses, while the enormous enamel coal-burning stove revives chilled extremities. The dining room is to the right, the beer hall (with a little more ambience) to the left and the small beer garden out front.

Colosseo ITALIAN €€
(Map p238; ☑528 09; Klammstrasse 7; mains €5.50-25.50; ⊙11.30am-2.30pm & 5-11.30pm) If you fancy an Alpine take on la dolce vita, with mountain views and a bit of faux archaeology thrown in, this much-lauded pasta-pizza parlour with a mammoth menu is the place to head.

Zirbel
PUB €€

(Map p238; ☎716 71; Promenadestrasse 2; mains €8-17; ⏱5pm-1am) Guarded by a grumpy-looking wood-carved bear, this popular music pub serves noodle dishes, salads and schnitzel, all washed down with Czech Urquell beer on tap.

Saigon City
VIETNAMESE €

(Map p238; Am Kurpark 17a; mains €6.50-11.50; ⏱11am-2.30pm & 5-10.30pm) No-frills Vietnamese diner serving crispy duck, egg noodles and seafood. Cheap lunch menus.

ⓘ Information

Hobi's Cyber Café (Zugspitzstrasse 2; per hr €3; ⏱5.45am-5.30pm Mon-Fri, to noon Sat, 7-11am Sun) Internet cafe within the town's best bakery.

Mountain Rescue (☎112; www.bergwacht bayern.de; Auenstrasse 7) Mountain rescue station.

Post Office (Bahnhofstrasse 31)

Sparda Bank (Hauptbahnhof)

Tourist Office (☎180 700; www.gapa.de; Richard-Strauss-Platz 2; ⏱8am-6pm Mon-Sat, 10am-noon Sun)

ⓘ Getting There & Around

Garmisch-Partenkirchen has hourly connections from Munich (€19, 1½ hours), and special packages, available from Munich Hauptbahnhof (p222), combine the return trip with a Zugspitze day ski pass (around €45).

RVO bus 9606 (www.rvo-bus.de) leaves at 9.40am, reaching the Füssen castles at Neuschwanstein and Hohenschwangau two hours later. On the way back take the 4.13pm or 5.13pm bus 73 and change onto the 9606 at Echelsbacher Brücke. The 9606 also runs hourly to Oberammergau (40 minutes).

The A95 from Munich is the direct road route. The most central parking is at the Kongresshaus (next to the tourist office) for €1 per hour.

Bus tickets cost €1.50 for journeys in town. For bike hire, try **Fahrrad Ostler** (☎3362; Kreuzstrasse 1; per day/week from €10/50).

Mittenwald
☎08823 / POP 7400

Nestled in a cul-de-sac under snowcapped peaks, sleepily alluring Mittenwald, 20km southeast of Garmisch-Partenkirchen, is the most natural spot imaginable for a resort. Known far and wide for its master violin makers, the citizens of this drowsy village seem almost bemused by its popularity. The air is ridiculously clean, and on the main street the loudest noise is a babbling brook.

The **tourist office** (☎339 81; www.mitten wald.de; Dammkarstrasse 3; ⏱8.30am-6pm Mon-Fri, 9am-noon Sat, 10am-noon Sun Jul & Aug, shorter hours Sep-Jun) has details of excellent hiking and cycling routes. Popular hikes with cable-car access will take you up the grandaddy Alpspitze (2628m), as well as the Wank, Mt Karwendel and the Wettersteinspitze. Return tickets to Karwendel, which boasts Germany's second-highest cable-car route, cost €22/13.50 per adult/child.

The Karwendel ski field has one of the longest runs (7km) in Germany, but it is primarily for freestyle pros. All-day ski passes to the nearby Kranzberg ski fields, the best all-round option, cost €24.50 per adult and €18.50 per child. For equipment hire and ski/snowboard instruction contact the **Erste Skischule Mittenwald** (☎3582; www.skischule-mittenwald.de; Bahnhofsplatz 14).

The only classic off-piste sight in town is the **Geigenbaumuseum** (☎2511; www.geigenbaumu seum-mittenwald.de; Ballenhausgasse 3; adult/concession €4.50/3.50; ⏱10am-5pm Tue-Sun Feb–mid-Mar, mid-May–mid-Oct & mid-Dec–early Jan, other months 11am-4pm Tue-Sun), a collection of over 200 locally crafted violins and the tools used to fashion them. It's also the venue for occasional concerts.

Behind a very pretty facade, **Hotel-Gasthof Alpenrose** (☎927 00; www.alpenrose -mittenwald.de; Obermarkt 1; s €29-48, d €89-96) has cosy, old-style rooms, a cute restaurant and live Bavarian music almost nightly. Around 1km south of the Obermarkt, **Restaurant Arnspitze** (☎2425; Innsbrucker Strasse 68; mains €16.50-22.50; ⏱Thu-Mon) serves award-winning gourmet fare.

Mittenwald is served by trains from Garmisch-Partenkirchen (€4.10, 20 minutes, hourly), Munich (€22.20, 1¾ hours, hourly) and Innsbruck (€11.10, one hour, seven daily), across the border in Austria. Otherwise **RVO bus 9608** (www.rvo-bus.de) connects Mittenwald with Garmisch-Partenkirchen (30 minutes) several times a day.

Oberstdorf
☎08322 / POP 9900

Spectacularly situated in the western Alps, the Allgäu region feels a long, long way from the rest of Bavaria, both in its cuisine (more *Spätzle* than dumplings) and the dialect, which is closer to the Swabian of Baden-Württemberg. The Allgäu's chief draw is the car-free resort of Oberstdorf, a major skiing centre a short hop from Austria.

🏃 Activities

Oberstdorf is almost ringed by towering peaks and offers some top-draw hiking. In-the-know skiers value the resort for its friendliness, lower prices and less-crowded pistes. The village is surrounded by 70km of well-maintained cross-country trails and three ski fields: the **Nebelhorn** (half-day/day passes €32/37.50), **Fellhorn/Kanzelwand** (half-day/day passes €33.50/39) and **Söllereck** (half-day/day passes €21.50/26). For ski hire and tuition, try **Alpin Skischule** (⌨952 90; www.alpinskischule.de; Am Bahnhofplatz 1a) opposite the train station or **Erste Skischule Oberstdorf** (⌨3110; www.skischule-oberstdorf.de; Freiherr-von-Brutscher-Strasse 4).

Gaisalpseen   HIKING
For an exhilarating day walk, ride the Nebelhorn cable car to the upper station, then hike down via the Gaisalpseen, two lovely Alpine lakes (six hours).

Eislaufzentrum Oberstdorf   ICE SKATING
(⌨700 510; Rossbichlstrasse 2-6) The Eislaufzentrum Oberstdorf, behind the Nebelhorn cable-car station, is the biggest ice-skating complex in Germany, with three separate rinks.

🛏 Sleeping

Oberstdorf is chock full with private guesthouses, but owners are usually reluctant to rent rooms for just one night, even in the quieter shoulder seasons.

Haus Edelweiss   APARTMENTS €€
(⌨959 60; www.edelweiss.de; Freibergstrasse 7; apt from €103; P🐾) As crisp and sparkling as freshly fallen Alpine snow, this new apartment hotel just a couple of blocks from the tourist office has 19 pristine, self-contained flats with fully equipped kitchens, ideal for stays of three nights or more. Generally the longer you tarry, the fewer euros per night you kiss goodbye.

Weinklause   GUESTHOUSE €€
(⌨969 30; www.weinklause.de; Prinzenstrasse 10; s €67, d €106-126; P) Willing to take one nighters at the drop of a felt hat, this superb lodge offers all kinds of rooms and apartments, some with kitchenette, others with jaw-dropping, spectacular Alpine views. A generous breakfast is served in the restaurant, which comes to life most nights with local live music.

DJH Hostel   HOSTEL €
(⌨987 50; www.oberstdorf.jugendherberge.de; Kornau 8; dm €18.90) A relaxed, 200-bed chalet-hostel with commanding views of the Allgäu Alps. Take bus 9742 from the bus station in front of the Hauptbahnhof to the Reute stop; it's in the suburb of Kornau, near the Söllereck chairlift.

🍴 Eating & Drinking

Weinstube am Frohmarkt   TYROLEAN €€
(⌨3988; Am Frohmarkt 2; mains €10-19; ⏱5pm-midnight) 'Where did Bavaria go?' you might exclaim at this intimate wine bar, where the musty-sweet aroma of wine, cheese and Tyrolean cured ham scents the air. Rub shoulders with locals downstairs over a plate of wild boar or Tessin-style turkey steak, or retreat upstairs for a quiet nip of wine.

Nordi Stüble   SWABIAN €€
(⌨7641; cnr Walserstrasse & Luitpoldstrasse; mains €8.50-21.50; ⏱4pm-late Tue-Sat, from noon Sun) Family owned and run, this intimate neighbourhood eatery, a small wood-panelled dining room bedecked in rural junk of yesteryear, is the place to enjoy local takes on schnitzel and *Maultaschen*. All dishes are prepared fresh, so be prepared to wait; swab the decks afterwards with a Stuttgart Dinkelacker beer.

Oberstdorfer Dampfbierbrauerei   BREWERY
(Bahnhofsplatz 8; ⏱11am-1am) Knock back a few 'steamy ales' at Germany's southernmost brewery, right next to the train station.

ℹ Information

The main **tourist office** (⌨7000; www.oberstdorf.de; Prinzregenten-Platz 1; ⏱9am-5pm Mon-Fri, 9.30am-noon Sat) and its **branch office** (Bahnhofplatz; ⏱10am-5pm daily) at the train station run a room-finding service.

ℹ Getting There & Away

There are at least five direct trains daily from Munich (€30, 2½ hours), otherwise change in Buchloe.

Andechs

Founded in the 10th century, the gorgeous hilltop monastery of **Andechs** (⌨08152-376 253; www.andechs.de; admission free; ⏱8am-6pm Mon-Fri, 9am-6pm Sat, 9.45am-6pm Sun) has long been a place of pilgrimage, though today more visitors come to slurp the Benedictines' fabled ales.

The church owns two relics of enormous importance: branches that are thought to come from Christ's crown of thorns, and a victory cross of Charlemagne, whose army overran much of Western Europe in the 9th century. In the Holy Chapel, the votive candles, some of them over 1m tall, are among Germany's oldest. The remains of Carl Orff, the composer of *Carmina Burana,* are interred here as well.

Outside, soak up the magnificent views of the purple-grey Alps and forested hills before plunging into the nearby **Bräustüberl** (☺10am-8pm), the monks' beer hall and garden. There are seven varieties of beer on offer, from the rich and velvety *Doppelbock* dark to the fruity unfiltered *Weissbier.* The place is incredibly popular and, on summer weekends, you may have to join a queue of day trippers at the door to get in.

The easiest way to reach Andechs from Munich is to take the S8 to Herrsching (€7.50, 49 minutes), then change to bus 951 or the private Ammersee-Reisen bus (€2.20, 11 times daily). Alternatively, it's a pleasant 4km hike south from Herrsching through the protected woodland of the Kiental.

Bad Tölz

☑08041 / POP 17,800

Situated some 40km south of central Munich, Bad Tölz is a pretty spa town straddling the Isar River. The town's gentle inclines provide a delightful spot for its attractive, frescoed houses and the quaint shops of the old town. At weekends thousands flock here from Munich to enjoy the ultramodern swimming complex, Alpine slide and hiking trips down the river. Bad Tölz is also the gateway to the Tölzer Land region and its emerald-green lakes, the Walchensee and the Kochelsee.

◎ Sights & Activities

Cobble-stoned and car-free, **Marktstrasse** is flanked by statuesque town houses with ornate overhanging eaves that look twice as high on the sloping street. Above the town, on Kalvarienberg, looms Bad Tölz' landmark, the twin-towered **Kalvarienberg-kirche** (Cavalry Church). This giant baroque structure stands side by side with the petite **Leonhardikapelle** (Leonhardi Chapel; 1718), the destination of the Leonhardi pilgrimage.

Stadtmuseum   MUSEUM
(☑793 5156; Marktstrasse 48; adult/child €2/1; ☺10am-4pm Tue-Sun) The Stadtmuseum touches on virtually all aspects of local culture and history, with a fine collection of painted armoires (the so-called Tölzer Kas-

ten), a 2m-tall, single-stringed *Nonnengeige* (marine trumpet), examples of traditional glass painting and a cart used in the Leonhardifahrt.

Alpamare   SPA
(☑509 999; www.alpamare.de; Ludwigstrasse 14; day pass adult/child €34/24; ☺9.30am-10pm) In the spa section of town, west of the Isar River, you'll find the fantastic water complex Alpamare. This huge centre has heated indoor and outdoor mineral pools, a wave and surfing pool, a series of wicked water slides (including Germany's longest, the 330m-long Alpabob-Wildwasser), saunas, solariums and its own hotel. Bus 9570 from the train station stops 100m away.

Blomberg   HIKING
Southwest of Bad Tölz, the Blomberg (1248m) is a family-friendly mountain that has a natural toboggan track in winter, plus easy hiking and a fun Alpine slide in summer.

Unless you're walking, getting up the hill involves, weather permitting, a chairlift ride aboard the **Blombergbahn** (top station adult/child return €8/3.50; ☺9am-5pm May-Oct, 9am-4pm Nov-Apr). Over 1km long, the fibreglass Alpine slide snakes down the mountain from the middle station. You zip down at up to 50km/h through the 17 hairpin bends on little wheeled bobsleds with a joystick to control braking. A long-sleeved shirt and jeans provide a little protection. Riding up to the midway station and sliding down costs €4 per adult (€3.50 concession), with discounts for multiple trips.

To reach Blomberg, take RVO bus (p234) 9612 or 9591 from the train station to the Blombergbahn stop.

✷✰ Festivals & Events

Leonhardifahrt   PILGRIMAGE
Every year on 6 November, residents pay homage to the patron saint of horses, Leonhard. The famous Leonhardifahrt is a pilgrimage up to the Leonhardi chapel, where townsfolk dress up in traditional costume and ride dozens of garlanded horse carts to the strains of brass bands.

🛏 Sleeping & Eating

Posthotel Kolberbräu   HOTEL €€
(☑768 80; www.kolberbraeu.de; Marktstrasse 29; s/d from €54/94) Very well-appointed digs amid the bustle of the main street, with a classic Bavarian restaurant and a tradition going back over four centuries.

Gasthof Zantl BAVARIAN €€
(Salzstrasse 31; mains €8-18; ⊘lunch & dinner Sat-Thu Jun-Dec, Sat-Wed Jan-May) One of Bad Tölz' oldest buildings, this convivial tavern has a predictably pork-heavy menu, with ingredients sourced from local villages as much as possible. There's a sunny beer garden out front.

Solo BISTRO €€
(⌚730 923; Königsdorfer Strasse 2; mains €8-16; ⊘9am-midnight) For a casual meal try Solo, right on the Isar, which draws an all-ages crowd with global bistro favourites (pasta, curries, enchiladas, salads).

❶ Information

Tourist Office (⌚793 5156; www.bad-toelz.de; Marktstrasse 48; ⊘10am-4pm Tue-Sun)

❶ Getting There & Away

The private **Bayerische Oberlandbahn** (BOB; ⌚08024-997 171; www.bayerischeoberland bahn.de) runs hourly trains between Bad Tölz and Munich Hauptbahnhof (€11.10, 50 minutes). Alternatively, take the S2 from central Munich to Holzkirchen, then change to the BOB. In Holzkirchen make sure you board the Bad Tölz–bound portion of the train.

Chiemsee

⌚08051
Most foreign visitors arrive at the shores of the Bavarian Sea – as Chiemsee is affectionately known – in search of King Ludwig II's Schloss Herrenchiemsee. The lake's natural beauty and water sports make the area popular with de-stressing city dwellers, and many affluent Müncheners own weekend retreats by its shimmering waters.

The towns of Prien am Chiemsee and, about 5km south, Bernau am Chiemsee (both on the Munich–Salzburg rail line) are perfect bases for exploring the lake. Of the two towns, Prien is by far the larger and livelier. If you're day tripping to Herrenchiemsee, conveniently interconnecting transport is available. To explore further, you'll probably need a set of wheels.

◉ Sights

Schloss Herrenchiemsee CASTLE
(⌚688 70; www.herren-chiemsee.de; adult/child/concession €8/free/7; ⊘tours 9am-6pm Apr-Oct, 9.40am-4.15pm Nov-Mar) An island just 1.5km across the Chiemsee from Prien, Herreninsel is home to Ludwig II's Versailles-inspired

Schloss Herrenchiemsee. Begun in 1878, it was never intended as a residence, but as a homage to absolutist monarchy, as epitomised by Ludwig's hero, the French Sun King, Louis XIV. Ludwig spent only 10 days here and even then was rarely seen, preferring to read at night and sleep all day.

The palace is typical of Ludwig's creations, its design and appearance the product of the Bavarian monarch's romantic obsessions and unfettered imagination. Ludwig splurged more money on this palace than on Neuschwanstein and Linderhof combined, but when cash ran out in 1885, one year before his death, 50 rooms remained unfinished.

The rooms that were completed outdo each other in opulence. The vast **Gesandtentreppe** (Ambassador Staircase), a double staircase leading to a frescoed gallery and topped by a glass roof, is the first visual knockout on the guided tour, but that fades in comparison to the stunning **Grosse Spiegelgalerie** (Great Hall of Mirrors). This tunnel of light runs the length of the garden (98m, or 10m longer than that in Versailles). It sports 52 candelabra and 33 great glass chandeliers with 7000 candles, which took 70 servants half an hour to light. In late July it becomes a wonderful venue for classical concerts.

The **Paradeschlafzimmer** (State Bedroom) features a canopied bed perching altarlike on a pedestal behind a golden balustrade. This was the heart of the palace, where morning and evening audiences were held. But it's the king's bedroom, the **Kleines Blaues Schlafzimmer** (Little Blue Bedroom), that really takes the cake. The decoration is sickly sweet, encrusted with gilded stucco and wildly extravagant carvings. The room is bathed in a soft blue light emanating from a glass globe at the foot of the bed. It supposedly took 18 months for a technician to perfect the lamp to the king's satisfaction.

Admission to the palace also entitles you to a spin around the **König Ludwig II Museum**, where you can see the king's christening and coronation robes, more blueprints of megalomaniac buildings and his death mask.

To reach the palace, take the hourly or half-hourly ferry from Prien-Stock (€7.10 return, 15 to 20 minutes) or from Bernau-Felden (€8.30, 25 minutes, May to October). From the boat landing on Herreninsel, it's about a 20-minute walk through pretty gardens to the palace. Palace tours, offered in German or English, last 30 minutes.

Fraueninsel   ISLAND

A third of this tiny island is occupied by **Frauenwörth Abbey** (www.frauenwoerth.de; admission free), founded in the late 8th century, making it one of the oldest abbeys in Bavaria. The 10th-century church, whose free-standing campanile sports a distinctive onion-dome top (11th century), is worth a visit.

Opposite the church is the AD 860 Carolingian **Torhalle** (admission €2; ⊙10am-6pm May-Oct). It houses medieval objets d'art, sculpture and changing exhibitions of regional paintings from the 18th to the 20th centuries.

Return ferry fare, including a stop at Herreninsel, is €8.20 from Prien-Stock and €8.40 from Bernau-Felden.

🏃 Activities

The swimming beaches at Chieming and Gstadt (both free) are the easiest to reach, on the lake's eastern and northern shores respectively. A variety of boats are available for hire at many beaches, for €10 to €25 per hour. In Prien, **Bootsverleih Stöffl** (☑2000; www.stoeffl.de; Strandpromenade) is possibly the best company to turn to.

Prienavera   SWIMMING

(☑609 570; Seestrasse 120; 4hr pass adult/child €9.90/5.50, day pass €11.90/6.50, sauna extra €3; ⊙10am-9pm Mon-Fri, 9am-9pm Sat & Sun) The futuristic-looking glass roof by the harbour in Prien-Stock shelters Prienavera, a popular pool complex with a wellness area, water slides and a restaurant.

🛏 Sleeping

Hotel Bonnschlössl   HOTEL €€

(☑965 6990; www.alter-wirt-bernau.de; Kirchplatz 9, Bernau; s/d €57/96) Built in 1477, this pocket-sized palace hotel with faux turrets once belonged to the Bavarian royal court. Rooms are stylish, if slightly overfurnished, and there's a wonderful terrace with a rambling garden.

Hotel Garni Möwe   HOTEL €€

(☑5004; www.hotel-garni-moewe.de; Seestrasse 111, Prien; s/d from €61/99) This traditional Bavarian hotel right on the lakefront is excellent value, especially the loft rooms. It has its own bike and boat hire, plus a fitness centre, and the large garden is perfect for travellers with children.

DJH Hostel   HOSTEL €

(☑687 70; www.prien.jugendherberge.de; Carl-Braun-Strasse 66; dm from €18.40) Prien's hostel organises lots of activities and has an environmental study centre for young people. It's in a bucolic spot, a 15-minute walk from the Hauptbahnhof.

Panorama Camping Harras   CAMPGROUND €

(☑904 613; www.camping-harras.de; Harrasser Strasse 135; per person/tent/car from €5.50/3.60/2) This campsite is scenically located on a peninsula with its own private beach, and catamaran and surfboard hire. The restaurant has a delightful lakeside terrace.

🍴 Eating

Alter Wirt   BAVARIAN €€

(☑965 6990; Kirchplatz 9, Bernau; mains €8-15; ⊙closed Mon) This massive half-timbered inn with five centuries of history, situated on the main drag through Bernau, serves up Bavarian meat slabs and international favourites to a mix of locals and tourists.

Badehaus   BAVARIAN €€

(☑970 300; Rathausstrasse 11; mains €6.50-17; ⊙10am-late) Near the Chiemsee Info-Center and the lakeshore, this contemporary beer hall and garden has quirky decor and gourmet fare enjoyed by all. A special attraction is the 'beer bath', a glass tub (sometimes) filled with a mix of beer and water.

Westernacher am See   MODERN BAVARIAN €€

(☑4722; Seestrasse 115, Prien; mains €8-16) This lakeside dining haven has a multiple personality, with a cosy restaurant, cocktail bar, cafe, beer garden and glassed-in winter terrace. Its speciality is modern twists on old Bavarian favourites.

ℹ Information

All the tourist offices have free internet for brief walk-in use.

Bernau Tourist Office (☑986 80; www.bernau-am-chiemsee.de; Aschauer Strasse 10; ⊙8.30am-6pm Mon-Fri, 9am-noon Sat Jul–mid-Sep, shorter hours Mon-Fri & closed Sat mid-Sep–Jun)

Chiemsee Info-Center (☑965 550; www.chiemsee.de; ⊙9am-6pm Mon-Fri) On the southern lake shore, near the Bernau-Felden autobahn exit.

Prien Tourist Office (☑690 50; www.tourismus.prien.de; Alte Rathausstrasse 11; ⊙8.30am-6pm Mon-Fri, to 4pm Sat May-Sep, 8.30am-5pm Mon-Fri Oct-Apr)

ⓘ Getting There & Around

Trains run hourly from Munich to Prien (€16.40, one hour) and Bernau (€18.10, 1¼ hours). Hourly RVO bus 9505 (p234) connects the two lake towns.

Local buses run from Prien Bahnhof to the harbour in Stock. You can also take the historic **Chiemseebahn** (one-way/return €2.60/3.60) (1887), the world's oldest narrow-gauge steam train.

Chiemsee Schifffahrt (☑6090; www.chiemsee-schifffahrt.de; Seestrasse 108) operates half-hourly to hourly ferries from Prien with stops at Herreninsel, Fraueninsel, Seebruck and Chieming on a schedule that changes seasonally. You can circumnavigate the entire lake and make all these stops (getting off and catching the next ferry that comes your way) for €12.40. Children aged six to 15 get a 50% discount.

Chiemgauer Radhaus (☑4631; Bahnhofsplatz 6) and **Chiemgau Biking** (☑961 4973; Chiemseestrasse 84) hire out mountain bikes for between €12 and €22 per day.

Berchtesgaden

☑08652 / POP 7600

Wedged into Austria and framed by six formidable mountain ranges, the Berchtesgadener Land is a drop-dead-gorgeous corner of Bavaria steeped in myths and legends. Local lore has it that angels given the task of distributing the earth's wonders were startled by God's order to get a move on and dropped them all here. These most definitely included the Watzmann (2713m), Germany's second-highest mountain, and the pristine Königssee, perhaps Germany's most photogenic body of water.

Much of the area is protected by law within the Berchtesgaden National Park, which was declared a 'biosphere reserve' by Unesco in 1990. The village of Berchtesgaden is the obvious base for hiking circuits into the park.

Away from the trails, the main draws are the mountaintop Eagle's Nest, a lodge built for Hitler and now a major dark-tourism destination, and Dokumentation Obersalzberg, a museum that chronicles the region's sinister Nazi past.

⊙ Sights

Eagle's Nest   HISTORIC SITE
(☑2969; www.kehlsteinhaus.de; ⊘mid-May–Oct) Berchtesgaden's most sinister draw is Mt Kehlstein, a sheer-sided peak at Obersalzberg where Martin Bormann, a key hench-

man of Hitler's, engaged 3000 workers to build a diplomatic meeting house for the Führer's 50th birthday. Perched at 1834m, the innocent-looking lodge (called Kehlsteinhaus in German) occupies one of the world's most breathtaking spots. Ironically, Hitler is said to have suffered from vertigo and rarely enjoyed the spectacular views himself. The Allies never regarded the site worth bombing and it survived WWII untouched. Today the Eagle's Nest houses a restaurant that donates its profits to charity.

To get there, drive or take half-hourly bus 838 from the Hauptbahnhof to the Hotel Intercontinental then walk to the Kehlstein bus departure area. From here the road is closed to private traffic and you must take a special **bus** (adult/child €15.50/9) up the mountain (35 minutes). The final 124m stretch to the summit is in a luxurious brass-clad elevator.

Königssee   LAKE
Crossing the serenely picturesque, emerald-green Königssee makes for some unforgettable memories and once-in-a-lifetime photo opportunities. Contained by steep mountain walls some 5km south of Berchtesgaden, it's Germany's highest lake (603m), with drinkably pure waters shimmering into fjordlike depths. Bus 841 makes the trip out here from the Berchtesgaden Hauptbahnhof roughly every hour.

Escape the hubbub of the bustling lakeside tourist village by taking an electric **boat tour** (www.seenschifffahrt.de; return adult/child €13.30/6.70) to St Bartholomä, a quaint onion-domed chapel on the western shore. At some point, the boat will stop while the captain plays a horn towards the Echo Wall – the sound will bounce back seven times. Pure magic! The effect only fails during heavy fog. From the dock at St Bartholomä, an easy trail leads to the wondrous **Eiskapelle** (Ice Chapel) glacier cave in about one hour.

You can also skip the crowds by meandering along the lake shore. It's a nice and easy 3.5km return walk to the secluded **Malerwinkel** (Painter's Corner), a lookout famed for its picturesque vantage point.

Dokumentation Obersalzberg   MUSEUM
(www.obersalzberg.de; Salzbergstrasse 41, Obersalzberg; adult/child & student €3/free; ⊘9am-5pm daily Apr-Oct, 10am-3pm Tue-Sun Nov-Mar) In 1933 the quiet mountain retreat of Obersalzberg (3km from Berchtesgaden) became the southern headquarters of Hitler's

HITLER'S MOUNTAIN RETREAT

Of all the German towns tainted by the Third Reich, Berchtesgaden has a burden heavier than most. Hitler fell in love with nearby Obersalzberg in the 1920s and bought a small country home, later enlarged into the imposing Berghof.

After seizing power in 1933, Hitler established a part-time headquarters here and brought much of the party brass with him. They bought, or often confiscated, large tracts of land and tore down farmhouses to erect a 7ft-high barbed-wire fence. Obersalzberg was sealed off as the fortified southern headquarters of the NSDAP (National Socialist German Workers' Party). In 1938, British prime minister Neville Chamberlain visited for negotiations (later continued in Munich) which led to the infamous promise of 'peace in our time' at the expense of Czechoslovakia's Sudetenland.

Little is left of Hitler's Alpine fortress today. In the final days of WWII, the Royal Air Force levelled much of Obersalzberg, though the Eagle's Nest, Hitler's mountaintop eyrie, was left strangely unscathed. The historical twist and turns are dissected at the impressive Dokumentation Obersalzberg.

government, a dark period that's given the full historical treatment at the Dokumentation Obersalzberg. It's a fascinating exhibit that will probably make you queasy and uneasy, but the experience provides another piece in the region's historical jigsaw. You'll learn about the forced takeover of the area, the construction of the compound and the daily life of the Nazi elite. All facets of Nazi terror are dealt with, including Hitler's near-mythical appeal, his racial politics, the resistance movement, foreign policy and the death camps. A section of the underground bunker network is open for perusal. Half-hourly bus 838 from Berchtesgaden Hauptbahnhof will get you there.

Salzbergwerk
HISTORIC SITE

(www.salzzeitreise.de; Bergwerkstrasse 83; adult/child €15.50/9.50; ⊙9am-5pm May-Oct, 11am-3pm Nov-Apr) Once a major producer of 'white gold', Berchtesgaden has thrown open its salt mines for fun-filled 90-minute tours. Kids especially love donning miners' garb and whooshing down a wooden slide into the depths of the mine. Down below, highlights include mysteriously glowing salt grottoes and crossing a 100m-long subterranean salt lake on a wooden raft.

🏃 Activities

Berchtesgaden National Park
HIKING

(www.nationalpark-berchtesgaden.de) The wilds of the 210-sq-km Berchtesgaden National Park offer some of the best hiking in Germany. A good introduction is a 2km trail up from St Bartholomä beside the Königssee to the notorious Watzmann-Ostwand, where

scores of mountaineers have met their deaths. Another popular hike goes from the southern end of the Königssee to the Obersee. For details of routes visit the national park office (☑643 43; Franziskanerplatz 7; ⊙9am-5pm), or buy a copy of the Berchtesgadener Land (sheet 794) map in the Kompass series.

Jenner-Königssee Area
SKIING

(☑958 10; www.jennerbahn.de; daily pass adult/child €29.20/15.50) The Jenner-Königssee area at Königssee is the biggest and most varied of five local ski fields. For equipment hire and courses, try Skischule Treff-Aktiv (☑979 707; www.treffaktiv.de; Jennerbahnstrasse 19).

Watzmann Therme
SPA

(☑946 40; www.watzmann-therme.de; Bergwerkstrasse 54; 2hr/4hr/day €9.70/12.20/13.90; ⊙10am-10pm) The Watzman Therme is Berchtesgaden's thermal wellness complex, with several indoor and outdoor pools and various hydrotherapeutic treatment stations, a sauna and inspiring Alpine views.

👉 Tours

Eagle's Nest Tours
TOUR

(☑649 71; www.eagles-nest-tours.com; Königsseer Strasse 2; adult/child €50/35; ⊙1.15pm mid-May–Oct) Experience the sinister legacy of the Obersalzberg area, including the Eagle's Nest and the underground bunker system, on a four-hour guided tour with Eagle's Nest Tours. Buses depart from the tourist office and reservations are advised.

🛏 Sleeping

Ask at the tourist office about private rooms in and around Berchtesgaden and campsites in Schönau near the Königssee. Advertised room rates normally don't include the local spa tax of €2.10 per adult per night.

Hotel Krone   HOTEL €€
(☏946 00; www.hotel-krone-berchtesgaden.de; Am Rad 5; s €44-54, d €82-108) Ambling distance from the town centre, this family-run gem provides almost unrivalled views of the valley and the Alps beyond. The wood-rich cabin-style rooms are generously cut affairs, with carved ceilings, niches and bedsteads all in fragrant pine. Take breakfast on the suntrap terrace for a memorable start to the day.

Hotel-Pension Greti   GUESTHOUSE €€
(☏975 297; www.pension-greti.de; Waldhauser Strasse 20; s €35-39, d €61-120) Warm and welcoming, and just a 15-minute walk from the Königssee, Greti's rooms are surprisingly voguish and all have balconies. The cellar bar and small sauna are perfect for some post-piste unwinding.

Hotel Bavaria   HOTEL €€
(☏660 11; www.hotelbavaria.net; Sunklergässchen 11; r €50-130; P) In the same family for over a century, this well-run hotel offers a romantic vision of Alpine life with rooms bedecked in frilly curtains, canopied beds, heart-shaped mirrors and knotty wood galore. Five of the pricier rooms have their own whirlpools. Breakfast is a gourmet affair, with sparkling wine and both hot and cold delectables.

Hotel Vier Jahreszeiten   HOTEL €€
(☏9520; www.hotel-vierjahreszeiten-berchtesgaden.de; Maximilianstrasse 20; s €50-68, d €85-101; P🐕) For a glimpse of Berchtesgaden's storied past, stay at this traditional in-town lodge where Bavarian royalty once entertained. Rooms are a bit long in the tooth but the spectacular mountain views (only from south-facing, ergo more expensive, rooms) more than compensate. Don't miss dinner in the atmospheric Hubertusstube restaurant.

DJH Hostel   HOSTEL €
(☏943 70; www.berchtesgaden.jugendherberge.de; Struberberg 6; dm from €17.60) This 265-bed hostel is situated in the suburb of Strub and has great views of Mt Watzmann. It's a 25-minute walk from the Hauptbahnhof or a short hop on bus 839.

🍴 Eating

Farmers markets selling meats, cheese and other produce are held on the Marktplatz every Friday morning between April and October.

Le Ciel   INTERNATIONAL €€€
(☏975 50; www.restaurant-leciel.de; Hintereck 1; mains €30-40; ⊙6.30-10.30pm Tue-Sat) Don't let the Hotel InterConti location turn you off: Le Ciel really is as heavenly as its French name suggests and it has the Michelin star to prove it. Testers were especially impressed by Ulrich Heimann's knack for spinning regional ingredients into such inspired gourmet compositions. Service is smooth and the circular dining room is magical. Only 32 seats, so book ahead if you can.

Gaststätte St Bartholomä   BAVARIAN €€
(☏964 937; St Bartholomä; mains €7-16) Perched on the shore of the Königssee, and reached by boat, this is a tourist haunt that actually serves delicious food made with ingredients picked, plucked and hunted from the surrounding forests and the lake. Savour generous platters of venison in mushroom sauce with dumplings and red sauerkraut in the large beer garden or indoors.

Bräustübl   BAVARIAN €€
(☏976 724; Bräuhausstrasse 13; mains €8-14; ⊙10am-1am) Enter through the arch painted in Bavaria's white and blue diamonds and pass the old beer barrels to reach the secluded beer garden belonging to the town's brewery. The vaulted hall is the scene of heel-whacking Bavarian stage shows every Saturday night.

Holzkäfer   CAFE, BAR €
(☏600 90; Buchenhöhe 40; dishes €4-9; ⊙11am-1am Wed-Mon) This funky log cabin in the Obersalzberg hills is a great spot for a night out with fun-loving locals. Cluttered with antlers, carvings and backwoods oddities, it's known for its tender pork roasts, dark beer and Franconian wines.

Dalmacija   BISTRO €
(☏976 027; Marktplatz 5; dishes €5-9; ⊙9am-late) Pizzas, pastas and a whiff of the Balkans in a contemporary-styled bistro-cafe.

ℹ Information

Post Office (Franziskanerplatz 2)

Tourist Office (www.berchtesgaden.de; Königsseer Strasse 2; ⊙8.30am-6pm Mon-Fri, to 5pm Sat, 9am-3pm Sun Apr–mid-Oct, reduced hours mid-Oct–Mar)

BAVARIA BERCHTESGADEN

ⓘ Getting There & Away

Travelling from Munich by train involves a change at Freilassing (€30.90, three hours, five connections daily). The best option between Berchtesgaden and Salzburg is RVO bus (p234) 840 (45 minutes) which leaves from the train station in both towns roughly twice hourly. Berchtesgaden is south of the Munich–Salzburg A8 autobahn.

THE ROMANTIC ROAD

From the vineyards of Würzburg to the foot of the Alps, the almost 400km-long Romantic Road (Romantische Strasse) draws two million visitors every year, making it by far the most popular of Germany's holiday routes. This well-trodden trail cuts through a cultural and historical cross-section of southern Germany as it traverses Franconia and clips Baden-Württemberg in the north before plunging into Bavaria proper to end at Ludwig II's crazy castles. Expect lots of Japanese signs and menus, tourist coaches and kitsch galore, but also a fair wedge of *Gemütlichkeit* and geniune hospitality from those who earn their living on this most romantic of routes.

ⓘ Information

The Romantic Road runs north–south through western Bavaria, covering 385km between Würzburg and Füssen near the Austrian border. It passes through more than two dozen cities and towns, including Rothenburg ob der Tauber, Dinkelsbühl and Augsburg.

ⓘ Getting There & Away

Though Frankfurt is the most popular gateway for the Romantic Road, Munich is a good choice as well, especially if you decide to take the bus.

With its gentle gradients and bucolic flavour between towns, the Romantic Road is ideal for the holidaying cyclist. Bikes can be hired at many train stations; tourist offices keep lists of bicycle-friendly hotels that permit storage, or check out **Bett und Bike** (www.bettundbike.de) predeparture.

Direct trains run from Munich to Füssen (€24, two hours) at the southern end of the Romantic Road every two hours, more often if you change in Buchloe. Rothenburg is linked by train to Würzburg (€12.20, one hour), Munich (from €37.30, three hours), Augsburg (€29.70, 2½ hours) and Nuremberg (€18, 1¼ to two hours), with at least one change needed in Steinach to reach any destination.

ⓘ Getting Around

It is possible to do this route using train connections and local buses, but the going is complicated, tedious and slow, especially at weekends. The ideal way to travel is by car, though many foreign travellers prefer to take Deutsche Touring's **Europabus** (☎069-790 3230; www.romanticroadcoach.de), which can get incredibly crowded in summer. From April to October the special coach runs daily in each direction between Frankfurt and Füssen (for Neuschwanstein); the entire journey takes around 12 hours. There's no charge for breaking the journey and continuing the next day.

Tickets are available for short segments of the trip, and reservations are only necessary during peak-season weekends. Reservations can be made through travel agents, Deutsche Touring, EurAide in Munich, and Deutsche Bahn's Reisezentrum offices in the train stations. If you stayed on the coach all the way from Frankfurt to Füssen (a pointless exercise), the total fare would be €158, The average fare from one stop to the next is around €3.

Coaches can accommodate bicycles (up to five stops cost €5; six to 11 stops, €8), but you must give three working days' notice. Students, children, pensioners and rail-pass holders qualify for discounts of between 10% and 50%.

For detailed schedules and prices, see www.romanticroadcoach.de.

Würzburg

 0931 / POP 133,500

'If I could choose my place of birth, I would consider Würzburg', wrote author Hermann Hesse, and it's not difficult to see why. This scenic town straddles the Main River and is renowned for its art, architecture and delicate wines. A large student population guarantees a lively scene, and plenty of hip nightlife pulsates through its cobbled streets.

Würzburg was a Franconian duchy when, in 686, three Irish missionaries tried to persuade Duke Gosbert to convert to Christianity and ditch his wife. Gosbert was mulling it over when his wife had the three bumped off. When the murders were discovered decades later, the martyrs became saints and Würzburg was made a pilgrimage city and, in 742, a bishopric.

For centuries the resident prince-bishops wielded enormous power and wealth, and the city grew in opulence under their rule. Their crowning glory is the Residenz, one of the finest baroque structures in Germany and a Unesco World Heritage Site.

Decimated in WWII when 90% of the city centre was flattened, the authorities originally planned to leave the ruins as a reminder of the horrors of war. But a valiant rebuilding project saw the city restored almost to its pre-war glory.

◉ Sights

Residenz
PALACE

(Map p250; www.residenz-wuerzburg.de; Balthasar-Neumann-Promenade; adult/child €7.50/6.50; ⊙9am-6pm Apr-Oct, 10am-4.30pm Nov-Mar) The Unesco-listed Residenz is one of Germany's most important and beautiful baroque palaces and is a great way to kick off or end a journey along the Romantic Road.

Johann Philipp Franz von Schönborn, unhappy with his old-fashioned digs up in Marienberg Fortress, hired young architect Balthasar Neumann to build a new palace in town. Construction started in 1720. It took almost 60 years before the interior was completed, but the prince-bishops only used the palace for 20 years before they were incorporated into Bavaria. During the British bombing of WWII, the central section miraculously escaped unharmed; the rest required extensive restoration. Today the 350 rooms are home to government institutions, flats, faculties of the university and a museum, but the grandest spaces have been restored for visitors to admire.

Visits are by guided tour only. German-language groups leave every half an hour; English tours leave at 11am and 3pm year-round and, additionally, at 4.30pm April to October.

In 1750, the ceiling above Neumann's brilliant Grand Staircase, a single central set of steps that splits and zigzags up to the 1st floor, was topped by what still is the world's largest fresco (667 sq metres), by Tiepolo. It allegorically depicts the four then-known continents (Europe, Africa, America and Asia).

Take in the ice-white stucco of the Weisser Saal (White Hall), a soothing interlude in mind-boggling stucco and papier mâché, before entering the Kaisersaal (Imperial Hall), canopied by yet another impressive Tiepolo fresco. Other meticulously restored staterooms include the gilded stucco Spiegelkabinett (Mirror Hall), covered with a unique mirrorlike glass painted with figural, floral and animal motifs that make you feel as if you're standing inside a Fabergé egg. Destroyed in WWII, this room

took eight years to recreate in the 1980s and contains 600 sq metres of gold leaf.

You're usually set free by the guide to explore the north-wing imperial apartments alone. Less impressive than the other parts of the palace, highlights include the velveteen-draped bed where Napoleon I slept in 1812 and a green lacquered room with an intricately inlaid parquet floor.

The bare corridors between the various restored rooms are given interest by fascinating exhibitions on the restoraion techniques used here in the postwar decades.

In the residence's south wing, the Hofkirche (Court Church) is another Neumann and Tiepolo co-production. Its marble columns, gold leaf and profusion of angels match the Residenz in splendour and proportions.

Behind the Residenz, the Hofgarten has whimsical sculptures of children, mostly by court sculptor Peter Wagner. Concerts, festivals and special events take place here during the warmer months. Enter through intricate wrought-iron gates into the French- and English-style gardens, partly built on the old baroque bastions.

Next to the main entrance, the Martin-von-Wagner Museum (Map p250; ☑312 288; Residenzplatz 2; admission free; ⊙Antikensammlung 1.30-5pm Tue-Sat, Gemäldegalerie 10am-1.30pm Tue-Sat, Graphische Sammlung 4-6pm Tue & Thu) is home to three collections. The Antikensammlung (Antiquities Collection) focuses on Greek, Roman and Egyptian ceramics, vases, figurines and marble sculptures from 1500 BC to AD 300. The Gemäldegalerie (Art Gallery) has primarily German, Dutch and Italian paintings from the 15th to the 19th centuries, including works by Tiepolo. Finally, the Graphische Sammlung (Graphics Collection) consists of drawings, copperplate etchings and woodcuts, including some by Albrecht Dürer.

Atmospherically housed in the cellar of the Residenz is a winery owned and run by the Bavarian government, Staatlicher Hofkeller Würzburg (Map p250; ☑305 0931; www.hofkeller.de; Residenzplatz 3; tours €7; ⊙tours 4.30pm & 5.30pm Fri, hourly from 10am Sat & Sun), Germany's second largest. It produces some exceptional wines; tours conclude with a tasting.

Festung Marienberg
FORTRESS

(Map p250) Panoramic views over the city's red rooftops and vine-covered hills extend from Festung Marienberg (Marienberg Fortress), which has presided over Würzburg

Würzburg

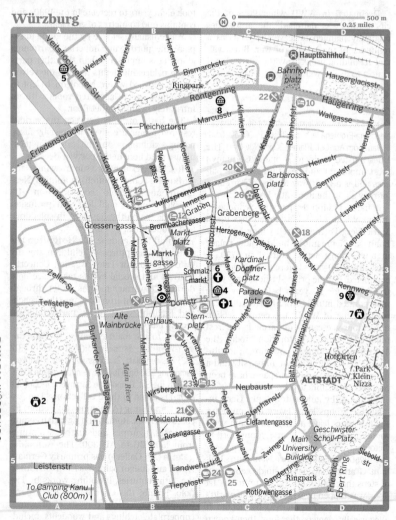

since the city's prince-bishops commenced its construction in 1201; they governed from here until 1719. At night floodlights dramatically illuminate the hulking structure, which has only been penetrated once, by Swedish troops in 1631 during the Thirty Years' War. In summer, the gently sloping lawns are strewn with picnickers.

The prince-bishops' pompous lifestyle is on show in the residential wing at the **Fürstenbaumuseum** (Map p250; adult/child €4.50/3.50; ☺9am-6pm Tue-Sun mid-Mar–Oct), the highlight of which is a huge tapestry showing the entire family of Julius Echter von Mespelbrunn. The city's history is laid out in the upper-level exhibition rooms.

A striking collection of Tilman Riemenschneider sculptures take pride of place in the **Mainfränkisches Museum** (Map p250; www.mainfraenkisches-museum.de; adult/child €4/2; ☺10am-5pm Tue-Sun). In another section, porcelain, glass, furniture and other such objects illustrate life during the baroque and rococo eras; from the same period are the sketches and drawings by Neumann and Tiepolo.

The fortress is a 30-minute walk up the hill from the Alte Mainbrücke via the **Tell-**

Würzburg

steige trail, which is part of the 4km-long **Weinwanderweg** (Wine Hiking Trail) through the vineyards around Marienberg.

Neumünster CHURCH
(Map p250; Schönbornstrasse; ⊙6am-6.30pm Mon-Sat, from 8am Sun) In the Altstadt, this satisfyingly symmetrical church stands on the site where the three ill-fated Irish missionaries who tried to convert Duke Gosbert to Christianity in 686 met their maker. Romanesque at its core, it was given a baroque makeover by the Zimmermann brothers. The interior has busts of the three martyrs (Kilian, Colonan and Totnan) on the high altar and the tomb of St Kilian lurks in the crypt.

Dom St Kilian CHURCH
(Map p250; www.dom-wuerzburg.de) Würzburg's Romanesque Dom St Kilian was built between 1040 and 1237, although numerous alterations have added Gothic, Renaissance and baroque elements. The whole ecclesiatical caboodle was under heavy renovation at the time of writing, but was set to reopen in early 2013.

FREE Grafeneckart MEMORIAL
(Map p250; Domstrasse) Adjoining the **Rathaus**, the 1659-built Grafeneckart houses a scale model of the WWII bombing, which starkly depicts the extent of the damage to the city following the night of 16 March 1945, when 5000 citizens lost their lives. Viewing it before you climb up to the fortress overlooking the city gives you an appreciation of Würzburg's astonishing recovery.

Museum Am Dom ART MUSEUM
(Map p250; www.museum-am-dom.de; Kiliansplatz; adult/concession €3.50/2.50; ⊙10am-6pm Tue-Sun Apr-Oct, to 5pm Nov-Mar) Housed in a beautiful building by the cathedral, this worthwhile museum displays collections of modern art on Christian themes. Works of international renown by Joseph Beuys, Otto Dix and Käthe Kollwitz are on show, as well as masterpieces of the Romantic, Gothic and baroque periods.

Museum im Kulturspeicher ART MUSEUM
(Map p250; ☎322 250; www.kulturspeicher.de; Veitshöchheimer Strasse 5; adult/concession €3.50/2; ⊙1-6pm Tue, 11am-6pm Wed & Fri-Sun, 11am-7pm Thu) In a born-again historic granary right on the Main River, you'll find this absorbing art museum with choice artworks from the 19th to the 21st centuries. The emphasis is on German impressionism, neo-realism and contemporary art, but the building also houses the post-1945 constructivist works of the Peter C Ruppert collection, a challenging assembly of computer art, sculpture, paintings and photographs.

Röntgen Gedächtnisstätte MUSEUM
(Map p250; ☎351 1102; www.wilhelmconradroentgen.de; Röntgenring 8; admission free; ⊙8am-8pm Mon-Fri, 8am-6pm Sat) Nobel Prize–winner Wilhelm Conrad Röntgen discovered X-ray in 1895; his laboratory forms the heart of this small exhibition where illuminating multimedia displays chart the emergence of the X-ray process.

BAVARIA WÜRZBURG

✳ Festivals & Events

Mozart Fest
MUSIC

(☑372 336; www.mozartfest-wuerzburg.de; ☺Jun) Germany's oldest Mozart festival takes place at the Residenz throughout June.

Africa Festival
CULTURE

(☑150 60; www.africafestival.org; ☺late May) Held on the meadows northwest of the river at Mainwiesen, complete with markets, food stalls and, if it rains, lots of mud.

Hoffest am Stein
WINE & MUSIC

(www.weingut-am-stein.de; ☺early Jul) Wine and music festival held in the first half of July at the Weingut am Stein.

🛏 Sleeping

Sleep in Würzburg comes slightly cheaper than in other Bavarian cities.

Hotel Rebstock
HOTEL €€

(Map p250; ☑309 30; www.rebstock.com; Neubaustrasse 7; s/d from €101/120; ✳@🖤) Don't be misled by the Best Western sign out front: Würzburg's top digs, in a squarely renovated rococo town house, has 70 unique, stylishly finished rooms, impeccable service and an Altstadt location. The list of illustrious former guests includes Franz Beckenbauer and Cliff Richard. Bike rental available.

Babelfish
HOSTEL €

(Map p250; ☑304 0430; www.babelfish-hostel. de; Haugerring 2; dm €17-23, s/d €45/70) With a name inspired by a creature in Douglas Adams' novel *The Hitchhiker's Guide to the Galaxy*, this uncluttered and spotlessly clean hostel has 74 beds spread over two floors, a sunny rooftop terrace, 24-hour reception (2nd floor), wheelchair-friendly facilities and little extras like card keys and a laundry room. The communal areas are an inviting place to down a few beers in the evening and there's a well-equipped guest kitchen.

Hotel Zum Winzermännle
GUESTHOUSE €€

(Map p250; ☑541 56; www.winzermaennle.de; Domstrasse 32; s €56-70, d €86-100; P@) This former winery in the city's pedestrianised heart was rebuilt in its original style after the war as a guesthouse by the same charming family. Well-furnished rooms and communal areas are bright and often seasonally decorated. Breakfast and parking are an extra €5 and €8 respectively.

Hotel Dortmunder Hof
HOTEL €€

(Map p250; ☑561 63; www.dortmunder-hof.de; Innerer Graben 22; s €42-65, d €76-100) This bike-friendly hotel occupies a brightly renovated building with spotless en-suite rooms with cable TV. Parking can be arranged close by, and there's live music in the cellar bar.

Hotel Residence
HOTEL €€

(Map p250; ☑3593 4340; www.wuerzburg-hotel. de; Juliuspromenade 1; s/d from €75/95; P) The grandly named Residence has box-ticking rooms, some in pale shades others warmer, plusher affairs. It could do with a bit of an update, but it's comfortable enough and very central.

DJH Hostel
HOSTEL €

(Map p250; ☑425 90; www.wuerzburg.jugendher berge.de; Fred-Joseph-Platz 2 ; dm from €21.30) At the foot of the fortress, this well-equipped, wheelchair-friendly hostel has room for 238 snoozers in three- to eight-bed dorms.

Camping Kanu Club
CAMPGROUND €

(☑725 36; www.kc-wuerzburg.de; Mergentheimer Strasse 13b; per person/tent €2.50/3.50) The closest campsite to the town centre. Take tram 3 or 5 to the Judenbühlweg stop, which is on its doorstep.

🍴 Eating

For a town of its size, Würzburg has an enticing selection of pubs, beer gardens, cafes and restaurants, with plenty of student hang-outs among them.

Bürgerspital Weinstube
WINE RESTAURANT €€

(Map p250; ☑352 880; Theaterstrasse 19; mains €7-23; ☺lunch & dinner) The cosy nooks of this labyrinthine medieval place are among Würzburg's most popular eating and drinking spots. Choose from a broad selection of Franconian wines (declared Germany's best in 2011) and wonderful regional dishes, including *Mostsuppe*, a tasty wine soup.

Alte Mainmühle
FRANCONIAN €€

(Map p250; ☑167 77; Mainkai 1; mains €7-21; ☺10am-midnight) Accessed straight from the old bridge, tourists and locals alike cram onto the double-decker terrace suspended above the Main River to savour modern twists on old Franconian favourites. Summer alfresco dining is accompanied by pretty views of the Festung Marienberg; in winter retreat to the snug timber dining room.

Backöfele
FRANCONIAN €€

(Map p250; ☎590 59; Ursulinergasse 2; mains €10-22; ☺noon-1am) Begin a memorable meal at this cobble-floored, candlelit restaurant with *Fränkische Mostsuppe* (frothy Franconian wine soup with cinnamon croutons) and follow up with Backöfele's innovative twists on traditional game, steak and fish dishes. Popular with the uni crowd and almost always full, so bookings are recommended.

Juliusspital
WINE RESTAURANT €€

(Map p250; ☎540 80; Juliuspromenade 19; mains €8-21; ☺10am-midnight) This attractive *Weinstube* (traditional wine tavern) features fabulous Franconian fish and even better wines. Ambient lighting, scurrying waiters and walls occupied by oil paintings make this the place to head to for a special do.

Uni-Café
CAFE €

(Map p250; ☎156 72; Neubaustrasse 2; snacks €2.50-7; ☺8am-1am) Hugely popular contemporary cafe strung over two levels, with a student-priced, daily-changing menu of burgers and salads and a buzzy bar.

Natur-Feinkostladen
VEGETARIAN €

(Map p250; Sanderstrasse 2a; dishes from €4; ☺8.30am-7.30pm Mon-Fri, 10am-2pm Sat) Come here for wholesome snacks and healthy fare enjoyed around simple wooden tables. Also runs the adjacent specialist grocery.

Capri & Blaue Grotto
ITALIAN €€

(Map p250; Elefantengasse 1; pizzas €6-8, other mains €6.50-14; ☺lunch & dinner) This outpost of the *bel paese* has been plating up pronto pasta and pizza since 1952, making it Germany's oldest Italian eatery.

Starback
BAKERY €

(Map p250; Kaiserstrasse 33; snacks from €0.69) No German-language skills are required to put together a budget breakfast or lunch at this no-frills self-service bakery opposite the train station.

☕ Drinking & Entertainment

For more options, grab a copy of the monthly listing magazine *Frizz* (in German). Look out for posters and flyers advertising big-name concerts that take place on the Residenzplatz.

Kult
CAFE, BAR

(Map p250; Landwehrstrasse 10; ☺9am-late Mon-Fri, 10am-late Sat & Sun) Enjoy a tailor-made breakfast, munch on a cheap lunch or party into the wee hours at Würzburg's hippest cafe. The unpretentious interior, with its salvaged tables and old beige benches, hosts regular fancy-dress parties, table-football tournaments and other off-beat events. DJs take over at weekends.

MUCK
CAFE, BAR

(Map p250; Sanderstrasse 29) One of the earliest openers in town, and serving a mean breakfast from 7am, the cafe morphs into something of an informal party after nightfall.

Standard
LIVE MUSIC

(Map p250; Oberthürstrasse 11a) Soulful jazz spins beneath a corrugated-iron ceiling and stainless-steel fans, while bands and DJs play a couple of times or more a week in a second, dimly lit downstairs bar.

❶ Information

Ferial Internet Cafe (Sanderstrasse 6a; per hr €1.80; ☺10am-11pm Mon-Fri, from 11am Sat & Sun) Cheap web access.

Post Office (Paradeplatz 4)

Tourist Office (☎372 398; www.wuerzburg.de; Marktplatz; ☺10am-6pm Mon-Fri, 10am-2pm Sat Apr-Dec, plus 10am-2pm Sun May-Oct, reduced hours Jan-Mar)

❶ Getting There & Away

BUS The Romantic Road Europabus stops at the main bus station next to the Hauptbahnhof, and at the Residenzplatz.

TRAIN Train connections from Würzburg:

» **Bamberg** €19, one hour, twice hourly

» **Frankfurt** €33, one hour, hourly

» **Nuremberg** €19.20 to €27, one hour, twice hourly

» **Rothenburg ob der Tauber** Change in Steinach; €12.20, one hour, hourly

❶ Getting Around

The most useful service is bus 9 (€1.60) which shuttles roughly hourly between the Residenz and the Festung Marienberg. Otherwise Würzburg can be easily tackled on foot.

Rothenburg ob der Tauber

☑09861 / POP 11,000

A well-polished gem from the Middle Ages, Rothenburg ob der Tauber (meaning 'above the Tauber River') is the main tourist stop along the Romantic Road. With its web of cobbled lanes, higgledy-piggledy houses and towered walls, the town is impossibly charming. Preservation orders here are the

Rothenburg ob der Tauber

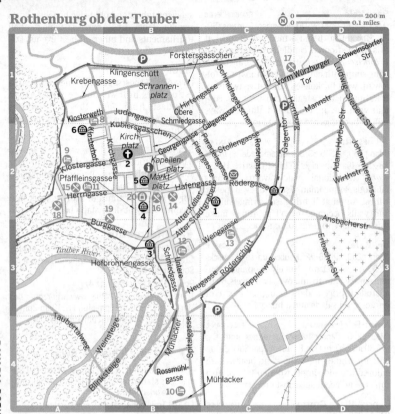

strictest in Germany – and at times it feels like a medieval theme park – but all's forgiven in the evenings, when the yellow lamplight casts its spell long after the last tour buses have left.

◉ Sights

Jakobskirche
CHURCH

(Map p254; Klingengasse 1; adult/child €2/0.50; ⏰9am-5pm) One of the few places of worship in Bavaria to charge cheeky admission, Rothenburg's Lutheran parish church was begun in the 14th century and finished in the 15th. The building sports some wonderfully aged stained-glass windows, but its real pièce de résistance is Tilman Riemenschneider's carved **Heilig Blut Altar** (Sacred Blood Altar). The gilded cross above the main scene depicting the Last Supper incorporates Rothenburg's treasured reliquary: a capsule made of rock crystal said to contain three drops of Christ's blood.

Mittelalterliches Kriminalmuseum
MUSEUM

(Map p254; ☑5359; www.kriminalmuseum.rothenburg.de; Burggasse 3-5; adult/child €4.20/2.60; ⏰10am-6pm May-Oct, shorter hours Nov-Apr) Brutal implements of torture and punishment from medieval times are on show at this gruesomely fascinating museum. Exhibits include chastity belts, masks of disgrace for gossips, a cage for cheating bakers, a neck brace for quarrelsome women and a beer-barrel pen for drunks, and there are also displays on local witch trials. Visitors can have their photo taken in the stocks outside.

Deutsches Weihnachtsmuseum
MUSEUM

(Map p254; ☑409 365; www.weihnachtsmuseum.de; Herrngasse 1; adult/child/family €4/2/7; ⏰10am-5.30pm daily Easter-Christmas, 11am-4pm Sat & Sun mid-Jan–Easter) If you're glad Christmas comes but once every 365 days, then stay well clear of the Käthe Wohlfahrt Weihnachtsdorf

Rothenburg ob der Tauber

(p257), a Yuletide superstore that also houses the Christmas Museum. This repository of all things 'Ho! Ho! Ho!' traces the development of various Christmas customs and decorations, and includes a display of 150 Santa figures, plus lots of retro baubles and tinsel – particularly surreal in mid-July when the mercury outside is pushing 30°C. Not as big a hit with kids as you might predict, as they can't get their hands on anything.

Town Walls   HISTORIC SITE
With time and fresh legs, a 2.5km circular walk around the unbroken ring of the town walls gives a sense of the importance medieval man put on defending his settlements. There are good views from the eastern tower, the **Röderturm** (Map p254; Rödergasse; adult/child €1.50/1; ⊙9am-5pm Mar-Nov), though it's staffed by volunteers and is often closed. For the most impressive views head to the west side of town, where a sweeping view of the Tauber Valley includes the **Doppelbrücke**, a double-decker bridge.

Reichsstadt Museum   MUSEUM
(Map p254; www.reichsstadtmuseum.rothenburg. de; Klosterhof 5; adult/concession €4/3.50; ⊙10am-5pm Apr-Oct, 1-4pm Nov-Mar) Highlights of the Reichsstadt Museum, housed in a former Dominican convent, include the *Rothenburger Passion* (1494), a cycle of 12 panels by Martinus Schwarz, and the oldest convent kitchen in Germany, as well as weapons and armour. Outside the main entrance (on your right as you're facing the museum), you'll see a spinning barrel, where the nuns distributed bread to the poor – and where women would leave babies they couldn't afford to keep. For a serene break between sightseeing, head to the **Klostergarten** behind the museum (enter from Klosterhof).

Rathaus   HISTORIC BUILDING
(Map p254; Marktplatz; Rathausturm adult/concession €2/0.50; ⊙Rathausturm 9.30am-12.30pm & 1-5pm daily Apr-Oct, noon-3pm daily Dec, shorter hours Sat & Sun Nov & Jan-Mar) The Rathaus on Marktplatz was begun in Gothic style in the 14th century, and was completed during the Renaissance. Climb the 220 steps to the viewing platform of the **Rathausturm** to be rewarded with widescreen views of the Tauber.

Alt-Rothenburger Handwerkerhaus   HISTORIC BUILDING
(Map p254; ☑5810; Alter Stadtgraben 26; adult/child €2.50/1; ⊙11am-5pm Mon-Fri, from 10am Sat & Sun Easter-Oct, 2-4pm daily Dec) Hidden down a little alley is the Alt-Rothenburger Handwerkerhaus, where numerous artisans – including coopers, weavers, cobblers and potters – have their workshops today, and have had their workshops for the house's more than 700-year existence.

Puppen-und Spielzeugmuseum   MUSEUM
(Map p254; ☑7330; Hofbronnengasse 13; adult/child €4/2.50; ⊙9.30am-6pm Mar-Dec, 11am-5pm Jan & Feb) A nostalgic collection of dollhouses, teddy bears, toy carousels, tin soldiers and infinite glass-eyed dolls awaits at this comprehensive museum, the work of collector Katharina Engels. All the exhibits are presented in traditional glass display cases.

BAVARIA ROTHENBURG OB DER TAUBER

ⓒ Tours

The tourist office (p257) runs 90-minute walking tours (€7; in English) at 11am and 2pm from April to October. Every evening a lantern-toting *Nachtwächter* dressed in traditional costume leads an entertaining tour of the Altstadt; English tours (€7) meet at the Rathaus at 8pm.

✱ Festivals & Events

Historisches Festspiel 'Der Meistertrunk'   FOLK DANCE

The Historisches Festspiel 'Der Meistertrunk' takes place each year on Whitsuntide, with parades, dances and a medieval market. The highlight, though, is the re-enactment of the mythical *Meistertrunk* story. The *Meistertrunk* play itself is performed three more times: once during the Reichsstadt-Festtage in early September, when the entire city's history is re-enacted in the streets, and twice during the Rothenburger Herbst, an autumn celebration in October.

Historischer Schäfertanz   DANCE

(Marktplatz) The Historischer Schäfertanz (Historical Shepherds' Dance), featuring colourfully dressed couples, takes places on Marktplatz several times between April and October.

Christmas Market   MARKET

Rothenburg's Christmas market is one of the most romantic in Germany. It's set out around the central Marktplatz during Advent.

🛏 Sleeping

Hotel Herrnschlösschen   HOTEL €€€

(Map p254; ☑873 890; www.herrnschloesschen.de; Herrngasse 20; r from €195) The most recent addition to Rothenburg's hotel stock has breathed life back into a 900-year-old mansion. The whole place is a blend of ancient and new, with Gothic arches leaping over faux-retro furniture and ageing oak preventing ceilings from crashing down onto chic 21st-century beds. The hotel's restaurant has established itself as one of the town's most innovative dining spots.

Altfränkische Weinstube   HOTEL €

(Map p254; ☑6404; www.altfraenkische-weinstube-rothenburg.de; Klosterhof 7; r €59-89; 🐭) Hiding in a quiet side street near the Reichsstad Museum, this enchantingly characterful inn has six atmosphere-laden rooms, all with bathtubs and most with four-poster or canopied beds. The restaurant (open for dinner only) serves up sound regional fare with a dollop of medieval cheer.

Hotel Raidel   HOTEL €

(Map p254; ☑3115; www.gaestehaus-raidel.de; Wenggasse 3; s/d €45/69; 🐭) With 500-year-old exposed beams studded with wooden nails, antiques throughout and a welcoming owner, as well as musical instruments for the guests to play, this is the place to check in if you're craving some genuine romance on the Romantic Road.

BOTTOMS UP FOR FREEDOM

In 1631 the Thirty Years War – pitching Catholics against Protestants – reached the gates of Rothenburg ob der Tauber. Catholic General Tilly and 60,000 of his troops besieged the Protestant market town and demanded its surrender. The town resisted but couldn't stave off the onslaught of marauding soldiers, and the mayor and other town dignitaries were captured and sentenced to death.

And that's about where the story ends and the legend begins. As the tale goes, Rothenburg's town council tried to sate Tilly's bloodthirstiness by presenting him with a 3L pitcher of wine. Tilly, after taking a sip or two, presented the men with an unusual challenge, saying 'If one of you has the courage to step forward and down this mug of wine in one gulp, then I shall spare the town and the lives of the councilmen!' Mayor Georg Nusch accepted – and succeeded! And that's why you can still wander though Rothenburg's wonderful medieval lanes today.

It's pretty much accepted that Tilly was really placated with hard cash. Nevertheless, local poet Adam Hörber couldn't resist turning the tale of the *Meistertrunk* into a play, which, since 1881, has been performed every Whitsuntide (Pentecost), the seventh Sunday after Easter. It's also re-enacted several times daily by the clock figures on the tourist office building.

Burg-Hotel
HOTEL €€

(Map p254; ☎948 90; www.burghotel.eu; Klostergasse 1-3; s €100-135, d €100-170; P🐾) Each of the 15 elegantly furnished guest rooms at this boutique hotel built into the town walls has its own private sitting area. The lower floors shelter a decadent spa with tanning beds, saunas and rainforest showers, and a cellar with a Steinway piano; while phenomenal valley views unfurl from the breakfast room and stone terrace. Garaged parking costs €7.50.

Kreuzerhof Hotel Garni
GUESTHOUSE €

(Map p254; ☎3424; www.kreuzerhof-rothenburg. de; Millergasse 2-6; s €45, d €59-72) Away from the tourist swarms, this quiet family-run B&B has charming, randomly furnished rooms with antique touches in a medieval town house and annexe. There's free tea and coffee and the generous breakfast is an energy-boosting set-up for the day.

DJH Hostel
HOSTEL €

(Map p254; ☎941 60; www.rothenburg.jugendherberge.de; Mühlacker 1; dm from €21.60) Rothenburg's youth hostel occupies two enormous old buildings in the south of town. It's agreeably renovated and extremely well equipped, but you can hear the screams of noisy school groups from outside.

✖ Eating

Bürgerkeller
FRANCONIAN €

(Map p254; ☎2126; Herrngasse 24; mains €6.80-12.80; ⊙dinner) Down a short flight of steps in a frescoed 16th-century cellar, this hidden spot serves local, seasonal produce, such as autumn mushrooms and spring asparagus, as part of classic Franconian mains. Service is clued up about the wines on offer and the food is some of the most authentically German you'll experience on the Romantic Road.

Zur Höll
GERMAN €€

(Map p254; ☎4229; Burggasse 8; dishes €6.50-18; ⊙dinner) This medieval wine tavern, with an appreciation for slow food, is in the town's oldest original building, dating back to the year 900. The menu of regional specialities is limited but refined, though it's the wine, some from nearby Würzburg, that people really come for.

Villa Mittermeier
FRANCONIAN €€€

(Map p254; ☎945 40; www.villamittermeier.de; Vorm Würzburger Tor 9; mains €18-26; ⊙dinner

Tue-Sat, lunch Sat) The kitchen ninjas at this classy establishment serve top-notch Michelin-starred cuisine in five settings, including a black-and-white tiled 'temple', an alfresco terrace and a barrel-shaped wine cellar. The artistic chefs rely on locally harvested produce, and the wine list (400-plus varieties) is probably Franconia's best.

Weinstube zum Pulverer
FRANCONIAN €€

(Map p254; ☎976 182; Herrngasse 31; mains €5-16.50; ⊙call ahead for hours) The ornately carved timber chairs in this ancient wine bar (allegedly Rothenburg's oldest) are works of art. Its simple but filling dishes, like soup in a bowl made of bread, gourmet sandwiches and cakes, are equally artistic.

Bosporus Döner
KEBABS €

(Map p254; Hafengasse 2; dishes €3-8) You haven't really been to Germany until you've devoured a takeaway kebab in a twee medieval setting.

🛍 Shopping

Käthe Wohlfahrt
Weihnachtsdorf
CHRISTMAS DECORATIONS

(Map p254; ☎4090; www.wohlfahrt.com; Herrngasse 1) With its mind-boggling assortment of Yuletide decorations and ornaments, this huge shop lets you celebrate Christmas every day of the year (to go with the local snowballs). Many of the items are handcrafted with amazing skill and imagination; prices are accordingly high.

ⓘ Information

Post Office (Rödergasse 11)

Tourist Office (☎404 800; www.rothenburg. de; Marktplatz 2; ⊙9am-6pm Mon-Fri, 10am-5pm Sat & Sun Apr-Oct, 9am-5pm Mon-Fri, 10am-1pm Sat Nov-Mar) Offers free internet access.

❶ Getting There & Away

BUS The Europabus (p248) stops in the main bus park at the Hauptbahnhof and on the more central Schrannenplatz.

CAR The A7 autobahn runs right past town.

TRAIN You can go anywhere by train from Rothenburg, as long as it's Steinach. Change there for services to Würzburg (€12.20, one hour and 10 minutes). Travel to and from Munich (from €37.30, three hours) can involve up to three different trains.

❶ Getting Around

The city has five car parks right outside the walls. The town centre is closed to non-resident vehicles from 11am to 4pm and 7pm to 5am weekdays, and all day at weekends; hotel guests are exempt.

Dinkelsbühl

📞 09851 / POP 11,500

Some 40km south of Rothenburg, immaculately preserved Dinkelsbühl proudly traces its roots to a royal residence founded by Carolingian kings in the 8th century. Saved from destruction in the Thirty Years' War and ignored by WWII bombers, this is arguably the Romantic Road's quaintest and most authentically medieval halt. For an overall impression of the town, walk along the fortified walls with their 18 towers and four gates.

◉ Sights

Haus der Geschichte   MUSEUM
(📞902 440; Altrathausplatz 14; adult/child €4/2; ⊙9am-6pm Mon-Fri, 10am-5pm Sat & Sun May-Oct, 10am-5pm daily Nov-Apr) Near the Wörnitzer Tor, Dinkelsbühl's history comes under the microscope at the Haus der Geschichte, which occupies the old town hall. There's an interesting section on the Thirty Years' War and a gallery with paintings depicting Dinkelsbühl at the turn of the century. Audioguides are included in the ticket price.

Münster St Georg   CHURCH
(Marktplatz 1) Standing sentry over the heart of Dinkelsbühl is one of southern Germany's purest late-Gothic hall churches. Rather austere from the outside, the interior stuns with an incredible fan-vaulted ceiling. A curiosity is the **Pretzl Window** donated by the bakers' guild; it's located in the upper section of the last window in the right aisle.

Museum of the 3rd Dimension   MUSEUM
(📞6336; www.3d-museum.de; Nördlinger Tor; adult/concession/under 12yr €10/8/6; ⊙10am-6pm daily Jul & Aug, 11am-5pm daily Apr-Jun, Sep & Oct, 11am-5pm Sat & Sun Nov-Mar) Located just outside the easternmost town gate, this is probably the first museum dedicated entirely to simulating acid trips. Inside there are three floors of holographic images, stereoscopes and attention-grabbing 3D imagery (especially in the nude section on the 3rd floor). The you-gotta-be-kidding admission includes a pair of red–green-tinted specs.

✦ Festivals & Events

Kinderzeche   FESTIVAL
(www.kinderzeche.de; ⊙Jul) In the third week of July, the 10-day Kinderzeche celebrates how, during the Thirty Years' War, the town's children persuaded the invading Swedish troops to spare Dinkelsbühl from a ransacking. The festivities include a pageant, re-enactments in the festival hall, lots of music and other merriment.

⌂ Sleeping

The tourist office can help find private rooms from around €30.

TOP CHOICE Dinkelsbühler Kunst-Stuben   GUESTHOUSE €€
(📞6750; www.kunst-stuben.de; Segringer Strasse 52; s €60, d €80-85, ste €90; @) Personal attention and charm by the bucketload make this guesthouse, situated near the westernmost gate (Segringer Tor), one of the best on the entire Romantic Road. Furniture (including the four-posters) is all handmade by Voglauer, the cosy library is perfect for curling up in with a good read, and the new suite is a matchless deal for travelling families. The artisan owner will show his Asia travel films if enough guests are interested.

Gasthof Goldenes Lamm   HOTEL €€
(📞2267; www.goldenes.de; Lange Gasse 26-28; s €47-62, d €76-90; ℗) Run by the same family for four generations, this stress-free, bike-friendly oasis has pleasant rooms at the top of a creaky staircase, and a funky rooftop garden deck with plump sofas. The attached wood-panelled restaurant plates up Franconian–Swabian specialities, including a vegie selection.

Deutsches Haus HOTEL €€
(2 6058; www.deutsches-haus-dkb.de; Weinmarkt 3; s €79-90, d €129;) Concealed behind the town's most ornate and out-of-kilter facade, the 19 elegant rooms at this central inn opposite the Münster St Georg flaunt antique touches and big 21st-century bathrooms. Downstairs Dinkelsbühl's hautiest restaurant serves game and fish prepared according to age-old recipes.

Campingpark 'Romantische Strasse' CAMPGROUND €
(2 7817; www.campingplatz-dinkelsbuehl.de; Kobeltsmühle 6; per tent/person €6.15/4.10) This camping ground is set on the shores of a swimmable lake 1.5km northeast of Wörnitzer Tor.

DJH Hostel HOSTEL €
(2 9509; www.dinkelsbuehl.jugendherberge.de; Koppengasse 10; dm from €19; closed Nov-Feb) Dinkelsbühl's hostel in the western part of the Altstadt occupies a beautifully restored 15th-century granary.

Eating

Haus Appelberg BAVARIAN €
(2 582 838; www.haus-appelberg.de; Nördlinger Strasse 40; dishes €5.20-10.50; 6pm-midnight Mon-Sat) At Dinkelsbühl's best-kept dining secret, owners double up as cooks to keep tables supplied with traditional dishes such as local fish, Franconian sausages and *Maultaschen* (pork and spinach ravioli). On warm days swap the rustic interior for the secluded terrace, a fine spot for some evening idling over a local Hauf beer or a Franconian white wine. There are well-appointed rooms upstairs for sleeping off any overindulgences.

Weib's Brauhaus PUB €
(2 579 490; Untere Schmiedgasse 13; mains €5-13.50; 11am-1am Thu-Mon, 6pm-1am Wed;) A female brewmaster presides over the copper vats at this sage-green half-timbered pub-restaurant, which has a good-time vibe thanks to its friendly crowd of regulars. Many dishes are made with the house brew, including the popular *Weib's Töpfle* ('woman's pot') – pork in beer sauce with croquettes.

Information
Tourist Office (2 902 440; www.dinkelsbuehl. de; Altrathausplatz 14; 9am-6pm Mon-Fri, 10am-5pm Sat & Sun May-Oct, 10am-5pm daily Nov-Apr)

Getting There & Away
Despite a railway line cutting through the town, Dinkelsbühl is not served by passenger trains. Regional bus 501 to Nördlingen (50 minutes, six daily) stops at the derelict train station. Reaching Rothenburg is a real test of patience without your own car. Change from bus 805 to a train in Ansbach, then change trains in Steinach. The Europabus stops right in the Altstadt at Schweinemarkt.

Nördlingen
09081 / POP 19,000
Charmingly medieval, Nördlingen sees fewer tourists than its better-known neighbours and manages to retain an air of authenticity, which is a relief after some of the Romantic Road's kitschy extremes. The town lies within the Ries Basin, a massive impact crater gouged out by a meteorite more than 15 million years ago. The crater – some 25km in diameter – is one of the best preserved on earth, and has been declared a special 'geopark'. Nördlingen's 14th-century walls, all original, mimic the crater's rim and are almost perfectly circular.

Incidentally, if you've seen the 1970s film *Willy Wonka and the Chocolate Factory*, you've already looked down upon Nördlingen from a glass elevator.

Sights
You can circumnavigate the entire town in around an hour by taking the sentry walk (free) on top of the walls all the way.

St Georgskirche CHURCH
(tower adult/child €2.50/1.70; tower 9am-6pm Apr-Jun, Sep & Oct, to 7pm Jul & Aug, to 5pm Nov-Mar) Dominating the heart of town, the immense late-Gothic St Georgskirche got its baroque mantle in the 18th century. To truly appreciate Nördlingen's circular shape and the dished-out crater in which it lies, scramble up the 350 steps of the church's 90m-tall Daniel Tower.

Bayerisches Eisenbahnmuseum MUSEUM
(www.bayerisches-eisenbahnmuseum.de; Am Hohen Weg 6a; adult/child €6/3; noon-4pm Tue-Sat, 10am-5pm Sun May-Sep, noon-4pm Sat, 10am-5pm Sun Oct-Mar) Half museum, half junkyard retirement home for locos that have puffed their last, this trainspotter's paradise occupies a disused engine depot across the tracks from the train station (no access from the platforms). The museum runs steam and old

BAVARIA NÖRDLINGEN

diesel trains up to Dinkelsbühl, Feuchtwangen and Gunzenhausen several times a year; see the website for details.

Rieskrater Museum
MUSEUM

(📞847 10; www.rieskrater-museum.de; Eugene-Shoemaker-Platz 1; adult/child €4/1.50; ⊙10am-4.30pm Tue-Sun May-Oct, 10am-noon Nov-Apr) Situated in an ancient barn, this unique museum explores the formation of meteorite craters and the consequences of such violent collisions with earth. Rocks, including a genuine moon rock (on permanent loan from NASA), fossils and other geological displays shed light on the mystery of meteors.

Stadtmuseum
MUSEUM

(Vordere Gerbergasse 1; adult/concession €4/1.50; ⊙1.30-4.30pm Tue-Sun Mar-early Nov) Nördlingen's worthwhile municipal museum covers an ambitious sweep of human existence on the planet, from the early Stone Age to 20th-century art, via the Battle of Nördlingen during the Thirty Years' War, Roman endeavours in the area and the town's once-bustling mercantile life.

Stadtmauermuseum
MUSEUM

(Löpsinger Torturm; adult/concession €2/1; ⊙10am-4.30pm Apr-Oct) A fascinating exhibition on the history of the town's defences is on show at this tower-based museum, the best place to kick off a circuit of the walls.

🛏 Sleeping & Eating

Hotel Altreuter
HOTEL €

(📞4319; www.hotel-altreuter.de; Marktplatz 11; s/d from €36/52; 🅿) Perched above a busy cafe and bakery, the bog-standard rooms here are of the could-be-anywhere type, but the epicentral location next to the Daniel Tower cannot be beaten. Bathrooms are private and breakfast is served downstairs in the cafe.

Jugend & Familengästehaus
GUESTHOUSE €

(📞275 0575; www.jufa.at/noerdlingen; Bleichgraben 3a; s/d €50/70; 🅿@🛜) Located just outside the town walls, this shiny, 186-bed hostel-guesthouse is spacious and clean-cut. There are two- to four-bed rooms, ideal for couples or families, and facilities include bicycle hire, a cafe with internet terminals and even a small cinema. Unless you are travelling with an entire handball team in tow,

dorms are off limits to individual travellers, no matter how hard you plead.

Kaiserhof Hotel Sonne
HOTEL €€

(📞5067; www.kaiserhof-hotel-sonne.de; Marktplatz 3; s €55-65, d €75-120; 🅿) Right on the main square, Nördlingen's top digs once hosted crowned heads and their entourages, but have quietly gone to seed in recent years. However, rooms are still packed with character, mixing modern comforts with traditional charm, and the atmospheric regional restaurant downstairs is still worth a shot.

Café Radlos
CAFE €€

(📞5040; www.cafe-radlos.de; Löpsinger Strasse 8; mains €4.50-14; ⊙10am-1am Thu-Tue; 🍴) More than just a place to tuck into tasty Bavarian dishes, this convivialy random cafe, Nördlingen's coolest haunt, parades cherry-red walls that showcase local art and photography exhibits. Kids have their own toy-filled corner, while you while away the hours with board games, soak up the sunshine in the beer garden, or surf the web (€2 per hour).

Sixenbräu Stüble
BAVARIAN €€

(Bergerstrasse 17; mains €5-17; ⊙10am-2pm Tue & Wed, 10am-2pm & 5pm-midnight Thu-Sat, 10am-10pm Sun) An attractive gabled town house near the Berger Tor houses this local institution, which has been plonking wet ones on the bar since 1545. The pan-Bavarian menu has heavy carnivorous leanings, and there's a beer garden where, in the words of the menu, you can take on some *bayerisches Grundnahrungsmittel* (Bavarian nutritional staple).

ⓘ Information

Geopark Ries Information Centre (www.geopark-ries.de; Eugene-Shoemaker-Platz; ⊙10am-4.30pm Tue-Sun) Free exhibition on the crater.

Tourist Office (📞841 16; www.noerdlingen.de; Marktplatz 2; ⊙9.30am-6pm Mon-Thu, to 4.30pm Fri, 10am-2pm Sat Easter-Oct, plus 10am-2pm Sun Jul & Aug, Mon-Fri only mid-Nov−Easter) Staff sell the Nördlinger Tourist-Card (€9.95) that saves you around €8 if you visit everything in town.

ⓘ Getting There & Away

BUS The Europabus stops at the Rathaus. Bus 501 goes to Dinkelsbühl (45 minutes, five daily).

TRAIN Train journeys to and from Munich (€24.50, two hours) and Augsburg (€14.40, 1¼ hours) require a change in Donauwörth.

Donauwörth

🕿 0906 / POP 18,240

Sitting pretty at the confluence of the Danube and Wörnitz rivers, Donauwörth rose from its humble beginnings as a 5th-century fishing village to its zenith as a Free Imperial City in 1301. Three medieval gates and five town wall towers still guard it today, and faithful rebuilding – after WWII had destroyed 75% of the medieval old town – means steep-roofed houses in a rainbow of colours still line its main street, Reichstrasse.

Reichstrasse is around 10 minutes' walk north of the train station. Turn right onto Bahnhofstrasse and cross the bridge onto Ried Island.

◎ Sights

Liebfraukirche   CHURCH
(Reichstrasse) At the western end of Reichstrasse rises this 15th-century Gothic church with original frescos and a curiously sloping floor that drops 120cm. Swabia's largest church bell (6550kg) swings in the belfry.

Käthe-Kruse-Puppenmuseum   MUSEUM
(Pflegstrasse 21a; adult/child €2.50/1.50; ⊙11am-5pm daily May-Sep, 2-5pm Tue-Sun Apr & Oct, Wed, Sat & Sun Nov-Mar,) This nostalgia-inducing museum fills a former monastery with old dolls and dollhouses by world-renowned designer Käthe Kruse (1883–1968).

Rathaus   HISTORIC BUILDING
(Rathausegasse) Work on Donauwörth's landmark town hall began in 1236, but it has seen many alterations and additions over the centuries. At 11am and 4pm daily, the carillon on the ornamented step gable plays a composition by local legend Werner Egk (1901–83) from his opera Die Zaubergeige (The Magic Violin). The building also houses the tourist office.

Heilig-Kreuz-Kirche   CHURCH
(Heilig-Kreuz-Strasse) Overlooking the grassy banks of the shallow Wörnitz River, this soaring baroque confection has for centuries lured the faithful to pray before a chip of wood, said to come from the Holy Cross, installed in the ornate-ceilinged Gnadenkappelle.

🛏 Sleeping & Eating

Drei Kronen   HOTEL €€
(🕿 706 170; www.hotel3kronen.com; Bahnhofstrasse 25; s/d €82/115; 🅿 🛜) Situated opposite the train station a little way along Bahnhofstrasse, the 'Three Crowns' has the town's most comfortable rooms and a lamplit restaurant. The reception is, inconveniently, closed in the evenings and all weekend, but staff are around in the restaurant.

Posthotel Traube   BAVARIAN €€
(Kapellstrasse 14-16; mains €5.50-17; ⊙11am-2pm & 5-10pm Mon-Fri & Sun, closed Sat) Choose from a cafe, coffee house, restaurant or beer garden at this friendly, multitasking hotel where Mozart stayed as a boy in 1777. The schnitzel, cordon bleu and local carp in beer sauce are where your forefinger should land on the menu.

Cafe Rafaello   ITALIAN €€
(Fischerplatz 1; mains €6.50-23.50) On Ried Island, this Italian job specialising in seafood uses Apennines kitsch to recreate La Dolce Vita to southern-German tastes.

ℹ Information

Tourist Office (🕿 789 151; www.donauwoerth. de; Rathausgasse 1; ⊙9am-noon & 1-6pm Mon-Fri, 3-6pm Sat & Sun May-Sep, shorter hours Mon-Fri, closed Sun Sat Oct-Apr)

ℹ Getting There & Away

BUS The Europabus stops by the Liebfraukirche.

CAR & MOTORCYCLE Donauwörth is at the crossroads of the B2, B16 and B25 roads.

TRAIN Train connections from Donauwörth:

DESTINATION	FARE	DURATION	FREQUENCY
Augsburg	€6	30 minutes	twice hourly
Harburg	€3.40	10 minutes	hourly
Ingolstadt	€11.10	45 minutes	hourly
Nördlingen	€5.50	30 minutes	hourly

Augsburg

🕿 0821 / POP 264,700

The largest city on the Romantic Road (and Bavaria's third largest), Augsburg is also one of Germany's oldest, founded by the stepchildren of Roman emperor Augustus over 2000 years ago. As an independent city state from the 13th century, it was also one of its

HARBURG

Looming over the Wörnitz River, the medieval covered parapets, towers, turrets, keep and red-tiled roofs of the 12th-century **Schloss Harburg** (www.burg-harburg.de; adult/child €5/3; ☺10am-5pm Tue-Sun mid-Mar–Oct) are so perfectly preserved they almost seem like a film set. Tours tell the building's long tale and evoke the ghosts that are said to use the castle as a hang-out.

From the castle, the walk to Harburg's cute, half-timbered **Altstadt** takes around 10 minutes, slightly more the other way as you're heading uphill. A fabulous panorama of the village and castle can be admired from the 1702 **stone bridge** spanning the Wörnitz.

The Europabus stops in the village (outside the Gasthof Grüner Baum) but not at the castle. Hourly trains run to Nördlingen (€4.10, 18 minutes) and Donauwörth (€3.40, 10 minutes). The train station is about a 30-minute walk from the castle. Harburg is on the B25 road.

wealthiest, free to raise its own taxes, with public coffers bulging from the proceeds of the textile trade. Banking families such as the Fuggers and the Welsers even bankrolled entire countries and helped out the odd skint monarch. However, from the 16th century, religious strife and economic decline plagued the city. Augsburg finally joined the Kingdom of Bavaria in 1806.

Shaped by Romans, medieval artisans, bankers, traders and, more recently, industry and technology, this attractive city of spires and cobbles is an easy day trip from Munich or an engaging stop on the Romantic Road, though one with a grittier, less quaint atmosphere than others along the route.

◉ Sights

Fuggerei   HISTORIC SITE
(www.fugger.de; Jakober Strasse; adult/concession €4/3; ☺8am-8pm Apr-Sep, 9am-6pm Oct-Mar) The legacy of Jakob Fugger 'The Rich' lives on at Augsburg's Catholic welfare settlement, the Fuggerei, which is the oldest of its kind in existence.

Around 200 people live here today and their rent remains frozen at 1 Rhenish guilder (now €0.88) *per year,* plus utilities and three daily prayers. Residents wave to you as you wander through the car-free lanes of this gated community flanked by its 52 pinneat houses (containing 140 apartments) and little gardens.

To see how residents lived before running water and central heating, one of the apartments now houses the **Fuggereimuseum**, while there's a modern apartment open for public viewing at Ochsengasse 51. Interpretive panels are in German but you

can ask for an information leaflet in English or download it from the website before you arrive.

Rathausplatz   SQUARE
The heart of Augsburg's Altstadt, this large, pedestrianised square is anchored by the **Augustusbrunnen**, a fountain honouring the Roman emperor; its four figures represent the Lech River and the Wertach, Singold and Brunnenbach brooks.

Rising above the square are the twin onion-domed spires of the Renaissance **Rathaus**, built by Elias Holl from 1615 to 1620 and crowned by a 4m-tall pine cone, the city's emblem (also an ancient fertility symbol). Upstairs is the **Goldener Saal** (Rathausplatz; adult/concession €3/2; ☺10am-6pm), a huge banquet hall with an amazing gilded and frescoed coffered ceiling.

For panoramic views over Rathausplatz and the city, climb to the top of the **Perlachturm** (Rathausplatz; adult/child €1.50/1; ☺10am-6pm daily Apr-Nov), a former guard tower, and also an Elias Holl creation.

St Anna Kirche   CHURCH
(Im Annahof 2, off Annastrasse; ☺10am-12.30pm & 3-6pm Tue-Sat, 10am-12.30pm & 3-4pm Sun) Often regarded as the first Renaissance church in Germany, the rather plain-looking (and well-hidden) St Anna Kirche contains a bevy of treasures, as well as the sumptuous **Fuggerkapelle**, where Jacob Fugger and his brothers lie buried, and the lavishly frescoed **Goldschmiedekapelle** (Goldsmiths' Chapel; 1420). The church played an important role during the Reformation. In 1518 Martin Luther, in town to defend his beliefs before the papal legate, stayed at what was then a Carmelite monastery. His rooms have been

turned into the **Lutherstiege**, a small museum about the Reformation, under renovation at the time of writing.

Maximilianmuseum   MUSEUM
(☑324 4102; Philippine-Welser-Strasse 24; adult/child €7/5.50; ☺10am-5pm Wed-Sun, to 8pm Tue) The Maximilianmuseum occupies two patrician town houses joined by a statue-studded courtyard covered by a glass-and-steel roof. Highlights include a fabulous collection of Elias Holl's original wooden models for his architectural creations, and a collection of gold and silver coins that can be viewed through sliding magnifying glass panels. Opening to the courtyard is a chic cafe where kids won't want to miss turning the pages of the 'magic book' that brings Augsburg's history to life.

Bertolt-Brecht-Haus   MUSEUM
(☑324 2779; Auf dem Rain 7; adult/concession €2.50/2; ☺10am-5pm Wed-Sun, to 8pm Tue) Opened in 1998 to celebrate local boy Bertolt Brecht's 100th birthday, this house museum is the birthplace of the famous playwright and poet, where he lived for the first two years of his life (from 1898 to 1900) before moving across town. Among the displays are old theatre posters and a great series of life-size chronological photos, as well as his mother's bedroom.

Dom Mariä Heimsuchung   CHURCH
(Hoher Weg; ☺7am-6pm) Augsburg's cathedral, the Dom Mariä Heimsuchung, has its origins in the 10th century but was Gothicised and enlarged in the 14th and 15th centuries. The star treasures here are the so-called 'Prophets' Windows'. Depicting David, Daniel, Jonah, Hosea and Moses, they are among the oldest figurative stained-glass windows in Germany, dating from the 12th century. Look out for four paintings by Hans Holbein the Elder, including one of Jesus' circumcision.

Jüdisches Kulturmuseum   JEWISH, MUSEUM
(www.jkmas.de; Halderstrasse 8; adult/concession €4/2; ☺9am-6pm Tue-Thu, to 4pm Fri, 10am-5pm Sun) About 300m east of the main train station, as you head towards the Altstadt, you'll come to the Synagoge Augsburg, an art-nouveau temple built between 1914 and 1917 and housing a worthwhile Jewish museum. Exhibitions here focus on Jewish life in the region, presenting religious artefacts collected from defunct synagogues across Swabia.

🛏 Sleeping

Augsburg is a good alternative base for Oktoberfest, though hotel owners pump up their prices just as much as their Munich counterparts.

⭐TOP CHOICE Dom Hotel   HOTEL €€
(☑343 930; www.domhotel-augsburg.de; Frauentorstrasse 8; s €70-135, d €90-155; P@🛜🏊) Augsburg's top choice packs a 500-year-old former bishop's guesthouse (Martin Luther and Kaiser Maxmilian I stayed here) with 57 rooms, all different but sharing a stylishly understated air and pristine upkeep; some have cathedral views. However the big plusses here are the large swimming pool, fitness centre and solarium, as well as the inviting lobby offering free English-language press, coffee and fruit. Parking is an extra €6.

Hotel am Rathaus   HOTEL €€
(☑346 490; www.hotel-am-rathaus-augsburg.de; Am Hinteren Perlachberg 1; s €79-98, d €98-125; 🛜) Just steps from Rathausplatz and Maximilianstrasse, this central boutique hotel hires out 31 rooms with freshly neutral decor and a sunny little breakfast room. Attracts a business-oriented clientele, so watch out for special weekend deals.

Jakoberhof   GUESTHOUSE €
(☑510 030; www.jakoberhof.de; Jakoberstrasse 41; s/d with shared bathroom from €27/39, with private bathroom from €49/64; P) This friendly *Pension* spans a collection of three buildings near the Fuggerei. Rooms are clean-cut if unimaginative, there's a decent Bavarian restaurant on the premises, and free parking and bike storage are available.

Steigenberger Drei Mohren Hotel   HOTEL €€€
(☑503 60; www.augsburg.steigenberger.de; Maximilianstrasse 40; r €125-280; P✳@🛜) A proud Leopold Mozart stayed here with his prodigious kids in 1766 and it remains Augsburg's oldest and grandest hotel. Recently renovated, the fully refreshed rooms are the last word in soothing design in these parts and come with marble bathrooms and original art. Dine in-house at the gastronomic extravaganza that is **Maximilians**, a great place to swing by for Sunday brunch.

Augsburger Hof   HOTEL €€
(☑343 050; www.augsburger-hof.de; Auf dem Kreuz 2; s €90-115, d €99-140; 🛜) All rooms are business standard, staff are well regimented

and there are two on-site eateries at this pretty window-boxed hotel near the Dom. The higher-priced rooms look out into the quiet courtyard.

✕ Eating

In the evening, Maximilianstrasse is the place to tarry, with cafes tumbling out onto the pavements and Augsburg's young and beautiful watching the world go by.

Bayerisches Haus am Dom BAVARIAN €€
(☑349 7990; Johannisgasse 4; mains €7-16) Enjoy an elbow massage from the locals at chunky timber benches while refuelling on Bavarian and Swabian dishes, cheap lunch options (€6) or a sandwich served by Dirndl-clad waitresses. Erdinger and Andechser are the frothy double act that stimulates nightly frivolity in the beer garden.

Barfüsser Café CAFE €
(☑450 4966; Barfüsserstrasse 10; snacks €1-6; ⊙11am-6pm Mon-Sat) Follow a short flight of steps down from the street through a covered passageway to uncover this pretty snack stop by a little canal. It's run by a team of staff with disabilities, for whom it provides work opportunities as part of a community project, and serves delectable homemade cakes, pastries, salads and light lunches.

Bauerntanz GERMAN €€
(Bauerntanzgässchen 1; mains €7-16; ⊙11am-11.30pm) Belly-satisfying helpings of creative Swabian and Bavarian food (*Spätzle,* veal medallions, and more *Spätzle*) are plated up by friendly staff at this prim Alpine tavern with lace curtains, hefty timber interior and chequered fabrics. When the sun makes an appearance, everyone bails for the outdoor seating.

Fuggereistube BAVARIAN €€
(☑308 70; Jakoberstrasse 26; mains €10-19; ⊙lunch & dinner Tue-Sat, lunch Sun) Old-fashioned fine dining involving expertly crafted Bavarian and Swabian dishes in an understated dining space with arching ceilings and terracotta-tiled floors. The reassuringly short and seasonal menu reboots on a daily basis.

Anno 1578 CAFE €
(Fuggerplatz 9; mains €4-10; ⊙8.30am-7pm Mon-Sat) Munch on blockbuster breakfasts, lunchtime burgers and sandwiches, or just pop by for a cappuccino or ice cream at this slick cafe under ancient neon-uplit vaulting.

🍷 Drinking

Elements CAFE, BISTRO
(☑508 0759; Frauentorstrasse 2) Knock back a cocktail or five at this trendy cafe-bistro which attracts the beautiful people of an eve. Weekend breakfast is ideal for those who rise at the crack of lunchtime.

Thing BEER GARDEN
(☑395 05; Vorderer Lech 45) Augsburg's coolest beer garden sports totem poles and often gets crowded in the evenings.

☆ Entertainment

Augsburger Puppenkiste THEATRE
(☑450 3450; www.augsburger-puppenkiste.de; Spitalgasse 15) The celebrated puppet theatre holds performances of modern and classic fairy tales that even non–German speakers will enjoy. Advance bookings essential.

❶ Information

Post Office (Halderstrasse 29) At the Hauptbahnhof.

Tourist Office (☑502 070; www.augsburg-tourismus.de; Rathausplatz; ⊙9am-6pm Mon-Fri, 10am-5pm Sat, 10am-3pm Sun)

❶ Getting There & Away

BUS The Romantic Road Europabus stops at the Hauptbahnhof and the Rathaus.

CAR & MOTORCYCLE Augsburg is just off the A8 northwest of Munich.

TRAIN Augsburg rail connections:

» **Füssen** €19.20, two hours, every two hours

» **Munich** €12.20 to €20, 30 to 45 minutes, three hourly

» **Nuremberg** €34, one hour, hourly

» **Ulm** €16.40 to €23, 45 minutes to one hour, three hourly

Landsberg am Lech

☑08191 / POP 28,100

Lovely Landsberg am Lech is often overlooked by Romantic Road trippers on their town-hopping way between Füssen to the south and Augsburg to the north. But it's for this very absence of tourists and a less commercial ambience that this walled town on the River Lech is worth a halt, if only a brief one.

Landsberg can claim to be the town where one of the German language's best-selling books was written. Was it a work by Goethe,

Remarque, Brecht? No, unfortunately, it was Hitler. It was during his 264 days of incarceration in a Landsberg jail, following the 1923 beer-hall putsch, that Adolf penned his hate-filled *Mein Kampf*, a book that sold an estimated seven million copies when published. The jail later held Nazi war criminals and is still in use; the rights to the text of *Mein Kampf* are owned by the Free State of Bavaria, but these run out in 2015, 70 years after the author's demise.

☉ Sights

Landsberg's hefty medieval defensive walls are punctuated by some beefy gates, the most impressive of which are the 1425 **Bayertor** to the east and the Renaissance-styled **Sandauer Tor** to the north. The tall **Schmalztor** was left centrally stranded when the fortifications were moved further out and still overlooks the main square and the 500 listed buildings within the town walls.

Stadtpfarrkirche
Mariä Himmelfahrt   CHURCH
(Georg-Hellmair-Platz) This huge 15th-century church was built by Matthäus von Ensingen, architect of Bern Cathedral. The barrel nave is stuccoed to baroque perfection, while a cast of saints populates the columns and alcoves above the pews. Gothic-era stained glass casts rainbow hues on the church's most valuable work of art, the 15th-century *Madonna with Child* by local sculptor Lorenz Luidl.

Johanniskirche   CHURCH
(Vorderer Anger) If you've already seen the Wieskirche (p235) to the south, you'll instantly recognise this small baroque church as a creation by the same architect, Dominikus Zimmermann, who lived in Landsberg and even served as its mayor.

Heilg-Kreuz-Kirche   CHURCH
(Von-Helfenstein-Gasse) Head uphill from the Schmalztor to view this beautiful baroque Jesuit church, the interior a hallucination in broodily dark gilding and glorious ceiling decoration.

Neues Stadtmuseum   MUSEUM
(www.museum-landsberg.de; Von-Helfenstain -Gasse 426; adult/concession €3.50/2; ☉2-5pm Tue-Fri, from 10am Sat & Sun May-Jan, closed Feb-Apr) Housed in a former Jesuit school, Landsberg's municipal museum chronicles the area's past from prehistory to the 20th century, and displays numerous works of local art, both religious and secular in nature.

🛏 Sleeping & Eating

Stadthotel Augsburger Hof   HOTEL €
(☏969 596; www.stadthotel-landsberg.de; Schlosser -gasse 378; s €32-43, d €69-72; P🔊) The 14 en-suite rooms at this highly recommended traditional inn are a superb deal, and have chunky pine beds and well-maintained bathrooms throughout. The owners and staff are a friendly bunch and the breakfast is a filling set-up for the day. Cycle hire and cycle friendly.

Schafbräu   INTERNATIONAL €€
(Hinterer Anger 338; mains €5-15) This cosy Bavarian-styled tavern has an international menu that leans firmly towards southern Europe. If you don't feel like moving far afterwards, there are rooms upstairs (€75).

Altstadt Cafe   CAFE €
(Ludwigstrasse 164; mains €5-8; ☉8am-5pm) Munch on the mainstays of central European cuisine amid brass statuary and mock Chinese vases at this central cafe.

❶ Information

Tourist Office (☏128 246; www.landsberg.de; Rathaus, Hauptplatz 152; ☉8am-6pm Mon-Fri May-Oct, 10am-5pm Sat & Sun Apr-Oct, shorter hours & closed weekends Nov-Mar)

❶ Getting There & Away

BUS The Europabus stops on request at the train station across from the old town.

TRAIN Landsberg has the following rail connections:

» **Augsburg** €7.50, 50 minutes, hourly

» **Füssen** Change at Kaufering; €14.40, 1½ hours, every two hours

» **Munich** Change at Kaufering; €12.20, 50 minutes, twice hourly

NUREMBERG & FRANCONIA

Somewhere between Ingolstadt and Nuremberg, Bavaria's accent mellows, the oompah bands play that little bit quieter and wine competes with beer as the local tipple. This is Franconia (Franken) and, as every local will tell you, Franconians, who inhabit the wooded hills and the banks of the Main River in Bavaria's northern reaches, are a breed apart from their brash and extrovert cousins to the south.

In the northwest, the region's winegrowers produce some exceptional whites, sold in a distinctive teardrop-shaped bottle, the *Bocksbeutel*. For outdoor enthusiasts, the Altmühltal Nature Park offers wonderful hiking, biking and canoeing. But it is Franconia's old royalty and incredible cities – Nuremberg, Bamberg and Coburg – that draw the biggest crowds.

Nuremberg

📞 0911 / POP 503,000

Nuremberg (Nürnberg), Bavaria's second-largest city and the unofficial capital of Franconia, is an energetic place where the nightlife is intense and the beer is as dark as coffee. As one of Bavaria's biggest draws it is alive with visitors year-round, but especially during the spectacular Christmas market.

For centuries, Nuremberg was the undeclared capital of the Holy Roman Empire and the preferred residence of most German kings, who kept their crown jewels here. Rich and stuffed with architectural wonders, it was also a magnet for famous artists, though the most famous of all, Albrecht Dürer, was actually born here. 'Nuremberg shines throughout Germany like a sun among the moon and stars,' gushed Martin Luther. By the 19th century, the city had become a powerhouse in Germany's industrial revolution.

The Nazis saw a perfect stage for their activities in working class Nuremberg. It was here that the fanatical party rallies were held, the boycott of Jewish businesses began and the infamous Nuremberg Laws outlawing German citizenship for Jewish people were enacted. On 2 January 1945, Allied bombers reduced the city to landfill, killing 6000 people in the process.

After WWII the city was chosen as the site of the war crimes tribunal, now known as the Nuremberg Trials. Later, the painstaking reconstruction – using the original stone – of almost all the city's main buildings, including the castle and old churches in the Altstadt, returned the city to some of its former glory.

⊙ Sights

Most major sights are within the Altstadt.

Kaiserburg   CASTLE

(Map p268; www.schloesser.bayern.de; adult/child incl museum €7/6; ⊙9am-6pm Apr-Sep, 10am-4pm Oct-Mar) Construction of Nuremberg's landmark, the immensely proportioned Kaiserburg, began during the reign of Hohenstaufen King Konrad III in the 12th century and dragged on for about 400 years. The complex, for centuries the receptacle of the Holy Roman Empire's treasures, consists of three parts: the Kaiserburg and Stadtburg (the Emperor's Palace and City Fortress), as well as the Burggrafenburg (Count's Residence), which was largely destroyed in 1420. Wedged between its surviving towers are the Kaiserstallung (Royal Stables), which today house the DJH hostel (p275).

The **Kaiserburg Museum** chronicles the history of the castle and provides a survey of medieval defence techniques. Other Tardis-like sections open to visitors include the royal living quarters, the Imperial and Knights' Halls, and the **Romanesque Doppelkapelle** (Twin Chapel). The latter poignantly illustrates the medieval hierarchy: common folk sat in the dimly lit lower section, with the royals entering up above directly from the palace.

Enjoy panoramic city views from atop the **Sinwellturm** (Sinwell Tower; 113 steps) or peer into the amazing 48m-deep **Tiefer Brunnen** (Deep Well) – guides lower a platter of candles so you can see its depth; it still yields drinking water.

The grassy knoll at the southeast corner of the **castle gardens** (open seasonally) is **Am Ölberg**, a favourite spot to sit and gaze out over the city's rooftops.

Deutsche Bahn Museum   MUSEUM

(Map p268; 📞0180-444 2233; www.db-museum. de; Lessingstrasse 6; adult/child €5/2.50, free with InterRail pass; ⊙9am-5pm Tue-Fri, 10am-6pm Sat & Sun) Forget Dürer and Nazi rallies, Nuremberg is a railway town at heart. Germany's first passenger trains ran between here and Fürth, a fact reflected in the unmissable German Railways Museum, which explores the history of Germany's legendary rail system.

If you have tots aboard, head straight for the **Eisenbahn-Erlebniswelt** (Railway World), where lots of hands-on, interactive choo-choo–themed attractions await. Here you'll also find a huge model railway, one of Germany's largest, set in motion every hour by a uniformed controller.

The main exhibition charting almost two centuries of rail history starts on the ground floor and continues with more recent exhibits on the first. Passing quickly through the historically inaccurate beginning (as every rail buff knows, the world's first railway was the Stockton–Darlington, not the Liverpool–Manchester), highlights include Germany's oldest railway carriage dating from 1835 and lots of interesting Deutsche Reichsbahn paraphernalia from East Germany.

However the real meat of the show are the two halls of locos and rolling stock. The first hall contains Ludwig II's incredible rococo rail carriage, dubbed the 'Versailles of the rails', as well as Bismarck's considerably less ostentatious means of transport. There's also Germany's most famous steam loco, the *Adler*, built by the Stephensons in Newcastle upon Tyne for the Nuremberg–Fürth line. The second hall across the road from the main building houses some mammoth engines, some with their Nazi or Deutsche Reichsbahn insignia still in place.

Hauptmarkt   SQUARE

This bustling square in the heart of the Altstadt is the site of daily markets as well as the famous Christkindlesmarkt. At the eastern end is the ornate Gothic **Pfarrkirche Unsere Liebe Frau** (Map p268; Hauptmarkt 14), built from 1350 to 1358, and also known simply as the **Frauenkirche**. The work of Prague cathedral builder Peter Parler, it's the oldest Gothic hall church in Bavaria and stands on the ground of Nuremberg's first synagogue. It was built as a repository for the crown jewels of Charles IV who, fearing theft, sent them instead to Prague for safe keeping. The western facade is beautifully ornamented and is where, every day at noon, crowds crane their necks to witness a spectacle called *Männleinlaufen*. It features seven figures, representing electoral princes, parading clockwise three times around Emperor Karl IV to chimed accompaniment.

Rising from the square like a Gothic spire, the gargoyle-adorned, 19m-tall **Schöner Brunnen** (Beautiful Fountain; Map p268) is a gilded replica of the 14th-century original, though it no longer spouts water. Look for the seamless golden ring in the ornate wrought-iron gate on the southwestern side. Local superstition has it that if you turn it three times, your wish will come true. (Be careful not to confuse it with the gold ring on the opposite side of the gate, which, it's claimed, will make you conceive – if you're female, of course.)

Memorium
Nuremberg Trials   HISTORIC BUILDING

(☑3217 9372; www.memorium-nuremberg.de; Bärenschanzstrasse 72; adult/concession €5/3; ⊙10am-6pm Wed-Mon) Nazis were tried from 1945 to 1946 for crimes against peace and humanity in Schwurgerichtssaal 600 (Court Room 600) of what is still Nuremberg's regional courthouse. These became known as the Nuremberg Trials, and were held by the Allies in the city for obvious symbolic reasons. Another factor in their choice of venue was that there was (and still is) a secure underground tunnel between the courthouse and adjacent prison (though today it only has female prisoners).

The initial and most famous trial, conducted by international prosecutors, saw 24 people accused, of whom 19 were convicted and sentenced. Following trials also resulted in the conviction, sentencing and execution of Nazi leaders and underlings until 1949. Hermann Göring, the Reich's field marshal, cheated the hangman by taking a cyanide capsule in his cell hours before his scheduled execution.

In addition to viewing the courtroom (if not in use), a new exhibition provides comprehensive background to the trials and their significance to the world today.

To get here, take the U1 towards Bärenschanze (get off at Sielstrasse). It's about 2km from the centre of the Altstadt.

Reichsparteitagsgelände   HISTORIC SITE

(Luitpoldhain) If you've ever wondered where the infamous black-and-white images of ecstatic Nazi supporters hailing their Führer were filmed, it was here in Nuremberg. This orchestrated propaganda began as early as 1927 but, after 1933, Hitler opted for a purpose-built venue, the **Reichsparteitagsgelände**. Much of the outsize grounds were destroyed during Allied bombing raids, but 4 sq km remain, enough to get a sense of the megalomania behind it.

At the northwestern edge was the **Luitpoldarena**, designed for mass SS and SA parades. The area is now a park. South of here, the half-built **Kongresshalle** (Congress Hall) was meant to outdo Rome's Colosseum in both scale and style.

A visit to the **Dokumentationszentrum** (☑231 7538; Bayernstrasse 110; adult/concession €5/3; ⊙9am-6pm Mon-Fri, 10am-6pm Sat & Sun) in the north wing of the Kongresshalle helps to put the grounds into some historical context. A stunning walkway of glass cuts diagonally through the complex, ending with an interior view of the congress hall. Inside, the *Fascination and Terror* exhibit examines the rise of the NSDAP, the Hitler cult, the party rallies and the Nuremberg Trials.

Nuremberg

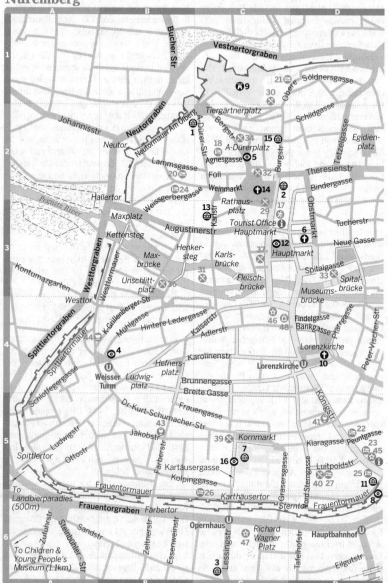

East of the Kongresshalle, across the artificial Dutzendteich (Dozen Ponds), is the **Zeppelinfeld**, fronted by a 350m-long grandstand, the **Zeppelintribüne**, where most of the big Nazi parades, rallies and events took place. It now hosts sport-

ing events and rock concerts, though this rehabilitation has caused controversy.

The grounds are bisected by the 60m-wide **Grosse Strasse** (Great Road), which culminates 2km to the south at the **Märzfeld** (March Field), which was planned as a mili-

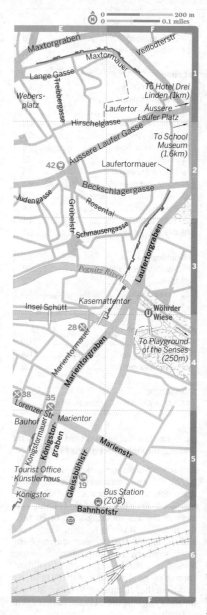

The Reichsparteitagsgelände is about 4km southeast of the centre. Take tram 9 from the Hauptbahnhof to Doku-Zentrum.

Germanisches Nationalmuseum MUSEUM
(Map p268; www.gnm.de; Kartäusergasse 1; adult/child €6/4; ⊙10am-6pm Tue & Thu-Sun, to 9pm Wed) Spanning prehistory to the early 20th century, the Germanisches Nationalmuseum is the country's most important museum of German culture. It features works by German painters and sculptors, an archaeological collection, arms and armour, musical and scientific instruments and toys. Among its many highlights is Dürer's anatomically detailed *Hercules Slaying the Stymphalian Birds*. The research library has over 500,000 volumes and 1500 periodicals.

At the museum's entrance is the inspired **Way of Human Rights** (Map p268), a symbolic row of 29 white concrete pillars (and one oak tree) bearing the 30 articles of the Universal Declaration of Human Rights. Each pillar is inscribed in German and, in succession, the language of peoples whose rights have been violated, with the oak representing languages not explicitly mentioned.

Neues Museum MUSEUM
(Map p268; www.nmn.de; Luitpoldstrasse 5; adult/child €4/3; ⊙10am-8pm Tue-Fri, to 6pm Sat & Sun) The aptly named Neues Museum showcases contemporary art and design, with resident collections of paintings, sculpture, photography, video art and installations, as well as travelling shows. Equally stunning is the building itself, with a dramatic 100m curved glass facade that, literally and figuratively, reflects the stone town wall opposite.

Albrecht-Dürer-Haus MUSEUM
(Map p268; Albrecht-Dürer-Strasse 39; adult/child €5/2.50; ⊙10am-5pm Fri-Wed, to 8pm Thu) Dürer, Germany's most famous Renaissance draughtsman, lived and worked at the Albrecht-Dürer-Haus from 1509 until his death in 1528. After a multimedia show there's an audioguide tour of the four-storey house, which is narrated by 'Agnes', Dürer's wife. Highlights are the hands-on demonstrations in the recreated studio and print shop on the 3rd floor and, in the attic, a gallery featuring copies and originals of Dürer's work.

Special tours led by an actress dressed as Agnes take place at 6pm Thursday, 3pm Saturday and 11am Sunday; there's an English-language tour at 2pm on Saturday.

tary exercise ground. The **Deutsches Stadion**, with a seating capacity of 400,000, was to have stood west of the Grosse Strasse. Things never got beyond the first excavation when the hole was filled with groundwater – today's Silbersee.

BAVARIA NUREMBERG

Nuremberg

Altes Rathaus　　HISTORIC BUILDING
(Map p268; Rathausplatz 2) Beneath the Altes Rathaus (1616–22), a hulk of a building with lovely Renaissance-style interiors, you'll find the macabre **Lochgefängnisse** (Medieval Dungeons; Map p268; ✆231 2690; adult/concession €3.50/1.50; ⊙tours 10am-4.30pm Tue-Sun Apr-Oct). This 12-cell death row and torture chamber must be seen on a 30-minute guided tour (held every half-hour) and might easily put you off lunch.

Stadtmuseum Fembohaus　　MUSEUM
(Map p268; ✆231 2595; Burgstrasse 15; museum adult/child €5/3, Noricama €4/2.50; ⊙10am-5pm Tue-Fri, 10am-6pm Sat & Sun) Offering an entertaining overview of the city's history, highlights of the Stadtmuseum Fembohaus include the restored historic rooms of this 16th-century merchant's house. Also here, **Noricama** takes you on a flashy Hollywood-esque multimedia journey (in German and English) through Nuremberg's history.

Jüdisches Museum Franken　　JEWISH, MUSEUM
(✆770 577; www.juedisches-museum.org; Königstrasse 89; adult/concession €3/2; ⊙10am-5pm Wed-Sun, to 8pm Tue) A quick U-Bahn ride away in the neighbouring town of Fürth is the Jüdisches Museum Franken. Fürth once had the largest Jewish congregation of any city in southern Germany and this museum, housed in a handsomely restored building, chronicles the history of Jewish life in the region from the Middle Ages to today. To reach the museum, take the U1 to the Rathaus stop in Fürth.

St Sebalduskirche　　CHURCH
(Map p268; www.sebalduskirche.de; Albrecht-Dürer-Platz 1; ⊙from 9.30am) Nuremberg's oldest church was built in rusty pink-veined sandstone in the 13th century. Its exterior is replete with religious sculptures and

symbols; check out the ornate carvings over the **Bridal Doorway** to the north, showing the Wise and Foolish Virgins. Inside, the bronze shrine of St Sebald (Nuremberg's own saint) is a Gothic and Renaissance masterpiece that took its maker, Peter Vischer the Elder, and his two sons more than 11 years to complete (Vischer is in it too, sporting a skullcap). The church is free to enter, despite the misleading sign on the door.

Felsengänge   HISTORIC SITE

(Underground Cellars; Map p268; www.felsengaenge -nuernberg.de; Bergstrasse 19; tours adult/concession €5/4; ⊙tours 11am, 1pm, 3pm & 5pm Mon-Fri, plus noon, 2pm & 4pm Sat & Sun) Beneath the Albrecht Dürer Monument on Albrecht-Dürer-Platz are the chilly Felsengänge. Departing from the brewery shop at Burgstrasse 19, tours descend to this four-storey subterranean warren, which dates from the 14th century and once housed a brewery and a beer cellar. During WWII it served as an air-raid shelter. Tours take a minimum of three people. Take a jacket against the chill.

Spielzeugmuseum   MUSEUM

(Toy Museum; Map p268; Karlstrasse 13-15; adult/child €5/3; ⊙10am-5pm Tue-Fri, to 6pm Sat & Sun) Nuremberg has long been a centre of toy manufacturing, and the Spielzeugmuseum presents toys in their infinite variety – from innocent hoops to blood-and-guts computer games, historical wooden and tin toys to Barbie et al. Kids and kids at heart will delight in the play area.

Ehekarussell Brunnen   FOUNTAIN

(Map p268; Am Weissen Turm) At the foot of the fortified Weisser Turm (White Tower; now the gateway to the U-Bahn station of the same name) stands this large and startlingly grotesque sculptural work depicting six interpretations of marriage (from first love to quarrel to death-do-us-part), all based on a verse by Hans Sachs, the medieval cobbler-poet. You soon realise why the artist faced a blizzard of criticism when the fountain was unveiled in 1984; it really is enough to put anyone off tying the knot.

Lorenzkirche   CHURCH

(Map p268; Lorenzplatz) Dark and atmospheric, the Lorenzkirche has dramatically downlit pillars, taupe stone columns, sooty ceilings and many artistic highlights. Check out the 15th-century tabernacle in the left aisle – the delicate carved strands wind up to the vaulted ceiling. Remarkable also are the stained glass (including a rose window 9m in diameter) and Veit Stoss' *Engelsgruss* (Annunciation), a wooden carving with life-size figures suspended above the high altar.

Handwerkerhof   MARKET

(Map p268; www.handwerkerhof.de; Am Königstor; ⊙9am-6.30pm Mon-Fri, 10am-4pm Sat mid-Mar–Dec) A recreation of an old-world Nuremberg crafts quarter, the Handwerkerhof is a self-contained tourist trap by the Königstor. It's about as quaint as a hammer on your thumbnail, but if you're cashed up you may find some decent merchandise (and the bratwurst aren't bad here either).

👉 Tours

English-language **Old Town walking tours** (Map p268; adult/child €10/free; ⊙1pm May-Oct) are run by the tourist office (p277) and include admission to the Kaiserburg. Tours leave from the Hauptmarkt branch and take 2½ hours.

Geschichte für Alle   CULTURAL TOUR

(☑307 360; www.geschichte-fuer-alle.de; adult/concession €7/6.) Intriguing range of themed English-language tours by a nonprofit association. The 'Albrecht Dürer' and 'Life in Medieval Nuremberg' tours come highly recommended.

Nuremberg Tours   WALKING TOUR

(www.nurembergtours.com; adult/concession €18/16; ⊙11.15am Mon, Wed & Sat Apr-Oct) Four-hour walking and public transport tours taking in the city centre and the Reichsparteitagsgelände (p267). Groups meet at the entrance to the Hauptbahnhof.

✷✷ Festivals & Events

Christkindlesmarkt   CHRISTMAS MARKET

(www.christkindlesmarkt.de) From late November to Christmas Eve, the Hauptmarkt is taken over by the most famous Christkindlesmarkt in Germany. Yuletide shoppers descend on the 'Christmas City' from all over Europe to seek out unique gifts at the scores of colourful timber trinket stalls that fill the square. The aroma of *Lebkuchen* (large, soft, spicy biscuits), mulled wine and roast sausages permeates the chilly air, while special festive events take place on the square and at other venues around town.

🛏 Sleeping

Accommodation gets tight and rates rocket during the Christmas market and the toy

NUREMBERG FOR KIDS

No city in Bavaria has more for kids to see and do than Nuremberg. In fact keeping the little 'uns entertained in the Franconian capital is child's play.

Museums

» **Children & Young People's Museum** (☑600 040; www.kindermuseum-nuernberg.de; Michael-Ende-Strasse 17; adult/family €7/19; ⊘2-5.30pm Sat, 10am-5.30pm Sun Sep-Jun) Educational exhibitions and lots of hands-on fun – just a pity it's not open more often.

» **School Museum** (☑231 3875; Äussere Sulzbacher Strasse 62; adult/child €5/3; ⊘9am-5pm Tue-Fri, 10am-6pm Sat & Sun) Recreated classroom plus school-related exhibits from the 17th century to the Third Reich.

» **Deutsche Bahn Museum** (p266) Feeds the kids' obsession with choo-choos.

Play

» **Playground of the Senses** (☑231 5445; www.erfahrungsfeld.nuernberg.de; Untere Talgasse 8; adult/child €6.10/4.40; ⊘9am-6pm Mon-Fri, 1-6pm Sat, 10am-6pm Sun May–mid-Sep) Some 80 hands-on 'stations' designed to educate children in the laws of nature, physics and the human body. Take the U2 or U3 to Wöhrder Wiese.

Toys

» **Playmobil** (☑9666 1700; www.playmobil-funpark.de; Brandstätterstrasse 2-10; admission €10; ⊘9am-7pm May-Sep, 9am-6pm Oct) This theme park has life-size versions of the popular toys. It's located 9km west of the city centre in Zirndorf; take the S4 to Anwanden, then change to bus 151. Free admission if it's your birthday. Special 'Kleine Dürer' (Little Dürer; €2.99) figures are on sale here and at the tourist office.

» **Käthe Wohlfahrt Christmas shop** (Map p268; www.bestofchristmas.com; Königstrasse 8) The Nuremberg branch of this year-round Christmas shop.

» **Spielzeugmuseum** (p271) Some 1400 sq metres of Matchbox, Barbie, Playmobil and Lego, plus a great play area.

» **Germanisches Nationalmuseum** (p269) Has a toy section and holds occasional tours for children.

Zoo

» **Nuremberg Zoo** (☑545 46; www.tiergarten.nuernberg.de; Am Tiergarten 30; adult/child €13.50/6.50; ⊘8am-7.30pm) An open-air zoo and dolphinarium, with enclosures as close as possible to the animals' natural habitats. Take tram 5 from the Hauptbahnhof.

fair (trade only) in late January to early February. At other times, cheap rooms can be found, especially if you book ahead.

TOP CHOICE Hotel Elch HOTEL €€
(Map p268; ☑249 2980; www.hotel-elch.com; Irrerstrasse 9; s/d from €75/95; ☎) Tucked up in the antiques quarter, this 14th-century, half-timbered house has morphed into the snuggest, most romantic 12-room gem of a hotel you could imagine. A couple of rooms (2 and 7) have half-timbered walls and ceilings, but modern touches include contemporary art, glazed terracotta bathrooms, rainbow-glass chandeliers and trendy multicoloured elk heads throughout (the name means 'elk'). The tiny, original wood-beamed

Schnitzelria restaurant downstairs serves guests breakfast in the morning, followed by numerous types of – yep, you guessed it – schnitzel later in the day. Rather surprisingly, rates come *down* at weekends.

Hotel Deutscher Kaiser HOTEL €€
(Map p268; ☑242 660; www.deutscher-kaiser-hotel. de; Königstrasse 55; s/d from €89/108; @☎) Epicentral in its location, aristocratic in its design and service, this treat of a historic hotel has been in the same family since the turn of the 20th century. Climb the castle-like granite stairs to find rooms of understated simplicity, flaunting oversize beds, Italian porcelain, silk lampshades and real period furniture (Biedermeier and Jugendstil). The

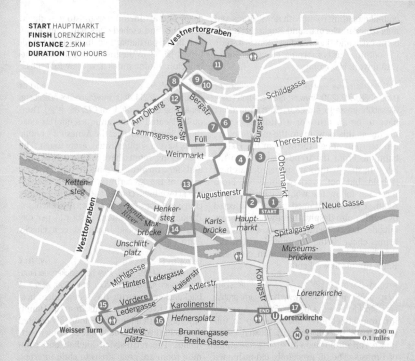

START HAUPTMARKT
FINISH LORENZKIRCHE
DISTANCE 2.5KM
DURATION TWO HOURS

Walking Tour
Nuremberg Altstadt

❯ This circuit covers the historic centre's key sights. With visits to all the attractions listed, it could take the best part of two days.

The tour starts at the Hauptmarkt, the main square. At the eastern end is the ornate Gothic ❶ **Pfarrkirche Unsere Liebe Frau**, also called the Frauenkirche. The church clock's figures spring into action every day at noon. Also here, the ❷ **Schöner Brunnen** rises from the cobblestones like a buried cathedral. Walk north to the Altes Rathaus, the old town hall, with its ❸ **Lochgefängnisse**, the medieval dungeons. Opposite stands the 13th-century ❹ **St Sebalduskirche**, with the bronze shrine of St Sebald inside. Just up Burgstrasse, the ❺ **Stadtmuseum Fembohaus** covers the highs and lows of Nuremberg's past.

Backtrack south to Halbwachsengässchen and turn right into Albrecht-Dürer-Platz, with the ❻ **Albrecht Dürer Monument**. Directly beneath are the ❼ **Felsengänge**, tunnels once used as a beer cellar and air-raid shelter. Up Bergstrasse you'll reach the ❽ **Tiergärtnertor**, a 16th-century tower. Nearby is the

half-timbered ❾ **Pilatushaus** and a strange, glassy-eyed hare dedicated to Dürer. A few steps east is the ❿ **Historischer Kunstbunker** where precious art was stored in WWII. Looming over the scene is the ⓫ **Kaiserburg** castle of medieval knights. Go south to the ⓬ **Albrecht-Dürer-Haus**, where the Renaissance genius lived and worked. Continue south along Albrecht-Dürer-Strasse, turn left on Füll and skirt the back of Sebalduskirche to Karlsstrasse, where you'll reach the ⓭ **Spielzeugmuseum**, with generations of nostalgia-inducing playthings.

Cross the Karlsbrücke to enjoy a view of the ⓮ **Weinstadel**, an old wine depot by the river. Continue across the Henkersteg (Hangman's Bridge) and south to Vordere Ledergasse, which leads west to the ⓯ **Ehekarussell Brunnen**, with its shocking images of married life. Head east on Ludwigplatz past the ⓰ **Peter-Henlein-Brunnen**, with a statue of the first watchmaker, and proceed along Karolinenstrasse to the massive ⓱ **Lorenzkirche**, with its 15th-century tabernacle and suspended carving of the Annunciation.

club-like reading room with newspapers and magazines in German and English is a welcome extra and the breakfast room is a study in soothing, early-morning elegance. Renovation work is ongoing.

Art & Business Hotel
HOTEL €€

(Map p268; ☎232 10; www.art-business-hotel.com; Gleissbühlstrasse 15; s/d €89/115; ☎) You don't have to be an artist or a business person to stay at this new, up-to-the-minute place, a retro sport shoe's throw from the Hauptbahnhof. From the trendy bar area to the latest in slate bathroom styling, design here is bold, but not overpoweringly so. From reception follow the wobbly carpet to your room, a well-maintained haven uninfected by traffic noise despite the city-centre frenzy outside. Local Technicolor art and design brings cheer to the communal spaces and there's a small sculpture garden out back. Rates tumble at weekends.

Probst-Garni Hotel
PENSION €

(Map p268; ☎203 433; www.hotel-garni-probst. de; Luitpoldstrasse 9; s/d €56/75; ☎) A creaky lift from street level takes you up to this realistically priced, centrally located guesthouse, run for 65 years by three generations of Probsts. The 33 gracefully old-fashioned rooms are multi-hued and high-ceilinged but some are more renovated than others. Furniture in the breakfast room is family made.

Burghotel
HOTEL €€

(Map p268; ☎238 890; www.burghotel-nuernberg. de; Lammsgasse 3; s/d from €56/100; @☎☒) The mock-Gothic reception area and lantern-lit corridors (watch your head) indicate you're in for a slightly different hotel experience here. The small singles and doubles have strange '50s-style built-in timber furniture reminiscent of yesteryear train carriages, old-fashioned bedhead radios and chunky TVs, while some much larger 'comfort' rooms under the eaves have spacious sitting areas and more up-to-date amenities. However the big draw here is the basement heated swimming pool, where all guests are free to make a splash.

Hotel Drei Raben
HOTEL €€€

(Map p268; ☎274 380; www.hotel3raben.de; Königstrasse 63; s/d €130/150; ☎) The design of this original hotel builds upon the legend of the three ravens perched on the building's chimney stack, who tell stories from Nuremberg lore. Each of the 'mythology' rooms uses decor and art including sandstone-sculpted bedheads and etched-glass bathroom doors to reflect a particular tale, from the life of Albrecht Dürer to the history of the local football club. Junior suites have claw-foot tubs.

Agneshof
HOTEL €€

(Map p268; ☎214 440; www.agneshof-nuernberg. de; Agnesgasse 10; s/d from €73/86; P@) Tranquilly located in the antiques quarter near the St Sebalduskirche, the Agneshof's public areas have a sophisticated, artsy touch. The box-ticking rooms have whitewashed walls and '90s furniture; some at the top have views of the Kaiserburg. There's a state-of-the-art wellness centre, and a pretty summer courtyard garden strewn with deckchairs. Parking (by reservation) costs €15 per day and the farmhouse breakfast is a cheeky extra €7.

Lette'm Sleep
HOSTEL €

(Map p268; ☎992 8128; www.backpackers.de; Frauentormauer 42; dm €16-20, r from €50; @☎) A backpacker favourite, this independent hostel is just five minutes' walk from the Hauptbahnhof, with a laundry, colourfully painted dorms and some groovy self-catering apartments. The retro-styled kitchen and common room are great areas to chill; internet, tea and coffee are free, and staff are wired into what's happening around town.

Hotel Victoria
HOTEL €€

(Map p268; ☎240 50; www.hotelvictoria.de; Königstrasse 80; s/d from €78/99; P@☎) A hotel since 1896, the Victoria is a solid option with a central location. With its early 21st-century bathrooms and now ever-so-slightly dated decor, the price is about right. Popular with business travellers. Parking costs €11.

Hotel Drei Linden
HOTEL €

(☎506 800; www.hotel-drei-linden-nuernberg.de; Äussere Sulzbacher Strasse 1-3; s/d €40/60; ☎) Persistently the cheapest deal in town, rooms are comfortable though not at all chic, and there's round-the-clock free tea and coffee. Breakfast is a whopping €9.50 extra. Located 1km east of the Altstadt; take tram 8 to Deichlerstrasse.

Knaus-Campingpark
CAMPGROUND €

(☎981 2717; www.knauscamp.de; Hans-Kalb-Strasse 56; per tent/person €5.30/6.30; ☎) A camping ground near the lakes in the Volkspark, southeast of the city centre. Take the U1 to Messezentrum, then walk about 1km.

DJH Hostel
HOSTEL €

(Map p268; ☎230 9360; www.nuernberg.jugendher berge.de; Burg 2; dm from €21.90) A 20-minute walk north of the Hauptbahnhof, this spotless, recently renovated youth hostel in the former castle stables has 382 beds in bright airy dorms. Open year-round.

✕ Eating

⌂TOP CHOICE⌂ Goldenes Posthorn
FRANCONIAN €€

(Map p268; ☎225 153; Glöckleinsgasse 2, cnr Sebalder Platz; mains €6-19; ⊘11am-11pm; ☑) Push open the heavy copper door to find a real culinary treat that has been serving the folk of Nuremberg since 1498. The miniature local sausages are big here, but there's plenty else on the menu including many an obscure rural dish and some vegie options. The choice of dining spaces ranges from formal to folksy, chunky wood to wood panelled. Cash only.

⌂TOP CHOICE⌂ Bratwursthäusle
GERMAN €€

(Map p268; http://die-nuernberger-bratwurst.de; Rathausplatz 2; meals €6-14; ⊘closed Sun) Seared over a flaming beech-wood grill, the little links sold at this rustic inn arguably set the standard for *Rostbratwürste* across the land. You can dine in the timbered restaurant or on the terrace with views of the Hauptmarkt. Service can be flustered at busy times.

Hütt'n
GERMAN €€

(Map p268; Bergstrasse 20; mains €5.50-15; ⊘4pm-midnight Mon-Fri, 11am-12.30am Sat, 11am-10.30pm Sun) Successfully and confusingly relocated from Burgstrasse to Bergstrasse, this local haunt perpetually overflows with admirers of *Krustenschäufele* (roast pork with crackling, dumplings and sauerkraut salad) and the finest bratwurst put to work in various dishes, though menus change daily (Friday is fish day). It's also not the worst place to try a tankard or three of Franconian *Landbier*.

Heilig-Geist-Spital
BAVARIAN €€

(Map p268; ☎221 761; Spitalgasse 16; mains €7-17; ⊘lunch & dinner) Lots of dark carved wood, a herd of hunting trophies and a romantic candlelit half-light make this former hospital, suspended over the Pegnitz, one of the most atmospheric dining rooms in town. Sample the delicious, seasonally changing menu inside or out in the pretty courtyard, where the tinkle of cutlery on plate competes with a dribbling fountain.

Marientorzwinger
GERMAN €€

(Map p268; Lorenzer Strasse 33; mains €8-17; ⊘lunch & dinner) The last remaining *Zwinger* eatery (taverns built between the inner and outer walls when they relinquished their military use) in Nuremberg is an atmospheric place to chomp on sturdy Franconian staples or a vegie dish in the simple wood-panelled dining room or the leafy beer garden. Swab the decks with a yard of Fürth-brewed Tucher.

Restaurant Oberkrainer
FRANCONIAN €€

(Map p268; Hauptmarkt 7; mains €7-21.50; ⊘lunch & dinner) Blending tradition and nutrition for 35 years, central Oberkrainer is the place to explore Franconia with a knife and fork. You might want to skip a meal before tackling the strapping portions of goose, beef steak, *Schäufele*, schnitzel and the house speciality of tenderloin in paprika and garlic sauce, all served in the timber-rich dining room.

Café am Trödelmarkt
CAFE €

(Map p268; Trödelmarkt 42; dishes €4-8.50; ⊘9am-6pm Mon-Sat, 11am-6pm Sun) A gorgeous place on a sunny day, this multilevel waterfront cafe overlooks the covered Henkersteg bridge. It's especially popular for its continental breakfasts, and has fantastic cakes, as well as good blackboard lunchtime specials between 11am and 2pm.

Burgwächter
FRANCONIAN, INTERNATIONAL €€

(Map p268; ☎222 126; Am Ölberg 10; mains €9-15; ⊘11am-11pm; ☑) Refuel after a tour of the Kaiserburg with prime steaks, bratwurst with potato salad, and vegetarian-friendly Swabian filled pastas and salads, as you feast your eyes on the best terrace views from any Nuremberg eatery or drinking spot. With kiddies in tow, ask for *Kloss*, a simple dumpling with sauce.

Sushi Glas
SUSHI €

(Map p268; ☎205 9901; Kornmarkt 5-7; sushi from €5; ⊘noon-11pm Mon-Wed, noon-midnight Thu-Sat, 6-10pm Sun) Take a pew in this 21st-century sugar cube to watch the sushi chef deftly craft your order. When the mercury climbs high, enjoy your nigiri, sashimi and American sushi beneath the huge sunshades on the Kornmarkt.

Schäufelewärtschaft
BAVARIAN €

(Schweiggerstrasse 19; mains €6-8.50; ⊘noon-2pm & 5-10pm Mon-Fri, 5-10pm Sat, 11am-10pm Sun) It's easy to maintain best-kept-secret status with such an unpronounceable name and a dodgy location on the wrong side of the tracks behind the Hauptbahnhof. But most Nürnbergers agree that this rough-hewn eatery plates up the best shoulder of pork in the business. Take tram 6, 7, 8 or 9 from the train station to the Schweigger-strasse stop.

Naturkostladen Lotos   ORGANIC, BUFFET €
(Map p268; www.naturkostladen-lotos.de; Unschlittplatz 1; dishes €3-6; ☺noon-6pm Mon-Fri; ✍) Unclog arteries and blast free radicals with a blitz of grain burgers, spinach soup or vegie pizza at this health-food shop. The fresh bread and cheese counter is a treasure chest of nutritious picnic supplies.

Souptopia   SOUP €
(Map p268; ☎240 6697; Lorenzer Strasse 27; soups €3-7.50; ☺closed Sun) This fragrantly spicey place has a weekly changing menu, outdoor seating and a choice of non-liquid mains (sandwiches, salads) if you don't fancy a bowl of broth. Very popular lunch spot, so get there early.

American Diner   AMERICAN €€
(Map p268; Gewerbemuseumsplatz 3; burgers €9-12; ☺11am-1am Sun-Thu, 11am-2am Fri & Sat) For the juiciest burgers in town, head for this retro diner in the Cinecitta Cinema, Germany's biggest multiplex.

Wurst & Durst   GERMAN €
(Map p268; Luitpoldstrasse 13; dishes €3-5; ☺11am-6pm Tue & Wed, 11am-6pm & 9pm-3am Thu, 1-6pm & 9pm-5am Fri & Sat) Wedged between the facades of Luitpoldstrasse, this tiny snack bar offers munchies relief in the form of Belgian fries, sausages and trays of *Currywurst*.

🍷 Drinking

Landbierparadies   PUB
(☎468 882; www.landbierparadies.com; Wodanstrasse 15; mains €6-9; ☺evenings Mon-Fri, from noon Sat, from 10am Sun) This spit 'n sawdust saloon stocks an incredible wellspring of obscure country ales, some of which are only available here and in the village where they are brewed.

Barfüsser Brauhaus   BEER HALL
(Map p268; Königstrasse 60) This beer hall is a popular spot to hug a mug of site-brewed ale, bubbling frothily in the copper kettles that occupy the cavernous vaulted cellar. Traditional trappings have been done away with, yellow polo shirts having replaced Dirndl and local kitsch kept to a minimum.

Treibhaus   CAFE
(Map p268; ☎223 041; Karl-Grillenberger-Strasse 28; snacks €3.80-8.20; ☎) Well off the path of most visitors, this bustling cafe is a Nuremberg institution. It serves breakfast till evening and caffeinated comfort to students and weary-legged shoppers.

Sausalitos   BAR
(Map p268; ☎200 4889; Färber Strasse 10) This busy Santa Fe–themed bar draws all sorts, from mums with prams and business people during the day to a slicker crowd the later the hour, who come for the long cocktail menu.

Meisengeige   BAR
(Map p268; Am Laufer Schlagturm 3) This long-established hole-in-the-wall bar draws an intense crowd of film intellectuals.

☆ Entertainment

The excellent *Plärrer*, available at newsstands throughout the city, is the best source of information on events around town. Otherwise the free monthly listings magazine *Doppelpunkt* (www.doppelpunkt.de), found in bars, restaurants and the tourist office, does an adequate job.

Hirsch   LIVE MUSIC
(☎429 414; www.der-hirsch.de; Vogelweiherstrasse 66) This converted factory, 2.5km south of the Hauptbahnhof, hosts live alternative music almost daily, both big-name acts and local names. Take the U1 or U2 to Plärrer, then change to tram 4, alighting at Dianaplatz.

Staatstheater   THEATRE
(Map p268; www.staatstheater-nuernberg.de; Richard-Wagner-Platz 2) Nuremberg's magnificent state theatre serves up an impressive mix of dramatic arts. The renovated art-nouveau opera house presents opera and ballet, while the Kammerspiele offers a varied program of classical and contemporary plays. The Nürnberger Philharmoniker also performs here.

Filmhaus   CINEMA
(Map p268; ☎231 5823; www.kubiss.de; Königstrasse 93) This small indie picture house shows foreign-language movies, plus reruns of cult German flicks and films for kids.

Loop Club   CLUB
(☎686 767; www.loopclub.de; Klingenhofstrasse 52) With three dance areas and a languid chill-out zone with lounge music, this place attracts a slightly more mature crowd, meaning

'80s and '90s hits plus student nights. Take the U2 to Herrnhütte, turn right and it's a five-minute walk.

Mach1
CLUB

(Map p268; ☑246 602; www.mach1-club.de; Kaiser-strasse 1-9; ☺Thu-Sat) This legendary dance temple has been around for decades, but still holds a spell over fashion victims. Line up and be mustered.

Roxy
CINEMA

(☑488 40; www.roxy-nuernberg.de; Julius-Loss-mann-Strasse 116) This cinema shows first-run films in the original English version, a rarity in Nuremberg. Take tram 8 to the Südfried-hof stop.

Rockfabrik
CLUB

(☑565 056; Klingenhofstrasse 56; ☺Thu-Sat; ☎) Safely out of earshot of the centre, 3.5km to the northeast, this citadel of rock heaves with longhairs, who flock here for the week-end 'AC/DC', 'Oldies' and 'Heroes of Rock' nights. Take the U2 to Herrnhütte.

ⓘ Information

Main Post Office (Bahnhofplatz 1)

ReiseBank (Hauptbahnhof)

S-Flat (Hauptbahnhof; per 15min €1; ☺24hr) Web access upstairs in the train station.

Tourist Office (www.tourismus.nuernberg. de) Künstlerhaus (☑233 60; Königstrasse 93; ☺9am-7pm Mon-Sat, 10am-4pm Sun) Haupt-markt (Hauptmarkt 18; ☺9am-6pm Mon-Sat, 10am-4pm Sun May-Oct)

ⓘ Getting There & Away

AIR Nuremberg airport (NUE; www.airport -nuernberg.de), 5km north of the centre, is served by regional and international carriers, including Lufthansa, Air Berlin and Air France.

BUS Buses to destinations across Europe leave from the **main bus station** (ZOB) near the Hauptbahnhof. There's a Touring/Eurolines office nearby. Special Deutsche Bahn express coaches to Prague (€50, 3½ hours, seven daily) leave from outside the Hauptbahnhof.

TRAIN Rail connections from Nuremberg:

» **Berlin** €93, five hours, at least hourly

» **Frankfurt** €51, two hours, at least hourly

» **Hamburg** €122, 4½ hours, nine daily

» **Munich** €52, one hour, twice hourly

» **Vienna** €94.20, five hours, every two hours

ⓘ Getting Around

TO/FROM THE AIRPORT U-Bahn 2 runs every few minutes from the Hauptbahnhof to the air-port (€2.40, 12 minutes). A taxi to the airport will cost you about €16.

BICYCLE Nuremberg has ample bike lanes along busy roads and the Altstadt is pretty bike friendly. For bike hire, try the excellent **Ride on a Rainbow** (☑397 337; www.ride-on-a-rainbow. de; Adam-Kraft-Strasse 55; per day from €10).

PUBLIC TRANSPORT The best transport around the Altstadt is at the end of your legs. Timed tickets on the VGN bus, tram and U-Bahn/S-Bahn networks cost from €1.60. A day pass costs €4.80. Passes bought on Saturday are valid all weekend.

Bamberg

☑0951 / POP 70,000

A disarmingly beautiful architectural mas-terpiece with an almost complete absence of modern eyesores, Bamberg's entire Alt-stadt is a Unesco World Heritage Site and one of Bavaria's unmissables. Generally re-garded as one of Germany's most attractive settlements, the town is bisected by rivers and canals, and was built by archbishops on seven hills, earning it the sobriquet of 'Fran-conian Rome'. Students inject some liveli-ness into its streets, pavement cafes and pubs and no fewer than 10 breweries cook up Bamberg's famous smoked beer, but it's usually wide-eyed tourists who can be seen filing through its narrow medieval streets. The town can be tackled as a day trip from Nuremberg but, to really do it justice and to experience the romantically lit streets once most visitors have left, consider staying the night.

Bamberg

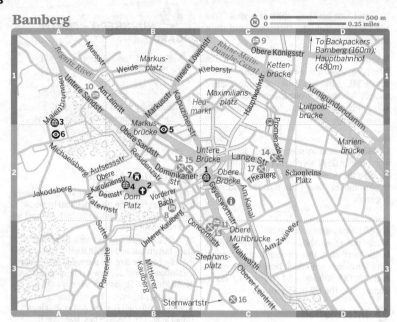

Sights

Bamberger Dom CATHEDRAL
(Map p278; www.erzbistum-bamberg.de; Domplatz; ⊗8am-6pm Apr-Oct, to 5pm Nov-Mar) The quartet of spires of Bamberg's Dom soars above the cityscape. Founded by Heinrich II in 1004, its current appearance dates to the early 13th century and is the outcome of a Romanesque-Gothic duel between church architects after the original and its immediate successor burnt down in the 12th century. The pillars have the original light hues of Franconian sandstone thanks to Ludwig I, who eradicated all postmedieval decoration in the early 19th century.

The interior contains superb and often intriguing works of art. In the north aisle, you'll spot the **Lächelnde Engel** (Smiling Angel), who smirkingly hands the martyr's crown to the headless St Denis.

In the west choir is the marble tomb of **Pope Clemens II**, the only papal burial place north of the Alps. Of the several altars, the **Bamberger Altar**, carved by Veit Stoss in 1523, is worth closer inspection. Because its central theme is the birth of Christ, it's also called the Christmas Altar.

However, the Dom's star attraction is the statue of the knight-king, the **Bamberger Reiter**. Nobody has a clue as to either the name of the artist or the young king on the steed. The canopy above the statue represents the heavenly Jerusalem, suggesting the mysterious figure may have been revered as a saint.

Altes Rathaus HISTORIC BUILDING
(Map p278; Obere Brücke) The best views of the Gothic 1462 Altes Rathaus, which perches on a tiny artificial island between two bridges like a ship in dry dock, are from the small Geyerswörthsteg footbridge across the Regnitz. Look for the cherub's leg sticking out from the fresco on the east side.

For closer views, turning at the end of the Geyerswörthsteg then right again onto Obere Brücke brings you face to facade with the imposing tower, a baroque addition by Balthasar Neumann. It provides access to the precious porcelain and faiences – mostly from Strasbourg and Meissen – housed in the **Sammlung Ludwig Bamberg** (Map p278; ☏871 871; Obere Brücke 1; adult/concession €3.50/2.50; ⊗9.30am-4.30pm Tue-Sun).

Historisches Museum MUSEUM
(Map p278; ☏519 0746; www.museum.bamberg.de; Domplatz 7; adult/concession €5/4.50; ⊗9am-5pm Tue-Sun May-Oct) Bamberg's main museum fills the **Alte Hofhaltung** (Old Court Hall), a former prince-bishops' palace near

Bamberg

the cathedral, with a mixed bag of exhibits. These include a model of the pilgrimage church Vierzehnheiligen and the Bamberger Götzen, ancient stone sculptures found in the region. Often of greater interest are the expertly curated special exhibitions (some of which run through the winter), which examine aspects of the region's past in more detail.

Neue Residenz PALACE
(Map p278; ☑519 390; www.schloesser.bayern.de; Domplatz 8; adult/child €4.50/3.50; ⊙9am-6pm Apr-Sep, 10am-4pm Oct-Mar) Home to Bamberg's prince-bishops from 1703 until secularisation in 1802, 45-minute guided tours of Neue Residenz take in some 40 stuccoed rooms crammed with furniture and tapestries from the 17th and 18th centuries.

The palace also hosts a small branch of the **Bayerische Staatsgalerie** (Bavarian State Gallery). Its strengths are in medieval, Renaissance and baroque paintings, with works by Anthony Van Dyck, Hans Baldung Grien and Cranach the Elder.

The third attraction here is the small but exquisite baroque **Rosengarten** (Rose Garden), from where the Altstadt's sea of red rooftops spread out below.

Fränkisches Brauereimuseum MUSEUM
(Map p278; ☑530 16; www.brauereimuseum.de; Michaelsberg 10f; adult/concession €3/2.50; ⊙1-5pm Wed-Fri, 11am-5pm Sat & Sun Apr-Oct) Located next to the Kloster St Michael, this comprehensive brewery museum exhibits heaps of period mashing, boiling and bottling implements, as well as everything to do with local suds, such as beer mats, tankards, enamel beer signs and lots of photos and documentation. If the displays have left you dry mouthed, quench your thirst in the small pub.

Kloster St Michael MONASTERY
(Map p278; Franziskanergasse 2; ⊙9am-6pm) Above Domplatz, at the top of Michaelsberg, is the Benedictine Kloster St Michael, a former monastery and now an aged people's home. The monastery church is a must-see, both for its baroque art and the meticulous depictions of nearly 600 medicinal plants and flowers on the vaulted ceiling. The manicured garden terrace boasts a splendid city panorama.

☞ Tours

BierSchmecker Tour WALKING TOUR
(adult €20) Possibly the most tempting tour of the amazingly varied offerings at the tourist office (p281) is the self-guided BierSchmecker Tour. The price includes entry to the Franconian Brewery Museum (depending on the route taken), plus five beer vouchers valid in five pubs and breweries, an English information booklet, a route map and a souvenir stein.

⊨ Sleeping

Hotel Sankt Nepomuk HOTEL €€
(Map p278; ☑984 20; www.hotel-nepomuk.de; Obere Mühlbrücke; r €95-145; 🖓) Aptly named after the patron saint of bridges, this is a classy establishment in a half-timbered former mill right on the Regnitz. It has a superb restaurant (mains €15 to €30) with a terrace, 24 comfy rustic rooms and bikes for rent.

Barockhotel am Dom HOTEL €€
(Map p278; ☑540 31; www.barockhotel.de; Vorderer Bach 4; s/d from €77/99; 🅿🖓) The sugary facade, a sceptre's swipe from the Dom, gives a hint of the baroque heritage and original details within. The 19 rooms have sweeping views of the Dom or the roofs of the Altstadt, and breakfast is served in a 14th-century vault.

DON'T MISS

KLEIN VENEDIG

A row of diddy, half-timbered cottages once inhabited by fishermen and their families makes up Bamberg's **Klein Venedig** (Little Venice; Map p278), which clasps the Regnitz' east bank between Markusbrücke and Untere Brücke. The little homes balance on poles set into the water and are fronted by tiny gardens and terraces (wholly unlike Venice, but who cares). Klein Venedig is well worth a stroll but looks at least as pretty from a distance, especially when red geraniums tumble from the many window boxes.

Hotel Residenzschloss   HOTEL €€€
(Map p278; ☑609 10; www.residenzschloss.com; Untere Sandstrasse 32; r €109-199; ⓅⓈⓇ) Bamberg's grandest digs occupy a palatial building formerly used as a hospital. But have no fear, as the swanky furnishings – from the Roman-style steam bath to the flashy piano bar – have little in common with institutional care. High-ceilinged rooms are business standard though display little historical charm. Bus 916 from the ZOB stops nearby.

Hotel Europa   HOTEL €€
(Map p278; ☑309 3020; www.hotel-europa-bamberg.de; Untere Königstrasse 6-8; r €89-119) The Europa is a spick-and-span but unfussy affair above the town's most respected Italian restaurant, just outside the Altstadt. Ask for a room at the front with views of the Dom and the red-tiled roofs of the Altstadt. Breakfast is in the restaurant or out in the sunny courtyard.

Backpackers Bamberg   HOSTEL €
(☑222 1718; www.backpackersbamberg.de; Heiliggrabstrasse 4; dm €15-18, s/d €27/40; Ⓡ) Bamberg's backpacker hostel is a funky but well-kept affair, with clean dorms, a fully functional kitchen and a quiet, family-friendly atmosphere. Make sure you let staff know when you're arriving, as it's left unmanned for most of the day. Located around 400m north along Luitpoldstrasse from the Luitpoldbrücke.

Campingplatz Insel   CAMPGROUND €
(☑563 20; www.campinginsel.de; Am Campingplatz 1; tents €4-8, adult/car €5/4) If rustling nylon is your abode of choice, this well-equipped site, in a tranquil spot right on the river, is the sole camping option. Take bus 918 to Campingplatz.

✕ Eating & Drinking

Messerschmidt   FRANCONIAN €€
(Map p278; ☑297 800; Lange Strasse 41; mains €12-25; ⊙lunch & dinner) This stylish gourmet eatery may be ensconced in the house where aviation engineer Willy Messerschmidt was born, but there's nothing 'plane' about dining here. The place oozes old-world charm, with dark woods, white linens and traditionally formal service. Sharpen your molars on platters of roast duck and red cabbage out on the alfresco terrace overlooking a pretty park, or in the attached wine tavern.

Schlenkerla   FRANCONIAN €
(Map p278; ☑560 60; Dominikanerstrasse 6; dishes €5-10; ⊙9.30am-11.30pm) At the foot of the cathedral, this local legend is a dark, rustic 14th-century tavern with hefty wooden tables groaning with scrumptious Franconian fare and its own superb *Rauchbier,* poured straight from oak barrels.

Kornblume   ORGANIC €€
(☑917 1760; Kapellenstrasse 22; mains €7-22; ⊙5.30pm-midnight Wed-Mon, plus 11.30am-2pm Sun; Ⓙ) Don't be deterred by the somewhat style-absent decor at this family-run place 1.5km east of the centre, as the tasty food is lovingly prepared and strict organic and ecofriendly principles impeccably upheld. The menu reads like a vegetarian's antioxidant bible, though the occasional meat dish also makes an appearance. Take bus 905 to Wunderburg.

Zum Sternla   FRANCONIAN €
(Map p278; ☑287 50; Lange Strasse 46; mains €4-12.50; ⊙10am-11pm) Bamberg's oldest *Wirtshaus* (inn), Zum Sternla was established in 1380 and the camaraderie among its patrons has seemingly changed little in the intervening years. Bargain-priced staples include pork dishes, steaks, dumplings and sauerkraut, as well as specials, but it's a great, non-touristy place for traditional *Brotzeit* (snack) or just a pretzel and a beer. The menu is helpfully translated from Franconian into German.

Spezial-Keller   BREWERY €
(Map p278; ☑548 87; Sternwartstrasse 8; dishes €5-12; ⊙3pm-late Tue-Sat, from 10am Sun) Quite a hike out of town, but the superb *Rauchbier* served here is your reward, along with

great views of the Dom and the Altstadt from the beer garden.

Klosterbräu
BREWERY €

(Map p278; ☑522 65; Obere Mühlbrücke 1-3; mains €6-12; ⊙10.30am-11pm Mon-Fri, 10am-11pm Sat, 10am-10pm Sun) This beautiful half-timbered brewery is Bamberg's oldest. It draws *Stammgäste* (regular local drinkers) and tourists alike who wash down filling slabs of meat and dumplings with its excellent range of ales. English-language brewery tours on request.

Ambräusianum
PUB €

(Map p278; ☑509 0262; Dominikanerstrasse 10; dishes €7-15; ⊙11am-11pm Tue-Sat, 11am-9pm Sun) Bamberg's only brewpub does a killer *Weisswurst* breakfast – parsley-speckled veal sausage served with a big freshly baked pretzel and a *Weissbier* – as well as schnitzel, pork knuckle and *Flammkuchen* (Alsatian pizza) that'll have you waddling out the door like a Christmas goose.

⊙ Information

Post Office (Ludwigstrasse 25)

Tourist Office (☑297 6200; www.bamberg. info; Geyerswörthstrasse 5; ⊙9.30am-6pm Mon-Fri, to 4pm Sat, to 2.30pm Sun) Slightly visitor-weary office in a new purpose-built complex. Staff sell the three-day Bambergcard (€12) which provides admission to city attractions, use of city buses and a Unesco-themed walking tour.

⊙ Getting There & Around

BUS Several buses, including 901, 902 and 931, connect the train station with the **central bus station** (ZOB). Bus 910 goes from the ZOB to Domplatz.

TRAIN Bamberg has the following rail connections:

» **Berlin** €76, 4¼ hours, every two hours

» **Munich** €59, two to 2½ hours, every two hours

» **Nuremberg** €12 to €21, 40 to 60 minutes, four hourly

» **Würzburg** €19, one hour, twice hourly

Bayreuth

☑0921 / POP 72.600

Even without its Wagner connections, Bayreuth would still be an interesting detour from Nuremberg or Bamberg for its baroque architecture and curious palaces. But it's for the annual Wagner Festival that 60,000 opera devotees make a pilgrimage to this neck of the *Wald*.

Bayreuth's glory days began in 1735 when Wilhelmine, sister of King Frederick the Great of Prussia, was forced to marry stuffy Margrave Friedrich. Bored with the local scene, the cultured Anglo-oriented Wilhelmine invited the finest artists, poets, composers and architects in Europe to court. The period bequeathed some eye-catching buildings, still on display for all to see.

⊙ Sights

Outside of the Wagner Festival (see box, p282) from late July to the end of August, the streets of Bayreuth slip into a kind of provincial slumber, although the town's strong musical traditions ensure there are good dramatic and orchestral performances all year.

Markgräfliches Opernhaus
OPERA HOUSE

(☑759 6922; Opernstrasse 14; tours adult/concession €5.50/4.50; ⊙tours 9am-6pm daily Apr-Sep, occasional weekends Oct-Mar) Designed by Giuseppe Galli Bibiena, a famous 18th-century architect from Bologna, Bayreuth's opera house is one of Europe's most stunningly ornate baroque theatres. Germany's largest opera house until 1871, it has a lavish interior smothered in carved, gilded and marbled wood. However, Richard Wagner considered it too modest for his serious work and conducted here just once. The 45-minute sound-and-light multimedia show is in German only but, even if you don't speak the local lingo, tours are still worth it just to ogle at the show-stopping auditorium.

Neues Schloss
PALACE

(☑759 6920; Ludwigstrasse 21; adult/concession €5.50/4.50; ⊙9am-6pm daily Apr-Sep, 10am-4pm Tue-Sun Oct-Mar) The Neues Schloss, which opens into the vast **Hofgarten** (admission free; ⊙24hr), lies a short distance to the south of the main shopping street, Maxmilianstrasse. A riot of rococo style, the margrave's residence after 1753 features a vast collection of 18th-century porcelain made in Bayreuth. The annual VIP opening of the Wagner Festival is held in the Cedar Room. Also worth a look is the Spiegelscherbenkabinett (Broken Mirror Cabinet), which is lined with irregular shards of broken mirror – supposedly Wilhelmine's response to the vanity of her era.

Richard Wagner
Museum – Haus Wahnfried
MUSEUM

(www.wagnermuseum.de; Richard-Wagner-Strasse 48) In the early 1870s King Ludwig II, Wagner's most devoted fan, gave the great composer

WAGNER FESTIVAL

The **Wagner Festival** (www.bayreuther-festspiele.de) has been a summer fixture in Bayreuth for over 130 years and is generally regarded as the top Wagner event anywhere in the world. The festival lasts for 30 days (from late July to late August), with each performance attended by an audience of just over 1900. Demand is insane, with an estimated 500,000 fans vying for less than 60,000 tickets. Until recently all tickets were allocated in a shady lottery with preference given to 'patrons' and 'Wagner enthusiasts'. Ordinary, unconnected fans sometimes had to wait five to 10 years before 'winning' a seat. However, in a bid to introduce a bit more transparency into proceedings, the festival organisers recently decided to release some tickets onto the open market through travel agencies, making the procedure of bagging a seat considerably less frustrating and angering many a Wagner society in the process. Alternatively, it is still possible to lay siege to the box office two and a half hours before performances begin in the hope of snapping up cheap returned tickets, but there's no guarantee you'll get in.

Once in the Festspielhaus, ticket holders to one of Germany's premier classical music festivals face uncomfortable hard wood seats and poor ventilation – all part of the experience, diehards claim.

the cash to build Haus Wahnfried, a mini-mansion on the northern edge of the Hofgarten. The building now houses the Richard Wagner Museum, but at the time of research it was closed for renovation and would remain that way until at least 2013.

Despite the ongoing building work, you can still sneak around the back of the house to see the unmarked, ivy-covered tomb containing Wagner and his wife Cosima. The sandstone grave of his loving canine companion Russ stands nearby.

Festspielhaus OPERA HOUSE

(☎787 80; www.bayreuther-festspiele.de; Festspielhügel 1-2; adult/concession €5/3) North of the Hauptbahnhof, the main venue for Bayreuth's annual Wagner Festival is the Festspielhaus, constructed in 1872 with King Ludwig II's backing. The structure was specially designed to accommodate Wagner's massive theatrical sets, with three storeys of mechanical works hidden below stage. It's still one of the largest opera venues in the world. Tours are available daily most of the year; check the website for details. Take bus 305 to Am Festspielhaus.

Eremitage PARK

Around 6km east of the centre lies the Eremitage, a lush park girding the **Altes Schloss** (☎759 6937; adult/concession €4.50/3.50; ⊙9am-6pm Apr-Sep), Friedrich and Wilhelmine's summer residence. Visits to the palace are by guided tour only and take in the Chinese Mirror Room where Countess Wilhelmine penned her memoirs.

Also in the park is horseshoe-shaped Neues Schloss (not to be confused with the one in town), which centres on the amazing mosaic Sun Temple with gilded Apollo sculpture. Around both palaces you'll find numerous grottoes, follies and gushing fountains. To get there take bus 302 from Markt.

Maisel's Brauerei-und-Büttnerei-Museum MUSEUM, BREWERY

(☎401 234; www.maisel.com/museum; Kulmbacher Strasse 40; tours adult/concession €4/2; ⊙tours 2pm daily) For a fascinating look at the brewing process, head to this enormous museum next door to the brewery of one of Germany's top wheat-beer producers. The 90-minute guided tour takes you into the bowels of the 19th-century plant, with atmospheric rooms filled with 4500 beer mugs and amusing artefacts. Visits conclude with a glass of cloudy *Weissbier* (wheat beer).

Sleeping

Don't even think of attempting a sleepover in Bayreuth during the Wagner Festival as rooms are booked out months in advance.

Hotel Goldener Anker HOTEL €€€

(☎787 7740; www.anker-bayreuth.de; Opernstrasse 6; s €98-128, d €148-198; P 🛜) The refined elegance of this hotel, owned by the same family since the 16th century, is hard to beat. It's just a few metres from the opera house, in the pedestrian zone. Many of the rooms are decorated in heavy traditional style with swag curtains, dark woods and antique touches. Parking is €15 a day.

Hotel Goldener Hirsch
HOTEL €€

(☎1504 4000; www.bayreuth-goldener-hirsch.de; Bahnhofstrasse 13; s €65-85, d €85-110; ☏@☎) Just across from the train station, the 'Golden Reindeer' looks a bit stuffy from the outside, but once indoors you'll discover crisp, well-maintained rooms with contemporary furniture and unscuffed, whitewashed walls. Some of the 40 rooms have baths. Parking is free.

Gasthof Hirsch
GUESTHOUSE €

(☎267 14; St Georgen Strasse 6; dm/d €25/50) Though a bit of a hike from the train station, some of it uphill, this guesthouse is a decent budget option with well-furnished doubles or a three-bed dorm with its own piano. Bathrooms are shared but there are hot- and cold-water basins in all rooms. Calling ahead is advised as there's no reception.

DJH Hostel
HOSTEL €

(☎764 380; www.bayreuth.jugendherberge.de; Universitätsstrasse 28; dm €17.60) This excellent 140-bed hostel near the university has comfortable, fresh rooms, a relaxed atmosphere and heaps of guest facilities.

✗ Eating & Drinking

Oskar
FRANCONIAN, BAVARIAN €€

(☎516 0553; Maximilianstrasse 33; mains €6-15; ⊙8am-1am Mon-Sat, from 9am Sun) At the heart of the pedestrianised shopping boulevard, this multitasking, open-all-hours bar-cafe-restaurant is Bayreuth's busiest eatery. It's good for a busting Bavarian breakfast, a light lunch in the covered garden cafe, a full-on dinner feast in the dark-wood restaurant, or a *Landbier* and a couple of tasty Bayreuth bratwursts anytime you feel.

Kraftraum
CAFE €

(Sophienstrasse 16; mains €6-8; ⊙8am-1am Mon-Fri, from 9am Sat & Sun; ☏) This vegetarian eatery has plenty to tempt even the most committed meat eaters, including pastas, jacket potatoes, soups and huge salads. The retroish, shabby-chic interior empties on sunny days when everyone plumps for the alfresco seating out on the cobbles. Tempting weekend brunches (€12.50) always attract a large crowd.

Rosa Rosa
BISTRO, BAR €

(☎685 02; Von-Römer-Strasse 2; mains €3-7.50; ⊙5pm-1am Mon-Fri, from 11am Sat, from 4pm Sun; ☏) Join Bayreuth's chilled crowd at this bistro-cum-pub for belly-filling portions of salad, pasta and vegie fare, as well as seasonal dishes from the big specials board, or just a Friedenfelser beer in the evening. The poster-lined walls keep you up to date on the latest acts to hit town.

Hansl's Wood Oven Pizzeria
PIZZERIA €

(☎543 44; Friedrichstrasse 15; pizzas from €4.30) The best pizza in town is found at this hole in the wall. A checklist menu lets you choose your own toppings and, voila, you can name your creation.

RICHARD WAGNER

With the backing of King Ludwig II, Richard Wagner (1813–83), the gifted, Leipzig-born composer and notoriously poor manager of money, turned Bayreuth into a mecca of opera and high-minded excess. Bayreuth profited from its luck and, it seems, is ever grateful.

For Wagner, listening to opera was meant to be work and he tested his listeners wherever possible. *Götterdämmerung, Parsifal, Tannhäuser* and *Tristan and Isolde* are grandiose pieces that will jolt any audience geared for light entertainment. Four days of *The Ring of the Nibelung* are good for limbering up.

After poring over Passau and a few other German cities, Wagner designed his own festival hall in Bayreuth. The unique acoustics are bounced up from a below-stage orchestra via reflecting boards onto the stage and into the house. The design took the body density of a packed house into account, still a remarkable achievement today.

Wagner was also a notorious womaniser, an infamous anti-Semite and a hardliner towards 'non-Europeans'. So extreme were these views that even Friedrich Nietzsche called Wagner's works 'inherently reactionary, and inhumane'. Wagner's works, and by extension Wagner himself, were embraced as a symbol of Aryan might by the Nazis and, even today, there is great debate among music lovers about the 'correctness' of supporting Wagner's music and the Wagner Festival in Bayreuth.

Underground BAR

(☎633 47; Von-Römer-Strasse 15; ⊙from 7pm Tue-Sun Sep-May, Mon-Sun Jun-Aug) Squeezed into a cellar space shaped like a London Underground train, and decked out as such with hard seats and Tube logos, this bar-cafe has a gay clientele, though the crowd's usually as mixed as the cocktails.

❶ Information

Bayreuth Card (72hr €11.50) Good for unlimited trips on city buses, museum entry and a two-hour guided city walk (in German).

Post Office (Hauptbahnhof)

Sparkasse (Opernstrasse 12)

Tourist Office (☎885 748; www.bayreuth-tourismus.de; Opernstrasse 22; ⊙9am-7pm Mon-Fri, 9am-6pm Sat year-round, plus 10am-2pm Sun May-Oct) Has a train ticket booking desk and a worthwhile gift shop.

❶ Getting There & Away

Most rail journeys between Bayreuth and other towns in Bavaria require a change in Nuremberg:

» **Munich** Change in Nuremberg; €65, 2½ hours, hourly

» **Nuremberg** €19, one hour, hourly

» **Regensburg** Change in Nuremberg; €26 to €41, 2¼ hours, hourly

Coburg

☎09561 / POP 41,000

If marriage is diplomacy by another means, Coburg's rulers were surely masters of the art. Over four centuries, the princes and princesses of the house of Saxe-Coburg intrigued, romanced and ultimately wed themselves into the dynasties of Belgium, Bulgaria, Denmark, Portugal, Russia, Sweden and, most prominently, Great Britain. The crowning achievement came in 1857, when Albert of Saxe-Coburg-Gotha took his vows with first cousin Queen Victoria, founding the present British royal family. The British royals quietly adopted the less-German name of Windsor during WWI.

Coburg languished in the shadow of the Iron Curtain during the Cold War, all but closed in by East Germany on three sides, but since reunification the town has undergone a revival. Its proud Veste is one of Germany's finest medieval fortresses. What's more, some sources contend that the original hot dog was invented here.

◉ Sights & Activities

Coburg's epicentre is the magnificent Markt, a beautifully renovated square radiating a colourful, aristocratic charm. The fabulous Renaissance facades and ornate oriels of the **Stadthaus** (town house) and the **Rathaus** vie for attention, while a greening bronze of Prince Albert, looking rather more flamboyant and Teutonic medieval than the Brits are used to seeing him, calmly surveys the scene.

Veste Coburg FORTRESS, MUSEUM
(www.kunstsammlungen-coburg.de; adult/concession €5/2.50; ⊙9.30am-5pm daily Apr-Oct, 1-4pm Tue-Sun Nov-Mar) Towering above Coburg's centre is a story-book medieval fortress, the Veste Coburg. With its triple ring of fortified walls, it's one of the most impressive fortresses in Germany but, curiously, has a dearth of foreign visitors. It houses the vast collection of the **Kunstsammlungen**, with works by star painters such as Rembrandt, Dürer and Cranach the Elder. The elaborate Jagdintarsien-Zimmer (Hunting Marquetry Room) is a superlative example of carved woodwork.

Protestant reformer Martin Luther, hoping to escape an imperial ban, sought refuge at the fortress in 1530. His former quarters have a writing desk and, in keeping with the Reformation, a rather plain bed.

The **Veste-Express** (one-way/return €3/4; ⊙10am-5pm Apr-Oct), a tourist train, leaves from the tourist office (p285) and makes the trip to the fortress every 30 minutes. Otherwise it's a steep 3km climb on foot.

Schloss Ehrenburg CASTLE
(☎808 832; www.sgvcoburg.de; Schlossplatz; adult/child €4.50/free; ⊙tours hourly 9am-5pm Tue-Sun Apr-Sep, 10am-4pm Tue-Sun Oct-Mar) The lavish Schloss Ehrenburg was once the town residence of the Coburg dukes. Albert spent his childhood in this sumptuous, tapestry-lined palace, and Queen Victoria stayed in a room with Germany's first flushing toilet (1860). The splendid **Riesensaal** (Hall of Giants) has a baroque ceiling supported by 28 statues of Atlas.

Coburger Puppenmuseum MUSEUM
(www.coburger-puppenmuseum.de; Rückerstrasse 2-3; adult/child €4/2; ⊙10am-4pm daily Apr-Oct, 11am-4pm Tue-Sun Nov-Mar) Spanning 33 rooms, this delightfully old-fashioned museum displays a collection of 2000 dolls, dollhouses, miniature kitchens and chinaware,

some from as far away as England and all dating from between 1800 and 1956. Aptly named 'Hallo Dolly', the stylish cafe next door is ideally situated for restoring calm after all those eerie glass eyes.

⭐ Festivals & Events

Samba Festival DANCE
(www.samba-festival.de) Believe it or not, Coburg hosts Europe's largest Samba Festival every year in mid-July, an incongruous venue if ever there was one. This orgy of song and dance attracts almost 100 bands and up to 200,000 scantily-clad, bum-wiggling visitors. Now what would Queen Vic have made of that?

🛏 Sleeping & Eating

Romantik Hotel Goldene Traube HOTEL €€
(🕿8760; www.goldenetraube.com; Am Viktoriabrunnen 2; s €89-99, d €109-129; P🅿🛜) Owner Bernd Glauben is president of the German Sommelier's Union, and you can taste and buy over 400 wines in the charming hotel **wine bar**. These can also be sampled in the two eateries, the Michelin-starred Esszimmer and the less fancy Victora Grill. Rooms are splashed with bright Mediterranean yellows and oranges or else decked out Laura Ashley style. Located in the Altstadt.

Hotelpension Bärenturm GUESTHOUSE €€
(🕿318 401; www.baerenturm-hotelpension.de; Untere Anlage 2; s €85, d €110-130; P🛜) For those who prefer their complimentary pillow pack of gummy bears served with a touch of history, Coburg's most characterful digs started life as a defensive tower that was expanded in the early 19th century to house Prince Albert's private tutor. Each of the 15 rooms is a gem boasting squeaky parquet floors, antique-style furniture and regally high ceilings.

DJH Hostel HOSTEL €
(🕿153 30; www.coburg.jugendherberge.de; Parkstrasse 2) Housed in a mock redbrick castle, Schloss Ketschendorf (some 2km from town), Coburg's youth hostel was receiving a comprehensive makeover at the time of research and it wasn't clear when it would be back online. Check the website for details.

Café Prinz Albert CAFE €
(Ketschengasse 27; snacks & cakes €2-5; ⏰7.30am-6pm Mon-Fri, from 8am Sat, from 1pm Sun) Coburg's links with the British royals are reflected here in both the decor and menu.

The Prince Albert breakfast (€7.60) – a cross-cultural marriage of sausage, egg and Bamberger croissants – is fit for a queen's consort.

Tie VEGETARIAN €€€
(Leopoldstrasse 14; mains €15-23; ⏰from 5pm Tue-Sun; 🍽) Heavenly (if pricey) food is crafted from fresh organic ingredients at this vegetarian restaurant, where the focus is firmly on the food and not gimmicky decor. Dishes range from vegetarian classics to Asian inspirations, with the odd fish or meat dish for the unconverted.

Ratskeller FRANCONIAN €
(Markt 1; mains €4.50-13.50; ⏰10am-midnight) Munch on regional dishes from Thuringia and Franconia while kicking back on well-padded leather benches under the heftily vaulted ceiling of Coburg's spectacular town hall.

ℹ Information

Tourist Office (🕿898 000; www.coburg -tourist.de; Herrengasse 4; ⏰9am-6.30pm Mon-Fri, 10am-3pm Sat, 10am-2pm Sun Apr-Oct, 9am-5pm Mon-Fri, 10am-3pm Sat Nov-Mar) Helpful office where staff sell the CObook (€14.90), a five-day ticket good for 13 sights in Coburg and around as well as local public transport. English audioguides (€3.50) to the city are also available here.

ℹ Getting There & Away

Coburg has the following rail connections:

» **Bamberg** €11.10, 40 minutes, hourly

» **Bayreuth** €16.40, 1½ hours, hourly

» **Nuremberg** €21.50, 1¾ hours, hourly

Altmühltal Nature Park

The Altmühltal Nature Park is one of Germany's largest nature parks and covers some of Bavaria's most eye-pleasing terrain. The Altmühl River gently meanders through a region of little valleys and hills before joining the Rhine–Main Canal and eventually emptying into the Danube. Outdoor fun on well-marked hiking and biking trails is the main reason to head here, but the river is also ideal for canoeing. There's basic camping in designated spots along the river, and plenty of accommodation in the local area.

The park takes in 2900 sq km of land southwest of Regensburg, south of Nuremberg, east of Treuchtlingen and north of

Eichstätt. The eastern boundaries of the park include the town of Kelheim.

North of the river, activities focus around the towns of Kipfenberg, Beilngries and Riedenburg.

🏃 Activities

Canoeing & Kayaking

The most beautiful section of the river is from Treuchtlingen or Pappenheim to Eichstätt or Kipfenberg, about a 60km stretch that you can do lazily in a kayak or canoe in two to three days. There are lots of little dams along the way, as well as some small rapids about 10km northwest of Dollnstein, so make sure you are up for little bits of portaging. Signs warn of impending doom, but locals say that, if you heed the warning to stay to the right, you'll be safe.

You can hire canoes and kayaks in just about every town along the river. Expect to pay about €15/25 per day for a one-/two-person boat, more for bigger ones. Staff will sometimes haul you and the boats to or from your embarkation point for a small fee.

You can get a full list of boat-hire outlets from the Informationszentrum Naturpark Altmühltal (p286).

San-Aktiv Tours   CANOE RENTAL
(☑09831-4936; www.san-aktiv-tours.com; Otto-Dietrich-Strasse 3, Gunzenhausen) San-Aktiv Tours are the largest and best-organised of the canoe-hire companies in the park, with a network of vehicles to shuttle canoes, bicycles and people around the area. Trips through the park run from April to October, and you can canoe alone or join a group. Packages generally include the canoe, swim vests, maps, instructions, transfer back to the embarkation point and, for overnight tours, luggage transfer and lodgings.

Cycling & Hiking

With around 3000km of hiking trails and 800km of cycle trails criss-crossing the landscape, foot and pedal are the best ways to strike out into the park. Cycling trails are clearly labelled and have long rectangular brown signs bearing a bike symbol. Hiking-trail markers are yellow. The most popular cycling route is the Altmühltal Radweg, which runs parallel to the river for 166km. The Altmühltal-Panoramaweg stretching 200km between Gunzenhausen and Kelheim is a picturesque hiking route that crosses the entire park from west to east.

You can hire bikes in almost every town within the park, and prices are more or less uniform. Most bike-hire agencies will also store bicycles. Ask for a list of bike-hire outlets at the Informationszentrum Naturpark Altmühltal.

In Eichstätt, **Fahrradgarage** (☑08421-2110; www.fahrradgarage.de; Herzoggasse 3) hires out bicycles for €10 per day. Staff will bring the bikes to you or take you and the bikes to anywhere in the park for an extra fee.

Rock Climbing

The worn cliffs along the Altmühl River offer some appealing terrain for climbers of all skill levels. The medium-grade 45m-high rock face of Burgsteinfelsen, located between the towns of Dollnstein and Breitenfurt, has routes from the fourth to eighth climbing levels, with stunning views of the valley. The Dohlenfelsen face near the town of Wellheim has a simpler expanse that's more suitable for children. The Informationszentrum Naturpark Altmühltal can provide more details on the region's climbing options.

ℹ️ Information

The park's main information centre is in Eichstätt, a charmingly historic town at the southern end of the park that makes an excellent base for exploring.

For information on the park and for help with planning an itinerary, contact the **Informationszentrum Naturpark Altmühltal** (☑08421-987 60; www.naturpark-altmuehltal.de; Notre Dame 1; ⊙9am-5pm Mon-Sat, 10am-5pm Sun Apr-Oct, 8am-noon & 2-4pm Mon-Thu, 8am-noon Fri Nov-Mar) in Eichstätt. The website is tricky to navigate but does have a lot of brochures for free download.

ℹ️ Getting There & Around

There are bus and train connections between Eichstätt and all the major milestones along the river including, from west to east, Gunzenhausen, Treuchtlingen and Pappenheim.

BUS From mid-April to October the FreizeitBus Altmühltal-Donautal takes passengers and their bikes around the park. Buses normally run three times a day from mid-April to early October (see www.naturpark-altmuehltal.de to download the timetable). Route 1 runs from Regensburg and Kelheim to Riedenburg on weekends and holidays only. Route 2 travels between Eichstätt, Beilngries, Dietfurt and Riedenburg, with all-day service on weekends and holidays and restricted service on weekdays. All-day tickets, which cost €10.50/7.50 for passengers with/without bicycles, or €23.50/17.50 per family, are bought from the driver.

TRAIN Hourly trains run between Eichstätt Bahnhof and Treuchtlingen (€5.50, 25 minutes), and between Treuchtlingen and Gunzenhausen (€4, 15 minutes). RE trains from Munich that run through Eichstätt Bahnhof also stop in Dollnstein, Solnhofen and Pappenheim.

Eichstätt

📞 08421 / POP 13,800

Hugging a tight bend in the Altmühl River, Eichstätt radiates a tranquil Mediterranean-style flair. Cobbled streets meander past elegantly Italianate buildings and leafy piazzas, giving this sleepy town a general sense of refinement. Italian architects, notably Gabriel de Gabrieli and Maurizio Pedetti, rebuilt the town after Swedes razed the place during the Thirty Years' War (1618–48) and it has since remained undamaged. Since 1980 many of its baroque facades have concealed faculties belonging to Germany's sole Catholic university.

Eichstätt is pretty enough, but is really just a jumping off and stocking up point for flits into the wilds of Altmühltal Nature Park. You'll be chomping at the bit, eager to hit a trail or grab a paddle, if you stay more than a day.

◉ Sights

Dom CHURCH
(www.bistum-eichstaett.de/dom; Domplatz; ⊗7.15am -7.30pm) Eichstätt's centre is dominated by the richly adorned Dom. Standout features include an enormous 16th-century stained-glass window by Hans Holbein the Elder, and the carved sandstone **Pappenheimer Altar** (1489–97), depicting a pilgrimage from Pappenheim to Jerusalem. The seated statue is of St Willibald, the town's first bishop.

The adjoining **Domschatzmuseum** (Cathedral Treasury; 📞507 42; Residenzplatz 7; adult/concession €3/1.50, Sun €1; ⊗10.30am-5pm Wed-Fri, 10am-5pm Sat & Sun Apr-Nov) includes the robes of 8th-century English-born bishop St Willibald and baroque Gobelin tapestries.

Willibaldsburg CASTLE
(📞4730; Burgstrasse 19; ⊗9am-6pm Tue-Sun Apr-Oct, 10am-4pm Tue-Sun Nov-Mar) The walk or drive up to the hilltop castle of Willibaldsburg (1355) is worth it for the views across the valley from the formally laid-out **Bastiongarten**; many locals also head

up here on sunny days for the nearby beer garden. The castle itself house two museums, the most interesting of which is the **Jura-Museum** (Burgstrasse 19; adult/concession €4.50/3.50; ⊗9am-6pm Apr-Sep, 10am-4pm Oct-Mar, closed Mon) specialising in fossils and containing a locally found archaeopteryx (the oldest-known fossil bird), as well as aquariums with living specimens of the fossilised animals.

Kloster St Walburga CONVENT
(www.abtei-st-walburg.de; Westenstrasse; ♿) The final resting place of St Willibald's sister, the Kloster St Walburga is a popular local pilgrimage destination. Every year between mid-October and late February, water oozes from Walburga's relics in the underground chapel and drips down into a catchment. The nuns bottle diluted versions of the so-called *Walburgaöl* (Walburga oil) and give it away to the faithful. A staircase from the lower chapel leads to an off-limits upper chapel where you can catch a glimpse through the grill of beautiful ex-voto tablets and other trinkets left as a thank you to the saint. The main **St Walburga Church** above has a glorious rococo interior.

Residenz PALACE
(Residenzplatz; admission €1; ⊗tours 10.15am, 11am, 11.45am, 2pm, 2.45pm & 3.30pm Sat & Sun Apr-Oct) The prince-bishops lived it up in the baroque Residenz, built between 1725 and 1736 by Gabriel de Gabrieli. Inside the stunning main staircase and a hall of mirrors stick in the mind, though you'll have to arrive on a weekend to see them. In the square outside rises a late 18th-century golden statue of the Madonna atop a 19m-high column.

🛏 Sleeping & Eating

Hotel Adler HOTEL €€
(📞6767; www.adler-eichstaett.de; Marktplatz 22; s €67-75, d €91-115; 🅿) A superb ambience reigns in this ornate 300-year-old building, Eichstätt's top digs. Sleeping quarters are bright and breezy, and the generous breakfast buffet a proper set up for a day on the trail or river. Despite the posh feel, this hotel welcomes hiker and bikers.

Fuchs HOTEL €
(📞6789; www.hotel-fuchs.de; Ostenstrasse 8; s €40-48, d €60-80; 🕿) This central, family-run hotel, with under-floor heating in the

bathrooms, adjoins a cake shop with a sunny dining area. It's convenient to a launch ramp on the river where you can put in, and you can lock your canoe or kayak in the garage.

DJH Hostel
HOSTEL €

(☎980 410; www.eichstaett.jugendherberge.de; Reichenaustrasse 15; dm from €19, d €46.60) This comfy, 122-bed youth hostel provides pretty views of the Altstadt. The double rooms, if available, have their own shower and toilet.

Municipal Camp Site
CAMPGROUND €

(☎908 147; www.eichstaett.info/wohnmobilstell platz; Pirkheimerstrasse; per site €7) This basic campground is on the northern bank of the Altmühl River, about 1km southeast of the town centre. It's open year-round but closes for 10 days during the Volksfest (a mini-Oktoberfest) in late August or early September.

Café im Paradeis
CAFE €€

(☎3313; Markt 9; mains €5-17; ⊗8am-midnight) This open-all-hours cafe on Markt is a prime spot for people watching wherever the hands of the clock may be. Recharge with a home-cooked meal or just a coffee, either in the antique-lined interior or out on the terrace.

Gasthof Krone
BAVARIAN €€

(☎4406; Domplatz 3; mains €7-18; ⊗lunch & dinner) Traditionally garbed waitresses bang down monster platters of local nosh in the beer garden and two-tiered dining room of this lively tavern. Altmühltaler lamb is the speciality here, its meat infused with special flavour by the park's herb-rich meadows.

ⓘ Information

Post Office (Domplatz 7)

Raiffeisenbank (Domplatz 5)

Tourist Office (☎600 1400; www.eichstaett. info; Domplatz 8; ⊗9am-6pm Mon-Sat, 10am-1pm Sun Apr-Oct, 10am-noon & 2-4pm Mon-Thu, 10am-noon Fri Nov-Mar)

ⓘ Getting There & Away

Eichstätt has two train stations. Mainline trains stop at the Bahnhof, 5km from the centre, from where coinciding diesel services shuttle to the *Stadtbahnhof* (town station). Trains run hourly between Ingolstadt and Eichstätt (€5.50, 25 minutes) and every two hours to Nuremberg (€18.10, 1½ hours).

REGENSBURG & THE DANUBE

The sparsely populated eastern reaches of Bavaria may live in the shadow of Bavaria's big-hitting attractions, but they hold many historical treasures to rival their neighbours. Top billing goes to Regensburg, a former capital, and one of Germany's prettiest and liveliest cities. From here the Danube gently winds its way to the Italianate city of Passau. Landshut was once the hereditary seat of the Wittelsbach family, and the region has also given the world a pope, none other than incumbent Benedict XVI who was born in Marktl am Inn. Away from the towns, the Bavarian Forest broods in semi-undiscovered remoteness.

Eastern Bavaria was a seat of power in the Dark Ages, ruled by rich bishops at a time when Munich was but a modest trading post. A conquering Napoleon lumped Eastern Bavaria into river districts, and King Ludwig I sought to roll back these changes by recreating the boundaries of a glorified duchy from 1255. Though it brought a sense of renewed Bavarian identity, the area remained very much on the margins of things, giving rise to the odd and appealing mixture of ancient Roman cities, undulating farmland and rugged wilderness that it is today.

Regensburg

☎0941 / POP 135,500

A Roman settlement completed under Emperor Marcus Aurelius, Regensburg was the first capital of Bavaria, the residence of dukes, kings and bishops, and for 600 years an Free Imperial City. Two millennia of history bequeathed the city some of the region's finest architectural heritage, a fact recognised by Unesco in 2006. Though big on the historical wow factor, today's Regensburg is a laid-back and unpretentious sort of place, and a good springboard into the wider region.

◉ Sights

Schloss Thurn und Taxis
CASTLE

(Map p289; www.thurnundtaxis.de; Emmeramsplatz 5; tours adult/concession €11.50/9; ⊗tours 11am, 1pm, 2pm, 3pm, 4pm Mon-Fri, additionally 10am & noon Sat & Sun, closed Dec-Mar) In the 15th century, Franz von Taxis (1459-1517) assured his place in history by setting up the first

Regensburg

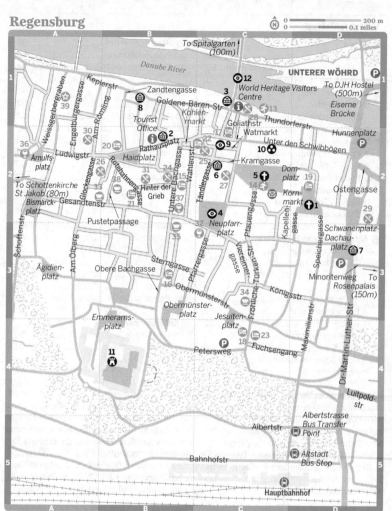

European postal system, which remained a monopoly until the 19th century. In recognition of his services, the family was given a new palace, the former Benedictine monastery St Emmeram, henceforth known as Schloss Thurn und Taxis. It was soon one of the most modern palaces in Europe and featured such luxuries as flushing toilets, central heating and electricity. Tours include a look into the Basilika St Emmeram.

The palace complex also contains the **Schatzkammer** (Map p289; adult/concession €4.50/3.50; ⏰11am-5pm Mon-Fri, 10am-5pm Sat & Sun). The jewellery, porcelain and precious furnishings on display belonged, for many years, to the wealthiest dynasty in Germany. The fortune, administered by Prince Albert II, is still estimated at well over €1 billion.

Dom St Peter
CHURCH

(Map p289; Domplatz; ⏰6.30am-6pm Apr-Oct, to 5pm Nov-Mar) It takes a few seconds for your eyes to adjust to the dim interior of Regensburg's soaring landmark, the Dom St Peter, one of Bavaria's grandest Gothic cathedrals. Impressive features inside are the kaleidoscopic stained-glass windows above the choir and in the south transept, and the intricately

Regensburg

gilded altar. Construction dates from the late 13th century, but the distinctive filigree spires weren't added until the 19th century; the extravagant western facade also dates from this period and is festooned with sculptures.

The **Domschatzmuseum** (Map p289; adult/child €2/1; ⊙10am-5pm Tue-Sat, noon-5pm Sun) brims with monstrances, tapestries and other church treasures.

Altes Rathaus & Reichstagsmuseum HISTORIC BUILDING
(Map p289; Rathausplatz; adult/concession €7.50/4; ⊙English tours 3pm Apr-Oct, 2pm Nov-Mar) The seat of the Reichstag for almost 150 years, the Altes Rathaus is now home to Regensburg's mayors and the **Reichstagsmuseum**. Tours take in not only the lavishly decorated **Reichssaal** (Imperial Hall), but also the original **torture chambers** in the basement. The interrogation room bristles with tools such as the rack, the Spanish donkey (a tall wooden wedge on which the victim was made to sit naked) and spiked chairs. Ask at the nearby tourist office about tickets and times of German-language tours.

Steinerne Brücke BRIDGE
(Map p289) An incredible feat of engineering for its day, Regensburg's 900-year-old Steinerne Brücke (Stone Bridge) was at one time the only fortified crossing of the Danube. Ensconced in its southern tower is the **Brückturm-Museum** (Map p289; Weisse-Lamm-Gasse 1; adult/concession €2/1.50; ⊙10am-7pm Apr-Oct), a small historical exhibit about the bridge.

Historisches Museum MUSEUM
(Map p289; ☎507 2448; Dachauplatz 2-4; adult/concession €2.20/1.10; ⊙10am-4pm Tue, Wed & Fri-Sun, 10am-8pm Thu) A medieval monastery provides a suitably atmospheric backdrop for the city's history museum. The collections plot the region's story from cave dweller to Roman, and medieval trader to 19th-century burgher.

Schottenkirche St Jakob CHURCH
(Jakobstrasse 3) The sooty 12th-century main portal of the Schottenkirche St Jakob is considered one of the supreme examples of Romanesque architecture in Germany. Its reliefs and sculptures form an iconography

that continues to baffle the experts. Sadly it's protected from further pollution by an ageing glass structure that makes the whole thing an eyesore. However, this is more than made up for inside, where pure, tourist-free Romanesque austerity prevails.

Golf Museum MUSEUM
(Map p289; www.golf-museum.com; Tändlergasse 3; adult/concession €7.50/5; ⊙10am-6pm Mon-Sat) Claiming to be the second most important golf museum in Europe (after the British Golf Museum in Scotland), this unexpected repository of club, tee and score card (including one belonging to King George V of England) backswings its way through golf's illustrious past – interesting, even if you think a green fee is something to do with municipal recycling.

Document Neupfarrplatz HISTORIC SITE
(Map p289; ☑507 3454; Neupfarrplatz; adult/concession €5/2.50; ⊙tours 2.30pm Thu-Sat Sep-Jun, Thu-Mon Jul & Aug) Excavations in the mid-1990s revealed remains of Regensburg's once-thriving 16th-century Jewish quarter, along with Roman buildings, gold coins and a Nazi bunker. The subterranean Document Neupfarrplatz only provides access to a small portion of the excavated area, but tours feature a nifty multimedia presentation (in German) about the square's history. Back up above, on the square itself, a work by renowned Israeli artist Dani Karavan graces the site of the former synagogue.

Tickets are purchased from Tabak Götz at Neupfarrplatz 3.

Kepler-Gedächtnishaus MUSEUM
(Kepler Memorial House; Map p289; Keplerstrasse 5; adult/concession €2.20/1.10; ⊙10.30am-4pm Sat & Sun) Disciples of astronomer and mathematician Johannes Kepler should visit the house he lived in while resident in Regensburg.

Alte Kapelle CHURCH
(Map p289; Alter Kornmarkt 8) South of the Dom, the humble exterior of the graceful Alte Kapelle belies the stunning interior with its rich rococo decorations. The core of the church, however, is about 1000 years old, although the Gothic vaulted ceilings were added in the Middle Ages. The church is open only during services but you can always peek through the wrought-iron grill.

Roman Wall HISTORIC SITE
The most tangible reminder of the ancient Castra Regina (Regen Fortress), where the name 'Regensburg' comes from, is the remaining Roman wall, which follows Unter den Schwibbögen and veers south onto Dr-Martin-Luther-Strasse. Dating from AD 179 the rough-hewn **Porta Praetoria** (Map p289; Unter den Schwibbögen) arch is a key reminder of the city's heritage.

Tours

Schifffahrt Klinger BOAT
(Map p289; ☑521 04; www.schifffahrtklinger.de; cruises adult/child from €7.50/4.80) Offers short cruises (50 minutes) on the Danube (available April to late October) and to the Walhalla monument.

Tourist Train Tours TRAIN
(Map p289; departs Domplatz; adult/family €8/19; ⊙8 tours daily) Multilingual tourist train tours of the city centre take 45 minutes to complete a circuit from the south side of the cathedral. Fares include a free coffee at Haus Heuport.

Festivals & Events

Dult BEER
Oktoberfest-style party with beer tents, carousel rides, entertainment and vendors on the Dultplatz, in May and late August/early September.

Weihnachtsmarkt CHRISTMAS MARKET
The Christmas market has stalls selling roasted almonds, gingerbread and traditional wooden toys. Held at Neupfarrplatz and Schloss Thurn und Taxis during December.

Sleeping

Regensburg has an unexpectedly wide choice of places to achieve REM, from blue-blooded antique-graced apartments to blood-red suites for fired up honeymooners.

Hotel Elements
HOTEL €€

(Map p289; 3819 8600; www.hotel-elements.de; Alter Kornmarkt 3; apt €135-155) Four elements, four rooms, and what rooms they are! This tiny theme hotel breaks new ground with its imaginative design and is the best-kept secret in Eastern Bavaria. 'Fire' blazes in plush crimson and is just the thing for honeymooning couples, while nautically themed 'Water' is splashed with portholes and a Jacuzzi. 'Air' is spacious and light, as opposed to 'Earth' where colonial chocolate browns and bamboo reign. Reception and breakfast are in the adjoining Caffè Rinaldi.

Petit Hotel Orphée
HOTEL €€

(Map p289; 596 020; www.hotel-orphee.de; Wahlenstrasse 1; s €35-125, d €70-135) Behind a humble door in the heart of the city lies a world of genuine charm, unexpected extras and real attention to detail. The striped floors, wrought-iron beds, original sinks and common rooms with soft cushions and well-read books give the feel of a lovingly attended home. Another somewhat grander branch of the hotel is located above the Café Orphée (p293).

Hotel Goldenes Kreuz
HOTEL €€

(Map p289; 558 12; www.hotel-goldeneskreuz. de; Haidplatz 7; r €75-125;) Surely the best deal in town, the nine fairy-tale rooms each bear the name of a crowned head and are fit for a kaiser. Huge mirrors, dark antique and Bauhaus furnishings, four-poster beds, chubby exposed beams and parquet flooring produce a stylishly aristocratic opus in leather, wood, crystal and fabric. Yes, those prices are correct!

Altstadthotel am Pach
HOTEL €€

(Map p289; 298 610; www.regensburghotel.de; Untere Bachgasse 9; s €98-124, d €118-144; @) Those who have shaped Regensburg history, from Marcus Aurelius to Emperor Karl V, are commemorated in the 20 rooms of this sleek hotel. Quarters vary in size in size but all are warmly furnished with thick carpets, comfy mattresses and a minibar with complimentary beer and water. If you're tall, you might want to avoid the beamed and slanted rooms in the attic.

Goliath Hotel
HOTEL €€€

(Map p289; 200 0900; www.hotel-goliath.de; Goliathstrasse 10; s/d from €125/155;) Right in the heart of the city centre, the 41 rooms at the Goliath are all differently conceived and pristinely serviced. Some have little extras, such as bathroom–bedroom windows

and big baths. Funky, but doesn't go the whole boutique hog and staff are surprisingly old school. Parking costs €12.

Brook Lane Hostel
HOSTEL €

(Map p289; 696 5521; www.hostel-regensburg.de; Obere Bachgasse 21; dm/s/d from €16/40/50, apt per person €55;) Regensburg's only backpacker hostel has its very own convenience store, which doubles up as reception; it isn't open 24 hours, so late landers should let staff know in advance. Dorms do the minimum required, but the apartments and doubles here are applaudable deals, especially if you're travelling in a twosome or more. Access to kitchens and washing machines throughout.

Hotel Roter Hahn
HOTEL €€

(Map p289; 595 090; www.roter-hahn.com; Rote-Hahnen-Gasse 10; s/d €100/120;) A bulky beamed ceiling and a glassed-in Roman stone well (of which staff are oblivious) greet you in the lobby of the 'Red Rooster', contrasting with streamlined rooms offering freshly minted amenities. Parking costs €12; request a room on the 2nd floor to access the free wi-fi.

Zum Fröhlichen Türken
HOTEL €€

(Map p289; 536 51; www.hotel-zum-froehlichen -tuerken.de; Fröhliche-Türken-Strasse 11; s/d €59/ 84;) With its comfortable, clean quarters, unstinting breakfast and mild-mannered staff, the 'Jolly Turk' will bring a smile to any budget-minded traveller's face. The pricier rooms have private bathrooms.

Azur-Campingplatz
CAMPGROUND €

(270 025; www.azur-camping.de/regensburg; Weinweg 40; per person/tent €8.50/9) A pretty site about 3km from the Altstadt on the southern bank of the Danube. Take bus 6.

DJH Hostel
HOSTEL €

(466 2830; www.regensburg.jugendherberge. de; Wöhrdstrasse 60; dm from €21) Regensburg's 186-bed hostel occupies a beautiful old building on a large island about a 10-minute walk north of the Altstadt.

Hotel Am Peterstor
HOTEL €

(Map p289; 545 45; www.hotel-am-peterstor.de; Fröhliche-Türken-Strasse 12; s/d €38/48; reception 7-11am & 4-10.30pm;) The pale-grey decor might be grim, and the recpetion hours silly, but the location is great, the price is right and staff go out of their way to assist. Make sure you get a non-smoking room as

some pong of secondhand smoke. Breakfast is an optional €5 extra.

Eating

'In Regensburg we ate a magnificent lunch, had a divine musical entertainment, an English hostess and a wonderful Moselle wine,' wrote Mozart to his wife Constance in 1790. Available in Mozart's day, but better washed down with a local Kneitinger Pils, is the delectable bratwurst (grilled sausage) and *Händlmaier's Süsser Hausmachersenf,* a distinctive sweet mustard.

Haus Heuport   INTERNATIONAL €€
(Map p289; 599 9297; Domplatz 7; mains €7-23; from 9am;) Enter an internal courtyard (flanked by stone blocks where medieval torches were once extinguished) and climb up the grand old wooden staircase to this space-rich Gothic dining hall for eye-to-eye views of the Dom St Peter and an internationally flavoured culinary celebration. The Sunday breakfast buffet runs to a hangover-busting 3pm. Always busy.

Spaghetteria   ITALIAN €
(Map p289; Am Römling 12; dishes €4.50-10; lunch & dinner) Get carbed up at this former 17th-century chapel, where you can splatter six types of pasta with 23 types of sauce, and get out the door for the cost of a cocktail in Munich. The all-you-can-eat buffet (€5 to €6.50) is a cheap way to fill up at lunchtime.

Historische Wurstkuchl   GERMAN €
(Map p289; Thundorfer Strasse 3; 6 sausages €7.80; 8am-7pm) Completely submerged several times by the Danube's fickle floods, this titchy eatery has been serving the city's traditional finger-size sausages, grilled over beech wood and dished up with sauerkraut and sweet grainy mustard, since 1135, making it the world's oldest sausage kitchen.

Dicker Mann   BAVARIAN €€
(Map p289; www.dicker-mann.de; Krebsgasse 6; mains €6.50-20; 9am-11pm) Stylish, very traditional and serving all the staples of Bavarian sustenance, the 'Chubby Chappy' is one of the oldest restaurants in town, allegedly dating back to the 14th century. On a balmy eve, be sure to bag a table in the lovely beer garden out back.

Vitus   FRENCH €€
(Map p289; 526 46; Hinter der Grieb 8; mains €8-18; 9am-11pm;) Colourful canvasses mix with ancient beamed ceilings at this bustling place serving provincial French food, including delicious *Flammkuchen* (Alsatian pizza), quiche, salads, meat and fish dishes, as well as a commendable number of meat-free options. Sit in the rustic bar area, the restaurant with linen-draped tables or the child-friendly cafe section.

Café Orphée   FRENCH €€
(Map p289; 529 77; Untere Bachgasse 8; mains €7-18; 9am-1am) Claiming to be the most French bistro east of the Rhine, you do feel as though you've been teleported to 1920s Paris at this visually pleasing eatery, bedecked in red velvet, dark wood and mirrors aplenty. Pâtés, crêpes, baguettes and other light lunch fare populate a handwritten menu of appetising Gallic favourites with slight Bavarian touches for sturdiness.

Rosenpalais   BAVARIAN €€€
(0170-880 1333; Minoritenweg 20; mains €12-32; dinner Tue-Sat) If it's posh nosh you're after, try this refined place occupying a pinkish palace just off Dachauplatz and serving a well-heeled gourmet clientele. Service is first-rate, the admirable edibles as well prepared as they are beautifully presented.

Leerer Beutel   EUROPEAN €€
(Map p289; 589 97; Bertoldstrasse 9; mains €10-17; dinner Mon, lunch & dinner Tue-Sat, lunch Sun) Subscriber to the slow-food ethos, the cavernous restaurant at the multi-purpose Leerer Beutel centre offers an imaginatively mixed menu of Bavarian, Tyrolean and Italian dishes, served indoors or out on the car-free cobbles.

Dampfnudel Uli   CAFE €
(Map p289; 532 97; Watmarkt 4; dishes under €5; 10.01am-6.01pm Wed-Fri, to 3.01pm Sat) This quirky little noshery serves a mean *Dampfnudel* (steamed doughnut) with custard in a photo- and stein-filled Gothic chamber at the base of the Baumburger Tower.

Drinking

Spitalgarten   BEER GARDEN
(St Katharinenplatz 1) A veritable thicket of folding chairs and slatted tables by the Danube, this is one of the best places in town for some alfresco quaffing. It claims to have brewed beer (today's Spital) here since 1350, so it probably knows what it's doing by now.

Félix CAFE
(Map p289; Fröhliche-Türken-Strasse 6; ⊙9am-2am Sun-Thu, 10am-3am Fri & Sat) Early birds breakfast and after-dark trendoids leaf through the lengthy drinks menu behind the curvaceous neo-baroque frontage of this open-all-hours cafe with a welcoming air.

Kneitinger PUB
(Map p289; Arnulfsplatz 3) This quintessential Bavarian brewpub is the place to go for some hearty home cooking, delicious house suds and outrageous oompah frolics. It's been in business since 1530.

Hemingway's CAFE, BAR
(Map p289; Obere Bachgasse 5) Black wood, big mirrors and lots of photos of Papa himself add to the cool atmosphere of this art-deco-style cafe-bar.

Augustiner BEER GARDEN
(Map p289; Neupfarrplatz 15) This popular fairy-lit beer garden and restaurant is ideally located in the heart of the city. Leave your beer-glass ring and pack away some gorgeous grub in the sprawling garden or cavernous interior.

Paletti CAFE, BAR
(Map p289; Gesandtenstrasse 6, Pustetpassage) Tucked into a covered passageway off Gesandtenstrasse, this buzzy Italian cafe-bar is a hip hang-out, with seen-and-be-seen windows and art-clad walls.

Cafebar CAFE, BAR
(Map p289; Gesandtenstrasse 14) This time-warped, tightly squeezed blast from the past in tile, cast iron and stained glass fills with newspaper-reading caffeine fans at first rays and ethanol fans after sundown.

Moritz BAR
(Map p289; Untere Bachgasse 15) Take some Gothic cross vaulting, paint it high-visibility tunnel orange, throw in some killer cocktails and invite the iPad crowd – and you got Moritz!

☆ Entertainment

Film Galerie CINEMA
(Map p289; ✆298 4563; www.filmgalerie.de; Bertoldstrasse 9) Part of the Leerer Beutel cultural centre, this cinema concentrates on art-house films, often shown in the original language (including English).

Garbo-Filmtheater CINEMA
(Map p289; ✆575 86; Weissgerbergraben 11) This theatre shows German films on general release, as well as mainstream Hollywood and British movies in English.

ⓘ Information

Lok.in (Hauptbahnhof; per hr €4; ⊙6am-11pm Mon-Sat, from 7am Sun) Internet access in the 1st floor of the train station.

Sparkasse City Center (Neupfarrplatz 10)

Post Office (Domplatz) There's another branch next to the Hauptbahnhof.

Regensburg Card (www.regensburgcard.de; 24/48hr €9/17) For free public transport and discounts at local attractions and businesses. Available at the tourist office.

Tourist Office (www.regensburg.de; Altes Rathaus; ⊙9am-6pm Mon-Fri, to 4pm Sat & Sun)

World Heritage Visitors Centre (✆507 4410; www.regensburg-welterbe.de; Weisse-Lamm-Gasse 1; ⊙10am-7pm) Brand-new visitors centre by the Steinerne Brücke focusing on the city's Unesco World Heritage Sites. Interesting interactive multimedia exhibits.

ⓘ Getting There & Away

CAR Regensburg is about an hour's drive southeast of Nuremberg and northwest of Passau via the A3 autobahn. The A93 runs south to Munich.

TRAIN Train connections from Regensburg:

» **Frankfurt am Main** €67, three hours, every two hours or change in Nuremberg

» **Munich** €25.20, 1½ hours, hourly

» **Landshut** €12.20, 40 minutes, hourly

» **Nuremberg** €19, one to two hours, hourly

» **Passau** €22 to €27, one to 1½ hours, hourly or change in Plattling

ⓘ Getting Around

BICYCLE At **Bikehaus** (✆599 8193; www.bikehaus.de; Bahnhofstrasse 17; bikes per day €12; ⊙10am-2pm & 3-7pm Mon-Sat) you can hire anything from kiddies' bikes to fully saddled tourers and even a rickshaw for a novel city tour.

BUS On weekdays the **Altstadtbus** (€1) somehow manages to squeeze its way through the narrow streets between the Hauptbahnhof and the Altstadt every 10 minutes between 9am and 7pm. The **bus transfer point** is one block north of the Hauptbahnhof, on Albertstrasse. Tickets for all city buses (except the Altstadtbus) cost €2 for journeys in the centre; an all-day ticket costs €4.40 at ticket machines, €5.90 on the bus and €3.80 at weekends (valid for both days).

CAR & MOTORCYCLE The Steinerne Brücke and much of the Altstadt is closed to private vehicles. Car parks in the centre charge from €1.50 per hour and are well signposted.

Around Regensburg

WALHALLA

Modelled on the Parthenon in Athens, the Walhalla is a breathtaking Ludwig I monument dedicated to the giants of Germanic thought and deed. Marble steps seem to lead up forever from the banks of the Danube to this dazzling marble hall, with a gallery of 127 heroes in marble. It includes a few dubious cases, such as astronomer Copernicus, born in a territory belonging to present-day Poland. The latest addition (2009) was romantic poet Heinrich Heine, whose works were set to music by Strauss, Wagner and Brahms.

To get there take the Danube Valley country road (unnumbered) 10km east from Regensburg to the village of Donaustauf, then follow the signs. Alternatively, you can take a two-hour boat cruise with Schifffahrt Klinger (p291), which includes a one-hour stop at Walhalla, or take bus 5 from Regensburg Hauptbahnhof.

Ingolstadt

📞 0841 / POP 125,400

Even by Bavaria's standards, Danube-straddling Ingolstadt is astonishingly affluent. Auto manufacturer Audi has its HQ here, flanked by a clutch of oil refineries on the outskirts, but industry has left few marks on the medieval centre, with its cobblestone streets and historic, if slightly over-renovated, buildings. Ingolstadt's museum-church has the largest flat fresco ever made, and few people know that its old medical school figured in the literary birth of Frankenstein, the monster by which all others are judged.

⊙ Sights

Asamkirche Maria de Victoria CHURCH
(📞 305 1831; Neubaustrasse 11-12; adult/concession €2/1.50; ⊙ 9am-noon & 1-5pm Tue-Sun Mar-Oct, 1-4pm Tue-Sun Nov-Feb) The Altstadt's crown jewel is the Asamkirche Maria de Victoria, a baroque masterpiece designed by brothers Cosmas Damian and Egid Quirin Asam between 1732 and 1736. The church's mesmerising trompe l'œil ceiling, painted in just six weeks in 1735, is the world's largest fresco on a flat surface.

Visual illusions abound: stand on the little circle on the diamond tile near the door and look over your left shoulder at the archer with the flaming red turban – wherever you walk, the arrow points right at you. The fresco's Horn of Plenty, Moses' staff and the treasure chest also appear to dramatically alter as you move around the room.

Deutsches Medizinhistorisches Museum MUSEUM
(German Museum of Medical History; 📞 305 2860; www.dmm-ingolstadt.de; Anatomiestrasse 18-20; adult/concession €5/2.50; ⊙ 10am-5pm Tue-Sun) Located in the stately Alte Anatomie (Old Anatomy) at the university, this sometimes rather gory museum chronicles the evolution of medical science as well as the many (scary) instruments and techniques used. Unless you are, or have been, a medical student, pack a strong stomach for the visit.

The ground floor eases you into the exhibition with medical equipment such as birthing chairs, enema syringes, lancets used for bloodletting and other delightful paraphenalia guaranteed to make many go weak at the knees. Upstairs things get closer to the bone with displays of human skeletons, foetuses of conjoined twins, a pregnant uterus and a cyclops.

Neues Schloss PALACE, MUSEUM
The ostentatious Neues Schloss (New Palace) was built for Duke Ludwig the Bearded in 1418. Fresh from a trip to wealth-laden France, Ludwig borrowed heavily from Gallic design and created a residence with 3m-thick walls, Gothic net vaulting and individually carved doorways. One guest who probably didn't appreciate its architectural merits was future French president Charles de Gaulle, held as a prisoner of war here during WWI.

Today the building houses the Bayerisches Armeemuseum (Bavarian Military Museum; 📞 937 70; www.armeemuseum.de; Paradeplatz 4; adult/concession €3.50/3, Sun €2; combined ticket with Reduit Tilly & Turm Triva €7/5; ⊙ 9am-5.30pm Tue-Fri, 10am-5.30pm Sat & Sun) with exhibits on long-forgotten battles, armaments dating back to the 14th century and legions of tin soldiers filling the rooms.

The second part of the museum is in the Reduit Tilly (adult/concession/child €3.50/3/free, Sun €2; ⊙ 9am-5.30pm Tue-Fri, 10am-5.30pm Sat & Sun) across the river. This 19th-century fortress has an undeniable aesthetic, having been designed by Ludwig I's chief architect. It was named after Johann Tilly – a field

STRAUBING

Some 30km southeast of Regensburg, Straubing enjoyed a brief heyday as part of a wonky alliance that formed the short-lived Duchy of Straubing-Holland. As a result, the centre is chock-a-block with historical buildings that opened new horizons in a small town. In August, the demand for folding benches soars during the Gäubodenfest, a 10-day blow-out that once brought together grain farmers in 1812, but now draws over 20,000 drinkers.

Lined with pastel-coloured houses from a variety of periods, the pedestrian square is lorded over by the Gothic **Stadtturm** (1316). It stands next to the richly gabled **Rathaus**, originally two merchant's homes but repackaged in neo-Gothic style in the 19th century. Just east of the tower is the gleaming golden **Dreifaltigkeitssäule** (Trinity Column), erected in 1709 as a nod to Catholic upheavals during the War of the Spanish Succession.

Straubing has about half a dozen historic churches. The most impressive is **St Jakobskirche** (Pfarrplatz), a late-Gothic hall church with original stained-glass windows; it was the recipient of a baroque makeover, courtesy of the frantically productive Asam brothers. The pair also designed the interior of the **Ursulinenkirche** (Burggasse), their final collaboration. Its ceiling fresco depicts the martyrdom of St Ursula surrounded by allegorical representations of the four continents known at the time. Also worth a look is the nearby **Karmelitenkirche** (Hofstatt).

North of here is the former ducal residence **Herzogsschloss** (Schlossplatz), which overlooks the river. This rather austere 14th-century building was once the town's tax office.

One of Germany's most important repositories of Roman treasure is the intimate **Gäubodenmuseum** (☏974 10; www.gaeubodenmuseum.de; Frauenhoferstrasse 23; adult/concession €4/3; ☺10am-4pm Tue-Sun). Displays include imposing armour and masks for both soldiers and horses, probably plundered from a Roman store.

If you fancy staying over, the **tourist office** (☏944 307; www.straubing.de; Theresienplatz 2; ☺9am-5pm Mon-Wed & Fri, 9am-6pm Thu, 10am-2pm Sat) can find rooms.

Straubing has direct train connections to Regensburg (€9.10, 25 minutes, hourly). For Passau (€14.40, one hour and 10 minutes, hourly) and Munich (€24.90, two hours, twice hourly) change at Plattling or Neufahrn.

marshal of the Thirty Years' War who was known as the 'butcher of Magdeburg' – and features exhibits covering the history of WWI and post-WWI Germany.

The newest addition to the museum complex is the **Bayerisches Polizeimuseum** (Donaulände 1; adult/concession €3.50/3; ☺9am-5.30pm Tue-Fri, 10am-5.30pm Sat & Sun), housed in the Turm Triva, which was built at the same time as the Reduit Tilly. Exhibitions trace the story of Bavarian bobbies and their role in various episodes of history such as the Third Reich and the Cold War.

Museum Mobile   MUSEUM

This high-tech car museum is part of the **Audi Forum** (☏893 7575; www.audi.de/foren; Ettinger Strasse 40; adult/child €2/1, tours €4/2; ☺9am-6pm). Exhibits on three floors chart Audi's humble beginnings in 1899 to its latest dream machines, such as the R8. Some 50 cars and 20 motorbikes are on display, including prototypes that glide past visitors on an open lift. Bus 11 and 44 run every 30 minutes from the Hauptbahnhof or central bus station (ZOB) to the Audi complex.

The two-hour tours of the **Audi factory** (adult/concession €7/3.50; ☺tours hourly Mon-Sat, 11am, 1pm & 3pm Sun) take you through the entire production process, from the metal press to the testing station.

Liebfrauenmünster   CHURCH

(Kreuzstrasse; ☺8am-6pm) Ingolstadt's biggest church was established by Duke Ludwig the Bearded in 1425 and enlarged over the next century. This classic Gothic hall church has a pair of strangely oblique square towers that flank the main entrance. Inside, subtle colours and a nave flooded with light intensify the magnificence of the high-lofted vaulting and the blossoming stonework of several side chapels.

The high altar by Hans Mielich (1560) has a rear panel depicting St Katharina debating with the professors at Ingolstadt's new university, ostensibly in a bid to convert the Protestant faculty to Catholicism – a poke at Luther's Reformation. At the rear of the church, there's a small *Schatzkammer* (treasury) displaying precious robes, goblets and monstrances belonging to the diocese.

Museum für Konkrete Kunst   MUSEUM
(Museum of Concrete Art; ☑305 1871; Tränktorstrasse 6-8; adult/child €3/1.50; ☺10am-5pm Tue-Sun) This unique art museum showcases works and installations from the Concrete Movement, all of a bafflingly abstract nature. The movement was defined and dominated by interwar artists Max Bill and Theo van Doesburg whose works make up a large share of the collection.

Kreuztor   HISTORIC BUILDING
(Kreuzstrasse) The Gothic Kreuztor (1385) was one of the four main gates into the city until the 19th century and its redbrick fairy-tale outline is now the emblem of Ingolstadt. This and the main gate within the Neues Schloss are all that remain of the erstwhile entrances into medieval Ingolstadt, but the former fortifications, now flats, still encircle the city.

Lechner Museum   MUSEUM
(☑305 2250; www.lechner-museum.de; Esplanade 9; adult/concession €3/1.50; ☺11am-6pm Thu-Sun) This unusual art museum highlights works cast in steel, a medium that's more expressive than you might think. Exhibits are displayed in a striking glass-covered factory hall from 1953.

🛌 Sleeping

Kult Hotel   DESIGN HOTEL €€€
(☑951 00; www.kult-hotel.de; Theodor-Heuss-Strasse 25; s/d from €120/141; P🐕@🛜) Aping the Asamkirche, the most eye-catching feature of rooms at this exciting design hotel, 2km northeast of the city centre, are the painted ceilings, each one a work of art. Otherwise fittings and furniture come sleek, room gadgets are the latest toys, and the restaurant is a study in cool elegance.

Hotel Anker   HOTEL €€
(☑300 50; www.hotel-restaurant-anker.de; Tränktorstrasse 1; s/d €58/92) Bright rooms, a touch of surrealist art and a commendably central location make this family-run hotel a good choice, although the lack of English is a slight downside. Try to avoid arriving at mealtimes, when staff are busy serving in the traditional restaurant downstairs.

Enso Hotel   HOTEL €€
(☑885 590; www.enso-hotel.de; Bei der Arena 1; s/d from €79/99; P🛜) Located just across the Danube from the city centre, the 176 business-standard rooms at Ingolstadt's newest digs come in bold dashes of lip-smacking red and soot black, with acres of retro faux veneer providing a funky feel. Traffic noise is barely audible despite the location at a busy intersection. Amenities include sushi and pasta bars, and a fitness room.

Bayerischer Hof   HOTEL €€
(☑934 060; www.bayerischer-hof-ingolstadt.de; Münzbergstrasse 12; s €59-70, d €82-87) Located around a Bavarian eatery, the 34 rooms are a pretty good deal, and are filled with hardwood furniture, TVs and modern, renovated bathrooms. Rates come down at weekends when business traffic thins out.

DJH Hostel   HOSTEL €
(☑305 1280; www.ingolstadt.jugendherberge.de; Friedhofstrasse 41-42; dm under/over 27yr €16.60/20.60) This beautiful, well-equipped and wheelchair-friendly hostel is in a renovated redbrick fortress (1828), about 150m west of the Kreuztor.

THE BIRTH OF FRANKENSTEIN

Mary Shelley's *Frankenstein,* published in 1818, set a creepy precedent in the world of monster fantasies. The story is well known: young scientist Viktor Frankenstein travels to Ingolstadt to study medicine. He becomes obsessed with the idea of creating a human being and goes shopping for parts at the local cemetery. Unfortunately, his creature is a problem child and sets out to destroy its maker.

Shelley picked Ingolstadt because it was home to a prominent university and medical faculty. In the 19th century, a laboratory for scientists and medical doctors was housed in the Alte Anatomie (now the Deutsches Medizinhistorisches Museum (p295)). In the operating theatre, professors and their students carried out experiments on corpses and dead tissue, though perhaps one may have been inspired to work on something a bit scarier...

✕ Eating & Drinking

Local drinkers are proud that Germany's Beer Purity Law of 1516 was issued in Ingolstadt. To find out why, try a mug of frothy Herrnbräu, Nordbräu or Ingobräu.

For a quick bite head for the Viktualienmarkt, just off Rathausplatz, where fast-food stalls provide international flavour.

Zum Daniel   BAVARIAN €€
(☎352 72; Roseneckstrasse 1; mains €5-15; ⊙9am-1am Tue-Sun) Ingolstadt's oldest inn is a lovingly run local institution serving what many claim to be the town's best pork roast and seasonal specials.

Weissbräuhaus   PUB €€
(☎328 90; Dollstrasse 3; mains €4.20-16) This modern beer hall serves standard Bavarian dishes, including the delicious *Weissbräupfändl* (pork fillet with homemade *Spätzle*). There's a beer garden with a charming fountain out back.

Casa Rustica   ITALIAN €€
(☎333 11; Höllbräugasse 1; mains €6-19; ⊙11.30am-2.30pm & 5-11pm) Most agree that this is Ingolstadt's best Italian restaurant, with a melting cheese and herb aroma in the air and cosy half-circle box seating.

Kuchlbauer   PUB
(☎335 512; Schäffbräustrasse 11a) This unmissable brewpub, with oodles of brewing and rustic knick-knacks hanging from the walls and ceiling, really rocks (or, should we say, sways) when someone stokes up an accordion. Tipples include the house *Hefeweissbier* or you could try the *Mass Goass*, a 1L jug containing dark beer, cola and 4cL of cherry liqueur!

Neue Galerie Das MO   CAFE, BAR
(☎339 60; Bergbräustrasse 7; mains €5-21; ⊙from 5pm) This trendy, evening-only place puts on occasional art exhibitions, but it's the walled beer garden in the shade of mature chestnut trees that punters really come for. The international menu offers everything from cheeseburgers to schnitzel and baked potatoes, and vegies are well catered for.

ⓘ Information

Post Office (Am Stein 8; ⊙8.30am-6pm Mon-Fri, 9am-1pm Sat)
Sparkasse (Rathausplatz 6)

Surfen bei Yorma's (Hauptbahnhof; per hr €2.50) Internet access.
Tourist Office (☎305 3005; Elisabethstrasse 3; ⊙8.30am-6.30pm Mon-Fri, 9.30am-2pm Sat). The other branch is at **Rathausplatz** (☎305 3030; Rathausplatz 2; ⊙9am-6pm Mon-Fri, 10am-2pm Sat & Sun, shorter hours Nov-Mar).

ⓘ Getting There & Away

When arriving by train from the north (from Eichstätt and Nuremberg), Ingolstadt Nord station is nearer to the historical centre than the Hauptbahnhof. Trains from the south arrive at the Hauptbahnhof. Ingolstadt has the following rail connections:

DESTINA-TION	FARE	DURATION	FREQUENCY
Munich	€16.40 to €27	one hour	twice hourly
Nuremberg	€21.80 to €30	30 to 40 minutes	hourly
Regensburg	€14.40	one hour	hourly

ⓘ Getting Around

Buses 10, 11, 18, 16 and 31 (€1.20) run every few minutes between the city centre and the Hauptbahnhof, 2.5km to the southeast.

Landshut

☎0871 / POP 63,200

A worthwhile halfway halt between Munich and Regensburg, or a place to kill half a day before a flight from nearby Munich Airport, Landshut (pronounced 'lants-hoot') was the hereditary seat of the Wittelsbach family in the early 13th century, and capital of the Dukedom of Bavaria-Landshut for over a century. Apart from a brief episode as custodian of the Bavarian University two centuries ago, Landshuters have since been busy retreating into provincial obscurity, but the town's blue-blooded past is still echoed in its grand buildings, a historical pageant with a cast of thousands and one seriously tall church.

◉ Sights

Coming from the train station, you enter Landshut's historical core through the broken Gothic arch of the stocky **Ländtor**, virtually the only surviving chunk of the town's medieval defences. From here, Theaterstrasse brings you to the 600m-long **Altstadt**, one of Bavaria's most impressive medieval marketplaces. Pastel town houses lining its curving cobbled length hoist elaborate gables, every one a different bell-shaped or saw-toothed creation in brick and plaster.

Burg Trausnitz CASTLE
(924 110; www.burg-trausnitz.de; adult/child €4/free; 9am-6pm Apr-Sep, 10am-4pm Oct-Mar) Roosting high above the Altstadt is Burg Trausnitz, Landshut's top attraction. The 50-minute guided tour (in German with English text) takes you through the Gothic and Renaissance halls and chambers, ending at an alfresco party terrace with bird's-eye views of the town below. The ticket is also good for the **Kunst- und Wunderkammer**, a typical Renaissance-era display of exotic curios assembled by the local dukes.

St Martin Church CHURCH
(7.30am-6pm Apr-Sep, to 5pm Oct-Mar) Rising in Gothic splendour at the southern end of the Altstadt is Landshut's record-breaking St Martin Church; at 130.6m, its spire is the tallest brick structure in the world and it took 55 years to build.

Stadtresidenz PALACE
(924 110; Altstadt 79; adult/concession €3.50/2.50; tours in German hourly 9am-6pm Apr-Sep, 10am-4pm Oct-Mar, closed Mon) Gracing the Altstadt is the Stadtresidenz, a Renaissance palace built by Ludwig X which hosts temporary exhibitions on historical themes. Admission is by guided tour only.

Festivals & Events

Landshuter Hochzeit MEDIEVAL
Every four years in July, the town hosts the Landshuter Hochzeit (next held in 2013 and 2017), one of Europe's biggest medieval bashes. It commemorates the marriage of Duke Georg der Reiche of Bavaria-Landshut to Princess Jadwiga of Poland in 1475.

Sleeping & Eating

Goldene Sonne HOTEL €€
(925 30; www.goldenesonne.de; Neustadt 520; s/d from €89/125; P) True to its name, the 'Golden Sun' fills a magnificently gabled, six-storey town house with light. Rooms sport stylishly lofty ceilings, ornate mirrors, flat-screen TVs and renovated bathrooms. Bus 2 from the train station stops right outside the door.

Zur Insel HOTEL €€
(923 160; www.insel-landshut.de; Badstrasse 16; s €45-90, d €70-95) A good-value place to kip with simple folksy rooms and a wood-panelled restaurant.

DJH Hostel HOSTEL €
(234 49; www.landshut.jugendherberge.de; Richard-Schirrmann-Weg 6; dm from €15) This clean, well-run 100-bed hostel occupies an attractive old villa up by the castle, with views across town.

Alt Landshut BAVARIAN €€
(Isarpromenade 3; mains €6-14) Sunny days see locals linger over an Augustiner and some neighbourhood nosh outside by the Isar. In winter you can retreat to the simple white-washed dining room.

Augustiner an der St Martins Kirche BAVARIAN €€
(Kirchgasse 251; mains €7-17; 10am-midnight) This dark wood tavern at the foot of the St Martin's spire is the best place in town to sample a meat–dumpling combo, washed down with a frothy Munich wet one.

ⓘ Information

Tourist Office (922 050; www.landshut.de; Altstadt 315; 9am-6pm Mon-Fri, 10am-4pm Sat Mar-Oct, 9am-5pm Mon-Fri, 9am-2pm Sat Nov-Feb)

ⓘ Getting There & Away

TO/FROM THE AIRPORT The airport bus (€11, 35 minutes) leaves almost hourly from near the tourist office and the train station.

TRAIN Landshut is a fairly major stop on the Munich–Regensburg mainline.

» **Munich** €14.40, 45 minutes, twice hourly

» **Passau** €21.50, one hour and 20 minutes, hourly

» **Regensburg** €12.20, 40 minutes, at least hourly

Passau
0851 / POP 50,600
Water has quite literally shaped the picturesque town of Passau on the border with Austria. Its Altstadt is stacked atop a narrow peninsula that jabs its sharp end into the confluence of three rivers: the Danube, the Inn and the Ilz. The rivers brought wealth to Passau, which for centuries was an important trading centre, especially for Bohemian salt, central Europe's 'white gold'. Christianity, meanwhile, generated prestige as Passau evolved into the largest bishopric in the Holy Roman Empire. The Altstadt remains pretty much as it was when the powerful prince-bishops built its tight lanes, tunnels and archways with an Italiante flourish, but

the western end (around Nibelungenplatz) has received a modern makeover with shopping malls centred around the hang-glider-shaped central bus station (ZOB).

Passau is a Danube river cruise halt and is often bursting with day visitors. It's also the convergence point of several long-distance cycling routes.

⊙ Sights

Dom St Stephan
CHURCH

(⊙6.30am-7pm) The green onion domes of Passau's Dom St Stephan float serenely above the town's silhouette. There's been a church in this spot since the late 5th century, but what you see today is much younger thanks to the great fire of 1662, which ravaged much of the medieval town, including the ancient cathedral. The rebuilding job went to a team of Italians, notably the architect Carlo Lurago and the stucco master Giovanni Battista Carlone. The result is a rather top-heavy baroque interior with a pious mob of saints and cherubs gazing down at the congregation from countless cornices, capitals and archways.

The building's acoustics are perfect for its pièce de résistance, the world's largest organ above the main entrance, which contains an astonishing 17,974 pipes. Half-hour organ recitals take place at noon daily Monday to Saturday (adult/child €4/2) and at 7.30pm on Thursday (adult/child €5/3) from May to October and for a week around Christmas. Show up at least 30 minutes early to ensure you get a seat.

Veste Oberhaus
FORTRESS

(www.oberhausmuseum.de; adult/concession €5/4; ⊙9am-5pm Mon-Fri, 10am-6pm Sat & Sun mid-Mar–mid-Nov) A 13th-century defensive fortress, built by the prince-bishops, Veste Oberhaus towers over Passau with patriarchal pomp. Not surprisingly, views of the city and into Austria are superb from up here.

Inside the bastion is the Oberhausmuseum, a regional history museum where you can uncover the mysteries of medieval cathedral building, learn what it took to become a knight and explore Passau's period as a centre of the salt trade. Displays are labelled in English.

Altes Rathaus
HISTORIC BUILDING

(Rathausplatz 2; Grosser Rathaussaal adult/concession €2/1.50; ⊙Grosser Rathaussaal 10am-4pm Apr-Oct) Passau's Rathaus is a grand Gothic affair topped by a 19th-century landmark painted tower. A carillon chimes several times daily (hours are listed on the wall, alongside historical flood-level markers).

The entrance on Schrottgasse takes you to the Grosser Rathaussaal (Great Assembly Room), where large-scale paintings by 19th-century local artist Ferdinand Wagner show scenes from Passau's history with melodramatic flourish. If it's not being used for a wedding or a meeting, also sneak into the adjacent Small Assembly Room for a peek at the ceiling fresco, which again features allegories of the three rivers.

Passauer Glasmuseum
MUSEUM

(⊘350 71; www.glasmuseum.de; Hotel Wilder Mann, Am Rathausplatz; adult/concession €5/4; ⊙10am-5pm) Opened by Neil Armstrong, of all people, Passau's warren-like glass museum is filled with some 30,000 priceless pieces of glass and crystal from the baroque, classical, art-nouveau and art-deco periods. Much of what you see hails from the glassworks of Bohemia, but there are also works by Tiffany and famous Viennese producers. Be sure to pick up a floor plan as it's easy to get lost.

Dreiflusseck
PENINSULA

The very nib of the Altstadt peninsula, the point where the rivers merge, is known as the Dreiflusseck (Three River Corner). From the north the little Ilz sluices brackish water down from the peat-rich Bavarian Forest, meeting the cloudy brown of the Danube as it flows from the west and the pale jade of the Inn from the south to create a murky tricolour. The effect is best observed from the ramparts of the Veste Oberhaus.

Museum Moderner Kunst
ART MUSEUM

(⊘383 8790; www.mmk-passau.de; Bräugasse 17; adult/concession €5/3; ⊙10am-6pm Tue-Sun) Gothic architecture contrasts with 20th- and 21st-century artworks at Passau's Modern Art Museum. The rump of the permanent exhibition is made up of cubist and expressionist works by Georg Philipp Wörlen, who died in Passau in 1954 and whose architect son, Hanns Egon Wörlen, set up the museum in the 1980s. Temporary exhibitions normally showcase big-hitting German artists and native styles and personalities from the world of architecture.

Römermuseum
MUSEUM

(⊘347 69; Lederergasse 43; adult/concession €2/1; ⊙10am-4pm Tue-Sun Mar–mid-Nov) Roman Passau can be viewed from the ground up at this Roman fort museum. Civilian and military artefacts unearthed here and elsewhere in Eastern Bavaria are on show and the ruins of **Kastell Boiotro**, which stood here from AD 250 to 400, are still in situ; some of the towers are still inhabited. There's a castle-themed kids' playground nearby.

Activities

Wurm + Köck
BOAT TOUR

(929 292; www.donauschiffahrt.de; Höllgasse 26) From March to early November, Wurm + Köck operate cruises to the Dreiflusseck from the docks near Rathausplatz, as well as a whole host of other sailings to places along the Danube. The most spectacular vessel in the fleet is the sparkling Kristallschiff (Crystal Ship) decorated inside and out with Swarovski crystals.

Sleeping

Hotel Schloss Ort
BOUTIQUE HOTEL €€

(340 72; www.schlosshotel-passau.de; Im Ort 11; s €68-98, d €97-156; P) This 800-year-old medieval palace by the Inn conceals a tranquil boutique hotel, stylishly done out with polished timber floors, crisp white cotton sheets and wrought-iron bedsteads. Many of the 18 rooms enjoy river views and breakfast is served in the vaulted restaurant.

Pension Rössner
GUESTHOUSE €

(931 350; www.pension-roessner.de; Bräugasse 19; s/d €35/60; P) This immaculate Pension, in a restored mansion near the tip of the peninsula, offers great value for money and a friendly, cosy ambience. Each of the 16 rooms is uniquely decorated and many overlook the fortress. There's bike hire (€10 per day) and parking for €5 a day. Booking recommended.

Hotel König
HOTEL €€

(3850; www.hotel-koenig.de; Untere Donaulände 1; s €65-100, d €89-140; P🐾) This riverside property puts you smack in the middle of the Altstadt. The 41 timber-rich rooms – many of them enormous – spread out over two buildings and most come with views of the Danube and fortress. One slight disadvantage is the lack of English. Parking is €10 a night.

Hotel Wilder Mann
HOTEL €€

(350 71; www.wilder-mann.com; Am Rathausplatz 1; s €50-70, d €80-200; P) Sharing space with the glass museum, this historic hotel boasts former guests ranging from Empress Elizabeth (Sisi) of Austria to Mikhail Gorbachev and Yoko Ono. In the rooms, folksy painted furniture sits incongrously with 20th-century telephones and 21st-century TVs. The building is a warren of staircases, passage-

ways and linking doors, so make sure you remember where your room is. Guests receive a miserly discount to the glass museum.

HendlHouseHotel
HOTEL €

(330 69; www.hendlhousehotel.com; Grosse Klingergasse 17; s/d €55/78) With their light, unfussy decor and well-tended bathrooms, the 15 pristine rooms at this Altstadt new boy offer a high quality to price ratio. Buffet breakfast is served in the downstairs restaurant.

Rotel Inn
HOTEL €

(951 60; www.rotel-inn.de; Donauufer; s/d €30/50; ⊙closed Oct-Apr; P) An architectural abomination geared up for cyclists, rooms at this no-frills 'cabin hotel' near the train station are literally capsules equipped with an inbuilt futon and basic storage space. However it's not bad considering the bargain price. Breakfast is €6 extra.

Zeltplatz Ilzstadt
CAMPGROUND €

(414 57; Halser Strasse 34; adult/child €8/6.50; @) Tent-only campground idyllically set on the Ilz River, 15 minutes' walk from the Altstadt. Catch bus 1, 2 or 4 to Kleiner Exerzierplatz-Ilzbrücke.

DJH Hostel
HOSTEL €

(493 780; www.passau.jugendherberge.de; Veste Oberhaus 125; dm from €20.50) Beautifully renovated 127-bed hostel right in the fortress.

Eating & Drinking

Heilig-Geist-Stifts-Schenke
BAVARIAN €€

(2607; Heilig-Geist-Gasse 4; mains €9.50-20; ⊙closed Wed) Not only does the 'Holy Spirit Foundation' have a succession of walnut-panelled rooms, a candlelit cellar (open from 6pm) and a vine-draped garden, but the food is equally inspired. Specialities include Spiessbraten (marinated meat licked by a beechwood fire) and fish plucked live from the concrete trough. The garden's apricot tree produces the handmade jam incorporated in the Marillenpalatschinke (a rolled-up pancake) and fruit for the Marillenknödel (filled yeast dumplings); the schnapps are also homemade.

Diwan
CAFE €€

(490 3280; Niebelungenplatz 1, Stadtturm; mains €7.20-10.50; ⊙9am-7pm Mon-Thu, to midnight Fri & Sat, 1-6pm Sun) Climb aboard the high-speed lift from street level to get to this trendy, high-perched cafe-lounge at the top of the Stadtturm, with by far the best views in town. From the tangled rattan and plush cappuccino-culture sofas you can see it all –

the Dom St Stephan, the rivers, the Veste Oberhaus – while you tuck into the offerings of the changing seasonal menu.

Zum Grünen Baum
ORGANIC €€

(☎356 35; Höllgasse 7; mains €7.50-16.50; ☺10am-1am; ☒) Take a seat under the chandelier made from cutlery to savour risottos, goulash, schnitzel and soups, prepared as far as possible using organic ingredients. Cosy, friendly and tucked away in the atmospherically narrow lanes between the river and the Residenzplatz.

Café Kowalski
CAFE €

(☎2487; Oberer Sand 1; dishes €4-10; ☺10am-1am; ☎) Chat flows as freely as the wine and beer at this gregarious cafe, a kicker of a nightspot. The giant burgers, schnitzels and big breakfasts are best consumed on the terrace overlooking the Ilz.

Scharfrichter Haus
ITALIAN, BAVARIAN €€

(☎359 00; Milchgasse 2; mains €11-27; ☺noon-2pm & 5pm-1am) Cafe, cellar restaurant, jazz club and theatre rolled into one, this Passau institution draws a sophisticated crowd who enjoy seasonal specials on smooth white linen, before retiring to the intimate cabaret theatre with a glass of Austrian wine.

Zi'Teresa Pizzeria
ITALIAN €€

(Theresienstrasse 26; meals €6.40-26; ☺lunch & dinner) Italian hot spot serving outstanding thin-crust pizzas and tasty pastas, as well as a huge selection of mussel dishes and other seafood.

Andorfer Weissbräu
BEER GARDEN

(☎754 444; Rennweg 2) High on a hill 1.5km north of the Altstadt, this rural beer garden attached to the Andorfer brewery serves filling Bavarian favourites, but the star of the show is the outstanding *Weizen* and *Weizenbock* ales brewed metres away. Take bus 7 from the ZOB to Ries-Rennweg.

ⓘ Information

Post Office (Bahnhofstrasse 1)
Tourist Office (☎955 980; www.passau.de) Altstadt (Rathausplatz 3; ☺8.30am-6pm Mon-Fri, 9am-4pm Sat & Sun Easter–mid-Oct, 8.30am-5pm Mon-Thu, 8.30am-4pm Fri mid-Oct–Easter) Hauptbahnhof (Bahnhofstrasse 28; ☺9am-5pm Mon-Fri, 10.30am-3.30pm Sat & Sun Easter-Sep, reduced hours Oct-Easter) Passau tourist office has a main branch in the Altstadt and another smaller office opposite the Hauptbahnhof. Both branches sell the PassauCard (one day per adult/child €15.50/13, three days €29.50/21), valid

for several attractions, unlimited use of public transport and a city river cruise.

ⓘ Getting There & Away

BUS Buses leave at 7.45am and 4.45pm to the Czech border village of Železná Ruda (2½ hours), from where there are connections to Prague.

TRAIN Rail connections from Passau:

» **Munich** €32.70, 2¼ hours, hourly

» **Nuremberg** €46, 2¼ hours, every two hours

» **Regensburg** €27, one hour, every two hours or change in Plattling

» **Vienna** €48.20, 2¾ hours, six daily

» **Zwiesel** Change in Plattling; €20.60, 1½ hours, hourly

ⓘ Getting Around

Central Passau is sufficiently compact to explore on foot. The CityBus links the Bahnhof with the Altstadt (€0.80) up to four times an hour. Longer trips within Passau cost €1.50; a day pass costs €3.50 (€5 for a family).

The walk up the hill to the Veste Oberhaus or the DJH Hostel, via Luitpoldbrücke and Ludwigsteig path, takes about 30 minutes. From April to October, a shuttle bus operates every 30 minutes from Rathausplatz (one-way/return costs €2/2.50).

There are several public car parks near the train station, but only one in the Altstadt at Römerplatz (€0.60/€8.40 per 30 minutes/day).

Bikehaus (☺Mar-Oct) at the Hauptbahnhof hires out bikes from €12 per day.

Bavarian Forest

Together with the Bohemian Forest on the Czech side of the border, the Bavarian Forest (Bayerischer Wald) forms the largest continuous woodland area in Europe. This inspiring landscape of rolling hills and rounded tree-covered peaks is interspersed with little-disturbed valleys and stretches of virgin woodland, providing a habitat for many species long since vanished from the rest of central Europe. A large area is protected as the wild and remote Bavarian Forest National Park (Nationalpark Bayerischer Wald).

Although incredibly good value, the region sees few international tourists and remains quite traditional. A centuries-old glass-blowing industry is still active in many of the towns along the Glasstrasse (Glass Road), a 250km holiday route connecting Waldsassen with Passau. You can visit the

MARKTL AM INN

On a gentle bend in the Inn, some 60km southwest of Passau, sits the drowsy settlement of Marktl am Inn. Few people outside of Germany (or indeed Bavaria) had heard of it before 19 April 2005, the day when its favourite son, Cardinal Joseph Ratzinger, was elected Pope Benedict XVI. Overnight the community was inundated with reporters, devotees and the plain curious, all seeking clues about the pontiff's life and times. Souvenirs like mitre-shaped cakes, 'Papst-Bier' (Pope's Beer) and religious board games flooded the local shops.

The pope's **Geburtshaus** (☑08678-747 680; www.papsthaus.eu; Marktplatz 11; adult/child €3.50/free; ☉10am-noon & 2-6pm Tue-Fri, 10am-6pm Sat & Sun Easter-Oct) is the simple but pretty Bavarian home where Ratzinger was born in 1927 and lived for the first two years of his life before his family moved to Tittmoning. The exhibition kicks off with a film (in English) tracing the pontiff's early life, career and the symbols he selected for his papacy. You then head into the house proper, where exhibits expand on these themes.

The **Heimatmuseum** (Marktplatz 2; adult/child €2/1) is in possession of a golden chalice and a skullcap that was used by Ratzinger in his private chapel in Rome, but is only open to groups of five or more by prior arrangement; visitors should call the **tourist office** (☑08678-748 820; www.marktl.de; Marktplatz 1; ☉10am-noon Mon-Wed & Fri, 2-5pm Thu) at least a day ahead to arrange entry. His baptismal font can be viewed at the **Pfarrkirche St Oswald** (Marktplatz 6), which is open for viewing except during church services.

With immaculate rooms and a superb restaurant, family-run **Pension Hummel** (☑08678-282; www.gasthof-hummel.de; Hauptstrasse 34; s/d €44/63), a few steps from the train station, is the best sleeping spot. Wash down no-nonsense Bavarian fare with a Papst-Bier at **Gasthaus Oberbräu** (☑08678-1040; Bahnhofstrasse 2; mains €6-11; ☉10am-midnight).

Marktl is a brief stop on an Inn-hugging line between Simbach and Mühldorf (€5.50, 20 minutes), from where there are regular direct connections to Munich, Passau and Landshut.

BAVARIA BAVARIAN FOREST

studios, workshops, museums and shops, and stock up on traditional and contemporary designs.

The central town of Zwiesel is a natural base, but other settlements such as Frauenau and Grafenau are also worth considering if relying on public transport.

⊙ Sights

Bavarian Forest National Park
NATIONAL PARK

(www.nationalpark-bayerischer-wald.de) A paradise for outdoor fiends, the Bavarian Forest National Park extends for around 24,250 hectares along the Czech border, from Bayerisch Eisenstein in the north to Finsterau in the south. Its thick forest, most of it mountain spruce, is criss-crossed by hundreds of kilometres of marked hiking, cycling and cross-country skiing trails, some of which now link up with a similar network across the border. The three main mountains, Rachel, Lusen and Grosser Falkenstein, rise up to between 1300m and 1450m and are home to deer, wild boar, fox, otter and countless bird species.

Around 1km northeast of the village of Neuschönau stands the **Hans-Eisenmann-Haus**

(☑08558-961 50; www.nationalpark-bayerischer-wald.de; Böhmstrasse 35), the national park's main visitor centre. The free, but slightly dated, exhibition has hands-on displays designed to shed light on topics such as pollution and tree growth. There's also a children's discovery room, a shop and a library.

Glasmuseum
MUSEUM

(☑09926-941 020; www.glasmuseum-frauenau.de; Am Museumspark 1, Frauenau; adult/concession €5/4.50; ☉9am-5pm Mon-Fri, 10am-4pm Sat & Sun) Frauenau's dazzlingly modern Glasmuseum covers four millennia of glassmaking history. Demonstrations and workshops for kids are regular features.

Museumsdorf Bayerischer Wald
MUSEUM

(☑08504-8482; www.museumsdorf.com; Am Dreiburgensee, Tittling; adult/child €4/free; ☉9am-5pm Apr-Oct) Tittling, on the southern edge of the Bavarian Forest, is home to this 20-hectare open-air museum displaying 150 typical Bavarian Forest timber cottages and farmsteads from the 17th to the 19th centuries. Take frequent RBO bus 6124 to Tittling from Passau Hauptbahnhof.

Waldmuseum
MUSEUM

(☑09922-840 583; www.waldmuseum-zwiesel.de; Stadtplatz 29, Zwiesel; adult/concession €2.50/1; ☺9am-5pm Mon-Fri, 10am-noon & 2-4pm Sat & Sun mid-May–mid-Oct, reduced hours mid-Oct–mid-May) Housed in a former brewery, Zwiesel's 'Forest Museum' has exhibitions on local customs, flora and fauna, glassmaking and life in the forest.

🏃 Activities

Two long-distance hiking routes cut through the Bavarian Forest: the European Distance Trails E6 (Baltic Sea to the Adriatic Sea) and E8 (North Sea to the Carpathian Mountains). There are mountain huts all along the way. Another popular hiking trail is the Gläserne Steig (Glass Trail) from Lam to Grafenau. Whatever route you're planning, maps produced by Kompass – sheets 185, 195 and 197 – are invaluable companions. They are available from tourist offices and the park visitor centre.

The Bavarian Forest has seven ski areas, but downhill skiing is low-key, even though the area's highest mountain, the Grosser Arber (1456m), occasionally hosts European and World Cup ski races. The major draw here is cross-country skiing, with 2000km of prepared routes through the ranges.

🛏 Sleeping

Accommodation in this region is a bargain; Zwiesel and Grafenau have the best choices.

Hotel Zur Waldbahn
HOTEL €€

(☑09922-8570; www.zurwaldbahn.de; Bahnhofplatz 2, Zwiesel; s €58-64, d €76-96; P🅿🛜🏊) Opposite Zwiesel train station, many of the rooms at this characteristic inn run by three generations of the same family open to balconies with views over the town. The breakfast buffet is an especially generous spread and even includes homemade jams. The restaurant, serving traditional local nosh, is the best in town and is open to non-guests.

Hotel Hubertus
HOTEL €€

(☑08552-964 90; www.hubertus-grafenau.de; Grüb 20, Grafenau; s €66-75, d €108-138) This elegant hotel in Grafenau offers incredible value for the weary traveller. The rooms are spacious and most have balconies. Guests are treated to a pool and sauna, and delicious buffet meals. Prices are for half-board.

DJH Hostel
HOSTEL €

(☑08553-6000; www.waldhaeuser.jugendherberge. de; Herbergsweg 2, Neuschönau; dm from €19.30) The only hostel right in the Bavarian Forest National Park is an ideal base for hikers, bikers and cross-country skiers.

Ferienpark Arber
CAMPGROUND €

(☑09922-802 595; www.ferienpark-arber.de; Waldesruhweg 34, Zwiesel; per site €19.50) This convenient and well-equipped campground is about 500m north of Zwiesel train station.

ⓘ Information

Grafenau Tourist Office (☑08552-962 343; www.grafenau.de; Rathausgasse 1; ☺8am-5pm Mon-Thu, 8am-1pm Fri, 10-11.30am & 3-5pm Sat, 9.30-11.30am Sun)

Zwiesel Tourist Office (☑09922-840 523; www.zwiesel-tourismus.de; Stadtplatz 27; ☺8.30am-5pm Mon-Fri, 10am-1pm Sat)

ⓘ Getting There & Around

From Munich, Regensburg or Passau, Zwiesel is reached by rail via Plattling; most trains continue to Bayerisch Eisenstein on the Czech border, with connections to Prague. The scenic Waldbahn shuttles directly between Zwiesel and Bodenmais, and Zwiesel and Grafenau.

There's also a network of regional buses, though service can be infrequent. The Igel-Bus, operated by **Ostbayernbus** (www.ostbayern bus.de), navigates around the national park on five routes. A useful one is the Lusen-Bus (€4/10 per one/three days), which leaves from Grafenau Hauptbahnhof and travels to the Hans-Eisenmann-Haus, DJH Hostel and Lusen hiking area.

The best value is usually the **Bayerwald-Ticket** (www.bayerwald-ticket.com; €7), a day pass good for unlimited travel on bus and train throughout the forest area. It's available from the park visitor centre, stations and tourist offices throughout the area.

Stuttgart & the Black Forest

Best Places to Eat

» Irma la Douce (p313)

» Schwarzwaldstube (p339)

» Zur Forelle (p328)

» Rizzi (p333)

» Rindenmühle (p355)

Best Places to Stay

» Parkhotel Wehrle (p352)

» Hotel Schiefes Haus (p327)

» Die Halde (p348)

» Hotel am Schloss (p320)

» Villa Barleben (p360)

Why Go?

If one word could sum up Germany's southwesternmost region, it would be inventive. Baden-Württemberg gave the world relativity (Einstein), DNA (Miescher) and the astronomical telescope (Kepler). It was here that Bosch invented the spark plug; Gottlieb Daimler, the gas engine; and Count Ferdinand, the zeppelin. And where would we be without black forest gateau, cuckoo clocks and the ultimate beer food, the pretzel?

Beyond the high-tech, urbanite pleasures of 21st-century Stuttgart lies a region still ripe for discovery. On the city fringes, country lanes roll to vineyards and lordly baroque palaces, spa towns and castles steeped in medieval myth. Swinging south, the Black Forest (*Schwarzwald* in German) looks every inch the Grimm fairy-tale blueprint. Hills rise steep and wooded above church steeples, half-timbered villages and a crochet of tightly woven valleys. It is a perfectly etched picture of sylvan beauty, a landscape refreshingly oblivious to time and trends.

When to Go

Snow dusts the heights from January to late February and pre-Lenten *Fasnacht* brings carnival shenanigans to the region's towns and villages. Enjoy cool forest hikes, riverside bike rides, splashy fun on Lake Constance and open-air festivals galore during summer. From late September to October the golden autumn days can be spent rambling in woods, mushrooming and snuggling up in Black Forest farmhouses.

HAVE YOUR CAKE

True, there's more to the Black Forest than gateau but try saying that after a cherry-chocolate-cream fest at Café Schäfer in Triberg, guardian of the original 1915 recipe.

Need to Know

» Many museums close on Mondays.

» Family in tow? *Ferien-wohnungen* (holiday apartments) are often a better deal than hotels. Tourist offices have lists.

» Save on train fares with the good-value Baden-Württemberg Ticket.

Spa Time

» Friedrichsbad (p331) A palatial 19th-century spa for a Roman-style scrub-a-dub-dub.

» Sanitas Spa (p352) Broad forest views, few crowds, luscious treatments. Bliss.

» Badeparadies (p350) Palms, lagoons and Caribbean cocktails lift rainy-day moods.

Resources

» Schwarzwaldverein (www. schwarzwaldverein.de)

» Farmstays (www.bauern hofurlaub.de)

» Baden-Württemberg Tourism (www.tourism-bw. com)

» Local news and weather (www.swr.de)

Outdoor Adventures

Oh, we have nothing but fresh air, plenty of forest and peace and quiet, the self-effacing locals tell you with a shrug. One whiff of that cold piny air and a glimpse of those emerald forested hills and you'll be itching to grab your walking boots or cross-country skis and strike into the wilderness of the Black Forest. Great waterways like Lake Constance and the Danube invite languid days spent exploring by bike or kayak.

Baden-Württemberg practically coined the word 'wanderlust' as the founding father of the Schwarzwaldverein (www.schwarzwaldverein.de), whose well-marked paths crisscross the darkest depths of the Black Forest.

DRIVE TIME

The Schwarzwald (Black Forest) may be a forest but it sure is a big'un and you'll need a car to reach its out-of-the-way corners.

Schwarzwald-Hochstrasse (Black Forest Hwy; www.schwarzwaldhochstrasse.de) Swoon over views of the mist-wreathed Vosges Mountains, heather-flecked forests and glacial lakes like Mummelsee on this high-altitude road, meandering 60km from Baden-Baden to Freudenstadt on the B500.

Badische Weinstrasse (Baden Wine Rd; www.deutsche-weinstrassen.de) From Baden-Baden to Lörrach, this 160km route corkscrews through the vineyards of Ortenau, Kaiserstuhl, Tuniberg and Markgräflerland.

Schwarzwald-Tälerstrasse (Black Forest Valley Rd) What scenery! Twisting 100km from Rastatt to Alpirsbach, this road dips into the forest-cloaked hills and half-timbered towns of the Murg and Kinzig valleys.

Deutsche Uhrenstrasse (German Clock Rd; www.deutscheuhrenstrasse.de) A 320km loop starting in Villingen-Schwenningen that revolves around the story of clockmaking in the Black Forest. Stops include Furtwangen and cuckoo-crazy Triberg.

Grüne Strasse (Green Rd; www.gruene-strasse.de) Linking the Black Forest with the Rhine Valley and French Vosges, this 160km route zips through Kirchzarten, Freiburg, Breisach, Colmar and Münster.

Discount Passes

Check into almost any hotel in Baden-Württemberg, pay the nominal *Kurtaxe* (holiday tax) and you automatically receive the money-saving **Gästekarte** (Guest Card), often entitling you to free entry to local swimming pools and attractions, plus hefty discounts on everything from bike hire and spas to ski lifts and boat trips. Versions with the **Konus** symbol offer free use of public transport.

Most tourist offices in the Black Forest sell the three-day **SchwarzwaldCard** for admission to around 150 attractions. For details, visit www.blackforest-tourism.com.

ℹ️ Getting There & Around

Flights to the region serve Stuttgart airport (STG; www.stuttgart-airport.com), a major hub for Germanwings; **Karlsruhe-Baden-Baden airport** (Baden Airpark; www.badenairpark. de), a Ryanair base; and **Basel-Mulhouse EuroAirport** (BSL; www.euroairport.com), where easyJet operates.

Trains, trams and/or buses serve almost every town and village, though public transport across the Black Forest can be slow, and long-distance trips (for instance, Freiburg to Konstanz) may involve several changes. Plan your journey with the help of www.efa-bw.de and www.bahn.de.

By road, motorways blazing through the region include the A5 from Baden-Baden south to Freiburg and Basel, which can get hellishly congested because of ongoing roadworks; www.swr .de (in German) has up-to-date traffic news. The A81 runs south from Stuttgart to Lake Constance

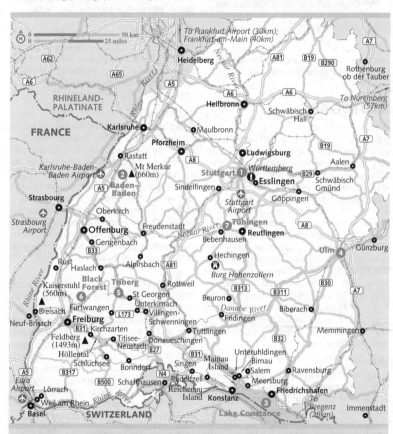

Stuttgart & the Black Forest Highlights

❶ Tune into modern-day **Stuttgart** (p308)

❷ Wallow in thermal waters and art nouveau grandeur in **Baden-Baden**, belle of the Black Forest (p329)

❸ Hop between borders on **Lake Constance** (p356), straddling Switzerland, Germany and Austria

❹ Be amazed by Einstein's birthplace, **Ulm**, crowned by the world's tallest cathedral steeple (p325)

❺ Go cuckoo for clocks, black forest gateau and waterfalls in **Triberg** (p352)

❻ Roam hill, dale and kilometre after pristine kilometre of woodland in the **Black Forest** (p336)

❼ Boat along the Neckar and live it up Goethe-style in postcard-pretty **Tübingen** (p318)

BADEN-WÜRTTEMBERG TICKET

Available at all train stations and online (www.bahn.de), the great-value **Baden-Württemberg Ticket** allows unlimited 2nd-class travel on IRE, RE, RB, S-Bahn trains and buses in the region. The one-day ticket costs €21 for an individual, plus €4 per extra person. Children aged 14 and under travel for free when accompanied by an adult.

via Villingen-Schwenningen, while the A8 links Stuttgart to Karlsruhe, Ulm and Munich.

STUTTGART

☎ 0711 / POP 581,100

Ask many Germans their opinion of Stuttgarters and they will go off on a tangent: they are road hogs speeding along the autobahn; they are sharp-dressed executives with a Swabian drawl; they are tight-fisted homebodies who slave away to *schaffe, schaffe, Häusle baue* (work, work, build a house). So much for the stereotypes.

The real Stuttgart is less superficial than legend. True, some good-living locals like their cars fast and their restaurants fancy but most are just as happy getting their boots dirty in the surrounding vine-clad hills and hanging out with friends in the rustic confines of a *Weinstube* (wine tavern). In the capital of Baden-Württemberg, city slickers and down-to-earth country kids walk hand in hand.

History

Whether with trusty steeds or turbocharged engines, Stuttgart was born to ride, founded as the stud farm Stuotgarten around 950 AD. Progress was swift: by the 12th century Stuttgart was a trade centre, by the 13th century a blossoming city and by the early 14th century the seat of the Württemberg royal family. Count Eberhard im Bart added sheen to Swabian suburbia by introducing the *Kehrwoche* in 1492, the communal cleaning rota still revered today.

The early 16th century brought hardship, peasant wars, plague and Austrian rulers (1520–34). A century later, the Thirty Years' War devastated Stuttgart and killed half its population.

In 1818, King Wilhelm I launched the first the Cannstatter Volksfest to celebrate the end of a dreadful famine. An age of industrialisation dawned in the late 19th and early 20th centuries, with Bosch inventing the spark plug and Daimler pioneering the gas engine. Heavily bombed in WWII, Stuttgart was painstakingly reconstructed and became the capital of the new state of Baden-Württemberg in 1953. Today it is one of Germany's greenest and most affluent cities.

◉ Sights

Stuttgart's main artery is the shopping boulevard Königstrasse, running south from the Hauptbahnhof. Steep grades are common on Stuttgart's hillsides: more than 500 city streets end in *Stäffele* (staircases).

Schlossplatz SQUARE
(Map p310) This regal plaza is crowned by the **König Wilhelm Jubilee Column** (Map p310), topped by a statue of winged Concordia and flanked by two fountains representing the eight rivers of Baden-Württemberg.

Rising majestically above the square is the exuberant three-winged **Neues Schloss**. Duke Karl Eugen von Württemberg's answer to Versailles, the baroque-neoclassical royal residence now houses state government ministries. A bronze statue of Emperor Wilhelm I graces nearby **Karlsplatz**.

Staatsgalerie GALLERY
(Map p310; www.staatsgalerie-stuttgart.de; Konrad-Adenauer-Strasse 30-32; adult/concession €5.50/4, special exhibitions €10/8, Wed & Sat free; ◷10am-6pm Tue-Sun, to 8pm Tue & Thu) The neoclassical-meets-contemporary Staatsgalerie bears British architect James Stirling's curvy, colourful imprint. Alongside big-name exhibitions, the gallery harbours a phenomenal collection of 20th-century art, showcasing works by Rembrandt, Picasso, Monet, Dalí and pop idols Warhol and Lichtenstein.

Kunstmuseum Stuttgart GALLERY
(Map p310; www.kunstmuseum-stuttgart.de; Kleiner Schlossplatz 1; adult/concession €5/3.50; ◷10am-6pm Tue-Sun, to 9pm Wed & Fri) Occupying a shimmering glass cube, this gallery is a romp through modern and contemporary art, with works by Otto Dix and Dieter Roth. For a 360-degree view over Stuttgart, head up to the Cube cafe. Out front, the primary colours and geometric forms of **Alexander Calder's mobile** (Map p310) catch the eye.

Schlossgarten
GARDEN

(Map p310) The fountain-dotted **Mittlerer Schlossgarten** (Middle Palace Garden; Map p310) draws thirsty crowds to its beer garden in summer. The **Unterer Schlossgarten** (Lower Palace Garden) is a ribbon of greenery rambling northeast to the Neckar River and the **Rosensteinpark**, home to the zoo. Sitting south, the **Oberer Schlossgarten** (Upper Palace Garden) is framed by eye-catching landmarks like the columned **Staatstheater** (State Theatre; Map p310) and the ultramodern glass-clad **Landtag** (State Parliament; Map p310).

FREE Aussichtsplatform
VIEWPOINT

(Viewing Platform; Map p310; ☺10am-6pm Fri-Wed, to 8pm Thu) A lift races up to the Hauptbahnhof's 9th floor, where a staircase spirals up to this viewing platform. You'll get close-ups of the revolving Mercedes logo and far-reaching views over Stuttgart, from the bauble-topped **Fernsehturm** (TV Tower) to vine-cloaked hills on the city fringes.

You also get a bird's-eye view of developments taking shape for Stuttgart 21, a huge – and hugely controversial – project to revamp the main train station and extend the city's high-speed rail network. Costing €4.5 billion, the project is due for completion in 2021.

Mercedes-Benz Museum
MUSEUM

(www.museum-mercedes-benz.com; Mercedesstrasse 100; adult/concession €8/4; ☺9am-6pm Tue-Sun; ⓡNeckarpark) A futuristic swirl on the cityscape, the Mercedes-Benz Museum takes a chronological spin through the Mercedes empire. Look out for legends like the 1885 Daimler Riding Car, the world's first gasoline-powered vehicle, and the record-breaking Lightning Benz that hit 228km/h at Daytona Beach in 1909. There's a free guided tour in English at 11am.

Porsche Museum
MUSEUM

(www.porsche.com; Porscheplatz 1; adult/concession €8/4; ☺9am-6pm Tue-Sun; ⓡNeuwirtshaus) Like a pearly white spaceship preparing for lift-off, the barrier-free Porsche Museum is every little boy's dream. Groovy audio-guides race you through the history of Porsche from its 1948 beginnings. Break to glimpse the 911 GT1 that won Le Mans in 1998.

Landesmuseum Württemberg
MUSEUM

(Map p310; www.landesmuseum-stuttgart.de; Schillerplatz 6; adult/concession €5.50/4.50; ☺10am-5pm Tue-Sun) An archway leads to the turreted 10th-century Altes Schloss, where this museum homes in on regional archaeology and architecture. The historic booty comprises Celtic jewellery, neolithic pottery, diamond-encrusted crown jewels and rare artefacts. Time your visit to see, from the arcaded courtyard, the rams above the clock tower lock horns on the hour.

Wilhelma Zoologisch-Botanischer Garten
GARDEN, ZOO

(www.wilhelma.de; Rosensteinpark; adult/concession €12/6, after 4pm & in winter €8/4; ☺8.15am-nightfall; Ⓢ Wilhelma) Wilhelma Zoologisch-Botanischer Garten is a quirky mix of zoo and botanical gardens. Kid magnets include semi-striped okapis, elephants, penguins and a petting farm. Greenhouses sheltering tree ferns, camellias and Amazonian species are among the botanical highlights. Sniff out the gigantic bloom of the malodorous titan arum in the Moorish Villa.

Württembergischer Kunstverein
GALLERY

(Map p310; www.wkv-stuttgart.de; Schlossplatz 2; adult/concession €5/3; ☺11am-6pm Tue-Sun, to 8pm Wed) Identified by its copper cupola, this gallery stages thought-provoking contemporary art exhibitions.

Schillerplatz
SQUARE

(Map p310) On the other side of the Renaissance **Alte Kanzlei** (Old Chancellery; Map p310), south of Schlossplatz, lies cobbled Schillerplatz, where the poet-dramatist **Friedrich Schiller** (Map p310) is immortalised in bronze.

FREE Stiftskirche
CHURCH

(Collegiate Church; Map p310; Stiftstrasse 12; ☺10am-7pm Mon & Thu, to 4pm Fri & Sat, to 6pm Sun) Topped by two mismatched towers, this largely 15th-century church has Romanesque origins.

☞ Tours

Sightseeing tours feature **Hop-on, Hop-off Bus Tours** (adult/concession € 18/15; ☺11am Apr-Oct), which depart roughly hourly from 11am to 6pm from Schlossplatz and trundle past icons like the Fernsehturm and Mercedes-Benz Museum. Pop into the tourist office for details on German-language guided tours, from vineyard ambles to after-work 'walk and wine' strolls.

From May to October, **Neckar-Käpt'n** (www.neckar-kaeptn.de) runs boat excursions on the Neckar River (€9 to €31), departing from its dock at Wilhelma in Bad Cannstatt on the U14.

Stuttgart

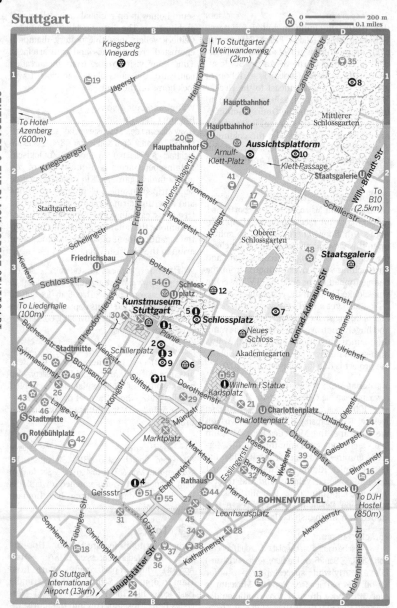

✿✿ Festivals & Events

Sommerfest
FESTIVAL

(www.sommerfest-stuttgart.de) Riverside parties, open-air gigs and alfresco feasting are what this four-day August shindig is all about.

Weindorf
WINE FESTIVAL

(www.stuttgarter-weindorf.de) A 10-day event where winemakers sell the year's vintages from hundreds of booths on Schlossplatz and the Oberer Schlossgarten. Begins on the last weekend in August.

Stuttgart

STUTTGART & THE BLACK FOREST STUTTGART

Cannstatter Volksfest   BEER FESTIVAL
(www.cannstatter-volksfest.de) Stuttgart's answer to Oktoberfest, this beer-guzzling bash, held over three consecutive weekends from late September to mid-October, lifts spirits with oompah music, fairground rides and fireworks.

Weihnachtsmarkt   CHRISTMAS MARKET
(www.stuttgarter-weihnachtsmarkt.de) One of Germany's biggest Christmas markets brings festive twinkle to Marktplatz, Schillerplatz and Schlossplatz from late November to 23 December.

🛏 Sleeping

Stuttgart is gradually upping the ante in slumberland but nondescript chains still reign supreme. Expect weekend discounts of 10% to 20% at hotels targeting business travellers. If you're seeking individual flair and a family welcome, stop by the tourist office for a list of private guesthouses and apartments.

Kronen Hotel   HOTEL $$$
(Map p310; ☑225 10; www.kronenhotel-stuttgart. de; Kronenstrasse 48; s €108-120, d €149-180; P❄@☎) Right on the lap of Königstrasse, this outclasses most of Stuttgart's hotels

with its terrific location, good-natured team, well-appointed rooms and funkily lit sauna. Breakfast is above par, with fresh fruit, egg and bacon, smoked fish and pastries to keep you going.

Hostel Alex 30

HOSTEL **$**

(Map p310; ☑838 8950; www.alex30-hostel.de; Alexanderstrasse 30; dm/s/d/q €24/36/58/100, breakfast €8; P🖻🖻) Backpackers find a relaxed base in these mellow digs with a bar, sun deck and communal kitchen. The spotless, citrus-bright rooms are light and contemporary.

Hotel Azenberg

HOTEL **$$**

(☑225 5040; www.hotelazenberg.de; Seestrasse 114-116; s €70-105, d €85-120; P🖻🖻🖼; 🖳43) This family-run pick has individually designed quarters with themes swinging from English country manor to Picasso. There's a pool, tree-shaded garden and mini spa for relaxing moments. Take bus 43 from Stadtmitte to Hölderlinstrasse.

Hotel am Schlossgarten

LUXURY HOTEL **$$$**

(Map p310; ☑202 60; www.hotelschlossgarten. com; Schillerstrasse 23; s €132-167, d €167-187, tasting menus €109-139; P🖼🖻) Sidling up to the Schloss, this hotel has handsome, park-facing rooms, which flaunt the luxuries that justify the price tag. Book a table at Michelin-starred Zirbelstube for classy

DON'T MISS

BOHEMIAN BEANS

To really slip under Stuttgart's skin, mosey through one of the city's lesser-known neighbourhoods. Walk south to **Hans-im-Glück Platz**, centred on a fountain depicting the caged Grimm's fairy-tale character **Lucky Hans** (Map p310), and you'll soon reach the boho-flavoured **Bohnenviertel** (Bean District; www.bohnenviertel.net), named after beans that were introduced in the 16th century. Back then they were grown everywhere as the staple food of the poor tanners, dyers and craftsmen who lived here.

A recent facelift has restored the neighbourhood's cobbled lanes and gabled houses, which harbour idiosyncratic galleries, workshops, bookshops, wine taverns and cafes. The villagey atmosphere is a refreshing tonic to the big-city feel of central Stuttgart.

French dining in subtly lit, pine-panelled surrounds.

City Hotel

HOTEL **$$**

(Map p310; ☑210 810; www.cityhotel-stuttgart. de; Uhlandstrasse 18; s €79-89, d €99-115; P🖻) Eschew the anonymity of Stuttgart's cookie-cutter chains for this intimate hotel just off Charlottenplatz. Rooms are light, clean and modern, if slightly lacklustre. Breakfast on the terrace in summer is a bonus.

Interhostel

HOSTEL **$**

(Map p310; ☑6648 2797; www.inter-hostel.com; Paulinenstrasse 16; dm/s/d €25/42/64; 🖻) A short toddle from Stadtmitte station, this hostel makes backpackers' hearts sing with its free coffee and wi-fi, bright and characterful digs, relaxed lounge and chipper team, plus handy stuff like luggage storage and a shared kitchen.

Der Zauberlehrling

BOUTIQUE HOTEL **$$$**

(Map p310; ☑237 7770; www.zauberlehrling.de; Rosenstrasse 38; s €135-180, d €180-290, ste €195-320; P🖻) The self-consciously cool Sorcerer's Apprentice reveals design-driven rooms, from Titanic and its waterbed to the high-tech wizardry of the Media Suite. Yet the place lacks a little soul. Nice, but not quite magic.

Steigenberger Graf Zeppelin

LUXURY HOTEL **$$$**

(Map p310; ☑204 80; www.stuttgart.steigenberger. de; Arnulf-Klett-Platz 7; r €170-260; P🖼🖻🖼) While its concrete facade won't bowl you over, inside is a different story. This five-star pad facing the Hauptbahnhof is luxury all the way with its snazzy rooms, Zen-style spa and Michelin-starred restaurant, Olivo.

Ochsen Hotel

HISTORIC HOTEL **$$**

(☑407 0500; www.ochsen-online.de; Ulmer Strasse 323; s €89-99, d €119-129; P🖻; 🖸Inselstrasse) It's worth going the extra mile to this charismatic 18th-century hotel. Some of the spacious, warm-hued rooms have whirlpool tubs for a post-sightseeing bubble. The wood-panelled restaurant dishes up appetising local fare.

Abalon Hotel

HOTEL **$$**

(Map p310; ☑217 10; www.abalon.de; Zimmermannstrasse 7-9; s €74-89, d €89-112; P🖻) Affable staff, a top location and wallet-friendly rates make Abalon a great pick. The bright parquet-floored rooms are large and spotless.

DJH Hostel

HOSTEL **$**

(☑6647470; www.jugendherberge-stuttgart.de; Haussmannstrasse 27; dm 1st/subsequent night €24.50/21.20; @🖻; 🖸Eugensplatz) This DJH hostel is a step above most others. Its squeaky-clean dorms have private bathrooms and a lounge and a terrace with fab city views add to the sociable vibe. It's 800m southeast of the Hauptbahnhof.

✗ Eating

Stuttgart has raised the bar in the kitchen, with chefs putting an imaginative spin on local, seasonal ingredients. The city's half-dozen Michelin-starred restaurants prepare cuisine with enough gourmet panache to satisfy a food-literate crowd. For intimate bistro-style dining, explore the backstreets and the alley-woven Bohnenviertel.

Self-caterers make for the **food market** (Map p310; Marktplatz; ⊘7.30am-1pm Tue, Thu & Sat) and the **Markthalle** (Map p310; Dorotheenstrasse 4, Market Hall; ⊘7am-6.30pm Mon-Fri, to 4pm Sat), which sells picnic fixings and has Italian and Swabian restaurants.

TOP CHOICE **Irma la Douce** MEDITERRANEAN $$$
(Map p310; ☏470 4320; www.irmaladouce.de; Katharinenstrasse 21b; lunch €11-14, dinner €25-39.50; ⊘closed lunch Sat & Sun) An ornate fireplace and chandeliers cast flattering light across the polished wood, book shelves and paintings at this 19th-century bistro. Inspired by the seasons and herby Mediterranean flavours, the menu might star quail breast on wild garlic and roast Iberian pork with spinach gnocchi – all beautifully cooked and expertly matched with wine.

Ochs'n'Willi SWABIAN $$$
(Map p310; ☏226 5191; www.ochsn-willi.de; Kleiner Schlossplatz 4; mains €10-22.50; ⊘daily) A warm,

GOING THE WHOLE HOG

Billing itself as the world's biggest pig museum, the **Schweinemuseum** (www.schweinemuseum.de; Schlachthofstrasse 2a; adult/concession €4.90/4; ⊘11am-7.30pm daily; ☐56) is one heck of a pigsty: 45,000 paintings, lucky trinkets, antiques, cartoons, piggy banks and a veritable mountain of cuddly toys cover the entire porcine spectrum. Since opening in 2010 in the city's 100-year-old former slaughterhouse, the kitsch-cool museum has drawn crowds to its exhibits spotlighting everything from pig worship to wild boar hunt rituals. In the adjacent beer garden (mains €12 to €19), you can pig out on schnitzel, fat stubby pork knuckles and more.

woody hunter's cottage of a restaurant just this side of twee, Ochs'n'Willi delivers gutsy portions of Swabian and Bavarian fare. Dig into pork knuckles with lashings of dumplings and kraut, spot-on *Maultaschen* (pasta pockets) or rich, brothy *Gaisburger Marsch*. There's a terrace for warm-weather dining.

Olivo MODERN EUROPEAN $$$
(Map p310; ☏204 8277; www.olivo-restaurant.de; Arnulf-Klett-Platz 7; mains €35-44, 4-course lunch/dinner €68/98; ⊘Tue-Sat) Young, sparky chef Nico Burkhardt works his stuff at Steigenberger's Michelin-starred restaurant. The minimalist-chic restaurant is lauded for

THE WAY TO A SWABIAN'S HEART...

As the Swabian saying goes: *Was der Bauer net kennt, frisst er net* (What the farmer doesn't know, he doesn't eat), so find out before you dig in:

Bubespitzle Officially called *Schupfnudeln*, these short, thick potato noodles – vaguely reminiscent of gnocchi – are browned in butter and tossed with sauerkraut. Sounds appetising until you discover that *Bubespitzle* means 'little boys' penises'.

Gaisburger Marsch A strong beef stew served with potatoes and *Spätzle*.

Maultaschen Giant ravioli pockets, stuffed with leftover ground pork, spinach, onions and bread mush. The dish is nicknamed *Herrgottsbeschieserle* (God trickster) because it was a sly way to eat meat during Lent.

Saure Kuddle So who is for sour tripe? If you haven't got the stomach, try potato-based, meat-free *saure Rädle* (sour wheels) instead.

Spätzle Stubby egg-based noodles. These are fried with onions and topped with cheese in the calorific treat *Käsespätzle*.

Zwiebelkuche Autumnal onion tart with bacon, cream and caraway seeds, which pairs nicely with *neuer Süsser* (new wine) or *Moschd* (cider).

exquisitely presented, French-inspired specialities such as Breton turbot with celery, peanuts and Champagne foam.

Weinhaus Stetter   SWABIAN $$

(Map p310; ✆240 163; Rosenstrasse 32; mains €8.50-13.50; ⏰3-11pm Mon-Fri, noon-3pm & 5.30-11pm Sat) No-nonsense Swabian cooking, such as flavoursome *Linsen und Saiten* (lentils with sausage), and wines are the mainstay of this Bohnenviertel tavern. The attached wine shop sells 650 different vintages.

Cube   INTERNATIONAL $$$

(Map p310; ✆280 4441; Kleiner Schlossplatz 1; mains lunch €9-17, dinner €28-31; ⏰daily) The food is good but it plays second fiddle to the dazzling view at this glass-fronted cube on Kleiner Schlossplatz. Bag a window table to see Stuttgart twinkle over winningly fresh dishes like yellow-fin tuna with wasabi-pepper crumble and black bean risotto. Come at lunchtime for a more relaxed vibe.

Weinstube Fröhlich   SWABIAN $$

(Map p310; ✆242 471; www.weinstube-froehlich. de; Leonhardstrasse 5; mains €12-23; ⏰5.30pm-12.30am daily) True, it's in the heart of the red-light district, but don't be put off. This softly lit, dark-wood-panelled restaurant is an atmospheric choice for well-executed Swabian fare (cheese-rich *Käsespätzle*, *Maultaschen* with potato salad) and regional wines.

Délice   MODERN EUROPEAN $$$

(Map p310; ✆640 3222; www.restaurant-delice. de; Hauptstätter Strasse 61; 5-course tasting menu €90; ⏰6.30pm-midnight Mon-Fri) At this vaulted Michelin-starred restaurant, natural, integral flavours sing in specialities like medley of tuna with lemon vinaigrette and fried egg with parsnips and Périgord truffles. The sommelier will talk you through the award-winning riesling selection.

Amadeus   SWABIAN $$

(Map p310; ✆292 678; Charlottenplatz 17; mains €9.50-22.50; ⏰daily) Once an 18th-century orphanage dishing up gruel, this chic, bustling restaurant now serves glorious Swabian food such as *Maultaschen* and riesling-laced *Kutteln* (tripe). The terrace is a big draw in summer.

Alte Kanzlei   GERMAN $$

(Map p310; ✆294 457; Schillerplatz 5a; mains €10.50-20.50; ⏰daily) Empty tables are gold-dust rare at this convivial, high-ceilinged restaurant on Schillerplatz. Feast on Swabian favourites like *Spannpferkel* (roast

suckling pig) and *Flädlesuppe* (pancake soup), washed down with regional tipples.

Takeshii's   VIETNAMESE $$

(Map p310; ✆2483 9559; Esslinger Strasse 12; mains €10.90-13.90; ⏰Tue-Sat) Subtly lit Vietnamese bolt-hole, rustling up faves like shrimp-and-herb summer rolls with hoisin sauce.

Café Nast   CAFE $

(Map p310; Esslingerstrasse 40; snacks €1.50-3.50; ⏰7am-6.30pm Mon-Sat) Great bakery for freshly prepared sandwiches or coffee and cake.

Reiskorn   INTERNATIONAL $

(Map p310; ✆664 7633; Torstrasse 27; mains €5.50-12.90; ⏰closed Sun lunch; ✔) With an easy-going vibe and bamboo-green retro interior, this culinary globetrotter serves everything from tangy Caribbean prawn salad to dim sum.

Forum Café   CAFE $

(Map p310; Gymnasiumstrasse 21; snacks €4-7.50; ⏰Mon-Sat; ✔👶) Wholesomely hip, kid-friendly cafe in the Forum Theatre, with yogi teas and organic snacks on the menu.

Imbiss Zum Brunnenwirt   FAST FOOD $

(Map p310; Leonhardsplatz 25; snacks €2.70-3.50; ⏰11am-2am Mon-Thu, to 3am Fri & Sat, 4pm-2am Sun) Join hungry Stuttgarter to chomp on wurst and fries at this hole-in-the-wall joint.

🍷 Drinking

Ciba Mato   LOUNGE

(Map p310; www.ciba-mato.de; Wilhelmsplatz 11; ⏰5pm-3am Mon-Sat, 10am-3am Sun) There's more than a hint of Buddha Bar about this scarlet-walled, Asia-infused space. It's a slinky spot to sip a gingertini or pisco punch, hang out Bedouin-style in the shisha tent and nibble on fusion food. The decked terrace is a summertime magnet.

Sky Beach   BAR

(Map p310; www.skybeach.de; Königstrasse 6, Galeria Kaufhof, top floor; ⏰noon-12.30am Mon-Sat, 11am-midnight Sun Easter-Sep) When the sun comes out, Stuttgarters live it up at this urban beach, complete with sand, cabana beds, DJs spinning mellow lounge beats and grandstand city views.

Biergarten im Schlossgarten   BEER GARDEN

(Map p310; www.biergarten-chlossgarten.de; ⏰10.30am-1am May-Oct; 🐕) Toast summer with beer and pretzels at Stuttgart's best-loved, 2000-seat beer garden in the green heart of the Schlossgarten. Regular live music gets steins a-swinging.

Hüftengold
CAFE

(Map p310; Olgastrasse 44; ⊙7am-midnight Mon-Thu, to 1am Fri & Sat, 10am-8pm Sun) Work on your own *Hüftengold* (love handles) with cake and locally roasted coffee at this sylvan wonderland of a cafe. The log stool and sheepskins create a wonderfully cosy vibe for brunch or evening chats by candlelight.

Zum Paulaner
PUB

(Map p310; Calwerstrasse 45; ⊙10am-midnight daily, to 1am Fri & Sat) Freshly tapped Paulaner brews in a buzzy, tree-shaded beer garden.

Fou Fou
COCKTAIL BAR

(Map p310; Leonhardstrasse 13; ⊙5pm-1am Mon-Wed, 6pm-2am Thu, 8pm-3am Fri & Sat) Intimate bar with expertly mixed cocktails.

Palast der Republik
BAR

(Map p310; Friedrichstrasse 27; ⊙3pm-1am) Bar staff didn't graduate from charm school but this public toilet reborn as a kiosk bar is still a pleasingly laid-back spot for a beer.

☆ Entertainment

For the events low-down, grab a copy of German-language monthly **Lift Stuttgart** (www.lift-online.de) from the tourist office or news kiosks, or listings magazine **Prinz** (www.prinz.de/stuttgart.html). Events tickets can be purchased at the **i-Punkt desk** (☑222 8243; Königstrasse 1a; ⊙9am-8pm Mon-Fri, to 6pm Sat, 11am-6pm Sun).

Liederhalle
CONCERT VENUE

(☑202 7710; www.liederhalle-stuttgart.de; Berliner Platz 1) Jimi Hendrix and Sting are among the stars who have performed at this culture and congress centre. The 1950s venue stages big-name classical and pop concerts, cabaret and comedy.

Staatstheater
PERFORMING ARTS

(Map p310; ☑203 20; www.staatstheater-stuttgart.de; Oberer Schlossgarten 6) Stuttgart's grandest theatre presents a top-drawer program of ballet, opera, theatre and classical music. The **Stuttgart Ballet** (www.stuttgart-ballet.de) is hailed one of Europe's best companies.

Bix Jazzclub
LIVE MUSIC

(Map p310; ☑2384 0997; www.bix-stuttgart.de; Leonhardsplatz 28; ⊙7pm-2am Tue-Wed, to 3am Thu-Sat) Suave chocolate-gold tones and soft lighting set the scene for first-rate jazz acts at Bix, swinging from big bands to soul and blues.

DON'T MISS

THROUGH THE GRAPEVINE

To taste the region's fruity Trollingers and citrusy rieslings, factor in a stroll through the vineyards surrounding Stuttgart. The **Stuttgarter Weinwanderweg** (www.stuttgarter-weinwanderweg.de) comprises several walking trails that thread through winegrowing villages. One begins at Pragsattel station (on the U5 or U6 line) and meanders northeast to Max-Eyth-See, affording fine views from Burgholzhofturm. Visit the website for alternative routes, maps and distances.

From October to March, look out for a broom above the door of **Besenwirtschaften** (*Besa* for short). Run by winegrowers, these rustic bolt-holes are atmospheric places to chat with locals while sampling the new vintage and Swabian home cooking. Some operate every year but most don't. Check the Besen Kalender website (www.besenkalender.de) during vintage times. Stuttgart-area *Besenwirtschaften* that open annually include the central **City-Besen** (Map p310; ☑470 4248; Wilhelmsplatz 1; ⊙daily), an atmospheric vaulted cellar serving home-grown wines.

Kiste
LIVE MUSIC

(Map p310; www.kiste-stuttgart.de; Hauptstätter Strasse 35; ⊙6pm-1am Mon-Thu, to 2am Fri & Sat) Jam-packed at weekends, this hole-in-the-wall bar is Stuttgart's leading jazz venue, with nightly concerts starting at 9pm or 10pm.

Wagenhallen
CLUB

(www.wagenhallen.de; Innerer Nordbahnhof 1; Eckhardtshaldenweg) Swim away from the mainstream at this post-industrial space, where club nights, gigs and workshops skip from Balkan beat parties to poetry slams. There's a relaxed beer garden for summertime quaffing.

Theaterhaus
THEATRE

(☑402 0720; www.theaterhaus.com; Siemensstrasse 11; Maybachstrasse) This dynamic theatre stages live rock, jazz and other music genres, plus theatre and comedy performances.

Shopping

Mooch around plane-tree-lined Königstrasse, Germany's longest shopping mile, for high-street brands and department stores, Calwer

THEODOR-HEUSS-STRASSE BAR CRAWL

Packed with clubs and hipper-than-thou lounges, Theodor-Heuss-Strasse is perfect for a late-night bar crawl. DJs spin house and electro at charcoal-black **7 Grad** (Map p310; Theodor-Heuss-Strasse 32). Next door **Barcode** (Map p310; Theodor-Heuss-Strasse 30) fuels the party with decadent cocktails in streamlined surrounds, while neighbouring **rohbau** (Map p310; Theodor-Heuss-Strasse 26) pumps out '80s disco and rock in retro-cool surrounds. Good-looking Stuttgarters dance to soul and funk at nouveau Alpine chic **Mutter-milch** (Map p310; Theodor-Heuss-Strasse 23) and ice-cool **Suite 212** (Map p310; Theodor-Heuss-Strasse 23). Further along is spacily lit, monochromatic **T-O12** (Map p310; Theodor-Heuss-Strasse 12), where RnB, house and electro dominate the decks.

Strasse for boutiques and Stifftstrasse for designer labels. The casual Bohnenviertel is the go-to quarter for antiques, galleries, vintage garb and Stuttgart-made crafts and jewellery.

Just north of Schlossplatz is the classical, colonnaded Königsbau, reborn as an upmarket shopping mall, the **Königsbau Passagen** (Map p310). For outdoor shopping, there's a bustling **flower market** (Map p310; Schillerplatz; ⏰7am-1pm Tue, Thu & Sat) and a **flea market** (Map p310; Karlsplatz; ⏰8am-4pm Sat).

Tausche   ACCESSORIES
(Map p310; Eberhardstrasse 51; ⏰11am-7pm Mon-Fri, to 6pm Sat) Berlin's snazziest messenger bags have winged their way south. Tausche's walls are a technicolour mosaic of exchangeable flaps: from *die blöde Kuh* (the silly cow) to Stuttgart's iconic Fernsehturm (TV Tower). Pick one to match your outfit and mood.

Brunnenhannes   FASHION
(Map p310; Geissstrasse 15; ⏰11am-7pm Tue-Fri, to 4pm Sat) Nothing to wear to Oktoberfest? Biker-meets-Bavaria Brunnenhannes has the solution, with lederhosen for strapping lads, dirndls for buxom dames and gingham lingerie that is half kitsch, half cool.

Feinkost Böhm   FOOD
(Map p310; Kronprinzstrasse 6) Böhm is a foodie one-stop shop with regional wine, beer, chocolate and preserves, and an appetising deli.

Stilwerk   DESIGN
(Map p310; www.stilwerk.de; Königsbau-Passagen) Some of Germany's top design stores cluster under an elliptical glass roof at Stilwerk, doing trade in everything from futuristic bathrooms to stylish rattan creations.

ⓘ Information

Königstrasse has many ATMs, including one in the tourist office. **ReiseBank & Western Union** (Hauptbahnhof, opposite track 11; ⏰8am-8.30pm) offers currency exchange.

City Call Internet Center (Eberhardstrasse 14; per hr €2; ⏰10am-midnight Mon-Sat, 11am-midnight Sun)

Coffee Fellows (per 10min €0.50; ⏰8am-9pm; 🛜) Up the stairs opposite track 4 in the Hauptbahnhof. Free wi-fi.

I-Punkt Tourist Information (📞222 8100; www.stuttgart-tourist.de; Königstrasse 1a; ⏰9am-8pm Mon-Fri, to 6pm Sat, 11am-6pm Sun) The staff can help with room bookings (for a €3 fee) and public transport enquiries. Has a list of vineyards open for tastings.

Klinikum Stuttgart (📞278 01; Kriegsberg-strasse 60) The city's largest hospital.

Post office (inside Königsbau Passagen) Slightly northwest of the Schlossplatz. There's also a branch in the **Hauptbahnhof**, up the stairs behind track 4.

StuttCard (72hr with/without VVS ticket €18/9.70) Free entry to most museums, plus discounts on events, activities and guided tours. Sold at the tourist office and some hotels.

Tourist office (⏰8am-7pm Mon-Fri, 9am-1pm & 2-6pm Sat & Sun) The tourist office branch at Stuttgart International Airport. Situated in Terminal 3, Level 2 (Arrivals).

VVS 3-Day Ticket (72hr inner city/metropolitan area €10.60/14.50) Three-day pass for unlimited use of public transport, available to guests with a hotel reservation.

ⓘ Getting There & Away

AIR Stuttgart International Airport (STG; www.stuttgart-airport.com), a major hub for **Germanwings** (www.germanwings.com), is 13km south of the city. There are four terminals, all within easy walking distance of each other.

CAR & MOTORCYCLE The A8 from Munich to Karlsruhe passes Stuttgart (often abbreviated to 'S' on highway signs) as does the A81 from

Singen (near Lake Constance) to Heilbronn and Mannheim. Stuttgart is an **Umweltzone** (Green Zone; www.umwelt-plakette.de), where vehicles are graded according to their emissions levels. Expect to pay €6 to €10 for an *Umweltplakette* (environment sticker), which is obligatory in green zones and can be ordered online.

TRAIN IC and ICE destinations include Berlin (€135, 5½ hours), Frankfurt (€59, 1¼ hours) and Munich (€49 to €54, 2¼ hours). There are frequent regional services to Tübingen (€12.20, one hour), Schwäbisch Hall (€16.40, 70 minutes) and Ulm (€18.10 to €25, one hour).

ⓘ Getting Around

TO/FROM THE AIRPORT S2 and S3 trains take about 30 minutes to get from the airport to the Hauptbahnhof (€3.50).

BICYCLE **Rent a Bike** (www.rentabike-stuttgart. de; Lautenschlagerstrasse 22; adult 6½hr/full day €12/18, concession €9/14) delivers and picks up bikes. Stuttgart has 50 **Call-a-Bike** (☎0700 0522 2222; www.callabike.de) stands. The first 30 minutes are free and rental costs €4.80 per hour thereafter (€15 per day). Visit the website for maps and details.

It's free to take your bike on *Stadtbahn* lines, except from 6am to 8.30am and 4pm to 6.30pm Monday to Friday. Bikes are allowed on S-Bahn trains (S1 to S6) but you have to buy a *Kinderticket* (child's ticket) from 6am to 8.30am Monday to Friday. You can't take bikes on buses or the *Strassenbahn* (tramway).

CAR & MOTORCYCLE Underground parking costs about €2.50 for the first hour and €2 for each subsequent hour. See www.parkinfo.com (in German) for a list of car parks. The Park & Ride ('P+R') options in Stuttgart's suburbs afford cheap parking; convenient lots include Degerloch Albstrasse (on the B27; take the U5 or U6 into town), which is 4km south of the centre; and Österfeld (on the A81; take the S1, S2 or S3 into the centre).

Avis, Budget, Europcar, Hertz, National and Sixt have offices at the airport (Terminal 2, Level 2). Europcar, Hertz and Avis have offices at the Hauptbahnhof (opposite track 16).

PUBLIC TRANSPORT From slowest to fastest, Stuttgart's **public transport network** (www. vvs.de) consists of a *Zahnradbahn* (rack railway), buses, the *Strassenbahn* (tramway), *Stadtbahn* lines (light-rail lines beginning with U; underground in the city centre), S-Bahn lines (suburban rail lines S1 through to S6) and *Regionalbahn* lines (regional trains beginning with R). On Friday and Saturday there are night buses (beginning with N) with departures from Schlossplatz at 1.11am, 2.22am and 3.33am.

For travel within the city, single tickets are €2.10 and four-ride tickets (*Mehrfahrtenkarte*)

cost €7.90. A day pass, good for two zones (including, for instance, the Mercedes-Benz and Porsche Museums), is better value at €6.10 for one person and €10.50 for a group of between two and five.

TAXI To order a taxi call ☎194 10 or ☎566 061.

Around Stuttgart

MAX-EYTH-SEE

When temperatures soar, Stuttgarters head to Max-Eyth-See, for pedalo fun on the lake and picnicking beside the Neckar River. Murky water rules out swimming but there's a worthwhile bike path, part of the Neckar-Radweg (www.neckar-radweg.com). The terraced-style vineyards rising above the river are scattered with *Wengerter-Häuschen* (tool sheds); some are over 200 years old and protected landmarks.

The lake is 9km northeast of Stuttgart Hauptbahnhof on the U14 line.

GRABKAPELLE WÜRTTEMBERG

When King Wilhelm I of Württemberg's beloved wife Katharina Pavlovna, daughter of a Russian tsar, died at the age of 30 in 1819, the king tore down the family castle and built this domed **burial chapel** (adult/concession €2.20/1.10; ⊙10am-noon & 1-5pm Tue-Sat, 10am-noon & 1-6pm Sun Mar-Oct). The king was also interred in the classical-style Russian Orthodox chapel decades later. Scenically perched on a vine-strewn hill, the grounds afford long views down to the valley.

Grapkapelle Württemberg is 10km southeast of Stuttgart's centre. Take bus 61 from Stuttgart-Untertürkheim station, served by the S1.

LUDWIGSBURG

☎07141 / POP 87,740

This neat, cultured town is the childhood home of the dramatist Friedrich Schiller. Duke Eberhard Ludwig put it on the global map in the 18th century by erecting a chateau to out-pomp them all: the sublime, Versailles-inspired Residenzschloss. With its whimsical palaces and gardens, Ludwigsburg is baroque in overdrive and a flashback to when princes wore powdered wigs and lords went a-hunting.

◉ Sights & Activities

[TOP CHOICE] **Residenzschloss**   PALACE

(www.schloss-ludwigsburg.de; 30min tour adult/concession €6.50/3.30, museums incl audioguide

€3.50/1.80; ⊘10am-5pm) Nicknamed the Swabian Versailles, the Residenzschloss is an extravagant 452-room baroque, rococo and Empire affair. The 90-minute chateau tours (in German; English tour at 1.30pm) begin half-hourly.

The 18th-century feast continues with a spin of the staggeringly ornate, scarlet and gold **Karl Eugen Apartment**, and three **museums** showcasing everything from exquisite baroque paintings to fashion accessories and majolica.

Blühendes Barock   GARDEN

(Mömpelgardstrasse 28; adult/concession €8/3.90; ⊘gardens 7.30am-8.30pm, Märchengarten 9am-6pm, both closed early Nov–mid-Mar) More appealing in summer is a fragrant stroll amid the herbs, rhododendrons and gushing fountains of the Blühendes Barock gardens.

Included in the admission price is entry to the **Märchengarten** (⊘9am-6pm), a fairytale theme park. Take your kids to see the witch with a Swabian cackle at the gingerbread house and admire their fairness in Snow White's magic mirror. Should you want Rapunzel to let down her hair at the tower, get practising: *Rapunzel, lass deinen Zopf herunter*. (The gold-tressed diva only understands German – accurately pronounced!).

Schloss Favorite   PALACE

(30min tour adult/concession €3.50/1.80; ⊘10am-noon & 1.30-5pm mid-Mar–Oct, 10am-noon & 1.30-4pm Tue-Sun Nov–mid-Mar) Sitting in parkland, a five-minute walk north of the Residenzschloss, is the petit baroque palace Schloss Favorite, graced with Empire-style furniture. Duke Eugen held glittering parties here.

ⓘ Information

Ludwigsburg's **tourist office** (☑910 2252; www.ludwigsburg.de; Marktplatz 6; ⊘9am-6pm Mon-Fri, to 2pm Sat) has excellent material in English on lodgings, festivals and events such as the baroque Christmas market.

ⓘ Getting There & Around

S-Bahn trains from Stuttgart serve the Hauptbahnhof, 750m southwest of the centre. The Residenzschloss, on Schlossstrasse (the B27) lies 400m northeast of the central Marktplatz.

Stuttgart's S4 and S5 S-Bahn lines go directly to Ludwigsburg's Hauptbahnhof (€3.50), frequently linked to the chateau by buses 421, 425 and 427. On foot, the chateau is 1km from the train station.

There are two large car parks 500m south of the Residenzschloss, just off the B27.

MAULBRONN

Billed as the best-preserved medieval monastery north of the Alps, the one-time Cistercian monastery **Kloster Maulbronn** (☑07043-926 610; www.schloesser-und-gaerten.de; adult/concession/family €6/3/15; ⊘9am-5.30pm Mar-Oct, 9.30am-5pm Tue-Sun Nov-Feb) was founded by Alsatian monks in 1147, born again as a Protestant school in 1556 and designated a Unesco World Heritage Site in 1993. Its famous graduates include the astronomer Johannes Kepler. Aside from the Romanesque-Gothic portico in the monastery church and the weblike vaulting of the cloister, it's the insights into monastic life that make this place so culturally stimulating.

Maulbronn is 30km east of Karlsruhe and 33km northwest of Stuttgart, near the Pforzheim Ost exit on the A8. From Karlsruhe, take the S4 to Bretten Bahnhof and from there bus 700; from Stuttgart, take the train to Mühlacker and then bus 700.

SWABIAN ALPS & AROUND

Tübingen

☑07071 / POP 88,360

Liberal students and deeply traditional *Burschenschaften* (fraternities) singing ditties for beloved Germania, eco-warriors, artists and punks – all have a soft spot for this bewitchingly pretty Swabian city, where cobbled lanes lined with half-timbered town houses twist up to a turreted castle. It was here that Joseph Ratzinger, now Pope Benedict XVI, lectured theology in the late 1960s; and here that Friedrich Hölderlin studied stanzas; Johannes Kepler planetary motions; and Goethe, the bottom of a beer glass.

The finest days unfold slowly in Tübingen: lingering in Altstadt cafes, punting on the plane-tree-lined Neckar River and pretending, as the students so diligently do, to work your brain cells in a chestnut-shaded beer garden.

⊙ Sights & Activities

TOP CHOICE **Schloss Hohentübingen**   CASTLE

(Burgsteige 11; museum adult/concession €5/3; ⊘castle 7am-8pm daily, museum 10am-5pm Wed-Sun, to 7pm Thu) On its perch above Tübingen, this turreted 16th-century castle has a terrace overlooking the Neckar and the

Altstadt's triangular rooftops to the vine-streaked hills beyond. An ornate Renaissance gate leads to the courtyard and the laboratory where Friedrich Miescher discovered DNA in 1869.

Inside, the **archaeology museum** hides the 35,000-year-old Vogelherd figurines, the world's oldest figurative artworks. These thumb-sized ivory carvings of mammoths and lions were unearthed in the Vogelherd-höhle caves in the Swabian Alps.

Am Markt SQUARE
Half-timbered town houses frame the Altstadt's main plaza Am Markt, a much-loved student hang-out. Rising above it is the 15th-century **Rathaus**, with a riotous baroque facade and an astronomical clock. Statues of four women representing the seasons grace the **Neptune Fountain** opposite. Keep an eye out for **No 15**, where a white window frame identifies a secret room where Jews hid in WWII.

Cottahaus LANDMARK
The Cottahaus is the one-time home of Johann Friedrich Cotta, who first published the works of Schiller and Goethe. A bit of a lad, Goethe conducted detailed research on Tübingen's pubs during his weeklong stay in 1797. The party-loving genius is commemorated by the plaque 'Hier wohnte Goethe' (Goethe lived here). On the wall of the grungy student digs next door is the perhaps more insightful sign 'Hier kotzte Goethe' (Goethe puked here).

FREE **Stiftskirche St Georg** CHURCH
(Am Holzmarkt; ⊙9am-5pm) The late-Gothic Stiftskirche shelters the tombs of the Württemberg dukes and some dazzling late-medieval stained-glass windows.

Platanenallee PROMENADE
Steps lead down from Eberhardsbrücke bridge to Platanenallee, a leafy islet on the Neckar River canopied by sycamore trees, with views up to half-timbered houses in a fresco painter's palette of pastels and turreted villas nestled on the hillsides.

Hölderlinturm MUSEUM
(Bursagasse 6; adult/concession €2.50/1.50; ⊙10am-noon & 3-5pm Tue & Fri, 2-5pm Sat & Sun) You can see how the dreamy Neckar views from this silver-turreted tower fired the imagination of Romantic poet Friedrich Hölderlin, resident here from 1807 to 1843.

It now contains a museum tracing his life and work.

Kunsthalle GALLERY
(www.kunsthalle-tuebingen.de; Philosophenweg 76; adult/concession €9/7; ⊙10am-6pm Tue-Sun) The streamlined Kunsthalle stages first-rate exhibitions of mostly contemporary art. At the time of writing, Beuys, Polke and Warhol were in the spotlight. Buses 5, 13 and 17 stop here.

FREE **Botanischer Garten** GARDEN
(Hartmeyerstrasse 123; ⊙8am-4.45pm daily, to 7pm Sat & Sun in summer) Green-fingered students tend to the Himalayan cedars, swamp cypresses and rhododendrons in the gardens and hothouses of the serene Botanischer Garten, 2km northwest of the centre. Take bus 5, 13, 15 or 17.

Wurmlinger Kapelle CHURCH, WALK
(⊙10am-4pm May-Oct) A great hike is the Kreuzweg (way of the cross) to the 17th-century Wurmlinger Kapelle, 6km southwest of Tübingen. A footpath loops up through well-tended vineyards to the whitewashed pilgrimage chapel, where there are

DON'T MISS

MESSING ABOUT ON THE RIVER

There's nothing like a languid paddle along the sun-dappled Neckar River in summer. At **Bootsvermietung Märkle** (Eberhardsbrücke 1; ⊙11am-6pm Apr-Oct, to 9pm in summer), an hour of splashy fun in a rowboat, canoe, pedalo or 12-person Stocherkähne (punt) costs €9, €9, €12 and €48 respectively.

Or sign up at the tourist office for an hour's **punting** (adult/child €6/3; ⊙1pm Sat & Sun May-Sep) around the Neckarinsel, beginning at the Hölderlinturm.

Students in fancy dress do battle on the Neckar at June's hilarious **Stocherkahnrennen** (www.stocherkahn rennen.com) punt race, where jostling, dunking and even snapping your rival's oar are permitted. The first team to reach the Neckarbrücke wins the race, the title and as much beer as they can sink. The losers have to down half a litre of cod-liver oil. Arrive early to snag a prime spot on Platanenallee.

long views across the Ammer and Neckar Valleys. The tourist office has leaflets (€1).

Sleeping

The tourist office has a free booklet listing private rooms, holiday homes, youth hostels and camping grounds in the area.

 Hotel am Schloss HISTORIC HOTEL **$$**
(929 40; www.hotelamschloss.de; Burgsteige 18; s €75, d €108-135; P) So close to the castle you can almost touch it, this flower-bedecked hotel has dapper rooms ensconced in a 16th-century building. Rumour has it Kepler was partial to the wine here; try a drop yourself before attempting the tongue twister above the bench outside: *dohoggeddiadiaemmerdohogged* (the same people sit in the same spot). And a very nice spot it is, too.

Hotel La Casa HOTEL **$$$**
(946 66; www.lacasa-tuebingen.de; Hechinger Strasse 59; d €156-182;) Tübingen's swishest digs are a 15-minute stroll south of the Altstadt. Contemporary rooms designed with panache come with welcome tea, coffee and soft drinks. Breakfast is a smorgasbord of mostly organic goodies. The crowning glory is the top-floor spa with tremendous city views.

DON'T MISS

TOP SNACK SPOTS

Eating on the hoof? Try these informal nosh spots.

» **Die Kichererbse** (Metzgergasse 2; snacks €3-5; closed Sun;) All hail the 'chickpea' for its scrummy falafel. Grab a table to chomp on a classic (€3).

» **X** (Kornhausstrasse 6; snacks €1.50-3; 11am-1am) Hole-in-the-wall joint rustling up Tübingen's crispiest fries, bratwurst and burgers.

» **Wochenmarkt** (7am-1pm Mon, Wed & Fri) Bag glossy fruit and veg, oven-fresh bread, local honey and herbs at Tübingen's farmers market.

» **Eiscafé San Marco** (Nonnengasse 14; ice cream cone €1; 8.30am-11pm Mon-Sat, 10.30am-11pm Sun) Italian-run, with hands-down the best gelati in town.

Hotel Hospiz GUESTHOUSE **$$**
(9240; www.hotel-hospiz.de; Neckarhalde 2; s/d €70/105;) Huddled away in the Altstadt, this candyfloss-pink guesthouse has old-school, immaculately kept rooms, many looking across Tübingen's gables. Pastries, smoked fish and eggs are nice additions to the breakfast buffet.

Eating

Mauganeschtle SWABIAN **$$$**
(929 40; Burgsteige 18; mains €10-19.50; daily) It's a stiff climb up to this restaurant at Hotel am Schloss but worth every step. Suspended above the rooftops of Tübingen, the terrace is a scenic spot for the house speciality, *Maultaschen*, with fillings like lamb, trout, porcini and veal.

Neckarmüller BREWPUB **$$**
(278 48; Gartenstrasse 4; mains €7.50-15; 10am-1am) Overlooking the Neckar, this cavernous microbrewery is a summertime magnet for its chestnut-shaded beer garden. Come for home brews by the metre and beer-laced dishes from (tasty) Swabian roast to (interesting) tripe stew.

Alte Weinstube Göhner SWABIAN **$$$**
(551 668; Schmiedtorstrasse 5; mains €10-17; closed Mon lunch, Sun) As down-to-earth and comfy as a Swabian farmer's boots, this 175-year-old haunt is Tübingen's oldest wine tavern. Join the high-spirited regulars to discuss the merits of *Maultaschen*, sip a glass of Trollinger and, if you're lucky, hear someone bashing out golden oldies on the piano.

Wurstküche GERMAN **$$$**
(927 50; Am Lustnauer Tor 8; mains €9-17.50; 11am-midnight daily) The rustic, wood-panelled Wurstküche brims with locals quaffing wine and contentedly munching *Schupfnudeln* (potato noodles) and *Spanpferkel* (roast suckling pig).

Drinking

Tangente-Night BAR
(Pfleghofstrasse 10; 6pm-3am, to 5am Fri & Sat) Totally chilled Tangente-Night enjoys a fierce student following. Belt out a classic at Monday's karaoke party under the motto 'drink faster and sing for your life'. The vibe is clubbier at weekends, with music skipping from rock to electro.

Weinhaus Beck BAR
(Am Markt 1; 9am-11pm) There's rarely an empty table at this wine tavern beside the

Rathaus, a convivial place to enjoy a local tipple or coffee and cake.

Storchen CAFE
(Ammergasse 3; ⊘3pm-1am, from 11am Sat) Mind your head climbing the stairs to this easygoing student hang-out, serving enormous mugs of milky coffee and cheap local brews under wood beams.

Schwärzlocher Hof BEER GARDEN
(Schwarzloch 1; ⊘11am-10pm Wed-Sun; ⚌) Scenically perched above the Ammer Valley, a 20-minute trudge west of town, this creaking farmhouse is famous for its beer garden and home-pressed *Most* (cider). Kids love the resident horses, rabbits and peacocks.

ⓘ Information

Find ATMs around the Hauptbahnhof, Eberhardsbrücke and Am Markt.
Post office (cnr Hafengasse & Neue Strasse) In the Altstadt.
Tourist office (☎913 60; www.tuebingen -info.de; An der Neckarbrücke 1; ⊘9am-7pm Mon-Fri, 9am-4pm Sat, plus 11am-4pm Sun May-Sep) South of Eberhardsbrücke. Has a hotel board outside and can provide details on hiking options (for example, to Bebenhausen or Wurmlinger Kapelle).

ⓘ Getting There & Around

The Neckar River divides Tübingen from east to west. Karlstrasse leads south to the Hauptbahnhof (500m) from Eberhardsbrücke.

Tübingen is an easy train ride from Stuttgart (€12.20, one hour, at least two per hour) and Villingen (€21, 1½ to two hours, hourly) in the Black Forest.

The centre is a maze of one-way streets with residents-only parking, so head for a multistorey car park. To drive into Tübingen, you need to purchase an environmentally friendly *Umweltplaketten* (emissions sticker).

Radlager (Lazarettgasse 19-21; ⊘9.30am-6.30pm Mon, Wed & Fri, 2-6.30pm Tue & Thu, 9.30am-2.30pm Sat) rents bikes for €10 per day.

If you'd rather let someone else do the pedalling, **Riksch-Radsch** (☎300 449; Aixer Strasse 198) organise a three-hour spin to Bebenhausen (€59 for a two-person rickshaw).

Naturpark Schönbuch

For back-to-nature hiking and cycling, make for this 156-sq-km **nature reserve** (www. naturpark-schoenbuch.de), 8km north of Tübingen. With a bit of luck you might catch a glimpse of black woodpeckers and yellow-bellied toads.

The nature reserve's beech and oak woods fringe the village of **Bebenhausen** and its well-preserved **Cistercian Abbey** (www.kloster-bebenhausen.de; adult/concession €4.50/2.30; ⊘guided tours hourly 11am-5pm Tue-Sun). Founded in 1183 by Count Rudolph von Tübingen, the complex became a royal hunting retreat post-Reformation. A visit takes in the frescoed **summer refectory**, the Gothic **abbey church** and intricate star vaulting and half-timbered facades in the **cloister**.

Bebenhausen, 3km north of Tübingen, is the gateway to Naturpark Schönbuch. Buses run at least twice hourly (€2.20, 15 minutes).

Burg Hohenzollern

Rising dramatically from an exposed crag, its medieval battlements and silver turrets often veiled in mist, **Burg Hohenzollern** (www.burg-hohenzollern.com; tour adult/concession €10/8, grounds admission without tour adult/concession €5/4; ⊘tour 10am-5.30pm, to 4.30pm Nov–mid-Mar) is impressive from a distance but up close it looks more contrived. Dating to 1867, this neo-Gothic castle is the ancestral seat of the Hohenzollern family, the first and last monarchical rulers of the short-lived second German empire (1871–1918).

History fans should take a 35-minute German-language **tour**, which takes in towers, overblown salons replete with stained glass and frescoes, and the dazzling *Schatzkammer* (treasury). The **grounds** command tremendous views over the Swabian Alps.

Frequent trains link Tübingen, 28km distant, with Hechingen (€4.40, 25 minutes, one or two per hour), about 4km northwest of the castle.

Schwäbisch Hall

☎0791 / POP 37,140
Out on its rural lonesome near the Bavarian border, Schwäbisch Hall is an unsung gem. This medieval time-capsule of higgledy-piggledy lanes, soaring half-timbered houses built high on the riches of salt, and covered bridges that criss-cross the Kocher River is storybook stuff.

Buzzy cafes and first-rate museums add to the appeal of this town, known for its rare black-spotted pigs and the jangling piggy banks of its nationwide building society.

Historic Marvels

Germany's history has been shaped by many players. Hear the whispers of the past as you nose around medieval castles, crane your neck to take in lofty cathedrals and explore the cobbled tangle of towns founded centuries before Columbus set sail. If only stones could talk...

Beauteous Bamberg

1 Germany teems with towns drenched in history, but Bamberg (p277) is a particularly delightful web of medieval lanes, with a lordly cathedral, well-kept historic buildings and some of Germany's best beer. Straddling the Regnitz River, the Altes Rathaus is a shutterbug favourite.

Europe's Roots

2 Few people have shaped Europe as much as Charlemagne. And few German cathedrals have as illustrious a history as Aachen's (p487), where the Frankish king-turned-emperor is buried and which witnessed the coronations of 30 German kings between AD 936 and 1531.

Joyful Sanctuaries

3 Lift your spirits at the heavenly rococo Wieskirche pilgrimage church (p235), rising like a vision from an emerald Bavarian meadow. With angels flitting across frescoed ceilings and an altar that is a symphony of colour, its beauty will resonate even with nonbelievers.

Fairy-tale Fantasy

4 Before touring Schloss Neuschwanstein in Füssen, glimpse an insight into 'Mad' King Ludwig II's mind on a spin around his childhood home, Schloss Hohenschwangau (p232). A romantic neo-gothic extravaganza, it is festooned with mythological murals and still furnished in the original 19th-century style.

Clockwise from top left
1 Altes Rathaus, Bamberg 2 Aachen Dom 3 Wieskirche, Bavaria 4 Schloss Hohenschwangau, Füssen

⊙ Sights & Activities

Altstadt   NEIGHBOURHOOD

A leisurely Altstadt saunter takes you along narrow alleys, among half-timbered hillside houses and up slopes overlooking the Kocher River. The islands and riverbank parks are great for picnics.

Am Markt springs to life with a farmers market every Wednesday and Saturday morning. On the square, your gaze is drawn to the baroque-style **Rathaus**, festooned with coats of arms and cherubs, and to the terracotta-hued **Widmanhaus** at No 4, a remnant of a 13th-century Franciscan monastery. The centrepiece is the late-Gothic **Kirche St Michael**.

Note the **Gotischer Fischbrunnen** (1509), next to the tourist office, a large iron tub once used for storing fish before sale.

Towering above Pfarrgasse is the steep-roofed, 16th-century **Neubau**, built as an arsenal and granary and now used as a theatre. Ascend the stone staircase for dreamy views over red-roofed houses to the former city fortifications, the covered **Roter Steg** bridge and the **Henkerbrücke** (Hangman's Bridge).

FREE **Kunsthalle Würth**   GALLERY

(www.kunst.wuerth.com; Lange Strasse 35; ⊙11am-6pm) The brainchild of industrialist Reinhold Würth, this contemporary gallery is housed in a striking limestone building that preserves part of a century-old brewery. Stellar temporary exhibitions have previously spotlighted the work of artists such as David Hockney, Edvard Munch and Georg Baselitz.

Hällisch-Fränkisches Museum   MUSEUM

(adult/student €2.50/1.50; ⊙10am-5pm Tue-Sun) Down by the river, this well-curated museum traces Schwäbisch Hall's history with its collection of shooting targets, Roman figurines, and rarities including an exquisite hand-painted wooden synagogue interior from 1738 and a 19th-century mouse guillotine.

Hohenloher Freilandmuseum   MUSEUM

(Wackershofen; adult/concession €6/4; ⊙9am-6pm daily; 🚻) One place you can be guaranteed of seeing a black-spotted pig is this open-air farming museum, a sure-fire hit with the kids with its traditional farmhouses, orchards and animals. It's 6km northwest of Schwäbisch Hall and served by bus 7.

🛏 Sleeping & Eating

Hotel Scholl   HOTEL $$

(☎975 50; www.hotel-scholl.de; Klosterstrasse 2-4; s/d €74/99; 🖧) A charming pick behind Am Markt, this family-run hotel has rustic-chic rooms with parquet floors, flat-screen TVs, granite bathrooms and free wi-fi.

Der Adelshof   HISTORIC HOTEL $$

(☎758 90; www.hotel-adelshof.de; Am Markt 12; s €80-100, d €110-150, mains €18-32; P🖧) This centuries-old pad is as posh as it gets in Schwäbisch Hall, with a wellness area and plush quarters, from the blue-and-white Wedgwood room to the four-poster Turmzimmer. Its beamed Ratskeller serves seasonally inspired French fare.

TOP CHOICE **Rebers Pflug**   GASTRONOMIC $$$

(☎931 230; www.rebers-pflug.de; Weckriedener Strasse 2; mains €17.50-36; ⊙closed lunch Mon & Tue, dinner Sun) Hans-Harald Reber mans the stove at this 19th-century country house, one of Schwäbisch Hall's two Michelin-starred haunts. Signatures such as veal in an oxtail crust are exquisitely cooked and presented. Dine in the chestnut-shaded garden in summer.

Entenbäck   BISTRO $$

(☎9782 9182; Steinerner Steg 1; mains €10-15.50; ⊙noon-2.30pm & 5-10pm Tue-Fri, 11am-10pm Sat & Sun) This inviting bistro receives high praise for its Swabian-meets-Mediterranean menu, from satisfying roast beef with Spätzle to salmon roulade with riesling sauce. Lunch is a snip at €7.50.

Brauerei-Ausschank Zum Löwen   BREWPUB $$

(☎2041 622; Mauerstrasse 17; mains €8-14.50; ⊙5-11pm Thu, 11.30am-2pm & 5-11pm Fri-Tue) Down by the river, this brewpub attracts a jovial bunch of locals, who come for freshly tapped Haller Löwenbrauerei brews and hearty nosh like pork cooked in beer-cumin sauce.

ⓘ Information

Tourist office (☎0791 751 246; www.schwae bischhall.de; Am Markt 9; ⊙9am-6pm Mon-Fri, 10am-3pm Sat & Sun May-Sep, 9am-5pm Mon-Fri Oct-Apr) On the Altstadt's main square.

ⓘ Getting There & Around

The town has two train stations: trains from Stuttgart (€14.40, 1¼ hours, hourly) arrive at Hessental, on the right bank about 7km south of the centre and linked to the Altstadt by bus 1; trains from Heilbronn go to the left-bank Bahnhof Schwäbisch Hall, a short walk along Bahnhofstrasse from the centre.

Ulm

☏0731 / POP 122,800

Starting with the statistics, Ulm has the crookedest house (as listed in *Guinness World Records*) and one of the narrowest (4.5m wide), the world's oldest zoomorphic sculpture (aged 30,000 years) and tallest cathedral steeple (161.5m high), and is the birthplace of the physicist Albert Einstein. Relatively speaking, of course.

This idiosyncratic city will win your affection with everyday encounters, particularly in summer as you pedal along the Danube and the Fischerviertel's beer gardens hum with animated chatter. One *Helles* too many and you may decide to impress the locals by attempting the tongue twister: '*In Ulm, um Ulm, und um Ulm herum.*'

◉ Sights & Activities

FREE **Münster** CATHEDRAL

(Map p326; www.ulmer-muenster.de; Münsterplatz; organ concerts €3.50-6, tower adult/concession €4/2.50; ⊙9am-7.45pm, to 4.45pm in winter) Ooh, it's so big... first-time visitors gush as they strain their neck muscles gazing up to the Münster. It is. And rather beautiful. Celebrated for its 161.5m-high steeple, the world's tallest, this Goliath of cathedrals took a staggering 500 years to build from the first stone laid in 1377. Note the hallmarks on each stone, inscribed by cutters who were paid by the block. Those intent on cramming the Münster into one photo, filigree spire and all, should lie down on the cobbles.

Only by puffing up 768 spiral steps to the 143m-high viewing platform of the tower can you appreciate the Münster's dizzying height. Up top there are terrific views of the Black Forest and, on cloud-free days, the Alps.

The **Israelfenster**, a stained-glass window above the west door, commemorates Jews killed during the Holocaust. The Gothic-style wooden pulpit canopy eliminates echoes during sermons. Biblical figures and historical characters such as Pythagoras embellish the 15th-century oak **choir stalls**. The Münster's regular organ concerts are a musical treat.

CITY SAVER

If you're planning on ticking off most of the major sights, consider investing in a good-value **UlmCard** (1/2 days €12/18), which covers public transport in Ulm and Neu-Ulm, a free city tour or rental of the itour audioguide and entry to all museums, plus numerous other discounts on tours, attractions and restaurants.

Marktplatz SQUARE

Lording it over the Marktplatz, the 14th-century, step-gabled **Rathaus** (Town Hall; Map p326) sports an ornately painted Renaissance facade and a gilded astrological clock. Inside is a replica of Albrecht Berblinger's flying machine. In front is the **Fischkastenbrunnen** (Map p326; Marktplatz), a fountain where fishmongers kept their catch alive on market days. The 36m-high glass pyramid behind the Rathaus is the city's main library, the **Zentralbibliothek** (Map p326; Marktplatz), designed by Gottfried Böhm.

Stadtmauer WALL

(Map p326) South of the Fischerviertel, along the Danube's north bank, runs the red-brick *Stadtmauer* (city wall), the height of which was reduced in the 19th century after Napoleon decided that a heavily fortified Ulm was against his best interests. Walk it for fine views over the river, the Altstadt and the colourful tile-roofed **Metzgerturm** (Butcher's Tower; Map p326), doing a Pisa by leaning 2m off-centre.

East of the Herdbrücke, the bridge to Neu-Ulm, a bronze **plaque** (Map p326) marks where Albrecht Berblinger, a tailor who invented a flying machine, attempted to fly over the Danube in 1811. The so-called 'Tailor of Ulm' made an embarrassing splash landing but his design was later shown to be workable (his failure was caused by a lack of thermals on that day).

Fischerviertel NEIGHBOURHOOD

(Map p326) The charming Fischerviertel, Ulm's old fishers' and tanners' quarter, is slightly southwest. Here beautifully restored half-timbered houses huddle along the two channels of the Blau River. Harbouring art galleries, rustic restaurants, courtyards and the crookedest house in the world – as well as one of the narrowest – the cobbled lanes are ideal for a leisurely saunter.

Ulm

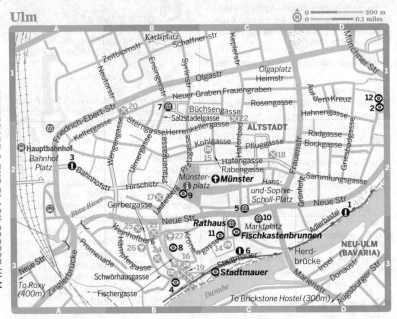

Ulmer Museum   MUSEUM
(Map p326; www.ulmer-museum.ulm.de; Marktplatz
9; adult/concession €5/3.50, Fri free; ⊙11am-5pm
Tue-Sun, to 8pm Thu) This museum is a fascinating romp through ancient and modern art,
history and archaeology. Standouts are the
20th-century **Kurt Fried Collection**, starring Klee, Picasso and Lichtenstein works.

Archaeological highlights include tiny Upper Palaeolithic figurines, unearthed in caves in the Swabian Alps, including the 30,000-year-old ivory *Löwenmensch* (lion man), the world's oldest zoomorphic sculpture.

Kunsthalle Weishaupt   GALLERY

(Map p326; www.kunsthalle-weishaupt.de; Hans-und-Sophie-Scholl-Platz 1; adult/concession €6/4; ⊙11am-5pm Tue-Sun, to 8pm Thu) The glass-fronted Kunsthalle Weishaupt unveils the private collection of Siegfried Weishaupt. The accent is on modern and pop art, with bold paintings by Klein, Warhol and Haring.

Museum der Brotkultur   MUSEUM

(Map p326; www.museum-brotkultur.de; Salzstadelgasse 10; adult/concession €3.50/2.50; ⊙10am-5pm) How grain grows, what makes a good dough and other bread-related mysteries are unravelled at the Museum of Bread Culture. The collection celebrates bread as the stuff of life over millennia and across cultures, displaying curios from mills to Egyptian corn mummies.

Stadthaus   LANDMARK

(Map p326) Designed by Richard Meier, the contemporary aesthetic of the concrete-and-glass Stadthaus is a dramatic contrast to the Münster. The American architect caused uproar by erecting a postmodern building alongside the city's Gothic giant but the result is striking. The edifice stages exhibitions and events, and houses the tourist office and a cafe.

Schwörhaus   LANDMARK

(Oath House; Map p326) On the third Monday of July, the mayor swears allegiance to the town's 1397 constitution from the 1st-floor loggia of the early 17th-century baroque Schwörhaus (Oath House), three blocks west of the Rathaus.

Einstein Fountain & Monument   LANDMARK

(Map p326) A nod to Ulm's most famous son, Jürgen Goertz's fiendishly funny bronze fountain shows a wild-haired, tongue-poking-out Albert Einstein, who was born in Ulm but left when he was one year old. Standing in front of the 16th-century Zeughaus (arsenal; Map p326), the rocket-snail creation is a satirical play on humanity's attempts to manipulate evolution for its own self-interest. Nearby, at Zeughaus 14, is a single stone bearing the inscription *Ein Stein* (One Stone).

On Bahnhofstrasse sits Max Bill's 1979 monument (Map p326) to the great physicist, a stack of red-granite pillars marking the spot where Einstein was born.

Legoland   THEME PARK

(www.legoland.de; adult/concession €38/34; ⊙10am-btwn 6pm & 8pm Apr-early Nov) A sure-fire kid-pleaser, Legoland Deutschland is a pricey Lego-themed amusement park, with shows, splashy rides and a miniature world built from 25 million Lego bricks. It's in Günzburg, 37km east of Ulm, just off the A8.

🛏 Sleeping

The tourist office lists apartments and guesthouses charging around €25 per person.

TOP CHOICE Hotel Schiefes Haus   B&B $$$

(Map p326; ☑967 930; www.hotelschiefeshausulm.de; Schwörhausgasse 6; s €125, d €148-160; ☎) There was a crooked man and he walked a crooked mile...presumably to the world's most crooked hotel. But fear not, ye of little wonkiness, this early-16th-century, half-timbered rarity is not about to topple into the Blau River. And up those creaking wood stairs, in your snug, beamed room, you won't have to buckle yourself to the bed thanks to spirit levels and specially made height adjusters. If you're feeling *really* crooked, plump straight for room No 6.

Brickstone Hostel   HOSTEL $

(☑708 2559; www.brickstone-hostel.de; Schützenstrasse 42; dm €18-22, s/d €30/44; ☎) We love the homely vibe at this beautifully restored art nouveau house in Neu-Ulm. The high-ceilinged rooms are kept spotless and backpacker perks include a self-catering kitchen with free coffee and tea, bike rental and a cosy lounge with book exchange. Take bus 7 to Schützenstrasse from the Hauptbahnhof.

Das Schmale Haus   B&B $$

(Map p326; ☑175 4940; Fischergasse 27; s/d €81/104) Measuring just 4.5m across, the half-timbered 'narrow house' is a one-off. The affable Heides have transformed this slender 16th-century pad into a gorgeous B&B, with exposed beams, downy bedding and wood floors in all three rooms.

Hotel Restaurant Löwen   HOTEL $$

(☑388 5880; www.hotel-loewen-ulm.de; Klosterhof 41; s €81-91, d €116-122; P☎) It's amazing what you can do with a former monastery and an eye for design. Exposed beams and stone add historic edge to streamlined rooms

DON'T MISS

SPOT THE SPARROW

You can't move for *Spatzen* (sparrows) in the German language. You can eat like one (*essen wie ein Spatz*) and swear like one (*schimpfen wie ein Rohrspatz*); there are *Spatzenschleuder* (catapults), *Spätzles* (little darlings) and *Spatzenhirne* (bird brains). Nicknamed *Spatzen*, Ulm residents are, according to legend, indebted to the titchy bird for the construction of their fabulous Münster.

The story goes that the half-baked builders tried in vain to shove the wooden beams for the minster sideways through the city gate. They struggled, until suddenly a sparrow fluttered past with straw for its nest. Enlightened, the builders carried the beams lengthways, completed the job and placed a bronze statue of a sparrow at the top to honour the bird.

Today there are sparrows everywhere in Ulm: on postcards, in patisseries, at football matches (team SSV Ulm are dubbed *die Spatzen*) and, above all, in the colourful sculptures dotting the Altstadt.

with parquet floors and flat-screen TVs. The chestnut-canopied beer garden is a boon in summer. Take tram 1 from central Ulm to Söflingen.

Hotel Bäumle HISTORIC HOTEL **$$**
(Map p326; ☑622 87; www.hotel-baeumle.de; Kohlgasse 6; s €70-89, d €90-103, tr €130; 🖥) Big on old-world flair, the Bäumle can trace its history way back to 1522 and houses smart, immaculately kept rooms. Unless you class cathedral bells as 'noise', you're going to love the location. No lift.

Hotel am Rathaus &
Hotel Reblaus HOTEL **$$**
(Map p326; ☑968 490; www.rathausulm.de; Kronengasse 10; s €70-110, d €88-130, q €130-170, s/d without bathroom €52/72; 🖥) Just paces from the Rathaus, these family-run twins ooze individual charm in rooms with flourishes like stucco and Biedermeier furnishings. Light sleepers take note: the walls are thin and the street can be noisy.

🍴 Eating

Zur Forelle GERMAN **$$$**
(Map p326; ☑639 24; Fischergasse 25; mains €12-22; ⊘daily) Since 1626, this low-ceilinged tavern has been convincing wayfarers (Einstein included) of the joys of seasonal Swabian cuisine. Ablaze with flowers in summer, this wood-panelled haunt by the Blau prides itself on its namesake *Forelle* (trout), kept fresh under the bridge.

Barfüsser BREWPUB **$$**
(Map p326; ☑602 1110; Lautenberg 1; mains €9-16.50; ⊘10am-1am Sun-Wed, to 2am Thu-Sat) Hearty fare like *Käsespätzle* (cheese noo-

dles) and pork roast soak up the prize-winning beer, microbrewed in Neu-Ulm, at this brewpub.

Da Franco ITALIAN **$$$**
(Map p326; ☑305 85; Neuer Graben 23; mains €13-24.50; ⊘closed Mon) If you fancy a break from the norm, why not give this little Italian a whirl. There is a seasonal touch to authentic dishes like swordfish with clams and veal escalope with asparagus, which are cooked and presented with style.

Gerberhaus MEDITERRANEAN **$$$**
(Map p326; ☑677 17; Weinhofberg 9; mains €10-18; ⊘daily) This warm, inviting woodcutter's cottage of a restaurant hits the mark with its Med-inspired dishes. Plump for a river-facing table for clean, bright flavours like home-smoked salmon carpaccio and lemongrass crème brûlée. Day specials go for as little as €7.

Zunfthaus der Schiffleute GERMAN **$$$**
(Map p326; ☑1755 771; www.zunfthaus-ulm.com; Fischergasse 31; mains €10-19; ⊘daily) Looking proudly back on a 600-year tradition, this timber-framed restaurant sits by the river. The menu speaks of a chef who loves the region, with Swabian faves like *Katzagschroi* (beef, onions, egg and fried potatoes) and meaty one-pot *Schwäbisches Hochzeitssüppchen*.

Zur Lochmühle GERMAN **$$$**
(Map p326; ☑673 05; Gerbergasse 6; mains €8.50-18.50; ⊘daily; 🖩) The watermill has been churning the Blau since 1356 at this rustic half-timbered pile. Plant yourself in the riverside beer garden for Swabian classics like crispy roast pork, *Schupfnudeln* and brook trout with lashings of potato salad.

Cafe Ulmer Münz CAFE $$
(Map p326; Schwörhausgasse 4; light meals €7-12; ☺closed Mon) Fischerviertel cafe with a happy buzz on the cobbled patio, daily specials and homemade cakes.

Yamas GREEK $$$
(Map p326; ☑407 8614; Herrenkellergasse 29; mains €12-23; ☺daily) Classy Greek food with a market-driven menu, lots of fresh seafood and a bulging wine cellar.

Café im Kornhauskeller CAFE $
(Map p326; Hafengasse 19; breakfast & snacks €4-8; ☺8am-midnight Mon-Sat, 9am-10pm Sun) Arty cafe with an inner courtyard for drinks, breakfast, light bites or ice cream.

Café im Stadthaus CAFE $
(Map p326; Münsterplatz 50; lunch special €8.40; ☺8am-midnight, to 1am Fri & Sat) Go for coffee or a good-value lunch special; linger for the mesmerising cathedral views at this glass cube opposite.

⬤ Drinking & Entertainment

Zur Zill BAR
(Map p326; Schwörhausgasse 19; ☺10am-2am daily, to 4am Fri & Sat) Join a happy-go-lucky crowd for a cold beer or cocktail by the river.

Wilder Mann PUB
(Map p326; Fischergasse 2; ☺11am-1am Mon-Thu, to 3am Fri-Sun) Service is a lucky dip and the food is mediocre but by all means head to the people-watching terrace for a drink.

Roxy ARTS CENTRE
(www.roxy.ulm.de; Schillerstrasse 1) A huge cultural venue, housed in a former industrial plant 1km south of the Hauptbahnhof, with a concert hall, cinema, disco, bar and special-event forum. Take tram line 1 to Ehinger Tor.

ⓘ Information

Internet cafe (Herdbruckerstrasse 26; per hr €1; ☺10am-9pm)

Post office (Bahnhofplatz 2) To the left as you exit the Hauptbahnhof.

Tourist office (☑161 2830; www.tourismus. ulm.de; Münsterplatz 50, Stadthaus; ☺9am-6pm Mon-Fri, to 4pm Sat, 11am-3pm Sun) Sells the Ulm Card and events tickets and has a free room-booking service.

ⓘ Getting There & Away

Ulm, about 90km southeast of Stuttgart and 150km west of Munich, is near the intersection of the north–south A7 and the east–west A8.

Ulm is well-served by ICE and EC trains; major destinations include Stuttgart (€18.10 to €25, 56 minutes to 1¼ hours, several hourly) and Munich (€30 to €36, 1¼ hours, several hourly).

ⓘ Getting Around

Ulm's ecofriendly trams run on renewable energy. There's a **local transport information counter** (www.swu-verkehr.de) in the tourist office. A single/day ticket for the bus and tram network in Ulm and Neu-Ulm costs €1.95/4.40.

Except in parking garages (€0.60 per 30 minutes), the whole city centre is metered; many areas are limited to one hour (€1.80). There's a Park & Ride lot at Donaustadion, a stadium 1.5km northeast of the Münster and on tram line 1.

You can hire bikes from **Fahrradhandlung Ralf Reich** (☑211 790 231; Frauenstrasse 34; per day €9; ☺9am-12.30pm & 2-6.30pm Mon-Fri, 9am-2pm Sat), a five-minute stroll northeast of the Münsterplatz. Bike paths shadow the Danube.

THE BLACK FOREST

Baden-Baden

☑07221 / POP 54,500

'So nice that you have to name it twice', enthused Bill Clinton about Baden-Baden, whose air of old-world luxury and curative waters have attracted royals, the rich and celebrities over the years – Obama and Bismarck, Queen Victoria and Victoria Beckham included. 'Nice', however, could never convey the amazing grace of this Black Forest town, with its grand colonnaded buildings and whimsically turreted art nouveau villas spread across the hillsides and framed by forested mountains.

The bon-vivant spirit of France, just across the border, is tangible in the town's open-air cafes, chic boutiques and pristine gardens fringing the Oos River. And with its temple-like thermal baths – which put the *Baden* (bathe) in Baden – and palatial casino, the allure of this grand dame of German spa towns is as timeless as it is enduring.

⊙ Sights

Trinkhalle LANDMARK
(Pump Room; Map p332; Kaiserallee 3; ☺10am-5pm Mon-Sat, 2-5pm Sun) Standing proud above a manicured park, this neoclassical pump room was built in 1839 as an attractive addition to the Kurhaus. The 90m-long portico is embellished with 19th-century frescoes of

Black Forest

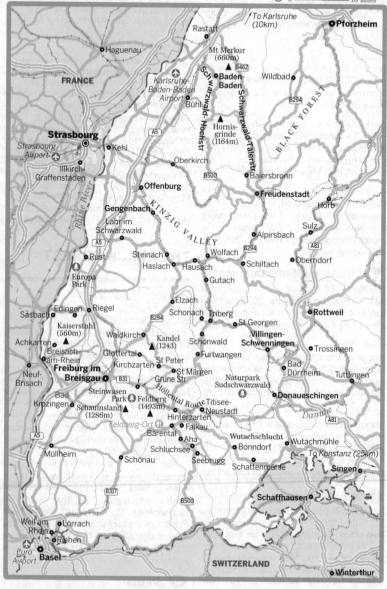

Kurhaus & Casino
LANDMARK

(Map p332; www.kurhaus-baden-baden.de; Kaiserallee 1; guided tour €5; ☺guided tour 9.30am-11.30am daily) Corinthian columns and a frieze of mythical griffins grace the belle époque facade of the Kurhaus, which towers above well-groomed gardens. An alley of chestnut trees, flanked by two rows of boutiques, links the Kurhaus with Kaiserallee.

Inside is the sublime casino (www.casino -baden-baden.de; admission €5; ⊘2pm-2am Sun-Thu, to 3am Fri & Sat), which seeks to emulate the gilded splendour of Versailles. Marlene Dietrich called it 'the most beautiful casino in the world'. Gents must wear a jacket and tie, rentable for €8 and €3 respectively. If you're not a gambler and don't fancy dressing up, join a 25-minute guided tour of the opulent interior.

Lichtentaler Allee   GARDENS

This 2.3km ribbon of greenery, threading from Goetheplatz to Kloster Lichtenthal, is quite a picture: studded with fountains and sculptures and carpeted with flowers (crocuses and daffodils in spring, magnolias and azaleas in summer). Shadowing the sprightly Oosbach, its promenade and bridges are made for aimless ambling.

The gateway to Lichtentaler Allee is Baden-Baden Theater (Map p332), a neobaroque confection whose grandiose interior resembles the Opéra-Garnier in Paris. About 1km south is the Gönneranlage (Map p332), a rose garden ablaze with more than 400 varieties. Almost Siberian is the Russische Kirche (Russian Church; Map p332; Maria-Victoria-Strasse; admission €1; ⊘10am-6pm), slightly to the east. Built in the Byzantine style in 1882, it's topped with a brilliantly golden onion dome.

Lichtentaler Allee concludes at the Kloster Lichtenthal, a Cistercian abbey founded in 1245, with an abbey church, open daily, where generations of the margraves of Baden lie buried.

Museum Frieder Burda   GALLERY

(Map p332; www.museum-frieder-burda.de; Lichtentaler Allee 8b; adult/concession €10/8; ⊘10am-6pm Tue-Sun) A Joan Miró sculpture guards the front of this architecturally innovative gallery, designed by Richard Meier. The star-studded collection of modern and contemporary art, featuring works by Picasso, Gerhard Richter and Jackson Pollock, is complemented by temporary exhibitions, such as the recent retrospective of American surrealist William Copley.

Staatliche Kunsthalle   GALLERY

(Map p332; www.kunsthalle-baden-baden.de; Lichtentaler Allee 8a; adult/concession €5/4; ⊘10am-6pm Tue-Sun) Sidling up to the Museum Frieda Burda is this sky-lit gallery, which showcases rotating exhibitions of contemporary art in neoclassical surrounds. Recently it zoomed in on Belgian visual artist Jan de Cock, postmodern painter Georg Baselitz and the collage-style works of Kenyan artist Wangechi Mut.

Stiftskirche   CHURCH

(Map p332; Marktplatz; ⊘8am-6pm daily) The centrepiece of cobbled Marktplatz is this pink church, a hotchpotch of Romanesque, late Gothic and, to a lesser extent, baroque styles. Its foundations incorporate some ruins of the former Roman baths. Come in the early afternoon to see its stained-glass windows cast rainbow patterns across the nave.

Römische Badruinen   ARCHAEOLOGICAL SITE

(Map p332; Römerplatz; adult/concession €2.50/1; ⊘11am-noon & 3-4pm mid-Mar–mid-Nov) The beauty-conscious Romans were the first to discover the healing properties of Baden-Baden's springs in the city they called Aquae Aureliae. Slip back 2000 years on a tour of the well-preserved ruins of their baths.

🏃 Activities

Baden-Baden is criss-crossed by scenic walking trails. Footpaths lead to the crumbling 11th-century Altes Schloss, 3km north of the centre, with Rhine Valley views; the Geroldsauer waterfalls, 6km south of Leopoldsplatz; and the overgrown Yburg castle ruins, in the vineyards southwest of town. The 40km Panoramaweg is an above-the-city delight.

🏆 TOP CHOICE Friedrichsbad   SPA

(Map p332; ✆275 920; www.roemisch-irisches-bad. de; Römerplatz 1; 3hr ticket €23, incl soap-and-brush massage €33; ⊘9am-10pm, last admission

---

DON'T MISS

TEN YEARS YOUNGER

Rheumatism, arthritis, respiratory complaints, skin problems – all this and a host of other ailments can, apparently, be cured by Baden-Baden's mineral-rich spring water. If you'd rather drink the stuff than bathe in it, head to the Fettquelle fountain at the base of a flight of steps near Römerplatz, where you can fill your bottle for free. It might taste like lukewarm bath water but who cares if it makes you feel 10 years younger?

Baden-Baden

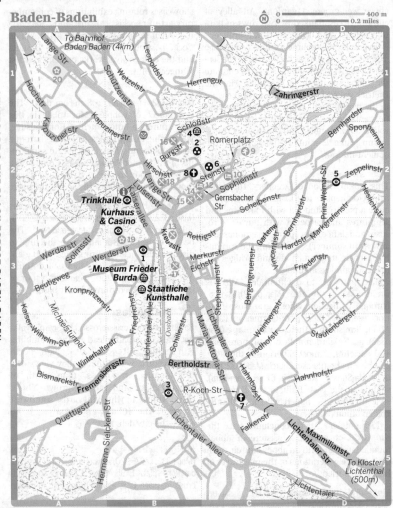

7pm) If it's the body of Venus and the complexion of Cleopatra you desire, abandon modesty (and clothing) to wallow in thermal waters at this sumptuous 19th-century spa. As Mark Twain put it, 'after 10 minutes you forget time; after 20 minutes, the world' as you slip into the regime of steaming, scrubbing, hot-cold bathing and dunking in the Roman-Irish bath. With its cupola, mosaics and Carrera marble pool, the bathhouse is the vision of a neo-Renaissance palace.

Caracalla Therme SPA
(Map p332; www.caracalla.de; Römerplatz 11; 2/3/4hr €14/17/20; ⊙8am-10pm, last admission 8pm) If you would prefer to keep your bathing togs on, this glass-fronted spa has a cluster of indoor and outdoor pools, grottos and surge channels, making the most of the mineral-rich spring water. For those who dare to bare, saunas range from the rustic 'forest' to the roasting 95°C 'fire' variety.

Baden-Baden

🛏 Sleeping

Baden-Baden is crammed with hotels but bargains are rare. The tourist office has a room-reservation service, for which a 10% fee is deducted from the cost of the room.

Hotel am Markt
HISTORIC HOTEL $

(Map p332; ☎270 40; www.hotel-am-markt-baden. de; Marktplatz 18; s €37-53 d €70-92; P@🖤) Sitting pretty in front of the Stiftskirche, this 250-year-old hotel has 23 homely, well-kept rooms. It's quiet up here apart from your wake-up call of church bells, but then you wouldn't want to miss out on the great breakfast.

Heiligenstein
HOTEL $$

(☎07223-961 40; www.hotel-heiligenstein.de; Heiligensteinstrasse 19a; s €78-82, d €113-118; P) It's worth going the extra mile (or seven) to this sweet hotel overlooking vineyards. Slick, earthy-hued rooms come with balconies and guests can put their feet up in the spa and gardens. The highly regarded **restaurant** (mains €15 to €27) serves local, seasonally inspired fare, from homemade *Maultaschen* to venison ragout.

Rathausglöckel
HOTEL $$

(Map p332; ☎906 10; www.rathausgloeckel.de; Steinstrasse 7; s €77-100, €110-139; @🖤) Down the hill from the Stiftskirche, this family-run hotel occupies a 16th-century town house. The recently renovated rooms (some with rooftop views) are dressed in muted tones with pine furniture.

Hotel Belle Epoque
LUXURY HOTEL $$$

(Map p332; ☎300 660; www.hotel-belle-epoque. de; Maria-Viktoria-Strasse 2c; s €170-245, d €225-299; 🖤) Nestling in manicured parkland, this neo-Renaissance villa is one of Baden-Baden's most characterful five-star pads. Antiques lend a dash of old-world opulence to the individually designed rooms. Rates include high tea, with scones and cakes and fine brews served on the terrace or by the fireplace.

Hotel Beek
B&B $$

(Map p332; ☎367 60; www.hotel-beek.de; Gernsbacherstrasse 44-46; s €85-95, d €109-119; @) On a tree-fringed street in the heart of town, this pretty-in-pink hotel doubles as an excellent patisserie, going strong since 1885. Facing either a courtyard or the Neues Schloss, the bright rooms sport comfy beds; the best ones (for a price hike) come with balconies.

🍴 Eating

Rizzi
ITALIAN $$$

(Map p332; ☎258 38; Augustaplatz 1; mains €18-25; ⊙noon-1am) A summertime favourite, this pink villa's tree-shaded patio faces Lichtentaler Allee. Italian-influenced dishes like osso buco (veal shanks braised with vegetables, garlic and wine) and scallops with truffle mash pair well with local wines. The €7.90 lunch is a steal.

La Provence
FRENCH $$$

(Map p332; ☎216 515; Schlossstrasse 20; mains €13.50-25; ⊙5pm-1am Mon-Fri, noon-1am Sat

DON'T MISS

SILENT HEIGHTS

Escape the crowds and enjoy the view at these Baden-Baden lookouts.

Neues Schloss (Map p332; Schlossstrasse) Vine-swathed steps lead from Marktplatz to the 15th-century Neues Schloss, the former residence of the Baden-Baden margraves, which is set to reopen as a luxury hotel in 2013. The lookout affords far-reaching views over Baden-Baden's rooftops and spires to the Black Forest beyond.

Mt Merkur Though modest in height, this 668m peak commands wide-screen views of Baden-Baden and the Murg Valley. It's a popular spot for paragliding, gentle hiking and family picnics. Buses 204 and 205 stop near the **funicular** (one-way/rtn €2/4 ⊙10am-10pm), which has been trundling to the top since 1913.

Florentinerberg (Map p332) The Romans used to cool off here; check out the ruins of the original baths at the foot of the hill. Nowadays, the serene botanical gardens nurture wisteria, cypress trees, orange and lemon groves.

Paradies am Annaberg (Map p332) These Italianate gardens are the perfect spot to unwind in, with their soothing fountains and waterfalls. There are fine views of the Altstadt and wooded hills from these heights. Bus 205 to Friedrichshöhe runs nearby.

& Sun) Housed in the Neues Schloss wine cellar, the vaulted ceilings, art nouveau mirrors and sense of humour at La Provence complement the French cuisine. Specialities like garlicky snails, frogs' legs and chateaubriand are spot-on.

Café König CAFE $
(Map p332; Lichtentaler Strasse 12; cake €3.50-5; ⊙9.30am-6.30am Mon-Sat, 10.30am-6.30pm Sun) Liszt and Tolstoy once sipped coffee at this venerable cafe, which has been doing a brisk trade in Baden-Baden's finest cakes, tortes, pralines and truffles for 250 years. Black forest gateau topped with clouds of cream, fresh berry tarts, moist nut cakes – oh, decisions!

La Casserole FRENCH $$$
(Map p332; ✆222 21; Gernsbacherstrasse 18; mains €12-18; ⊙closed Mon, Sun lunch) Lace curtains, cheek-by-jowl tables and flickering candles create the classic bistro tableau at intimate La Casserole. Go for satisfying Alsatian specialities like beef cheeks braised in Pinot noir until tender, served with *Spätzle* (thick egg-based noodles).

Weinstube im Baldreit GERMAN $$$
(Map p332; ✆231 36; Küferstrasse 3; mains €12.50-19; ⊙5-10pm Mon-Sat) Tucked down cobbled lanes, this wine cellar restaurant is tricky to find, but persevere. Baden-Alsatian fare such as *Flammkuchen* topped with Black Forest ham, Roquefort and pears is expertly matched with local wines. Eat in the ivyswathed courtyard in summer, the vaulted interior in winter.

Rathausglöckl GERMAN $$
(✆906 10; Steinstrasse 7; mains €10-16; ⊙6-11pm Mon-Sat, 11.30am-2pm & 6-11pm Sun, closed Wed; ✍🖶) Strong on old-school charm, this lowbeamed tavern is cosily clad in dark wood and oil paintings. Historic regional and German dishes are on the menu, from *Himmel und Erde* (black pudding, mashed potatoes, apple sauce and fried onions) to stuffed quail with *Schupfnudeln* (stubby potato noodles with sauerkraut).

Kaffeehaus Baden-Baden CAFE $
(Map p332; Gernsbacherstrasse 24; snacks €3-6; ⊙9.30am-6pm Mon-Fri, 10.30am-6pm Sat, 1-6pm Sun) The aroma of freshly roasted coffee fills this artsy cafe, a laid-back spot for an espresso and slice of tart. Its shop sells organic preserves and handmade ceramics.

☆ Entertainment

Ensconced in an historic train station and fabled for its acoustics, the **Festspielhaus** (Map p332; ✆301 3101; www.festspielhaus.de; Beim Alten Bahnhof 2, Robert-Schumann-Platz) is Europe's second biggest concert hall, seating 2500 theatre-goers, and a lavish tribute to Baden-Baden's musical heritage. Under the direction of Andreas Mölich-Zebhauser, the grand venue hosts a world-class program of concerts, opera and ballet.

The revered **Baden-Badener Philharmonie** (Map p332; ✆932 791; www.philharmonie.baden-baden.de; Solms-Strasse 1) frequently performs in the Kurhaus.

ℹ Information

Branch tourist office (Kaiserallee 3; ☺10am-5pm Mon-Sat, 2-5pm Sun) In the Trinkhalle. Sells events tickets.

Main tourist office (☏275 200; www.baden-baden.com; Schwarzwaldstrasse 52; ☺9am-6pm Mon-Sat, to 1pm Sun) Situated 2km northwest of the centre. If you're driving from the northwest (from the A5) this place is on the way into town. Sells events tickets.

Post office (Lange Strasse 44) Inside Kaufhaus Wagener.

ℹ Getting There & Away

Karlsruhe-Baden-Baden airport (p307), 15km west of town, is linked to London and other European cities by Ryanair.

Buses to Black Forest destinations depart from the bus station, next to the Bahnhof.

Baden-Baden is close to the A5 (Frankfurt–Basel autobahn) and is the northern starting point of the zigzagging Schwarzwald-Hochstrasse, which follows the B500.

Baden-Baden is on a major north–south rail corridor. Twice-hourly destinations include Freiburg (€19.20 to €28, 45 to 90 minutes) and Karlsruhe (€10 to €15, 15 to 30 minutes).

ℹ Getting Around

BUS Local buses run by **Stadtwerke Baden-Baden** (www.stadtwerke-baden-baden.de) cost €2.20/5.20 for a single/24-hour ticket. A day pass for up to five people is €8.20. Bus 201 (every 10 minutes) and other lines link the Bahnhof with Leopoldsplatz. Bus 205 runs roughly hourly between the Bahnhof and the airport, less frequently at weekends.

CAR & MOTORCYCLE The centre is mostly pedestrianised, so it's best to park and walk. There is a free Park & Ride at the Bahnhof. Closer to the centre, the cheapest car park is at the Festspielhaus (€0.70 per hour). Michaelstunnel on the D500 routes traffic away from the centre, ducking underground west of the Festspielhaus and resurfacing just south of the Russische Kirche.

Karlsruhe

☏0721 / POP 294,760

When planning this radial city in 1715, the Margraves of Baden placed a mighty baroque palace smack in the middle – an urban layout so impressive it became the blueprint for Washington DC.

Laid-back and cultured, Karlsruhe grows on you the longer you linger, with its rambling parks, museums crammed with futuristic gizmos and French Impressionist paintings. The suburbs dotted with art nouveau town houses are a reminder that France is just 15km away. Some 20,000 students keep the beer cheap and the vibe upbeat in the pubs and the wheels of innovation in culture and technology turning.

◉ Sights & Activities

TOP CHOICE Schloss   PALACE

From the baroque-meets-neoclassical Schloss, Karlsruhe's 32 streets radiate like the spokes of a wheel. Karl Wilhelm Margrave of Baden-Durlach named his epicentral palace Karlsruhe (Karl's retreat) when founding the city in 1715. Destroyed in the war, the grand palace was sensitively rebuilt. In warm weather, locals play pétanque on the fountain-strewn Schlossplatz parterre.

The treasure-trove **Badisches Landesmuseum** (www.landesmuseum.de; adult/concession €4/3, after 2pm Fri free; ☺10am-5pm Tue-Thu, to 6pm Fri-Sun), inside the Schloss, shelters the jewel-encrusted crown of Baden's grand-ducal ruling family, and spoils of war from victorious battles against the Turks in the 17th century. Scale the tower for a better look at Karlsruhe's circular layout and for views to the Black Forest.

Edging north, the Schlossgarten is a popular student hang-out and a relaxed spot for walks and picnics.

Kunsthalle Karlsruhe   GALLERY

(www.kunsthalle-karlsruhe.de; Hans-Thoma-Strasse 2-6; adult/concession €8/6, Orangerie €4/2.50; ☺10am-5pm Tue-Fri, to 6pm Sat & Sun) The outstanding State Art Gallery presents a world-class collection; from the canvases of late-Gothic German masters like Matthias Grünewald and Lucas Cranach the Elder to Impressionist paintings by Degas, Monet and Renoir. Step across to the Orangerie to view works by German artists like Georg Baselitz and Gerhard Richter.

Marktplatz   SQUARE

The grand neoclassical Marktplatz is dominated by the Ionic portico of the 19th-century Evangelische Stadtkirche and the dusky-pink Rathaus. The iconic red-stone pyramid is an incongruous tribute to Karl Wilhelm Margrave of Baden-Durlach and marks his tomb.

At its northern tip, Museum beim Markt (Karl-Friedrich-Strasse 6; adult/concession €2/1, after 2pm Fri free; ☺11am-5pm Tue-Thu, 10am-6pm

A WALK IN THE BLACK FOREST

As locals will tell you, you need to hit the trail to really see the **Black Forest** (www.black forest-tourism.com; SchwarzwaldCard adult/child/family €37/€27/€113). From gentle half-day strolls to multi-day treks, we've cherry-picked the region for a few of our favourites.

Panoramaweg (40km) If you want to appreciate Baden-Baden and the northern Black Forest from its most photogenic angles, walk all or part of this high-level ridge trail, weaving past waterfalls and viewpoints through orchards and woodlands.

Gütenbach-Simonswäldertal (13km) Tucked-away Gütenbach, 22km south of Triberg, is the trailhead for one of the Black Forest's most beautiful half-day hikes. From here a forest trail threads to Balzer Herrgott, where a sandstone figure of Christ has grown into a tree. Walking downhill from here to Simonswälder Valley, fir-draped hills rise like a curtain before you. Return by veering north to Teichsschlucht gorge, where a brook cascades through primeval forest lined by sheer cliffs and moss-strewn boulders. Head upstream to return to Gütenbach.

Westweg (280km) Up for an adventure? This famous long-distance trail, marked with a red diamond, stretches from Pforzheim in the Northern Black Forest to Basel, Switzerland. Highlights feature the steep Murg Valley, Titisee and Feldberg. See www.westweg.de (in German) for maps and details.

Wutachschlucht (13km) This wild gorge, carved out by a fast-flowing river and flanked by near-vertical rock faces, lies near Bonndorf, close to the Swiss border and 15km east of Schluchsee. The best way to experience its unique microclimate, where you might spot orchids, ferns, rare butterflies and lizards, is on this trail leading from Schatten-mühle to Wutachmühle. For more details, visit the website www.wutachschlucht.de (in German).

Feldberg Steig (12km) Orbiting Feldberg, the Black Forest's highest peak at 1493m, this walk traverses a nature reserve that's home to chamois and wildflowers. On clear days, the views of the Alps are glorious. It's possible to snowshoe part of this route in winter.

Martinskapelle (10km) A scenic and easygoing walk, this 10km loop begins at hilltop chapel Martinskapelle, which sits 11km southwest of Triberg. The well-marked path wriggles through forest to tower-topped Brendturm (1149m) which affords views reaching from Feldberg to the Vosges and Alps on cloud-free days. Continue via Brendhäusle and Rosseck for a stunning vista of overlapping mountains and forest.

Fri-Sun) contains a stash of post-1900 applied arts, from art nouveau to Bauhaus.

Zentrum für Kunst und Medientechnologie   MUSEUM

Set in a historic munitions factory, the **ZKM** (www.zkm.de; Lorenzstrasse 19; ⊙10am-6pm Wed-Fri, 11am-6pm Sat & Sun) is a mammoth exhibition and research complex fusing art and emerging electronic media technologies.

The interactive **Medienmuseum** (Media Museum; adult/concession €5/3, after 2pm Fri free) has media art displays, including a computer-generated 'legible city' and real-time bubble simulations. The **Museum für Neue Kunst** (adult/concession €5/3, incl the Medienmuseum €8/5, after 2pm Fri free) hosts first-rate temporary exhibitions of post-1960 art.

Served by tram 2E, the ZKM is 2km southwest of the Schloss and a similar distance northwest of the Hauptbahnhof.

Botanischer Garten   GARDEN

(Hans-Thoma-Strasse 6; garden admission free, greenhouses adult/concession €2.20/1.10; ⊙10am-6pm) Lush with exotic foliage, the Botanischer Garten is speckled with greenhouses – one with a giant Victoria waterlily.

Museum in der Majolika   MUSEUM

(Ahaweg 6; adult/concession €2/1; ⊙10am-1pm & 2-5pm Tue-Sun) A line of 1645 blue majolica tiles, called the **Blaue Linie**, connects the Schloss to the Museum in der Majolika, exhibiting glazed ceramics made in Karlsruhe since 1901.

🛏 Sleeping

Mainly geared towards corporate functions, Karlsruhe's hotels don't rank too highly on the charm-o-meter. Ask the tourist office for a list of private guesthouses.

Hotel Rio HOTEL **$$**
(📞840 80; www.hotel-rio.de; Hans-Sachs-Strasse 2; s €70-108, d €86-125; [P][🛜]) Service can be brusque but this is still one of your best bets for spotless, contemporary quarters in Karlsruhe. Breakfast is worth the extra €6 – eggs, salmon, the works. Take the tram to Mühlburger Tor.

Acora Hotel HOTEL **$$$**
(📞850 90; www.acora.de; Sophienstrasse 69-71; s €99-144, d €119-179; [P][🛜]) Chirpy staff make you feel right at home at this apartment-hotel, featuring bright, modern rooms equipped with kitchenettes.

Hotel Avisa HOTEL **$$**
(📞349 77; www.hotel-avisa.de; Am Stadtgarten 5; s/d from €85/120; [P][🛜]) Spruce rooms with free wi-fi are the deal at this family-run hotel, two blocks northeast of the Hauptbahnhof.

🍴 Eating & Drinking

Vogelbräu BREWPUB **$$**
(Kapellenstrasse 50; mains €6.50-13; ⊙10am-midnight Sun-Thu, to 1am Fri & Sat) Quaff a cold one with regulars by the copper vats or in the leafy beer garden of this microbrewery. The unfiltered house pils washes down hale and hearty food like Berlin-style beef liver with mash and onions.

Oberländer Weinstuben GERMAN **$$$**
(📞250 66; www.oberlaender-weinstube.de; Akademiestrasse 7; 3-course lunch €35, mains €34-37; ⊙Tue-Sat) Special occasion? Book a table at this Michelin-starred restaurant, combining a cosy wood-panelled tavern and a flowery courtyard. Fine wines marry perfectly with signatures like meltingly tender lamb with aubergines and peppers – cooked with flair, served with finesse.

Die Kippe PUB **$**
(Gottesauer Strasse 23; daily special €3.90; ⊙8am-1am, to 2am Fri & Sat) Every student has a tale about the 'dog end', named after the free tobacco behind the bar. Wallet-friendly daily specials skip from schnitzel to plaice with potato salad. There's live music a couple of times weekly, as well as bingo and quiz

nights. The beer garden has a great buzz in summer. Take tram 1 or 2 to Durlacher Tor.

Moccasin CAFE **$**
(Ritterstrasse 6; snacks €2-5; ⊙daily) Go for a mango smoothie, bagel or coffee with a cherry-studded Black Forest muffin.

Bray Head PUB **$**
(Kapellenstrasse 40; mains €5.90-7.90; ⊙4pm-btwn 1am & 3am; 🛜) Home-brewed stout goes down a treat with grub such as Irish stew and fish and chips at this convivial pub, with regular live music and quiz nights.

ℹ Information

Hauptbahnhof tourist office (📞3720 5383; www.karlsruhe-tourism.de; Bahnhofplatz 6; ⊙8.30am-6pm Mon-Fri, 9am-1pm Sat) Across the street from the Hauptbahnhof. The iGuide (€7.50) is a self-guided audiovisual walking tour of the centre lasting four hours. Also sells the Karlsruher WelcomeCard (24-/48-/72-hour card €5.50/10.50/15.50) for free or discounted entry to museums and other attractions.
Post office (Poststrasse) Just east of the Hauptbahnhof.

ℹ Getting There & Away

Destinations well-served by train include Baden-Baden (€10 to €15, 15 to 30 minutes) and Freiburg (€24.70 to €34, one to two hours).

Karlsruhe is on the A5 (Frankfurt–Basel) and is the starting point of the A8 to Munich. There are Park & Ride options outside of the city centre; look for 'P+R' signs.

ℹ Getting Around

The Hauptbahnhof is linked to the Marktplatz, 2km north, by tram and light-rail lines 2, 3, S1, S11, S4 and S41. Single tickets cost €2.20; a 24-Stunden-Karte costs €5.20 (€8.20 for up to five people).

A relaxed and ecofriendly way to explore Karlsruhe is by bike. Deutsche Bahn has Call-a-Bike stands across the city.

Freudenstadt

📞07441 / POP 23,550
Duke Friedrich I of Württemberg built a new capital here in 1599, which was bombed to bits in WWII. The upshot is that Freudenstadt's centre is underwhelming, though its magnificent setting in the Black Forest is anything but. That said, statistic lovers will delight in ticking off Germany's biggest square (216m by 219m, for the record),

dislocated by a T-junction of heavily trafficked roads.

Freudenstadt marks the southern end of the Schwarzwald-Hochstrasse and is a terminus of the gorgeous Schwarzwald-Tälerstrasse, which runs from Rastatt via Alpirsbach.

⊙ Sights

Stadtkirche
CHURCH

(⊘10am-5pm) In the southwest corner of Marktplatz looms the 17th-century red-sandstone Stadtkirche, with an ornate 12th-century Cluniac-style baptismal font, Gothic windows, Renaissance portals and baroque towers. The two naves are at right angles to each other, an unusual design by the geometrically minded duke.

🕴 Activities

While you won't linger for Freudenstadt's sights, the deep forested valleys on its fringes are worth exploring. Scenic hiking trails include a 12km uphill walk to Kniebis on the Schwarzwald-Hochstrasse, where there are superb Kinzig Valley views. Ask the tourist office for details.

Jump on a mountain bike to tackle routes like the 85km Kinzigtal-Radweg, taking in dreamy landscapes and half-timbered villages, or the 60km Murgtal-Radweg over hill and dale to Rastatt. Both valleys have bike trails and it's possible to return to Freudenstadt by train.

Intersport Glaser
BICYCLE RENTAL

(Katharinenstrasse 8; bike rental per day €14-20; ⊘9.30am-6.30pm Mon-Fri, to 4pm Sat) A couple of blocks north of Marktplatz, this outlet hires mountain bikes.

Panorama-Bad
SWIMMING

(www.panorama-bad.de; Ludwig-Jahn-Strasse 60; 3hr pass adult/concession €6.70/5.80; ⊘9am-10pm Mon-Sat, to 8pm Sun) The glass-fronted Panorama-Bad is a relaxation magnet with pools, steam baths and saunas.

🛌 Sleeping & Eating

At the heart of Freudenstadt, the sprawling, arcaded Marktplatz harbours rows of shops and cafes with alfresco seating.

Warteck
HOTEL $$

(☏919 20; www.warteck-freudenstadt.de; Stuttgarterstrasse 14; s €55-70, d €88-98, mains €14.50-39; 🛜) In the capable hands of the Glässel family since 1894, this hotel sports modern, gleamingly clean rooms. The real draw, however, is the wood-panelled restaurant, serving market-fresh fare like beetroot tortellini and rack of venison with wild mushrooms.

Hotel Adler
HOTEL $$

(☏915 20; www.adler-fds.de; Forststrasse 15-17; s €45-53, d €74-90, mains €12 to €17; P🛜) This family-run hotel near Marktplace has well-kept, recently renovated rooms and rents out e-bikes for €9/16 per half-/full day. The restaurant dishes up appetising regional grub such as Zwiebelrostbraten (roast beef with onions).

Camping Langenwald
CAMPGROUND $

(☏2862; www.camping-langenwald.de; Strasburger Strasse 167; per person/tent €7/8.50; ⊘Easter-Oct; ⊛) With a solar-heated pool and nature trail, this leafy site has impeccable eco credentials. It's served by bus 12 to Kniebis.

Turmbräu
GERMAN $$

(Marktplatz 64; mains €7-17; ⊘11am-midnight, to 3am Fri & Sat) This lively microbrewery doubles as a beer garden. Pull up a chair in ye-olde barn to munch Maultaschen and guzzle Turmbräu brews – a 5L barrel costs €14.

ⓘ Information

Tourist office (☏8640; www.freudenstadt.de; Marktplatz 64; ⊘9am-6pm Mon-Fri, 10am-3pm Sat & Sun; 🛜) Has an internet terminal (per 5/60min €0.50/6). Hotel reservations are free.

ⓘ Getting There & Away

Freudenstadt's focal point is the Marktplatz on the B28. The town has two train stations: the Stadtbahnhof, five minutes' walk north of Marktplatz, and the Hauptbahnhof, 2km southeast of Marktplatz at the end of Bahnhofstrasse.

Trains on the Ortenau line, serving Offenburg and Strasbourg, depart hourly from the Hauptbahnhof and are covered by the 24-hour Europass. The pass represents excellent value, costing €10.40 for individuals and €16.70 for families. Trains go roughly hourly to Karlsruhe (€16.40, 1½ to two hours) from the Stadtbahnhof and Hauptbahnhof.

Kinzigtal

Shaped like a horseshoe, the Kinzigtal (Kinzig Valley) begins south of Freudenstadt and shadows the babbling Kinzig River south to Schiltach, west to Haslach and north to Offenburg. Near Strasbourg, 95km downriver, the Kinzig is swallowed up by the mighty Rhine. The valley's inhabitants survived for centuries on mining and shipping goods by raft.

WORTH A TRIP

REACH FOR THE STARS

Swinging along country lanes 6km north of Freudenstadt brings you to Baiersbronn. It looks like any other Black Forest town, snuggled among meadows and wooded hills. But on its fringes sit two of Germany's finest restaurants, both holders of the coveted three Michelin stars.

First up is the Schwarzwaldstube (07442-4920; www.traube-tonbach.de; Tonbach-strasse 237, Baiersbronn-Tonbach; menus €155-189; closed Mon, Tue, lunch Wed), with big forest views from its rustically elegant dining room. Here Harald Wohlfahrt performs culinary magic, staying true to the best traditions of French cooking, sourcing carefully and adding his own creative flourishes. The tasting menu goes with the seasons but you might begin with a palate-awakening carpaccio of wild salmon and scallops with ginger-lime marinade, say, followed by saddle of venison served two ways. If you fancy getting behind the stove, sign up for one of the cookery classes (€140-180; 10am Mon & Tue), which revolve around a theme such as cooking with crustaceans, asparagus, goose or truffles, or techniques like pasta-making and preparing pâtés.

Equally legendary is the Restaurant Bareiss (07442-470; www.bareiss.com; Gärten-bühlweg 14, Baiersbronn-Mitteltal; menus €125-185; Wed-Sun). Claus-Peter Lumpp has consistently won plaudits for his brilliantly composed, French-inflected menus. On paper, dishes such as braised Bresse chicken with nut-butter foam and almond macaroon with pineapple and dill seem deceptively simple; on the plate they become things of beauty, rich in textures and aromas and presented with an artist's eye for detail.

This Black Forest valley is astonishingly pretty, its hills brushed with thick larch and spruce forest and its half-timbered villages looking freshly minted for a fairy-tale. For seasonal colour, come in in autumn (foliage) or spring (fruit blossom).

❶ Getting There & Away

The B294 follows the Kinzig from Freudenstadt to Haslach, from where the B33 leads north to Offenburg. If you're going south, pick up the B33 to Triberg and beyond in Hausach.

An hourly train line links Freudenstadt with Offenburg (€14.40, 1¼ hours), stopping in Alpirsbach (€3.25, 16 minutes), Schiltach (€5.50, 27 minutes), Hausach (€7.50, 43 minutes), Haslach (€9.10, 49 minutes) and Gengenbach (€12.20, one hour). From Hausach, trains run roughly hourly southeast to Triberg (€5.50, 22 minutes), Villingen (€11.10, 47 minutes) and Konstanz (€27.10, two hours).

Alpirsbach

07444 / POP 6580

Lore has it that Alpirsbach is named after a quaffing cleric who, when a glass of beer slipped clumsily from his hand and rolled into the river, exclaimed: *All Bier ist in den Bach!* (All the beer is in the stream!). A prophecy, it seems, as today Alpirsbacher

Klosterbräu is brewed from pure spring water. Brewery tours (670; www.alpirsbacher .com; Marktplatz 1; tours €6.90; 2.30pm daily) are in German, though guides may speak English. Two beers are thrown in for the price of a ticket.

A few paces north, you can watch chocolate being made and scoff delectable beer-filled pralines at Schau-Confiserie Heinzelmann (Ambrosius-Blarer-Platz 2; 9am-12pm & 2-6pm Mon-Fri, to 5pm Sat).

All the more evocative for its lack of adornment, the 11th-century former Benedictine Kloster Alpirsbach (adult/concession €4/3.30; 10am-5.30pm Mon-Sat & 11am-5.30pm Sun) sits opposite. The monastery effectively conveys the simple, spiritual life in its flat-roofed church, spartan cells and Gothic cloister, which hosts candlelit concerts (www.kreuzgangkonzerte.de) from June to August. It's amazing what you can find under the floorboards, as the museum reveals with its stash of 16th-century clothing, caricatures (of artistic scholars) and lines (of misbehaving ones).

The tourist office (951 6281; www.stadt -alpirsbach.de; Krähenbadstrasse 2; 10am-noon & 2-5pm Mon-Fri, closed Wed afternoon) can supply hiking maps and, for cyclists, information on the 85km Kinzigtalradweg from Offen-burg to Lossburg.

Schiltach

☎07836 / POP 3880

Sitting smugly at the foot of wooded hills and on the banks of the Kinzig and Schiltach Rivers, medieval Schiltach looks too perfect to be true. The meticulously restored half-timbered houses, which once belonged to tanners, merchants and raft builders, are a riot of crimson geraniums in summer.

Sights & Activities

Altstadt NEIGHBOURHOOD

Centred on a trickling fountain, the sloping, triangular **Marktplatz** is Schiltach at its picture-book best. The frescoes of the step-gabled, 16th-century **Rathaus** opposite depict scenes from local history. Clamber south up **Schlossbergstrasse**, pausing to notice the plaques that denote the trades of one-time residents, such as the *Strumpfstricker* (stocking weaver) at No 6, and the sloping roofs where tanners once dried their skins. Up top there are views over Schiltach's red rooftops. Because Schiltach is at the confluence of the **Kinzig** and **Schiltach Rivers**, logging was big business until the 19th century and huge rafts were built to ship timber as far as the Netherlands. The willow-fringed banks now attract grey herons and kids who come to splash in the shallows when the sun's out.

FREE **Museum am Markt** MUSEUM

(Marktplatz 13; ⏲11am-5pm daily Apr-Oct, Sat & Sun only Nov-Mar) Museum am Markt is crammed with everything from antique spinning wheels to Biedermeier costumes. Highlights include the cobbler's workshop and an interactive display recounting the tale of the devilish Teufel von Schiltach.

FREE **Schüttesäge Museum** MUSEUM

(Gerbegasse; ⏲11am-5pm daily Apr-Oct, Sat & Sun only Nov-Mar) The Schüttesäge Museum focuses on Schiltach's rafting tradition with reconstructed workshops, a watermill generating hydroelectric power for many homes in the area and touchy-feely exhibits for kids, from different kinds of bark to forest animals.

Sleeping & Eating

TOP CHOICE **Weysses Rössle** GUESTHOUSE $

(☎387; www.weysses-roessle.de; Schenkenzeller Strasse 42; s/d €52/75; P 📶) Rosemarie and Ulrich continue the tradition of 19 generations in this 16th-century inn. Countrified rooms decorated with rosewood and floral fabrics also feature snazzy bathrooms and wi-fi. Its restaurant uses locally sourced, organic fare.

Zur Alten Brücke GUESTHOUSE $$

(☎20 36; www.altebruecke.de; Schramberger Strasse 13; s/d/apt €59/89/109; P 📶) You'll receive a warm welcome from Michael, Lisa and dog Max at this riverside guest house. The pick of the bright, cheery rooms overlook the Schiltach. Michael cooks up seasonal, regional fare in the kitchen and there's a terrace for summer imbibing.

Campingplatz Schiltach CAMPGROUND $

(☎7289; Bahnhofstrasse 6; per person/tent/car €5/3.50/3; ⏲Apr-Oct) Beautifully positioned on the banks of the Kinzig, this campground has impeccable eco credentials and a playground and sandpit for kids.

Information

The **tourist office** (☎5850; www.schiltach.de; Marktplatz 6; ⏲9am-noon & 2-4pm Mon-Thu, 9am-noon Fri) in the Rathaus can help find accommodation and offers free internet access. Hiking options are marked on an enamel sign just opposite.

Gutach

☎07831 / POP 2180

Worth the 4km detour south of the Kinzig Valley, the **Schwarzwälder Freilichtmuseum** (www.vogtsbauernhof.org; adult/concession/child/family €8/7/4.50/18; ⏲9am-6pm late Mar-early Nov, to 7pm Aug) spirals around the Vogtsbauernhof, an early-17th-century farmstead. Farmhouses shifted from their original locations have been painstakingly reconstructed, using techniques such as thatching and panelling, to create this authentic farming hamlet and preserve age-old Black Forest traditions.

Explore barns filled with wagons and horn sleds, *Rauchküchen* (kitchens for smoking fish and meat) and the Hippenseppenhof (1599), with its chapel and massive hipped roof constructed from 400 trees. It's a great place for families, with inquisitive farmyard animals to pet, artisans on hand to explain their crafts and frequent demonstrations from sheep shearing to butter-making.

The self-controlled bobs of the **Schwarzwald Rodelbahn** (Black Forest Toboggan Run; Singersbach 4; adult/child €2.50/2; ⏲9am-6pm Mar-early Nov), 1.5km north of Gutach, are faster than they look. Lay off the brakes for extra speed.

Haslach

☑ 07832 / POP 6980

Back in the Kinzig Valley, Haslach's 17th-century former Capuchin monastery lodges the Schwarzwälder Trachtenmuseum (Black Forest Costume Museum; Im Alten Kapuzinerkloster; adult/concession €2/1.50; ☉10am-12.30pm & 1.30-5pm Tue-Sun), showcasing flamboyant costumes and outrageous hats, the must-have accessories for the well-dressed Fräulein of the 1850s. Look out for the Black Forest *Bollenhut*, a straw bonnet topped with pompons (red for unmarried women, black for married) and the *Schäppel*, a fragile-looking crown made from hundreds of beads and weighing up to 5kg.

DON'T MISS

BEHOLD THE SUPER BOG

If giant cuckoo clocks and black forest gateau no longer thrill, how about a trip to the world's largest loo? Drive a couple of minutes south of Gutach on the B33 to Hornberg and there, in all its lavatorial glory, stands the titanic toilet dreamed up by Philippe Starck. Even if you have no interest in designer urinals or home jacuzzis, it's worth visiting the Duravit Design Centre (www.duravit.de; Werderstrasse 36; ☉8am-6pm Mon-Fri, 12-4pm Sat) for the tremendous view across the Black Forest from the 12m-high ceramic loo.

Gengenbach

☑ 07803 / POP 11,020

If ever a Black Forest town could be described as chocolate box, it would surely be Gengenbach, with its scrumptious Altstadt of half-timbered town houses framed by vineyards and orchards. It's fitting, then, that director Tim Burton made this the home of gluttonous Augustus Gloop in the 2005 blockbuster *Charlie and the Chocolate Factory* (though less so that he called it Düsseldorf).

◉ Sights & Activities

The best way to discover Gengenbach's historic centre is with a saunter through its narrow backstreets, such as the gently curving Engelgasse, off Hauptstrasse, lined with listed half-timbered houses draped in vines and bedecked with scarlet geraniums. Between the town's two tower-topped gates sits the triangular Marktplatz, dominated by the Rathaus, an 18th-century, pink-and-cream confection. The fountain bears a statue of a knight, a symbol of Gengenbach's medieval status as a Free Imperial City.

Amble east along Klosterstrasse to spy the former Benedictine monastery. Opposite, the stuck-in-time Holzofen-Bäckerei Klostermühle (Klosterstrasse 7; ☉7am-6pm Mon-Fri, to noon Sat) fills the lanes with wafts of freshly baked bread from its wood-fired oven. Buy a loaf to munch in the calm Kräutergarten (Herb Garden; Benedikt-von-Nursia-Strasse) or stroll east to the flowery park.

The tourist office has info on the hour-long Weinpfad, a wine trail beginning in the Altstadt that threads through terraced vineyards to the Jakobskapelle, a 13th-century chapel commanding views that reach as far as Strasbourg on clear days. The free, lantern-lit Nachtwächterrundgang (night watchman's tour) starts at the Rathaus on Wednesday and Saturday at 10pm from May to July and at 9pm from August to October.

🛏 Sleeping & Eating

Pfeffermühle B&B $
(☑933 50; www.pfeffermuehle-gengenbach.de; Oberdorfstrasse 24; s/d €50/78, mains €14-22) In a snug half-timbered house dating to 1476, close to one of the Altstadt gate towers, this neat-and-tidy B&B is a bargain. Decorated with antique knick-knacks, the wood-panelled restaurant features among the town's best, dishing out regional favourites like Black Forest trout and *Sauerbraten* (sweet-sour pot roast).

DJH Hostel HOSTEL $
(☑0781-317 49; www.jugendherberge-schloss-ortenberg.de; Burgweg 21; dm €21.70) The Hogwarts gang would feel at home in 12th-century Schloss Ortenberg, rebuilt in whimsical neo-Gothic style complete with lookout tower and wood-panelled dining hall. A staircase sweeps up to dorms with Kinzig Valley views. Take bus 7134 to Ortenberger Hof, 500m from the hostel.

Pfeffer & Salz B&B $
(☑934 80; www.pfefferundsalz-gengenbach.de; Mattenhofweg 3; s/d €52/78) This forest farmhouse is a peaceful hideaway 10 minutes' stroll north of the Altstadt. The modern rooms are quite a bargain, jazzed up with warm colours and flat-screen TVs.

DON'T MISS

CHRISTMAS COUNTDOWN

Every December, Gengenbach rekindles childhood memories of opening tiny windows when the Rathaus morphs into the world's biggest advent calendar. At 6pm daily, one of 24 windows is opened to reveal a festive scene. In the past, the tableaux have been painted by well-known artists and children's-book illustrators such as Marc Chagall and Tomi Ungerer. From late November to 23 December, a Christmas market brings extra yuletide sparkle, mulled wine and carols to the Marktplatz.

Winzerstüble GERMAN $
(Hauptstrasse 18; Flammkuchen €6.50-9) In the cobbled courtyard next to the tourist office, this wine tavern serves local produce and wine. Visitors can sample light, crisp *Flammkuchen* with Müller-Thurgau and riesling wines.

 Information

The **tourist office** (☏930 143; www.stadt-gengenbach.de; Im Winzerhof; ☺9am-5pm Mon-Fri) is in a courtyard just off Hauptstrasse.

Freiburg

☏0761 / POP 224,190

Sitting plump at the foot of the Black Forest's wooded slopes and vineyards, Freiburg is a sunny, cheerful university town, its medieval Altstadt a story-book tableau of gabled town houses, cobblestone lanes and cafe-rimmed plazas. Party-loving students spice up the local nightlife.

Blessed with 2000 hours of annual sunshine, this is Germany's warmest city. Indeed, while neighbouring hilltop villages are still shovelling snow, the trees in Freiburg are clouds of white blossom, and locals are already imbibing in canalside beer gardens. This eco-trailblazer has shrewdly tapped into that natural energy to generate nearly as much solar power as the whole of Britain, making it one of the country's greenest cities.

 Sights

Freiburg's medieval past is tangible in back-streets like wisteria-draped Konviktstrasse and in the canalside Fischerau and Gerberau, the former fishing and tanning quarters.

The Dreisam River runs along the Altstadt's southern edge.

Keep an eye out for the cheerful pavement mosaics in front of many shops – a cow is for a butcher, a pretzel for a baker, a diamond marks a jewellery shop, and so on.

TOP CHOICE Münster CATHEDRAL
(Map p344; Münsterplatz; tower adult/concession €1.50/1; ☺10am-5pm Mon-Sat, 1pm-7.30pm Sun, tower 9.30am-5pm Mon-Sat, 1-5pm Sun) Freiburg's 11th-century Münster is the monster of all minsters, a red-sandstone giant that looms above the half-timbered facades framing the square. Its riot of punctured spires and gargoyles flush scarlet in the dusk light.

The main portal is adorned with sculptures depicting scenes from the Old and New Testaments. Nearby are medieval wall markings used to ensure that merchandise (eg loaves of bread) were of the requisite size.

Square at the base, the sturdy tower becomes an octagon higher up and is crowned by a filigreed 116m-high spire. Ascend the tower for an excellent view of the church's intricate construction; on clear days you can spy the Vosges Mountains in France.

Inside the Münster, the kaleidoscopic stained-glass windows dazzle. Many were financed by various guilds – in the bottom panels look for a pretzel, scissors and other symbols of medieval trades. The high altar features a masterful triptych of the coronation of the Virgin Mary by Hans Baldung.

Augustinermuseum MUSEUM
(Map p344; Augustinerplatz 1; adult/concession €6/4; ☺10am-5pm Tue-Sun) Following a recent makeover, this beautiful Augustinian monastery, with origins dating back to 1278, once again showcases a prized collection of medieval, baroque and 19th-century art. Baldung, Matthias Grünewald and Cranach masterpieces grace the gallery and the medieval stained glass ranks among Germany's finest. There is a cafe overlooking the cloister where you can sip a drink and soak up the monastic vibe.

Historisches Kaufhaus LANDMARK
(Map p344; Münsterplatz) Facing the Münster's south side and embellished with polychrome tiled turrets is the arcaded brick-red Historisches Kaufhaus, an early 16th-century merchants' hall. The coats of arms on the oriels and the four figures above the balcony

symbolise Freiburg's allegiance to the House of Habsburg.

City Gates
HISTORIC BUILDING

Freiburg has two intact medieval gates, one of which is the Martinstor (Martin's Gate; Map p344; Kaiser-Joseph-Strasse) rising above Kaiser-Joseph-Strasse. A block east of the Museum of Modern Art is the 13th-century Schwabentor (Map p344) on the Schwabenring, a massive city gate with a mural of St George slaying the dragon and tram tracks running under its arches.

Schlossberg
VIEWPOINT, WALK

(Schlossbergring; cable car one way/return €2.80/5; ⊙9am-10pm, shorter hours in winter) The forested Schlossberg dominates Freiburg. Take the footpath opposite the Schwabentor, leading up through sun-dappled woods, or hitch a ride on the recently restored Schlossbergbahn cable car. If you're keen to do some serious hiking, several trails begin here, including those to St Peter (17km) and Kandel (25km).

The little peak is topped by the ice-cream-cone-shaped Aussichtsturm (lookout tower). From here, Freiburg spreads photogenically before you – the spire of the Münster soaring above a jumble of red gables, framed by the dark hills of the Black Forest.

Rathausplatz
SQUARE

(Town Hall Square; Map p344) Freiburg locals hang out by the fountain in chestnut-shaded Rathausplatz. On its western side, note the red-sandstone, step-gabled Neues Rathaus (New City Hall; Map p344).

Across the way is the mid-16th-century Altes Rathaus (Old City Hall; Map p344; Universtitatstrasse), a flamboyant, ox-blood-red edifice, embellished with gilt swirls and crowned by a clock and a fresco of the twin-headed Habsburg eagle.

On its northern side, the medieval Martinskirche (Map p344) demands attention with its covered cloister. Once part of a Franciscan monastery, the church was severely damaged in WWII; it was rebuilt in the ascetic style typical of this mendicant order.

Haus zum Walfisch
LANDMARK

(House of the Whale; Map p344; Franziskanerstrasse) Across the street from the Martinskirche is its architectural antithesis, the marvellously extravagant Haus zum Walfisch, whose late-Gothic oriel is garnished with two impish gargoyles.

Archäologisches Museum
MUSEUM

(Map p344; www.museen.freiburg.de; Rotteckring 5; adult/concession €2/1; ⊙10am-5pm Tue-Sun) In a sculpture-dotted park sits the neo-Gothic Colombischlössle. Built for the Countess of Colombi in 1859, the whimsical red-sandstone villa now harbours this archaeology-focused museum. From the skylit marble entrance, a cast-iron staircase ascends to a stash of finds, from Celtic grave offerings to Roman artefacts.

Museum für Stadtgeschichte
MUSEUM

(Map p344; Münsterplatz 30; adult/concession €2/1; ⊙10am-5pm Tue-Sun) The sculptor Christian Wentzinger's baroque town house, east of the Historisches Kaufhaus, now shelters this museum, spelling out in artefacts Freiburg's eventful past. Inside, a wrought-iron staircase guides the eye to an elaborate ceiling fresco.

Museum für Neue Kunst
GALLERY

(Map p344; Marienstrasse 10; adult/concession €2/1; ⊙10am-5pm Tue-Sun) Across the Gewerbekanal, this gallery highlights 20th-century expressionist and abstract art, including emotive works by Oskar Kokoschka and Otto Dix.

☞ Tours

If you want to explore the Altstadt at your own pace, two-and-a-half-hour audioguides are available at the tourist office for €9.

Freiburg Kultour
GUIDED TOUR

(Map p344; www.freiburg-kultour.com; Rathausplatz 2-4; adult/concession €8/6; ⊙11.30am Sat) Based in the tourist office, Kultour offers 1½- to two-hour walking tours of the Altstadt and Münster in English. The website lists times for the more frequent tours in German.

> ### COLD FEET OR WEDDED BLISS?
>
> As you wander Freiburg's Altstadt, watch out for the gurgling *Bächle*, streamlets once used to water livestock and extinguish fires. Today they provide welcome relief for hot feet on sweltering summer days. Just be aware that you could get more than you bargained for: legend has it that if you accidentally step into the Bächle, you'll marry a Freiburger or a Freiburgerin.

Freiburg

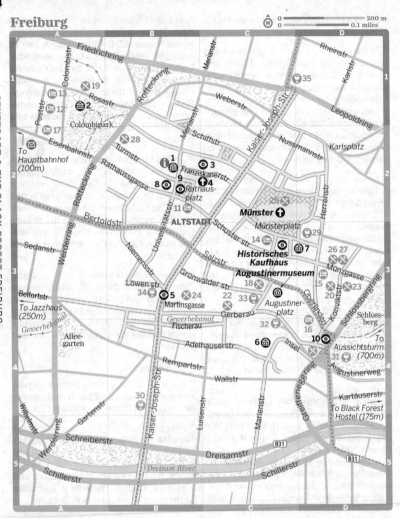

Fahrradtaxi

GUIDED TOUR

(☎947 9595; www.fahrradtaxi-freiburg.de; An der Höhlgasse 5; ☺mid-Apr–Oct) Fahrradtaxi charges €7.50 for a 15-minute, two-person spin of the Altstadt in a pedicab. Call ahead or look for one on Rathausplatz or Münsterplatz.

🛌 Sleeping

Charismatic hotels abound in the Altstadt but it's wise to book ahead in summer. The tourist office offers a booking service (€3) and has a list of good-value private guesthouses.

TOP CHOICE Hotel Oberkirch

HISTORIC HOTEL $$$

(Map p344; ☎202 6868; www.hotel-oberkirch.de; Münsterplatz 22; s €102-123, d €155-169, mains €13-23; P) Wake up to Münster views at this green-shuttered hotel. The country-style rooms feature floral wallpaper and half-canopies over the beds. Oberkirch has an intoxicating 250-year history; during a fire in WWII the hotelier doused the blaze with wine from his cellar. The dark-wood tavern downstairs does a roaring trade in hearty Badisch fare like venison ragout with *Knödel* (dumplings).

Freiburg

Park Hotel Post
HISTORIC HOTEL $$$

(Map p344; ☎385 480; www.park-hotel-post.de; Am Colombipark; s €99-159, d €129-199; P🖥) Slip back to the more graceful age of art nouveau at this refined pile overlooking Colombipark, with summery rooms decorated in pastel blues and yellows. Attentive service and generous breakfasts sweeten the deal.

Hotel Schwarzwälder Hof
HOTEL $$

(Map p344; ☎380 30; www.schwarzwaelder-hof. eu; Herrenstrasse 43; s/d/tr €65/99/120; @) This bijou hotel has an unrivalled style-for-euro ratio. A wrought-iron staircase sweeps up to snazzy rooms that are temples to chalk whites and chocolate browns. Some have postcard views of the Altstadt.

Hotel am Rathaus
HOTEL $$

(Map p344; ☎296 160; www.am-rathaus.de; Rathausgasse 4-8; s €85-95, d €119-129; P🖥) Just a step away from the bustle of Rathausplatz, this neat-and-tidy hotel has spacious, neutral-toned rooms with homely touches like CD and DVD players; ask for a back-facing room if you're a light sleeper. Breakfast is a treat, with smoked salmon and a wide array of bread, cheese and fruit.

Hotel Minerva
HOTEL $$

(Map p344; ☎386 490; www.minerva-freiburg.de; Poststrasse 8; s €85-100, d €115-150; P🖥) All curvaceous windows and polished wood, this art nouveau charmer is five minutes' trudge from the Altstadt. The convivial rooms are painted in sunny shades and feature free wi-fi. The sauna is another plus.

Hotel zum Roten Bären
HISTORIC HOTEL $$$

(Map p344; ☎387 870; www.roter-baeren.de; Oberlinden 12; s €90-133, d €129-184; P@) Billed as Germany's oldest guesthouse, this bubblegum-pink hotel near Schwabentor dates to 1120. Though the vaulted cellar is medieval, rooms are modern, with sleek wood furnishings.

Hotel Barbara
HISTORIC HOTEL $$

(Map p344; ☎296 250; www.hotel-barbara.de; Poststrasse 4; s €74-86, d €102-129, apt €124-189; 🖥) A grandfather clock, curvy staircases and high ceilings give this art nouveau town house a nostalgic feel. It's a homely, family-run place with old-fashioned, pastel-hued rooms and homemade jams at breakfast.

Black Forest Hostel
HOSTEL $

(☑881 7870; www.blackforest-hostel.de; Kartäuserstrasse 33; dm €14-23, s/d €30/50; @) Funky budget digs with chilled common areas, a shared kitchen, bike rental and spacey stainless-steel showers. It's a five-minute walk from the centre of town.

Hirzberg Camping
CAMPGROUND $

(☑350 54; www.freiburg-camping.de; Kartäuserstrasse 99; sites per adult/tent/car €7.80/5/2.50; P🖳🖥) This year-round campground sits in a quiet woodland spot 1.5km east of Schwabentor. It has cooking facilities and bike rental. Take tram 1 to Musikhochschule.

✕ Eating

The Altstadt is stacked with cafes, wine taverns, brewpubs and restaurants, many spilling out onto pavement terraces. You can find cheap bites on Martinstor and Kartäuserstrasse.

Zirbelstube
FRENCH $$$

(Map p344; ☑210 60; www.colombi.de; Rotteckring 16; mains €32-49; ☺Wed-Sun) Freiburg's bastion of fine dining is this candlelit restaurant, decorated in warm Swiss pine. A chef of exacting standards, Alfred Klink allows each ingredient to shine in specialities like poussin with Périgord truffles and Dover sole with caramelised capers, perfectly matched with top wines.

Drexlers
BRASSERIE $$$

(Map p344; ☑595 7203; www.drexlers-restaurant. de; Rosastrasse 9; mains €10-26; ☺closed Sat lunch, Sun; ☖) There's a great lunchtime buzz at this contemporary, high-ceilinged brasserie behind Colombipark. It's an unpretentious, kid-friendly choice, with an ingredient-focused menu homing in on dishes from homemade pasta to herb-crusted lamb.

Kreuzblume
FUSION $$$

(Map p344; ☑311 94; Konviktstrasse 31; mains €22.50-24.50, 3-course menu €36; ☺Wed-Sun) Clever backlighting and a menu fizzing with bright, sunny flavours attract a food-literate clientele to Kreuzblume. Dishes like homesmoked cod with beetroot and anise and zingy lemongrass tart with chilli, mango and yoghurt pack a taste-bud punch.

Wolfshöhle
MEDITERRANEAN $$$

(Map p344; ☑303 03; Konviktstrasse 8; mains €16-27; ☺closed Mon lunch, Sun) With tables set up on a pretty square, Wolfshöhle is a summer-evening magnet. The menu whisks you off on a gastro tour of the Mediterranean, with well-executed dishes like Iberian pork with wild-garlic purée and scampi with saffron-infused risotto.

Englers Weinkrügle
GERMAN $$

(Map p344; ☑383 115; Konviktstrasse 12; mains €9-16; ☺Tue-Sun) A warm, woody Baden-style *Weinstube* (wine tavern) with wisteria growing out front and regional flavours on the menu. The trout in various guises (for instance, with riesling or almond-butter sauce) is delicious.

Enoteca Trattoria
ITALIAN $$$

(Map p344; ☑389 9130; www.enoteca-freiburg. de; Schwabentorplatz 6; mains €15-28; ☺dinner Mon-Sat) This is the trattoria of the two Enoteca twins (the more formal restaurant is at Gerberau 21). The chef here always hits the mark, with authentic Italian dishes such as Taleggio ravioli with Frascati sauce and glazed pear.

Harem
TURKISH $$

(Map p344; Gerberau 7c; mains €6-12; ☺closed Sun) Friendly spot for good-value Turkish specialities such as crisp *börek* (filled pastries).

Chang
THAI $$

(Map p344; Grünwälderstrasse 21; mains €6-9.50; ☺daily) Sweet little Thai for inexpensive daily specials, from green curry to pad thai.

Martin's Bräu
MICROBREWERY $$

(Map p344; Fressgässle 1; mains €9-18; ☺11am-midnight, to 2am Fri & Sat) Homebrewed pilsners wash down meaty snacks like ox tongue salad and half-metre bratwursts.

Münsterplatz Food Market
MARKET $

(Map p344; ☺until 1pm Mon-Fri, to 1.30pm Sat) Bag local goodies sold here (honey, cheese, fruit and the like), or snack on a wurst-in-a-bun topped with fried onions.

Markthalle
FOOD HALL $

(Map p344; Martinsgasse 235; light meals €3-6; ☺8am-8pm, closed Sun) A food court whose Mexican, Italian, Indian, Korean and French counters offer fast, tasty lunches.

Rücker Käse und Wein
DELI $

(Map p344; Münzgasse 1; ☺10am-6.30pm Mon-Fri, 9am-3pm Sat) For wine and cheese.

Drinking & Entertainment

Freiburg's restless student population keep steins a-swinging in the beer gardens and bars and clubs pumping until the wee hours.

Schlappen PUB
(Map p344; Löwenstrasse 2; ⊙11am-btwn 1am & 3am Mon-Sat, 3pm-1am Sun) With its jazz-themed back room and poster-plastered walls, this pub is a perennial favourite. Try one of 10 absinthe varieties and you'll be away with the green fairies. Punters spill onto the terrace in summer.

Alte Wache WINE BAR
(Map p344; Münsterplatz 38; ⊙10am-7pm Mon-Fri, to 4pm Sat) Right on the square, this 18th-century guardhouse serves local Müller-Thurgau and Pinot noir wines at the tasting tables. If they sharpen your appetite, order a tasting plate of cheese and olives.

Freiburg Bar BAR
(Map p344; Kaiser-Joseph-Strasse 278; ⊙daily) This retro-cool bar attracts a mixed, fun-loving crowd with everything from karaoke and quiz nights to '80s and *Schlager* (German pop) parties. If you get hungry, you can also order decent grub here (mains €9 to €15).

Hausbrauerei Feierling BEER GARDEN
(Map p344; Gerberau 46; ⊙11am-midnight, to 1am Fri & Sat Mar-Oct) This stream-side beer garden is a relaxed spot to quaff a cold one under the chestnut trees in summer. Pretzels and sausages (snacks €3 to €7) soak up the malty brews.

Greiffenegg-Schlössle BEER GARDEN
(Map p344; Schlossbergring 3; ⊙11am-midnight Mar-Oct) All of Freiburg is at your feet from this chestnut-shaded beer garden atop Schlossberg. Perfect sunset spot.

Isle of Innisfree PUB
(Map p344; Atrium Augustinerplatz; ⊙daily) Find Guinness and the craic at this lively Irish watering hole, with a weekly line-up of quizzes, karaoke and live music.

White Rabbit Club CLUB
(Map p344; www.white-rabbit-club.de; Leopoldring 1) A student wonderland of cheap beers, DJs and gigs. Things get even curiouser at Wednesday night's open jam sessions.

Jazzhaus LIVE MUSIC
(☑349 73; www.jazzhaus.de; Schnewlinstrasse 1) Under the brick arches of a wine cellar, this venue hosts first-rate jazz, rock and world-music concerts (€15 to €25) at 7.30pm or 8pm at least three nights a week (see the website for details). It morphs into a club from 11pm to 3am on Friday and Saturday nights.

ℹ️ Information

Police station (Rotteckring)

Post office (Eisenbahnstrasse 58-62)

Tourist office (☑388 1880; www.freiburg. de; Rathausplatz 2-4; ⊙8am-8pm Mon-Fri, 9.30am-5pm Sat, 11am-4pm Sun) Well stocked with 1:50,000-scale cycling maps, city maps (€1) and the useful booklet *Freiburg – Official Guide* (€4.90). Can make room bookings (€3).

ℹ️ Getting There & Around

AIR Freiburg shares EuroAirport (p307) with Basel (Switzerland) and Mulhouse (France). Low-cost airline easyJet flies from here to destinations including London, Berlin, Rome and Alicante.

BICYCLE Bike paths run along the Dreisam River, leading westward to Breisach and then into France.

Mobile (Wentzingerstrasse 15; city bike 4hr/day €8/15, mountain/e-bike day €20/25; ⊙9am-7pm), in a glass-enclosed pavilion across the bridge from the Hauptbahnhof, rents bikes and sells cycling maps.

BUS The **airport bus** (☑500 500; www. freiburger-reisedienst.de; one-way/rtn €23/39) goes hourly from Freiburg's bus station to EuroAirport (55 minutes).

Südbaden Bus (www.suedbadenbus.de) and **RVF** (www.rvf.de) operate bus and train links to towns and villages throughout the southern Black Forest. Single tickets for one/two/three zones cost €2.10/3.60/5.10; a 24-hour Regio24 ticket costs €5.30 for one person and €9.50 for two to five people.

Bus and tram travel within Freiburg is operated by **VAG** (www.vag-freiburg.de) and charged at the one-zone rate. Buy tickets from the vending machines or from the driver and validate upon boarding.

CAR & MOTORCYCLE The Frankfurt–Basel A5 passes just west of Freiburg. The scenic B31 leads east through the Höllen Valley to Lake Constance. The B294 goes north into the Black Forest.

Car-hire agencies include **Europcar** (☑515 100; Lörracher Strasse 10) and **Avis** (☑197 19; St Georgener Strasse 7).

About 1.5km south of Martinstor, there's unmetered parking on some side streets (eg Türkenlouisstrasse). Otherwise, your best bet is to park at a free Park & Ride, such as the one at Bissierstrasse, a 10-minute ride from the centre on tram 1.

TRAIN Freiburg is on a major north–south rail corridor, with frequent departures for destinations such as Basel (€16.40 to €24.20, 42 to 69 minutes) and Baden-Baden (€19.20 to €28, 45 minutes to 1½ hours). Freiburg is also the western terminus of the Höllentalbahn to Donaueschingen via Titisee-Neustadt (€5.10, 38 minutes, twice an hour). There's a local connection to Breisach (€5.10, 26 minutes, at least hourly).

Schauinsland

Freiburg seems tiny as you drift up above the city and a tapestry of meadows and forest on the Schauinslandbahn (adult/concession return €12/11, one-way €8.50/8; ⊙9am-5pm, to 6pm Jul-Sep) to the 1284m Schauinsland peak (www.bergwelt-schauinsland.de). The lift provides a speedy link between Freiburg and the Black Forest highlands.

Up top there's a lookout tower commanding astounding views to the Rhine Valley and Alps, plus walking, cross-country and cycling trails that allow you to capture the scenery from many angles. Or you can bounce downhill on the 8km off-road scooter track (www. rollerstrecke.de; €20; ⊙2pm & 5pm Sun May-Jun, Sat & Sun Jul & Sep-Oct, Wed-Sun Aug), one of Europe's longest; it takes around an hour from top to bottom station. To reach Schauinslandbahn from Freiburg, take tram 2 to Günterstal and then bus 21 to Talstation.

On its quiet perch above the rippling hills of the Black Forest, Die Halde (☑07602-944 70; www.halde.com; Oberried-Hofsgrund; d €124-157, mains €16-26.50; P@☎) is a rustic-chic retreat, with an open fire crackling in the bar, calm rooms dressed in local wood and a glass-walled spa overlooking the valley. Martin Hegar cooks market-fresh dishes from trout to wild boar with panache in the wood-panelled restaurant.

Steinwasen Park

Buried deep in the forest, the nature-focused Steinwasen Park (www.steinwasen-park.de; Steinwasen 1; adult/concession €19/16; ⊙9am-6pm, closed early Nov-late Mar) is a big hit with families. A trail weaves past animal-friendly enclosures home to wild boar, ibex and burrowing marmots. One of the top attractions is a 218m-long hanging bridge, one of the world's longest. Not to be outdone by its rival, Europa-Park, Steinwasen has introduced whizzy rides such as Gletscherblitz and River Splash.

Todtnauer Wasserfall

Heading south on the Freiburg–Feldberg road, you'll glimpse the roaring Todtnauer Wasserfall (admission free; ⊙daylight hrs). While the 97m falls are not as high as those in Triberg, they're every bit as spectacular, tumbling down sheer rock faces and illuminating the velvety hills with their brilliance. Hike the circular 9km trail to Aftersteg for precipitous views over the cataract. Take care on paths in winter when the falls often freeze solid. The waterfall car park is on the L126.

St Peter

☑07660 / POP 2550

The folk of the bucolic village of St Peter, on the southern slopes of Mt Kandel (1243m), are deeply committed to time-honoured traditions. On religious holidays, villagers (from toddlers to pensioners) still proudly don colourful, handmade Trachten (folkloric costumes).

The most outstanding landmark is the Ehemaliges Benediktkloster (Former Benedictine Abbey; guided tours adult/concession €6/2; ⊙tours 11.30am Sun, 11am Tue, 2.30pm Thu), a rococo jewel designed by Peter Thumb of Vorarlberg. Many of the period's top artists collaborated on the sumptuous interior of the twin-towered red-sandstone church, including Joseph Anton Feuchtmayer, who carved the gilded Zähringer duke statues affixed to pillars. Guided tours (in German) to the monastery complex include the rococo library.

The tourist office (☑910 224; www.st-peter-schwarzwald.de; Klosterhof 11; ⊙9am-noon & 3-5pm Mon-Fri) is under the archway leading to the Klosterhof (the abbey courtyard). A nearby information panel shows room availability.

By public transport, the best way to get from Freiburg to St Peter is to take the train to Kirchzarten (13 minutes, twice hourly) and then bus 7216 (23 minutes, twice hourly).

St Peter is on the Schwarzwald Panoramastrasse, a 70km-long route from Waldkirch (17km northeast of Freiburg) to Feldberg with giddy mountain views.

Breisach

☑07667 / POP 14,500

Rising above vineyards and the Rhine, Breisach is where the Black Forest spills into Alsace. Given its geographical and cultural proximity to France, it's little surprise that the locals share their neighbours' passion for a good bottle of plonk.

From the cobbled streets lined with pastel-painted houses you'd never guess that 85% of the town was flattened in WWII, so successful has been the reconstruction. Vauban's star-shaped French fortress-town of Neuf-Brisach (New Breisach), which made the Unesco World Heritage list in 2008, sits 4km west of Breisach.

High above the centre, the Romanesque and Gothic St Stephansmünster shelters a faded fresco cycle, Martin Schongauer's *The Last Judgment* (1491), and a magnificent altar triptych (1526) carved from linden wood. From the tree-shaded square outside, the Schänzletreppe leads down to Gutgesellentor, the gate where Pope John XXIII was scandalously caught fleeing the Council of Constance in 1415.

Boat excursions along the Rhine are run by BFS (www.bfs-info.de; Rheinuferstrasse; ⊙Apr-Sep); the dock is 500m southwest of the tourist office.

Some of Breisach's hotels have seen better days but there is a great DJH hostel (☑7665; www.jugendherberge-breisach.de; Rheinuferstrasse 12; dm 1st/subsequent night €23/19.70) on the banks of the Rhine, whose facilities include a barbecue hut and volleyball court.

The tourist office (☑940 155; Marktplatz 16; ⊙9am-12.30pm & 1.30-6pm Mon & Wed-Fri, 10am-3pm Sat) can advise on wine tasting and private rooms in the area. You'll find the pick of the restaurants along Rheinuferstrasse and Richard-Müller-Strasse.

ⓘ Getting There & Around

Breisach's train station, 500m southeast of Marktplatz, serves Freiburg (€4.80, 25 minutes, at least hourly) and towns in the Kaiserstuhl. Buses go to Colmar, 22km west.

Breisach is a terrific base for free-wheeling over borders. Great rides include crossing the Rhine to the delightful French town of Colmar, or pedalling through terraced vineyards to Freiburg. Hire wheels from Funbike (☑7733; Metzgergasse 1; 1/3 days €10/25; ⊙9am-noon or on request) opposite the tourist office.

Kaiserstuhl

Squeezed between the Black Forest and French Vosges, these low-lying volcanic hills in the Upper Rhine Valley yield highly quaffable wines, including fruity *Spätburgunder* (Pinot noir) and *Grauburgunder* (Pinot gris) varieties.

The grapes owe their quality to a unique microclimate, hailed as Germany's sunniest, and fertile loess (clay and silt) soil that retains heat during the night. Nature enthusiasts should look out for rarities like sand lizards, praying mantis and European bee-eaters.

The Breisach tourist office can advise on cellar tours, wine tastings, bike paths like the 55km Kaiserstuhl-Tour circuit, and trails such as the Winzerweg (Wine Growers' Trail), an intoxicating 15km hike from Achkarren to Riegel.

The Kaiserstuhlbahn does a loop around the Kaiserstuhl. Stops (where you may have to change trains) include Sasbach, Endingen, Riegel and Gottenheim.

⊙ Sights & Activities

Vitra Design Museum   MUSEUM
(www.design-museum.de; Charles-Eames-Strasse 1, Weil am Rhein; adult/concession €8/6.50, architectural tour €10.50; ⊙10am-6pm, to 8pm Wed) Sharp angles contrast with graceful swirls on Frank Gehry's strikingly postmodern Vitra Design Museum. The blindingly white edifice hosts thought-provoking contemporary design exhibitions. Buildings on the nearby Vitra campus, designed by prominent architects like Nicholas Grimshaw, Zaha Hadid and Alvaro Siza, can be visited on a two-hour architectural tour, held in English at noon and 2pm daily.

Europa-Park   THEME PARK
(www.europapark.de; adult/concession €37.50/33; ⊙9am-6pm Apr-early Nov, 11am-7pm late Nov-early Jan) Germany's largest theme park, 35km north of Freiburg near Rust, is Europe in miniature. Get soaked fjord-rafting in Scandinavia before nipping across to England to race at Silverstone, or Greece to unravel the mysteries of Atlantis. Aside from white-knuckle thrills, Welt der Kinder amuses tots with labyrinths and Viking ships. When Mickey waltzed off to Paris, Europa-Park even got their own mousy mascot, Euromaus.

Shuttle buses (hourly in the morning) link Ringsheim train station, on the Freiburg–Offenburg line, with the park. By car, take the A5 exit Rust (57b).

Feldberg

☑07655 / POP 1880

At 1493m Feldberg is the Black Forest's highest mountain and one of the few places here with downhill skiing. The actual mountaintop is treeless and not particularly attractive but on clear days the view southward towards the Alps is mesmerising.

Feldberg is also the name given to a cluster of five villages, of which Altglashütten is the hub. Its Rathaus houses the tourist office (Kirchgasse 1; ⊙8am -12pm & 1-5pm Mon-Fri), which has the low-down on activities in the area and rents Nordic walking poles.

Sitting 2km north is the lushly wooded Bärental, where traditional Black Forest farmhouses snuggle against the hillsides. East of Bärental in the Haslach Valley is Falkau, a family-friendly resort with a small waterfall. Windgfällweiher, an attractive lake for a swim or picnic, is 1km southeast of Altglashütten.

Around 9km west of Altglashütten is Feldberg-Ort, in the heart of the 42-sq-km nature reserve that covers much of the mountain. Most of the ski lifts are here, including the scenic Feldbergbahn chairlift to the Bismarckdenkmal (Bismarck monument).

Activities

The eco-conscious Haus der Natur (07676-933 610; www.naturpark-suedschwarzwald.de; Dr-Pilet-Spur 4; ⊙10am-5pm, closed Mon) can advise on some of the area's great hiking opportunities, such as the rewarding 12km Feldberg–Steig to Feldberg summit.

The Feldberg ski area comprises 28 lifts, accessible with the same ticket. Four groomed cross-country trails are also available. To hire skis, look for signs reading 'Skiverleih'. A reliable outlet is Skiverleih Schubnell.

Come winter Feldberg's snowy heights are ideal for a stomp through twinkling woods. Strap on snowshoes to tackle the pretty 3km Seebuck-Trail or the more challenging 9km Gipfel-Trail. The Haus der Natur rents lightweight snowshoes for €10/5 per day for adults/children.

Sleeping

Landhotel Sonneck   HOTEL $$
(211; www.sonneck-feldberg.de; Schwarzenbachweg 5; d €90-100) Immaculate, light-filled rooms with pine furnishings and balconies are the deal at this hotel. The quaint restaurant (mains €8 to €15) rolls out hearty local fare.

Naturfreundehaus   HOSTEL $
(07676-336; www.jugendherberge-feldberg.de; Am Baldenweger Buck; dm €14.50) Lodged in a Black Forest farmhouse a 30-minute walk from Feldberg's summit, this back-to-nature hostel uses renewable energy and serves fair-trade and organic produce at breakfast. Surrounding views of wooded hills and comfy, pine-clad dorms make this a great spot for hiking in summer, and skiing and snowshoeing in winter.

ⓘ Getting There & Away

Bärental and Altglashütten are stops on the Dreiseenbahn, linking Titisee with Seebrugg (Schluchsee). From the train station in Bärental, bus 7300 makes trips at least hourly to Feldberg-Ort (€2.10, 10 minutes).

From late December until the end of the season, shuttle buses run by Feldberg SBG link Feldberg and Titisee with the ski lifts (free with a lift ticket or Gästekarte).

If you're driving, take the B31 (Freiburg–Donaueschingen) to Titisee, then the B317. To get to Altglashütten, head down the B500 from Bärental.

Titisee-Neustadt

07651 / POP 11,860

Titisee is a cheerful summertime playground with a name that makes English-speaking travellers giggle and a shimmering blue-green glacial lake, ringed by forest, which has them diving for their cameras.

◉ Sights & Activities

Sure, the village is touristy but tiptoe south along the flowery Seestrasse promenade and you'll soon leave the crowds and made-in-China cuckoo clocks behind to find secluded bays ideal for swimming and picnicking. For giddy views, head up to 1192m Hochfirst tower, which overlooks Titisee from the east.

A laid-back way to appreciate the lake's soothing beauty is to hire a rowing boat or pedalo at one of the set-ups along the lakefront; expect to pay around €6 per hour.

The forest trails around Titisee are hugely popular for Nordic walking which, for the uninitiated, is walking briskly with poles to simultaneously exercise the upper body and legs.

Snow transforms Titisee into a winter wonderland and a cross-country skiing magnet, with *Loipen* (tracks) threading through the hills and woods, including a 3km floodlit track for a starlit skate. The tourist office map pinpoints cross-country and Nordic walking trails in the area.

Badeparadies   DAY SPA
(www.badeparadies-schwarzwald.de; Am Badeparadies 1; 3hr €17, incl sauna complex €21; ⊙10am-10pm Mon-Thu, to 11pm Fri, 9am-10pm Sat & Sun) This huge glass-canopied leisure and wellness centre made a splash when it opened in December 2010. You can lounge, cocktail in hand, by palm-fringed lagoons in Pal-

menoase, race white-knuckle slides with gaggles of overexcited kids in Galaxy, or strip off in themed saunas with waterfalls and Black Forest views in the adults-only Wellnessoase.

🛏 Sleeping & Eating

Alemannenhof
HOTEL $$$

(☑911 80; www.hotel-alemannenhof.de; d €120-250, mains €22-34; P🅿🛜🅿) A pool, private beach and contemporary rooms with transparent shower stalls and balconies overlooking Titisee await at this farmhouse-style hotel. Opening onto a lakefront terrace, the all-pine restaurant serves regional cuisine with a twist, such as local beef with potato-rosemary puree and wild-garlic pasta.

Neubierhäusle
PENSION $

(☑8230; www.neubierhaeusle.de; Neustädterstrasse 79; d €64-82; P) Big forest views, piny air and pastures on the doorstep – this farmhouse is the perfect country retreat. Dressed in local wood, the light-filled rooms are supremely comfy. The hosts lay on a hearty spread at breakfast and you can help yourself any time to free tea and fruit. It's on the L156, 3km northeast of the station.

Bergseeblick
PENSION $

(☑8257; www.bergseeblick-titisee.de; Erlenweg 3; s €27-33, d €52-78, q €70; P) This welcoming, family-run cheapie near the church offers peaceful slumber in humble rooms decorated in pine and floral fabrics.

ℹ Information

The **tourist office** (☑07652-1206 8120; www.titisee-neustadt.de; Strandbadstrasse 4; ⊙9am-6pm Mon-Fri, 10am-1pm Sat & Sun) in the Kurhaus, 500m southwest of the train station, stocks walking and cycling maps.

ℹ Getting There & Around

Train routes include the twice-hourly Höllentalbahn to Freiburg (€5.10, 40 minutes) and hourly services to Donaueschingen (€9.10, 50 minutes), Feldberg (€2.10, 12 minutes) and Schluchsee (€2.10, 22 minutes).

From Titisee train station, there are frequent services on bus 7257 to Schluchsee (€2.10, 40 minutes) and bus 7300 to Feldberg–Bärental (€2.10, 13 minutes).

Ski-Hirt (☑922 80; Titiseestrasse 26) rents reliable bikes and ski equipment, and can supply details on local cycling options.

Schluchsee
☑07656 / POP 2540

Photogenically poised above its namesake petrol-blue lake – the Black Forest's largest – and rimmed by forest, Schluchsee tempts you outdoors with pursuits like swimming, windsurfing, hiking, cycling and, ahem, skinny-dipping from the western shore's secluded bays. The otherwise sleepy resort jolts to life with sun-seekers in summer and cross-country skiers in winter.

Popular with families, the lakefront lido, **Aqua Fun Strandbad** (Strandbadstrasse; adult/concession €4/2.70; ⊙9am-7pm Jun-Aug) has a heated pool, a sandy beach, a volleyball court and waterslides.

T Toth (www.seerundfahrten.de) runs boat tours around Schluchsee, with stops in Aha, Seebrugg and the Strandbad. An hour-long round trip costs €7.50 (less for single stops). You can hire rowing boats and pedalos for €4/6 per half/full hour.

🛏 Sleeping & Eating

Decent beds are pretty slim in Schluchsee, though there are a few good-value pensions and farmstays – ask the tourist office.

Gasthof Hirschen
GUESTHOUSE $

(☑989 40; www.hirschen-fischbach.de; Schluchseestrasse 9; s €45, d €54-80, mains €13-21) It's worth going the extra mile to this farmhouse prettily perched on a hillside in Fischbach, 4km north of Schluchsee. The simple, quiet rooms are a good-value base for summer hiking and modest winter skiing. There's also a sauna, playground and a restaurant dishing up regional fare.

Seehof
INTERNATIONAL $$$

(☑988 9965; Kirchsteige 4; mains €8-18; ⊙11.30am-10.30pm Mon-Sun) An inviting spot for a bite to eat, with a terrace overlooking the lake, Seehof has a menu packed with local fish and meat mains, salads, pizzas and ice cream.

ℹ Information

The train tracks and the B500 shadow the lake's eastern shore between the lakefront and the Schluchsee's town centre. The lake's western shore is accessible only by bike or on foot.

Tourist office (☑07652-1206 8500; www.schluchsee.de; Fischbacher Strasse 7, Haus des Gastes; ⊙8am-5pm Mon-Thu, 9am-5pm Fri) Situated 150m uphill from the church, with maps and info on activities and accommodation.

ⓘ Getting There & Around

Trains go hourly to Feldberg–Altglashütten (€2.10, 11 minutes) and Titisee (€2.10, 22 minutes). Bus 7257 links Schluchsee three or four times daily with the Neustadt and Titisee train stations (€2.10, 40 minutes).

City, mountain and e-bikes can be rented for €9/10/22 per day at **Müllers** (An der Staumauer 1; ⏱10am-6pm Apr-Oct). An hour's pedalo/motor boat/rowing boat hire costs €6/15/6.

Triberg

☑0722 / POP 5000

Home to Germany's highest waterfall, heir to the original 1915 black forest gateau recipe and nesting ground of the world's biggest cuckoos, Triberg leaves visitors reeling with superlatives. It was here that in bleak winters past folk huddled in snowbound farmhouses to carve the clocks that would drive the world cuckoo, and here that in a flash of brilliance the waterfall was harnessed to power the country's first electric street lamps in 1884.

◉ Sights & Activities

Triberger Wasserfälle WATERFALL
TOP CHOICE
(adult/concession €3.50/3; ⏱Mar-early Nov & 25-30 Dec) Niagara they ain't but Germany's highest waterfalls do exude their own wild romanticism. The Gutach River feeds the seven-tiered falls, which drop a total of 163m. It's annoying to have to pay to experience nature but the fee is at least worth it. The trail up through the wooded gorge is guarded by tribes of red squirrels after the bags of nuts (€1) sold at the entrance.

Weltgrösste Kuckucksuhr LANDMARK
Triberg is Germany's undisputed cuckoo-clock capital. Two timepieces claim the title of world's largest cuckoo clock, giving rise to the battle of the birds.

To the casual observer, the biggest is undeniably the commercially savvy **Eble Uhren-Park** (www.uhren-park.de; Schonachbach 27; admission €2; ⏱9am-6pm Mon-Sat, 10am-6pm Sun), listed in *Guinness World Records*, on the B33 between Triberg and Hornberg.

At the other end of town in Schonach is its underdog **rival clock** (Untertalstrasse 28; adult/concession €1.20/0.60; ⏱9am-noon & 1-6pm), nestled inside a snug chalet and complete with gear-driven innards. This giant timepiece – unable to compete in size alone – has taken to calling itself the world's oldest, largest cuckoo clock. It was built in the 1980s.

Haus der 1000 Uhren LANDMARK
(House of 1000 clocks; www.hausder1000uhren.de; Hauptstrasse 79; ⏱9am-5pm Sat, 10am-5pm Sun) A glockenspiel bashes out melodies and a cuckoo greets his fans with a hopelessly croaky squawk on the hour at the kitschy House of 1000 Clocks, a wonderland of clocks from traditional to trendy. The latest quartz models feature a sensor that sends the cuckoo to sleep after dark!

Sanitas Spa SPA
(☑860 20; www.sanitas-spa.de; Gartenstrasse 24; admission half/full-day €24/40; ⏱9.30am-8pm) Fronted by wrap-around windows overlooking Triberg's forested hills, Parkhotel Wehrle's day spa is gorgeous. This is a serene spot to wind down, with its spacily lit kidney-shaped pool, exquisitely tiled hammams, steam rooms, whirlpool and waterbed meditation room. Treatments vary from rhassoul clay wraps to reiki.

🛏 Sleeping & Eating

Parkhotel Wehrle HISTORIC HOTEL $$$
TOP CHOICE
(☑860 20; www.parkhotel-wehrle.de; Hauptstrasse 51; s €95-105, d €149-169, mains €12-23; P🅿🛜🐕) Hemingway once waxed lyrical about this 400-year-old hotel and it remains a rustically elegant place to stay today. Often with a baroque or Biedermeier touch, quarters are roomy and beautifully furnished with antiques; the best have Duravit whirlpool tubs. All guests get free entry to the hotel's Sanitas Spa. The well-regarded restaurant serves seasonal delicacies like gilthead sea bream with market-fresh veg and oxtail jus in wood-panelled, softly lit surrounds.

Kukucksnest B&B $
(☑869 487; Wallfahrtstrasse 15; d €58) Below is the shop of master woodcarver Gerald Burger, above is the beautiful nest he has carved for his guests, featuring blonde-wood rooms with flat-screen TVs. The *Wurzelsepp* (faces carved into fir tree roots) by the entrance supposedly ward off evil spirits.

Café Schäfer BAKERY $
(www.cafe-schaefer-triberg.de; Hauptstrasse 33; cake €3-4; ⏱9am-6pm Mon-Fri, 8am-6pm Sat, 11am-6pm Sun, closed Wed) The black forest gateau here is the real deal and confectioner Claus Schäfer has Josef Keller's original 1915 recipe for *Schwarzwälder Kirschtorte* to prove it. The aroma draws you to the glass counter showcasing the masterpiece: layers of moist sponge, fresh cream and sour cher-

LOCAL KNOWLEDGE

CLAUS SCHÄFER, CONFECTIONER

Want to whip up your own black forest gateau back home? Claus Schäfer reveals how.

All About Cake Baking a black forest gateau isn't rocket science but it involves time, practice and top-quality ingredients. Eat the cake the day you make it, when it is freshest, and never freeze it or you will lose the aroma.

Secrets in the Mix Whip the cream until silky, blend in gelatine and two shots of quality kirsch. Mine comes from a local distillery and is 56% proof. The compote needs tangy cherries, sugar, cherry juice and a pinch of cinnamon. The bottom layer of sponge should be twice as thick as the other two, so it can support the compote without collapsing.

Finishing Touches These are important: spread the gateau with cream, then decorate with piped cream, cherries, chocolate shavings and a dusting of icing sugar.

Other Regional Flavours When in the Black Forest, try the fresh trout, smoked ham and *Kirsch* sold locally by farmers. Their quality is higher and prices lower than elsewhere.

ries, with a mere suggestion of *Kirsch* (cherry brandy) and heavenly dusting of chocolate.

❶ Information

Triberg's main drag is the B500, which runs more or less parallel to the Gutach River. The town's focal point is the Marktplatz, a steep 1.2km uphill walk from the Bahnhof.

Triberg markets itself as **Das Ferienland** (The Holiday Region; www.dasferienland.de) to visitors.

Tourist office (☑866 490; www.triberg.de; Wahlfahrtstrasse 4; ◷10am-5pm Oct-Apr, to 6pm May-Sep) Inside the Schwarzwald-Museum, 50m uphill from the river.

❶ Getting There & Away

The Schwarzwaldbahn train line loops southeast to Konstanz (€23.30, 1½ hours, hourly), and northwest to Offenburg (€11.10, 46 minutes, hourly).

Bus 7150 travels north through the Gutach and Kinzig Valleys to Offenburg; bus 7265 heads south to Villingen via St Georgen. Local buses operate between the Bahnhof and Marktplatz, and to the nearby town of Schonach (hourly).

Stöcklewaldturm

Triberg's waterfall is the trailhead for an attractive 6.5km walk to Stöcklewaldturm (1070m). A steady trudge through spruce forest and pastures brings you to this 19th-century lookout tower (admission €0.50), where the 360-degree views stretch from the Swabian Alps to the snowcapped Alps. Footpaths head off in all directions from

the summit, where the woodsy cafe (snacks €2.50-7; ◷10am-8pm, closed Tue) is an inviting spot for a beer and snack or, in winter, hot chocolate. The car park on the L175 is a 10-minute stroll from the tower.

Martinskapelle

Named after the tiny chapel at the head of the Bregtal (Breg Valley), Martinskapelle attracts cross-country skiers to its forested trails in winter and hikers when the snow melts. The steep road up to the 1100m peak negotiates some pretty hairy switchbacks, swinging past wood-shingle farmhouses that cling to forested slopes.

Höhengasthaus Kolmenhof (☑07723-931 00; www.kolmenhof.de; An der Donauquelle; mains €9.50-16; ◷closed Wed dinner, Thu) fills up with ruddy-cheeked skiers and walkers, who pile into this rustic bolt-hole for *Glühwein* (mulled wine) and soul food. Despite what critics (who have argued until blue in the face since 1544) may say, the Danube's main source is right here. This accounts for the freshness of the trout, served smoked, roasted in almond butter, or poached in white wine.

Bus 7270 runs roughly hourly from the Marktplatz in Triberg to Escheck (€1.90, 25 minutes); from here it's a 4.5km walk to Martinskapelle. If you're driving, take the B500 from Triberg following signs to Schwarzenbach, Weissenbach and the K5730 to Martinskapelle.

Villingen-Schwenningen

07221 / POP 81,020

Villingen and Schwenningen trip simultaneously off the tongue, yet each town has its own flavour and history. Villingen once belonged to the Grand Duchy of Baden and Schwenningen to the duchy of Württemberg, conflicting allegiances that apparently can't be reconciled. Villingen, it must be said, is the more attractive of the twin towns.

Encircled by impenetrable walls that look as though they were built by the mythical local giant, Romäus, Villingen's Altstadt is a late medieval time capsule, with cobbled streets and handsome patrician houses. Though locals nickname it the *Städtle* (little town), the name seems inappropriate during February's mammoth weeklong *Fasnet* celebrations.

⊙ Sights & Activities

Münsterplatz   SQUARE
The main crowd-puller in Villingen's Altstadt is the red-sandstone Münster with disparate spires: one overlaid with coloured tiles, the other spiky and festooned with gargoyles. The Romanesque portals with haut-relief doors depict dramatic biblical scenes.

Right opposite is the step-gabled Altes Rathaus (Old Town Hall) and Klaus Ringwald's Münsterbrunnen, a bronze fountain and a tongue-in-cheek portrayal of characters that have shaped Villingen's history. The square throngs with activity on Wednesday and Saturday mornings when market stalls are piled high with local bread, meat, cheese, fruit and flowers.

Franziskaner Museum   MUSEUM
(Rietgasse 2; adult/concession €3/2; ⊙1-5pm Tue-Sat, 11am-5pm Sun) Next to the 13th-century Riettor and occupying a former Franciscan monastery, the Franziskaner Museum skips merrily through Villingen's history and heritage. Standouts include Celtic artefacts unearthed at Magdalenenberg, 30 minutes' walk south of Villingen's centre. Dating to 616 BC, the mystery-enshrouded site is one of the largest Hallstatt burial chambers ever discovered in Central Europe and is shaded by a 1000-year-old oak tree.

Spitalgarten   GARDEN
Tucked behind the Franziskaner is the Spitalgarten, a park flanked by the original city walls. Here your gaze will be drawn to Romäusturm, a lofty 13th-century thieves' tower named after fabled local leviathan Remigius Mans (Romäus for short).

Kneippbad   SWIMMING
(Am Kneippbad 1; adult/child €3.70/2.50; ⊙6.30am-8pm Mon-Fri, 8am-8pm Sat & Sun mid-May-early Sep) If the sun's out, take a 3km walk northwest of the Altstadt to this forest lido, a family magnet with its outdoor pools, slides and volleyball courts.

WORTH A TRIP

NATURPARK OBERE DONAU

Theatrically set against cave-riddled limestone cliffs, dappled with pine and beech woods that are burnished gold in autumn, and hugging the Danube's banks, the Upper Danube Valley Nature Reserve (www.naturpark-obere-donau.de) bombards you with rugged splendour. Stick to the autobahn, however, and you'll be none the wiser. To explore the nature reserve, slip into a bicycle saddle or walking boots and hit the trail.

One of the finest stretches is between Fridingen and Beuron, a 12.5km ridge-top walk of three to four hours. The signposted, easy-to-navigate trail runs above ragged cliffs, affording eagle's-eye views of the meandering Danube, which has almost 2850km to go before emptying into the Black Sea. The vertigo-inducing outcrop of Laibfelsen is a great picnic spot. From here, the path dips in and out of woodlands and meadows flecked with purple thistles. In Beuron the big draw is the working Benedictine abbey, one of Germany's oldest, dating to 1077. The lavish stucco-and-fresco church (⊙5am-8pm daily) is open to visitors. See the website www.beuron.de (in German) for sleeping options.

Fridingen and Beuron lie on the L277, 45km east of Villingen. Frequent trains link Beuron to Villingen (€7.50, one hour).

📖 Sleeping & Eating

Rindenmühle
HOTEL $$

(📞886 80; www.rindenmuehle.de; Am Kneippbad 9; r €99-125, mains €16-32; P🐾) Next to the Kneippbad, this converted watermill houses one of Villingen's smartest hotels, with forest walks right on its doorstep. Rooms are slick and decorated in muted hues. In the kitchen, Martin Weisser creates award-winning flavours using home-grown organic produce, including chicken, geese and herbs from his garden.

Haus Bächle
GUESTHOUSE $

(📞597 29; Am Kneippbad 5; s/d €15/32; P) This half-timbered house overlooks the flowery Kurgarten. The tidy rooms are an absolute bargain and the Kneippbad is next door for early-morning swims.

Kapuzinerhof
ITALIAN $$$

(📞506 084; Färberstrasse 18; mains €10-24; ⊙11.30am-10pm Sun-Thu, to 11pm Fri & Sat, closed Wed) Gathered around a courtyard in a restored 17th-century Capuchin monastery, this Altstadt restaurant emphasises Italian flavours, from antipasti to sea bass.

Zampolli
CAFE $

(Rietstrasse 33; ice cream cone €0.80; ⊙9.30am-11pm Mon-Sat, 10.30am-11pm Sun Feb–mid-Nov) For an espresso or creamy gelati, make for this Italian-run cafe. By night, the pavement terrace facing Riettor is a laid-back spot for a drink.

ℹ️ Information

Post office (Bahnhofstrasse 6)
Villingen Tourist Office (📞822 525; www.tourismus-vs.de; Rietgasse 2; ⊙9am-5pm Mon-Sat, 11am-5pm Sun) In the Franziskaner Museum. You can pick up the itour audio guide in English; two hours costs €5.

ℹ️ Getting There & Around

Villingen's Bahnhof is on the scenic Schwarzwaldbahn train line from Konstanz (€18.10, 70 minutes) to Triberg (€7.50, 23 minutes) and Offenburg (€16.40, 70 minutes). Trains to Stuttgart (€28.50, 1¾ hours) involve a change in Rottweil, and to Freiburg (€18.10 to €27.10, two hours) a change in Donaueschingen.

From Villingen, buses 7265 and 7270 make regular trips north to Triberg. Frequent buses (for example, line 1) link Villingen with Schwenningen.

Villingen-Schwenningen is just west of the A81 Stuttgart–Singen motorway and is also crossed by the B33 to Triberg and the B27 to Rottweil.

Rottweil

📞0741 / POP 25.660

Baden-Württemberg's oldest town is the strapline of Roman-rooted Rottweil, founded in AD 73. Yet a torrent of bad press about the woofer with a nasty nip means that most folk readily associate it with the Rottweiler, which was indeed bred here as a hardy butchers' dog until recently. Fear not, the Rottweiler locals are much tamer.

The sturdy 13th-century Schwarzes Tor is the gateway to Hauptstrasse and the well-preserved Altstadt, a cluster of red-roofed, pastel-painted houses. Nearby at No 6, the curvaceous Hübschen Winkel will make you look twice with its 45-degree kink. Just west on Münsterplatz, the late Romanesque Münster-Heiliges-Kreuz features some striking Gothic stonework and ribbed vaulting. Equally worth a peek about 1km south is the Roman bath (Hölderstrasse; admission free; ⊙daylight hrs), a 45m-by-42m bathing complex unearthed in 1967.

The tourist office (📞494 280; www.rottweil.de; Hauptstrasse 21; ⊙9.30am-5.30pm Mon-Fri, to 12.30pm Sat) can advise on accommodation, tours and biking the Neckartal-Radweg.

Rottweil is just off the A81 Stuttgart–Singen motorway. Trains run at least hourly to Villingen (€3, 25 minutes) and Stuttgart (€20.80, 1½ hours).

Unterkirnach

📞07721 / POP 2730

Nestled among velvety green hills, low-key Unterkirnach appeals to families and outdoorsy types. Kids can slide and climb to their heart's content at the all-weather Spielscheune (Schlossbergweg 4; admission €4; ⊙1-7pm Mon-Fri, 11am-7pm Sat & Sun), or toddle uphill to the farm to meet inquisitive goats and Highland cattle (feeding time is 3pm). In summer, the village is a great starting point for forest hikes, combed with 130km of marked walking trails, while in winter there are 50km of *Loipen* (cross-country ski tracks) and some terrific slopes to sledge.

Picturesquely perched above Unterkirnach, Ackerloch Grillschopf (www.ackerloch.de; Unteres Ackerloch; light meals €4-11; ⊙11.30am-midnight, closed Tue) is a rickety barn, brimming with rustic warmth in winter and with a beer garden overlooking a broad valley in summer. Occasionally there is a suckling pig

DON'T MISS

CELEBRATE THE FIFTH SEASON

Boisterous and totally bonkers, the **Swabian-Alemannic Fasnacht** or *Fasnet* (not to be confused with Carnival) is a 500-year-old rite to banish winter and indulge in pre-Lenten feasting, parades, flirting and all-night drinkathons. Starting on Epiphany, festivities reach a crescendo the week before Ash Wednesday. Dress up to join the party, memorise a few sayings to dodge the witches, and catch the flying sausages – anything's possible, we swear. For *Fasnacht* at its traditional best, try the following:

Rottweil (www.narrenzunft.rottweil.de) At Monday's 8am *Narrensprung*, thousands of jester-like Narros in baroque masques ring through Baden-Württemberg's oldest town. Look out for the devil-like *Federhannes* and the *Guller* riding a cockerel.

Schramberg (www.narrenzunft-schramberg.de) Protagonists include the *hoorige Katz* (hairy cat) and the hopping *Hans*.

Elzach (www.schuttig.com) *Trallaho!* Wearing a hand-carved mask and a tricorn hat adorned with snail shells, *Schuttige* dash through Elzach's streets cracking *Saublodere* (pig bladders) – dodge them unless you wish for many children! Sunday's torchlit parade and Shrove Tuesday's afternoon *Schuttigumzug* are the must-sees.

roasting on the spit and you can grill your own steaks and sausages on the barbecue.

Bus 61 runs roughly hourly between Unterkirnach and Villingen (€3, 18 minutes).

LAKE CONSTANCE

Nicknamed the *schwäbische Meer* (Swabian Sea), Lake Constance is Central Europe's third largest lake and it straddles three countries: Germany, Austria and Switzerland. Formed by the Rhine Glacier during the last ice age and fed and drained by that same sprightly river today, this whopper of a lake measures 63km long, 14km wide and up to 250m deep. Vital statistics aside, there is definite novelty effect in the fact that this is the only place in the world where you can wake up in Germany, cycle across to Switzerland for lunch and make it to Austria in time for afternoon tea, strudel and snapshots of the Alps.

Taking in meadows and vineyards, orchards and wetlands, beaches and Alpine foothills, the lake's landscapes are like a 'greatest hits' of European scenery. Culture? It's all here, from baroque churches to Benedictine abbeys, Stone Age dwellings to Roman forts, medieval castles to zeppelins.

Come in spring for blossom and autumn for new wine, fewer crowds and top visibility when the warm *Föhn* blows. Summers are crowded, but best for swimming and camping. Almost everything shuts from November to February, when fog descends and the first snowflakes dust the Alps.

❶ Getting There & Around

The most enjoyable way to cross the lake is by ferry. Konstanz is the main hub but Meersburg and Friedrichshafen also have plentiful ferry options.

Although most towns have a train station (Meersburg is an exception), in some cases buses provide the only land connections. **Euregio Bodensee** (www.euregiokarte.com), which groups all Lake Constance–area public transport, publishes a free *Fahrplan* with schedules for all train, bus and ferry services.

The **Euregio Bodensee Tageskarte** (www.euregiokarte.com) gets you all-day access to land transport around Lake Constance, including areas in Austria and Switzerland. It's sold

BODENSEE ERLEBNISKARTE

The three-day **Bodensee Erlebniskarte** (adult/child €72/36, not incl ferries €40/21), available at area tourist and ferry offices from early April to mid-October, allows free travel on almost all boats and mountain cableways on and around Lake Constance (including its Austrian and Swiss shores) and gets you free entry to around 180 tourist attractions and museums. There are also seven-day (adult/child €92/46) and 14-day (adult/child €130/66) versions.

at train stations and ferry docks and costs €16.50/22/29 for one/two/all zones.

CAR FERRIES The roll-on-roll-off **Konstanz–Meersburg car ferry** (www.sw.konstanz.de; car up to 4m incl driver/bicycle/pedestrian €8.40/2.20/2.60) runs 24 hours a day, except when high water levels prevent it from docking. The ferry runs is every 15 minutes from 5.30am to 9pm, every 30 minutes from 9pm to midnight and every hour from midnight to 5.30am. The crossing, affording superb views from the top deck, takes 15 minutes.

The dock in Konstanz, served by local bus 1, is 4km northeast of the centre along Mainaustrasse. In Meersburg, car ferries leave from a dock 400m northwest of the old town.

PASSENGER FERRIES The most useful lines, run by German **BSB** (www.bsb-online.com) and Austrian **OBB** (www.bodenseeschifffahrt.at), link Konstanz with ports such as Meersburg (€5.30, 30 minutes), Friedrichshafen (€11.70, 1¾ hours), Lindau (€15.40, three hours) and Bregenz (€16.40, 3½ hours); children aged six to 15 years pay half-price. The website lists full timetables.

Der Katamaran (www.der-katamaran.de; adult/6-14yr €9.80/4.90) is a sleek passenger service that takes 50 minutes to make the Konstanz–Friedrichshafen crossing (hourly from 6am to 7pm, plus hourly from 8pm to midnight on Fridays and Saturdays from mid-May to early October).

Konstanz

☎ 07531 / POP 84,690

Sidling up to the Swiss border, bisected by the Rhine and outlined by the Alps, Konstanz sits prettily on the northwestern shore of Lake Constance. Roman emperors, medieval traders and the bishops of the 15th-century Council of Constance have all left their mark on this alley-woven town, mercifully spared from the WWII bombings that obliterated other German cities.

When the sun comes out to play, Konstanz is a feel-good university town with a lively buzz and upbeat bar scene, particularly in the cobbled Altstadt and the harbour where the voluptuous *Imperia* turns. In summer the locals, nicknamed *Seehasen* (lake hares), head outdoors to the leafy promenade and enjoy lazy days in lakefront lidos.

◉ Sights

TOP CHOICE Münster   CATHEDRAL
(Map p358; tower adult/child €2/1; ⊙10am-6pm Mon-Sat, to 6pm Sun, tower 10am-5pm Mon-Sat, 12.30am-5.30pm Sun) Crowned by a filigree spire and looking proudly back on 1000 years of history, the sandstone Münster was the church of the diocese of Konstanz

Lake Constance

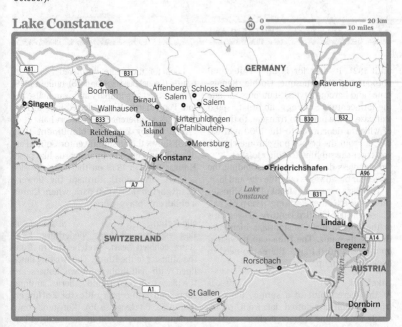

Konstanz

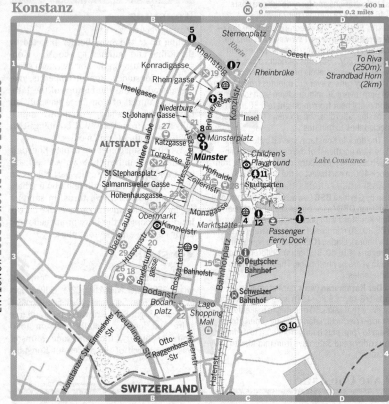

until 1821. Its interior is an architectural potpourri of Romanesque, Gothic, Renaissance and baroque styles. Standouts include the 15th-century **Schnegg**, an ornate spiral staircase in the northern transept, to the left of which a door leads to the 1000-year-old **crypt**. From the crypt's polychrome chapel, you enter the sublime **Gothic cloister**.

On cloudless days, it's worth ascending the **tower** for broad views over the city and lake.

The glass pyramid in front of the Münster shelters the **Römersiedlung** (Map p358; tour €1; ☺6pm Sun), the 3rd-century-AD remains of the Roman fort Constantia, which gave the city its name. The ruins can be visited on a brief guided tour – there's no need to book; just turn up.

Lakefront   HARBOUR

At the merest hint of a sunray, the tree-fringed, sculpture-dotted lakefront promenade lures inline skaters, cyclists, walkers and ice-cream-licking crowds.

Look for the white dormered **Konzilgebäude** (Council Building; Map p358), built in 1388, which served as a granary and warehouse before Pope Martin V was elected here in 1417. Today it's a conference and concert hall.

The nearby **Zeppelin Monument** (Map p358) shows the airship inventor Count Ferdinand von Zeppelin in an Icarus-like pose. He was born in 1838 on the Insel, an islet a short stroll north through the flowery **Stadtgarten** (Map p358) park, where there's a **children's playground**.

Niederburg   NEIGHBOURHOOD

Best explored on foot, Niederburg, Konstanz' cobbled heart, stretches north from the Münster to the Rhine. The twisting lanes lined with half-timbered town houses are the place to snoop around galleries, antique shops and 13th-century **Kloster Zoffingen** (Map p358; Brückengasse 15), Konstanz' only remaining convent, still in the hands of Dominican nuns.

Konstanz

On the Rheinsteig is the medieval **Rheintorturm** (Rhine Gate Tower; Map p358), a defensive tower with a pyramid-shaped red-tile roof. About 200m west along the river is the more squat, 14th-century **Pulverturm** (Gunpowder Tower; Map p358), with 2m-thick walls.

Cross the street to the orange-red, baroque **Domprobstei** (Map p358; Rheingasse 20), once the residence of the cathedral provosts.

Rathaus   LANDMARK
(City Hall; Map p358; Kanzleistrasse) Slightly south of the Münster, the flamboyantly frescoed Renaissance Rathaus occupies the former linen weavers' guildhall. Behind you'll find a peaceful arcaded courtyard.

Rosgartenmuseum   MUSEUM
(Map p358; www.rosgartenmuseum-konstanz.de; Rosgartenstrasse 3-5; adult/concession €3/1.50, 1st Sun of the month & after 2pm Wed free; ⏱10am-6pm Tue-Fri, to 5pm Sat & Sun) The one-time butchers' guildhall now harbours the Rosgartenmuseum, spotlighting regional art and history, with an emphasis on medieval panel painting and sculpture.

Sea Life   AQUARIUM
(Map p358; www.visitsealife.com/konstanz; Hafenstrasse 9; adult/child €15.95/10.95; ⏱10am-btwn 5pm & 7pm) Running a dragnet through your wallet, the borderline-kitsch Sea Life immerses you in an underwater world. Highlights include a shipwreck where you can handle starfish and get stingray close-ups, a shark tunnel, penguins, and a creepy corner blubbing with oddities like frogfish and, ugh, giant isopods.

🏃 Activities

For some ozone-enriched summer fun, grab your bathers and head to the lake.

FREE **Strandbad Horn**   BEACH
(Eichhornstrasse 100; ⏱mid-May–Sep) This lakefront beach, 4km northeast of the centre, has sunbathing lawns, a kiddie pool, playground, volleyball courts and even a naturist area.

La Canoa   BOAT HIRE
(www.lacanoa.com; Robert-Bosch-Strasse 4; canoe/kayak 3 hr €14/18, per day €21/27; ⏱10am-12.30pm & 2-6pm Tue-Fri, 10am-4pm Sat) Rents high-quality canoes and kayaks in Konstanz and from various other Lake Constance locations, including Lindau and Friedrichshafen. Visit the website for canoe tour details.

Bootsvermietung Konstanz   BOAT HIRE
(Map p358; per hr €9-17; ⏱11am-sunset Easter–mid-Oct) This boat rental in the Stadtgarten has pedalos for trundling across the lake.

ONE LAKE, TWO WHEELS, THREE COUNTRIES

When the weather warms, there is no better way to explore Bodensee (Lake Constance) than with your bum in a saddle. The well-marked Bodensee Cycle Path (www.bodensee-radweg.com) cycling path makes a 273km loop of Lake Constance, taking in vineyards, meadows, orchards, wetlands and historic towns. There are plenty of small beaches where you can stop for a refreshing dip in the lake. See the website for itineraries and maps. Bike hire is available in most towns for between €10 and €20 per day. While the entire route takes roughly a week, ferries and trains make it possible to cover shorter chunks, such as Friedrichshafen–Konstanz–Meersburg, in a weekend.

A day suffices to cover some highlights in three countries on a 30km stretch of the route. Begin in Lindau's storybook old town in Germany, then pedal along the lakeshore to Bregenz, in Austria, famous for its Festpiele (www.bregenzerfestspiele.com), an open-air opera festival held on the lake from mid-July to mid-August. Rearing above the town is the 1064m peak of Pfänder, which commands a breathtaking panorama of Lake Constance and the not-so-distant Alps. A cable car (round-trip adult/concession €11/8.80; ☺8am-7pm) glides to the summit. Continue southwest along a woodland path to the broad banks of the Bregenzerach, a beautiful meltwater river where locals bathe and fly-fish on hot days. From here it's just a short pedal to the Rheindelta wetlands and the wide bay of Rorschach in Switzerland, where you can stop for Swiss chocolate before catching a ferry back to Lindau.

🛏 Sleeping

Rock up between November and mid-March and you may find some places closed. The tourist office has a free booking service and a list of private rooms.

Villa Barleben   HISTORIC HOTEL $$$
(Map p358; ☑942 330; www.hotel-barleben.de; Seestrasse 15; s €135-230, d €195-255; 🐾) Gregariously elegant, this 19th-century villa's sunny rooms and corridors are sprinkled with antiques and ethnic art. The rambling lakefront gardens are ideal for dozing in a Strandkorb (wicker beach lounger), G&T in hand, or enjoying lunch on the terrace.

Hotel Barbarossa   HISTORIC HOTEL $$
(Map p358; ☑128 990; www.barbarossa-hotel.com; Obermarkt 8-12; s €55-75, d €95-130; 🐾) This 600-year-old patrician house harbours parquet-floored, individually decorated rooms, which are bright and appealing, if a tad on the small side. The terrace has views over Konstanz' rooftops and spires.

Riva   BOUTIQUE HOTEL $$$
(☑363 090; www.hotel-riva.de; Seestrasse 25; s €110-150, d €200-240; 🅿🐾🌊) This ultra-chic contender has crisp white spaces, glass walls and a snail-like stairwell. Zen-like rooms with hardwood floors feature perks such as (like it!) free minibars. The rooftop pool and Mediterranean-style restaurant (mains €18 to €25) overlook the lake.

Pension Gretel   B&B $$
(Map p358; ☑455 825; www.hotel-gretel.de; Zollernstrasse 6-8; s €45, d €60-98, tr/q €126/180) Sure, the rooms are basic, but they are light, tidy and a snip given the Altstadt location. There's a cosy Weinstube if you fancy a glass of wine and bite to eat, and handy bike storage for cyclists.

Hotel Halm   HOTEL $$
(Map p358; ☑12 10; www.hotel-halm-konstanz.de; Bahnhofplatz 6; s/d €110-130; 🐾) A joyous hop and skip from the lake and Altstadt, this late 19th-century pile has warm, elegantly furnished rooms with marble bathrooms; upgrade if you want a balcony with lake view. Skip the €16 breakfast and hit a nearby bakery instead.

🍴 Eating

Münsterplatz and Markstätte are peppered with pizzerias, snack bars and gelaterias. Watch out for rip-offs around Stadtgarten.

Münsterhof   GERMAN $$$
(Map p358; ☑3638 427; Münsterplatz 3; mains €8.50-17; ☺daily; ✏🚼) Tables set up in front of the Münster, a slick bistro interior and a lunchtime buzz have earned Münsterhof a loyal local following. The two-course €6.90 lunch is a bargain. Dishes from cordon bleu with pan-fried potatoes to asparagus-filled Maultaschen in creamy chive sauce are substantial and satisfying.

Tolle Knolle
INTERNATIONAL $$$

(Map p358; ☑175 75; Bodanplatz 9; mains €9-17; ☺daily) On a fountain-dotted square with alfresco seating, this art-slung restaurant lives up to its 'great potato' moniker. Potatoes come in various guises: with *Wiener Schnitzel*, beer-battered fish and on the signature pizza. There's always a good-value €5.50 lunch special.

Voglhaus
CAFE $

(Map p358; Wessenbergstrasse 8; light meals €2.50-6; ☺9am-6.30pm Mon-Sat, 11am-6pm Sun; ☑) Locals flock to the 'bird house' for its chilled vibe and contemporary wood-and-stone interior, warmed by an open fire in winter. Wood-oven bread with spreads, wholegrain bagels and cupcakes pair nicely with smoothies and speciality coffees like Hansel and Gretel (with gingerbread syrup).

Zeitlos
GERMAN $

(Map p358; St Stephansplatz 25; snacks €4-10; ☺10am-1am Mon-Sat, to 6pm Sun) Behind Stephanskirche, this beamed, stone-walled bistro overflows with regulars. It's a cosy spot for brunch or filling snacks like *Wurstsalat* (sausage salad) and *Maultaschen*, the local take on ravioli. Sit in the ivy-draped courtyard in summer.

La Bodega
TAPAS $$

(Map p358; ☑277 88; Schreibergasse 40; tapas €3.50-10.50; ☺dinner Tue-Sat) Squirrelled away in Niederburg, this candy-bright bodega with a pocket-sized terrace whips up tapas from *papas canarias* (Canarian potatoes) to stuffed calamari.

Hexenkuche
STEAKHOUSE $$

(Map p358; ☑245 60; Bodanstrasse 30; mains €10-23; ☺dinner Wed-Mon) Rump, fillet and Charolais – the rustic-look 'witches' kitchen' hits the mark with well-seasoned steaks.

Maximilian's
DELI $

(Map p358; Hussenstrasse 9; cake around €2.50; ☺10am-7pm Mon-Fri, to 6.30pm Sat) Fancy a picnic by the lake? Stop by this central deli for fresh bread, cheese, ham, wine and other goodies. It's also a snug spot for coffee and cake.

Drinking & Entertainment

A vibrant student population fuels Konstanz' after-dark scene. For the low-down, see www.party-news.de (in German). Head to the harbour for drinks with a lake view.

K9
CULTURAL CENTRE

(Map p358; www.k9-kulturzentrum.de; Obere Laube 71) Once a medieval church, this is now Konstanz' most happening cultural venue, with a line-up skipping from salsa nights and film screenings to gigs, club nights and jive nights. See the website for times.

Klimperkasten
BAR

(Map p358; Bodanstrasse 40; ☺10am-1am, to 3am Sat) Indie kids, garage and old-school fans all hail this retro cafe, which gets clubbier after dark when DJs work the decks. Occasionally hosts gigs.

Schwarze Katz
BAR

(Map p358; Katzgasse 8; ☺6pm-1am Mon-Thu, to 2am Fri & Sat) Found the 'black cat'? You're in luck. A relaxed mood, friendly crowd and reasonably priced drinks (including Black Forest Alpirsbacher beer) make this a Konstanz favourite.

Brauhaus Johann Albrecht
BREWPUB

(Map p358; Konradigasse 2; ☺11.30am-1pm) This step-gabled microbrewery is a relaxed haunt for quaffing wheat beer or hoppy lager by the glass or metre, with a terrace for summer imbibing.

Seekuh
PUB

(Map p358; Konzilstrasse 1; ☺6pm-btwn 1am & 3am) The rough and ready 'lake cow' is a Konstanz favourite for its beer garden, cheapish drinks and occasional gigs.

ⓘ Information

ReiseBank (Hauptbahnhof; ☺8am-12.30pm & 1.30-6pm Mon-Fri, 8am-3pm Sat) Currency exchange, including Swiss francs.

DON'T MISS

IMPERIA RULES

At the end of the pier in Konstanz, giving ferry passengers a come-hither look from her rotating pedestal, stands **Imperia** (Map p358). Peter Lenk's 9m-high sculpture of a buxom prostitute, said to have plied her trade in the days of the Council of Constance, is immortalised in a novel by Honoré de Balzac. In her clutches are hilarious sculptures of a naked (and sagging) Pope Martin V and Holy Roman Emperor Sigismund, symbolising religious and imperial power.

Tourist office (133 030; www.konstanz-tourismus.de; Bahnhofplatz 43; ⊙9am-6.30pm Mon-Fri, to 4pm Sat, 10am-1pm Sun Apr-Oct, 9.30am-6pm Mon-Fri Nov-Mar) Just north of the train stations. Inside you can pick up a walking-tour brochure (€1) and city map (€0.50); outside there's a hotel reservation board and free hotel telephone.

❶ Getting There & Away

Konstanz is Lake Constance's main ferry hub.

By car, Konstanz can be reached via the B33, which links up with the A81 to and from Stuttgart near Singen. Or you can take the B31 to Meersburg and then catch a car ferry.

Konstanz' Hauptbahnhof is the southern terminus of the scenic Schwarzwaldbahn, which trundles hourly through the Black Forest, linking Offenburg with towns such as Triberg and Villingen. To reach Lake Constance's northern shore, you usually have to change in Radolfzell. The Schweizer Bahnhof has connections to destinations throughout Switzerland.

❶ Getting Around

The city centre is a traffic headache, especially at weekends. Your best bet is the free Park & Ride lot 3km northwest of the Altstadt, near the airfield on Byk-Gulden-Strasse, where your only outlay will be for a bus ticket.

Local buses (www.sw.konstanz.de) cost €2.10 for a single ticket; day passes are €4/6.80 for an individual/family. Bus 1 links the Meersburg car-ferry dock with the Altstadt. If you stay in Konstanz for at least two nights, your hotelier will give you a Gästekarte entitling you to free local bus travel.

Bicycles can be hired from **Kultur-Rädle** (273 10; Bahnhofplatz 29; per day €12; ⊙9am-12.30pm & 2.30-6pm Mon-Fri, 10am-4pm Sat year-round, plus 10am-12.30pm Sun Easter-Sep), close to the tourist office.

Mainau Island

Jutting out over the lake and bursting with flowers, the lusciously green islet of Mainau (www.mainau.de; adult/concession €16.90/9.50; ⊙dawn-dusk) is a 45-hectare Mediterranean garden dreamed up by the Bernadotte family, relatives of the royal house of Sweden.

Around two million visitors flock here every year to admire sparkly lake and mountain views from the baroque castle, and wander sequoia-shaded avenues and hothouses bristling with palms and orchids. Crowd-pullers include the Butterfly House, where hundreds of vivid butterflies flit amid the dewy foliage, an Italian Cascade integrating patterned flowers with waterfalls, and a petting zoo. Tulips and rhododendrons bloom in spring, hibiscus and roses in summer. Avoid weekends, when the gardens get crowded.

You can drive, walk or cycle to Mainau, 8km north of Konstanz. Take bus 4 from Konstanz' train station or hop aboard a passenger ferry.

Reichenau Island

☑07534 / POP 3200

In AD 724 a missionary named Pirmin founded a Benedictine monastery on Reichenau (www.reichenau.de), a 4.5km-by-1.5km island (Lake Constance's largest) about 11km west of Konstanz. During its heyday, from 820 to 1050, the so-called Reichenauer School produced stunning illuminated manuscripts and vivid frescoes. Today, three surviving churches provide silent testimony to Reichenau's Golden Age. Thanks to them, the island was declared a Unesco World Heritage Site in 2000.

Bring walking boots and binoculars, as this fertile isle of orchards and wineries is home to Wollmatinger Ried (www.nabu-wollmatingerried.de), a marshy nature reserve whose reed wetlands attract butterflies, migratory birds including kingfishers, grey herons and cuckoos, and even the odd beaver.

A 2km-long tree-lined causeway connects the mainland with the island, which is served by bus 7372 from Konstanz. The Konstanz–Schaffhausen and Konstanz–Radolfzell ferries stop off at Reichenau.

Marienschlucht

Well worth the 15km trek north of Konstanz, Marienschlucht (⊙daylight hrs) is a deep ravine wedged between the villages of Bodman and Wallhausen. A wooden staircase zigzags up through the chasm, past a babbling stream and 30m-high cliffs thick with lichen and ferns. The top rewards you with snapshot views of Lake Constance through the beech trees. Bear left to follow the trail along the ridge and back down to Wallhausen. There are picnic areas and a kiosk en route, as well as pebbly bays for refreshing dips in the lake.

Coming from Konstanz, Wallhausen is the best place to access the gorge, either by bicycle or bus 4 from the Hauptbahnhof (€2.30, 30 minutes). From Wallhausen it's a 3km walk to Marienschlucht.

Meersburg

07532 / POP 5630

Tumbling down vine-streaked slopes to Lake Constance and crowned by a perkily turreted medieval castle, Meersburg lives up to all those clichéd knights-in-armour, damsel-in-distress fantasies. And if its tangle of cobbled lanes and half-timbered houses filled with jovial banter doesn't sweep you off your feet, the local Pinot noir served in its cosy *Weinstuben* (wine taverns) will, we swear.

Sights & Activities

Altes Schloss   CASTLE
(adult/concession €8.50/6.50; ⊙9am-6.30pm Mar-Oct, 10am-6pm Nov-Feb) Looking across the Lake Constance from its lofty perch, the Altes Schloss is an archetypal medieval stronghold, complete with keep, drawbridge, knights' hall and dungeons. Founded by Merovingian king Dagobert I in the 7th century, the fortress is among Germany's oldest, which is no mean feat in a country with a *lot* of castles. The bishops of Konstanz used it as a summer residence between 1268 and 1803.

Neues Schloss   CASTLE
(www.schloesser-und-gaerten.de; adult/concession €5/2.50; ⊙9am-6.30pm May-Oct, 11am-4pm Sat & Sun Nov-Apr) In 1710 Prince-Bishop Johann Franz Schenk von Stauffenberg, perhaps tired of the dinginess and rising damp, swapped the Altes Schloss for the dusky-pink, lavishly baroque Neues Schloss. A visit to the now state-owned palace takes in the extravagant bishops' apartments replete with stucco work and frescoes, Bathasar Neumann's elegant staircase, and gardens with inspirational lake views.

Lakefront   HARBOUR
Stroll the harbour for classic snaps of Lake Constance or to hire a pedalo. On the jetty, you can't miss – though the pious might prefer to – Peter Lenk's satirical Magische Säule (Magic Column). The sculpture is a hilarious satirical depiction of characters who have shaped Meersburg's history, including buxom wine-wench Wendelgart and poet Annette von Droste-Hülshoff (the seagull).

Meersburg Therme   DAY SPA
(440 2850; www.meersburg-therme.de; Uferpromenade 12; thermal baths 3hr adult/concession €9/8.50, incl sauna 3hr €16.50/16; ⊙10am-10pm Mon-Thu, to 11pm Fri & Sat, 9am-10pm Sun) It's a five-minute walk east along the Uferpromenade to this lakefront spa, where the 34°C thermal waters, water jets and Swiss Alp views are soothing. Those who dare to bare all can skinny-dip in the lake and steam in saunas that are replicas of Unteruhldingen's Stone Age dwellings.

Sleeping & Eating

Meersburg goes with the seasons, with most places closing from November to Easter. Pick up a brochure listing good-value apartments and private rooms at the tourist office.

Characterful wine taverns line Unterstadtstrasse, while the lakefront Seepromenade has wall-to-wall pizzerias, cafes and gelaterias with alfresco seating.

Gasthof zum Bären   GUESTHOUSE $$
(432 20; www.baeren-meersburg.de; Marktplatz 11; s €49, d €98-110, mains €9-17.50) Straddling three 13th- to 17th-century buildings, this guest house near Obertor receives glowing reviews for its classic rooms, spruced up with stucco work, ornate wardrobes and lustrous wood; corner rooms No 13 and 23 are the most romantic. The rustic tavern serves Lake Constance fare like *Felchen* (whitefish).

Romantik Residenz
am See   LUXURY HOTEL $$$
(800 40; www.hotel-residenz-meersburg.com; Uferpromenade 11; s €80-120, d €150-200; tasting menus €80-135; ⊛) Sitting aplomb the promenade, this romantic hotel is a class act. The higher you go, the better the view in the warm-hued rooms facing the vineyards or lake. In the hotel's Michelin-starred restaurant, Casala, chef Markus Philippi brings sophisticated Mediterranean cuisine to the table.

Aurichs   GUESTHOUSE $
(445 9855; www.aurichs.com; Steigstrasse 28; s €44, d €72-76, mains €16.50-32) Choose from lake or castle views in stylish rooms with flourishes like slanted beams and wool rugs. In the art-filled restaurant, chef Christian Aurich pairs market-fresh dishes such as wild boar with chestnut purée and Lake Constance lamb with rosehip jus with Meersburg wines.

Gasthaus zum Letzten Heller   GUESTHOUSE $
(6149; www.zum-letzten-heller.de; Daisendorfer Strasse 41; s/d €38/58, mains €9-12.50) This family-friendly guest house keeps it sweet 'n' simple in bright, cottage-like

rooms with pine trappings. The restaurant serving home-grown food and wine has a tree-shaded patio. It's 1km north of the old town.

Winzerstube zum Becher GERMAN $$$
(☎9009; Höllgasse 4; mains €10.50-25.80; ☺closed Mon) Vines drape the facade of this wood-panelled bolt-hole, run by the same family since 1884. Home-grown Pinot noirs accompany Lake Constance classics such as whitefish in almond-butter sauce. The terrace affords Altes Schloss views.

Weinhaus Hanser GERMAN $
(☎9128; Unterstadtstrasse 28; Flammkuchen €7-8) Exposed red-brick and barrel tables create a cosy vibe at this 500-year-old *Torkel* (wine press), where you can taste local wines and chomp pizza-like *Flammkuchen*.

Gutsschänke GERMAN $$
(☎807 630; Seminarstrassse 6; mains €10-15; ☺daily) On a perch above the lake and vineyards, this restaurant's terrace is a beautiful spot to sip a glass of Meersburg Pinot noir or blanc or dig into hearty mains like *Zwiebelrostbraten* (beef and onions in gravy).

❶ Information

Tourist office (☎440 400; www.meersburg. de; Kirchstrasse 4; ☺9am-12.30pm & 2-6pm Mon-Fri, 10am-3pm Sat, 10am-1pm Sun, shorter hours in winter) Housed in a one-time Dominican monastery. Internet access costs €3 per hour.

❶ Getting There & Away

Meersburg, which lacks a train station, is 18km west of Friedrichshafen.

From Monday to Friday, eight times a day, express bus 7394 makes the trip to Konstanz (€3.25, 40 minutes) and Friedrichshafen (€3.10, 26 minutes). Bus 7373 connects Meersburg with Ravensburg (€5, 40 minutes, four daily Monday to Friday, two Saturday). Meersburg's main bus stop is next to the church.

❶ Getting Around

The best and only way to get around Meersburg is on foot. Even the large pay car park near the car-ferry port (€1.20 per hour) is often full in high season. You might find free parking north of the old town along Daisendorfer Strasse.

Hire bikes at **Hermann Dreher** (☎5176; Stadtgraben 5; per day €4.50; ☺rental 9am-noon), down the alley next to the tourist office.

Pfahlbauten

Awarded Unesco World Heritage status in 2011, the **Pfahlbauten** (Pile Dwellings; www. pfahlbauten.de; Strandpromenade 6, Unteruhldingen; adult/concession €7/5; ☺9am-btwn 5pm & 7pm; ⏹) 6km north of Meersburg, represent one of 111 Prehistoric Pile dwellings around the Alps. Based on the findings of local excavations, the carefully reconstructed pile dwellings catapult you back to the Stone and Bronze Age, from 4000 to 850 BC. A spin of the lakefront complex takes in stilt dwellings that give an insight into the prehistoric lives of farmers, fishermen and craftsmen. Kids love the hands-on activities, from axe-making to starting fires using flints.

Birnau

The exuberant, powder-pink **Wahllfahrtskirche Birnau** (Pilgrimage Church; Uhldingen-Mühlhofen; ☺7.30am-btwn 5.30pm & 7pm) is one of Lake Constance's architectural highlights. It was built by the rococo master Peter Thumb of Vorarlberg in 1746. When you walk in, the decor is so intricate and profuse that you don't know where to look first. At some point your gaze will be drawn to the ceiling, where Gottfried Bernhard Göz worked his usual fresco magic. It's situated 9km north of Meersburg on the B31.

Affenberg Salem

No zoo-like cages, no circus antics – just happy Barbary macaques free to roam in a near-to-natural habitat is the concept behind the conservation-oriented **Affenberg Salem** (www.affenberg-salem.de; adult/child €8/5; ☺9am-btwn 5pm & 6pm). Trails interweave the 20-hectare woodlands, where you can feed tail-less monkeys one piece of special popcorn at a time, observe their behaviour (you scratch my back, I'll scratch yours...) and get primate close-ups at hourly feedings. The park is also home to storks: listen for bill clattering and look out for their nests near the entrance. The Affenburg is on the K7765, 10km north of Meersburg.

Schloss Salem

Founded as a Cistercian monastery in 1134, the immense estate known as **Schloss Salem** (www.salem.de; adult/concession €7/3.50; ◷9.30am-6pm Mon-Sat, 10.30am-6pm Sun Apr-Oct) was once the largest and richest of its kind in southern Germany. The Grand Duchy of Baden sold out to the state recently but you can still picture the royals swanning around the hedge maze, gardens and extravagant rococo apartments dripping with stucco. The west wing shelters an elite boarding school, briefly attended by Prince Philip (Duke of Edinburgh and husband of Queen Elizabeth II). Schloss Salem sits 12km north of Meersburg.

Friedrichshafen

📞07541 / POP 59,000

Zeppelins, the cigar-shaped airships that first took flight in 1900 under the stewardship of high-flying Count Ferdinand von Zeppelin, will forever be associated with Friedrichshafen. An amble along the flowery lakefront promenade and a visit to the museum that celebrates the behemoth of the skies are the biggest draws of this industrial town, which was heavily bombed in WWII and rebuilt in the 1950s.

◉ Sights & Activities

TOP CHOICE **Zeppelin Museum**   MUSEUM
(www.zeppelin-museum.de; Seestrasse 22; adult/concession €7.50/4; ◷9am-5pm daily May-Oct, 10am-5pm Tue-Sun Nov-Apr) Near the eastern end of Friedrichshafen's lakefront promenade, Seestrasse, is the Zeppelin Museum, housed in the Bauhaus-style former Hafenbahnhof, built in 1932.

The centrepiece is a full-scale mock-up of a 33m section of the *Hindenburg* (LZ 129), the largest airship ever built, measuring an incredible 245m long and outfitted as luxuriously as an ocean liner. The hydrogen-filled craft tragically burst into flames, killing 36, while landing in New Jersey in 1937.

Other exhibits provide technical and historical insights, including an original motor gondola from the famous *Graf Zeppelin*, which made 590 trips and travelled around the world in 21 days in 1929.

The top-floor art collection stars brutally realistic works by Otto Dix.

Lakefront   PROMENADE
A promenade runs through the lakefront, sculpture-dotted **Stadtgarten** park along Uferstrasse, a great spot for a picnic or stroll. Pedal and electric boats can be rented at the Gondelhafen (€9 to €23 per hour).

The western end of Friedrichshafen's promenade is anchored by the twin-onion-towered, baroque **Schlosskirche**. It's the only accessible part of the Schloss and is still inhabited by the ducal family of Württemberg.

🛏 Sleeping & Eating

The tourist office has a free booking terminal. For lake-view snacks, hit Seestrasse's beer gardens, pizzerias and ice-cream parlours.

Hotel Restaurant Maier   HOTEL **$$**
(📞4040; www.hotel-maier.de; Poststrasse 1-3, Friedrichshafen-Fischbach; s €59-95, d €89-120; 🅿🛜) The contemporary, light-drenched rooms are immaculately kept at this family-run hotel, 5km west of Friedrichshafen and an eight-minute hop on the train. The mini spa invites relaxing moments, with its lake-facing terrace, steam room and sauna.

Gasthof Rebstock   GUESTHOUSE **$**
(📞950 1640; www.gasthof-rebstock-fn.de; Werasstrasse 35; s/d/tr/q €55/75/90/100; 🛜) Geared up for cyclists and offering bike rental (€7 per day), this family-run hotel has a beer garden and humble but tidy rooms with pine furnishings. It's situated 750m northwest of the Stadtbahnhof.

DON'T MISS

COME FLY WITH ME

Real airship fans will justify the splurge on a trip in a high-tech, 12-passenger **Zeppelin NT** (📞590 00; www.zeppelinflug.de). Flights lasting 30/45/60/90/120 minutes cost €200/295/395/565/745. Shorter trips cover lake destinations such as Schloss Salem and Lindau, while longer ones drift across to Austria or Switzerland. Take-off and landing are in Friedrichshafen. The flights aren't cheap but little beats floating over Lake Constance with the Alps on the horizon, so slowly that you can make the most of legendary photo ops.

Brot, Kaffee, Wein
CAFE $

(Karlstrasse 38; snacks €3-8; ⊘8.30am-8pm Mon-Fri, 9am-8pm Sat, 9.30am-8pm Sun) Slick and monochrome, this deli-cafe has a lakeside terrace for lingering over a speciality coffee, breakfast, homemade ice cream or sourdough bread sandwich.

Beach Club
LOUNGE BAR $

(Uferstrasse 1; snacks €6-8; ⊘11am-midnight Apr-Oct) This lakefront shack is the place to unwind on the deck, mai tai in hand, and admire the *Klangschiff* sculpture and the not-so-distant Alps. Revive over tapas, salads and antipasti.

ⓘ Information

Post office (Bahnhofplatz) To the right as you exit the Stadtbahnhof.

Tourist office (⌀300 10; www.friedrichshafen. info; Bahnhofplatz 2; ⊘9am-1pm & 1-6pm Mon-Fri, 9am-1pm Sat) On the square outside the Stadtbahnhof. Has a free internet terminal. Can book accommodation and zeppelin flights.

ⓘ Getting There & Around

There are ferry options, including a catamaran to Konstanz. Sailing times are posted on the waterfront just outside the Zeppelin Museum.

From Monday to Friday, seven times a day, express bus 7394 makes the trip to Konstanz (1¼ hours) via Meersburg (30 minutes). Birnau and Meersburg are also served almost hourly by bus 7395.

Friedrichshafen is on the Bodensee–Gürtelbahn train line, which runs along the lake's northern shore from Radolfzell to Lindau. There are also regular services on the Bodensee–Oberschwaben–Bahn, which runs to Ravensburg (€3.95, 20 minutes).

Ravensburg

⌀0751 / POP 49,780

Ravensburg has puzzled the world for the past 125 years with its jigsaws and board games. The medieval Altstadt has toy-town appeal, studded with turrets, robber-knight towers and gabled patrician houses. For centuries dukes and wealthy merchants polished the cobbles of this Free Imperial City – now it's your turn.

⊙ Sights

Marienplatz
SQUARE

The heart of Altstadt is the elongated, pedestrianised Marienplatz, framed by sturdy towers, frescoed patrician houses and cafes.

The 51m-high **Blaserturm** (adult/concession €1.50/1; ⊘2-5pm Mon-Fri, 10am-3pm Sat April-early Nov), part of the original fortifications, has superb views over the Altstadt from up top. Next door is the late-Gothic, step-gabled **Waaghaus**, while on the opposite side of Marienplatz sits the 15th-century **Lederhaus**, with its elaborate Renaissance facade, once the domain of tanners and shoemakers.

At the northern end of Marienplatz is the round **Grüner Turm**, with its lustrous tiled roof, and the weighty, late-Gothic church **Liebfrauenkirche**.

Ravensburger Spieleland
THEME PARK

(www.spieleland.de; Mecklenbeuren; adult/concession €25.50/23.50; ⊘10am-6pm Apr-Oct) Kids in tow? Take them to this board-game-inspired theme park, with attractions from giant-rubber-duck racing and cow milking against the clock to rodeo and Alpine rafting. It is a 10-minute drive south of Ravensburg on the B467.

Museum Humpis
MUSEUM

(www.museum-humpis-quartier.de; Marktstrasse 45; adult/concession €4/2; ⊘11am-6pm Tue-Sun, to 8pm Thu) Seven exceptional late-medieval houses set around a glass-covered courtyard shelter a permanent collection and rotating exhibitions focusing on Ravensburg's past as a trade centre.

Mehlsack
TOWER

The all-white Mehlsack (Flour Sack) is a tower marking the Altstadt's southern edge. From there a steep staircase leads up to the **Veitsburg**, a quaint baroque castle, which now harbours the restaurant of the same name, with outlooks over Ravensburg's mosaic of red-tiled roofs.

🛏 Sleeping & Eating

Waldhorn
HISTORIC HOTEL $$

(⌀361 20; http://waldhorn.de; Marienplatz 15; s €75-125, d €135-150, mains €12-25; 🕏) The Waldhorn creaks with history and its light, appealingly restored rooms make a great base for exploring the Altstadt. Lodged in the 15th-century vintners' guildhall, its wood-beamed restaurant, **Rebleutehaus**, turns out spot-on seasonal dishes like tender corn-fed chicken with herb gnocchi. The three-course lunch is a bargain at €19.80.

Gasthof Obertor
GUESTHOUSE $$

(⌀366 70; www.hotelobertor.de; Marktstrasse 67; s €72-90, d €112-125; 🅿🕏) The affable Rimpps take pride in their lemon-fronted patrician house. Obertor stands head and shoulders above most Altstadt guesthouses, with spotless rooms, a sauna area and generous breakfasts.

Veitsburg
INTERNATIONAL $$$

(☑366 1990; www.restaurant-veitsburg.de; Veitsburg 2; mains €11-18; ☺11am-midnight, closed Wed Oct-Mar; ☑☺) Welf and Hohenstaufen dukes once lorded it over this castle, now a highly atmospheric restaurant. Gaze across Ravensburg to the hills beyond while tucking into dishes like Bavarian pork roast in dark beer sauce and tagliatelle in wild mushroom sauce.

ⓘ Information

Tourist office (☑828 00; www.ravensburg.de; Kirchstrasse 16; ☺9am-5.30pm Mon-Fri, 10am-1pm Sat) A block northeast of Marienplatz.

ⓘ Getting There & Away

The train station is six blocks to the west along Eisenbahnstrasse. Ravensburg is on the train line linking Friedrichshafen (€3.95, 16 minutes, at least twice hourly) with Ulm (€16.40, 57 minutes, at least hourly) and Stuttgart (€38, two hours, at least hourly).

Lindau

☑08382 / POP 24,800

Brochures rhapsodise about Lindau being Germany's 'Garden of Eden' and the 'Bavarian Riviera'. Paradise and southern France it ain't but it is, well, pretty special. Cradled in the southern crook of Lake Constance and almost dipping its toes into Austria, this is a good-looking, outgoing little town, with a candy-coloured postcard of an Altstadt, clear-day Alpine views and lakefront cafes that use every sunray to the max.

◉ Sights

Seepromenade
PROMENADE

In summer the harbourside promenade has a happy-go-lucky air, with its palms, bobbing boats and folk sunning themselves in pavement cafes.

Out at the harbour gates, looking across to the Alps, is Lindau's signature 33m-high **Neuer Leuchtturm** (New Lighthouse) and, just in case you forget which state you're in, a statue of the Bavarian lion. The square tile-roofed, 13th-century **Mangturm** (Old Lighthouse) guards the northern edge of the sheltered port.

Altes Rathaus
LANDMARK

(Old Town Hall; Bismarckplatz) Lindau's biggest architectural stunner is the 15th-century step-gabled Altes Rathaus, a frescoed frenzy of cherubs, merry minstrels and galleons.

Stadtmuseum
MUSEUM

(Marktplatz 6; adult/concession €3/1.50; ☺11am-5pm Tue-Fri & Sun, 2-5pm Sat) Lions and voluptuous dames dance across the trompe l'oeil facade of the flamboyantly baroque Haus zum Cavazzen, which contains this museum, showcasing a fine collection of furniture, weapons and paintings.

Peterskirche
CHURCH

(Schrannenplatz; ☺daily) Looking back on a 1000-year history, this enigmatic church is now a war memorial, hiding exquisite time-faded frescoes of the Passion of Christ by Hans Holbein the Elder. The cool, dimly lit interior is a quiet spot for contemplation. Next door is the turreted 14th-century **Diebsturm**, once a tiny jail.

🛏 Sleeping

Lindau virtually goes into hibernation from November to February, when many hotels close. Nip into the tourist office for a list of good-value holiday apartments.

Hotel Garni-Brugger
HISTORIC HOTEL $$

(☑934 10; www.hotel-garni-brugger.de; Bei der Heidenmauer 11; s €56-78, d €92-106; @) Our readers rave about this 18th-century hotel, with bright rooms done up in floral fabrics and pine. The family bends over backwards to please. Guests can unwind in the little spa with steam room and sauna (€10) in the cooler months.

Reutemann & Seegarten
LUXURY HOTEL $$$

(☑9150; www.reutemann-lindau.de; Seepromenade; s €87-240, d €138-342; ☞☒) Wow, what a view! Facing the harbour, lighthouse and lion statue, this hotel has plush, spacious rooms done out in sunny shades, as well as a pool big enough to swim laps, a spa, gym and refined restaurant.

Hotel Anker
GUESTHOUSE $

(☑260 9844; www.anker-lindau.de; Bindergasse 15; s/d €55/78; ☞) Shiny parquet floors, citrus colours and artwork have spruced up the bargain rooms at this peach-coloured guesthouse. Rates include a hearty breakfast.

Alte Post
HOTEL $$

(☑934 60; www.alte-post-lindau.de; Fischergasse 3; s €60-75, d €120-150, mains €8-15) Sitting on cobbled Fischergasse, this 300-year-old coaching inn was once a stop on the Frankfurt–Milan mail run. Well-kept, light and spacious, the rooms have chunky pine furnishings and perks like free tea. Downstairs is a beer garden and a dark-wood tavern pairing dishes like *Tafelspitz* (boiled beef) and *Maultaschen* with fruity local wines.

Hotel Medusa GUESTHOUSE $$
(☑932 20; www.medusa-hotel.com; Schafgasse 10; s €49-69, d €98-138) The Greek mythology link is tenuous, but this guesthouse pleases with lovingly renovated, high-ceilinged rooms, jazzed up with bursts of red or aquamarine and flat-screen TVs.

✖ Eating & Drinking

For a drink with a cool view, head to Seepromenade. The crowds on the main thoroughfare, Maximilianstrasse, can be dodged in nearby backstreets, where your euro will stretch further.

Valentin MEDITERRANEAN $$$
(☑504 3740; In der Grub 28; mains €8-23.50; ⊙Tue-Sat) Markus Allgaier carefully sources the local ingredients that go into his Med-style dishes at this sleek vaulted restaurant. Signatures like leg of lamb with parmesan beans and pistachio-plum risotto and grilled scallops on balsamic-beluga lentils are beautifully cooked and presented.

37° CAFE $$
(Bahnhofplatz 1; snacks €4-11; ⊙10am-8pm Tue-Wed & Sun, to 11pm Thu-Sat) Part boutique, part boho-chic cafe, 37° combines a high-ceilinged interior with a lake-facing pavement terrace. Pull up a chair for cold drinks and light bites like tapas, quiche and soups.

Weinstube Frey GERMAN $$$
(☑947 9676; Maximilianstrasse 15; mains €13-22; ⊙closed Mon) This 500-year-old wine tavern oozes Bavarian charm in its wood-panelled tavern full of cosy nooks. Dirndl-clad waitresses serve up regional wines and fare such as beer-battered Lake Constance trout. Sit on the terrace when the sun's out.

Marmor Saal BAR
(Bahnhofplatz 1e; ⊙9am-2am or 3am) The lakefront 'marble hall' once welcomed royalty and still has a feel of grandeur with its soaring columns, chandeliers and Biedermeier flourishes. Nowadays it's a relaxed cafe-bar with occasional live music and a chilled terrace.

❶ Information

Post office (cnr Maximilianstrasse & Bahnhofplatz)

Tourist office (☑260 030; www.lindau.de; Alfred-Nobel-Platz 1; ⊙10am-6pm Mon-Sat, to 1pm Sun, shorter hours in low season) Can make hotel bookings.

❶ Getting There & Away

Lindau is on the B31 and connects to Munich by the A96. The precipitous **Deutsche Alpenstrasse** (German Alpine Rd), which winds giddily eastward to Berchtesgaden, begins here.

Lindau is at the eastern terminus of the train line, which goes along the lake's north shore via Friedrichshafen (€5.50, 20 minutes) westward to Radolfzell and the southern terminus of the Südbahn to Ulm (€23.50, 1¾ hours) via Ravensburg (€9.10, 44 minutes).

❶ Getting Around

The compact, walkable Insel (island), home to the town centre and harbour, is connected to the mainland by the Seebrücke, a road bridge at its northeastern tip, and by the Eisenbahndamm, a rail bridge open to cyclists and pedestrians. The Hauptbahnhof lies to the east of the island, a block south of the pedestrianised, shop-lined Maximilianstrasse.

Buses 1 and 2 link the Hauptbahnhof to the main bus hub, known as ZUP. A single ticket costs €2, a 24-hour pass is €5.20.

To get to the island by car follow the signs to 'Lindau-Insel'. It's easiest and cheapest to park at the large metered car park (€0.60 per hour) just before you cross the bridge to the island.

Bikes and tandems can be rented at **Unger's Fahrradverleih** (Inselgraben 14; per day €6-12; ⊙9am-1pm & 3-6pm Mon-Fri, 9am-1pm Sat & Sun).

Frankfurt & Southern Rhineland

Best Places to Eat

» Adolf Wagner (p390)
» Kleinmarkthalle (p389)
» Zur Kanzel (p409)
» Zur Herrenmühle (p420)
» Zum Stiefel (p458)

Best Places to Stay

» Fleming's Hotel (p386)
» Hip Hotel (p419)
» Arthotel (p419)
» Deidesheimer Hof (p432)
» Hotel Bellevue (p443)

Why Go?

Frankfurt is best known as a banking powerhouse, trade-fair venue and air hub, but ask the residents of Germany's most cosmopolitan city what they like about living there and they'll mention the excellent quality of life, flowery parkland, laid-back cafes and pulsating nightlife. Just an hour west – past the cathedral city of Mainz, where Gutenberg invented printing – flows the Romantic Rhine, whose storied castles and snug wine villages have drawn artists and tourists since the early 19th century. Vineyards also stretch along the dramatic hillsides above the serpentine Moselle River and, just north of Alsace (France), along the German Wine Route – in both areas, crisp rieslings can all be sampled in a multitude of ambience-laden wine taverns. For sheer romance, though, it's hard to beat the ancient university city of Heidelberg, where something is always brewing – beer, of course, but also deep thoughts and culture both high and popular.

When to Go

Frankfurt's many charms can be enjoyed at any time of the year, but you'll pay a fortune for accommodation if your visit coincides with a big trade fair – see the Frankfurt section for further advice. The Moselle and the Rhine are particularly popular from May to August and very quiet – almost dead, in fact – from November to March, except in places that have Christmas markets in December. Along the German Wine Route – Germany's warmest region – village wine festivals are held on weekends from March to mid-November.

FEDERAL STATES

This chapter covers parts of four German states:

» **Hesse** (Hessen) – Frankfurt, Wiesbaden, Rüdesheim

» **Baden-Württemberg** – Heidelberg, Mannheim

» **Rhineland-Palatinate** – Romantic Rhine, Moselle, German Wine Road, Speyer, Worms

» **Saarland** – Saarbrücken

Need to Know

All of Frankfurt's museums are closed on Monday except:

» Goethe-Haus (p378)

» Senckenberg Museum (p381)

» Explora (p381)

Advance Planning

» During Frankfurt's major trade fairs, arrange your accommodation well in advance. Rooms are *much* cheaper outside the city.

» If a trade fair's in town, book restaurants ahead.

» Check with the Deidesheim tourist office (p433) for details on Weinfeste (wine festivals) in German Wine Route villages.

Resources

» **Frankfurt Tourist Office** (www.frankfurt-tourismus.de)

» **Romantic Rhine** (www.welterbe-mittelrheintal.de)

» **Cycling Routes** (www.radwanderland.de)

Cycling Paradise

Delightful long-distance bike trails (www.radwanderland.de and www.radroutenplaner.hessen.de) – many following decommissioned rail lines, with their mellow gradients – can be found along the Rhine, the Moselle, the German Wine Route and in the Saarland. Almost all the cities and towns mentioned in this chapter (Saarbrücken is an exception) have bike rental options, listed under Getting Around.

Tourist offices can supply you with cycling maps that include elevation charts, and can outline your public transport options (eg so you can catch a ride up the hill and cycle back).

Bicycles can be taken aboard all trains for no charge except before 9am from Monday to Friday, when you need a special ticket, and for a small charge on passenger boats.

TRAIN DISCOUNTS

Various day passes often work out costing *much* less than standard one-way fares, especially for groups:

» **Baden-Württemberg-Ticket** For travel in the Heidelberg area. Same prices and conditions as the Rheinland-Pfalz-Ticket.

» **Hessenticket** (1 day €31) Allows a group of up to five people travelling together to take regional trains (those designated RB, RE and IRE, ie any trains except D, IC, EC or ICE) anywhere within the German federal state of Hesse plus Mainz and Worms any time after 9am (all day on Saturday, Sunday and holidays) – an incredible deal!

» **Rheinland-Pfalz-Ticket** (1 day for 1 person €21, additional person €4) Valid from 9am to 3am the following day (all day on weekends and holidays) for up to five people travelling together in both Rhineland-Palatinate and Saarland, plus adjacent parts of Hesse (eg Wiesbaden) and Baden-Württemberg (eg Mannheim). Parents and grandparents can bring along their own children or grandchildren under age 15 for free.

Jewish Sites

In the Middle Ages, the Rhineland was home to the most illustrious Jewish communities in Ashkenaz (the Hebrew name for Germany). The brilliant Talmudic scholar Rashi (Raschi; Rabbi Shlomo Yitzhaqi, 1040–1105), whose commentaries are still considered indispensable, studied in Worms and Mainz. These days, Speyer and Worms have some of Europe's most important medieval Jewish sites.

Most towns and villages along the Romantic Rhine and the Moselle River had Jewish communities from the Middle Ages until 1942. Vestiges include cemeteries, alleys called 'Judengasse', repurposed synagogue buildings and commemorative plaques.

FRANKFURT AM MAIN

📞 069 / POP 680,000

Unashamedly high-rise, Frankfurt-on-the-Main (pronounced 'mine') is unlike any other German city. Bristling with jagged sky-scrapers, 'Mainhattan' – the focal point of a conurbation with some 5 million inhabitants – is a true capital of finance and business, home base for one of the world's largest stock exchanges as well as the European Central Bank. It also hosts some of Europe's most important trade fairs, including the largest book and motorcar fairs anywhere.

Yet Frankfurt consistently ranks as one of the world's most liveable cities, with a rich collection of museums (second in Germany only to Berlin's), lots of parks and greenery, a lively student scene, excellent public transport, fine dining and plenty to do in the evening. Nightspots range from cosy neighbourhood apple-wine taverns to some of Europe's most thumping techno-discos.

Frankfurt's airport, the region's biggest employer, is the third-largest in Europe, handling over 56 million passengers per year.

Hotel prices rise precipitously during major trade fairs, so plan ahead if you don't want to spend €350 a night for a very average double. For the trade-fair schedule, go to www.messefrankfurt.com or www.frankfurt-tourismus.de, or see the boxed text on p386.

History

Around 2000 years ago Frankfurt was a site of Celtic and Germanic settlement and then, in the area known today as the Römerberg, a Roman garrison town.

Mentioned in historical documents as far back as AD 794, Frankfurt was an important centre of power in the Holy Roman Empire. With the election of Frederick I (Barbarossa) in 1152, the city became the customary site of the selection of German kings. International trade fairs – attracting business from the Mediterranean to the Baltic – were held here, beginning in the 12th century.

In 1372 Frankfurt became a 'free imperial city', a status it enjoyed almost uninterruptedly until the Prussian takeover of 1866. A stock exchange began operating in Frankfurt in 1585, and it was here that the Rothschild banking family began its ascent in the 1760s.

About 80% of the medieval city centre was destroyed – and 1000 people were killed – by Allied bombing raids in March 1944.

◉ Sights & Activities

ALTSTADT

Frankfurt's historic core, known as the Altstadt (old city), is centred on the Dom and the lively, tourist-mobbed Römerberg, a medieval public square.

Frankfurter Dom
CATHEDRAL

(Frankfurt Cathedral; Map p374; www.domkonzerte.de; Domplatz 14; ☺church 9am-noon & 2.30-8pm) Dominated by an elegant Gothic tower (95m), begun in the 1400s and completed in the 1860s, Frankfurt's red sandstone cathedral is an island of calm amid the bustle of the city centre. From 1356 to 1792, the Holy Roman Emperors were elected (and, after 1562, consecrated and crowned) in the Wahlkapelle and the adjacent transept, now the site of a modern high altar. The structure was rebuilt both after an 1867 fire and after the bombings of 1944, which left it a burnt-out shell.

For information (in German) on the frequent concerts here, including organ recitals, see the Dom's website or pick up the brochure *Frankfurter Domkonzerte*. Frankfurt Ticket (p394) sells tickets.

The Dommuseum (cathedral museum; Map p374; www.dommuseum-frankfurt.de; adult/student €3/2, tours adult/student €4/2; ☺10am-5pm Tue-Fri, 11am-5pm Sat, Sun & holidays, tours 3pm Tue-Sun except during weddings), to the left as you enter the cathedral, has a small collection of precious liturgical objects and sells tickets for Dom tours (in German).

Römerberg
PLAZA

(Map p374; ☒Dom/Römer) The Römerberg, a long block west of the Dom, is Frankfurt's old central square. Buildings from the 14th and 15th centuries, reconstructed after the war, give an idea of how beautiful the city's medieval core once was. In the centre is the Gerechtigkeitsbrunnen (Font of Justice; Map p374); in 1612, at the coronation of Matthias, the fountain ran with wine! At the time of writing, the southern part of the plaza was being rebuilt. The Römerberg is especially lovely during December's Weihnachtsmarkt (Christmas market).

Alte Nikolaikirche
CHURCH

(Map p374; www.alte-nikolaikirche.de; Römerberg; ☺10am-8pm Apr-Sep, 10am-6pm Oct-Mar; ☒Dom/Römer) Topped by a single spire, this compact Protestant church – built of red sandstone, starting in the 13th century – was one of the few Altstadt structures to survive the war

(Continued on page 376)

FRANKFURT & SOUTHERN RHINELAND FRANKFURT AM MAIN

Frankfurt & Southern Rhineland Highlights

1 Checking out **Frankfurt am Main's** trademarks: a big-city skyline, first-class museums, apple wine and smelly cheese (p371)

2 Hiking or cycling through vineyards along the castle-studded **Romantic Rhine** (p434)

3 Wandering the ruins and gardens of Heidelberg's impossibly romantic **Schloss** (p416)

4 Marvelling at the towering Romanesque cathedrals of **Mainz** (p407), **Speyer** (p423) and **Worms** (p429)

5 Wandering towel-clad between the pools of Wiesbaden's Jugendstil **thermal baths** (p403)

6 Travelling back to the time of the gladiators at the remarkable Roman ruins in **Trier** (p451)

7 Exploring Darmstadt's Jugendstil artists' colony **Mathildenhöhe** (p411) and its gold-domed **Russian chapel** (p412)

8 Visiting 12th-century synagogues and Jewish ritual baths in **Worms** (p429) and **Speyer** (p424).

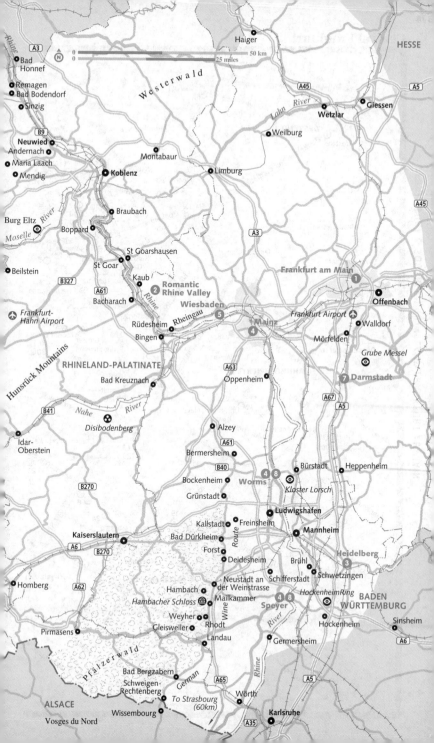

Central Frankfurt

WESTEND

Westend

Bockenheimer Landstr

Liebigstr

Reuterweg

Kettenhofweg

Guiollettstr

Westendplatz

Savignystr

Niedenau

Mainzer Landstr

Taunusanlage

Taunusanlage

Bockenheimer Anlage

Escherheimer Landstr

Opernplatz

2 56

Eschenheimer Tor

Eschenheimer Turm

39

Hochstr

Alte
Oper

Gr Bockenheimer
Str

Kleine
Hochstr

Kaiserhofstr

57
86

12

4

Börsenplatz

Schillerstr

Grosse

Eschenheimer Str

87

76

Goethestr

Börsenstr

15 Biebergasse

Hauptwache

65

Kalbächer
Gasse

Junghofstr

Goetheplatz

Rossmarkt

75

3

An der
Hauptwache

22

Neue Mainzer Str

Am Salzhaus

Kaiserplatz

62

17 Berliner Str

Grosser
Hirschgraben

Tourist Office

30

See Frankfurt - Messe, Westend & Bockenheim Map (p382)

Düsseldorferstr

50

14

Niddastr

Weserstr

11

Friedenstr

Bethmannstr

BAHNHOFSVIERTEL

43

37

71

Karlstr

Taunusstr

Moselstr

Elbestr

Kaiserstr

74

9

34

Willy-
Brandt-
Platz

Untermainkai

46

Poststr

Hauptbahnhof

Münchener Str

Untermainanlage

81

Tourist Office
Hauptbahnhof

91

36

20

29

Untermainbrücke

49

45

Eurolines

Wiesenhüttenplatz

Windmühlstr

Schaumainkai

23

Mannheimer Str

Stuttgarter Str

Baseler Str

Wilhelm-Leuschner-Str

19

Holbeinsteg

90

72

Museumsufer

6

5

Schweizer Str

24

Stadelstr

47

Baselerplatz

Untermainkai

MUSEUMSUFER

Guteutstr

Main River

**Städel
Museum**

Dürerstr

48

70

Gartenstr

Schweizer
Platz

Speicherstr

Schaumainkai

Liebieghaus

26

Steinlestr

Holbeinstr

Friedensbrücke

Gartenstr

Kennedyallee

Theodor-Stern-Kai

Schwanthaler Str

Textorstr

To Messe
(500m)

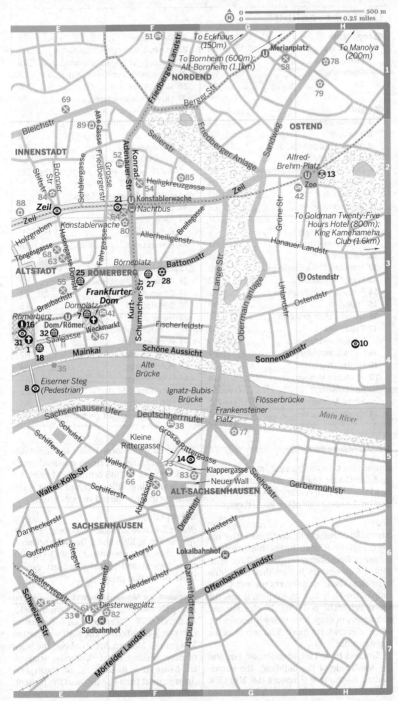

Central Frankfurt

⊙ Top Sights

Frankfurter Dom	E4
Liebieghaus	C6
Städel Museum	C6
Zeil	E2

⊙ Sights

1	Alte Nikolaikirche	E4
2	Alte Oper	C2
3	An der Hauptwache	D3
4	Bulle und Bär Statue	D2
5	Deutsches Architekturmuseum	D5
6	Deutsches Filmmuseum	D5
7	Dommuseum	E3
8	Eiserner Steg	E4
9	Euro Symbol	C4
10	European Central Bank HQ (under construction)	H4
11	Eurotower	C4
12	Frankfurt Stock Exchange	D2
13	Frankfurt Zoo	H2
14	Frau Rauscher Brunnen	F5
15	Fressgass'	D2
16	Gerechtigkeitsbrunnen	E4
17	Goethe-Haus	D3
	Halligalli Kinderwelt	(see 57)
18	Historisches Museum	E4
19	Holbeinsteg	C5
20	Jüdisches Museum	C4
	Kaisersaal	(see 30)
	Kinder Museum	(see 75)
21	Konstablerwache	F2
22	Main Tower	C3
23	Museum für Angewandte Kunst	D5
24	Museum für Kommunikation	D5
25	Museum für Moderne Kunst	E3
26	Museum Giersch	C6
27	Museum Judengasse	F3
28	Old Jewish Cemetery	F3
29	Riverfront Promenade	C5
30	Römer	D4
31	Römerberg	E4
32	Schirn Kunsthalle	E4
	Wand der Namen	(see 28)

⊙ Activities, Courses & Tours

33	Goethe Institut	E7
34	Inlingua	C4
	Kulturothek	(see 63)
35	Primus Linie	E4

⊜ Sleeping

36	Adina Apartment Hotel	C4
37	Concorde Hotel	A4
38	DJH Hostel	F5
39	Fleming's Hotel	D2
40	Frankfurt Hostel	B4
41	Hotel am Dom	E3
42	Hotel am Zoo	H2
43	Hotel Carlton	A4
44	Hotel Domicil	A4
45	Hotel Excelsior	B5
46	Hotel Hamburger Hof	A4
47	Hotel Ibis Frankfurt Centrum	B6

(Continued from page 371)

almost intact. In the tranquil interior, under neat late-Gothic vaulting, are stone carvings and 14th- and 15th-century gravestones. Situated on the south side of the Römerberg.

Römer   HISTORIC BUILDING

(Map p374; Römerberg; 🚇Dom/Römer) The old town hall, or Römer, in the northwestern corner of Römerberg, consists of three step-gabled 15th-century houses that were little more than shells at the end of the war. In the time of the Holy Roman Empire, it was the site of celebrations during the election and coronation of emperors; today it houses the office of Frankfurt's mayor and serves as the registry office.

Reached from Limpurgerstrasse (around the south side of the building), the barrel-vaulted **Kaisersaal** (Emperor's Hall; Map p374; adult/child €2/0.50; ⊙10am-1pm & 2-5pm, closed during events) is adorned with the mid-19th-century portraits of 52 rulers who made their mark between the 8th century and 1806. Access is via a fine little courtyard and a spiral staircase made of carved red sandstone.

Schirn Kunsthalle   MUSEUM

(Map p374; www.schirn.de; Römerberg; ⊙10am-7pm Tue-Sun, to 10pm Wed & Thu; 🚇Dom/Römer) This museum puts on some of Germany's most topical and talked-about art exhibitions. Admission prices vary.

Museum für Moderne Kunst   MUSEUM

(Map p374; www.mmk-frankfurt.de; Domstrasse 10; adult/child €8/4; ⊙10am-6pm Tue & Thu-Sun, to 8pm Wed; 🚇Dom/Römer) The highly respected Museum of Modern Art – dubbed the 'slice of cake' because of its distinctive triangular footprint – focuses on European and American art from the 1960s to the present, with frequent temporary exhibits. The permanent collection (not always on display) includes works by Roy Lichtenstein, Claes Oldenburg and Joseph Beuys.

Historisches Museum MUSEUM
(Map p374; www.historisches-museum.frankfurt. de; Römerberg; adult/child €4/2; ⊙10am-5pm Tue-Sun; ⓡDom/Römer) Established to showcase Frankfurt's long and fascinating history, Frankfurt's Historical Museum spent almost four decades in a concrete monstrosity – built, unsurprisingly, in 1972 – that was recently razed and is now in the process of being rebuilt. Parts reopened in May 2012; the rest should be operational by 2014.

INNENSTADT
The Innenstadt (inner city), Frankfurt's financial, business and commercial heart, is bounded by the park-lined Main River to the south and, on its other sides, by a narrow, semicircular strip of parks – lovely for a stroll

– that follow the route of the city's medieval walls, torn down between 1806 and 1812.

Zeil PEDESTRIAN MALL
(Map p374) For some truly grand (window) shopping, stroll along the pedestrianised Zeil, Frankfurt's great commercial precinct, which is unendingly animated by day and brightly lit by night. It is anchored to the east by a public square known as **Konstablerwache** (Map p374; ⓡKonstablerwache) and to the west by a square called **An der Hauptwache** (Map p374; ⓡHauptwache), named after a baroque-style building (now a cafe) that once housed the city's main guardhouse. West of there, you can continue through the pedestrianised restaurant district known as **Fressgass'** (officially Biebergasse, Kalbächer Gasse and Grosse Bockenheimer Strasse) to the Alte Oper.

Riverfront Promenade
PARK

(Map p374; ⌂Willy-Brandt-Platz) The parkland along both banks of the Main River is ideal for strolling, especially on a sunny day. The most popular section is between the two pedestrian bridges, Holbeinsteg (Map p374) and Eiserner Steg (Map p374). The latter is adorned with thousands of little locks, many of them engraved with the names of lovers who, to express the permanence of their commitment, attached them to the fence and then tossed the key into the river.

FREE Frankfurt Stock Exchange
BUILDING

(Börse; Map p374; ☎2111 1515; visitors.center@ deutsche-boerse.com; Börsenplatz; admission free; ⏱guided tour 9am, 10am, 11am & noon Mon-Fri; ⌂Hauptwache) The famous old Börse, built in 1843, is an impressively colonnaded neoclassical structure. The porch is decorated with allegorical statues of the five continents. Frenzied buying and selling are a thing of the past but you can see the all-electronic trading floor on a free tour (in German and English). Make reservations by telephone or email at least a day ahead; office hours are 9am to 5pm Monday to Friday. Bring ID.

In the square out front, a sculpture entitled Bulle und Bär (Map p374) depicts a showdown between a bull and a bear in which the former clearly has the upper hoof.

Alte Oper
OPERA HOUSE

(Map p374; Opernplatz 1; ⌂Alte Oper) Inaugurated in 1880, the Italian Renaissance-style Alte Oper anchors the western end of the Zeil-Fressgass' pedestrian zone. Burnt out in 1944, it narrowly avoided being razed and replaced with 1960s cubes and was finally reconstructed (1976–81) to resemble the original, its ornate facade graced with statues of Goethe and Mozart. Except for the mosaics in the lobby, the interior (closed except during concerts) is modern.

Main Tower
SKYSCRAPER

(Map p374; www.maintower.de; Neue Mainzer Strasse 52-58; elevator/lift adult/child/family €5/3.50/13.50; ⏱10am-9pm Sun-Thu, to 11pm Fri & Sat late-Mar–late-Oct, closes 2hr earlier late-Oct–late-Mar, cocktail lounge 9pm-midnight or 1am Tue-Sat; ⌂Alte Oper) A good place to get a feel for 'Mainhattan' is 200m above street level, on the observation platform of the 56-storey Main Tower. The lift takes just 45 seconds to save you climbing about 1000 stairs. Be prepared for airport-type security. Closes during thunderstorms.

You can also admire the cityscape from the 53rd-story restaurant (Map p374; ☎3650 4777; www.maintower-restaurant.de; ⏱noon-3pm Tue-Fri, 6pm-midnight Tue-Sat), for which reservations are required, or the cocktail lounge, where the minimum order is €25. The dress code for both is 'business casual'.

Eurotower
SKYSCRAPER

(Map p374; Kaiserstrasse 29; ⏱Info Shop 10am-7.30pm Mon-Fri; ⌂Willy-Brandt-Platz) You can't go inside the 148m-high Eurotower, home of the European Central Bank until its new headquarters (Map p374) east of the Innenstadt is ready in 2014, but outside you can see the enormous blue-and-gold euro symbol (Map p374), beloved of TV talking heads reporting on EU financial news. The ground-floor Info Shop sells euro coins from all over the Eurozone.

In 2012, the park adjacent to the euro symbol was the site of protests by Occupy Frankfurt, its motley tent city festooned with signs displaying punchy anti-capitalist slogans.

Goethe-Haus
HISTORIC BUILDING

(Map p374; www.goethehaus-frankfurt.de; Grosser Hirschgraben 23-25; adult/student/family €7/3/11; ⏱10am-6pm Mon-Sat, 10am-5.30pm Sun; ⌂Willy-Brandt-Platz) Completely rebuilt after the war (only the cellar survived Allied bombing), the birthplace of Johann Wolfgang von Goethe (1749–1832) is furnished in the haut-bourgeois style of Goethe's time, based on an inventory taken when Goethe's family sold the place. One of the few pieces that actually belonged to the great man is a puppet theatre given to him at age four. Laminated information cards provide background in a variety of languages. The Gemäldegalerie (in the same building as the ticket counter) displays 18th-century paintings. PDA tours (€2) are available in German, English, Chinese, Japanese and Korean.

Jüdisches Museum
MUSEUM

(Jewish Museum; Map p374; www.jewishmuseum. de; Untermainkai 14-15; adult/child €4/2, incl same-day entry to Museum Judengasse €5/2.50; ⏱10am-5pm Tue-Sun, to 8pm Wed; ⌂Willy-Brandt-Platz) Nine centuries of Jewish life in Frankfurt are explored with chronologically arranged artefacts, paintings (including a Matisse confiscated by the Nazis), photographs and documents, housed in the one-time residence of the Rothschild family. In 1933, Frankfurt's Jewish community, with 30,000 members, was Germany's second largest.

FRANKFURT FOR CHILDREN

Frankfurt is an easy and enjoyable place to travel if you've got the little ones along. The city has plenty of parks and playgrounds where kids can blow off steam, several museums have exhibits that are likely to captivate tweens and teens, and restaurants are happy to have young'uns as clients – some even offer child-sized portions.

Destinations likely to interest children include the Senckenberg Museum (p381), with its dinosaurs; the zoo (p381); the optical illusions of Explora (p381); the parkland and fountains of the PalmenGarten (p381); and, a bit out of town, the hands-on museum inside Wiesbaden's Schloss Freudenberg (p404).

Attractions specifically designed for kids:

» **Kinder Museum** (Children's Museum; Map p374; www.kindermuseum.frankfurt.de; An der Hauptwache 15; adult/child 6-18yr €4/2; ⊙10am-6.30pm Tue-Sun, also open Mon during school holidays; ⓇHauptwache) Puts on creative, year-long exhibits for children aged six to 13. Kids five and under can hang out in a fabulous playroom (admission free) off the lobby. Situated at the entrance to the Hauptwache U-Bahn station, one storey below street level.

» **Halligalli Kinderwelt** (Map p374; www.halligalli-myzeil.de; Zeil 106, 5th & 6th floors; adult/child 2-16yr/1-2yr €4/7.50/4.50, Fri-Sun €1 more; ⊙11am-8pm) A 1500-sq-m indoor playground and restaurant complex for kids, on the top floor of the My Zeil shopping mall.

An audioguide (€2) is available in German, English, French and Spanish. English translations of explanatory text can be found in binders or spiral booklets next to each exhibit. The lobby has a small cafe.

Museum Judengasse
MUSEUM

(Map p374; www.jewishmuseum.de; Kurt-Schumacher-Strasse 10; adult/student €2/1, incl same-day entry to Jüdisches Museum €5/2.50; ⊙10am-5pm Tue-Sun, to 8pm Wed; ⓇKonstablerwache) Most of Frankfurt's medieval Jewish ghetto, situated along narrow Judengasse (Jews' Street), was destroyed by a French bombardment in 1796, but you can get a sense of local Jewish life during the 15th to 18th centuries from the excavated remains of houses and ritual baths. Laws confining Frankfurt's Jews to the ghetto were repealed in 1811. Ask at the ticket counter for information in English.

Old Jewish Cemetery
JEWISH

(Map p374; Battonstrasse; ⊙closed on Saturday and Jewish holidays; ⓇKonstablerwache) About a third of the cemetery's original tombstones, dating from the 13th century to 1828, survived Nazi depredations; many still lean at crazy angles. The key can be picked up half a block to the west at the Museum Judengasse (you'll be asked to leave ID as a deposit).

The exterior of the cemetery's western wall is known as the **Wand der Namen** (Wall of Names; Map p374) because it is studded with row upon row of metal cubes bearing the names of 11,000 Frankfurt Jews who died in the Holocaust. Visitors often place pebbles atop the cubes to indicate, in accordance with Jewish tradition, that the deceased is still remembered.

Around town, you may see brass squares the size of a cobblestone embedded in the sidewalk. Known as **Stolpersteine** ('stumbling blocks'), they serve as memorials to Jews deported by the Nazis by marking their last place of residence.

SACHSENHAUSEN

Situated across the Main River from the Innenstadt, Sachsenhausen stretches from the **Museumsufer** (Museum Embankment), Frankfurt's famed, riverside 'museum row', east to the restaurants and bars of Alt Sachsenhausen and south to the Südbahnhof train station.

The periphery of Sachsenhausen has a few U-Bahn and S-Bahn stations (Schweizer Platz, Südbahnhof, Lokalbahnhof) but for many areas the easiest transport is provided by trams 14 and 16 and, along the river, bus 46 (three times an hour Monday to Friday, twice an hour Saturday and Sunday).

The Museumsufer museums include (from east to west):

Museum für Angewandte Kunst
MUSEUM

(Museum of Applied Arts; Map p374; www.angewandte kunst-frankfurt.de; Schaumainkai 17; adult/student €8/4; ⊙10am-5pm Tue & Thu-Sun, to 9pm Wed) Displays sublimely beautiful furniture, textiles, metalwork, glass and ceramics from

GETTING ORIENTED IN FRANKFURT

The Main River flows from east to west, with the Altstadt (old city) and the Innenstadt (city centre) to the north and the Sachsenhausen district, including the Museumsufer (Museum Embankment), to the south. Frankfurt's Hauptbahnhof (the main train station), on the eastern side of the partly sleazy Bahnhofsviertel (train station quarter), is about 1.3km west of the Römerberg, a historic public square marking the centre of the Altstadt. About 500m to the north of the Römerberg, the pedestrianised, east-west Zeil is the city's main shopping street; it links the city's two most important public squares, An der Hauptwache and Konstablerwache.

Head northwest from the Innenstadt along Bockenheimer Landstrasse and you get to the well-off Westend neighbourhood and then, 2km northwest of Hauptwache, to Bockenheim, home to the university's new and old campuses, respectively. North and northeast of Konstablerwache are the Nordend and Bornheim districts.

The airport is 12km southwest of the city centre.

Europe (including Jugendstil/art nouveau) and Asia. Set in lovely gardens, with a smart cafe and outdoor seating.

Deutsches Filmmuseum MUSEUM

(Map p374; ☎961 220 220; www.deutschesfilmmuseum.de; Schaumainkai 41; adult/student €5/2.50; ⏲10am-6pm Tue-Sun, to 8pm Wed) A dynamic place with permanent and changing exhibitions on the history of cinema, how films are made, and specific genres or artists. Has an in-house art cinema. Signs are in English and German.

Deutsches Architekturmuseum MUSEUM

(DAM; Map p374; www.dam-online.de; Schaumainkai 43; adult/child €7/3.50; ⏲11am-6pm Tue-Sun, to 8pm Wed) Puts on first-rate temporary exhibits (three at a time – see the website for details) on architecture, often with a focus on a particular architect or firm. Not much relates to Frankfurt, though. Signs are in German and English.

Städel Museum MUSEUM

(Map p374; www.staedelmuseum.de; Schaumainkai 63; adult/student/family €12/10/20, child under 12yr free; ⏲10am-5pm Tue & Fri-Sun, to 9pm Wed & Thu; [R]Schweizer Platz) Founded in 1815, this world-renowned institution has a truly outstanding collection of works by 14th- to 20th-century painters, including Botticelli, Dürer, Van Eyck, Rembrandt, Renoir, Rubens, Vermeer and Cézanne, plus Frankfurt natives such as Hans Holbein. The contemporary art section reopened in 2012 after extensive renovations.

Liebieghaus MUSEUM

(Map p374; www.liebieghaus.de; Schaumainkai 71; adult/student & senior/family €7/5/16, child under 12yr free; ⏲10am-6pm Tue-Sun, to 9pm Wed & Thu) *The* place to come to see sculpture. Housed in a gorgeous 1890s villa, the superb collection encompasses Greek, Roman, Egyptian, medieval, Renaissance and baroque works, plus some items from East Asia. Special exhibitions (extra charges may apply) sometimes displace parts of the permanent collection.

Museum Giersch MUSEUM

(Map p374; www.museum-giersch.de; Schaumainkai 83; adult/student €5/3, under 12yr free; ⏲noon-7pm Tue-Thu, 10am-6pm Fri-Sun) Puts on special exhibitions of works by lesser-known Frankfurt-area artists from the 19th and early 20th centuries.

MESSE, WESTEND & BOCKENHEIM

Head northwest from the Innenstadt (eg along Bockenheimer Landstrasse) and you come to the leafy Westend neighbourhood, known for its parks and upscale residential streets, many lined with impressive 19th-century apartment blocks and mansions. The area's southwestern edge is formed by the Messe (fairgrounds), which is pretty desolate except during events. To the north lies the monumental IG-Farbenhaus, which anchors the new Westend campus of Goethe Universität (Frankfurt University).

Bockenheimer Landstrasse leads – as its name implies – to Bockenheim, which was, and to some extent still is, Frankfurt's student stomping ground. Most university faculties, however, have already moved to the new campus.

Messe FAIRGROUND

(Fairgrounds; Map p382; www.messefrankfurt.com; [S]Festhalle/Messe, [R]Messe) Spread out between 1km and 2km northwest of the

Hauptbahnhof, Frankfurt's famous fairgrounds are anchored by the instantly recognisable **MesseTurm** (Messe Tower; Map p382; www.messeturm.com), a 256m-high skyscraper nicknamed *der Bleistift* (the pencil) because its round body is topped by a 36m-high pyramid that makes its silhouette look like a stubby pencil. The Messe grounds have absolutely nothing of interest to offer visitors except during trade fairs, which famously wreak periodic havoc on the local tourist economy.

PalmenGarten   PARK

(Map p382; www.palmengarten.de; Siesmayerstrasse 63; adult/child/family €5/2/9.50; ⊘9am-6pm Feb-Oct, 9am-4pm Nov-Jan; 🚇Westend) The lovely PalmenGarten ('palm garden'), established in 1871, is a botanical garden with historic tropical hothouses, rose gardens, playgrounds for kids, a pond with rowboats (May to September) and a mini-gauge train. Hosts open-air concerts in summer. There's a second entrance on Palmengartenstrasse.

Old University Campus   NEIGHBOURHOOD

(Map p382; 🚇Bockenheimer Warte) To see some strikingly ugly 1960s buildings that have aged badly and may not be around for long (and a few solid Wilhelmian ones), head to the old campus of Johann-Wolfgang-Goethe-Universität (Frankfurt University), which is situated south of Bockenheimer Warte, a big public square named after a medieval guard tower, between Gräfstrasse and Senckenberganlage.

Leipziger Strasse   SHOPPING STREET

(🚇Bockenheimer Warte or Leipziger Strasse) This is Bockenheim's lively main shopping street.

Senckenberg Museum   MUSEUM

(Map p382; www.senckenberg.de; Senckenberganlage 25; adult/student/senior/family €6/3/5/15, audioguide €3; ⊘9am-5pm Mon, Tue, Thu & Fri, to 8pm Wed, to 6pm Sat, Sun & holidays; 🚇Bockenheimer Warte) A solid neo-baroque building from the early 1900s houses Frankfurt's fine natural history museum, which has full-sized dinosaur mock-ups out front – great for the kiddies – and, inside, exhibits on palaeontology (including fossils from the Grube Messel site), biology and geology. Most have English signs.

NORDEND & BORNHEIM

Quiet residential streets, comfortable but unpretentious, stretch northward from the Innenstadt, forming the Nordend neighbourhood and, to the northeast (past Höhenstrasse), Bornheim, with its lively pub zone.

Berger Strasse   SHOPPING STREET

(www.bornheim-mitte.de; 🚇Merianplatz, Höhenstrasse & Bornheim Mitte) Lively, youthful Berger Strasse, Frankfurt's longest street, is the commercial heart of both Nordend and Bornheim. Well-off but not stuffy, it's lined with eateries, cafes, wine bars, pubs and shops, and is ideal for a leisurely, well-irrigated stroll. The U4 U-Bahn line runs underneath.

Explora   MUSEUM

(📞788888;www.explora.info;Glauburgplatz1;adult/child/student €16/8/10; ⊘11am-6pm; 🚇Glauburgstrasse) This 'science centre', which survives without government subsidies, features mesmerising optical illusions and extraordinary images of all sorts.

Highlights, which are likely to delight teens and tweens, include stunning stereoscopic slides of insects and mammals; mind-boggling holograms; 3D X-ray photos of flowers; and feels-like-you're-there 3D photos of turn-of-the-20th-century Frankfurt, most of it destroyed during WWII. There's a **children's playground** out front. Situated 1.6km north of Konstablerwache.

OTHER AREAS

Frankfurt Zoo   ZOO

(Zoologisher Garten; Map p374; www.zoo-frankfurt. de; Alfred-Brehm-Platz 16; adult/student/family €8/4/20; ⊘9am-7pm late-Mar–late-Oct, 9am-5pm

MUSEUM CARDS & TIPS

The **Museumsufer Ticket** (www.kultur-frankfurt.de; adult/concession/family €15/8/23) gets you into 34 museums over the course of two days; a version valid for a whole year costs €75 for one person. Both are sold wherever they're valid and at the tourist office, Frankfurt Ticket and the Verkehrsinsel.

Many museums are free on the last Saturday of the month; exceptions include the Goethe Haus, the Senckenberg and Städel Museums, the Schirn Kunsthalle and Explora.

For details on museums not covered in this chapter, as well as other aspects of the city's cultural life, see www.kultur-frankfurt.de.

Frankfurt - Messe, Westend & Bockenheim

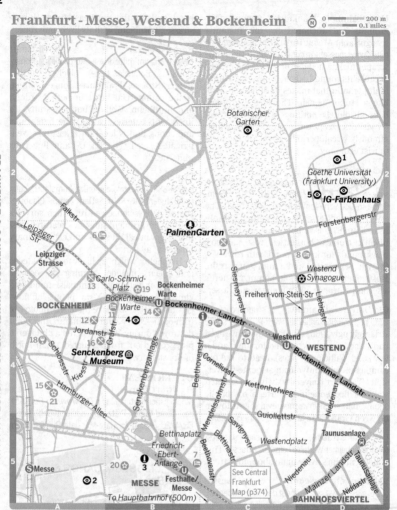

late-Oct–late-Mar; ☒Zoo) The zoo, at this site since 1874, isn't Germany's prettiest but it does have kid-friendly houses for primates, nocturnal creatures, birds and amphibians.

🎓 Courses

Language institutes offering German classes include:

Goethe Institut COURSE
(Map p374; ☎961 2270; www.goethe.de; Diesterwegplatz 72; ☒Südbahnhof) At the venerable Goethe Institute, options include 'superin-

tensiv' German language courses (40 academic hours a week) lasting one (€875) or two (€1590) weeks and eight-week courses that meet three times a week in the morning or evening (€1085).

Inlingua COURSE
(Map p374; ☎242 9200; www.inlingua-frankfurt.de; Kaiserstrasse 37; ☒Willy-Brandt-Platz) Offerings include classes that meet for four academic hours each morning from Monday to Friday (€395 to €460 for four weeks).

Frankfurt - Messe, Westend & Bockenheim

☞ Tours

Tourist Office
WALKING TOURS

(www.frankfurt-tourismus.de; Römerberg 27; adult/child 4-14yr/student €12/6/10; ⊙tours depart 2.30pm; ⊠Dom/Römer) Two-hour walking tours of the city start every day at the Römer tourist office; no need to reserve ahead. The tourist office also has other walking tours, especially in the warm season, and audiovisual iPod tours (four hours/all-day €7.50/10).

Primus Linie
BOAT TOURS

(Map p374; www.primus-linie.de; Mainkai, Altstadt; ⊙hourly 11am-5pm Mon-Sat, half-hourly 11am-6.30pm Sun & holidays Apr-Oct, also Sat & Sun Mar; ⊠Dom/Römer) Runs 50-minute sightseeing cruises (adult €8.40) both upstream and down; for the best skyline views, take the full 100-minute circuit (€10.40). The dock is across the Eisener Steg from the Museumsufer.

Kulturothek
WALKING TOURS

(Map p374; ☎281 010; www.kulturothek-frankfurt.de; An der Kleinmarkthalle 7-9; adult €8-15; ⊠Hauptwache) Runs engaging cultural tours of the city and its cultural institutions, some in English. Book ahead.

✿ Festivals & Events

Some of Frankfurt's many festivals:

Christopher Street Day
GAY FESTIVAL

(www.csd-frankfurt.de; ⊙Fri-Sun in mid-Jul) Colourful gay pride parade, plus a *Strassenfest* (street festival) at Konstablerwache.

Frankfurt Book Fair
TRADE FAIR

(Frankfurter Buchmesse; www.frankfurt-book-fair.com; ⊙5 days early or mid-October) World's largest book fair, with 7800 exhibitors from over 100 countries. A mind-bogglingly diverse celebration of the written word.

Christmas Market
MARKET

(Weihnachtsmarkt; ⊙late Nov-23 Dec) Christmas fair in the Altstadt, with choirs, ornament stalls, traditional foods and, of course, hot *Glühwein* (mulled wine).

⊨ Sleeping

When it comes to accommodation prices, supply and demand reign supreme in Frankfurt. The city's hotels cater mainly to business travellers and so tend to drop rates on weekends (Friday, Saturday and Sunday nights), on holidays and in July and August. But during major trade fairs, prices can triple or even quadruple, with modest doubles going for €300 or more. The easiest way to find out if your trip coincides with one of the larger fairs is go to almost any hotel website and plug in specific dates. Sky-high prices mean that you've got a big *Messe* on your hands.

To avoid paying a fortune for accommodation during trade fairs, many travellers stay outside the city and commute using Frankfurt's fast, easy-to-use public transport system. In neighbouring cities such as Darmstadt, Wiesbaden and Mainz, which are an hour or less by S-Bahn from the fairgrounds, prices rise by only a few tens of per

IG-FARBENHAUS – FROM NAZI INDUSTRIAL HQ TO BASTION OF HUMANISM

The monumental **IG-Farbenhaus** (Map p382; Furstenbergerstrasse 200, Westend; ⊙7am-10pm Mon-Sat; ⓡHolzhausenstrasse), seven storeys tall and slightly curved, was erected in 1931 as the prestigious headquarters of IG-Farben (pronounced 'ee geh *far*-behn'), the mammoth German chemicals conglomerate whose constituent companies included Agfa, BASF, Bayer and Hoechst. After Hitler came to power, Jewish scientists and executives were fired, and the company's products soon became central to the Nazi war effort. From 1941 to 1944, white-collar staff based in this building kept the Final Solution running smoothly by carrying out the work of coordinating the production of the company's most notorious product, Zyklon-B, the cyanide-based killing agent used in the gas chambers of Auschwitz.

After the war, IG-Farbenhaus served briefly as the headquarters of General Dwight D Eisenhower, Supreme Commander of Allied Forces in Europe, and later as the headquarters of US occupation forces ('the Pentagon in Europe') and as a CIA bureau. The 'Casino' building was bombed by the Red Army Faction terrorist group in the 1970s.

In 1995, with the Cold War over, US forces handed the building back to Germany's federal government. After refurbishment, it became the focal point of the new Westend campus of **Johann-Wolfgang-Goethe-Universität** (Frankfurt University; Map p382; www.goethe-universitaet.de) – and thus a bastion of the spirit of free inquiry and humanism that Nazism tried so hard to extinguish. North of IG-Farbenhaus (now officially called IG-Hochhaus), shiny new university buildings are being constructed.

Inside the Bauhaus-influenced building, you can check out an informative **historical exhibit** (in German and English) on IG Farben and its erstwhile headquarters. It's displayed on the walls to either side of the main entrance (in sectors Q3 and Q4) on floors one to five.

To get from floor to floor, you can hop (literally) onto one of the two **paternoster lifts**, whose open cabins keep cycling around like rosary beads (thus the name). Stay on board after you pass the top or bottom floor and see what happens! Signs warn, reasonably enough, that these historic elevators are not safe for children, pets and people wearing backpacks or roller skates.

About 50m from the southwest corner of the building (to the left as you approach the main entrance) stands the **Wollheim Memorial** (Map p382; www.wollheim-memorial.de; ⊙8am-6pm) in a little pavilion marked '107984' (Norbert Wollheim's prisoner number). Inside you can watch 24 masterfully done video testimonials, a few in English (go to 'menu', then 'en' for English; also viewable on the excellent website) by survivors of IG Farben's corporate slave-labour camp, Buna/Monowitz (Auschwitz III). IG-Farben slave labourers who lived to write about their experiences include Primo Levi and Elie Wiesel.

Under the trees in front of IG-Farbenhaus, panels show **photographs** of German Jews, later sent to Buna/Monowitz, enjoying life in the years before the Holocaust, unaware of what was to come.

---

cent during even the largest fairs, and each has a lot more to offer visitors than the suburbs out by the airport.

Major hotel chains with outposts in Frankfurt include Hilton, Holiday Inn, Ibis, Intercontinental, Le Méridien, Mercure, Mövenpick (on the Messe grounds), Ramada and Sheraton.

The **tourist office** (www.frankfurt-tourismus .de) has a free hotel booking service but arranges private rooms only during trade fairs. At the airport, help with hotel reservations (including during trade fairs) is available from **Hotels & Tours** (☎6907 0402; www .hotels.frankfurt-airport.de; Terminal 1, Arrival Hall B; ⊙7am-10.30pm).

You can find furnished rooms and apartments in Frankfurt through a *Mitwohnzentrale* (accommodation finding service), such as www.city-residence.de and www.mitwohnzentrale-mainhattan.de (in German; free registration required).

TRAIN STATION AREA

The Bahnhofsviertel (the area around the main train station, the Hauptbahnhof) has lots of moderately priced places to stay, few of them noteworthy but all of them just a short walk from most of the city's major sights. The Hauptbahnhof is a major S-Bahn (commuter rail), U-Bahn (metro) and Strassenbahn (tram) hub so good transport links it with both the airport and the Messe.

Hauptbahnhof-area streets with respectable hotels include Baseler Strasse and, north of the station, Poststrasse, Düsseldorferstrasse and Karlstrasse. Frankfurt's sleazy red-light area, a hang-out of drug addicts, is a few blocks northeast of the station, on and around Elbestrasse and Taunusstrasse.

Frankfurt Hostel
HOSTEL **$**

(Map p374; ☏247 5130; www.frankfurt-hostel. com; Kaiserstrasse 74, 3rd fl; dm €19-25, s/d from €35/45, during fairs up to €80/100; @🖨; ☒Frankfurt Hauptbahnhof) Popular with young travellers (and families, too), this lively, 200-bed establishment is a great place to meet other travellers. Reached via a pre-war marble-and-tile lobby and a mirrored lift, it has a chill-out area for socialising, a small shared kitchen, squeaky wooden floors and free, all-you-can-eat spaghetti, served nightly at 8pm. Dorm rooms, two of which are women-only, have three to 10 metal bunks. Use of lockers is free (deposit required for the key).

Twenty-Five Hours
BOUTIQUE HOTEL **$$**

(25h; Map p374; ☏256 6770; www.25hours-hotels. com; Niddastrasse 58; d without breakfast weekday/weekend from €107/77, during fairs up to €390; ✳@🖨; ☒Frankfurt Hauptbahnhof) Inspired by Levi's (yes, the jeans), the 76 rooms are themed by decade, with each floor representing 10 years between the 1930s and 1940s (calm, conservative colours) through the 1980s (brace yourself for tiger-print walls and optical-illusion carpets). The staff are young and friendly; clients often come from creative sectors of the economy. In the basement Musik-Raum (music room), designed by Gibson, guests are welcome to jam on the drums and guitars. The roof terrace offers skyline views.

Le Méridien Parkhotel
LUXURY HOTEL **$$$**

(Map p374; ☏26970; www.lemeridienparkhotelfrank furt.com; Wiesenhüttenplatz 28-38; s weekday/weekend from €139/125, d weekday/weekend €199/145, during fairs up to €600/600; P✳@🖨; ☒Frankfurt Hauptbahnhof) Midway between the train station and the river, this stylish luxury hotel has 80 rooms in an ornate Wilhelmian-era structure, built in 1905 with high ceilings and broad hallways, and another 217 rooms in its modern business wing. The former are decorated with English-style antiques and have marble bathrooms, while the latter come with light-coloured wood furnishings and, sometimes, great skyline views. Some of the singles are very small.

Hotel Excelsior
HOTEL **$**

(Map p374; ☏256 080; www.hotelexcelsior-frank furt.de; Mannheimer Strasse 7-9; s/d from €61/75, during fairs €199/239; P@🖨; ☒Frankfurt Hauptbahnhof) Behind a light-green facade, this 197-room place offers excellent value, with a free business centre, free landline phone calls throughout Germany, and free coffee, tea, fruit and cakes in the lobby.

Concorde Hotel
HOTEL **$$**

(Map p374; ☏242 4220; www.hotelconcorde.de; Karlstrasse 9; s/d weekday from €110/130, weekend from €65/80, during fairs up to €400; ✳@🖨; ☒Frankfurt Hauptbahnhof) Understated and friendly, this establishment – in a restored century-old building – has compact singles and spacious, sleek doubles with trendy washbasins and art photos on the wall.

Hotel Domicil
HOTEL **$$**

(Map p374; ☏0800-212 5888, 271 110; www.best western.com; Karlstrasse 14; d without breakfast weekday/weekend from €89/55, during fairs up to €255; ✳@🖨; ☒Frankfurt Hauptbahnhof) The 64 rooms, renovated in 2012, are unsurprising

---

ⓘ EBBELWEI-EXPRESS

Run by Frankfurt's public transport company, the **Ebbelwei-Express** (Apple Wine Express; www.ebbelwei -express.com; adult/child under 14yr €7/3; ⏱half-hourly 1.30-5.30pm Sat, Sun & holidays Apr-Oct & Sat Nov-Mar, approx hourly 1.30-5pm Sun & holidays Nov-Mar) is a historic tram whose 70-minute circuit takes in both banks of the Main between the Zoo and the Messe. Jump on at any stop marked with the letters EE – clockwise from the east, Zoo, Frankensteiner Platz, Lokalbahnhof, Südbahnhof, Hauptbahnhof and Börneplatz are convenient ones. As you'd expect, the price includes apple wine (Ebbelwei) or juice and pretzels.

TRADE FAIRS

Frankfurt is famous around the world for its *Messen* (trade fairs), held at the southern edge of the Westend district on the ground of Messe Frankfurt (p380).

If you're in Frankfurt during one of the really big trade fairs, you'll experience a city transformed. Accommodation prices skyrocket, getting a table at many restaurants requires advance booking, and you'll overhear conversations – in strange jargon, sprinkled with obscure acronyms – about parts of the global economy that usually fly under the radar. The largest such events include:

» **Heimtextil Frankfurt** (☉2nd week of Jan) – home and commercial textiles

» **Christmasworld, Paperworld & Creativeworld** (☉late Jan) – consumer goods

» **Ambiente** (☉mid-Feb) – interior design and consumer goods

» **ISH** (☉mid-Mar) – bathrooms, heating and air-conditioning

» **Prolight & Sound** (☉mid-Apr) – events and entertainment technology

» **Achema** (www.achema.de; ☉mid-Jun every three years) – chemical engineering, environmental protection and biotechnology

» **Tendence** (☉3rd week of Aug) – consumer goods

» **Automechanika Frankfurt** (☉mid-Sep in even-numbered years) – automotive industry

» **IAA** (☉mid-Sep in odd-numbered years) – automotive industry

» **Frankfurt Book Fair** (p383) – books

but quite decent. Breakfast costs €14. Best Western–affiliated.

Hotel Hamburger Hof
HOTEL $$
(Map p374; ☏2713 9690; www.hamburgerhof. com; Poststrasse 10-12; s/d weekday from €85/95, weekend €65/85, during fairs up to €240; @🖤; 🚊Frankfurt Hauptbahnhof) A practical hotel with a spiffy white-and-maroon lobby and 66 comfortable rooms.

Hotel Carlton
HOTEL $
(Map p374; ☏241 8280; www.carlton-hotel-frankfurt.de; Karlstrasse 11; s/d €50/70, weekend from €40/50, during fairs up to €190/250; @🖤; 🚊Frankfurt Hauptbahnhof) The Carlton's 28 rooms, in a century-old building, are neat, practical and fairly large, but hardly romantic.

Hotel Ibis Frankfurt Centrum
HOTEL $
(Map p374; ☏273 030; www.ibishotel.de; Speicherstrasse 4; d without breakfast weekday/weekend €79/59, during fairs up to €199; P@🖤; 🚊Frankfurt Hauptbahnhof) You won't be swinging cats in the rooms of this 233-room chain hotel, but they are bright and some have nice views to the river or the quiet yard. An electronic scoreboard out front shows the day's prices. Breakfast costs €10; wi-fi in your room costs €9 for 24 hours.

ALTSTADT
The centre of the centre offers easy access to the Dom, the parks along the river and the Innenstadt.

Hotel am Dom
HOTEL $$
(Map p374; ☏138 1030; www.hotelamdom.de; Kannengiessergasse 3; s/d €90/120, during fairs €165/199; 🖤; 🚊Dom/Römer) Just a few paces from the cathedral, this unprepossessing hotel has 29 unexciting rooms, family suites and apartments with kitchenettes.

INNENSTADT
Stay in this part of town and you'll be near the historic sites of the Altstadt, the city's tallest buildings, some fine shopping and plenty of cultural venues and restaurants.

🔝 Fleming's Hotel
HISTORIC HOTEL $$$
(Map p374; ☏0800-373 7700, 427 2320; www.flemings-hotels.com; Eschenheimer Tor 2; d without breakfast from €168, during fairs €398; ❄@🖤; 🚊Eschenheimer Tor) Classic 1950s elegance stretches from the stainless steel, neon and black-and-white marble of the lobby all the way up to the 7th-floor panoramic restaurant, linked by a rare, hop-on hop-off Paternoster elevator/lift. The 200 rooms are quietly luxurious, and some are huge. The sexy, see-through showers, set in the middle of the room, are not for the prudish.

Amenities include a fitness room, sauna and steam bath.

Westin Grand
BUSINESS HOTEL $$$

(Map p374; ✆29810; www.westin.com; Konrad-Adenauer-Strasse 5-7; d €200-300, ste €500-1500; P✻@🖥🏊; ⓡKonstablerwache) An international-standard business hotel whose 371 rooms, large and very comfortable, come with sparkling marble bathrooms. There's a candlelit bar in the classy, granite-floored lobby, which displays two classic motorcars. The fitness room has a sauna.

Adina Apartment Hotel
HOTEL $$

(Map p374; ✆247 4740; www.adina.eu; Wilhelm-Leuschner-Strasse 6; d without breakfast from €84-135, during fairs up to €377; 🖥🏊; ⓡWilly-Brandt-Platz) If you'd like to do some of your own cooking and have a bit more space, or are travelling with kids, it's well worth considering the Adina's studio, one and two-bedroom apartments, all with kitchenettes.

SACHSENHAUSEN

There's art along the Museumsufer and plenty of places to eat and drink in Alt Sachsenhausen.

Hotel Kautz
HOTEL $$

(Map p374; ✆618 061; www.hotelkautz.de; Gartenstrasse 17; s/d without breakfast weekday from €85/99, weekend €69/79, during fairs €159; 🖥; ⓡSchweizer Platz) In the heart of Sachsenhausen's shopping district, this quiet, family-run hotel has 17 pretty rooms, a living-room-like lobby and a breakfast room decked out in white, pink and red. Breakfast costs €10. Reception is on the 1st floor; there's no elevator/lift.

DJH Hostel
HOSTEL $

(Map p374; ✆610 0150; www.jugendherberge-frankfurt.de; Deutschherrnufer 12, Sachsenhausen; dm €19-26.50, s/d €42/74, age 26 & under €37.50/65; @🖥) Advance bookings are advisable for Frankfurt's bustling, 434-bed Jugendherberge, situated within easy walking distance of the city centre and Alt Sachsenhausen's nightspots. Dorm rooms are single-sex. Family rooms have three or four beds. Has washing machines but no cooking facilities. From the Hauptbahnhof, take bus 46 to Frankensteiner Platz.

MESSE, WESTEND & BOCKENHEIM

The area right around the Messe is home to surprisingly few hotels, so even fair-goers who can afford Frankfurt's sky-high 'fair rates' usually stay elsewhere in the centre, nearer amenities such as restaurants.

Hotel Liebig
TOP CHOICE
HOTEL $$

(Map p382; ✆2418 2990; www.hotelliebig.de; Liebigstrasse 45; s €112-175, d €143-205, q €360, weekend s/d/q from €95/115/295, d during fairs up to €295; ✻🖥; ⓡWestend) Two blocks from Goethe Universität's new Westend campus, this Italian-run family hotel, in a late 19th-century building, has 19 bright rooms with wood floors and stylish bathrooms. Prices include a buffet breakfast (€15) only on the weekend.

Hotel Hessischer Hof
LUXURY HOTEL $$$

(Map p382; ✆75 400; www.hessischer-hof.de; Friedrich-Ebert-Anlage 40; d without breakfast weekday/weekend from €225/160, during fairs up to €465; P✻@🖥; ⓡFesthalle/Messe) Owned by the descendants of the Landgraves, Electors and Grand Dukes of the House of Hessen, this classy business hotel is renowned for its old-world luxury and superb service (some staff members have worked here for 30 or 40 years). Opened in 1952, it is decorated with over 1500 antiques from the family collections. Breakfast costs €28. Situated right across the avenue from the Messe.

Hotel Palmenhof
HOTEL $$$

(Map p382; ✆753 0060; www.palmenhof.com; Bockenheimer Landstrasse 89-91; s €125-159, d €165-195, weekends s/d from €80/90, breakfast €16; P🖥; ⓡWestend or Bockenheimer Warte) In the heart of the leafy Westend, this old-time establishment, constructed in 1890, offers 45 understated rooms with mixed modern and classical furnishings. Also rents out residential apartments (from €860 a month plus taxes) for stays of at least two weeks.

Hotel West
HOTEL $$

(Map p382; ✆247 9020; www.hotelwest.de; Gräfstrasse 81; s weekday/weekend from €68/59, d from €84/72; ⏱reception 7am-10pm; 🖥; ⓡBockenheimer Warte) A family-run hotel whose 15 attractive rooms come with modern styling, TV and hairdryers. Has a cute breakfast room with white tablecloths and red candles.

Hotel Falk
HOTEL $$

(Map p382; ✆7191 8870; www.hotel-falk.de; Falkstrasse 38a; s/d €100/130, weekend €65/85, during fairs up to €225/275; P✻@🖥; ⓡLeipziger Strasse) Near the Bockenheim shops and student eateries, this modern hotel has 29 rooms that are smallish but practical and comfy.

Hotel Pension Backer
HOTEL $

(Map p382; ✆747 992; www.hotel-backer.de; Mendelssohnstrasse 92; s/d/tr with shared bathroom €25/40/45, during fairs €30/50/60; ☒Westend) This no-frills, internet-challenged pension – it lacks both an email address and wi-fi – has 30 basic rooms that share five bathrooms, one on each floor. The Backer is clean and has a great location but don't expect an effusive welcome. Old-time cheapies like this are a dying breed.

NORDEND & BORNHEIM

This part of town, northeast of the Innenstadt, is a favourite destination of locals in the mood for a traditional Frankfurt-style meal, a mug of beer or a glass of apple wine.

TOP CHOICE Villa Orange
HOTEL $$

(Map p374; ✆405 840; www.villa-orange.de; Hebelstrasse 1; s/d without breakfast weekday from €118/138, with breakfast weekend from €90/115; P✳@🖙; ☒Musterschule) Offering a winning combination of tranquility, modern German design and small-hotel comforts (eg a quiet corner library), this century-old villa has 38 spacious rooms. The buffet breakfast (€10) is organic.

OSTEND

The neighbourhoods east of the Innenstadt and the Nordend are known as the Ostend. Hanauer Landstrasse runs through the Osthafen ('eastern harbour') area.

Goldman Twenty-Five Hours
BOUTIQUE HOTEL $$

(Goldman 25h; ✆4058 6890; www.25hours-hotel.com; Hanauer Landstrasse 127; d weekday/weekend from €107/75, during fairs up to €350; @🖙; ☒Ostbahnhof) This quirky, creative establishment won't remind you of anywhere else you've ever stayed. Each of the 49 original rooms (22 sq m) was designed by a local personality, while the 49 rooms opened in 2012 commemorate famous or infamous people from around the world. Has a comfortable sitting room with free coffee and an outstanding Mediterranean restaurant. Beehives on the roof produce house-brand honey. Guests get free use of two bicycles. Situated 2.5km east of the Dom area (take Battonnstrasse, then Hanauer Landstrasse).

Hotel am Zoo
HOTEL $$

(Map p374; ✆949930; www.hotel-am-zoo.com; Alfred-Brehm-Platz 6; s €50-70, d €70-90, s/d during fairs up to €190/220; P@🖙; ☒Zoo) This unpretentious hotel has 79 unexciting but serviceable rooms, some of them hypo-allergenic, with tile bathrooms in colours they don't make any more. Prices do not include breakfast (€6.50). Situated across the square from the zoo and just a block east of the Zeil's eastern end.

AIRPORT

The hotels at and right around Frankfurt's airport tend to be pricey. Nearby suburbs (eg Kelsterbach, Walldorf and Mörfelden) have places to stay but their public transport links with the city centre, including the Messe, are often less convenient than hotels in attractive, neighbouring cities such as Wiesbaden, Mainz and Darmstadt, which are linked to the airport and the city centre by speedy S-Bahn trains.

Sheraton Frankfurt Airport
BUSINESS HOTEL $$$

(✆69770; www.sheraton.com; Hugo-Eckener-Ring 15; d €220, during fairs up to €345; ✳@🖙; ☒Flughafen Regionalbahnhof) Unbelievably convenient if you arrive by air – it's right across the street from Terminal 1 – but the prices can be sky-high. The whopping 1008 rooms, which come with six layers of glass to ensure peace and quiet, are attractive but bland. There's a fitness centre with sauna and steam bath. Wi-fi costs US$8/19 for one/24 hours. Prices drop to as low as €122 on weekends and during holidays (eg July and August).

✗ Eating & Drinking

Locals in search of a restaurant recommendation often consult *Frankfurt Geht Aus!* (Frankfurt Goes Out; www.journal -frankfurt.de; €5.80), an annual booklet that details 260 restaurants by category; the lists are useful even if you don't read German. It's available at news stands.

During trade fairs restaurants fill up fast so be sure to reserve ahead.

TRAIN STATION AREA

Plenty of eateries, including ethnic places, can be found along Kaiserstrasse and parallel Münchnerstrasse. There's also a Rewe (Map p374; Karlstrasse 4; ⊙7am-10pm Mon-Sat; ☒Frankfurt Hauptbahnhof) supermarket, handy for picnic supplies.

ALTSTADT

The places right around the Römerberg cater mainly to tourists, but nearby you'll find some very local – and atmospheric – dining options.

TOP CHOICE Kleinmarkthalle MARKET **$**

(Map p374; Hasengasse 5-7; ⏱7.30am-6pm Mon-Fri, to 3pm Sat; ✍; ⓇDom/Römer) This traditional covered food market has fruit and vegie stands, ethnic specialities, wine and beer places (along the glass northern wall) and several wurst (sausage) places, including the renowned **Gref Völslings Rindswurst** (Map p374) at the western end – it's not far from a large mural depicting impressions of Frankfurt. You can eat at narrow tables along the walls.

Bitter & Zart CAFE **$**

(Map p374; www.bitterundzart.de; Braubachstrasse 14; ⏱10am-8pm Mon-Sat, 10am-6pm Sun; ⓇDom/Römer) Walk past the wing chair made of solid chocolate (is it real?) – turn left and you're in a delightful shop whose shelves are piled high with the finest chocolates, turn right and you can sit down and order espresso (€2.20), light meals (soup, salad), scrumptious chocolate pralines (€1 each) and (until noon) breakfast. The cakes in the glass case look as delicious as they taste.

Metropol BISTRO **$$**

(Map p374; ☎288 287; Weckmarkt 13-15; mains €9.50-14.50; ⏱9am-1 or 2am Tue-Sat, 9am-midnight Sun; ⓇDom/Römer) Serves dishes from a changing menu that ranges from bistro staples to inspired. Has a lovely courtyard out the back where children can chill out. Cash only.

Mozart Café CAFE **$$**

(Map p374; Töngesgasse 23-25; cakes €2.90-3.80, lunch mains €9.80-12.90; ⏱8 or 9am-9pm; ⓇHauptwache) Join Frankfurt's highly civilised 'granny scene' for coffee and cake or a proper meal. The menu changes every few weeks depending on what's available fresh in the markets. Sit on red leather wing chairs inside or at Paris-cafe-style tables out front.

Karin CAFE **$$**

(Map p374; ☎295 217; Grosser Hirschgraben 28; mains €8-14; ⏱9am-midnight Mon-Sat, 10am-7pm Sun, 10am-midnight holidays; ⓇWilly-Brandt-Platz) Across from the Goethe-Haus, this Frankfurt-style cafe serves German and international dishes and nine different breakfasts (from €3; available until 6pm). Changing exhibits by local artists grace the walls. Cash only.

INNENSTADT

The Innenstadt has some of Frankfurt's best dining options. The pedestrianised avenue linking the Alte Oper and the western end of the Zeil – officially called Kalbächer Gasse and Grosse Bockenheimer Strasse – is known affectionately as **'Fressgass'** (Munch Alley; Map p374; ⓇHauptwache) because of its generous selection of eateries. Many places offer outdoor seating in the warm season.

For cheap eats, check out the underground galleries attached to the Hauptwache U-Bahn and S-Bahn station.

TOP CHOICE Fleming's Club INTERNATIONAL **$$$**

(Map p374; ☎427 2320; www.flemings-hotels.com; Eschenheimer Tor 2; mains €14-58; ⏱6am-11pm; ❋🅵; ⓇEschenheimer Tor) Great city views and equally great food await at this 7th-floor restaurant and bar, reached from the lobby of Fleming's Hotel via a Paternoster lift/elevator that will make you feel like you're in a 1930s movie. Serves tasty fish, seafood, steak and vegie dishes, a good-value *plat du jour* (€18.50) and Sunday brunch.

Buffalo STEAK **$$$**

(Map p374; ☎285 796; Kaiserhofstrasse 18-20; mains €10.80-39; ⏱11.30am-11pm Mon-Sat; ⓇOpernplatz) Founded way back in 1973, this renowned steakhouse serves some of Frankfurt's most mouth-watering sirloin (180/300/400gr €10.80/17/22), tenderloin (€19.50/30/39) and rib-eye steak, all shipped fresh from Argentina. Also boasts an impressive wine list. Unless you'll be dining from 3pm to 6pm, reservations are a must, daily all year. Situated down the stairs that lead to tiny Zwingerstrasse.

Pulse BAR **$$**

(Map p374; ☎1388 6802; www.pulse-frankfurt.de/page; Bleichstrasse 38a; mains €9.80-16.80; ⏱11am-1am Sun-Thu, 11am-4am Fri, 10am-4am or later Sat; ⓇKonstablerwache) This laid-back restaurant, bar and weekend nightclub is more than just 'gay-friendly' but ends up very mixed, especially on weekends. The cuisine is seasonal and international (including Mediterranean). Has a wonderful warm-season patio out back. Turns into a disco – house music is a speciality – on Friday and Saturday after about 11pm.

Die Leiter FRENCH & ITALIAN **$$$**

(Map p374; ☎292 121; www.dieleiter.de; Kaiserhofstrasse 11; mains €19.50-29.50; ⏱noon-3pm

& 6-11pm Mon-Fri, noon-11pm Sat; ⓇOpernplatz)
Dine on veal, steak and fish amid old-world,
bistro-style elegance. The chef, who hails
from Vienna, is deft with his signature
French and Italian dishes but is especially
proud of his 'Original Wiener Schnitzel'.
Veggie options include soups, risotto and
spagettini. A three-course lunch costs €30,
a four-course dinner €46.

Leonhard's Restaurant & Skylounge
FOOD COURT **$$**

(Map p374; Zeil 116-26, 7th fl; mains €9.95-12.95;
⊙9.30am-9pm Mon-Sat; ✈; ⓇHauptwache) High
atop the upscale Galeria Kaufhof depart-
ment store, this gourmet food court serves
up everything from coffee (€1.95) and baked
goods to cafeteria-style fish and meat meals.
The outdoor deck, offering over-the-rooftops
views of the city, is a great place to catch a
few rays or sip beer (€2.20) or wine (€3.80).

Brasserie
BISTRO **$$**

(Map p374; ☑9139 8634; Opernplatz 8; mains
€11.50-26.80; ⊙10am-1am; ⓇOpernplatz) One of
four cosy little eateries facing the east side of
the Alte Oper, Brasserie serves red meat, fish
and pasta of German, Italian and French inspiration. Often crowded, with a burble of
voices permeating the small indoor eating
area, decorated with murals of the flapper
era. The front terrace affords fine views of
the Alte Oper and surrounding skyscrapers.

Ariston
GREEK **$$$**

(Map p374; ☑9203 9950; www.ariston-restaurant.
de; Heiligkreuzgasse 19; mains €13.90-24.50;
⊙11.30am-midnight; ⓇKonstablerwache) Deli-
cious Greek dishes, both traditional and cre-
ative, are served in an elegant corner dining
room. Specialities include beef, lamb and
wild-caught fish and, of course, *souvlákion*
(kebabs; €16.90). A two/three-course busi-
ness lunch costs €11.50/13.50.

Konstablerwache Farmers Market
MARKET **$**

(Map p374; www.erzeugermarkt-konstablerwache.
de; Konstablerwache; ⊙10am-8pm Thu, 8am-
5pm Sat; ⓇKonstablerwache) A great place to
assemble a picnic of fresh fruits, veggies,
bread, wurst and cheeses.

Rewe
SUPERMARKET **$**

(Map p374; Zeil 106; ⊙7am-midnight Mon-Sat) In
the basement of the My Zeil shopping mall.

SACHSENHAUSEN

Frankfurt's biggest cluster of places to drink
and eat is in Sachsenhausen's northeast-
ern corner in an area called **Alt-Sachsen-
hausen** (Old Sachsenhausen; ⓇLokalbahnhof).
Head to bar- and eatery-packed streets such
as Grosse Rittergasse, Kleine Rittergasse,
Klappergasse and Wallstrasse for a meal, a
glass of apple wine, a beer or a shisha smoke.
People do imbibe to excess – the sheer pro-
fusion of establishments makes a pub crawl
hard to resist – but the area is fairly safe and
everyone-friendly (gays, lesbians, heteros,
students, baked sun-studio worshippers,
naked men dancing to their ear buds). Seven
long blocks to the southwest, the southern
end of shop-lined Schweizer Strasse also has
its share of restaurants.

At the **Frau Rauscher Brunnen** (Map p374;
Klappergasse; ⊙warm season; ⓇLokalbahnhof),
the statue of a bulky, nasty-looking Haus-
frau periodically spews a stream of water
onto the footpath – when the street's busy,
you often see pedestrians get drenched. The
idea comes from a popular Frankfurt song
about apple wine.

TOP CHOICE Adolf Wagner
APPLE-WINE TAVERN **$$**

(Map p374; ☑612 565; www.apfelwein-wagner.com;
Schweizer Strasse 71; mains €4.50-13.90; ⊙11am-
midnight; ✈; ⓇSüdbahnhof) Hang up your coat
at one of the hooks along the wood-panelled
wall, take a seat at a long table and order
something local – a great beginning to a traditional, Frankfurt-style night out. Opened
in 1931, this warm, woody tavern specialises in local dishes such as *handkäse mit
Musik* (€2.90), *Grüne Sosse* (€8.20) and
Würstchen mit Sauerkraut (sausage with
sauerkraut; €4.50). Apple wine costs €1.80
(€1.60 standing at the bar).

Lobster
BISTRO **$$$**

(Map p374; ☑612 920; www.lobster-weinbistrot.
de; Wallstrasse 21; mains €15-20; ⊙6pm-1am
Mon-Sat, hot dishes until 10.30pm; ⓇSüdbahnhof)
In a one-time grocery and milk shop from
the 1950s, this cosy, friendly 'wine bistro'
is renowned for mouth-watering meat and
fish dishes that are 'a little bit French'; of-
ferings are listed on chalkboards. Three
dozen wines are available by the glass
(€1.50 to €3.50). Reservations are highly
recommended (there are just seven tables),
especially from Thursday to Saturday and
during fairs.

Fichtekränzi
APPLE WINE TAVERN **$$**

(Map p374; ☑612 778; www.fichtekraenzi.de; Wallstrasse 5; mains €7.20-15.50; ⊙5-11pm; ✈; ⓇLoka-
lbahnhof) Founded in 1849, Fichte Kränzi is

an authentic Frankfurt *Lokal* (pub) with wood-panelled walls, smoke-stained murals, long tables, long benches and great atmosphere. Serves a good selection of German and Frankfurt-style favourites, including *Handkäse mit Musik*, schnitzel and apple strudel. Cash only. Situated on the corner of Abstgässchen.

Maincafé CAFE $
(Map p374; Shaumainkai; ⊘10am-about 2am Marlate Oct; ⓡSchweizer Platz) A good spot to order a beer (€4), a glass of apple wine (€3.20), a coffee (€2) or a sandwich right on the river, in a grassy park with dazzling views of the downtown skyline. Maincafé is hidden away between the embankment and the water's edge, across the street from the **Museum für Kommunikation**.

O'Dwyers Pub IRISH PUB
(Map p374; Klappergasse 19; ⊘5pm-1am or later, until 3.30am or later Fri & Sat; ⓡLokalbahnhof) Irish-owned (though not particularly Irish in ambience), this establishment features on Frankfurt's drinking topography because it's loud and lively – even hellish sometimes. Monday is quiz night (at 9.30pm), and there's karaoke at 10pm on Thursday. Serves Guinness and Kilkenny on tap and screens footy and rugby.

Food Market MARKET $
(Diesterwegplatz; ⊘8am-6pm Tue & Fri; ⓡSüdbahnhof) Colourful food stalls sell fresh fruits and vegies, bread, wurst and other picnic-worthy edibles, all with a very local, Sachsenhausen vibe. In front of the Südbahnhof.

Rewe SUPERMARKET $
(Map p374; Schweizer Strasse 33-37; ⊘8am-8pm Mon-Sat; ⓡSchweizer Platz) Two blocks south of the Museumsufer, in the basement of Woolworth. Buy the picnic fixin's here and then head to the riverbank to dine.

MESSE, WESTEND & BOCKENHEIM
In Bockenheim, a string of inexpensive eateries and ethnic take-aways can be found along **Leipziger Strasse** (ⓡBockenheimer Warte or Leipziger Strasse). The streets southwest of Bockenheimer Warte are sprinkled with reasonably priced restaurants and bars.

Near the Westend campus of Goethe Universität (whose cafeterias are only open to students) several restaurants can be found along **Feldbergstrasse** (ⓡWestend), which is lined with impressive Wilhelmian-era buildings.

Few places to eat are located right around the Messe because custom in this part of the city fluctuates so wildly, with throngs during fairs and nary a soul the rest of the time.

Albatros GERMAN $
(Map p382; www.cafe-albatros.de; Kiesstrasse 27; mains €6.50-8.50; ⊘9am-midnight Mon-Sat, 9am-7pm Sun; ⓙ; ⓡBockenheimer Warte) The favourite old-time student cafe of many Frankfurters, Albatros – decorated with anti-nuclear stickers and Green Party posters – offers exceptionally good value. This is a fine place to try Frankfurt specialities such as *Grüne Sosse* (€7.50) and *Handkäse mit Musik* (€3.50). Great brunches are served on Sunday and holidays from 9am to 2.30pm; the cost for adults is €11, while children up

FRANKFURT SPECIALITIES

Frankfurt delicacies are best experienced in the city's traditional apple-wine taverns such as Fichtekränzi (p390) and Adolf Wagner (p390) in Sachsenhausen and Apfelwein Solzer (p393) in Bornheim.

Many old-time Frankfurters derive great pleasure from savouring a glass of *Ebbelwei* (or *Ebbelwoi*; Frankfurt dialect for *Apfelwein*), a tangy, slightly carbonated apple wine with the alcohol content of a strong beer. Visitors, though, may find that the tart golden liquid, served straight up or *gespritzt* (with sparkling water), is something of an acquired taste.

Handkäse mit Musik ('hand-cheese with music') is the sort of dish you could only find in Germany. The name refers to a round cheese marinated in oil and vinegar with chopped onions and cumin seeds, served with dark bread and butter and (traditionally) no fork. As you might imagine, this potent mixture tends to give one a healthy dose of wind – the release of which, ladies and gentlemen, is the music part.

Frankfurter Grüne Sosse (Frankfurt green sauce) is made from parsley, sorrel, dill, burnet, borage, chervil and chives mixed with mayonnaise, sour cream or yoghurt. It is usually slathered on boiled potatoes, eggs or ox meat, and was Goethe's favourite food.

to 12 pay €0.50 for each year they've been alive. Has a warm-season patio out back.

Pielok
GERMAN $$

(Map p382; ☎776 468; www.restaurant-pielok.de; Jordanstrasse 3; lunch mains €5.90-10.80, dinner mains €10.80-24.80; ⏱11.30am-2.30pm & 5.30-midnight Mon-Fri & during trade fairs Sun, 5.30pm-midnight Sat, hot dishes until 10.30pm; ⓡBockenheimer Warte) Without claiming to be special, this place – run by the same family since 1945 – somehow is: loyal regulars, students and workers tread a path here for hearty *bürgerlich* German fare (including seasonal specialities) at reasonable prices. It has a lovely grape-shaded back *Sommergarten*.

Orfeo's Erben
ITALIAN $$

(Map p382; ☎7076 9100; www.orfeos.de; Hamburger Allee 45; mains €11-19.50; ⏱noon-3pm & 6pm-midnight Mon-Fri, 6pm-midnight Sat; ⓡWestbahnhof) Inside an art-house cinema, this restaurant-bar – great for an informal, romantic meal – has wood-slab tables, backlit beers and dishes with an Italian inflection.

Bockenheimer Weinkontor
WINE BAR

(Map p382; ☎702 031; www.bockenheimer-weinkontor.de; Schlossstrasse 92; ⏱7pm-2am; ⓡWestbahnhof) Hidden away in a courtyard in a 19th-century cellar workshop, this mellow, friendly wine bar attracts a very mixed crowd, both after work and late at night. In winter you can warm yourself by the fireplace and in summer enjoy the fresh air in a lovely vine-shaded courtyard, but the window ledge and the bar are the places to hang your buttocks and start gabbing. Serves about 40 wines by the glass (€3.50 to €6) and snacks.

Siesmayer
CAFE $$

(Map p382; www.palmengarten-gastronomie.de; Siesmayerstrasse 59; mains €7.95-20.50; ⏱8am-7pm; ⓡBockenheimer Warte) Experience highly civilised, haut-bourgeois Westend life at this bright and very proper cafe, pastry shop and restaurant whose lovely patio is surrounded by the greenery of the Palmen-Garten. Yummy French-style pastries can be selected from a glass case; meal options include soups and schnitzel. It's located on a street lined with 19th-century mansions.

Bastos
CAFE $

(www.bastos.de; Gräfstrasse 45; mains €6.50-9.50; ⏱9am-1am or later Sun-Thu, 9am-3am Fri & Sat; ⓡⓐ; ⓡBockenheimer Warte) This contemporary style cafe and night-owl drinking spot

– cocktails are a speciality – serves tapas (€2.50 to €6.90) and a small selection of salads, pasta and mains.

Food Market
MARKET $

(Map p382; Bockenheimer Warte; ⏱8am-6pm Thu; ⓡBockenheimer Warte) A great place to pick up supplies for a fresh, healthy picnic.

Alnatura
SUPERMARKET $

(Map p382; Leipziger Strasse 19; ⏱8am-9pm Mon-Sat; ⓡBockenheimer Warte) A block northwest of Bockenheimer Warte.

NORDEND & BORNHEIM

Berger Strasse, the kind of shopping street where locals go to buy bread, eyeglasses or a bottle of aspirin, heads northeast from the Innenstadt through Nordend and into Bornheim. Offering a slice of everyday Frankfurt life, it is home to some of the city's most authentic and atmospheric cafes and eateries, especially out past **Merianplatz** (ⓡMerianplatz). Sandweg, which runs parallel to Berger Strasse, also has a number of reasonably priced restaurants. The pub-lined stretch of Berger Strasse north of No 249 (just north of Rendeler Strasse) is known as **Alt-Bornheim** (Old Bornheim; ⓡBornheim Mitte)

TOP CHOICE Wein-Dünker
WINE CELLAR

(www.weinkellerei-duenker.de; Berger Strasse 265; ⏱2pm-1am Mon-Thu, 2pm-3am Fri & Sat, 6pm-midnight Sun; ⓡBornheim Mitte) This little wine cellar, down the stairs to the right as you enter the courtyard, is not retro, it's real. Descend, rub your eyes and try some of Germany's finest wines (per glass €2.50). They don't serve food (other than snacks) but you can bring your own and picnic atop an upturned barrel. A good place to meet real Frankfurters. Situated in Alt Bornheim, 2.7km northeast of Konstablerwache.

Paparazzi
ITALIAN $$

(☎6897 7340; www.paparazzi-ffm.de; Seckbacher Landstrasse 48; mains €7-19.50; ⓟ; ⓡSeckbacher Landstrasse) Serves truly outstanding Italian food, which arrives piping hot and with the courses perfectly timed. The atmosphere is relaxed, with romantic red lanterns at each table. A three-course menu costs €15.50 (with a meat or fish main €25.50); a succulent steak is €19. The perfect coda to your meal: a delicious Italian dessert. Situated 3km northeast of Konstablerwache, midway between the two exits of the Seckbacher Landstrasse U-Bahn station.

Apfelwein Solzer APPLE-WINE TAVERN $$
(☏452 171; www.solzer-frankfurt.de; Berger Strasse 260; mains €4.90-17.50; ⊙4 or 5pm-midnight Mon-Sat, 12.30-10pm Sun; 圓Bornheim Mitte) For authentic regional and German dishes, served in the wood-panelled precincts of a traditional *Apfelweinwirtschaft* (apple-wine tavern), it's hard to beat Apfelwein Solzer, run by the same family since 1893. Warm and cosy, with wood-panelled walls and a summertime courtyard, this is an ideal place to sample home-made *Ebbelwei* (apple wine; €1.55). Situated in Alt-Bornheim 2.5km northeast of Konstablerwache.

Café Kante CAFE $
(Map p374; Kantstrasse 13; breakfast €3-7; ⊙7am-7 or 8pm; 圓Merianplatz) Walk into this classic neighbourhood cafe and you'll be overwhelmed by the delicious aroma of fantastic coffee, breads, cakes and croissants. Situated 1.5km northeast of Konstablerwache, half a block east of Berger Strasse 48.

Eckhaus GERMAN $$
(☏491 197; Bornheimer Landstrasse 45; mains €8-17.90; ⊙5pm-midnight or 1am; 圓Merianplatz) The smoke-stained walls and ancient floorboards suggest an inelegant, long-toothed past. We love this place, though some say the noise level can be a bit much. The hallmark *Kartoffelrösti* (shredded potato pancake; €9 or €10.90) has been served here for over 100 years. Situated in the Nordend neighbourhood 1.3km north-northeast of Konstablerwache.

Harvey's RESTAURANT $$
(☏4800 4878; www.einfach-mal-gut-essen-gehen.de; Bornheimer Landstrasse 64; mains €11.90-15.80; ⊙10am-midnight or later; 🕸; 圓Merianplatz) In a great corner location with windows on three sides, this family-friendly place is modern but cosy, romantic but also great for a glass of apple wine (€3.40), a glass of grape wine (€4) or beer (€4) with friends. Edibles, served at heavy wooden tables, include salads, schnitzel, burgers and *Flammkuchen* (Alsatian pizza). Has warm-season outdoor seating. Located 1km north of Konstablerwache (take Friedberger Landstrasse).

Manolya TURKISH $$
(☏494 0162; Habsburger Allee 6a; mains €9.50-19.80; ⊙5pm-1 or 2am; 🕸; 圓Höhenstrasse) A Frankfurt favourite for two decades, this unpretentious Turkish restaurant has a convivial atmosphere, outdoor seating and delicious Anatolian specialities, including several vegie options. Situated 1.5km north-

east of Konstablerwache along the Zeil and then Sandweg.

Best Worscht in Town GERMAN $
(www.bestworschtintown.de; Berger Strasse 80; wurst €2.60-3; ⊙11am-10 or 11pm Mon-Sat, 1-7pm Sun; 圓Merianplatz) A worthy pun as this hugely popular place – which in recent years has become a regional chain – does indeed serve some of Frankfurt's finest hot *Worscht* (known to people from other regions of Germany as wurst). The level of *Schärfehölle* (hellish hotness) goes from A up to F (for 'FBI') – we've tried D and it feels like a blowtorch. Situated 1.2km northeast of Konstablerwache.

Food Market MARKET
(Map p374; Berger Strasse 177; ⊙8am-6.30pm Wed, 8am-4pm Sat; 圓Bornheim Mitte) A lively street market with plenty of fresh, healthy tidbits that make it easy to assemble a romantic picnic on a bench. Situated in Bornheim 2km northeast of Konstablerwache.

Food Market MARKET
(Friedberger Platz; ⊙10am-8pm Fri; 圓Musterschule) Yuppies drop by late Friday afternoon to chat each other up. Very social. Situated 1km north of Konstablerwache (take Friedberger Landstrasse).

Rewe Supermarket SUPERMARKET $
(Berger Strasse 161; ⊙8am-10pm Mon-Sat; 圓Bornheim Mitte) For self caterers. Situated in Bornheim 2km northeast of Konstablerwache.

☆ Entertainment

Frankfurt is a cultural magnet for the whole Rhine-Main region, and this is reflected in the variety, verve and velocity of its concerts, clubs and cabarets. Thursday is a big night out for workers who commute to Frankfurt for the week and go 'home' on Friday with drooping eyelids, scuffed dance shoes and wretched hangovers. Several dance clubs have summertime beach clubs along the Main River.

Several entertainment magazines (in German), available at newsstands and kiosks (or online), provide day-by-day listings of cultural events and nightlife, including lesbian and gay venues: comprehensive *Journal Frankfurt* (www.journal-frankfurt.de; €1.80), *Prinz Frankfurt* (http://frankfurt.prinz.de; €2.90), student-oriented *Frizz* (www.frizz-frankfurt.de; free) and *Strandgut* (www.strandgut.de; free).

TICKETS FOR CULTURAL EVENTS

Tickets for rock, pop and classical concerts, operas, musicals, plays and sports events (except football/soccer) are available from **Frankfurt Ticket** (☎134 0400; www.frankfurtticket.de), whose **main office** (Map p374; ☺9.30am-7pm Mon-Fri, 9.30am-4pm Sat, longer hrs Dec, shorter hrs Jul & Aug) is underground in the Hauptwache U-Bahn/S-Bahn station, on the B Level facing KFC. Posters and brochures announcing upcoming events line the walls, making this a good place to assess your options for going out. Tickets ordered through their internet site (€5 surcharge) are sent out by post. Other Frankfurt Ticket offices:

Messe (Map p382; Ludwig Erhard Anlage 1 in the Festhalle, Messe; ☺11am-6pm Mon-Fri; 🚇Festhalle/Messe)

Alte Oper (Map p374; Opernplatz 1, Alte Oper; ☺10am-6.30pm Mon-Fri, 10am-2pm Sat; 🚇Alte Oper)

Last-minute tickets can generally be purchased an hour or so before performance time at each venue's *Abendkasse* (evening ticket window).

Cabaret

Tigerpalast CABARET
(Map p374; ☎restaurant 9200 2225, tickets 9200 220; www.tigerpalast.com; Heiligkreuzgasse 16-20; adult €58.75-64.25, child half-price; ☺shows 7pm & 10pm Tue-Thu, 7.30pm & 10.30pm Fri & Sat, 4.30pm & 8pm Sun, closed mid-Jun–mid-Aug; 🚇Konstablerwache) A top venue for cabaret and *Varieté* theatre, with programs that often include acrobats and circus and magic performances. Hugely enjoyable even if you don't speak German. Reserve by phone or through the website.

Mouson PERFORMING ARTS
(Künstlerhaus Mousonturm; Map p374; ☎405 8950; www.mousonturm.de; Waldschmidtstrasse 4; 🚇Merianplatz) This rambling former soap factory serves as a forum for younger artists and hosts contemporary dance, theatre (sometimes in English) and cabaret, as well as concerts by up-and-coming bands.

Cinemas

Films in the original language (ie non-dubbed) are denoted by the abbreviations 'OV' (original version), 'OmU' (*Original mit Untertiteln*, ie subtitled) or the cryptic 'O.m.dt.Ut.' (*Original mit deutschen Untertiteln*, ie with German subtitles). Look for posters in U-Bahn stations; if the description is in English, so is the movie. Listings appear in the free *Kino Journal Frankfurt* (www.kinojournal-frankfurt.de), which comes out every Thursday and is available around town (eg at the tourist office).

Kino im Deutschen Filmmuseum CINEMA
(Map p374; ☎961 220 220; www.deutsches-film institut.de; Schaumainkai 41; adult/student €7/5; ☺closed Mon; 🚇Schweizer Platz) This art cinema is attached to Frankfurt's cinema museum.

Orfeo's Erben CINEMA
(Map p382; ☎7076 9100; www.orfeos.de; Hamburger Allee 45; 🚇Westbahnhof) A few blocks northeast of the Messe, Orfeo's Erben screens non-dubbed art-house films (celluloid and digital) and has a charming restaurant.

Kino Mal Seh'n CINEMA
(☎597 0845; www.malsehnkino.de; Adlerflycht strasse 6; admission €7; 🚇Musterschule) An 80-seat art-house cinema with offbeat non-dubbed movies from around the world and an engaging wine bar. Situated 1.2km due north of Konstablerwache, just off Eckenheimer Landstrasse.

Nightclubs

King Kamehameha CLUB
(☎4800 9610; www.king-kamehameha.de; Hanauer Landstrasse 192; admission Thu €8, Fri & Sat €10; ☺9pm-4am or later Thu, 10pm-4am or later Fri & Sat) A strapping Leonardo DiCaprio-type guy might dash out and unexpectedly plough the length of the ornamental pool (clothed, take note) – it's been known to happen here. And much more too, for 'KingKa' is legendary, with DJ dance beats on weekends and its own live club band on Thursday (this is *the* place in Frankfurt to usher in Friday). Draws a mixed crowd, most in their 20s and early 30s, that come nicely turned-out (jeans are OK, though). Often full – the

earlier you arrive, the better your chance of getting in. Or you can reserve by phone a day or two ahead. Situated about 2km southeast of the zoo; accessible by tram 11. Runs a warm-season 'beach club' across the river at Hafeninsel 2 in Offenbach.

Nachtleben
CLUB

(Map p374; www.nachtleben.net; Kurt Schumacher Strasse 45; disco €3-8, concerts €5-25; ☺cafe 11am-2am Mon-Thu, 11am-4 or 5am Fri & Sat, disco 11pm-4am or later Fri & Sat; ☒Konstablerwache) Tucked away in the southeastern corner of Konstablerwache, Nachtleben has a sedate cafe with a terrace on the ground floor and a downstairs disco that reaches its full pulsating potential at about 1am. Concerts showcase alternative and independent music, parties often feature house, electro and hip-hop. The dress code is relaxed – jeans are fine but jogging pants are not.

Living XXL
CLUB

(Map p374; ☎242 9370; www.livingxxl.de; Kaiserstrasse 29; ☺6pm-1am Wed, 7pm-3am Thu, 7pm-4am Fri, 7pm-5am or later Sat; ☒Willy-Brandt-Platz) If the euro ever goes into freefall, it'll land here – this large, mainstream club, with a restaurant and six bars, is in the basement of the Eurotower, home of the European Central Bank. No surprise, then, that it's popular with bankers (and wannabes) in their 20s, 30s and 40s. On Wednesday it has a hugely popular after-work party (€7), with buffet and happy hour from 6pm to 8pm. On Thursday there's either live music (€10 or €15; from 9pm) or, on the first Thursday of the month, salsa (€7.50), with a class (9pm to 10pm) followed by dancing until 2am. On Friday and Saturday (€10) the party begins at 10pm and hits full blast at about midnight; DJs spin house, R&B and pop. As for the dress code: on Wednesday, t-shirts are banned but jeans are OK; on Friday t-shirts are fine; Saturday is a bit chic-er, with button-down shirts a must for men.

Südbahnhof
CLUB

(Map p374; www.suedbahnhof.de; inside Südbahnhof, Sachsenhausen; ☒Südbahnhof) This *Musik-Lokal*, inside the Südbahnhof S-Bahn station, is known for its '30-Plus' parties (€7, Saturday from 9pm to 3am), open to anyone who's been around for at least three decades. Often hosts dances for seniors (Monday from 5.30pm to 8pm) and live music (eg Sunday

from noon to 12.30pm). Set to reopen in late 2012 after renovations.

The Cave
CLUB

(Map p374; www.the-cave.de; Brönnerstrasse 11; admission after 11pm Fri & Sat €5; ☺10pm-3am Thu, 10pm-6.30am Fri-Sun; ☒Hauptwache or Konstablerwache) At Frankfurt's number one rock club, DJs (who take requests) feature alternative rock as well as punk and metal in two barrel-vaulted cellars. Things really get going at midnight or 1am. No dress code. Ages range from 18 to 50. Has a Facebook page.

Cocoon Club
CLUB

(www.cocoon.net; Carl-Benz-Strasse 21, Fechenheim) This postmodern pulsating membrane-like miracle, about 5km east of the centre (off Hanauer Landstrasse), is the home of techno legend Sven Väth. It throbs with music from the man himself or his guests on Friday and Saturday. To get there take tram 11 or 12 to Dieselstrasse.

Robert Johnson
CLUB

(www.robert-johnson.de; Nordring 131, Kaiserlai, Offenbach) This renowned club, minimalist in décor, attracts the best names in German electronic music. Situated on the south bank of the river just over the line in Offenbach (and just east of the B661), about 5.5km southeast of downtown.

Gay & Lesbian Venues

Frankfurt's gay life is concentrated north of the Zeil around Schäfergasse (☒Konstablerwache) and, a block farther north, Alte Gasse, with a bevy of clubs and cafes. For details on the scene, see the free monthly magazine *Gab* (www.inqueery.de), www.frankfurt.gay-web.de or www.up-cityguide.de (in German).

TUESDAY NIGHT SKATING

Thousands of experienced in-line skaters come out on Tuesday nights (starting at 8.30pm) in late March to late October for a sociable, 2½-hour (35km to 42km) circuit – with police escort. It begins in Sachsenhausen, on the riverfront, at the southern end of Ignatz-Bubis-Brücke (served by trams 14 and 18). For more information check out the website www.tns-frankfurt.de.

La Gata
LESBIAN

(Map p374; www.club-la-gata.de; Seehofstrasse 3, Sachsenhausen; ⏰8pm-1am Mon, Wed & Thu, 9pm-3am Fri & Sat, 6pm-1am Sun; ⓡLokalbahnhof) Opened in 1971, this is Frankfurt's only women-only lesbian bar.

Rock & Jazz

Batschkapp
LIVE MUSIC

(www.batschkapp.de; Maybachstrasse 24; ⓡEschersheim) In its 35-plus years of staging live bands (rock, soul, hip-hop etc), the legendary 'Batsch' has seen 'em come, go, burn out, gloriously self-destruct or simply rust to dust. May relocate in the near future, but until then it's 6km north-northwest of Konstablerwache, next to the Eschersheim S-Bahn stop.

Jazzkeller
JAZZ

(Map p374; www.jazzkeller.com; Kleine Bockenheimer Strasse 18a; admission €5-25; ⏰8pm-2am Tue-Thu, 10pm-3am Fri, 9pm-2am Sat, 8pm-1am Sun; ⓡAlte Oper) A great jazz venue with mood, since 1952. Check out the walls for photos of jazz greats who've played here over the years. Concerts begin an hour after opening except on DJ night (Friday) when there's dancing to Latin and funk. Hidden away in a cellar across from Goethestrasse 27.

Mampf
JAZZ

(Map p374; ☎448 674; www.mampf-jazz.de; Sandweg 64, Merianplatz; ⏰6pm-1am Sun-Thu, 6pm-2am Fri & Sat) Great jazz permeates this tiny jazz-club-cum-pub, running since 1972. Hosts live concerts two or three times a week, often from 8.30pm to 11pm on Wednesday and Saturday.

FREE Summa Summarum
LIVE MUSIC

(Map p374; Klappergasse 3; admission free; ⏰8pm-1am Tue-Sat) This *Musikkeller* (music cellar), an intimate basement venue with vaulted stone ceilings and just a half-dozen tables, features traditional New Orleans jazz on Wednesday and Friday and singer-songwriters (blues, rock etc) on Thursday and Saturday; Tuesday is open-mike night. The music lasts from about 9pm to midnight. A beer (0.5L) costs €4.50; a big glass of apple wine is €3.80.

Theatre, Classical & Dance

The Frankfurt theatre scene has all the hallmarks of high art – it barks, bites back, and occasionally an offended ego spontaneously and publicly explodes. There are over 30 different venues around town.

Städtische Bühnen
PERFORMING ARTS

(Map p374; ☎2124 9494; www.buehnen-frankfurt.de; Untermainanlage 11; ⓡWilly-Brandt-Platz) A huge cultural complex that includes **Oper Frankfurt** (Map p374; www.oper-frankfurt.de), the city's main opera company, and **Schauspiel Frankfurt** (Map p374; www.schauspielfrankfurt.de), Frankfurt's largest theatre company. Tickets can be ordered by phone or via the websites.

Alte Oper
CLASSICAL MUSIC

(Map p374; www.alteoper.de; Opernplatz 1; ⏰closed mid-Jul–late-Aug; ⓡAlte Oper) The 'old opera house' hosts frequent concerts of symphonic and chamber music in its two halls, which seat 2450 and 720 respectively.

English Theatre
THEATRE

(Map p374; ☎2423 1620; www.english-theatre.org; Kaiserstrasse 34, entrance on Gallusanlage; tickets €22-47; ⏰season runs late Aug-Jun, box office noon-6pm Mon, 11am-6.30pm Tue-Fri, 3-6.30pm Sat, 3-5pm Sun; ⓡWilly-Brandt-Platz) Continental Europe's largest English-language theatre company stages first-rate plays and musicals, with top actors hired after casting calls in London and New York.

Bockenheimer Depot
DANCE

(Map p382; ☎2124 9494; www.bockenheimer-depot.de; Carlo-Schmid-Platz 1; ⓡBockenheimer Warte) This century-old former tram depot hosts innovative dance productions by the **Forsythe Company** (www.theforsythecompany.com; tickets €22 to €32) as well as Städtische Bühnen theatre and opera productions.

🔒 Shopping

When it comes to shopping, Frankfurt is not Berlin, Paris or Milan, but the city still has plenty to offer the shopping aficionado. The eminently strollable **Zeil** (ⓡHauptwache or Konstablerwache) is the main shopping precinct, but the really serious splurging takes place along **Goethestrasse** (Hauptwache) and other streets just west of Goetheplatz, where you'll find the city's chic-est fashion boutiques and most glamorous jewellery stores. Young clothing designers have shops in Sachsenhausen around the intersection of Brückenstrasse and Wallstrasse.

Galeria Kaufhof
DEPARTMENT STORE

(Map p374; www.galeria-kaufhof.de; Zeil 116-26; ⏰9.30am-8pm Mon-Wed, 9.30am-9pm Thu-Sat; ⓡHauptwache) Upscale wares in the heart of the Zeil shopping zone. The basement supermarket has a superb selection of gourmet chocolates.

My Zeil
SHOPPING MALL

(Map p374; www.myzeil.de; Zeil 106; ⊙10am-8pm Mon-Wed, 10am-9pm Thu-Sat; ⓡHauptwache) Behind the vortex facade, the Zeil's newest mega project (opened 2009) has over 100 shops.

Schaumainkai
MARKET

(Map p374; ⊙8am-2pm Sat) Hundreds of tables and blankets spread out on the pavement are piled high with an incredible array of both worthless junk and valuable junque. Come early for finds. Some stalls sell sausages. Takes place on alternate weeks in Sachsenhausen, along the riverfront Schaumainkai between the two pedestrian bridges, Eiserner Steg and Hobeinsteg; and at the Osthafen, along Lindleystrasse, about 1km southeast of the zoo.

British Bookshop
BOOKSHOP

(Map p374; ⏹280 492; www.british-bookshop.de; Börsenstrasse 17; ⊙9.30am-7pm Mon-Fri, to 6pm Sat; ⓡHauptwache) Largest selection of English-language books in town, including LP guides.

Oscar Wilde Bookshop
BOOKSHOP

(Map p374; www.oscar-wilde.de; Alte Gasse 51; ⊙11am-7pm Mon-Fri, 10am-4pm Sat; ⓡKonstablerwache) Gay and lesbian books, plus information on Frankfurt's LGBT community.

ⓘ Information

Dangers & Annoyances

The area northeast of the Hauptbahnhof (ie north of Kaiserstrasse, itself quite safe) is a base for Frankfurt's trade in sex and illegal drugs, and has *Druckräume*, centres where needles are distributed and the drug-dependent can shoot up. Women in particular might want to avoid Elbestrasse and Taunusstrasse, which play host to the city's largest concentration of sex shows, go-go bars, short-time hotels, sleazy casinos and shifty characters. Frequent police and private security patrols of the station and the surrounding streets keep things under control, but it's always advisable to use big-city common sense.

Discount Cards

Frankfurt Card (1/2 days €9.20/13.50, for up to 5 people €19/28) Benefits include free public transport (including to/from the airport – a big saving); 50% off at 26 museums, the PalmenGarten and the zoo; 15% off for the opera; and all sorts of other discounts. Available at the airport's Hotels & Tours desk (so you can use it for the train ride into the city), the tourist office, the Verkehrsinsel and some hotels.

Emergency

Fire/Ambulance (⏹112)

Police (⏹110)

Women's Hotline (Frauennotruf; ⏹709 494; www.frauennotrufe-hessen.de)

Internet Access

CybeRyder Internet Lounge (Töngesgasse 31, Innenstadt; per 15min €1.60; ⊙9.30am-10pm Mon-Fri, 10am-8pm Sat, noon-7pm Sun, 2-8pm holidays; ⓡKonstablerwache) Frankfurt's first internet cafe, founded way back in 1995. Has cupcakes, snacks, scanners and QUERTY keyboards.

PTT Shop (Baseler Strasse 35-37; per hr €2; ⊙8am-midnight; ⓡFrankfurt Hauptbahnhof) Bright and pleasant. Inside the ReiseBank; the entrance is on Mannheimerstrasse.

Internet Resources

» **www.frankfurt-tourismus.de** Frankfurt tourist office.

» **www.frankfurt.de** Municipal website.

» **www.frankfurt-handicap.de** Information for travellers with limited mobility (mostly in German).

» **www.frankfurthigh.com** For a fascinating collection of historical engravings, photos, maps and links, click 'Eagle Information', then 'History' and finally 'Frankfurt History'.

Laundry

SB Waschsalon (⊙6am-11pm except Sun & holidays)

Sachsenhausen (Wallstrasse 8, Sachsenhausen; ⓡLokalbahnhof)

Bornheim (Sandweg 41, Bornheim; ⓡMerianplatz)

Bockenheim (Grosse Seestrasse 46, Bockenheim; ⓡBockenheimer Warte).

Medical Services

To find a *Notdienstapotheke* (duty pharmacy) open after-hours, check the window of any pharmacy, check out www.aponet.de (in German) or consult the *Frankfurter Rundschau* newspaper. Pharmacies at the Hauptbahnhof and the airport are open until late at night.

Vertragsärztlicher Bereitschaftsdienst (VBF; ⏹192 92; www.bereitschaftsdienst-frankfurt. de) A 24-hour doctor service. Physicians make house (or hotel) calls.

Unfallklinik (Centre for Trauma Surgery; ⏹4750; www.bgu-frankfurt.de; Friedberger Landstrasse 430) Accident treatment, 4km northeast of the centre. Served by bus 30.

Uni-Klinik (University Hospital; ⏹630 11, 630 10; www.kgu.de; Theodor-Stern-Kai 7; ⊙24hr;

Stresemannallee) About 1.5km due south of the Hauptbahnhof, across the river. Served by trams 12, 15 or 21.

Money

ReiseBank (⊙7am-9pm; ⓡFrankfurt Hauptbahnhof) Inside the Hauptbahnhof, behind track 1. Exchanges cash (commission €2.10, plus 2.5%) and travellers cheques (minimum commission €8) and does Visa and MasterCard cash advances.

Post Office

Hauptbahnhof (Hauptbahnhof; ⊙7am-7pm Mon-Fri, 9am-6pm Sat; ⓡFrankfurt Hauptbahnhof) Behind track 23.

Innenstadt (Goetheplatz 4, Innenstadt; ⊙9.30am-7pm Mon-Fri, 9am-2pm Sat; ⓡHauptwache)

Tourist Office (🖉2123 8800, for hotel reservations 2123 0808; www.frankfurt-tourismus.de) The Hauptbahnhof (Hauptbahnhof; ⊙8am-9pm Mon-Fri, 9am-6pm Sat, Sun & holidays; ⓡFrankfurt Hauptbahnhof) branch is behind track 13 at the far end of the barrel-vaulted hall; the Altstadt (Römerberg 27, inside Römer, Altstadt; ⊙9.30am-5.30pm Mon-Fri, 9.30am-4pm Sat, Sun & holidays; ⓡDom/Römer) branch is very helpful, with oodles of useful information and brochures.

Verkehrsinsel (🖉01801-069 960; www.rmv. de; Zeil 129; ⊙9am-8pm Mon-Fri, 9.30am-6pm Sat; ⓡHauptwache) In a round, glass pavilion. Provides public transport information including timetables, and sells local and DB tickets. Staff are also happy to provide general tourist information.

Wheelchair Accessibility

Frankfurt is becoming more and more accessible for visitors with limited mobility. For nuts-and-bolts details of access to sights, activities, the Messe and public transport, download the outstanding 89-page booklet *Barrier-free Frankfurt* (English version published in 2012), from www.frankfurt-tourismus.de/barrier-free.html. The website www.frankfurt-handicap.de also has some useful information. Details of using public transport appears in the brochure *Barrierefrei Unterwegs* (in German), available from any traffiQ (p400) office.

ⓘ Getting There & Away

Air

Frankfurt Airport (FRA; www.frankfurt-airport. com), 12km southwest of downtown, is Germany's busiest airport, with the highest cargo turnover and the third-highest passenger numbers in Europe (after London's Heathrow and Paris' Charles de Gaulle).

Halls A, B and C are in **Terminal 1**, whose tenants include Lufthansa, while Halls D and E are in the newer **Terminal 2**. Terminal 3 will someday be built on land that was once part of the American Rhein-Main Air Base, closed in 2005.

Terminals 1 and 2 are linked by a driverless elevated railway, the **SkyLine**, which runs every two minutes. Finding it is harder than you might expect – the maps printed in official brochures are very schematic, and the airport's signposting is nothing to write home about, either.

Frankfurt airport has two train stations accessible via underground passages from Terminal 1. The **Regionalbahnhof** (Regional Train Station) handles regional train and S-Bahn connections; services begin at about 4.30am and end at 12.30am. The **Fernbahnhof** (Long-Distance Train Station), underneath a new shopping area called **The Squaire**, is used by long-haul IC, ICE and EC trains. The easiest way to get from the train stations to Terminal 2 or vice versa, especially if you've got lots of luggage, is to take one of the yellow shuttle buses (rather than the SkyLine).

Amenities and services available at the airport:

Children's Play Area (Terminal 2, next to Food Plaza & Visitors' Terrace, Frankfurt Airport) Shaped like a spaceship.

Currency Exchange (Frankfurt Airport; ⊙approx 6am-9 or 10pm) Available at desks (eg Travelex) all over the airport. The commission for cash is generally €2 or €3, for traveller's cheques 3% (minimum €10).

Food Courts In Terminal 1, in Area A of the Airport City Mall (one floor below the Arrival level); in Terminal 2, next to the Visitors' Terrace.

Hotels & Tours (🖉6907 0402; https://hotels. frankfurt-airport.de; Terminal 1, Arrival Hall B, Frankfurt Aiport; ⊙7am-10.30pm) This desk can help with hotel bookings. Sells the FrankfurtCard.

Information (⊙24hr) Airport, transport and tourist information is available from several Fraport (Frankfurt Airport) counters and mobile stands, including one 24-hour counter in each terminal.

Internet Terminals (per minute approx €0.17) Computer terminals with stainless steel keyboards are sprinkled around the airport.

Last-Minute Plane Tickets (Terminal 1, between Departure Halls B & C, Frankfurt Airport; ⊙24hr) Sometimes cheaper than advance-purchase tickets, these are available at a row of travel agency counters in Terminal 1. Arrive at least two hours before you hope to travel.

Lufthansa Buses (www.lufthansa.com; Frankfurt Airport) Link Terminal 1 with Mannheim (€19.90), Heidelberg (€23) and Strasbourg, France (€49).

Luggage Carts (deposit €2) You can pay with €1 or €2 coins, or with €5 or €10 banknotes; the deposit is returned when you return the cart. Carts are designed to go up and down escalators but cannot be taken on the SkyLine.

Luggage Storage (Gepäckaufbewahrung; Frankfurt Airport; up to 2/24hr €4.50/7; ⊙6am-10pm) Situated in Terminal 1, Arrival Hall B (open 24 hours); Terminal 1, between Departure Halls B and C; and in Terminal 2, Hall D.

Medical Services (Medizinische Dienste; ✆6906 6767; Terminal 1, between Arrival Halls B & C, Frankfurt Airport; ⊙24hr) Medical care, including prescriptions for lost medications.

Post Office (Terminal 1, Arrival Hall B, Frankfurt Airport; ⊙9am-7pm Mon-Fri, 11am-6pm Sat) Can ship those extra kilos if your baggage is overweight.

Rewe City Supermarket (The Squaire; ⊙5am-1am) Picnic supplies, located above the Fernbahnhof (Long-Distance Train Station).

Showers (Duschen; Terminal 1, Departure Hall B & Terminal 2, Hall D, Frankfurt Airport; €6 or US$8; ⊙6am-10 or 11pm)

Tegut Supermarket (Terminal 1, Hall C, one floor below Arrival level, Frankfurt shop; ⊙6am-10pm) Take the down escalator in front of the USO office. There's no supermarket in Terminal 2.

Travellers Aid (Kirchlicher Sozialdienst; ✆50201, 47131; Terminal 1, between Departure Halls B & C, counter 700.1, frankfurt airport; ⊙8am-4.30pm Mon-Fri) Run jointly by the Catholic and Evangelical Churches, this counter, staffed by volunteers, can help travellers in distress, eg by helping them contact the police or their embassy.

USO (✆691 581; www.uso.org; Terminal 1, Arrival Hall C, Frankfurt Airport; ⊙7am-3pm) For active duty US military personnel and their families, offers information and a small lounge with free internet, wi-fi, phone calls to the USA, drinks and snacks.

Wi-fi To get 30 minutes of free wi-fi, go to a hotspot, connect and enter your mobile phone number; a code will be sent to your cellphone. After your free time (available once a day), the charge is €4.95 an hour. The German word for 'wi-fi' is 'WLAN' (pronounced 'veh lahn').

If your flight (eg on Ryanair) is to **Frankfurt-Hahn Airport** (HHN; www.hahn-airport.de) – a US Air Force base during the Cold War – you'll land about 110km west of Frankfurt. **Buses** (www.bohr.de; €14) link Frankfurt-Hahn with the real Frankfurt airport (Terminal 2 only) and Frankfurt's Hauptbahnhof (Mannheimer Strasse; 1¾ hours).

Bus

Eurolines (✆790 3253; www.eurolines.eu; Mannheimer Strasse 15; ⊙7.30am-7.30pm Mon-Fri, 7.30am-2pm Sat, 7.30am-1pm Sun; ☒Frankfurt Hauptbahnhof) can take you inexpensively to cities all around Europe (but not within Germany).

Car & Motorcycle

Car rental desks at the airport:

Terminal 1 (in the underground Airport City Mall, Area A) – Avis/Budget, Europcar, Hertz, National/Alamo and Sixt.

Terminal 2 (Car Rental Center) – Avis/Budget, Dollar/Thrifty, Enterprise, Europcar, Hertz/Advantage and Sixt.

At the Hauptbahnhof, Avis, Europcar, Hertz and Sixt have offices next to the tourist office.

ADAC (✆01805-101 112; www.adac.de; Schillerstrasse 12; ⊙9.30am-6.30pm Mon-Fri, 10am-1pm Sat; ☒Hauptwache) Germany's automobile association provides free maps and route advice to members of partner automobile clubs, including the AAA in the US, the AA in the UK and eight state AAA groups in Australia (membership card required). Also sells safety equipment (snow chains, child car seats) and insurance.

Ride Service

The **Mitfahrzentrale** (✆194 40; Baselerplatz; ⊙9.30am-6.30pm Mon-Fri, 10am-2pm Sat; ☒Frankfurt Hauptbahnhof) matches travellers with drivers going to the same destination. Typical all-up fares, including fees: Berlin (€35), Cologne (€19), London (€45), Munich (€30), Paris (€47) and Stuttgart (€20). It's best to make reservations (by phone or in person) two or three days ahead, but last-minute bookings are often possible. Drivers meet passengers at the office.

You can also find drivers going your way on the internet – try www.mfz.de or www.mitfahrgelegenheit.de or www.drive2day.de, all in German.

Train

The **Hauptbahnhof**, about 1km west of the Altstadt and 1km southeast of the Messe, handles more departures and arrivals than any other station in Germany, which means that there are convenient trains to pretty much everywhere, including Berlin (€118, four hours). For train information call ✆01805-996 633 (not toll-free). Details on travel to destinations in the greater Frankfurt region is available from www.rmv.de.

ATMs Look for a sign reading 'Geldautomat'.

Luggage Lockers (Schliessfacher; Hauptbahnhof; small/large for 72 hr €3/5) At three locations, including 50m behind track 18.

Model Train Layout (€1) Behind track 1. Likely to please the kids.

Schmitt & Hahn (Map p374; Hauptbahnhof; ⊙5 or 6am-11pm or midnight) Sells international newspapers and mags behind track 7, and English-language books (including LP guides) behind track 17.

Reisezentrum (information office; www.bahn.de; Hauptbahnhof; ⊙6 or 7am-10pm) Can explain DB's many discount options (you can often travel for much less than the full-fare prices quoted in this chapter). In the barrel-vaulted hall behind track 11.

Toilets (Hauptbahnhof; €0.70) Down the stairs behind track 9.

Wi-fi hotspots There's one behind track 4.

From Frankfurt Airport's **Fernbahnhof** (Long-Distance Train Station), destinations served at least hourly, often by superfast IC and ICE trains, include Basel (€79.20, three hours), Cologne (€64, one hour), Hamburg (€92 to €115, four to five hours), Hannover (€69 to €86, 2½ hours) and Stuttgart (€59, 1¼ hours).

ⓘ Getting Around

To/From the Airport

S-Bahn lines S8 and S9 shuttle between the airport's regional train station, Flughafen Regionalbahnhof, and the city centre (one-way €4.10, 15 minutes), stopping at the Hauptbahnhof, Hauptwache and Konstablerwache, as well as (in the other direction) Wiesbaden and Mainz. To get to Darmstadt, change to the S3. Intercity trains use the airport's modern, glass-roofed Fernbahnhof (Long-Distance Train Station).

Bus 61 links the Südbahnhof in Sachsenhausen with Terminals 1 and 2 every 15 minutes (every 30 minutes on Saturday and Sunday).

A taxi from the airport to the city centre costs about €26 or €27 (a bit more from 10pm to 6am).

Many airport-area hotels operate free shuttle buses from Terminal 1 and/or Terminal 2.

Bicycle

Cycling is a great way to get around Frankfurt, which is well endowed with designated bike lanes.

Call-a-Bike (☑07000-522 5522; www.callabike-interaktiv.de) Run by Deutsche Bahn. You register by phone with your credit card number and then, each time you want a bicycle, you go to one of Frankfurt's 72 Call-a-Bike Stations and phone to get the lock code. Costs are €0.08 a minute and up to €15 for 24 hours (€9 for students).

Next Bike (☑030-6920 5046; www.nextbike.de; per hr/24hr €1/8) After registering with a credit card, you go to a pick-up point (eg next to the Römer tourist office or at Hauptwache) and phone to get the lock code; phone again when you return the bike.

Velotaxi (☑715 888 55, 8356 8294; www.frankfurt.velotaxi.de; 1/2 people per km €3/4, per hr €22/33; ⊙noon-8pm Apr-Oct) In some parts of the Altstadt and Innenstadt, you can flag down (or reserve by phone) a pedal-powered, three-wheel cycle-taxi.

Car & Motorcycle

Traffic flows smoothly in central Frankfurt, but if you're behind the wheel the many one-ways may drive you to distraction. To preserve your sanity (even if you have a GPS), you may be better off parking your vehicle and proceeding on foot. Throughout the centre you'll see signs indicating the way to the nearest **Parkhaus** (parking garage; www.parkhaus-frankfurt.de; per hr €2, overnight €3-5) and the number of spaces left. City-centre street parking costs €1 per 30 minutes and is generally limited to one hour.

In many areas, parking on one side of the street is reserved for Bewohner (local residents) whose cars have a special sticker. Signs explain (in German, of course) the hours during which restrictions apply.

Public Transport

Frankfurt's excellent transport network, run by **traffiQ** (☑01801-069 960; www.traffiq.de) integrates all bus, Strassenbahn (tram), S-Bahn (commuter rail) and U-Bahn (metro/subway) lines; in general the U-Bahn is underground only in the city centre. The city centre's main transport hubs are Hauptwache, Konstablerwache and Frankfurt Hauptbahnhof; each has a traffiQ office that can supply you with transport maps, including a Gesamtlinienplan (system-wide route map). Details on how the system works are spelled out in a very useful free brochure called Travelling in Frankfurt.

Each site mentioned in the Frankfurt am Main section – provided it's within about 500m of a U-Bahn or S-Bahn station – has the nearest station indicated after the address. Some areas (eg northern Sachsenhausen) are most conveniently accessed by tram and/or bus.

Tickets can be purchased from the Fahrkartenautomaten (ticket machines) at transit stops; press the little UK flag for English. Zone 50 encompasses most of Frankfurt, excluding the airport. Machines accept euro coins and bills (up to €10 or €20) and credit cards that have an embedded computer chip (ie cards that require a PIN code to use), a requirement that excludes many US-issued cards.

An Einzelfahrt (single-ride) ticket costs €2.50 (for children age six to 14 €1.50); it's time-stamped when you buy it and so is valid only for travel you begin immediately. For trips of less than 2km, buy a *Kurzstrecke* (short-distance journey) ticket (€1.60).

A *Tageskarte* (all-day ticket), valid from the start of service until 3.30am the next day, costs €6.20 (€8 including the airport); a *Gruppentageskarte* (all-day collective ticket), the version valid for up to five people, is just €9.50 (€14.50 including the airport) – a superb deal. A *Wochenkarte* (weekly pass, valid for any seven consecutive days), sold at the airport's DB ticket office and available from some ticket machines, costs €23.10 (including the airport) and is also a wildly great deal.

Nachtbus (night bus; www.nachtbus -frankfurt.de) lines, whose numbers begin with 'n', leave from Konstablerwache (to be precise, from both sides and the middle of Kurt Schumacher Strasse) half-hourly (hourly for some suburban destinations) from 1.30am to 3.30am daily. For destinations outside of the city, the Nachtbus service runs only on Friday and Saturday nights and holiday eves. Tickets cost the same as for daytime transport, or you can use an all-day ticket or weekly pass.

Inspectors frequently check to make sure passengers have valid tickets. The fine for travelling *schwarz* ('black', ie without a ticket) is €40.

Frankfurt's public transport system is being made *barrierefrei* (barrier-free, ie wheelchair accessible) but while buses have ramps, not all U-Bahn and S-Bahn stations have elevators/lifts yet.

Taxi

Taxis are quite expensive. There's a €2.75 hire charge (€3.25 at night); travel costs €1.65 per kilometre (€1.75 at night), with a waiting charge of €21 per hour (€28 at night). A fifth passenger costs €7 extra. A helpful hint: don't look for a cab at the Thurn-und-Taxis-Palais, named after a German princely family!

There are taxi ranks throughout the city, or you can contact:

Taxi Frankfurt (☑250 001, 230 001; www. taxi-frankfurt.de)

Time Car (☑203 04; www.yellow-cab-taxi.de)

SGS Taxi (☑7930 7999; www.sgs-service office.de)

AROUND FRANKFURT

Wiesbaden

☑0611 / POP 276,000

The spa-town capital of Hesse, 40km west of Frankfurt and across the Rhine from Mainz, is a handsome city with a lively commercial centre, several historic attractions, green parks to calm the weariest of urban eyes, and a century-old thermal bath.

Dostoyevsky messed himself up badly here in the 1860s when he amassed huge debts at the city's gambling tables, events that inspired his masterpiece, *The Gambler*.

Wiesbaden is at the eastern edge of the Rheingau wine-growing region, which stretches along the right (northern) bank of the Rhine west to the Rüdesheim area of the Romantic Rhine. The tourist office can provide details on wine-tasting opportunities.

The US military presence in Wiesbaden (www.wiesbaden.army.mil) is set to expand in 2013 when the European headquarters of the US Army moves here from Heidelberg.

FRANKFURT & SOUTHERN RHINELAND WIESBADEN

ROAD-TRIP RADIO IN ENGLISH

Thanks to the 50,000 American military personnel stationed on German soil, you can listen to a variety of often surprising radio programs while tooling around Germany's southwest.

To feel like you're in Middle America (or to find out the weather at Baghram Air Base in Afghanistan), just tune to a station run by **AFN Europe** (American Forces Network Europe; www.afneurope.net) whose intended audience serves at places like Ramstein Air Base near Kaiserslautern and the US Army Garrison Wiesbaden. Programming you might come across includes NPR (National Public Radio) favourites such as *Car Talk*, pearls of populism from Rush Limbaugh, and news from AP Radio and the Pentagon Channel. Peppered with nanny-state public service announcements and unfathomable acronyms, the broadcasts give a taste of US military life in Germany. The most powerful relay frequencies to check are 873kHz AM (transmission from Frankfurt), 1107kHz (from Kaiserslautern) and 1143kHz (from Stuttgart). There are also a variety of local FM options.

When atmospheric conditions are right (as they often are at night), **BBC Radio 4** – including a late-late relay of the BBC World Service – can be heard on 198kHz long wave.

Wiesbaden

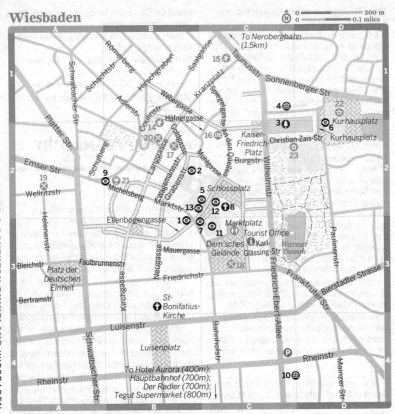

Wiesbaden

◉ Sights & Activities

CITY CENTRE

Wiesbaden's strollable city centre is 1km north (along Bahnhofstrasse) from the Hauptbahnhof. The main shopping precinct is around the pedestrianised **Langgasse**, lined with impressive 19th-century buildings, and its southern continuation, Kirchgasse.

Schlossplatz   SQUARE

(Map p402) A good place to start exploring Wiesbaden is the Schlossplatz, where you'll find the **Marktbrunnen** (Löwenbrunnen; Market Fountain; 1537), the **Altes Rathaus** (Old Town Hall; 1610) and, across the square, the **Neues Rathaus** (New Town Hall; 1884-87). On the north side is the neoclassical **Stadtschloss** (Schlossplatz 1-3) built in 1840 for Duke Wilhelm von Nassau and now home of the Hessischer Landtag (Hessian state parliament).

The Protestant neo-Gothic **Marktkirche** (www.marktkirche-wiesbaden.de), built of bright red bricks from 1852 to 1862, has a **Glockenspiel** (carillon; ⊘rings 9am, noon, 3pm & 5pm, concerts noon-12.30pm Sat) – the 49 bronze bells weigh between 13kg and 2300kg – and hosts **organ concerts** (see website for details).

Kurhaus Wiesbaden   CASINO

(Map p402; www.wiesbaden.de; Kurhausplatz 1; ⊘24hr, closed during events) Built in 1907, the neoclassical Kurhaus now serves as the city's convention centre. Pop inside to see some incredibly ornate spaces, including the **main hall**, with its marble floor, granite columns, Greco-Roman–style statuary and sparkling dome mosaics, and the **casino** (Spielbank; www.casino-wiesbaden.de; admission €2.50; ⊘2.45pm-3 or 4am). To do a gambling Dostoevsky (or have a drink at the casino bar), men will need a jacket (you can borrow one for €4.10), a button-down shirt (€2.70) and non-sports shoes; ties are no longer required. Everyone must have ID.

The neoclassical plaza out front, graced by three fountains, is tastefully illuminated at night – great for a romantic walk, especially around dusk. The **Bowling Green** (a lawn for which locals have chosen a name that's as appropriate as it is English) is flanked by an elegant, 129m-long **colonnade** and, opposite, the Hessisches Staatstheater (p405), whose arcade shelters some interesting shop windows.

Museum Wiesbaden   MUSEUM

(Map p402; www.museum-wiesbaden.de; Friedrich-Ebert-Allee 2; adult/student €5/3, child under 18yr free; ⊘10am-5pm Wed & Fri-Sun, 10am-8pm Tue & Thu) Wiesbaden's art museum specialises in painting, sculpture and installations, including works by the old masters, 20th-century American minimalists and the Russian expressionist Alexei Jawlensky (1864–1941), who lived in Wiesbaden for the last 20 years of his life. The natural sciences section is set to reopen in 2013. In the hall to the left of the reception desk, look up to see a dazzling gilded mosaic dating from just before WWI.

Michelsberg
Synagogue Memorial   MEMORIAL

(Map p402; www.am-spiegelgasse.de; Michelsberg 24) Since 2011, the site of Wiesbaden's largest pre-war synagogue, built in 1869 and destroyed in 1938, has been marked by a memorial that includes an outline of the structure (in dark paving stones on the sidewalks and street) and an interactive screen displaying historic photos and biographical information on 1507 Wiesbaden Jews who perished in the Holocaust; their names appear on one of the memorial's walls.

Kaiser-Friedrich-Therme   THERMAL BATHS

(Map p402; Langgasse 38-40; per hr May-Aug €4.50, Sep-Apr €6; ⊘10am-10pm, to midnight Fri & Sat Sep-Apr) Built in 1913 as a municipal bathhouse on the site of a Roman steam bath, the gorgeous Kaiser-Friedrich-Therme, still run by the city, lets you experience 'Irish-Roman' spa culture by availing yourself of a succession of saunas and pools fed by water naturally heated to 66.4°C. Bathrobes (€8.20) and towels (from €3.10) can be rented; swimsuits are unnecessary as, in keeping with *Saunakultur,* this place is 'textile-free'. Actually, bathing suits are banned only in the sauna (you just wear a towel); elsewhere, nudity is merely a recommendation. Tuesday is for women only. Shower before entering the pools. The minimum age is 16. Payment is made at the end – the wristband they give you tells the cashier your arrival time.

Kochbrunnen   HOT SPRINGS

(Map p402; Kranzplatz; ⊘24hr) Want to actually taste the hot spa waters for which the city is known (and, indeed, named), said to have wonderful pharmacological powers? Head to the Kochbrunnen – inside the stone pavilion are four free-flowing spouts. A sign recommends drinking no more than 1L a day,

TOUCH, FEEL, SMELL, TASTE & MAKE NOISE

Astonishing things happen – but only with your active participation – at **Schloss Freudenberg** (www.schloss-freudenberg.de; Freudenbergstrasse 220-226, Dotzheim, Wiesbaden; adult/child 7-17yr €12/6; ⊙Tue-Fri 9am-5pm, Sat & Sun 11am-6pm), a century-old mansion that's been turned into a hands-on, experiential *Erhfahrungsfeld* ('Experience Field') designed to engage and challenge all your senses. Inspired by the ideas of Rudolf Steiner, the exhibits feature a Geruchsorgel ('odour organ'), where you try to identify different smells; ceramic jars you put your hand into and try to figure out what you're touching (there are some surprises); a gong room, where you can produce all manner of banging and clanging; and the **Dunkelcafé** ('darks cafe'), in which you can order a drink (eg coffee, €2.50) in absolute, total darkness. Great for tweens and teens.

The museum, surrounded by a 50ha park, is 3.5km southwest of Wiesbaden's city centre in the suburb of Dotzheim. To get there from the city centre, take bus 23 or 24 (20 minutes, four to six times an hour) to the Märchenland stop.

though if you can down more than a mouthful you deserve a beer.

There's another hot springs tap at the **Bäckerbrunnen** (Map p402; Grabenstrasse; ⊙24hr), a little brick building a block south of Goldgasse.

NEROBERG

About 2km northwest of the centre, the Neroberg is a hill that's great for rambling. The grassy expanses are ideal for sunbathing, or you can visit one of the oldest vineyards in the area.

Nerobergbahn   HISTORIC RAILWAY
(www.nerobergbahn.de; one-way/return €2.50/3.30, under 14yr €1.25/1.65; ⊙9am-8pm May-Aug, 10 or 11am-7pm Apr, Sep & Oct) The easiest way to get up the Neroberg is to take this historic funicular railway. Inaugurated in 1888, it's powered by water ballast: the car at the top is filled with up to 7000L of water, making it heavier than the car at the bottom, to which it's attached by a 452m-long cable. When the heavier car reaches the bottom, the water is pumped out – and then pumped back up the hill. Elegant, ecological, ingenious! The lower station is linked to the train station (stop B) and the city centre (Dern'sches Gelände) by bus 1.

Russian Orthodox Church   CHURCH
(Christian-Spielmann-Weg 2; adult/child €0.60/0.30; ⊙10am-5pm Sat, Sun & holidays May-Oct, noon-4pm Sat, Sun & holidays Nov-Apr) A five-domed church built between 1847 and 1855.

Kletterwald   ADVENTURE PARK
(☎580 2246; www.kletterwald-neroberg.de; adult/child 4-18yr €19/12; ⊙9 or 10am-dusk Sat, Sun & school holidays, 1pm-dusk Wed-Fri mid-Mar–early-

Nov) Spend three challenging hours climbing from tree to tree with the help of ladders, ropes, harnesses and zip-lines! Great for kids who don't have a fear of heights.

Opelbad   SWIMMING POOL
(adult/student €8.20/4; ⊙7am-8pm May-Sep) Attractions on the Neroberg include this Bauhaus-style outdoor swimming pool complex, built in 1934.

☞ Tours

The tourist office runs **walking tours** (adult/under 12yr €6.50/3.50; ⊙10.30am Sat, also 2.30pm Sat Jul-Oct).

Free tours (in German) of the **Hessischer Landtag** (Hessian State Parliament; Map p402; Schlossplatz; ⊙3pm Sat) begin at the corner of the Stadtschloss that faces the Marktbrunnen.

🛏 Sleeping

Room rates rise during Frankfurt's trade fairs but not by much, making Wiesbaden a pleasant and reasonably priced base.

TOP CHOICE Hotel Aurora   HOTEL $$
(☎373 728; www.aurora-online.de; Untere Albrechtsstrasse 9; s/d €69/89, during fairs €79/99; P@🖁) Friendly, bright, quiet and Italian-run, this 31-room gem, in a late 19th-century building with high ceilings, is just three blocks north along Bahnhofstrasse from the Hauptbahnhof.

Trüffel   BOUTIQUE HOTEL $$
(Map p402; ☎990550; www.trueffel.net; Webergasse 6-8; s/d without breakfast weekdays from €115/145, weekends €95/125, during fairs €145/165; ❄@🖁) An ultra-stylish business hotel whose 27 modern rooms, equipped with huge bathrooms,

are sleek, spacious and more than a little romantic.

DJH Hostel
HOSTEL $

(☑486 57; www.wiesbaden.jugendherberge.de; Blücherstrasse 66; dm/s €19.90/33; ☞) The functional exterior belies clean rooms and staff who are as helpful as they are strict. Has 220 beds. Situated 1.2km west of the city centre. From the Hauptbahnhof or the centre, take bus 14 to Gneisenaustrasse.

✖ Eating

Restaurant-lined Goldgasse, a block north of the Stadtschloss, is the heart of Wiesbaden's dining district. For Turkish baked goods and cuisine, head south west to Wellritzstrasse.

Aurum
ITALIAN $$

(Map p402; Goldgasse 16; pizzas €5.50-11, mains €7.50-13.50; ☺9.30am-1am) Serves excellent stone-oven pizza and tasty Italian dishes.

Harput Restaurant
TURKISH $$

(Map p402; ☑406 196; www.harputrestaurant. de; Wellritzstrasse 9; mains €7.50-11.50; ☺7am-1 or 2am) A hugely popular sit-down Turkish restaurant where you can feast on delectable Anatolian breads and a variety of main dishes, including skewers of grilled meat. In the heart of Wiesbaden's Turkish quarter.

Feinkostladen
DELI $$

(Map p402; Webergasse 6-8; ☺9am-7pm Mon-Fri, 8am-4pm Sat) Cheeses, salamis and ready-to-eat dishes – perfect for a gourmet picnic.

Food Market
MARKET $

(Map p402; Dern'sches Gelände; ☺7am-2pm Wed & Sat) Food stalls next to the tourist office.

Rewe
SUPERMARKET $

(Map p402; Langgasse 32; ☺7am-10pm Mon-Sat) Picnic supplies.

Tegut
SUPERMARKET $

(☺7am-9pm Mon-Sat) Edibles next to the Hauptbahnhof, in the Lilien Carré shopping mall (exit the train station next to Track 11).

🍷 Drinking & Entertainment

Events tickets can be purchased at the tourist office.

Irish Pub
PUB

(Map p402; www.irish-pub-wiesbaden.de; Michelsberg 15; ☺5pm-1am Sun-Thu, 5pm-2am Fri, 3pm-2am Sat; ☞) Expats congregate at this sprawling, Irish-run basement establishment for live music (from 10pm on Thursday, Friday and Satur-day), karaoke (from 10pm on Tuesday and Sunday), open mic night (Wednesday), beer pong (Monday) and, of course, Guinness (€4).

Hessisches Staatstheater
PERFORMING ARTS

(Hessian State Theatre; Map p402; ☑132 325; www. staatstheater-wiesbaden.de; Christian Zais Strasse 3) Puts on operas, operettas, ballet, classical music, musicals, plays and events for children.

Kulturzentrum Schlachthof
LIVE MUSIC

(☑974 450; www.schlachthof-wiesbaden.de; Murnaustrasse 1) Live music, top-name DJs and a tumultuous program make this venue a huge draw for music lovers and party animals. Has events four or five nights a week. Situated on the east side of the train tracks 500m south of the Hauptbahnhof.

Murnau Filmtheater
CINEMA

(www.deutsches-filmhaus-wiesbaden.de; Murnaustrasse 6, Deutsches Filmhaus) An art theatre opened in 2009. Situated on the east side of the train tracks 500m south of the Hauptbahnhof.

ℹ Information

Eco-Express Laundrette (Dotzheimer Strasse 96) Situated 1.2km west of the centre.

Planet Callnet (Wellritzstrasse 22; per hr €1; ☺11am-9pm) Internet access and computer repair.

Post Office (Kaiser-Friedrich-Ring 98) Facing the Hauptbahnhof. Has an ATM.

ReiseBank (Hauptbahnhof; ☺9am-5.30 or 6.30pm, closed some days 12.30-1.30pm) Currency exchange inside the train station, behind Track 1.

Tourist Office (☑172 9930; www.wiesbaden. de; Marktplatz 1; ☺10am-6pm Mon-Fri, 9.45am-3pm Sat, 11am-3pm Sun & holidays Apr-Sep) Can help you find a hotel room, supply you with a Leisure Guide for Families and issue events tickets.

ℹ Getting There & Around

S-Bahn trains link Wiesbaden with Frankfurt's Hauptbahnhof (€7.30, every 15 minutes). S1 (42 minutes) goes direct; S8 and S9 go via Frankfurt Airport (€4.30). S8 also serves Mainz (13 minutes), a major rail hub. DB trains run by **Vias** take just 38 minutes to Frankfurt (€7.30). An all-day ticket for travel between Wiesbaden and Frankfurt, including the use of local trams and buses, costs €14.25.

Buses (www.eswe-verkehr.de) linking the Hauptbahnhof with the city centre include 1, 4, 8, 14, 27 and 47. A single ticket costs €2.50; a day pass for one/up to five people costs

Mainz

0 — 0.2 miles
0 — 400 m

Rhine River

Riverside Promenade

Adenauerufer

Peter-Altmeier-Allee

Rheinstr

Stresemannufer
Lauterenstr
Holzstr

Am Fischtorplatz
Rheinstr

Augustinerkirche

Weintorstr
Grebenstr
Augustinerstr

Kapuzinerstr
Neutorstr

Windmühlenstr
Kartäuserstr
Kirschgarten

4
3

Bruckenturm
am Rathaus
Mailandsgasse
Rathaus
Rötekopfgasse

**Gutenberg
Museum**

Liebfrauenplatz

**Dom St
Martin**

1

2

19

Tourist
Office

Am Brand

Seilergasse
Markplatz
Quintinstr

Schusterstr

Gutenbergplatz

Bischofsplatz

Ballplatz

Weissliliengasse

Stefansstr

Eisgrubweg

20

Bauerngasse

Petersstr

5
Flachsmarktstr

Löwenhofstr
Synagogenstr
Stadthausstr
Am Kronberger Hof

Kötherhofstr

23

Emmeranstr
Steingasse

Grosse Langgasse

Kirschgarten
Kartäuserstr

Kleine
Weissgasse

6

Gaustr

Landesmuseum Mainz

16

Bleiche

Grosse Bleiche

Mittlere Bleiche

Klarastr

Lotharstr

Schillerstr

Schillerplatz

13

Neue Universitätsstr

Münsterstr

Emmerich-Joseph-Str
Walpodenstr

Terrassenstr

Kupferbergterrasse

Augustusstr

Römer-Wall

Langenbstr

Am Linsenberg Str

Hintere Bleiche

Kaiserstr

Neubrunnenstr

Gartnergasse

Bahnhofstr

Binger Str

Parcusstr

Boppstr

Kaiser-Wilhelm-Ring

Mombacher Str

Bahnhofplatz

Verkehrs
Center
Mainz

Schottstr

Bonifaziusstr

10

8

7

Hauptbahnhof

€5.90/8.80. You can pick up a city map at the **Eswe Verkehr bus information office** (⊙6am-8pm Mon-Fri, 10am-5.30pm Sat) just outside the train station.

For a cab, contact **Taxi Wiesbaden** (☑99999; www.taxi-wiesbaden.de).

Bicycles can be rented from **Der Radler** (☑0171-222 7888; Hauptbahnhof; per hr/day €2/10, electric bikes 24hr €20; ⊙8am-6pm Mon-Fri year-round, 9am-1pm Sat May-Sep). Helmets and child seats cost €3 each. To get there from the train station, walk out the exit next to Track 11, turn left and go 50m.

Mainz

☑06131 / POP 199,000

Strategically situated at the confluence of the Rhine and Main Rivers, Mainz has a sizable university, fine pedestrian precincts and a certain *savoir vivre* (knowledge of how to live well) whose origins go back to Napoleon's occupation (1797–1814). Strolling along the Rhine and sampling local wines in a half-timbered Altstadt tavern are as much a part of any Mainz visit as viewing the fabulous Dom, Chagall's ethereal windows in St-Stephan-Kirche, or the first printed Bible in the Gutenberg Museum, a bibliophile's paradise. Mainz has been the capital of the German federal state of Rhineland-Palatinate since 1946.

In the 15th century, native son Johannes Gutenberg ushered in the information age here by perfecting moveable type.

⊙ Sights

The broad **Marktplatz**, Mainz' central market square, and the adjacent **Liebfrauenplatz** are the focal point of the Altstadt. South of there, pedestrian-only **Augustinerstrasse**, lined with handsome five-storey houses (some of them half-timbered), is great for a window-shopping stroll. Along the Rhine, the grassy **riverfront promenade** (Adenauer-Ufer and Stresemann-Ufer) affords fine views of a parade of passing barges.

TOP CHOICE Dom St Martin CHURCH

(Map p406; Marktplatz; ⊙9am-6.30pm Mon-Fri, 9am-4pm Sat, 12.45-3pm & 4-6.30pm Sun & holidays Mar-Oct, to 5pm Sun-Fri & to 3pm Sat Nov-Feb) Topped by an octagonal tower, Mainz' world-famous cathedral, built of deep red sandstone in the 12th century, is quintessentially Romanesque. Its predecessor went through a literal baptism by fire when it burned down in 1009 on the very day of its consecration. Over the centuries seven coronations were held here.

Off the delicate, late-Gothic cloister, accessible from inside the Dom, is the **Dom-und Diözesanmuseum** (Cathedral & Diocesan Museum; Map p406; www.dommuseum-mainz.de;

FRANKFURT & SOUTHERN RHINELAND MAINZ

Mainz

adult/student/family €5/3.50/10; ⊘10am-5pm Tue-Fri, 11am-6pm Sat & Sun), which displays artwork from the cathedral, including sculptures from the rood screen (1239) – an ornate partition separating the priests, in the choir, from the congregation and the work of the renowned Master of Naumburg – that portray the saved and the, well, not-so-saved. In the **Schatzkammer** (Domschatz) you can see bejewelled ritual objects from as far back as the 10th century (English-language pamphlet available).

Gutenberg Museum   MUSEUM

(Map p406; www.gutenberg-museum.de; Liebfrauenplatz 5; adult/child €5/3; ⊘9am-5pm Tue-Sat, 11am-5pm Sun) A heady experience for anyone excited by books, the Gutenberg Museum takes a panoramic look at the technology that made the world as we know it possible. Highlights include very early printed masterpieces – kept safe in a walk-in vault – such as three extremely rare (and valuable) examples of Gutenberg's original 42-line Bible. Many of the signs are in English; a quarter-hour film is available in seven languages.

In the museum's **Druckladen** (Map p406; 122 686; www.gutenberg-druckladen.de; individual admission free, group admission per person incl tour €5; ⊘9am-5pm Tue-Fri, 10am-3pm Sat) across tiny Seilergasse, you can try out Gutenberg's technology yourself on the condition that you're at least five years old. You'll be instructed in the art of hand-setting type – backwards, of course. Nearby, master craftsmen produce elegant posters, certificates and cards using the labour-intensive technologies of another age. Fascinating, especially if you grew up in an era when 'print' usually means 'Ctrl+P'.

Landesmuseum Mainz   MUSEUM

(Map p406; www.landesmuseum-mainz.de; Grosse Bleiche 49-51; adult/student €5/3.50, child 6-18yr free; ⊘10am-8pm Tue, 10am-5pm Wed-Sun) One of Germany's most enjoyable state museums, with every object superbly presented. Highlights include an ensemble of Jugendstil (art nouveau) pieces so exquisite they may leave you speechless, outstanding collections of Renaissance and 20th-century German paintings, and some fine baroque porcelain and furniture. Rare artefacts from the Merovingian and Carolingian periods include 4th- to 7th-century tombstones in Latin. Mainz' illustrious medieval Jewish community, whose members included Rashi, is represented by gravestones from the 11th to 13th centuries. An audioguide (€1) is available in five languages.

St-Peterskirche   CHURCH

(Map p406; Petersstrasse 3; ⊘9am-6pm) The Church of St Peter, built in 1748, is a worthy showcase for the exuberant glory of the rococo

FORTY-TWO LINES THAT CHANGED THE WORLD

Johannes Gutenberg, the inventor of printing with moveable type, is one of those rare epochal figures whose achievements truly changed the course of human history.

Little is known about Gutenberg the man, who was born in Mainz in the very late 1300s, trained as a goldsmith and then, in the late 1420s, left for Strasbourg (now in France), where he first experimented with printing technology. By 1448 he was back in Mainz, still working on his top-secret project and in debt to some rather impatient 'venture capitalists'. But eventually his perseverance paid off and he perfected a number of interdependent technologies:

» Metal type that could be arranged into pages.

» Precision moulds to produce such type in large quantities.

» A metal alloy from which type could be cast.

» A type of oil-based ink suitable for printing with metal type.

» Press technology derived from existing wine, paper and bookbinding presses.

Despite several lawsuits, by 1455 Gutenberg had produced his masterpiece, the now-legendary Forty-Two-Line Bible, so-named because each page has 42 lines. Thus began a new era in human history, one in which the printed word – everything from Martin Luther's *Ninety-Five Theses* to the *Declaration of the Rights of Man* to Nazi propaganda – was to become almost universally accessible. In all of human history, arguably only two other inventions have come close to having the same impact on the availability of information: the alphabet and the internet.

style. It is noted for its richly adorned and gilded pulpit and altars, putti-decorated columns and white-and-pink colour scheme.

Augustinerkirche CHURCH
(Map p406; Augustinerstrasse 34; ☺8am-5pm Mon-Fri) Part of the local Catholic seminary, the classically baroque Augustinerkirche, built from 1768 to 1772, was left unscathed by WWII so all its rich decor is original. Features an elaborate organ loft and a delicate ceiling fresco by Johann Baptist Enderle.

St-Ignazkirche CHURCH
(Map p406; Kapuzinerstrasse 40; ☺10am-7pm) Completed in 1773, this church marks the transition from rococo to neoclassicism – note, for instance, that the baroque baldachin (over the altar) and organ sit in a space defined by Corinthian columns and a neoclassical dome.

St-Stephan-Kirche CHURCH
(Map p406; Kleine Weissgasse 12; ☺10am-4.30 or 5pm) This would be just another Gothic church rebuilt after WWII were it not for the nine brilliant, stained-glass windows created by the Russian-Jewish artist Marc Chagall (1887–1985) in the final years of his life. Bright blue and imbued with a mystical, meditative quality, they serve as a symbol of Jewish–Christian reconciliation.

FREE Museum für Antike Schiffahrt MUSEUM
(Map p406; www.rgzm.de; Neutorstrasse 2b; admission free; ☺10am-6pm Tue-Sun) The extraordinary remains of five wooden ships of the Romans' Rhine flotilla, used around AD 300 to thwart the Germanic tribes then threatening Roman settlements, are the centrepiece of the Museum of Ancient Seafaring, which was totally renovated in 2011. Also on display are two full-size replicas of Roman ships and a collection of scale-model ships (sure to please the kids). Signs are in English.

☞ Tours
The tourist office runs **walking tours** (adult/student/family €7/4/15; ☺2pm Sat year-round, also at 2pm Mon, Wed, Fri & Sun May-Oct) of the city in English and German.

☞ Sleeping
During Frankfurt's trade fairs, room prices in Mainz rise only moderately. The half-a-dozen or so hotels around the train station

(full disclosure: the area is a tiny bit seedy) make for an easy commute to Frankfurt.

The tourist office has a **room reservations hotline** (☎286 2128; ☺9am-6pm Mon-Fri, 10am-4pm Sat, 11am-3pm Sun); bookings can be made in person, by phone or via www.touristik-mainz.de (under Accommodation).

Hotel Hof Ehrenfels HOTEL $$
(Map p406; ☎971 2340; www.hof-ehrenfels.de; Grebenstrasse 5-7; s/d/tr €80/100/120, €10 less Fri-Sun) Just steps from the cathedral, this 22-room place, housed in a 15th-century, one-time Carmelite nunnery, has Dom views that are hard to beat. A real treat if you love the tintinnabulation of the bells, bells, bells. Rooms are spacious, practical and modern.

Hotel Schwan HOTEL $$
(Map p406; ☎144 920; www.mainz-hotel-schwan.de; Liebfrauenplatz 7; s/d €87/114, during fairs €98/149; ☎) You can't get any more central than this family-run place, around since 1463. The 22 well-lit rooms have baroque-style furnishings. Kaiser Joseph II stayed here in 1777.

Hotel Hammer HOTEL $$
(Map p406; ☎965 280; www.hotel-hammer.com; Bahnhofplatz 6; d weekday/weekend €110/89, during fairs €155; ✳@☎) Convenient to the train station, the 37-room, business-oriented Hammer offers 37 rooms, attractive and sound-proofed, with upbeat colours and bright bathrooms. The free sauna is a welcome bonus. Solid value.

Hotel Königshof HOTEL $$
(Map p406; ☎960 110; www.hotel-koenigshof-mainz.de; Schottstrasse 1-5; s/d from €63/77, during fairs €87/107; ✳☎) The lobby is modest but upstairs the 60 rooms are attractive and very spacious. Very near the train station. Excellent value.

✕ Eating & Drinking
Cheap eateries can be found near the Hauptbahnhof (eg along Bahnhofstrasse) and, south of the Dom, along Augustinerstrasse.

TOP CHOICE Zur Kanzel FRENCH $$$
(Map p406; ☎237 137; www.zurkanzel.de; Grebenstrasse 6; mains €11.50-21.50; ☺5pm-1am Mon-Fri, noon-3pm & 6pm-1am Sat) A classy place with a distinctly French flair and a lovely courtyard, this *Weinstube* (wine bar) serves upmarket French and regional cuisine, including dishes made with *grüne Sosse* (a light sauce made with fresh herbs, sour cream

FRANKFURT & SOUTHERN RHINELAND MAINZ

and soft white cheese). All ingredients are fresh, so the menu evolves with the seasons.

TOP CHOICE **Weinstube Hottum** GERMAN $$
(Map p406; ☑223 370; Grebenstrasse 3; mains €7.80-15.50; ☺4pm-midnight, may close earlier Jul & Aug) One of the best of the Altstadt wine taverns (despite its plain facade), this eight-table wine tavern has a cosy, traditional atmosphere and a menu – half of which appears on a tiny slate tablet – with regional dishes such as *Saumagen* (pig's stomach stuffed with meat, potatoes and spices, then boiled, sliced and briefly fried) and *Winzersteak* (vintner-style pork steak). Serves a dozen delectable local wines by the glass.

El Chico STEAK $$$
(Map p406; ☑238 440; Kötherhofstrasse 1; mains €13.90-26.90; ☺6pm-11pm; ☎) Widely believed to serve Mainz' finest steaks (from Argentina) and lamb chops (from New Zealand); dessert options include delicious apple strudel (€4.90). Bright but intimate, it has the feel of a modern bistro, with a red rose and a candle on every table. Reservations are a good idea, especially on Friday, Saturday and Sunday.

Eisgrub-Bräu BEER TAVERN $
(Map p406; ☑221 104; www.eisgrub.de; Weissliliengasse 1a; weekday lunch €5.90, mains €8.40-18.90; ☺11.30am-midnight Mon-Fri, 9am-midnight Sat & Sun) Grab a seat in this down-to-earth microbrewery's warren of vaulted chambers, order a mug of *Dunkel* (dark) or *Hell* (light) – or even a 3L/5L *Bierturm* (beer tower; €18.90/29.40) – and settle in for people watching. The Monday-to-Friday lunch (€5.90) and the weekend breakfast buffet (€6.90; available 9am to 11.30am) offer great value. It's a good idea to make reservations (by phone or internet), especially for dinner on Thursday, Friday and Saturday.

Specht GERMAN $$
(Map p406; ☑231 770; www.gasthausspecht.de; Rotekopfgasse 2; mains €9.80-18.80; ☺5pm-midnight or later Mon-Fri, 11.30am-midnight or later Sat & Sun) Thanks to its ancient wood beams and smoked walls, the 'Woodpecker' has a 19th-century feel, though the building itself dates from 1557. Serves German and regional cuisine made with fresh produce from the nearby market. If the ancient beam ceiling *doesn't* look uneven and wavy, you've had too much to drink.

Heiliggeist CAFE $$
(Map p406; www.heiliggeist-mainz.de; Mailandsgasse 11; mains €9.80-19.80; ☺4pm-1am Mon-Fri, 9am-1am or 2am Sat, Sun & holidays) Sit beneath the soaring Gothic vaults of a 15th-century hospital and enjoy a beer, glass of wine, snack or full meal from a menu filled with dishes of German and Italian inspiration. On weekends breakfast is served until 4pm.

Irish Pub IRISH PUB
(Map p406; www.irish-pub-mainz.de; Weissliliengasse 5; ☺5pm-1am Sun-Thu, to 2am Fri & Sat; ☎) A candle-lit basement watering hole – Irish owned and staffed – with open-mic nights on Sunday and Tuesday, karaoke on Monday, Wednesday and Thursday, and bands on Friday and Saturday (all from 9.30pm). Screens Bundesliga, Irish and American football, rugby and hurling so may open earlier weekends if there's a big game. Attracts a very international crowd, including lots of flight crews.

Food Market MARKET
(Map p406; Marktplatz & Liebfrauenplatz; ☺7am-2pm Tue, Fri & Sat) Along the north and east sides of the Dom. A big, open-air market with stalls selling fruit, vegetables and ready-to-eat dishes.

Rewe City SUPERMARKET $
(Map p406; Augustinerstrasse 55; ☺8am-10pm Mon-Sat) The best place in the heart of the city centre to pick up picnic supplies.

Lidl SUPERMARKET $
(Map p406; Grosse Bleiche 41) Edibles on one of central Mainz' main commercial streets.

☆ Entertainment

Mainz has exceptionally rich and varied cultural offerings.

Four free monthly mags, available at the tourist office and in cafes and pubs, have listings (in German) of cultural events: *Frizz* (www.frizz-mainz.de), *Der Mainzer* (www.dermainzer.net), *Sensor* (www.sensor-magazin.de) and *Stuz* (www.stuz.de).

Tickets for most events can be purchased at the tourist office.

TOP CHOICE **KuZ** LIVE MUSIC
(Map p406; ☑286 860; www.kuz.de; Dagobertstrasse 20b) Concerts by German and international bands, dance parties, theatre for kids...the happening *KulturZentrum* (cultural centre) has something for almost everyone. Housed in a red-brick building that

began life in the 19th century as a military laundry.

Frankfurter Hof LIVE MUSIC
(Map p406; 220 438; www.frankfurter-hof-mainz. de; Augustinerstrasse 55) Hosts and organises concerts both by up-and-coming artists and by big-name international acts such as Chris de Burgh. Some events take place at other venues around the city.

Staatstheater PERFORMING ARTS
(Map p406; 285 1222; www.staatstheater-mainz. com; Gutenbergplatz 7) The state theatre stages plays, opera and ballet. Students get significant discounts.

ⓘ Information

Several ATMs are situated in the Hauptbahnhof and along Grosse Bleiche.

ConAction (Grosse Bleiche 25; per hr €2; ☺9am-midnight or later) Internet cafe.

Eco-Express (Parcusstrasse 12; ☺6am-10pm Mon-Sat, closed Sun & holidays) Self-service laundry.

Internet Cafe (Bahnhofstrasse 11; per hr €1; ☺9am-11pm) One of several internet cafes near the Hauptbahnhof.

Mainz Card (individual/group of 5 €9.95/25) Valid for two days, it gets you admission to museums (some are free anyway), a walking tour, unlimited public transport plus various discounts. Available at the tourist office.

Post Office (Bahnhofstrasse 2) Has an ATM.

ReiseBank (☺8am-6pm Mon-Fri, 7.30am-noon & 12.30-3pm Sat) Currency exchange in the Hauptbahnhof.

Teleinternet Cafe (Kartäuserstrasse 13; per hr €2; ☺10am-9.30pm) Internet.

Tourist Office (286 210; www.touristik -mainz.de; Brückenturm am Rathaus; ☺9am-6pm Mon-Fri, 10am-4pm Sat, 11am-3pm Sun) Touristik Centrale Mainz is across the pedestrian bridge (ie over the highway) from the Rathaus (town hall). Excellent English brochures include a self-guided tour map.

ⓘ Getting There & Away

Commuting to/from Frankfurt, eg for a trade fair, is easy. From the Hauptbahnhof, S-Bahn line S8 goes via Frankfurt airport to Frankfurt's Hauptbahnhof (€7.30, 35-42 minutes, several times hourly).

Details of public transport in the Mainz region are available at the **Verkehrs Center Mainz** (127 777; www.mvg-mainz.de; Bahnhofplatz 6a; ☺7am-7pm Mon-Fri, 9am-2pm Sat).

A major rail hub, Mainz's Hauptbahnhof has at least hourly regional services to Bingen (€6.20, 15 to 40 minutes) and other Romantic Rhine towns, Koblenz (€18.10 to €21, 50 to 90 minutes), Saarbrücken (€21, 2¼ hours) and Worms (€8.30, 26 to 43 minutes).

At some city parking garages, the ticket issued when you pull in allows unlimited use of public transport.

ⓘ Getting Around

S-Bahn line S8 links the Hauptbahnhof with Frankfurt Airport (€4.10, 19-27 minutes, several times hourly). Buses to Hahn Airport (www. hahn-airportshuttle.de; adult/child €12.50/7, 70 minutes, seven to 10 times a day) depart from in front of the Hauptbahnhof. A day ticket that takes in both Mainz and Frankfurt, including local trams and buses, costs €14.25.

Mainz operates its bus and tram system jointly with Wiesbaden (www.mvg-mainz.de). Single tickets cost €2.50; day passes are €5.90/8.80 for individuals/groups of up to five.

Mainzer Radverleih (Map p406; 336 1225; Binger Strasse 19; bicycle per day €8.90, deposit €50; ☺8am-7.30pm Mon-Fri, 8am-4pm Sat Apr-Oct) hires out bikes and sells cycling maps. It's located across the tracks from the Hauptbahnhof, next to the round tower atop the CityPort Parkhaus.

Darmstadt

06151 / POP 144,000

Jugendstil (art nouveau) architecture, fine museums and a world-renowned technical university are the hallmarks of this modest but interesting city about 35km south of Frankfurt. Despite some atrocious post-war architecture (the university has some real zingers), Darmstadt is a pretty city, and just the right size for strolling.

The super-heavy element Darmstadtium (Ds; atomic number: 110) was first created here in 1994. The city's glass-and-stone conference centre is also called the Darmstadtium.

Thanks to the S-Bahn commuter rail line, Darmstadt makes an easy day trip from Frankfurt – and Frankfurt makes an easy day trip from Darmstadt.

ⓞ Sights & Activities

Mathildenhöhe AREA
(www.mathildenhoehe.info) Darmstadt's biggest attraction is the former *Künstlerkolonie* (artists colony) at Mathildenhöhe, surrounded by a lovely hilltop park with fountains. Famous for its Darmstädter Jugendstil architecture and creations, it was established

FRANKFURT & SOUTHERN RHINELAND DARMSTADT

GRUBE MESSEL

Die-hard fossil fans might want to check out Grube Messel (Messel Pit), a Unesco World Heritage Site and one-time coal and oil shale quarry, famed for its superbly preserved animal and plant remains from the Eocene era (around 49 million years ago). Early horses found here illustrate the evolutionary path towards the modern beast. Many of the most interesting finds can be seen at the Hessisches Landesmuseum in Darmstadt and the Senckenberg Museum in Frankfurt, but some are at Grube Messel's own **museum** (www.messelmuseum.de; Langgasse 2, Messel; admission free; ⊙11am-5pm Apr-Oct, 11am-5pm Sat, Sun & holidays Nov-Mar), in a pretty half-timbered house.

Messel is about 10km northeast of Darmstadt.

in 1899 at the behest of Grand Duke Ernst Ludwig. On site, the **Museum Künstlerkolonie** (Olbrichweg 13; adult/student €5/3; ⊙10am-5pm Tue-Sun) displays supremely elegant Jugendstil furniture, tableware, textiles, ceramics and jewellery, while the **Ausstellungsgebäude Mathildenhöhe** (adult €5-8, student €3-6; ⊙10am-6pm Tue, Wed & Fri-Sun, to 9pm Thu) puts on temporary art exhibitions.

Mathildenhöhe's western slope is graced by the three golden onion domes of a mosaic-adorned **Russian Orthodox chapel** (☑424 235; Nikolaiweg 18; ⊙10am-1pm & 2-4pm Tue-Sat, 2-4pm Sun). It was built from 1897 to 1899 for the last Russian Tsar, Nicholas II, who married a local gal, Princess Alix von Hessen (Grand Duke Ernst Ludwig's younger sister), in 1894.

The area is linked to the centre by bus F.

Luisenplatz
SQUARE

Darmstadt's focal point is the 18th-century Luisenplatz, a hive of activity thanks to the tram lines running down the middle and the adjacent shopping precinct, which stretches south from the **LuisenCenter shopping mall** for several pedestrianised blocks.

In the centre of Luisenplatz, a 39m-high column, erected in 1844, holds aloft a statue of Grand Duke Ludwig I of Hesse and the Rhine (1753–1830). The square itself is named after his wife, Grand Duchess Louise (1761–1829).

Luisenplatz is connected to the Hauptbahnhof by a long eastward walk (1.5km) or a short tram ride.

Herrngarten
PARK

(Karolinenplatz) This English-style park is where students from the adjacent campus of Darmstadt's **Technische Universität Darmstadt** (TU Darmstadt; www.tu-darmstadt.de; Karolinenplatz 5), renowned for its science and engineering faculties, come to play frisbee. Situated two blocks northeast of Luisenplatz.

Hessisches Landesmuseum
MUSEUM

(☑165 703; www.hlmd.de; Friedensplatz 1) The Hesse State Museum has a wide-ranging art collection that includes an exceptional selection of works by Joseph Beuys. Closed for renovations until 2013. Situated two blocks northeast of Luisenplatz.

Schlossmuseum
MUSEUM

(☑24035; www.schlossmuseum-darmstadt.de; Marktplatz 15; adult/student €4/2.50; ⊙tours begin 10am, 11.30am, 1pm, 2.30pm & 4pm Mon-Fri) The Schlossmuseum is packed with ornate furnishings, carriages and paintings. It occupies the southeast corner of the Schloss complex, one-time residence of the landgraves and grand dukes of Hessen-Darmstadt; rebuilt after WWII damage, it is now part of the university. It's situated a long block east of Luisenplatz.

Jugendstilbad
SWIMMING POOL

(www.jugendstilbad.de; Mercksplatz 1; swimming pools 2hr/4hr/all day €5.50/7.50/9.50, incl spa €8.50/11/13, incl spa & saunas €12.50/15/18, child under 1m tall free, child 1m-17yr 25% discount; ⊙10am-10pm, 1st Fri of month to midnight) This historic swimming and spa complex looks just as gorgeous as it did when it opened in 1909. It has a year-round outdoor pool, a superb Jugendstil indoor pool, children's pools and 10 dry and wet saunas. Some areas are *textilfrei* (clothing-free). You can rent a towel (€5) and a bathrobe (€5). Situated a long block east of the Schloss along Landgraf-Georg-Strasse.

Grosser Woog
LAKE

Situated four blocks south of Mathildenhöhe, this natural lake offers open-air swimming in the warm season. From the city centre, take bus L.

☞ Tours

The tourist office runs **tours** (adult/student €7/5; ⊙11am Sun Apr-Oct) of the city and Matildenhöhe.

🛌 Sleeping

If you visit the Frankfurt area during a big trade fair, staying in Darmstadt will save you money; local prices rise only moderately during fairs and train travel to Frankfurt's Hauptbahnhof can take as little as 20 minutes. Book early, though, as rooms fill up fast.

Best Western Hotel   DARMSTADT HOTEL **$$**
(📞281 00; www.hotel-darmstadt.bestwestern.de; Grafenstrasse 31, 3rd fl; s/d weekday €112/132, weekend €85/100, during fairs €139/159; P❋@🛜) The entrance, through a parking garage, is unpromising, but inside the lobby is pristine and the 77 quiet rooms are spacious, modern and comfortable. Situated two blocks southwest of Luisenplatz – very central.

Hotel Prinz Heinrich   HOTEL **$**
(📞813 70; www.hotel-prinz-heinrich.de; Bleichstrasse 48; s/d/tr without breakfast weekdays €59/76/82, weekends €50/60/70, during fairs up to €50 more; 🛜) A traditional feel, modern furnishings and overall comfort make this 60-room hotel a good-value choice. Singles are small but serviceable. Breakfast costs €9. Located in a slightly forlorn area midway between the Hauptbahnhof and Luisenplatz.

DJH Hostel   HOSTEL **$**
(📞45293; www.darmstadt.jugendherberge.de; Landgraf-Georg-Strasse 119; dm/s €24.90/34.90; 🛜) This 130-bed hostel is on the shores of the Grosser Woog, 1km west of Luisenplatz and four blocks south of Matildenhöhe. From the city centre take bus L to the 'Woog' stop.

🍴 Eating & Drinking

In the warm season, outdoor cafes can be found two blocks southeast of Luisenplatz on the Marktplatz. For cheap eats, head to the area around the Technische Universität, east of the Schloss along Landgraf-Georg-Strasse.

City Braustübl   GERMAN **$$**
(📞255 11; www.city-braustuebl.de; Wilhelminenstrasse 31; mains €5.70-16.90; ⊘11am-midnight Mon-Sun; 🛜) A classic brewery-affiliated restaurant, with hops hanging from the rafters. Strong on regional dishes to wash down with a Darmstädter beer (€2.20) brewed nearby. Has a beer garden out back. Reservations can be made through the website. Situated three short blocks south of Luisenplat

Tegut   SUPERMARKET **$**
(cnr Marktplatz & Ludwigstrasse; ⊘7am-9pm Mon-Sat) At the southern end of Marktplatz, facing the Altes Rathaus.

An Sibin Irish Pub   PUB
(www.ansibin.com; Landgraf-Georg-Strasse 25; ⊘6pm-1am Sun-Wed, 6pm-3am Thu-Sat) An Irish pub and live concert venue good for a few rounds and a yarn or four. Tuesday is quiz night, Wednesday is open mic night and on Thursday there's karaoke, all from 9pm. For live music, come by on Friday or Saturday after 9.30pm.

☆ Entertainment

Thanks to its science and engineering students, some of whom party as hard as they study, Darmstadt has plenty of student-oriented nightspots and concert venues.

Goldene Krone   CLUB
(📞213 52; www.goldene-krone.de; Schustergasse 18; ⊘7pm-very late Mon-Sat) An old student favourite, this bar is known for its concerts and disco dance parties, many held on Friday and Saturday nights starting at 9pm or 10pm. The entrance is on Holzstrasse, a block east of the Marktplatz..

Centralstation   LIVE MUSIC
(📞366 8899; www.centralstation-darmstadt.de; Im Carree; ⊘cafe 11am-1am Mon-Thu, 11am-5pm Fri & Sat) Housed in the city's first electric power plant (built 1888), this cultural venue has a good-value midday buffet (open noon to 2.30pm except Sunday), an upstairs cocktail lounge and concerts (especially jazz but also pop and classical). On Friday and Saturday nights from 10pm to 4am it turns into a disco. Situated in the courtyard across Luisenstrasse from the tourist office.

ℹ Information

ATMs There are several around Luisenplatz.

Call Shop & Internet Cafe (Wilhelminenstrasse 8; internet access per hr €1; ⊘10am-11pm Mon-Sat, 11am-11pm Sun) Facing the west side of the Luisencenter shopping mall, in the same covered passageway as the CityDome cinema.

Darmstadt Card (1/2 days €6/9) Buys you unlimited use of public transport and reduced-price entry to museums. Sold at the tourist office and via their website.

Post Office (Luisenplatz) On the northwest corner.

Tourist Office (📞134 513; www.darmstadt-marketing.de; Luisenplatz 5; ⊘10am-6pm Mon-Fri, & 10am-4pm Sat, plus 10am-2pm Sun Apr-Sep) Located in the northeast corner of the Luisencenter shopping mall, with direct access from Luisenplatz; look for a sign reading 'Darmstadt Shop'. Sells cultural events tickets and a handsome booklet on Mathildenhöhe (€3).

Heidelberg Altstadt

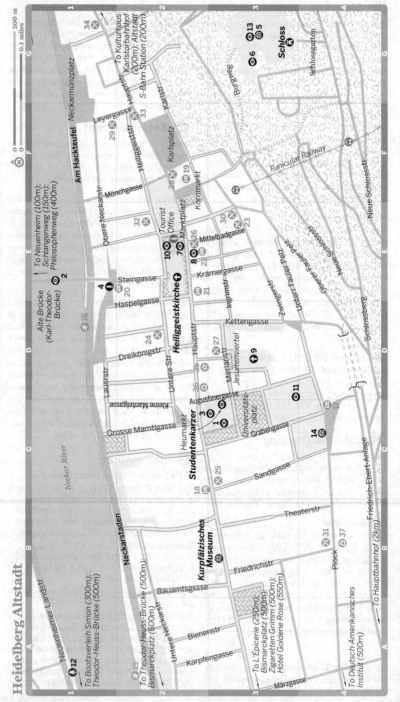

ⓘ Getting There & Around

Frequent S-Bahn (S3) trains link Darmstadt with Frankfurt's Hauptbahnhof (€7.30, 38 minutes), but it's faster to take one of DB's RB, IC or ICE trains (€8, 16 minutes). A day ticket that takes in both cities, including local trams and buses, costs €14.25.

In Darmstadt, the DB Service counter inside the Hauptbahnhof can supply you with a free map of the city. Trams 2, 3 and 5 link the Hauptbahnhof with Luisenplatz.

HEIDELBERG & AROUND

Heidelberg

☏ 06221 / POP 147,300

Germany's oldest and most famous university town is renowned for its baroque old town, lively university atmosphere, excellent pubs and evocative half-ruined castle, which draw 3½ million visitors a year. They are following in the footsteps of the late 18th- and early 19th-century romantics, most notably

the poet Goethe. Britain's William Turner also loved Heidelberg, which inspired him to paint some of his greatest landscapes.

Less-starry eyed was Mark Twain, who in 1878 began his European travels with a three-month stay in Heidelberg, recounting his bemused observations in *A Tramp Abroad*. For some deliciously acerbic excerpts from his writing, see www.mark-twain-in-heidelberg.de.

Heidelberg's Altstadt has a red-roofed townscape of remarkable architectural unity. After having been all but destroyed by French troops under Louis XIV (1690s), it was built pretty much from scratch during the 18th century. Unlike the vast majority of German cities, it emerged from WWII almost unscathed. Today, Heidelberg is one of Germany's most romantic cities – and the romance builds the longer you stay: the more you wander around, the more unexpected beauty and heartstopping panoramas you'll discover.

Heidelberg Altstadt

◎ Top Sights
Heiliggeistkirche	E2
Kurpfälzisches Museum	B3
Schloss	G3
Studentenkarzer	C3

◎ Sights
1	Alte Aula	C3
2	Alte Brücke	E1
3	Alte Universität	C3
4	Brass Monkey	E1
5	Deutsches Apotheken-Museum	G3
6	Grosses Fass	G3
7	Hercules Fountain	E2
8	Hofapotheke	E2
9	Jesuitenkirche	D3
10	Marktplatz	E2
11	Neue Universität	D3
12	Neuenheim River Bank	A1
	Ruprecht-Karls-Universität	(see 3)
13	Schlosshof	G3
	Universitäts Museum	(see 1)
14	Universitätsbibliothek	C4

⊕ Activities, Courses & Tours
15	Rhein-Neckar Fahrgastschifffahrt	A2
16	Solarschiff	D1

⊕ Sleeping
17	Arthotel	C4
18	Hip Hotel	C2
19	Hotel am Kornmarkt	F2
20	Hotel Goldener Hecht	E2
21	Hotel zum Ritter St Georg	E2
22	Pension Jeske	E2

⊗ Eating
23	Alte Gundtei	E3
24	Café Burkardt	D2
25	City-Markt	C3
26	City-Markt	E2
27	Falafel	D3
28	Gundel	F2
29	KulturBrauerei	F1
30	Persepolis	E3
31	Raja Rani	B4
32	Schiller's Café	E2
	Soltana	(see 18)
33	Wirthaus Zum Sepp'l	F2
34	Zur Herrenmühle	G1

⊛ Entertainment
35	Gloria und Gloriette	D2

⊜ Shopping
36	Bären Treff	D2
37	Heidelberger Zuckerladen	B4

⊙ Sights

Heidelberg's Altstadt runs along the left (south) bank of the Neckar River from Bismarckplatz east to the hillside Schloss. One of Europe's longest pedestrian zones, the 1600m-long Hauptstrasse, runs east-to-west through the Altstadt, about 200m south of the Neckar.

SCHLOSS

TOP CHOICE **Schloss** CASTLE

(Map p414; www.schloss-heidelberg.de; adult/child incl Bergbahn €5/3, Audioguides €4, 1½ hours; ⊙24hr, ticket required 8am-5.30pm) Sticking up above the Altstadt like a picture-book pop-up, Heidelberg's ruined Schloss is one of the most romantic spots in Germany. Palatinate princes, stampeding Swedes, rampaging French, Protestant reformers and lightning strikes – this Renaissance castle has seen the lot. Its tumultuous history, lonely beauty and changing moods helped inspire the German Romantic movement two centuries ago.

To reach the red-sandstone castle, perched about 80m above the Altstadt, you can either hoof it up the steep, cobbled **Burgweg** in about 10 minutes, or take the **Bergbahn** (Funicular Railway; www.bergbahn-heidelberg.de; ⊙every 10min 9am-about 5pm), opened in 1890, from the Kornmarkt station. Schloss tickets include travel on the Bergbahn – or, to put it another way, Bergbahn tickets include entry to the Schloss. The Schloss' courtyard and terrace are accessible 24 hours a day – tickets are required only from 8am to 5.30pm.

Audioguides that cite Goethe's poems and Mark Twain's stories can be hired at the **Ticket Office**, to the right as you enter the gardens from the Bergbahn station. They are available in eight languages, including Chinese, Japanese and Korean. You'll be asked to leave ID as a deposit.

Except for the museum, almost the entire Schloss is wheelchair accessible, though the cobblestones can make for rough rolling.

The **Schlosshof** (Map p414; ⊙24hr), the castle's central courtyard, is surrounded by Gothic and Renaissance buildings so elaborate they often elicit gasps from visitors, as do the breathtaking views of the Altstadt and the Neckar Valley from the terrace (through the archway at the bottom of the courtyard). The terrace's benches are perfect for a picnic.

The only way to see the less-than-scintillating interior of the **Friedrichsbau**, rebuilt (or, more accurately, built) a century ago, is on a guided tour (€4). Psalm 118 is inscribed on the facade in Hebrew and Latin.

With a capacity of about 228,000L, the mid-18th-century **Grosses Fass** (Great Wine Barrel; Map p414), shaped from 130 oak trees, is the world's largest wine cask. Describing it as being 'as big as a cottage', Mark Twain bemoaned its emptiness and mused on its possible functions as a dance floor and a gigantic cream churn.

The adjacent cafe serves beer, wine and, in winter, Glühwein (hot mulled wine). Sampling three different wines costs €5.50.

The surprisingly interesting **Deutsches Apotheken-Museum** (German Pharmacy Museum; Map p414; ⊙10am-5.30 or 6pm), off the Schlosshof, illustrates the history of Western pharmacology, in which Germany played a central role. Exhibits include pharmacies from the early 1700s and the Napoleonic era. Kids can use a mortar and a pestle to blend their own herbal tea (details available at the entrance). Most signs are in English.

The grassy, flowery **Schlossgarten** (Castle Garden; ⊙24hr), on the hillside south and east of the Schloss, is a lovely spot for a stroll or a picnic. The cracked Pulver Turm (Gunpowder Tower) was damaged by French forces in 1693.

ALTSTADT

The Hauptstrasse passes by a series of attractive public squares, many with historic or modern fountains.

Marktplatz SQUARE

(Map p414) The Marktplatz is the focal point of Altstadt street life. The trickling **Hercules fountain** (Map p414; Marktplatz) – that's him up on top of the pillar – in the middle is where petty criminals were chained and left to face the mob in the Middle Ages. Across the street at Hauptstrasse 190 stands the baroque **Hofapotheke** (Court Pharmacy; Map p414), built in the early 1700s and still sporting a gilded coat-of-arms.

Heiliggeistkirche CHURCH

(Map p414; Marktplatz; spire adult/student €2/1; ⊙11am-5pm Mon-Sat, 12.30-5pm Sun & holidays mid-Mar–Oct, 11am-3pm Fri & Sat, 12.30-3pm Sun Nov–mid-Mar) Heidelberg's most famous church, the Gothic-style Church of the Holy Spirit, was built from 1398 to 1441. Starting in 1706 it was used by both Catholics and Protestants, with a wall separating the two congregations; since 1936 it's been Protestant. See if you can spot the late-medieval markings on the facade, used to ensure that pretzels were of the requisite shape and size. For a bird's-eye view of Heidelberg, climb 208 stairs to the top of the spire.

Heiliggeistkirche is often used for concerts (www.studentenkantorei.de; organ concerts adult/student €4/2; ◷organ concerts 5.15pm), including half-hour organ concerts held every summer evening, except possibly Saturday. Stop by at 12.30pm from Monday to Saturday (except in winter) for 10 minutes of exquisite organ music.

Ruprecht-Karls-Universität   UNIVERSITY

(Map p414; www.uni-heidelberg.de) Despite witty observations about student duels and boisterous public drunkenness, Mark Twain points out that 'idle students are not the rule' in Heidelberg in his 1880 travelogue *A Tramp Abroad*. Indeed, Germany's oldest university, established in 1386 by Count Palatinate Ruprecht I, has plenty of gravitas, with a student hall of fame that ranges from Chancellor Helmut Kohl (history and political science, 1956) to composer Robert Schumann (law, 1829) to Nazi propagandist Joseph Goebbels (PhD, 1921). Today it comprises 12 faculties with over 29,000 students from 80 nations. Fifty-five winners of the Nobel Prize have been in some way connected to Heidelberg University.

The most historic facilities are around Universitätsplatz, dominated by the Alte Universität (1712–28; on the south side) and the Neue Universität (1931; on the north side), the 'old' and 'new' university buildings respectively. The latter was built largely with American donations. Nearby stands the Löwenbrunnen (Lions Fountain).

Studentenkarzer   HISTORIC SITE

(Map p414; Augustinergasse 2; adult/student incl Universitäts Museum €3/2.50; ◷10am-6pm Tue-Sun Apr-Sep, 10am-4pm Tue-Sat Oct-Mar) From 1823 to 1914, students convicted of misdeeds such as public inebriation, loud nocturnal singing, freeing the local pigs or duelling were sent to the Student Jail, where they were 'inkarzerated' for at least 24 hours and, for the first two days, fed only bread and water. Delinquents were let out to attend lectures or take exams. In certain circles, a stint in the Karzer was *de rigueur* to prove one's manhood. Judging by the inventive graffiti and creative inscriptions, some found their stay highly entertaining.

Universitäts Museum   MUSEUM

(Map p414; Grabengasse 1; adult/student incl Studentenkarzer €3/2.50; ◷10am-6pm Tue-Sun Apr-Sep, 10am-4pm Tue-Sat Oct-Mar) The three-room University Museum, inside the Alte Universität building, has paintings, portraits, documents and photos documenting the university's mostly-illustrious history. Only the signs on the Third Reich period are in English but the admission fee includes an English audioguide.

Except during academic events, you can visit the adjacent Alte Aula (Old Assembly Hall), a neo-Renaissance hall whose rich decoration dates from 1886.

Jesuitenkirche   CHURCH

(Map p414; ◷9.30am-6pm May-Sep, to 5pm Oct-Apr) The red-sandstone Jesuits' church, rising above an attractive square just east of Universitätsplatz, is a fine example of 18th-century baroque. This part of town was once the focal point of Heidelberg's Jewish quarter. The Schatzkammer (Treasury; admission €3; ◷10am-5pm Tue-Sat, 1-5pm Sun Jun-Oct, Sat & Sun Nov-May) displays precious religious artefacts.

Alte Brücke   BRIDGE

(Karl-Theodor-Brücke; Map p414; Neckarstaden) The 200m-long 'Old Bridge', built in 1788, connects the Altstadt with the river's right bank and the Schlangenweg (Snake Path), whose switchbacks head up the hill to the Philosophenweg (Philosophers' Way). In March 1945, as American troops approached Heidelberg, retreating German troops blew up the bridge. The crests of historic floods are marked on the bridge supports.

On the Altstadt side of the bridge stands a brass sculpture of a monkey (1979) holding a mirror and accompanied by some mice: touch the mirror for wealth, the outstretched fingers to ensure you return to Heidelberg, and the mice for many children.

Kurpfälzisches Museum   MUSEUM

(Map p414; www.museum-heidelberg.de; Hauptstrasse 97; adult/child up to 16yr €3/free; ◷10am-6pm Tue-Sun) The city-run Palatinate Museum has well-presented exhibits on Heidelberg's eventful history and is especially strong on the Roman period – exhibits include original wood beams from a 3rd-century bridge. To learn about really ancient local life, check out the replica of the 600,000-year-old jawbone of *Homo heidelbergensis* (Heidelberg Man), unearthed about 18km southeast of here in 1907 (the original is stored across the river at the university's palaeontology institute).

FREE **Universitätsbibliothek** MUSEUM
(Map p414; Plöck 107-109; ⊙exhibition 10am-6pm, closed holidays) The University Library was built in massive Wilhelmian style from 1901 to 1905. Upstairs you can see rare books and prints from its superb collections in the corner **Ausstellungsraum** (exhibition room).

NEUENHEIM
The north (right) bank of the Neckar has some worthwhile sights.

Philosophenweg TRAIL
Passing through steep fields and orchards on the slopes across the river from the Altstadt, the Philosophers' Way commands panoramic views of the Schloss as it wends its way through the forest to various monuments, towers, ruins, a beer garden and the **Thing-stätte**, a Nazi-era amphitheatre. The views are especially captivating around sundown, when the city is often bathed in a reddish glow. The walkway is a well-known lovers' haunt, and many a young local is said to have lost their heart – and virginity – here!

The Philosophenweg is linked to the Alte Brücke by the **Schlangenweg** (Snake Path), a series of switchbacks.

Neuenheim River Bank PARK
(Map p414; Uferstrasse; 🚌) The grassy Neckar's northern bank between Theodor-Heuss-Brücke and Ernst-Walz-Brücke, whose eastern end is about 500m northwest of Bismarckplatz, is a favourite student hang-out when the weather is warm. Small cafes sell snacks, drinks and beer.

FREE **Botanischer Garten der Universität** PARK
(http://botgart.hip.uni-heidelberg.de; Im Neuenheimer Feld 340; admission free; ⊙outdoor areas open all day, hothouses 9am-4pm Mon-Thu, 9am-2.30pm Fri, 9 or 10am to 4 or 5pm Sun & holidays, closed Sat) Orchids, ferns and Madagascan succulents thrive in the verdant University Botanical Garden, part of the university's right-bank Neuenheimer Feld campus. Situated 2.5km northwest of Bismarckplatz; served by trams 4 and 5.

Activities

Bootsverleih Simon BOAT RENTAL
(📞411 925; 3-/4-person pedalos per 30min €9/11; ⊙2pm-sundown Mon-Fri, noon-sundown Sat & Sun Apr-Oct, closed during storms) A leisurely way to soak up that special Heidelberg atmosphere is to hire a pedalo (pedal boat) on the north shore of the Neckar, just east of Theodor-Heuss-Brücke.

Solarschiff RIVER CRUISE
(Map p414; www.hdsolarschiff.com; Alte Brücke; adult/3-14yr/student €7/3/5; ⊙Tue-Sun Mar-Oct) For carbon-neutral sailing, you can't beat this glass-topped boat, powered by 12-tonne batteries juiced up by 56 sq m of solar panels. It was extended by 12m – yes, chopped in half and lengthened – in 2010. The engine is silent – all you hear during a 50-minute excursion is the water and the distant sounds of the city. Docks just west of the Alte Brücke.

Rhein-Neckar Fahrgastschifffahrt RIVER CRUISE
(Weisse Flotte; Map p414; 📞201 81; www.weisse-flotte-heidelberg.de; adult/child 5-14yr to Neckarsteinach return €14/8; ⊙mid-Apr–late-Nov) Offers boat trips up and down the Neckar. Free on your birthday. Boats dock on the south bank midway between the two Altstadt bridges.

☞ Tours

The tourist office runs English-language **walking tours** (adult/concession €7/5; ⊙10.30am Fri & Sat Apr-Oct) of the Altstadt; departures are from the Marktplatz (Rathaus) tourist office.

✷✷ Festivals & Events

For festival dates, see the tourist office website www.heidelberg-marketing.de.

Schlossbeleuchtung FIREWORKS
(Castle Illumination; ⊙10.15pm on 1st Sat Jun, 2nd Sat Jul & 1st Sat Sep) The Schloss, the Alte Brücke and the Altstadt are lit up by fantastic fireworks that commemorate the French assault on the Schloss in 1693. The best views are from both banks of the Neckar, west of the Alte Brücke.

Heidelberger Herbst STREET PARTY
(⊙10am-11pm last Sat in Sep, flea market from 7am) A huge street party with music, arts and crafts, buskers, food and a great deal of merrymaking.

Weihnachtsmarkt   CHRISTMAS MARKET
(⊙approx 21 Nov-22 Dec) Heidelberg's colourful Christmas market, with 140 stalls, takes over many of the Altstadt's public squares, including the Marktplatz, Universitätsplatz and the Kornmarkt.

🛏 Sleeping

Bargains are thin on the ground in Heidelberg and finding a bed can be tricky, so it's worth booking ahead. Many hotels set their room rates according to demand. The local low season runs from January to March and from late October to November.

TOP CHOICE **Hip Hotel**   BOUTIQUE HOTEL **$$$**
(Map p414; ☎208 79; www.hip-hotel.de; Hauptstrasse 115; s €135-180, d €150-210, breakfast €12; @🛜) Snooze in a Fijian beach shack complete with sandy bay, a woodsy Canadian hunter's cottage, or a topsy-turvy Down Under room where everything (paintings, doors, bed) is upside down. In an age in which cities are awash with 'theme hotels', this 27-room place is both genuinely creative and heaps of fun. The Amsterdam room is wheelchair-accessible.

TOP CHOICE **Arthotel**   BOUTIQUE HOTEL **$$**
(Map p414; ☎650 060; www.arthotel.de; Grabengasse 7; d without breakfast €115-198; P✳🛜) If you're in the mood to experience 21st-century German interior design at its most stylish, the Arthotel won't disappoint. The red and black lobby, lit by a wall of windows, sets the tone, while the 24 rooms, equipped with huge bathrooms, are spacious and cleanly minimalist – except for three, which come with painted ceilings that date from 1790. Has wheelchair-accessible rooms.

Steffis Hostel   HOSTEL **$**
(☎778 2772; www.hostelheidelberg.de; Alte Eppelheimer Strasse 50; dm without breakfast from €18, d with hall bathroom €52; ⊙reception 8am-10pm; P@🛜) Hidden away in a 19th-century tobacco factory, Steffis offers bright, well-lit rooms (all with shared bathrooms), a colourful lounge that's ideal for meeting fellow travellers, a spacious kitchen and an ineffable old-time hostel vibe. The buffet breakfast costs €3. Perks include free wi-fi, tea, coffee and bicycles (deposit €20). Situated a block north of the Hauptbahnhof, three floors above a Lidl supermarket; access is via an industrial-size lift.

Hotel zum Ritter St Georg   HISTORIC HOTEL **$$$**
(Map p414; ☎1350; www.ritter-heidelberg.de; Hauptstrasse 178; s €72-134, d €144-206; 🛜) Set in an ornate, late-Renaissance mansion built by a Huguenot cloth merchant in 1592. The cheaper rooms are an anticlimax after the opulent facade, but the spacious Superior (28 sq m) and De Luxe (35 sq m) rooms, some with church views, are bright and really lovely.

Hotel am Kornmarkt   HOTEL **$$**
(Map p414; ☎905 830; www.hotelamkornmarkt.de; Kornmarkt 7; s/d from €65/85, without bathroom €40/70, breakfast €9; 🛜) Just a block from the Marktplatz, this hotel is a beacon to euro-conscious travellers. The 20 rooms are no-frills but they're comfortable and spotless; the priciest have Kornmarkt views. Parking is available nearby at parking garage P12 (€8 per 24 hours with a hotel voucher). Great value.

Hotel Regina   HOTEL **$$**
(☎53640; www.hotel-regina.de; Luisenstrasse 6; s/d from €70/98; 🛜) Central but quiet, the welcoming Regina occupies a brick-and-stone building built a century ago. The 15 attractive rooms, decked out in tones of orange, green and white, are all outfitted with bright, all-tile bathrooms. Has a cute breakfast room. Situated just west of the Altstadt, 200m west of Bismarckplatz.

Hotel Goldene Rose   HOTEL **$$**
(☎905 490; www.hotel-goldene-rose.de; St-Anna-Gasse 7; d €99-149; 🛜) In a great location at the western end of the Hauptstrasse. The 37 rooms are compact but quiet, attractive and especially well-kept. Wheelchair-accessible.

Hotel Goldener Hecht   HOTEL **$$**
(Map p414; ☎166 025; www.hotel-goldener-hecht.de; Steingasse 2; d without breakfast €73-94; 🛜) This atmospheric hotel, just a few paces from the Alte Brücke, has just 13 rooms, six with bridge views; the three corner rooms are bright and gorgeous. One drawback to being so central: it can be a bit noisy at night, especially on summer weekends. Goethe was once turned away for lack of space so book ahead.

Denner Hotel   HOTEL **$$**
(☎604 510; www.denner-hotel.de; Bergheimer Strasse 8; s/d weekday from €90/110, weekend from €70/90; 🛜) An almost-boutique hotel whose 18 rooms come with modern furniture, hardwood floors and creatively painted

walls; two feature neoclassical balconies overlooking Bismarckplatz, one block west of the Altstadt's western edge.

Pension Jeske
HOTEL $

(Map p414; 237 33; www.pension-jeske-heidelberg.de; Mittelbadgasse 2; s/d without bathroom €25/55, d with bathroom €65; reception 11am-1pm & 5-7pm;) If you're on a tight budget, consider Pension Jeske, which enjoys a great location but whose rooms are outfitted with fake parquet floors and cheap furnishings. Reception is staffed (for both check-in and phone enquiries) only from 11am to 1pm and 5pm to 7pm (to 6.30pm on Saturday, Sunday and holidays); let them know ahead if you'll be arriving at another time. No lift/elevator.

DJH Hostel
HOSTEL $

(651 19; www.jugendherberge-heidelberg.de; Tiergartenstrasse 5; dm €28.50, 26yr & under €24.50) Although the schoolkids here are often as night-active as the nocturnal critters in the neighbouring zoo, this modern hostel is very comfortable, with impeccable dorms and the occasional passing elephant. Situated 5km northwest of the Altstadt, on the north bank of the river. From the Hauptbahnhof, take bus 33.

Eating

The Altstadt, especially around Steingasse and Untere Strasse, is chock-full of restaurants, cafes, pubs and beer gardens, serving everything from classic German dishes to fresh falafel and spicy curries. Cosy restaurants frequented by students and locals can be found along the side streets south of the Hauptstrasse and west of the Kornmarkt. The Hauptstrasse is the place to go for ice cream.

For a pub crawl, you can't beat pedestrianised Untere Strasse, which student revellers keep lively until very late on weekends.

TOP CHOICE Zur Herrenmühle
GERMAN $$$

(Map p414; 602 909; www.herrenmuehle-heidelberg.de; Hauptstrasse 237-239; mains €14.50-28.50; 6-10pm Mon-Sat) A flour mill from 1690 has been turned into an elegant and highly cultured place to enjoy traditional 'country house' cuisine, including fish, under 300-year-old wood beams, a candle flickering romantically at each table. A five-course menu costs €36.50.

Gundel
CAFE $

(Map p414; www.gundel-heidelberg.de; Hauptstrasse 212; pastries €2.50-4; 8 or 8.30am-6 or 6.30pm Tue-Sun) Gundel is everything a classic modern cafe should be, with fresh flowers on the tables and unbelievably, orgasmically delicious pastries and breads. Also serves sandwiches and light meals. The bakery section sells 30 different kinds of bread and rolls.

Café Burkardt
CAFE $

(Map p414; Untere Strasse 27; cake & snacks €3-8; 9am-11pm Tue-Sat, 9am-6pm Sun) Full of doily-draped tables and dark-wood crannies, this friendly cafe serves salads, German dishes, pasta and some of Heidelberg's scrummiest tarts and cheesecakes. Also on offer are great breakfasts (€4.20 to €11.50) and about 20 wines (available by the glass) from villages right around Heidelberg. The courtyard abuts the house where Friedrich Ebert, German President during the Weimar Republic, was born.

Schiller's Café
CAFE $

(Map p414; Heiliggeiststrasse 5; cakes €2.50; 10am-8pm Sun-Wed, 10am-midnight Thu-Sat) Housed in one of Heidelberg's oldest residential buildings – the cellar and first floor date from the 1500s – this homey, wholesome cafe serves reasonably priced hot chocolate (over 60 kinds!), homemade cakes, quiche and wines; most are organic and some are gluten-free.

Falafel
FALAFEL $

(Map p414; Merianstrasse 3; snacks €3.50-6.50; 11.30am-11pm;) Serves some of the tastiest Syrian-style falafel – always served steaming hot – anywhere in Germany. Also has kebab, hummus, baba ganoush and Middle Eastern salads.

Café Gekko
CAFE, BAR $$

(Bergheimer Strasse 8; mains €7.20-17.80; 7am-1am Mon-Thu, 7am-3am Fri, 8am-5am Sat;) This bistro-bar-cafe, relaxed but stylishly so, is groovy for breakfast (served until 6pm), lunch (daily specials cost €7.80 to €9.80), dinner (salads, pasta and meat dishes are served until 11pm), tapas and a drink. Situated at the southwestern corner of Bismarckplatz.

KulturBrauerei
CAFE $$

(Map p414; 502 980; Leyergasse 6; mains €10.50-26.50; 7am-11pm or later) With its wood-plank floor, black iron chandeliers and time-faded ceiling frescoes, this microbrewery – in a hall that dates from 1903 – is an atmospheric spot to tuck into salad, soup or regional dishes such as *Schäufele* (pork shoulder) with sauerkraut (€10.50), or to quaff home-brews in the beer garden.

Soltana
MEDITERRANEAN **$$**
(Map p414; ✆20879; Hauptstrasse 115, 1st fl; mains €12-22.50; ⊗5pm-1am Mon & Wed-Fri, noon-1am Sat & Sun) Keyhole arches, *tadelakt*-style walls and bursts of hot colour whisk you to Marrakech at this restaurant, inside the Hip Hotel. Dishes from Spain, Italy, Greece, Turkey and Morocco are served at elegant tables set with crystal.

Wirthaus Zum Sepp'l
GERMAN **$$**
(Map p414; Hauptstrasse 217; mains €11.90-24.50; ⊗5pm-12.30am Tue-Sat) Heidelberg's most-historic student pub has black-and-white frat photos on the dark wooden walls and names carved into the tables, though these days students are outnumbered by tourists. Dishes are a mix of German and Italian.

Alte Gundtei
TURKISH **$$**
(Map p414; ✆29395; www.alte-gundtei.com; Zwingerstrasse 15a; mains €11.50-19.80; ⊗5pm-midnight) Enjoy the rich flavours of Anatolia under multi-coloured Oriental lamps at this excellent Turkish restaurant, whose offerings include charcoal-grilled meats, half-a-dozen fish dishes, two excellent veggie options and Turkish wines. Has belly-dancing on Wednesday.

Persepolis
PERSIAN **$$**
(Map p414; Zwingerstrasse 21; mains €5.90-10.80; ⊗11am-5pm Mon-Fri, noon-8pm Sat, 1-7pm Sun) A tiny place serving tasty, inexpensive Persian cuisine based on chicken, lamb and/or veggies. Good value.

Raja Rani
INDIAN **$**
(Map p414; Friedrichstrasse 15; mains €7.90; P❊🗲) Not bad for a cheap, fast korma or curries. The mango lassis (€1) are superb.

City-Markt
SUPERMARKET **$**
(Map p414; Hauptstrasse 198; ⊗8am-8pm Mon-Sat) Picnic supplies at the Marktplatz.

City-Markt
SUPERMARKET **$**
(Map p414; Hauptstrasse 116; ⊗9am-9pm Mon-Sat) Picnic supplies at the Hauptstrasse's midpoint.

☆ Entertainment

Heidelberg's student population fuels the party at the weekend. The city's effervescent cultural scene includes concerts, films and dance and theatre performances. **Zigaretten Grimm** (✆20909; Sophienstrasse 11; ⊗9am-7pm Mon-Fri, 10am-5pm Sat), a tobacco shop at Bismarckplatz (east of the Alstadt), sells tickets for concerts and other cultural events.

TOP CHOICE ✩ **Kulturhaus Karlstorbahnhof**
LIVE MUSIC
(✆978 711; www.karlstorbahnhof.de; Am Karlstor 1; ⊗closed Aug) This cutting edge cultural centre offers a variety of nightlife options including: **concerts** (⊗9pm; tickets €8-30), **art-house cinema** (✆tickets 978 918; www.karlstorkino.de), screening non-dubbed films, and theatre performances (some of which are in English). There's also a hugely popular disco, **Klub K** (⊗10 or 11pm-5 or 6am Thu-Sat), whose DJs play everything from techno and dubstep to indie rock for a mixed crowd, most in the 18-to-40 age group. There's no dress code. Germany's largest Jazz festival, **Enjoy Jazz** (www.enjoyjazz.de), also takes place here every fall.

Kulturhaus Karlstorbahnhof is situated next to the train tracks 100m east of the Karlstor, the towering stone gate at the eastern end of the Altstadt. To get there, take bus 35 or, from the Hauptbahnhof, the S-Bahn one stop to the Altstadt station.

Nachtschicht
CLUB
(www.nachtschicht.com; Bergheimerstrasse 147; admission €3-6; ⊗10pm-4am Thu, 8pm-1am Fri, 11pm-5am Sat) Situated two blocks north of the Hauptbahnhof, on the right beyond the Lidl supermarket, is Nachtschicht, part of an old tobacco factory turned into one of Heidelberg's most-popular student discos. Friday night is Schools Club night, open only to 16- to 18-year-olds. The door policy is laidback.

Gloria und Gloriette
CINEMA
(Map p414; ✆253 19; www.gloria-kamera-kinos.de; Hauptstrasse 146) Screens non-dubbed films, some in English.

Deutsch-Amerikanisches Institut
CULTURAL CENTRE
(German-American Institute; ✆607 30; www.dai-heidelberg.de; Sofienstrasse 12; ⊗ticket office 1-6pm Mon-Fri) Puts on concerts, lectures and films several times a week.

Shopping

Amble down the mile-long, traffic-free Hauptstrasse for souvenirs, brand-name shops and fine window displays, or find one-off galleries and speciality shops in the Altstadt's backstreets (eg Plöck).

WORTH A TRIP

HOCKENHEIMRING

Host of some of Germany's most-famous car races, including the Formula One German Grand Prix (in even-numbered years), the historic **HockenheimRing** (☑06205-9500; www.hockenheimring.de) has three circuits and stands that can accommodate up to 120,000 fans. Formula One cars have reached speeds of up to 330km/hr here.

Motorsports fans can get a look behind the scenes on an **Insider Tour** (adult/child incl museum 6-16yr €12/6.50; ☉11am except during races), conducted in English and German; there's no need to book ahead. Tickets are sold at the **Motor Sport Museum** (adult/child €6/3; ☉10am-5pm Mar-Dec, longer hours on race days), which has a fantastic collection of historic motorcycles, some a century old, and a fine ensemble of historic race cars. Upstairs, check out the reconstruction of the world's first motorcycle, built of wood by Maybach and Daimler in 1885.

If roaring along on a speedlimitless Autobahn doesn't get the adrenalin pumping any more, you can try out the Hockenheim track yourself when it isn't being used for a race:

» **Renntaxi** (per person €150 to €269) Three laps on the Grand Prix course with a professional driver in a superfast racing car, eg a Porsche GT3, a Mercedes SLK 350 or an Audi R8 V10.

» **Drifttaxi** (€269) Lets you experience high-speed skids with a professional driver.

» **Race'n'roll** (€399) Drive a superfast race car yourself.

» **Touristenfahrten** (per 15 minutes €12) Drive your own car around the track.

For information on available dates and for reservations, see the website or call ☑06205-950 183/222.

The HockenheimRing is 22km southwest of Heidelberg, just across (east of) the A6 from the town of Hockenheim.

TOP CHOICE / **Heidelberger Zuckerladen**   CANDY
(Map p414; Plöck 52; ☉noon-7pm Mon-Fri, 11.15am-3pm Sat) The dentures and dentist's chair in the window of this old-time sweet shop hint at what will happen to your gnashers if you overindulge on the Zuckerladen's bonbons, liquorice laces and fizzy sherbet. Marion Brecht is the eccentric candy man who adds magic to the pick 'n' mix.

L'Épicerie   GOURMET FOODS
(Hauptstrasse 35; ☉1-7pm Mon, 11am-7pm Tue-Fri, 10am-7pm Sat) In a courtyard off Hauptstrasse, L'Épicerie is a haven for foodies thanks to its luscious pralines, spices, oils and preserves.

Bären Treff   CANDY
(Map p414; Hauptstrasse 144) An entire store dedicated to chewy gummi bear candies! A poster on the wall shows how they're made.

ⓘ Information

Ärztlicher Bereitschaftsdienst (☑192 92; Alte Eppenheimer Strasse 35; ☉7pm-7am, from 1pm Wed, 24hr Sat & Sun) For medical care when most doctors' offices are closed. Situated one block north of the Hauptbahnhof.

Heidelberg Card (1/2/4 days €11/13/16, 2-day family pass €28) Entitles you to unlimited pub-

lic transport use, free admission to the Schloss (including the Bergbahn) and discounts at most museums, for bike and boat rental, and for tours. Available at the tourist office.

Heidelberger Internet C@fe (Plöck 8; per hr €1; ☉10am-midnight) Internet access.

Internet Lounge (per hr €5; ☉6.30am-midnight) Pricey internet inside the Hauptbahnhof.

Police Post (☑991 700, emergency 110; Bismarckplatz; ☉noon-8pm Mon-Sat) In a little pavilion in the middle of the square. The much larger Heidelberg Mitte police station is at Römerstrasse 2–4.

Post Office (Sofienstrasse 8-10)

ReiseBank (☉7.30am-8pm Mon-Fri, 9am-5pm Sat, 9am-1pm Sun) Currency exchange inside the Hauptbahnhof.

Tourist Office (☑194 33, 584 4444; www.heidelberg-marketing.de) Has loads of useful information and sells a useful walking-tour map (€1.50). The **Hauptbahnhof** (Willy-Brandt-Platz 1; ☉9am-7pm Mon-Sat, 10am-6pm Sun & holidays Apr-Oct, 9am-6pm Mon-Sat Nov-Mar) branch is right outside the train station; the **Marktplatz** (Marktplatz 10; 8am-5pm Mon-Fri, 10am-5pm Sat) branch is inside the red-sandstone Rathaus.

Waschsalon (Kettengasse 17; per 6kg €10; ☉9am-5pm Mon, Tue, Thu & Fri early Oct-Jun, 9am-2pm Mon, Tue, Thu & Fri Jul-early Oct,

9am-1pm Wed & Sat year-round) A full-service laundry; wash and dry takes three to four hours.

ⓘ Getting There & Away

Heidelberg is 93km south of Frankfurt, 20km southeast of Mannheim and 120km northwest of Stuttgart.

From the **Hauptbahnhof** (Willy-Brandt-Platz), 3km west of the Schloss, there are at least hourly train services to/from Frankfurt (€16.40 to €27, one hour to 1½ hours) and Stuttgart (€21.20 to €37, 40 minutes to 1½ hours), as well as frequent S-Bahn services to Mannheim (€4.90, 19 minutes), Speyer (€8.70, 50 minutes) and, with a change in Neustadt an der Weinstrasse, the German Wine Route towns of Deidesheim (€8.70, 1¼ hours) and Bad Dürkheim.

ⓘ Getting Around

TO & FROM THE AIRPORTS The fastest way to get to Frankfurt airport (€23, one hour, every hour or two) is to take the eight-seat **Lufthansa's Airport Shuttle** (☑06152-976 9099; www.transcontinental-group.com). In Heidelberg, it stops at the Crowne Plaza Hotel (Kurfürstenanlage 1-3), three blocks southwest of Bismarckplatz; at the airport, you can catch it outside Terminal 1's Arrival Hall B (exit B4). Book at least a day ahead.

To get to Hahn airport (adult/child €20/10, 3½ hours, five daily), you can take the **Hahn Express** (☑01805-225 287; www.hahn-express.de), which stops at the Hauptbahnhof (next to McDonald's)

BICYCLE Places that rent out bicycles:

Radhof (☑893 7345; www.fahrrad-heidelberg.de; Hauptbahnhof; per day/overnight €5/10; ☺7am-6pm Mon & Fri, 10am-6pm Tue-Thu) Weekday bike rental, repair and second-hand sales at the Hauptbahnhof, next to Track 1, at Platform 1b.

Fahrradverleih (☑654 4460; www.fahrrad verleih-heidelberg.de; Neckarstaden 52; per day €18; ☺10am-1pm & 2-6pm Tue-Fri, 10am-6pm Sat, 2-6pm Sun) Has cycling maps.

CAR Street parking in the city centre is reserved for residents so there's no way to avoid the fees at the city's 19 **parking garages** (http://parken.heidelberg.de; per hr €0.50-1.50, per day €9-18). Some hotels offer discount vouchers.

To figure out how to drive to your hotel, find out which parking garage is closest and follow the signs.

PUBLIC TRANSPORT Tram 5 and buses 32, 33 and 34 link the Hauptbahnhof with Bismarckplatz, the main hub for public transport (www.vrn.de), and various parts of the Altstadt. The quickest way from the Hauptbahnhof to the eastern part of the Altstadt is to take an S-Bahn train one stop to the Altstadt station. The tourist office can supply you with a *Linienplan*, a useful, pocket-sized city map that indicates bus and tram lines.

Single tickets cost €2.30; for travel within the city centre (ie within the area between the Hauptbahnhof, the Schloss and the start of the Philosphenweg), a ticket costs just €1.10. A Ticket 24 (also valid on Sunday if stamped Saturday) for one/five people, valid for 24 hours in up to three zones, costs €5.50/9.60; a 3-Tages-Karte, valid for three days, costs €13.70 per person. Tickets are sold at tram-stop ticket machines and by bus drivers.

TAXI Taxis (☑302 030) line up outside the Hauptbahnhof. Count on paying about €9 or €10 from the Hauptbahnhof to the Alte Brücke.

Speyer

☑06232 / POP 50,000

The handsome town of Speyer, about 50km south of Worms, has an eminently walkable centre – hardly damaged during WWII – distinguished by a magnificent Romanesque cathedral, high-quality historical museums and a medieval synagogue. Another highlight is the extraordinary Technik Museum, guaranteed to awe kids and adults alike.

First a Celtic settlement, then a Roman market town, Speyer gained prominence in the Middle Ages under the Salian emperors, hosting 50 imperial parliament sessions (1294–1570).

In 1076 the king and later Holy Roman Emperor Heinrich IV, having been excommunicated by Pope Gregory VII, launched his penitence walk to Canossa in Italy from Speyer. He crossed the Alps in the middle of winter, an action that warmed the heart of the pope, who revoked his excommunication. He lies buried in the Kaiserdom.

In 1529 pro-Luther princes 'protested' a harsh anti-Luther edict issued by the Diet of Speyer, thereby starting the use of the term 'Protestant'.

◉ Sights

Kaiserdom CHURCH
(crypt adult/child €3/free; ☺9am-7pm Mon-Sat, 11.30am-5.30pm Sun Apr-Oct, 9am or 10am-5pm daily Nov-Mar) A Unesco World Heritage Site since 1981, this extraordinary Romanesque cathedral is instantly recognisable thanks to its square red towers and green copper dome, which float majestically above Speyer's rooftops. Begun in 1030 by Emperor Konrad II of the Salian dynasty, its interior is startling for its awesome dimensions (it's an astonishing 134m long) and austere, dignified

DISCOUNT CARD

The **Rheinland-Pfalz & Saarland Card** (FreizeitCard; www.freizeitcard.info; 24hr/3-day/6-day €14/41/66; ☺Apr-Oct) sold at most tourist offices in the states of Rhineland-Palatinate and Saarland, gets you a slew of freebies and discounts (eg to 73 museums and 22 castles) and some great discounts.

symmetry; walk up the side aisles to the elevated altar area to get a true sense of its vastness.

Another set of steps, to the right of the altar, leads down to the darkly festive **crypt**, whose candy-striped Romanesque arches – like those on the west front – recall Moorish architecture (ask for an English-language brochure). Stuffed into a side room, up some stairs, are the sandstone sarcophagi of eight emperors and kings, along with some of their queens. You can rent a 45-minute audioguide (€4) at the crypt entrance. By the time you read this it may be possible to climb the **southwest tower** and see some huge 19th-century paintings in the **Kaisersaal**.

The most scenic way to approach the Dom is from Maximilianstrasse. Behind the Dom, the large **Domgarten** (cathedral park) stretches towards the Rhine.

The cathedral often hosts **organ concerts** (www.dommusik-speyer.de; admission €10-20).

Maximilianstrasse   PEDESTRIAN STREET

Roman troops and medieval emperors once paraded down 'Via Triumphalis'. Now known as Maximilianstrasse, Speyer's pedestrian-only shopping precinct is 800m long, linking the Dom with the 55m-high, 13th-century **Altpörtel** (adult/child €1/0.50; ☺10am-noon & 2-4pm Mon-Fri, 10am-5pm Sat & Sun Apr-Oct), the city's western gate and the only remaining part of the town wall. The clock (1761) has separate dials for minutes and hours. The views from up top are breathtaking.

A favourite with window-shoppers and strollers alike, Maximilianstrasse is lined with baroque buildings, among which the **Rathaus** (at No 13), with its red-orange facade and lavish rococo 1st floor (open for concerts and events), and the **Alte Münze** (Old Mint; at No 90) are worth a look.

The numbering of the buildings along Maximilianstrasse (from 1 to 100) begins at the Dom, runs sequentially along the south

side to the Altpörtel, and then continues along the north side back to the Dom - be prepared for confusion!

Judenhof   SYNAGOGUE

(Kleine Pfaffengasse 21; adult/student/family €3/1.50/7.50; ☺10am-5pm daily Apr-Oct, 10am-4pm Tue-Sun Nov-Mar) The 'Jews' Courtyard', a block south of the Rathaus, is one of the most important medieval Jewish sites in Germany. The remains of a Romanesque-style synagogue, it was consecrated in 1104 and used until 1450. Its 13th-century women's section, a **Mikwe** (ritual bath) from the early 1100s – the oldest, largest and best preserved north of the Alps – and a small **museum** (opened in 2010) hint at the glories of the city's storied medieval Jewish community. Signs are in German, English and French. A new synagogue, **Beith Schalom** (Am Weidenberg 3), opened 1km to the northwest in 2011. A curious fact: everyone with the surname of Shapira (or Shapiro) is descended from Jews who lived in Speyer during the Middle Ages.

Dreifaltigkeitskirche   CHURCH

(Grosse Himmelsgasse 3a; ☺10.30am-4pm Wed & Sat, 2-5pm Sun) Consecrated in 1717, 200 years to the day after Luther posted his 95 Theses, this harmonious church is a superb example of Protestant baroque. Almost all the rich, if restrained, interior decor is original. The front pews (installed in 1890) face both ways so worshippers can see the pulpit during the sermon. English brochures offer historical background. There's 30 minutes of organ music every Saturday starting at 11.30am. When the church is closed, the interior can be glimpsed through the glass doors. Situated half-a-block north of Maximilianstrasse.

Historisches Museum der Pfalz   MUSEUM

(Historical Museum of the Palatinate; ☎620 222; http://museum.speyer.de; Domplatz; adult/student incl audioguide €7/4, incl special exhibitions €13/4; ☺10am-6pm Tue-Sun) Some of the exhibits here will leave you quite simply speechless. Highlights include the **Goldener Zeremonialhut von Schifferstadt**, an ornate, perfectly preserved gilded hat, shaped like a giant thimble, that dates back to the Bronze Age (circa 1300 BC), and Celtic artefacts such as **two bronze wheels** (about 800 BC). In the **Wine Museum** you can see an amphora from about AD 325 containing unappetising blobs that may be the world's oldest wine. Two floors below is the **Domschatz** (cathedral treasury), whose prized exhibit is Emperor Konrad II's surprisingly simple 11th-century bronze crown.

Technik Museum
MUSEUM

(www.technik-museum.de; Am Technik Museum 1; adult/6-14yr €14/12; ⊙9am-6pm) At this truly amazing technology extravaganza, you can climb aboard a Boeing 747-230 (like most visitors, you'll probably wonder: how in the world did they get the aircraft here and then mount it 28m off the ground?), a 1960s U-boat that's claustrophobic even on dry land, and a mammoth Antonov An-22 cargo plane with an all-analogue cockpit and a nose cone you can peer out of. Other highlights include the Soviet space shuttle *Buran,* a superb collection of vintage automobiles and fire engines, and military jets and helicopters from both sides of the Iron Curtain.

The **Wilhelmsbau** showcases some truly extraordinary automated musical instruments – all in working order – including a Hupfeld Phonoliszt-Violina, a player-piano that also bows and fingers two violins, and a Roland orchestrion (1928), which simulates the sound of a soprano accompanying an orchestra. The **Technik Museum**, which is sure to please the kids, is 1km south of the Dom, on the other side of the A61 highway.

🛏 Sleeping

Hotel Domhof
HOTEL **$$**

(☑132 90; www.domhof.de; Bauhof 3; s/d €98/121, cheaper Sun night; P✷@☎) A hotel has stood on this spot next to the Dom – an unbeatable location – since the Middle Ages, once hosting emperors, kings and councillors. Wrapped around an ivy-covered, cobbled courtyard, the 49 comfortable rooms have calming views and bright bathrooms.

Hotel Zum Augarten
HOTEL **$**

(☑754 58; www.augarten.de; Rheinhäuser Strasse 52; s/d from €59/79; P) A cosy, family-run, family-friendly hotel with 16 rooms where you can enjoy German guest-house hospitality and observe suburban German life up close. Situated 1.7km south of the Dom – from the Technik Museum take Industriestrasse and turn right on Am Flugplatz.

Maximilian
APARTMENT **$**

(☑100 2500; www.mein-maximilian.de; Korngasse 15; d€50-100) Cafe-bistro Maximilian rents out three very modern two-person apart-ments and two attractive rooms. Excellent value.

DJH Hostel
HOSTEL **$**

(☑615 97; www.jugendherberge.de; Geibstrasse 5; dm/d €21/54) A bright, cheery hostel on the Rhine, a few hundred metres east of the Technik Museum and next door to the Bademaxx swimming complex. Has 51 rooms, including 13 bunk doubles, all with private bathroom. Linked to the Hauptbahnhof and city centre by the City-Shuttle bus.

Hotel Speyer
HOTEL **$$**

(☑671 00; www.hotel-speyer.de; Am Technik Museum 1; s/d from €64/89; P) Part of the Technik Museum complex, this motel-like establishment has 108 practical, workaday rooms. Linked to the Hauptbahnhof and city centre by the City-Shuttle bus.

🍴 Eating

A selection of dining options, including Italian eateries and, in the warm months, outdoor cafes, can be found along Maximilianstrasse and nearby streets, such as Kleine Pfaffengasse (near the Judenhof).

Domhof-Hausbrauerei
GERMAN **$$**

(Grosse Himmelsgasse 6; mains €7.50-23.10; ⊙11.30am-11pm or later) Speyer's loveliest beer garden, shaded by chestnut trees, is just steps west of the Dom. The menu features regional and German favourites, some prepared using the four beers brewed on the premises. Has a small children's playground.

ℹ CYCLING AROUND SPEYER

The circular **Kaiser-Konrad-Radweg** (Kaiser Konrad bicycle path) links Speyer's Dom with Bad Dürkheim's Rathaus (about 30km each way), on the German Wine Route; the 129km **Salier-Radweg** circuit also includes Worms. **Veloroute Rhein** follows the Rhine north to Worms. The tourist office has free brochures on various local cycling paths.

The excellent 1:150,000-scale cycling map *Radtouren rund um Speyer* (Bicycle Touring Around Speyer; €2) is sold at the tourist office and bookshops.

Maximilian   INTERNATIONAL **$**
(Korngasse 15; mains €6.30-18.90; ⊙8 or 9am-midnight or 1am; ⊘) Just inside the Altpörtel, this buzzing cafe-bistro with an Italian vibe serves up soups, salads, grilled meats, pasta, two good-value dinner specials (€4.90) and a dozen different breakfasts. No credit cards accepted except EC.

Backmulde   MEDITERRANEAN **$$$**
(⊘715 77; www.backmulde.de; Karmeliterstrasse 11-13; mains €13-32; ⊙11.30am-2.30pm & 7-11pm, closed Sun dinner & Mon) Owner-chef Gunter Schmidt has a knack for spinning fresh, all-local products into creative gourmet dishes with a Mediterranean flavour – thus his motto, *cuisine sans frontières*. A block south of the western side of the Altpörtel.

Rewe City   SUPERMARKET **$**
(Maximilianstrasse 50; ⊙7am-10pm Mon-Sat) Next to the Altpörtel.

❶ Information

ATMs (Maximilianstrasse 47 & 49) Near the Altpörtel.

City-Call-Center (Bahnhofstrasse 3; per hr €1; ⊙10am-9pm Mon-Sat, noon-9pm Sun) Internet access half-a-block north of the Altpörtel.

Post Office (Wormser Strasse 4) A block north of Maximilianstrasse 61.

Tourist Office (⊘142 392; www.speyer.de; Maximilianstrasse 13; ⊙9am-5pm Mon-Fri year-round, 10am-3pm Sat, 10am-2pm Sun & holidays Apr-Oct, 10am-noon Sat Nov-Mar) Situated 200m west of the Dom, next to the historic Rathaus.

❶ Getting There & Around

S-Bahn (S3 and S4) trains link the Hauptbahnhof (on Bahnhofstrasse), about 700m north of the Altpörtel and 1.5km northwest of the Dom, with Mannheim (€4.90, 25 minutes), a key rail hub, and Heidelberg (€8.70, 50 minutes). Change at Schifferstadt and Neustadt an der Weinstrasse to get to the German Wine Route towns of Deidesheim (€6.20) and Bad Dürkheim.

The convenient City-Shuttle minibus (bus 565; day pass €1) links the Hauptbahnhof, Maximilianstrasse, the Dom, Festplatz, the Technik Museum and the youth hostel at 10- or 15-minute intervals from 6am (9am on Sunday) to 8pm.

At the Festplatz, 500m south of the Dom and across (under) the A61 from the Technik Museum, parking costs €2 per day, including a free City-Shuttle ride for one person.

You can rent a bicycle, borrow cycling maps and discuss pedal-driven touring options at English-speaking **Radsport Stiller** (⊘759 66; www.

stiller-radsport.de; Gilgenstrasse 24; bike/tandem per day €10/20; ⊙9.30am-12.30pm & 2-6.30pm Mon-Fri, 9am-2pm Sat, 1-5pm Sun), a first-rate bike shop a block southwest of the Altpörtel.

Schwetzingen

⊘06202 / POP 21,800

The enchanting gardens of **Schloss Schwetzingen** (Schwetzingen Palace; www.schloss-schwetzingen.de; adult/student/family gardens €5/2.50/12.50, incl Schloss tour €9/4.50/22.50, cheaper in winter; ⊙gardens 9am-7.30pm late-Mar–late-Oct, 9am-4pm late-Oct–late-Mar), the grand baroque-style summer residence of Prince-Elector Karl Theodor (1724–99), are wonderful for a family outing or a romantic stroll-à-deux, especially on a sunny spring or summer day.

Of Versaillian proportions and inspiration, the gardens are a beguiling mix of exquisite French formality and meandering, English-style landscaping. Scattered around the gardens are burbling **fountains** and 'follies', architectural flights of fancy – among them an ersatz **Moschee** (mosque), an extraordinary complex in pink, decorated with Turkish crescents, that mixes 18th-century German baroque with 'exotic' styling inspired by Constantinople. As you wander, keep an eye out for strutting peacocks.

The only way to see the furnished **Schloss interior** is on a tour (in German with printed text in English and French). From late March to late October, tours begin on the hour from 11am to 4pm or 5pm; in winter, there are tours at 11am, 2pm and 3pm on Saturday, Sunday and holidays.

The map-brochure *Schwetzingen Castle Garden* (€1.50), sold at the ticket desk, is a good investment. Schloss Schwetzingen is 10km west of Heidelberg and 8km south of Mannheim, just east of the A6.

✗ Eating

The Schloss has a couple of cafes, or head for the **Kaufhof** supermarket (Carl Theodor Strasse 37; ⊙7am-10pm Mon-Sat) for picnic supplies, situated 150m to the right as you exit Schwetzingen's train station.

❶ Getting There & Away

Schwetzingen's train station is linked to Speyer (€4.90, one hour) and Heidelberg's Hauptbahnhof by bus 717 (€3.60, 30 minutes) and to Mannheim's Hauptbahnhof by bus 710 (€3.60, 35 minutes); both run twice an hour (hourly on

Saturday and Sunday). The Schloss is 600m northwest of the train station along Carl Theodor Strasse.

Mannheim

📞 0621 / POP 309,800

Situated near the confluence of the Rhine and Neckar Rivers, industrial Mannheim isn't Germany at its prettiest, but it compensates with a big-city sense of fun, an energetic cultural scene and decent shopping.

Two important transportation firsts took place in Mannheim: Karl Drais created the world's first bicycle in 1817, and Karl Benz built the world's first production motorcar in 1885.

Sights & Activities

Barockschloss Mannheim   PALACE
(www.schloss-mannheim.de; cnr Bismarckstrasse & Breite Strasse) Mannheim's most famous sight is the mustard-yellow-and-red sandstone Schloss, Germany's largest baroque palace. Now occupied by the University of Mannheim, the 450m-long structure was built over the course of 40 years in the mid-1700s but was almost completely destroyed during WWII.

In the **Schloss Museum** (Ehrenhof; adult/student incl audioguide €6/3; 10am-5pm Tue-Sun), off the main courtyard, you can see the impressively rococo **Kabinettsbibliothek**, saved from wartime destruction thanks to having been stored off-site, and several go-for-baroque halls – each a feast of stucco, marble, porcelain and chandeliers – rebuilt after the war.

Across the courtyard stands the baroque **Schlosskirche** (⊙daily), built from 1720 to 1731 and rebuilt after the war. Mozart performed here in 1777. It belongs to the Alt-Katholiken (Old Catholics), a movement that split with Rome over papal infallibility in the 1870s and is now part of the Anglican Communion.

Jesuitenkirche   CHURCH
(A4, 2; ⊙9am-7pm) For over-the-top baroque, head to the lavishly gilded Jesuitenkirche, meticulously restored to its 18th-century glory, and check out the altar, the pulpit and the organ over the entrance (used for concerts).

Friedrichsplatz   PARK
Friedrichsplatz, five blocks northeast of the Hauptbahnhof, is an oasis of manicured lawns, lovely flower beds and art-nouveau fountains. Its centrepiece is the 60m-high **Wasserturm** (Water Tower), a bit of 19th-century civil architecture that has become one of the city's symbols. A handsome ensemble of red sandstone edifices, many with arcades, lines the perimeter.

Kunsthalle Museum   ART MUSEUM
(www.kunsthalle-mannheim.de; Friedrichsplatz 4; adult/concession/family €7/5/8; ⊙11am-6pm Tue & Thu-Sun to 8pm Wed) A vast repository of modern and contemporary art by masters such as Cézanne, Degas, Manet, Kandinsky and Rodin. The permanent collection is sometimes stored away to make space for blockbuster exhibitions.

Sleeping

Central Hotel   HOTEL $$
(📞12300; www.centralhotelmannheim.de; Kaiserring 26-28; s/d weekday €96/106, weekend €75/85; P☎) Offers snazzy modern design at reasonable prices. The 35 rooms are bright and modern, though singles can be small. For a cityscape panorama, ask for one of the three corner rooms. Situated two blocks north of the Hauptbahnhof.

ℹ NAVIGATING MANNHEIM

Mannheim is famous for its quirky – indeed, unique – chessboard street layout. The city centre, which measures 1.5km by 1.5km, is divided into four quadrants by two perpendicular, largely pedestrianised shopping streets, the north-south Breite Strasse and the east-west Planken. At their intersection is the grassy Paradeplatz, with a fountain in the middle.

The streets don't have names. Instead, each rectilinear city block has an alphanumeric designation. Starting at the Schloss, as you move north the letters go from A up to K for blocks west of Breite Strasse and from L to U for blocks east of it. The numbers rise from 1 to 7 as you move away – either east or west – from Breite Strasse. The result is addresses such as 'Q3, 16' or 'L14, 5' (the latter numeral specifies the building) that sound a bit like galactic sectors.

Maritim Parkhotel LUXURY HOTEL $$$
(☑158 80; www.maritim.de; Friedrichsplatz 2; d without breakfast €120-280; P✳@☞☎) Built in 1901 in the sumptuous style of the Renaissance, this 173-room hotel offers 1st-class elegance plus pool, sauna, steam bath, fitness gadgets and, often, live lobby music in the evenings. Faces Friedrichsplatz.

Arabella Pension HOTEL $
(☑230 50; www.pension-arabella-mannheim.de; M2, 12; s/d without breakfast from €28/46) Super-centrally situated just two blocks north of the Schloss, the Arabella has 18 bright, spacious rooms with shared bathrooms. Reception is closed Sunday afternoon – call ahead if you'll be arriving then.

✕ Eating

The attractive Marktplatz is flanked by cafes with alfresco seating.

TOP CHOICE Café Prag CAFE $
(E4, 17; cake €3.50; ☺10am-6.30pm Sun & Mon, 10am-10pm or later Tue-Sat) A one-time tailor's shop and cigar store, built in 1902, is now an arty cafe with Jugendstil woodwork, cranberry-red walls and a pre-war Central European feel. The jazz on the PA system is as smooth as the espresso and as sweet as the great rhubarb cake. Belgian-style croissants cost €3.

Gasthaus Zentrale RESTAURANT $
(N4, 15; mains €6.30-19.50; ☺9.30am-1am) Once a student dive, this dark, rustic pub rustles up decent salads, noodle dishes, pizza, steaks and schnitzel, and has a warm-weather terrace. Great-value daily specials (not available Sunday) cost €4.50 to €6.30. Situated three blocks east of Paradeplatz.

Taksim TURKISH $
(H3, 21; sweets & snacks €1-2; ☺8am-10am) There's often a snaking queue for the goodies at this authentic Turkish bakery, opened in 1979. Wait your turn for spinach-cheese *gözleme* (rolled pastry) made fresh in front of you, savoury *pides* (Turkish-style pizza) and sticky baklava (per kg €14.90).

Rewe City SUPERMARKET $
(Paradeplatz, south side; ☺7am-midnight Mon-Sat) For a picnic.

🔒 Shopping

Breite Strasse is lined with shops, but some of the city's most stylish shopping can be found along Kunststrasse and the parallel Planken. The areas east of Breite Strasse are more stylish than those to the west.

❶ Information

Tourist Office (☑293 8700; www.tourist-mannheim.de; Willy-Brandt-Platz 3; ☺9am-7pm Mon-Fri, 10am-1pm Sat) Just across the square from the Hauptbahnhof. Has information (but not tickets) for cultural events. An audioguide tour of the city costs €7.50 (plus €2.50 for a 2nd earbud).

❶ Getting There & Around

Mannheim is a major rail hub on the Hamburg-Basel line. Destinations include Frankfurt (€19 to €27, 37 to 70 minutes, several times hourly) and Freiburg (€24 to €47, 1½ hours, twice hourly). Frequent S-Bahn trains link the Hauptbahnhof with Heidelberg (€4.90, 19 minutes), making for an easy day trip.

Worms

☑06241 / POP 82,300

Worms (starts with a 'V' and rhymes with 'forms') has played a pivotal role at various moments in European history. In AD 413 it became capital of the legendary, if short-lived, Burgundian kingdom whose rise and fall was creatively chronicled in the 12th-century *Nibelungenlied*. Later hijacked by Wagner and the Nazis, the epic is featured in a local museum and the annual **Nibelungen-Festspiele** (www.nibelungenfestspiele.de) a two-week festival usually held sometime between late June and mid-August

After the Burgundians, just about every other tribe in the area had a go at ruling Worms, including the Huns, the Alemans and finally the Franks, and it was under the Frankish leader, Charlemagne, that the city flourished in the 9th century. The most impressive reminder of the city's medieval heyday is its majestic, late-Romanesque Dom. A Jewish community, renowned for the erudition of its rabbis, thrived here from the 10th century until the 1930s, earning Worms the moniker 'Little Jerusalem'.

◎ Sights

From the Hauptbahnhof, pedestrianised Wilhelm-Leuschner-Strasse leads 500m southeast to Lutherplatz, on the northwest edge of the half-oval-shaped Altstadt, where the impressive **Luther Memorial** honours the Protestant reformer. From there, it's 150m southeast to pedestrianised **Kämmererstrasse**, the old city's main commercial thoroughfare, and 300m south to the Dom.

Kaiserdom
CHURCH

(www.wormser-dom.de; ⊙9am-6pm Apr-Oct, 10am-5pm Nov-Mar, closed during Sun morning Mass) Worms' skyline, such as it is, is dominated by the four towers and two domes of the magnificent Kaiserdom (Dom St Peter und St Paul), built in the 11th and 12th centuries in the late-Romanesque style. Inside, the lofty dimensions impress as much as the lavish, canopied high altar (1742) in the east choir, designed by the baroque master Balthasar Neumann. In the south transept, a scale model shows the enormity of the original complex. Nearby stairs lead down to the stuffy crypt, which holds the stone sarcophagi of several members of the Salian dynasty of Holy Roman emperors.

See the website (in German) for details on concerts.

FREE Alte Synagoge
SYNAGOGUE

(Rashi Shul; Synagogenplatz, Judengasse; admission free; ⊙10am-12.30pm & 1.30-5pm Apr-Oct, 10am-noon & 2-4pm Nov-Mar, closed to visitors Sat morning) Worms' famous Old Synagogue, founded in 1034, was destroyed by the Nazis, but in 1961 it was reconstructed using, as much as possible, stones from the original. Inside, men are asked to cover their heads.

In the garden, stone steps lead down to an extraordinary, Romanesque-style Mikwe (ritual bath) built in the 1100s.

Jüdisches Museum
MUSEUM

(Raschi-Haus; Hintere Judengasse 6; adult/student €1.50/0.80; ⊙10am-12.30pm & 1.30-5pm Tue-Sun Apr-Oct, to 4.30pm Nov-Mar) A good place to start a visit to Worms' Jewish sites is the Jewish Museum, whose exhibits and a 10-minute film introduce the city's storied Jewish community. Signs are in English and German. Sells several informative and useful English booklets on Jewish Worms. Situated behind the Alte Synagoge.

Alter Jüdenfriedhof
CEMETERY

(Willy-Brandt-Ring 21; ⊙8am-dusk Sep-Jun, to 7 or 8pm Jul & Aug, closed Jewish holidays) Inaugurated in 1076, the Old Jewish Cemetery, also known as the Heiliger Sand ('sacred sand'), is one of the oldest Jewish burial grounds in Europe. It is situated 250m west of the Dom; turn left at the fountain roundabout on Andreasstrasse. Ring the bell of the keeper's house (to the left just inside the gate)

JEWISH WORMS

Starting in the 900s, Jewish life in Worms – known as Varmaiza in medieval Jewish texts – was centred on Judengasse, in the northeast corner of the Altstadt, 1km northeast of the Dom (on foot, take Kämmererstrasse). Today, that's where you'll find a medieval synagogue, a 12th-century ritual bath and Worms' Jewish museum.

Before 1933, 1100 Jews lived in the city. A Jewish community was re-established in the late 1990s and now numbers 140 souls, almost all of them from the former USSR.

For more information, go to www.worms.de, switch to English and click 'Jewish Worms'.

to purchase an excellent historical brochure (€2.50).

The most-revered gravestone is that of Rabbi Meir of Rothenburg (1215–93), a Talmudic commentator, still read today, who died in captivity after being imprisoned by King Rudolf of Habsburg for attempting to lead a group of persecuted Jews to Palestine (emigration would have cut the king's income from a special tax only Jews had to pay). It's on the left just after you enter, the left-hand gravestone of the two that are topped with large piles of pebbles (left by visitors as tokens of respect) and Western Wall–style prayer notes.

Nibelungen Museum
MUSEUM

(www.nibelungen-museum.de; Fischerpförtchen 10; adult/child €5.50/3.50; ⊙10am-5pm Tue-Fri, 10am-6pm Sat & Sun) The *Nibelungenlied* is the ultimate tale of love and hate, treasure and treachery, revenge and death, with a cast including dwarves, dragons and bloodthirsty *Überfrauen* (superwomen). Richard Wagner set it to music, Fritz Lang turned it into a masterful silent movie (in 1924) and the Nazis abused its mythology, seeing in Siegfried the quintessential German hero. The state-of-the-art Nibelungen Museum seeks to rescue the epic from the Nazi manipulations, bringing it to life in a surprisingly interesting multimedia exhibit.

Museum der Stadt Worms
MUSEUM

(City Museum; Weckerlingplatz 7; adult/student/ family €2/1/5, special exhibitions extra; ⊙10am-5pm Tue-Sun) Chronicles Worms' turbulent

DON'T MISS

FALCONS IN THE TOWER

Live **webcam feed** (10am-9pm) from a peregrine falcon nest in the Kaiserdom's northeast tower in Worms can be seen in the window of the shop nearest the tower. From the tourist office, cross the street – the screen is behind and to the left of the six stainless steel bike racks.

history. Highlights include Bronze Age women's jewellery and a superb collection of delicate Roman glass excavated from local graves. A section on the Middle Ages opened in 2011. Signs are in German. Situated two blocks south of the Dom, behind the youth hostel.

Sleeping

Hotel Kriemhilde HOTEL $
(911 50; www.hotel-kriemhilde.de; Hofgasse 2-4; s/d/tr €54/76/100;) Wake up to the peal of the Dom bells at this friendly, family-run inn. It faces the north side of the mighty cathedral, which can be glimpsed from some of the 18 rooms. The breakfast room is cosy, with a very German vibe.

DJH Hostel HOSTEL $
(257 80; www.jugendherberge.de; Dechaneigasse 1; dm/s/d €20/34/51; P) A 150-bed hostel in an unbeatable location facing the south side of the Dom. The well-kept rooms have two to six beds and private bathrooms. Has free parking out front.

Parkhotel Prinz Carl HOTEL $$
(3080; www.parkhotel-prinzcarl.de; Prinz-Carl-Anlage 10-14; s/d from €85/125; P) Housed in handsome barracks built – and built to last – during the reign of the last Kaiser, this place has 90 pastel rooms that are spacious, comfortable and businesslike. Situated on the northern edge of town, 500m north – through a chestnut-shaded park – from the Hauptbahnhof.

Eating

Local culinary options have changed quite a bit since the Diet of Worms in 1521. A cluster of Italian restaurants can be found a block southeast of the Dom at the corner of Gerberstrasse and Wollstrasse. Cheap eats are available up towards the Hauptbahnhof, along pedestrianised Wilhelm-Leuschner-Strasse.

Trattoria-Pizzeria Pepe e Sale ITALIAN $
(258 36; Wollstrasse 12; pizzas €3-8.50; 11am-11.30pm;) Serves 201 kinds of delicious pizza, as well as pasta (including Spaghetti Robinson, made with tuna and garlic), in a homey, Mediterranean ambience. Excellent value.

Café TE INTERNATIONAL $
(Bahnhofstrasse 5; mains €4-13.50; 8am-1am Mon-Thu, 8am-2am Fri & Sat, 9am-1am Sun;) Just south of the Hauptbahnhof, this place – 'TE' stands for 'Trans Europa' – is chic in an Italian sort of way. Popular with students, it features pizza, pasta, meat mains, salads, veggie dishes, 14 breakfast options and a different special each night. There's a non-smoking room upstairs.

Nah und Gut SUPERMARKET $
(Kämmerer Strasse 22; 8.30am-6.30pm Mon-Fri, 8.30am-4pm Sat) Self-catering in the city centre. The entrance is 20m around the corner.

Information

Internet & Telefonhaus (Siegfriedstrasse 31; per hr €1; 9.30am-11.30pm) Internet across the street from the train station.
Tourist Office (250 45; www.worms.de; Neumarkt 14; 9am-6pm Mon-Fri, 10am-2pm Sat, Sun & holidays Apr-Oct, 9am-5pm Mon-Fri Nov-Mar) Has excellent brochures in English. Sells local-events tickets.

Getting There & Around

Worms, about 75km southwest of Frankfurt, has frequent train connections with Frankfurt (from €12.20, 1¼ hours), Mainz (€13.50, 26 to 44 minutes), Darmstadt (from €12, one hour) and Deidesheim (€8.70). Going to Speyer (€8.70) requires a change in Ludwigshafen.

Bicycles can be rented at **Radhaus-Mihm** (242 08; Von Steubenstrasse 8; 5-speed per day/weekend €5/7.50; 9.30am-12.30pm & 1.30-6pm Mon-Fri, 10am-1pm Sat, shorter hrs in winter), under the tracks from the Hauptbahnhof. The tourist office sells cycling maps.

Lorsch

Founded in about AD 760 and Unesco-listed in 1991, Lorsch Abbey (Kloster Lorsch; www.kloster-lorsch.de; Nibelungenstrasse 35, Lorsch; adult/student/family €5/3/12; 10am-5pm Tue-Sun) was an important religious site in its Carolingian heyday (8th to 10th centuries). A handful of medieval buildings have been preserved; the rare, Carolingian-era Königshalle and the Altenmünster are the most accessible. The complex – which, alas, is not all that interesting – has three museum sections, on the history of the abbey, on life in Hesse, and on tobacco, which was cultivated in Lorsch in the late 17th century.

By car, Lorsch is easily reached from Darmstadt along the A5 or the A67 south, or via the picturesque Bergstrasse (B3).

GERMAN WINE ROUTE

The **Deutsche Weinstrasse** (www.deutsche -weinstrasse.de), inaugurated in 1935, is a collection of roughly parallel rural roads, only sporadically signposted, that wend their way through the heart of the Palatinate (Pfalz) – a region of vine-covered hillsides, gentle forests, ruined castles, picturesque hamlets and welcoming wine estates. Starting in Bockenheim, about 15km west of Worms, it winds south – through Germany's largest contiguous winegrowing area – for 85km to Schweigen-Rechtenbach, on the French border (adjacent to the Alsatian town of Wissembourg). Especially pretty towns and villages include (from north to south) **Freinsheim**, **Kallstadt**, **Bad Dürkheim**, **Forst**, **Deidesheim**, **Meilkammer** and **Rhodt**. Hiking and cycling options are legion.

Blessed with a moderate climate that allows almonds, figs, kiwi fruit and even lemons to thrive, the German Wine Route is especially pretty during the spring bloom (March to mid-May). **Weinfeste** (wine festivals) run from March to mid-November (especially on the weekends). The grape harvest (September and October) is also an especially eventful time to visit.

In part because of its proximity to France, the Palatinate is a renowned culinary destination, with restaurants serving everything from gourmet German nouvelle cuisine to traditional regional specialities such as *Saumagen*. Tourist offices can supply lists of visitable wineries.

The **Pfälzerwald** (www.pfaelzerwald.de), the hilly forest that runs along the western edge of the Wine Road, was declared (along with France's adjacent Vosges du Nord area) a Unesco Biosphere Reserve in 1993. Locals often plan a day outdoors around dining in a rustic **Waldhütte** (year-round), a traditional rustic eatery found along forest trails such as the **Pfälzer Weinsteig**; tourist offices can supply maps to find them.

ⓘ Getting There & Away

The **Rhein-Haardtbahn** (RHB; www.rhein -haardtbahn.de) light rail line links Bad Dürkheim with Mannheim (€7.50, 50 minutes, at least hourly); the **RNV-Express** (www.rnv-online.de) goes all the way to Heidelberg's Hauptbahnhof and Bismarckplatz (€8.70, 1¼ hours). The trip from Speyer requires a change at Schifferstadt. Travel to/from Frankfurt (€19.80 to €31, 2½ hours) requires at least two connections.

ⓘ Getting Around

The German Wine Route is most easily explored by car or – thanks to a multitude of *Radwanderwege* (bike paths and cyclable back roads; www.radwanderland.de) such as the **Radweg Deutsche Weinstrasse** – bicycle. Area tourist offices sell various excellent cycling maps and have details of places that rent bicycles (www.fahrradverleih-pfalz.de).

Thanks to Germany's superb public transport system, however, it's possible to get almost everywhere – including *to* trail heads and *from* hike destinations – by public transport. Twice an hour, local trains that take bicycles (free except before 9am Monday to Friday) link Deidesheim and Bad Dürkheim with each other (€2.30, seven minutes) and head – parallel to the variants of the German Wine Route – south to Landau (and beyond, including the French town of Wissembourg) and north to Grünstadt. Tourist offices have schedules and can suggest routes.

Deidesheim

☏06326 / POP 3700

Awash in wisteria, diminutive Deidesheim is one of the German Wine Route's most picturesque – and upscale – villages. Perfect for a romantic getaway, it offers plenty of opportunities for wine tasting, relaxed strolling and excellent dining.

◉ Sights

Marktplatz   SQUARE

Deidesheim is centred on the historic Marktplatz, where you'll find a late Gothic church, **Pfarrkirche St Ulrich** (⊘daily), built from 1440 to 1480, and the 16th-century **Altes Rathaus**, noted for the canopied outdoor staircase. Inside is the three-storey **Museum für Weinkultur** (Museum of Wine Culture; Marktplatz 8; admission free; ⊘4-6pm Wed-Sun & holidays), featuring displays on winemakers' traditional lifestyle and naive-art portrayals of the German Wine Route (English brochure available).

FREE **Deutsches Film-und Fototechnik Museum** MUSEUM
(www.dftm.de; Weinstrasse 33; ☉2-6pm Wed-Sun & holidays Mar-Dec) Down an alleyway across from the Rathaus, the German Film & Photography Museum has an impressive collection of historic photographic and movie-making equipment. Veteran shutterbugs may be able to spot every film camera they've ever used.

Geissbockbrunnen FOUNTAIN
(Bahnhofstrasse) Near the tourist office, the whimsical 'Goat Fountain' (1985), celebrates a quirky local tradition. For seven centuries, the nearby town of Lambrecht has had to pay an annual tribute of one goat for using pastureland belonging to Deidesheim. The presentation of this goat, which is auctioned off to raise funds for local cultural activities, culminates in the raucous **Geissbockfest** (Goat Festival), held on Pentecost Tuesday.

Erlebnisgarten PARK
(off Bahnhofstrasse; ☉11am-6pm Wed-Sun & holidays) Kids will love the 'experience garden', a public park with 20 creative installations.

Jüdischer Friedhof CEMETERY
(Platanenweg) Established in 1712, Deidesheim's tiny Jewish cemetery is five blocks west of the Marktplatz, just north of the much larger Christian cemetery.

 Activities

Deidesheim is home to 16 **winemakers** (some closed Sun) that welcome visitors – look for signs reading *Weingut* (winery), *Verkauf* (sale) and *Weinprobe* (wine tasting) and ring the bell. Many can be found along the small streets west of Pfarrkirche St Ulrich.

Galleries and artisans' studios (eg jewellery makers and potters) can be visited along the **Kunst und Kultur** (Art and Culture) Circuit; look for dark-blue-on-yellow 'K' signs.

The tourist office has maps for several signposted **walking routes** through vineyards and the Pfälzerwald.

FESTIVAL
Deidesheim is famed for its **Weihnachtsmarkt** (Christmas market), the region's largest, held on the four weekends (Friday evening, Saturday and Sunday) before Christmas.

Sleeping & Eating

Culinary capital of the Palatinate, Deidesheim is one of only nine German towns that have earned membership in the Cittaslow ('slow city'; www.cittaslow.org) movement, inspired by the Slow Food movement.

TOP CHOICE **Deidesheimer Hof** LUXURY HOTEL $$$
(☏968 70; www.deidesheimerhof.de; Am Marktplatz; s/d from €110/155; P❄@☎) This renowned hostelry has 28 supremely elegant rooms, each unique, and two fine restaurants: **St Urban** (mains cost €14.80 to €23.90), whose regional offerings include *Saumagen*, made with chestnuts in autumn; and, in the basement, the gourmet **Schwarzer Hahn** (mains cost €40 to €50; open 6.30pm to 9pm Tuesday to Saturday), which specialises in creative French- and Palatinate-style *haute cuisine* prepared with a Japanese touch. Check out the photos of kings and presidents who have dined here.

Ketschauer Hof BOUTIQUE HOTEL $$$
(☏70000; www.ketschauerhof.com; Ketschauerhofstrasse 1; d €200-780, breakfast €25; ❄☎) A one-time winemaker's mansion has been turned into a supremely romantic boutique hotel that mixes traditional luxury with elegant modern styling. Has 18 rooms and a gourmet restaurant. Reserve well ahead for Friday and Saturday.

Gästehaus Ritter von Böhl GUESTHOUSE $$
(☏972 201; www.ritter-von-boehl.de; Weinstrasse 35; s €49, d €75-89; ☉reception 8am-6pm; P) Set around a wisteria-wrapped courtyard, this guesthouse belongs to, and occupies part of the grounds of, a charity hospital (now an old-age home) founded in 1494. It has 22 rooms with pastel walls and parquet floors and a bright breakfast atrium.

Turmstüb'l GERMAN $$
(☏981 081; www.turmstuebel.de; Turmstrasse 3; mains €8.60-16.80; ☉6pm-midnight Tue-Sat, noon-11pm Sun & holidays) This artsy wine cafe, down an alley opposite the church, serves tasty regional specialities such as *Saumagen* (€12.60) and over a dozen wines by the glass (€3.20 to €5.40). Excellent value.

Gasthaus zur Kanne GERMAN $$$
(☏966 00; www.gasthauszurkanne.de; Weinstrasse 31; mains €19-27; ☉noon-2pm & 6-10pm Wed-Sun) Serves fresh, refined regional cuisine, with a menu that changes daily. Three-/four-/five-course menus cost €44/50/64.

ℹ️ Information

Tourist Office (📞967 70; www.deidesheim. de; Bahnhofstrasse 5; ⏰9am-noon & 2-5pm Mon-Fri Nov-Jul, 9am-12.30pm & 1.30-5pm Mon-Thu, to 6pm Fri Aug-Oct, 9am-12.30pm Sat Apr-Oct) Very helpful, with useful English brochures. Situated 150m across the car park from the Bahnhof.

ℹ️ Getting Around

Owned by Olympic cycling champion Stefan Steinweg, **Gepäckservice Pfalz** (📞982 284; www .gsp1.de; Kirschgartenstrasse 49; ⏰daily Apr-Oct), 500m southwest of the tourist office, rents bikes (€10 per day) and arranges cycling tours.

Bad Dürkheim

📞06322 / POP 18,800

Adorned with plenty of splashy fountains, the attractive spa town of Bad Dürkheim is famous for its salty thermal springs and lovely parks – and for the annual **Dürkheimer Wurstmarkt** ('sausage market'; www. duerkheimer-wurstmarkt.de; ⏰2nd & 3rd weekends in Sep), which bills itself as the world's largest wine festival. Much of the action takes place around the **Dürkheimer Riesenfass,** a gargantuan wine cask that's had a restaurant inside since a master cooper built it out of 200 pine trees in 1934.

◎ Sights & Activities

Shops line the perimeters of two town-centre squares, the Stadtplatz and the Obermarkt. The **Kaiser-Konrad-Radweg** bike path to Speyer starts here too.

Kurpark   PARK
Between the Hauptbahnhof and the tourist office lies the grassy Kurpark, an azalea- and wisteria-filled public garden where you'll find the tiny **Isenach River**, its banks recently re-landscaped; a **children's playground**, in the corner nearest the Hauptbahnhof; and most of the town's spa and wellness facilities. In the lobby of the modern **Kurzentrum** (spa centre; 📞9640; www.kurzentrum-bad-duerkheim. de; Kurbrunnenstrasse 14; ⏰9am-8pm Mon-Fri, 9am-5pm Sat, 9am-2.30pm Sun, closed holidays), warm spring water flows from a fountain; for a free taste – it's said to be good for your digestion – ask at reception for a conical cup.

Salinarium   SWIMMING POOL
(www.salinarium.de; pools adult/child over 6yr €5.95/3.25, saunas €12.30/9.70; ⏰9am-8.30pm, to 6pm Mon, to 10.30pm Fri) The city-run Salinarium is a year-round complex of outdoor (April to September) and indoor swimming pools (only one of which is saltwater) that includes a 100m-long spiral water slide, whirlpools, a children's pool and seven saunas. Great for kids. Lockers require a €1 deposit. Situated a few hundred metres northeast of the tourist office.

Vineyard Trails   HIKING
Walking options are legion and include **Weinwanderwege** (vineyard trails) from St Michaelskapelle, a chapel atop a little vine-clad hill northeast of the tourist office, to Honigsäckel and the Hochmess vineyards (a 6km circuit); and **forest trails** to two historic ruins, **Limburg** and **Hardenburg** (4km west of town). The tourist office has maps.

🛏️ Sleeping & Eating

Bad Dürkheim has a good selection of reasonably priced hotels. Restaurants with warm-season terraces can be found on Römerplatz and along nearby Kurgartenstrasse.

Hotel Weingarten   PENSION $$
(📞940 10; www.hotelweingarten.de; Triftweg 11a-13; s/d from €69.80/96; 🅿🄰) Welcoming and very aptly named, the 'wine garden' has 18 lovingly cared-for rooms, most with balconies. Reception closes at 2pm on Sunday – call ahead if you'll be arriving after that. The same family runs a winery next door. Situated 1km northeast of the Bahnhof along Manheimerstrasse.

Kurparkhotel   HOTEL $$$
(📞7970; www.kurpark-hotel.de; Schlossplatz 1-4; s/d from €128/164; 🅿🄰🄰🄰) Occupying a yellow, neoclassical building on the edge of the Kurpark, this casino-affiliated hotel has 113 spacious, well-lit and very attractive rooms, many with balconies affording lovely views of the Kurpark's immaculate gardens.

Marktschänke   HOTEL $
(📞952 60; www.marktschaenke-badduerkheim. de; d from €62, weekends Mar-Oct €84; 🄰) Seven simple rooms about 250m southwest of the Hauptbahnhof, off the Obermarkt.

ℹ️ Information

Billard Café Valentino (Weinstrasse Sud 16; per hr €2; ⏰2pm-1 or 2am) A pool hall and sports bar with internet access. One block up the hill (southeast) of the Obermarkt.

Tourist Office (📞935 140; www.bad -duerkheim.com; ⏰9am-5 or 6pm Mon-Fri year-round, 10am-2.30pm Sat, Sun & holidays

THE RHINE

The Rhine River meanders for a total of 1390km, rising in the Swiss Alps and emptying into the North Sea at Rotterdam.

May-Oct) In the Kurzentrum building. Has a useful walking-tour map in English.

ⓘ Getting Around

Fahrradverleih im Salinencafe (⌐0800-228 8440, 947 2373; www.fahrradverleih-pfalz.de; Salinenstrasse 17; ⊘mid-May–Oct) Bike rental 600m northeast of the train station.

THE ROMANTIC RHINE VALLEY

Between Rüdesheim and Koblenz, the Rhine cuts deeply through the Rhenish slate mountains, meandering between hillside castles and steep fields of wine to create a magical mixture of beauty and legend. This is Germany's landscape at its most dramatic – muscular forested hillsides alternate with craggy cliffs and nearly-vertical terraced vineyards. Idyllic villages appear around each bend, their neat half-timbered houses and Gothic church steeples seemingly plucked from the world of fairy tales.

High above the river, busy with barge traffic, and the rail lines that run along each bank are the famous medieval castles, some ruined, some restored, all mysterious and vestiges of a time that was anything but tranquil. Most were built by a mafia of local robber barons – knights, princes and even bishops – who extorted tolls from merchant ships by blocking their passage with iron chains. Time and French troops under Louis XIV laid waste to many of the castles but several were restored in the 19th century, when Prussian kings, German poets and British painters discovered the gorge's timeless beauty. Today, some have been reincarnated as hotels and, in the case of Burg Stahleck, as a hostel.

In 2002 Unesco designated these 67km of riverscape, more prosaically known as the **Oberes Mittelrheintal** (Upper Middle Rhine Valley; www.welterbe-mittelrheintal.de), as a World Heritage Site. The *World Heritage Atlas* (published 2011), a 220-page book

available at tourist offices for a bargain €2, has reams of information on everything between the river's Kilometre 526 (Rüdesheim and Bingen) and Kilometre 593 (Koblenz).

One of Germany's most popular tourist destinations, the area is often deluged with visitors, especially in summer and early autumn, but it all but shuts down in winter. Hotel prices are highest on weekends from May to mid-October but are still remarkably reasonable.

🏃 Activities

Cycling

The **Rhein-Radweg** (Rhine Cycle Route; www.rheinradweg.eu) stretches for 1230km from Switzerland to Rotterdam. Between Bingen and Koblenz it runs along the left (more-or-less west) bank, as well as on a growing number of sections of the right bank, and links up with two other long-distance bike paths: the **Nahe-Hunsrück-Mosel-Radweg** (www.naheland-radtouren.de) which follows the Nahe River from Bingen southwest through the Eifel; and the 311km **Mosel-Radweg** (www.mosel-radweg.de) which runs along the banks of the Moselle River from Koblenz to Traben-Trarbach, Bernkastel-Kues, Trier and beyond.

Bicycles can be taken on regional trains, car ferries and river ferries, making it possible to ride one way (eg down the valley) and take public transport the other way.

Hiking

The Rhine Valley is great hiking territory. Almost every village has hiking options – tourist offices can supply suggestions and maps. A one-way hike can be turned into a circuit by mixing walking with ferries, trains and buses.

Two challenging but achingly beautiful long-distance hiking trails run along the Bamberg, with variants continuing downriver to Bonn and upriver to Mainz and beyond:

RheinBurgenWeg HIKING
(www.rheinburgenweg.com) Mainly on the left bank. Passes by some 40 castles.

Rheinsteig HIKING
(www.rheinsteig.de) On the right bank, linking Wiesbaden with Bonn (320km). Some say the prettiest section of this challengingly hilly trail is between Rüdesheim and Loreley.

Romantic Rhine Valley

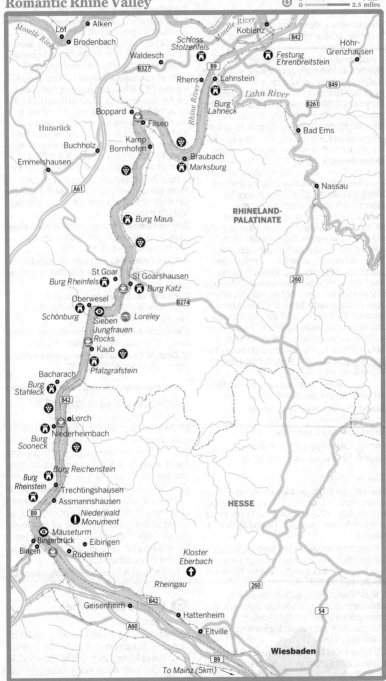

0   5 km
0   2.5 miles

Moselle River

Löf
Alken
Brodenbach

Koblenz
B42

Moselle River

Schloss
Stolzenfels

Festung
Ehrenbreitstein

Höhr-
Grenzhausen

Waldesch
B327
B9

Rhens
Lahnstein

Lahn River
B261

Rhine River
Burg
Lahneck

B49

Boppard
Filsen

Bad Ems

Hunsrück

Kamp
Bornhofen

Buchholz

Braubach
Marksburg

Emmelshausen

Nassau

A61

RHINELAND-
PALATINATE

Burg Maus

260

St Goar
Burg Rheinfels

St Goarshausen
Burg Katz

Oberwesel

B274

Schönburg

Loreley

Sieben
Jungfrauen
Rocks

Kaub

Bacharach

Pfalzgrafstein

Burg
Stahleck

B42

Lorch

Niederheimbach

Burg
Sooneck

Burg Reichenstein

Burg
Rheinstein

Trechtingshausen
Assmannshausen

HESSE

B9

Niederwald
Monument

Mäuseturm
Bingerbrück
Eibingen

Bingen
Rüdesheim

Kloster
Eberbach

Rheingau

260

Geisenheim
B42

Hattenheim

54

Eltville

Wiesbaden

A60

B9

To Mainz (5km)

ⓘ Getting Around

Boat

River travel is a relaxing and very romantic way to see the castles, vineyards and villages of the Romantic Rhine.

Because of fast currents, shallows, narrow channels and the many passing barges (the Rhine is still a hugely important trade artery), some more than 100m long, manoeuvering a passenger ferry is a very tricky business – and a fascinating one to see up close. Vessels zipping downriver have priority over those steaming slowly upriver.

From about Easter to October (winter services are very limited), passenger ships run by **Köln-Düsseldorfer** (KD; ☎0221-2088 318; www.k-d.com) link Rhine villages on a set timetable. You can travel to the next village or all the way from Mainz to Koblenz (€55.40, downstream/upstream 5½/8 hours). Within the segment you've paid for (for example, Boppard–Rüdesheim, which costs €26 return), you can get on and off as many times as you like, but make sure to ask for a free stopover ticket each time you disembark. Many rail passes (such as Eurail) get you a free ride on normal KD services, although you still need to register at the ticket counter. Children up to the age of four travel for free, while those up to age 13 are charged a flat fee of €6 regardless of distance. Students under 27 get a 50% discount, and seniors (over 60) get 30% off. Travel on your birthday, for you and one other person, is free. Return tickets usually cost only slightly more than one-way. To bring along a bicycle/dog, there's a supplement of €2.80/3.80.

Several smaller companies also send passenger boats up and down the river:

Bingen-Rüdesheimer (www.bingen -ruedesheimer.com)

Hebel Linie (www.hebel-linie.de)

Loreley Linie (www.loreley-linie.com)

Rössler Linie (www.roesslerlinie.de)

Bus & Train

Bus and train travel, perhaps combined with mini-cruises by boat and car ferry, are a convenient way to go village-hopping, get to a trailhead or return to your lodgings at the end of a hike or bike ride.

Villages on the Rhine's **left bank** (eg Bingen, Bacharach, Oberwesel and Boppard) are served hourly by local trains on the Koblenz–Mainz run, inaugurated in 1859.

Right-bank villages such as Rüdesheim, Assmannshausen, Kaub, St Goarshausen and Braubach are linked hourly to Koblenz' Hauptbahnhof and Wiesbaden by the RheingauLinie, operated by Vias.

It takes about 1½ hours to travel by train from Koblenz, along either riverbank, to either Mainz or Wiesbaden.

Car Ferry

Since there are no bridges over the Rhine between Koblenz and Mainz (though there are controversial plans to build one near St Goar, possibly endangering the area's Unesco World Heritage status), the only way to cross the river along this stretch is by *Autofähre* (car ferry).

Prices vary slightly but you can figure on paying about €3.50 per car, including the driver; €1 per car passenger; €1.50 per pedestrian (€0.70 for a child); and €2.20 for a bicycle, including the rider. This being well-organised Germany, the fare tables take into account the possibility, however remote, that you might want to bring along a horse or head of cattle (€3 or €4) or a horse-drawn cart (€4.50, including the driver).

The following services, listed from south to north, operate every 15 or 20 minutes during the day and every 30 minutes early in the morning and late at night:

Bingen-Rüdesheim (www.bingen-ruedesheimer .com/rheinfaehren; ⏱6 or 7am-9.45pm Nov-Apr, to midnight or later May-Oct)

Niederheimbach-Lorch (www.mittelrhein -faehre.de; ⏱6am-6.50pm Nov-Mar, to 7.50pm Apr-Oct)

Boppard-Filsen (www.faehre-boppard.de; ⏱6.30am-8pm Oct-Mar, to 9pm Apr, May & Sep, to 10pm Jun-Aug)

Oberwesel-Kaub (www.faehre-kaub.de; ⏱6 or 8am-6.50pm Oct-Mar, to 7.50pm Apr-Sep)

St Goar-St Goarshausen (www.faehre-loreley. de; ⏱5.30 or 6am-midnight)

Rüdesheim & Around

♫06722 / POP 10,000

Rüdesheim, part of the Rheingau wine region (famous for its superior rieslings), is deluged by some three million day-tripping coach tourists a year. Depending on how you look at it, the town centre – and especially its most famous feature, an alley know as Drosselgasse – is either a 'mass tourism nightmare from hell' or a lot of silly, kitschy, colourful fun. If you're looking for a souvenir thimble, this is definitely the place to come, but Rüdesheim also offers a variety of delightful vineyard walks.

Rüdesheim is famous for its **Weihnachtsmarkt** (Christmas market).

◉ Sights & Activities

Drosselgasse   ALLEY

Drosselgasse, a tunnel-like alley so overloaded with signs that it looks like it could be in Hong Kong (some of the signs are, in fact, in Chinese), is the Rhine at its most colourfully touristic – bad German pop wafts out of the pubs, which are filled with rollicking crowds. The Oberstrasse, at the top of Drosselgasse, is similarly overloaded with eateries and drinkeries, though to get away from the drunken madness all you have to do is wander a few blocks in any direction.

Siegfried's Mechanisches Musikkabinett
MUSEUM

(www.smmk.de; Oberstrasse 29; tour adult/student €6/3; ⊙10am-6pm Mar-Dec) Has a fun and often surprising collection of 18th- and 19th-century mechanical musical instruments that play themselves as you're shown around. Situated 50m to the left from the top of Drosselgasse.

Weinmuseum
MUSEUM

(www.rheingauer-weinmuseum.de; Rheinstrasse 2; adult/student incl audioguide €5/3; ⊙10am-6pm mid-Mar–Oct) The 1000-year-old Brömserburg castle now houses the Wine Museum, filled with wine-making and wine-drinking paraphernalia from Roman times onwards. The tower offers great river views. Situated near the Bingen car-ferry dock.

Assmannshausen
CIRCUIT WALKING

For a stunning river panorama, head up to the Niederwald Monument (erected 1877 to 1883, renovated 2012), a bombastic monument on the wine slopes west of town starring Germania and celebrating the Prussian victory in the Franco-Prussian War and the creation of the German Reich, both in 1871. You can walk up here via the Rüdesheimer Berg vineyards – signposted trails include one that begins at parking lot P2 (one short block above Oberstrasse) – but it's faster (you save 203 vertical metres) to glide above the vineyards aboard the 1400m-long Seilbahn (Kabinenbahn; www.seilbahn-ruedesheim. de; Oberstrasse 30; adult/5-13yr one-way €4.50/2, return €6.50/3; ⊙late Mar–11 Nov & late Nov–23 Dec) cable car.

From the monument, a network of trails leads to destinations such as the Jagdschloss (2km), a one-time hunting lodge that's now a hotel and restaurant; and, down the hill, the romantic ruin of Burg Ehrenfels (Ruine Ehrenfels).

A bit north of the Jagdschloss, you can catch a viewless trail (part of the Rheinsteig long-distance path) down to Assmannshausen, a sedate burg 5km downriver from Rüdesheim that's known for its *Spätbur-*

KLOSTER EBERBACH

If you saw the 1986 film *The Name of the Rose*, starring Sean Connery, you've already seen parts of this one-time Cistercian monastery (www.kloster-eberbach.de; adult/student incl audioguide €6.50/4.50; ⊙10am-6pm Apr-Oct, 11am-5pm Nov-Mar), in which many of the interior scenes were shot. Dating from as far back as the 12th century and once home to 150 or more monks and perhaps 400 lay brothers, this graceful complex – in an idyllic little valley – went through periods as a lunatic asylum, jail, sheep pen and accommodation for WWII refugees. Today visitors can explore the 13th- and 14th-century Kreuzgang (cloister), the monks' baroque refectory and their vaulted Gothic Monchdormitorium (dormitory), as well as the austere Romanesque Klosterkirche (basilica).

At the Vinothek (www.weingut-kloster-eberbach.de) you can taste and buy the superb wines produced by the government-owned Hessische Staatsweingüter (Hessian State Winery).

Kloster Eberbach is about 20km northeast of (ie towards Wiesbaden from) Rüdesheim.

gunder (Pinot noir) red wines. Or you can head down to Assmannshausen on the Sesselbahn (Sessellift; adult/child incl the Seilbahn €6.50/3) and return to Rüdesheim on foot (via hillside vineyards and Burg Ehrenfels), by train or by passenger ferry. A round-trip Ring-Ticket (adult/child €11/5.50) includes the Seilbahn, the Sesselbahn and the ferry, and even lets you stop across the river in Bingen.

ⓘ Information

Tourist Office (☑906 150; www.ruedesheim. de; Rheinstrasse 29a; ⊙8.30am-6.30pm Mon-Fri & 10am-4pm Sat, Sun & holidays Apr-Oct, 11am-4.30pm Mon-Fri Nov-Mar) At the eastern edge of the town centre.

ⓘ Getting There & Away

Rüdesheim is connected to Bingen by passenger and car ferries.

Bingen

📞06721 / POP 24,600

Thanks to its strategic location at the confluence of the Nahe and Rhine Rivers, Bingen has been coveted by warriors and merchants since its founding by the Romans in 11 BC. These days it's an attractive, flowery town that's less touristy – and less cute – than its smaller neighbours.

Bingen was the birthplace of the writer Stefan George (1868–1933) and the adopted home of Hildegard von Bingen.

⊙ Sights

The area between the train tracks and the Rhine has been turned into a delightful **riverside promenade,** with lawns, flower beds, a children's playground, a beer garden and a stylish wine bar. The monumental statue on the wine slopes across the Rhine portrays a triumphant **Germania.**

Museum am Strom   MUSEUM
(Museumsstrasse 3; adult/concession/family €3/2/6; ⊙10am-5pm Tue-Sun) On the riverside promenade, this museum – in a one-time power station – has worthwhile exhibits on Rhine romanticism, both engraved and painted, and on the life and achievements of Hildegard von Bingen. Another highlight is a set of surgical instruments – from scalpels and cupping glasses to saws – left behind by a Roman doctor in the 2nd century AD.

Mäuseturm   CASTLE
(⊙closed to the public) The Mouse Tower, on an island near the confluence of the Nahe and Rhine, is where – according to legend – Hatto II, the 10th-century archbishop of Mainz, was devoured alive by mice as punishment for his oppressive rule. In fact, the name is probably a mutation of *Mautturm* (toll tower), which reflects the building's medieval function.

🛏 Sleeping

Hotel-Café Köppel   HOTEL $
(📞147 70; www.hotel-koeppel.de; Kapuzinerstrasse 12; s/d from €48/78; 🛜) In the heart of town across from the Kapuzinerkirche, this place is above a stylish *Konditorei* (cake cafe) whose products will make your eyes go wide. The 22 rooms are quiet, modern and attractive, decorated in calming, lighter hues. The hotel entrance is around the side.

DJH Hostel   HOTEL $
(📞06721-321 63; www.jugendherberge.de; Herterstrasse 51; dm/d €21.50/54) A modern hostel with 121 beds in rooms for one to four. Situated 10 minutes on foot from the Hauptbahnhof.

ℹ Information

Tourist Office (📞184 205; www.bingen.de; Rheinkai 21; ⊙9am-6pm Mon-Fri, 9am-5pm Sat Easter-Oct, 10am-1pm Sun May-Oct, 9am-4pm Tue-Thu, to 6pm Mon, to 1pm Fri Nov-Easter) Facing the Rhine 250m west of the Bahnhof Bingen Stadt train station. Has brochures and

---

HILDEGARD VON BINGEN

She's hip and holistic, a composer, a dramatist and a courageous campaigner for the rights of women. She heals with crystals and herbs, her music frequently hits the New Age charts...and she's been dead for more than 800 years.

Hildegard von Bingen (1098–1179) was born in Bermersheim (near Worms), the 10th child of a well-off and influential family. At the age of three, she experienced the first of the visions that would occur over the course of her extraordinary – and extraordinarily long – life. As a young girl, she entered the convent at Disibodenberg on the Nahe River and eventually became an abbess, founding two abbeys of her own. During her preaching tours – an unprecedented activity for a woman in medieval times – she lectured both to the clergy and the common people, attacking social injustice and ungodliness.

Pope Eugene III publicly endorsed Hildegard, urging her to write down both her theology and her visionary experiences. This she did in a remarkable series of books that encompass ideas as diverse as cosmology, natural history and female orgasm. Her overarching philosophy was that humankind is a distillation of divinity and should comport itself accordingly. Her accomplishments are even more remarkable considering her lifelong struggle against feelings of worthlessness and the physical effects of her mysterious visions, which often left her near death.

maps for hikers and cyclists, helps find accommodation and sells events tickets.

ℹ Getting There & Away

Bingen has two train stations: the Hauptbahnhof, just west of the Nahe in Bingerbrück; and the more central Bahnhof Bingen Stadt, just east of the town centre.

Passenger ferries to Rüdesheim leave from the town centre's riverfront promenade; car ferries dock about 1km upriver (east) from the centre.

Burg Rheinstein

In the 1820s privately-owned Burg Rheinstein (www.burg-rheinstein.de; adult/5-13yr €4.50/3; ⏰9.30am-6pm mid-Mar–Oct, 10am-5pm Sat & Sun mid-Nov–mid-Mar) became the first Rhine castle to be converted – by Prussian royalty (a branch of the Hohenzollerns) – into a romantic summer residence complete with turrets and battlements. Today, the mostly neo-Gothic interior is furnished more-or-less as it was over a century ago. Highlights include a tiny chapel, the Rittersaal (knights' hall) and 14th- to 19th-century stained-glass windows brought from churches in Cologne and Düsseldorf. Entry fees help fund upkeep. Has two apartments for rent (minimum stay two nights).

The castle, 90 vertical metres above the river, is 6km downriver from Bingen. A short switchback path leads up the slope from a row of parking places along the B9.

Burg Reichenstein

Looming above the village of Trechtingshausen is the mighty Burg Reichenstein (☎06721-6117; www.burg-reichenstein.de; adult/under 12yr €4.50/; ⏰10am-6pm Tue-Sun Mar–mid-Nov, call for winter hours), which harbours a lavish collection of furnishings, armour, hunting trophies and even cast-iron oven slabs. Has rooms for rent (doubles cost €94 to €153). Situated 8km downriver from Bingen.

Bacharach

☎06743 / POP 2250
One of the prettiest of the Rhine villages, tiny Bacharach – 24km downriver from Bingen – conceals its considerable charms behind a 14th-century wall. From the B9, go through one of the thick arched gateways under the train tracks and you'll find yourself in a medieval old town graced with half-timbered mansions such as the Altes Haus, the Posthof and the off-kilter Alte Münze – all are along Oberstrasse, the main street, which runs parallel to the Rhine, and all now house places to eat, drink and be merry.

⊙ Sights & Activities

Peterskirche   CHURCH
(Oberstrasse; ⏰10am-5 or 6pm Apr-Oct) This late Romanesque-style Protestant church has some columns with vivid capitals – look for the naked woman with snakes sucking her breasts (a warning about the consequences of adultery), at the altar end of the left aisle.

Stadtmauer Rundweg   WALKING
The best way to get a sense of the village and its hillside surrounds is to take a stroll on top of the walls – it's possible to walk almost all the way around the centre. The lookout tower on the upper section of the wall affords panoramic views. The filigreed ruins of the Gothic Wernerkapelle were built between 1289 and 1430; the 12th-century Burg Stahleck is now a hostel.

🛏 Sleeping

TOP CHOICE Rhein Hotel   HOTEL $$
(☎1243; www.rhein-hotel-bacharach.de; Langstrasse 50; s €39-65, d €78-130; ❄🖥) Right on the town's medieval ramparts, this very welcoming, family-run hotel has 14 well-lit rooms with original artwork and compact bathrooms. Those facing the river, and thus the train tracks, have double double-glazing. Guests can borrow bikes for no charge.

DJH Burg Stahleck   HOSTEL $$
(☎1266; www.jugendherberge.de; Burg Stahleck; dm/d €20.50/52) In a dream setting inside a hillside medieval castle, Burg Stahleck, this hostel has 168 beds in rooms for one to six people, almost all with private bathrooms. To get there, walk along the town walls or drive up Blücherstrasse for 1km.

🍴 Eating & Drinking

Eateries can be found along Oberstrasse.

Stübers Restaurant   GERMAN $$
(☎1243; Langstrasse 50; mains €9.50-24.50; ⏰11.30am-2.15pm & 5.30-9.15pm except Tuesday; 🖥) Specialises in regional dishes such as Rieslingbraten (riesling-marinated braised beef); a four-course vegan menu costs €27. The chef is happy to pack you a delicious picnic lunch (€19 for two). Situated in the Rhein Hotel.

Nahkauf GROCERY $
(Koblenzerstrasse 2; ⊙8am-12.30pm & 2-6pm Mon
-Fri, 8am-12.30pm Sat) About 150m north along
Oberstrasse from the church.

Zum Grünen Baum WINE BAR
(Oberstrasse 63; snacks & light meals €2.90-9.80;
⊙noon-11pm except Thu) An unpretentious
wine tavern serving some of Bacharach's
best whites, 18 of them by the glass (€2.90-
4.10). Order the *Weinkarussel* (€19.50) and
you can sample 15 of them!

 Information

There's an ATM on Oberstrasse facing the
church.
Tourist Office (☑919 303; www.rhein-nahe
-touristik.de; Oberstrasse 45; ⊙9am-5pm Mon-
Fri, 10am-3pm Sat, Sun & holidays Apr-Oct,
9am-1pm Mon-Fri Nov-Mar) Has handy information about the entire area, including day hikes
through the vineyards. May move to a site near
the train station in 2013.

Kaub

Across the river from Bacharach and about
8km upriver from Loreley, near the village
of Kaub, stands the fairly-tale **Pfalzgrafstein** (www.burg-pfalzgrafenstein.de; adult/under
18yr/family €3/1.50/6; ⊙10am-6pm Tue-Sun Apr-
Oct, to 5pm Mar, 10am-5pm Sat & Sun Nov, Jan
& Feb, closed Dec), a boat-shaped toll castle
perched on a narrow island – perfect for
picnics – in the middle of the Rhine. To get
out to there, hop on a **Fährboot** (ferry boat;
adult/4-11yr/family €2.50/1/6) next to the Kaub
car ferry dock; there are departures every
half-hour.

Oberwesel

☑06744 / POP 3300
Oberwesel is known for its 3km-long medieval **town wall**, sporting the remains of
16 guard towers, that wraps around much
of the picturesque Altstadt; a path lets you
walk along the top of most of it. The old
town is separated from the river by the rail
line laid way back in 1857.

⊙ Sights

Churches CHURCH
Easily spotted on a hillside at the northern
end of town is the 14th-century **St-Martins-
Kirche**, popularly known as the 'white
church', which has painted ceilings, a richly

sculpted main altar and a tower that once
formed part of the town's defences. In the
southern Altstadt, the High Gothic **Liebfrauenkirche**, known as the 'red church' for
the colour of its facade, is older by about 100
years and boasts an impressive gilded altar.

Oberwesel Kulturhaus MUSEUM
(www.kulturhaus-oberwesel.de; Rathausstrasse 23;
adult/child/student €3/1/2; ⊙10am-5pm Tue-Fri,
2-5pm Sat, Sun & holidays Apr-Oct) Every April,
Oberwesel crowns not a *Weinkönigin* (wine
queen), as in most Rhine towns, but a *Wein-
hexe* (wine witch) – a good witch, of course
– who is said to protect the vineyards. Photos of all the *Weinhexen* crowned since 1946
are on display in the cellar of Oberwesel's
Kulturhaus, a cultural centre whose local
history exhibits feature 19th-century engravings of the Romantic Rhine, models of
Rhine riverboats and five films, one of them
about what happened when the Rhine froze
solid in 1963. An excellent English visitors'
guide is available at reception.

Schönburg CASTLE
High above the town's upriver edge is the
majestic Schönburg, saved from total ruin
when a New York real-estate millionaire
purchased it in 1885. It's now a hotel.

Legend has it that this was once the home
of seven beautiful but haughty sisters who
ridiculed and rejected all potential suitors
until all seven were turned into stone and
submerged in the Rhine. You may be able
to spot them from the **Siebenjungenfrau-
blick** (Seven Virgins Viewpoint), reached
via a lovely vineyard trail beginning at the
town's downriver edge.

🛏 Sleeping & Eating

There's a fancy hotel inside the **Schönberg**
(www.hotel-schoenburg.com; d €130-180). Places
to eat can be found around the Rathaus.

TOP CHOICE **Hotel Römerkrug** HOTEL $$
(☑7091; www.hotel-roemerkrug.rhinecastles.com;
Marktplatz 1; s/d €52.50/82.50, restaurant mains
€12.50-20; ⊙restaurant closed Wed & most of Nov
& Feb; 🐭) Facing the Rathaus in the prettiest
part of town, the half-timbered Römerkrug
is run by three generations of a friendly local
family. The 10 rooms, including three under
ancient roof beams, have an antique feel. At
the excellent **restaurant**, traditional Ger-
man specialities include trout.

DJH Hostel HOSTEL **$**
(☑933 30; www.jugendherberge.de; dm/d from
€21.50/54) This modern, 206-bed place has
commanding views from its perch up near
the Schönburg.

Nah und Gut SUPERMARKET
(Koblenzstrasse 1; ⊙8am-7pm Mon-Fri, 8am-2pm
Sat) Picnic supplies a block from the Rathaus.

ⓘ Information
Tourist Office (☑710 624; www.oberwesel.de;
Rathausstrasse 3; ⊙9am-1pm & 2-5pm Mon-
Fri year-round, to 2pm Fri Nov-Mar, also open
9am-1pm Sat Jun-Oct) Across the street from
the Rathaus.

ⓘ Getting Around
Bicycles can be rented from **Hans Höhn** (☑336;
Liebfrauenstrasse 38; per day €7.50-13; ⊙8am-
noon Mon-Sat, 2-6pm Mon & Fri), three blocks
south of the Rathaus.

Loreley & St Goarshausen
☑06771 / POP 1300
Loreley, the most fabled spot along the
Romantic Rhine, is an enormous, almost
vertical slab of slate that owes its fame to
a mythical maiden whose siren songs are
said to have lured sailors to their death in
the river's treacherous currents. Heinrich
Heine told the tale in his 1824 poem *Die
Lorelei*.

A **sculpture** of the blonde, buxom beauty
in question perches lasciviously below the
outcrop, at the very tip of a narrow breakwater jutting into the Rhine.

◎ Sights & Activities
Loreley Besucherzentrum VISITORS CENTRE
(☑599 093; www.loreley-besucherzentrum.de;
adult/student €2.50/1.50; ⊙10am-6pm Apr-Oct,
10am-5pm Mar, 11am-4pm Sat & Sun Nov-Feb) On
the edge of the agricultural plateau stretching away from the cliff, Loreley's Visitors
Centre takes an engaging, interactive look
at the region's geology, flora and fauna,
shipping and winemaking; the Loreley
myth; and early Rhine tourism (signs are
in English and German). It also screens an
18-minute 3-D film. The tourist office desk
sells hiking maps for the trails that pass by
here.

Loreleyspitze VIEWPOINT
A gravel path leads from the Loreley visitors centre through the forest to the tip of

the Loreley outcrop, where you suddenly
come upon a breathtaking panorma. About
190 vertical metres below, teeny-tiny trains
slither along both banks of the Rhine, while
miniature barges negotiate its turbulent
waters.

Burg Katz & Burg Maus CASTLES
On either side of the village of St Goarshausen stand two rival castles. Burg Peterseck was built by the archbishop of Trier
in an effort to counter the toll practices of
the powerful Katzenelnbogen family. In a
show of medieval muscle flexing, the latter
responded by building a much bigger castle
high on the other side of town, Burg Neu-
katzenelnbogen, which became known as
Burg Katz (Cat Castle; ⊙closed to the public)
for short. And so, to highlight the obvious
imbalance of power between the Katzenel-
nbogens and the archbishop, Burg Peterseck
was soon nicknamed **Burg Maus** (Mouse Castle; ⊙closed to the public).

ⓘ Getting Around
The Loreley outcrop can be reached:
By car – it's a 4km uphill drive from St Goars-
hausen; parking costs €2.
By shuttle bus – one-way from St Goars-
hausen's Marktplatz costs €2.65; runs hourly
from 10am to 5pm April to October.
On foot – the Treppenweg, a strenuous, 400-
step stairway, begins about 2km upriver from St
Goarshausen at the base of the breakwater.

St Goar
A car ferry connects St Goarshausen with
its twin across the river, St Goar, which is
lorded over by the sprawling ruins of **Burg
Rheinfels** (www.st-goar.de; adult/child €4/2;
⊙9am-6pm mid-Mar–early Nov, 11am-5pm Sat
& Sun in good weather early Nov–mid-Mar), once
the mightiest fortress on the Rhine. Built in
1245 by Count Dieter V of Katzenelnbogen
as a base for his toll-collecting operations,
its size and labyrinthine layout – guard towers, battlements, casemates, subterranean
galleries – are truly astonishing. The views
are stupendous. A brochure in English costs
€2. The last entry is one hour before closing.

Part of the castle complex is occupied by
the **Romantik Hotel Schloss Rheinfels**
(☑06741-8020; www.schloss-rheinfels.de; d €115-
265, cheaper in winter; @🔊≋) – great for a
honeymoon – with 64 rooms and suites that
range in size from a tiny 12 sq m to a palatial

CLASSIC, MODERN & TIMELESS

Faced with fickle fashion trends, few furniture styles retain their freshness and popularity for long. A rare exception is bentwood furniture, invented by a Boppard-born cabinet-maker named Michael Thonet (1796–1871).

Whether in modern-day Paris cafes or Toulouse-Lautrec paintings of Paris cafes, we've all seen Thonet's minimalist Chair Number 14 looking curvaceous, elegant and sturdy. The secret of this model – of which tens of millions have been produced – and all other bentwood pieces lies in a production process that involves stacking strips of veneer, soaking them in hot glue so they become pliable, and then drying them in the desired shape in metal moulds. Thonet began experimenting in his Boppard shop in about 1830, but it was the 1851 Great Exhibition in London's Crystal Palace that catapulted him and his Vienna-based firm, soon to be known as Gebrüder Thonet, into prominence.

Exquisite bentwood furniture produced by Thonet during the 19th century can be seen in Boppard in the Museum der Stadt Boppard (p442). **Gebrüder Thonet** (www. thonet.de) is now run by its founders' great-great-grandchildren.

38 sq m. All have antique-style furnishings and a luxurious feel; pricier pads come with a river view. The hotel has three fine restaurants: one rustic, one semi-formal and one gourmet.

St Goar is 10km upriver from Boppard and 28km downriver from Bingen. To get to the castle by car, head up the hill from the downstream edge of St Goar. On foot, it's a 20-minute walk.

Boppard

☑ 06742 / POP 15,750

Thanks to its scenic location on a horseshoe bend in the river – and the fact that the riverfront and historic centre are both on the same side of the train tracks – Boppard (pronounced bo-*part*) is one of the Romantic Rhine's prettiest and most enjoyable getaways. A gateway to lots of great hikes (eg in the Hunsrück), it's also a proper town, complete with a small cinema. Be sure to sample the excellent riesling from grapes grown near here in some of the Rhine's steepest vineyards.

◉ Sights

Marktplatz   SQUARE
(◷8am-1pm Fri, food market 8am-1pm Fri) Just off Boppard's main commercial street, the pedestrianised, east–west oriented **Oberstrasse**, is the ancient Marktplatz, whose modern fountain is a favourite local hangout. Still home to a weekly **food market**, it's dominated by the pointy twin towers of the late-Romanesque **Severuskirche** (◷8am-6pm) an elegant 13th-century Catholic church built on the site of Roman military baths. Inside are polychrome wall paintings,

a hanging cross from 1225 (in the choir) and spiderweb-like vaulted ceilings.

Teehäusje   HISTORIC BUILDING
(Untere Marktstrasse 10; ◷9.30am-6pm Mon-Fri, 10am-1pm Sat) The oldest and cutest of Boppard's half-timbered buildings, built in 1519, now houses a delightful tea shop with a tiny tearoom called Teehäusje. Situated half a block east of the church.

Museum der Stadt Boppard   MUSEUM
(Burgstrasse) In a 14th-century palace, the city museum has exhibits on local history and an entire floor dedicated to bentwood furniture. Undergoing renovations but set to reopen in early 2014.

Rheinallee   PROMENADE
A pedestrian promenade with a turn-of-the-20th-century vibe, lined with boat docks, neatly painted hotels and wine taverns, runs along the riverfront. There are grassy areas and a **children's playground** a bit upriver from the car-ferry dock.

FREE **Römer-Kastell**   ARCHAEOLOGY
(Roman Fort; cnr Angertstrasse & Kirchgasse; ◷24hr) A block south of the Marktplatz, the Roman Fort (also known as the Römerpark) has 55m of the original 4th-century Roman wall and graves from the Frankish era (7th century). A wall panel shows what the Roman town of Bodobrica looked like 1700 years ago.

🏃 Activities

Vierseenblick   HIKING
The peculiar geography of the Four-Lakes-View panoramic outlook creates the illu-

sion that you're looking at four separate lakes rather than a single river. The nearby **Gedeonseck** affords views of the Rhine's hairpin curve. To get up there you can either hike or – to save 240 vertical metres – take the 20-minute **Sesselbahn** (chairlift; www.sesselbahn-boppard.de; adult/child under 14yr return €7/4.50, up only €4.20/3, bicycle €1.50; ⏰10am-5 or 6pm Apr-Oct) over the vines from the upriver edge of town.

Klettersteig   HIKING

This 2½- to three-hour cliffside adventure hike begins at the upriver edge of town right next to the Sesselbahn (chairlift). Decent walking or climbing shoes are a must; optional climbing equipment can be rented at the Aral petrol station for €5 (plus €20 deposit). If you chicken out at the critical vertical bits, some of which involve ladders, less vertiginous alternatives are available – except at the *Kletterwand*, a hairy section with steel stakes underfoot. It's possible to walk back to town via the Vierseenblick.

Hunsrück Trails   HIKING

The dramatically steep **Hunsrückbahn** (adult/child one-way €2.65/1.50; ⏰10 minutes, rides depart hourly) travels through five rail tunnels and across two viaducts on its 8km journey from Boppard's Bahnhof to Buchholz. From there, many people hike back via the Mörderbachtal to Boppard, but Buchholz is also the starting point for an excellent 17km hike via the romantic Ehrbachklamm (Ehrbach gorge) to Brodenbach (on the Moselle), from where you can get back to Boppard by taking bus 301 (hourly) to Koblenz and then the train or bus 650 to Boppard.

Wine Tastings   WINE TASTING

(5 wines €7; ⏰8pm Thu Apr-Oct) Sessions organised by the tourist office are hosted each month by a different *Weingut* (winegrowing estate).

🛏 Sleeping & Eating

Cafes, restaurants and great-value hotels line the Rheinallee, Boppard's riverfront promenade along the Rhine.

⌈TOP⌉ Hotel Günther   HOTEL $$
   ⌊CHOICE⌋

(☑890 90; www.hotelguenther.de; Rheinallee 40; s/d from €72/82, cheaper Nov-Apr; ⏰closed most of Dec; @🐾) Watch boats and barges glide along the mighty Rhine from your balconied room at this bright, welcoming waterfront

hotel. It's owned by an American fellow and his German wife, which makes communication a cinch – and explains why the breakfast buffet includes peanut butter.

Hotel Bellevue   HOTEL $$

(☑1020; www.bellevue-boppard.de; Rheinallee 41; s/d from €96/142, cheaper Nov-Apr; P@🐾) This classy, Best Western–affiliated hotel, built with art-nouveau flair in 1910, has 94 highly civilised rooms, half with views of the Rhine.

Hotel Rebstock   HOTEL $

(☑4876; www.rheinhotel-rebstock.de; Rheinallee 31; s €35-52, d €63-85; ⏰closed Nov-Mar) On the Rhine facing the car-ferry landing, this family-run hotel has 10 bright, spacious rooms, many with river views and some with balconies. The **restaurant** (mains €10.90-18.90; ⏰noon-9pm Wed-Sun) serves delicious Rhenish and German dishes.

Severus Stube   GERMAN $$

(☑3218; www.severus-stube.de; Untere Marktstrasse 7; mains €6.30-14.90; ⏰11.30am-2pm & 5pm-midnight, closed Thu) Serves up tasty German food, reasonably priced, in a cosy, rustic dining room.

Penny Markt   SUPERMARKET $

(Oberstrasse 171; ⏰7am-9pm Mon-Sat) One of several food shops along Oberstrasse.

🍷 Drinking

Weinhaus Heilig Grab   WINE BAR $

(www.heiliggrab.de; Zelkesgasse 12; snacks €3.50-7; ⏰3-11pm or later Wed-Mon) Across the street from the Hauptbahnhof, Boppard's oldest wine tavern offers a cosy setting for sipping 'Holy Sepulchre' rieslings. When it's warm, you can sit outside under the chestnut trees. Also has snacks and five **rooms for rent** (d €59-79).

Weingut Felsenkeller   WINE BAR $

(www.felsenkeller-boppard.de; Mühltal 21; ⏰3-10pm or later Wed-Mon) Across the street from the Sesselbahn (chairlift) station and next to a little stream, this homely place serves its own and other local growers' wines (per glass €2.70 to 4.30) and light meals.

❶ Information

ATMs On the parking-permitted part of the Marktplatz, behind the tourist office.

Post Office (Heerstrasse 177; ⏰9am-noon & 2-5.30pm Mon-Fri, 9am-noon Sat) Facing the train station. Sells train tickets.

Tourist Office (☑3888; www.boppard
-tourismus.de; Marktplatz; ☺9am-6.30pm
Mon-Fri, 10am-2pm Sat May-Sep, 9am-5pm
Mon-Fri Oct-Apr) Inside the Altes Rathaus. Has
good English brochures and an internet computer, both free, and sells event tickets, as well
as walking and cycling maps. Lists of hotels
and cultural events and a town map are posted
outside. When closed, brochures are available
across the Marktplatz at the Chocobar cafe.

❶ Getting There & Around

Boppard is about 20km upriver from Koblenz. If
you're travelling by car, the best way to get to the
riverfront is to follow the signs on the B9 to the
Autofähre – that is, turn onto Mainzer Strasse at
the upriver (eastern) edge of town. Parking lot
P2, about 500m upriver (east) of the centre, is
the only town centre lot offering free parking.

Bikes can be hired from **Fahrrad Studio**
(☑4736; Oberstrasse 105; per day €7.50;
☺9am-6pm Mon-Fri, 9am-1pm Sat). The tourist
office has lots of material on cycling options.

Braubach

☑02627 / POP 3050

Framed by forested hillsides, vineyards and
Rhine-side rose gardens, the 1300-year-
old town of Braubach, about 8km south
of Koblenz on the right bank, is centred
on the small, half-timbered **Marktplatz**.
High above are the dramatic towers, turrets and crenellations of the 700-year-old
Marksburg, (☑206; www.marksburg.de; adult/
student/6-18yr €6/5/4; ☺10am-5pm mid-Mar–
Oct, 11am-4pm Nov–mid-Mar) one of the area's
most interesting castles because, unique
among the Rhine fortresses, it was never destroyed. Tours (often held in English at noon
and 4pm – call for details) take in the citadel, the Gothic hall and the large kitchen,
plus a grisly torture chamber, with its hair-
raising assortment of pain-inflicting nasties.

Koblenz

☑0261 / POP 106,000

The modern, flowery, park-filled city of
Koblenz sits at the confluence of the Rhine
and Moselle Rivers. Its roots go all the way
back to the Romans, who founded a military
stronghold here (calling it Confluentes) because of the site's supreme strategic value.

Today, Koblenz is the northern gateway
to the Romantic Rhine and also affords access to the outdoor charms of the three low

mountain ranges – the Hunsrück, the Eifel
and the Westerwald – that converge here.

⊙ Sights

Koblenz' core is shaped like the bow of a
ship seen in profile, with the Rhine to the
east, the Moselle to the north and the Deutsches Eck at the tip of the bow, right where
Leonardo DiCaprio would be kissing Kate
Winslet if this were the *Titanic*.

Deutsches Eck   PLAZA
At the point of confluence of the Moselle and
the Rhine, the 'German Corner' is dominated
by a statue of Kaiser Wilhelm I on horseback, in the bombastic style of the late 19th
century. After the original was destroyed in
WWII, the stone pedestal remained empty –
as a testament to lost German unity – until,
post-reunification, a copy was re-erected in
1993. Lovely, flowery parks stretch southwest
from here for several hundred metres, linking
up with a grassy riverfront promenade that
runs southward along the Rhine – great for a
bracing, fresh-air stroll.

Ludwig Museum   MUSEUM
(www.ludwigmuseum.org; Danziger Freiheit 1;
adult/student & senior €2.50/1.50; ☺10.30am-
5pm Tue-Sat, 11am-6pm Sun & holidays) About
300m south of the Deutsches Eck, the
Deutschherrenhaus, once the property of
the Order of the Teutonic Knights, is now
home to the Ludwig Museum, which showcases post-1945 and contemporary art from
France and Germany.

Across a lovely formal garden stands
Koblenz' oldest church, **Basilika St Kastor**
(☺9am-6pm), established in the 9th century
and rebuilt in the 12th century; the entrance
is on the west side.

Altstadt   OLD CITY
Koblenz' Altstadt, most of it rebuilt after the
war, surrounds the northern end of shop-
lined, pedestrians-only **Löhrstrasse**, the
city's main shopping street. Its intersection
with Altengraben is known as **Vier Türme**
(Four Towers) because each of the 17th-
century corner buildings sports an ornately
carved and painted oriel.

The arched walkway at Am Plan's northeastern corner leads to the Catholic **Liebfrauenkirche** (www.liebfrauen-koblenz.de; ☺8am or
8.30am-6pm), built in a hotchpotch of somehow harmonious styles: of Romanesque
origin, it has a Gothic choir (check out the
stained glass) and baroque onion-domed

turrets. Note the fancy painted vaulting above the central nave.

Mittelrhein-Museum
MUSEUM

(www.mittelrhein-museum.de; Florinsmarkt 15; adult/student & senior €3.50/2; ⊙10.30am-5pm Tue-Sat, 11am-6pm Sun & holidays) Has eclectic displays reflecting the region's history and a collection of 19th-century landscape paintings of the Romantic Rhine by German and British artists. For a bit of whimsy, check out the Augenroller (Eye Roller) figure beneath the clock over the entrance, which rolls its eyes and, on the hour and half-hour, sticks out its tongue. There are plans to move the museum at some point to the new Kulturbau (Zentralplatz), a huge cultural complex whose construction is supposed to be completed in early 2013.

Historiensäule
SCULPTURE

At Josef-Görres-Platz, six blocks southeast of Florinsmarkt, the History Column portrays 2000 years of Koblenz history in 10 scenes perched one on top of the other – the WWII period, for instance, is represented by a flaming ruin. A panel explains all (in English).

Festung Ehrenbreitstein
FORTRESS

(www.diefestungehrenbreitstein.de; adult/child €6/3; ⊙10am-6pm Apr-Oct, to 5pm Nov-Mar) On the right bank of the Rhine opposite the Deutsches Eck, looming 118m above the river, the mighty Ehrenbreitstein Fortress proved indestructible to all but Napoleonic troops, who levelled it in 1801. A few years later the Prussians, to prove a point, rebuilt it as one of Europe's mightiest fortifications. Today, its once-top-secret ramparts offer excellent views. Audioguides (€2) may soon be available in English.

The huge complex is too vast and the buildings too overbearingly massive for the scattered exhibits of the Landesmuseum, (State Museum; www.landesmuseum-koblenz.de) which range from photography to Celtic and Roman archaeology.

Festung Ehrenbreitstein is accessible by car; on foot (the Felsenweg begins across Hofstrasse, ie the B42, from the Koblenz-Ehrenbreitstein train station); and by a Schrägaufzug (www.schraegaufzug-ehrenbreitstein.de; adult/child return €5/3, incl fortress €8.80/4.80), a sort of angled elevator/lift. To get to the Rhine's right bank, you can hop on a Personenfähre (passenger ferry; adult/child €2/1, bicycle €1.50; ⊙to 6pm or 7pm in warm months) 500m south of the Deutsches Eck.

But by far the most spectacular way to get up there from the city centre is to take the 850m-long Seilbahn (aerial cable car; www.seilbahn-koblenz.de; adult/6-14yr return €8/4, incl fortress €11.20/5.60; bicycle one-way €3; ⊙10am-6pm or 7pm Apr-Oct, to 5pm Nov-Mar) from near the Deutsches Eck. Intended, like the Eiffel Tower, to be temporary, it's theoretically going to be dismantled in 2013 to avoid running foul of Unesco's World Heritage designation.

Schloss Stolzenfels
CASTLE

(www.schloss-stolzenfels.de; adult/child €14/2; ⊙9am-6pm Apr-Sep, to 5pm Oct, Nov & Jan-Mar, closed Dec) With its crenellated towers, ornate gables and medieval-style fortifications, Schloss Stolzenfels, 5km south of the city centre above the Rhine's left bank, exudes the timeless, sentimental beauty for which the Romantic Rhine is famed. In 1823, the future Prussian king Friedrich Wilhelm IV fell under its spell and had the castle – ruined by the French – rebuilt as his summer residence; during the Victorian era, guests included Queen Victoria. Today, the rooms remain largely as the king left them, with paintings, weapons, armour and furnishings from the mid-19th century.

To get there, take bus 650 from the Hauptbahnhof to the castle car park, from where it's a 15-minute walk.

🛏 Sleeping

Hotel Morjan
HOTEL $$

(☎304 290; www.hotel-morjan.de; Konrad Adenauer Ufer; s/d €65/95, with Rhine view €10 more; P@🖢) In a great spot facing the Rhine about 300m south of the Deutsches Eck, this late-20th-century hotel has 42 bright rooms, half with river views. Some of Koblenz' loveliest gardens are right nearby.

Hotel Jan van Werth
HOTEL $

(☎365 00; www.hoteljanvanwerth.de; Von-Werth-Strasse 9; s/d €45/66, without bathroom €25/53; @🖢) This long-time budget favourite, with a lobby that feels like someone's living room, offers exceptional value – no surprise that the 17 rooms are often booked out. Conveniently situated four long blocks north of the Hauptbahnhof and several blocks south of the Altstadt.

Contel Koblenz
HOTEL $$

(☎406 50; www.contel-koblenz.de; Pastor-Klein-Strasse 19; s/d from €79.50/89.50, buffet breakfast €11; P@🖢) This 185-room hotel's exuberant bad taste begins with the electric-blue facade and gets wilder inside – some amusing outrage against bourgeois good taste awaits around every corner. Some rooms have kitchenettes and three rooms come with waterbeds. Situated 1km west along the Moselle from the Altstadt; served by bus 3, whose nearest stop is Ludwig-Erhard-Strasse.

Eating & Drinking

Many of Koblenz' restaurants and pubs are in the Altstadt (eg along the streets south of Florinsmarkt) and along the Rhine.

Cafe Miljöö
CAFE $$
(www.cafe-miljoeoe.de; Gemüsegasse 12; mains €7.90-11.90; ⊙9am-1am or later; 🛜🐾) 'Milieu' (pronounce it like the French) is a cosy cafe-restaurant with fresh flowers, changing art exhibits, salads, healthy mains and a great selection of coffees, teas and homemade cakes. Breakfast is available until 5pm.

Kaffeewirtschaft
CAFE $$
(www.kaffeewirtschaft.de; Münzplatz 14; mains €8-15.90, salads €6.20-9.80; ⊙9am-midnight Mon-Thu, 9am-2am Fri & Sat, 10am-midnight Sun & holidays; 🐾) An old-fashioned cafe-restaurant with marble tables and weekly specials that take advantage of whatever's in season.

Aldi
SUPERMARKET $
(Bahnhofstrasse 50; ⊙8am-8pm Mon-Sat) Self-catering two blocks north of the Hauptbahnhof.

Irish Pub
IRISH PUB
(www.irishpubkoblenz.de; Burgstrasse 7; ⊙4pm-1am or later Mon-Fri, 1pm-2am or later Sat & Sun) A Koblenz institution since 1985, this Irish-owned and run drinking establishment screens major sports events, hosts live music (usually on Friday and Saturday from 9pm) and has karaoke (Wednesday from 8.30pm), quiz nights (Tuesday at 9pm) and student nights (Thursday).

ⓘ Information

The **Tourist office** (www.touristik-koblenz.de) has a branch at the **Hauptbahnhof** (🖉313 04; Bahnhofplatz 17; ⊙9am-6pm Mon-Fri), across the square and a bit to the right as you exit the train station, and one at the **Rathaus** (🖉130 920; Jesuitenplatz 2, Rathaus; ⊙9am-6pm Mon-Fri, 10am-4pm Sat & Sun). Both have excellent maps in English, sell event tickets and help with hotel reservations. A branch is supposed to open in the new Kulturbau complex (Zentralplatz) in early 2013.

Eco-Express Waschsalon (Bahnhofstrasse 22; ⊙6am-10pm Mon-Sat, closed Sun & holidays) Self-service laundry 400m north of the Hauptbahnhof.

LöwenPlay (Bahnhofplatz 5; per hr €3; ⊙6am-midnight Mon-Sat, 11am-midnight Sun & holidays) Internet access in a casino.

ⓘ Getting There & Away

Koblenz has two train stations, the main **Hauptbahnhof** on the Rhine's left bank about 1km south of the city centre, and **Koblenz-Ehrenbreitstein** on the right bank (right below Festung Ehrenbreitstein). The Hauptbahnhof is served by frequent regional/IC trains going north to destinations such as Bonn (€11.10/15, 29 to 63 minutes) and Cologne (€18.10/21, one to 1½ hours), south to Mainz and Frankfurt (€24/30, 1½ to 2¼ hours), and southwest to Traben-Trarbach (€14.40, 1¼ hours) and Trier (€20.80/25, 1½ to two hours). Regional trains serve villages on both banks of the Romantic Rhine, including Bingen (€12.20, 50 minutes).

Some Romantic Rhine villages are also served by buses (www.rmv-bus.de) that stop outside the Hauptbahnhof. Bus 650 goes to Boppard via Schloss Stolzenfels, while bus 570 goes to Braubach/Marksburg.

Several boat companies have docks on Konrad-Adenauer-Ufer, which runs along the Rhine south of the Deutsches Eck.

ⓘ Getting Around

Bus 1 (twice an hour, after 8pm hourly) links the Hauptbahnhof with the Deutsches Eck.

Bicycles can be rented from **Fahrrad Zangmeister** (🖉9887 2450; www.fz-24.de; Am Löhrrondell; ⊙9am-6.30pm Mon-Fri, 10am-4pm Sat), one of Germany's oldest bike shops (it was founded, unbelievably, way back in 1898). Situated half a block east of Löhnstrasse 89a.

THE MOSELLE VALLEY

While plenty of places in Germany demand that you hustle, the Moselle (in German, Mosel) gently suggests that you should, well...just mosey. The German section of the river, which rises in France and then traverses Luxembourg, runs for 195km from Trier to Koblenz on a slow, serpentine course, revealing new scenery at every bend. Unlike the Romantic Rhine, it's spanned by plenty of bridges.

Exploring the wineries of the Moselle Valley (www.mosellandtouristik.de) is an ideal way to get to know German culture, interact with locals and, of course, sample some wonderful wines. To experience the sublime pleasures of serial sipping, look for signs reading *Weingut, Weinprobe, Wein Probieren, Weinverkauf* and *Wein zu Verkaufen*. In spring luscious purple wisteria flowers, dangling from stone village houses, anticipate the bunches of grapes that will ripen in the fall.

Lots of walking trails allow you to explore the Moselle's banks and hillsides, where you'll find Europe's steepest vineyard (the Bremmer Calmont near Bremm, with a 68% gradient) and Germany's most expensive one (the Bernkasteler Doctor in Bernkastel-Kues). Attractive villages worth a wander include (heading upriver) **Ediger-Eller, Bremm, Zell, Enkirch, Traben-Trarbach, Kröv, Ürzig, Zeltingen-Rachtig** and **Bernkastel-Kues.**

From November to about Easter, most Moselle towns are very quiet, and some hotels shut down. Accommodation can be booked via www.mosellandtouristik.de. Almost all Moselle towns have a camping ground.

The listings in this section are organised in the order you'd come upon them if travelling upriver from Koblenz. If you're starting in Trier, read backwards from p451.

🏃 Activities

Cycling

Many superb cycling paths traverse the countryside along and near the Moselle. Tourist offices have brochures and maps.

Hiking

The Moselle Valley is especially scenic walking country. Variants of the **Mosel Erlebnis Route** (www.mosel-erlebnis-route.com) follow the entire Moselle Valley along both banks of the river. Expect some steep climbs if you venture away from the river (eg on the long-distance **Moselhöhenweg**, which sticks to high ground), but the views are often both sublime and breathtaking. Bookshops and tourist offices carry good maps, including *Mosel Erlebnis Route* (€9.50).

ℹ Getting There & Around

AIR Frankfurt-Hahn Airport is just 22km east of Traben-Trarbach and 17km east of Bernkastel-Kues. A **shuttle bus** (☏0180-506 6735; www.hahn-airport.de; ⊙eight times daily) links the airport with the railhead of Bullay (€6.80, 51 minutes).

BUS & TRAIN The rail line linking Koblenz with Trier (€19.20, 1½ to two hours, at least hourly) – most people begin their visit to the area in one of these cities – follows the Moselle (and stops at its villages) only as far upriver as Bullay (€11.10, 49 to 65 minutes from Koblenz, 38 to 53 minutes

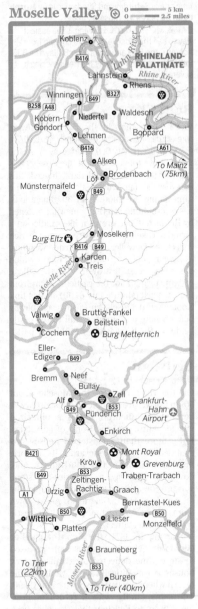

Moselle Valley

from Trier). From there, hourly shuttle trains head upriver to Traben-Trarbach (€3.40, 20 minutes, hourly). The villages between Traben-Trarbach and Trier, including Kröv, Ürzig and Bernkastel-Kues, are served by bicycle-carrying bus 333 (six times daily Monday to Friday, three times daily Saturday and Sunday), run by **Moselbahn buses** (www.moselbahn.de)

CAR & MOTORCYCLE Driving is the easiest way to see the Moselle. If you're coming from Koblenz, the B49 and then, after Bullay, the B53 follow the river all the way to Trier, crossing it several times.

Burg Eltz

Victor Hugo thought the Burg Eltz (www.burg-eltz.de; tour adult/student/family €8/5.50/24; ⊙9.30am-5.30pm Apr-Oct), hidden away in the forest above the left bank of the Moselle, was 'tall, terrific, strange and dark'. Indeed, this 850-year-old fairy-tale castle, owned by the same family for more than 30 generations, has a forbidding exterior somewhat softened by the turrets that crown it like candles on a birthday cake. The treasury features a rich collection of jewellery, porcelain and weapons.

By car, you can reach Burg Eltz – which has never been destroyed – via the village of Münstermaifeld; the castle is 800m from the car park (shuttle bus €1.50). Trains link Koblenz and Moselkern (also reachable by boat), where a 35-minute trail to the castle begins at the Ringelsteiner Mühle car park.

Beilstein

☑02673 / POP 140

On the right bank of the Moselle about 50km upriver from Koblenz, Beilstein (www.beilstein-stadtfuehrung.de) is a pint-sized village right out of the world of fairy tales. Little more than a cluster of houses surrounded by steep vineyards, its historic highlights include the Marktplatz and, down an alleyway, a centuries-old stone synagogue (Weingasse 13), now occupied by an art shop called Galerie 13. Above town looms Burg Metternich, a hilltop castle reached via a staircase.

Starting in 1574, the Zehnthauskeller (Marktplatz; ⊙11am-evening Tue-Sun) was used to store wine delivered as a tithe; it now houses a romantically dark, vaulted wine tavern where you can try six wines for €8.90. The same family, with a record of hosting visitors to Beilstein that stretches back to 1795, runs two flowery hotels (☑1850; www.hotel-lipmann.de). The area has plenty of hiking trails.

Traben-Trarbach

☑06541 / POP 5850

Perhaps the most attractive of the Moselle towns, Traben-Trarbach is perfect for a relaxing, turn-of-the-20th-century-style rivertown holiday – and makes an excellent base for exploring the valley by bike or car. A major centre of the wine trade a century ago, the town's winemakers still welcome visitors for tasting and sales.

Traben lost its medieval look to three major fires but was well compensated with beautiful Jugendstil (art nouveau) villas – and lots of wisteria. It united with Trarbach, across the river, in 1904.

◉ Sights & Activities

The banks of the Moselle are delightful for strolling.

Hotel Bellevue HOTEL
(Am Moselufer 11, Traben) Of Traben's sinuous art-nouveau villas, the most seductive – and the only one open to the public – is the riverfront Hotel Bellevue, built in 1903 and easily recognised by its Champagne-bottle-shaped slate turret. The oak staircase in the lobby and the restaurant's stained-glass windows are deliciously sinuous examples of the style, brought to town by Berlin architect Bruno Möhring. Hotel reception sells an illustrated brochure about local Jugendstil buildings (€3). Historic flood crests are marked on the wall near the entrance.

Möhring also designed the medieval-style Brückentor (1898) above the bridge on the Trarbach side.

Buddha Museum MUSEUM
(www.buddha-museum.de; Bruno-Möhring-Platz 1, Trarbach; adult/student €15/8; ⊙10am-6pm Tue-Sun) This museum has a gorgeous – and beautifully presented – collection of over 2000 wood, bronze and paper statues of the Buddha from all over Asia. Upstairs there's a peaceful rooftop garden with river views.

Mittelmosel-Museum MUSEUM
(Casinostrasse 2, Trarbach; adult/youth €2.50/1; ⊙10am-5pm Tue-Sun Easter-Oct) If you'd like to learn more about Traben-Trarbach and its castles, head to this homey local history museum, housed in a furnished baroque villa proud of having hosted Johann Wolfgang von Goethe for a few hours in 1792.

FREE **Fahrradmuseum** MUSEUM
(Moselstrasse 2, Trarbach; ⊙2-6pm Mon-Fri, 10am-3pm Sat, 10am-1pm Sun May-Oct, 10am-1pm Sat & Sun Apr) To check out a collection of historic bicycles, head up the stairs from the Wein-Kontor wine shop.

Grevenburg RUINS
The Grevenburg castle, built in the mid-1300s, sits high in the craggy hills above Trarbach. Because of its strategic importance, it changed hands 13 times, was besieged six times and was destroyed seven times. No wonder two walls are all that are left! It can be reached via a steep footpath, the Sponheimer Weg, that begins a block north of the bridge.

Mont Royal RUINS
Above Traben stand the remains of the vast Mont Royal fortress (1690s), designed by Vauban for Louis XIV as a base from which to project French power. Ruinously expensive, it was dismantled before completion by the French themselves under the Treaty of Ryswick. The footpath up to the site begins at the upper end of Römerstrasse.

Wine Tasting WINE TASTINGS
(€4-8) The tourist office can supply details of daily wine tastings and cellar tours.

🛏 Sleeping & Eating

Trarbach has plenty of restaurants and wine taverns in the area upriver from the bridge, eg along Moselstrasse and Weiherstrasse. Across the bridge in Traben, eateries can be found along Bahnhofstrasse and tiny parallel Neue Rathausstrasse. If you're thirsty, try a bottle of the local spring water, Trarbacher.

TOP CHOICE **Hotel Bellevue** HISTORIC HOTEL $$$
(☎7030; www.bellevue-hotel.de; Am Moselufer 11, Traben; d €150-190; @ 🛜 🏊) Classy, romantic and historic, this exquisite Jugendstil (art nouveau) hotel, facing the river, offers perks that include bike and canoe hire, pool and sauna. The elegant gourmet restaurant (mains €19 to €27), adorned with exquisite stained glass, serves regional and Mediterranean-inspired cuisine.

Central Hotel HOTEL $
(☎6238; www.central-hotel-traben.de; Bahnstrasse 43, Traben; s €37-42, d €64-68; P 🛜) In the same family for three generations, this super-welcoming hotel has 32 modest but spotless rooms. The owner, Iris, lived in Texas for eight years but somehow returned twangless. Great budget value. Situated 200m south of the train shelter.

DJH Hostel HOSTEL $
(☎9278; www.jugendherberge.de; Hirtenpfad 6, Traben; dm/d €20.50/52) All rooms at this modern, 172-bed hostel have private bathrooms. It's a 1.2km walk up the hillside from the train station, past the fire station.

TOP CHOICE **Weingut Caspari** GERMAN $$
(☎5778; www.weingut-caspari.de; Weiherstrasse 18, Trarbach; mains €6.50-16.90) Six short blocks inland from the bridge, this rustic, old-time *Strausswirtschaft* (winery-cum-eatery) serves hearty local pork specialities, such as *Feiner Grillschinken Moselart* (boiled ham with potato puree and sauerkraut), and their own delicious rieslings.

Alte Zunftscheune GERMAN $$
(☎9737; www.zunftscheune.de; Neue Rathausstrasse 15, Traben; mains €7.20-19.60; ⊙5-11pm or later Tue-Sun, also open 11am-3pm Sat & Sun; 🐾) Serves Moselle-style dishes in a series of wonderfully atmospheric rooms choc-full of rustic bric-a-brac. Warm and very welcoming. The cellar still has its original 1890s lighting. Has a weekend salad buffet from May to October.

Brücken-Schenke GERMAN $$
(☎818 435; www.bruecken-schenke.de; Brückentor, Trarbach; mains €8.20-16.80; ⊙2-9pm Mon & Wed-Fri, 11am-10pm Sat & Sun, open Tue & longer hours May-Oct; 🛝) A range of solid, good-value German and regional favourites are served up inside the tower at the Trarbach end of the bridge. Offers great river views.

Edeka Neukauf SUPERMARKET $
(Am Bahnhof 44, Traben; ⊙8am-9pm Mon-Sat, bakery also open 8-11am Sun) This supermarket is situated diagonally across the tracks from the train shelter.

🛈 **BOAT & BIKE COMBO**

From May to October, boats run by Kolb (☎06531 4719; www.kolb-mosel.de) link Bernkastel with Traben-Trarbach (one-way/return €13/19, two hours, five daily). You can take along a bicycle for €2, making it easy to sail one way and ride the 24km back.

ℹ Information

Traben, on the Moselle's left bank, is where you'll find the tourist office, the end-of-the-line train shelter (linked by shuttle trains to the railhead of Bullay), the adjacent bus station, the commercial centre and several ATMs. Trarbach is across the bridge on the right bank.

Tourist Office (☎839 80; www.traben -trarbach.de; Am Bahnhof 5, Traben; ⏰10am-5pm Mon-Fri May-Aug, to 6pm Sep & Oct, to 4pm Nov-Apr, 11am-3pm Sat May-Oct; 🛜) Sells walking and cycling maps and events tickets. In the 24-hour lobby, you can pick up excellent English-language brochures (including a map-guide) and use an interactive information screen. Situated in the Alter Bahnhof (old train station) 100m west along Bahnhofstrasse from the train shelter.

ℹ Getting There & Around

Bernkastel-Kues is 24km upriver by car but, because of the Moselle's hairpin curve, just 6.5km over the hill on foot.

Zweirad Wagner (☎1649; www.zweirad -wagner.de; Brückenstrasse 42, Trarbach; city/mountain bike per day €8.50/10; ⏰8.30am-12.30pm & 2-6pm Mon-Fri, 8.30am-1pm Sat year-round, also 10-11am Sun & holidays approx Mar-Oct) A friendly bike shop that hires out bicycles and loans out cycling maps. Situated next to the bridge.

Bernkastel-Kues

☎06531 / POP 6500

This charming twin town, some 50km downriver from Trier, is the hub of the 'Middle Moselle' region. Bernkastel, on the right bank, is a symphony in half-timber, stone and slate and teems with wine taverns – and tour groups. Kues, the birthplace of theologian Nicolaus Cusanus (1401–64), has little fairy-tale flair but is home to the town's most important historical sights.

◉ Sights

The Kues shore has a lovely riverfront promenade.

Marktplatz   SQUARE
(Bernkastel) Bernkastel's pretty Marktplatz, a block inland from the bridge, is enclosed by a romantic ensemble of half-timbered houses with beautifully decorated gables. Note the medieval iron handcuffs, to which criminals were attached, on the facade of the old Rathaus.

On Karlstrasse, the alley to the right as you face the Rathaus, the tiny Spitzhäuschen resembles a giant bird's house, its narrow base topped by a much larger, precariously leaning, upper floor. More such crooked gems line Römerstrasse and its side streets.

Pfarrkirche St Michael   CHURCH
(⏰9am-6pm) Facing the bridge, this partly 14th-century-Gothic church has an ornate interior and has some colourful stained glass. The tower was originally part of the town's fortifications.

Burg Landshut   RUIN
(Bernkastel; ⏰beer garden 10am-6pm except Thu Easter-Nov) A rewarding way to get your heart pumping is by hoofing it from the Marktplatz up to Burg Landshut, a ruined 13th-century castle – framed by vineyards and forests – on a bluff above town; allow 30 minutes. You'll be rewarded with glorious river valley views and a refreshing drink in the beer garden.

FREE **St-Nikolaus-Hospital**   HISTORIC BUILDING
(Cusanusstrasse 2, Kues; guided tour €5; ⏰9am-6pm Sun-Fri, 9am-3pm Sat, guided tour 10.30am Tue & 3pm Fri Apr-Oct) Most of Kues' sights are conveniently grouped near the bridge in the late-Gothic St-Nikolaus-Hospital, an old-age home founded by Cusanus in 1458 for 33 men (one for every year of Jesus' life). You're free to explore the cloister and Gothic Kapelle (chapel) at leisure, but the treasure-filled library can only be seen on a guided tour.

Mosel-Weinmuseum   MUSEUM
(www.moselweinmuseum.de; Cusanusstrasse 2, Kues; adult/13-18yr €5/3; ⏰10am-6pm Apr-Oct, 11am-5pm Nov, Dec, Feb & Mar) Part of the St-Nikolaus-Hospital complex, the multimedia Moselle Wine Museum has interactive terminals (in German, English and Dutch) and attractions such as an Aromabar (you have to guess what you're smelling). In the adjacent Vinothek (www.moselvinothek.de), you can sample 10 Moselle wines by the glass (about €2) or, in the cellar, indulge in an 'all you can drink' wine tasting (€15) with about 150 vintages to choose from.

☞ Tours

The tourist office rents out an audioguide (three hours/all day €6/8, 2nd earphone €2). If you have a smartphone, you can download the audio file for free from www.itour.de.

🛏 Sleeping & Eating

In Bernkastel, places to eat can be found along the waterfront and on the Altstadt's squares and narrow, pedestrian-only streets. In Kues there are several restaurants near the bridge.

Hotel Moselblümchen HOTEL $$
(☎2335; www.hotel-moselbluemchen.de; Schwanenstrasse 10, Bernkastel; s €42-79, d €69-129; P@🖥) This traditional, family-run hotel is situated on a narrow alley behind the tourist office. It has 20 tasteful rooms and a small sauna, and can arrange bike rental. In the **restaurant**, German and local specialities include sauerkraut and homemade wurst.

DJH Hostel HOSTEL $
(☎2395; www.jugendherberge.de; Jugendherbergsstrasse 1, Bernkastel; dm/d €16/39) Fairly basic by today's standards, with 96 beds. Scenically but inconveniently located above town next to Burg Landshut.

Edeka Aktiv SUPERMARKET $
(facing Cusanusstrasse 4a; ⊙8am-10pm Mon-Sat) Self-catering deep inside the ugly commercial centre across the street from St-Nikolaus-Hospital.

ℹ Information

Tourist Office (☎500 190; www.bernkastel.de; Am Gestade 6, Bernkastel; ⊙9 or 10am-4 or 5pm Mon-Fri year-round, also open 10am-5pm Sat & 10am-1pm Sun May-Oct) Reserves hotel rooms, sells hiking and cycling maps, offers internet access (per hour €2) and has a 24-hour ATM. A hotel reservation board with a free phone is just outside. Situated 100m downriver from the bridge.

ℹ Getting There & Around

The bus station is at Forumsplatz, on the Kues side behind the commercial centre situated across the street from St-Nikolaus-Hospital.

The **Mosel-Maare-Radweg** (Mosel Maare cycycle route; www.maare-moselradweg.de), linking Bernkastel-Kues with Daun (in the Eifel), follows an old train line so the gradients are reasonable. From April to October, you can take RegioRadler bus 300 up and ride the 57km back down to Bernkastel-Kues.

Hire bikes at **Fun Bike Team,** (☎940 24; www.funbiketeam.de; Schanzstrasse 22; 7-speed/tandem per day €11/19; ⊙9am-6.30pm Mon-Wed, 9am-7pm Thu, 9am-6:30pm Fri, 9am-2pm Sat) 500m upriver from the bridge.

Trier

☎0651 / POP 105,250

A Unesco World Heritage Site since 1986, the handsome, leafy university city of Trier is home to Germany's finest ensemble of Roman monuments – including several elaborate thermal baths – as well as architectural gems from later ages. Its proximity to both Luxembourg and France can be tasted in the cuisine and felt in the local esprit. About 25,000 students do their part, contributing to keeping things snappy.

◉ Sights & Activities

Trier has a handsome, mostly pedestrianised city centre with plenty of cafes and restaurants, some inside gorgeous Gothic or baroque buildings.

At most sites, children up to age 17 get in free if accompanied by an adult. Excellent free brochures on the Roman monuments are available in English and French.

Porta Nigra ROMAN GATE
(Map p452; adult/student €3/2.10, incl Stadtmuseum Simeonstift €7.20/5.80; ⊙9am-6pm Apr-Sep, to 5pm Mar & Oct, to 4pm Nov-Feb) Top billing among Trier's Roman monuments goes to the Porta Nigra, a brooding 2nd-century city gate that's been blackened by time (hence the name, Latin for 'black gate'). A marvel of engineering and ingenuity, it's held together by nothing but gravity and iron rods. In the 11th century, Archbishop Poppo converted the structure into St Simeonkirche, a church named in honour of a Greek hermit who spent a stint holed up in its east tower.

Stadtmuseum Simeonstift MUSEUM
(Map p452; adult/student €5.50/4, incl Porta Nigra €7.20/5.80; ⊙10am-6pm Tue-Sun) Housed in a one-time monastery, this museum brings alive two millennia of local history with carefully chosen objects, many of them exquisite. Highlights include the **Trier Kino** (Trier Cinema), where you can see 78 short films of Trier, some made as far back as 1904. Admission includes a free audioguide in German, English or French. Situated right next to the Porta Nigra (and reached via the same entrance).

Hauptmarkt SQUARE
(Map p452) Anchored by a festive **fountain** (1595) dedicated to St Peter and the Four Virtues, Trier's central market square is surrounded by medieval and Renaissance architectural treasures such as the **Rotes**

Trier

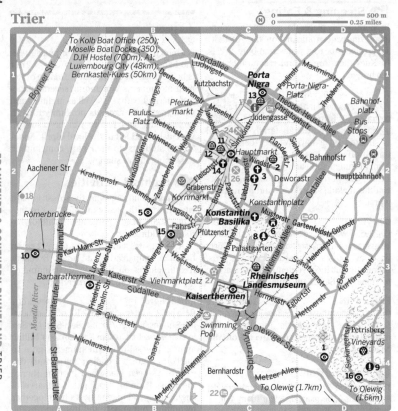

Haus (Red House; Map p452) and the Steipe, which now house an attractive cafe and the Spielzeugmuseum (Toy Museum; Map p452; www.spielzeugmuseum-trier.de; Dietrichstrasse 51, 2nd fl; adult/child/family €4.50/2.50/12; ⊙11am-6pm Tue-Sun Apr-Oct, to 5pm Nov-Mar) chock full of miniature trains, dolls and other childhood delights. To get up there, take the elevator/lift in the back of the cafe, Zur Steipe.

On the south side, St-Gangolf-Kirche (Map p452; ⊙8 or 9am-6.30pm), a Gothic church built in the 14th and 15th centuries, is reached via an angel-bedecked, 18th-century baroque portal.

The Hauptmarkt hosts a small market daily except Sunday.

Dom CHURCH
(Map p452; www.dominformation.de; Liebfrauenstrasse 12; ⊙10am-5pm Mon-Sat, 12.30-5pm Sun, shorter hrs Nov-Mar; ⊕) Built above the palace of Constantine the Great's mother, Helena, this fortress-like cathedral is mostly Roman-

esque, with some soaring Gothic and eye-popping baroque embellishments.

To see some dazzling ecclesiastical equipment and peer into early Christian history, head upstairs to the Domschatz (cathedral treasury; Map p452; adult/child €1.50/0.50; ⊙10am-5pm Mon-Sat, 12.30-5pm Sun Apr-Oct, 11am-4pm Tue-Sat, 12.30-4pm Sun & Mon Nov-Mar) or go around the corner to the Bischöfliches Dom-und Diözesanmuseum (Map p452; ☑710 5255; www.bistum-trier.de/museum; Windstrasse 6-8; adult/student €3.50/2; ⊙9am-5pm Tue-Sat, 1-5pm Sun) The prized exhibit here is a 4th-century Roman ceiling from Helena's palace, in vivid colours, that was pieced together from countless fragments.

Liebfrauenbasilika CHURCH
(Map p452; Liebfrauenstrasse; ⊙8am-7pm Mon-Sat, to 6pm Sun Apr-Oct, 8am-5pm Nov-Mar) One of Germany's earliest Gothic churches. The cruciform structure is supported by a dozen pillars symbolising the 12 Apostles and, de-

Trier

spite its strict symmetry, has a light, mystical quality. Has some colourful post-war stained glass. Completely renovated in 2011.

Konstantin Basilika CHURCH

(Map p452; www.konstantin-basilika.de; Konstantinplatz; ⊙10am-6pm Apr-Oct, 10 or 11am-noon and 2 or 3pm-4pm Tue-Sat, noon-1pm Sun Nov-Mar) Constructed around AD 310 as Constantine's throne hall, the brick-built Konstantin Basilika (Aula Palatina) is now a typically austere Protestant church. Its dimensions (67m long and 36m high) are truly mind-blowing considering that it was built by the Romans. A new organ, with 87 registers and 6500 pipes, is being installed and should be ready in 2014.

Palastgarten PARK

(Map p452) Stretching south from Konstantinplatz, the lawns, daffodil beds, statues and fountains of the formal Palace Garden are perfect for a stroll or sunbathing, especially on warm summer days. The pink and gold rococo confection at the northern end is the **Kurfürstliches Palais** (Prince Electors' Palace; Map p452; interior closed to the public).

Rheinisches Landesmuseum MUSEUM

(Roman Archaeological Museum; Map p452; www.landesmuseum-trier.de; Weimarer Allee 1; adult/student

incl audioguide €6/4; ⊙10am-5pm Tue-Sun) This museum affords an extraordinary look at local Roman life. Highlights include a scale model of 4th-century Trier and rooms filled with tombstones, mosaics, rare gold coins and some fantastic glass.

Kaiserthermen ROMAN SITE

(Imperial Baths; Map p452; Palastgarten; adult/student €3/2.10) On the southern edge of the Palastgarten, the Kaiserthermen is a vast thermal bathing complex created by Constantine. The striped brick-and-stone arches, once part of the caldarium, make you feel like you're at the Forum in Rome. You can get a sense of the layout from the corner lookout tower.

Amphitheater ROMAN SITE

(Map p452; Olewiger Strasse; adult/child €3/2.10; ⊙9am-6pm Apr-Sep, to 5pm Mar & Oct, to 4pm Nov-Feb) Trier's Roman *Amphitheater*, built in the late 2nd century AD, was once capable of holding 20,000 spectators during gladiator tournaments and animal fights – or when Constantine the Great crowned his battlefield victories by feeding his enemies to voracious animals. Situated about 700m to the southeast of the Kaiserthermen.

CYCLE TOURING: FIVE RIVERS IN FIVE DAYS

Trier makes an ideal base for day trips by bike, with five different riverside bike paths (www.radwanderland.de) to choose from. Trains and RegioRadler buses (www.regio-radler.de; ☺Apr–Oct, internet reservations recommended) make it possible to ride one way (eg downhill) and take public transport the other. Esterbauer (www.esterbauer.com) publishes Bikeline cycling guides (€10.90), which include 1:50,000-scale maps.

» **Kylltal-Radweg** Heads 115km north along the Kyll (pronounced *kool*) River, paralleling the rail line to Cologne. Take the train between Erdorf and Kyllburg (five to seven minutes) to avoid a killer (or should we say Kyller) hill. Very romantic.

» **Mosel-Radweg** (www.mosel-radweg.de) Hugely popular. From Trier, heads down the Moselle River all the way to Koblenz and upriver along the Luxembourg border and into the French region of Lorraine. Parts are served by RegioRadler bus 333.

» **Ruwer-Hochwald-Radweg** (www.ruwer-hochwald-radweg.de) Opened in 2011, this 50km bike path runs along a one-time rail line south along the Ruwer River and then west. Served by RegioRadler bus 200.

» **Saar-Radweg** (VeloRoute SaarLorLux) Heads south from Trier along the mostly gorgeous, partly industrial Saar River to Saarbrücken and, at Sarreguemines, into France.

» **Sauertal-Radweg** This 53km path heads north from Trier, following a decommissioned rail line along the Sauer River into Luxembourg. Northern variants follow the Prüm and Nims Rivers. Parts are served by RegioRadler bus 441.

Weinkulturpfad
HIKING

(Wine Culture Path; Map p452) Halfway up Petrisberg, the vine-covered hill just east of the *Amphitheater*, you come to the Wine Culture Path, which leads through the grapes to Olewig (1.6km). Further up the slope, next to the stop for bus 14, a multilingual panel (Map p452) traces local history from the first known human habitation (30,000 years ago) through the last ice age to the Romans. The panoramic views are tremendous.

Thermen am Viehmarkt
ROMAN SITE

(Map p452; Viehmarktplatz; adult/student €3/2.10; ☺9am-5pm) Found by accident in the 1980s during the construction of a parking garage, these thermal baths are sheltered by a dramatic glass cube. The site is closed on Monday (or Tuesday when Monday is a public holiday).

Karl Marx Haus
HISTORIC SITE

(Map p452; www.fes.de/karl-marx-haus; Brückenstrasse 10; adult/child €3/2; ☺10am-6pm daily Apr-Oct, 2-5pm Tue-Sun Nov-Mar) The early-18th-century baroque town house in which the author of *Das Kapital* was born in 1818 now houses exhibits that take a highbrow, dialectical look at Marx, the meaning of his intellectual and political legacy, and social democracy. Admission includes a free audioguide that opens with the stirring cadences of *L'Internationale;* it's available in six languages, including that spoken by fully one quarter of visitors, Chinese (not at all surprising if you think about it). The gift shop sells busts of Marx (from €21.95), Marx coffee mugs and a wine - a red, of course - called Karl Marx Rotwein (€7.99). Run by a foundation affiliated with the SPD (Social Democratic Party of Germany), whose historical perspectives inform the exhibits.

Römerbrücke
ROMAN SITE

(Map p452; western end of Karl Marx Strasse) This Mosel bridge still uses five of the 2nd-century support columns (out of seven) that have been holding it up since legionnaires crossed on chariots. Parts of the arches date from the 1300s.

🎓 Courses

The Europäische Kunstakademie (European Academy of Fine Arts; Map p452; ☎998 460; www.eka-trier.de; Aachener Strasse 63) offers a wide variety of courses, ranging from four days to six months, in painting, sculpture, drawing, printmaking, photography and ceramics.

👉 Tours

City Walking Tour
WALKING TOUR

(Map p452; adult/6-14yr €8.50/5; ☺1.30pm Sat Apr-Oct) Two-hour tours in English begin at the tourist office.

Wine Tasting

WINE TASTING

(Map p452; 4/6/6 wines €6.50/8.50/9.50; ☉5pm)
Each week a different vintner plays host.
Contact the tourist office for a schedule.

🛏 Sleeping

Hotel prices rise on Friday and Saturday.

TOP
CHOICE Becker's Hotel   BOUTIQUE HOTEL $$

(☏938 080; www.beckers-trier.de; Olewiger
Strasse 206; d €110-220; P✳@🖥) Affiliated
with Design Hotels, this classy establish-
ment pairs 31 supremely tasteful rooms
– some ultramodern, others rustically tra-
ditional – with stellar dining. Situated 3km
southeast of the centre in the quiet wine
district of Olewig, across the creek from the
old monastery church. Served by buses 6, 16
and 81.

Hotel Villa Hügel   BOUTIQUE HOTEL $$
(Map p452; ☏937 100; www.hotel-villa-huegel.de;
Bernhardstrasse 14; d €142-194; P@🖥🏊) A stylish, 33-room hillside villa where you can begin the day with *Sekt* (sparkling wine) at a
lavish breakfast buffet and end it luxuriating
in the 12m indoor pool and Finnish sauna.
Rooms, decorated with honey-toned woods,
are calming and create a sense of well-being.
Served by buses 2 and 82.

Hille's Hostel   HOSTEL $
(Map p452; ☏710 2785, outside office hrs 0171-
329 1247; www.hilles-trier.de; Gartenfeld-
strasse 7; dm from €14, s/d €40/50, breakfast €8;
☉reception 9am-noon & 4-6pm or later; @🖥) An
independent hostel with a 1970s vibe, this
laid-back place has a piano in the common
kitchen and 12 attractive, spacious rooms,
most with private bathrooms. If you'll
be arriving when reception is closed, call
ahead and they'll leave the door code and
the key.

Hotel Römischer Kaiser   HOTEL $$
(Map p452; ☏977 00; www.friedrich-hotels.de; Por-
ta-Nigra-Platz 6; s/d from €73.50/111; 🖥) Built in
1894, this hotel – convenient to the train sta-
tion and the old city – offers 43 bright, com-
fortable rooms with solid wood furnishings,
parquet floors and spacious bathrooms.

DJH Hostel   HOSTEL $
(☏146 620; www.jugendherberge.de; An der Ju-
gendherberge 4; dm/d €21.50/54; P🖥) A spick-
and-span, 228-bed hostel right on the Mo-
selle, about 1km northeast of the tourist
office. Rooms have bathrooms and up to six

beds. Served by bus 12 from the Hauptbahn-
hof or Porta Nigra.

🍴 Eating

In the warm months, cafes fill the old city's
public squares, including the Kornmarkt.
The Olewig district, 3km southeast of the
centre, is home to several traditional *Wein-
stuben* (wine taverns).

TOP
CHOICE Weinhaus Becker   GOURMET $$$

(☏938 080; Olewiger Strasse 206; 1-/3-course
lunch with wine €15/28, 3-/4-course dinner
€36/48; ☉noon-2pm & 6-10pm) Serves German bourgeois cuisine as well as modern
interpretations of French and Italian classics – and even goes in for bit of molecular
gastronomy. Everything is made with fresh
regional products – the wines are very local,
the grapes having been grown on the hillside opposite. Also inside the Becker's Hotel
complex (situated 3km southeast of the centre) is the gourmet **Becker's Restaurant**
(5/8 courses €105/125; ☉7-9pm Tue-Sat), which
holds two Michelin stars.

Zum Domstein   ROMAN $$
(Map p452; www.domstein.de; Hauptmarkt 5; mains
€8.90-18.50, Roman dinner €17-35) A German-
style bistro where you can either dine like
an ancient Roman or feast on more con-
ventional German and international fare.
Roman dishes are based on the recipes of
Marcus Gavius Apicius (1st century AD).

Kartoffel Kiste   POTATOES $$
(Map p452; www.kiste-trier.de; Fahrstrasse 13-14;
mains €7.20-17; ☉11am-midnight; 🖥) A local favourite, this place specialises in baked, breaded, gratineed, soupified and sauce-engulfed
potatoes, as well as schnitzel and steaks.
Check out the extraordinary bronze fountain
out front. Situated 400m south of the Hauptmarkt, half a block west of Brotstrasse.

Textorium   RESTAURANT $$
(Map p452; Wechselstrasse 4-6; meals €5.90-16.90;
☉noon-2.30pm Mon-Fri, 6pm-1am or 2am daily) A
popular, industrial-chic eatery with outdoor
seating and daily specials. Attached to the
TuFa cultural events venue.

Food Market   MARKET $$
(Map p452; Viehmarktplatz; ☉7am-1 or 2pm Tue &
Fri) The city centre's largest outdoor market
makes it easy to assemble a tasty picnic.

Karstadt   SUPERMARKET $

(Map p452; Simeonstrasse 46; ⏱9.30am-8pm Mon-Sat) The city centre's Karstadt department store has this supermarket in the basement.

☆ Entertainment

The tourist office can provide details of concerts and other cultural activities and sells tickets.

TuFa   PERFORMING ARTS

(Map p452; ☎718 2412; www.tufa-trier.de; Wechselstrasse 4-6) This vibrant cultural events venue, housed in a former *Tuchfabrik* (towel factory) – thus the name – hosts cabaret, live music of all sorts, theatre and dance performances.

ℹ Information

ATMs At the Kornmarkt; also in the Hauptbahnhof.

Antiquities Card (two/four Roman sites & Rheinisches Landesmuseum €9/14) A great deal for Trier's most interesting antiquities. Sold at the tourist office and each site.

Falconet (Bahnhofplatz 1; per hr €1; ⏱9am-11pm) Internet access next to the Hauptbahnhof.

ITS Internet Cafe (Porta-Nigra-Platz 4; per hr €1; ⏱10am-9pm Mon-Fri, 11am-9pm Sat, noon-9pm Sun) Internet access and computer repair.

Post Office (Bahnhofplatz) Just north of the Hauptbahnhof.

Tourist Office (☎978 080; www.trier-info.de; just inside Porta Nigra; ⏱9 or 10am-5 or 6pm Mon-Sat, 9 or 10am-1pm or later Sun) Next to the Porta Nigra. Has excellent brochures in English and sells Moselle-area walking and cycling maps, concert tickets and boat excursions.

TrierCard (adult/family €9/19) For three consecutive days you get 10% to 25% off museum and monument admissions, unlimited use of public transport and other discounts. Sold only at the tourist office.

Waschsalon (Brückenstrasse 19-21; ⏱8am-10pm) Self-service laundry.

ℹ Getting There & Away

Trier has train connections to Saarbrücken (€16.40, one to 1½ hours) and Koblenz (€20.80, 1½ to two hours) at least every hour. There are also frequent trains to Luxembourg (same-day return €10.80, 50 minutes, at least hourly), with onward connections to Paris.

ℹ Getting Around

The city centre is easily explored on foot. A bus ride (see www.swt.de) costs €1.90, a public transport day pass costs €5.20. The Olewig wine district is served by buses 6, 16 and 81.

Bikes in tip-top condition can be rented at the Hauptbahnhof's excellent **Radstation** (Fahrradservicestation; Map p452; ☎148 856; per 24hr €12; ⏱9am-6pm mid-Apr–Oct, 10am-6pm Mon-Fri Nov–mid-Apr) next to track 11. Staff are enthusiastic about cycling and can provide tips on routes.

SAARLAND

The tiny, often-overlooked federal state of Saarland (www.visitsaarland.co.uk), long a land of coal and heavy industry, has in recent decades cleaned up its air and streams and reoriented its struggling economy towards high-techology and ecotourism. The capital, Saarbrücken, is a vibrant city with excellent museums and a fine, French-influenced culinary scene. Rolling hills and forest cover much of the countryside, which can be explored not only by car or public transport but also on foot or by bicycle; cycling paths include the 356km, circular Saarland-Radweg and the 98km Saar-Radweg (VeloRoute SaarLorLux), along the (mostly) beautiful Saar River. The region's industrial heritage is celebrated in places such as the historic Völklinger Hütte ironworks.

Over the centuries, France and Germany have played ping pong with the Saarland, coveting it for its valuable natural resources. In the 20th century, the region came under French control twice – after each of the world wars – but in both cases (in referendums held in 1935 and 1955) its people voted in favour of rejoining Germany.

Although now solidly within German boundaries, the influence of the land of the baguette is still felt in all sorts of subtle ways. Many locals are bilingual and the standard greeting is not ' *hallo'* but ' *salü'*, from the French ' *salut'*. Their French heritage, although somewhat imposed, has softened the Saarlanders, who tend to be pretty relaxed folk with an appreciation of good food, wine and company – ' *Saarvoir vivre'*, it's been called.

Saarbrücken

☎0681 / POP 175,750

The Saarland capital, though a thoroughly modern city, has considerable historical charm. Vestiges of its 18th-century heyday as a royal residence under Prince Wilhelm Heinrich (1718–68) survive in the baroque town houses and churches designed by his prolific court architect, Friedrich Joachim Stengel.

The historic centre around St Johanner Markt brims with excellent restaurants and cafes.

⊙ Sights

RIGHT BANK

From the Hauptbahnhof, at the northwestern end of the city centre, pedestrian-only Reichsstrasse and its continuation Bahnhofstrasse – the attractive main shopping street – lead 1km southeast to St Johanner Markt.

St Johanner Markt   SQUARE

The heart of Saarbrücken (and its nightlife hub) is the historic St Johanner Markt, a long, narrow public square anchored by an ornate fountain designed by Stengel and flanked by some of the town's oldest buildings.

Basilika St Johann   CHURCH

(Katholisch-Kirch-Strasse 26; ⊙8.30 or 9.30am-7.15pm, Wed to 5pm) This dazzlingly baroque Catholic church, designed by Stengel, will wow you with its gleaming gold altars, *pulpit*, organ case and overhead rayburst design – and with its legions of über-cute putti. As you face the facade, the entrance is to the left around the side.

 Moderne Galerie   MUSEUM

(www.saarlandmuseum.de; Bismarckstrasse 11-15; admission free; ⊙10am-6pm Tue & Thu-Sun, 10am-10pm Wed) One of Saarland's cultural highlights, the Saarland Museum's Moderne Galerie covers European art from the late 1800s to the present and is especially noteworthy for its works of German Impressionism (eg Slevogt, Corinth and Liebermann), French Impressionism (eg Monet, Sisley and Renoir) and expressionism (eg Kirchner, Marc and Jawlensky). The brand new Galerie der Gegenwart focuses on contemporary art. Set to reopen after a complete renovation in late 2012.

LEFT BANK

Schlossplatz   SQUARE

Crossing the Saar River via the pedestrians-only Alte Brücke takes you over the autobahn and up to the Stengel-designed baroque Schlossplatz, around which you'll find all the city's museums that deal with history and pre-19th-century art. The dominant building here is the Saarbrücker Schloss, which mixes several architectural styles from Renaissance to baroque to neoclassical. The northern wing was once used by the Gestapo as offices and detention cells.

Historisches Museum Saar   MUSEUM

(www.historisches-museum.org; Schlossplatz 15; adult/student €5/3; ⊙10am-6pm Tue, Wed, Fri & Sun, 10am-8pm Thu, noon-6pm Sat) The Saarbrücker Schloss' basement and a modern annex house the well-designed Museum of Regional History. The section covering Saarland from 1870 to 1914 includes a 1904 film of Saarbrücken street life with cameo appearances by a surprising number of dogs. From here you can descend to the castle's massive bastions and Kasematten (casemates; English brochure available). Other exhibits look at Saarland under French rule (1920–1935) and during the Nazi era. Signs are in German and French.

Kreisständehaus   MUSEUM

(Schlossplatz 16; ⊙10am-6pm Tue & Thu-Sun, 10am-10pm Wed) The Kreisständehaus provides access to three free museums. The Saarland Museum's Alte Sammlung (Old Collection; www.saarlandmuseum.de) displays a millennium's worth of paintings, porcelain, tapestries and sculptures from southwest Germany and the Alsace and Lorraine regions of France. Fans of the Romans, the Celts and their predecessors won't want to miss the Museum für Vor- und Frühgeschichte (Museum of Early History & Prehistory; www.vorgeschichte.de). The star exhibit here features resplendent gold jewellery from around 400 BC, discovered in the tomb of a Celtic princess at Bliesbruck-Reinheim. The Museum in der Schlosskirche (☑954 0518; admission free; ⊙10am-6pm Tue & Thu-Sun, 10am-10pm Wed), inside a desanctified late Gothic church, features religious art from the 13th to 19th centuries.

Ludwigskirche   CHURCH

(www.ludwigskirche.de; Ludwigsplatz; ⊙10am-6pm Tue-Sun Apr-Sep, noon-5pm Tue & 10am-5pm Wed-Sat Jan-Mar, closed during weddings) The star at Stengel's handsome Ludwigsplatz, flanked by stately baroque town houses, is Stengel's masterpiece, Ludwigskirche, a Protestant church built in 1775 and rebuilt after WWII. It sports a facade festooned with biblical figures and a brilliant white interior with stylish stucco decoration. When it's closed, you can sneak a peek through the windows of the vestibule.

☞ Tours

You can download a free, 1½-hour MP3 **audioguide** to the city (available in English, French and German) from www.saarbruecken.tomis.

mobi. The tourist office rents out MP3 players with the audioguide already loaded (€3).

🛏 Sleeping

Hotel Stadt Hamburg
HOTEL $$
(☎379 9890; www.hotel-stadt-hamburg-saarbru ecken.de; Bahnhofstrasse 71-73, 3rd fl; s/d from €63/89, weekend €4 less; [P][❤]) An unpromisingly small street door leads to a cheerful, well-kept establishment decorated with original watercolours, oils and collages (the owner is an artist). The 24 cheerful rooms are decorated in shades both pastel and saturated. Very central, but quiet.

Hotel Madeleine
HOTEL $$
(☎322 28; www.hotel-madeleine.de; Cecilienstrasse 5; d/q Mon-Thu €89/130, Fri-Sun €74/125; [@][❤]) Central and friendly, this family-run hotel has 28 well-kept rooms that are bright and comfortable but compact (doubles are 12 to 14 sq m). Half the rooms have church views. Breakfasts are organic.

DJH Hostel
HOSTEL $
(☎0681 330 40; www.jugendherberge.de; Meerwiesertalweg 31; dm/d €21.50/54; [P][❤]) This modern, 192-bed hostel, 1.5km northeast of the city centre (ie Kaiserstrasse), is a 20-minute walk from the Hauptbahnhof and 100m from a supermarket. Served by buses 101, 102 and 150 from the Rathaus and, Monday to Friday, by buses 112 and 124 from the Hauptbahnhof.

🍴 Eating & Drinking

Many local dishes revolve around the humble potato – look for *Hoorische* (potato dumplings, literally 'hairy ones'), *Gefüllde* (*Hoorische* filled with minced meat and liver sausage) and *Dibbelabbes* (a potato casserole with dried meat and leeks). In the French tradition, meals are often served with a basket of crunchy French bread.

Saarbrücken's lively restaurant, cafe and bar scene centres on St Johanner Markt and nearby streets Saarstrasse, Am Stiefel and Kappenstrasse, with cheaper eats along Kaltenbachstrasse.

The city's lively student nightlife district is four long blocks northeast of St Johanner Markt around the intersection of Nauwieserstrasse and Cicilienstrasse. Some of the bars (eg very popular **Kurze Eck** at Nauwieserstrasse 15) are open until the wee hours.

On the Left Bank, cafes can be found around the Schlossplatz.

TOP CHOICE Zum Stiefel
GERMAN $$
(☎936 450; www.stiefelgastronomie.de; Am Stiefel 2; restaurant mains €8.50 to €23; ⊘restaurant open 11.45am-2pm and 5.30pm-11pm except Sun, Stiefel-Bräu open 11.30am-1am Mon-Sat and 5.30-11pm Sun) Zum Stiefel's two very German eateries share a kitchen. The restaurant features good-value classic German and *saarländische* dishes, including Gefüllde. Next door (the entrance is around the corner), Stiefel-Bräu, Saarbrücken's oldest microbrewery, serves quicker meals and three beers brewed according to an old Broch family recipe.

Rewe
SUPERMARKET $
(Reichstrasse 1; ⊘8am-8pm Mon-Sat) Picnic fixin's on the lower level of the huge, new Europa-Galerie shopping mall.

Wally's Irish Pub
PUB
(Katholisch-Kirch-Strasse 1; ⊘2pm-midnight or later Sun-Thu, to 3am or later Fri & Sat) Popular with locals who hail from the English-speaking lands, this welcoming pub – a great place to meet people – is owned by an Irish fellow whose name is *not* Wally.

☆ Entertainment

Tickets for concerts and other cultural events are available at the **Ticketshop** (☎936 990; St Johanner Markt 27; ⊘9am-7pm Mon-Fri, 10am-4pm Sat).

ℹ Information

ATMs Sprinkled along Kaiserstrasse.

Evangelisches Krankenhaus (EvK; ☎388 60; Grossherzog-Friedrich-Strasse 44; ⊘24hr) A city centre hospital whose main entrance is on Neikestrasse.

Tele-Med Internet Cafe (Cicilienstrasse 11; per hr €1; ⊘10am-11pm Mon-Sat, noon-11pm Sun) Internet access and international phone calls.

Tourist Office (☎938 090; www.die-region -saarbruecken.de; Rathausplatz 1; ⊘9am-6pm Mon-Fri, 10am-4.30pm Sat) Has some excellent English brochures on Saarbrücken and the Saarland. Sells tickets for cultural events and cycling guides. Offers free internet access. Situated inside Rathaus St-Johann, a red-brick neo-Gothic structure built from 1897 to 1900.

Waschhaus (Nauwieserstrasse 22; ⊘8am-10pm) Self-service laundry.

ℹ Getting There & Away

Saarbrücken's Hauptbahnhof has at least hourly rail connections to Mainz (€21 to €35, two hours) and, via Völklingen, to Trier (€16.40, 1¼ hours). Every two hours there's a train south to the lovely French city of Metz (€15.80, one hour) – ideal for a trans-border day trip.

ℹ Getting Around

Saarbrücken has an extensive, integrated **bus and rail network** (☎500 3377; www.saarbahn. de) that includes one tram line, called S1. Tickets within the city (Zone 111) cost €2.40 (€1.80 for up to five stops); a day pass for one/five people costs €5.20/9.50.

You can book a taxi on ☎330 33.

At press time, there was nowhere in Saarbrücken to rent bicycles.

Around Saarbrücken

⊙ Sights

Völklinger Hütte   HISTORICAL SITE
(www.voelklinger-huette.org; adult/7-16yr/student/family €12/3/10/25; ⊙10am-7pm Apr-Oct, 10am-6pm Nov- Mar) Both Dickensian and futuristic, dystopian and a symbol of renewal, the hulking former ironworks of Völklinger Hütte, located in Völklingen, about 10km northwest of Saarbrücken, are one of Europe's great heavy-industrial relics. Opened in 1873, 17,000 people worked here by 1965 – the height of Germany's post-WWII boom. The plant blasted its last pig iron in 1986 and was declared a World Heritage Site by Unesco in 1994.

The plant's massive scale dwarfs mere humans, who nevertheless, managed to master the forces of fire, wind and earth in order to smelt iron, without which civilisation as we know it could not exist. Fine views of the whole rusty ensemble can be had from atop a 45m **blast furnace** (helmet required). Parts of the vast complex are being reclaimed by trees, shrubs and mosses. Brochures and all signs are in German, English and French.

Colourful works of modern art make a particularly cheerful impression amid the ageing concrete and rusted pipes, beams, conveyors and car-sized ladles. Check out the website for details on exhibitions and events (eg summertime jazz concerts). At night the compound is luridly lit up like a vast science-fiction set.

Trains link the town of Völklingen with Saarbrücken (€3, 10 minutes, twice an hour) and Trier (€13.30, one hour, at least hourly); the ironworks are a three-minute walk from the Bahnhof.

By car, take the A620 to Völklingen and follow the signs to the 'Weltkulturerbe'.

Saarschleife   AREA
The most scenic spot along the Saar River is the Saarschleife, where the river makes a spectacular, almost unbelievable hairpin turn, flowing 10km to return to a point just 2km from where it started. In a large nature park about 5km northwest of Mettlach (towards Nennig), the best viewing point is Cloef, a short walk through the forest from the village of Orscholz.

The Saarschleife is 55km northwest of Saarbrücken along the A620 and A8.

GÜNTER GRÄFENHAIN / HUBER / 4CORNERS©

Landscapes

Like a fine wine, Germany's landscapes want to be savoured. Remember this as you revel in the rustic grandeur of the Alps, sample the mellifluous meanderings of the Moselle or ramble in an enchanted forest that inspired fairy tales.

Bewitching Forests

1 Germany's ancient and inky forests captivate with enough drama and grace to convert even a dedicated loafer to the great outdoors. The Black Forest (p329) – fabled, fabulous and family friendly – is just one such green oasis exerting its siren call.

Coastal Charisma

2 Germany's coast is a tale of two seas. Undulating dunes hem the tranquil Baltic (p702), punctuated by candy-striped lighthouses. Fierce and raw, the North Sea is dotted with scores of wind-whipped offshore islands, like glamorous Sylt (p688).

Sinuous Streams

3 Germany's rivers course vividly through the imagination, and none more so than the Romantic Rhine (p434). Rife with mythology, artist-inspiring scenery and legend-shrouded castles, its mystique will carve deeply into your memory.

PETER ADAMS / GETTY IMAGES ©

Magic Mountains

4 The big-shouldered Bavarian Alps (p230) are Germany's 'upper storey'. Hike among fragrant pines in summer, through hamlets serenaded by the bells of onion-domed churches, or try snowshoeing through a winter wonderland.

Languorous Lakes

5 Germany's shimmering lakes are fantastic summer destinations. From sea-sized Lake Constance (p356) to pristine mountain pools and the 'land of a thousand lakes' (p698) in the north, you'll find plenty of ways to frolic in or out on the water.

Clockwise from top left
1 Hotzenwald in the Black Forest 2 Ellenbogen, Sylt
3 The Rhine Valley 4 Bavarian Alps

Cologne & Northern Rhineland

Best Places to Eat

» Salon Schmitz (p474)

» Päffgen (p475)

» Brauerei im Füchschen (p498)

» Altes Gasthaus Leve (p515)

Best Places to Stay

» Hotel Résidence (p505)

» Galerie-Hotel Abingdorf (p522)

» Hotel Hopper et cetera (p473)

» Hotel Drei Könige (p490)

Why Go?

Cologne's iconic Dom has twin towers that might as well be twin exclamation points after the word 'welcome'. Flowing behind the cathedral, the Rhine River provides a vital link for some of the region's highlights: Düsseldorf, with its great nightlife and fabulous shopping, and Bonn, which has retained its air of Cold War mystery. Away from the river, Aachen still echoes with the beat of the Holy Roman Empire and Charlemagne.

Much of Germany's 20th-century economic power stemmed from the Northern Rhineland industrial region known as the Ruhrgebiet. Now cities such as Essen are transforming old steelworks and coal mines into cultural centres and more, Dortmund is embracing its amazing football record and literally scoring with it, while ancient Münster is a hive of students on bikes day and night, making it endlessly interesting and vibrant.

When to Go

Sure it's cold in December but Cologne's Christmas market will warm you up. And then just a couple of months later, the city's Carnival is one of Europe's best. Although the region has plenty of beer gardens and restaurants that delight in the warm weather, much of what's best happens indoors so you really can visit any time. The best reason to come in summer might be for walks along the Rhine, hikes in the Eifel National Park or partying in Münster's parks.

The Region's Beers

» **Kölsch** From Cologne and unlike any other beer in Germany. It's light, clear, hoppy and slightly sweet,

» **Altbier** Düsseldorf's special: a dark, hoppy beer that's just slightly heavy.

» **Pinkus Müller** A fabulous microbrewery in Münster, with a splendid range of seasonal beers.

DON'T MISS

What may be most rewarding about your trip to Cologne and the surrounding region are the surprises. In the big city itself, you may be trying to get your jaw back in place for days after seeing the incredible Roman mosaics in Cologne's **Römisch-Germanisches Museum**.

Equally lavish but 1700 years newer, are the over-the-top **Brühl Palaces** in their namesake town. Just up the Rhine, Bonn has a wonderful trip down memory lane to when it was the capital of West Germany. The **Haus der Geschichte der Bundesrepublik Deutschland** recalls a time when you could expect a spy to be lurking around every corner. Also in Bonn, where better to hear the works of local-boy-made-good Beethoven than in the concert hall named after him, **Beethovenhalle**.

Vast amounts of wealth have been produced in the region and it has gone to funding such cultural heavyweights as Düsseldorf's **Kunstsammlung Nordrhein-Westfalen**, which is three art museums in one.

In the once-mighty industrial Ruhr region, the Ruhrgebiet, you can easily spend a day at the Unesco-recognised **Zollverein** near Essen. A vast coal mine and coke-producing plant has been turned into an adventureland of museums, galleries and more. Just up the road, you can get a sense of the sweat that helped make the region what it is at the restored **Zollern Colliery** near Dortmund.

Regional Train Passes

There are several deals available for getting around Cologne and the surrounding state of North Rhine–Westphalia by public transport. The **SchönerTagTicket** buys one day of unlimited travel within the state from 9am to 3am the following day (midnight to 3am the next day on weekends). You can only use RE, RB and S-Bahn trains as well as buses, U-Bahn and trams. The ticket costs €27 for single travellers and €37.50 for groups of up to five people.

ON YOUR KNEES

If you need to repent, consider these churches:

» Kölner Dom (Cologne)

» Münster Basilica (Bonn)

» Dom (Aachen)

» Dom St Paul (Münster)

» St Patrokli (Soest)

Fast Facts

» Population: 17.8 million (North Rhine–Westphalia)

» Area: 34,080 sq km (North Rhine–Westphalia)

Score!

The region is football mad, as shown with:

» Gelsenkirchen's hugely popular club FC Schalke 04

» Dortmund's winning club Borussia

» The 2014 opening of the German Football Museum in Dortmund.

Resources

» Ruhr Tourismus (www.ruhr-tourismus.de)

» Industrial Heritage Trail (www.route-industrie kultur.de)

» 100 Schlösser Route (www.100-schloesser-route.de)

» Route Charlemagne Information Centre (www.route-charlemagne.eu)

COLOGNE & NORTHERN RHINELAND

Cologne & Northern Rhineland Highlights

1 Feel your spirits soar as you climb the majestic loftiness of Cologne's **Dom** (p466)

2 Live the good life in the comfy surrounds of **Düsseldorf** (p492)

3 Experience a 21st-century spin on the industrial age at the **Zollverein coal mine** (p504) in Essen

4 Step back to the Middle Ages in **Aachen** (p487), with memories of Charlemagne around every corner

5 Enjoy the vibrant life of **Münster** (p511), where great history combines with youthful pleasures

6 Taste the unique beers of the region in the many **splendid old restaurants** (p475)

7 Realise that Germany's Roman history almost rivals Italy's in **Xanten** (p501)

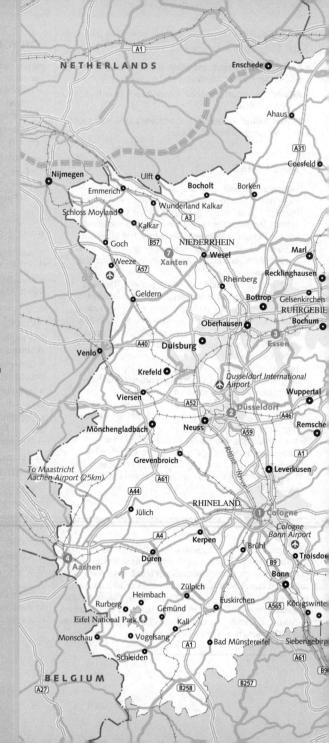

COLOGNE

☎0221 / POP 1 MILLION

Cologne (Köln) offers seemingly endless attractions, led by its famous cathedral with filigree twin spires that dominate the skyline. The city's Dom is regularly voted the country's single most popular tourist attraction. Cologne's museum landscape is especially strong when it comes to art but also has something in store for fans of chocolate, sports and even Roman history. Its people are well known for their liberalism and joie de vivre and it's easy to have a good time right along with them year-round in the beer halls of the Altstadt (old town) or during the springtime Carnival.

Cologne is like a 3D textbook on history and architecture. Drifting about town you'll stumble upon an ancient Roman wall, medieval churches galore, nondescript postwar buildings, avant-garde structures and even a new postmodern quarter right on the Rhine. Germany's fourth-largest city was founded by the Romans in 38 BC and given the lofty name Colonia Claudia Ara Aggripinensium. It grew into a major trading centre, a tradition it solidified in the Middle Ages and continues to uphold today.

⊙ Sights

ALTSTADT

The Altstadt hugs the river bank between two bridges, Hohenzollernbrücke and Deutzer Brücke. You can spend half a day in Cologne or a couple of days, just strolling and soaking it in. The city maintains an excellent website (www.museenkoeln.de) with info on most of Cologne's museums.

Cologne's medieval heyday is reflected in its wealth of Romanesque churches, which were constructed between 1150 and 1250, and survived largely intact until WWII. About a dozen have been rebuilt since and offer many unique architectural and artistic features. Even if you're pushed for time, try seeing at least a couple of the ones mentioned here.There's a good website (www.romanische-kirchen-koeln.de) with info on all the churches.

Kölner Dom   CHURCH

(Cologne Cathedral; Map p468; ☎1794 0200; www .koelner-dom.de; ⊙6am-10pm May-Oct, to 7.30pm Nov-Apr) Cologne's geographical and spiritual heart – and its single-biggest tourist draw – is the magnificent Kölner Dom. With its soaring twin spires, this is the Mt Everest of cathedrals, jam-packed with art and treasures. Its loftiness and dignified ambience leave only the most jaded of visitors untouched.

Construction began in 1248 in the French Gothic style but proceeded slowly and was eventually halted in 1560 when funds ran out. The half-built church lingered for nearly 300 years and even suffered a stint as a horse stable and prison when Napoleon occupied the town. A few decades later, a generous cash infusion from Prussian King Friedrich Wilhelm IV finally led to its completion in 1880. Luckily, it escaped WWII bombing raids with nary a shrapnel wound and has been a Unesco World Heritage Site since 1996.

The Dom is Germany's largest cathedral and must be circled to truly appreciate its dimensions. Note how its lacy spires and flying buttresses create a sensation of lightness and fragility despite its mass and height. This sensation continues inside, where a phalanx of pillars and arches supports the lofty nave. Soft light filters through the dazzling stained-glass windows, including the spectacular new one by Gerhard Richter in the transept. A kaleidoscope of 11,500 squares in 72 colours, Richter's abstract design has been called a 'symphony of light'. In the afternoon especially, when the sun hits it just so, it's easy to understand why.

Among the cathedral's numerous treasures, the *pièce de résistance* is the Shrine of the Three Kings behind the main altar, a richly bejewelled and gilded sarcophagus said to hold the remains of the kings who followed the star to the stable in Bethlehem where Jesus was born. The bones were spirited out of Milan in 1164 as spoils of war by Emperor Barbarossa's chancellor and instantly turned Cologne into a major pilgrimage site.

Other highlights include the Gero Crucifix (970), notable for its monumental size and an emotional intensity rarely achieved in those early medieval days; the choir stalls from 1310, richly carved from oak; and the altar painting by local artist Stephan Lochner from around 1450.

To get more out of your visit, invest €1 in the information pamphlet or join a guided tour (adult/child €7/5; ⊙tours in English: 10.30am & 2.30pm Mon-Sat, 2.30pm Sun Apr-Oct, less often other times).

For an exercise fix, climb the 509 steps up the Dom's south tower (adult/child €3/1.50;

⊙9am-4pm Nov-Feb, to 5pm Mar-Apr & Oct, to 6pm May-Sep) to the base of the steeple that dwarfed all buildings in Europe until Gustave Eiffel built a certain tower in Paris. A good excuse to take a breather on your way up is the 24-tonne Peter Bell (1923), the largest free-swinging working bell in the world. Views from the 95m platform are so wonderful, you'll forget your vertigo.

Cologne is justifiably proud of its Domschatz-kammer (Cathedral Treasury; Map p468; ☑1794 0300; adult/child €5/2.50; ⊙10am-6pm), whose reliquaries, robes, sculptures and liturgical objects are handsomely presented in medieval vaulted rooms. Standouts include a Gothic bishop's staff from 1322 and a 15th-century sword.

TOP CHOICE Museum Schnütgen   MUSEUM
(Map p468; ☑2212 3620; www.museenkoeln.de; Cäcilienstrasse 29; adult/child €5/3; ⊙10am-6pm Tue-Sun, to 8pm Thu) East of the Neumarkt, the Cultural Quarter encompasses the Museum Schnütgen, a repository of medieval religious art and sculpture. Part of the exhibit shows the beautiful setting of the Romanesque Cäcilienkirche (Cecily Church). Also part of the atrium complex is the Rautenstrauch-Joest-Museum.

Rautenstrauch-Joest-Museum   MUSEUM
(Map p468; ☑2213 1301; www.museenkoeln.de; Cäcilienstrasse 29-33; adult/child €6/4; ⊙10am-6pm Tue-Sun, to 8pm Thu) Opened in 2010, this museum boldly makes a statement with a huge rice boat from Sulawesi that fills the lobby. Over three floors there are exhibits on the cultures of the world; fear not about getting your knuckles rapped, these are interactive and you're encouraged to touch.

Chocolate Museum   MUSEUM
(Schokoladen Museum; Map p468; ☑9318880; www.schokoladenmuseum.de; Am Schokoladenmuseum 1a; adult/concession €8.50/6; ⊙10am-6pm Tue-Fri, 11am-7pm Sat & Sun) You don't have to have a sweet tooth to enjoy the Schokoladen Museum, which looks like, well, a box of chocolates on its little island in the river. At this high-tech temple to the art of chocolate-making, exhibits on the origin of the 'elixir of the gods', as the Aztecs called it, and the cocoa-growing process are followed by a live-production factory tour and a stop at a chocolate fountain for a sample. Upstairs are exhibits on the cultural history of chocolate, as well as advertising, and porcelain

and other accessories. Stock up on your favourite flavours at the downstairs shop.

Deutsches Sport &
Olympia Museum   MUSEUM
(German Sport & Olympic Games Museum; Map p468; ☑0221 336 090; Im Zollhafen 1; adult/child €6/3; ⊙10am-6pm Tue-Fri, 11am-7pm Sat & Sun) In a 19th-century customs building, the Deutsches Sport & Olympia Museum is an imaginative, if Germany-focused, tribute to the sporting life from antiquity to today. There are exhibits on the 1936 Berlin and 1972 Munich Olympic Games and on such modern-day heroes as Steffi Graf and Michael Schumacher. Interactive displays allow you to experience a bobsled run or a bike race, and on the miniature football field on the rooftop you can kick with a view of the cathedral.

NS Dokumentationszentrum   MUSEUM
(Map p468; ☑2212 6332; www.museenkoeln.de; Appellhofplatz 23-25; adult/child €5/2; ⊙10am-6pm Tue-Fri, 11am-6pm Sat & Sun) Cologne's Third Reich history is poignantly documented in the NS Documentation Centre. In the basement of this otherwise mundane-looking building was the local Gestapo prison where scores of people were interrogated, tortured and killed. Inscriptions on the basement cell walls offer a gut-wrenching record of the emotional and physical pain endured by inmates. Executions often occurred in the courtyard.

Kolumba   MUSEUM
(Map p468; ☑933 1930; www.kolumba.de; Kolumbastrasse 4; adult/child €5/free; ⊙noon-5pm Wed-Mon, to 7pm Thu) Art, history, architecture and spirituality form a harmonious tapestry in this spectacular collection of religious treasures of the Archdiocese of Cologne. Called Kolumba, the building encases the ruins of the late-Gothic church of St Kolumba, layers of foundations going back to Roman times and the Madonna in the Ruins chapel, built on the site in 1950. It's yet another magnificent design by Swiss architect Peter Zumthor, 2009 winner of the Pritzker Prize, the 'architectural Oscar'. Exhibits span the arc of religious artistry from the early days of Christianity to the present. Coptic textiles, Gothic reliquary and medieval painting are juxtaposed with works by Bauhaus legend Andor Weininger and edgy room installations. Don't miss the 12th-century carved ivory crucifix.

Cologne

Brusseler Str

Schmalbeinstr

20

Hildebold-platz

Gereonshof

Gereonsdriesch

Steinfelder Gasse

Mohrenstr

62

Bismarckstr

Venloer Str

Au dem Berlich

18

To Underground (1.8km)

Friesen-platz

Friesenstr

52

43

Am Römerturm

Antwerpener Str

46

Helenenstr

44

Brüsseler Str

BELGISCHES VIERTEL

Hohenzollernring

Frieserwall

St-Apern-Str

Gertrudenstr

Wolfstr

Richmodstr

Brüsseler Platz

Maastricher Str

Ehrenstr

Flandrische Str

Lütticher Str

38

45

Mittelstr

Pfeilstr

Mittelstr

36

40

65

Aachener Str

55

Hahnenstr

7

Rudolf-platz

Neumarkt

34

Richard-Wagner-Str

Cäcilienstr

Handelstr

Engelbertstr

Schaafenstr

Mauritiussteinweg

Clemensstr

30

Moltkestr

53

28

ZÜLPICHER VIERTEL

Rubenstr

Mauritiuswall

31

Bayardsgasse

Jülicher Str

58

33

Mozartstr

64

Thieboldsgasse

Lindenstr

Roonstr

Rathenau-platz

Kleiner Griechenmarkt

Görresstr

39

Hohenstaufenring

Friedrichstr

Zülpicher Platz

Rothgerberbach

Dasselstr

43

Hochstadenstr

41

Zülpicher Str

37

Barbarossa-platz

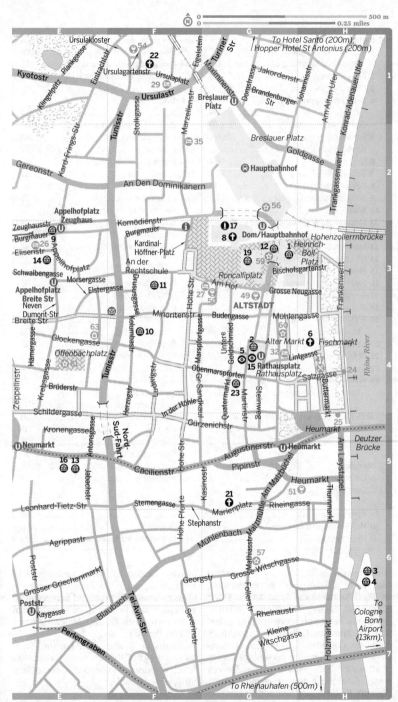

N 0 —————— 500 m
0 —————— 0.25 miles

COLOGNE & NORTHERN RHINELAND COLOGNE

To Hotel Santo (200m);
Hopper Hotel St Antonius (200m)

Ursulakloster

Kyotostr

Ursulagartenstr

29

22

Ursulaplatz

Ursulastr

Breslauer
Platz

Gereonstr

35

Breslauer Platz

Goldgasse

An Den Dominikanern

Hauptbahnhof

56

Appelhofplatz
Zeughaus

Zeughausstr

Komödienstr
Burgmauer

17

Burgmauer

26

Elisenstr

Kardinal-
Höffner-Platz
An der
Rechtschule

8

Dom/Hauptbahnhof

Hohenzollernbrücke

12

1

Heinrich-
Böll-
Platz

14

Appelhofplatz

Schwalbengasse

Morsergasse

Elstergasse

19

59

Bischofsgartenstr

Appelhofplatz
Breite Str
Neven
Dumont-Str

11

27

Roncalliplatz
Am Hof

50

49

Grosse Neugasse

ALTSTADT

Breite Str

Minoritenstr

Budengasse

Mühlengasse

Glockengasse

10

60

6

Alter Markt

Fischmarkt

Offenbachplatz

63

Untere
Goldschmied

2

32

Lintgasse

Rhine River

15

Rathausplatz
Rathausplatz

24

Obenmarspforten

Salzgasse

Buttermarkt

Schildergasse

Gr. Sandkaul

Marspfortengasse

In der Höhle

23

Martinstr

Steinweg

25

Kronengasse

Gürzenichstr

Heumarkt

Deutzer
Brücke

Neumarkt

16

13

Cäcilienstr

Augustinerstr

Heumarkt

Pipinstr

Leonhard-Tietz-Str

Sternengasse

21

Marienplatz

Rheingasse

Heumarkt

51

Stephanstr

Mühlenbach

Agrippastr

57

Grosser Griechenmarkt

Georgstr

Grosse Witschgasse

3

4

Poststr

Kaygasse

Rheinaustr

Kleine
Witschgasse

To
Cologne
Bonn
Airport
(13km);

Perlengraben

To Rheinauhafen (500m)

Cologne

Museum Ludwig   MUSEUM
(Map p468; ☎2212 6165; www.museenkoeln.
de; Bischofsgartenstrasse 1; adult/child €10/7;
◔10am-6pm Tue-Sun) The distinctive building facade and unorthodox roofline signal
that the Museum Ludwig is no ordinary
museum. Considered a mecca of postmodern art, it actually presents a survey
of all major 20th-century genres. There's
plenty of American pop art, including Andy
Warhol's *Brillo Boxes,* alongside a comprehensive Picasso collection and plenty of
works by Sigmar Polke. Fans of German expressionism will get their fill here as much
as those with a penchant for such Russian
avant-gardists as Kasimir Malewitsch and
Ljubow Popowa.

Admission is also good for the Foto-
Museum Agfa Foto-Historama (Map p468),
which comprises a collection of compelling
historic photographs.

Wallraf-Richartz-Museum & Fondation Corboud
MUSEUM

(Map p468; ☑2212 1119; www.museenkoeln.de; Obenmars-pforten; adult/child €9/6; ⊙10am-6pm Tue-Sun, to 9pm Thu) A famous collection of paintings from the 13th to the 19th centuries, the Wallraf-Richartz-Museum occupies a postmodern cube designed by the late OM Ungers. Works are presented chronologically, with the oldest on the 1st floor where standouts include brilliant examples from the Cologne School, known for its distinctive use of colour. Upstairs are Dutch and Flemish artists, including Rembrandt and Rubens, Italians such as Canaletto and Spaniards such as Murillo. The 3rd floor focuses on the 19th century, with evocative works by Caspar David Friedrich and Lovis Corinth. There's also a respectable collection of impressionist paintings, including canvases by Monet and Cézanne.

Gross St Martin
CHURCH

(Map p468; ☑1642 5650; An Gross-St-Martin 9; ⊙8.30am-7.30pm Tue-Sat, 1-7pm Sun) Winning top honours for Cologne's most handsome exterior is Gross St Martin, whose ensemble of four slender turrets grouped around a central spire towers above Fischmarkt in the Altstadt. Its striking clover-leaf choir is an architectural feature pioneered by St Maria im Kapitol (Map p468; ☑214 615; Marienplatz 19; ⊙10am-6pm Mon-Sat, noon-6pm Sun), where major treasures include a carved door from the original 11th-century church and a spectacularly ornate Renaissance rood screen.

Museum für Angewandte Kunst
MUSEUM

(Museum of Applied Arts; Map p468; ☑2212 6735; www.makk.de; An der Rechtschule; adult/child €5/3; ⊙11am-5pm Tue-Sun) The Museum für Angewandte Kunst consists of a series of period rooms tracing European design from the Middle Ages to today. Keep an eye out for a 15th-century Venetian wedding goblet, a silver service by Henry van de Velde and life-sized animals made of Meissen porcelain.

Käthe Kollwitz Museum
MUSEUM

(Map p468; ☑227 2899; www.kollwitz.de; Neumarkt 18-24; adult/child €4/2; ⊙10am-6pm Tue-Fri, 11am-6pm Sat & Sun) The Käthe Kollwitz Museum has graphics and sculptures by the acclaimed socialist artist. A highlight is the haunting cycle called Ein Weberaufstand (A Weavers' Revolt, 1897). Enter through an arcade, then take the glass-walled lift to the 4th floor.

Kölnisches Stadtmuseum
MUSEUM

(Cologne City Museum; Map p468; ☑2212 5789; www.museenkoeln.de; Zeughausstrasse 1-3; adult/child €3.50/1.50; ⊙10am-8pm Tue, to 5pm Wed-Sun) The Kölnisches Stadtmuseum, in the former medieval armoury, explores all facets of Cologne history. There are exhibits on Carnival, Kölsch (the local beer), eau de cologne and other things that make the city unique.

St Gereon
CHURCH

(Map p468; ☑474 5070; Gereonskloster 2-4; ⊙10-noon, 3-5pm Tue-Fri, 10am-noon Sat) Cologne's most eccentric-looking church is St Gereon, which grew from a late-Roman chapel into a massive complex lidded by a 10-sided dome decorated with delicate ribbed vaulting.

St Ursula
CHURCH

(Map p468; ☑133 400; Ursulaplatz 24; ⊙10am-6pm Mon-Sat, 3-4.30pm Sun) If you look at Cologne's coat of arms, you'll see what looks like 11 apostrophes but in fact represents the Christian martyrs St Ursula and 10 virgins. The church of St Ursula stands atop the Roman graveyard where the virgins' remains were allegedly found. In the 17th century, the richly ornamented baroque Goldene Kammer (Golden Chamber; Map p468; www.heilige-ursula.de; adult/child €2/1) was built to house their relics.

ALTES RATHAUS & AROUND

Cologne's Altes Rathaus (old town hall) and the surrounding area have been a major construction site while a new U-Bahn line is built. During this time, massive archeological excavations have taken place, which have produced many new discoveries about Cologne's Roman and even Jewish past. Work will continue through 2014 but eventually there will be two museums and a new U-Bahn stop.

Altes Rathaus
HISTORIC BUILDING

(Map p468; Rathausplatz; ⊙8am-4pm Mon & Wed-Thu, to 6pm Tue, to noon Sat) Dating to the 15th century and much restored, the old city hall has fine bells that ring daily at noon and 5pm. The Gothic tower is festooned with newly cleaned statues of old city notables.

Future Jüdisches Museum
HISTORIC SITE

(Jewish Museum; Map p468; www.museenkoeln.de; Rathausplatz) Cologne had a large Jewish population in the 12th and 13th centuries, and the foundations of a large neighbourhood have been uncovered as part of the new U-Bahn line construction as well as

HARBOUR REDUX: RHEINAUHAFEN

London has its Docklands, Düsseldorf its Medienhafen, Hamburg its building HafenCity and now Cologne has joined the revitalised-harbour trend with the Rheinauhafen. South of the Altstadt, a new urban quarter has sprung up along a 2km stretch between the Severinsbrücke and Südbrücke bridges. Dozens of 19th-century brick buildings are taking on a second life as office, living and entertainment spaces, juxtaposed with contemporary designs ranging from bland to avant-garde. The most dramatic change to Cologne's skyline comes courtesy of a trio of Kranhäuser (Crane Houses), huge inverted L-shaped structures that are an abstract interpretation of historic harbour cranes. There are some shops, restaurants and cafes as well as a riverside promenade but, as with all projects of this type, it'll be a while before the quarter's true character and personality make it a compelling place to visit.

improvements to the Roman Praetorium site and exhibit in the same area. A new Jewish museum based on these discoveries is set to rise behind the Rathaus, with work begun in 2012. In the meantime, at times the subterranean parts of a medieval synagogue here are open to the public. Visit the work site for more details.

TOP CHOICE Römisch-Germanisches Museum   MUSEUM
(Roman Germanic Museum; Map p468; ☎2212 2304; www.museenkoeln.de; Roncalliplatz 4; adult/child €8/4; ☺10am-5pm Tue-Sun) If you've never seen actual Roman mosaics before, be prepared to exclaim 'wow!' at the extraordinary Römisch-Germanisches Museum, adjacent to the Dom. Sculptures and ruins displayed outside are merely the overture to a full symphony of Roman artefacts found along the Rhine. Highlights include the giant Poblicius tomb (AD 30–40), the magnificent 3rd-century Dionysus mosaic around which the museum was built, and astonishingly well preserved glass items. Insight into daily Roman life is gained from such items as toys, tweezers, lamps and jewellery, the

designs of which have changed surprisingly little since.

Plenty of remnants of the Roman city survive around the museum, including a street leading to the harbour and two wells. Other vestiges from the ancient settlement include a Roman arch (Map p468) from the former town wall outside the Dom and the Römerturm (Map p468), a tower standing among buildings at the corner of St-Apern-Strasse and Zeughausstrasse.

Praetorium   HISTORIC SITE
(Map p468; ☎2212 2394; Kleine Budengasse 2; adult/child €3.50/free; ☺10am-5pm Tue-Sun) The Praetorium has relics of a Roman governor's palace below the Altes Rathaus. It will be part of the much larger subterranean archaeological area that will include the new Jewish Museum. Visitors will be able to get close-ups of remnants, ruins and foundations of both Roman Cologne. There have been many delays to the project but some form of access to the ruins has been maintained throughout.

BRÜSSELER PLATZ
The heart of the ever-so-lively-and-trendy Belgisches Viertel neighbourhood, Brüsseler Platz is a lush square surrounding St Michael's Church. Locals play chess, make out, sip a beer or catch up on the gossip. It's a good place for a picnic from one of the many ethnic markets on the surrounding streets.

☞ Tours

For an excellent DIY walking tour, start at the Dom and walk down to the river, turn south and head to the bridge over the Rhine River, the Deutzer Brücke. Cross east, watching the boat traffic below. On the east bank, follow the river promenade north, soaking up the sweeping view of the Cologne skyline across the water. Take the pedestrian path along the side of the Hohenzollernbrücke, the busy railway bridge, back west across the Rhine. All manner of trains will pound past you, just a few metres away. Return to the Dom and you will have walked about 2km.

Rent-A-Bike   BIKE TOUR
(Map p468; ☎0171-629 8796; www.koelnerfahrrad verleih.de; Marksmann-gasse; tours €15; ☺10am-6pm Apr-Oct) This bike rental place runs German/English three-hour bicycle tours daily at 1.30pm from April to October. Tours start in the Altstadt right below the Deutzer Brücke.

KD River Cruises · BOAT TOUR

(Map p468; ☑258 3011; www.k-d.com; Frankenwerft 35; tour €10; ☺10.30am-5pm) One of several companies offering one-hour spins taking in the splendid Altstadt panorama; other options include sunset cruises.

🛏 Sleeping

Cologne often hosts trade shows, which can cause hotel rates to double and triple. Otherwise, you'll find good-value options across the walkable central area.

TOP CHOICE Hotel Hopper et cetera · HOTEL €€

(Map p468; ☑924 400; www.hopper.de; Brüsseler Strasse 26; s €95-120, d €135-180; P@☜) A wax monk welcomes you to this former monastery, where the 49 rooms sport eucalyptus floors, cherry furniture and marble baths, along with lots of little pampering touches like iPod docks. The sauna and bar, both in the vaulted cellars, are great places for reliving the day's exploits. The cheapest singles are dubbed by the hotel 'monastic cells'.

Cerano Hotel · HOTEL €€

(Map p468; ☑925 7300; www.cerano-hotels.de; Elisenstrasse 16; r incl breakfast €60-120; ☜) This unassuming five-storey hotel is a short walk from the train station and is peppered with extra touches: mineral water, juices and more apples than you'd find in an orchard are always available. Many of the rooms have large work desks and windows that provide much natural light. The staff are uncommonly helpful and the breakfast is a delight.

Dom Hotel · LUXURY HOTEL €€€

(Map p468; ☑20240; www.starwoodhotels.com; Domkloster 2a; s/d from €170/195; ✳@☜) This temple to overnight stays is right on the plaza with Cologne's iconic cathedral. Built in 1857, and renovated and rebuilt innumerable times since, the 120 rooms drip with traditional luxury and most have views of the namesake Dom – where you can always drop by to renew your vow of poverty.

Pension Otto · PENSION €

(Map p468; www.pensionotto.de; Pension Otto Richard-Wagner-Strasse 18; s €30-65, d €60-90) This five-room *Pension* occupies the 1st floor of a beautiful 100-year-old apartment building. The five rooms have terrazzo floors and share bathrooms. There's no TV but you might just enjoy pondering the elaborate wall tiles in many rooms. This is excellent-value, basic accommodation.

Hotel Chelsea · HOTEL €€

(Map p468; ☑207 150; www.hotel-chelsea.de; Jülicher Strasse 1; s €60-130, d €90-160; P✳@☜) Those fancying an artsy vibe will be well sheltered in this self-proclaimed 'hotel different'. Originals created by international artists in exchange for lodging grace the public areas and 38 rooms and suites. The eye-catching deconstructivist rooftop extension houses a spectacular penthouse.

Hotel Cristall · HOTEL €€

(Map p468; ☑163 00; www.hotelcristall.de; Ursulaplatz 9-11; s €70-180, d €90-250; ✳@☜) This stylish boutique hotel makes excellent use of colour, customised furniture and light accents, and manages to appeal both to the suit brigade and city-breakers. Some rooms are rather compact, though, and light sleepers should get one facing away from the busy street.

Hopper Hotel St Antonius · HOTEL €€€

(☑166 00; www.hopper.de; Dagobertstrasse 32; s €105-290, d €150-320; P⊖@☜; Ebertplatz) History and high-tech mix nicely at this 54-room posh retreat with plenty of eye candy for the style-conscious. The romantic courtyard garden and small wellness area in the brick-vaulted cellar are great bliss-out spots. Main drawback: the bland setting near the Hauptbahnhof.

DON'T MISS

COLOGNE'S LOVE LOCKS

What at first looks like so much confetti in Cologne's iconic **Hohenzollernbrücke** railway bridge over the Rhine are in reality tens of thousands of locks in myriad shapes and colours. Almost all are engraved with some romantic slogan, proclamation of love or simply the names of people meant to be locked together for the ages.

On sunny weekends, you'll see people engaging in rituals grand and humble as they affix new 'love locks' to the railings and – inevitably – you might catch a delocking ceremony, whereby evidence of someone's now unpermanent love is removed and usually tossed in the drink, followed by much of same.

Hotel Santo
HOTEL €€

(913 9770; www.hotelsanto.de; Dagobertstrasse 22-26; s €95-140, d €120-160; P⊖❄🐾; Ebertplatz) Despite the drab location near the Hauptbahnhof, this 69-room boutique hotel is an island of sassy sophistication. The design flaunts an edgy, urban feel tempered by playful light effects, soothing colours and natural materials. Bonus: a gourmet breakfast is included.

Hotel Leonet
HOTEL €€

(Map p468; 272 300; www.hotel-leonet-koeln. de; Rubensstrasse 33; s €45-160, d €65-225; P⊖@🐾) This modern hotel has 78 rooms that vary between tiny economy singles and quite spacious doubles. The six floors are served by elevators. A good choice if you want a drama-free night's rest, with breakfast included.

Lint Hotel
HOTEL €€

(Map p468; 920 550; www.lint-hotel.de; Lintgasse 7; s €60-90, d €90-130; 🐾) Cute, contemporary and ecoconscious (solar-panelled roof) hotel in the heart of the Altstadt. The 18 rooms have hardwood floors and the breakfast buffet (included) has organic foods.

Station Hostel for Backpackers
HOSTEL €

(Map p468; 912 5301; www.hostel-cologne. de; Marzellenstrasse 44-56; dm €17-20, s/d from €32/48; @🐾) Near the Hauptbahnhof, this is a hostel as hostels should be: central, convivial and economical. A lounge gives way to clean, colourful rooms sleeping one to six people. There's lots of free stuff, including linen, internet access, lockers, city maps and guest kitchen. Some private rooms have their own bathrooms.

Meininger City Hostel & Hotel
HOSTEL €

(Map p468; 355 332 014; www.meininger-hostels .com; Engelbertstrasse 33-35; dm €18-24, s/d from €48/70; @🐾) In a former hotel, this charming hostel in the cool Zülpicher Viertel is loaded with retro appeal coupled with modern rooms that feature lockers, reading lamps, a small TV and private bathrooms. Freebies include linen, towels and pasta that you can whip up in the small basement kitchen. Room rates soar during trade shows.

✕ Eating

Cologne's multiculturalism lets you take a culinary journey around the world. The Belgisches Viertal and streets in and around Zülpicher Platz and Ehrenstrasse are ideal areas for making a tasty discovery.

TOP CHOICE Salon Schmitz
MODERN EUROPEAN €

(Map p468; Aachener Strasse 28; snacks €4-8) No matter whether you prefer sidling up to the long bar or grabbing an ultracomfy sofa in the retro lounge, Schmitz is a perfect pit stop for relaxed chats over coffee, cocktails or its house-brand *Kölsch*. If hunger strikes, pop next door to Metzgerei Schmitz, an elaborately tiled deli in a former butcher's shop. There's good casual take-out fare here.

Bei Oma Kleinmann
GERMAN €€

(Map p468; www.beiomakleinmann.de; Zülpicher Strasse 9; mains €12; ⏰5pm-1am Tue-Sun, kitchen to 11pm) Named for its long-time owner, who was still cooking almost to her last day at age 95 in 2009, this cosy traditional restaurant has a timeless menu of 14 kinds of schnitzel. Pull up a seat at the small wooden tables for a classic Cologne night out.

Feynsinn
INTERNATIONAL €€

(Map p468; 240 9210; www.cafe-feynsinn.de; Rathenauplatz 7; mains €7-18) What used to be a small cafe, famous for its eccentric glass-chard chandelier, has morphed into a well-respected restaurant where organic ingredients are woven into sharp-flavoured dishes. The owners raise their own meat. Get a table overlooking the park for a meal or just a drink.

Belgischer Hof
FRENCH €€

(Map p468; www.belgischer-hof.de; Brüsseler Strasse 54; mains €8-12) *Flammenkuchen,* the flat pizza-like tarts popular in France's Alsace region and Belgium, are the stars at this most-inviting bistro. At the first hint of warmth, the front opens to the street. The plant-filled courtyard is a more intimate place to sit. As suggested by the name, there are many fine Belgian beers on offer.

Sorgenfrei
MODERN EUROPEAN €€€

(Map p468; 355 7327; www.sorgenfrei-koeln.com; Antwerpener Strasse 15; mains €8-25; ⏰noon-3pm Mon-Fri, 6pm-midnight Mon-Sat) A huge wine-by-the-glass menu is but one draw of this Belgische Viertel fine dining treasure. Dishes are prepared with the same attention to detail (yet lack of pretension) found throughout this small restaurant. Hardwood floors encourage a casual vibe that goes well with salads and simple mains at lunch and more complex creations for dinner.

Engler's
MODERN EUROPEAN €€€

(Map p468; 990 6041; www.englerskoeln.de; Benesistrasse 57; mains €15-25; ⏰lunch & dinner Mon-Sat) A charming neighbourhood restaurant with a dedication to serving excellent meals. It's in a small midblock location, but the service and flavours are big. The menu changes daily and reflects the season; in late spring, for instance, you might enjoy fresh asparagus with pasta. Book, as this part of town around the Ehrenstrasse is as trendy as you can get.

Madame Miammiam
PASTRIES €

(Map p468; madamemiammiam.de; Antwerpener Strasse 39; treats from €3; ⊙11am-7pm Tue-Thu, to 10pm Fri & Sat, 1-5pm Sun) A luscious and spunky bakery that captures the Belgisches Viertel vibe, come here for amazing cupcakes, tarts, cookies and more. Then repair to Brüsseler Platz to sit back and enjoy.

Sünner im Walfisch
GERMAN €€€

(Map p468; www.walfisch.net; Salzgasse 13; mains €13-20) In a building that can trace its foundation back to at least 1626, this traditional German restaurant does a fine job with all the classics and is a cut above the often humdrum Altstadt tourist experience. It serves its own brand of *Kölsch* beer.

Engelbät
EUROPEAN €€

(Map p468; ☑246 914; www.engelbaet.de; Engelbertstrasse 7; crepes €3-9; ⊙11am-1am) This cosy restaurant-pub is famous for its habit-forming crepes, which come in 50 varieties – sweet, meat or vegetarian. It's also popular for weekend breakfast (served until 3pm). Outside of summer, there's often live jazz at night. The pavement tables are popular for drinks.

La Bodega
TAPAS €

(Map p468; ☑257 3610; www.la-bodega-koeln.de; Friesenstrasse 51; tapas €3-7; ⊙5pm-1am Sun-Thu, to 3am Fri & Sat) Tapas is served until late in this cosy vaulted cellar and romantic courtyard. Gobble up the *jamón* (air-cured ham), stuffed peppers, nut-encrusted goat's cheese and other authentic tapas or order a heaping paella.

Falafel Salam
FALAFEL €

(Map p468; ☑240 2933; Zülpicher Platz 7; felafel €4; ⊙11.30am-2am or later) The mother of all Cologne felafel snack bars. Get one with extra 'hommos'.

🍷 Drinking

Cologne's thirst parlours range from grungy to grand. Centres of action include the Altstadt, the student-flavoured Zülpicher Viertel and the more grown-up Belgisches Viertel, zinging bar and pub quarters.

KÖLSCH BEER

Cologne has its own style of beer, *Kölsch*, which is unlike any other in Germany. It's light and hoppy and slightly sweet, always crisp, and served cool. Unlike the vast steins used elsewhere for suds serving, in Cologne your *Kölsch* comes in *stangen*, skinny, straight glasses that only hold 0.2L.

In traditional Cologne beer halls and pubs you don't order beer so much as subscribe. The constantly prowling waiters will keep dropping off the little glasses of beer until you indicate you've had enough by placing a beer mat on top of your glass.

A ceaseless flow of *stangen* filled with *Kölsch*, along with earthy humour and platters of meaty local foods are the hallmarks of Cologne's iconic beer halls. Look for the days when each place serves glorious potato pancakes (*Kartoffelpuffer* or *Reibekuchen* in local dialect).

🏆 Päffgen
BEER HALL

(Map p468; www.paeffgen-koelsch.de; Friesenstrasse 64-66) Busy, loud and boisterous, Päffgen has been pouring *Kölsch* since 1883 and hasn't lost a step since. In summer you can enjoy the refreshing brew and local specialities beneath starry skies in the beer garden. Potato pancakes are served on Fridays.

Brauhaus Peters
BEER HALL

(Map p468; ☑257 3950; www.peters-brauhaus. de; Mühlengasse 1; dishes €4-13; ⊙11am-12.30am) This relative youngster draws a somewhat less raucous crowd knocking back their *Kölsch* in a web of highly individualistic nooks, including a room lidded by a kaleidoscopic stained-glass ceiling. On Tuesday, insiders invade for the freshly made potato pancakes. The wood carving over the main entrance translates as: 'Hops and malt, God preserves'.

Früh am Dom
BEER HALL

(Map p468; ☑258 0394; www.frueh.de; Am Hof 12-14; mains €5-12) This warren of a beer hall near the Dom epitomises Cologne earthiness. Sit inside amid loads of knick-knacks or on the flower-filled terrace next to a fountain. It's also known for great breakfasts.

Schreckenskammer
BEER HALL

(Mapp468;☑132581;www.schreckenskammer.com; Ursula-gartenstrasse 11; mains €7-15; ☺11am-1.45pm & 4.30-10.30pm Mon-Sat) Empty chairs are a rare sight at this locals' favourite that has excellent food. There's a fine beer garden and should you need divine inspiration for just one more *stangen,* Romanesque St Ursula is just across the square.

Malzmühle
BEER HALL

(Map p468; ☑210 117; www.muehlenkoelsch.de; Heumarkt 6; mains €6-15; ☺10am-midnight) Expect plenty of local colour at this convivial beer hall off the beaten tourist track. It brews *Kölsch* with organic ingredients and is also known for its lighter *Malzbier* (malt beer, 2% alcohol).

TOP
CHOICE **Biergarten**

Rathenauplatz
BEER GARDEN

(Map p468; www.rathenauplatz.de; Rathenauplatz; ☺noon-10pm) A large, leafy park is the site of one of Cologne's best places for a drink: a community-run beer garden. Tables sprawl

---

GAY & LESBIAN COLOGNE

Next to Berlin, Cologne is Germany's gayest city, with the rainbow flag flying especially proudly in the so-called 'Bermuda Triangle' around Rudolfplatz, which explodes into a nonstop fun zone at weekends. Another major romping ground is the Heumarkt area (especially Pipinstrasse), which draws more sedate folks and leather and fetish lovers. The Cologne Pride in June basically serves as a warm-up for the Christopher Street Day (www.csd-cologne.de; ☺usually in July), which brings more than a million people to Cologne.

A good source of info is Checkpoint (www.checkpoint-cologne.de).

Places worth checking out:

» Blue Lounge (Map p468; ☑271 7117; blue-lounge.com; Mathiasstrasse 4-6; ☺from 9pm Wed-Sun) A smooth dance and cocktail bar with a mixed crowd.

» Ixbar (Map p468; www.i-like-x.de; Mauritiuswall 84) Hard driving music bar with top DJs.

» Barflo (Map p468; ☑257 3239; Friesenwall 24d; ☺10.30am-1am) Ever-popular cafe near Rudolfplatz with a great scene outside.

---

under huge, old trees next to a playground. From a tidy and distinctive serving hut, you are offered a range of simple snacks such as salads and some very good *frikadelle* (spiced hamburger). Prices are dirt cheap, even for the various beers brewed just up the street at Hellers Brewery – try the organic lager. Proceeds help maintain the park.

Scheinbar
BAR

(Map p468; ☑923 9048; Brüsseler Strasse 10; ☺from 8pm) If you needed any proof that Cologne's nightlife is the bomb, stop by this bar. It's decorated with red satin and lava lamps, and has sitting areas perfect for chilling.

Six Pack
BAR

(Map p468; ☑254 587; Aachener Strasse 33; ☺8pm-5am) This is a must-stop on any Belgian Quarter pub crawl. Pass through the battered door and belly up to the super-long bar and pick from several dozen varieties of beer, all served by the bottle from a giant fridge. Things can get seriously jammed after midnight.

☆ Entertainment

Major listings are in *Kölner Illustrierte* (mainstream, www.koelner.de) and *StadtRevue* (alternative, www.stadtrevue.de).

Nightclubs & Live Music

Gebäude 9
CLUB

(☑814 637; www.gebaeude9.de; Deutz-Mülheimer Strasse 127-129) This ex-factory is an essential indie-rock concert venue in town. DJs take over at other times, and there's also an eclectic programme of nonmainstream plays and films. Take tram 3 or 4 to KölnMesse/Osthallen.

Stadtgarten
CLUB

(Map p468; ☑952 9940; www.stadtgarten.de; Venloer Strasse 40) Surrounded by a small park, this Belgian Quarter favourite hosts vibrant dance parties and live jazz, soul and world music concerts in its cellar hall. It's also a great spot just for a drink (with a summer beer garden).

Underground
LIVE MUSIC

(☑542 326; www.underground-cologne.de; Vogelsanger Strasse 200; ☺Mon & Wed-Sat) This complex combines a pub and two concert halls where indie and alternative rock bands hold forth several times a week. Otherwise there's different music nightly (no cover). There's a beer garden in summer. To get here, take U3 or U4 to Venloer Strasse/Gürtel.

FOOLS, FLOATS & REVELRY: COLOGNE CARNIVAL

Carnival in Cologne is one of the best parties in Europe and a thumb in the eye of the German work ethic. Every year at the onset of Lent (late February/early March), a year of painstaking preparation culminates in the 'three crazy days' – actually more like six.

It all starts with *Weiberfastnacht*, the Thursday before Ash Wednesday, when women rule the day (and do things like chop off the ties of their male colleagues/bosses). The party continues through the weekend, with more than 50 parades of ingenious floats and wildly dressed lunatics dancing in the streets. By the time it all comes to a head with the big parade on *Rosenmontag* (Rose Monday), the entire city has come unglued. Those still capable of swaying and singing will live it up one last time on Shrove Tuesday before the curtain comes down on Ash Wednesday.

'If you were at the parade and saw the parade, you weren't at the parade,' say the people of Cologne in their inimitable way. Translated, this means that you should be far too busy singing, drinking, roaring the Carnival greeting '*Alaaf!*' and planting a quick *Bützchen* (kiss) on the cheek of whoever strikes your fancy, to notice anything happening around you. Swaying and drinking while crammed like sardines in a pub, or following other costumed fools behind a huge bass drum leading to God-only-knows-where, you'll be swept up in one of the greatest parties the world knows.

Alter Wartesaal   CLUB
(Map p468; ☑912 8850; www.wartesaal.de; Johannisstrasse 11; ⊗Thu-Sat) In a former train station waiting hall, this is a stylish bar-disco-restaurant combo. Themed nights range from the erotic KitKatClub to SoulChannel. There are cafe tables out front in the shadow of the Dom where you can take a pause. Note that the entrance is near the train station entrance and not in the noxious passage under the tracks.

Papa Joe's Klimperkasten   LIVE MUSIC
(Map p468; ☑258 2132; www.papajoes.de; Alter Markt 50) A piano player tickles the ivories nightly in this museum-like place where the smoky brown walls are strewn with photographs from yesteryear. By day the tables outside on the Markt are among the better.

Theatre & Classical Music

Kölner Philharmonie   CLASSICAL MUSIC
(Map p468; ☑280 280; www.koelner-philharmonie.de; Bischofsgartenstrasse 1) The famous Kölner Philharmoniker is the 'house band' in this grand, modern concert hall below the Museum Ludwig. Buy tickets at www.koelnticket.de, by phone or at the box office.

Schauspiel   THEATRE
(Map p468; ☑2212 8400; www.buehnenkoeln.de; Offenbachplatz) Repertory theatre based at the Schauspiel, in the same complex as the Opernhaus (opera). The box office for both is in the Opernhaus foyer.

 Shopping

Cologne is a fantastic place to shop, with lots of eccentric boutiques, designer and vintage stores, plus the usual selection of chain and department stores.

Hohe Strasse is one of Germany's oldest pedestrianised shopping strips, and along with its side street **In der Höhle**, it's where you'll find all the mainstream chains and department stores. Smaller fashion and shoe shops culminate in **Schildergasse** in the Neumarkt, where the **Neumarkt-Galerie** mall is easily recognised by the upturned ice-cream cone on the roof, designed by Claes Oldenburg and Coosje van Brugge.

Mittelstrasse and **Pfeilstrasse** are lined with exclusive fashion, jewellery and home-accessory shops, while **Ehrenstrasse** is easily Cologne's most creative strip, with designer boutiques mixing with more offbeat fare. Funky music shops, vintage clothing dealers and the-next-hot-designer shops are scattered about the streets near **Belgisches Viertel** and **Brüsseler Platz**.

4711   PERFUME
(Map p468; www.4711.com; cnr Glockengasse & Schwertnergasse) A classic gift for Mum is a bottle of eau de cologne, the not terribly sophisticated but refreshing perfume, which was created – and is still being produced – in its namesake city. The most famous brand is called 4711, named after the number of the house where it was invented, which now houses this shop. Outside, up on the facade, note the cutesy carillon with characters

from Prussian lore parading hourly from 9am to 9pm.

Mayersche Buchhandlung BOOKS
(Map p468; ☎203 070; Neumarkt 2) Large bookstore with a good English-language selection.

Gleumes BOOKS
(Map p468; ☎211 550; Hohenstaufenring 47-51) Travel and map specialist.

ⓘ Information

Giga-Byte (☎6502 6442; www.giga-byte.info; Hohenzollernring 7-11; per hr €0.50-1.50; ⓧ24hr) Huge entertainment centre with 130 high-speed computers.

Köln Welcome Card (24hr €9) Offers free public transport and discounted admission, tours, meals and entertainment. It's available at the tourist office and participating venues.

Post Office (☎925 9290; Breite Strasse 6-26, WDR Arkaden shopping mall; ⓧ9am-7pm Mon-Fri, to 2pm Sat)

ReiseBank (☎134 403; Hauptbahnhof; ⓧ7am-10pm) Exchange services and money transfers.

Tourist Office (☎0221 2213 0400; www.koelntourismus.de; Kardinal-Höffner-Platz 1; ⓧ9am-8pm Mon-Sat, 10am-5pm Sun) Excellent location in the shadow of the Dom; sells event tickets.

ⓘ Getting There & Away

AIR About 18km southeast of the city centre, **Cologne-Bonn Airport** (CGN; www.airport-cgn.de) has direct flights to 130 cities and is served by numerous airlines, with destinations across Europe.

BUS Eurolines runs buses in all directions, including Paris (7½ hours) and Amsterdam (5¼ hours). The central bus station is on Breslauer Platz, behind the Hauptbahnhof.

TRAIN Cologne's beautiful Hauptbahnhof sits just a frisbee toss away from the landmark Dom. Services are fast and frequent in all directions. Domestic connections include Berlin (€113, 4¼ hours), Frankfurt (€67, 1¼ hours) and Munich (€134, 4½ hours). In addition there are fast trains to Brussels (where you can connect to the Eurostar for London) and Paris.

ⓘ Getting Around

TO/FROM THE AIRPORT The S13 train connects the airport and the Hauptbahnhof every 20 minutes (€2.80, 15 minutes). Taxis charge about €30.

BICYCLE Radstation (☎139 7190; www.radstationkoeln.de; Am Hauptbahnhof/Breslauerplatz; per 3hr/1/3/7 days €5/10/20/40; ⓧ5.30am-10.30pm Mon-Fri, 6.30am-8pm Sat, 8am-8pm

Sun) is convenient when you get to town. Rent-A-Bike (p472) has similar rates.

CAR & MOTORCYCLE Central Cologne is now a low-emission zone, meaning that your car needs to display an *Umweltplakette* (emission sticker). Rental cars automatically have the sticker, but if you're driving your own vehicle, you'll need to obtain one. Your best option is to stash the car in one of the many large parking buildings and forget it.

PUBLIC TRANSPORT Cologne's comprehensive mix of buses, trams, and U-Bahn and S-Bahn trains is operated by **VRS** (☎01803-504 030; www.vrsinfo.de) in cooperation with Bonn's system. Short trips (up to four stops) cost €1.80, longer ones €2.60. Day passes are €7.50 for one person and €11.10 for up to five people travelling together. Buy your tickets from the orange ticket machines at stations and aboard trams; be sure to validate them.

TAXI Call ☎2882 or 194 10.

THE RHINELAND

Linked by the iconic river, a host of cities and towns are worth your time.

Brühl
☎02232 / POP 44,300

Brühl wraps an astonishing number of riches into a pint-size package. The town, halfway between Cologne and Bonn, languished in relative obscurity until the 18th century, when archbishop-elector Clemens August (1723–61) – friend of Casanova and himself a lover of women, parties and palaces – made it his residence. His two made-to-impress rococo palaces, at opposite ends of the elegant Schlosspark, landed on Unesco's list of World Heritage Sites in 1984.

⊙ Sights & Activities

TOP CHOICE Brühl Palaces PALACES
(www.schlossbruehl.de; combined ticket for all sites adult/child €7/4.50; ⓧ9am-1pm & 1.30-5pm Tue-Fri, 10am-6pm Sat & Sun, last admission 1hr before closing, closed Dec & Jan) The larger and flashier of the two palaces, **Schloss Augustusburg** (☎440 00; Max-Ernst-Allee; adult/child €5/4.50) is a little jewel box inside a moat. It was designed by François Cuvilliés. On guided tours you'll learn fascinating titbits about hygiene, dating and other aspects of daily life at court. The architectural highlight is a ceremonial staircase by Balthasar Neumann, a dizzying symphony in stucco, sculpture and faux marble.

Cuvilliés also dreamed up Jagdschloss Falkenlust (Otto-Weis-Strasse; adult/child €3.50/3), a hunting lodge where Clemens August liked to indulge his fancy for falconry. Though small, it's almost as opulent as the main palace. A particular gem is the adjacent chapel, which is awash in shells, minerals and crystals.

The two palaces are a wonderful 30-minute stroll apart on a wide 2.5km promenade through the Schlosspark. Schloss Augustusburg is close to the train station and presents a dramatic vision as you arrive.

Max Ernst Museum   MUSEUM
(☑579 3110; www.maxernstmuseum.com; Comesstrasse 42; adult/child €6/3.50; ⊘11am-6pm Tue-Sun) A short stroll from the palaces is the Max Ernst Museum, where nine rooms trace all creative phases of the Brühl-born Dadaist and surrealist (1891–1976). We especially enjoyed examples of his artistic innovations such as frottage (floor-board rubbings) and the spooky collage novels, which are graphic works exploring the darkest crevices of the subconscious.

Phantasialand   THEME PARK
(☑362 00; www.phantasialand.de; Berggeiststrasse 31-41; day pass adult/child €38.50/18; ⊘9am-6pm Apr-Oct, last admission 4pm) Brühl's other big drawcard is Phantasialand, one of Europe's earliest, most popular and best Disneyland-style amusement parks (since 1967). The park has six themed areas – Chinatown, Berlin, Mexico, Fantasy, Mystery and Deep in Africa – each with their own roller coasters, gondolas, flight simulators, water rides and other thrills, plus song and dance shows. To be admitted as a child you have to be shorter than 145cm; if you're younger than seven or it's your birthday, admission is free.

❶ Getting There & Around
Brühl is regularly served by regional **trains** from Cologne (€3.30, 15 minutes) and Bonn (€4.20, 10 minutes). The Hauptbahnhof is opposite Schloss Augustusburg, with the compact town centre behind the palace. Shuttle buses to Phantasialand leave from outside the station. You can rent **bikes** at the station.

Bonn
☑0228 / POP 324,900
When this friendly, relaxed city on the Rhine became West Germany's 'temporary' capital in 1949 it surprised many, including its own residents. When in 1991 a reunited German government decided to move to Berlin, it shocked many, *especially* its own residents.

A generation later, Bonn is doing just fine, thank you. It has a healthy economy and lively urban vibe. For visitors, the birthplace of Ludwig van Beethoven has plenty in store, not least the great composer's birth house, a string of top-rated museums, a lovely riverside setting and the nostalgic flair of the old government quarter.

◉ Sights
Bonn can be seen on an easy day trip from Cologne or as a stop on the busy Rhine railway line. There is a concentration of sights in the Altstadt but others are rather removed from the centre.

ALTSTADT
You can easily explore all of Bonn's old town on foot.

TOP CHOICE Münster Basilica   CHURCH
(☑985 880; www.bonner-muenster.de; Münsterplatz; ⊘7am-7pm) A good place to start exploring Bonn's historic centre is on Münsterplatz, where the landmark Münster Basilica was built on the graves of the two martyred Roman soldiers who later got promoted to be the city's patron saints. It got its Gothic look in the 13th century but the Romanesque origins survive beautifully in the ageing cloister (open till 5pm). It's interior is redolent with centuries of burnt incense. On the square outside the church, a buttercup-yellow baroque Palais (palace; now the post office) forms a photogenic backdrop for the Beethoven Monument (1845).

Beethoven-Haus   MUSEUM
(☑981 7525; www.beethoven-haus-bonn.de; Bonngasse 24-26; adult/child €5/4; ⊘10am-6pm Mon-Sat, 11am-6pm Sun Apr-Oct, to 5pm Nov-Mar) The famous composer first saw the light of day in 1770 in the rather plain Beethoven Haus. It's now the repository of a pretty static array of letters, musical scores, instruments and paintings. The highlights – his last grand piano, the huge ear trumpets he used to combat his growing deafness and a famous portrait – are all on the 2nd floor.

Tickets are also good for the Digitales Beethoven-Haus next door, where you can experience the composer's genius during a spacey, interactive 3D multimedia show or deepen your knowledge in the digital archive. You can contemplate his life in a near-hidden garden out back, and stroke your inner-Schroeder (of Peanuts fame) in the Beethoven-bust-filled gift shop.

Altes Rathaus   HISTORIC BUILDING
Situated on the Altstadt's triangular Markt, the baroque Altes Rathaus absolutely glistens with silver and gold trim. Politicians from Charles de Gaulle to John F Kennedy have waved to the crowds from its double-sided staircase.

Kurfürstliche Residenz   HISTORIC BUILDING
(Electoral Residence; Regina-Pacis-Weg) The palatial 1705 Kurfürstliche Residenz was once the immodest home of the archbishop-electors of Cologne and has been part of Bonn's university since 1818. Its south side opens up to the expansive Hofgarten (Palace Garden), a popular gathering place for students.

Arithmeum   MUSEUM
(738 790; www.arithmeum.uni-bonn.de; Lennéstrasse 2; adult/child €3/2; 11am-6pm Tue-Sun) The Arithmeum explores the symbiosis of science, technology and art. On view are hundreds of mechanical calculators and historic mathematics books but also an out-there exhibit on the aesthetics of microchips. Design your own or study their beauty through a polarisation microscope. Work your way down from the top floor of this minimalist glass-and-steel cube. It's on the southeast corner of the Altstadt by the Hofgarten.

LandesMuseum Bonn   MUSEUM
(Rhineland Regional Museum; 207 00; www.landesmuseum-bonn.lvr.de; Colmantstrasse 14; adult/child €8/6; 11am-6pm Tue-Fri & Sun, from 1pm Sat) South of the Hauptbahnhof, the LandesMuseum presents its rich collections in such themed exhibits as Epochs, Gods and Power. Highlights include a 40,000-year-old Neanderthal skull and a rare blue Roman glass vessel from the 1st century AD. The museum restaurant, DelikArt (mains €11-17), enjoys a fine reputation.

BUNDESVIERTEL
From 1949 to 1999, the nerve centre of West German political power lay about 1.5km southeast of the Altstadt along Adenauerallee. These days the former government quarter has reinvented itself as the home for UN and other international and federal institutions. The airy and modern Plenary Hall, where the Bundestag (German parliament) used to convene, now hosts international conferences. Nearby, the high-rise nick-named Langer Eugen (Tall Eugen), where members of parliament kept their offices, is now a UN campus. Officially retaining their former purposes are the stately Villa Hammerschmidt, still a secondary official residence of the federal president, and the neoclassical Palais Schaumburg, now serving as the chancellor's Bonn office.

A good way to explore the district is by following the Weg der Demokratie (Path of Democracy; www.wegderdemokratie.de), a self-guided walking tour taking in 18 key historic sites. It starts at the Haus der Geschichte der Bundesrepublik Deutschland. Explanatory panelling in English is provided.

TOP CHOICE Haus der Geschichte der Bundesrepublik Deutschland   MUSEUM
(FRG History Museum; 916 50; www.hdg.de; Willy-Brandt-Allee 14; 9am-7pm Tue-Fri, 10am-6pm Sat & Sun) The Haus der Geschichte der Bundesrepublik Deutschland presents a highly engaging and intelligent romp through recent German history, starting when the final bullet was fired in WWII. Walk through the fuselage of a Berlin Airlift Rosinenbomber, watch classic clips in a 1950s movie theatre, examine Erich Honecker's arrest warrant, stand in front of a piece of the Berlin Wall or see John F Kennedy's famous 'Ich bin ein Berliner' speech. U-Bahns 16, 63 and 66 stop here.

MUSEUMSMEILE
Bonn's Museum Mile sits opposite the government quarter, on the western side of the B9. U-Bahns 16, 63 and 66 stop here.

Museum Koenig   MUSEUM
(912 20; www.zfmk.de; Adenauerallee 160; adult/concession €4.50/2; 10am-6pm Tue & Thu-Sun, to 9pm Wed) Across from the Villa Hammerschmidt, the Museum Koenig is a natural history museum but it's hardly your usual dead-animal zoo. The 'Savannah' exhibit recreates an entire habitat with theatrical flourishes: elephants drinking at a watering hole, a jaguar holed up with its kill and vultures surveying the scene from above. Other highlights include a talking baobab tree in the 'Rainforest', a colossal sea elephant in the 'Arctic' and a condor with a 3m wingspan in the 'World of Birds'.

Kunstmuseum Bonn   MUSEUM
(776 260; www.kunstmuseum-bonn.de; Friedrich-Ebert-Allee 2; adult/concession €7/3.50; 11am-6pm Tue & Thu-Sun, to 9pm Wed) Beyond its

dramatic foyer, the Kunstmuseum Bonn presents 20th-century works, especially by August Macke and other Rhenish expressionists, as well as such avant-gardists as Beuys, Baselitz and Kiefer.

Bundeskunsthalle   EXHIBITION SPACE
(Art and Exhibition Hall of the Federal Republic of Germany; ☑917 1200; www.bundeskunsthalle.de; Friedrich-Ebert-Allee 2; ☉10am-9pm Tue & Wed, to 7pm Thu-Sun) Adjoining the Kunstmuseum Bonn, the Kunst-und Ausstellungshalle der Bundesrepublik Deutschland is another striking space with a name that's a mouthful. It has special exhibitions of everything from serious art to the works of Pixar (admission fees vary).

Deutsches Museum Bonn   MUSEUM
(☑302 255; www.deutsches-museum-bonn.de; Ahrstrasse 45; adult/child €5/2.50; ☉10am-6pm Tue-Sun) Did you know that the air bag and MP3 technology were invented in Germany? You will, after visiting the Deutsches Museum Bonn. This pint-size subsidiary of the blockbuster Munich mother ship highlights German technology since WWII with plenty of buttons to push and knobs to pull. It's some 2km south of the other museums; take U-Bahn 16 or 63.

NORDSTADT
Also referred to as Northern Altstadt, Nordstadt is a former working-class quarter whose web of narrow streets has grown pockets of hipness. Cafes, restaurants, boutiques and galleries have sprouted along Breite Strasse, Heerstrasse and the connecting side streets. The quarter is prettiest in spring when the cherry trees are in bloom.

August-Macke-Haus   MUSEUM
(☑655 531; www.august-macke-haus.de; Bornheimer Strasse 96; adult/child €4/3; ☉2.30-6pm Tue-Fri, 11am-5pm Sat & Sun) The expressionist painter August Macke (1887–1914) lived in this neighbourhood in the three years before his untimely death on the battlefields in WWI. His neoclassical home is now the August-Macke-Haus, where you can soak up the master's aura in his recreated studio and see some originals; the finest works, though, are not far away at the Kunstmuseum Bonn. The house is about 1km from the train station.

POPPELSDORF & AROUND
About 2km south of the Altstadt, elegant and leafy Poppelsdorf is anchored by Schloss Poppelsdorf, another electoral palace now used by the university. Students and neighbourhood folk populate the bars and restaurants along Clemens-August-Strasse, which runs south of the palace towards the hillside Kreuzbergkirche (www.kreuzberg-bonn.de; Stationsweg 21; ☉9am-6pm Apr-Oct, to 5pm Nov-Mar). This rococo gem is lavishly decorated with gilded faux marble, frescos and a Balthasar Neumann–designed version of the Holy Steps.

Doppelkirche Schwarzrheindorf   CHURCH
(☑461 609; Dixstrasse 41; ☉9am-6.30pm Tue-Sat, 11.30am-6.30pm Sun, upper church Sat & Sun only) The 12th-century Doppelkirche Schwarzrheindorf is a magnificent 'double church' where the nobility sat on the upper level and the parishioners on the lower. The beautiful Romanesque architecture is impressive, as is the restored Old Testament fresco cycle in the lower church. It is across the river from Poppelsdorf in the suburb of Schwarzrheindorf; take bus 550 or 640 from the Hauptbahnhof to Schwarzrheindorf-Kirche.

☞ Tours

Beethoven fans can follow in his footsteps, either via a free Beethoven Walk pamphlet or an iTour audio guide (rental €7.50), both available at the tourist office.

If you fancy taking to the water, Boats heading upriver to Königswinter and beyond leave from the Alter Zoll landing docks at the Brassertufer between April and October.

Big City Tour   TOUR
(www.bonn.de; Bonn Information, Windeckstrasse 1; adult/concession €16/8; ☉2pm daily Apr-Nov, Sat Dec-Mar) A combination bus and walking tour run by the tourist office, this 2½-hour tour takes in almost everything.

🛌 Sleeping

Accommodation – like Bonn – is spread out. There are some decent places in the Altstadt and some more atmospheric hotels along the Rhine.

Hotel Pastis   PENSION €€
(☑969 4270; www.hotel-pastis.de; Hatschiergasse 8; s/d from €60/95) This little hotel-restaurant combo is so fantastically French you'll feel like donning a beret and affecting a silly accent. After dining on unfussy gourmet cuisine – paired with great wines, *bien sûr* – you'll sleep soundly in the basic comfortable rooms.

Altes Treppchen   GUESTHOUSE €€
(☑625 004; www.treppchen.de; Endenicher Strasse
308; s/d from €70/100; ℗) In the suburb of
Endenich, this rustic inn is a true gem that's
been in the same family for 500 years. The
nine rooms are simple but squeaky clean
and most of them are decent sized. The restaurant, a winter-time gem with its wooden
booths, is loaded with old-world ambience.

Ameron Hotel Königshof   HOTEL €€€
(☑260 10; www.hotel-koenigshof-bonn.de; Adenauerallee 9; r €100-250; ℗✳@☎) Sit back on the
leafy terrace and enjoy sweeping views of
the Rhine from this luxurious understated
hotel that dates to the 1950s. Rooms have
some bold colour combinations. There are
good walks along the river and strolls in
the neighbouring Stadtgarten. The stylish
restaurant, Oliveto, is known for its Med-
influenced fare.

Hotel Löhndorf   HOTEL €€
(☑634 726; www.hotel-loehndorf-bonn.de; Stock-
enstrasse 6; s/d from €55/95; ⊝@☎) This 13-
room property is wonderfully quiet and
atmospherically close to the Hofgarten as
well as the Rhine. The cheery breakfast
room and the bamboo-lined patio are great
for munching your morning croissants. Bonus: a handy honour bar in the lounge and
free access to the adjacent gym and sauna.

DJH Hostel   HOSTEL €
(☑289 970; www.bonn.jugendherberge.de; Haager
Weg 42; dm/s/d from €27/49/50; ℗⊝@) Bonn's
modern hostel has 249 beds and is about
4km south of the city centre, next to a nature
park. From the Hauptbahnhof, take bus 600
to Jugendherberge.

✕ Eating & Drinking

The largely pedestrianised historic Altstadt
brims with options, including all of those
listed below.

Cafe Spitz   CAFE €€
(☑697 430; www.spitz-bonn.de; Sterntorbrücke
10; mains €5-16; ⊝9am-1am Mon-Thu, to 2am Fri &
Sat, 10am-midnight Sun) This spare and stylish
place is often mobbed, especially during the
after-work cocktail happy hour. The menu
revolves around salad, pizza and pasta supplemented by changing – and inspired –
blackboard specials.

Brauhaus Bönnsch   BREWERY €€
(☑650 610; www.boennsch.de; Sterntorbrücke 4;
mains €7-15; ⊝11am-1am) The unfiltered ale

is a must at this congenial brew-pub where
the walls are adorned with photographs of
famous politicians from Willy Brandt to, yes,
Arnold Schwarzenegger. Schnitzel, various
pork cuts and sausage dominate the menu,
but the *Flammkuchen* is a crowd pleaser.

Zum Gequetschten   GERMAN €€
(☑638 104; Sternstrasse 78; mains €9-18; ⊝noon-
1am, kitchen to 11am) This traditional restaurant-pub is festooned with eye-catching blue
tiles and is one of the most storied inns in
town. The menu is mostly back-to-basics
German, although some salads that *don't*
contain sausage and a few sandwiches make
appearances.

Cassius Garten   CAFE €
(☑652 429; www.cassiusgarten.de; Maximilianstrasse 28, Cassius-Passage; dishes per 100g €1.50;
⊝8am-8pm Mon-Sat; ✍) Barely the distance
your average chef can hurl a courgette from
the train station, this vegetarian cafe manages to put mellow style ahead of worthiness
(eat your peas!). The menu changes daily
and it truly is cheap and cheerful. Breakfasts
are simply yummy.

TOP CHOICE Weinkommissar   WINE BAR
(www.weinkommissar.de; Friedrichstrasse 20; wines
from €5; ⊝noon-11pm Mon-Sat) In the heart of
the Altstadt, pause from your stroll, stop
humming Beethoven's 5th and sit back to
enjoy one of many wines sold by the glass
at this simple little spot that opens to the
street. There are little tasty nibbles to wash
it down.

Pawlow   BAR
(☑653 603; Heerstrasse 64; ⊝11am-1am Sun-Thu,
11am-to late Fri & Sat) Generations of bon
vivants have followed the Pavlovian bell to
this northern Altstadt institution. A cafe in
the daytime, it morphs into a DJ bar at night
with electro, punk and '60s sounds heating
up a chatty, boozy crowd.

Stadtgarten Biergarten   BEER GARDEN
(Stadtgarten, Adenauerallee; snacks from €3;
⊝noon-11pm Apr-Oct) Here's a Bonn drinking
game: every time a barge passes below this
beer garden with views of the Rhine, have a
drink. You won't last an hour. Bonn's Stadtgarten is a little leafy gem next to the Altstadt with an old bastion overlooking the
river. The beer and sausages here are standard but the surroundings are anything but.

⭐ Entertainment

It won't surprise you to learn that Bonn's entertainment scene is strong in the field of classical music. A calendar highlight is the Beethovenfest (www.beethovenfest.de) in September with several dozen concerts held in venues around town.

Kammermusiksaal   VENUE
(☎981 7515; www.beethoven-haus-bonn.de; Bonn gasse 24-26) This chamber-music hall is part of the Beethoven House complex.

Beethovenhalle   CONCERT HALL
(☎722 20; www.beethovenhalle.de; Wachsbleiche 17) The Beethovenhalle is Bonn's premier concert hall.

ℹ Information

Bonn Information (☎775 000; www.bonn.de; Windeckstrasse 1; ⊙10am-6pm Mon-Fri, to 4pm Sat, to 2pm Sun) Has excellent free information and tours in English.

Bonn Regio WelcomeCard (www.bonn-region. de; one-person/family 24hr €9/19) Unlimited public transport, admission to over 20 museums, plus discounts on tours, thermal baths and more in Bonn and beyond. Sold at the tourist office and some hotels.

Internet Several telephone-call shops near the Hauptbahnhof offer internet access.

Post Office (Münsterplatz 17; ⊙9am-8pm Mon-Fri, 9am-4pm Sat)

ℹ Getting There & Away

AIR The **Cologne Bonn Airport** (CGN; www .airport-cgn.de) has flights across Europe.

TRAIN Bonn is linked by train to Cologne many times hourly by **U-Bahn** lines U16 and U18, regional trains (€7, 30 minutes) and even ICs. There are frequent trains across the region including the scenic ride upriver to Koblenz (€12, 45 minutes).

BOAT You can also travel the Rhine by boat, to/ from Cologne and south to/from Koblenz and beyond on **KD** (www.k-d.com; to Cologne €16, to Koblenz €35). Boats are also operated by **Bonner Personen Schiffahrt** (www.b-p-s.de).

ℹ Getting Around

TO/FROM THE AIRPORT Cologne-Bonn Airport (CGN; www.airport-cgn.de) is about 25km northeast of the city centre. Express bus SB60 makes the trip between the airport and Hauptbahnhof every 20 or 30 minutes between 4.45am and 12.30am (€7.10, 26 minutes). For a taxi to/ from the airport budget between €35 and €40.

PUBLIC TRANSPORT Buses, trams and the U-Bahn make up the public transport system, which is operated by the **VRS** (☎01803-504 030; www.vrsinfo.de). It extends as far as Cologne and is divided into zones. All you need to travel within Bonn is a City Ticket for €2.60 per trip or €7.50 for the 24-hour pass. All tickets must be validated when boarding.

BICYCLE Radstation (☎981 4636; Quantiusstrasse 26; per day from €8; ⊙6am-10.30pm Mon-Fri, 7am-10.30pm Sat, 8am-10.30pm Sun), on the south side of the Hauptbahnhof.

TAXI ☎555 555.

Around Bonn

Steeped in legend, the densely forested hills of the Siebengebirge (Seven Mountains) rise above the right bank of the Rhine, just a few kilometres south of Bonn. Closer inspection actually reveals about 40 peaks, but only the seven most prominent give the region its name.

At 461m, the Ölberg may be the highest, but the 321m Drachenfels is the most heavily visited of these 'mountains'. Since 1883, some 32 million peak-baggers have reached the top aboard the Drachenfelsbahn (☎02223-920 90; www.drachenfelsbahn-koenigs winter.de; Drachenfelsstrasse 53, Königswinter; one-way/return €7.50/9; ⊙9am-7pm May-Sep, shorter hr Oct-Apr), a nostalgic cogwheel train that rattles along for 1.5km. Prices are a bit steep, but so is the paved path, should you prefer to walk.

The walking route leads past restaurants and various attractions, including the 1913 Nibelungenhalle (☎02223-241 50; www.nibe lungenhalle.de; adult/child €5/3; ⊙10am-6pm mid-Mar-Nov), a templelike shrine to the composer Richard Wagner decorated with scenes from his opera cycle *Ring of the Nibelungen*. Tickets include access to the Drachenhöhle, a cave inhabited by a 13m-long stone dragon, and, strangely enough, a small reptile zoo.

Further uphill loom the fairy-tale turrets of the neo-Gothic Schloss Drachenburg (☎02223-901 970; www.schloss-drachenburg.de; adult/concession €6/4; ⊙11am-6pm Apr-Oct, shorter hr other times), which looks medieval but was actually built in the 1880s. It houses exhibits on the building's rather short history. More interesting are the lovely grounds with their terraces, fountains, and tower that can be climbed for expansive views.

Views are at least as nice (and free) from the medieval Burg Drachenfels at the top of the mountain, which has remained a ruin since the Thirty Years War (1618–48).

The Drachenfels rises above the town of Königswinter, which is served by the U66 from Bonn Hauptbahnhof. A more atmospheric approach is by one of the boats that leave from Bonn between April and October. Bonner Personen Schiffahrt (www.b-p-s.de; one-way/return €8.50/11.50) and KD (☎0221-208 8318; www.k-d.com; one-way/return €9.20/11.50) are the main operators.

Remagen

☎02642 / POP 16.100

Remagen, 20km south of Bonn, was founded by the Romans in AD 16 as Rigomagus, but the town would hardly figure in the history books were it not for one fateful day in early March 1945. As the Allies raced across France and Belgium to rid Germany of Nazism, the Wehrmacht tried frantically to stave off defeat by destroying all bridges across the Rhine.

But the Brücke von Remagen (the steel rail bridge at Remagen) lasted long enough for Allied troops to cross the river, contributing significantly to the collapse of Hitler's western front. One of the bridge's surviving basalt towers now houses the Friedensmuseum (Peace Museum; ☎218 63; www.bruecke-remagen.de; adult/child €3.50/1; ☉10am-5pm early Mar-mid-Nov, to 6pm May-Oct), with a well-presented exhibit on Remagen's pivotal role in WWII. Note the many memorial plaques to the battle placed by a generation of soldiers now all but passed.

The bridge and museum are a 15-minute walk along the Rhine promenade south from the train station, which has frequent services towards both Cologne and Koblenz.

The Ahr Valley & the Eifel

The Eifel, a rural area of gentle hills, tranquil villages and volcanic lakes, makes for a good respite from the mass tourism of the Moselle and Rhine Valleys. Its subtle charms are best sampled on a bike ride or a hike, though it also has a few headline attractions, including a world-class car-racing track, a stunning Romanesque abbey and a lovely wine region, the Ahr Valley.

The Ahr River has carved a scenic 90km valley stretching from Blankenheim, in the High Eifel, to its confluence with the Rhine near Remagen. This is one of Germany's few red-wine regions – growing *Spätburgunder* (pinot noir), in particular – with vineyards clinging to steeply terraced slopes along both banks. The quality is high but the yield

small, so very few wine labels ever make it beyond the area – all the more reason to visit and try them for yourself.

BAD NEUENAHR-AHRWEILER

☎02641 / POP 27,400

Bad Neuenahr and Ahrweiler are a bit of an odd couple: two small towns joined together by government edict. The spouse listed second, Ahrweiler, should come first in terms of appeal. It's an attractive medieval town encircled by a wall and criss-crossed by pedestrianised lanes lined with half-timbered houses.

Bad Neuenahr, by contrast, is a spa town, Although its healing waters have been sought out by the moneyed and the famous (including Karl Marx and Johannes Brahms) for a century and a half, it's rather on the bland side.

◉ Sights & Activities

The two towns are about 3km apart; you can walk between the two along the narrow Ahr River. There's myriad more hikes amidst the hillside vineyards. The tourist office has info.

AHRWEILER

Ahrweiler has a delightful, pedestrianised Altstadt, almost entirely encircled by a medieval town wall with four gates. The focal point is the Marktplatz and its yellow Gothic church, Pfarrkirche St Laurentius, beautifully decorated with floral frescos from the 14th century, old wood carvings and luminous stained-glass windows, some of which show farmers working their vineyards.

Museum Roemervilla   MUSEUM
(☎5311; Am Silberberg 1; adult/child €4/2; ☉10am-5pm Tue-Sun Apr-mid-Nov, closed mid-Nov-Mar) Ahrweiler's Roman roots spring to life at the Museum Roemervilla on the northwest edge of town. Protected by a lofty glass and wood structure are the surprisingly extensive 1st- to 3rd-century ruins – a veritable Rhenish Pompeii – which reveal the remarkable standard of living enjoyed by wealthy Romans.

Dokumentationsstätte Regierungsbunker   HISTORIC SITE
(Government Bunker Documentation Site; ☎917 10; www.regbu.de; adult/child €8/3.50; ☉10am-5pm Wed, Sat, Sun & holidays early Mar-mid-Nov, closed mid-Nov-early Mar) During the Cold War, there was no vast, top-secret bunker complex bored into the hillside 500m up the slope

from the Museum Roemervilla – at least not officially. Since 2008, though, you can see the truth for yourself – at a 200m section of the nuclear-proof 'Emergency Seat of the Constitutional Organs of the Federal Republic of Germany', rechristened (in inimitable bureaucratese) as the Dokumentationsstätte Regierungsbunker. There's a real Dr Strangelove quality to what comforts the bureaucrats thought would be good to have at hand as the world ended.

BAD NEUENAHR

The focal point of Bad Neuenahr, bisected by the Ahr, is the stately **Kurhaus**, an art nouveau structure built in 1903; next door is the casino. The nearby **riverbanks** are great for strolling.

Ahr Resort SPA
(☑801100; www.ahr-resort.de; Felix-Rütten-Strasse 3; weekday/weekend day pass €20/22; ☺9am-11pm or midnight) Neuenahr owes its 'Bad' reputation' (ie its spa status) to its mineral springs; their soothing qualities can be experienced in the Ahr Resort. Besides swimming pools, options include a surge channel, massage jets and all sorts of saunas. Various discounts are available.

🍽 Sleeping & Eating

Ahrweiler (in particular around Marktplatz) teems with traditional restaurants and Weinstuben, all serving the tasty local red.

Hotel Garni Schützenhof PENSION €€
(☑902 83; www.schuetzenhof-ahrweiler.de; Schützenstrasse 1, Ahrweiler; s/d incl breakfast from €50/80; P☺☎) Facing the Ahrtor, one of Ahrweiler's landmark town gates, this unpretentious, welcoming family-run hotel has 14 spacious rooms. Excellent value.

Kleine Herberge GUESTHOUSE €
(☑378 1024; www.kleineherberge.de; Adenbachhutstrasse 8, Ahrweiler; s €42-48, d €52-63) Just inside the Adenbachtor, the gate closest to the train stop, this 1898 house has been turned into a stylish little guesthouse. There's a garden out back where you can chill out after hillside wanderings. Rates include breakfast.

Hotel & Restaurant Hohenzollern HOTEL €€
(☑9730; www.hotelhohenzollern.com; Am Silberberg 50; s/d from €75/90; P☺☎) This elegant hillside hotel, right on the Rotweinwanderweg, has unbeatable valley views and a top-end restaurant (menus from €60) with local, French and Italian dishes. From Ahrweiler's

A RHINE DAY OUT

You can experience the sweeping beauty of the Rhine River fully on this circular day trip from Cologne, which includes a short ferry ride and a good walk.

Catch a train south (hourly, one hour) on the right bank of the Rhine to the small riverside village of **Erpel**. Walk about 200m down to the waterfront and catch a small **ferry** (€1, every 30 minutes) across the river to **Remagen**. Check out the remains of the famous bridge, then begin your walk north along the Rhine path. The views of passing boats are endlessly engaging and there is a sharp bend in the river to add interest. After about 5km you'll reach another small riverside village, **Oberwinter**, which has frequent trains back to Cologne (40 minutes).

Museum Roemervilla, head up the narrow road 700m through the forest.

Bell's WeinRestaurant GERMAN €€
(☑900 243; www.bells-restaurant.de; Niederhutstrasse 27a, Ahrweiler; mains €9-18) In fine weather, the chestnut-shaded beer garden has the nicest tables, where you can kick back and drink the house-brewed beer. There's also a fine selection of the local wine, so try a few.

Eifelstube GERMAN €€€
(☑348 50; www.eifelstube-ahrweiler.de; Ahrhutstrasse 26, Ahrweiler; mains €13-25; ☺Thu-Mon, plus Wed Sep & Oct) Sample upmarket German and regional specialities in this cosy dining room, with its beam ceiling and tiled stove, run by the same family since 1905.

ℹ Information

Ahrweiler tourist office (☑917 10; www.ahrtaltourismus.de; Blankartshof 1; ☺9am-5.30pm Mon-Fri, 10am-3pm Sat & Sun) sells walking and cycling maps of the area.

ℹ Getting There & Away

TRAIN By train, skip the 'Ahrweiler' stop and use 'Ahrweiler Markt', which is just north of the old town. From the proper Bahnhof in Bad Neuenahr, it's a five-minute walk to the centre, which is around car-free Poststrasse.

Hourly trains serve the paired towns from Bonn (€5, 40 minutes) and Remagen, where you change for travel south to Koblenz.

ALTENAHR
📞 02643 / POP 1700

Surrounded on all sides by craggy peaks, steep vineyards and rolling hills, Altenahr may just be the most romantic spot in the Ahr Valley. The landscape is best appreciated by taking a 20-minute uphill walk from the Bahnhof to the 11th-century **Burgruine Are**, a ruined hilltop castle, whose weather-beaten stone tower stands guard over the valley.

Altenahr is the western terminus of the **Rotweinwanderweg**. A dozen more **trails** can be picked up in the village centre (eg the 7km **Geologischer Wanderweg**) or at the top of the **Ditschardhöhe** (354m), the 'peak' of which is most easily reached by the **Seilbahn** (chairlift; 📞 8383; ascent/return adult €4/6, child €3/4; ⊙ 10am-5pm or later Easter-Oct). In the town centre, parts of the Romanesque **Pfarrkirche Maria Verkündigung** (Church of the Annunciation) date from the late 1100s.

Altenahr's **tourist office** (Haus des Gastes; 📞 8448; www.altenahr-ahr.de; ⊙ 9am-4.30pm Mon-Fri, 10am-2pm Sat May & Aug-Oct, 10am-3pm Mon-Fri rest of yr), inside the former Bahnhof building, sells hiking and cycling maps.

🛏 Sleeping & Eating

DJH hostel HOSTEL €
(📞 02643 1880; www.jugendherberge.de; Langfigtal 8; dm €21-27) Altenahr's 92-bed hostel is beautifully located in the Langfigtal nature park, overlooking the Ahr.

Hotel-Restaurant Zum Schwarzen Kreuz HOTEL €€
(📞 02643 1534; www.zumschwarzenkreuz.de; Brückenstrasse 5-7; s €35-60, d €65-110) In the heart of town, this stolid-looking 30-room place offers retro flair, a quiet library with overstuffed chairs and rooms with balconies, groovy tapestries and remodelled bathrooms. The restaurant does Eifel specialities (mains €9 to €20) and *Flammkuchen*.

Campingplatz Altenahr CAMPGROUND €
(📞 8503; www.camping-altenahr.de; Im Pappelauel; per tent & car/person €9/4.50; ⊙ Apr-Oct) A grassy camping ground on the banks of the Ahr.

DON'T MISS

MARIA LAACH ABBEY CHURCH

Abteikirche Maria Laach (Maria Laach Abbey Church; 📞 02652-590; www.maria-laach.de; Maria Laach; admission free; ⊙ 9.30-11.15am & 1.15-4.45pm Mon-Sat, 1.15-4.45pm Sun) is one of the finest examples of a Romanesque church in Germany. Part of a nine-century-old Benedictine abbey, it is next to a volcanic lake, the **Laacher See**, surrounded by a 21-sq-km nature reserve.

You enter the church via a large **Vorhalle** (portico; restored in 2009), a feature not usually found north of the Alps. Note the quirky carvings on and above the capitals and the **Löwenbrunnen** (Lion Fountain), reminiscent of Moorish architecture. The interior is surprisingly modest, in part because the original furnishings were lost during the 1800s. In the west apse lies the late-13th-century, recumbent statue-adorned **tomb** of abbey founder Heinrich II of Palatine (laminated information sheets in six languages are available nearby). The east apse shelters the high altar with its wooden canopy; overhead is an early-20th-century Byzantine-style mosaic of Christ donated by Kaiser Wilhelm II. The entrance to the 11th-century **crypt** is to the left of the choir.

Across the path from the **Klostergaststätte** (restaurant), a 20-minute **film** looks at the life of the 46 monks, who take the motto *Ora et labora* (pray and work) very seriously indeed. They earn a living from economic activities such as growing organic apples and raising house plants, available for purchase in the **Klostergärtnerei** (nursery); and they pray five times a day. Attending Gottesdienst (prayer services; hours posted at the church entrance) is worthwhile if only to listen to the ethereal chanting in Latin and German.

Various **trails** take walkers up the forested hill behind the abbey; options for circum-ambulating the Laacher See include the lakefront **Ufer-Rundweg** (8km) and two hillier trails (15km and 21km). You can swim near the camping ground.

Next to the car park, the **Bioladen** (organic grocery; ⊙ 8.30am-6pm Mon-Sat, 10am-6pm Sun) sells fruits and vegies grown by the monks, as well as other organic edibles.

Maria Laach is about 25km northwest of Koblenz and 18km southeast of Ahrweiler. It is served hourly by bus 312 from Mendig, the nearest town with a train station.

Getting There & Away

Trains run on the line through Ahrweiler (€4, 20 minutes).

NÜRBURGRING

The **Nürburgring** (www.nuerburgring.de), a historic Formula One race car track, has hosted many spectacular races with legendary drivers since its completion in 1927. The 20.8km, 73-curve **Nordschleife** (North Loop) was not only the longest circuit ever built but also one of the most difficult, earning the respectful moniker 'Green Hell' from racing legend Jackie Stewart. After Niki Lauda's near-fatal crash in 1976, the German Grand Prix moved to the Hockenheimring near Mannheim, but in 1995 Formula One returned (in odd-numbered years) to the 5148m **Grand-Prix-Strecke** (South Loop), built in 1984. The complex hosts 100 races a year.

You can get a glimpse behind the scenes with a one-hour **Backstage Tour** (tour €7.50; ⏱11am, 1pm & 3pm), usually in German with printed material in English.

If you have your own car or motorcycle, you can discover your inner Michael Schumacher by taking a spin around the Nordschleife for €26 per circuit. The Grand-Prix-Strecke costs €40 per 20 minutes (motorcycles forbidden). Check the website for Open Nordschleife times and dates.

There are all sorts of options for joining a driver in a very high-performance machine like an Aston Martin that start at €300 and are limited to nonrace periods.

The **Ring-Werk** (www.ring-werk.com; adult/child €19.50/11; ⏱10am-6pm) theme park features interactive, 3D and tunnel-projection technologies. It also includes the Ring-Racer, which takes less than 2.5 seconds to accelerate from 0km/h to over 200km/h.

The Nürburgring is off the B258, reached via the B257 from Altenahr. It is 60km west of Koblenz.

Aachen

📞0241 / POP 258,700

Aachen has been firmly on the map for millennia. The Romans nursed their war wounds and stiff joints in the steaming waters of Aachen's mineral springs, but it was Charlemagne who put the city firmly on the European map. The emperor too enjoyed a dip now and then, but it was more for strategic reasons that, in 794, he made Aachen the geographical and political capital of his vast

REDECORATING THE DOM

Like the stereotypical suburban housewives who never know when to leave well enough alone, the caretakers of the Dom in Aachen have been on a centuries-long remodelling binge. The result is that very little of what you see dates to Charlemagne's time. For instance, the interior of the main part of the church was redone for the the umpteenth time in the 19th century. At that time, churches across Europe thought to be as old as the Dom were scoured for design ideas, which explains why you can see echoes of Hagia Sophia in Istanbul.

The inside of the dome overhead dates from the 17th century and on it goes. Other than possibly the hidden relics and Charlemagne's bones, the oldest authenticated item in the Dom is the 12th-century chandelier that was a gift from Emperor Friedrich Barbarossa.

Frankish Empire – arguably the first empire with European dimensions.

Today, Aachen should be on any visitor's map. It is still very much an international city, and has a unique appeal thanks to its location in the border triangle with the Netherlands and Belgium. And Charlemagne's legacy lives on in the stunning Dom, which in 1978 became Germany's first Unesco World Heritage Site.

◉ Sights

Appreciating the Dom and wandering Aachen's medieval streets can easily fill a day. Everything is reachable by foot.

TOP CHOICE **Dom** CHURCH
(Map p488; www.aachendom.de; ⏱10am-7pm Apr-Dec, to 6pm Jan-Mar) It's impossible to overestimate the significance of Aachen's magnificent cathedral. The burial place of Charlemagne, it's where more than 30 German kings were crowned and where pilgrims have flocked since the 12th century.

The oldest and most impressive section is Charlemagne's palace chapel, the **Pfalzkapelle**, an outstanding example of Carolingian architecture. Completed in 800, the year of the emperor's coronation, it's an octagonal dome encircled by a 16-sided ambulatory

Aachen

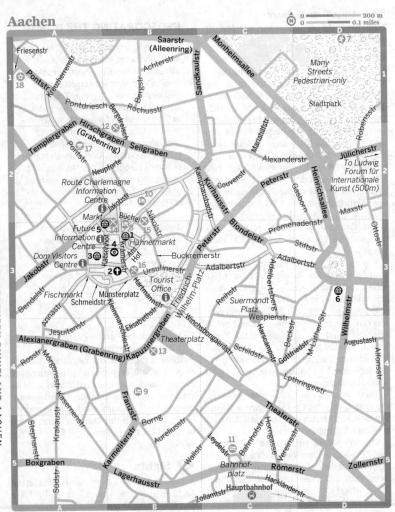

supported by antique Italian pillars. The colossal brass **chandelier** was a gift from Emperor Friedrich Barbarossa during whose reign Charlemagne was canonised in 1165.

Pilgrims have poured into town ever since that time, drawn in as much by the cult surrounding Charlemagne as by his **prized relics**: Christ's loincloth when he was crucified, Mary's cloak, the clothes used for John the Baptist when he was beheaded and swaddling clothes from when Jesus was an infant. These are displayed once every seven years (next in 2014) and draw 100,000 or more faithful.

To accommodate these regular floods of the faithful, a Gothic **choir** was docked to the chapel in 1414 and filled with such priceless treasures as the **pala d'oro**, a gold-plated altar-front depicting Christ's Passion, and the jewel-encrusted gilded copper **pulpit**, both fashioned in the 11th century. At the far end is the gilded **shrine of Charlemagne** that has held the emperor's remains since 1215. In front, the equally fanciful **shrine of St Mary** shelters the cathedral's four prized relics.

Unless you join a **guided tour** (adult/child €5/4; ⊙11am-4.30pm Mon-Fri, 1-4pm Sat & Sun, tours in English 2pm), you'll barely catch

Aachen

a glimpse of Charlemagne's white marble **imperial throne** in the upstairs gallery. Reached via six steps – just like King Solomon's throne – it served as the coronation throne of those 30 German kings between 936 and 1531. The tours themselves are fascinating for the level of detail they reveal about the church.

Before entering the church, stop by the new **Dom Visitors Centre** (☎4770 9127; Klosterplatz 2; ☺10am-1pm Mon, to 5pm Tue-Sun Jan-Mar, 10am-1pm Mon, to 6pm Tue-Sun Apr-Dec) for info and tickets for tours and the Schatzkammer.

Domschatzkammer MUSEUM
(Cathedral Treasury; Map p488; ☎4770 9127; adult/child €6.50/5.50; ☺10am-1pm Mon, to 5pm Tue-Sun Jan-Mar, 10am-1pm Mon, to 6pm Tue, Wed & Fri-Sun, to 9pm Thu Apr-Dec) The cathedral treasury is a veritable mother lode of gold, silver and jewels. Focus your attention on the **Lotharkreuz**, a 10th-century processional cross, and the **marble sarcophagus** that held Charlemagne's bones until his canonisation; the relief shows the rape of Persephone.

Rathaus HISTORIC BUILDING
(Map p488; Markt; adult/concession €5/3; ☺10am-6pm) The Dom gazes serenely over Aachen's Rathaus, a splendid Gothic pile festooned with 50 life-size statues of German rulers, including the 30 kings crowned in town. It was built in the 14th century atop the foundations of Charlemagne's palace, of which only the eastern tower, the **Granusturm**, survives. Inside, the undisputed highlights are the **Kaisersaal** with its epic 19th-

century **frescos** by Alfred Rethel and the replicas of the **imperial insignia**: a crown, orb and sword (the originals are in Vienna). The Rathaus sits proudly facing the **Markt**.

Katschhof SQUARE
(Map p488) It's worth finding a comfy spot to sit and contemplate this deeply historic square. On the north end is the backside of the Rathaus; across from it is the Dom and its complex of buildings. To the west is a mishmash of old buildings that have parts dating back to when this was part of Charlemagne's palace. This is the future site of the Route Charlemagne information centre.

Couven Museum MUSEUM
(Map p488; www.couven-museum.de; Hühnermarkt 17; adult/child €5/3; ☺10am-6pm Tue-Sun) A small applied arts museum which re-creates the living spaces and lives of 17th- and 18th-century patricians.

Suermondt Ludwig Museum MUSEUM
(Map p488; ☎479 800; www.suermondt-ludwig -museum.de; Wilhelmstrasse 18; adult/child €5/3; ☺noon-6pm Tue, Thu & Fri, noon-8pm Wed, 10am-6pm Sat & Sun) Of Aachen's two art museums, the Suermondt Ludwig Museum is especially proud of its medieval sculpture but also has fine works by Cranach, Dürer, Macke, Dix and other masters.

Ludwig Forum für Internationale Kunst MUSEUM
(Ludwig Forum for International Art; ☎180 7104; www.ludwigforum.de; Jülicherstrasse 97-109; adult/child €5/3; ☺noon-6pm Tue, Wed & Fri, noon-8pm Thu, 11am-6pm Sat & Sun) In a former umbrella factory, the Ludwig Forum für Internationale

ROUTE CHARLEMAGNE

The Route Charlemagne is designed to showcase Aachen's 1200-year tradition as a European city of culture and science. The city's sites are linked together and many have special exhibits related to the theme.

A large future information centre with displays is planned for the old building on the west side of the Katschhof. It is hoped it will open by 2014. In the meantime, the **Route Charlemagne Information Centre** (www.route-charlemagne.eu; Haus Löwenstein, Markt; ⏱10am-6pm) is in one of Aachen's few surviving medieval townhouses.

Kunst trains the spotlight on contemporary art (Warhol, Immendorf, Holzer, Penck, Haring etc) and also stages progressive changing exhibits.

Activities

In fine weather, get off the asphalt and onto the trails of the densely forested spa garden north of the Altstadt.

A brisk 20-minute walk takes you up the 264m-high **Lousberg hill**, where the entire city panorama unfolds below you. Get there by cutting north on Kupferstrasse from Ludwigsallee, then left on Belvedereallee.

Carolus Thermal Baths   SPA
(Map p488; ☑182 740; www.carolus-thermen.de; Stadtgarten/Passstrasse 79; with/without sauna from €24/12; ⏱9am-11pm) Oriental pools, honey rubs, deep-tissue massages and soothing saunas are among the relaxation options at the Carolus-Thermen, a snazzy bathing complex on the edge of the Stadtpark (city park).

Tours

Old Town Guided Tour   WALKING TOUR
(adult/child €8/4; ⏱11am Sat Apr-Dec) The tourist office runs 90-minute English-language walking tours.

Sleeping

There are good choices around the Dom and the historic quarters. Chain hotels dot the ring roads.

TOP CHOICE ⧉ **Hotel Drei Könige**   HOTEL €€
(Map p488; ☑483 93; www.h3k-aachen.de; Büchel 5; s €90-130, d €120-180, apt €140-240; 🖥) The radiant Mediterranean decor is an instant mood enhancer at this family-run favourite, with its doesn't-get-more-central location. Some rooms are a tad twee but the two-room apartment sleeps up to four. Breakfast is served on the 4th floor, with dreamy views over the rooftops and the cathedral.

Aquis Grana City Hotel   HOTEL €€
(Map p488; ☑4430; www.hotel-aquis-grana.de; Büchel 32; r from €100/150; P🖥) The best quarters at this gracious hotel have terrace and balcony views of the Rathaus. But even in the most modest of the 98 rooms, you couldn't be any closer to the heart of town. The hotel offers a full range of services.

Hotel Benelux   HOTEL €€
(Map p488; ☑400 030; www.hotel-benelux.de; Franzstrasse 21-23; s/d incl breakfast from €90/130; 🖥) Though on a busy street, this well-run place has 33 quiet, uncluttered rooms reached via art-filled floors. Fuel up with a generous breakfast served tableside and wrap things up with a sunset drink in the rooftop garden. There's even a small gym to work out the kinks.

DJH Hostel   HOSTEL €
(☑0241 711 010; www.aachen.jugendherberge.de; Maria-Theresia-Allee 260; dm/s/d from €26/45/68) Aachen's modernised 180-bed hostel is nicely located in a park overlooking the city. About a third of the 55 rooms have private bathrooms. Take bus 2 (direction Preuswald) to the Ronheide stop.

Hotel Stadtnah   HOTEL €
(Map p488; ☑474 580; www.hotelstadtnah.de; Leydelstrasse 2; s/d from €56/68; ⬅🖥) The rate reflects the basic decor and amenities, but this 16-room cheapie near the Hauptbahnhof should do in a snap. It shares ownership with the Hotel Am Bahnhof around the corner, which has similar prices and amenities.

Eating & Drinking

Aachen is the birthplace of the famous *Printen*, crunchy spiced cookies spiked with herbs or nuts and drenched in chocolate or frosting. You'll find them sold in bakeries across town.

Ponstrasse is a good place to go restaurant browsing.

TOP CHOICE **Leo van den Daele** CAFE €

(Map p488; www.van-den-daele.de; Büchel 18; treats from €3) Leather-covered walls, tiled stoves and antiques forge the yesteryear flair of this rambling cafe institution. Come for all-day breakfast, a light lunch or divine cakes (the strudel and the Belgian Reisfladen, made with rice, are specialities), which are shown off in the front window.

Am Knipp GERMAN €€

(Map p488; ☑331 68; www.amknipp.de; Bergdri-esch 3; mains €8-18; ⊘dinner Wed-Mon) Hungry grazers have stopped by this traditional inn since 1698, and you too will have a fine time enjoying hearty German cuisine served amid a flea market's worth of twee knick-knacks. A vast, lovely beer garden as well.

Gaststätte Postwagen GERMAN €€

(Map p488; ☑350 01; www.postwagen-aachen. de; Krämerstrasse 2; mains €10-20) This oh-so-evocative old place, tacked onto the Rathaus, oozes old-world flair from every nook and cranny and is a good place for classic German meals. The downstairs is made to look like an 18th-century postal coach (hence the name). Tables spill onto the cafe-ringed Markt.

Noblis BAKERY €

(Map p488; Münsterplatz; snacks from €3; ⊘8am-7pm) This gorgeous bakery is right across from the Dom. It has a stunning array of sandwiches and other goods ready to eat at tables on the square or as a picnic in the nearby parks. Get your *Printen* here.

Magellan CAFE

(Map p488; www.magellan-ac.de; Pontstrasse 78; mains €8-12) This cocktail bar and cafe has a surprising garden setting right near the centre of town. There's even a little stream running past tables where you can enjoy the Mediterranean-style food and refreshments under the stars.

Friture Belge BELGIAN €

(Map p488; Kapuzinergraben; snacks from €2) If you can't go over the nearby border into Belgium, you can at least enjoy some classic and perfectly presented Belgian-style *frites* here, with mayonnaise of course.

☆ Entertainment

For listings, pick up the free *Klenkes* in cafes, pubs and the tourist office. The main bar-hopping drag is student-flavoured Pontstrasse (locals say 'Ponte').

Apollo Kino & Bar BAR/CLUB

(Map p488; ☑900 8484; www.apollo-aachen.de; Pontstrasse 141-149) This cavernous basement joint does double duty as an art-house cinema and a sweaty dance club for the student brigade. Alt-sounds rule on Mondays, salsa on Wednesdays, but on other nights it could be anything from dancehall to disco, house to power pop.

ⓘ Information

Reisebank (☑0241 912 6872; Lager-hausstrasse 9; ⊘9.45am-2pm & 2.45-5.45pm Mon-Fri) Currency exchange.

Tourist Office (☑0241 180 2961, 0241 180 2960; www.aachen-tourist.de; Friedrich-Wil-helm-Platz; ⊘9am-6pm Mon-Fri, to 2pm Sat, also 10am-2pm Sun Easter-Dec)

ⓘ Getting There & Away

Regional **trains** to Cologne (€16, one hour) run twice hourly, with some proceeding beyond. Aachen is a stop for high-speed trains to/from Brussels and Paris.

ⓘ Getting Around

The Hauptbahnhof is a 10- to 15-minute signed walk to the tourist office and the Altstadt.

Bus tickets for travel within central Aachen cost €1.60; drivers sell tickets.

For bike hire, try **Cycle** (☑408 363; Heinrich-sallee 66; per day €9.50).

Eifel National Park

Wild cats, beavers, kingfishers, bats and owls are just some of the critters you might spot in **Eifel National Park** (☑02444-951 00; www.na tionalpark-eifel.de), North Rhine–Westphalia's only national park. It protects about 110 sq km of beech forest, rivers and lakes, and is filled with interesting plants and wildlife. In spring, a sea of wild narcissus floods the valleys. It's hard to imagine now that, until recently, Belgian troops used much of the area for military exercises.

A focal point of the park is **Forum Vogel-sang** (☑02444-915 790; www.nationalpark-eifel. de; guided tour adult/child €4/free; ⊘8am-8pm Apr-Oct, 10am-5.30pm Nov-Mar, guided tour 2pm, also 11am Sun, visitor centre 10am-5pm), a vast complex built by the Nazis as a party leadership training centre and later used as military barracks by the Belgians. It has exhibits on the national park and the Eifel region as well as a documentation centre about the indoctrination and educational system in the Nazi state.

Forum Vogelsang is also a good starting point for hikes in the national park. Staff at its visitor centre hand out suggestions and maps. Information is also available inside the **Kall train station** (☎02441-777 545; Bahnhofstrasse 13; ☺6am-6pm Mon-Fri, 8am-6pm Sat, 9am-5pm Sun).

❶ Getting There & Away

The park is some 50km southeast of Aachen and 70km southwest of Cologne near the border with Belgium.

From Cologne, regional **trains** make the trip to Kall several times hourly, where you can switch to the **Nationalpark Shuttle Bus SB82** (☺Sat & Sun) to Vogelsang. The park website has details of additional options.

Düsseldorf

☑0211 / POP 589,000

Düsseldorf dazzles with boundary-pushing architecture, zinging nightlife and an art scene to rival many higher-profile cities. It's a posh and modern city that seems all buttoned-up business at first glance: banking, advertising, fashion and telecommunications are among the fields that have made North Rhine–Westphalia's capital one of Germany's wealthiest cities. Yet all it takes is a few hours of bar-hopping around the Altstadt, the historical quarter along the Rhine, to realise that locals have no problem letting their hair down once they shed those Armani jackets.

The Altstadt may claim to be the 'longest bar in the world' but some attention has strayed to Medienhafen, a redeveloped harbour area and a feast of international avant-garde architecture. Older neighbourhoods are also changing. Case in point: Flingern, which has gone from drab to fab in recent years and is has a multifaceted arty boho scene. Highbrow types, meanwhile, can get more than their fill at the city's many world-class art museums and cultural institutions.

⊙ Sights

Düsseldorf has long had a love affair with art, dating back to Jan Wellem's generous patronage, and the city has several high-calibre museums to prove it. Those museums and a stroll through the reconstructed Altstadt can easily fill a day – and that's before you allow time for some *Altbier*.

ALTSTADT & AROUND

Düsseldorf's Altstadt, a mostly pedestrianised web of lanes cuddling up to the Rhine, is rightly (in)famous for its lively nightlife. But it has some interesting sights that recall its age-old wealth.

Marktplatz SQUARE
The historic Marktplatz is framed by the Renaissance **Rathaus** (town hall; Map p494; Marktplatz), built in 1573 and accented by an equestrian **statue** of the art-loving elector Jan Wellem, who lies buried nearby in the early baroque **Andreaskirche** (Map p494; www.dominikaner-duesseldorf.de; Andreasstrasse 27; ☺8am-6.30pm). The church is drenched in fanciful white stucco. Six baroque saint sculptures from the original altar are integrated into the sanctuary. More religious art awaits in the **treasury** in the upstairs gallery. A great time to visit is for the free organ concert at 4.30pm on Sundays.

St Lambertuskirche CHURCH
(Church of St Lambert; Map p494; www.lambertus kirche.de; Stiftsplatz; ☺8am-5pm) The twisted tower of the 14th-century St Lambertuskirche shadows treasures that span several centuries. Look for the Gothic tabernacle, the Renaissance marble tombs, baroque altars and modern windows.

Kunstsammlung Nordrhein-Westfalen MUSEUM
(Art Collection of North Rhine–Westphalia; www.kunstsammlung.de; Combined ticket for 3 museums adult/child €20/5; ☺10am-6pm Tue-Fri, 11am-6pm Sat & Sun) The regional art museum is spread over three separate buildings. Its diversity and richness reflect the high importance art has in local life. During opening hours, a shuttle bus runs every 20 minutes between K20 and K21.

K20 Grabbeplatz (Map p494; ☑838 1130; Grabbeplatz 5; adult/child €12/9.50) A collection that spans the arc of 20th-century artistic vision gives the K20 an enviable edge in the art world. Paul Klee is well represented, but walls are also graced by plenty of other Western European and American bigshots, including Picasso, Matisse, Robert Rauschenberg, Jasper Johns and Düsseldorf's own Joseph Beuys. A recent revamp has made things even more impressive.

K21 Ständehaus (Map p494; ☑838 1630; Ständehausstrasse 1; adult/child €10/2.50) A stately 19th-century parliament building forms the incongruous setting of the cutting-edge K21, which brims with canvases, photographs, installations and video art created after 1980 by an international cast of artists. Look for works by Andreas Gursky, Candida Höfer, Bill Viola and the late Nam June Paik.

Schmela Haus (Map p494; Mutter-Ey-Strasse 3) Designed by noted Dutch architect Aldo van Eyck, the Schmela Haus opened in 1971 as a private gallery. It's now part of the state museum and its angular grey pumice exterior is an architectural landmark. It closed in 2012 for renovations that should allow more of the permanent collection to be exhibited along with special shows.

Kunsthalle
MUSEUM

(Art Hall; Map p494; ☎899 6243; www.kunsthalle-duesseldorf.de; Grabbeplatz 4; adult/child €5/free; ☺11am-6pm Tue-Sun) Across the square from K20, a Brutalist '60s cube houses the Kunst-halle, which hosts headline-grabbing contemporary art shows.

Schifffahrt Museum
MUSEUM

(Navigation Museum; Map p494; ☎899 4195; www .freunde-schifffahrtmuseum.de; Burgplatz 30; adult/child €3/free; ☺11am-6pm Tue-Sun) The **Schlossturm** (Palace Tower) is all that's left of the electors' palace, which burned down in 1872. Now it makes an atmospheric backdrop for the Schifffahrt Museum, where nifty multimedia exhibits chronicle Rhine shipping from the Middle Ages until today. The 4th-floor cafe offers panoramic views.

Rheinuferpromenade
PROMENADE

(Rhine River Walk; Map p494) Burgplatz marks the beginning of the Rheinuferpromenade, whose cafes and benches fill with people in fine weather, creating an almost Mediterranean flair.

Rheinturm
TOWER

(Map p494; Stromstrasse 20; adult/child €4/2.50; ☺10am-11.30pm) Spearing the sky at the southern end of the Rhine promenade, the Rheinturm has an observation deck at the 168m level of its overall height of 240m. The views are as sweeping as you'd expect, although the phrase 'on a clear day you can see Essen' may not inspire. There are also various cafes, bars and a revolving restaurant should the mere thought of Essen get you hungry. Near the base is the Landtag, the state parliament.

Elvis Presley Exhibition
MUSEUM

(Map p494; www.elvis-duesseldorf.de; Flinger-strasse 11; adult/child €8.50/4; ☺11am-7pm Mon-Fri, from 10am Sat & Sun) The connec-tion between 'the King' and Düsseldorf isn't even tenuous – there is none. But three avid local collectors of anything Presley have opened this museum with their collections anyway. The ostensible peg is Elvis's time on an US Army base some 200km southeast of here. To that end there's the guitar he used while in Germany and literally thousands more objects relating to him (his alarm clock even!).

Hetjens Museum
MUSEUM

(Map p494; ☎899 4210; www.duesseldorf.de; Schulstrasse 4; adult/child €4/2; ☺11am-5pm Tue & Thu-Sun, to 9pm Wed) A short detour off the Rheinuferpromenade takes you to the Hetjens Museum, known for its survey of 8000 years of ceramic art from around the world. An extension houses the **Filmmuseum** (Map p494; ☎899 2232; www.duesseldorf.de; adult/concession €5/2.50; ☺11am-5pm Tue & Thu-Sun, to 9pm Wed), which trains the spotlight on the technology, history and mystery of movie-making. The Black Box art-house cinema presents retrospectives, rare flicks and silent movies with live organ accompaniment.

Heinrich Heine Institut
MUSEUM

(Map p494; ☎899 2902; www.duesseldorf.de; Bilker Strasse 12-14; adult/child €4/2; ☺11am-5pm Tue-Fri & Sun, 1-5pm Sat) For a literary kick, swing by the Heinrich Heine Institut, where letters, portraits, first editions and manuscripts document this famed Düsseldorfer's career. **Heine's birth house** at Bolkerstrasse 53 now contains a literary bookshop and reading room.

Mahn- und Gedenkstätte für die Opfer des Nationalsozialismus
MEMORIAL

(Memorial Exhibit to the Victims of the Nazi Regime; Map p494; ☎899 6205; www.ns-gedenkstaetten. de; Mühlenstrasse 29) A few steps west of Marktplatz is this memorial with exhibits on local persecution and resistance during the Third Reich. It closed beginning in 2011 so the building could be repaired and the exhibits improved. Check for a reopening date.

NRW-Forum Düsseldorf
GALLERY

(Map p494; ☎892 6690; www.nrw-forum.de; Ehrenhof 2; adult/concession €8/5.50; ☺11am-8pm Tue-Thu, Sat & Sun, to midnight Fri) For Zeitgeist-capturing exhibits, swing by the NRW-Forum Düsseldorf. It targets the life-style-savvy crowd with changing exhibits on fashion, media, design and architecture.

Düsseldorf

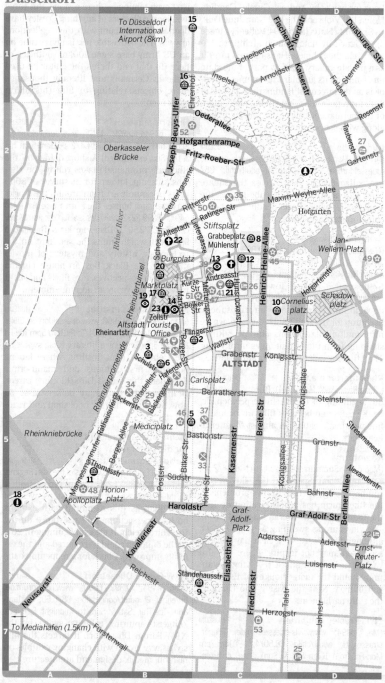

Museum Kunstpalast

MUSEUM

(Map p494; ☑899 0200; www.smkp.de; Ehrenhof 5; adult/child €7/5.50; ⊙11am-6pm Tue-Sun, to 9pm Thu) The once-stuffy Kunstpalast now takes an unconventional approach to presenting its well-respected collection. Old masters find themselves juxtaposed with contemporary artists and nonWestern works to reveal unexpected connections between the ages and artistic trends. Temporary exhibitions further reinforce the theme.

KIT – Kunst im Tunnel

GALLERY

(Map p494; ☑892 0769; www.kunst-im-tunnel.de; Mannesmannufer 1b; adult/concession €4/3; ⊙11am-6pm Tue-Sun) Young artists – many from the local art academy – get the nod in this underground exhibition space housed in a spectacularly adapted tunnel below the Rhine promenade. The entrance is via a glass pavilion.

MEDIENHAFEN

South of the Altstadt, the Medienhafen (Media Harbour) is an office quarter that's been wrought from the remains of the old city harbour. It's Düsseldorf's largest and most progressive urban construction project, yet despite a few trendy restaurants and design shops, there's a lack of life in the streets as yet.

Modern architecture fans, however, will want to head right down. The most eye-catching structure is clearly the warped **Neuer Zollhof**, a typically sculptural design by Frank Gehry. Moored nearby is Claude Vasconi's **Grand Bateau**, built to resemble an ocean liner. A new pedestrian bridge links to another quay dominated by William Alsop's **Colorium**, easily recognised by its kaleidoscopic glass facade. New additions include Hafen by Helmut Jahn while the huge **Casa Stupenda** by Renzo Piano remains in a holding pattern.

KÖNIGSALLEE & HOFGARTEN

Banks and boutiques are the ammo of the Königsallee (Kö for short), one of Germany's most expensive shopping strips. Otherwise, there's little of actual merit here, although the art nouveau facade of the **Kaufhof** (Map p494; Königsallee 1-9) department store and the landmark **Triton fountain** deserve a look.

When you've had your shopping fill, head on over to the pleasant **Hofgarten** (Map p494) dotted with statues of Heinrich Heine, Robert Schumann and other German greats. Thespians might get a kick out of the

COLOGNE & NORTHERN RHINELAND DÜSSELDORF

Düsseldorf

Theatermuseum, which looks back on Düsseldorf's centuries-old theatre tradition.

Goethe Museum MUSEUM
(Map p494; ☏899 6262; www.goethe-museum.com; Jacobistrasse 2; adult/concession €4/2; ⊙11am-5pm Tue-Fri & Sun, 1-5pm Sat) On the northern edge of the Hofgarten, this modest museum dedicated to the great man of letters is housed in the pretty-in-pink 18th-century Schloss Jägerhof on the park's northern edge.

SCHLOSS BENRATH
Schloss Benrath MUSEUM
(☏899 3832; www.schloss-benrath.de; Benrather Schlossallee 100-106; ⊙11am-5pm Tue-Sun) Elector Carl Theodor was a man of deep pockets and good taste, as reflected in his exquisite pleasure palace and gardens, where he came to relax and frolic. Designed by Frenchman Nicolas de Pigage, the three-winged palace centres on the **Corps de Logis** (adult/child €7.50/2), the former residential tract, where tours (in German) offer a glimpse of the elector's lifestyle. The other wings contain an old-school **natural history museum** (adult/child €5/2) and a museum of **European garden history** (adult/child €5/2) that will probably grow on you.

The complex is about 10km south of the city centre and reached by tram 701 in about 30 minutes.

Tours

Hop On Hop Off City Tour BUS TOUR
(www.duesseldorf-tourismus.de; Immermannstrasse 65; adult child from €12/5) The city's tourist office operates a daytime bus tour of the city

that's a good way to get a handle on the sprawl that is Düsseldorf in 90 minutes. Although there are a few caveats: the 'Hop On Hop Off' aspect is optional and costs an extra €3 (outside of summer you may wait a long time to hop between buses), the roof may stay closed even on nice days and if you want *clean* headphones for the narration, it's an extra €1.50.

🛌 Sleeping

Düsseldorf's hotels cater primarily for the business brigade, which explains prices that can triple during big trade shows held not only here but as far away as Cologne and Essen. On the bright side, bargains abound at weekends and in summer. Prices quoted here are applicable outside trade-show times.

Stage 47 BOUTIQUE HOTEL €€
(Map p494; ☎388 030; www.stage47.de; Graf-Adolf-Strasse 47; s/d from €130/145; P❄@🛰) Behind the drab exterior, movie glamour meets design chic at this urban boutique hotel. Rooms are named for famous people, who appear in enormous black-and-white prints framed on the wall, so let's hope you like who you sleep with! Nice touches: an iHome and a Nespresso coffeemaker.

Hotel Orangerie HOTEL €€€
(Map p494; ☎866 800; www.hotel-orangerie-mcs.de; Bäckergasse 1; s €110-165, d €130-210; ⊜🛰) Ensconced in a neoclassical mansion in a quiet corner of the Altstadt, this place puts you within staggering distance of pubs, the river and museums, yet offers a quiet and stylish refuge to retire to. Some of the 27 rooms skimp somewhat on size but all are as bright, modern and uncluttered as the lobby and breakfast room (rates include breakfast).

Max Hotel Garni HOTEL €€
(Map p494; ☎386 800; www.max-hotelgarni.de; Adersstrasse 65; s/d from €70/85; @🛰) Upbeat, contemporary and run with personal flair, this charmer is a Düsseldorf favourite. The 11 rooms are good-sized and decked out in bright hues and warm woods. Rates include coffee, tea, soft drinks and a regional public-transport pass. The reception isn't always staffed, so call ahead to arrange an arrival time.

Backpackers-Düsseldorf HOSTEL €
(Map p494; ☎302 0848; www.backpackers-duesseldorf.de; Fürstenwall 180; dm incl breakfast €15-23; @🛰) Düsseldorf's adorable indie hostel sleeps 60 in clean four- to 10-bed dorms, which are fitted with individual backpack-sized lockers. It's a low-key place with a kitchen and a relaxed lounge where cultural and language barriers melt quickly. The reception is generally staffed from 8am to 9pm. The vending machine is filled with beer.

Sir & Lady Astor HOTEL €€
(Map p494; ☎173 370; www.sir-astor.de; Kurfürstenstrasse 18 & 23; s €85-170, d €95-250; @🛰) Never mind the ho-hum setting on a residential street near the Hauptbahnhof: this unique twin boutique hotel brims with class, originality and charm. Check-in is at Sir Astor, furnished in 'Scotland-meets-Africa'-style, while Lady Astor across the street goes more for French floral sumptuousness. With a huge fan base and only 20 rooms total, book early.

Hotel Mondial HOTEL €€
(Map p494; ☎173 9920; www.nk-hotels.de; Graf-Adolf-Strasse 82; s €60-80, d €85-120; 🛰) In a veritable ghetto of mid-priced hotels near the Hauptbahnhof, the Mondial stands out for having small but very clean rooms and service that borders on the jolly. Try for a room facing the street on the 5th floor and you'll get a small terrace.

DON'T MISS

GROOVY FLINGERN

Once all working-class, Flingern, a neighbourhood near the Hauptbahnhof, is now the centre of Düsseldorf's boho-chic hipness. The main strip is a 1km stretch of leafy **Ackerstrasse**, where retail therapy gets a unique twist in indie boutiques stocked with vintage frocks, edgy jewellery, whimsical tees, handmade accessories and gourmet foods.

There are cafes by the dozen. Try **Café Hüftgold** (www.cafehueftgold.de; Ackerstrasse 113; snacks from €3), renowned for its amazing cakes, tortes and more baked goodness. The coffee and sandwiches are good as well.

Getting there is easy: from the Hauptbahnhof it's either a 15-minute walk via Worringer Strasse or a short ride on tram 709 to Wetterstrasse (head north for a couple of minutes to get to Ackerstrasse).

DJH Hostel
HOSTEL €

(☑557 310; www.duesseldorf.jugendherberge.de; Düsseldorfer Strasse 1; dm/s/d from €22/36/56; P☺@☺) Offering fine views of the Altstadt across the Rhine, this contender scores highly for cleanliness, security, location and comforts. Each of the 96 rooms has its own shower and toilet. Take U70, U74, U75, U76 or U77 to Luegplatz; from there walk seven minutes on foot along Kaiser-Wilhelm-Ring.

Hotel Berial
HOTEL €

(Map p494; ☑490 0490; www.hotelberial.de; Gartenstrasse 30; s/d incl breakfast from €50/70; @☺) This well-kept property is a fine choice for wallet-watching nomads who have outgrown hostels. Room decor is nothing to tweet about, but all the expected comforts and amenities are here. The Hofgarten is a couple of minutes away – perfect for jogging off your jet lag.

Hotel Alt-Düsseldorf
HOTEL €€

(Map p494; ☑133 604; www.alt-duesseldorf.de; Hunsrückenstrasse 11; s €50-120, d €70-160; @) If you're happy to trade genericness for centrality, this family-run hotel should do in a snap. It's a small, good-value place where days start with a big breakfast buffet served in sun-yellow surroundings.

✗ Eating

The heart of the Altstadt is a mass of places to eat, of widely variable quality. Head over to Ratinger Strasse and Hohe Strasse for choices that are less swamped by visitors.

TOP CHOICE Brauerei im Füchschen
GERMAN €€

(Map p494; ☑137 470; www.fuechschen.de; Ratinger Strasse 28; mains €5-15; ☺9am-1am) Boisterous, packed and drenched with local colour – the 'Little Fox' in the Altstadt is all you expect a Rhenish beer hall to be. The kitchen makes a mean *Schweinshaxe* (roast pork leg). The high-ceilinged interior echoes with the mirthful roar of people enjoying their meals. This is one of the best *Altbier* breweries.

Weinhaus Tante Anna
MODERN EUROPEAN €€€

(Map p494; www.tanteanna.de; Andreasstrasse 2; mains/menus from €25/45) If you've ever wondered what it might be like to have a baroness as an aunt, you'll find out at Aunt Anna. Silver serving plates, subdued carved wood interior, wines decanted and poured properly, the details do go on. The menu changes constantly and shows the range of the kitchen, whether it is boar piglet loin with celery and potato gnocchi or a simply superb springtime asparagus special.

Bistro Zicke
BISTRO €€

(Map p494; ☑324 056; www.bistro-zicke.de; Bäckerstrasse 5a; dishes €6-14; ☺9am-1am) Arty types jam this staple eatery, tucked away from the Altstadt bustle in a quiet corner. Linger over breakfast (served until 3pm, on weekends till 4pm) or come for fresh and tasty soups, salads and various hot plates that change daily. Marble tables add class.

Robert's Bistro
FRENCH €€€

(☑304 821; www.robertsbistro.de; Wupperstrasse 2; mains €12-22; ☺Tue-Sat) Tables are squished together as tightly as lovers at this *très* French restaurant in the Mediahafen. Bring both an appetite for hearty Gallic fare (the fish soup is highly recommended) and some patience – it doesn't take reservations and a queue is guaranteed. The rosemary pine-nut creme has people swooning.

Libanon Express
MIDDLE EASTERN €

(Map p494; Berger Strasse 19-21; mains €3-20) Crammed with mirrors and tiles, this cafe serves great kebabs, felafel and other Middle Eastern specialities. Its takeaway is a standout amongst competitors counting on customers too drunk to notice their poor fare. Outdoor tables have a front seat on endless Berger Strasse frivolity.

Zum Schiffchen
GERMAN €

(Map p494; ☑132 421; www.brauerei-zum-schiffchen.de; Hafenstrasse 5; mains €7-20) History pours from every nook and cranny in this almost ridiculously cosy Altstadt restaurant specialising in hearty German and Rhenish meals. Were portions as huge when Napoleon dropped by a couple of centuries ago? Reservations recommended (he didn't need any); slightly more restrained than some of the other traditional joints.

Sila Thai
THAI €€€

(Map p494; ☑860 4427; www.sila-thai.com; Bahnstrasse 76; mains €17-25; ☺noon-3pm & 6pm-1am) Even simple curries become culinary poetry at this Thai gourmet temple with its fairytale setting of carved wood, rich fabrics and imported sculpture. Like a trip to Thailand without the passport. Reservations advised.

Münstermann Delikatessen
DELI €

(Map p494; www.muenstermann-delikatessen.de; Hohe Strasse 9-13; snacks from €3) This is the kind of beautiful deli filled with so much goodness that people stand outside window-shopping in hushed tones. Meats, cheeses, prepared foods, sandwiches and much more.

Bäckerei Hinkel
BAKERY €

(Map p494; www.baeckerei-hinkel.de; Hohe Strasse 31; treats from €2) This traditional bakery is an institution that has people queuing patiently for its excellent breads and cakes. Buy the fixings for a perfect picnic – it blows away anything you've had from a train station chain bakery.

Drinking

Düsseldorf's beverage of choice is *Altbier,* a dark, hoppy beer that's just slightly heavy. Think of it as the pepper to rival city Cologne's salt *(Kölsch).*

Zum Uerige
BEER HALL

(Map p494; ☎866 990; www.uerige.de; Berger Strasse 1) This cavernous beer hall is the best place to soak it all up. The suds flow so quickly from giant copper vats that the waiters – called *Köbes* – simply carry huge trays of brew and plonk down a glass whenever they spy an empty. Even on a cold day, there are groups all over the street outside.

Anaconda Lounge
LOUNGE

(Map p494; ☎869 3939; www.anaconda-lounge.de; Andreasstrasse 11; ⊙8pm-2am Wed & Thu, to 5am Fri & Sat) The living room of hipsters, this designer cave is great for chilling or launching a bar hop. Strong drinks from an L of a bar, kick-ass music and complexion-friendly decor further loosen inhibitions.

Cafe Seitensprung
GAY

(Map p494; www.seitensprung-cafe.de; Grupellostrasse 5; ⊙6pm-late Tue-Sat) Great convivial gay and lesbian bar which has been welcoming visitors to Düsseldorf for years. Management cheerfully call themselves a 'living room' for locals and anyone who wanders in the door.

Melody Bar
BAR

(Map p494; ☎329 057; Kurze Strasse 12; ⊙Tue-Sun) After 10pm you may have to shoehorn your way into this jewel of a cocktail bar; it's an island of sophistication amid the boisterous Altstadt thirst parlours. The drinks are excellent, the owner couple gracious, the crowd mixed and the house dog a cute pooch.

Salon des Amateurs
LOUNGE

(Map p494; ☎899 6243; www.salondesamateurs. de; Grabbeplatz 4; ⊙noon-1am Tue-Sun, to 5am Fri & Sat) Tucked into the Kunsthalle, this

WHERE TO DRINK IN THE ALTSTADT

What with the world's longest bar hype, Düsseldorf's Altstadt may seem like one big festive drunk but there are actually distinct personalities to various streets. Here's a guide as you go on the prowl.

» **Andreasstrasse** A good place to find a cafe or restaurant with a free table outside.

» **Berger Strasse** Excellent casual restaurants and what seems like a hectare of outdoor tables.

» **Bolker Strasse** A nightmare of fake ethnic restaurants geared towards the undiscerning.

» **Hunsrückenstrasse** Fake Irish bars – need we say more?

» **Rheinartstrasse** The merry crowds spilling out of Zum Uerige set the tone.

» **Kurze Strasse** Slightly mellow, restaurants with tables outside, not a mob scene.

» **Mertensgasse** Quieter than others, few outside tables, several late-night clubs.

tunnel-shaped cafe-lounge pulls off an artsy vibe without a single canvas. Museum-goers arrive in the afternoon for tea and chat, while hipsters keep the bar and little dance floor hopping after dark.

☆ Entertainment

Check listings site **Coolibri** (www.coolibri.de) for current goings-on in 'D-Town'.

Nightclubs & Live Music

Stone Im Ratinger Hof
CLUB

(Map p494; ☎210 7828; www.stone-club.de; Ratinger Strasse 10; cover varies; ⊙Wed, Fri & Sat) The venerable Ratinger Hof has returned to its rock roots and is now the 'it' place for lovers of indie and alt sounds. Depending on the night, tousled hipsters, skinny-jean emos and sneaker-wearing students thrash it out to everything from noise pop to neo-garage to punk and roll.

Pretty Vacant
CLUB

(Map p494; www.prettylush.net; Mertensgasse 8; ⊙from 8pm) It may be named for a Sex Pistols song, but this Altstadt haunt ain't no punk club. It's a shape-shifter really, whose cellar walls vibrate to different sounds nightly. Live bands, too.

Sub CLUB
(Map p494; ☑865 890; www.sub-dc.de; Bolker Strasse 16; ⊙from 10pm Fri & Sat) Getting past the door wolf can be tough, but if you succeed you'll have a fine time inside this hip basement haunt designed to look like a subway station. Tip: dress nicely, smile and don't arrive drunk.

Theatre

Marionetten-Theater THEATRE
(Map p494; ☑328 432; www.marionettentheater -duesseldorf.de; Bilker Strasse 7; tickets €14-24) Generations of kids and adults have been enthralled by the adorable marionettes that sing, dance and act their way through beautifully orchestrated operas and fairy tales at this venerable venue. Pure magic.

Roncalli's Apollo Varieté THEATRE
(Map p494; ☑828 9090; www.apollo-variete.de; Apolloplatz 1; tickets €14-39) No German skills are needed to enjoy the line-up of acrobats, comedians, magicians, artists and other variety acts performing under the starry-sky ceiling of this nostalgic theatre hall.

Schauspielhaus THEATRE
(Map p494; ☑369 911; www.duesseldorfer-schaus pielhaus.de; Gustaf-Gründgens-Platz 1; tickets €14-41) The main venue for drama and comedies, the Schauspielhaus enjoys a solid reputation nationwide.

Classical Music

Tonhalle CLASSICAL MUSIC
(Map p494; ☑899 6123; www.tonhalle-duesseldorf. de; Ehrenhof 1) The imposing domed Tonhalle, in a converted 1920s planetarium, is the home base of the Düsseldorfer Symphoniker (Düsseldorf Symphony Orchestra).

Deutsche Oper Am Rhein OPERA
(Map p494; ☑892 5211; www.rheinoper.de; Heinrich-Heine-Allee 16a; tickets €12-90) Mozart to Monteverdi are the bread and butter of Düsseldorf's renowned opera house.

🔒 Shopping

The big noise is all about the big names with the big prices in the **Königsalle**. Think of it as duty-free luxury goods without the savings.

More fun (and not just because of the namesake **market** (www.carlsplatz.net; Carlsplatz; ⊙8am-6pm Mon-Sat)) is the area

around **Carlsplatz**. Check out streets like **Benratherstrasse** for interesting and creative boutiques. **Lorettostrasse**, near the Mediahafen, is where you'll find D-town's thriving indie desginer scene.

Finally, there is the already mentioned Flingern, with everything for sale you can imagine along **Ackerstrasse**.

Buchhaus Stern-Verlag BOOKS
(Map p494; ☑388 10; Friedrichstrasse 24-26; ⊙9.30am-8pm Mon-Sat) Awesome bookshop with huge international selection, a cafe and internet access.

ℹ Information

Düsseldorf Tourist Information (www. duesseldorf-tourismus.de) has two offices: **Altstadt Tourist Office** (Marktstrasse/Ecke Rheinstrasse; ⊙10am-6pm) and **Hauptbahnhof Tourist Office** (Immermannstrasse 65b; ⊙9.30am-7pm Mon-Fri, to 5pm Sat)
Düsseldorf Welcome Card (24/48/72hr €9/14/19) Discount card offering free public transport and discounted museum admission. Available from the tourist office.
ReiseBank (☑364 878; Hauptbahnhof; ⊙7am-10pm Mon-Sat, 8am-9pm Sun) Exchange and money transfer services.

ℹ Getting There & Away

AIR **Düsseldorf International Airport** (DUS; www.dus-int.de) has three terminals and is served by a wide range of airlines.

BUS Düsseldorf's central bus station is on Worringer Strasse, about 250m north of the Hauptbahnhof main exit. From here, Eurolines services include daily buses to Paris (7½ hours), Warsaw (20 hours) and London (13½ hours).

TRAIN Düsseldorf is part of a dense S-Bahn and regional train network in the Rhine-Ruhr region, including Cologne (€12, 30 minutes). ICE/IC train links include Berlin (€107, 4¼ hours), Hamburg (€78, 3¾ hours) and Frankfurt (€78, 1¾ hours).

ℹ Getting Around

The Hauptbahnhof is on the southeastern edge of the city centre. From here it's about a 20-minute walk along Bismarckstrasse and Blumenstrasse to the Königsallee, with the Altstadt just beyond. Alternatively, any U-Bahn from the Hauptbahnhof to Heinrich-Heine-Allee will put you right in the thick of things.

TO/FROM THE AIRPORT The airport is about 7km north of the Altstadt.

S-Bahns, regional RE and long-distance trains connect the airport with Düsseldorf Hauptbahnhof, and cities beyond, every few minutes. The free SkyTrain links the airport terminals with the station. A taxi into town costs about €16.

CAR & MOTORCYCLE Central Düsseldorf is now a low-emission zone, meaning that your car needs to display an *Umweltplakette* (emission sticker). Rental cars automatically have the sticker, but if you're driving your own vehicle you'll need to obtain one.

PUBLIC TRANSPORT **Rheinbahn** (www.rheinbahn.de) operates an extensive network of U-Bahn trains, trams and buses throughout Düsseldorf. Most trips within the city cost €2.40. Day passes are €5.70. Tickets are available from bus drivers and orange vending machines at U-Bahn and tram stops, and must be validated upon boarding.

TAXI (☏212 121, 333 33)

Lower Rhine

North of Düsseldorf, the Rhine widens and embarks on its final headlong rush towards the North Sea, traversing the sparsely populated Lower Rhine (Niederrhein). It's a flat, windswept plain that feels like Holland without the windmills and even yields a few off-beat surprises.

The region has its own airport, the tiny **Niederrhein airport** (NRN; www.flughafen-niederrhein.de) in Weeze, which is a hub for RyanAir (which, in its own inimitable fashion, calls the airport 'Düsseldorf' even though D-town is over 80km away).

XANTEN
☏02801 / POP 21,600

Some of the region's most interesting museums capture Xanten's role as the hub of the Lower Rhine, going all the way back to when it was founded as a Roman military camp in 12 BC. Within a century it grew into a respectable settlement called Colonia Ulpia Traiana. At its peak, some 15,000 people milled about town, enjoying a surprisingly high standard of living.

Xanten's next heyday – in medieval times – is best symbolised by the majestic Dom that dominates the tangled old town with its stately gates, cheerful mills and historic fountains. The town is also the mythological birthplace of Siegfried, the dragon-slaying hero of the 12th-century Nibelungen epic, which became the subject of Richard Wagner's *Ring* opera cycle 700 years later.

With its new and upgraded museums, many would say Xantan is enjoying another heyday now.

◉ Sights

RömerMuseum & Grosse Thermen
TOP CHOICE
MUSEUM

(☏9881 7110; www.apx.lvr.de; Siegfriedstrasse 39; incl Archäologischer Park adult/child €9/free; ⊙9am-6pm Mar-Oct, 10am-4pm Nov-Feb) The grand building west of the park houses the RömerMuseum, which takes you on a journey through 400 years of Roman presence in the Lower Rhine region. Modern and interactive, the exhibit kicks off with the arrival of the Roman legions and ends with the colony's 4th-century demise at the hands of marauding Germanic tribes. Make your way along the floating ramps to learn how the Roman folk earned their money, how they worshipped, educated their kids, played and buried their dead. A highlight among the locally excavated treasures is the Roman ship.

The museum was built on the foundations of the **Grosse Thermen** thermal baths, which have been partly excavated and can be admired in an adjacent hall.

Archäologischer Park
MUSEUM

(Archaeological Park; ☏2999; www.apx.lvr.de; Wardter Strasse 2; incl RömerMuseum & Grosse Thermen adult/child €9/free; ⊙9am-6pm Mar-Oct, 10am-4pm Nov-Feb) The old Roman colony has been reborn as an archaeological park, an open-air museum that features faithfully reconstructed structures to help amateurs visualise what the Roman town looked like. The originals were torn down and used in building the medieval town.

The self-guided tour takes you past such sites as the **Amphitheatre**, which seats 12,000 people during Xanten's summer music festival; the **Spielehaus**, where you can play early versions of backgammon and Nine Men's Morris; a Roman **hostel** complete with hot baths and restaurant; and the majestic **Hafentempel** (harbour temple). Kids will also enjoy the two imaginative playgrounds, one a Roman fort, the other a water-themed one (bring a towel). To get the most out of your visit, use the audioguide.

The Archaeological Park is a 15-minute walk northwest of the centre.

Dom St Viktor
CHURCH

(☏71310; www.stviktor-xanten.de; Kapitel 8; ⊙10am-6pm Mon-Sat, 12.30-6pm Sun Apr-Oct, to 5pm Nov-Mar) The crown jewel of Xanten's Altstadt is the Dom St Viktor, which has Romanesque roots but is now largely Gothic. It is framed by a walled close, called an 'Immunity', which can only be entered from the Markt.

COLOGNE & NORTHERN RHINELAND LOWER RHINE

The soaring five-nave interior brims with treasures, reflecting the wealth Xanten enjoyed in the Middle Ages. Foremost among them is the **Marienaltar**, halfway down the right aisle, whose base features an intricately carved version of the *Tree of Jesse* by Heinrich Douvermann (1535). The **candelabrum** in the central nave, with its *Doppelmadonna* (Double Madonna, 1500), is another masterpiece. A stone sarcophagus in the crypt holds the remains of St Viktor, the Roman martyr who became Xanten's patron saint.

Museum Nibelungen(h)ort
MUSEUM

(www.nibelungen-xanten.de; Kurfürstenstrasse 9; adult/child €5/3; ⊘10am-6pm Mar-Oct, to 5pm Nov-Feb) Lost in the mists of time, the role of the House of Burgundy and Norse settlers who flowed into northern German starting in about the 6th century is operatic, involving tales of kings, rivalries, invasions and even dwarfs. So operatic, in fact, that Wagner turned it into an opera – *Der Ring des Nibelungen* (The Ring of the Nibelung) – which is something of a legend for its length: 15 hours over four nights. The opera, and the story of the Nibelungen, have become an obsession for many and this new museum in the Altstadt lays out the tales and myths in all their melodramatic glory.

Stiftsmuseum
MUSEUM

(Monastic Museum; www.stiftsmuseum-xanten.de; Kapitel 21; adult/child €4/3; ⊘10am-5pm Tue-Sat, to 6pm Sun) Having undergone a major renovation, this museum in the 1000-year-old abbey near the Dom contains treasures, including reliquaries, sculptures and graphics. The illuminated manuscripts always amaze with their detailed, hand-drawn beauty.

🛏 Sleeping & Eating

TOP CHOICE Neumaier
HOTEL €€

(☑715 70; www.hotel-neumaier.de; Orkstrasse 19-21; s €62-72, d €82-92; P🐕⏰) The 16 rooms are sprightly at this family-run hotel that's very close to the Markt in the Altstadt. Cute touches abound, including rubber ducks for rooms with bathtubs. Back in a courtyard there's a beautiful beer garden that makes a perfect pause between the town's fab museums.

Hotel van Bebber
HOTEL €€

(☑6623; www.hotelvanbebber.de; Klever Strasse 12; s €70-90, d €100-180; P🐕⏰) Both Queen Victoria and Churchill have slept in this old-school 35-room hotel where waiters wear tuxedos. Reception is past a gallery of mounted animal heads. Rooms reflect the hotel's history, with open beams and antiques.

Cafe de Fries
CAFE €

(☑2068; Kurfürstenstrasse 8; dishes €3.50-8; ⊘8.30am-6.30pm Tue-Fri, 9am-6pm Sat & Sun) This cafe has a 180-year pedigree and is famous for its filled pancakes. Kids love the chocolate fountain and the Easter-bunny centrifuge in the one-room museum (admission free; open 11am to 5pm). Great tables out front.

Gotisches Haus
AUSTRIAN €€

(☑706 400; www.gotisches-haus-xanten.de; Markt 6; mains €9-20; ⊘9am-1am; 🍴) Xanten's top restaurant offers creative Austrian cuisine and artsy design flourishes within the wood-panelled confines of a centuries-old merchant house. The three-course lunch is a steal at €10 and tots love picking out their favourite dish from a menu designed just for them. Try the strudel!

ⓘ Information

The **tourist office** (☑02801 983 00; www.xanten.de; Kurfürstenstrasse 9; ⊘9am-5pm) is right in the Altstadt, close to the Markt and Dom.

ⓘ Getting There & Around

Trains run on a branch line from Duisberg (45 minutes, hourly), which has good connections.

Xanten's compact Altstadt is about a 10-minute walk northeast of the train station via Hagenbuschstrasse or Bahnhofstrasse.

Zweirad Reineke in the pedestrian zone near the Markt rents **bikes** from €10 per day.

KALKAR & AROUND
☑02824 / POP 11,500

About 15km north of Xanten, Kalkar boasts a pretty medieval core centred on a proud **Rathaus** and the **St Nikolaikirche** (Jan-Joest-Strasse 6; ⊘10am-noon & 2-6pm Apr-Oct, 2-5pm Nov-Mar), famous for its nine masterful altars chiselled by members of the Kalkar woodcarving school. Top billing goes to the **High Altar**, which depicts the Passion of Christ in heart-wrenching detail. For a little comic relief, lift the first seat on the left in the back row of the choir chairs (with you facing the altar) to reveal a monkey on a chamber pot. Another eye-catcher is the Seven Sorrows Altar by Henrik Douvermann at the end of the right aisle. Note the oak-carved Jesse's root, which wraps around the entire altar. Bus 44 makes regular trips from Xanten's Bahnhof to the Markt in Kalkar, but the service is infrequent at weekends.

With its Rapunzel towers, Romeo-and-Juliet balcony and creeping ivy, **Schloss Moyland** (☏02824-951 00; www.moyland.de; Am Schloss 4; adult/child €7/3; ⊙11am-6pm Tue-Fri, 10am-6pm Sat & Sun Apr-Sep, 11am-5pm Tue-Sun Oct-Mar) is a most unexpected sight amid the sweeping pastures and sleepy villages of the Lower Rhine flatlands. Medieval in origin, the palace got its fairy-tale looks in the 19th century and since 1997 has housed a private modern-art collection that includes the world's largest assortment of works by Joseph Beuys. 'Less is more' is definitely not a curatorial concept here, as every wall of the labyrinthine interior is smothered in drawings, paintings and etchings. If you need to clear your head, take a spin around the lovely park with its old trees and wacky sculptures. The Schloss is about 4km northwest of Kalkar off the B57 and well signposted. Bus 44 heads out here from the Xanten Bahnhof or the Markt in Kalkar, but service is sketchy at weekends.

THE RUHRGEBIET

When the Ruhrgebiet – a sprawling postindustrial region of 53 cities and 5.3 million people – was named the Cultural Capital of Europe in 2010, eyebrows were raised across the continent. What kind of culture could there possibly be in a region that, until recently, was primarily known for its belching steelworks and filthy coal mines? Plenty.

Old masters? World-class opera and drama? Great architecture from Gothic to Bauhaus to postmodern? Music festivals that draw visitors by the hundreds of thousands? Check, check, check and check again.

Since the demise of the coal and steel industry in the 1960s, the Ruhrgebiet has tried to completely reinvent itself. These days hopes are pinned on information technology, biomedicine, robotics and logistics, to name just a few 21st-century industries that it's hoped will revive the region's economy.

In the meantime, rather than eschew the Ruhrgebiet's heritage, the people have embraced it. Many of the dormant furnaces, steel works, coking plants and other vestiges of the industrial age have been rebooted in creative ways. You can see cutting-edge art in a huge converted gas tank or free-climb around a blast furnace. Sip a martini in a former turbine house, go clubbing in a former coal-mine boiler room or listen to Mozart in a converted compressor machine hall.

For travellers, the Ruhrgebiet delivers a trainload of surprises and unique sights, locations and experiences.

ℹ Information

The **Ruhr.TopCard** (www.ruhrtopcard.de; adult/child €48/33) gives free public transport and free and discounted admission to 90 attractions, including theme parks, museums and tours, during the course of a calendar year. It's available from local tourist offices.

The region's tourist authority, **Ruhr Tourismus** (www.ruhr-tourismus.de), has an excellent range of information in English.

ℹ Getting Around

The Ruhrgebiet has an efficient and comprehensive web of **public transport** systems made up of U-Bahns, buses and trams. Cities are connected to each other by S-Bahn and regional trains.

The region is divided into zones by the transport authority **VRR** (www.vrr.de; Single tickets from €2.40 for one zone, day passes from €5.70 for one zone). Check the displays on ticket machines to determine how much you'll pay for your ticket.

All cities covered in the Ruhrgebiet section have introduced low-emission zones in their city centres, meaning that your **car** needs to display an *Umweltplakette* (emission sticker). Rental cars automatically have the sticker, but if you're driving your own vehicle you'll need to obtain one.

Essen

☏0201 / POP 575,000

It's taken a few decades, but Germany's seventh-largest city has mastered the transition from industrial powerhouse to city of commerce and culture like few others. Van Gogh, anyone? Go to the Museum Folkwang. Fancy a look at Emperor Otto III's gem-studded childhood crown? Head for the cathedral treasury. A Unesco-listed Bauhaus-style coal mine with a a fabulous museum? Look no further than Zollverein.

◉ Sights

Essen's sights are scattered about. If you only have time for one, make it Zollverein, with its myriad attractions. If you have time, give the city centre a wander. All this can be done on an easy day trip from Düsseldorf or Cologne.

ZOLLVEREIN

The former Zollverein coal mine was recognised as a Unesco World Heritage Site in 2001. In operation until 1986, the sprawling site has since been rebooted as a cultural hub with museums, performance spaces, artist studios, cafes and some unusual playgrounds. The centrepiece is the old coal-washing plant, a beautiful Bauhaus-style behemoth that houses the main museum and the visitors centre (☑246 810; www.zollverein.de; Gelsenkirchener Strasse 181; ☺10am-8pm Apr-Sep, to 6pm Oct-Mar). Start your visit with a ride on the giant exterior escalator that points your way like a huge orange arrow.

You can wander the grounds, which encompass dozens of large industrial buildings spread out over a wooded expanse with some parklike areas. The attractions are grouped into three main areas. In the vast former coking plant there is a Sonnenrad (Ferris wheel) and an ice-skating rink on the old barge canal that operate seasonally.

Tram 107 travels to Zollverein from the Hauptbahnhof.

TOP CHOICE Ruhr Museum
MUSEUM
(☑884 5200; www.ruhrmuseum.de; adult/child €6/2; ☺10am-8pm Apr-Sep, to 6pm Oct-Mar) The former coal-washing plant provides an edgy setting for the Ruhr Museum. Exhibits span the history of the Ruhr Region in an easily accessible and engaging fashion. Just as

the coal was transported on conveyor belts, a long escalator whisks you up to the foyer from where you descend into the dark bowels of the building. With its raw stone walls, steep steel stairs, shiny aluminium ducts and industrial machinery, the space itself has all the drama and mystique of a movie set (*Blade Runner* comes to mind). Don't miss the section showing the poor conditions of the workers and how an effort to strike for better conditions in the 1920s was brutally crushed. It has echoes today.

Panorama
VIEWPOINT
(Coal-Washing Plant; adult/child €2/free; ☺10am-8pm Apr-Sep, 10am-6pm Oct-Mar) Feel like a coal miner as you climb dozens of steps up from the Ruhr Museum to the summit of the coal-washing building, where a large viewing platform lets you ponder the vast scope of Zollverein, with the Ruhrgebiet as a backdrop. There's also a multimedia presentation on industrial culture.

Red Dot Design Museum
MUSEUM
(☑301 0425; www.red-dot.org; Gelsenkirchener Strasse 181; adult/child €6/free; ☺11am-6pm Tue-Sun) The Red Dot Design Museum is in the stoker's hall, creatively adapted by Lord Norman Foster. In a perfect marriage of space and function, this four-storey maze showcases the best in contemporary design right amidst the original fixtures: bathtubs balancing on grated walkways, bike helmets

THE KRUPP DYNASTY – MEN OF STEEL

Steel and Krupp are virtual synonyms. So are Krupp and Essen. It's this bustling Ruhrgebiet city that is the ancestral seat of the Krupp family and the headquarters of one of the most powerful corporations in Europe.

It all began rather modestly in 1811 when Friedrich Krupp and two partners founded a company to process 'English cast steel', but, despite minor successes, he left a company mired in debt upon his death in 1826. Enter his son Alfred, then at the tender age of 14, who would go on to become one of the seminal figures of the industrial age.

It was through the production of the world's finest steel that the 'Cannon King' galvanised a company that by 1887 employed more than 20,000 workers. In an unbroken pattern of dazzling innovation, coupled with ruthless business practices, Krupp produced steel and machinery that was essential to the world economy.

But Krupp also provided womb-to-tomb benefits to its workers at a time when the term 'social welfare' had not yet entered the world's vocabulary.

However, Krupp will forever be associated with the Third Reich. Not only did the corporation supply the hardware for the German war machine, it also provided much of the financial backing that Hitler needed to build up his political power base. Krupp plants were prime targets for Allied bombers. After the war, the firm slowly lost its way and in 1999 merged with once arch-rival Thyssen.

An excellent source for an understanding of what the Krupp family has meant to Germany is William Manchester's brilliant chronicle *The Arms of Krupp* (1964).

dangling from snakelike heating ducts, and beds perching atop a large oven. All objects are winners of the Red Dot award, the Oscar of the design world.

CITY CENTRE

Dom CHURCH

(☑220 4206; www.domschatz-essen.de; Burgplatz 2; treasury adult/child €4/2; ☺6.30am-6.30pm Mon-Fri, 9am-7.30pm Sat, 9am-8pm Sun, treasury 10am-5pm Tue-Sat, 11.30am-5pm Sun) Essen's medieval Dom is an island of quiet engulfed by the commercialism of pedestrianised Kettwiger Strasse, the main shopping strip. It has a priceless collection of Ottonian works, all about 1000 years old. Not to be missed is a hauntingly beautiful Golden Madonna, set in her own midnight-blue chapel that matches the colour of her eyes. The treasury presents more fancy baubles, including a crown worn by Holy Roman Emperor Otto III, in a modern, intimate fashion.

Alte Synagoge SYNAGOGUE

(☑884 5218; www.alte-synagoge.essen.de; Steeler Strasse 29; ☺10am-6pm Tue-Sun) East of the cathedral, the grand Alte Synagoge miraculously survived WWII largely intact. A memorial site since 1980, today it is a Jewish cultural centre and meeting place. It's worth wandering in.

Museum Folkwang MUSEUM

(☑884 5314; www.museum-folkwang.de; Goethestrasse 41; adult/child €5/3.50; ☺10am-6pm Tue-Sun, to 10.30pm Fri) A grand dame among Germany's art repositories, the Museum Folkwang has sparkling new digs designed by British star architect David Chipperfield. Galleries radiate out from inner courtyards and gardens of the glass-fronted building, providing a progressive setting for such 19th- and 20th-century masters as Gauguin, Caspar David Friedrich and Mark Rothko.

WERDEN

On the southern Ruhr bank, the half-timbered houses and cobbled lanes of the suburb of Werden hint at what a preindustrial Ruhrgebiet must have looked like. Students of the prestigious Folkwang School for Music, Dance and Drama fill the many pubs, cafes and restaurants, and the DJH hostel is here as well.

The S6 goes straight to Werden from the Hauptbahnhof.

INDUSTRIAL HERITAGE TRAIL

Most of the smokestacks and mines are eerily silent today, but many of the Ruhr region's 'cathedrals of industry' have taken on a new life as museums, concert halls, cinemas, restaurants, lookouts, playgrounds and other such venues. Dozens of them are linked along the 400km Industrial Heritage Trail (www.route-industriekultur.de) that takes in such cities as Dortmund, Essen, Duisburg and Bochum. Most sites are also served by public transport.

The route has several dedicated visitors centres, including one at the Ruhr Museum (p504) at the Zollverein coal mine in Essen. Information is also available at the visitors centre (☑429 1942; ☺10am-5pm Mon-Thu, 10am-9pm Fri-Sun Apr-Oct, reduced hr in winter) in the Landschaftspark Duisburg-Nord.

Abteikirche St Liudger CHURCH

(☑491 801; www.schatzkammer-werden.de; Brückstrasse 54; treasury adult/concession €3/2; ☺treasury 10am-noon & 3-5pm Tue-Sun) Werden's main sight is the 1175 Abteikirche St Liudger, a beautiful late-Romanesque church named for the Frisian missionary buried here. It has an impressive exterior as well as a commendable treasury housed in the old abbey.

🛏 Sleeping

Hotels in the centre cater for business visitors and are mostly nondescript and overpriced. The more charming places are in the suburbs.

TOP CHOICE Hotel Résidence BOUTIQUE HOTEL €€€

(☑02054-955 90; www.hotel-residence.de; Auf der Forst 1; s/d from €95/125; P🅿🐕🛜) Posh and petite, this 17-room hotel in an art nouveau villa in the historic suburb of Kettwig appeals to refined tastes. Dinner in the vaunted namesake restaurant (menus from €120), which boasts two Michelin stars for chef Berthold Buehler, is a special delight during summer when you can dine in the garden.

DJH Hostel HOSTEL €

(☑0201 491 163; www.essen.jugendherberge.de; Pastoratsberg 2; dm/s/d incl breakfast €26/44/66) Essen's updated hostel is in the pretty but outlying suburb of Werden. Many rooms have private bathrooms. Take the S6 to Essen-Werden, then bus 190 to Jugendherberge. Rates include breakfast.

Mintrops City Hotel Margarethenhöhe HOTEL €€€
(☑438 60; www.mmhotels.de; Steile Strasse 46; r €120-190; P⊛☎) A former Krupp guesthouse has been reborn as a cheerful hotel, filled with youthful flair, art and designer touches. It's about 5km south of the centre in the Margarethenhöhe, a gardenlike art nouveau workers' colony. Take the U17 to Laubenweg.

✕ Eating

There's a dearth of interesting restaurants in the city centre, which is also dead after dark. Head south to the Rüttenscheider Strasse (known as 'Rü' locally), where you have your pick from dozens of eateries. Take the U11 or tram 107 to Martinstrasse.

TOP CHOICE Miamamia CAFE €
(www.miamamia.de; Rüttenscheider Strasse 183; ☺9am-10pm Mon-Sat) An Italian treasure! This cafe is beautifully housed in an old house and offers easily the best coffees in the region. Also enjoy paninis and other simple Med classics. The tables in the garden are a pure delight.

Eigelstein MODERN EUROPEAN €€
(www.eigelstein-ruettenscheid.de; Rüttenscheider Strasse 199; mains €8-20) Boisterous and fun, this large Cologne-style eatery (the *Kölsch* is from Sion) is a classic Rü eatery. The menu has a mix of casual fare from salads to steaks. Eat at long tables or at more intimate corners.

🍺 Drinking & Entertainment

Zeche Carl CLUB
(☑834 4410; www.zechecarl.de; Wilhelm-Nieswandt-Allee 100; ☺cafe 5-11pm) The machine hall and washrooms of a former coal mine have been restyled as an alternative cultural centre with live concerts, parties, cabaret, theatre and art exhibits. The cafe has a beer garden plus a wide range of small and large plates. Take U11 or U17 to Karlsplatz.

Hotel Shanghai LOUNGE
(☑747 4756; www.hotelshanghai.de; Steeler Strasse 33; ☺Wed, Fri & Sat) Electronic-music fans invade for ravetastic nights in this unpretentious joint where DJs spin in a lotus-shaped

console, while you dance beneath Chinese lanterns. When your legs need a break, plonk down into a red leather booth and scan the crowd.

ℹ Information

Tourist Office (☑0201 194 33, 0201 887 2048; www.essen.de; Am Hauptbahnhof 2; ☺9am-6pm Mon-Fri, 10am-4pm Sun)

ℹ Getting There & Around

TRAIN There are frequent ICE and IC trains in all directions and RE and S-Bahn trains to other Ruhrgebiet cities departing every few minutes and other cities in the region such as Düsseldorf (€10, 30 minutes).

The Hauptbahnhof's Nord (north) exit drops you right onto the centre's main drag, the pedestrianised Kettwiger Strasse.

TRAM Essen's major sights are spread out, but all are accessible by U-Bahn, S-Bahn or trams. The handiest line is tram 107, which shuttles between the Zollverein coal mine, the Museum Folkwang and the Rüttenscheid restaurant and pub mile.

TAXI (☑866 55)

Dortmund

☑0231 / POP 580,400

Football (soccer) is a major Dortmund passion. Borussia Dortmund, the city's Bundesliga (Germany's first league) team, has been national champion a ridiculous eight times, including the 2010–11 and 2011–12 seasons. So it's appropriate that the city will be home to the new German Football Museum starting in 2014.

As the largest city in the Ruhrgebiet, Dortmund built its prosperity on coal, steel and beer. Now, the mines are closed, the steel mills quiet and more Zeitgeist-compatible high-tech industries have taken their place. Only the breweries are going as strong as ever, churning out huge quantities of delicious beer and ale, much of it for export.

◎ Sights

Ignoring the imminent arrival of the megaattraction, the German Football Museum, Dortmund continues the Ruhrgebiet theme of industrial resuse with a brewery-turned-art-centre right by the station and a string of beautiful churches in its centre. You can easily take it all in in a few hours.

Commerce coexists with religious treasures in Dortmund's city centre, just south of the Hauptbahnhof. The trio of churches described below conveniently line up along the pedestrianised Westenhellweg.

Dortmunder U · GALLERY
(www.dortmunder-u.de; Leonie-Reygers-Terrasse; ☺Tue-Wed & Sat-Sun 11am-6pm, to 8pm Thu-Fri) You can see it from afar – the golden 'U' atop the tower of the defunct Union Brauerei. Once one of Dortmund's largest and most famous breweries, the protected landmark has been reborn as a cultural centre. Three upper floors are home to the Museum am Ostwal (www.museumamostwall.dortmund.de; Dortmunder U, Leonie-Reygers-Terrasse; adult/child €5/2.50)l, an art-world star thanks to its far-reaching collection of all major 20th- and 21st-century genres, from expressionism to art informel, fluxus to op art and concrete art. This translates into works by Macke, Nolde, Beuys and Paik, and living artists including Jochen Gerz, and Anna and Bernhard Blume. Many exhibitions outside the museum are free and there are great views from the top-floor cafe. It's a five-minute walk east of the train station.

Museum Für Kunst & Kulturgeschichte · MUSEUM
(Museum of Art & Cultural History; ☎ 502 6028; www.museendortmund.de; Hansastrasse 3; adult/concession €5/2.50; ☺10am-5pm Tue, Wed, Fri & Sun, to 8pm Thu, noon-5pm Sat) In a rambling art deco bank building, this museum is a repository of the kind of stuff that tracks the cultural history of a city. That might be a snooze, were it not for such standout exhibits as sparkling Roman gold treasure, a Romanesque triumphal cross, period rooms and paintings by Caspar David Friedrich, Lovis Corinth and other outstanding artists.

Mahn- und Gedenkstätte Steinwache · MEMORIAL
(☎502 5002; www.ns-gedenkstaetten.de; Steinstrasse 50; ☺10am-5pm Tue-Sun) This municipal memorial uses the original rooms and cells of a Nazi prison as a backdrop for a grim exhibit about Dortmund during the Third Reich. Over 66,000 people were imprisoned here, many tortured and killed. It's north of the Hauptbahnhof, just beyond the multiplex cinema.

TOP CHOICE Zollern Colliery · MUSEUM
(☎0231 696 1111; www.lwl-industriemuseum.de; Grubenweg 5; adult/child €5/2; ☺10am-6pm Tue-Sun; ☐462, 378, ☒Bövinghausen Bahnhof) The Zollern II/IV Coal Mine was considered a model mine when operation began in 1902. It boasted state-of-the-art technology and fantastic architecture, including an art nouveau machine hall and a castlelike administration building adorned with gables and onion-domed towers. An innovative exhibit documents the harsh realities of life as a miner, with plenty of interactive and child-oriented programs. It's one of eight industrial museums across the region linked under the banner LWL Industrial Museum. To get here, take the U47 from Hauptbahnhof to Dortmund-Huckarde Bushof, then bus 462 direction Dortmund-Marten to Industriemuseum Zollern.

German Football Museum · MUSEUM
Classic scenes of German football triumphs will play across the facade of this vast new shrine to the nation's passion. Right outside the Hauptbahnhof, the museum will have 6900 sq m of exhibits. Opening is planned for 2014.

Petrikirche · CHURCH
(www.stpetrido.de; Westenhellweg; ☺10am-5pm) The 14th-century Petrikirche's show-stopper is the massive Antwerp Altar (1520), featuring 633 individually carved and gilded figurines in scenes depicting the Easter story. Note that the altar is closed in summer, exposing only the panels' painted outer side.

Reinoldikirche · CHURCH
(www.sanktreinoldi.de; Ostenhellweg 2; tower admission €1; ☺10am-4pm Tue-Sun, tower noon-3pm Sat) Dating to 1280, this church is named after the city's patron saint. As the story goes, after Reinold was martyred in Cologne, the carriage containing his coffin rolled all the way to Dortmund, stopping on the spot of the church. There's a statue of him, opposite Charlemagne, at the entrance to the choir. Of outstanding artistic merit is the late-Gothic high altar. There are good views from the bell tower.

Marienkirche · CHURCH
(www.st-marien-dortmund.de; Ostenhellweg; ☺10am-noon & 2-4pm Tue-Fri, to 1pm Sat) Marienkirche is the oldest of Dortmund's churches, and its Romanesque origins are still visible in the round-arched nave. The star exhibit here is the Marienaltar (1420), with a delicate triptych by local son Conrad von Soest. In the northern nave is the equally impressive Berswordt Altar (1385). Both were saved

from wartime destruction; the churches all needed massive reconstruction.

🛏 Sleeping

Hotel Fürst Garden   HOTEL €€
(📞477 3210; www.hotelfuerstgarden.de; Beurhausstrasse 57; s/d incl breakfast from €70/90; P) A bit outside the city centre, but not far from the stadium, this low-key 16-room place is mod in cheerful shades. The bathrooms are tiny but rooms have all the expected amenities and the breakfast is a generous spread best enjoyed in the charming garden.

Cityhotel Dortmund   HOTEL €€
(📞477 9660; www.cityhoteldortmund.de; Silberstrasse 37-43; s/d incl breakfast from €75/85; P@🛜) A mousy grey facade hides this jewel of a hotel where a palette evoking the ocean, sun and sand gives rooms and public areas a cheerful and fresh look. The 50 rooms are quiet.

🍴 Eating & Drinking

Hövel's Hausbrauerei   GERMAN
(📞0231 914 5470; www.hoevels-hausbrauerei.de; Hoher Wall 5-7; mains €8-15; ⏱11am-midnight Sun-Thu, to 1am Fri & Sat) This brewpub makes up for its bland neighbourhood surrounds with a vast number of tables outside. The menu is custom-made for hardcore meat lovers (try the suckling pig or the roast pork knuckle), washed down with the libation of choice, the tasty house-brewed *Bitterbier*.

Zum Alten Markt   GERMAN €€
(📞572 217; www.altermarkt-dortmund.de; Markt 3; mains €8-15) Traditional Westphalian fare is served to hordes of appreciative locals in the very centre of the city. Pray to the gods of digestion at one of the nearby churches.

☆ Entertainment

Borussia Dortmund   FOOTBALL
(📞01805-309 000; www.bvb.de; Strobelallee 50; tickets €12-60) Dortmund's famous, massively popular *and* succesful Bundesliga soccer team plays its home games at the legendary Westfalenstadion, now branded **Signal Iduna Park** (www.signal-iduna-park.de; tours adult/child €6/4; ⏱tours noon Tue, 4pm Fri, 2pm Sat & Sun). Guided tours of the 80,000-seat stadium, Germany's largest, are popular. Take U-Bahn 45.

ⓘ Information

Tourist Office (📞0231 189 990; www.dortmund-tourismus.de; Königswall 18a; ⏱9am-6pm Mon-Fri, to 1pm Sat) Opposite the Hauptbahnhof's south exit.

ⓘ Getting There & Around

There are frequent ICE and IC **trains** in all directions and RE and S-Bahn trains to other Ruhrgebiet cities departing every few minutes.

The centre, art museums and churches are all close to the train station.

Elsewhere in the Ruhrgebiet

The Ruhrgebiet has plenty of other places of interest, many of them on the Industrial Heritage Trail. All of the cities listed below have frequent train service from across the region.

BOCHUM
📞0234 / POP 374,000

Industrial cities are not exactly the stuff of heartfelt anthems, but that didn't stop singer-songwriter Herbert Grönemeyer from rhapsodising about his home town in the 1984 song 'Bochum'. The homage not only boosted Grönemeyer's career but also the image of this classic Ruhrgebiet city, halfway between Essen and Dortmund.

Though indeed no beauty, as one of Grönemeyer's lyrics says, Bochum is also a Ruhrgebiet party hub, with most of the action concentrated in the so-called **Bermuda Dreieck** (Bermuda Triangle). Formed by Kortumstrasse, Viktoriastrasse and Brüderstrasse, it's just a five-minute walk from the Hauptbahnhof. Nearby, the Bochum Symphony will get new digs in the emerging **Viktoria Quartier** around the Marienkirche, a church that's being converted into a cultural centre.

⊙ Sights

Deutsches Bergbau-Museum   MUSEUM
(German Mining Museum; 📞587 70; www.bergbaumuseum.de; Am Bergbaumuseum 28; adult/child €6.50/3; ⏱8.30am-5pm Tue-Fri, 10am-5pm Sat & Sun) Bochum is worth a quick stop if only to get down and dirty in the German mining museum, one of the nation's most-visited museums. Besides learning about all aspects of life *unter Tage* (below ground), you can descend into the earth's belly for a

spin around a demonstration pit followed by a ride up the landmark winding tower for commanding views. The U-Bahn 35 goes to the museum from the Hauptbahnhof.

Eisenbahnmuseum MUSEUM
(Train Museum; ☑492 516; www.eisenbahnmuseum-bochum.de; Dr-C-Otto-Strasse 191; adult/child €6.50/3.50; ☺10am-5pm Tue-Fri & Sun Mar–mid-Nov) It's a bit away from the centre, but fans of historic 'iron horses' have plenty to admire at this vast train museum. It displays around 180 steam and electric locomotives, coaches and wagons dating back as far as 1853. From the Hauptbahnhof take tram 318 to Bochum-Dahlhausen, then walk for 1200m or take the historic shuttle (Sundays only).

OBERHAUSEN
☑0208 / POP 213,000
Part of a blast furnace is now one of Germany's most innovative exhibition spaces; a gallery that's not just a metaphor for the revival of Oberhausen, but the entire Ruhrgebiet as well.

⊙ Sights

Gasometer Oberhausen GALLERY
(☑850 3730; www.gasometer.de; Arenastrasse 11; ☺10am-6pm Tue-Sun) A barrel-shaped tower that once stored gas to power blast furnaces, the Gasometer Oberhausen has been reborn as one of Germany's most exciting and popular art and exhibition spaces. Since 1994 it has drawn sizeable crowds, with its site-specific installations by top artists, Bill Viola and Christo and Jeanne-Claude included. Top off your visit – literally – by riding a pair of elevators to a 117m-high platform for sweeping views over the entire western Ruhrgebiet.

From Oberhausen's train station, take any bus or tram from Terminal 1 to Neue Mitte.

DUISBURG
☑0203 / POP 490,000
Duisburg, about 25km west of Essen, is home to Europe's largest inland port, whose immensity is best appreciated on a leisurely **boat tour** (Weisse Flotte; ☑713 9667; www.wf-duisburg.de; Schwanentor; adult/child €12/6; ☺Apr-Nov). Embarkation is at the Schwanentor, which is also the gateway to the **Innenhafen Duisburg** (inner harbour), now an increasingly dynamic urban quarter with restaurants, bars, clubs and attractions set up in the old storage silos.

⊙ Sights

TOP CHOICE **Landschaftspark Duisburg-Nord** PARK
(Landscape Park Duisburg-Nord; ☑429 1942; www.landschaftspark.de; Emscherstrasse 71; admission free, activities vary; ☺park 24hr, visitor centre 9am-6pm Mon-Fri, 11am-6pm Sat & Sun) Molten iron used to flow 24/7 from the fiery furnaces of this decommissioned iron works that's now a unique performance space and an all-ages adventure playground. You can free-climb its ore bunkers, take a diving course in the former gas tank, climb to the top of the blast furnace, picnic in a flower garden and visit a petting zoo. On Friday, Saturday and Sunday, a light installation by British artist Jonathan Park illuminates the complex after sundown.

From Duisburg train station take bus 903 to the stop Landschaftspark-Nord, then walk along Emscherstrasse (around seven minutes).

Wilhelm-Lehmbruck-Museum MUSEUM
(☑2833294; www.lehmbruckmuseum.de; Friedrich-Wilhelm-Strasse 40; adult/child €8/5; ☺noon-6pm Wed, Fri & Sat, noon-8pm Thu, 11am-6pm Sun) Great art awaits at this renowned modern art museum, which presents a survey of 20th-century international sculpture – think Giacometti, Calder, Ernst and Chillida. About 40 sculptures alone are planted throughout the lovely surrounding park.

It's a five-minute walk from the Hauptbahnhof.

Museum Küppersmühle MUSEUM
(☑3019 4811; www.museum-kueppersmuehle.de; Philosophenweg 55; adult/child €6/free, incl special exhibit €8/free; ☺2-6pm Wed, 11am-6pm Thu, Sat & Sun) A half-century of German art is on display at the Museum Küppersmühle in a mill storage building converted by Swiss Pritzker Prize–winning architects Herzog & de Meuron. From Baselitz to Kiefer to Richter, all the big names are showcased beneath the lofty ceilings, as are up to six international art exhibits annually.

From the train station, take bus 934 to Hansegracht.

BOTTROP
☑02041 / POP 117,000
About 13km north of Essen, Bottrop is the birthplace of Josef Albers (1888–1976), the Bauhaus artist famous for his explorations of colour and spatial relationships, squares in particular.

⊙ Sights

FREE Josef Albers Museum   MUSEUM

(✆297 16; www.bottrop.de/mq/; Im Stadtgarten 20; ⊙11am-5pm Tue-Sat, 10am-5pm Sun) With the Josef Albers Museum, the city honours its famous son, who fled the Nazis for the US in 1933 and later taught such notables as Robert Rauschenberg and John Cage. Presented in a starkly minimalist space are examples from Albers' key series 'Homage to the Square', as well as early lithographs from the Bottrop period.

From Bottrop Hauptbahnhof take bus SB16 to Im Stadtgarten.

FREE Tetraeder   SCULPTURE

(Tetrahedron; Beckstraße; ⊙24hr) The Tetraeder is one of the striking stops on the Industrial Heritage Trail. This 60m-high installation made from steel pipes and open space graces the top of a former slag heap turned landscape park, complete with trees, trails and benches. You can climb the Tetraeder via 'floating' staircases suspended from steel cables (yes, they swing when the wind's up), which lead to three viewing platforms. Not an experience recommended for vertigo sufferers! Views of the surprisingly green yet undeniably industrial surrounds are impressive rather than conventionally beautiful. At night, the Tetraeder becomes a light installation that you can see glowing from afar.

Alpincenter Bottrop   AMUSEMENT PARK

(✆709 50; www.alpincenter.com; Prosperstrasse 299; day pass weekday/weekend €30/40; ⊙9.30am-midnight Wed-Sun) The Alpincenter Bottrop is the world's longest indoor alpine ski run (630m); it's especially popular with teens and the Dutch (and Dutch teens, for that matter). Tickets include ski rental, unlimited food and drink, including beer and wine (now there's an idea...). Take bus 262 from Bottrop Hauptbahnhof to Brakerstrasse to get to both the centre and the Tetraeder.

Movie Park Germany   AMUSEMENT PARK

(✆02045-8990; www.movieparkgermany.de; Warner Allee 1; adult/child €34/28; ⊙10am-6pm, closed Nov-Mar) Silly fun awaits at the Movie Park Germany, the Ruhrgebiet's version of Universal Studios, with thrill rides, live-action shows, restaurants and shops. There are

direct RE train connections hourly from Essen; get off at Feldhausen.

GELSENKIRCHEN

✆0209 / POP 262,000

Gelsenkirchen's story is typical of the region: in the early 19th century it was still an agricultural backwater but then the industrial revolution swept through the Ruhr region and it became a major source of coal to power the region's factories and mills. Its population had increased 20-fold and it was nicknamed the 'city of a thousand fires' for all the smokestacks burning off waste mining gasses.

Today there are no coal mines operating and there is chronic high unemployment. Like other cities in the Ruhrgebiet, it is looking for a new future.

⊙ Sights & Activities

Zoom Erlebniswelt   ZOO

(✆954 50; www.zoom-erlebniswelt.de; Bleckstrasse 47; adult/child €17.50/11.50; ⊙9am-6pm Mar & Oct, to 6.30pm Apr-Sep, to 5pm Nov-Feb) The animals here don't roam in cages but in habitats that recreate their natural surroundings as closely as possible. 'Alaska', for instance, has rivers, a gushing waterfall, canyons and rock formations where grizzly bears lumber, timber wolves prowl, otters tumble and elks strut. Fencing is minimal and unobtrusive – you can get surprisingly close to even the fiercer animals thanks to ditches and glass walls. Africa and Asia are the other continents represented.

From Gelsenkirchen Hauptbahnhof, tram 301 goes straight to the zoo.

FC Schalke 04   FOOTBALL

(✆tickets 01805-150 810; www.schalke04.com; tickets €15-60) To football (soccer) fans, Gelsenkirchen is of course synonymous with FC Schalke 04, the legendary club that's long been a mainstay in the Bundesliga and which is the second most popular in Germany (after Dortmund's...). The team plays home games at the modern **Veltins Arena** (✆tour times 389 2900; www.veltins-arena.de; Ernst-Kuzorra-Weg 1; tour adult/child €9/7; ⊙tours Tue-Sun). Stadium tours include a visit to the club's **museum** (✆389 2900; adult/child €5/3; ⊙10am-7pm Tue-Fri, to 5pm Sat & Sun).

To get to the stadium, take tram 302 to Veltins Arena from Gelsenkirchen Hauptbahnhof.

MÜNSTER & OSNABRÜCK

Catholic Münster and protestant Osnabrück are forever linked – at least in the minds of suffering middle-school history students – as the dual sites chosen to sign the Peace of Westphalia, the series of treaties that ended the Thirty Years War (one of the longest and comparatively most destructive wars in history). Today you can find echoes of the event in both towns.

Münster

☏0251 / POP 279,800

Watch out! You might get run down by a bike in Münster and that's just one example of the exuberance found in this entrancing town. In fact, when strolling around Münster's Altstadt, it's hard to imagine that nearly everything you see is only 60 years or so old. After near-total destruction in WWII, the cultural capital of Westphalia opted for creating a carbon copy of its medieval centre rather than embracing the ideas of modern town planning.

Yet Münster is not mired in nostalgia. Its 50,000 students keep the cobwebs out and civic pride is great – both of the town's main cultural treasures are emerging from ambitious renovations and enhancements. More than anything, though, it's the 500,000 bicycles – called *Leeze* in local dialect – that quite literally bring energy and movement to this pretty city.

◉ Sights

Münster's Altstadt is encircled by the 4.8km **Promenade**, a car-free ring trail built through parkland on top of the former city fortifications; it's hugely popular with cyclists, joggers, lovers and walkers.

On any warm days, especially the first ones of spring, you'll find thousands of locals sunbathing, partying, barbecueing and much more on the grassy **parkland** along the Aasee near Adenauerallee.

The architect who left his mark on Münster more than any other was Johann Conrad Schlaun (1695–1773). He was a master of the Westphalian baroque, a more subdued, less exuberant expression of the style than in southern Germany. A most exquisite example of Schlaun's vision is the 1757 **Erbdrostenhof** (Map p512; Salzstrasse 38), a

lavish private mansion. Nearby, the equally stunning 1753 **Clemenskirche** (Map p512; Klemensstrasse) boasts a domed ceiling fresco supported by turquoise faux-marble pillars. Less pristinely preserved is the 1773 **Schloss** (Map p512; Schlossplatz), the former residence of the prince-bishops and now the main university building.

You can find weblinks to many of Münster's sites at www.muenster.de.

Dom St Paul   CHURCH
(Map p512; www.paulusdom.de; Domplatz; ⏱6.30am-6pm Mon-Sat, to 7.30pm Sun) The two massive towers of Münster's cathedral, Dom St Paul, match the proportions of this 110m-long structure and the vast square it overlooks. It's a three-nave construction built in the 13th century, a time when Gothic architecture began overtaking the Romanesque style in popularity. Enter from Domplatz via the porch (called the 'Paradise'), richly festooned with sculptures of the apostles. Inside, pay your respects to the **statue of St Christopher**, the patron saint of travellers, then make your way to the southern ambulatory with its **astronomical clock**. This marvel of 16th-century ingenuity indicates the time, the position of the sun, the movement of the planets, and the calendar. Crowds gather daily at noon (12.30pm Sunday) when the carillon starts up.

The **Domkammer** (Cathedral Treasury; Map p512; ☏495 333; www.domkammer-muenster.de; adult/child €3/free; ⏱11am-4pm Tue-Sun), which is reached via the cloisters, counts an 11th-century, gem-studded golden head reliquary of St Paul among its finest pieces.

Note: the Dom and the Domkammer are due to reopen in 2013 after a multiyear reconstruction that saw the former get a new roof among other improvements (work was delayed after the first new roof's copper was found to have the wrong shade of green). Archeological excavations at the same time found parts of previous cathedrals on the site, predating the current structure.

AROUND DOMPLATZ

Northwest of the Dom, the **Überwasser-kirche** (officially known as Liebfrauen-kirche) is a 14th-century Gothic hall church with handsome stained-glass windows. The nickname was inspired by its location right by the Aa, a tiny stream with a tree-lined promenade perfect for relaxed strolling.

Münster

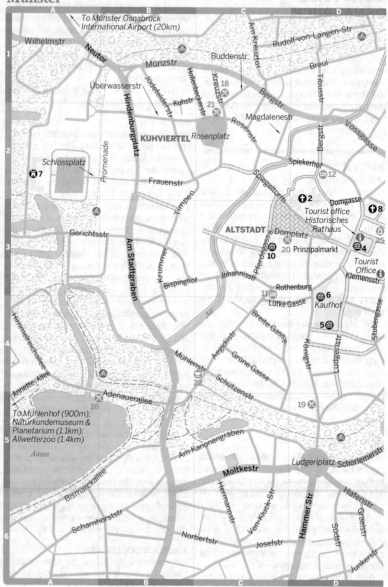

To Münster Osnabrück International Airport (20km)

Wilhelmstr

Neutor

Münzstr

Buddenstr

Rudolf-von-Langen-Str

Breul

Überwasserstr

Jüdefelderstr

Hindenburgplatz

Hollenbeckerstr

Kuhstr

Kreuzstr

18

21

Bergstr

Tibusstr

Vossgasse

Magdalenestr

KUHVIERTEL

Rosenplatz

Rosenstr

Spiekerhof

Bergstr

12

Schlossplatz

7

Promenade

Frauenstr

Spiegelturm

2

Domgasse

8

Tourist office
Historisches
Rathaus

Timpen

ALTSTADT

Domplatz

i

25

Gerichtsstr

Am Stadtgraben

Krummer

10

20

Prinzipalmarkt

4

Tourist
Office

Klemensstr

i

Pferdegasse

Bispinghof

Johannisstr

Rothenburg

Aa

11

Lütke Gasse

Kaufhof

6

Stubengasse

Breite Gasse

5

Himmelreichallee

Mühlenstr

Aegidiistr

Grüne Gasse

Königstr

Ludgeristr

Annette-Allee

Schützenstr

22

Adenauerallee

16

19

To Mühlenhof (900m);
Naturkundemuseum &
Planetarium (1.1km);
Allwetterzoo (1.4km)

Aasee

Am Kanonengraben

Ludgeriplatz

Schorlemerstr

Bismarckallee

Moltkestr

Hermannstr

Von-Kluck-Str

Hammer Str

Hafenstr

Graelstr

Scharnhorststr

Norbertstr

Josefstr

Südstr

Junkerstr

Westfälisches Landesmuseum MUSEUM
(State Museum; Map p512; ☎590 701; Domplatz 10) Many of the sculptures purged from the churches by the Anabaptists miraculously ended up at the state museum, where the collection spans from the Middle Ages to the latest avant-garde creations. The painters Conrad von Soest, August Macke and other expressionists also get their due. However, that's not until 2014, when a vast new wing adjoining the 1908 building is complete and the museum reopens.

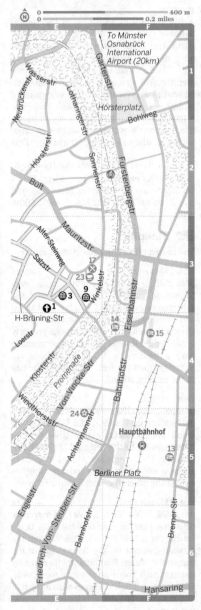

ing exhibits are drawn from the collection of some 800 graphic works, including a near complete series of Picasso's lithographs.

PRINZIPALMARKT

The most interesting street in Münster's Altstadt is the Prinzipalmarkt, lined by restored Patrician town houses with arcades sheltering elegant boutiques and cafes. The key building here is the Gothic **Historisches Rathaus** (Map p512), with its elegant filigree gable. In 1648, an important subtreaty of the Peace of Westphalia was signed here, marking the first step in ending the calamitous Thirty Years War.

To the left, the beautifully porticoed Renaissance building is the **Stadtweinhaus** (City Wine House).

Just south of Prinzipalmarkt is the **Münster Arkaden** (Map p512), a small and elegant shopping mall with striking marble flooring and a central glass dome.

Friedenssaal   HISTORIC SITE
(Hall of Peace; Map p512; ☑492 2724; Rathaus, Prinzipalmarkt 8-9; adult/child €2/1.50; ☺10am-5pm Tue-Fri, to 4pm Sat & Sun) The spot where the subtreaty was signed is a splendidly woodcarved hall in the Rathaus.

St Lambertikirche   CHURCH
(Map p512; ☑448 93; www.st-lamberti.de; ☺9am-5pm) One of Münster's finest churches, the late-Gothic St Lambertikirche, was built in 1450. See those three wrought-iron cages dangling from the openwork spire? They once displayed the corpses of the Anabaptist leader Jan van Leyden and his cohorts after they were defeated in 1535 by troops of the prince-bishop. Before their execution, the trio was publicly tortured with red-hot tongs.

FREE **Stadtmuseum**   MUSEUM
(City Museum; Map p512; ☑492 4503; Salzstrasse 28; ☺10am-6pm Tue-Fri, 11am-6pm Sat & Sun) The city's museum has a fascinating collection of town models showing how Münster grew and changed from the 16th century onwards. Also included are the once-red-hot tongs used on Jan van Leyden and his unlucky colleagues.

AASEE

Southwest of the Altstadt, the Aasee is another recreational getaway. Come for a picnic by the lake, a stroll along its promenade or go for a spin on the water itself. Family-friendly attractions include the **Mühlenhof** (☑981 200; www.bockwindmuel.de; Theo-Breider-Weg 1;

Kunstmuseum Picasso   MUSEUM
(Map p512; ☑414 4710; www.kunstmuseum-picasso-muenster.de; Königsstrasse 5; adult/child €10/4; ☺10am-6pm Tue-Sun) One of the 20th century's most famous artists gets the spotlight in this 18th-century nobleman's house. Chang-

adult/child €5/3; ⊙10am-6pm Mar-Oct, 11am-4pm Sun-Fri Nov-Feb), an open-air museum where you can stroll among historical Westphalian buildings, including a windmill and bakery. Dinosaurs and the universe are the stars at the **Naturkundemuseum & Planetarium** (Natural History Museum; ☑0251 591 05; Sentruper Strasse 285; museum adult/child €5.50/3, planetarium €5.50/3, both €9.50/5; ⊙9am-6pm Tue-Sun), while highlights of the **Allwetterzoo** (☑890 40; www.allwetterzoo.de; Sentruper Strasse 315; adult/child €14/7; ⊙9am-6pm Apr-Sep, 9am-5pm Oct & Mar, 9am-4pm Nov-Feb) include the horse museum with fun exhibits on the region's equestrian heritage.

HAFEN

A 10-minute walk southeast of the Hauptbahnhof takes you to the Hafen, Münster's partly revitalised **old harbour**. What were once derelict halls and brick warehouses have been updated with avant-garde architectural elements and now house artist studios and creative offices in a string of buildings called the **Kreativkai**. There are a few cafes and nightspots; you can promenade along the waterfront and watch cargo barges cutting along the Dortmund–Ems canal.

To get to the Hafen, exit the Hauptbahnhof to the east via Bremer Platz, follow Bremer Strasse south, cross Hansaring and it will be on your left. It's about a 500m walk.

⏹ Sleeping

The tourist office has a reservation service.

Hotel Mauritzhof HOTEL €€
(Map p512; ☑417 20; www.mauritzhof.de; Eisenbahnstrasse 17; r €90-150; ⊛❋☎) Bold hues, a harmonious interplay of glass and wood and extravagant designer furniture (Vitra, Driade, Kartell) give this 39-room property a mod edge. Rooms facing the promenade have a balcony, and XXL-sized beds are available upon request. Wind down the day in the reading room.

Central Hotel HOTEL €€
(Map p512; ☑510 150; www.central-hotel-muenster.de; Aegidiistrasse 1; s €90-140, d €110-190; ℗❋☎) Small and personably run, this 20-room hotel lives up to the geographic promise of its name. The owners are avid art supporters and you'll find bold prints and other touches amidst the otherwise starkly white rooms.

Hotel Marco Polo HOTEL €€
(Map p512; ☑960 920 013; www.hotel-marcopolo.de; Bremer Platz 36; r incl breakfast €60-120; ☎) On the far side of the train tracks from the Altstadt but not on the wrong side of the tracks, the Marco Polo honours its name by naming each room after a city worldwide. For instance, 'Madrid' comes with a toy bull and matador. The decor is basic, the breakfast is good.

Hotel Busche am Dom HOTEL €€
(Map p512; www.hotel-busche.de; Bogenstrasse 10; s/d from €60/110) A family-run hotel with a fantastic location, this central hotel has 13 comfortable rooms in muted pastels. You'll hear the bells ringing on the hour and if

you're the imaginative sort you could picture yourself running late for a treaty signing.

Factory Hotel
HOTEL €€

(☑418 80; www.factoryhotel-muenster.de; An der Germania Brauerei 5; s/d from €90/110; P🚗❄🁢) This sleek hotel marries the historical with the contemporary in the defunct Germania Brewery. The 144 large and modern rooms feature wood, leather and concrete, and come with a balcony overlooking an artificial lake. Entertainment includes three restaurants, a lounge and a club. It's about 2km north of the city centre.

Sleep Station
HOSTEL €

(Map p512; ☑482 8155; www.sleep-station.de; Wolbecker Strasse 1; dm €16-24, s/d €40/56; 🚗@) Münster's hostel is 200m from the Hauptbahnhof. Dorms are clean but basic and sleep three to eight; only a few singles and doubles have private bathrooms. Perks include free coffee and tea, and kitchen use. Check-in is from 8am to 12.30pm and 5pm to 9pm.

✖ Eating & Drinking

Most places in Münster are good just for a drink or vice-versa. Besides its namesake pub, look for the local brew Pinkus Müller on better taps around town.

TOP CHOICE Altes Gasthaus Leve
GERMAN €€

(Map p512; ☑455 95; www.gasthaus-leve.de; Alter Steinweg 37; mains €7-18; ⊙11.30am-11pm) Münster's oldest inn (since 1607) has painted tiles, oil paintings and copper etchings that form a suitably rustic backdrop to the hearty Westphalian fare. Dishes such as lima-bean stew and sweet-and-sour beef are delicious. Despite being ever busy, the staff are lovely. In spring try a surprising *Altbierbowle* (dark Pinkus Müller beer with strawberries) – it's almost addictive.

TOP CHOICE Pinkus Müller
BREWERY €€

(Map p512; ☑451 51; www.pinkus-mueller.de; Kreuzstrasse 4; mains €8-15; ⊙closed Sun) One of Germany's best small brewers, Pinkus Müller has a namesake pub and restaurant in the heart of the nightlife-filled Kuhviertel. It has a swath of tables out front under a big tree. Enjoy German standards along with great beers such as the *honig malz* (honey malt).

Kleines Restaurant im Oer'schen Hof
MODERN EUROPEAN €€€

(Map p512; www.kleines-restaurant-im-oerschen hof.de; menus from €40; ⊙lunch & dinner Tue-Sat) Housed in a 1798 courtyard building with a regal past, this beautiful restaurant has a

COLOGNE & NORTHERN RHINELAND MÜNSTER

THE ANABAPTISTS

They did like to argue. The Anabaptists were a religious movement that swept through Europe in the early 16th century. Starting in Zurich, Anabaptists spread through much of Germany and beyond. But like many cultish groups, its true believers had sharp disagreements among themselves. The name alone was cause for strife as it referred to the core tenet that adults should be 'rebaptised' into the faith. However, many claimed that any original baptism as an infant hadn't counted because nonAnabaptist religions were not valid, thus your Anabaptist baptism was the first. And so it went.

Other beliefs included polygamy and community ownership of goods. The movement reached its apex at Münster in 1534, when a Dutchman named Jan van Leyden and a crew of followers managed to take over the town. Soon they had baptised over 1000 new followers.

Some rather extreme personalities also emerged: Jan Matthys marched out to confront a vast army of besiegers from the Catholic church who planned to retake the city. He was promptly beheaded and his genitals nailed to a town gate. Meanwhile, van Leyden proclaimed himself king and took 16 wives, which worked out to be about one for each month he was in power; besiegers overran the Münster in 1535 and had van Leyden and many Anabaptists tortured and killed. Three of the bodies ended up in the cages you can still see today in St Lambertikirche.

After the defeat at Münster, the movement was never the same. It had managed to bring both Catholics and Protestants together as both mercilessly tortured and killed Anabaptists. Splinters of the old faith eventually formed what later became Amish and Mennonites, among others.

series of spaces inside and outside that are casual without being fussy. The fare is seasonal and usually drawn from the region. In summer, opt for a candle-lit table outside under the stars and enjoy the refined service and fine wine list.

Marktcafe
CAFE €€

(Map p512; ☎575 85; Domplatz 7; mains €5-13; ☺9am-1am) In good weather, there's no better place to soak up the street action than the terrace of this been-here-forever cafe with free views of the Dom. The food is fresh and tasty, and Sunday's brunch buffet is an institution. Note: despite the view, true gentlemen take the seats facing in...

A2am See
CAFE €€

(Map p512; ☎284 6840; www.a2amsee.de; Annette-Allee 3; mains €8-20; ☺11am-midnight Sun-Thu, to late Fri & Sat) Location, location, location. A2, right on the Aasee, has certainly got it. The glass walls and designer furniture scream trendy, but this bar-bistro-restaurant actually appeals as much to lifestyle-savvy types as to hip families and salt-and-pepper couples. The vast waterside terrace is a must at sunset.

Cavete
GERMAN €€

(Map p512; ☎457 00; Kreuzstrasse 38; mains €8-11) For a relaxed pint, steer to the Kuhviertel, the traditional student quarter north of the Dom. Cavete has been a classic for generations. Find a seat at one of the battered old wood tables and enjoy housemade noodles with schnitzel.

Cafe Gasolin
CAFE

(Map p512; ☎510 5897; www.cafe-gasolin.de; Aegidiistrasse 45; snacks from €3; ☺11am-3am) This cleverly converted 1950s gas station has yummy cakes and latte macchiatos for a potent sugar fix, and is also a good place for that final drink when everything else is closed. Prices are low, quality is not; huge patio.

Pension Schmidt
CAFE

(Map p512; Alter Steinweg 37; snacks from €3) Given the quality of the coffee at this hipster cafe, it's unlikely you'll wish it was a real *Pension*, even if the sofas for lounging on are very comfortable. The clientele are the kinds of students who get a Beemer from Dad for college. Get them to buy a round.

☆ Entertainment

Münster's party-happy students fuel an eclectic pub and club scene. The Haven's Kreativkai quarter is breeding a few interesting places.

TOP CHOICE Hot Jazz Club
BAR

(☎6866 7909; www.hotjazzclub.de; Hafenweg 26b) The best reason to head out to the Hafen, this subterranean bar keeps it real with live music of all stripes, not only jazz. Check the schedule before you walk over in case it's an off night.

Hafen Bar
BAR

(☎289 7810; Hafenweg 26) For a glamour vibe without the velvet rope, beat a trail to this stylish glass cube in the Hafen's Kreativkai. Soft lighting gives even pasty-faced hipsters a healthy glow. Good tunes.

Black Box
CULTURAL CENTRE

(Map p512; www.blackbox-muenster.de; Achtermannstrasse 10-12) This performance venue and cultural centre sees a huge range of acts in any given week. Classical mixes with jazz, which mixes with house; well-known DJs often appear to try out something experimental.

🄰 Shopping

The least appealing part of Münster is the main, chain-filled shopping drag Königstrasse. You'll find much more appealing retails action amidst the colonnades on Prinzipalmarkt.

Poertgen Herder
BOOKS

(Map p512; ☎490 140; Salzstrasse 56) Fine selection of English books as befits a university town.

❶ Information

Stadtbücherei (☎492 4242; Alter Steinweg 11; per hr €0.50; ☺10am-7pm Mon-Fri, to 3pm Sat) Public library with internet access.

Tourist Office (☎492 2710; www.tourismus.muenster.de; Heinrich-Brüning-Strasse 9; ☺9.30am-6pm Mon-Fri, to 1pm Sat) Main office.

Tourist office Historisches Rathaus (☎492 2724; Prinzipalmarkt 10; ☺10am-5pm Tue-Fri, to 4pm Sat & Sun)

❶ Getting There & Away

Münster Osnabrück International Airport (FMO; www.fmo.de) has mostly internal German flights and a few charters to holiday spots.

Münster is on an IC **train** line with regular links to points north including Hamburg (€56, 2¼ hours) and south to Cologne (€33, 1¾ hours). Like the cathedral, the Hauptbahnhof is getting a complete reconstruction through 2013.

ⓘ Getting Around

Buses connect the airport and the Hauptbahnhof every half-hour (40 minutes).

Bus drivers sell single tickets for €1.40 or €2.50, depending on the distance, as well as day passes for €4.40 (valid after 9am).

Hire bikes at **Radstation** (☑484 0170; Berliner Platz 27a; 1/3 days €9/19; ☺5.30am-11pm Mon-Fri, 7am-11pm Sat & Sun) at the Hauptbahnhof. The tourist office has cycling maps.

Münsterland

Münster is surrounded by Münsterland, a flat and rural region that's home to about 100 castles and palaces, some of which are still owned and inhabited by the landed gentry. Many are protected by water-filled moats, which today offer little protection from tax assessors.

The region is a dream for cyclists, with over 4500km of well-signposted trails (called *Pättkes* in local dialect), including the scenic **100 Schlösser Route** (www.100 -schloesser-route.de), which links, well, 100 palaces. Bicycles can be hired in Münster and at practically all local train stations. Many castles are also served by public transport, though service can be sketchy or convoluted, especially at weekends. The route website has downloadable maps and much more info for cyclists.

◉ Sights

The following quartet of castles offer the greatest tourist appeal and, except for Schloss Nordkirchen, are relatively accessible from Münster.

Burg Hülshoff   CASTLE
(☑02534-1052; www.burg-huelshoff.de; Schonebeck 6; adult/child incl audio guide €5/4.50, park and castle free; ☺11am-6.30pm Apr-Oct) In Havixbeck, about 10km west of Münster, Burg Hülshoff is the birthplace of one of Germany's preeminent women of letters, Annette von Droste-Hülshoff (1797–1848). The red-brick Renaissance chateau is embedded in a lovely – partly groomed, partly romantic – park. The interior, which consists of period rooms furnished in the style of the poet's day, can be explored with an English-language audioguide. Alas, there's no public transport out here.

Haus Rüschhaus   HISTORIC BUILDING
(☑02533-1317; www.rueschhaus.de; Am Rüschhaus 81; adult/child €5/2.50; ☺tours hourly 10am-noon & 2-5pm Tue-Sun May-Oct, 11am, noon, 2pm & 3pm Tue-Sun Apr) Annette von Droste-Hülshoff did some of her finest writing at the smaller Haus Rüschhaus, where she lived for 20 years from 1826. The building was once the private home of star architect Johann Conrad Schlaun, who magically morphed a farmhouse into a baroque mini mansion backed by a formal garden (always open). It's in the suburb of Nienberge, about 3km north of Burg Hülshoff, and served by bus 5 from Münster's Hauptbahnhof (€2.50, 20 minutes).

Burg Vischering   CASTLE
(☑02591-799 00; www.burg-vischering.de; Berenbrok 1; adult/child €2.50/1; ☺10am-12.30pm & 1-5.30pm Tue-Sun Apr-Oct, to 4.30pm Nov-Mar) The quintessential medieval moated castle, Burg Vischering is Westphalia's oldest (1271), and the kind that conjures romantic images of knights and damsels. Surrounded by a system of ramparts and ditches, the complex consists of an outer castle and the main castle, now a **museum**.

Burg Vischering is in Lüdinghausen, about 30km south of Münster. Catch bus S90/91 or S92 at the Hauptbahnhof to Lüdinghausen (€6, 45 minutes), then walk for about 10 minutes.

Schloss Nordkirchen   PALACE
(☑02596-9330; www.schloss.nordkirchen.net; castle tours adult/child €3/1, gardens free; ☺castle tours 11am-5pm Sun May-Sep, 2-4pm Sun Oct-Apr, park 9am-6pm) On an island surrounded by a sprawling, manicured park, Schloss Nordkirchen is an imposing baroque red-brick structure nicknamed the 'Westphalian Versailles'. On a nice day, the palace is well worth visiting for the gardens and the exterior alone. Since it's used as a state college for financial studies, the interior – with its stuccoed ceilings, festival hall and dining room – can only be seen on guided tours.

Schloss Nordkirchen is 8km southeast of Lüdinghausen in the hamlet of Nordkirchen, which is poorly served by public transport. Consult your bike map to find the route from Burg Vischering.

Osnabrück

📞 0541 / 164,100

'Zum Glück komm' ich aus Osnabrück', locals boast of their good luck to come from this city; and that's something you might understand at night, wandering the winding lamp-lit streets of the old town. However, the main attraction here is a museum dedicated to the locally born Jewish painter Felix Nussbaum.

● Sights

TOP CHOICE **Felix-Nussbaum-Haus**   MUSEUM
(📞 323 2207, 323 2237; www.osnabrueck.de/fnh; Lotter Strasse 2; adult/concession €5/3; ⊙ 11am-6pm Tue-Fri, to 8pm Thu, 10am-6pm Sat & Sun) Shaped like an interconnected series of concrete shards, with slit windows and sloping floors, the Felix-Nussbaum-Haus predates Libeskind's famous Jewish Museum Berlin. Inside is a collection of works by the Osnabrück-born Jewish painter Felix Nussbaum (1904–44). His works reveal shades of Van Gogh and Henri Rousseau, and Libeskind's 1998 building uses space magnificently to illustrate the absence of orientation in the artist's eventful and tragic life.

In 1944, after several years in exile, arrest in Belgium and successful escape in France, Nussbaum was denounced and finally deported from Belgium to Auschwitz, where he died. Today the museum shares an entrance with the **Kulturgeschichtliches Museum** (entry included in price), which has graphics cabinets, also designed by Libeskind, holding works by Albrecht Dürer. The local **Museum of Cultural History** adjoins.

MARKT & AROUND

Much of the Altstadt is a humdrum shopping district but wander around and you'll find some gems.

Rathaus   HISTORIC BUILDING
(Markt; ⊙ 8am-6pm Mon-Fri, 9am-4pm Sat, 10am-4pm Sun) It was on the Rathaus steps that the Peace of Westphalia was proclaimed on 25 October 1648, ending the Thirty Years' War. The preceding peace negotiations were conducted partly in Münster, about 60km south, and partly in the Rathaus' **Friedenssaal** (Peace Hall). On the left as you enter the Rathaus are portraits of the negotiators. Also have a look around the **Schatzkammer** (Treasure Chamber) opposite, especially for the 13th-century *Kaiserpokal* (Kaiser goblet).

Marienkirche   CHURCH
(Markt) The four richly ornamented cross gables of the Marienkirche loom above the square, painstakingly rebuilt after burning down during WWII.

WORTH A TRIP

KALKRIESE

You needn't be a history buff to come to the **Varusschlacht Museum & Park Kalkriese** (📞 05468-920 4200; www.kalkriese-varusschlacht.de; Bramsche-Kalkriese; adult/child €7/4.50; ⊙ 10am-6pm Apr-Oct, 10am-5pm Tue-Sun Nov-Mar), although by the time you leave you'll have probably acquired an interest. It was long known that rebellious Germanic tribes had won a major victory over their Roman masters somewhere in the Osnabrück region in AD 9 – defeating three of military commander Publius Quinctilius Varus' legions.

But it wasn't until 1987 that this likely candidate for the site of the so-called **Battle of Teutoberg Forest** was uncovered near Kalkriese. In 2000, the battlefield was opened as an archaeological park to display the Germans' dirt ramparts and explain how they did it. Since then, facilities have expanded steadily and you'll find exhibits on the artefacts dug up so far, as well as much contextual coverage of how the Germanic tribes had such good luck against the otherwise proud Romans.

The surrounding park and battlefield features three quirky pavilions, called 'seeing', 'hearing' and 'questioning'. Using a camera obscura, huge ear trumpet and video technology respectively, they give you an unusual perspective on the battlefield.

If you try to visit the museum and park without your own vehicle, you may well feel like the Romans trying to defend against the Germanic tribes: defeated (public transport is sparse). The site is about 16km north of Osnabrück, off the N218.

FREE **Erich Maria Remarque Friedenszentrum** MUSEUM
(Erich Maria Remarque Peace Centre; ☎323 2109; www.remarque.uos.de; Markt 6; ⏰10am-1pm & 3-5pm Tue-Fri, 11am-5pm Sat & Sun) The small Erich Maria Remarque Friedenszentrum uses photos and documents to chronicle the writer's life (1898–1970) and work.

Half-Timbered Houses HISTORIC BUILDINGS
Various half-timbered houses survived WWII. At **Bierstrasse 24** is the baroque Romantik Hotel Walhalla, with a portal flanked by cheeky cherubs. There's a good row of shops at **Hackenstrasse 3**. At **Krahnstrasse 4** you'll find a beautiful house (1533), with a cafe taking up the ground floor. At **Krahnstrassehe 7** is the best of the bunch, the Renaissance **Haus Willmann** (1586), with its carved circular motifs and small relief of Adam and Eve. It's now a wine shop.

Bucksturm TOWER
(Bucksturm; ☎323 2152; Bocksmauer; adult/concession €3/1; ⏰11am-5pm Sun) Just north of Heger Tor and Felix-Nussbaum-Haus you'll find the 28m-high Bucksturm, built as a watchtower inside the town wall in the 13th century and later used as a prison. Then, in the 16th and 17th centuries, those accused of being witches were tortured here. Today, a small exhibition here on the persecution of 'witches' explains why and how this took place.

🛏 Sleeping

Intour Hotel HOTEL €€
(☎963 860; www.intourhotel.de; Maschstrasse 10; s €51-60, d €84-90; P🐕) Situated just outside the historic centre and handy to Felix-Nussbaum-Haus, this hotel looks unprepossessing from the outside but is modern, cosy and clean inside. It is a 10-minute walk to the eating and drinking spots in the lively Heger-Tor-Viertel. Take buses 31, 32 or 33 to Weissenburgstrasse from the train station or Neuer Markt.

Penthouse Backpackers HOTEL €€
(☎600 9606; www.penthousebp.com; Möserstrasse 19; dm €14-16, s €28-32, d €36-40; @🐕) The furniture looks like it's been cobbled together from friends of the owner (because it has been!). Check-in is only from 8am to 11am and 4pm to 9pm, so call ahead. Close to the train station, this 4th-floor establishment has a kitchen, big guest lounge room, a sauna and a rooftop terrace.

Romantik Hotel Walhalla HOTEL €€
(☎349 10; www.hotel-walhalla.de; Bierstrasse 24; s €93-105, d €120-130; P🐕) If you're looking for historic atmosphere, this hotel has it aplenty. The half that's housed in a traditional half-timbered building has higgledy-piggledy rooms with low-beamed ceilings and rustic features. Even rooms in the more modern half continue the theme.

🍴 Eating & Drinking

Not far west of the Markt, the Heger-Tor-Viertel area around the namesake old tower is a good place to scout out a good meal and a drink.

Tristan ITALIAN €€
(☎350 2401; www.tristan-restaurant.de; Heger Strasse 12; pizza €6-11, mains €15-24; ⏰lunch & dinner Tue-Sun; 🐕) This homely, family-friendly Italian *osteria* (inn) has chunky dark-wood tables and white walls hung with art. Beyond the pizza and pasta, the menu is small, changing and meat focused; the house red wine is very decent.

Hausbrauerei Rampendahl GERMAN €€
(☎245 35; www.rampendahl.de; Hasestrasse 35; meals €7-22) This restaurant and micro-brewery is about as hearty as they come, serving substantial dishes to accompany the house beers. It has various cheaper and ever-changing lunch or dinner deals like a *Stammessen* (staple; €5.95) – typically a beef goulash with cabbage and dumplings. Its unfiltered lager is excellent.

Konditorei Ulrich Läer CAFE €
(Krahnstrasse 4; treats from €3; ⏰9am-6pm Mon-Sat) In one of Osnabrück's prettiest authentic half-timbered houses, this bakery and cafe is suitably luxe. Pastries and cakes will make you accidentally wimper. Watch the passing parade of locals from one of the tables out front.

ℹ Information

Tourist Information (☎0541 323 2202; www.osnabrueck.de; Bierstrasse 22/23; ⏰9.30am-6pm Mon-Fri, 10am-4pm Sat) Close to the Rathaus.

ℹ Getting There & Away

Münster Osnabrück International Airport (FMO; www.fmo.de) has mostly internal German flights and a few charters to holiday spots.

Trains to Hanover (€27, 1¼ hours) and Münster (€12, 35 minutes) leave at least twice an hour.

 Getting Around

The **airport** is 30km southwest of the centre, and reached by Schnellbus X150 (€9, 40 minutes).

Single **bus** tickets cost €2.40 and day tickets €5.10.

The Hauptbahnhof is on the town's eastern edge. The Altstadt is a bland 15-minute walk along Möserstrasse, turning left at the Kaufhof building into Wittekindstrasse.

OSTWESTFALEN

The rolling hills and forests make for pleasant and scenic driving. Both terrain and elevations get more dramatic in the Sauerland, where there are winter sports. Nestled within it all are some interesting towns such as church-filled Soest.

Soest

☎ 02921 / POP 48,600

Soest is a tranquil town of half-timbered houses and a clutch of treasure-filled churches that reflect the wealth it enjoyed during its Hanseatic League days. Although heavily bombed in WWII, this maze of idyllic, crooked lanes has been beautifully rebuilt and preserves much of its medieval character.

If Soest seems green, it's the shimmering greenish shades of the local sandstone used in building its town wall, churches and other public structures.

Only 45km southeast of Münster, Soest is compact enough to be explored on a day trip or as a side trip en route to somewhere else.

⊙ Sights

Much of Soest's historic centre lies within a **moated defensive wall**, which today has a park-like appearance and is great for strolling and picnicking. The town is home to some of Westphalia's most important churches. Three are near the **Markt**, which features the **Rathaus**, a baroque confection with an arched portico on the western side. The **Grosser Teich** is a placid duck pond and park where the tourist office occupies an old water mill.

St Patrokli   CHURCH

(www.sankt-patrokli.de; Propst-Nübel-Strasse 2; ⊙10am-6pm) Ponder the balance and beauty of the soaring yet dignified tower of St Patrokli, a three-nave Romanesque structure partly adorned with delicate frescos. The west side is especially elaborate.

Nikolaikapelle   CHURCH

(Thomästrasse; ⊙11am-noon Tue-Thu & Sun) The tiny Nikolaikapelle is a few steps southeast of St Patrokli. It's a pity it's rarely open, for its almost mystical simplicity is enlivened by a masterful altar painting attributed to 15th-century master Conrad von Soest (who was born in Dortmund).

St Maria zur Höhe   CHURCH

(www.hohnegemeinde.de; Hohe Gasse; ⊙10am-5.30pm Apr-Sep, to 4pm Oct-Mar) St Maria zur Höhe, better known as Hohnekirche, is a squat, older and architecturally less refined 13th-century hall church. Its sombreness is brightened by beautiful ceiling frescos, an altar ascribed to the Westphalian painter known as the Master of Liesborn, and the *Scheibenkreuz*, a huge wooden cross on a circular board more typically found in Scandinavian churches; in fact, it's the only such cross in Germany. Look for the light switch on your left as you enter to shed a little light on the matter.

Petrikirche   CHURCH

(Petrikirchhof 10; ⊙9.30am-5pm Tue-Sat, 2-5.30pm Sun) Petrikirche has Romanesque origins in the 8th century and a choir from Gothic times, all topped by a baroque onion dome. It's adorned with wall murals and features an unusual modern altar made from the local green sandstone, glass and brushed stainless steel.

St Maria zur Wiese   CHURCH

(Wiesenstrasse; ⊙11am-4pm Mon-Sat, noon-4pm Sun) Close to the train station, this exquisite late-Gothic hall church is also known as Wiesenkirche and easily recognised by its lacy neo-Gothic twin spires. These are undergoing restoration and will remain under wraps until sometime after 2020. Note the 1520 **stained-glass window** showing Jesus and his disciples enjoying a Westphalian Last Supper of ham, beer and pumpernickel bread, which is native to Soest.

FREE **Grünsandstein-Museum**   MUSEUM

(Green Sandstone Museum; ☎ 15011; www.gruensand steinmuseum.de; Walburgerstrasse 56; ⊙10am-5pm

Mon-Sat, 2-5pm Sun) The church of St Maria zur Wiese's restoration workshop operates this museum, where you can learn about the origin of Soest's mysteriously green stone.

🍴 Sleeping & Eating

Local specialities include the Soester pumpernickel, a rough-textured rye bread made entirely without salt, and the *Bullenauge* (bull's eye), a creamy mocha liqueur.

Hotel Im Wilden Mann   HOTEL €€

(☑150 71; www.im-wilden-mann.com; Am Markt 11; s/d from €55/90; P🐕) This central landmark in a portly half-timbered town house offers the opportunity to connect to the magic of yesteryear in a dozen comfortable rooms furnished in white minimalist style. The casual timbered restaurant is all about traditional local foods.

Pilgrim Haus   HOTEL €€

(☑1828; www.pilgrimhaus.de; Jakobistrasse 75; s/d/tr €79/105/128; P🐕) This darling inn has been in the hospitality business since 1304 and hasn't lost its lustre. Pack your tummy with fancy German fare in the popular restaurant (mains €9 to €20), which has a terrace. The 14 rooms decked out in soothing colours and attractive art.

Brauerei Christ   BREWERY €€

(☑155 15; www.brauerei-christ.com; Walburger Strasse 36; mains €10-20) History oozes from every nook and cranny of this warren of living-room-style rooms stuffed with musical instruments, oil paintings and unique knick-knacks. Hunker down at polished tables for Westphalian specialities or any of its 15 schnitzel variations. Nice beer garden.

ℹ Information

Tourist Office (☑02921 6635 0050; www. soest.de; Teichsmühlengasse 3; ⏰9.30am-4.30pm Mon-Fri, 10am-3pm Sat year-round, 11am-1pm Sun Apr-Oct)

ℹ Getting There & Around

Soest is easily reached by **train** from Dortmund (€12, 45 minutes) and is also regularly connected to Paderborn (€12, 40 minutes) and Münster (€15, 50 minutes).

The train station is on the north side of the ring road enclosing Soest's historic centre. Follow the pedestrianised Brüderstrasse south to the Markt, tourist office and the churches.

Paderborn

☑05251 / POP 146.300

About 50km east of Soest, Paderborn is the largest city in eastern Westphalia. It derives its name from the Pader which, at 4km, is Germany's shortest river.

Charlemagne used Paderborn as a power base to defeat the Saxons and convert them to Christianity, giving him the momentum needed to rise to greater things. A visit by Pope Leo III in 799 led to the establishment of the Western Roman Empire, a precursor to the Holy Roman Empire, and Charlemagne's coronation as its emperor in Rome the following year.

Paderborn remains a pious place to this day – churches abound, and religious sculpture and motifs adorn facades, fountains and parks. Many of the city's 14,000 students are involved in theological studies. It's a good stop if you're passing by on the train.

⊙ Sights

Most sights cluster in the largely pedestrianised Altstadt, which is small enough to explore on foot.

Should you weary of walking, however, at the foot of the Abdinghofkirche lies the **Paderquellgebiet**, a small park perfect for relaxing by the astonishing 200 springs that feed the Pader.

Dom   CHURCH

(Markt 17; ⏰10am-6.30pm) Paderborn's massive Dom, a three-nave Gothic hall church, is a good place to start your explorations. Enter through the southern portal (called 'Paradise'), adorned with delicate carved figures, then turn your attention to the **high altar** and the pompous **memorial tomb of Dietrich von Fürstenberg**, a 17th-century bishop. Signs point the way to the Dom's most endearing feature, the so-called **Dreihasenfenster**, a unique trompe l'oeil window in the cloister. Its tracery depicts three hares, ingeniously arranged so that each has two ears, even though there are only three ears in all.

The hall-like **crypt**, one of the largest in Germany, contains the grave and relics of St Liborius, the city's patron saint. A 4th-century priest in today's France, his remains were sent to Paderborn in the 8th century as a gift.

Erzbischöfliches Diözesanmuseum
MUSEUM

(Museum of the Archdiocese; ☑125 1400; www.dioezesanmuseum-paderborn.de; Markt 17; adult/child €3.50/1.50; ☺10am-6pm Tue-Sun) The famous 1627 Liborius shrine is housed in an attractive modernist structure outside the Dom. It brims with church treasures, the most precious of which are kept in the basement, including the gilded shrine and prized portable altars. Upstairs, the one piece not to be missed is the Imad Madonna, an exquisite 11th-century linden-wood statue.

Rathaus
HISTORIC BUILDING

(Rathausplatz) Paderborn's proud Rathaus (1616) with ornate gables, oriels and other decorative touches is typical of the Weser Renaissance architectural style.

Marktkirche
CHURCH

(Market Church; Rathausplatz; ☺9am-6pm) South of the Rathaus is the Marktkirche, aka Jesuitenkirche, a galleried basilica where pride of place goes to the dizzyingly detailed baroque high altar. A soaring symphony of wood and gold, it's an exact replica of the 17th-century original destroyed in WWII.

Marienplatz
SQUARE

Rathausplatz blends into Marienplatz with its delicate Mariensäule (St Mary's Column) and Heising'sche Haus, an elaborate 17th-century patrician mansion that shares a wall with the tourist office. The Abdinghofkirche (Am Abdinghof; ☺11am-6pm) is easily recognised by its twin Romanesque towers. Once a Benedictine monastery, it's been a Protestant church since 1867 and is rather austere with its whitewashed and unadorned walls and flat wooden ceiling.

Carolingian Kaiserpfalz
HISTORIC SITE

East along Am Abdinghof to the north of the Dom are the remnants of the Carolingian Kaiserpfalz, Charlemagne's palace where that historic meeting with Pope Leo took place. It was destroyed by fire and replaced in the 11th century by the Ottonian-Salian Kaiserpfalz, which has been reconstructed as faithfully as possible atop the original foundations. Inside is the Museum in der Kaiserpfalz (☑105 110; www.kaiserpfalz-paderborn.de; Am Ikenberg 2; adult/child €3.50/1.50; ☺10am-6pm Tue-Sun), which presents excavated items from the days of Charlemagne, including drinking vessels and fresco remnants. The only original palace building is

the twee Bartholomäuskapelle next door. Consecrated in 1017, it's considered the oldest hall church north of the Alps and enjoys otherworldly acoustics.

Schloss Neuhaus
PALACE

(www.schlosspark-paderborn.de;Schlosspark)Schloss Neuhaus, a moated palace, can be reached by a lovely riverside walk about 5km northwest of the Paderquellgebiet. It hosts frequent cultural events in summer.

Heinz Nixdorf Museumsforum
MUSEUM

(HNF; ☑306 600; www.hnf.de; Fürstenallee 7; adult/child €7/4; ☺9am-6pm Tue-Fri, 10am-6pm Sat & Sun) You don't have to be a techie to enjoy this museum, a high-tech romp through 5000 years of information technology, from cuneiform to cyberspace. Established by the local founder of Nixdorf computers (since swallowed by bigger corporations), it displays all manner of once-high-tech gadgets from the predigital age but most memorable is the replica of Eniac, a room-sized vacuum-tube computer developed for the US Army in the 1940s. These days, the data it held would fit onto a barely-there microchip.

There are plenty of machines to touch, push and prod, as well as computer games and a virtual-reality theatre. Catch bus 11 from the Hauptbahnhof to Museumsforum.

🛏 Sleeping & Eating

Near the Rathaus, the Rathauspassage has delis and markets where you can assemble a fine picnic to enjoy in the Paderquellgebiet.

ⓉⓄⓅ CHOICE Galerie-Hotel Abdinghof
HOTEL €€

(☑122 40; www.galerie-hotel.de; Bachstrasse 1; s/d incl breakfast from €80/100; P🖨🛜) The best option if you bed down in Paderborn is this hotel in a 1563 stone building overlooking the Paderquellgebiet. Famous artists – Michelangelo to Picasso – inspired the decor of the 11 rooms, furnished in styles ranging from country and rustic to elegant and feminine. Original art graces the downstairs cafe-restaurant.

Le Maison
BISTRO €€

(www.lamaison-paderborn.de; Rathauspassage, Rosenstrasse 13-15; mains €8-16) A very appealing thoroughly French bistro hidden away in the modern warren of the Rathauspassage. Tables inside spill outside and you can linger over one of many coffee drinks. Plates include excellent salads, pasta and various meaty mains. Snacks too.

Curry Company   SAUSAGES €

(☑387 7414; Kamp 10; dishes €2.50-9; ☺11am-midnight) 'Gourmet snack' is not an oxymoron in this artsy sausage parlour where you can pair your wurst with freshly made gourmet sauces like truffle mayonnaise.

ⓘ Information

Tourist Office (☑05251 882 980; www.paderborn.de; Marienplatz 2a; ☺10am-6pm Mon-Fri, to 4pm Sat Apr-Oct, to 5pm Mon-Fri, to 2pm Sat Nov-Mar)

ⓘ Getting There & Away

Paderborn has direct **trains** every two hours to Kassel-Wilhelmshöhe (€27, 1¼ hours) and regional connections to Dortmund (€22, 1¼ hours) and other Ruhrgebiet cities. Trains to Soest (€12, 40 minutes) leave several times hourly.

ⓘ Getting Around

To get to the Dom, the tourist office and other sights from the Hauptbahnhof, exit right onto Bahnhofstrasse and continue straight via the Westernstrasse, the main shopping street.

Radstation (☑870 740; www.paderborner-radstation.de; Bahnhofstrasse 29; per 24hr €10; ☺5.30am-10.30pm) at the Hauptbahnhof rents bicycles.

SAUERLAND

This hilly forested region is popular as an easy getaway for nature-craving Ruhrgebiet residents and hill-craving Dutch tourists. There are a few museums and castles sprinkled about, but the Sauerland's primary appeal lies in the outdoors. Some 20,000km of marked hiking trails, mostly through beech and fir forest, spread across five nature parks. Cyclists and mountain bikers can pick their favourites from dozens of routes. In winter some of the steeper slopes come alive with downhill skiiers.

The Sauerland is best explored with your own wheels; you can get loads of info from the **regional tourist office** (☑01802-403 040; www.sauerland.com).

Altena

☑02352 / POP 18,300

In a steep, narrow valley carved by the Lenne River, Altena has built its fortune on producing industrial wire since making mail-shirts for medieval knights.

The main reason to stop is the majestic **Burg Altena** (☑966 7033; www.burg-altena.de; Fritz-Thomee-Strasse 80; museum adult/child €5/2.50; ☺9.30am-5pm Tue-Fri, 11am-6pm Sat & Sun). This fairy-tale medieval castle started out as the home of the local counts, then served military purposes under the Prussians before becoming, in 1912, the birthplace of the youth hostel movement as the world's first hostel. Dark dorms sporting wooden triple bunks can be seen in the **museum**. There is a series of 31 themed rooms, each zeroing in on a different aspect of regional history, often in a visually pleasing and engaging fashion. You'll see some fancy historic weapons and armour, but also an exhibit on the Sauerland under the Nazis. Plan on spending at least 90 minutes to see it all.

Admission is also good at the nonelectrifying **Deutsches Drahtmuseum**, about 300m downhill, which covers wire and all its uses.

The castle and hostel are about a 15-minute walk from the train station. Altena is served by regional trains running between Hagen and Siegen.

Attendorn

☑02722 / POP 24,700

The main attraction of Attendorn is underground: the **Atta-Höhle** (☑937 50; www.atta-hoehle.de; Finnentroper Strasse 39; adult/child €7.50/4.50; ☺10am-4.30pm May-Aug, reduced hr Sep-Apr) is one of Germany's largest and most impressive caves. A 40-minute tour takes you past a subterranean lake and stalagmites and stalactites shaped into curtains, domes, columns and shields.

The town is on the **Biggesee** which is great for water sports. Lake cruises are operated by **Personenschiffahrt Biggesee.** (☑02761-965 90; www.biggesee.de; cruises adult/child €9.50/4.50; ☺Apr-Oct)

To get to Attendorn by regional train requires changing in Hagen and in Finnentrop.

Winterberg

☑02981 / POP 14,500

Winterberg, the main town in the **Rothaargebirge nature park**, is the Sauerland's winter sports centre.

The primary ski mountain is the 843m-high **Kahler Asten**. It is home to **Skiliftkarussell Winterberg** (www.skiliftkarussell.de; lift ticket adult/child from €26/17), a 32-run piste that sprawls over four mountains above town and includes nine chairlifts. Other winter attractions include a 1600m-long **bobsled run** that hosts international competitions and an **indoor skating rink**. In good winters, the season runs from December to March, helped along by snow-making machines if nature fails to perform. In summer, there's lots of good hiking, including a popular and moderately strenuous 5km trail to the top of the Kahler Asten.

Wintersport-Arena Sauerland (www.wintersport-arena.de/en) has excellent info in English. For more ideas, stop by the Winterberg **tourist office** (☎02981 925 00; www.winterberg.de; Am Kurpark 6; ☉9am-5.30pm Mon-Fri, to 3pm Sat).

Winterberg is at the end of a branch line and has trains from Dortmund (€17, 1¾ hours).

SIEGEN

☎0271 / POP 103,000

Wedged into a valley hemmed by dense forest, Siegen is the commercial hub of the Siegerland and birthplace of the painter Peter Paul Rubens (1577–1640).

For centuries it was ruled by the counts of Nassau-Oranien, the family that ascended to the Dutch throne in 1813. One of two palaces from those glory days that survived the bombing squadrons of WWII is well worth a stop if you're in the area. Otherwise Siegen is short on charm. Pause for refreshment at cafes on the Markt.

◉ Sights

Oberes Schloss PALACE

From Markt, Burgstrasse slopes up to the Oberes Schloss, a classic medieval fortress and the ancestral home of the rulers of Nassau-Oranien. Its labyrinth of rooms now houses the **Siegerlandmuseum** (☎230 410; Burgstrasse 10; adult/child €3/1.50; ☉10am-5pm Tue-Sun), which would be a mediocre collection of old paintings were it not for its **nine Rubens originals**, including a self-portrait and a large-scale work viscerally depicting a lion hunt. Other rooms cover aspects of local history.

Nikolaikirche CHURCH

(Markt; ☉10am-6pm Mon-Fri, to noon Sat Apr-Oct) Halfway up the hill looms Siegen's signature landmark, the late-Romanesque Nikolaikirche. It's easily recognised by the golden crown atop the steeple, placed there by a local ruler in 1652 to commemorate his promotion from count to prince. The church itself has an unusual hexagonal floor plan but is otherwise rather plain on the inside.

ⓘ Information

Tourist Office (☎404 1316; www.tourismus.gss-siegen.de; Rathaus, Markt 2; ☉9am-5pm Mon-Fri, 11am-3pm Sat & Sun)

ⓘ Getting There & Away

Direct **trains** depart hourly for Cologne (€21, 1½ hours).

Central Germany

Best Places to Eat

» Rattenfängerhaus (p538)
» Zwiesel (p543)
» Jo Hanns (p550)
» Turmschänke (p557)
» Osteria da Salvatore (p593)

Best Places to Stay

» Schlosshotel Münch-hausen (p538)
» Opera Hostel (p542)
» Hotel auf der Wartburg (p557)
» Hotel Gothisches Haus (p570)
» Grüne Zitadelle (p589)

Why Go?

Central Germany consists of parts of former East Germany, the Harz Mountains and some of northern Germany. The region is very much a cultural heartland, taking in towns like Weimar (famous for Germany's figures from the Enlightenment), Erfurt, Lutherstadt Eisleben and Lutherstadt Wittenberg. The latter two cities earned their 'Luther' prefixes because in these places the religious reformer Martin Luther was born and died (Eisleben) or he ushered in the Reformation from there (Wittenberg). During the Reformation, Luther went into hiding in Eisenach's Wartburg castle. The region has some great landscapes, with the bucolic Thuringian Forest – best known for its excellent hiking trails – the picturesque riverside vineyards of the Saale-Unstrut region (famous for its sparkling and red wines) and the Harz Mountains (brimming with spa towns). The Harz is also known for its excellent cross-country skiing and hiking in mixed deciduous and conifer forests.

When to Go

Spring or summer is the best time, because the museums and sights have long opening hours, the leafless landscapes lose their brown tones and burst back to life, and the hiking and cycling are at their finest. An exception is the Harz, where cross-country skiing or hikes on skis are popular in winter. The Saale-Unstrut wine region, the Harz and the Thuringian Forest are picturesque and colourful in autumn if the weather plays along, and for anyone dressed for conditions, hiking here can be invigorating on a snappy winter's day under blue skies and upon frozen ground.

Central Germany Highlights

1 Spend an hour chasing the water as it cascades down the slope from Kassel's towering **Herkules statue** (p532)

2 Study the origins of modernist architecture by touring Dessau's **Bauhaus** (p584) gems

3 Hike to the top of the highest mountain in the Harz, the **Brocken** (p572), and soak up the kitsch mythology of the region

4 Explore the mining history of the Harz region in Goslar or visit the town's medieval **Kaiserpfalz** (p565) residence

5 Walk in the footsteps of Martin Luther in **Eisleben** (p594) and **Wittenberg** (p578)

6 Sample the local product while hopping between small wine estates around **Freyburg** (p563)

7 Check out the medieval musical instruments at Jörg Dahms' Lutherstadt Wittenberg **workshop** (p582) or visit Halle's **Beatles Museum** (p592)

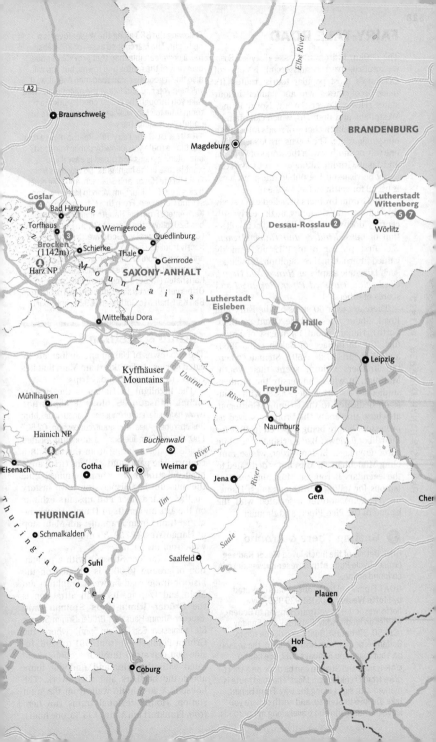

FAIRY-TALE ROAD

The 600km **Märchenstrasse** (Fairy-Tale Road; www.deutsche-maerchenstrasse.com) is one of Germany's most popular tourist routes. It's made up of cities, towns and hamlets in four states (Hesse, Lower Saxony, North Rhine-Westphalia and Bremen), which can often be reached by using a choice of roads rather than one single route. The towns are associated in one way or another with the works of Wilhelm and Jakob Grimm. Although most towns can easily be visited using public transport, a car is useful for getting a feel for the route.

The Grimm brothers travelled extensively through central Germany in the early 19th century documenting folklore. Their collection of tales, *Kinder- und Hausmärchen*, was first published in 1812 and quickly gained international recognition. It includes such fairy-tale staples as *Hansel and Gretel, Cinderella, The Pied Piper, Rapunzel* and scores of others.

There are over 60 stops on the Fairy-Tale Road. Major ones include (from south to north): Hanau, about 15km east of Frankfurt, the birthplace of Jakob (1785–1863) and Wilhelm (1786–1859); Steinau, where the Brothers Grimm spent their youth; Marburg, in whose university the brothers studied for a short while; Kassel, with a museum dedicated to the Grimms; Göttingen, at whose university the brothers served as professors before being expelled in 1837 for their liberal views; Bad Karlshafen, a white baroque village; Bodenwerder, whose rambling Münchhausen Museum is dedicated to the legendary Baron von Münchhausen, (in)famous for telling outrageous tales; Hamelin (Hameln), forever associated with the legend of the Pied Piper; and Bremen.

ⓘ Getting There & Around

BIKE Details of the much-loved **Weser Radweg** (Weser Cycle Path; http://weser-radweg.de) can be found online.

BOAT From April to October, boats operated by **Flotte Weser** (☏05151-939 999; www.flotte-weser.de) travel from Hamelin to Bodenwerder on Wednesday, Saturday and Sunday (€13.50, 3½ hours). Boats also do the run to Bodenwerder to/from Holzminden in the season on Thursdays and Sundays (€17, five hours).

CAR Hanau and Steinau can be done on a short drive from Frankfurt am Main. The road route is marked with signs along the way. From Hanau, take the A66 to Steinau, and north of here you leave the autobahn and travel along minor roads.

Following the B83 along the Weser River is a highlight. The Märchenstrasse (p528) website has a downloadable map that provides a good overview of the routes and towns, but you will also find a good German road map useful, as it will help you find and follow the minor roads that take you through the nicest countryside. Factor in time to stop, walk around and explore the countryside along the way.

TRAIN & BUS The Fairy-Tale Road is more a road trip than a route you follow by public transport, but catching trains and buses is easy if you want to take in the highlights. Do day trips from Frankfurt to Hanau and Steinach, and take other trains from Frankfurt am Main to Marburg, Kassel and Göttingen. From there, trains run to Bad Karlshafen. From the Hauptbahnhof at Hamelin, bus 520 follows the Weser to/from Holzminden (€11.65, 1½ hours) via Bodenwerder (€6.05) hourly from 6.50am to 7.50pm during the week and every couple of hours on weekends. From Holzminden at least five trains leave daily for Bad Karlshafen (€7.50, 50 minutes), with a change at Ottbergen. Direct trains run every two hours from Bad Karlshafen to Göttingen (€9.55, one hour).

Hanau & Steinau

The two towns of Hanau and Steinau are located so close to Frankfurt am Main that it is easiest to visit them on day trips.

The highlight in Hanau is the **Historisches Museum Schloss Philippsruhe** (www.hanau.de/kultur/museen/hanau/index.htm; Philippsruher Allee 45; adult/concession €2.50/1.50; ⏰11am-6pm Tue-Sun), a museum located inside a palace dating from the early 18th century. The parks and gardens (free) are a beautiful stroll in snow or in summer, while the museum has displays on town history on the ground floor and upstairs exhibits on the arts and crafts in Hanau. Hourly regional trains from Frankfurt am Main stop at Hanau West (€7.50, 30 minutes), a short walk from the palace.

Steinau (an der Strasse), with a population of around 10,000, is situated on the historic trade road between Frankfurt am Main and Leipzig. Its main attraction is the **Brüder-Grimm-Haus Steinau** (www.Brueder-Grimm-Haus.de; Brüder-Grimm-Strasse 80; admission €3; ⏰10am-5pm), where the Grimm family lived from 1791 to 1796. Inside you can stroll through sections decorated with the tales and find out more about the brothers and their work. The house is a 20-minute walk from the train station. Hourly regional trains run here from Frankfurt am Main (€13.50, one hour).

Marburg

06421 / POP 80,600

Hilly and historic, the university town of Marburg is situated some 90km north of Frankfurt. Narrow lanes wind through its vibrant Altstadt (old town), which has a castle above it and a spectacular Gothic church below. Founded in 1527, Philipps-Universität – the world's oldest Protestant university – once counted the Brothers Grimm among its students, of whom there are now 18,000. Thanks to them you'll find some relaxed cafes and nightspots.

◎ Sights & Activities

Elisabethkirche CHURCH
(www.elisabethkirche.de; Elisabethstrasse; adult/concession €2/1.50; ⊙9am-6pm) Built between 1235 and 1283, and later given its two high spires, the Protestant Elisabethkirche is considered to be Germany's earliest pure-Gothic church. The highlight inside is the Hohe Chor (high choir), where you can see beautiful Gothic stained glass behind an astounding stone Hochaltar (high altar). The cathedral also houses the elegant Elisabeth-Schrein (Elisabeth Shrine), dedicated to St Elisabeth, whose burial here made the church a site of pilgrimage in the Middle Ages. The church is located about 100m south of Bahnhofstrasse.

Altstadt NEIGHBOURHOOD
One of the nicest things to do in Marburg is to stroll around the small Altstadt. Its focal point is the Marktplatz; on the south side is the historic Rathaus (1512). From there it's a steep climb to the Lutheran St-Marien-Kirche, an imposing red-brick church with great views over the lower town. The terrace on the south side is the place to come at sunrise, particularly on weekends, when you'll often be joined by a motley crowd of students, late-night drinkers, early-morning dog walkers and rough sleepers. At the base of the Altstadt's Reitgasse are the Universitätskirche (early 1300s), a former Dominican monastery, and the neo-Gothic Alte Universität (1891), still a well-used and well-loved part of the university.

Landgrafenschloss CASTLE
(Landgraves' Castle; www.uni-marburg.de/uni-museum; Schloss 1; adult/concession €4/3; ⊙10am-6pm Tue-Sun) Perched at the highest point in town, a steep walk up from St-Marien-Kirche or the Marktplatz, is the huge Margrave Castle, built between 1248 and 1300. It offers panoramic views of bucolic hills, jumbled Marburg rooftops and the Schlosspark, whose amphitheatre hosts concerts and open-air films. The museum inside the castle has exhibits on cultural history from prehistoric to modern times.

Universitätsmuseum für Bildende Kunst GALLERY
(University Fine Arts Museum; 282 2355; www.uni-marburg.de/uni-museum; Biegenstrasse 11) Focuses on 20th-century art. Closed until 2014.

FREE Marburger Kunstverein GALLERY
(www.marburger-kunstverein.de; Biegenstrasse 1; ⊙11am-5pm Tue & Thu-Sun, to 8pm Wed) Temporary exhibits of contemporary art.

Synagoge SYNAGOGUE
(Willy-Sage-Platz) These excavated remains of a 13th- and 14th-century synagogue are under a giant glass cube.

Boating BOAT HIRE
Row boats and pedal boats (per hour €8) can be hired on the east bank of the Lahn, just south of Weidenhäuser Brücke.

🛌 Sleeping

Hostaria Del Castello HOTEL $
(243 02; www.del-castello.de; Marktplatz 19; s €49-74, d €69-95) In the thick of things, 50m up the hill from the Markt, this Italian-run establishment has seven rooms and a downstairs restaurant.

Stadthotel Marburg HOTEL $$
(685 880; www.village-hotels.de; Bahnhofstrasse 14; s/d/tr from €79/99/129; P@) The functional, modern furnishings at this family-run place are pleasant, if bland. Ask for a room away from the busy street.

Hotel am Schlossberg HOTEL $$
(9180; www.welcome-hotels.com; Pilgrimstein 29; s €90-110, d €110-130; ❈@✿) Just below the Altstadt, this hotel has 147 bright, spacious rooms with large windows.

DJH Hostel HOSTEL $
(234 61; www.jugendherberge.de; Jahnstrasse 1; dm €21, s with/without bathroom € 33/31, d with/without bathroom €56/52; @✿) This clean, well-run youth hostel is located 500m south of the centre on the river and the Lahntal Radweg (Lahntal Bike Route). Staff can help plan outings, rent canoes and arrange bike hire. Take bus 3 to the Auf der Weide bus stop.

✕ Eating

TOP CHOICE Café Barfuss   CAFE **$**

(Barfüsserstrasse 33; meals €5-8; ⏱10am-1am; ✍)
This off-beat place attracts a sociable student crowd and serves up good vegetarian
dishes.

KostBar   HEALTH FOOD **$$**

(www.kostbar-marburg.de; Barfüsserstrasse 7; mains
€6.90-15.90; ⏱10am-1am; ✍) This modern res-
taurant and bar offers well-prepared soups,
salads, potatoes, vegie dishes, fish and
meats, all concocted from a creative blend
of ingredients.

Local Central   GERMAN **$$**

(Marktplatz 11; mains €6.90-16.90; ⏱9.30am-mid-
night) The service here is young and friendly, the rump steak is especially delicious,
and the room warbles with the sounds of
lively conversation. The kitchen is open all
day.

🍸 Drinking & Entertainment

For listings, look no further than the free
Marburger Magazin Express (www.marbuch
-verlag.de).

Delirium mit Frazzkeller   PUB

(Steinweg 3; ⏱8pm-3am) Delirium is upstairs,
Frazzkeller is downstairs – both of these
student hang-outs scream '1970s' and have
great views over the Unterstadt (yes, even
from the cellar). The house drink is Roter
Korn, a redcurrant liqueur.

Café Vetter   CAFE

(Reitgasse 4; chocolate cake €2.80; ⏱9am-6pm)
The same family has been tending to tipplers
in this tearoom for five generations, amid
wicker-back chairs and classic 1970s lamps.
The house-speciality chocolate cream cake is
best enjoyed with the fine panoramas.

Hugo's   BAR

(www.hugos-marburg.de; Gerhard-Jahn-Platz 21a;
⏱9am-midnight Mon-Fri, from 10am Sat & Sun; 🛜)
This modern, Lahn-side beer garden, bar
and finger-food place offers watery views
through glass walls.

Jazzclub Cavete   JAZZ

(www.jazzini.de; Steinweg 12; ⏱8pm-1am or 2am)
A prime port of call for jazz-lovers, with
open-stage nights (no cover charge) on Monday and frequent concerts.

ℹ️ Information

Post Office (Bahnhofstrasse 6)

Tourist Office (☎991 20; www.marburg.de;
Pilgrimstein 26; ⏱9am-6pm Mon-Fri, 10am-
2pm Sat) Books inexpensive private rooms and
has free maps of town. In summer an information point is also open on the Markt.

ℹ️ Getting There & Away

BICYCLE The 245km Lahntal Radweg runs
along the Lahn all the way to the Rhine.

CAR From Marburg the next major stop on the
Fairy-Tale Road is Kassel. Follow the B3/B62
north out of town towards Neustadt and Bad Wildungen for the Nationalpark Kellerwald-Edersee
or Fritzlar (direct route) to Kassel.

TRAIN Frequent connections with Frankfurt am
Main (€22, one hour, frequent) and Kassel (€24,
one hour).

ℹ️ Getting Around

BICYCLE Velociped (☎886 890;
www.velociped.de; Alte Kasseler Strasse 43;
touring bikes per day €10; ⏱9am-5.30pm Mon-
Fri), located 400m north of the Hauptbahnhof,
organises individual and guided cycling tours
and rents out bicycles.

BUS The Hauptbahnhof is linked to Rudolphs-
platz (where Pilgrimstein meets Universitätsstrasse) by buses 2 and 6.

LIFT About 100m north of the tourist office, **free
lifts** (inside Parkhaus Oberstadt, Pilgrimstein;
⏱6am-2am) whisk you up to Wettergasse in
the Altstadt. A thigh-toughening alternative is
nearby Enge Gasse, a monstrously steep stone
staircase that was once a sewage sluice.

Fulda

📞0661 / POP 65,000

Although it's not on the Fairy-Tale Road,
Fulda is well worth a side trip for those interested in baroque architecture, historic
churches and religious reliquaries. A Benedictine monastery was founded here in
744, and today Fulda has its own bishop.
The Hauptbahnhof is about 600m east of
the main sights, at the northeastern end of
Bahnhofstrasse.

👁 Sights

Stadtschloss   CASTLE

(Town Castle; ☎102 1469) Across the street from
the tourist office, the Stadtschloss was built
from 1706 to 1721 as the residence of Fulda's
prince-abbots. It now houses the city administration and function rooms. Worth visiting

are the ornate **Historische Räume** (Historic Room; adult/student €3.50/2.30; ☺10am-5pm Mon-Thu, to 2pm Fri), which is a grandiose banquet hall, and the octagonal **Schlossturm** (Tower; ☺Apr-Oct) for great views of the town and the baroque and English-style **Schlossgarten** (palace gardens), where locals play *pétanque* (boules) and sunbathe in summer. On its northern edge are the baroque **Floravase** sculpture and the neoclassical **Orangerie** (now occupied by the Maritim Hotel).

Dom   CHURCH
(Cathedral; ☺10am-6pm Mon-Fri, to 3pm Sat, 1pm-6pm Sun) Inside the baroque Dom, built from 1704 to 1712, you'll find gilded furnishings, plenty of *putti* (figures of infant boys), some dramatic statues (eg to the left of the altar) and the tomb of St Boniface, who died a martyr in 754. There are **organ recitals** (www.orgelmusik.bistum-fulda.de; adult/concession €3.50/2.50) here at noon every Saturday during May, June, September, October and December.

Dommuseum   MUSEUM
(adult/student €2.10/1.30; ☺10am-5.30pm Tue-Sat, 12.30-5.30pm Sun) Reached through a delightful garden, reliquaries include the spectacular Silver Altar and a spooky object reported to be part of the skull of St Boniface.

Michaelskirche   CHURCH
(☺10am-6pm) The rotunda and crypt are 9th-century Carolingian.

🛏 Sleeping & Eating
Wiesenmühle   HOTEL $$
(☎928 680; www.wiesenmuehle.de; Wiesenmühlenstrasse 13; s €63, d €83-93; P🖤) Situated four blocks down the hill (southwest) of the Stadtschloss on the banks of the Fulda, this one-time mill is a hotel with beer garden, restaurant (mains €8 to €20, open 11am to 2.30pm and 5.30pm to 11pm), a waterwheel and copper vats for brewing house beers.

Hotel Goldener Karpfen   HOTEL $$$
(☎868 00; http://www.hotel-goldener-karpfen.de; Simpliziusbrunnen 1; s €115-155, d €165-250, ste €280-450; P🖤@🖤) An elegant, historic hotel with traditional and designer rooms (only the designer rooms have air-conditioning), and a restaurant (mains €16 to €32, open 11am to 11pm).

ℹ Information
Tourist Office (☎102 1813; www.tourismus-fulda.de; Bonifatiusplatz 1; ☺8.30am-6pm Mon-Fri, 9.30am-4pm Sat & Sun) Near Fulda's Stadtschloss.

ℹ Getting There & Around
BIKE Bike path options are signposted down by the river. **Hahner Zweiradtechnik** (☎933 9944; www.hahner-zweirad.de; Beethovenstrasse 3; touring/mountain bikes per day €12/20; ☺9am-6pm Mon-Fri, 9am-1pm Sat) rents out bicycles.

TRAIN Frequent ICE connections with Frankfurt am Main (€30, one hour), Kassel (€30, 30 minutes) and Erfurt (€37, 1¼ hours).

Nationalpark Kellerwald-Edersee

Hesse's first **national park** (www.nationalpark-kellerwald-edersee.de), established in 2004, encompasses one of the largest extant red beech forests in Central Europe – the **Kellerwald** – in addition to the **Edersee**, a serpentine artificial reservoir 55km northeast of Marburg and about the same distance southwest of Kassel. In 2011 this national park, along with Hainich National Park in Thuringia and a cluster of other parks or reserves with large beech forests, became a Unesco World Cultural Heritage site.

For information and insights into the area's ecosystems, head to the **NationalparkZentrum** (☎05635-992 781; www.nationalparkzentrum-kellerwald.de; B252, Vöhl-Herzhausen; e-bikes per day €19; ☺10am-6pm Apr-Oct, to 5pm Nov-Mar), a striking modern visitors centre at the western end of the Edersee, on the northern edge of Kirchlotheim. Here and at other points you can rent e-bikes and ride around the lake on a comfortable day tour, changing the battery at points along the way. Bike trails also run through the forest itself.

The national park's lush forests and flowery meadows offer excellent hiking. Hiking trails include the **Kellerwaldsteig** (marked 'K') and the **Urwaldsteig-Edersee** (marked 'UE'). Shorter hiking circuits include animal or plant icons. The lake has swimming, canoeing and sailing.

The park is easiest to visit if you've got your own wheels but public transport using the local **Nordhessische Verkehrsbund** (☎0180 234 0180; www.nvv.de) is also an option. Buses lead into the park from the train stations in Bad Wildungen, Frankenberg and from Korbach, which is linked to Kassel-Wilhelmshöhe by the RE04 train. Bus 555 (runs every hour or two Monday to Friday, six times on Saturday, two or three times on Sunday and holidays) links the NationalparkZentrum with both Frankenberg and Korbach. A one-way ticket with the train and bus from Kassel to Korbach-Süd and on to the national park office costs €13; the trip takes 2¾ hours. Bus 521 goes from Bad Wildungen to the Edersee.

Kassel

📞 0561 / POP 195.500

Although wartime bombing and postwar reconstruction have left Kassel with lots of unattractive 1950s buildings, visitors to this city on the Fulda River will find a glorious baroque park – Schlosspark Wilhelmshöhe – and several interesting and unusual museums.

Most of the museums are located in the centre, whereas Wilhelmshöhe and its attractions are at the western end of 4.5km-long Wilhelmshöher Allee, which runs straight as an arrow from the centre, westward to the Schloss.

◉ Sights

CENTRE

Neue Galerie GALLERY
(www.museum-kassel.de; Schöne Aussicht 1; adult/concession €4/2; ⊙10am-5pm Tue-Wed & Fri-Sun, to 8pm Thu) The recently restored Neue Galerie showcases paintings and sculptures by German artists from 1750 to the present, as well as exhibits from past dOCUMENTA exhibitions.

Brüder Grimm-Museum MUSEUM
(Museum of the Brothers Grimm; www.grimms.de; Schöne Aussicht 2; adult/children €3/free; ⊙10am-5pm, to 8pm Wed) Wilhelm and Jakob Grimm began compiling folk stories while living in Kassel. Their lives and stories are told in a recently revamped permanent exhibiton, complemented by changing exhibitions on the ground floor.

Museum für Sepulkralkultur MUSEUM
(Museum of Sepulchral Culture; www.sepulkral museum.de; Weinbergstrasse 25-27; adult/child €6/4; ⊙10am-5pm Tue & Thu-Sun, to 8pm Wed) Billed as 'a meditative space for funerary art', this museum aims at burying the taboo of discussing death. The permanent collection includes headstones, hearses, dancing skeleton bookends and sculptures depicting death. Take trams 1 or 3 to Weigelstrasse.

Museum Fridericianum MUSEUM
(www.fridericianum-kassel.de; Friedrichsplatz 18) Has changing exhibitions.

Documenta Halle GALLERY
(www.documentahalle.de; Du-Ry-Strasse 1) Changing exhibitions on modern art.

WILHELMSHÖHE

Schlosspark Wilhelmshöhe PARK
(Wilhelmshöhe; www.museum-kassel.de; ⊙Teufelsbrücke 3.10pm, Aquädukt 3.20pm, Grosse Fontäne 3.30pm) Situated 7km west of the centre, in the enchanting Habichtswald (Hawk Forest nature park), this spectacular baroque parkland takes its name from Schloss Wilhelmshöhe, the late-18th-century palace situated inside the expanse. You can spend an entire day here walking through the forest, enjoying a romantic picnic and exploring the castles, fountains, grottoes and a massive 8.25m-high copper **Herkules statue** (adult/concession €3/2.25; ⊙10am-5pm Tue-Sun mid-Mar–mid-Nov) atop a towering stone pyramid atop an octagonal amphitheatre atop an imposing hill, 600m above sea level. Erected between 1707 and 1717, the statue offers spectacular views over the park. A one-hour water cascade known as the **Wasserspiele** takes place every Wednesday, Sunday and public holidays from May to 3 October. The water begins its tumble at 2.30pm from up top, near Herkules. From there, you can walk down via the **Teufelsbrücke** (Devil's Bridge) and the **Aquädukt** to the **Grosse Fontäne** (Large Fountain) to watch the water emerge in a 50m-high jet.

Schloss Wilhelmshöhe MUSEUM, PALACE
(www.museum-kassel.de; Schlosspark Wilhelmshöhe; Gemäldegalerie adult/concession €6/2; ⊙10am-5pm Tue-Sun) Home to Elector Wilhelm and later Kaiser Wilhelm II, Wilhelmshöhe Palace (1786–98) at the foot of the Wilhelmshöhe Schlosspark today houses one of Germany's best art collections (especially of Flemish and Dutch baroque painting). It features works by Rembrandt, Rubens, Jordaens, Lucas Cranach the Elder, Dürer and many others in the Gemäldegalerie (painting gallery). The 23 rooms of the **Weissensteinflügel** (adult/concession €4/2; ⊙tours hourly 10am-4pm Tue-Sun) wing comprise the oldest part of the palace, dating from 1790, and are filled with original furnishings and paintings. The **Antikensammlung** is an excellent collection of Egyptian, Etruscan, Greek and Roman statuary and vases.

🛏 Sleeping

The tourist office books private rooms from around €25.

Schlosshotel Bad Wilhelmshöhe   HOTEL $$
(☎30 880; www.schlosshotel-kassel.de; Schlosspark 8; s €79-129, d €99-149, ste €199-299; P🐕🛜) Situated a stone's throw from Kassel's prime attractions, Schlosspark Wilhelmshöhe and Schloss Wilhelmshöhe, this hotel is built in the Bauhaus style but is rather unflattering from the outside. Inside, however, it has stylish, comfortable rooms with large windows. Take tram 1 to the terminus.

Hotel Domus   HOTEL $$
(☎703 330; www.markhoteldomus.de; Erzbergerstrasse 1-5; s €59-99, d €69-109; P@🛜) Quality hotel with bright, modern rooms situated 500m northeast of Kassel Hauptbahnhof or 600m north of Scheidemannplatz. Take bus 52 or tram 7 from Kassel-Wilhelmshöhe train station to Scheidemannplatz.

DJH Hostel   HOSTEL $
(☎776 455; www.jugendherberge.de; Schenkendorfstrasse 18; dm/s €22.90/32.90; P@🛜) Situated about 1km west of Kassel Hauptbahnhof, or you can take tram 4 or 7 from Königsplatz to Queralee.

🍴 Eating & Drinking

The free monthly *Frizz* (www.frizz-kassel.de) has listings.

TOP
CHOICE Restaurant Santé
& Gourmet   GERMAN $$$
(☎940 480; Konrad-Adenauer-Strasse 117; €10-28; ☺Santé lunch & dinner, Gourmet dinner Wed-Sat) Santé is the mainstay of two quality restaurants inside the Zum Steinernen Schweinchen hotel, under the tutelage of the highly acclaimed chef Jürgen Richter; the other restaurant, Gourmet, is more eclectic. They're 5km southwest of Kassel-Wilhelmshöhe station (take bus 51 or 52 to the stop Brasselsberg).

Lohmann   GERMAN $
(www.lohmann-kassel.de; Königstor 8; mains €7-16; ☺11am-1am, closed lunch Sat) With roots that go back to 1888, this family-run *Kneipe* (pub) has an old-style birch- and maple-shaded beer garden with an outdoor grill. Schnitzel (always pork) features heavily on

---

ⓘ GETTING TO SCHLOSSPARK WILHELMSHÖHE

Getting to Kassel's palace park is very easy. Tram 1 to the Wilhelmshöhe terminus drops you near the the park itself if you just want to stroll around. To get to the Herkules statue, take tram 3 to the Druseltal terminus and then bus 22 (runs once or twice an hour from 8am to 7pm or 8pm) to the Herkules stop. To reach Schloss Wilhelmshöhe, you can either walk down from the hilltop Herkules statue or, from the city, take tram 1 to the Wilhelmshöhe terminus. From there it's a short walk, or you can take bus 23 for one stop.

---

the menu. Situated five blocks southwest of Kassel Hauptbahnhof.

Bolero   MEXICAN $
(www.bolerobar.de; Schöne Aussicht 1a; mains €7.90-13; ☺10am-midnight Mon-Fri, 9am-1am Sat & Sun) This sleek and modern restaurant is part of a chain serving Tex-Mex and Mediterranean dishes – the menu is enormous and there are lots of cocktails. It's situated behind Kassel's Neue Galerie.

Cafe-Bar Suspekt   GAY
(www.cafe-suspekt.de; Fünffensterstrasse 14; ☺6pm-1am Tue-Thu, 1pm-2am Fri & Sat, 1pm-1am Sun) This hetero-friendly gay bar, painted in primary colours, has hip marble tables and mellow music. Situated five blocks south of Kassel Hauptbahnhof, at the southwestern edge of the pedestrian zone.

ⓘ Information

Kassel Card (1 or 2 people for 24/72hr €13/16, 4 people €18/23) Gets you discounts on attractions and free use of public transport. Sold only at the tourist office. An excellent deal.

Mercur Spielothek (Wilhelmshöher Allee 256; per hr €3; ☺11am-2am) Internet, opposite Kassel-Wilhelmshöhe train station.

Tourist office There are tourist information offices at the Kassel-Wilhelmshöhe **train station** (☎340 54; www.kassel-tourist.de; Kassel-Wilhelmshöhe train station; ☺9am-6pm Mon-Fri, to 2pm Sat) and **Rathaus** (☎707 707; Obere Königsstrasse 8; ☺9am-6pm Mon-Fri, to 2pm Sat).

ℹ️ Getting There & Away

Kassel has two main train stations. Kassel Hauptbahnhof, on the northwest edge of the city centre, is served by regional (RE) trains, while the more important Kassel-Wilhelmshöhe (Fernbahnhof), 3km west of the centre, handles both regional and IC/ICE trains. ICE or IC connections from Kassel-Wilhelmshöhe include Fulda (€30, 30 minutes), Marburg (€19, one hour), Göttingen (€19.50, 18 minutes) and Frankfurt am Main (€51, 1½ hours).

ℹ️ Getting Around

BICYCLE You can rent city and trekking bikes and buy bike maps at **Fahrradhof** (☎313 083; www.fahrradhof.de; per 24hr/week €10/50; ⏰9am-1pm & 2-6.30pm Mon-Fri, 9am-3pm Sat), on the east side of Kassel-Wilhelmshöhe train station, just past track 11.

TRAM Tram 1 runs the length of Wilhelmshöher Allee, linking the city centre with Wilhelmshöhe. Trams 1, 3 and 4 go from Kassel-Wilhelmshöhe train station to the centre. Almost all the city's tram lines stop at Königsplatz.

Göttingen

☎0551 / POP 121,500

Though short on sights, this historic town nestled in a corner of Lower Saxony near the Hesse border offers a good taste of university-town life in Germany's north. Since 1734, the year the Georg-August Universität was established here, Göttingen has sent more than 40 Nobel Prize winners into the world.

As well as all those award-winning doctors and scientists, alumni include the fairy-tale-writing Brothers Grimm (who worked here as German linguistic teachers) and Prussian chancellor Otto von Bismarck (who attended as a student).

◎ Sights & Activities

Gänseliesel   MONUMENT
The city's symbol, the Gänseliesel (little goose girl) statue, located on the Markt, is hailed locally as the most kissed woman in the world. Not a flattering moniker, you might think, but enough to make her iconic. After graduating, doctoral students climb up to peck her on the cheek.

Altes Rathaus   HISTORIC BUILDING
(Markt; ⏰9.30am-6pm Mon-Sat, 10am-4pm Sun) The Altes Rathaus was built in 1270 and once housed the merchants' guild. Inside, later decorations added to its Great Hall include frescos of the coats of arms of the Hanseatic cities and local bigwigs, grafted onto historic scenes.

Göttinger Wald   FOREST
Göttinger Wald (Göttingen Forest) is one of the best mixed forest stands of predominantly beech and oak in the region. It's easily reached by following Herzberger Landstrasse east from the centre of town to the point near where it forms a hairpin bend, and turning into Borheckstrasse. From there, a bitumen track open to hikers and cyclists winds towards Am Kehr, 45 minutes away, where there's a small Bavarian-style beer garden open in summer and weekends when the weather is good, and a small game enclosure with snorting wild boars and Bambis.

Bismarckturm   TOWER
(www.bismarcktuerme.de; adult/concession €2/1; ⏰11am-6pm weekends & holidays Apr-Sep) From Am Kehr, a path leads to the Bismarckturm, a stone tower with pretty views over the Leine Valley.

Schillerwiese Park   PARK
(Merkelstrasse) Göttingen's largest park backs onto forest. To reach it, follow Herzberger Landstrasse east for 20 minutes, then turn right into Merkelstrasse.

Junkernschänke   HISTORIC BUILDING
(Barfüsser-strasse 5) The colourful 16th-century Renaissance facade makes this the finest of local half-timbered houses.

Haus Börner   HISTORIC BUILDING
(Barfüsserstrasse 12) A house built in 1536, with the interesting Börnerviertel alley behind it.

City Wall   WALKING
The town wall has been converted into an attractive path, lined with trees, that takes you past **Bismarckhäuschen** (Bismarck Cottage; between Nikolai & Angerstrasse), where the city fathers reputedly banished 18-year-old Otto for rowdy behaviour in 1833. Nearby are two old **water mills**.

✨ Festivals & Events

The **Händel Festival**, held in late May or early June, will interest those keen on music. Enquire about tickets at the tourist office.

🛌 Sleeping

TOP CHOICE Gebhards Hotel   HOTEL $$$
(📞496 80; www.romantikhotels.com/goettingen; Goetheallee 22-23; s €119-169, d €173-248; 🅿@🛜) This quaint, elegant four-star hotel has art-deco touches, wellness facilities like a large whirlpool and small sauna, and a 24-hour bar in its excellent restaurant. You can take breakfast any time of day here, so it's actually possible to stay up all night in the bar sipping champagne, sleep all day, sweat in the sauna, plunge into the whirlpool, and breakfast in the evening, if that's your style.

Hotel Stadt Hannover   HOTEL $$
(📞547 960; www.hotelstadthannover.de; Goetheallee 21; s €82-102, d €116-126, tr €168-177; 🅿@🛜) Beyond the art nouveau etched-glass door and quaint entrance hall here, you'll find modern, comfortable rooms with free wi-fi. There's a choice of bathtub or shower. Prices vary according to the size of the room and standard of furnishings.

Kasseler Hof   HOTEL $$
(📞720 812; www.kasselerhof.de; Rosdorfer Weg 26; s €57-61, d €83-93; 🅿) This appealing alternative to more expensive places in town is located outside the centre but within easy walking distance. Rooms are modern and refurbished.

Hotel Central   HOTEL $$
(📞571 57; www.hotel-central.com; Jüdenstrasse 12; s €79-85, d €99-190; 🅿🛜) The more-expensive rooms here have baths not shower cubicles, while those at the top of the doubles range are junior suites. Free wi-fi access is available in all but a couple of rooms (ask ahead if this is important).

DJH Hostel   HOSTEL $
(📞576 22; www.djh-niedersachsen.de/jh/goettingen; Habichtsweg 2; dm under/over 27yr €24/28, s €26/30, d €50/58; 🅿@🛜) In a pleasant spot about 3km east of the centre, this large, slightly older hostel is popular with cyclists and youth groups. To get here, take bus 6 or 9 to Jugendherberge.

🍴 Eating & Drinking

TOP CHOICE Gauss   GERMAN $$$
(📞566 16; www.restaurant-gauss.de; Obere Karspüle 22, enter on Theaterstrasse; 3-5-course menu €38-61; ⏰6pm-midnight Tue-Sat; 🅿) This is Göttingen's finest gourmet experience, with exquisite (and changing) haute cuisine from chef Jaqueline Amirfallah; there's an emphasis on seasonal ingredients.

Myer's   INTERNATIONAL $
(Lange-Geismar-Strasse 47; dishes €5-16; ⏰9am-midnight Mon-Sat, 10am-11pm Sun, closed Sun Jul-Aug; 🅿) This rambling cafe-bar and restaurant is great if you can handle the noise. Every now and again the skilled chefs whip up a delicious surprise or two to complement pastas, salads, pancakes, pizzas and vegetarian or meat dishes that feature on its large year-round (or smaller seasonal) menus. Smokers can sit upstairs.

Einstein   INTERNATIONAL $$
(www.meineinstein.de; Kurze Geismarstrasse 9; €7-20; ⏰11-1am Mon-Thu, 10-2am Fri, 10-2am Sat, 10-1am Sun) Attracting a mixed crowd, many of whom cruise in from satellite towns, Einstein has an OK atmosphere and chefs who prepare good homemade pasta, meats of all types, burgers and salads.

Junkernschänke   GERMAN $$
(www.junkernschaenke.de/; Barfüsserstrasse 5; lunch special €7, mains €12-27; ⏰11.30am-11pm Mon-Thu, to 1am Fri & Sat, noon-3pm & 6pm-10pm Sun; 🅿) Behind the colourful timbers of one of the city's oldest buildings, you find a restaurant and an upstairs lounge where you can hang off the bar in fine style, sipping delicious wines and more. Food is well-prepared traditional fare, including game and sometimes kangaroo and bison steaks, all served in moderately sized portions. It has frequent events Fridays and Saturdays.

Cron & Lanz   CAFE $
(Weender Strasse 25; cake €3.50; ⏰8.30am-7pm Mon-Sat, 1pm-6.30pm Sun) This ornate Viennese-style cafe is Göttingen's dignified haunt for connoisseurs of chocolate and other calorie bombs.

TOP CHOICE Apex   PUB
(www.apex-goe.de; Burgstrasse 46; light dishes €7-12; ⏰from 5.30pm Mon-Sat) Apex is a trumvirate of art gallery, performance venue and – since Jaqueline Amirfallah from Gauss, the town's best restaurant, took over the kitchen – an eatery serving quality light dishes. The winter goulash is highly recommended, and the wines are top quality.

Monster   BAR
(Goetheallee 13a; ⏰11am-midnight Mon-Thu, to 1.30am Fri & Sat, noon-midnight Sun) Lively student bar with an arty edge. While on Goetheallee, also

check out the other options near the small bridge.

☆ Entertainment

Savoy CLUB
(www.club-savoy.de; Berliner Strasse 5; entry €4-8; ⊙Wed, Fri & Sat) Göttingen's leading nightclub plays mainstream and house music; it's spread over a couple of levels.

Junges Theater THEATRE
(✆495 015; www.junges-theater.de; Hospitalstrasse 6) Göttingen's Junges Theater has been on the scene since the late 1950s and enjoys a high reputation throughout Germany; this was where Switzerland's most famous contemporary actor, Bruno Gans, began his career.

ℹ Information

Post Office (Groner Strasse 15-17)

Tourist Office (✆499 800; www.goettingen -tourismus.de; Markt 9, Altes Rathaus; ⊙9.30am-6pm Mon-Sat, 10am-4pm Sun) Free bilingual English-German brochures describing walks.

Waschsalon (Ritterplan 3; per wash from €3.50; ⊙7am-10pm Mon-Sat)

ℹ Getting There & Away

CAR Göttingen is on the A7 running north– south. The closest entrance is 3km southwest along Kasseler Landstrasse, an extension of Groner Landstrasse. Pick up the B27 southwest to the Weser River and northeast to the Harz Mountains for Fairy-Tale Road towns.

TRAIN Frequent direct ICE services to Hanover (€33, 35 minutes), Kassel (€19.50, 18 minutes), Hamburg (€64, two hours), Frankfurt (€61, 1¾ hours), Munich (€106, 3¾ hours) and Berlin-Hauptbahnhof (€77, 2¼ hours). Direct regional services go to Kassel (€14.40, one hour), Weimar (€28.30, two hours) and Goslar (€16.40, 1¼ hours).

ℹ Getting Around

Bikes can be hired from **Voss Fahrräder/ Parkhaus am Bahnhof** (✆488 759 13; Am Bahnhof; per day €11; ⊙5am-10pm Mon-Sat, 8am-11pm Sun). Single bus tickets cost €2, 24-hour tickets €4.60. For a taxi, call ✆340 34.

Bad Karlshafen

✆05672 / POP 3800
You'd be forgiven for thinking you'd stumbled into 18th-century France in this sleepy spa town. It's little wonder – Bad Karlshafen's orderly streets and whitewashed baroque buildings were built at that time for the local earl Karl by Huguenot refugees. The town was planned with an impressive harbour and a canal connecting the Weser with the Rhine to attract trade, but the earl died before his designs were completed. All that exists today is a tiny *Hafenbecken* (harbour basin) trafficked only by white swans.

The town is small and easily covered on foot. Most of it lies on the south bank of the Weser River, with the *Hafenbecken* and surrounding square, Hafenplatz, at its western end.

To reach the **tourist office** (✆999 922; www.bad-karlshafen.de; Hafenplatz 8; ⊙9am-5pm Mon-Fri, 9.30am-noon Sat, 2.30-5pm Sun) from the Hauptbahnhof, follow the road left for a few minutes after exiting the station and cross the bridge, right, over the river. Turn right again on the other side and continue straight ahead to Hafenplatz.

Take a stroll around the *Hafenbecken* and pop into the **Deutsches Huguenotten Museum** (German Huguenot Museum; www.hugenot tenmuseum.de; Hafenplatz 9a; adult/concession €4/2; ⊙10am-5pm Tue-Sun, 11am-6pm Sat & Sun), which explains the history of the Huguenots in Germany.

🛏 Sleeping

Helmarshausen DJH Hostel HOSTEL $
(✆1027; www.djh-hessen.de/jh/helmarshausen; Gottsbürener Strasse 15; dm/s/d €19/26/47; P🖢) This hostel is 3km from Hafenplatz (take bus 180 to Helmarshausen-Mitte) in the suburb of Helmarshausen. It's situated on the edge of the forest and the forest trails in a lovely half-timbered building. There are cheaper singles and doubles with a shared bathroom.

Hotel-Pension Haus Fuhrhop HOTEL $
(✆404; www.pension-fuhrhop.de; Friedrichstrasse 15; s/d/tr €39/80/90) This charming *Pension* has spacious and comfortable rooms with a modern, stylish character, right in the centre of town.

Hotel zum Schwan HOTEL $$
(✆104 445; www.hotel-zum-schwan-badkarlshafen. de; Conradistrasse 3-4; s/d €48/86; P🖢) Earl Karl's former hunting lodge is now one of the better hotels in towns, with views of the harbour and a lovely rococo dining room. There's wi-fi in the bar.

Bodenwerder

📞 05533 / POP 5600

If Bodenwerder's most famous son were to have described his small hometown, he'd probably have painted it as a huge, thriving metropolis on the Weser River. But then Baron Hieronymous von Münchhausen (1720–97) was one of history's most shameless liars. He gave his name to a psychological condition – Münchhausen's syndrome, or compulsive exaggeration of physical illness – and inspired the cult film of British comedian Terry Gilliam, *The Adventures of Baron Munchausen*.

Bodenwerder's principal attraction is the **Münchhausen Museum** (📞409 147; Münchhausenplatz 1; adult/child €2.50/1.50; ☺10am-5pm Apr-Oct), which struggles a little with the difficult task of conveying the chaos and fun associated with the 'liar baron' – a man who liked to regale dinner guests with his Crimean adventures, claiming he had, for example, tied his horse to a church steeple during a snow drift and ridden around a dining table without breaking one teacup.

The museum houses a cannonball to illustrate the baron's most famous tale: he claimed to have hitched a lift on one in an attempt to spy on a battlefield enemy. It also has paintings and displays of Münchhausen books in many languages.

The **tourist office** (📞405 41; www.muenchhausenland.de; Münchhausenplatz 1; ☺9am-noon & 2-5pm Mon-Fri, 10am-12.30pm Sat) has information on canoe and bicycle hire in town, arranges accommodation and can answer other queries. No trains run to Bodenwerder.

Hamelin

📞 05151 / POP 57,800

If you have a phobia about rats, you might give this picturesque town on the Weser River a wide berth. According to *The Pied Piper of Hamelin* fairy tale, in the 13th century the Pied Piper (*Der Rattenfänger*) was employed by Hamelin's townsfolk to lure its nibbling rodents into the river. When they refused to pay him, he picked up his flute and led their kids away. Today the rats rule once again – rats that are stuffed, fluffy and cute, wooden rats, and even little rats that adorn the sights around town. In 2009 the town celebrated the 725th anniversary of the 'rat event', and since then work has been going on to revamp the centre. As well as having rats, Hamelin is a pleasant town with half-timbered houses and opportunities for cycling along the Weser River.

On the eastern bank of the Weser River lies Hamelin's circular Altstadt. The main streets are Osterstrasse, which runs east–west, and Bäckerstrasse, the north–south axis.

◉ Sights & Activities

Museum Hamelin   MUSEUM
(Osterstrasse 8-9; adult/concession €5/4; ☺11am-6pm Tue-Sun) Many of Hamelin's finest buildings were constructed in the Weser Renaissance style, which has strong Italian influences. Today two of the best provide the location for the town's revamped museum, which has an excellent permanent exhibition on regional history from the earliest times to the present. The two buildings are joined by a walkway. The **Leisthaus** at No 9 was built for a patrician grain trader in 1585–89, whereas the **Stiftsherrenhaus** dates from 1558 and is the only surviving building in Hamelin decorated with figures. It depicts two themes: one of planetary gods from classical times and the other of biblical figures.

Rattenfängerhaus   HISTORIC BUILDING
(Rat Catcher's House; Osterstrasse 28) Among the finest of the houses built in the ornamental Weser Renaissance style – prevalent throughout the Altstadt – is the Rattenfängerhaus, from 1602, with its typically steep and richly decorated gable.

Hochzeitshaus   HISTORIC BUILDING
(Osterstrasse 2) Situated on the corner of Markt and Osterstrasse is the Hochzeitshaus (1610–17), partly used today as city council offices and as a police station. The **Rattenfänger Glockenspiel** at the far end of the building chimes daily at 9.35am and 11.35am, while a carousel of Pied Piper figures twirls at 1.05pm, 3.35pm and 5.35pm.

Pferdemarkt   SQUARE
The heart of Hamelin is the Markt and its northern continuation, Pferdemarkt (Equestrian Square) where, during the Middle Ages, knights fought it out in tournaments. On the eastern side of Pferdemarkt is a sculpture by the eastern German artist Wolfgang Dreysse, *The Opening of the Iron Curtain*, dealing with the collapse of the East German border.

DON'T MISS

SOMETHING SPECIAL

Schlosshotel Münchhausen

(☎05154-706 00; www.schlosshotel -muenchhausen.com; Schwöbber 9, Aerzen bei Hameln; s/d in Tithe barn from €110/140, in castle from €135/180, ste €345-445; P❋) 15km outside Hamelin, is well worth staying at if you're driving through this region. As the name implies, it's set in a castle – the rooms are stylish and contemporary with historic touches, while the suites have tasteful period furnishings. Rooms in the adjacent Tithe barn are entirely modern. Two restaurants, one in the castle cellar with a traditional focus and the other Mediterranean, as well as spa facilities and two golf courses set in 8 hectares of parkland round off this luxurious option.

Schloss Hämelschenburg   CASTLE

(☎05155-951 690; www.schloss-haemelschenburg. de; Schlossstrasse 1, Emmerthal; tours adult/concession €6.50/3.50; ⏰tours 11am, noon, 2pm, 3pm & 4pm Tue-Sun Apr-Sep) Some 15km southwest of Hamelin near a tributary of the Weser River is Schloss Hämelschenburg, a Renaissance residence dating from 1588–1613 set in pretty parkland. This is among the best of its ilk in Germany, and was built on a former pilgrimage road that eventually led to Santiago de Compostella in Spain. Tours, which are the only way to see the palace, take you through rooms decked out with original Renaissance furnishings and paintings. Getting there can be half the fun if you cycle along the Weser – follow the Weser River **bicycle path** (www.weser-radweg.de) south, then the signs near Emmerthal – or take bus 40 (€2.60, 30 minutes) to the residence from the train station.

🛏 Sleeping & Eating

Ask the tourist office about camping; there's a camp ground a 15-minute walk north of town.

TOP CHOICE Hotel La Principessa   HOTEL $$

(☎956 920; www.laprincipessa.de; Kupferschmiedestrasse 2; s/d €78/99; P🛜) Cast-iron balustrades, tiled floors, and gentle Tuscan pastels and ochre shades make this Italian-themed hotel an unusual and distinguished option

in Hamelin. There's a junior suite (€129), and out the back are some giant rats for the kids to mess with.

Hotel-Garni Christinenhof   HOTEL $$

(☎95080; www.christinenhof-hameln.de; Alte Markt -strasse 18; s/d €77/99; P🛜🏊) Historic on the outside but totally modern in attitude, this hotel likes to pamper its guests, providing a small swimming pool in the vaulted cellar with a current so you can simulate laps, a sauna, a generous buffet breakfast and compact but uncluttered rooms.

Hotel Garni Altstadtwiege   HOTEL $

(☎278 54; www.hotel-altstadtwiege.de; Neue Marktstrasse 10; s/d/tr €47/70/90; P@) This central hotel has charming, individually decorated rooms. The singles are narrow but the doubles are large and some have stained-glass windows – No 14 even has a four-poster bed. Power LAN is available.

DJH Hostel   HOSTEL $

(☎3425; www.jugendherberge.de/jh/hameln; Fisch beckerstrasse 33; dm under/over 27yr €20/24) Although there's not a lot of space in the dorms or bathrooms, this hostel enjoys excellent river views out the back. Take bus 2 from the Hauptbahnhof to Wehler Weg.

TOP CHOICE Rattenfängerhaus   GERMAN $$

(Osterstrasse 28; mains €10-23; ⏰11am-10pm) Hamelin's traditional restaurants are unashamedly aimed at tourists, such as this cute half-timbered tavern with a speciality of 'rats' tails' flambéed at your table (fortunately, like most of the theme dishes here, it's based on pork). Schnitzels, herrings, vegie dishes and 'rat killer' herb liquor are also offered.

ℹ Information

Tourist Office (☎957 823; www.hameln.de; Diesterallee 1; ⏰9am-6pm Mon-Fri, 9.30am-3pm Sat, 9.30am-1pm Sun) On the eastern edge of the Altstadt (bus stop Bügergarten). Look for the rat symbols cropping up throughout the streets, along with information posts (currently only in German) offering a glimpse into the history of Hamelin and its restored 16th- to 18th-century architecture.

ℹ Getting There & Around

BICYCLE Bikes can be hired from the **Jugendwerkstatt Hameln** (☎609 770; Ruthenstrasse 10; per day €5; ⏰7am-5pm Mon-Fri, 9am-1pm Sat).

BUS Buses 1 to 7 are just some of the bus lines that will take you into town from Hauptbahnhof.
CAR By car, take the B217 to/from Hanover.

TRAIN Frequent S-Bahn trains (S5) go to Hamelin from Hanover's Hauptbahnhof (€11.10, 45 minutes). Regular direct trains connect Hanover's airport with Hamelin (€14.40, one hour).

ERFURT, WEIMAR & THURINGIA

Taking in the towns of Erfurt, Weimar, Gotha and the Kyffhäuser Mountains, as well as smaller places in Thuringia such as Mühlhausen, this part of central Germany offers the traveller an interesting blend of culture and bucolic nature. The major attractions in the region include Weimar, the centre of the German Enlightenment and home to literary giants Goethe, Schiller and others. Erfurt, the capital of Thuringia, is a lively medium-sized town, Mühlhausen has a charming medieval atmosphere and access to the nearby Hanich National Park, and Bad Frankenhausen in the Kyffhäuser Mountains has an enormous monument.

ⓘ Getting There & Around

Erfurt and Weimar are easily reached by ICE or regional train along a line that runs from Fulda to Leipzig; without your own wheels you will be dependent on buses to get to Hainich or the Kyffhäuser Mountains. The A4 autobahn leads into the region here between Fulda and Kassel.

Erfurt

🎵 0361 / POP 205.000

Thuringia's capital is a scene-stealing combo of sweeping squares, time-worn alleyways, perky church towers, idyllic river scenery, and vintage inns and taverns. On the little Gera River, Erfurt was founded by the indefatigable missionary St Boniface as a bishopric in 742, and was catapulted to prominence and prosperity in the Middle Ages when it began producing a precious blue pigment from a woad plant. In 1392 rich merchants founded the university, allowing students to study common law, rather than religious law. Its most famous graduate was Martin Luther, who studied philosophy here before becoming a monk at the local Augustinian monastery in 1505.

Today Erfurt's looks still reflect its medieval roots. The city's university is thriving

and it's also a small media hub as the seat of KI.KA, a popular children's TV channel.

⊙ Sights

Mariendom CHURCH
(St Mary's Cathedral; Map p540; Domplatz; ⊙9am-6pm Mon-Sat, 1-6pm Sun) Erfurt is at its most striking in the vast Domplatz, where the Mariendom and Severikirche form a photogenic ensemble. The Dom began life as a simple chapel founded in 742 by St Boniface, but the Gothic pile you see today has the hallmarks of the 14th century. Look for the superb stained-glass windows (1370–1420) featuring biblical scenes; the Wolfram (1160), a bronze candelabrum in the shape of a man; the Gloriosa bell (1497); a Romanesque stucco Madonna; and the 14th-century choir stalls. The steps buttressing the cathedral make for a dramatic backdrop for the popular **Domstufen-Festspiele** (www.domstufen.de), a classical music festival held in July or August.

Krämerbrücke BRIDGE
(Map p540) Even if it could not claim to be the only bridge north of the Alps that's lined with houses on both sides, the medieval Merchant Bridge would still be a most charming spot. You can watch chocolate makers, potters, jewellers and other artisans at work in their teensy studios or enjoy a coffee or glass of wine in a cafe. The 1325 stone bridge used to be bookended by two churches, of which only the **Ägidienkirche** (Map p540) remains. The tower has irregular hours but a sign indicates whether it's open.

Severikirche CHURCH
(Map p540; Domplatz; ⊙9am-6pm Mon-Sat, 1-6pm Sun) The Severikirche, together with Erfurt's Dom forming the ensemble on Domplatz, is a five-aisled hall church (1280) with prized treasures that include a stone Madonna (1345), a 15m-high baptismal font (1467) and the sarcophagus of St Severus.

Zitadelle Petersberg FORTRESS
(guided tours adult/concession €8/4; ⊙7pm Fri & Sat May-Oct) Situated on the Petersberg hill northwest of Domplatz, this citadel ranks among Europe's largest and best-preserved baroque fortresses. It sits above a honeycomb of tunnels, which can be explored on two-hour guided tours run by the tourist office. Various other tours go here throughout the year; ask at the tourist office.

Erfurt

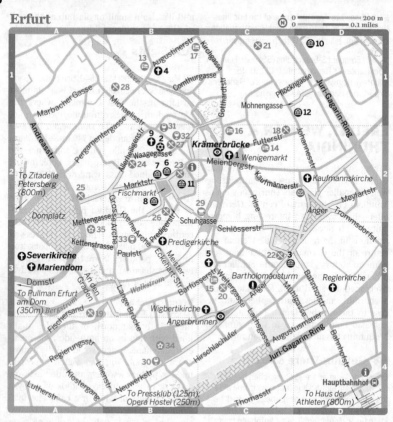

Augustinerkloster
CHURCH

(Augustinian Monastery; Map p540; Augustiner-strasse 10, enter on Comthurgasse; tours adult/concession €6/4; ☺tours hourly 10am-noon & 2-5pm Mon-Sat, 11am & noon Sun) It's Luther lore galore at the Augustinerkloster. This is where the reformer lived from 1505 to 1511, and where he was ordained as a monk and read his first mass. You're free to roam the grounds, visit the church with its ethereal Gothic stained-glass windows, and attend the prayer services held by the resident Protestant sisters at 7am, noon and 6pm daily except Tuesday. Guided tours get you inside the monastery itself, including the cloister, a recreated Luther cell and an exhibit on the history of the Bible and Luther's life in Erfurt. You can sleep here too.

Alte Synagoge
SYNAGOGUE

(Old Synagogue; Map p540; http://alte-synagoge.erfurt.de; Waagegasse 8; adult/concession €5/3; ☺10am-5pm Tue-Thu, 11am-5pm Fri-Sun) The Alte Synagoge in Erfurt is one of the oldest Jewish houses of worship in Europe, with roots in the 12th century. After the pogrom of 1349, it was converted into a storehouse and, after later standing empty for decades, has been restored as an exhibition space and museum. Exhibits document the history of the building and include the Erfurt Treasure, unearthed during excavations in Erfurt's Jewish quarter. This includes 600 pieces in all: rings, brooches, cutlery and, most famously, a super-rare golden Jewish marriage ring from the early 14th century.

Angermuseum
MUSEUM

(Map p540; www.angermuseum.de; Anger 18; adult/concession €5/3; ☺1-7pm Tue-Fri, 11am-7pm Sat & Sun) Housed inside a fully restored baroque building dating from the early 18th century, the Angermuseum has a strong collection of medieval art, paintings ranging from the 17th century to contemporary times and Thuringian faience (glazed earthenware).

Erfurt

A highlight is the Heckelraum on the ground floor, which has expressionist frescos by the artist Erich Heckel.

Stadtmuseum MUSEUM
(City Museum; Map p540; Johannesstrasse 169; adult/concession €5/3; ◎10am-5pm Tue-Sun) Inside the magnificent **Haus am Stockfisch**, the Stadtmuseum has exhibits ranging from a medieval bone-carver's workshop to displays on Erfurt in GDR times.

Museum für Thüringer Volkskunde MUSEUM
(Thuringian Folklore Museum; Map p540; Juri-Gagarin-Ring 140a; adult/concession €5/3; ◎10am-5pm Tue-Thu & Sat-Sun, to 2pm Fri) This museum is one of the largest of its ilk in Germany, with an interesting collection that focuses on the applied arts, with household objects, furnishings and tools of all sorts. Its centrepiece is an exhibit on 19th-century village life.

Egapark Erfurt GARDENS
(Erfurter Gartenausstellung; www.ega-erfurt.com; Gothaer Strasse 38; adult/concession €6/4.80,

Nov-Feb free; ◎9am-6pm) It's easy to spend hours amid the kaleidoscopic flower beds, romantic rose garden, Japanese rock garden and greenhouses of the rambling Egapark, about 4km west of the city centre (take tram 2 from Anger). It's so huge that there's even a little trolley to whisk around the foot-weary. Part of the park is the medieval **Cyriaksburg** citadel, now home to a horticultural museum. Climb to the top for fantastic views.

Michaeliskirche CHURCH
(Map p540; cnr Michaelisstrasse & Allerheiligenstrasse; ◎11am-4pm Mon-Sat) The old university church boasts a magnificent organ (1652), made by local master Ludwig Compenius, and was a key gathering place of leading local dissidents during the final days of the GDR.

Barfüsserkirche CHURCH
(Map p540; Barfüsserstrasse 20; adult/concession €3/2; ◎10am-6pm Tue-Sun Apr-Oct) This church ruin has a small collection of medieval art and hosts a summer theatre in its courtyard.

Kunsthalle Erfurt
GALLERY

(Map p540; www.kunsthalle-erfurt.de; Fischmarkt 7; adult/concession €3/1.50; ⊘11am-5pm Tue, Wed & Fri, to 8pm Thu, to 6pm Sat & Sun) Art gallery inside the historic Haus zum Roten Ochsen.

Rathaus
HISTORIC BUILDING

(Map p540; Rathausplatz; ⊘8am-6pm Mon, Tue & Thu, to 4pm Wed, to 2pm Fri, 10am-5pm Sat & Sun) Neo-Gothic town hall built in 1870–75, with a series of murals depicting scenes from Luther's life, as well as the Tannhäuser and Faust legends. On the 3rd floor is an extravagant festival hall.

Haus zum Breiten Herd
HISTORIC BUILDING

(Map p540; Fischmarkt 13-16) Built in 1584. Features a rich Renaissance facade and a frieze depicting the five human senses.

Gildehaus
HISTORIC BUILDING

(Map p540; Fischmarkt 13-16) Dating from 1892, and decorated with depictions of the four virtues, it's now a restaurant and cafe.

🛏 Sleeping

The Erfurt tourist office has access to a large contingent of private rooms (☎664 0110), starting at €20 per person. Visitors pay a 5% tax on accommodation to fund cultural upkeep.

TOP CHOICE / Re_4 Hostel
HOSTEL $

(☎600 0110; www.re4hostel.de; Puschkinstrasse 21; dm €13-16, s/d without bathroom €20/40, with bathroom €26/52, linen €2; P @) If you've ever spent a night in a police lock-up, staying in this former police station might give you flashbacks – or not. It's run by an energetic, clued-in crew, happy to help you make the most out of your stay in Erfurt. Breakfast costs an extra €4.50. Room 13 has a chilling surprise. The hostel's about 1.5km southwest from the Hauptbahnhof (tram 5 to Pushkinstrasse).

TOP CHOICE / Opera Hostel
HOSTEL $

(☎6013 1360; www.opera-hostel.de; Walkmühlstrasse 13; dm €13-18, s/d/tr without bathroom €37/48/66, with bathroom €45/54/75, linen €2.50; @⊛) Run with smiles and aplomb, this upmarket hostel in a historic building scores big with wallet-watching global nomads. Rooms are bright and spacious, many with an extra sofa for chilling, and you can make friends in the communal kitchen and on-site lounge-bar. Take bus 51 from Hauptbahnhof to Alte Oper.

Pension Rad-Hof
PENSION $

(Map p540; ☎602 7761; www.rad-hof.de; Kirchgasse 1b; s €33-53, d/tr €66/89; @⊛) The owners of this cyclist-friendly guesthouse, next to the Augustinian monastery and near the pub quarter, have gone the extra mile in renovating the building with natural materials, such as wood and mud. No two rooms are alike. Take tram 1 or 5 to Augustinerstrasse.

Pullman Erfurt am Dom
LUXURY HOTEL $$

(☎644 50; www.pullmanhotels.com; Theaterplatz 2; s €100-125, d €128-153; P⊛⊛) Situated about 300m west of Domplatz (off Lauentor), Erfurt's only full-on luxury address has 160 rooms that exude effortless sophistication thanks to classy decor and a soothing natural-hued colour scheme. Sightseeing fatigue quickly fades in the impeccable Zen-inspired wellness area. Wi-fi is in some rooms. Prices vary significantly according to demand. The restaurant inside the hotel is among the best in town. Take tram 4 from Hauptbahnhof to Theater.

Evangelisches Augustinerkloster zu Erfurt
GUESTHOUSE $

(Map p540; ☎664 0110; www.augustinerkloster.de; Augustinerstrasse 10; s/tw €50/80; P) This venerable monastery offers an unusual retreat from the rat race of everyday life – a bible, but no television, telephones or internet, in rooms barely larger than a monk's cell. It's undeniably a special and tranquil place where you can allow your social networking accounts to digitally rust. Take tram 1 or 5 to Augustinerstrasse.

Hotel Ibis
HOTEL $$

(Map p540; ☎664 10; www.accorhotels.com; Barfüsserstrasse 9; s/d from €75; P@⊛) If you've stayed at other Ibis hotels, you'll be pleasantly surprised by the larger-than-usual rooms and decent bathrooms at this entry in a quiet yet central setting opposite the Barfüsserkirche. Price doesn't include breakfast. Take tram 1, 2, 3, 4, 5 or 6 to Anger.

Hotel am Kaisersaal
HOTEL $$

(Map p540; ☎658 560; www.bachmann-hotels.de; Futterstrasse 8; s/d €89/104; P⊛) Rooms are tip-top and appointed with all expected mod cons in this highly rated hotel. Request a room facing the yard, though, if street noise disturbs. Prices can be higher or lower according to day and demand. Take tram 1 or 5 to Futterstrasse.

IBB Hotel   HOTEL **$$**
(Map p540; ☑674 00; www.ibbhotels.com; Gott-
hardtstrasse 27; s/d €95/120; Ⓟ✳@⋧) This
saucy lifestyle hotel, near a willow-fringed
arm of the Gera River, gets thumbs up from
design-minded travellers. Rooms are spread
over two buildings, one an annex on the
historic Krämerbrücke with cheaper rooms.
Prices vary by demand. Take tram 3, 4 or 6
to Fischmarkt.

Hotel & Gasthof Nikolai   HOTEL **$$**
(Map p540; ☑5981 7119; www.hotel-nikolai-erfurt.
com; Augustinerstrasse 30; s €78-81, d €94-110;
Ⓟ) The location alongside the river and the
overall good standard of rooms make this a
prime choice, even though some rooms are
small. Take tram 1 or 5 to Augustinerstrasse.

Haus der Athleten   APARTMENT **$**
(www.haus-der-athleten-erfurt.de; Friedrich-Ebert-
Str. 61; s €32) Nine single apartments with
a small kitchen area in a complex housing
sportspeople south of the train station. Take
tram 3 from Hauptbahnhof two stops to
Tschaikowskistrasse.

✕ Eating

TOP CHOICE **Zwiesel**   GERMAN **$**
(Map p540; Michaelisstrasse 31; mains €6-9;
⊗6pm-late Mon-Thu, 3pm-late Fri, Sat & Sun) Been
cut out of the family will? No problem at this
reliable cheapie choice, which has 25 mains
costing just €6 and drinks prices to match.
Even the rump steak is only €9. Any of the
350 cocktails cost €5.

TOP CHOICE **Alboth's**   GERMAN **$$$**
(Map p540; ☑568 8207; www.alboths.de; Futter-
strasse 15-16; 5-/7-course menu €67/87; ⊗dinner
Tue-Sat, closed most of Feb & Aug) Alboth's rates
consistently among the top restaurants in
Thuringia. The choice of dishes is limited to
a couple of menus, but you can order any
main dish for €27, or any other course for
€11. One menu has local specialities.

Il Cortile   ITALIAN **$$**
(Map p540; ☑566 4411; www.il-cortile.de; Johan-
nesstrasse 150; mains €18.50-23.50; ⊗lunch &
dinner Tue-Sat) Less expensive than Erfurt's
other gourmet restaurants, Il Cortile offers
game and other meats, as well as fish, all
prepared creatively – the steak comes with
a walnut crust and calf's liver is served with
vanilla-laced carrots.

Trattoria la Grappa   ITALIAN **$$$**
(Map p540; ☑562 3315; www.la-grappa-erfurt.de;
Schuhgasse 8-10; 5-course menu €28-35; ⊗lunch &
dinner; ⓐ) This cosy Italian trattoria wends
and winds over two floors and is almost
bursting at the seams with homely decora-
tions. The pasta is homemade and you can
also order veal, lamb, beef and lamb dishes à
la carte, but the set menus are the best value.

Henner   FAST FOOD **$**
(Map p540; Weitergasse 8; dishes €3-7; ⊗9am-5pm
Mon-Fri; ⓐ) This upbeat bistro makes a great
daytime pit stop for freshly made sandwich-
es, homemade soups and crisp salads.

Altstadt Cafe   CAFE **$**
(Map p540; Fischersand 1; dishes €4-8; ⊗11.30am-
11pm Mon-Fri, noon-10pm Sat, 2-7pm Sun) Chatty
mothers, foot-weary sightseers and people
catching up on their reading gather at this
historic cafe in a 14th-century building. The
terrace overlooking the Gera is an enchant-
ing spot in fine weather.

Zum Goldenen Schwan   GERMAN **$$**
(Map p540; Michaelisstrasse 9; snacks €3-7, mains
€8-17; ⊗11am-1am) This authentic inn serves
all the usual Thuringian classics, but, if
you're up to mounting your own *Survivor* challenge, try something called *Puff-
bohnenpfanne* (fried broad beans with roast
bacon), an Erfurt speciality. Excellent house
brews wash everything down well.

Si Ju   INTERNATIONAL **$$**
(Map p540; Fischmarkt 1; mains €7-20; ⊗9am-late
Mon-Sat, 10am-late Sun; ⋧) This restaurant-
lounge combo is a fashionable stop any time
for diners and drinkers of all ages. Steals in-
clude the breakfast buffet for €7 and other
deals.

Steinhaus   GERMAN **$**
(Map p540; Allerheiligenstrasse 20-21; mains €4-8;
⊗from 11am-late, food till midnight) The ceil-
ing beams may be ancient, but the crowd
is intergenerational at this rambling gastro
pub-cum-beer garden in the historic En-
gelsburg. Dips, baguettes, pasta and gratins
should keep your tummy filled and your
brain balanced.

Rewe   SUPERMARKET **$**
(Map p540; Anger 1) In the Anger 1 shopping
mall.

Tegut   SUPERMARKET **$**
(Map p540; cnr Marktstrasse and Domplatz) With
a large selection of organic products.

Drinking

Just north of Fischmarkt, Erfurt's former university quarter is a hub of nightspots, pubs and bars, especially along Michaelisstrasse and Futterstrasse.

Hemingway BAR
(Map p540; www.hemingway-erfurt.de; Michaelis-strasse 26) Everything the macho scribe loved is here in abundance: cigar humidors with personal drawers, 148 types of rum and 30 different daiquiri cocktails. The Africa Lounge has a local Bambi, though, not an elephant bagged beneath Kilimanjaro.

Modern Masters BAR
(Map p540; Michaelisstrasse 48; ⊘Mon-Sat) Urbane and sophisticated, this cocktail bar has been shaking up Erfurt with liquid flights of fancy. There's an impressive range of more than 220 concoctions.

Weinstein LeBar WINE BAR
(Map p540; Kleine Arche 1; ⊘from 7pm Sun-Fri, 8pm Sat) This unassuming wine bar has soft music, candlelight and as many as 50 wines by the glass, including some hard-to-get bottles from the nearby Saale-Unstrut Valley. A basic snack menu is available.

Dubliner PUB
(Map p540; Neuwerkstrasse 47a; ⊘from 4pm) On weekends it seems everybody's popping by to knock back pints of Kilkenny or Guinness at this boisterous Irish thirst parlour. Smokers can sit downstairs.

Barista CAFE
(Map p540; Schlösserstrasse 32; coffee & muffin €4; ⊘8am-7.30pm Mon-Fri, 9am-8pm Sat, 2-7pm Sun; ⓐ) Small but stylish coffee shop with free wi-fi.

Entertainment

Consult the free zines *Dates, Takt* (www.takt-magazin.de) and *Blitz* (www.blitz-world.de) for nightlife and event listings. Throughout summer, from the end of May, classical concerts take place beneath the linden trees in the romantic courtyard of Michaeliskirche (on Fridays). Organ concerts are held year-round in the Predigerkirche and Michaeliskirche (at noon Wednesdays), and in the Dom (Saturdays).

Engelsburg CLUB
(Map p540; www.eburg.de; Allerheiligenstrasse 20-21) Good times are pretty much guaranteed at this venerable venue, no matter whether you hunker down for beer and talk in the **Steinhaus** pub (also an eating option), report to the dance floor of the medieval cellar labyrinth or go highbrow at the upstairs **Café DuckDich** cultural forum.

Presseklub CLUB
(www.presseklub.net; Dalbergsweg 1) A former gathering spot for media types, this club is now a delightful dance party location with a chic interior.

DasDie Brettl PERFORMING ARTS
(Map p540; ☑551 166; www.dasdielive.de; Lange Brücke 29) Cabaret, musicals, concerts, transvestite shows and poetry slams heat up the stage of this cultural centre.

Theater Waidspeicher THEATRE
(Map p540; ☑598 2924; www.waidspeicher.de; Domplatz 18) Not only children will be enchanted by the adorable marionettes and puppets that perform at this cute theatre in a historic woad storehouse (reached via Mettengasse).

ℹ Information

Internet Café (☑262 3834; Fischmarkt 5, Ratskellerpassage; per 30min €1.50; ⊘10am-6pm Mon-Fri, 11am-6pm Sat, 3-8pm Sun)

Post Office (Anger 66; ⊘9am-7pm Mon-Fri, to 1pm Sat)

ReiseBank (Hauptbahnhof; ⊘8am-8pm Mon-Fri, 9am-6pm Sat) Currency exchange.

Thuringia Tourist Office (☑37 420; Willy-Brandt-Platz 1; ⊘9am-7pm Mon-Fri, 10am-4pm Sat & Sun) Opposite the Hauptbahnhof.

Tourist Office (www.erfurt-tourismus.de) The **Benediktsplatz** (☑664 00; www.erfurt-tourismus.de; Benediktsplatz 1; ⊘10am-7pm Mon-Fri, to 6pm Sat, to 4pm Sun) and **Petersberg** (☑6015 384; www.erfurt-tourismus.de; ⊘11am-6.30pm mid-Apr-Oct, to 4pm Nov & Dec, closed Jan-mid-Apr) branches of the tourist office sell the ErfurtCard (€12.90 per 48 hours), which includes a city tour, public transport and free or discounted admissions.

ℹ Getting There & Away

AIR Flughafen Erfurt (☑656 2200; www.flughafen-erfurt.de; Binderslebener Landstrasse 100) is about 6km west of the city centre, and is served by Air Berlin, Lufthansa and a few charter airlines.

CAR Erfurt is just north of the A4 and is crossed by the B4 (Hamburg to Bamberg) and the B7 (Kassel to Gera). The A71 autobahn runs south to Schweinfurt via Ilmenau, Oberhof and Meiningen.

TRAIN Frequent IC/ICE connections with Berlin (€60, 2½ hours, change in Leipzig) and direct ICE connections with Dresden (€51, 2½ hours) and Frankfurt am Main (€54, 2¼ hours). Direct trains also go to Meiningen (€18.10, 1½ hours) and Mühlhausen (€12.20, 45 minutes). Regional trains to Weimar (€5, 15 minutes) and Eisenach (€11.10, 45 minutes) run at least once hourly.

Getting Around

BIKE Bikes can be hired at **Fahrradstation** (Bahnhofstrasse; ⊙10am-7pm Mon-Fri, to 2pm Sat) for €12 per 24 hours and at **Radhaus am Dom** (☑602 0640; Andreasstrasse 28; ⊙10am-6pm Mon-Fri, to 2pm Sat) from €9 per 24 hours.

BUS & TRAM Tram 4 directly links the airport and Anger in the city centre (€1.80, 25 minutes). Trams 3, 4 and 6 run from Hauptbahnhof via Anger and Fischmarkt to Domplatz. Tickets in the central (yellow) zone for trams and buses cost €1.80, or €4.20 for a day pass.

TAXI Call ☑511 11 or 555 55.

Weimar

☑03643 / POP 65,500

Neither a monumental town nor a medieval one, Weimar appeals to those whose tastes run to cultural and intellectual pleasures. After all, this is the epicentre of the German Enlightenment, a symbol for all that is good and great in German culture. An entire pantheon of intellectual and creative giants lived and worked here: Goethe, Schiller, Bach, Cranach, Liszt, Nietzsche, Gropius, Herder, Feininger, Kandinsky, Klee...the list goes on (and on, and on). You'll see reminders of them wherever you go – here, a statue; there, a commemorative plaque decorating a house facade – plus scores of museums and historic sites. In summer, Weimar's many parks and gardens lend themselves to taking a break from the intellectual onslaught.

Internationally, of course, Weimar is better known as the place where the constitution of the Weimar Republic was drafted after WWI, though there are few reminders of this historical moment. Nearby, the ghostly ruins of the Buchenwald concentration camp provide haunting evidence of the terrors of the Nazi regime. The Bauhaus and classical Weimar locations are protected as Unesco World Heritage Sites.

It's about a 20-minute walk south from the Hauptbahnhof to the start of the historic centre at Goetheplatz. Bus 1 runs between Hauptbahnhof and Goetheplatz.

Sights

Goethe Nationalmuseum MUSEUM
(Map p546; Frauenplan 1; combined ticket Goethe Haus & permanent museum exhibition adult/concession €10.50/8.50, permanent museum exhibition only adult/concession €6.50/5.50; ⊙9am-6pm Tue-Fri & Sun, to 7pm Sat) No other individual is as closely associated with Weimar as Johann Wolfgang von Goethe, who lived in this town from 1775 until his death in 1832, the last 50 years in what is now the **Goethe Haus** (Map p546; ☑545 401; Frauenplan 1; adult/concession €8.50/7; ⊙9am-6pm Tue-Fri & Sun, to 7pm Sat Apr-Sep, 9am-6pm Tue-Sun Oct, to 4pm Tue-Sun Nov-Mar).

This is where he worked, studied, researched and penned *Faust* and other immortal works. If you're a Goethe fan, you'll get the chills when seeing his study and the bedroom where he died, both preserved in their original state. To get the most from your visit, use the audioguide (free). To preserve the exhibits, the number of visitors is limited and you purchase a ticket for a specific time.

Part of the museum complex adjoining Goethe's house is now a modern exhibition space that was being revamped at the time of research. In this section you'll find a permanent exhibition called 'Floods of Life – Storms of Action', which focuses on the life and works of Goethe (no visitor restrictions).

Schiller Haus MUSEUM
(Map p546; Schillerstrasse 12; adult/concession €5/4; ⊙9am-6pm Tue-Fri & Sun, to 7pm Sat) The dramatist Friedrich Schiller lived in Weimar from 1799 until his early death in 1805. Study up on the man, his family and life in Thuringia in a new permanent exhibit before plunging on to the private quarters, including the study with his deathbed and the desk where he wrote *Wilhelm Tell* and other famous works.

Fürstengruft MAUSOLEUM
(Map p546; Am Poseckschen Garten; adult/concession €3.50/3; ⊙10am-6pm) Both Goethe and to a lesser extent Schiller (more about that soon) are interred at the **Historischer Friedhof** (Historical Cemetery) in the neoclassical mausoleum along with Duke Carl August. The neoclassical mausoleum dates from 1828 and houses almost 50 sarcophagi. Schiller's, however, is empty today, after tests showed that his remains originated from several different people. He was a great writer, but no magician!

Weimar

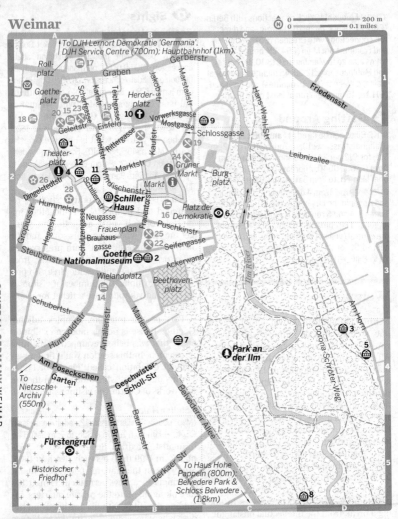

Park an der Ilm
PARK

(Map p546) The sprawling Park an der Ilm, just east of the Altstadt, is as inspiring and romantic now as it was in Goethe's time. As well as providing a bucolic backdrop to the city, the park is home to several historic houses that can be visited separately. The highlights are: **Goethes Gartenhaus** Goethe's Garden House; adult/concession €4.50/3.50; ⊙10am-6pm Wed-Mon), where the writer lived from 1776 to 1782; **Römisches Haus** (Roman House; adult/concession €3.50/3; ⊙10am-6pm Wed-Mon), built under Goethe's supervision as the duke Carl August's summer retreat, with period rooms and an exhibit on the park; and the **Liszt-Haus** (Marienstrasse 17, Liszt House; adult/concession 16 €4/3; ⊙10am-6pm Tue-Sun Apr-Sep, to 4pm Sat & Sun Oct-Mar), where the composer resided in 1848 and again from 1869 to 1886, and wrote the *Faust Symphony*).

The park was created between 1778 and 1828.

Herzogin Anna Amalia Bibliothek
LIBRARY

(Map p546; www.klassik-stiftung.de; Platz der Demokratie 1; adult/concession incl audioguide €6.50/5.50; ⊙9.30am-2.30pm Tue-Sun) The phoenix-like rebirth of Anna Amalia's precious library

Weimar

following a disastrous fire in 2004 is nothing short of a miracle. The magnificent Rokokosaal (Rococo Hall) is crammed with 40,000 tomes once used for research purposes by Goethe, Schiller and other Weimar hot shots. Scholars may still borrow the books; for others, the fine busts and paintings of these men offer an interesting backdrop. Entry is by timed ticket and capped at 290 people per day, so book in advance or start queuing before the ticket office opens at 9.30am.

Schloss Belvedere PALACE
(Belvedere Park; adult/concession €5/4; ◉10am-6pm, closed Jan-Mar) Set in the lovely Belvedere Park, this palace has displays of glass, porcelain, faience and weapons from the late 17th and 18th centuries. The easiest way to reach it is by bus 1 from Goetheplatz.

Schloss Tiefurt PALACE
(☑545 401; Hauptstrasse 14, Weimar-Tiefurt; adult/concession €5/4; ◉10am-6pm Tue-Sun Apr-Sep) Originally, this (relatively) small house from 1800 was leased to the tennant who ran the estate of the duchess Anna Amalia, but Anna took it over and turned it into her 'temple of the muses'. The period rooms give you an impression of the age and her intellectual round-table gatherings where Goethe, Schiller and Herder were regulars. Bus 3 from Goetheplatz goes out here.

Weimar Haus MUSEUM
(Map p546; www.weimarhaus.de; Schillerstrasse 16; adult/concession €6.50/5.50; ◉9.30am-6.30pm) The Weimar Haus is a history museum for people who hate history museums. Sets, sound-and-light effects, wax figures and even an animatronic Goethe accompany you on your 30-minute journey into Thuringia's past, from prehistory to the Enlightenment. The production values can be comical, but the entertainment factor is inarguably high.

Haus Hohe Pappeln HISTORIC BUILDING
(Belvederer Allee 58; adult/concession €2.50/2; ◉11am-4pm Tue-Sun Apr-Oct) Belgian art nouveau architect, designer and painter, Henry van de Velde is considered a pioneer of modernity. In 1902 he founded the arts and crafts seminar in Weimar that Walter Gropius later developed into the Bauhaus. For nine years, starting in 1908, van de Velde and his family lived in this house, which looks a bit like a ship on its side and features natural stone, stylised chimneys, loggias and oversized windows. One floor is open for touring and includes furniture that van de Velde designed for a local family. There's also a cluster of splendidly restored art nouveau buildings (though not by van de Velde) on Cranachstrasse, Gutenbergstrasse and Humboldtstrasse, just west of the Histor-

HOW THE WEIMAR REPUBLIC GOT ITS NAME

Despite its name, the Weimar Republic (1919–33), Germany's first dalliance with democracy, was never actually governed from Weimar. The town on the Ilm River was merely the place where, in 1919, the National Assembly drafted and passed the country's first constitution.

Assembly delegates felt that the volatile and explosive political climate rocking post-WWI Berlin would threaten the democratic process if it took place there, and looked for an alternative location. Weimar had several factors in its favour: a central location, a suitable venue (the Deutsches Nationaltheater) and a humanist tradition entirely antithetical to the militaristic Prussian spirit that had led to war.

Weimar's spot in the democratic limelight, however, lasted only briefly. With the situation in Berlin calming down, the delegates returned to the capital just one week after passing the constitution on 31 July.

ischer Friedhof. To get to Haus Hohe Pappeln, take bus 1 or 12 to Papiergraben.

Nietzsche Archiv   HISTORIC BUILDING
(Humboldtstrasse 36; adult/concession €2.50/2; ⊙11am-4pm Tue-Sun Apr-Oct) Belgian architect, designer and painter Henry van de Velde added some art-nouveau touches to this house, where the philosopher Friedrich Nietzsche spent his final years in illness.

Bauhaus Museum   MUSEUM
(Map p546; www.das-bauhaus-kommt.de; Theaterplatz; adult/concession €4.50/3.50; ⊙10am-6pm) Considering that Weimar is the birthplace of the influential Bauhaus school, this is a rather modest affair. Plans are to move to newer, larger premises, so check the situation again from 2013.

Haus am Horn   HISTORIC BUILDING
(Map p546; www.hausamhorn.de; Am Horn 61; ⊙11am-5pm Wed, Sat & Sun Apr-Oct) Weimar's only truly Bauhaus building. Today, it's used for exhibitions and events.

Stadtkirche St Peter und Paul   CHURCH
(Map p546; Herderplatz; ⊙closed for restoration until 2017) Popularly known as the Herderkirche after Johann Gottfried Herder, who's buried inside, this church has a famous altarpiece (1555), painted by the Cranach father-and-son team, and a triptych showing Martin Luther as a knight, professor and monk.

Schlossmuseum   MUSEUM
(Palace Museum; Map p546; Burgplatz 4; adult/concession €6/5; ⊙10am-6pm Tue-Sun) Situated in the former residential palace, which was rebuilt in 1789–1803 after a fire, the Schlossmuseum houses works of art dating from the Middle Ages to the turn of the 20th cen-

tury. Not to be missed is the gallery containing the works of Lukas Cranach the Elder and of other European masters such as Rodin, Tischbein and Caspar David Friedrich.

Wittumspalais   MUSEUM
(Map p546; Theaterplatz; adult/concession €5/4; ⊙10am-6pm) This is the palace in which the duchess Anna Amalia lived from 1774, after the residiential palace (today the Schlossmuseum) burned. Rooms contain period furniture and paintings, culminating in the Green Salon, the living room of the duchess.

🛏 Sleeping

Visitors to Weimar pay a supplement of €1 to €2 per person per overnight stay for the upkeep of cultural sites.

TOP CHOICE Casa dei Colori   PENSION $$
(Map p546; ✆489 640; www.casa-colori.de; Eisfeld 1a; r €84-114; P🐾) Possibly Weimar's most charming boutique *Pension,* the Casa convincingly imports cheerfully exuberant Mediterranean flair to central Europe. The mostly good-sized rooms are dressed in bold colours and come with a small desk, a couple of comfy armchairs and a stylish bathroom.

TOP CHOICE Hotel Amalienhof   HOTEL $$
(Map p546; ✆5490; www.amalienhof-weimar.de; Amalienstrasse 2; s €67-75, d €97-105, ste €115-130; P🐾) The charms of this hotel are manifold: classy antique furnishings, richly styled rooms that point to history without burying you in it, and a late breakfast buffet for those who take their holidays seriously. It's a splendid choice.

Hotel zur Sonne
HOTEL $$

(Map p546; ☎862 90; Rollplatz 2; s €52, d €78-86; P🐕) Although rooms are small and non-descript in this friendly, traditional hotel, it's clean, reliable and right in town. It also has a downstairs restaurant.

Hotel Anna Amalia
HOTEL $$

(Map p546; ☎495 60; www.hotel-anna-amalia.de; Geleitstrasse 8-12; s €65-110, d €95-120, 1-/2-/3-4-bed apt €115/125/145/170; P🐕) The Mediterranean look, with its nice, fresh colour scheme, exudes feel-good cheer in this family-run hotel near Goetheplatz. For more panache and elbow room, book one of the apartments.

Hotel Elephant Weimar
LUXURY HOTEL $$$

(Map p546; ☎8020; www.luxurycollection.com/elephant; Markt 19; r €109-221, ste €291; P@🐕) The moment you make your entrance in the elegant art deco lobby of this charmer, you sense that it's luxury all the way from here to the top. For over 300 years, this classic has wooed statesmen, artists, scholars and the merely rich with first-class service and amenities. These prices are averages and vary by demand and day; check the website.

Romantik Hotel
Dorotheenhof Weimar
HOTEL $$

(☎4590; www.dorotheenhof.com; Dorotheenhof 1; s €69-87, d €105-145, ste €165-185; P🐕) Located 3km north of Weimar in the suburb of Schöndorf, this excellent conference and tourist hotel is set in its own large park and gardens; rooms are modern and tastefully decorated. It's best if you have your own transport (take Friedrich-Ebert-Strasse north), but bus 7 from Hauptbahnhof runs out here daily.

DJH Lernort Demokratie
Germania'
HOSTEL $

(☎850 490; Carl-August-Allee 13; dm under/over 27yr €25/28, s €33/36, d €70/76; @🐕) Weimar has four DJH hostels, which are usually crawling with teens on school excursions. Inside this building is the **DJH Service Centre** (☎850 000; www.djh-thuringen.de); it can book any of the other hostels.

Labyrinth Hostel
HOSTEL $

(Map p546; ☎811 822; www.weimar-hostel.com; Goetheplatz 6; dm €14-21, s/d €35/46, linen €2.50, breakfast €3; @🐕) Loads of imagination has gone into this professionally run hostel with artist-designed rooms. In one double, for example, the bed perches on stacks of books, while another comes with a wooden platform bed. Bathrooms are shared and so are the kitchen and lovely rooftop terrace.

Eating

TOP CHOICE **Estragon**
HEALTH FOOD $

(Map p546; Herderplatz 3; soups €3-5.50; ⏰10am-7pm Mon-Sat, noon-6pm Sun) There are days when a bowl of steamy soup feels as warm and embracing as a hug from a good friend. This little soup kitchen turns mostly organic

---

GOETHE – THE LITERARY LION

Johann Wolfgang von Goethe bestrides German culture like a colossus. He's often called the 'German Shakespeare', but not even Shakespeare lived to be 82, having written novels, essays, literary criticism, philosophical treatises, scientific articles and travelogues, as well as plays and poetry. Goethe was also a consummate politician, town planner, architect, social reformer and scientist. In short, he was a Renaissance man, able to do everything.

Born in Frankfurt am Main and trained as a lawyer, Goethe quickly overcame the disadvantages of a wealthy background and a happy childhood to become the driving force of the 1770's *Sturm und Drang* (Storm and Stress) literary movement. Though he worked and experimented in various styles throughout his life, his work with Friedrich Schiller fostered the theatrical style known as Weimar classicism. Goethe himself once described his work as 'fragments of a great confession'.

Goethe's defining work was *Faust*, a lyrical but highly charged retelling of the classic legend of a man selling his soul for knowledge. It took Goethe almost his entire life to complete it to his own satisfaction, and it's still a much-performed piece of theatre in Germany today; a fitting legacy for a genuine giant. A statue dedicated to Goethe and Schiller, the **Goethe-Schiller Denkmal** (Goethe-Schiller Monument; Map p546), is directly in front of Weimar's Deutsches Nationaltheater.

ingredients into delicious flavour combos served in three sizes. It shares digs with a small organic supermarket.

TOP CHOICE Jo Hanns
GERMAN $$
(Map p546; 493 617; Scherfgasse 1; mains €11.50-17.50; 11am-midnight) The food is satisfying but it's the 130 wines from the Saale-Unstrut Region – many served by the glass – that give Jo Hanns a leg up on the competition. No matter whether you order the classic steak, roast lamb or scallops and shrimp with mint-lime spaghetti, there's a bottle to suit.

TOP CHOICE Versilia
ITALIAN $$
(Map p546; 770 359; www.versilia-weimar.de; Frauentorstrasse 17; mains €17.50-23.50, pasta €6-8.50; 11am-midnight) Goethe is quoted as saying that Tuscany isn't in Italy, Italy was in Tuscany. In any case, he'd approve of this *Vinothek* and restaurant, which has 300 wines on sale (and a white, red and *rosado* by the glass) and serves delicious antipasti, home-made pasta dishes and pan-Italian mains in a spacious setting.

ACC
GERMAN $
(Map p546; www.acc-cafe.de; Burgplatz 1; dishes €5-10; 11-1am;) Goethe had his first pad after arriving in Weimar in this building, now home to an alt-vibe, artsy hang-out, where the food and wine are organic whenever possible and the upstairs gallery delivers a primer on the local art scene. The owners also rent out a room and a holiday flat (www.goethezimmer.de), both handsomely furnished.

Residenz-Café
INTERNATIONAL $$
(Map p546; Grüner Markt 4; mains €5-18; 8-1am;) The 'Resi', one of Weimar's enduring favourites, is a jack of all trades: everyone should find something to their taste here. The Lovers' Breakfast is €19.50 for two, but the inspired meat and vegetarian dishes may well have you swooning, too.

Gasthaus zum Weissen Schwan
GERMAN $$
(Map p546; Frauentorstrasse 23; mains €11-22; lunch & dinner Tue-Sat) At this venerable inn, you can fill your tummy with Goethe's favourite dish, which actually hails from his home town of Frankfurt (boiled beef with herb sauce, red beet salad and potatoes). The rest of the menu, though, is mid-range Thuringian.

Anno 1900
INTERNATIONAL $$$
(Map p546; Geleitstrasse 12a; mains €16-19; 11am-midnight Mon-Fri, 9am-midnight Sat & Sun) Send your taste buds on a wild ride in this elegant art nouveau pavilion. How about emu fillet with carrot-and-rocket fettucine followed by tonka-bean crème brûlée? It's adventurous, but most of the time it works. Breakfast on Sunday is all you can eat from 9am to 1pm (€10.50).

Anna Amalia
INTERNATIONAL $$$
(Map p546; 8020; www.restaurant-anna-amalia.com; Markt 19; 8-course menu with wine €148; dinner Tue-Sat, closed Jan–mid-Mar) Weimar's highly acclaimed gourmet act, inside the Hotel Elephant Weimar.

Drinking & Entertainment

Planbar
BAR
(Jakobsplan 6) Past the heavy door awaits this good-looking bar with an unpretentious, all-ages crowd that likes to knock back the mojitos, flirt with the bartenders and wave to the DJs.

Studentenclub Schützengasse
CLUB
(Map p546; www.schuetzengasse.de; Schützengasse 2) The grunge factor is high at this student club, which may be just what the doctor ordered as an antidote to highbrow burnout. Monday movie nights and salsa nights also provide diversions.

Kasseturm
CLUB
(Map p546; www.kasseturm.de; Goetheplatz 10) Hip Kasse is a student club, with an assorted bag of parties, concerts, drum workshops and whatever else gets people off the couch. Three floors of action, for young and old.

Deutsches Nationaltheater
THEATRE
(German National Theatre; Map p546; 755 334; www.nationaltheater-weimar.de; Theaterplatz 2; tickets €8-55; closed Jul-Aug) Expect a grab bag of classic and contemporary theatre, opera and concerts at this venerable space.

E-Werk
CULTURAL CENTRE
(748 868; www.ewerkweimar.de; Am Kirschberg 4) The Deutsches Nationaltheatre and others perform in this former tram depot, which also has a cinema, live music, cultural events and an excellent exhibit of works by contemporary avant-garde artist Rebecca Horn.

Information

Buchenwald Information (☎747 540; Markt 10; ⏰9.30am-7pm Mon-Sat, to 3pm Sun) Desk for visitors, inside the tourist office (p551) building.

Post Office (Goetheplatz 7-8; ⏰9am-6.30pm Mon-Fri, to noon Sat)

Roxanne Internet Café (Markt 21; per 30min €1; ⏰10.30am-late Mon-Fri, 2pm-late Sat & Sun) Internet terminals and wi-fi. Smoking is permitted.

Sparkasse (Graben 4) Bank with ATM.

Stiftung Weimarer Klassik (☎545 407; www.klassik-stiftung.de; ⏰9.30am-7pm Mon-Sat, to 3pm Sun) Visitor information desk, inside the tourist office (p551).

Tourist Office The **central** (☎7450; www.weimar.de; Markt 10, centre; ⏰9.30am-7pm Mon-Sat, 3pm Sun) and **Friedenstrasse** (☎7450; Friedensstrasse 1; ⏰10am-6pm Mon-Sat) tourist offices sell the WeimarCard (€14.50 for 48 hours) for free or discounted museum admissions and travel on city buses and other benefits.

Getting There & Away

CAR Weimar is situated on the A4 autobahn that connects Eisenach and Erfurt in the west with Dresden in the east.

TRAIN Most ICE services to Frankfurt am Main (€58, 2¾ hours) require a change in Fulda. Direct IC trains run to Leipzig (€22, 1¼ hours, every two hours) and Dresden (€43, 2½ hours). There are a few direct services to Berlin (€54, 2¼ hours) but most require a change in Naumburg. Frequent regional and IC trains go to Erfurt (€8, 15 minutes), Eisenach (€18, 45 minutes) and Gotha (€12, 30 minutes) and regional trains to Jena-West.

Getting Around

BICYCLE **Grüne Liga** (☎492 796; Goetheplatz 9b; ⏰9am-3pm Mon-Fri, to noon Sat) rents out city bikes from €6 per 24 hours (enter from Rollplatz). Call ahead from November to March.

BUS A single costs €1.80; a day pass €4.20. Bus 1 connects Goetheplatz in the centre with Hauptbahnhof.

CAR Note that driving in the Altstadt is severely restricted; it's best to park outside the centre. There's a free lot at Hermann-Brill-Platz, about a 10-minute walk northwest from the Altstadt.

TAXI Call ☎903 600.

Buchenwald

The Buchenwald concentration camp **museum and memorial** (☎03643-4300; www.buchenwald.de; Ettersberg; ⏰buildings & exhibits 10am-6pm Tue-Sun Apr-Oct, to 4pm Tue-Sun Nov-Mar, grounds open until sunset) are 10km north-

west of Weimar. You first pass the memorial erected above the mass graves of some of the 56,500 victims from 18 nations that died here – including Jews, German antifascists, and Soviet and Polish prisoners of war. The concentration camp and museum are 1km beyond the memorial. Many prominent German communists and social democrats, Ernst Thälmann and Rudolf Breitscheid among them, were murdered here. After 1943, prisoners were exploited in the production of weapons. Many died during medical experimentation. Shortly before the end of the war, some 28,000 prisoners were sent on death marches. Between 1937 and 1945, more than one-fifth of the 250,000 people incarcerated here died. On 11 April 1945, as US troops approached and the SS guards fled, the prisoners rebelled (at 3.15pm – the clock tower above the entrance still shows that time), overwhelmed the remaining guards and liberated themselves.

After the war, the Soviet victors established Special Camp No 2, in which 7000 so-called anticommunists and ex-Nazis were literally worked to death. Their bodies were found after the Wende in mass graves north of the camp and near the Hauptbahnhof.

Pamphlets and books in English are sold at the bookshop, where you can also rent an excellent multilanguage audioguide for €3 (€5 with images). Last admission is 30 minutes before closing.

To get here, take bus 6 (direction Buchenwald) from Goetheplatz in Weimar. By car, head north on Ettersburger Strasse from Weimar train station and turn left onto Blutstrasse.

Gotha

☎03621 / POP 45,600

Gotha was once described in historic documents as Thuringia's wealthiest and most beautiful city. Although it can no longer lay claim to either accolade, it remains a pleasant town, dominated by the grand and gracious Schloss Friedenstein, built by Duke Ernst I (1601–75), the founder of the House of Saxe-Coburg-Gotha. His descendants reinvented themselves as the House of Windsor after WWI and now occupy the British royal throne. The Schloss is Gotha's blockbuster attraction, but the town is also useful as a gateway to the Thuringian Forest and is the northern terminus of the quirky Thüringerwaldbahn.

THROUGH THE TREES TO THE CAVE

Thuringia's most unusual ride has to be the **Thüringerwaldbahn** (www.waldbahn-gotha.de; one way €4). Starting out as ordinary city tram 4 at Gotha's Hauptbahnhof, it curves around the city ring road, crawls through some unlovely suburbs and then just keeps on going – like a local version of the Hogwarts Express – straight into the fairy-tale world of the Thuringian forest, as far as Tabarz. The tram departs Gotha every 30 to 60 minutes and takes one hour, winding for about 45 minutes to Friedrichroda, a town of some 7400 people located 20km south of Gotha. One stop further and you reach the prime attraction near Friedrichroda, the **Marienglashöhle** (☑311 667; www.tropfsteinhoehlen.de; tour adult/child €6/2.50; ☺tours 9am-5pm), a large gypsum cave featuring an underwater lake and a crystal grotto, replete with a few special effects to heighten the experience.

An alternative approach is to disembark at **Friedrichroda** itself and make your way to neo-Gothic **Schloss Reinhardsbrunn** (1828), situated in the northern part of town. This is hemmed in by a lavish English park with ancient trees. It was here that Queen Victoria of England first laid eyes on her cousin and future husband, Duke Albert of Saxe-Coburg-Gotha. Unfortunately, the palace is fenced off and you can only walk around the park.

The Schloss abuts the lovely landscaped **Kurpark**, home to the Ludowinger spring, where excellent mineral water bubbles up from a depth of 58m. Much of it is bottled, but you're free to fill up from the taps in one of the park's glass pavilions.

If you would like to stay in town, go no further than the family-run **Pension Feierabend** (☑03623-304 386; www.pension-feierabend.de; Büchig 1; s €25-30, d €36-40; ℙ), in a small but beautiful half-timbered house near the Kurpark.

The **tourist office** (☑03623-332 00; www.friedrichroda.info; Marktstrasse 13-15; ☺9am-5pm Mon-Thu, to 6pm Fri, to noon Sat) is in the centre of town.

The tram continues on from Friedrichsroda through the nicest part of the journey to the terminus in **Tabarz**.

It's a brisk 15-minute walk from the Hauptbahnhof via Schloss Friedenstein to the Neumarkt and Hauptmarkt central squares.

◉ Sights

Schloss Friedenstein　　　PALACE, MUSEUM
(www.stiftungfriedenstein.de; adult/concession €7/3, audioguide €2.50; ☺10am-5pm Tue-Sun) This horseshoe-shaped palace is the largest surviving early baroque palace in Germany. Much of the compound is now the **Schlossmuseum** (Palace Museum), a glorious assembly of art collections displayed in lavish baroque and neoclassical apartments. The picture gallery features priceless works by Rubens, Tischbein, Cranach and other old masters as well as the radiant *Gothaer Liebespaar* (Pair of Lovers) painted around 1480 by an anonymous artist known only as Master of the Housebook. Upstairs is the exuberantly stucco-ornamented **Festsaal** (Festival Hall) as well as the neoclassical wing, which has a sculpture collection that includes a famous Renaissance work by Conrad Meit called *Adam und Eva*.

Other highlights include the **Kunstkammer**, a curio cabinet jammed with exotica,

and the **Schlosskirche** (Palace Church) in the northeastern corner. The southwest tower contains the stunning **Ekhof-Theater**, one of the oldest baroque theatres in Europe, dating from the late 1700s. This hosts performances during the popular **Ekhof Festival** (www.ekhof-festival.de) in July and August.

Tickets double as the Friedenstein-Karte, which gives you admission to several other sights in Gotha.

Rathaus　　　HISTORIC BUILDING
(Hauptmarkt; admission to tower €0.50; ☺11am-6pm) Boasts a colourful Renaissance facade and 35m-tall tower. Other houses on Hauptmarkt also reward exploration.

❶ Information

Tourist Office (☑5078 5712; www.gotha.de; Hauptmarkt 33; ☺9am-6pm Mon-Fri, 10am-3pm Sat, 10am-2pm Sun) In Hauptmarkt central square.

❶ Getting There & Away

CAR Gotha is just north of the A4 and is crossed by the B247 and B7.

TRAIN Gotha is linked by IC to Eisenach (€8, 13 minutes), Erfurt (€8, 16 minutes), Weimar (€12, 35 minutes) and Mühlhausen (€7.50, 20 minutes), and by slower but cheaper regional trains.

Mühlhausen

📞 03601 / POP 36,500

Mühlhausen flaunts medieval charisma. Its historic centre is a warren of cobbled alleyways linking proud churches and encircled by nearly intact fortifications. In the early 16th century, the town became a focal point of the Reformation and a launch pad for the Peasants' War of 1525, led by local preacher Thomas Müntzer. The decisive battle took place on the Schlachtberg in nearby Bad Frankenhausen, where the rebellion was quickly crushed. Müntzer was decapitated outside the Mühlhausen town gates.

The GDR regime hailed the reformer as a great hero and an early social revolutionary who fought for the rights of the common man. There are still numerous sites in and around the town that uphold his memory. With reunification, Mühlhausen became united Germany's most central town, located a mere 5km north of the country's precise geographical centre in Niederdorla.

◉ Sights

Town Fortification   TOWER
(Am Frauentor; adult/concession €3/2; ⊙10am-5pm mid-Apr–Sep) The nicest thing to do in Mühlhausen is to admire the old town, and one of the best places to get an overview of its beauty is from this 330m section of the town fortification. Originally, the 12th-century fortification ran for 2.8km around the town, from which a remarkable 2km remain today. Eventually you reach the the **Rabenturm** (Raven's Tower), where you can chart the rest of your explorations of Mühlhausen's fascinating web of medieval lanes from the viewing platform. Access to the walk is from Inneres Frauentor.

Divi-Blasii-Kirche   CHURCH
(Untermarkt/Bachplatz; ⊙10am-5pm Mon-Thu & Sat, 1-5pm Sun) The Gothic Divi-Blasii-Kirche was built by the Teutonic Knights in the 13th and 14th centuries, based on the style of French Gothic cathedrals. It was here that in 1707–08 Johann Sebastian Bach worked as an organist.

Kornmarktkirche   MUSEUM
(Ratsstrasse; adult/concession €3/2; ⊙10am-5pm Tue-Sun) This former church is today a museum about the German Peasants' War and the Reformation. It can be easily reached from the nearby Divi-Blasii-Kirche via the pedestrianised Linsenstrasse.

Rathaus   HISTORIC BUILDING
(Ratsstrasse 19; ⊙10am-4pm Tue-Sun) Mühlhausen's town hall is an architecturally intriguing hotchpotch of Gothic, Renaissance and baroque styles. Inside, pay special attention to the Great Hall and the Councillors' Chamber. It's located just north of Kornmarkt.

Marienkirche   CHURCH
(St Mary's Church; 📞870 023; adult/concession €3/2; ⊙10am-5pm Tue-Sun) Thuringia's second-largest church after the Dom in Erfurt, it's now used as a memorial museum to Thomas Müntzer who preached here to his rebel followers in 1525 before the disastrous Schlachtberg battle. Located just north of the Rathaus and tourist office.

🍴 Sleeping & Eating

An Der Stadtmauer   HOTEL $
(📞465 00; www.hotel-an-der-stadtmauer.de; Breitenstrasse 15; s/d €52/72; 🅿🐕) The tasteful fittings, comfort and old-town location make this a very good choice. Some rooms open onto a courtyard, and there's a small bar and beer garden as well.

DJH Hostel   HOSTEL $
(📞813 318; www.muehlhausen.jugendherberge.de; Auf dem Tonberg 1; dm under/over 27yr €19.50/22.50; 🅿@🐕) This small hostel is about 2.5km west of the Hauptbahnhof. Take bus 5 to Blobach, then walk 500m.

Brauhaus zum Löwen   HOTEL $$
(📞4710; www.brauhaus-zum-loewen.de; Felchtaer Strasse 2-4; s/d €60/90; 🅿🐕) Conversation flows as freely as the beer at this classic brewery-pub, where you can get fed and fuelled among the copper vats before retiring to boldly pigmented, country-style rooms. Still in a party mood? Join the local cool kids in the adjacent Leo disco (Wednesday to Saturday).

Landhaus Frank Zum Nachbarn   GERMAN $$
(📞812 513; Eisenacher Landstrasse 34; mains €12-20; ⊙11.30am-10pm) One of the best local restaurants for regional cuisine, but book ahead. Take bus 151, 152 or 153 to the *Friedhof*

(cemetery) nearby if you haven't got your own wheels.

ⓘ Information

The **tourist office** (☏404 770; www.muehl hausen.de; Ratsstrasse 20; ☺9am-5pm Mon-Fri, 10am-4pm Sat & Sun) is about 1km west of the Hauptbahnhof, between Obermarkt and Untermarkt. Steinweg (near Obermarkt) is the main shopping street.

ⓘ Getting There & Away

Mühlhausen is at the crossroads of the B249 from Sondershausen and the B247 from Gotha. Regional trains link Mühlhausen with Erfurt (€12.20, 45 minutes) and Gotha (€7.50, 25 minutes), where you have to change if headed for Eisenach (€12.20, 50 minutes).

Around Mühlhausen

About 15km southwest of Mühlhausen, the **Hainich National Park** (Nationalpark Hainich; www.nationalpark-hainich.de) protects the largest continuous deciduous forest in Germany. There's hiking and cycling, of course, but the main reason to swing by is to take a walk through the treetops on the **Baumkronenpfad** (Treetop Trail; adult/concession/family €8.50/3/20; ☺10am-7pm). Two wooden paths meander some 44m above ground, giving you a unique perspective on the forest's flora and fauna, not to mention great views over the park itself. The trail is near Thiemsburg castle, also the site of the park information centre, which has a **nature exhibit** (adult/concession/family €8.50/3/20).

On Saturday and Sunday from April to October, a Wanderbus (Hiking Bus) leaves the town of Bad Langensalza at 11.20am and runs to the Tree Top Trail, returning at 3.53pm. Call ☏03625-481 001 to check the schedule. Bad Langensalza can be reached in 15 minutes by train from Mühlhausen or 45 minutes from Erfurt.

Kyffhäuser Mountains

It's not particularly mighty or large, but there's an undeniable mystique to the densely forested Kyffhäuser low-mountain range. Historically, this rural area is famous as the site of a bloody key battle in the Peasants' War of 1525 that left at least 6000 peasants dead and resulted in the capture and execution

of their leader, the radical reformer Thomas Müntzer.

Because the area is so sparsely populated, it's poorly served by public transportation, but bike trails and roads lead to all the main sights. The main town is Bad Frankenhausen.

⊙ Sights

Kyffhäuser Denkmal MONUMENT
(Kyffhäuser Monument; www.kyffhaeuser-denkmal. de; adult/concession/family €5/2.50/13; ☺9.30am-6pm) The Kyffhäuser was once home to one of Germany's largest medieval castles, the massive Reichsburg, built in the 12th century during the reign of Emperor Friedrich Barbarossa. It's now merely a romantic ruin but, according to legend, Barbarossa lies in eternal sleep in the belly of the mountain, awaiting the time when he'll be needed to bring honour and prosperity back to his people. In the 19th century, Emperor Wilhelm I was seen as Barbarossa's spiritual successor and a bombastic statue was erected in 1896 atop the foundations of the medieval castle. Showing the emperor on horseback, the Kyffhäuser Denkmal stands below a 60m-high tower and above a sculpture of Barbarossa sitting on a stone throne. To get to it, follow the B85 north from Bad Frankenhausen for about 10km, turn right at the sign and continue for another 2km.

Barbarossahöhle CAVE
(☏034671-545 13; www.hoehle.de; Mühlen 6, Rottleben; adult/child/family €7.50/4/21; ☺10am-5pm) This gypsum cave is on a grand scale, being one of the largest of its type in Europe. Hourly tours last about 50 minutes and take you past shimmering underground lakes and bizarre gypsum sheets that hang from the ceiling, as well as slabs described by legend as Barbarossa's table and chair. The caves are 7km west of Bad Frankenhausen, north of Rottleben.

Panorama Museum MUSEUM
(http://panorama-museum.de; Am Schlachtberg 9; adult/concession €5/4; ☺10am-6pm Tue-Sun) The Panorama Museum looms on the very site where thousands of peasants were slaughtered in 1525 during the Peasants' War. There's just one painting inside the giant cylindrical structure, but what a painting it is! Called *Frühbürgerliche Revolution in Deutschland* (Early Civil Revolution in Germany), it measures an astonishing 14m by 123m and

was inaugurated in 1989. The museum is on the Schlachtberg, about 3km north of Bad Frankenhausen.

ℹ Information

Regional Tourist Office (☑034671-717 16; www.kyffhaeuser-tourismus.de; Anger 14, in Bad Frankenhausen; ☺9.30am-6pm Mon-Fri, to 12.30pm Sat, 10-11.30am Sun) Can help with maps, directions and general information.

ℹ Getting There & Around

Bad Frankenhausen is no longer served by train. To get there from, say, Erfurt, first catch a regional train to Sondershausen (€11.10, one hour), Heldrungen, Artern or some other village and then switch to a bus or rent a bicycle. In Sondershausen, **Radwanderzentrum Kyffhäuserkreis** (☑03632-509 38; August-Bebel-Strasse 27; ☺7.30am-1.30pm Mon-Fri & by arrangement) rents bikes for €5 per 24 hours. In Bad Frankenhausen, bikes are rented in summer, but ask at the tourist office as the location tends to change. Bad Frankenhausen is 60km by road north of Erfurt (take the B4 north).

THURINGIAN FOREST & THE SAALE VALLEY

If most of the larger towns of Thuringia are about culture, the Thuringian Forest and the Saale Valley are about tradition, bucolic landscapes and – along the Saale River – winegrowing. This region takes in Eisenach, which is best known as the place where Luther sought protection after being excommunicated, the Saale-Unstrutt wineland, Jena – an important centre of optics and a lively university town – as well as a cluster of small, historic towns dotting the countryside. Hiking, especially along the Rennsteig, is excellent here. Follow the trail far enough south and you will end up on the border of Bavaria.

Eisenach

☑03691 / POP 42.750

Eisenach is a small town on the edge of the Thuringian forest whose modest appearance belies its association with two German heavyweights: Johann Sebastian Bach and Martin Luther. Luther went to school here and later returned to protective custody in the Wartburg, now one of Germany's most famous castles and a Unesco World Heritage Site. A century later, Bach, the grandest of all baroque musicians, was born in a wattle-and-daub home and attended the same school as Luther had. Eisenach also has a century-old automotive tradition – the world's first BMW rolled off the local assembly line in 1929. And when it's time to shake off culture and civilisation, remember that the famous Rennsteig hiking trail is only a hop, skip and jump away.

◉ Sights

Wartburg   CASTLE

(www.wartburg-eisenach.de; tour adult/concession €9/5, museum & Luther study only €5/4; ☺tours 8.30am-5pm, in English 1.30pm) When it comes to medieval castles and their importance in German history, the Wartburg is the mother lode. According to legend, the first buildings were put up in 1067 by the hilariously named local ruler Ludwig the Springer in an effort to protect his territory. In 1206, Europe's best minstrels met for the medieval version of *Pop Idol*, a song contest later immortalised in Richard Wagner's opera *Tannhäuser*. Shortly after, Elisabeth, the most famous Wartburg woman, arrived. A Hungarian princess, she was married off to the local landgrave at age four and later chose to abandon court life for charitable work, earning canonisation quickly after her death in 1235. Another famous resident was Martin Luther, who went into hiding here in 1521 under the assumed name of Junker Jörg after being excommunicated and placed under papal ban. During his 10-month stay, he translated the New Testament from Greek into German, contributing greatly to the development of the written German language.

Give yourself at least two hours: one for the guided tour, the rest for the museum and the grounds (views!).

To get to the Wartburg from the Markt, walk one block west to Wydenbrugkstrasse, then head southwest along Schlossberg through the forest via Eselstation (this takes about 40 minutes, and parts are rather steep). A more scenic route is via the Haintal (50 minutes).

From April to October, bus 10 runs hourly from 9am to 5pm from the Hauptbahnhof (with stops at Karlsplatz and Mariental) to the Eselstation, from where it's a steep 10-minute walk up to the castle. In winter, buses are available on demand; call ☑228 822 for a pick-up.

Bachhaus   MUSEUM

(www.bachhaus.de; Frauenplan 21; adult/concession €7.50/4; ☺10am-6pm) Johann Sebastian Bach,

CENTRAL GERMANY EISENACH

RENNSTEIG RAMBLE

Germany's oldest (first mentioned in public records in 1330) and most popular long-distance trail, the 169km Rennsteig winds southeast from Hörschel (near Eisenach) along forested mountain ridges to Blankenstein on the Saale River. This is one place where it pays to pack away the guidebook and simply explore the small towns you ramble close to along the way. In fact, following it is a bit like pushing into a Thuringian heart of darkness – distance closes up behind you, and if you press ahead as far as the Bavarian border region, the local dialect becomes incomprehensible even to many Germans. It's about as backwoodsy as the backwoods get.

The trail is marked by signposts reading 'R', and is best hiked in May/June and September/October. You should be moderately fit, but otherwise no special skills or equipment are needed – just good shoes and a set of strong thighs to carry you for six or seven days. Day hikes offer a taste of the trail, and hiker-geared lodging options abound in the villages and towns down below. The Rennsteig bike trail also begins in Hörschel and travels over asphalt, soft forest soil and gravel, mostly paralleling the hiking trail.

The tourist office in Eisenach has cycling and hiking brochures and maps. A time-honoured tradition for Rennsteig ramblers is to pick up a pebble from the Werra River at the beginning of your hike, carry it with you and throw it back into the Saale River upon completing the trail.

Eisenach is a handy gateway to the Thuringian Forest and Rennsteig. Bus 11 or regional bus 31 drops you at the Hohe Sonne trail head, right on the Rennsteig hiking trail, although you could also hike there (or back) via the craggily romantic Drachenschlucht gorge. From April to October, bus 11 departs seven times on Saturday and four times on Sunday. Regional bus 31 leaves year-round hourly (reduced services weekends; €1.30, 10 minutes).

who was born in Eisenach in 1685, takes the spotlight in the revamped and enlarged Bachhaus, one of the best biographical museums in Germany. Exhibits are set up in the type of wattle-and-daub town house where the Bach family lived (the original was destroyed) and trace both his professional and private life through concise, intelligent and engaging bilingual panelling. Your journey culminates in a modern annexe, where you can sit in suspended bubble chairs and listen to the wide range of musical contributions made by this versatile genius. Admission also includes a 20-minute concert played on antique instruments.

Automobile Welt Eisenach MUSEUM
(Friedrich-Naumann-Strasse 10; adult/concession €5/3.50; ⊙11am-5pm Tue-Sun) Cars, cars, cars! Production revved up in Eisenach in 1896 with the Wartburg, a model based on the French Decauville. The Automobile Welt Eisenach celebrates this history by displaying pretty much the entire product range, including an 1899 Wartburg Dixi, a 1936 BMW 328 sports car and other rare vintage vehicles and assorted memorabilia, many from the GDR era.

Georgenkirche CHURCH
(Pfarrberg 2; ⊙10am-noon & 2-4pm) The baptismal church of St Elizabeth and Johann Sebastian Bach. The reformer Martin Luther preached here while under papal ban. From June to September, free half-hour organ concerts take place at 11am Monday to Saturday.

Lutherhaus HISTORIC BUILDING
(www.lutherhaus-eisenach.de; Lutherplatz 8; adult/concession €4.50/2.50; ⊙10am-5pm) Displays in the house where the religious reformer Martin Luther lived as a schoolboy.

Reuter-Wagner Museum MUSEUM
(Reuterweg 2; adult/concession €4/2; ⊙11am-5pm Tue-Sun) Exhibits on the composer Richard Wagner's life and times, housed in a villa once owned by writer Fritz Reuter located at the foot of the Wartburg; it inspired Wagner's *Tannhäuser*.

Predigerkirche MUSEUM
(Predigerplatz 2; adult/concession €4/2; ⊙11am-5pm Tue-Sun) Exquisite collection of medieval sculpture, paintings and liturgical objects.

📖 Sleeping

TOP CHOICE **Hotel Villa Anna**   BOUTIQUE HOTEL **$$**
(☑239 50; www.hotel-villa-anna.de; Fritz-Koch-Strasse 12; s €76, d €99-119; P🅿🛜) This boutique hotel at the foot of the Wartburg has modern, good-sized rooms outfitted with ultracomfy beds and a big desk. Take bus 3, 10 or 11 to Prinzenteich.

TOP CHOICE **Hotel auf der Wartburg**   HOTEL **$$$**
(☑7970; http://wartburghotel.arcona.de; Auf der Wartburg; s €140-180, d €235-355; P) Built in 1914, this hotel has subdued colours and furnishings to match the location on the historic Wartburg. The singles at this luxury address are called 'Luther' rooms, but, for serious opulence, book one in the 'Prince' category.

Hotel Haus Hainstein   HOTEL **$$**
(☑2420; www.hainstein.de; Am Hainstein 16; s €55-65, d €78-85; P) A stately art nouveau villa in the leafy, hilly area south of town provides the charismatic setting of this small hotel, which has bright, stylish rooms, its own chapel, a restaurant and views of the Wartburg. Buses 3, 10 and 11 to Wandelhalle drop you within 500m.

Schlosshotel Eisenach   HOTEL **$$**
(☑214 260; www.schlosshotel-eisenach.de; Marktplatz 10; s €80, d €114-124, ste €130-195; P🛜) Most rooms, the nicest with balconies, face the quiet inner courtyard in this sprawling central complex. Its upmarket amenities lure business types during the week, but the sauna is perfect any time for unwinding or soothing post-hike muscles. Take any bus to Markt.

Gasthof Am Storchenturm   PENSION **$**
(☑733 263; www.gasthof-am-storchenturm.de; Georgenstrasse 43a; 3-6-bed dm €24, s/d €24/48, breakfast €5; P) Lots of long-socked hikers pad down the trails for simple but comfortable rooms here. It's a hostel-type guesthouse in a spiffed-up barn. Take any bus to Markt.

Residenzhaus   PENSION **$**
(☑214 133; www.residenzhaus-eisenach.de; Auf der Esplanade; s/d without bathroom €25/50, d with bathroom €60, breakfast €6) If you're into hip decor, fancy linen and chocolate on your pillow, you're better off elsewhere. But if you want modern comforts in a historic, central setting without shelling out big money, lug your luggage up the spiral stone staircase here. Some rooms share bathrooms. Take any bus to Markt.

🍴 Eating & Drinking

TOP CHOICE **Turmschänke**   GERMAN **$$**
(☑213 533; Karlsplatz 28; mains €19-24, 3-/4-course menu €32/38; ⊙dinner Mon-Sat) This hushed hideaway in Eisenach's only surviving medieval city gate scores a perfect 10 on the romance meter. Walls panelled in polished oak, beautiful table settings and immaculate service are a nice foil for Ulrich Rösch's flavour-packed concoctions that teeter between trendy and traditional.

Zucker + Zimt   ORGANIC **$**
(Markt 2; dishes €2.90-9.90; ⊙10am-8pm) A whiff of urbanity in stuffy Eisenach, this upbeat cafe, dressed in mod apple green, fully embraces the 'bio' trend. Organic and fair-trade ingredients find their destination in light creative mains, bagel sandwiches, stuffed crêpes and homemade cakes.

Brunnenkeller   GERMAN **$$**
(Markt 10; mains €7.50-14.60; ⊙lunch & dinner) Linen-draped tables beneath an ancient vaulted brick ceiling set the tone of this traditional chow house in a former monastery cellar. Quite predictably, the food is honest-to-goodness German and regional classics.

ℹ Information

Internet (cnr Bahnhofstrasse & Gabelsbergstrasse; per 30min €0.50; ⊙11am-11pm Mon-Fri, noon-11pm Sat & Sun) Two terminals inside a train station shop.

Post Office (Markt 6)

Sparkasse (Karlstrasse 2-4; ⊙9am-4pm Mon & Fri, to 6pm Tue & Thu, to 12.30pm Wed) Bank with ATM.

Tourist Office (☑792 30; www.eisenach.de; Markt 24; ⊙10am-6pm Mon-Fri, to 5pm Sat & Sun) Staff sell the Classic Card (€19 for 72 hours), which is good for public transport and admission to all the important sights, including the Wartburg.

ℹ Getting There & Around

BIKE Zweirad Henning (☑784 738; Schmelzerstrasse 4-6; ⊙9am-6pm Mon-Fri, to 1pm Sat) rents out bikes for €10 per day and also does repairs. You need to book two days ahead. Pick up a cycling map from the tourist office.

BUS Buses 1, 2, 5 and 12 run from the bus station opposite Hauptbahnhof to Markt.

CAR If you're driving, Eisenach is right on the A4 and is crossed by the B7, B19 and B84.

TRAIN Direct regional trains run frequently to Erfurt (€11.10, 45 minutes), Gotha (€5.50, 25 minutes) and Weimar (€14.40, one hour). ICE trains are faster and also serve Frankfurt am Main (€47, 1¾ hours) while IC trains go to Berlin-Hauptbahnhof (€65, 3¼ hours).

Schmalkalden

☑03683 / POP 20,000

Schmalkalden's old town groans and creaks under the sheer weight of its half-timbered houses and is crowned by a handsome hilltop castle, Schloss Wilhelmsburg. About 40km south of Eisenach, the little town played a big role during the Reformation. It was here in 1531 that the Protestant princes established the Schmalkaldic League to counter the central powers of Catholic emperor Charles V. Although they suffered a daunting military defeat in 1546, they managed to regroup and eventually got the emperor to sign the Peace of Augsburg in 1555 that allowed each of the German states to choose between Lutheranism and Catholicism.

It's about a 10-minute walk from the train and bus stations to the Altmarkt central square and another seven minutes to Schloss Wilhelmsburg.

⊙ Sights & Activities

Schloss Wilhelmsburg
PALACE

(www.museumwilhelmsburg.de; Schlossberg 9; adult/concession €3.50/2; ⊙10am-6pm Apr-Oct) Overlooking the town, the late-Renaissance Schloss Wilhelmsburg is easily Schmalkalden's most imposing building. Landgrave Wilhelm IV of Hessen conceived it as a hunting lodge and summer residence in the 1580s. Since then, the Schloss has largely kept its original design, with lavish murals and stucco decorating most rooms, of which the Riesensaal, with its coffered and painted ceiling, is the most impressive. The playfully decorated Schlosskirche (palace church) has a rare wooden organ that is thought to be the oldest working organ of its type in Europe. There's also an exhibit on life during the Renaissance and Schmalkalden's role in the Reformation, as well as an animated 3-D journey into the world of the Middle Ages.

Altmarkt
SQUARE

The incongruous towers of the late-Gothic Stadtkirche St. Georg (1437–1509) overlook the square. The Rathaus (1419) on Altmarkt functioned as the meeting place of the Schmalkaldic League, whom Luther preached to here in 1537.

⭐ Activities

Mart-Luther-Weg
HIKING

Schmalkalden is the western terminus of this 17km easy-to-moderate hiking trail that ends at Tambach-Dietharz, from where there are bus services back to town (weekdays only; the tourist office can help with times).

Mommelstein-Radweg
CYCLING

A recommended route is the 28km Mommelstein Bike Trail that follows a former railway line and some forest trails through a tunnel and viaduct (the tourist office has maps and directions).

🛏 Sleeping & Eating

Teichhotel
HOTEL $

(☑402 661; www.teichhotel.de; Teichstrasse 21; s/d €49/72; P) Expect plain but comfortable rooms in this hotel located just outside the Altstadt. The restaurant serves well-priced hearty fare, and the Wunderbar (closed Monday) has cocktails and occasional events.

Stadthotel Patrizier
HOTEL $$

(☑604 514; www.stadthotel-patrizier.de; Weidebrunner Gasse 9; s/d €55/82) Fourteen well-appointed, rooms in a historic hotel.

Maykel's
GERMAN $$

(www.maykels.eu; Lutherplatz 1; mains €9.50-18.90; ⊙10am-midnight Mon-Sat, closed Sun) Relaxed bar and restaurant with good salads, pasta, Flammkuchen and meat mains. Come to eat as well as to hang out over coffee or a drink.

ⓘ Information

The tourist office (☑403 182; www.schmalkalden.de; Mohrengasse 1a; ⊙10am-5pm Mon-Fri, to 1pm Sat) is just off Altmarkt.

ⓘ Getting There & Around

BICYCLE Fahrrad Anschütz (☑403 909; www.fahrrad-anschuetz.de; Stiller Gasse 17; per day €10; ⊙9am-6pm Mon-Fri, to noon Sat) rents out city, touring and mountain bikes.

TRAIN Schmalkalden is served by the private Süd-Thüringen-Bahn (www.sued-thueringen-bahn.de). Going to Erfurt (€16.40, two hours) requires a change in Zella-Mehlis; for Eisenach (€9.10, one hour), you need to change in Wernshausen. Schmalkalden is about 6km east of the B19, which connects Eisenach and Meiningen.

Saalfeld

☑03671 / POP 27,000

Gables, turrets and gates provide a cheerful welcome to Saalfeld, which has been sitting prim and pretty along the Saale River for 1100 years. Aside from the handsome medieval town centre, it lures visitors with one of Thuringia's most engrossing natural attractions, the Feengrotten (Fairy Grottoes).

◉ Sights

Feengrotten   CAVE
(Fairy Grottoes; www.feengrotten.de; Feengrottenweg 2; tour adult/child €8.80/5.50, combined ticket with Grottoneum exhibition & Fairy World adult/child €13.80/8.80; ⊙9.30am-5pm) About 3km southwest of Saalfeld's train station, the Feengrotten are the town's prime attraction. Formerly alum slate mines (from 1530 to 1850), they were opened for tours in 1914 and rank as the world's most colourful grottoes according to no less an authority than *Guinness World Records*. 'Colour' here refers mostly to different shades of brown, ochre and sienna, with an occasional sprinkling of green and blue. Small stalactite and stalagmite formations add to a bizarre and subtly impressive series of grottoes, with names like Butter Cellar and Blue-Green Grotto. The highlight is the Fairytale Cathedral and its Holy Grail Castle.

The **Feenweltchen**, only open from May to October, is a kingdom of elves, fairies and nature spirits, while the **Grottoneum** is open all year and has interactive exhibits on mining, the caves and how they came about.

❶ Information

Tourist Office (☑522 181; www.saalfeld.de; Markt 6; ⊙9am-6pm Mon-Fri, to 1pm Sat) Can help with accommodation.

❶ Getting There & Around

Regional trains run frequently to Rudolstadt (€2.20, 11 minutes) and Jena (Jena-Paradies; €9.10, 45 minutes). There are also a couple of direct ICE connections to Berlin-Hauptbahnhof (€66, three hours). Saalfeld is linked to Rudolstadt and Weimar via the B85 and to Jena by the B88.

The Hauptbahnhof is east of the Saale River, about a 10-minute walk from the Markt. Bus A makes the trip from Saalfeld Bahnhof and Markt to the grottoes every half-hour. For a taxi, call ☑511 115.

Jena

☑03641 / POP 105,150

Jena enjoys a lovely setting on the Saale River, flanked by muscular limestone hills and blessed with a climate mild enough for orchids and vines to thrive. A university town since 1558, it may not be as pretty as Weimar, some 20-odd kilometres to the west, but it did attract its own share of 18th-century cultural giants, Schiller and Goethe among them. However, it's really Jena's pedigree as a city of science that sets it apart from other Thuringian towns. This is, after all, the 19th-century birthplace of optical precision technology, pioneered by Carl Zeiss, Ernst Abbe and Otto Schott. Today, several museums and the world's oldest public planetarium attest to this legacy. Although it bears the scars of WWII and GDR aesthetics, Jena's still a beguiling town, with some 20,000 students injecting a large dose of liveliness. Outside the city centre, you'll find lovely art nouveau neighbourhoods, challenging trails leading to glorious viewpoints and the best nightlife in eastern Thuringia.

All sights are within a 10-minute walk from Markt.

◉ Sights

Optisches Museum   MUSEUM
(Optical Museum; www.optischesmuseum.de; Carl-Zeiss-Platz 12; adult/concession €5/4, combination ticket with Zeiss Planetarium €11/9; ⊙10am-4.30pm Tue-Fri, 11am-5pm Sat) The three pioneers who put Jena on the scientific map were Carl Zeiss, Ernst Abbe and Otto Schott. Zeiss began building rudimentary microscopes in 1846 and, with Abbe's help, developed the first scientific microscope in 1857. Together with Otto Schott, the founder of Jenaer Glasswerke (glass works), they pioneered the production of optical precision instruments, which eventually propelled Jena to global prominence in the early 20th century. Their life stories and the evolution of optical technology are the themes of this interactive museum with mind-bending 3D holograms. An English-language pamphlet is available. Outside is a commemorative pavilion built by Henry van de Velde, with a bust of Abbe by Max Klinger.

Rathaus   HISTORIC BUILDING
(Markt 1) Situated at the southern end of the town square, Jenn's Rathaus (1380) is graced with an astronomical clock in its baroque tower. Every hour, on the hour, a little door

opens and a devil/fool called Schnapphans appears, trying to catch a golden ball (representing the human soul) that dangles in front of him. The square itself is anchored by a statue of Prince-Elector Johann Friedrich I, founder of Jena's university and popularly known as 'Hanfried'.

Stadtmuseum & Kunstsammlung Jena
MUSEUM, GALLERY

(City Museum & Art Collection; www.stadtmuseum. jena.de; Markt 7; Kunstsammlung adult/concession €8/5, Stadtgeschichte €4/2.40; ⊙10am-5pm Tue, Wed & Fri, 3-10pm Thu, 11am-6pm Sat & Sun) This handsome building with the half-timbered upper section at the northern end of the town square houses the **Stadtmuseum**, where you can learn how the city evolved into a centre of philosophy and science, and the **Kunstsammlung** with changing exhibitions and a permanent collection of mostly 20th-century works.

Goethe Gedenkstätte
HISTORIC BUILDING

(Goethe Memorial; Fürstengraben 26; adult/concession €1/0.50; ⊙11am-3pm, closed Nov-Mar) As minister for the elector of Saxe-Weimar, Goethe visited Jena many times, regulating the flow of the Saale, building streets, designing the botanic garden, cataloguing the university library or discovering the obscure human central jawbone. Most of the time, he stayed in the tiny house that's now the Goethe Memorial. Exhibits illustrate his accomplishments as a natural scientist, poet and politician.

Botanischer Garten
GARDENS

(Botanic Garden; Fürstengraben 26; adult/concession €3/1.50; ⊙10am-7pm) Goethe himself planted the ginkgo tree in these gardens, the second-oldest in Germany, with more than 12,000 plants from every climatic zone on earth.

Schillers Gartenhaus
HISTORIC BUILDING

(Schiller's Garden House; Schillergässchen 2; adult/concession €2.50/1.30; ⊙11am-5pm Tue-Sun) Goethe is credited with recruiting Schiller to Jena University in 1789. The playwright enjoyed Jena so much that he stayed for 10 years, longer than anywhere else, in what is now known as Schillers Gartenhaus. He wrote *Wallenstein* in the little wooden shack in the garden, where he and Goethe liked to wax philosophical. To get to it, go south along Leutragraben.

JenTower
TOWER

(lift €3; ⊙11am-midnight) The 128m-tall cylindrical JenTower was intended to be a Zeiss research facility but proved unsuitable. Today it has a shopping mall at ground level and an observation platform and the upmarket Scala restaurant at the top.

Universität Jena – Collegium Jenense
UNIVERSITY

(Kollegiengasse) Jena's university faculties are spread throughout town, but this was where the university was founded as Collegium Jenense in 1558, in a former monastery. Enter the courtyard to admire the coat of arms of Johann Friedrich I and to check out the free exhibit (in German) on the university's illustrious history.

Zeiss Planetarium
PLANETARIUM

(www.planetarium-jena.de; Am Planetarium 5; adult/concession €8/6.50, combination ticket with Jena's Optical Museum €11/9, laser show €9/7.50) The world's oldest public planetarium (1926). Its state-of-the-art dome projection system makes it a heavenly setting for cosmic laser shows paying tribute to music legends Pink Floyd and Queen. Hours vary.

Stadtkirche St Michael
CHURCH

(Parish Church; Kirchplatz; ⊙12.30-5pm Mon, 10am-5pm Tue-Sun May-Sep) This Gothic church one block north of the town square is famous for having Martin Luther's original engraved tombstone (there's another in the Schlosskirche in the town of Wittenberg that is actually a 19th-century replica).

FREE Schott Glasmuseum
MUSEUM

(Otto-Schott-Strasse 13; ⊙1-5pm Tue-Fri) An interactive multimedia exhibition with audioguides in English on the history, production and technology of glass.

University Headquarters
UNIVERSITY

(Füstengraben 1) The highlight here is a Minerva bust by Rodin and a wall-sized painting showing Jena students going off to fight against Napoléon.

Universität Jena – Main Campus
UNIVERSITY

(Ernst-Abbe-Platz) The main campus of the Friedrich Schiller Universität Jena is located on Ernst-Abbe-Platz in a building that formerly belonged to the Carl Zeiss optics factory. The square is dotted with abstract sculptures by Frank Stella.

JENA FROM ABOVE

There's plenty of hiking and biking around Jena, but, for a rewarding thigh burner, scoot up the 500 steps to the **Landgrafenturm**, an ancient tower on a hill north of town (approach via Philosophenweg). Called 'Balcony of Jena', this lofty perch treats you to a glorious panorama of the town and surroundings, high above the din of the city and practically at eye level with the top of the JenTower. There are benches for resting and a restaurant, the **Landgrafen Jena** (☎507 071; www.landgrafen.com; mains €13.50-26.50; ⏱11am-11pm Wed-Sun), for refreshments or light seasonal dishes. Several trails radiate in all directions from up here as well. Less than 3.5km away, for instance, there's the **Papiermühle** (☎459 80; www.papiermuehle-jena.de; Erfurter Strasse 102; s/d €56/89, mains €10-27; ⏱11.30am-midnight), a charming brewery-pub and beer garden that's a welcome refuelling stop; it even has a few rooms in case you feel like spending the night. Otherwise, it's an easy ride on bus 16 back into town.

✿ Festivals & Events

A great time to be in town is for **Kulturarena Jena** (☎498 060; www.kulturarena.com), an international music festival – with blues, rock, classical and jazz – that gets the town rocking in July and August.

🛏 Sleeping

Gasthaus Zur Noll   PENSION $$
(☎597 710; www.zur-noll.de; Oberlauengasse 19; s €70-75, d €75-95; P🐾) You'll find classic Thuringian hospitality galore in this historic charmer that is well known for its breakfast buffet bonanza. Rooms teeter between elegant and rustic, and are endowed with all the expected modern trappings. For extra character and space, ask to stay in the wood-clad *Bohlenstube*. The restaurant-pub is perfect for sampling rustic fare (mains €9 to €17). Take any transport to Markt.

Ibis Hotel City Am Holzmarkt   HOTEL $$
(☎8130; www.ibishotel.com; Teichgraben 1; r from €69, breakfast €10; P🐾) This chain contender has all the prerequisites to give you a good night's sleep and puts you right in the thick of things. Wi-fi is free in the lobby. Bus 15 from Jena-West runs to Holzmarkt. From Jena-Paradies it's a short walk north.

Alpha One Hostel Jena   HOSTEL $
(☎597 897; www.hostel-jena.de; Lassallestrasse 8; dm €15-18, s/d €25/40, linen €2.50, breakfast €3.50; @) Jena's indie hostel is in a quiet street, yet within staggering distance of the Wagnergasse pubs. The decent-sized rooms are splashed in bright colour; those on the 3rd floor have great views and room 16 even has a balcony. The closest tram stop is Ernst-Abbe-Platz (tram 5, 25 or 35).

Steigenberger Esplanade Jena   LUXURY HOTEL $$$
(☎8000; www.jena.steigenberger.de; Carl-Zeiss-Platz 4; P🐾@🐾) Jena's premier abode has been recently revamped. Take tram 5, 25 or 35 to Ernst-Abbe-Platz.

🍴 Eating & Drinking

Café Immergrün   BISTRO $
(Jener Gasse 6; mains €2.50-5; ⏱11am-late) Sink deep into a plump sofa for intense tête-à-têtes or gather your posse in the leafy garden at this self-service bistro-pub, tucked off a quiet side street just north of the JenTower. The cheap meals (mostly pasta, rice and baguettes) make it popular with students.

Roter Hirsch   GERMAN $$
(Holzmarkt 10; mains €5-13; ⏱9am-midnight Mon-Sat, 10am-11pm Sun) About 500 years of wood-panelled charm and the perfect backdrop for hearty home cooking.

Scala   INTERNATIONAL $$$
(☎356 666; www.scala-jena.de; Leutragraben 1, JenTower; mains €18-29; ⏱11am-midnight) Excellent food with fantastic views from the top of JenTower.

Café Stilbruch [TOP CHOICE]   INTERNATIONAL $$
(www.stilbruch-jena.de; Wagnergasse 2; dishes €9-24; ⏱8.30-1am Mon-Thu, 9-2am Sat, 9-1am Sun) The competition is great on Wagnergasse, Jena's pub mile, but this multilevel contender is a fascinating stop for drinks and a bite from the something-for-everybody menu. For privacy, snag the table atop the spiral staircase; for people-watching, sit outside. Most dishes are under €12.

☆ Entertainment

Rosenkeller   CLUB
(http://rosenkeller.org; Johannisstrasse 13) This
historic club in a network of cellars has plied
booze and music to generations of students
and is still among the best places in town to
meet some friendly locals.

Kassablanca Gleis 1   CLUB
(www.kassablanca.de; Felsenkellerstrasse 13a) Near
Jena-West train station, this joint feeds the
cultural cravings of the indie crowd with a
potpourri of live concerts, dance parties,
readings, experimental theatre, movies and
other distractions. Cheap drinks fuel the fun.

Volksbad Jena   LIVE MUSIC
(www.volksbad-jena.de; Knebelstrasse 10) You can't
swim in this century-old public pool any
longer; instead you'll be showered by cultural
events ranging from the mainstream to the
offbeat. Opposite Jena-Paradies station.

ℹ Information

Bagels & Beans (Leutragraben 2-4; internet
per min €0.04, wi-fi per 30min €1.50; ⊗8am-
8.30pm Mon-Fri, 9am-7pm Sat, 10am-6pm
Sun) Internet and cheap bagels in a pleasant
atmosphere.

Tourist Office (☑498 050; www.jena.de;
Markt 16; ⊗10am-7pm Mon-Fri, to 4pm Sat
& Sun) In Jena's oldest building, dating from
1384. Sells the JenaCard (€8.90) for 48 hours
of public transport and free and discounted
tours and admissions.

ℹ Getting There & Away

CAR Jena is just north of the A4 from Dresden
to Frankfurt, and west of the A9 from Berlin to
Munich. The B7 links it with Weimar, while the
B88 goes south to Rudolstadt and Saalfeld.

TRAIN Direct trains depart from Jena-West to
Weimar (€5, 15 minutes) and Erfurt (€8.50, 30
minutes); for Eisenach (€19, 1½ hours) change
in Weimar. Two-hourly ICE trains to Berlin-
Hauptbahnhof (€59, 2¼ hours) depart from
Jena-Paradies, as do at least hourly services
to Rudolstadt (€7.90, 50 minutes) and Saalfeld
(€9.10, 30 minutes).

ℹ Getting Around

Jena has two train stations. Long-distance
trains arrive at Jena-Paradies, a 10-minute walk
south of Markt. Regional trains from Erfurt or
Weimar stop at the tiny Jena-West station, a
20-minute walk from Markt. To get to Markt from
Jena-West, turn left onto Westbahnhofstrasse
and turn right into Kollegienstrasse. Bus 15 runs

twice-hourly from Jena-West to Holzmarkt,
150m south of Markt along Löbderstrasse

BICYCLE Fahrrad Kirscht (☑441 539; Löbder-
graben 8; ⊗9am-7pm Mon-Fri, to 4pm Sat) rents
out bikes for €15 for the first 24 hours and €10
per day thereafter.

BUS Single bus or tram tickets cost €1.80, while
a day pass is €4.20.

TAXI Call ☑458 888.

SAALE-UNSTRUT REGION

The winegrowing region along the rivers
Saale and Unstrut provides a wonderfully
rural summer retreat. Europe's most north-
erly wine district produces crisp whites
and fairly sharp reds, which you can enjoy
at wine tastings, sometimes right at the estates. The 60km bicycle-friendly Weinstrasse
(Wine Road) meanders through the region,
past steeply terraced vineyards, castle-
topped hills and small family-owned farms.
Local tourist offices can help with information and maps.

Naumburg
☑03445 / POP 34,300

At the confluence of the Saale and Unstrut
Rivers, Naumburg has a handsome Altstadt
with the striking Renaissance Rathaus and
the Marientor double gateway. Its most famous sight, however, is the medieval cathedral. In late June, this normally sedate town
goes wild during the **Kirschfest** (Cherry Festival; www.kirschfest.de), a celebration of food,
drink, music, a parade and fireworks.

◉ Sights

Dom   CHURCH
(www.naumburger-dom.de; Domplatz 16-17; adult/
concession €6.50/4.50; ⊗9am-6pm Mon-Sat,
noon-6pm Sun) The enormous Cathedral of
Sts Peter & Paul is a masterpiece of medieval
architecture and a treasure trove of superb
sculpture. While the crypt and the east choir
feature elements of the Romanesque, the
famous west choir is a prime example from
the early Gothic period. This is where you
find the dozen monumental statues of the
cathedral founders, the work of the so-called
Master of Naumburg.

Medieval stained-glass windows are augmented by ruby-red modern panes by Neo
Rauch, one of the premier artists of the

New Leipzig School. Admission includes the **Domschatzgewölbe** (Cathedral treasury; adult/concession €2/1; ⊘9am-6pm Mon-Sat, noon-6pm Sun) (cathedral treasury), where highlights include an altar painting by Lucas Cranach the Elder and a heart-wrenching 14th-century pietà.

Nietzsche Haus   MUSEUM
(Weingarten 18; adult/concession €2.50/1.50; ⊘2-5pm Tue-Fri, 10am-5pm Sat & Sun) Friedrich Nietzsche (1844–1900) spent most of his childhood in this modest home, acquired by his mother after the death of her husband. In 1890 she brought her son back here to nurse him as he was going slowly mad, allegedly as a result of syphilis. The exhibit consists mostly of photos, documents and reams of biographical text about one of Germany's greatest philosophers.

🛏 Sleeping & Eating

Zur Alten Schmiede   HOTEL **$$**
(☑243 60; www.hotel-zur-alten-schmiede.de; Lindenring 36-37; s/d €78/105; P@⊛) All rooms are well sized and have been recently renovated. This is the snazziest place to stay in Naumburg.

Hotel Stadt Aachen   HOTEL **$$**
(☑2470; www.hotel-stadt-aachen.de; Markt 11; s €62-69, d €83-95, tr €105) Comfortable traditional hotel on the bustling main square.

Camping Blütengrund   CAMPGROUND **$**
(☑261 144; www.campingnaumburg.de; Blütengrund 6; adult/tent/car €5/4.65/2.40) Situated 1.5km northeast of Naumburg at the river confluence, with canoe and bicycle rentals.

DJH Hostel   HOSTEL **$**
(☑703 422; www.jugendherberge.de/jh/naumburg; Am Tennisplatz 9; dm incl breakfast under/over 27yr €17/20, s/d €23/32, linen €3.50; P⊛) Naumburg's large and well-equipped hostel is 1.5km south of the town centre.

Bocks   INTERNATIONAL **$$**
(www.bocks-restaurant.de; €10.50-24; ⊘10am-9pm; ⚹) Charming decor in the town's top eatery – it has two rooms, a cafe area and excellent meat dishes, pasta and other fare.

ℹ Information

Tourist Office (☑273 125; www.naumburg-tourismus.de; Markt 12; ⊘9am-6pm Mon-Fri, to 4pm Sat, 10am-1pm Sun) Audio tours €5.

ℹ Getting There & Around

BICYCLE **Radhaus Steinmeyer** (☑203 119; www.radhaus-naumburg.de; Bahnhofstrasse 46) rents bikes in summer from €10 per day.

BOAT The **MS Fröhliche Dörte** (☑03445-202 830; www.froehliche-doerte.de) runs to Freyburg between April and October, taking 70 minutes one way (one way adult/child €8/4, return €14/7). It departs Naumburg at 11am, 1.30pm and 4pm.

CAR From Halle or Leipzig, take the A9 to either the B87 or the B180 and head west; the B87 is less direct and more scenic, though it's the first exit from the A9.

TRAIN Regional trains chug to Naumburg from Halle (€7.50, 45 minutes), Jena (€7.50, 45 minutes) and Weimar (€9.10, 35 minutes). A local line runs to Freyburg (€2.50, eight minutes). For Leipzig, hop on the fast ICE train (€19, 40 minutes).

TRAM Don't dawdle after arrival – head straight out of the train station to the Naumburger Strassenbahn, a GDR-era tram (€1.50) that drops you at Theaterplatz, near Markt. By foot, walk along Rossbacher Strasse (keep bearing left and uphill) past the cathedral.

Freyburg

☑034464 / POP 4950

With its cobblestone streets and medieval castle clinging to vine-covered slopes, Freyburg has a vaguely French atmosphere. It's the sort of village that puts the 'r' in rustic. Sparkling wine production has been the main source of income here since the middle of the 19th century, and to this day, Freyburg is home to Germany's most famous bubbly brand, Rotkäppchen Sekt (named for the Little Red Riding Hood from the Grimm fairy tale). The town seriously comes alive for its wine festival in the second week of September.

⊙ Sights

Rotkäppchen Sektkellerei   WINERY
(www.rotkaeppchen.de; Sektkellereistrasse 5; 45min tours €5; ⊘tours 11am & 2pm daily, also 12.30pm & 3.30pm Sat & Sun) Established in 1856, and the biggest sparkling-wine producer in Germany, the Rotkäppchen Sektkellerei is one of the few companies that survived the GDR and, since reunification, has acquired enough muscle to buy other brands, including Mumm. Tours include the historic cellars and the production facilities. Between 10am and 5pm, you can also taste and buy a whole range of Sekt at the shop out front.

Schloss Neuenburg CASTLE

(www.schloss-neuenburg.de; Schloss 25; adult/concession €6/3.50, with tour €8/6.50, audioguide €2, tower €1.50/1; ⊙10am-6pm, tower Tue-Sun) The large medieval Schloss Neuenburg, on the hill above town, is one of Naumburg's highlights. It houses an excellent museum that illuminates various aspects of medieval life. The complex includes a rare Romanesque two-storey (or 'double') chapel and a freestanding tower, the Dicker Wilhelm, which has further historical exhibitions and splendid views.

ⓘ Information

Tourist Office (☎272 60; www.freyburg-info .de; Markt 2; ⊙9am-5pm Mon-Thu, to 6pm Fri, 8am-2pm Sat)

ⓘ Getting There & Around

BICYCLE The well-marked bicycle route between Naumburg and Freyburg makes for a wonderful ride.

BOAT The most scenic way to get to Freyburg is by boat from Blütengrund, at the confluence of the Saale and Unstrut Rivers, just outside Naumburg. The 19th-century **MS Fröhliche Dörte** (☎03445-202 830; www.froehliche-doerte.de) tootles its way along the Unstrut between April and October. The 40-minute one-way journey from Freyburg to Naumburg costs €7/3.50, and €14/7 return. It departs Freyburg at 12.15pm, 2.45pm and 5.15pm, returning from Naumburg at 11am, 1.30pm and 4pm.

CAR The B180 to Naumburg follws the river.

TRAIN & BUS Freyburg is about 9km north of Naumburg and served by trains (€2.50, eight minutes) and buses (€2.20, 23 minutes).

HARZ MOUNTAINS

Northern Germany's only serious upland lacks the spectacular peaks of Bavaria, rising scarcely to 1142m on the highest peak, the Brocken. What the Harz Mountains lack in alpine dramatics, however, they make up for by being easily and inexpensively reached from Berlin and other north German cities. Here you will find excellent hiking trails and spas. For instance, it's possible to spend a day hiking through deciduous or mixed beech and conifer forest, ease the aching muscles for a few hours in a sauna and salt grotto, and eat well in a local restaurant. Downhill skiers will consider the pistes scarcely worthy of the ride back up, but cross-country skiers will find some excellent loops and trails. Mountain bikers can also hit some good trails and cyclists will enjoy simply cruising the mountain roads.

The prettiest of the hikes is through the spectacular Bodetal from the former East German town of Thale. The most famous hike, however, is to the Brocken – a mountain that was a magnet for literary greats such as Wolfgang von Goethe and Heinrich Heine, and today draws hiking masses, especially on Walpurgis Night, the night of 30 April, when all and sundry hit the trails in the evening and celebrate a pagan festival.

ⓘ Information

The main information centre for the Harz Mountains is the Harzer Verkehrsverband (p568) in Goslar, but information on the Eastern Harz is best picked up in towns there, particularly in Wernigerode.

The kind of map that you choose will depend on the type of activity you have planned. *Der Harz und Kyffhäuser* 1:50,000 map (€5.80) provides a good overview of trails and major sites in the entire Harz.

A local *Kurtaxe* (resort tax; ranging from €0.75 to €3 per night) is charged in most towns. Your resort card will give various discounts.

ⓘ Getting There & Away

BUS BerlinLinienBus (www.berlinlinienbus.de) runs between Berlin via Magdeburg to/from Goslar (one way €22, six hours) and some smaller towns twice daily except on Wednesdays. There are plenty of regional bus services to take you further into the mountains.

CAR If you're driving, the area's main arteries are the east–west B6 and the north–south B4, which are accessed via the A7 (skirting the western edge of the Harz on its way south from Hanover) and the A2 (running north of the Harz between Hanover and Berlin).

TRAIN The area's main towns of Goslar, Wernigerode and Quedlinburg are serviced by frequent trains; see **Deutsche Bahn** (www. bahn.de).

ⓘ Getting Around

The Harz is one part of Germany where you'll rely on buses as much as trains, and the various local networks are fast and reliable. Narrow-gauge steam trains run to the Brocken and link major towns in the Eastern Harz.

Goslar

📞 05321 / POP 41,000

A hub of tourism and the most important town west of the former border running between the Western and Eastern Harz, Goslar has a charming medieval Altstadt, which, together with its historic Rammelsberg mine, is a Unesco World Heritage Site.

Founded by Heinrich I in 922, the town's early importance centred on silver and the Kaiserpfalz, the seat of the Saxon kings from 1005 to 1219. It fell into decline after a second period of prosperity in the 14th and 15th centuries, reflecting the fortunes of the Harz as a whole, and relinquished its mine to Braunschweig in 1552 and then its soul to Prussia in 1802. The Altstadt, Rammelsberg mine and Kaiserpfalz attract visitors by the busload in summer, when it's always best to reserve ahead.

◎ Sights

Altstadt   NEIGHBOURHOOD
(Map p566) One of the nicest things to do in Goslar is to wander through the historic streets around the Markt. **Hotel Kaiserworth** (Map p566) on Markt was erected in 1494 to house the textile guild, and sports almost life-size figures on its orange facade. The **market fountain**, crowned by an ungainly eagle symbolising Goslar's status as a free imperial city, dates from the 13th century; the eagle itself is a copy – the original is on show in the Goslarer Museum. Opposite the Rathaus is the **glockenspiel**, a chiming clock depicting four scenes of mining in the area. It plays at 9am, noon, 3pm and 6pm.

Kaiserpfalz   CASTLE
(Map p566; Kaiserbleek 6; adult/concession €4.50/2.50; ☺10am-5pm) Goslar's pride and joy is the reconstructed 11th-century Romanesque palace, Kaiserpfalz. After centuries of decay into a historic pile of rubble, this palace was resurrected in the 19th century and adorned with interior frescos of idealised historical scenes. On the southern side is **St Ulrich Chapel**, housing a sarcophagus containing the heart of Heinrich III. Below the Kaiserpfalz is the recently restored **Domvorhalle** (Map p566), displaying the 11th-century Kaiserstuhl, the throne used by Salian and Hohenstaufen emperors. Behind the palace, in pleasant gardens, is an excellent sculpture by Henry Moore called the *Goslarer Krieger* (Goslar Warrior).

Rammelsberger Bergbau Museum   MUSEUM
(www.rammelsberg.de; Bergtal 19; admission €12; ☺9am-6pm, last admission 4.30pm) About 1km south of the town centre, the shafts and buildings of this 1000-year-old mine are now a museum and Unesco World Heritage Site. Admission to the mine includes a German-language tour and a pamphlet with English explanations of the 18th- and 19th-century Roeder Shafts, the mine railway and the ore processing section. Bus 803 stops here.

Rathaus   HISTORIC BUILDING
(Map p566; Markt; admission to Huldigungssaal adult/child €3.50/1.50; ☺11am-3pm Mon-Fri, 10am-4pm Sat & Sun, closed Nov & Jan-Mar) The impressive late-Gothic Rathaus is most beautiful at night, when light shining through stained-glass windows illuminates the stone-patterned town square. The highlight inside is a beautiful cycle of 16th-century religious paintings in the **Huldigungssaal** (Hall of Homage).

Goslarer Museum   MUSEUM
(Map p566; König-strasse 1; adult/concession €4/2; ☺10am-5pm Tue-Sun) The Goslarer Museum offers a good overview of the natural and cultural history of Goslar and the Harz. One room contains the treasures from the former Goslar Dom, and there's also a cabinet with coins dating from the 10th century. The original golden eagle from the market fountain is also here.

Mönchehaus Museum   GALLERY
(Map p566; Mönchestrasse 3; admission €5; ☺10am-5pm Tue-Sat) The Mönchehaus Museum, in a 16th-century half-timbered house, has changing exhibits of modern art, including works by the most recent winner of the prestigious Kaiserring art prize; past winners include Henry Moore, Joseph Beuys and Rebecca Horn. Look for the interesting sculptures in the peaceful garden.

Museum im Zwinger   MUSEUM
(Map p566; Mönchestrasse 3; admission €5; ☺11am-4pm Tue-Sat mid-Mar–Oct) A 16th-century tower with a collection of such late-medieval delights as torture implements, coats of armour and weapons used during the Peasant Wars.

Zinnfiguren-Museum   MUSEUM
(Map p566; www.zinnfigurenmuseum-goslar.de; Klapperhagen 1; adult/concession €4/2; ☺10am-5pm Tue-Sun) Has a colourful collection of painted pewter figures.

Goslar

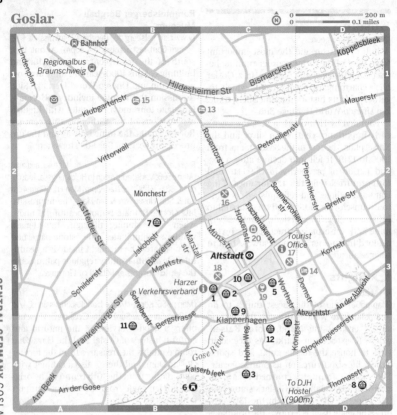

Musikinstrumenten- und
Puppenmuseum
MUSEUM

(Map p566; Hoher Weg 5; adult/child €3/1.50; ⊙11am-5pm) A private museum sprawling over five floors, with musical instruments, dolls and also a porcelain collection housed in the cellar.

Siemenshaus
HISTORIC BUILDING

(Map p566; Schreiberstrasse 12) This baroque 17th-century building is the ancestral home of the Siemens industrial family, but the interior is unfortunately closed to visitors.

Brusttuch
HISTORIC BUILDING

(Map p566; Hoher Weg 1) Dating from 1521 and today a hotel.

Bäckergildehaus
HISTORIC BUILDING

(Map p566; cnr Marktstrasse & Bergstrasse) A 16th-century historic house with the emblem of the bakers' guild on the eastern side.

🛏 Sleeping

TOP CHOICE Hotel Kaiserworth
HOTEL $$$

(Map p566; ☑7090; www.kaiserworth.de; Markt 3; s €71-101, d €122-182, tr €172-207; P🐕😊🔊) This magnificent 500-year-old former merchant guild building has tasteful rooms and a good restaurant open daily from 6am to 11pm. Insomniacs should head for the hotel's Café Nouvelle, which is open till 2am or the last customer.

Gästehaus Schmitz
GUESTHOUSE $

(Map p566; ☑234 45; www.schmitz-goslar.de; Kornstrasse 1; s/d/tr €45/60/75; P) This slightly eccentric guesthouse is an excellent choice in the heart of town, especially for those on low budgets or looking for an apartment. Book ahead.

Das Brusttuch
HOTEL $$

(Map p566; ☑346 00; www.brusttuch.de; Hoher Weg 1; s €81, d €119-152; P🔊😊) The soft colours

Goslar

and smart rooms in this historic hotel make it a comfortable snooze zone. It's very central and some rooms have double doors to the hallway.

Niedersächsischer Hof HOTEL $$
(Map p566; ☎3160; www.niedersaechsischer-hof-goslar.de; Rosentorstrasse 20; s €79-89, d €109-119; P☏) Opposite the train station, the 'Hof' toys with the idea of being an art hotel (the kids will love the piece near the foyer with the cindered toy cars) and has light rooms well insulated against the bustle outside. Prices fluctuate according to date, so call ahead.

Der Achtermann HOTEL $$
(Map p566; ☎700 00; www.der-achtermann.de; Rosentorstrasse 20; s €84-94, d €109-159; P@☏☎) The only drawbacks with this otherwise very good hotel are its sprawling size and the number of business conference guests buzzing between its ample amenities.

DJH Hostel HOSTEL $
(☎222 40; www.djh-niedersachsen.de/jh/goslar; Rammelsberger Strasse 25; under/over 27yr dm €23.40/27.40, r €28.40/31.40; P@☎) Take bus 803 to Theresienhof to reach this pretty hostel out near the mining museum. Facilities are excellent, with single and twin rooms and six- to eight-bed dorms, as well as barbecue and sports areas.

Hotel & Campingplatz Sennhütte CAMPGROUND, HOTEL $
(☎225 02; Clausthaler Strasse 28; adult/child €5/2, car/tent €3/2, s/d €25/50) This camping ground is 3km south of Goslar via the B241 (bus 830 to Sennhütte). Rooms are comfortable and have been renovated; it's advisable to reserve through the tourist office before setting out.

✕ Eating & Drinking

TOP CHOICE Henry's INTERNATIONAL $$
(Map p566; www.henrys-erleben.de; Markt 6; mains €14.60-21; ⊙7am-late; ☎) This stylish restaurant, bar and lounge has a comfortable minimalist edge with sofas for chilling out day and night. Henry's also has stylish rooms for €145 per night.

Das Schwarze Schaf INTERNATIONAL $
(Map p566; Jakobikirchhof 7; dishes €4.50-10.90; ⊙11am-8.30pm; ☎) This sleek eatery has a large menu of salads, pasta, *Flammkuchen* (Alsatian pizzas), stir-fries and grills, all served at wooden tables in a bright Asian-European crossover atmosphere. Dishes can be ordered takeaway.

Die Butterhanne GERMAN $$
(Map p566; www.butterhanne.de; Marktkirchhof 3; mains €8.50-14; ⊙from 8.30am) The fare is traditional and regular here, the outdoor seating is nice and on the first Saturday of the month the tables are cleared and the place morphs into a throbbing nightspot from 10pm. The name refers to a famous local frieze showing a milkmaid churning butter while clutching her buttock to insult her employer – don't try it on disco night.

Restaurant Aubergine
MEDITERANEAN $$

(Map p566; 421 36; www.aubergine-goslar.de; Marktstrasse 4; mains €16.90-19.50; noon-2.30pm & 6-11.30pm) Good-quality nontraditional cuisine, crisp tablecloths and service, and a classy atmosphere.

Brauhaus
GERMAN

(Map p566; www.brauhaus-goslar.de; Marktkirchhof 2; dishes €7.80-23.50; from 11am) A newcomer to Goslar's gastronomic and drinking scene, this gastro pub brews four types of beer in its copper vats beyond the bar and serves meals focusing mostly on steaks and other meats, some of them organic and locally produced.

🔒 Shopping

Hoher Weg has shops selling souvenirs, especially puppets and marionettes, many of which are witches.

Schnaps und So
SOUVENIRS

(Map p566; Hokenstrasse 3) This is a great local booze store, but approach the Harz fruit wines and herbal schnapps with caution – some of them may leave you the worse for wear.

🛈 Information

Asklepios (440; Kösliner Strasse 12) The hospital is about 6km north of town.

City-Textilpflege (Petersilienstrasse 9; 8am-6pm Mon-Fri, 9am-1pm Sat)

Harzer Verkehrsverband (340 40; www.harzinfo.de; Marktstrasse 45, Bäckergildehaus; 8am-5pm Mon-Thu, to 2pm Fri) Regional tourist information.

Post Office (Klubgartenstrasse 10)

Sparkasse (Bäckerstrasse/Jakobikirchhof 5) Bank services and ATM.

Telecenter & Internetcafe (Breite Strasse 79; per hr €1.80; 10am-8pm Mon-Sat)

Tourist Office (780 60; www.goslar.de; Markt 7; 9.15am-6pm Mon-Fri, 9.30am-4pm Sat, 9.30am-2pm Sun)

🛈 Getting There & Away

BUS The office of **Regionalbus Braunschweig** (RBB; 194 49; www.rbb-bus.de; Bahnhof), from where buses depart, has free timetables for services throughout the Harz region. Bus 831 runs between Goslar and Altenau in the south via Clausthal-Zellerfeld; 830 runs to Clausthal-Zellerfeld via Hahnenklee. Change to the 840 at Clausthal-Zellerfeld for St Andreasberg. Trains are easier to get to Bad Harzburg, where you can take bus 820 to Torfhaus. BerlinLinienBus (p564) runs daily to Berlin (one way €22, 4¼

hours, via Magdeburg). For timetables and bookings, refer to **DER-Reisebüro** (757 90; www.der.net; Bahnhof).

CAR & MOTORCYCLE The B6 runs north to Hildesheim and east to Bad Harzburg, Wernigerode and Quedlinburg. The north–south A7 is reached via the B82. For Hahnenklee, take the B241. Car rental is available at **Europcar** (251 38; Lindenplan 3).

TRAIN Bad Harzburg–Hanover trains stop here often, as do trains on the Braunschweig–Göttingen line. There are direct trains to Wernigerode (€9.10, 45 minutes, every two hours) and other services requiring a change at Vienenburg.

🛈 Getting Around

Local bus tickets cost €2.20. To book a taxi, ring 1313. **Hans Speed** (685 734; www.hans-speed.de; Kuhlenkamp 1c) rents mountain and city bikes for €13 per day.

Bad Harzburg

05322 / POP 22,000

This pretty spa town just 9km from Goslar is a magnet for visitors seeking health and curative spas. If you're not one of the many cure seekers, the main attraction will be the nearby Harz National Park and trails, which offer excellent access to some typically picturesque Harz landscapes.

🏃 Activities

Grosser Burgberg
FORTRESS

(cable car adult/child return €3/2; 9am-5pm) A nice thing to do in Bad Harzburg is to walk, or ride the cable car, to this hill above town with ruins of an 11th-century fortress built by Heinrich IV. It's a 3km walk. From there you can stroll around the fortress ruins or set out on longer hikes or mountain bike rides.

Hiking & Skiing
HIKING, SKIING

Marked hiking trails lead into the national park from Berliner Platz and Grosser Burgberg, the latter just over 3km from Berliner Platz on foot. Among the many walks are those from Berliner Platz to Sennhütte (1.3km), Molkenhaus (3km) and scenic Rabenklippe (7km), overlooking the Ecker Valley. All destinations except Sennhütte have restaurants; a board inside the cable-car station indicates which ones are open. From Grosser Burgberg you can take the Kaiserweg trail, which leads to Torfhaus and connects to the Brocken. If snow conditions are good, it's possible to ski cross-country to/from Torfhaus, which has equipment-hire facilities.

Sole Therme
SPA

(www.sole-therme-bad-harzburg.de; Nordhäuser Strasse 3; sauna & therme adult/child €12/7.50; ⊙8am-9pm Mon-Sat, to 7pm Sun) The local spa is one of the best around and has been partly the reason for a renaissance of this historic spa town. It has heated indoor and outdoor saltwater pools, and six types of saunas, including a salt grotto: rub a handful of white gold onto your skin, let it do the trick, then wash it off in the water cascade. Wednesday and Thursday mornings are respectively men- and women-only sauna days.

🛏 Sleeping & Eating

TOP CHOICE **Hotel Tannenhof-Solehotel** HOTEL **$$**
(☑968 80; www.solehotels.de; Nordhäuser Strasse 6; s €54-77, d €94-124; P🖥) This friendly and comfortable hotel alongside the tourist office has two adjacent buildings and its own access to the town's Sole Therme spa directly behind the hotel, with reductions for use of the spa and sauna all day. Rooms are spacious, if not always in newest condition.

Ringhotel Braunschweiger Hof HOTEL **$$**
(☑7880; www.hotel-braunschweiger-hof.de; Herzog-Wilhelm-Strasse 54; s €68-99, d €138-158; P🖥❄) Fine rooms, lots of wellness deals, a lovely garden and an extremely good restaurant (mains €9.50 to €29) downstairs. The cheapest rooms are in the guesthouse next door, where there's no wi-fi.

PlumbohmS Bio-Suiten Hotel HOTEL **$$**
(☑3277; www.plumbohms.de; Herzog-Wilhelm-Strasse 97; ste €85-110, plus one-off cleaning charge €30-40; P🖥❄) Upmarket suites based on natural fittings and fibres. Cafe Saxe (snacks and light meals €5.90 to €11.90) in the same building does strudels and *Kaiserschmarn* (pancakes sliced into strips, with raisins) and excellent soup, salads and cold platters.

ℹ Information

Haus der Natur (☑784 337; Berliner Platz; adult/concession €2/1; ⊙10am-5pm Tue-Sun) Harz National Park information centre, with a small interactive exhibition that kids will enjoy.

Spielpunkt (Herzog-Wilhelm-Strasse 42; per hr €2.50; ⊙9am-11pm Mon-Sat, 11am-11pm Sun)

Tourist-Information (☑753 30; www.bad-harzburg.de; Nordhäuser Strasse 4; ⊙9am-6pm Mon-Fri, 10am-4pm Sat & Sun)

ℹ Getting There & Around

BICYCLE **Bike House Harz** (☑987 0623; www.bikehouseharz.de; Ilsenburger Strasse 112) rents mountain bikes from €25 per day.

BUS Bus 810 leaves here regularly for Goslar (€3.50, 20 minutes) and goes via the cable-car station; bus 260/874 heads for Wernigerode (€4.10, one hour). Bus 820 shuttles almost hourly to Torfhaus (€3.50, 25 minutes).

CAR Bad Harzburg is on the A395 to Braunschweig; the B4 and B6 lead to Torfhaus and Wernigerode, respectively.

TRAIN Frequent train services link Bad Harzburg with Goslar (€3.50, 12 minutes), Hanover (€19, 1¼ hours), Braunschweig (€12.20, 45 minutes) and Wernigerode (€7.50, 30 minutes).

Wernigerode
☑03943 / POP 34,400

The Central Harz area is mostly within former East Germany and the major hub here is Wernigerode. A bustling, attractive town on the northern edge of the Harz, Wernigerode is a good starting point for exploring the eastern regions of the Harz National Park. The winding streets of the Altstadt are flanked by pretty half-timbered houses, and high above the Altstadt hovers a romantic ducal castle from the 12th century. This is the northern terminus of the steam-powered narrow-gauge Harzquerbahn, which has chugged along the breadth of the Harz for almost a century; the line to the summit of the Brocken (1142m), the highest peak in northern Germany, also starts here.

⊙ Sights

Schloss CASTLE
(www.schloss-wernigerode.de; adult/concession €6/5, tower €1; ⊙10am-6pm, closed Mon Nov-Apr) Originally built in the 12th century to protect German Kaisers on hunting expeditions, Schloss Wernigerode was enlarged over the years to reflect late-Gothic and Renaissance tastes. Its fairy-tale facade came courtesy of Count Otto of Stolberg-Wernigerode in the 19th century. The museum inside includes portraits of Kaisers, beautiful panelled rooms with original furnishings, the opulent **Festsaal** (Banquet Hall) and stunning **Schlosskirche** (1880) with its altar and pulpit made of French marble. You can walk (1.5km) or take a Bimmelbahn wagon ride (adult/child return €5/2) from Marktstrasse. In summer, horse-drawn carts make the trek from Marktplatz.

NARROW-GAUGE RAILWAYS

Fans of old-time trains or unusual journeys will be in their element on any of the three narrow-gauge railways crossing the Harz. This 140km integrated network – the largest in Europe – is served by 25 steam and 10 diesel locomotives, which tackle gradients of up to 1:25 (40%) and curves as tight as 60m in radius. Most locomotives date from the 1950s, but eight historic models, some from as early as 1897, are proudly rolled out for special occasions.

The network, a legacy of the GDR, consists of three lines. The **Harzquerbahn** runs 60km on a north–south route between Wernigerode and Nordhausen. The serpentine 14km between Wernigerode and Drei Annen Hohne includes 72 bends; you'll get dropped off on the edge of Harz National Park.

From the junction at Drei Annen Hohne, the **Brockenbahn** begins the steep climb to Schierke and the Brocken. Direct services to the Brocken can also be picked up from Wernigerode and Nordhausen, or at stations en route; single/return tickets cost €17/26 from all stations. One option is to take the train to Schieke and then follow a trail or the bitumen track to the Brocken, northern Germany's highest mountain.

The third service is the **Selketalbahn**, which begins in Quedlinburg and runs to Eisfelder Talmühle or Hasselfelde. At Eisfelder Tal, you can change trains for other lines. The picturesque Selketalbahn crosses the plain to Gernrode and follows Wellbach, a creek with a couple of good swimming holes, through deciduous forest to Mägdesprung, before joining the Selke Valley and climbing past Alexisbad to high plains around Friedrichshöhe, Stiege and beyond.

Passes for three/five days cost €44/49 per adult (children half-price). Timetables and information can be picked up from **Harzer Schmalspurbahnen** (☎03943-5580; www. hsb-wr.de; Hauptbahnhof, Wernigerode) or in Quedlinburg.

Marktplatz SQUARE
Dominating Wernigerode's town square, the colourful and spectacular towered **Rathaus** has an unusual provenance. It began life as a theatre around 1277, only to be given its mostly late-Gothic features in the 16th century. The artisan who carved the town hall's 33 wooden figures was said to have fallen foul of the authorities, and if you look closely you can see a few of his mocking touches. The neo-Gothic **fountain** (1848) was dedicated to charitable nobles, whose names and coats of arms are immortalised on it.

Oberpfarrkirchhof NEIGHBOURHOOD
By following the small Klint south from Marktplatz (the street on the right-hand side if you face the town hall), you pass some historic buildings and eventually reach Oberpfarrkirchhof, which surrounds the **Sylvestrikirche**. Here you'll find **Gadenstedtsches Haus** (1582) on the south side of Oberpfarrkirchhof, with its Renaissance oriel.

Breite Strasse NEIGHBOURHOOD
Essentially the main street of Wernigerode, Breite Strasse is where you find the pretty **Café Wien** building (1583) at No 4, today a dignified cafe and worthwhile stopover for both architectural and gastronomical reasons. It's almost impossible to miss the carved facade of the **Krummelsches Haus** at No 72, as it depicts various countries symbolically; America is portrayed, reasonably enough, as a naked woman riding an armadillo.

🏃 Activities

The deciduous forest behind the castle is crisscrossed with lovely **trails** and Forstwege (forestry tracks). Pick up maps from the toursit office. Wernigerode is also a good starting point for hikes and bike rides into the Harz National Park.

🛌 Sleeping

TOP CHOICE **Hotel Gothisches Haus** LUXURY HOTEL $$
(☎6750; www.travelcharme.com; Am Markt 1; s €89-129, d €122-258, ste €250-420; P✳🖤) The warm Tuscan colours and thoughtful design of this luxury hotel make it literally a very attractive option, and the wellness area is hard to beat, with three saunas and a 'beach' with real sand. One suite has a waterbed.

Parkhotel Fischer
HOTEL $$

(☑691 350; www.parkhotel-fischer.de; Mauergasse 1; s/d €65/105; P🅿🛗🏊) Rooms here are comfortable and modern, but it's extras like the tranquil indoor swimming pool with fake Roman pillars and the sauna that give this hotel the edge on others in town.

Hotel am Anger
HOTEL $$

(☑923 20; www.hotel-am-anger.de; Breite Strasse 92; s €50-60, d €90-100; P) Labyrinthine it may be, and there's an awful lot of pine in the 40 rooms, but this courtyard hotel is pleasant and some rooms have views of the castle.

DJH Hostel
HOSTEL $

(☑606 176; www.jugendherberge.de/jh/wernigerode; Am Eichberg 5; dm under/over 27yr €19/22, linen €3.50, s €32; 🕿) On the edge of the forest about 2.5km west of town in Hasserode, the DJH hostel has two-, three- and four-bed dorms with bathrooms. There's also a sauna and solarium here, and nearby is the large Brockenbad swimming complex. Take bus 1 or 4 to Hochschule Harz and follow the signs for 500m.

✕ Eating & Drinking

TOP CHOICE Casa Vita
MEDITERRANEAN $$

(www.casa-vita-wr.de; Marktstrasse 35; mains €10-18; ☉dinner Tue-Sun; ☑) This bistro and bar has an attractive, spacious interior as well as a courtyard and beer garden – all rounded off by a homely Mediterranean ambience. Like the salad with beef strips, many dishes cost less than €10.

Die Stuben
GERMAN, INTERNATIONAL $$

(☑6750; Am Markt 1; mains €19.50-23.50; ☉lunch & dinner daily, Bohlenstube dinner Wed-Sat Feb-Jun & Sep-Dec; ☑) Located inside Gothisches Haus hotel, Die Stuben consists of several restaurant rooms, including the Bohlenstube, a gourmet act that is one of the best in the region.

Bodega
SPANISH $$

(www.bodega-wernigerode.de; Marktstrasse 12; mains €12.80-16-80, tapas €2-11.50; ☉from 5pm Sun-Fri, from noon Sat) Decent tapas and meats from a relative newcomer on Wernigerode's scene.

Café am Markt & Lounge
CAFE, ITALIAN $$

(Marktplatz 6-9; mains €9.50-15.90; ☉8am-6.30pm Mon-Sat, Baldini brunch 9am-2pm Sun) This cafe has an Italian restaurant attached (same menu) and a lounge area upstairs for smokers.

Brauhaus
PUB

(www.brauhaus-wernigerode.de; Breite Strasse 24; mains €8.50-13.40; ☉11.30am-late) This enormous, multilevel pub and bistro serves fairly standard German meat and vegetarian dishes, but – on Saturday from 9pm – it also has a dance floor upstairs. German football is shown live here.

ℹ Information

Post Office (Burgstrasse 19)

Tourist Office (☑553 7835; www.wernigerode-tourismus.de; Marktplatz 10; ☉9am-7pm Mon-Fri, 10am-4pm Sat, 10am-3pm Sun) Tourist information, free map and room-booking service.

ℹ Getting There & Around

BICYCLE Bad-Bikes (☑626 868; www.bad-bikes-online.de; Breite Strasse 48a) rents good mountain and city bikes for between €20 and €25 per day. Entrance behind the shops.

BUS The timetable (€2) available from the **WVB bus office** (☑5640; www.wvb-gmbh.de; Hauptbahnhof) includes a train schedule. Bus 253 runs to Blankenburg and Thale, while bus 257 serves Drei Annen Hohne and Schierke.

CITY BUS Numbers 1 and 2 run from the bus station to the Rendezvous bus stop just north of the Markt, connecting with bus 3. Tickets cost €1.20 or are free with the Kurkarte, which your hotel will give you on checking in.

TAXI Call ☑633 053.

TRAIN There are frequent trains to Goslar (€9.10, 45 minutes) and Halle (€21.20, 1¼ hours). Change at Halberstadt for Quedlinburg (€9.10, 45 minutes) and Thale (€11.10, one hour).

Schierke

☑039455 / POP 700

Situated at 650m in the hills at the foot of the Brocken and just 16km west of Wernigerode, Schierke is a rambling, mostly modern village and the last stop for the Brockenbahn before it climbs the summit. It has an upper town on the main road to the Brocken and a lower town down in the valley of the Kalte Bode River. Schierke is also a popular starting point for exploring the Harz National Park, with opportunities for excellent hiking through deciduous or mixed beech and spruce forests, and it's the home of the ubiquitous 'Schierker Feuerstein' *digestif*.

⚡ Activities

Schierke is a good departure point for hikes to Brocken (1142m), Northern Germany's highest mountain, as well as cross-country skiing on trails through the forests of the Oberharz. Winter **cross-country ski hire** (☑409; Brockenstrasse 14a; per day €10; ☺9am-5pm Mon-Fri) is available from an outlet alongside the Stöber Eck store.

You can hike to the Brocken via the bitumen Brockenstrasse (12km), closed to private cars and motorcycles. More interesting is the 7km hike via Eckerloch. Marked trails also lead to the rugged rock formations of Feuersteinklippen (30 minutes from the Kurverwaltung) and Schnarcherklippen (1½ hours).

Horse-drawn wagons travel from Schierke to the Brocken and cost €25 return per person.

On the night of 30 April, Walpurgisnacht, Schierke attracts a veritable throng of visitors, most of whom set off on walking tracks to the Brocken.

ℹ Information

The **Kurverwaltung** (☑8680; www.schierke-am-brocken.de; Brockenstrasse 10; ☺9am-noon & 1-4pm Mon-Fri, 10am-noon & 2-4pm Sat, 10am-noon Sun) has tourist information and can help with accommodation in town. **National-parkhaus Schierke** (☑477; Brockenstrasse; ☺8.30am-4.30pm) has hiking brochures and information on the national park. It is situated 1km north of the tourist office towards Brocken.

ℹ Getting There & Around

The frequent bus 257 connects Schierke with Wernigerode (€2.90, 30 to 45 minutes). Narrow-gauge railway services run between Wernigerode and Schierke (single/return €7/11, one hour). Driving from the west, take the B27 from Braunlage and turn off at Elend. From Wernigerode, take Friedrichstrasse.

Brocken & Torfhaus

There are prettier landscapes and hikes in the Harz, but the 1142m Brocken is what draws the crowds: about 50,000 on a summer's day. There are several approaches, including one from Schierke, but the Goetheweg is the main trail up the mountain from the west.

GOETHEWEG FROM TORFHAUS

The 8km Goetheweg trail to the Brocken from the Western Harz starts at Torfhaus. Easier than other approaches, it initially takes you through bog, follows a historic aqueduct once used to regulate water levels for the mines, then crosses the Kaiserweg, a sweaty 11km trail from Bad Harzburg. The trail becomes steep as you walk along the former border between East Germany and West Germany. From 1945 to 1989 the Harz region was a frontline in the Cold War, and the Brocken was used by the Soviets as a military base. For 28 years the summit was off limits and was virtually the only mountain in the world that couldn't be climbed. Today you can hike along the train line above soggy moorland to reach the open, windy summit, where you can enjoy the view, eat pea soup and *Bockwurst* (boiled sausage), and think of Wolfgang von Goethe, Heinrich Heine and other literary greats who have written about the Harz.

Once at the top, you'll find the **Brocken-haus** (www.nationalpark-harz.de; adult/concession €4/3; ☺9.30am-5pm), with a cafe, interactive displays and a viewing platform. In summer (but only in snow-free conditions) rangers conduct one-hour tours of the plateau.

Torfhaus itself is a good starting point for **cross-country skiing** or winter ski treks, with plenty of equipment available for hire. Downhill skiing is limited to 1200m (on two pistes); one recommended route is the Kaiserweg. Make sure you pack a good map and take all precautions. The **Nationalparkhaus** (www.nationalpark-harz.de; Torfhaus 21; ☺9am-5pm) has information on the park.

ℹ Getting There & Away

Bus 820 stops at Torfhaus (€3.50, 20 minutes) on the well-served Bad Harzburg–Braunlage route. Otherwise, approach from Schierke.

Quedlinburg

☑03946 / POP 28,400

Quedlinburg, situated on a fertile plain at the northern cusp of the Harz Mountains, is the most spectacular of the historic towns in the Harz region.

Its intact Altstadt and over 1400 half-timbered houses dating from six centuries ago are a highlight of any trip to the Harz. In 1994 the city became a Unesco World Heritage Site; since then, work to save the crumbling treasures lining its romantic cobblestone streets has gradually progressed.

In the 10th century the Reich was briefly ruled from here by two women, Theophano and Adelheid, successive guardians of the 10th-century child-king Otto III, and Quedlinburg itself is closely associated with the *Frauenstift*, a medieval foundation for widows and daughters of the nobility that enjoyed the direct protection of the Kaiser.

Although the Altstadt can get crowded in summer and on weekends, any time of year is nice for a visit. You can also pick up the narrow-gage railway from here.

⊙ Sights

Stiftskirche St Servatius   CHURCH
(Schlossberg 1; adult/concession €4.50/3, combined ticket Dom, treasury, crypt & Schlossmuseum adult/concession €8.50/5.50; ⊙10am-6pm Tue-Sat) The 12th-century Stiftskirche St Servatius is one of Germany's most significant from the Romanesque period. Its treasury contains valuable reliquaries and early bibles. The crypt has some early religious frescos and contains the graves of Heinrich and his widow, Mathilde, along with those of the abbesses.

Schlossmuseum   MUSEUM
(Schlossberg 1; adult/concession €4/2.50, combined ticket Dom, treasury, crypt & Schlossmuseum adult/concession €8.50/5.50; ⊙10am-6pm Tue-Sun) The Schlossberg, on a 25m-high plateau above Quedlinburg, was first graced with a church and residence under Henry the Fowler. The present-day Renaissance Schloss contains the Schlossmuseum, with some fascinating Ottonian-period exhibits dating from 919 to 1056. A multimedia display explains how the Nazis used the site for propaganda by staging a series of events to celebrate Heinrich – whose life they skewed to justify their own ideology and crimes.

Fachwerkmuseum Ständebau   MUSEUM
(Wordgasse 3; adult/concession €3/2; ⊙10am-5pm Fri-Wed) Germany's earliest half-timbered houses were built using high perpendicular struts. The building from 1310 that now houses the Fachwerkmuseum Ständebau is a perfect illustration of this, and inside there are exhibits on the style and construction technique. Nearby is **Finkenherd** and a cluster of more recent half-timbered houses, built where Heinrich der Vogler (Henry the Fowler, also Heinrich I; r 919–36) was said to be trapping finches when told he had been elected king.

Lyonel-Feininger-Galerie   GALLERY
(www.feininger-galerie.de; Finkenherd 5a; adult/concession €6/3; ⊙10am-6pm Tue-Sun) This purpose-built gallery exhibits the work of influential Bauhaus artist Lyonel Feininger (1871–1956). Feininger was born in New York and came to Germany at the age of 16, later fleeing the Nazis and returning to the US in 1937. The original graphics, drawings, watercolours and sketches on display are from the period 1906 to 1936, and were hidden and saved from the paws of the Nazis by a Quedlinburg citizen.

CENTRAL GERMANY QUEDLINBURG

QUEDLINBURG'S HISTORIC BUILDINGS

With so many historic buildings, Quedlinburg is one town in which it's nice just to stroll the streets and soak up the atmosphere. The **Rathaus** (1320) dominates Markt, and in front of this is a **Roland statue** from 1426. Just behind the Rathaus is the **Marktkirche St Benedikti** (1233), and nearby is the Gildehaus zur Rose (p575) (1612) at Breite Strasse 39. Running off Markt is the tiny **Schuhhof**, a shoemakers' courtyard, with shutters and stablelike 'gossip doors'. **Alter Klopstock** (1580), which is found at Stieg 28, has scrolled beams typical of Quedlinburg's 16th-century half-timbered houses.

From Stieg 28 (just north of Schuhhof), it's a short walk north along Pölle to **Zwischen den Städten**, a historic bridge connecting the old town and Neustadt, which developed alongside the town wall around 1200 when peasants fled a feudal power struggle on the land. Behind the Renaissance facade, tower and stone gables of the **Hagensches Freihaus** (1558) is now the Hotel Quedlinburger Stadtschloss. Many houses in this part of town have high archways and courtyards dotted with pigeon towers. A couple of other places of special note are the **Hotel zur Goldenen Sonne** building (1671) at Steinweg 11 and **Zur Börse** (1683) at No 23.

Klopstockmuseum MUSEUM

(Schlossberg 12; adult/concession €3.50/2.50; ⊙10am-5pm Wed-Sun) The early classicist poet Friedrich Gottlieb Klopstock (1724–1803) is one of Quedlinburg's most celebrated sons. He was born in this 16th-century house, which is now a museum containing some interesting exhibits on Klopstock himself and Dorothea Erxleben (1715–62), Germany's first female doctor.

⭐ Festivals & Events

A program of classical music is held in the Stiftskirche every year from June to September. For tickets and information, contact the tourist office.

🛏 Sleeping

TOP CHOICE Hotel Quedlinburger Stadtschloss HOTEL $

(☑526 00; quedlinburgerstadtschloss@precise hotels.com; Bockstrasse 6/Klink 11; s €69-109, d €94-174; P🖧) Tasteful features and the wellness area (Finnish sauna, steam bath and whirlpool) of this hotel in a restored Renaissance residence make it a great choice in the town centre. Most rooms are designed to accommodate those in wheelchairs.

TOP CHOICE Romantik Hotel Theophano HOTEL $$

(☑963 00; www.hoteltheophano.de; Markt 13-14; s €69, d €99-140; P@🖧) Each room is decorated in an individual style at this rambling, rustic hotel. Most are spacious and very comfortable, but the many staircases (no lift) and low thresholds might be a problem for some. Double rooms are reduced Sunday to Thursday.

Hotel zur Goldenen Sonne HOTEL $

(☑962 50; www.hotelzurgoldenensonne.de; Steinweg 11; s €49-64, d €69-92; P) Both the old and new buildings of this hotel have decent rooms, but those in the old building are better furnished, have better windows and are mostly away from the restaurant's interior yard.

Hotel am Hoken HOTEL $

(☑525 40; www.hotel-am-hoken.de; Hoken 3; s €49-71, d €69-110, apt €89-140; P🖧) This highly recommended hotel off Markt has elegance, lots of traditional style and some light decorative touches. Floors and furnishings are in attractive timber.

Hotel Zum Bär HOTEL $$

(☑7770; www.hotelzumbaer.de; Markt 8-9; s €58-90, d €90-145; P) Expect spacious, well-styled rooms and a good mid-priced restaurant downstairs in this traditional hotel in the heart of the old town.

Schlosshotel Zum Markgrafen HOTEL $$$

(☑81140;www.schlosshotel-zum-markgrafen.de; Wallstrasse 96; s €105, d €150-180; P) Some rooms have a whirlpool, most have leadlight windows, and all are cosy in this neo-Gothic mansion from 1904. You can chill out on the cafe terrace or eat and drink in the hotel restaurant and cocktail bar. Its park is locked after dark and reserved for guests.

DJH Hostel HOSTEL $

(☑03946-811 703; www.jugendherberge.de; Neuendorf 28; dm €16.50-19.50, bedding €3) This excellent DJH hostel offers four- and 10-bed dorms in a quiet and very central location. It's relatively small and fills quickly in summer.

🍴 Eating & Drinking

TOP CHOICE Café Münzenberg CAFE $

(Münzenberg 1/17; snacks €4-8; ⊙11am-6pm Fri-Wed Easter-Oct) Perched upon the cliff of Münzenberg, a hilltop settlement above town, this sleek little cafe has outdoor seating, a few snacks and wonderful views. It's well worth the hike up here but hours are subject to change, so ask at the Zum Roland cafe to find out if it's currently open.

Brauhaus Lüdde GERMAN, PUB $$

(☑705 206; Blasiistrasse 14; mains €9-16; ⊙11am-midnight Mon-Sat, to 10pm Sun) After the arrival of a coach group, the average age can soar to 70 years, decreasing slowly as the night grinds on in this lively microbrewery. Decent food and good boutique beer (despite some rather flatulent names for the local drop) are the order of the day in Lüdde.

Zum Roland CAFE, INTERNATIONAL $$

(Breite Strasse 2-6; mains €6-15, cakes €3, meals €7.90-14.40; ⊙10am-10pm) Sprawling through seven houses, this cafe does decent, if unspectacular, international nosh and a delicious apple strudel. There's a kids' table and small play area.

Hössler SEAFOOD $

(Steinbrücke 21; meals €6.80-12.60, fish roll €3; ⊙8am-7.30pm Mon-Fri, 9am-8pm Sat, 2-7pm Sun) This is an excellent fish cafeteria with a restaurant through the passage. The same meals are cheaper in the front section.

Restaurant Theophano
im Palais Salfeldt
INTERNATIONAL $$

(963 00; www.palaissalfeldt.de; Kornmarkt 6; mains €12-35, 3-/6-course menu €32/49; 6pm-midnight Tue-Sat, closed Jan) Associated with the Romantik Hotel Theophano, this restaurant is housed in a mansion, where it serves fine seasonal, regional and Mediterranean dishes.

Kartoffelhaus No 1
GERMAN $

(Breite Strasse 37; mains €3.80-10.50; 11am-midnight) Tasty potato and grill dishes – nothing more, nothing less – are served here in large quantities. Enter from Klink.

☆ Entertainment

Gildehaus Zur Rose
LIVE MUSIC

(Breite Strasse 39; from 9pm Fri & Sat) In a town that's pretty close to being an entertainment-free zone, the Gildehaus is your best bet. It's an occasional venue with DJs and various parties, but the panelled interior alone justifies a visit whenever it's open.

❶ Information

Harzerschmalspurbahnen (527 191; www.hsb-wr.de; Marktstrasse 1; 10am-5pm) Narrow-gauge railway information.

Post Office (Bahnhofstrasse; 9am-6pm Mon-Fri, to noon Sat)

Sparkasse (Markt 15) ATM and banking services.

Spielstube (Breite Strasse 39; per hr €2; 9am-10pm Mon-Sat, 2-10pm Sun)

Tourist Office (905 625; www.quedlinburg.de; Markt 2; 9.30am-6pm Mon-Fri, to 3pm Sat, to 2pm Sun) Tourist information, maps and guided tours to sights.

❶ Getting There & Away

BUS QBus (2236; www.qbus-ballenstedt.de; Hauptbahnhof) office inside the hall has timetables and information on its frequent regional services. Buses to Thale (€2.90, 35 minutes) leave from the bridge in front of the train station (stop 8 and 9).

CAR The **Strasse der Romanik** (Romanesque Road; not to be confused with the Romantic Road in Bavaria) leads south to Gernrode. This theme road follows the L239 south to Gernrode and connects towns that have significant Romanesque architecture. The B6 runs west to Wernigerode, Goslar, the A395 (for Braunschweig) and the A7 between Kassel and Hanover. For Halle take the B6 east, and for Halberstadt the B79 north.

TRAIN Frequent services to Thale (€2.20, 12 minutes). For trains to Wernigerode (€9.10, 45 minutes), change at Halberstadt. The narrow-gauge Selketalbahn runs to Gernrode (€3, 15 minutes) and beyond. There are no left-luggage lockers, and the station hall isn't always open.

❶ Getting Around

Cars can be hired from **Avis** (8805; www.avis.de; Gernroeder Weg 5b). There are numerous **taxi services** (702 525, 707 777) in town. **2Rad Pavillon** (709 507; Bahnhofstrasse 1b) rents out bicycles from €6 per day.

Gernrode
039485

Only a short 8km hop south of Quedlinburg, Gernrode makes an ideal day trip. Its Stiftskirche St Cyriakus is a magnificent piece of Romanesque architecture, while hikers, picnickers and steam-train enthusiasts will also enjoy this pretty town, which boasts the largest thermometer and *Skat* (a card game) table in the world. It's also a nice place to pick up the narrow-gauge railway if you're planning to travel deeper into the mountains.

The **tourist office** (354; www.gernrode.de; Marktstrasse 20; 9.30am-3.30pm Mon-Fri, to 2pm Sat) is a 10-minute walk from the Hauptbahnhof (follow Bahnhofstrasse). It has information on summer organ concerts and tours in the town's major highlight, the Stiftskirche St Cyriakus.

◉ Sights & Activities

Stiftskirche St Cyriakus
CHURCH

(guided tour €3; 9am-5pm Mon-Sat, noon-5pm Sun Apr-Oct, tours 3pm daily) Stiftskirche St Cyriakus is one of the purest examples of Romanesque architecture from the Ottonian period. Construction of the basilica, which is based on the form of a cross, was begun in 959. Especially noteworthy is the early use of alternating columns and pillars, later a common Romanesque feature. The octagonal **Taufstein** (Christening stone), whose religious motifs culminate in the Ascension, dates from 1150. You can also see enclosed in glass **Das Heilige Grab**, an 11th-century replica of Christ's tomb in Jerusalem.

❶ Getting There & Away

Regular QBus services for Thale and Quedlinburg stop at the Hauptbahnhof and in the town centre. The Selketalbahn passes through Gernrode from Quedlinburg; buy tickets at the Hauptbahnhof.

Thale

☑ 03947 / POP 19,150

Situated below the northern slopes of the Harz Mountains, Thale is a dying industrial town and a thriving tourist centre. The main attraction for visitors is the sensational landscape of rugged cliffs flanking the Bode River, and a lush river valley that makes for ideal hiking.

The two cliffs at the head of the valley are known as Hexentanzplatz and Rosstrappe. These once had Celtic fortresses and were used by Germanic tribes for occult rituals and sacrifices. The landscape also inspired the myth of Brunhilde, who escaped a loveless marriage to Bohemian prince Bodo by leaping the gorge on horseback; her pursuing fiancé couldn't make the jump and plunged into the valley that now bears his name, turning into a hellhound on the way. The impact of Brunhilde's landing supposedly left the famous hoof imprint in the stone on Rosstrappe.

Postmodern pagans gather in grand style and numbers each year on 30 April to celebrate Walpurgisnacht here.

◎ Sights

Hexentanzplatz   LOOKOUT

(cable car return €5.50; ⊘9.30am-6pm) Of the two rocky bluffs flanking the Bode Valley (Rosstrappe is the other), Hexentanzplatz is the most developed and popular. It is most easily reached by cable car, which was completely rebuilt in 2012.

Rosstrappe   LOOKOUT

(chairlift return €3.80; ⊘9.30am-6pm Easter-Sep, 10am-4.30pm Oct-Easter) Rosstrappe takes its name from what is supposedly the horse's hoof imprint left by the mythical Brunhilde when she sprang over the gorge on horseback to avoid marrying the giant Bodo – the imprint can be seen in the stone on the cliff. Considering that Bodo, who leapt after her, landed in a watery grave, horse and all, you're probably better off taking the chairlift up here or one of the trails. Go early or late in the day to avoid crowds. Signs direct you to the chairlift from the Hauptbahnhof, near where the **Presidentenweg** hiking trail also begins.

✦ Activities

The hiking brochures *Wanderführer* (€1) and *Führer durch das Bodetal* (€2) are excellent if your German is up to it. Highly recommended is the Bode Valley **Hexenstieg walk** between Thale and Treseburg (blue triangle, 10km). If you take the bus from Thale to Treseburg, you can walk downstream and enjoy the most spectacular scenery at the end. WVB bus 264 does the trip from April to early November, and QBus 18 runs via Hexentanzplatz from April to October. Another 10km trail (red dot) goes from Hexentanzplatz to Treseburg; combine with the valley walk to make a round trip.

ⓘ Information

The **tourist office** (☑2597; www.thale.de; Bahnhofstrasse 3; ⊘7am-5pm Mon-Fri, 9am-3pm Sat & Sun) is in Friedenspark opposite the Hauptbahnhof. Pick up the English-language brochure *Legendary Thale*, or book a themed tour with a witch in German (€5).

ⓘ Getting There & Around

BUS The bus station is located alongside the train station. For Wernigerode, take bus WVB 253; to get to Treseburg, take QBus 18. WVB bus 264 goes to Treseburg and Blankenburg via Rosstrappe.

CAR Karl-Marx-Strasse leads to the main junction for roads to Quedlinburg and Wernigerode.

TAXI Call ☑2505 or 2435.

TRAIN Frequent trains travel to Quedlinburg (€2.20, 12 minutes) and Wernigerode (change in Halberstadt; €11.10, one hour).

Mittelbau Dora

From late in 1943, thousands of slave labourers (mostly Russian, French and Polish prisoners of war) toiled under horrific conditions digging tunnels in the chalk hills north of Nordhausen. From a 20km labyrinth of tunnels, they produced the V1 and V2 rockets that rained destruction on London, Antwerp and other cities during the final stages of WWII, when Hitler's grand plan became to conduct war from production plants below the ground.

The camp, called Mittelbau Dora, was created as a satellite of the Buchenwald concentration camp after British bombers destroyed the missile plants in

WITCHES & WARLOCKS

The Bodetal was first inhabited by Celts, whose fortresses were conquered by Germanic tribes and used for pagan rituals before Charlemagne embarked upon campaigns to subjugate and Christianise the local population during the 8th-century Saxon Wars. Today Harz mythology blends these pagan and Christian elements.

One popular – but misleading – explanation for the Walpurgisnacht festival (a pagan festival held on the night of 30 April, when everyone dresses up as witches and warlocks) is that it was an invention of the tribes who, pursued by Christian missionaries, held secret gatherings to carry out their rituals. They are said to have darkened their faces one night and, armed with broomsticks and pitchforks, scared off Charlemagne's guards, who mistook them for witches and devils. In fact the name 'Walpurgisnacht' itself probably derives from St Walpurga, but the festival tradition may also refer to the wedding of the gods Wodan and Freya.

According to local mythology, witches and warlocks gather on Walpurgisnacht at locations throughout the Harz before flying off to the Brocken on broomsticks or goats. There they recount the year's evil deeds and top off the stories with a Bacchanalian frenzy, said to represent copulation with the devil. Frightened peasants used to hang crosses and herbs on stable doors to protect their livestock; ringing church bells or cracking whips were other ways to prevent stray witches from dropping by.

One of the best places to celebrate Walpurgisnacht is Thale, where not-so-pagan hordes of 35,000 or more arrive for colourful variety events and the Walpurgishalle (Hexentanzplatz; adult/child €1.50/1; ☉10am-6pm May-Oct) tells you all you need to know about sacrifices, rituals and local myths. Schierke, also popular, is a starting point for Walpurgisnacht treks to the Brocken. Wherever you are, expect to see the dawn in with some very strange characters!

Peenemünde in far northeastern Germany. During the last two years of the war, at least 20,000 prisoners died at Dora, many having survived Auschwitz only to be worked to death here.

The US army reached the gates in April 1945, cared for survivors and removed all missile equipment before turning the area over to the Russians two months later. Much of the technology was later employed in the US space program.

After years of mouldering away in the GDR period, the memorial has gradually been improved to give a deeper insight into the horror of Hitler's undertaking. Today the memorial complex includes a permanent exhibition in a modern museum (☎03631-495 820; www.dora.de; admission free; ☉10am-6pm Tue-Sun Apr-Sep, to 4pm Oct-Mar) to explain the background of the camp and the experiences of those who were interned here; there's also a multilanguage library and a cafe.

The horrible truth of the place permeates the memorial, and a visit may be among the most unforgettable experiences you have in Germany.

Visitors have independent access to the grounds, crematorium and museum. The tunnels, which are the diameter of an aircraft hangar, are accessible by guided tour. Within the dank walls you can see partially assembled rockets that have lain untouched for over 50 years.

ℹ Information

Visitor Service (☎03631-495 820; www.dora.de; ☉10am-6pm Tue-Sun) Free 90-minute tours operate at 11am and 2pm from Tuesday to Friday, and at 11am, 1pm and 3pm on weekends (also 4pm March to October).

ℹ Getting There & Around

The narrow-gauge Harzquerbahn (p570) links Nordhausen with Wernigerode (single/return €11/17, 1½ hours). The nearest stop to Dora is Nordhausen-Krimderode, which is served by almost hourly trains from Nordhausen-Nord (11 minutes), next to the main station. Trains run to Halle (€18.10, 2 hours) and to Göttingen (€18.10, 1½ hours) from Nordhausen.

From the Krimderode stop, cross the tracks and walk south along Goetheweg, which curves and becomes Kohnsteinweg. Follow this for 1km towards the unassuming hill and you are at the camp.

LUTHERSTADT WITTENBERG & SAXONY-ANHALT

This otherwise unprepossessing region in former East Germany is renowned for two towns closely associated with the religious reformer Martin Luther – Lutherstadt Wittenberg and Lutherstadt Eisleben. Enthusiasts of Bauhaus architecture should not miss the chance to visit Dessau, whereas Halle is successfully morphing from a former chemicals centre to a lively university town. Magdeburg, the capital of Saxony-Anhalt, is a rather dour city that lacks the vibrancy of Halle and is best known for its cathedral.

Lutherstadt Wittenberg

☑ 03491 / POP 49,500

As its full name suggests, Wittenberg is first and foremost about Martin Luther (1483–1546), the monk who triggered the German Reformation by publishing his 95 theses against church corruption in 1517. A university town since 1502, Wittenberg back then was a hotbed of progressive thinking that also saw priests get married and educators like Luther's buddy Philipp Melanchthon argue for schools to accept female pupils. Today Wittenberg retains its significance for the world's 340 million Protestants, including 66 million Lutherans, as well as for those who simply admire Luther for his principled stand against authority. Sometimes called the 'Rome of the Protestants', its many Reformation-related sites garnered it the World Heritage Site nod from Unesco in 1996.

As a result, Wittenberg's popularity has steadily grown since reunification and – like it or not – even a nascent Luther industry has developed. *'Hier stehe ich. Ich kann nicht anders'* (Here I stand. I can do no other), Luther had declared after being asked to renounce his Reformist views at the Diet of Worms. Today, you can buy souvenir socks bearing the same credo.

◉ Sights

Lutherhaus MUSEUM

(Map p579; www.martinluther.de; Collegienstrasse 54; adult/concession €5/3; ◉9am-6pm) Even those with no previous interest in the Reformation will likely be fascinated by the state-of-the-art exhibits in the Lutherhaus, the former monastery turned Luther family home. Through an engaging mix of accessible narrative (in German and English), spotlit artefacts (eg his lectern from the Stadtkirche, indulgences chests, Bibles, cloaks), famous oil paintings and interactive multimedia stations, you'll learn about the man, his times and his impact on world history. Highlights include Cranach's *Ten Commandments* in the refectory and an original room furnished by Luther in 1535. Kids love the exhibit in the cellar, which uses wooden models and sensor-activated sound effects to depict everyday scenes from the life of the Luther family.

Luthereiche LANDMARK

(Luther Oak; cnr Lutherstrasse and Am Bahnhof) This oak tree marks the spot where the preacher burned the 1520 papal bull threatening his excommunication; the tree itself, though, was only planted around 1830.

Melanchthon Haus MUSEUM

(Map p579; www.martinluther.de; Collegienstrasse 60; ◉10am-6pm) An expert in ancient languages, Philipp Melanchthon helped Luther translate the Bible into German from Greek and Hebrew, becoming the preacher's friend and his most eloquent advocate. Where he lived is now known as Melanchthon Haus, which was being renovated and its exhibition reshaped at the time of research. Plans are to create two sections. One will be the historic house itself with authentic rooms in which you can soak up the mood of the great man, and the second, the new annex section, will house an exhibition on Melanchthon's life, work and influence. It should be open by the time you read this.

FREE Schlosskirche CHURCH

(Castle Church; Map p579; Schlossplatz; ◉10am-6pm Mon-Sat, 11.30am-6pm Sun) Did or didn't Luther nail those 95 theses to the door of the Schlosskirche? We'll never know for sure, because the original portal was destroyed by fire in 1760 and replaced in 1858 with a massive bronze version inscribed with the theses in Latin. Luther himself is buried inside below the pulpit, opposite his friend and fellow reformer Philipp Melanchthon. Pick up an information sheet from the desk so you don't walk past the other eye-catchers, such as the bronze memorial of Frederick the Wise, by Peter Vischer of Nuremberg, in a niche to the left of the altar.

Unfortunately, you are unable to climb the **Schlossturm** due to fire hazard.

Lutherstadt Wittenberg

Lutherstadt Wittenberg

FREE Stadtkirche St Marien   CHURCH
(Map p579; Jüdenstrasse 35; ◷10am-6pm Mon-Sat, 11.30am-6pm Sun) This church was where Martin Luther's ecumenical revolution began, with the world's first Protestant worship services in 1521. It was also here that Luther preached his famous Lectern sermons in 1522, and where he married ex-nun Katharina von Bora three years later.

The centrepiece is the large altar, designed jointly by Lucas Cranach the Elder and his son. The side facing the nave shows Luther, Melanchthon and other Reformation figures, as well as Cranach himself, in biblical contexts. The altar is also painted on its reverse side. On the lower rung, you'll see a seemingly defaced painting of heaven and hell; medieval students etched their initials into the painting's divine half if they passed their final exams – and into purgatory if they failed.

Cranachhöfe   GALLERY
(Map p579; Markt 4, Cranach Courtyards; admission €4/3; ◷10am-5pm Mon-Sat, 1-5pm Sun) Lucas Cranach's old residential and work digs have been rebooted as a beautifully restored cultural complex built around two courtyards that often echo with music and readings.

LUTHER LORE

'When the legend becomes fact, print the legend,' a journalist famously tells Jimmy Stewart in the classic Western movie *The Man Who Shot Liberty Valance*, and that is exactly what has happened with Martin Luther and his 95 theses. It's been so often repeated that Luther nailed a copy of his revolutionary theses to the door of Wittenberg's Schlosskirche on 31 October 1517, only serious scholars continue to argue to the contrary.

Certainly, Luther did write 95 theses challenging some of the Catholic practices of the time, especially the selling of 'indulgences' to forgive sins and reduce the buyer's time in purgatory. However, it's another question entirely as to whether he publicised them in the way popular legend suggests.

Believers point to the fact that the Schlosskirche's door was used as a bulletin board of sorts by the university, that the alleged posting took place the day before the affluent congregation poured into the church on All Saints' Day (1 November), and the fact that at Luther's funeral, his influential friend Philipp Melanchthon said he witnessed Luther's deed.

But Melanchthon didn't arrive in town until 1518 – the year *after* the supposed event. It's also odd that Luther's writings never once mentioned such a highly radical act.

While it's known that he sent his theses to the local archbishop to provoke discussion, some locals think it would have been out of character for a devout monk, interested mainly in an honest debate, to challenge the system so publicly and flagrantly without first exhausting all his options.

In any event, nailed to the church door or not, the net effect of Luther's theses was the same. They triggered the Reformation and Protestantism, altering the way that large sections of the world's Christian population worship to this day.

There's a permanent exhibit on the man, his life and his contemporaries.

Historische Druckerstube
GALLERY
(Historical Print Shop; Map p579; Schlossstrasse 1; tour €2.50; ☺9am-noon & 1-5pm Mon-Fri, 10am-1.30pm Sat) This gallery is part of the Cranachhöfe complex of courtyards (accessed separately from the main courtyards). It sells ancient-looking black-and-white sketches of Martin Luther, both typeset and printed by hand. Take a tour to hear the owner explain the sketches and early printing techniques.

Haus der Geschichte
MUSEUM
(House of History; Map p579; www.pflug-ev.de; Schlossstrasse 6; adult/concession €6/4.50; ☺10am-6pm) If you want to catch a glimpse of daily life in the region, especially life beyond the former Iron Curtain, pop by the Haus der Geschichte. The ground floor has a long-running special exhibition on German–Russian relations (many Russian soldiers were stationed in Lutherstadt Wittenberg during the GDR era), and other sections have living rooms, kids' rooms and kitchens from the GDR era and before. The top floor is dedicated to children's toys from this same 60-year period.

Hundertwasserschule
ARCHITECTURE
(Hundertwasser School; Strasse der Völkerfreundschaft 130; tours adult/concession €2/1; ☺1.30-4pm Tue-Fri, 10am-4pm Sat & Sun) How would you like to study grammar and algebra in a building where trees sprout from the windows and gilded onion domes balance above a rooftop garden? This fantastical environment is everyday reality for the lucky 1300 pupils of Wittenberg's Hundertwasserschule. It was the penultimate work of eccentric Viennese artist, architect and eco-visionary Friedensreich Hundertwasser, who was famous for quite literally thinking 'outside the box'. In Wittenberg, he transformed a boxy GDR-era concrete monstrosity into a colourful and curvy dreamscape. You can view the exterior any time, but tours of the interior wait for at least four participants before they start. Ring ahead for tours in English.

The school is a 20-minute walk northeast of the centre. From the Markt, head east on Jüdenstrasse, turn left into Neustrasse and continue into Geschwister-Scholl-Strasse. Turn left into Sternstrasse, right into Schillerstrasse, and the school is at the next intersection on the left.

🏃 Activities

Wittenberg is a key stop on the 860km Elberadweg (p585) (Elbe River Bike Trail) and a great departure point for shorter excursions along the idyllic river. The tourist office can help with logistics and suggestions. One particularly fine route is the 43km round trip to the Garden Realm Dessau-Wörlitz.

☞ Tours

City Tours   CULTURAL TOURS
(☑498 610; Schlossplatz 2, tourist office; adult €5; ⊗several daily Easter-Oct) The tourist office offers various tours, including its standard tour of the sights. DIY types might prefer renting a portable audioguide (€6 and your passport as deposit) with commentary in English and other languages. You can also rent a Segway from the tourist office (per hour €25, driver's licence required). If you have your own mobile phone, you can get the nitty-gritty on key sights by dialling ☑08122-9999 5682 plus a dedicated extension. The tourist office (p583) has a flyer on this particular scheme.

MS Lutherstadt Wittenberg   RIVER CRUISE
(Map p579; ☑769 0433; www.ms-wittenberg.de; Schlossstrasse 16; €11-17; ⊗booking office 10am-5pm Tue-Fri) Two-hour panoramic river cruises run on the Elbe from March to October. Check with the booking office or website about sailings and how to find the pier in Dessauer Strasse.

Trabant Tours   TOUR
(☑498 610; Schlossplatz 2; per 3hr from €45) *Good Bye, Lenin!* fans might get a kick out of negotiating Wittenberg's streets squeezed behind the wheel of a tinny East German Trabant car. The tourist office can arrange these through the Event & Touring company (www.trabant-mieten.de).

★★ Festivals & Events

Wittenberg is busiest during **Luthers Hochzeit** (Luther's Wedding Festival; www.lutherhochzeit.de) in early or mid-June, and for **Reformationsfest** (Reformation Festival) held on 31 October.

🛏 Sleeping

The tourist office operates a free room reservation service in person or by phone at ☑498 610. Private rooms start at €19 per person.

TOP CHOICE **Alte Canzley**   HOTEL $
(Map p579; ☑429 190; www.alte-canzley.de; Schlossplatz 3-5; s €70-125, d €85-139; ▣@🛜) The nicest place in town, for our money, is in a 14th-century building opposite the Schlosskirche. Each of the eight spacious units is furnished in dark woods and natural hues, named for a major historical figure and equipped with a kitchenette. The vaulted downstairs harbours Saxony-Anhalt's first certified organic restaurant (dishes €7.20 to €23.90).

Luther-Hotel   HOTEL $$
(Map p579; ☑4580; www.luther-hotel-wittenberg.de; Neustrasse 7-10; s/d/ste from €83/102/140; ▣🛜) You'll sleep like an angel in this sparkling, modern place affiliated with a Christian charity organisation. Expect good-sized and cheerfully coloured rooms, most of them with unimpeded Stadtkirche views. Some rooms have several beds, and there are also double junior suites. A sauna invites post-sightseeing unwinding. Prices vary according to demand. Wi-fi is in some rooms and the public areas.

DJH Hostel   HOSTEL $
(Map p579; ☑505 205; www.jugendherberge-wittenberg.de; Schlossstrasse 14/15; dm under/over 27yr €19/22, s/d €28.50/34, linen €3.50; ▣@🛜) Wittenberg's excellent youth hostel has 40 bright rooms sleeping up to six people. They come with bathrooms, bedside reading lamps and private cabinets.

Pension am Schwanenteich   PENSION $
(Map p579; ☑402 807; www.wittenberg-schwanenteich.de; Töpferstrasse 1; s from €39.50, d €71; ▣✳🛜) At these prices you know you're not getting the Ritz, but if you want friendly and familiar ambience and simple but comfy rooms, this humble *Pension* fits the bill.

WITTENBERG WORSHIP

From May to October, a changing roster of Lutheran guest preachers, usually from the US, hold free English-language services in Wittenberg's Schlosskirche or Stadtkirche, organised by the **Wittenberg English Ministry** (☑498 610; www.wittenberg-english-ministry.com; Schlossplatz 2). From Wednesday to Friday, half-hour services are also offered at 4.30pm in the tiny **Fronleichnamskapelle** (Corpus Christi Chapel; Map p579) attached to the Stadtkirche.

Stadthotel Wittenberg

Schwarzer Baer HOTEL **$$**

(Map p579; ☑420 4344; www.stadthotel-wittenberg.
de; Schlossstrasse 2; s/d €65/85; P@☎) The
modern rooms in this 500-year-old heritage-
listed building (no lift) are light and airy,
with wooden floors and cork headboards.

Brückenkopf Hotel Marina-

Camp Elbe CAMPGROUND **$**

(☑4540; www.marina-camp-elbe.de; Brückenkopf
1; adult/child €5/4, tent €7-10, car €4, hotel s/d
€43/66, breakfast €7; P@) How many camp-
ing grounds come with their own wine
cellar? This riverside one does, along with
a marina, a restaurant, a hotel, holiday
apartments, beach volleyball, table tennis,
a sauna, laundry facilities and other useful
amenities. Bonus: the dreamy views of the
town silhouette.

✕ Eating & Drinking

TOP CHOICE In Vino

Veritas GERMAN, MEDITERANNEAN **$$**

(Map p579; Mittelstrasse 3; dishes €6.90-18.50,
antipasti €2.50-9; ☺dinner) Antipasti, tapas,
salads or pasta dishes form the perfect accompaniment to the global wine menu at
this upmarket modern bistro.

Brauhaus Wittenberg GERMAN **$$**

(Map p579; Markt 6, Im Beyerhof; mains €6.90-
15.90; ☺11am-11pm) This place – with a cob-
bled courtyard, indoor brewery and shiny
copper vats – thrums with the noise of peo-
ple having a good time. The menu is hearty
but also features smaller dishes for waist-
watchers. Upstairs are a few simple rooms
with air-con (singles/doubles €57/79).

Tante Emmas Bier- & Caféhaus GERMAN **$$**

(Map p579; Markt 9; mains €8.90-16; ☺9am-5pm
Mon, to midnight Tue-Sun) Take a step back to
the 'good old times' in this German country kitchen, where servers wear frilly white
aprons and the room is chock-full of bric-a-
brac – from dolls and books to irons and a
gramophone.

Marc de Café CAFE

(Map p579; Pfaffengasse 5; ☺1-6pm) This French
cafe with its literary and music vibe is a delightful find, with house-roasted coffee or
cakes. When the sun's out, the idyllic courtyard is the place to be. In the yard is a **workshop** (☑03491- 404 011; Pfaffengasse 5; 1hr tour
€60) run by Jörg Dahms, who restores and
makes copies of historical musical instruments (maximum group size 20 persons;
book ahead).

Flower Power BAR

(Map p579; www.flowerpower.eu; Bügermeister-
strasse 21; ☺7pm-3am Mon-Thu, 9pm-5am Fri &
Sat) Catch live bands, croon karaoke or hit
the floor for a party in the town's grooviest
venue.

Independent BAR

(Map p579; Collegienstrasse 44) Alt-style pub;
one of several interesting venues along Collegienstrasse.

☆ Entertainment

Barrik CABARET

(Map p579; www.barrik.eu; Collegienstrasse 81;
☺Mon-Sat) Entertains the troops with live
comedy, dance, cabaret and transvestite
shows.

LOCAL KNOWLEDGE

JOERG DAHMS – CRAFTER & RESTORER OF MUSICAL INSTRUMENTS

About the workshop The workshop is in the centre of Wittenberg, close to the castle
church, where we make replicas of older stringed instruments like lutes, baroque gui-
tars, gitterns and cisterns as well as different viols and hurdy-gurdies.

Medieval instruments When the Arabic Moors came to Spain they brought with them
numerous instruments which had a great influence on the development of the lute and
the hurdy-gurdy throughout Europe. The organistrum is the ancestor which developed
over later centuries into the hurdy-gurdy as we know it today. Even Haydn used it in his
music. It didn't disappear completely, and in France, for instance, the hurdy-gurdy is still
used for playing 19th-century folk dance music together with bagpipes.

Favourite places to relax I go to the Stadtpark (city park), which is the former town
fortification, with views of the castle church. The other place where I like to relax is in my
own courtyard – there's a cafe (Marc de Café) just outside the workshop.

Stadtkirche St Marien   ORGAN MUSIC
(Map p579; Jüdenstrasse 35; ⊙May-Oct) Meditate to organ music in summer at 6pm Friday.

Schlosskirche   ORGAN MUSIC
(Map p579; Schlossplatz; ⊙May-Oct) Organ music at 2.30pm on Tuesdays in summer.

ⓘ Information

Hospital (⌀500; Paul-Gerhardt-Strasse 42, Paul-Gerhard-Stiftung)

Post Office (Wilhelm-Weber-Strasse 1)

Tourist Office (⌀498 610; www.wittenberg.de; Schlossplatz 2; ⊙9am-6pm Mon-Fri, 10am-4pm Sat & Sun)

Wittenberger Bierstuben (Jüdenstrasse 27; per hr €3; ⊙9am-10pm) Smoky pub with internet.

ⓘ Getting There & Away

Wittenberg is on the main train line to Halle and Leipzig (both €12.20, one hour). ICE (€30, 45 minutes) and RE trains (€21.50, 1¼ hours) travel to Berlin. Coming from Berlin, be sure to board for 'Lutherstadt Wittenberg', as there's also a Wittenberge west of the capital.

ⓘ Getting Around

Lutherstadt Wittenberg is tiny and best explored on foot or by bike. Parking enforcement is quite stringent, so use the car parks on the fringes of the Altstadt (such as near Elbtor and along Fleischerstrasse). For bike rental, head to **Fahrradhaus Kralisch** (Map p579; ⌀403 703; www.fahrradhaus-kralisch.de; Jüdenstrasse 11; per 24hr €7; ⊙9am-noon Mon-Sat, 1-6pm Mon-Fri).

Dessau-Rosslau

⌀0340 / POP 86,900

For Bauhaus junkies, Dessau hits the jackpot. Nowhere else in the world will you find a greater concentration of original 1920s Bauhaus structures than in this city on the Elbe River. Dessau was the home of the most influential design school of the 20th century during its most creative period from 1925 to 1932.

You could just stop off and see all major Bauhaus sights in the course of a day, or stay a bit longer to explore the city's four parks, which form part of the Gartenreich Dessau-Wörlitz (Garden Realm). Alas, the townscape itself is mostly defined by the grey concrete GDR-era aesthetic.

In 2007, Dessau merged with the smaller town of Rosslau across the Elbe, resulting in an official name change to Dessau-Rosslau.

The leading Bauhaus sights are west of the Hauptbahnhof, all within easy walking distance. The town centre lies southeast, about a 15-minute walk away. Pedestrianised Zerbster Strasse is the main drag, leading to the Markt, the Rathaus and the Rathaus-Center shopping mall.

◉ Sights

FREE **Bauhausgebäude**   ARCHITECTURE
(Bauhaus Bldg; www.bauhaus-dessau.de; Gropiusallee 38; exhibition adult/concession €6/4, tours €4/3; ⊙10am-6pm, tours 11am & 2pm daily, also noon & 4pm Sat & Sun) It's almost impossible to overstate the significance of the building, erected in 1925–26 as a school of Bauhaus art, design and architecture. Two key pioneers of modern architecture, Walter Gropius and Ludwig Mies van der Rohe, served as the school's directors. Gropius claimed that the ultimate of all artistic endeavours was architecture, and this building was the first real-life example of his vision. It was revolutionary, bringing industrial construction techniques such as curtain walling and wide spans into the public domain and influencing untold buildings worldwide. The school also disseminated the movement's ideals of functionality and minimalism.

Today a smattering of postgrads from an urban studies program use some of the building but much of it is open to the public. The gift shop sells cool trinkets, books, posters and postcards.

You can hire an English-language audioguide (adult/concession €4/3) and tour the building by yourself but you will only see inside the rooms on the guided tour.

Meisterhäuser   ARCHITECTURE
(Masters' Houses; www.meisterhaeuser.de; Ebertallee 63, 65-67 & 69-71, Masters' Houses; admission to all 3 houses adult/concession €7.50/5.50, tours €11.50/8.50; ⊙11am-6pm Tue-Sun, tours 12.30pm & 3.30pm daily, also 1.30pm Sat & Sun) You'll find the three remaining Meisterhäuser on leafy Ebertallee, a 15-minute walk west of the Hauptbahnhof. The leading lights of the Bauhaus movement lived together as neighbours in these white cubist structures that exemplify the Bauhaus aim of 'design for living' in a modern industrial world.

Originally there was a stand-alone home for Gropius, plus three duplexes, each half of which provided a living/working space for a senior staff member and his family. Gropius' home was destroyed in WWII, along

BAUHAUS TOURS

If you'd like to take in all the Bauhaus sights in Dessau, buy a **day ticket** (adult/concession €15/10), which covers the exhibitions in the Bauhaus Building, German-language guided tours of the Masters' Houses and a guided tour of the Törten Estate. Tours of the estate take you to the **Konsumgebäude** (Co-Op Building; admission without tour €2; ⊙10am-6pm Tue-Sun), which today houses a permanent exhibition on the history of the Törten housing estate, to the **Stahlhaus** (Steel House), which you can only visit on a tour, and to various other houses on the estate. You can also opt for a separate **tour** (€4; ⊙3pm Tue-Sun) of the Törten Estate.

The website www.bauhaus-dessau.de suggests visiting the exhibition in the Bauhaus Building at 10am, at 11am taking the guided tour of the building, at 12.30pm joining the tour of the Masters' Houses (meeting point is at the cash point in the Bauhaus Building), then doing the Törten tour at 3pm (meeting point is the Konsum building at Am Dreieck 1). For more information, call ☑650 8250.

with one-half of the neighbouring duplex (at the time of research both Gropius' home and the duplex were being reconstructed using original plans). In the 1920s, you could have sat at home here with the Kandinskys, on furniture donated by Marcel Breuer, and with the possibility that Paul Klee or László Moholy-Nagy might drop by for tea.

Haus Feininger, former home of Lyonel Feininger, now pays homage to Dessau-born Kurt Weill, who later became playwright Bertolt Brecht's musical collaborator in Berlin, and composed *The Threepenny Opera* and its hit 'Mack the Knife', later immortalised by a rasping Louis Armstrong.

Haus Muche/Schlemmer (☑882 2138; Ebertallee 65/67) could be said to demonstrate how the room proportions used, and experiments such as low balcony rails, don't really cut it in the modern world. The partially black bedroom here is intriguing, though; look out for the leaflet explaining the amusing story behind it – Marcel Breuer apparently burst in to paint it when reluctant owner Georg Muche was away on business.

Haus Kandinsky/Klee (☑661 0934; Ebertallee 69/71) is most notable for the varying pastel shades in which Wassily Kandinsky and Paul Klee painted their walls (recreated today). There's also biographical information about the two artists and special exhibitions about their work.

Törten Estate   ARCHITECTURE
(Am Dreieck 1) If the term 'housing estate' conjures up an image of grim tower blocks, rubbish-blown courtyards and shutters flapping on abandoned shops, leafy Törten, in Dessau's south, might make you think again. Built in the 1920s, it is a prototype of the modern working-class estate. Although many of the 300-plus homes have been altered in ways that would have outraged their purist creator Walter Gropius (with patios and rustic German doors added to a minimalist facade), others retain their initial symmetry. To reach Törten, take tram 1 towards Dessau Süd, get off at Damaschkestrasse and follow the signposts saying 'Bauhaus Architektur'.

Moses-Mendelssohn-Zentrum   MUSEUM
(www.mendelssohn-dessau.de; Mittelring 38; adult/child €2/1; ⊙10am-5pm) Located within the Törten Estate, the prototype housing estate from the 1920s, this exhibition tracks the life and accomplishments of the Dessau-born humanist philosopher Moses Mendelssohn, the godfather of the Jewish Enlightenment.

Kornhaus   ARCHITECTURE
(Kornhausstrasse 146) This striking Bauhaus riverside beer-and-dance hall was designed by Carl Flieger, an assistant of Gropius. It's about a 20-minute walk north of the Meisterhäuser (via Elballee) and, sadly, was a disused restaurant with Elbe views that was seeking a new owner when we visited.

Umweltbundesamt   ARCHITECTURE
(Federal Environmental Agency; Wörlitzer Platz 1; ⊙6am-10pm Mon-Fri, to 4pm Sat, 8.30am-4pm Sun) The brightly coloured and textured facade of this modern building makes a striking sight. Public art graces the parklike outdoor areas, while the lofty, light-flooded forum has exhibitions and is also open to visitors.

Technikmuseum Hugo Junkers MUSEUM

(www.technikmuseum-dessau.de; Kühnauer Strasse 161a; adult/concession €4/1.50; ⊘10am-5pm) Aviation fans will be wowed by the vintage aircraft at the Technikmuseum Hugo Junkers. Tram 1 goes straight to the museum (get off at Junkerspark) from the Hauptbahnhof.

🏃 Activities

Elberadweg CYCLING

(Elbe River Bike Trail; www.elberadweg.de) Dessau is ideal for cycling part of this bike trail, among Germany's top three cycling routes. This wends its way some 860km west alongside the river, from the Czech border to Cuxhaven. The scenic 360km stretch in Saxony-Anhalt is particularly popular. The tourist office in Dessau can give you information on the Fürst Franz Garden Realm Tour (68km), which travels between all the palaces around Dessau and Wörlitz, and passes along the Elbe River and the biosphere reserve information office.

🎆 Festivals & Events

Although more closely associated with Berlin, and later New York, the composer Kurt Weill was born in Dessau. From late February to early March the city hosts a **Kurt Weill Festival** (www.kurt-weill.de), reprising and updating his collaborations with Bertolt Brecht, such as *The Threepenny Opera*. Performances take place in Dessau and surrounds.

🛌 Sleeping

TOP CHOICE / Hotel-Pension An den 7 Säulen HOTEL $

(☑619 620; www.pension7saeulen.de; Ebertallee 66; s €47-56, d €62-74; ℗) Rooms at this small *Pension* are clean and nicely renovated; the owners are friendly, the garden is pleasant and the breakfast room overlooks the Meisterhäuser across the leafy street. Take bus 11 to Kornerhaus from Hauptbahnhof and walk back to Ebertallee.

NH Dessau HOTEL $$

(☑251 40; www.nh-hotels.com; Zerbster Strasse 29; r €65-99, breakfast €16; ℗ ✳ @ 🛜) This modern hotel in white-grey tones is set in the pedestrianised strip leading to the Rathaus and tourist office. Wrap up a day on the tourist track with a session in the rooftop sauna with attached terrace. Prices vary according to demand. Take bus 12 from the train station to Zerberstrasse.

Radisson Blu Hotel Fürst Leopold HOTEL $$

(☑251 50; www.hotel-dessau-city.de; Friedensplatz; r from €65; ℗ ✳ 🛜) Dessau's grandest hotel is modern and offers excellent facilities and value, with a bar, restaurant, fitness area and beauty spa. Prices vary by demand, mostly between €75 and €110. Take tram 1, 2 or 3 one stop from the train station to Theater or follow Fritz-Hesse-Strasse.

Bauhaus 'Prellerhaus' HOSTEL $

(☑650 8318; unterkunft@bauhaus-dessau.de; Gropiusallee 38; s/d €35/55; ℗) Channel your modernist dream into something highly functional by staying in the former students' rooms. Showers and toilets are shared.

DJH Hostel HOSTEL $

(☑619 803; www.jugendherberge.de/jh/dessau; Ebertallee 151; dm under/over 27yr €19/22, linen €3.50; ℗ @ 🛜) Cheerful dorms sleeping from two to seven people, each with their own bathroom. Close to the main Bauhaus sights. Take bus 11 to Ebertallee from the train station.

🍴 Eating

TOP CHOICE / Pächterhaus GERMAN $$

(☑650 1447; www.paechterhaus-dessau.de; Kirchstrasse 1; mains €18-25; ⊘lunch & dinner Tue-Sun) Foodies on a mission won't mind making the small detour to this gorgeously restored half-timbered farm house where seasonal and locally sourced ingredients get the gourmet treatment. In fine weather do anything to bag a table on the idyllic terrace beneath a canopy of vines. Take bus 11 to Kirchstrasse.

L'Appart FRENCH $$

(☑661 5975; www.appartdessau.de; Zerbster Strasse 8; 2-/3-course lunch €9.90/12.90, 3-/5-course evening menu €22.90/27.90, mains €9.90-22; ⊘lunch & dinner) The jazzy decor is a great foil for the tasty fare at this upbeat French brasserie with a nice terrace overlooking the market square and town hall.

Bauhaus Klub CAFE $

(Gropiusallee 38; light dishes €3.50-8.90; ⊘8am-midnight Mon-Fri, 9am-midnight Sat, 8am-6pm Sun; 🛜) Breakfasts, salads, snacks and Flammkuchen are served downstairs in the congenial cafe and snack bar in the Bauhaus Building.

Bauhaus Mensa CAFETERIA $

(Gropiusallee 38; dishes €3-7; ⊘8am-3pm Mon-Fri) Student cafeteria.

BAUHAUS: DESIGN FOR LIFE

'Less is more' said the third and final Bauhaus director, Ludwig Mies van der Rohe. Given that this school survived fewer than 15 years yet exerted more influence on modern design than any other, van der Rohe was probably right. As Frank Whitford put it in *Bauhaus: World of Art* (1984): 'Everyone sitting on a chair with a tubular steel frame, using an adjustable reading lamp or living in a house partly or entirely constructed from prefabricated elements is benefiting from a revolution...largely brought about by the Bauhaus.'

Founded in Weimar in 1919 by Berlin architect Walter Gropius, this multidisciplinary school aimed to abolish the distinction between 'fine' and 'applied' arts, and to unite the artistic with daily life. Gropius reiterated that form follows function and exhorted his students to craft items with an eye towards mass production. Consequently, Bauhaus products stripped away decoration and ornamentation and returned to the fundamentals of design, with strong, clean lines.

From the very beginning, the movement attracted a roll call of the era's greatest talents, including Lyonel Feininger, Wassily Kandinsky, Paul Klee, László Moholy-Nagy, Oskar Schlemmer, plus now legendary product designers Marianne Brandt, Marcel Breuer and Wilhelm Wagenfeld. After conservative politicians closed the Weimar school in 1925, the Bauhaus crew found a more welcoming reception in industrial Dessau.

Even here, though, right-wing political pressure continued against what was seen as the Bauhaus' undermining of traditional values, and Gropius resigned as director in 1928. He was succeeded by Swiss-born Hannes Meyer, whose Marxist sympathies meant that he, in turn, was soon replaced by Ludwig Mies van der Rohe. The latter was at the helm when the school moved to Berlin in 1932 to escape Nazi oppression. To no avail. Just one year later, the Nazis dissolved the school and its leading lights fled the country.

But the movement never quite died. After WWII, Gropius took over as director of Harvard's architecture school, while Mies van der Rohe (the architect of New York's Seagram Building) held the same post at the Illinois Institute of Technology in Chicago. Both men found long-lasting global fame as purveyors of Bauhaus' successor, the so-called International Style.

Nordsee SEAFOOD $ (Kavalierstrasse 49, Rathaus-Center; fish roll & drink €5; ☺9.30am-8pm Mon-Sat) Inside the Rathaus-Center shopping complex near the tourist office.

ⓘ Information

Bauhaus Stiftung (Bauhaus Foundation; ☎650 8250; www.bauhaus-dessau.de; Gropiusallee 38; ☺10am-6pm) For info on, and tours of, Bauhaus buildings (also in English).

Internet Cafe (Hauptbahnhof, 1st fl) Up the spiral stairs near the DB service point at the train station; closed for renovation at the time of research.

Post Office (Kavalierstrasse 30-32; ☺8.30am-6.30pm Mon-Fri, 9am-12.30pm Sat)

Tourist Office (☎204 1442, accommodation 220 3003; www.dessau-rosslau-tourismus.de; Zerbster Strasse 2c; ☺10am-6pm Mon-Fri, to 1pm Sat)

ⓘ Getting There & Around

BICYCLE Mobilitätszentrale (☎213 366; per day €5-8; ☺9am-5pm Mon-Fri, to 1pm Sat) bike hire is outside the Hauptbahnhof. Also try **Beckers Radhaus** (☎216 0113; Wilhelm-Feuerherdt-Strasse 13; per day from €8.50; ☺9am-6pm Mon-Fri, 10am-3pm Sat) for bike hire.

BUS Single bus and tram tickets cost €1.50; day passes are €4.50.

CAR The Berlin–Munich autobahn (A9) runs east of town.

TRAIN For Berlin (€36, 1½ hours), change in Lutherstadt Wittenberg (€7.50, 30 minutes). Direct regional services go to Leipzig (€11.10, 45 minutes), Halle (€11.10, 55 minutes) and Magdeburg (€11.10, 50 minutes).

Gartenreich Dessau-Wörlitz

Aside from being a mecca of modern architecture, Dessau and surrounds are home to the Gartenreich Dessau-Wörlitz (Garden Realm), one of the finest garden ensembles in Germany. The parks reflect the vision of Prince Leopold III Friedrich Franz von Anhalt-Dessau (1740–1817). A highly educated man, he travelled to Holland, Italy, France and Switzerland for inspiration on how to apply the philosophy of the Enlightenment to the design of a landscape that would create a harmony between nature, architecture and art. He was so successful that in 2000 Unesco recognised his efforts by putting the gardens onto its list of World Heritage Sites. Each of the six English-style gardens comes with its own palace and other buildings, in styles ranging from neoclassical to baroque to neo-Gothic.

The Garden Realm is embraced by the Unesco-protected **Biosphärenreservat Mittlere Elbe** (Biosphere Reserve Middle Elbe; www.biosphaerenreservatmittlereelbe.de). Nature-lovers should stop at the **information centre** (☑034904-4060; Am Kapenschlösschen 3, Oranienbaum) on the way to Schloss Oranienbaum.

The six parks are scattered over 142 sq km. The most central is Georgium, just five minutes' walk from Dessau Hauptbahnhof. The most impressive, Wörlitz, is situated about 18km east of Dessau, making it also the most distant. Mosigkau is about 7km southwest of central Dessau, while Luisium lies 3km east. Oranienbaum is 14km southeast of Dessau or 6km south of Wörlitz. Finally, Grosskühnau is about 5km northwest of central Dessau.

All parks are free and can be roamed during daylight hours (most aren't fenced off), but the palaces charge admission and have their own opening hours.

◉ Sights

Wörlitz Park & Schloss Wörlitz
GARDENS, PALACE
(www.woerlitz-information.de; Schloss tours €5; ⊙10am-6pm Tue-Sun Apr-Oct) With peacocks feeding on the lawn before a neo-Gothic house, a tree-lined stream flowing towards a Grecian-style temple and a gap in a hedge framing a distant villa, the 112-hectare English-style Wörlitz Park is the pinnacle of Prince Leopold's garden region. Take your sweet time to saunter among this mosaic of paths, hedges and follies, but don't even think about having a picnic on the sprawling lawns: even walking on them is very much *Verboten*, as is bicycling within park grounds.

On the edge of the park nearest the town lies Prince Leopold's former country house, the neoclassical **Schloss Wörlitz** (☑034905-4090; tours €4.50; ⊙10am-6pm Tue-Sun May-Sep, to 5pm Apr & Oct, closed Nov-Mar), which is still filled with original late-18th-century furniture and decorations.

Bus 334 does the 30-minute trip from Dessau to Wörlitz roughly every two hours between 6am and 5.30pm. From late March to early October, there's also a 35-minute train service on Wednesday, Saturday and Sunday. Check the timetable carefully before heading out or, better yet, check with the information kiosk Mobilitätszentrale (see Getting There & Around) outside the train station. By road from Dessau, take the B185 east to the B107 north, which brings you right into town.

Schloss & Park Georgium
PALACE, GARDENS
(www.gartenreich.com; Puschkinallee 100; Schloss adult/concession €3/2; ⊙10am-5pm Tue-Sun) Just a five-minute walk from Dessau Hauptbahnhof, the sprawling 18th-century Park Georgium is anchored by the neoclassical palace, now a picture gallery showcasing German and Dutch old masters, including Rubens and Cranach the Elder. The leafy grounds are also dotted with ponds and fake Roman ruins, including a triumphal arch and a round temple. Restoration of the palace, which was ongoing in 2012, might continue into 2013.

Schloss & Park Mosigkau
PALACE, GARDENS
(www.gartenreich.com; Knobelsdorffallee 3, Dessau; Schloss €4.50; ⊙10am-6pm Tue-Sun May-Sep, to 5pm Sat & Sun only Apr & Oct) Southwest of central Dessau, Schloss Mosigkau is a petite rococo palace that's been called a 'miniature Sanssouci'. Many of the 17 rooms retain their original furnishings, although the highlight is the **Galleriesaal** with paintings by Rubens and Van Dyck. In summer, play hide-and-seek in the leafy labyrinth. To get there, take bus 16 to Schloss.

Schloss & Park Luisium
PALACE, GARDENS
(www.gartenreich.com; Dessau; Schloss €4.50; ⊙10am-6pm Tue-Sun Apr-Oct) East of central Dessau, towards Wörlitz, Schloss Luisium is an intimate neoclassical refuge framed by an idyllic English garden scattered with

BOATING ON THE WÖRLITZER SEE

Things get very quaint in Wörlitz. This is where hand-cranked ferries (tickets €0.60; ⏱10am-6.30pm, limited or no service Nov-Mar) cross the Wörlitzer See, which lies between garden sections of Wörlitz Park. There are also 45-minute gondola tours (tickets €7; ⏱10am-6pm, limited or no service Nov-Mar) plying the lake, departing when eight people or more gather at the dock – this doesn't take long in summer; indeed the problem is more often too many garden-goers gathering for gondolas. If boats aren't your thing, weekend concerts are another highlight in summer.

neo-Gothic and classical follies; it's reached via bus 13 to Vogelherd.

Schloss & Park Oranienbaum
PALACE, GARDENS

(Oranienbaum; admission €4.50; ⏱10am-6pm Tue-Sun May-Sep) The baroque Schloss Oranienbaum is south of Wörlitz and reached by bus 331.

ⓘ Information

The Dessau tourist office has all the information you need, or stop by **Wörlitz-Information** (☏034905-310 09, room reservations 194 33; www.woerlitz.de; Förstergasse 26; ⏱9am-6pm)

Magdeburg

☏0391 / POP 231,500

Few people could deny that Magdeburg is aesthetically challenged, thanks to WWII bombs and socialist city planners in love with wide boulevards and prefab concrete apartment blocks, the so-called *Plattenbauten*. Yet this is one of the country's oldest cities, founded some 1200 years ago and home to the first Gothic cathedral on German soil. Magdeburg's newest architectural attraction, meanwhile, is the whimsical Grüne Zitadelle (Green Citadel), the last building of eccentric artist-architect Friedensreich Hundertwasser.

The Elbe River, too – demoted to industrial waterway in GDR times – is again a vital part of Magdeburg's green side, lined by beer gardens, beach bars, a promenade and paved bikeway. The most historic parts of town are Hegelstrasse and nearby Hasselbachplatz.

Sights & Activities

Dom
CHURCH

(Map p590; www.magdeburgerdom.de; Am Dom 1; tours adult/concession €3/1.50; ⏱10am-6pm Mon-Sat, 11.30am-6pm Sun, tours 2pm Mon-Sat, 11.30am Sun) Magdeburg's main historical landmark traces its roots to 937 when Otto I (912–73) founded a Benedictine monastery and had it built up into a full-fledged cathedral within two decades. After a fire destroyed the original a couple of centuries later, it was rebuilt as a Gothic three-aisled basilica with transept, choir and pointed windows. Today it's the burial place of Otto I and his English wife Editha, and is packed with artistic highlights ranging from the delicate 13th-century Magdeburg Virgins sculptures to a haunting antiwar memorial by Ernst Barlach.

Learn more during German-language tours or ask for an English booklet (€3.90).

Grüne Zitadelle
ARCHITECTURE

(Green Citadel; Map p590; ☏620 8655; www.gruene-zitadelle.de; Breiter Weg 9; tours adult/concession €6/5; ⏱information office 10am-6pm, tours 11am, 3pm & 5pm Mon-Fri, hourly 10am-5pm Sat & Sun) Completed in 2005, this piglet-pink building with trees growing from its facade and meadows sprouting on its rooftops was the final design of Viennese artist Friedensreich Hundertwasser. It reflects his philosophy of creating highly unique spaces in harmony with nature, an 'oasis for humanity'. Inside are offices, flats and shops, as well as a small hotel and a cafe. If you understand German, join the one-hour guided tours to learn more about the man and his intriguing vision.

Elbauenpark & Jahrtausendturm
PARK, TOWER

(www.elbauenpark.de; adult/concession incl Jahrtausendturm & butterfly house €3/2; ⏱park 9am-8pm, butterfly house 10am-6pm, Jahrtausenturm 10am-6pm Tue-Sun Apr-Oct) The Elbauenpark was carved out of the landscape for a 1999 garden exhibition and has rose, sculpture and other gardens, plus a butterfly house. Its most unusual attraction, though, is the conical, 60m-high Jahrtausendturm (Millennial Tower), which bills itself as the world's tallest wooden tower. Inside is a display on history from ancient times to the present, including a Foucault's pendulum. Take tram 5 to Herrenkrug or tram 6 to Messegelände.

Kunstmuseum Kloster
Unser Lieben Frauen   MUSEUM
(Map p590; www.kunstmuseum-magdeburg.de; museum adult/concession €2/1; ⊘10am-5pm Tue-Sun) Magdeburg's oldest building, a decommissioned medieval monastery, is now a museum presenting regional sculptures and contemporary art from Saxony-Anhalt. The front door, designed by popular local artist Heinrich Apel (b 1935), is fun: you knock with the woman's necklace and push down on the man's hat to enter. Admission to the cloister is free.

Kunsthistorisches Mueum   MUSEUM
(Map p590; www.khm-magdeburg.de; Otto-von-Guericke-Str. 68-73; adult/concession €3/2; ⊘10am-5pm Tue-Sun) This recently restored and enlarged museum is home to the original **Magdeburger Reiter** statue from 1240. A gilded copy is on Alter Markt.

Rathaus   HISTORIC BUILDING
(Map p590; Alter Markt) The local artist Heinrich Apel designed the relief bronze door of the Rathaus on Alter Markt square. It was recreated in its 17th-century form in the 1960s after total damage during WWII.

🛏 Sleeping

TOP CHOICE Grüne Zitadelle   BOUTIQUE HOTEL $$
(Map p590; ☑620 780; www.hotel-zitadelle.de; Breiter Weg 9; s €105-135, d €125-145, breakfast €11; P✳🔊) Housed inside the Green Citadel, a design by the Austrian architect Friedenreich Hundertwasser, this hotel has bold colours, organic shapes and all natural materials. The nicest rooms face the inner courtyard and provide access to a grassy terrace. Those facing the street are air-conditioned.

Herrenkrug Parkhotel   HOTEL $$
(☑850 80; www.herrenkrug.de; Herrenkrug 3; s €95-135, d €124-210; P@🔊≋) Rise to chirping birds at this art deco riverside mansion, then start the day with a wake-up stroll through the lush surrounding park. Rooms in this conference hotel are spacious and stylish, and its restaurant, Die Saison, is very good. Sauna and steam bath are included in the price. Wi-fi is extravagant (per hour €8) but internet on the house computer is free. Prices vary considerably by demand. Take tram 6 to Herrenkrug.

Hotel Sleep & Go   HOTEL $
(☑537 791; www.hotel-sleep-and-go.de; Rogätzer Strasse 5a; s/d €54/108; P@🔊) Filling a gap somewhere between student apartments and a hotel, this comfortable place has plain generic rooms (but feather duvets!), many with their own balcony. There's free wi-fi in the public areas. It's a 10-minute walk northeast along Ernst-Lehmann-Strasse from the Listemannstrasse stop (tram 2).

Residenz Joop   BOUTIQUE HOTEL $$
(☑626 20; www.residenzjoop.de; Jean-Burger-Strasse 16; s €89-114, d €114-144; P✳@🔊) Nothing is too much trouble for your hosts in this boutique hotel with very tastefully appointed rooms in a small villa. Take tram 3 or 9 to Am Fuchsberg.

DJH Hostel   HOSTEL $
(Map p590; ☑532 1010; www.jugendherberge.de/jh/magdeburg; Leiterstrasse 10; dm/s/tw €21/33/45, over 27yr extra €3; P@🔊) Rooms in this large, modern hostel have shower and toilet attached, and there's a family floor with a kiddie romper room.

🍴 Eating

TOP CHOICE Qilin   ASIAN $$
(Map p590; www.qilin-md.de; Leiterstrasse 1; lunch special €5.50-8.20, mains €9.50-15; ⊘11.30am-2.30pm & 5-11pm Mon-Fri, noon-9pm Sun) Magdeburg's culinary scene won't blow you out of the Elbe, but this small, sleek pan-Asian eatery is excellent – it serves soups, sushi variations, fried seafoods, salads, noodles and superb stir-fries (all without monosodium

CANAL IN THE SKY

You'll rub your eyes in disbelief when you first see it: a massive water-filled bridge straddling the Elbe River. About 15km northeast of central Magdeburg, the **Wasserstrassenkreuz** is Europe's longest canal bridge and a miracle of modern engineering. The 918m-long 'bathtub' links two major shipping canals and has made life a lot easier for barge captains navigating between Berlin and western Germany.

You can drive yourself there (take Magdeburg-Rothensee exit off the A2), take a 4½-hour boat trip with **Weisse Flotte** (Map p590; ☑532 8891; www.weisseflotte-magdeburg.de; Petriförder 1; adult/child €22.50/15; ⊘mid-Mar–Oct) or rent a bicycle and pedal along the scenic Elberadweg (p585) (Elbe River Bicycle Trail).

Magdeburg

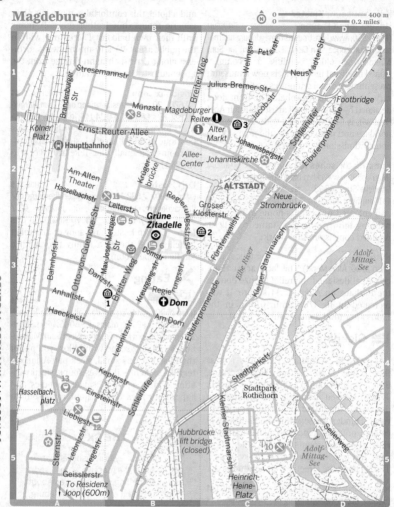

glutamate), complemented by a strong wine and cocktail list.

House of Steaks Ortega   STEAK $$
(Map p590; Otto-von-Guericke-Strasse 104; mains €7.25-15; ☺lunch & dinner) Surrender helplessly to your inner carnivore at this woodsy pub-style eatery where you'll join a mostly local crowd tucking into yummy cuts of aged Argentine steaks. Otherwise, choose from a variety of pizza, pasta and salads.

Die Saison   INTERNATIONAL $$$
(Herrenkrug 3; mains €24-28; ☺lunch & dinner) Classic German cuisine gets a modern inter-national twist within the ornately detailed dark-green walls of the Herrenkrug Parkhotel's art deco dining room.

Petriförder   ITALIAN, INTERNATIONAL $$
(Mapp590; ☎5979600;www.restaurant-petrifoerder -magdeburg.eu; Petriförder 1; mains €8-24; ☺from 11.30am Mon-Fri, from 10am Sat & Sun) Situated directly on the Elbe River, this restaurant and bar has a toe in all doors, with pasta, pizza, schnitzel and a good range of well-prepared poultry, fish and red-meat dishes, including lamb. Most dishes cost around €12. A beach bar sets up nearby in summer.

Magdeburg

Liebig INTERNATIONAL $$
(Map p590; Liebigstrasse 1-3; snacks €4.50-11, mains €8-15; ⊙from 10am, food until midnight) Tattooed hipsters to helmet-headed grannies eat or drink in this trendy cafe-bar-restaurant with large outdoor terrace.

Bingöl Grill TURKISH $
(Map p590; Breiter Weg 231; dishes €2-5; ⊙10am-3am Mon, Tue & Sun, to 5am Wed-Sat) Great salad selection, felafel and doner kebabs, and even better hours.

🍷 **Drinking & Entertainment**

The nightlife action revolves around the Hasselbachplatz. For listings, pick up a copy of *DATEs,* **Urbanite** (www.urbanite.de/magdeburg) or *Kulturfalter* (all free, all in German).

Café Central CAFE, BAR
(Map p590; www.cafecentral.cc; Leibnitzstrasse 34; ⊙from 7.30pm) This hip bar-cum-literary salon recreates the early 1900s with antique velvet sofas, flock wallpaper and Persian carpets. There are comedy shows, public readings, films or lectures on many evenings. It's worth visiting just for the cosy decor.

Deep BAR, CLUB
(Map p590; Breiter Weg 231; ⊙from 7pm) Dimly lit basement bar with DJs nightly and killer cocktails. Enter via Einsteinstrasse.

Stern CLUB
(Map p590; Sternstrasse 9; ⊙from 7pm Mon-Sat, from 8pm Sun) Cheap beer and alt-chic *boîte* with two floors of lounges and a dance floor. High flirt-factor, the rest is up to you.

Factory CLUB
(www.factory-magdeburg.de; Karl-Schmidt-Strasse 26-29) Live music and parties here in all musical directions.

ℹ **Information**

Anne's Waschparadies (Walther-Rathenau-Strasse 60; wash €4; ⊙9am-9pm Mon-Fri, to 3pm Sat) Inexpensive laundry.

City Café (Leiterstrasse 1; per 30min €1.90; ⊙10am-10pm) Smoky but convenient internet.

Post Office (Breiter Weg 203-206; ⊙9am-7pm Mon-Fri, to noon Sat)

Tourist Office (☎194 33; www.magdeburg-tourist.de; Ernst-Reuter-Allee 12; ⊙10am-6.30pm Mon-Fri, to 4pm Sat) Helpful office. Throughout town, bilingual information panels provide background about key sights and instructions for accessing additional details via your mobile phone.

ℹ **Getting There & Away**

Magdeburg is directly connected to Berlin-Hauptbahnhof (€27, two hours), Leipzig (€27, 1¼ hours) and Dessau (€11.10, 50 minutes). For Lutherstadt Wittenberg (€16.40, 70 minutes), change in Rosslau. Magdeburg is just south of the A2 to Berlin or Hanover and also served by the A14 to Leipzig.

ℹ **Getting Around**

BICYCLE Little John Bikes (☎733 0334; Alter Markt 13-14; ⊙10am-7pm Mon-Fri, to 4pm Sat) is a full-service bike shop that also rents two-wheelers for €10 per day. Book ahead, as the wheels aren't stored on the premises.

BUS & TRAM Single tickets cost €1.80, day tickets €3.60. Buy them from vending machines at each stop and punch on-board.

TAXI Call ☎737 373.

Halle

☎ 0345 / POP 233,000

Halle, once notoriously a hotbed for the GDR's chemical industry, is most famous for being the birthplace of Georg Friedrich Händel. With the collapse of the GDR, the chemical industries gradually sank into oblivion and the smoke began to clear from the skies. Change, however, was slow for many years, but some intelligent town planning and major projects in the lead-up to the celebration of Halle's 1200th anniversary in 2006 turned what was once a rather drab city into a surprisingly vibrant place. Much of this unexpected vibrancy comes from the some 20,000 students who attend the Martin Luther University of Halle-Wittenberg. For the casual visitor, however, it has a handful of interesting sights, including a museum dedicated to the Beatles.

◎ Sights

Marktkirche Unser Lieben Frauen CHURCH
(Marktplatz 12; Luther exhibit €2; ⊙10am-5pm Mon-Sat, 3-5pm Sun, organ music: noon Tue & Thu, also noon Sat May-Sep) Halle's central square has no fewer than five towers. One of these is the freestanding belltower known as Roter Turm, but the other four rise up from the bulky late-Gothic Marktkirche. Inside is its prized possession, Luther's original death mask of wax (ask the attendant to take you into the separate room). It also has a Renaissance pulpit from which he preached. A statue of Händel, who was baptised in the church, graces the square itself, and a new fountain recalls Halle's medieval heyday as a major salt-mining and -trading town.

Händel-Haus MUSEUM
(www.haendelhaus.de; Grosse Nikolaistrasse 5; adult/concession €4/2.50; ⊙10am-6pm Tue-Sun) The house in which Georg Friedrich Händel (1685–1759) was born is now the Händel-Haus. An exhibit charts the composer's life, achievements and impact on the evolution of classical music, with an emphasis on his wider European career. Descriptions are in German and English, and the free audioguide is also useful. In the second week of June, Halle hosts a prestigious **Händel Festival** (www.haendelfestspiele.halle.de).

Landeskunstmuseum GALLERY
(State Art Museum; www.kunstmuseum-moritzburg.de; Friedemann-Bach-Platz 5; adult/concession €7/5; ⊙10am-7pm Tue, to 6pm Wed-Sun) The late-Gothic Moritzburg castle forms a fantastic setting for the superb art collection of the Kunstmuseum des Landes Sachsen-Anhalt. The addition of a glass and aluminium roof over the north and west wings, which had been ruined since the Thirty Years' War (1618–48), nearly doubled the exhibition area. Airy and skylit, the new space is entirely dedicated to modern art. Older parts of the castle showcase works from medieval times to the 19th century. Take tram 3, 7 or 8 to Moritzburgring.

Beatles Museum MUSEUM
(www.beatlesmuseum.net; Alter Markt 12; adult/child €5/3; ⊙10am-8pm Tue-Sun) Take a 'magical mystery tour' through the life and music of the Fab Four at the Continent's only full-time Beatles Museum. Uberfan Rainer Moers has amassed enough knick-knacks to cram three floors with baby photos, birth certificates, album covers, film posters, wigs, jigsaws and even talcum powder – nothing is too trivial to be displayed. The gift shop sells many Beatles souvenirs. It's a few minutes' walk south of Markt.

🛏 Sleeping

Ankerhotel Halle [TOP CHOICE] HOTEL $$
(☎232 3200; www.ankerhofhotel.de; Ankerstrasse 2a; s €70-100, d €105-125; P✳@) Walls clad in local stone and ceilings supported by heavy wooden beams hark back to the 19th century when this was the Royal Customs Office. Completely modernised, it's now one of Halle's most charming hotels, with stylish and good-sized rooms; the nicest have river views. There's even a gym and saunas for sweating it out. Take tram 2, 5, 10 or 11 to Ankerstrasse.

Hotel-Pension Zum Ratshof HOTEL $
(☎202 5632; www.hotel-am-ratshof.de; Rathausstrasse 14; s/d €52/77) Rooms are large and decorated in bland beige-brown tones in this unspectacular but clean and conveniently located hotel spread over four floors. The quietest ones are on the top floor. It's just east of Markt.

Apart-Hotel Halle HOTEL $
(☎525 90; www.apart-halle.de; Kohlschütter Strasse 5-6; s/d/ste from €72/89/115; P@☎) Classic rooms but also fantastical prop-filled and mural-swathed themed suites, including 'Serengeti', 'Martin Luther' and 'King Ludwig II'. Take tram 3 or 12 to Hegelstrasse.

Dorint Charlottenhof Halle   HOTEL **$$$**
(☑292 30; www.dorint.com/halle; Dorotheen-
strasse 12; r without breakfast €80-130; P❄🕏)
This chain hotel is modern and efficient and
has lots of amenities – including a whirl-
pool, gym and sauna for post-sightseeing
relaxation. Prices vary significantly by de-
mand. Walk from Hauptbahnhof or take any
tram one stop to Riebeckplatz.

Domero Rotes Ross   HOTEL **$$$**
(☑233 430; www.dormero-hotel-rotes-ross.de/;
Leipziger Strasse 76; r €100-190, breakfast €17;
P❄🕏) Four-star hotel with excellent amenities, including a sauna and wellness area
with whirlpools. Prices vary significantly according to demand.

✕ Eating

Osteria da Salvatore   ITALIAN **$$**
(Bergstrasse 7; pasta €8-14, mains €13-28; ⊙11am-
midnight) There are several Italian places
along the main restaurant strip, Kleine Ul-
richstrasse, but this *osteria* on the corner of
Bergstrasse is the local favourite for its deli-
cious homemade pastas and cross-regional
selection of mains. Students, office workers
and anyone else with an appetite for good
Italian food come here. Lone diners will also
feel very comfortable.

Immergrün   INTERNATIONAL **$$**
(☑521 6056; www.restaurant-immergruen.de; Klei-
ne Klausstrasse 2; mains €19-24; ⊙dinner Tue-Sat)
Reserve two days ahead for a table at this
quality addition to Halle's restaurant scene.
Creatively prepared seasonal fish, poultry
and red-meat dishes are served from a small
menu that changes monthly.

Café NT   CAFE **$**
(☑205 0232; Grosse Ulrichstrasse 51; dishes
€4.90-9.10; ⊙9am-midnight Mon-Thu, to 1am Fri,
10-1am Sat, 10am-8pm Sun) Exuding the casual
charm of a Viennese coffeehouse, this artsy
spot is affiliated with the Neues Theater. As
well as cocktails and other drinks, it does
good pasta, salads and a worthy club sandwich with organic beef.

Ökoase   VEGETARIAN **$**
(Kleine Ulrichstrasse 2; mains €5-10; ⊙9.30am-
7.30pm Mon-Sat; 🖉) Vegetarian eatery with
soup, salads, curries and other dishes, which
change on a weekly basis.

Hallesches Brauhaus   GERMAN **$$**
(Grosse Nikolaistrasse 2; mains €8.70-13.90; ⊙from
11am Mon-Fri, 10am Sat & Sun) Sure, they make

their own beer, but that's not the only reason
to steer towards this contemporary brewpub
with food – expect hearty pub fare.

🍷 Drinking & Entertainment

Finding a party pen to match your mood is
easy in Halle's trifecta of fun strips: Kleine
Ulrichstrasse, Sternstrasse and the Bermu-
dadreieck (around Seebener Strasse and
Burgstrasse near Burg Giebichstein). Also
consult the free magazines *Blitz* or *Frizz*.

Potemkin   CAFE
(Kleine Ulrichstrasse 27; ⊙9am-midnight) Potem-
kin is a sleek and fashionable drinking spot
with an extraordinary selection of teas,
breakfasts and the occasional snack. It can
get a little smoky in the main room, though.

Objekt 5   LIVE MUSIC
(www.objekt5.de; Seebener Strasse 5) This clas-
sic venue has folk, rock, occasional avant-
garde concerts and regular DJs. Check the
program for times. Take tram 8 to Burg Gie-
bichenstein, the castle ruin nearby.

Turm   CLUB
(www.turm-halle.de; Friedemann-Bach-Platz 5;
⊙Wed, Fri & Sat) In the Moritzburg, this old
student club has DJs pressing out the latest
sounds and various events, including poetry
slams some Sundays.

❶ Information

Internet (Talamstrasse 4; per 30min €0.50;
⊙10.30am-10pm Mon-Sat, 11.30am-11pm Sun)
Cheap and smoky.

Bahnhofslounge Bastian (1st floor, Hauptbahn-
hof; ⊙24hr; 🕏) A 24/7 lounge with free wi-fi,
as well as internet access.

Post Office (Marktplatz 20; ⊙9.30am-8pm
Mon-Sat)

Tourist Office (☑122 9984; www.stadtmarket
ing-halle.de; Marktplatz 13; ⊙9am-7pm Mon-
Fri, 10am-4pm Sat) Sells the Halle Welcome
Card (one/three days €7.50/15), which in-
cludes public transport and discounts on tours
and museum admissions.

❶ Getting There & Around

AIR **Leipzig-Halle Airport** (LEJ; www.leipzig
-halle-airport.de) lies about equidistant between
both cities, which are about 45km apart. It is
served by domestic and international flights.
The airport is linked with Halle Hauptbahnhof at
least twice hourly by RE (€3.80, 11 minutes) and
hourly IC (€6, 10 minutes) trains.

CAR From Leipzig, take the A14 west to the
B100. The A14 connects Halle and Magdeburg in

about one hour. The B91 runs south from Halle and links up with the A9 autobahn, which connects Munich and Berlin.

TRAIN Leipzig and Halle are linked by frequent IC trains (€10, 25 minutes) and cheaper regional trains. Magdeburg is served by IC trains (€19.50, 50 minutes) and RE trains (€16.40, 70 minutes). A couple of direct ICs also go to Berlin (€38, 1¼ hours) but you need to change trains in Leipzig for frequent ICE/RB connections (€45, two hours). Local trains serve Lutherstadt Eisleben (€7.50, 40 minutes) and Wittenberg (€12.20, one hour).

TRAM Trams 2, 5, 7 and 9 run from the train station to the Marktplatz. Rides cost €1.80 (€1.30 for up to four stops) or €4 for day cards. Buy tickets from machines at many stops.

Lutherstadt Eisleben

☎ 03475 / POP 25,500

It seems odd for a well-travelled man whose ideas revolutionised Europe to have died in the town where he was born. However, as native son Martin Luther (1483–1546) himself put it before spinning off his mortal coil here, '*Mein Vaterland war Eisleben*' (Eisleben was my fatherland). This former mining town focuses almost exclusively on the devout follower. Every where you turn, it's Luther, Luther, Luther.

⊙ Sights

Luthers Sterbehaus   MUSEUM
(Luther Death House; Andreaskirchplatz 7; adult/concession €4/2.50; ⊙10am-6pm) Luther returned to Eisleben in January 1546 to help settle a legal dispute for the Count of Mansfeld, but he was already ill and died on 18 February, a day after finalising an agreement. It was long believed that Luther died here, but today we know he actually died on the site occupied by the Hotel Graf von Mansfeld. At the time of research, Luther's Death House was being upgraded with new exhibitions and double the exhibition space, focusing on three themes: the last 24 hours in Luther's life; his thoughts about death itself (obviously, while he was still alive); and thirdly, how the culture of death has evolved over the centuries. The museum exhibits a death mask from Luther (a 19th-century mask made from the wax mask kept in Halle's Marktkirche) and the original pall that covered his coffin. Its prize literary exhibit is a bible from 1541 – the last Luther worked on. Historic rooms have been restored to their original form in this museum,

which the Luther Memorial Foundation says is the only one in Germany that dispenses with the atheistic approach of the GDR era to take a theological view of Luther and his life.

Luthers Geburtshaus   MUSEUM
(www.martinluther.de; Lutherstrasse 15; adult/concession €4/2.50; ⊙10am-6pm) The house where the reformer was born, Luthers Geburtshaus has been a memorial site since 1693. The house is furnished period-style, while exhibits in the annex focus on the family of Luther and aspects of the society in which he grew up.

St Andreaskirche   CHURCH
(Andreaskirchplatz; admission €1; ⊙10am-4pm Mon-Sat, 11am-4pm Sun, closed Nov-Apr) Luther delivered his last sermons in the St Andreaskirche, a late-Gothic hall church on the hill behind the central Markt.

St Annenkirche   CHURCH
(⊙10am-4pm Mon-Sat, noon-4pm Sun, closed Nov-Apr) While district vicar, Martin Luther stayed in the apartments of the St Annenkirche, 10 minutes west of the Markt. This church also features a stunning Steinbilder-Bibel (Stone-picture Bible; 1585), the only one of its kind in Europe, and a wittily decorated pulpit.

St Petri Pauli Kirche   CHURCH
(Andreaskirchplatz; admission €1; ⊙10am-4pm Mon-Sat, 11am-4pm Sun, closed Nov-Apr) Remarkable for being the church where Luther was baptised.

⊨ Sleeping & Eating

TOP CHOICE Hotel Graf von Mansfeld   HOTEL $$
(☎663 00; www.hotel-eisleben.de; Markt 56; s/d/ste €65/95/125; ▣@🖙) Eisleben's premier in-town hotel is a classic outpost of charm and tradition. Although over 500 years old, it has seriously slicked-up rooms with four-poster beds, and bright and airy flair. No two rooms are alike. The partner-run wellness area has three saunas (€10 extra). The restaurant serves modern international cuisine (mains €8.50 to €18).

Mansfelder Hof   HOTEL $
(☎612 620; www.mansfelderhof.de; Hallesche Strasse 33; s/d without bathroom €43/57, with bathroom €49/69; ▣🖙) Behind its vine-covered, faded green stucco facade, the Mansfelder Hof turns out to have modern if rather generic rooms. The restaurant serves Greek

food. The quietest rooms are those facing the rear of the hotel.

Plan B   BAR, CAFE **$**
(Markt 33; snacks €3.50-7.50; ⊘from noon Mon-Sat) This sleek new bar offers a contrast to the historic aspects of Eisleben. As well as serving wine and cocktails it does Flamm-kuchen, antipasti and salads.

❶ Information

Tourist Office (🕿602 124; www.eisleben-tourist.de; Hallesche Strasse 4; ⊘10am-5pm Mon & Wed-Fri, to 6pm Tue, to 1pm Sat)

❶ Getting There & Around

There are frequent trains to Halle (€7.50, 40 minutes), where you can change for Lutherstadt Wittenberg (€22.50, 1¾ hours), Leipzig (€14.50, 70 minutes), Magdeburg (€24.50, 1½ hours) and Weimar (€21, 2¼ hours). Eisleben is a half-hour drive west of Halle on the B80.

Most sights are knotted together around the Markt, just north of Hallesche Strasse, the main thoroughfare. To get there from the station, it's a 15-minute walk via Bahnhofsring (turn left on leaving the station) and Bahnhofstrasse. Buses going past Markt usually meet the trains.

Lower Saxony & Bremen

POP 8.46 MILLION / AREA 47,960 SQ KM

Best Places to Eat

» Markthalle (p605)

» Ox (p616)

» Restaurant Brodocz (p616)

» Vini D'Italia Marrone (p620)

» Le Gril (p628)

Best Places to Stay

» Hotel Überfluss (p626)

» City Hotel am Thielenplatz (p603)

» Best Western Stadtpalais (p616)

» Hotel Goya (p619)

» Hotel Bölts am Park (p626)

Why Go?

In terms of size, the two German states of Lower Saxony and Bremen could not be more of a contrast. Lower Saxony is the largest German state after Bavaria and, outside its capital Hanover (Hannover), a patchwork of interesting regional centres each of a few hundred thousand inhabitants or less. Museums even in these smaller places are excellent, encouraging a stopover of a day or two for exploration. Outside the cities, the coast, river plains, tidal flats, moors and heath of Lower Saxony lend themselves perfectly to cycling or walking.

Bremen, the smallest of the German states, brings together culture and nightlife in a compact but lively format. Within minutes, you can explore an unusual expressionist street, move on to a quaint district of winding medieval lanes and continue to an alternative student quarter via a small but interesting 'museum mile'. Meanwhile, the port of Bremerhaven offers extraordinary insight into the region's seafaring tradition.

When to Go

Because Lower Saxony and Bremen are located in a lowlands region without mountains for winter sports, there are few outdoor advantages to travelling the region in winter. Expect some grey weather or even double-digit subzero temperatures in a cold year. Winter, however, is a good time to visit the museums, galleries and theatres of this region. From April to September, life moves outdoors and temperatures are high enough to cycle and hike comfortably, walk the Wadden Sea (tidal flats), visit the East Frisian Islands or enjoy picnics and outdoor eating.

HANOVER & THE EAST

The state capital of Hanover forms the urban hub of this region, which reaches out into towns such as Braunschweig and Wolfenbüttel, and to Wolfsburg – the headquarters of Volkswagen vehicle manufacturing. Towns like Celle and Hildesheim can easily be visited on day trips from Hanover. This region dissolves in the east into Brandenburg, and beyond that into Berlin, which is only two hours by train from Hanover and can be reached within an hour from Wolfsburg.

Hanover

📞 0511 / POP 522,700

Lacking the high profile of the Hanse city states Hamburg and Bremen to its north, Hanover (Hannover in German) is perhaps best known for its CeBit information and communications technology fair. Less well-known but buried deep within its identity is a British connection – for over 100 years from the early 18th century, monarchs from the house of Hanover also ruled Great Britain and everything that belonged to the British Empire. Perhaps it's this paradox – of being an incredibly influential part of something much larger than itself – that makes Hanover's character so difficult to pin down. Perhaps it belongs to the character of the Hanoverians and this lowlands region (the so-called *Tiefebene*) to be so low-key about such a powerful history.

As well as having its huge CeBit and providing monarchs that ruled half the world for some time, Hanover has acres of greenery and its spectacularly baroque Herrenhäuser Gärten (gardens), which is a mini Versailles. The compact centre, partially reconstructed in a medieval style after WWII bombing, is complemented in the east by the Eilenriede forest, and you can enjoy some good museums – and some football culture at Hanover's stadium – en route to the southern lake Maschsee.

History

Hanover was established around 1100 and became the residence of Heinrich der Löwe (p720) later that century. An early Hanseatic city, by the Reformation it had developed into a prosperous seat of royalty and a power unto itself.

A link was created with the monarchy of Britain in 1714, when the eldest son of Electress Sophie of Hanover (a granddaughter of James I of England; James VI of Scotland), ascended the British throne as George I while simultaneously ruling Hanover. This British–German union lasted until 1837.

In 1943, up to 80% of the centre and 50% of the entire city was destroyed by Allied bombing. The rebuilding plan included creating sections of reconstructed half-timbered houses and painstakingly rebuilding the city's prewar gems, such as the Opernhaus (Opera House), the Marktkirche and the Neues Rathaus (New Town Hall).

⊙ Sights & Activities

The city has painted a *Roter Faden* (red line) on pavements around the centre. Follow it with the help of the multilingual *Red Thread Guide* (€2.50), available from the tourist office, for a quick 4.2km, do-it-yourself tour of the city's 36 highlights.

CENTRE

TOP CHOICE ⟩ **Sprengel Museum**   MUSEUM
(www.sprengel-museum.de; Kurt-Schwitters-Platz; adult/concession €7/4, Fri free; ⊙10am-6pm Wed-Sun, to 8pm Tue) The Sprengel Museum is held in extremely high esteem, both for the design of the building as well as for the art housed inside. Its huge interior spaces are perfectly suited to displaying its modern figurative, abstract and conceptual art, including a few works by Nolde, Chagall and Picasso. At the core of the collection are 300 works by the artist Niki de Saint Phalle, a selection of which is usually on show. Take bus 100 from Kröpcke to the Maschsee/Sprengel Museum stop.

Neues Rathaus   HISTORIC BUILDING
(Map p602; Trammplatz 2; elevator adult/concession €3/2; ⊙9.30am-6.30pm Mon-Fri, 10am-6.30pm Sat & Sun, elevator closed mid-Nov–Mar) An excellent way to get your bearings in Hanover is to visit the Neues Rathaus (built in 1901-13) and travel 98m to the top in the curved lift inside its green dome. There are four viewing platforms here. The cabin can take only five people at a time, so queues are inevitable in summer.

In the downstairs lobby are four city models showing Hanover from the Middle Ages to today.

Maschsee   LAKE
(www.uestra-reisen.de; Rudolf-von-Bennigsen-Ufer; adult/child full tour €6/3, half-tour €3/1.50) This artificial lake, built by the unemployed in one of the earliest Nazi-led public-works

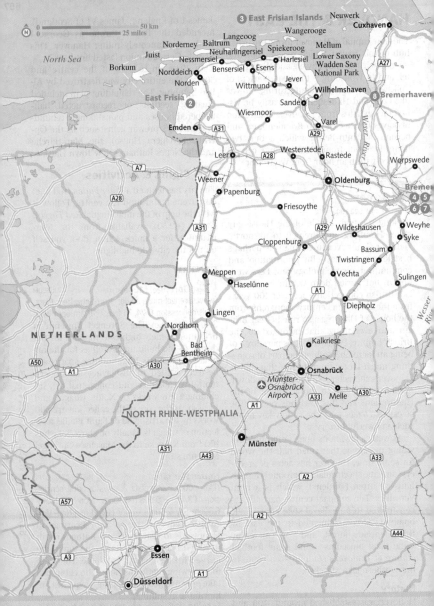

Lower Saxony & Bremen Highlights

1 Pay your respects to Anne Frank at the **Bergen-Belsen** (p612) concentration camp

2 Grab a bicycle or kayak and ride or paddle through **East Frisia** (p641)

3 Hike across tidal flats to an **East Frisian Island** (p639)

4 Marvel at the golden archangel and red-brick angles of **Böttcherstrasse** (p622)

5 Catch a ferry to **Café Sand** (p629) for a coffee on the golden sands of the Weser River 'beach'

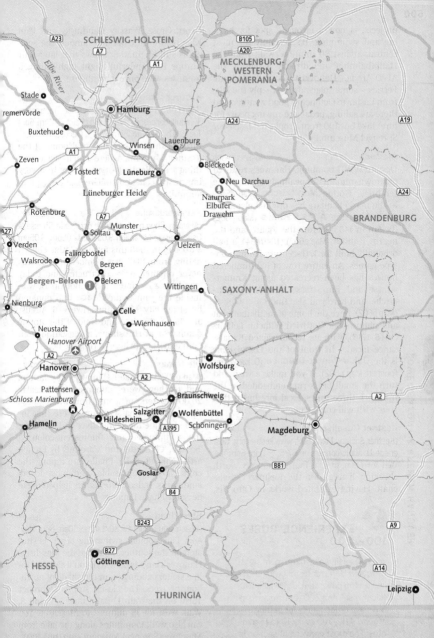

projects, is now a favourite spot for boating and swimming. It's certainly the most central, at just 30 minutes' walk from the Hauptbahnhof and directly alongside the AWD-Arena, Hanover's football stadium. Ferries – some solar-powered – ply the lake from Easter to October in good weather, and there are sailing, pedal and rowing boats for hire. Take bus 100 from Kröpke to Maschsee/Sprengel Museum.

Altstadt
NEIGHBOURHOOD

Despite WWII bombing, Hanover's restored old town remains appealingly quaint. The red-brick, Gothic Marktkirche (Map p602) in the market square has original elements, as do both the Altes Rathaus (Map p602) (begun in 1455), across the square, and the nearby Ballhof (Map p602) (1649–64), a hall originally built for 17th-century badminton-type games. An entire row of half-timbered houses has been recreated along Kramerstrasse and Burgstrasse near the Marktkirche, and here you also find Leibnizhaus (Map p602), once the home of mathematician and philosopher Gottfried Wilhelm Leibniz (1646–1716), with its reconstructed Renaissance facade. In front of the Leibnizhaus is the Oskar-Winter-Brunnen (Oskar Winter Fountain; Map p602). If you make a wish and turn the small brass ring embedded in the ironwork three times, local lore has it that your wish will come true.

Kestner Gesellschaft
GALLERY

(Kestner Society; Map p602; www.kestner.org; Goseriede 11; adult/concession €7/5; ⊕11am-6pm Tue, Wed & Fri-Sun, to 8pm Thu) It's always worth checking listings for the Kestner Gesellschaft. Having exhibited works by Otto Dix,

'EXPERIENCE' BUSES 100 & 200

You can easily take in the main sights by foot in Hanover by following the red line on the pavement, but buses 100 (clockwise) and 200 (anticlockwise) are sometimes handy for getting around. They run every 10 to 15 minutes. The most convenient section is bus 100 south from Hauptbahnhof to the Maschsee. Good places to pick up the 100/200 are Lister Meile, Kröpke and Maschsee/Sprengel Museum near the football stadium.

Georg Grosz, Wassily Kandinsky and Paul Klee before they became famous, the society is still originating shows that later tour Europe. Its wonderfully light, high-ceilinged premises were once a bathhouse.

Kestner Museum
MUSEUM

(Map p602; www.hannover.de/kestner; Trammplatz 3; adult/concession €7/5, Fri free; ⊕11am-6pm Tue & Thu-Sun, to 8pm Wed) Decorative arts through the ages are the focal point of the Kestner Museum, where you'll see everything from Bauhaus-style cutlery to a very impressive collection of Greek and Egyptian antiquities.

Aegidienkirche
MEMORIAL

(Aegidius Church; Map p602; cnr Breite Strasse & Osterstrasse; ⊕carillon 9.05am, 12.05pm, 3.05pm & 6.05pm) In 1943 this former Gothic church dating from 1347 was bombed out. It was never repaired or reconstructed and today stands as a reminder to the horrors of war. Inside the ruin is the Peace Bell donated by sister city Hiroshima. Every 6 August at 8.15am, the date and time of the atomic detonation at Hiroshima, a delegation from both cities meets here to ring the bell.

Die Nanas
SCULPTURE

(Map p602; Leibnizufer) Hanover's city fathers and mothers were inundated with nearly 20,000 letters of complaint when these three earth-mama sculptures were first installed beside the Leine River in 1974. Now, the voluptuous and fluorescent-coloured 'Sophie', 'Charlotte' and 'Caroline', by French artist Niki de Saint Phalle, are among the city's most recognisable, and most loved, landmarks. Indeed, *Die Nanas* helped make de Saint Phalle famous.

Strandbad
BEACH

(Beach; adult/child €2.30/1.40; ⊕10am-8pm May-Aug) This popular swimming beach is situated on the southeast bank of the Maschsee, Hanover's large lake, where you'll also find in-line skaters gliding by in the shade of neighbouring trees. The closest stop is Döhrener Turm on the tram/U-Bahn lines 1, 2 and 8. Walk west for 15 minutes to Maschsee. You can also walk 15 minutes along the lake from Maschsee/Sprengel Museum stop (bus 100).

Waterloo Memorial
MONUMENT

(Map p602) This 46.3-metre column commemorates the victory of German, British and Prussian forces over Napoleon in the Battle of Waterloo in June 1815.

ALL THE FUN OF THE TRADE FAIR

Coming to Hanover for a trade fair *(Messe)*? You're part of a time-honoured tradition. The first export fair was held in August 1947 in the midst of all the rubble from WWII. As most hotels had been destroyed, the mayor made an appeal to citizens to provide beds for foreign guests. The people did, the money came and it's become a tradition; about a third more beds are available in private flats at fair time (the only time they're offered) than in hotels.

The pre-eminent fair today is CeBit, a telecommunications and office information gathering that organisers claim is 'the largest trade show of any kind, anywhere in the world'. It's held every March and during the dotcom boom of the late 1990s had as many as 800,000 attendees. (More recent shows have attracted smaller crowds of around half a million visitors.) Another biggie is Hannover Messe, an industrial show in late April.

The **Messegelände**, the main trade fairgrounds, are in the city's southeast, served by tram/U-Bahn 8 (and during fair times 18, both to Entrance Nord) as well as the S4 S-Bahn, and IC and ICE trains. Tram/U-Bahn 6 and 16 serve the eastern part of the fairgrounds near the former Expo site.

During major fairs there's a full-service tourist office at the airport and an information pavilion at the fairgrounds, in addition to the main tourist office.

Pressure on accommodation means you really need to book ahead – and be prepared for phenomenal price hikes too. Indeed, some visitors choose to stay instead in Hildesheim, Celle (both of which up their own prices during these times) or even in Hamburg, and commute.

As a first step, the website www.hannovermesse.de has full information in English. To organise a private room or hotel in Hanover, call ☎1234 5555 or email the tourist office at hotel@hannover-tourismus.de.

NORTH OF THE CENTRE

Situated about 5km northwest of the centre, **Herrenhäuser Gärten** (☎1684 7576; www. herrenhaeuser-gaerten.de; ⊙9am-sunset) (Herrenhausen Gardens) are a remarkable ensemble of parks and gardens largely modelled on those at Versailles, outside Paris. Four gardens make up the ensemble, the oldest of which is the baroque Grosser Garten. Berggarten – like the Grosser Garten – is pay-for-admission; Georgeangarten (George Garden) and Welfengarten (Welf Garden) are free and open to the public any time of day or night. To get to the district, take tram/U-Bahn 4 or 5 from Kröpke to Herrenhäuser Gärten.

The pretty Eilenriede Forest northeast of the centre is ideal for cycling – a bicycle route to Lunebürg begins here.

Grosser Garten   GARDENS
(www.herrenhaeuser-gaerten.de; incl entry to Berggarten late-Mar–Oct adult/concession €5/3, Nov–late-Mar €3.50/1.50) The jewel in the crown of the Herrenhäuser Gärten (Herrenhausen Gardens), Grosser Garten is grand both in format and history, having been laid out as a baroque garden in 1714 under the tutelage of the French landscape gardener Martin Charbonnier. The garden contains statues,

fountains and the coloured tile walls of the **Niki de Saint Phalle Grotto** (creator of the city's much-loved *Die Nanas* sculptures, and opened after her death in 2002), providing a magical showcase of the artist's work. There's a maze near the northern entrance of the Grosser Garten, while the **Grosse Fontäne** (Great Fountain; the tallest in Europe) at the southern end jets water up to 80m high. From early 2013 the reconstructed Schloss Herrenhausen (Herrenhausen Palace) should be open – based on the original early-19th-century palace that was destroyed by bombing in 1943. The palace will mostly be used for conferences and events, but a Schlossmuseum, which should be open from spring 2013, will have temporary exhibitions on a Hanover theme and eventually will house a permanent exhibition. The cost of admission will be combined with park admission.

In summer a highlight is the **Wasserspiele** (Fountain Display; ⊙11am-noon & 3-5pm Mon-Fri, 11am-noon & 2-5pm Sat & Sun Apr-Oct), water fountains that are synchronised to do some spectacular spurting.

The **Illuminations** (www.hannover.de/herren hausen; adult/concession €5/3) are another popular summer attraction. Usually in August and September at 10pm or 9pm, the Grosser

Hanover

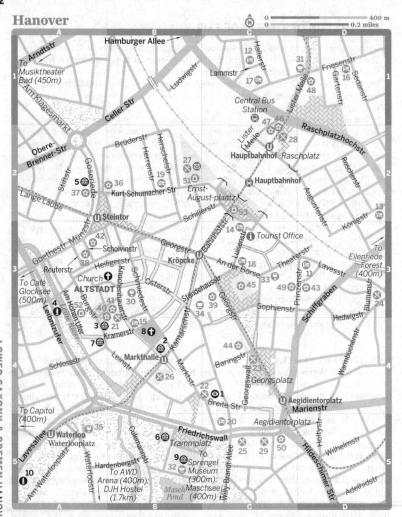

Garten is lit up for between one and two hours. Days vary, but the 'Events' section of the website gives dates and times. There are summer concerts, Shakespearean dramas and more, some also with illuminations.

Berggarten GARDENS
(www.herrenhaeuser-gaerten.de; adult/concession late-Mar–Oct €3.50/1.50, incl entry to Grosser Garten adult/concession €5/3, Nov–late-Mar €3.50/1.50) This botanical garden, which along with Grosser Garten is one of the pay-for-entry gardens in the Herrenhäuser Gärten ensemble, is the oldest in Germany

and has 300-year-old lime trees lining an avenue leading to a mausoleum holding the remains of George I of England.

Wilhelm-Busch-Museum MUSEUM
(www.wilhelm-busch-museum.de; Georgengarten; adult/concession €4.50/2.50; 11am-6pm Tue-Sun) Contains a wealth of caricature, including works by caricature greats Busch, Honoré Daumier and William Hogarth.

Eilenriede Forest FOREST
(Fritz-Behrens-Allee) Beginning about 1km northeast of the train station, this large parkland was the forested playground of the

Hanover

Hanoverians. Bus 100 going north to Emmichplatz stops at the entrance arch.

🎉 Festivals & Events

The annual **Maschsee festival**, which includes drinking, performances and an enormous fireworks display, runs annually from early August.

Each year in summer, pyrotechnic experts stage a handful of shows at the international **fireworks festival** and competition at Herrenhäuser Gärten.

People come to Hanover from afar for the Enercity Swinging Hannover (www.swinging hannover.de) international jazz festival, held over two days around Ascension Day in May/June.

🛏 Sleeping

The tourist office books rooms for a €2.50 fee. Prices given here are those outside trade-show periods. During shows, they can double, triple and even quadruple. Check the city website (www.hannover.de) or better yet ask the tourist office directly to ensure you're not unintentionally arriving during a trade-fair period.

City Hotel am Thielenplatz HOTEL $
(Map p602; ☎327 691; www.smartcityhotel.com; Thielenplatz 2; s/d from €59/69, breakfast €9.50; P🖥) This very central 'budget boutique' beauty has a reception and bar (open until 5am) restyled with leather seating, black-and-white

leaf-patterned wallpaper and lots of wood laminate. All rooms have been renovated, mostly in a minimalist style. Prices rise according to day of the week and demand.

[TOP CHOICE] **Loccumer Hof** HOTEL **$$**
(Map p602; ☎126 40; www.loccumerhof.de; Kurt-Schumacher-Strasse 14/16; s €99, d €139-159, ste €169; [P]@📶) Some of the stylish and well-decorated rooms here are themed by nations ('Australia'), elements ('Air') and feng shui. Others are low-allergy. As well as these walk-in prices, rates are often much less for advance or internet bookings (from €59 for singles).

Lühmanns Hotel am Rathaus HOTEL **$$**
(Map p602; ☎326 268; www.hotelamrathaus.de; Friedrichswall 21; s/d from €89/120; @📶) Posters from the nearby Kestner Museum and artwork adorn the halls here, and the rooms themselves are tastefully decorated. Although the hotel's on a busy street, good double-glazing makes the rooms very quiet.

Hanns-Lilje-Haus HOTEL **$$**
(Map p602; ☎124 1698; www.hanns-lilje-haus.de; Knochenhauerstrasse 33; s/d €66/82; 📶) Though Church-owned, this hotel is fine about unmarried or gay couples staying. Decorations are neutral, but rooms are large and make interesting use of space to create a bright and pleasant atmosphere.

Hotel Wiehberg HOTEL **$$**
(☎879 990; www.hotel-wiehberg.de; Wiehbergstrasse 55a; s/d €78/95; [P]📶; [S]1 to Wiehbergstrasse) Modernistic and evoking a 'Zen' feel, this hotel makes excellent use of natural lighting and shadow, and even features low Japanese-style beds set on rails. These are designed for trade-fair guests who want to share rooms without getting too snug. If guests do get snug, though, they can push the beds together. The hotel's in a leafy residential neighbourhood.

Hotel Königshof am Funkturm HOTEL **$$**
(Map p602; ☎339 80; www.koenigshof-hannover.de; Friesenstrasse 65; s €59-89, d €79-99; [P]@📶) Quirky religious statues and ethnic sculptures (plus an old Rolls-Royce) greet you in the foyer of this unusual hotel. You'll find 'economy', 'comfort', 'business' (with balcony) and 'deluxe' rooms (with sofa), decorated attractively with bright furnishings and subtle Toscana tones. The location is reasonably safe, but this is a small red-light club district.

🌿 **Schlafgut Hotel im Werkhof** HOTEL **$$**
(☎353 560; www.hotel-schlafgut.de; Kniesestrasse 33; s/d €85/109; [P]@📶; [S]6 or 11 to Kopernikusstrasse) Located in the Nordstadt in a former lift factory (remodelled along ecological principles), Schlafgut has a bright, open and colourful feel, along with a 1970s retro breakfast room. Rooms have large writing surfaces and high-speed internet through the power socket – but bring your own cable or you'll need to buy one from reception for €5. There's wi-fi in the foyer.

Hotel Alpha HOTEL **$$**
(Map p602; ☎341 535; www.hotelalpha.de; Friesenstrasse 19; s €79-94, d €112-124, tr €136; 📶) Situated at the end of the street away from the red-light clubs, this pleasant hotel's rooms are lovely and homey, complemented by an assortment of sweet and quirky statues and marionettes. There's a startling trompe l'oeil Italian piazza in the breakfast room.

Arabella Sheraton Pelikan HOTEL **$$$**
(☎909 30; pelikanhotel@arabellasheraton.com; Podbielskistrasse 145; r from €145, breakfast €20; ❄@📶; [S]3, 7 or 9 to Pelikanstrasse) Fat beds with thick mattresses and plump cushions dominate the rooms of this luxury hotel, where high ceilings alleviate any feeling of being cramped. Set on a redeveloped factory site in the suburbs, it feels like a hideaway village, with the renowned restaurant 5th Ave and Harry's New York bar. There's a fitness centre (free use) next door, too.

Kastens Hotel Luisenhof HOTEL **$$$**
(Map p602; ☎304 40; www.kastens-luisenhof.de; Luisenstrasse 1-3; s/d/junior ste/ste from €97/107/189/290, breakfast €18; [P]❄@📶) This *grande dame* looks pretty good in spite of being over 150 years old, possibly from the myriad wellness offerings such as massages and its upper-level spa and fitness centre. The Piano Suite comes literally with a piano. Prices rise especially on the singles and doubles according to demand, but early and internet bookers can get good deals.

Grand Hotel Mussmann HOTEL **$$$**
(Map p602; ☎36 560; www.grandhotel.de; Ernst-August-Platz 7; s €119, d €149-229, ste €279; ❄@📶) The four-star Mussmann is one of Hanover's old dames that has been given a facelift and completely revamped into a stylish, modern hotel with rooms named after famous Hanover landmarks. Rooms and suites are spacious and well appointed, with ample pillows

for comfort. Many of the doubles are junior suites, but each floor has a fully fledged grand suite with music (eg the song 'It's Raining Men') when you use the shower. There's LAN internet access in the rooms and wi-fi in the lobby (both €17 per day).

DJH Hostel
HOSTEL $

(☑131 7674; www.jugendherberge.de/jh/hannover; Ferdinand-Wilhelm-Fricke-Weg 1; 4-bed dm under/over 27yr from €21.80/25.80, s/d €38.50/57; P☺@🛜; ⓢ3 or 7 to Bahnhof Linden/Fischerhof) This huge, space-lab-like structure houses a modern hostel with breakfast room and terrace bar overlooking the river. It's only a short walk from here to the Maschsee.

City Hotel Flamme
HOTEL $$

(Map p602; ☑388 8004; www.city-hotel-flamme.de; Lammstrasse 3; s/d €70/125; P@🛜) Most of the 24 rooms of this attractively mural-painted hotel-*Pension* open onto balconies facing a large atrium courtyard, which has a quirky eating area and glassed-in front wall. If you don't like the area around the train station, they will pick you up from there for free.

GästeResidenz PelikanViertel
APARTMENT $

(☑399 90; www.gaesteresidenz-pelikanviertel.de; Pelikanstrasse 11; s €49-83, d €69-105, tr €100-125; P🛜; ⓢ3, 7 or 9 to Pelikanstrasse) Upmarket student residence meets budget hotel, this well-managed complex alongside the Arabella Sheraton Pelikan hotel has a wide range of very pleasant Ikea-ish rooms, some split over two levels. Per apartment an additional €8 (plus €50 deposit) is charged on the given prices for use of the kitchen utensils. Long-term stays for seven days or longer are excellent value.

City Hotel Königstrasse
HOTEL $$

(Map p602; ☑410 2800; www.smartcityhotel.com; Königstrasse 12; s/d/tr €60/69/99, breakfast €9.50; P@🛜) This convenient business hotel is a few minutes by foot from Hauptbahnhof. Prices rise according to day of week and demand.

Campingplatz Arnumer See
CAMPGROUND $

(☑05101-3534; http://camping-hannover.de; Oster-bruchweg 5, Arnum-Hemmingen; adult €6, car €2-4, tent €5; @🛜) In a leafy lakeside location south of the city, this extremely well-equipped camping ground has a playground and separate areas for tents and caravans. Take bus 300 to Arnum Mitte, from where it's a five-minute walk. By road, take A7 south to Laatzen, or B3 from Arnum, and follow the signs.

Eating

TOP CHOICE Pier 51
INTERNATIONAL $$

(☑807 1800; www.pier51.de; Rudolf von Bennigsen Ufer 51; starters €10-13, mains €21-22; ☺noon-midnight) One of Hanover's loveliest restaurants, and very romantic at sundown, Pier 51 is walled with glass and juts out over the Maschsee. Expect light pasta dishes and a small selection of fish, poultry and red meats on a changing menu. All dishes can be ordered in half-servings for little over half the price. Book at least a few days ahead if you want a window seat at dinner. Alongside it is a boat hire and snack stands with outdoor seating. Take tram/U-Bahn 1, 2 or 8 to Altenbeken Damm and walk 10 minutes to the Maschsee.

TOP CHOICE Spandau
INTERNATIONAL $

(www.spandauprojekt.de; Engelbosteler Damm 30; lunch special €6.50, mains €7.90-9.90; ☺from noon Mon-Fri, from 10am Sat & Sun; 🛜☑) Retro-'70s Spandau in Hanover's Nordstadt is more like a place in Berlin's Kreuzberg – where students from the nearby university and the local Turkish community rub shoulders. The menu is smallish and features cheeseburgers, salads, soups and mostly pasta as mains, many of these with meats.

TOP CHOICE Markthalle
MARKET $

(Map p602; www.hannover-markthalle.de; Kamarschstrasse 49; dishes €3.50-10; ☺7am-8pm Mon-Wed, to 10pm Thu & Fri, to 4pm Sat; ☑) This huge covered market of food stalls and gourmet delicatessens is fantastic for a quick bite, both carnivorous and vegetarian.

Georxx
INTERNATIONAL $$

(Map p602; www.georxx-hannover.de; Georgsplatz 3; pasta €8.50-13.50, mains €9.50-28.80; ☺from 9am) Popular with businesspeople, office workers, shoppers, tired travellers and even an arty crowd, Georxx has pleasant outdoor seating in summer, a menu offering a taste for everyone (a bit of Asia, a bit of the Balkans etc) and good lunch specials (€6.50 to €9.50). Breakfast is a staple and served until 5pm.

Ichiban
SUSHI $$

(Map p602; Friedrichswall 10; all-you-can-eat sushi €11.90-19-50; ☺lunch & dinner; ☑) The prime attraction here is the all-you-can-eat sushi: lunch costs €11.90, lunch or dinner on Sunday €16, and dinner €19.50 any other day. Tick your sushi choice on the menu card over a maximum sitting of two hours. Maximum order per round is five (lunch) or eight (dinner) pieces, and to prevent diners overordering, an extra €1 is charged on uneaten sushi pieces or €2 on anything warm left on your plate.

Basil
FUSION $$$

(☎622 636; Dragonerstrasse 30; menus €26.50-49.50; ⊗6.30pm-2am Mon-Sat) These former stables to the north of town now house a hip fusion restaurant, with a high arched ceiling and pressed tablecloths. The menus offer the best value. Take tram/U-Bahn 1 or 2 to Dragonerstrasse.

Ständige Vertretung
GERMAN $$

(Map p602; www.staev-hannover.de; Friedrichswall 10; mains €7.50-113; ⊗11am-midnight) One in a chain of seven Rhineland restaurants that have sprung up throughout Germany. Its mainstay is Rhineland chow served between walls that tell the story of German politics through its key figures. Kölsch beer from Cologne is on tap here.

Hiller
VEGETARIAN $

(Map p602; www.hannover-vegetarisch.de; Blumenstrasse 3; mains €7.70-10.50, lunch menu €7.90-10.70; ⊗lunch & dinner Mon-Sat; ⏸) Germany's oldest vegetarian restaurant is a tad hushed and old-fashioned but the interior, with colourful draped cloth on the walls, is cheery. Food is well prepared and excellent value.

Sonderbar
INTERNATIONAL $

(Map p602; http://sonderbar-hannover.de; Raschplatz 6; mains €4.90-16.50; ⊗from 10am Mon-Fri, from noon Sat, from 3pm Sun; ⏹⏸) This well-styled place has an assortment of Tex-Mex, Spanish and Italian snacks and mains, as well as oven potatoes in the upstairs, up-market sports-bar section (large screens) or downstairs in a lounge. It's aimed at a business and pleasure crowd, and is close enough to the station to duck into between trains.

Os Amigos
SPANISH $

(Map p602; www.osamigos.de; Ernst-August-Galerie; tapas €2.90-7.90, mains €7.90-12.90; ⊗8am-7.45pm Mon-Sat; ⏸) This Spanish place is one of several inexpensive options alongside Hauptbahnhof inside the large Ernst-August-Galerie shopping centre.

Denn's Biomarkt
SUPERMARKET $

(Map p602; Marktstrasse 45; ⊗8am-8pm Mon-Sat; ⏸) A large organic supermarket, Denn's has everything from fruit and vegies to wines, aquaculture fish and meats – perfect for a wholesome picnic in one of Hanover's parks.

🍷 Drinking

Many of the cultural centres, clubs and music venues listed under Entertainment are also good places to go just for a drink.

Cafe & Bar Celona
CAFE, TAPAS

(Map p602; www.cafe-bar-celona.de; Lister Meile 15; ⊗9-1am; ☎) A triple act that does decent-priced tapas, soups, salads and breakfasts as well as being good for coffee and drinks.

Brauhaus Ernst August
PUB

(Map p602; www.brauhaus.net; Schmiedestrasse 13; ⊗8am-3am Mon-Thu, to 5am Fri & Sat, 9am-3pm Sun) A Hanover institution, this sprawling brewpub makes a refreshing unfiltered Pilsner called Hannöversch. A party atmosphere reigns nightly, helped along by a varied roster of live bands and DJs.

Café Mezzo
CAFE, BAR

(Map p602; www.cafe-mezzo.de; Lister Meile 4; ⊗9am-2am Tue-Thu, to 3am Fri & Sat, to midnight Sun & Mon; ☎) This classic bar and cafe used to be a student hang-out, but today gets a balance of ages. It's popular any time of day (including for breakfast), but doubles well as a place to warm up in the evening before moving on to a club or performance.

Bronco's
BAR, LOUNGE

(Schwarzer Bär 7; ⊗from 5pm Mon-Sat) Bronco's brings together the features of a bar, club and lounge in decor that snaps up the best of the 1960s and '70s. You'll find a good selection of cocktails here, as well as DJs and a small dance floor. Take tram 9 or 17 to Schwarzer Bär.

HeimW
BAR, CAFE

(Map p602; www.heim-w.de; Theaterstrasse 6; ⊗10am-1am Mon-Thu & Sun, to 2am Fri & Sat) This long, narrow bar has lights shaped like huge droplets of water about to land on your head, an atrium ceiling, potted palms beside cream leather banquettes, and intriguing artwork on the walls. Salads, pasta, tapas, breakfast, burgers and classic German meat dishes are also served here (€5 to €17.90).

Der Gartensaal
CAFE

(Map p602; Trammplatz 2, Neues Rathaus; coffee with cake from €5.20; ⊗11am-10pm mid-May–mid-Sep, to 6pm mid-Sep–mid-May) A great place to sit and have a summer-afternoon coffee overlooking the central Stadtpark.

Holländische Kakaostube
CAFE

(Map p602; Ständehausstrasse 2-3; hot chocolate with cake €5; ⊗9am-7.30pm Mon-Fri, to 6.30pm

Sat) With the blue-and-white square-patterned floor matching the Delft pottery, and a curved ship's staircase and maritime paintings creating a subtle nautical feel, this historic Dutch coffeehouse has many fans, young and old.

Acanto   BAR, DISCO
(www.acantohannover.de; Dragonerstrasse 28; ⊘from 8pm Thu-Sat) This upbeat place is one of Hanover's trendiest DJ bars, where fashionably dressed beautiful people sip caipirinhas under chandeliers and mirror balls. Take tram 1 or 2 to Dragonerstrasse.

Waterloo   BEER GARDEN
(Map p602; www.waterloo-biergarten.de; Waterloostrasse 1; ⊘from 11am) Hanover's most-popular beer garden has a lovely stand of trees, low prices and a large screen that shows German League football (soccer) matches, and always the Hannover 96 game.

☆ Entertainment

For listings, check out the local edition of *Prinz*, in German.

Nightclubs

Hanover has two main clusters of clubs and bars. One place to head for is the red-light district of Steintor (cheekily nicknamed Stöhntor by locals, meaning 'Moaning Gate'), in a former strip- and sex-club stronghold. The other is around the revamped Raschplatz, behind the Hauptbahnhof. Many of the clubs around Steintor have free admission, so you can look inside and pick and choose if you like.

Eve Klub   CLUB
(Map p602; www.eve-klub.de; Reuterstrasse 3-4; ⊘mostly Fri & Sat) This former striptease bar has kept the red lamps over the tables and red corduroy sofas.

200 Ponies   CLUB
(Map p602; Goseriede 4, Tiedthof; ⊘Wed, Fri & Sat) This club pulling in a young crowd is the best of a couple in and at the entrance to the Tiedthof courtyard.

Kiez Klub   CLUB
(Map p602; www.kiez-klub.de; Scholvinstrasse 5; ⊘Mon-Sat) Minimal house, techno house and electro house, situated in a yard off the street.

Intensivstation   CLUB
(Map p602; www.intensivstation-hannover.de; Scholvinstrasse 9; ⊘Fri & Sat) This club in Hanover's red-light district has staff dressed as nurses

and medically themed surrounds – kinky for a place that has classic house and Black Charts music.

Osho Diskothek   CLUB
(Map p602; www.osho-disco.de; Raschplatz 7l) Fondly called 'Baggi' by the Hanoverians, Osho offers classic disco hits for the over-25s.

Palo Palo   CLUB
(Map p602; www.palopalo.de; Raschplatz 8a) On Hanover's nightlife calendars for over two decades, this club spins dance classics, soul, R&B and hip hop, with a very high see-and-be-seen factor.

3Raum   BAR, CLUB
(Map p602; www.3raum-ballhof.de; Ballhofstrasse 5; ⊘Thu-Sat) A crossover place for the 25-to-40 age group, where during the week you can enjoy drinks or theatre, and get down in the club on Friday and Saturday.

Cinema

Anzeiger Hochhaus   CINEMA
(Map p602; http://hochhaus-kino-hannover.kino-zeit.de; Goseriede 9) This spacious art-house cinema is on the top floor of a magnificent expressionist building designed by Fritz Höger, the architect of Hamburg's Chilehaus. Check listing times, as the box office only opens just before screenings.

Theatre & Classical Music

Staatsoper Hannover   PERFORMING ARTS
(Map p602; ☑tickets 9999 1111; www.staatsoper hannover.de; Opernplatz 1) Housed in the 19th-century Opernhaus (Opera House; Map p602; ☑268 6240; Opernplatz 1). Classical music as well as ballet and opera are performed.

Schauspielhaus   THEATRE
(Map p602; ☑tickets 9999 1111; www.schauspiel hannover.de; Prinzenstrasse 9) Home to the Staatstheater Hannover and sometimes used to host international performances.

Junges Schauspiel Hannover   THEATRE
(☑tickets 9999 1111; www.schauspielhannover.de; Ballhofplatz 5) Mainly uses two spaces on Ballhofplatz: Ballhof eins (Map p602; Ballhofplatz 5), directly on the square, and Ballhof zwei (Map p602; Knochenhauerstrasse 28), which adjoins it.

GOP Varieté Theatre   THEATRE
(Map p602; ☑301 8670; www.variete.de/hannover; Georgstrasse 36) An old-school type of variety theatre with dancing, acrobatics, circus-style

GAY & LESBIAN VENUES

Café Konrad (Map p602; www.cafekonrad.de; Knochenhauerstrasse 34; weekly specials €6.90-9.90; 10am-midnight Sun-Thu, to 1am Fri & Sat, breakfast to 4pm) Convivial cafe frequented by both gays and lesbians. It has a choice of four dishes each week.

Schwule Sau (www.schwulesauhannover.de; Schaufelder Strasse 30a) This alternative gay and lesbian centre regularly hosts concerts, theatre and club nights. Every second Friday in the month is lesbian. Take the U6 or 11 to Kopernikusstrasse from Kröpcke.

Martinos (http://martinos-hannover.de; Gretschenstrasse 16; 5pm-3am Sun-Thu, to 5am Fri & Sat) A cafe and bar with lots of events. Take the tram 3, 7 or 9 to Sedanstrasse/Listermeile.

More information can be found at http://hannover.gay-web.de (in German) and, for lesbians, at www.hannoverfrauen.de (in German), or head to the lesbian and gay hang-outs.

acts, magic, music and more, housed in the Georgspalast. It also boasts a much-lauded restaurant.

Marlene Bar & Bühne PERFORMING ARTS
(Map p602; 368 1687; www.marlene-hannover.de; cnr Alexanderstrasse & Prinzenstrasse; free-€15) Hanover's popular cabaret venue.

Neues Theater THEATRE
(Map p602; 363 001; www.neuestheater-hannover.de; Georgstrasse 54) Excellent performances of contemporary theatre.

Theater am Aegi THEATRE
(Map p602; 989 3333; www.theater-am-aegi.de; Aegidientorplatz) Comedies and theatre with musical accompaniment.

Live Music
Check the websites of the following venues (usually under 'Programm'), or listings, for dates and prices of events.

Café Glocksee CLUB
(www.cafe-glocksee.de; Glockseestrasse 35) Part live-music venue, part club, the Glocksee has everything from techno and trance DJs to grungy gigs. Take tram 10 or 17 to Goetheplatz.

Capitol LIVE MUSIC
(444 066; www.capitol-hannover.de; Schwarzer Bär 2) This former movie theatre has rock, pop, house, soul and more on weekends and frequently during the week. Take tram 9 or 17 to Schwarzer Bär.

Kulturzentrum Faust PERFORMING ARTS
(www.kulturzentrum-faust.de; Zur Bettfedernfabrik 1-3, Linden) Ska from Uruguay, Chinese new year festivals, disco, reggae, heavy-metal gigs, hip hop, multimedia installations, quiz evenings, book readings and film evenings – this all happens and more, in this former factory complex. The 1960s concert hall is complemented by a pub-bar, Mephisto, beer garden and cafe. Take tram 10 to Leinau-strasse.

Musiktheater Bad PERFORMING ARTS
(www.musiktheater-bad.de; Am Grossen Garten 60) In this large old building and its surrounding grounds, you'll find a mixed bag of live music, music theatre and dance offerings. It's great in summer when there's an outdoor stage. Take tram 5 to Herrenhäuser Markt and walk for 20 minutes.

Jazz Club Hannover JAZZ
(www.jazz-club.de; Am Lindener Berg 38) Hanover's premier jazz club, with top acts from Germany and abroad. Take tram 9 to Nieschlagstrasse.

Pavillon PERFORMING ARTS
(Map p602; www.pavillon-hannover.de; Lister Meile 4) This huge circular venue has a cafe-bar, theatre and various rooms used as venues where you can catch a wide program of jazz, off-beat rock, world music and whatever else anyone decides to put on there.

Sport
AWD Arena STADIUM
(www.hannover96.de) This football (soccer) stadium with a capacity of 49,000 is home turf for Hannover 96 football club. You can pick up available tickets at the ground on the same day for league matches or anytime from the DB service point inside Hauptbahnhof. Those with extra tickets (scalpers if it's a big match) sell them on the tree-lined alley leading to the ground. Follow the stream of fans or take tram 3, 7 or 9 from Hauptbahnhof to Waterloo and follow the signs for about 500m, or bus 100 from Kröpke to Maschsee/Sprengel Museum.

🛍 Shopping

Hanover's compact city centre makes it ideal for shopping, although most of what you will find is modern, international fashion. A pedestrianised zone full of shops extends south from the Hauptbahnhof, along Bahnhofstrasse, Georgstrasse and Karmarschstrasse.

Niki de Sainte Phalle Promenade   MALL
(Map p602; Bahnhofstrasse) A subterranean shopping strip running below the street.

Ernst-August-Galerie   SHOPPING CENTRE
(Map p602; Ernst-August-Platz 2) A large, modern complex alongside the train station.

Flea Market   MARKET
(Map p602; Am Hohen Ufer; ☺8am-4pm Sat) Behind the Historisches Museum, along the Leine River Canal near Die Nanas.

ℹ Information

DISCOUNT CARDS Available from the tourist office and DB service point inside the main train station, **HannoverCard** (1/2/3 days €9.50/13/16) offers unlimited public transport and discounted admission to museums etc.

EMERGENCY **Hospital** (☑304 31; Marienstrasse 37)

Medical emergency service (☑314 044)

Police (☑110; Raschplatz) Beneath the overpass on the north side of the Hauptbahnhof.

INTERNET ACCESS Go online at **Teleklick Hannover** (Kurt-Schumacher-Strasse 11; per hr €1.50; ☺9am-11pm Mon-Sat, 11am-11pm Sun).

LAUNDRY **Wasch-Treff** (cnr Friesenstrasse & Eichstrasse; per wash €4; ☺6am-11pm) is conveniently opposite an organic bakery-cafe.

MONEY **Reisebank** (Hauptbahnhof; ☺8am-10pm Mon-Sat, 9am-10pm Sun) has ATMs plus currency exchange services, inside the station.

POST The **post office** (Ernst-August-Platz 2; ☺9.30am-7.30pm Mon-Fri, to 3pm Sat) is inside the Ernst-August-Galerie.

TOURIST INFORMATION Information and brochures are available from a staffed desk at the Neues Rathaus. The **tourist office** (☑information 1234 5111, room reservations 123 45555; www.hannover.de; Ernst-August-Platz 8; ☺9am-6pm Mon-Fri, 10am-3pm Sat & Sun) is especially useful during trade fairs.

ℹ Getting There & Away

AIR **Hanover Airport** (HAJ; www.hannover-airport.de) has many connections, including **Lufthansa** (www.lufthansa.com), and the carriers **Air Berlin** (www.airberlin.com) to/from London-Stansted, **German Wings** (www.germanwings.com) to/from the UK, Moscow and many other destinations, and **TuiFly** (www.tuifly.com), flying to/from Moscow as well as many holiday destinations. The S-Bahn (S5) takes 18 minutes from the airport to the Hauptbahnhof (€3).

BUS Long-distance and international services leave from the **central bus station** close to the train station. **Eurolines Touring Ticket Center** (☑940 4269; Platform 5, Central Bus Station; ☺9am-8.30pm Mon, 8am-8.30pm Tue-Fri, 8.30am-2pm & 4-9.30pm Sat) has Europe-wide connections, including at least one direct bus daily to Warsaw (Poland; return €87) and a daily service to Moscow (return €193) with a change in Minsk (Belarus visa required).

CAR & MOTORCYCLE Nearby autobahns run to Hamburg, Munich, Frankfurt and Berlin, with good connections to Bremen, Cologne, Amsterdam and Brussels. Major car rental firms are in the Hauptbahnhof, including **Sixt** (☑01805-252 525; www.sixt.com; ☺6am-9pm Mon-Fri, 9am-6pm Sat, 9am-9pm Sun) and **Europcar** (☑363 2993; www.europcar.de; ☺7.30am-9pm Mon-Fri, 9am-4.30 Sat, 11am-8pm Sun).

TRAIN Hanover is a major rail hub for European and national services, with frequent ICE trains to/from Hamburg Hauptbahnhof (€43, 1¼ hours), Bremen (€31, one hour), Munich (€125, 4¼ hours), Cologne (€68, 2¾ hours) and Berlin (€65, 1¾ hours), among others. Left-luggage lockers are accessible 24 hours.

ℹ Getting Around

BIKE For bicycle hire, try **Fahrradstation am Bahnhof** (☑353 9640; Fernroder Strasse 2; bicycle per day €7.50; ☺6am-11pm Mon-Fri, 8am-11pm Sat & Sun) alongside the Hauptbahnhof.

PUBLIC TRANSPORT The transit system of buses and tram/U-Bahn lines (so-called *Stadtbahn* or 'city rail' because some are trams on lines underground) is run by **Üstra** (☑166 80; www.uestra.de; ☺6am-11pm Mon-Fri, to 8pm Sat, 7am-8pm Sun). Most U-Bahn lines from the Hauptbahnhof are boarded in the station's north (follow signs towards Raschplatz), including U-Bahn 8 to the *Messe* (fairgrounds; €2.30, 19 minutes). Lines U10 and U17 are different. These are overground trams leaving south of the station near the tourist office. Note that the late-night service of the U10 also begins on the north side. Most visitors only travel in the central 'Hannover' zone, where single tickets are €2.30 and day passes €4.50. If you wish to travel in two/three zones, singles cost €3/3.70, while day passes cost €5.70/7.

TAXIS Call ☑8484, 2143 or 3811. From the centre to the fairgrounds, a taxi costs about €35; to the airport it's about €20.

Around Hanover

Nobles the world over will tell you that ancestral homes can be such a huge financial burden to maintain, especially when they're turreted castles. In late 2005, the family of Prince Ernst August of Hanover (Princess Caroline of Monaco's husband) auctioned off some 25,000 household objects to raise money for the upkeep of their 130-room neo-Gothic fancy. Now a small part of the palace, Schloss Marienburg (www.schloss -marienburg.de; tour adult/under 16yr €7/56; ⏱10am-6pm early Mar-Oct), is open to members of the public interested in a behind-the-scenes glimpse of German aristocratic life. Admission is by a one-hour tour, either with a tour guide or using an audioguide (English, French, Polish, Russian and Spanish available). Tours include the Knight's Hall, Queen's Library and more.

From Hanover, you can take the B3 28km south or alternatively the A7 south and exit 62 to Hildesheim. Take the B1 out of Hildesheim and continue 7km until you come to Mahlerten. Turn right for Nordstemmen and you should see the castle. By public transport, the best way out is to take bus 300 to the stop 'Pattensen', then change to bus 310 to stop 'Marienburg Abzweig Nord'. From there it's 1.5km to the castle (day card €7).

Celle

🎵05141 / POP 70,250

With 400 half-timbered houses and its Ducal Palace dating back to the 13th century, Celle is graced with a picture-book town centre that is among the most attractive in the region. The white-and-pink Ducal Palace, Celle's centrepiece set in small gardens, contrasts with the ultramodern Kunstmuseum, which is illuminated at night into a '24-hour' museum and successfully creates an interesting contrast of old and new.

To reach the centre from the train station, follow Bahnhofstrasse and turn left at the end of the street.

◉ Sights

Altstadt   NEIGHBOURHOOD

Among the highlights of the Altstadt are the Old Town Hall from 1561–79 at Markt 14–16, built in the Weser Renaissance style with a stepped gable. One block south of here, on the corner of Poststrasse and Runde Strasse, is the ornate Hoppener Haus (1532). If you go another block southwards along Poststrasse and stop in the square in the corner, look for the tiny alley between the two buildings: you'll see a little box with a window that was a baroque toilet. Highlights in Neue Strasse include the Green House (1478) with the crooked beam at No 32 and the Fairy-Tale House at No 11. The facade of the latter is decorated with characters, such as a jackass crapping gold pieces.

Schloss   PALACE

(Ducal Palace; Schlossplatz; Residenzmuseum €5, combined Residenzmuseum, Bomann Museum & Kunstmuseum €8, Fri free, guided tours adult €6; ⏱10am-5pm Tue-Sun) Celle's wedding-cake Schloss was built in 1292 by Otto Der Strenge (Otto the Strict) as a town fortification and in 1378 was expanded and turned into a residence. The last duke to live here was Georg Wilhelm (1624–1705), and the last royal was Queen Caroline-Mathilde of Denmark, who died here in 1775. Today it houses administrative offices and the Palace Museum. One-hour guided tours depart at 11am, 1pm and 3pm from Tuesday to Friday and Sunday, and hourly from 11am to 3pm on Saturday. These take you into sections of the palace you can't otherwise visit, such as the Renaissance Schlosskapelle (Palace Chapel), the 19th-century Schlossküche (Palace Kitchen) and – rehearsals permitting – the baroque Schlosstheater (Palace Theatre; 🎫tickets 127 14; www.schlosstheater-celle. de; Schlossplatz; ⏱closed Jul & Aug).

Kunstmuseum & Bomann Museum   MUSEUM

(www.kunst.celle.de; Schlossplatz 7; incl Bomann Museum €5, Fri free; ⏱10am-5pm Tue-Sun) Situated across the road from Celle's Schloss, the Kunstmuseum (Art Museum) is dedicated to contemporary German artists. During the regular daytime opening hours, you can stroll around and admire a collection of modern art that includes work from the early 20th century to the present. A 'light room' is the work of the artist Otto Piene, and outside you find his tame *Firework for Celle* sculptures, which are most effective at night. As night slowly descends, the 'nocturnal museum' glows and oozes different colours, morphing into its own quaint work of 'art' with light and a few sounds.

In the older building adjacent, the Bomann Museum (🎫125 44; www.bomann-museum.de; Schlossplatz 7; adult/concession incl Kunstmuseum €5/3; ⏱10am-5pm Tue-Sun, last entry 4.15pm) is gradually upgrading its exhibitions by augmenting historic rooms with a permanent collection on the work, lives and times of ordinary people in the region. Most sections are already open.

Stadtkirche
CHURCH

(www.stadtkirche-celle.de; An der Stadtkirche 8; tower adult/concession €1/0.50; ⊙church 10am-6pm Tue-Sat year-round, tower 10-11.45am & 2-4.45pm Tue-Sat Apr-Oct) The highlight of the 13th-century Stadtkirche is the 235 steps you can climb to the top of the church steeple for a view of the city. The city trumpeter climbs 220 steps to the white tower below the steeple for a trumpet fanfare in all four directions at 9.30am and 5.30pm daily.

FREE Synagogue
SYNAGOGUE

(Im Kreise 24; ⊙3-5pm Tue-Thu, 9-11am Fri, 11am-noon Sun) Dating back to 1740, Celle's synagogue is the oldest in northern Germany. It was partially destroyed during Kristallnacht (p727) and looks just like any other half-timbered house from the outside. Once a new Jewish congregation formed in 1997, services began to be held here regularly. Changing exhibitions on Jewish history take place next door. The synagogue is at the southeastern end of the Altstadt, in the town's former ghetto.

🛏 Sleeping & Eating

The tourist office can help with camping, 4km from the centre.

You can find numerous eating and drinking options along Schuhstrasse and Neue Strasse, as well as on Am Heiligen Kreuz.

TOP CHOICE Hotel Celler Hof
HOTEL $$

(☎911 960; www.cellerhof.de; Stechbahn 11; s €75-80, d €110-115, tr €130-150; P@🖙) The friendly staff, Finnish sauna, tasteful furnishings and above all central location make this a good all-round option. All rooms have a writing desk, and there's a small lobby bar for relaxing.

Hotel Neun ¾
HOTEL $

(☎909 0731; www.hotel934.de; Bahnhofstrasse 46; s/d/tr without breakfast €35/60/75; P🖙) The exterior of this budget abode near the main train station is unattractive and a few of the rooms still have old window frames but it's a very clean and well-run place. It only does breakfast during a Hanover trade fair, but cafes are nearby. Call ahead if arriving between 11am and 3pm or after 8pm.

Hotel Fürstenhof
HOTEL $$$

(☎2010; www.fuerstenhof.de; Hannoversche Strasse 55/56; s €110-225, d €150-280, ste from €305; P❋🖙) In a converted baroque palace, this luxury hotel has floors featuring themes ranging from 'Hunting' to 'Golf'. In the latter you get a putter and carpet green for practising your shots.

DJH Hostel
HOSTEL $

(☎532 08; www.jugendherberge.de/jh/celle; Weghausstrasse 2; dm under/over 27yr €18.70/22.70; P🖙) This rambling youth hostel inside a former school building gets mostly school groups in its four- to six-bed dorms. It's a 25-minute walk from the train station, or take bus 2 to Jugendherberge from the top of Bahnhofstrasse, opposite the station.

Pasta
ITALIAN $

(www.pasta-celle.de; Neue Strasse 37; soup €3-4, pasta €5.70-7.70, pizza €4.90-8.50; ⊙9am-5pm Mon- Fri, to 4pm Sat; ✎) Fresh antipasti, pizza and pasta for which you can choose one of several sauces; it's all freshly homemade.

Restaurant Bier Akademie
GERMAN $$

(www.bier-akademie-celle.de; Weisser Wall 6; mains €11.10-22.50; ⊙lunch Mon-Thu, dinner Mon-Sat) This family-run restaurant serves an excellent range of beef, poultry and lamb as well as pork, but its speciality is a roral roulade, which you can order as a starter or main course. It's just northeast of Schlossplatz.

ℹ Information

Adunni Callshop & Internet (Bahnhofstrasse 38; internet per hr €2; ⊙10am-10pm Mon-Sat, noon-9pm Sun)

Tourist Office (☎1212; www.region-celle.com; Markt 14-16; ⊙9am-6pm Mon-Fri, 10am-4pm Sat, 11am-2pm Sun) Has a free map of town with a walking route and runs guided tours (€5; in German) at 11am Saturday to Thursday, 4.30pm Friday much of the year.

ⓘ Getting There & Away

CAR If you're driving, take the B3 straight into the centre.

TRAIN Several trains each hour to Hanover take from 20 minutes (IC; €11) to 45 minutes (S-Bahn; €9.10). There are also IC (€19.50, 40 minutes) and regional (€16.40, 1¼ hours) services to/from Lüneburg.

ⓘ Getting Around

BIKE Try **Fahrradhaus Jacoby** (☑254 89; Bahnhofstrasse 27; bicycle hire per day €8.50; ☺9am-1pm & 3-6pm Mon-Fri, 9am-1pm Sat) for bike hire.

BUS City buses 2 and 4 run between the Hauptbahnhof and Schlossplatz, the two main stations. Single tickets are €1.85 and day passes €5.20.

HORSE Horse-drawn carriage rides (from €5 per person) depart between April and October from the corner of Bergstrasse and Poststrasse.

TAXI Call ☑444 44 or 280 01. Expect to pay €35 from Celle to Bergen-Belsen concentration camp memorial.

Bergen-Belsen

Unlike Auschwitz in Poland, none of the original buildings remain from the most infamous concentration camp on German soil. Yet the large, initially peaceful-looking lumps of grassy earth – covered in beautiful purple heather in summer – soon reveal their true identity as mass graves. Signs indicate approximately how many people lie in each – 1000, 2000, 5000, an unknown number...

In all, 70,000 Jews, Soviet soldiers, political hostages and other prisoners died here. Among them was Anne Frank, whose posthumously published diary became a modern classic.

Bergen-Belsen (www.bergenbelsen.de; Lohheide; ☺10am-6pm) began its existence in 1940 as a POW camp, but was partly taken over by the SS from April 1943 to hold Jews as hostages in exchange for German POWs held abroad. Many Russian and Allied soldiers, then later Jews, Poles, homosexuals, Sinti and Roma all suffered here – beaten, tortured, starved and worked to death, or used as medical guinea pigs.

Tens of thousands of prisoners from other camps near the front line were brought to Belsen in the last months of WWII, causing overcrowding, an outbreak of disease and even more deaths. Despite attempts by the SS to hide evidence of their inhumane practices by destroying documents and forcing prisoners to bury or incinerate their deceased fellow inmates, thousands of corpses still littered the compound when British troops liberated the camp on 15 April 1945.

After WWII, Allied forces used the troop barracks here as a displaced persons' (DP) camp, for those waiting to emigrate to a third country (including many Jews who went to Israel after its establishment in 1948). The DP camp was closed in September 1950.

The **Documentation Centre** today is one of the best of its kind and deals sensitively but very poignantly with the lives of the people who were imprisoned here – before, during and after incarceration. The exhibition is designed to be viewed chronologically, and part of it focuses on the role of Bergen-Belsen in the early years as a POW camp for mostly Soviet prisoners of war. About 40,000 POWs died here in 1939–42, largely due to atrocious conditions. As you move through the exhibition, you listen to original-language descriptions through headphones (also subtitled on the screens), read documents and explanations, and watch a 25-minute documentary about the camp. This film includes a moving testimony from one of the British cameramen who filmed the liberation. Subtitled screenings rotate between different languages.

Also inside the centre, there's a book of names of those who were interned here, as well as guides and books for sale, including *The Diary of Anne Frank* (1947), plus the outline *Historical Information* (by donation).

In the several hectares of **cemetery** within the gates is a large stone obelisk and memorial, with inscriptions to all victims, a cross on the spot of a memorial initially raised by Polish prisoners and the **Haus der Stille**, where you can retreat for quiet contemplation.

A **gravestone for Anne Frank** and her sister, Margot, has also been erected (not too far from the cemetery gates, on the way to the obelisk). The entire family was initially sent to Auschwitz when their hiding place in Amsterdam was betrayed to police, but the sisters were later transferred to Belsen. Although no-one knows exactly where Anne lies, many pay tribute to their 15-year-old heroine at this gravestone.

Other monuments to various victim groups, including a Soviet memorial, are dotted across the complex.

ⓘ Getting There & Away

BUS Getting to the memorial by bus is possible but difficult, and it's best to either have your own transport or find people to share a taxi. On Saturdays, a direct bus departs Schlossplatz in Celle at 9am but you need to take a taxi back. The tourist office in Celle has a timetable sheet with a sketch map.

CAR Driving from Celle, take Hehlentorstrasse north over the Aller River and follow Harburger Strasse north out of the city. This is the B3; continue northwest to the town of Bergen and follow the signs to Belsen.

TAXI Call ☏05051-5555. Expect to pay €15 one way from the village of Bergen to the camp or €35 one way from Celle.

Hildesheim

☏05121 / POP 102,800

Though not an overly attractive or exciting city, Hildesheim has a couple of important sights that have visitors flocking to this former bishopric and market town: a pretty, post-WWII 'medieval' town centre, and genuinely ancient cathedral-door bas-reliefs, which were cleverly saved from the firebombing that razed Hildesheim to the ground on 22 March 1945.

◎ Sights & Activities

Markt   NEIGHBOURHOOD
One of the tragedies of Hitler's excursion into megalomania was the horrendous damage inflicted upon once-magnificent architectural gems such as Hildesheim. After WWII, key parts of the old town were lovingly reconstructed, and the result of this is especially visible on Markt. Clockwise (from north) you find the **Rokokohaus**, **Wollenweberhaus**, **Wedekindhaus**, **Knochenhauerhaus** (Butchers' Guild Hall) and **Bäckeramtshaus** (Bakers' Guild Hall), today containing the town museum). The **Marktbrunnen**, a fountain in front of the **Rathaus** on the east side of the square, has bells that play folk songs at noon, 1pm and 5pm daily. Bus 1 from Hauptbahnhof to Rathaustrasse drops you close.

Stadtmuseum   MUSEUM
(www.stadtmuseum-hildesheim.de; Markt 7-8; adult/concession €2.50/2; ☉10am-6pm Tue-Sun) This town museum is located in the reconstructed Knochenhauerhaus, one of Germany's most intricate half-timbered houses. Exhibits are spread over five floors, starting with changing exhibitions on the ground floor, leading into the town's history, and finally a silverware collection on the top floor.

Dom   CHURCH
(Hildesheim Cathedral; www.welterbe-hildesheim.de; Domhof; ☉closed for restoration until mid-2014) Hildesheim's cathedral took its present form in 1061 and was virtually rebuilt after WWII bombing. It's famous for the almost 5m-high **Bernwardstüren**, bronze doors with bas-reliefs dating from 1015. These depict scenes from the Bible's Old and New Testaments. The church's **wheel-shaped chandelier** and the **Christussäule** (Column of Christ) are also from the original cathedral. Current work on the cathedral to restore and protect it with a glass entrance means that it will be closed at least until August 2014. Until the church reopens, the Bernwardstüren and the reliquaries from the cathedral museum are on display in the Roemer- und Pelizaeus-Museum. To reach the Dom from Hauptbahnhof, take bus 1 to Bohlweg.

Tausend-Jähriger Rosenstock   RELIQUARY
(1000-year-old rosebush; adult/concession €0.50/0.30; ☉10am-5pm Mon-Sat, from noon Sun) Located in the cloister of the Hildesheimer Dom – and accessible despite building work on the cathedral lasting until mid-2014 – this is literally a rosebush that has survived for 1000 years and rose phoenixlike from the burnt-out cathedral remains after 1945. Take bus 1 or 2 from Hauptbahnhof to Bohlweg.

Roemer-und Pelizaeus-Museum   MUSEUM
(www.rpmuseum.de; Am Steine 1-2; adult/concession €10/8; ☉10am-6pm Tue-Sun) This museum houses one of Europe's best collections of Egyptian art and artefacts. There are dozens of mummies, scrolls, statues and wall hangings, but the life-size re-creation of an Egyptian tomb (of Sennefer) is a particular highlight. Take bus 1 from Hauptbahnhof to Museum.

FREE **St Michaeliskirche**   CHURCH
(www.welterbe-hildesheim.de; Michaelisplatz; ☉8am-6pm Mon & Wed-Sat, 10am-6pm Tue, 11am-6pm Sun) The Unesco-protected Church of St Michael was built in the Romanesque style in 1022 and reconstructed after war damage. Unusual features inside are the alternation of round columns and square pillars as supports, its painted wooden ceiling, a late-12th-century chancel barrier decorated with angels, the cloisters and a crypt containing Bernward, the bishop of Hildesheim

from 993 to 1022, who commissioned many artists and strove to make Hildesheim a cultural centre in his day. Bus 1 to Museum drops you within a few minutes' walk.

Dom-Museum MUSEUM
(www.dommuseum-hildesheim.de; Domhof; ⊙closed until mid-2014) Located inside Hildesheim's Dom (cathedral), with reliquaries and a changing exhibition. Take bus 1 from Hauptbahnhof to Bohlweg.

🛌 Sleeping

Its proximity to Hanover means Hildesheim often takes overspill guests during trade fairs, when accommodation prices rise phenomenally.

TOP CHOICE Van der Valk
Hotel Hildesheim HOTEL $$
(☑3000; www.vandervalk.de; Markt 4; s €95-155, d €115-165; @🖭🖥🌊) Behind its historic frontage on the central market place, this luxury hotel reveals a surprisingly large interior, with a flagstone-floored atrium entrance giving way to tasteful rooms in subtle tones. The pool and wellness areas (Finnish sauna) are a bonus.

Gästehaus-Café Timphus PENSION $
(☑346 86; www.timphus-conditorei-hotel.de; Braunschweiger Strasse 90/91; s €53.60, d €77.20-87.20, tr €120.80; 🖭) This small *Pension* has walls bedecked with photos of artful chocolate displays, which might mean you keep going next door to the associated cafe for supplies. Reserve ahead, especially if arriving after 6pm, as you will need a code for the key dispenser.

Novotel Hotel HOTEL $$
(☑171 70; www.accorhotels.com; Bahnhofsallee 38; r without breakfast from €84; 🅿@🖭) Prices vary by demand and day, and if you book early on the internet you can even pick up doubles for less than the room price we've noted, in this spacious cloister building with exposed stone walls, gentle tones and cosy designer-chic style. It is set back from the street in quiet grounds and has excellent dining and bar facilities.

DJH Hostel HOSTEL $
(☑427 17; www.djh-niedersachsen.de/jh/hildesheim; Schirrmannweg 4; dm under/over 27yr €21.10/25.10, s/d €32.10/57.20; 🅿@) This hostel is inconveniently located on the edge of town and close to forest, but it's well run and modern. From Hauptbahnhof, take bus 1 to Schuhstrasse

and change to 4 in the direction of Im Koken-Hof. Get off at the Triftstrasse stop and walk the remaining 750m uphill.

🍴 Eating & Drinking

There are quite a few eating and drinking options along the popular Friesenstrasse (just behind Schuhstrasse), where the pubs and bars usually sell cheap meals.

Café Desseo MEDITERRANEAN $
(www.cafedeseo.de; Hindenburgplatz 3; tapas €2.90-8.70, other dishes €5.60-17.50; ⊙from 8am Mon-Sat, from 9am Sun; 🖭) Generally billed as a tapas bar, this excellent venue is actually more of an all-rounder, with sandwiches, delicious wraps, pasta, pizza and other dishes right up to the top-of-the-range steak. In summer there's outdoor seating.

TOP CHOICE Nil im Museum INTERNATIONAL $$
(www.nil-restaurant.de; Am Steine 1; lunch mains €7.50-12, evening mains €9.80-17.90; ⊙5pm-midnight Mon, 11am-midnight Tue-Sat, 10am-midnight Sun) This relaxed restaurant in the Roemer- und Pelizaeus-Museum serves delicious antipasti, pasta and salads, along with poultry and red-meat main courses. Each Monday it has music ('anything but mainstream').

Schlegels Weinstuben INTERNATIONAL $$
(☑331 33; Am Steine 4-6; mains €11.50-22.50; ⊙dinner Mon-Sat) The lopsided walls of this rose-covered, 500-year-old house hunkering beside the Roemer- und Pelizaeus-Museum add to the sheer magic of the place. Inside are historic rooms and, in one corner, a round, glass-topped table fashioned from a well, where you can dine overlooking the water below. Select the changing seasonal and regional cuisine from the blackboard brought to your table; book ahead.

ⓘ Information

Il Giornale (Judenstrasse 3-4; per hr €2; ⊙8am-8pm Mon-Sat) Internet access in an Italian cafe atmosphere.

Post Office (Bahnhofsplatz 3-4; ⊙8.30am-6pm Mon-Fri, to 1pm Sat)

Tourist Office Hildesheim (☑179 80; www.hildesheim.de; Rathausstrasse 20; ⊙10.30am-6pm Mon-Fri, 9am-3pm Sat, 11am-3pm Sun) Information and accommodation bookings. Stocks the *Hildesheimer Rosenroute*, a very comprehensive guide to all of Hildesheim's sights (€2). The current version is in German but an English version is planned.

ⓘ Getting There & Around

CAR For those driving, the A7 runs right by town from Hanover, while the B1 goes to Hamelin.

CITY BUS Most sights in Hildesheim are within walking distance, but from Hauptbahnhof bus 1 is useful as it passes Schuhstrasse (for Markt and the tourist office), Bohlweg (for the cathedral sights) and Museum (for the Roemer- und Pelizaeus-Museum). Single tickets cost €2.15 (60 minutes), day tickets for the city cost €4.60.

TRAIN Frequent regional and suburban train services operate between Hildesheim and Hanover (€7.50, 30 minutes), while ICE trains to/from Braunschweig (€14, 25 minutes) and Göttingen (€25.50, 30 minutes) stop here on the way to/from Berlin (€64, 1¾ hours).

Braunschweig

☑ 0531

Still famous as the city of Heinrich der Löwe (Henry the Lion), nine centuries after this powerful medieval duke made it his capital, Braunschweig (Brunswick) reveals its past with a slightly meandering but pleasant historic old town. Today, despite a provincial feel, it can be an interesting place to while away a day or two, not least because of its handful of museums and impressive buildings. These give a good insight into the history and lives of people in this part of Germany.

⊙ Sights & Activities

Braunschweiger Löwe MONUMENT
(Burgplatz) Braunschweig's identity is intricately tied up with Heinrich der Löwe, a duke who was responsible for colonising the eastern regions of Germany beyond the Elbe and Saale. The Brunswick lion statue is based on the original lion Heinrich ordered to be made in 1166 as a symbol of his power and jurisdiction, and today it's the symbol of the city; you can see the original at Burg Dankwarderode.

Dom St Blasii CHURCH
(St Blasius Cathedral; www.braunschweigerdom.de; Domplatz 5; crypt admission €1; ⊙10am-5pm) The tomb of Heinrich der Löwe, the powerful duke who made Braunschweig his capital in the 12th century, can be found lying alongside his wife Mathilde in the crypt of Dom St Blasii. The Nazis decided to co-opt his image and in 1935 exhumed his tomb to conduct an 'archaeological investigation'. Even Hitler paid a visit. However, the corpse found inside had one leg shorter than the other

(it's known that Heinrich suffered a terrible horse-riding accident late in life) and dark hair, and the master-race propagandists went very quiet on the subject after that. There were also questions about the body's gender and some doubt as to whether it's really Heinrich in the sarcophagus.

Burg Dankwarderode MUSEUM
(www.museum-braunschweig.de; Burgplatz; adult/concession €5/2.50; ⊙10am-5pm Tue & Thu-Sun, 1-8pm Wed) This former castle of Heinrich der Löwe is now a museum housing a glittering medieval collection, including golden sculptures of arms, medieval capes and Braunschweig's symbol, the original bronze lion statue cast in 1166. Upstairs is a huge, spectacularly adorned Knights' Hall which at the time of research temporarily contained the pick of the crop from the Herzog Anton Ulrich Museum while it was being restored.

Schlossmuseum MUSEUM
(Schlossplatz 1; admission incl audioguide €2/1; ⊙10am-5pm Tue-Sun) Housed in the north wing of the Residential Palace immediately east of Burgplatz, the Palace Museum has two sections: one mostly consisting of a banquet hall with multilingual, interactive screens positioned like plates to explain the region's rulers and history, and a second section of four rooms with original furnishings from the 19th century. The courtyard of this 19th-century palace (which has hints of London's Buckingham Palace) has been cleverly turned into an enormous shopping centre.

Herzog Anton Ulrich Museum MUSEUM
(www.museum-braunschweig.de; Museumstrasse 1) Braunschweig's Duke Anton Ulrich (1633–1714) had an eye for miniature porcelain figures – as well as for crockery, furniture and all types of painting, from Chinese to European. Thousands of pieces he assembled in his lifetime are usually found in this building, which was closed for restoration at the time of research. Until restoration is completed (unlikely before 2013), prized works from artists such as Rembrandt, Rubens and Vermeer, as well as porcelain, graphics and sculptures, are housed inside the Knight's Hall of Burg Dankwarderode.

Landesmuseum MUSEUM
(State Museum; Burgplatz; adult/concession €4/3; ⊙10am-5pm Tue-Sun) This museum has lots of engaging exhibits that speak for themselves, starting with a large Foucault pendulum

illustrating the principle of the Earth's rotation, augmented by myriad artefacts assembled chronologically to tell the story of Germany's past. It is a fascinating place, not least because of eclectic objects like the strands of hair allegedly belonging to Heinrich der Löwe and his wife Mathilde. They are in cases of silver, gold and marble, specially constructed in 1935 as part of Hitler's propaganda offensive to present Heinrich posthumously as one of his own.

Altstadtmarkt
SQUARE

Braunschweig's former marketplace is an appealing square with the step-gabled Renaissance Gewandhaus (built 1303; facade redesigned 1590) and the Gothic Altstadt Rathaus.

Magniviertel
NEIGHBOURHOOD

(Am Magnitor) This arty precinct-cum-traditional quarter is nestled around the 11th-century Magnikirche. Some restaurants and bars have colonised the area's many restored half-timbered houses and there are occasional boutique stores.

🛏 Sleeping

Braunschweig has few budget options. A youth hostel should open here sometime in 2014; ask the tourist office about private rooms.

TOP CHOICE ⟩ Best Western Stadtpalais
HOTEL $$$

(☎241 024; www.palais-braunschweig.bestwestern.de; Hinter Liebfrauen 1a; s €82-114, d €102-165, ste €345; P⊗❋@🖙) This former 18th-century palace is now a four-star hotel that strikes a perfect balance between the historic and modern. Lots of cream, gilt and blue furnishings create interest, while great care has been taken to ensure comfort and functionality. The central, but fortunately quiet, location is another plus. Top of the range is the splendid Kaiser Suite. Tram M5 to Münzstrasse or Friedrich-Wilhelm-Strasse drops you very close.

Frühlings-Hotel
HOTEL $$

(☎243 210; www.fruehlingshotel.de; Bankplatz 7; s €70-90, d €90-130; P@🖙) Friendly staff with a good sense of humour, a stylish ground floor with reception and guest lounge, plus varying categories of comfortable rooms, make this an excellent choice. Tram M5 from Hauptbahnhof to Friedrich-Wilhelm-Strasse will get you near.

Hotel am Wollmarkt
HOTEL $$

(☎244 400; www.hotelamwollmarkt.de; Wollmarkt 9-12; s €49-60, d €75-93; P🖙) This comfortable and relaxed Church-affiliated hotel offers some of the best value in town, with clean and modern no-frills rooms a 10-minute walk north of the pedestrianised centre. Expect to pay top of the price range during the week. Alte Waage (tram M4) is the closest stop, but you can take M11 from the Hauptbahnhof to Radeklint and walk northeast 400m along Neuer Weg.

Hotel Café am Park
HOTEL $

(☎730 79; www.hotel-cafeampark.de; Wolfenbüttler Strasse 67; s/d/tr €60/75/83; P) This pleasant *Hotel garni* is near the Bürgerpark (take tram M2 to Bürgerpark) to the south of town. It has cheaper rooms with shared showers and toilets.

🍴 Eating

TOP CHOICE Ox
STEAKHOUSE $$$

(☎243 900; www.oxsteakhouse.com; Güldenstrasse 7; mains €19.90-45; ⊙lunch & dinner) Ox bills itself as the best steakhouse in town, and there can be little doubt about this for its prime and choice American beef and lamb. Connoisseurs of schnapps will soon be hailing the waiter for the trolley, which is filled with excellent, often lesser-known local and international varieties. Rooms in the comfortable hotel cost €95 and €120 for singles and doubles, respectively; less on weekends.

Restaurant Brodocz
VEGETARIAN, INTERNATIONAL $$

(www.restaurant-brodocz.de; Stephanstrasse 1; soups €3-4.80, mains €9.50-23.50; ⊙11.30am-10pm Mon & Wed-Sat, lunch Tue; 🍴) This excellent organic and vegetarian restaurant serves delicious salads, vegetarian soups and mains all day most days, augmented by a strong selection of fish – including fish and chips – and organic red-meat dishes, all based on quality ingredients.

Mutter Habenicht
GERMAN $

(Papenstieg 3; mains €5.95-18.85, weekday lunch menus €5.80; ⊙lunch & dinner) This 'Mother Hubbard' dishes up filling portions of schnitzels, potatoes, steaks, spare ribs and the occasional Balkan dish in the dimly lit, bric-a-brac-filled front room, or in the small beer garden out the back.

🍷 Drinking & Entertainment

The Magniviertel has a smattering of traditional pubs, whereas Kalenwall has a string of clubs that are mostly open on Friday and Saturday. Useful listings of these can be found in the tourist office's *Braunschweig Bietet* or the quarterly *Hin & Weg*.

Merz   BAR, CLUB
(www.merz-bs.de; Gieselerstrasse 3; ⊙Thu-Sat)
Spacious and relaxed, Merz is a long-standing favourite especially among the student crowd, with table football, a beer garden, and a few snacks to nibble with inexpensive drinks.

Staatstheater Braunschweig
'Grosses Haus'   PERFORMING ARTS
(✓ticket office 123 4567; www.staatstheater-braun schweig.de; Am Theater/Steinweg) This historic venue is used for classical music, theatre, dance and opera. The tourist office also sells tickets, or turn up an hour before the event for rush tickets.

Staatstheater Braunschweig
'Kleines Haus'   PERFORMING ARTS
(✓ticket office 123 4567; www.staatstheater-braun schweig.de; Magnitorwall 18) One of the performance spaces of the Staatstheater Braunschweig. You can get tickets from the tourist office, or rush tickets one hour before the performance.

ℹ️ Information

Main Post Office (Berliner Platz 12-16; ⊙9am-7pm Mon-Fri, 10am-1pm Sat) Alongside the Hauptbahnhof.

Post Office (Friedrich-Wilhelm-Strasse 3; ⊙9am-6.30pm Mon-Fri, 9.30am-1pm Sat)

Telecallshop (Friedrich-Wilhelm-Strasse 33; per hr €1.50; ⊙10am-8pm Mon-Sat, noon-8pm Sun)

Tourist Service Braunschweig (✓470 2040; www.braunschweig.de; Vor der Burg 1; ⊙10am-7pm Mon-Fri, to 4pm Sat)

ℹ️ Getting There & Away

CAR The A2 runs east–west between Hanover and Magdeburg across the northern end of the city. This connects with the A39 about 25km east of the city, which heads north to Wolfsburg. The A39 also heads south from the city.

TRAIN There are regular RE services to Hanover (€12.20, 45 minutes) and IC trains to Leipzig (€43, two hours). ICE trains go to Berlin (€56, one hour 20 minutes) and Frankfurt (€85, 2¾ hours).

ℹ️ Getting Around

Braunschweig is at the heart of an integrated transport network that extends throughout the region and as far south as the Harz Mountains. Ninety-minute bus and tram tickets cost €2.20, 24-hour tickets €5.50. Any bus or tram going to 'Rathaus' from the Hauptbahnhof will get you to the centre in 10 minutes; these leave from the same side as the public transport information booth just outside the train station. Trams 1 or 2 and bus 420 are among these. The M5 tram is useful, connecting the train station with Friedrich-Wilhelm-Platz via Am Magnitor and passing the Herzog Anton Ulrich Museum.

If driving, be aware that there are one-way systems all around the Altstadt. Alternatively, there's parking by the train station.

Wolfenbüttel

✓05331 / POP 53,400

'Alles mit Bedacht' (everything with prudence) was the expression favoured by Duke August II (1579–1666), who founded Wolfenbüttel's famous library and turned the town into a cultural centre in the mid-17th century. This friendly, charming little city, about 10 minutes by train from Braunschweig, is worlds away in terms of its feel and architecture. First mentioned in 1118, Wolfenbüttel was virtually untouched by WWII, and it's almost a time capsule of half-timbered houses – there are over 600 of them, nearly all beautifully restored.

Stadtmarkt, the town centre, is a five-minute walk northeast of Hauptbahnhof.

◉ Sights

Schloss Museum   MUSEUM
(www.schlosswolfenbuettel.de; Schlossplatz 13; adult/child €3.50/free; ⊙10am-5pm Tue-Sun) Wolfenbüttel's pretty Palace Museum showcases the living quarters of the Braunschweig-Lüneburg dukes, which have been preserved in all their glory of intricate inlaid wood, ivory walls, brocade curtains and chairs. A highlight is the large collection of porcelain.

Herzog August Bibliothek   MUSEUM, LIBRARY
(Herzog August Library; www.hab.de; Lessingplatz 1; adult/concession €5/2; ⊙10am-5pm Tue-Sun) Not only is this hushed building one of the world's best reference libraries for 17th-century books (if you're a member, that is), its collection of 800,000 volumes also includes what's billed as the 'world's most expensive book' (€17.50 million at the time of purchase in the 1980s). This is the *Welfen*

WALKING WOLFENBÜTTEL

Wolfenbüttel's tourist office has some excellent resources to help you explore town. You can download an English, French or German MP3 guide from the website www.wolfenbuettel.tomis.mobi (click on the appropriate flag for your preferred language). The free tourist office brochure, *A Walk Through Historic Wolfenbüttel*, takes you on a walk through town lasting around one hour (2km), excluding visits.

Evangelial, a gospel book once owned by Heinrich der Löwe. The original is only on show sporadically, but an impressive facsimile is permanently displayed in the vault on the 1st floor.

Klein Venedig   NEIGHBOURHOOD

In the late 16th century, Dutch workers came to Wölfenbüttel and built an extensive canal system, remnants of which today survive in a quarter of town known as Little Venice. To reach it from Schlossplatz, walk east along Löwenstrasse to Krambuden and north up Kleiner Zimmerhof.

ⓘ Information

Tourist Office (☎862 80; www.wolfenbuettel. com; Stadtmarkt 7; ⓞ10am-6pm Mon-Fri, to 2pm Sat & Sun) Take Bahnhofstrasse north to Kommisstrasse. This joins Kornmarkt, the main bus transfer point.

ⓘ Getting There & Away

Trains connect Wolfenbüttel with Braunschweig's Hauptbahnhof.

Wolfsburg

☎05361 / POP 121,450

Arriving in Wolfsburg by train, the first thing you see is an enormous, almost surreal, VW emblem on a building in a scene that could have come from Fritz Lang's classic film *Metropolis*. This is part of the Volkswagen company's nation-sized global headquarters. Wolfsburg is indeed a company town, and because of this it also has an earthy, working-class atmosphere that sets it apart from other cities in the region.

Volkswagen is the world's second-largest vehicle manufacturer, and about 40% of Wolfsburg works for it. As well as the hugely successful Autostadt theme park, the town boasts a Phaeno science centre, a sleek piece of futuristic architecture by celebrity architect Zaha Hadid.

◉ Sights & Activities

Autostadt   THEME PARK

(Car City; www.autostadt.de; Stadtbrücke; adult/child/concession/family €15/6/12/38, car tower discovery adult/child/concession €8/4/6; ⓞ9am-6pm) Spread across 25 hectares, Autostadt is a celebration of all things VW. A visit to this theme park kicks off with a broad view of automotive design and engineering in the **Konzernforum**. In the neighbouring **Zeithaus** you can find out about the history of the Beetle and other VW models. Then, in various outlying pavilions, you can learn more about individual marques, including VW itself, Audi, Bentley, Lamborghini, Seat and Skoda. Many exhibits are interactive and most have signage in German and English. Included in the tour is a 45-minute return **Maritime Panorama Tour** along the Aller River to the outlying district of Fallersleben. Unfortunately, you can't get off the boat.

For a pure, competitive adrenaline rush, ring ahead to organise an English-speaking instructor for the park's **obstacle courses** and **safety training** (costing between €25 and €28 each). You'll need a valid licence, of course, and to be comfortable with a left-hand-drive car. The park even has a mini-course, with toy models that can be driven by kids.

Phaeno   MUSEUM

(www.phaeno.de; Willy Brandt-Platz 1; adult/child/concession/family €12/7.50/9/26.50; ⓞ9am-5pm Tue-Fri, 10am-6pm Sat & Sun, last entry 1hr before closing) The glass-and-concrete building that houses the science centre Phaeno was designed by British-based Iraqi architect Zaha Hadid and houses 300 hands-on physics exhibits and experiments (with instructions and explanations in both German and English). It's a couple of minutes by foot from the train station.

AutoMuseum   MUSEUM

(http://automuseum.volkswagen.de; Dieselstrasse 35; adult/concession/family €6/3/15; ⓞ10am-6pm Tue-Sun) The Car Museum has a collection that includes a vehicle used in the *Herbie, the Love Bug* movie, a Beetle built from wood, the original 1938 Cabriolet presented to Adolf Hitler on his 50th birthday, and the bizarre 'See-Golf', a Golf Cabriolet from 1983 with hydraulic pontoons that extend outwards to make it amphibious. Take bus 208 to Automuseum.

Hoffmann Museum
MUSEUM

(☺due to reopen in early 2013) In 1841, Fallersleben native August Heinrich Hoffman (1798–1874) wrote the lyrics to what would become the German national anthem (music courtesy of Joseph Haydn). Here you'll find discussion of how his words '*über alles*' ('above everything') were simply a call for an end to petty inter-German fiefdoms, and how they were expunged after the Third Reich's nationalistic excesses. The museum is housed inside Fallersleben Schloss (Fallersleben Castle). Take bus 203, 204, 206 or 214 to Fallersleben, about 6km west of the centre.

Kunstmuseum
GALLERY

(www.kunst museum-wolfsburg.de; Porschestrasse 53; adult/concession €8/4; ☺11am-8pm Tue, to 6pm Wed-Sun) Wolfsburg's excellent art gallery stages temporary exhibitions of modern art. Buses 201 and 202 from the bus station run there.

Planetarium Wolfsburg
PLANETARIUM

(www.planetarium-wolfsburg.de; Uhlandweg 2; adult/concession/family €7/5/15) Built in 1982 after VW bartered Golfs for Zeiss projectors with the GDR, this planetarium stages laser and rock shows, star shows and spoken-word performances set to the stars. Show times vary; see the website.

🛏 Sleeping

The city's accommodation is mostly geared towards business travellers.

TOP CHOICE Hotel Goya
HOTEL $$

(☎266 00; www.goya-hotel.de; Poststrasse 34; s €78-83, d €93-105; P✿) Rooms in this very central and comfortable hotel are nicely furnished in subdued colours, with clever use of mirrors. Each room has a writing surface; while Goya caters for business guests, it actually does a very tasteful double-act as a quality tourist hotel.

Global Inn
HOTEL $$

(☎2700; www.globalinn.de; Kleiststrasse 46; s €62.50-69.50, d €83-96.50; P@✿) This hotel is very much aimed at the corporate customer but furnishings are comfortable and the rooms a decent size. Book ahead. It's a 20-minute walk or €5 by taxi from the train station. Buses 203 and 214 to Schubertring stop close by.

Ritz-Carlton
HOTEL $$$

(☎607 000; www.ritzcarlton.com; Stadtbrücke; r from €305, ste from €405; P✿✿✿) This hotel is a hard act to beat. The hotel swimming pool is integrated into the harbour basin of the canal, giving the hotel a lakeside feel, while the building forms a stunning arc on one side of Autostadt. The decor is elegant

BITTEN BY THE BUG

Cast-iron proof that Germans *do* have a sense of humour, the Volkswagen Beetle is truly greater than the sum of its parts. After all, the parts in question initially comprised little more than an air-cooled, 24-horsepower engine (maximum speed 100km/h) chucked in the back of a comically half-egg-shaped chassis. Yet somehow this rudimentary mechanical assembly added up to a global icon – a symbol of Germany's postwar *Wirtschaftswunder* (economic miracle) that owners the world over fondly thought of as one of the family.

Indeed, it's a testament to the vehicle's ability to run on the smell of an oily rag while rarely breaking down that few would even begrudge its Nazi provenance. Yes, in 1934 Adolf Hitler asked Ferdinand Porsche to design a 'Volkswagen' (people's car) affordable for every German household and, yes, the *Käfer* (bug) was the result. However, Beetle production only really began in the new Wolfsburg factory under British occupation in 1946.

Did the company realise then what a hit it had on its hands? By the early 1960s, the chugging, spluttering sound of VW engines could be heard across 145 nations. Long after VW withdrew its bucket-of-bolts old Beetle (essentially the same beast despite improvements) from Western markets, the car remained a best seller in the developing world. Only on 31 July 2003 did the last one roll off the assembly line in Mexico, the 21,529,464th of its breed.

and breathes natural tones. Expect full five-star facilities, complemented by a Michelin-starred restaurant and numerous bars. You can take high tea overlooking the harbour.

DJH Hostel HOSTEL $
(☑133 37; www.djh-niedersachsen.de/jh/wolfsburg; Kleiststrasse 18-20; dm under/over 27yr €24.40/ 28.40; P@☎) This hostel inside a former fire department building has bright dorms furnished in light-coloured woods. Each dorm has its own bathroom as well as a table with seating. Buses 201, 202, 203 and 204 stop close by.

✕ Eating & Drinking

Wolfsburg's Autostadt complex has a wide range of restaurants, including a couple in the foyer that you can eat in without having to pay admission.

Wolfsburgers do much of their drinking in Kaufhof – not the department store, but a small strip of bars, pubs and a few eateries west of Porschestrasse. The best thing is to wander along and see what appeals.

TOP CHOICE Vini D'Italia Marrone ITALIAN $$
(www.viniditalia-marrone.de; Schillerstrasse 25; dishes €9.50-21.50; ☉10am-8pm Mon-Sat) This Italian *bottega* does a double act as a wine store and a small eatery where antipasti and salads cost €5 to €8. You can choose from the main menu, do the daily lunch menu (€9.50), or simply treat yourself to the daily specialities.

Aalto Bistro INTERNATIONAL $
(Porschestrasse 51; mains €6.50-14.50; ☉lunch & dinner Mon-Sat) Part of the Kulturhaus designed by star Finnish architect Alvar Aalto, this relaxing place serves pasta and seafood in a modern bistro environment.

Trattoria Incontri ITALIAN $$
(☑437 254; Goethestrasse 53-55; blackboard mains €20-24, pasta €10-15; ☉lunch & dinner Mon-Sat, 4pm-midnight Sun) On a patch of Goethestrasse with several restaurants and bars, this Italian trattoria is one of the most popular and offers mains from a changing blackboard menu.

Altes Brauhaus PUB $
(www.brauhaus-fallersleben.de; Schlossplatz; mains €9.20-18.50; ☉from 11am) If you're visiting the Hoffmann Museum in Fallersleben or simply dying for a German beer-hall atmosphere, come here. There's a good house brew

and hearty fare including salads, sausages, potatoes and sauerkraut.

ℹ Information

Babylon Tele- and Internet Shop (Porschestrasse 23; per hr €1.80; ☉9.15am-10pm Mon-Fri, 10am-10pm Sat & Sun) Internet access.

Main Post Office (Porschestrasse 22-24; ☉8.30am-6.30pm Mon-Fri, 9am-1pm Sat)

Tourist Office (☑899 930; www.wolfsburg. de; Willy Brandt-Platz 3; ☉9am-6pm Mon-Sat, 10am-3pm Sun) In the train station. Books hotels and has maps.

ℹ Getting There & Away

CAR Vehicles can be hired from **Europcar** (☑815 70; Dieselstrasse 19). From Braunschweig, take the A2 east to the A39 north, which brings you right into town. Alternatively, take the B248 north to the A39.

TRAIN Frequent ICE train services go to Berlin (€47, one hour). IC trains to Hanover (€17.50, 30 minutes) are cheaper and barely slower than the ICE. Frequent ICE trains, including some Berlin and Hanover ones, pass through Braunschweig (€12, 16 minutes). Regional trains for Braunschweig take scarcely longer and are cheaper.

ℹ Getting Around

BIKE **Zweirad Schael** (☑140 64; Kleiststrasse 5) hires out bicycles from €10 per day. The tourist office also rents out bikes for €7.50 per day (book ahead).

BUS Single bus tickets, valid for 90 minutes, cost €2 and a day pass costs €5.50. The major bus transfer point (ZOB) is at the northern end of Porschestrasse, near the train station. Buses 203, 204, 206 and 214 go regularly to Fallersleben from here.

TAXI There are taxi ranks at the Hauptbahnhof and at the northern end of Porschestrasse. Alternatively, call **City Taxi** (☑230 23)

BREMEN & THE EAST FRISIAN COAST

Those of you who love peat bogs, walking on tidal flats, going to sea or blustery bike rides will especially enjoy visiting Bremen and the East Frisian coast. It's a place ideally suited to taking the pace off travel and to immersing yourself in flat, verdant countryside. If not for its focal point Bremen, it wouldn't even have a city of notable size to write home about. But Bremen, an outward-looking, very friendly cultural and industrial capital of its own city state, is the clear urban highlight and also includes the port of Bremerhaven and the artists' colony of Worpswede. While rail connections in the eastern parts are excellent, you will find buses and boats necessary for exploring outlying regions of East Frisia and of course the islands.

Bremen City

📞 0421 / POP 548,000

Bremen, one of Gemany's city-states, has a highly justified reputation for being among the country's most outward-looking and hospitable places, with a local population that seems to strike a very good balance between style, earthiness and good living.

Nature is never far away here, but Bremen is better known for its fairy-tale character, a unique expressionist quarter and (it must be said, because the Bremen folk are avid football fans) one of Germany's most exciting football teams. That nature would get its chance to win back a few urban patches did seem likely from the late 1960s, when the population, having peaked at over 600,000, began to decline. Something else happened, however, to clinch it: in 1979 Bremen – the city-state – was the first to elect Green Party candidates to its state parliament, unwittingly becoming the cradle of a worldwide movement to put 'Greens' in parliaments.

Today, Bremen just scrapes in among Germany's largest 10 cities and offers an unhurried and relaxed lifestyle, some very lively areas where you can enjoy good food, culture and a drink, a lovely old town with one section where the streets are way too narrow to risk swinging cats, and some tall tales to complement its history – likely proof that the people of Bremen are also among Germany's most gregarious.

History

Bremen's origins go back to a string of settlements that developed near today's centre from about 100 AD, and one settlement in particular that in 787 was given its own bishop's seat by Charlemagne. In its earliest days, it was known as the 'Rome of the North' and developed as a base for Christianising Scandinavia. Despite this, it gradually shed its religious character, enjoying the greater freedom of being an imperial city from 1186, joining the Hanseatic League in 1260, and in 1646 coming directly under the wing of the Kaiser as a free imperial city; today it is a 'Free Hanseatic City'.

◉ Sights & Activities

Most of Bremen's major sights are directly in the centre, notably the neighbourhoods Markt & Böttcherstrasse, Schnoor and Schlachte. The latter is a waterfront street with lots of bars and restaurants. Sights on the Weser River that are outside the centre can be quickly reached by public transport. The Kulturmeile & Das Viertel neighbourhood is a walk or short tram ride east of the centre and is one of Bremen's liveliest and most interesting areas, also packed with restaurants and lots of bars. The areas North & East of the Centre have a sprinkling of sights that are usually best reached by tram or bus.

MARKT & BÖTTCHERSTRASSE

Markt SQUARE

(Map p622) With high, historic buildings rising up from this very compact square, Bremen's Markt is one of the most remarkable in northern Germany. The two towers of the 1200-year-old **Dom St Petri** (p621) dominate the northeastern edge, beside the ornate and imposing **Rathaus**, which was erected in 1410. The Weser Renaissance balcony in the middle, crowned by three gables, was added between 1595 and 1618. In front of the Rathaus is one of the hallmarks of Bremen, the city's 13m-high **Knight Roland statue** (1404). As elsewhere, Roland stands for the civic freedoms of a city, especially the freedom to trade independently. On the western side of the Rathaus – in front of the **Kirche Unser Lieben Frauen** (Church of our Beloved Lady) – you find the city's even more-famous symbol: the **Town Musicians of Bremen** (1951) by the sculptor Gerhard Marcks. This depicts a dog, cat and rooster, one on top of the other, on the shoulders of a donkey. The donkey's nose and front legs are incredibly shiny after being touched by visitors for good luck.

The one obviously modern building on the Markt is the **Haus der Bürgerschaft** (State Assembly; 1966), whose geometrical steel-and-concrete structure features artfully moulded pieces of metal attached to its facade, suggesting a Gothic style that blends in with the other architecture of this historic square.

Dom St Petri CHURCH

(St Petri Cathedral; Map p622; tower €1; ⊙10am-4.45pm Mon-Fri, to 1.30pm Sat, 2-4.45pm Sun, tower closed Nov-Easter) Bremen's Dom St Petri is situated on the northeastern side of Markt. Construction began in 1041 in the style of an

Bremen City

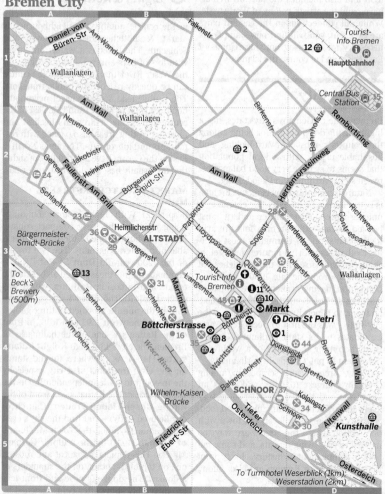

early Gothic basilica, on the site of Bremen's original wooden cathedral that was located here in the late-8th century. Today's stone incarnation was given ribbed vaulting inside, chapels and its two high towers in the 13th century. For views over Bremen, climb the 265 steps to the top of the southern tower.

Bleikeller   CRYPT
(Lead Cellar; Map p622; adult/child €1.40/1; ⏰10am-5pm Mon-Fri, to 1.45pm Sat, noon-4.45pm Sun Apr-Oct) Located inside Dom St Petri but accessed via a separate entrance south of

the main door, the Lead Cellar was formerly the cathedral's cellar and today is a crypt in which bodies have mummified in the incredibly dry air. You can see eight preserved bodies in open coffins here, including a Swedish countess, a soldier with his mouth opened in a silent scream, and a student who died in a duel in 1705.

Böttcherstrasse   NEIGHBOURHOOD
(Map p622) This charming lane with a golden entrance and staggered red-brick walls is a superb example of expressionism. The 110m-long street was commissioned in 1931

multicoloured, glass-walled spiral staircase. Hoetger worked around the existing, 16th-century Roselius Haus, and the Paula Modersohn-Becker Haus, with its rounded edges and wall reliefs, is his own design too. Today these two adjoining houses are museums comprising the Kunstsammlungen Böttcherstrasse (p623).

Kunstsammlungen Böttcherstrasse
MUSEUM

(Art Collection Böttcherstrasse; Map p622; www.pmbm.de; Böttcherstrasse 6-10; combined ticket adult/concession €5/3; ⊙11am-6pm Tue-Sun) Two adjoining houses make up the Art Collection Böttcherstrasse. One of these is the **Roselius-Haus Museum** (Map p622; ☑336 5077; combined ticket adult/concession €5/3; ⊙11am-6pm Tue-Sun), which is inside a historic patrician house from the 16th century and contains a collection of art from medieval times to the baroque era.

The collection belonged to Ludwig Roselius, the man who gave the world decaffeinated coffee and used the money from his beans and other ventures to bankroll the expressionist Böttcherstrasse in the 1930s.

The second house is the work of Bernhard Hoetger, the creative mind behind much of Böttcherstrasse. This house is now the **Paula Modersohn-Becker Haus Museum** (Map p622; ☑336 5077; combined ticket adult/concession €5/3; ⊙11am-6pm Tue-Sun) and showcases the art of the eponymous painter, Paula Modersohn-Becker (1876–1907), an early expressionist and member of the Worpswede colony.

Glockenspiel
CARILLON

(Map p622; Böttcherstrasse; ⊙hourly noon-6pm May-Dec, noon, 3pm & 6pm Jan-Apr) This carillon typifies Bremen's seafaring tradition, chiming while a rotating panel honours great sea explorers, such as Leif Eriksson and Christopher Columbus.

SCHNOOR

This part of Bremen's centre was once its maritime quarter and then its red-light district. Over the years, however, the district transmogrified into a quaint maze of restaurants, cafes and boutique shops. It's a honey-pot for tourists, but its restaurants are also popular with locals in the evenings. The name 'Schnoor' is north German for 'string', and refers to the way the 15th- and 16th-century cottages – once inhabited by

by Ludwig Roselius, a merchant who made his fortune by inventing decaffeinated coffee and founding the company Hag in the early 20th century.

Most of the street was designed by Bernhard Hoetger (1874–1959), including the **Lichtbringer** (Bringer of Light), the golden relief at the northern entrance, showing a scene from the Apocalypse with the Archangel Michael fighting a dragon.

Hoetger's **Haus Atlantis** (Map p622; ⊙free guided tours 10am-noon & 2-4pm Mon), now the Bremen Hilton, features a show-stopping,

Bremen City

fisherfolk, traders and craftspeople – are 'strung' along the alleyways.

SCHLACHTE & THE WESER

Weserburg Museum für Moderne Kunst   GALLERY
(Weserburg Museum of Modern Art; Map p622; www.weserburg.de; Teerhof 20; adult/concession €8/5; ⊙10am-6pm Tue, Wed & Fri, to 9pm Thu, 11am-6pm Sat & Sun) Situated on an island in the Weser River, across from the Schlachte promenade, the Weserburg Museum for Modern Art showcases German and interna-

tional artists in changing, hot-off-the-press exhibitions.

Hafenmuseum Speicher XI   MUSEUM
(Harbour Museum Warehouse 11; www.speicherelf. de; Am Speicher XI; adult/concession €4.50/3.50; ⊙11am-6pm Tue-Sun) This former harbour warehouse has a strong permanent exhibition focusing on Bremen's waterside history and the workers who have made it happen, including a section on forced labourers during WWII. Special exhibitions elaborate

on the waterside theme. Take bus 26 to Speicher XI.

Beck's Brewery
BREWERY

(☎01805 101 030; www.becks.de/besucherzentrum; Am Deich; tours €10.50; ☺1pm & 3pm Thu & Fri, 11.30pm, 1pm, 3.30pm & 4.30pm Sat Jan-Apr, 10am, 11.30am, 1pm, 3pm, 4.30pm & 6pm Thu-Sat May-Dec) Germany has well over 1200 breweries, and about half of these are found in Bavaria, not the north. The beer of one brewery in particular, though, has long washed beyond the shores of Germany to establish itself as an international brand. You can see where the wares come from during a two-hour tour of the Beck's brewery, run in conjunction with the tourist office. Book online or by telephone and meet at the brewery by taking tram 1 or 8 to Am Brill. *Prost!*

KULTURMEILE & DAS VIERTEL

TOP CHOICE Kunsthalle
GALLERY

(Map p622; www.kunsthalle-bremen.de; Am Wall 207; adult/concession €11/9; ☺10am-6pm Wed-Sun, to 9pm Tue) For art-lovers, the highlight of Bremen's *Kulturmeile* (Cultural Mile) is the Kunsthalle, which presents a large permanent collection of paintings, sculpture and copperplate engraving from the Middle Ages into the modern, as well as changing exhibitions. This gallery bills itself as having masterpieces from over 600 years – and it's as good as its word, especially after expanding exhibition space with a new wing in 2011.

Gerhard Marcks Haus
GALLERY

(Map p622; www.marcks.de; Am Wall 208; adult/concession €5/3.50; ☺10am-6pm Tue-Wed & Fri-Sun, to 9pm Thu) Gerhard Marcks (1889–1981), the man responsible for Bremen's famous Stadtmusikanten sculpture on Markt, is among Germany's greatest sculptors. He was born in Berlin and was one of the artists condemned as 'degenerate' by the Nazis in the 1930s and forbidden from exhibiting his work until after WWII. In 1966 he transferred much of his work into a foundation in Bremen, culminating in this excellent museum with exhibits of his own works as well as those of modern and contemporary sculptors.

Wilhelm Wagenfeld Haus
MUSEUM

(Map p622; www.wwh-bremen.de; Am Wall 209; adult/concession €3.50/1.50; ☺3-9pm Tue, 10am-6pm Wed-Sun) Wilhelm Wagenfeld (1900–90) was a Bauhaus luminary whose foundation today promotes contemporary design in its many facets and forms in special exhibitions, including, for instance, through photography.

NORTH & EAST OF THE CENTRE

Universum Science Center
MUSEUM

(www.universum-bremen.de; Wiener Strasse 1a; adult/child €16/11; ☺9am-6pm Mon-Fri, 10am-6pm Sat & Sun) Bremen has a strong aerospace industry, and space buffs will enjoy the eye-catching, oyster-shaped Universum Science Center, where you can make virtual trips to the stars, as well as to the ocean floor or the centre of the earth. Take tram 6 from the main train station to Universität/NW1 stop.

Übersee Museum
MUSEUM

(Overseas Museum; Map p622; www.uebersee-museum.de; Bahnhofplatz 13; adult/concession €6.50/4.50; ☺9am-6pm Tue-Fri, from 10am Sat & Sun) The Übersee Museum takes you to all continents of the world and offers an insight

---

THE FANTASTIC FOUR

In the Brothers Grimm fairy tale, the *Bremer Stadtmusikanten* (Town Musicians of Bremen) never actually make it to Bremen, but when you arrive in the city you might enjoy a quick reminder of what the fuss is about. Starting with a donkey, four overworked and ageing animals, fearing the knacker's yard or the Sunday roasting pan, run away from their owners. They head for Bremen intending, like many young dreamers, to make their fortune as musicians.

On their first night on the road, they decide to shelter in a house. It turns out to be occupied by robbers, as our heroes discover when they climb on the donkey to peer through the window. The sight of a rooster atop a cat, perched on a dog, which is sitting on a donkey – and the 'musical' accompaniment of braying, barking, meowing and crowing – startles the robbers so much, they flee. The animals remain and make their home 'where you'll probably still find them today'.

On Sunday from May to September, this story is charmingly re-enacted (at noon) in Bremen's Markt.

SAMBA ON THE WESER

As weird as it sounds, every year in January or February, Bremen celebrates a popular *Karneval* that has become the largest samba carnival in Europe. Okay, so the competition for samba carnivals in Europe isn't exactly enormous, but you can expect about 10,000 people to take to the streets in Bremen. It all began when the 1st Bremer Samba Group swung into action in 1986, and today this merrymaking continues, as the www.bremer-karnival.de (in German) website puts it, to celebrate 'the road from the dark, cold time to brightness and warmth', when 'the foreign, the bizarre, the grotesque and the exotic invade the streets'. Each year the carnival takes a different theme. In 2012 it was 'Metamorphosis'. To get into the swing of things, follow the parade from Markt along Ostertorsteinweg and into Das Viertel. Open-air stages are set up, mostly on Ostertorsteinweg. Dress up warm, weird and inappropriately, and get down to the beat!

into natural evolution with its dazzling collection of exotic artefacts. It can call on about 1.1 million objects, including African art, tropical plants and gold from South America.

Dutch windmill　　HISTORIC BUILDING
(Map p622; Am Wall) The city's typical Dutch windmill today houses a restaurant and adds a pleasant rural flavour to the parkland tracing the part of town where Bremen's city fortifications once were.

Botanika　　GARDENS
(www.botanika.net; Deliusweg, in Rhododendron-Park; adult/concession €8/6; ⊙9am-6pm Mon-Fri, 10am-6pm Sat & Sun) If you're a plant-lover, don't miss a trip to Botanika and its replicated Asian landscapes from the Himalayas to New Guinea. Admission to the rhododendron park itself, where you find 2000 rhododendrons and azaleas, is free. To get here, take tram 4 to Horner Kirche.

☞ Tours

City Tour　　BUS TOUR
(Map p622; adult/child under 12yr €17.90/12; ⊙10.30am Tue-Sun) Two-hour tours leaving from platform M outside the Hauptbahnhof

are run by the tourist office with English and German commentary. Otherwise, ask the office about its many German-language tours.

Hal Över Schreiber Reederee　　TOUR
(Map p622; www.hal-oever.de; Schlachte 2, Martinianleger; harbour & Weser tour adult/child €9.90/5.60; ⊙office 9am-5pm Mon-Fri) Operates a 75-minute **Weser and harbour tour** three to five times daily from January to November. Also runs scheduled services along the river in summer, the ferry across the river to Café Sand (p629) and – surely a unique way of getting to a football game – can even take you by boat from the Martinianleger to Werder Bremen's stadium during home matches.

🛏 Sleeping

Note that in mid-2012 Bremen introduced a City Tax of €1 to €3 per guest and per night on rooms that will need to be added to the prices below, varying according to the category of accommodation.

TOP CHOICE Hotel Bölts am Park　　HOTEL $$
(Map p622; ☑346110; www.hotel-boelts.de; Slevogtstrasse 23; s/d €65/85; ᴾ🛜) This cosy family-run hotel in a leafy neighbourhood has real character, from the wonderfully old-fashioned breakfast hall to its well-proportioned doubles.

TOP CHOICE Hotel Überfluss　　BOUTIQUE HOTEL $$$
(Map p622; ☑322 860; www.hotel-ueberfluss. com; Langenstrasse 72/Schlachte 36; s €120-160, d €131-195, ste from €339; ❄🛜🛁) Quite literally 7m above river level, this designer hotel has black bathrooms (some with transparent shower areas) and stunning views from its more-expensive rooms. For splashy fun, the magnificently designed suite has its own sauna and whirlpool – perfect for a honeymoon.

Turmhotel Weserblick　　HOTEL $$
(☑790 3054; www.turmhotel-weserblick-bremen. de; Osterdeich 53; s €70-80, d €85-95; ᴾ🛜) This tower-topped hotel right on the Weser River foreshore has heaps of atmosphere, with bare floorboards and Persian carpets in extremely spacious rooms. The tower rooms overlook the river and have a kitchen. Take tram 2 or 3 to Sielwall.

Hotel Residence　　HOTEL $$
(Map p622; ☑348 710; www.hotelresidence.de; Hohenlohestrasse 42; s €66-133, d €88-155; ᴾ@🛜)

Many celebrities, including Destiny's Child and writer Harry Rowohlt, have stayed in this century-old terrace converted into a charming hotel – check out the photos near reception. The main building has rooms to the street, while the newer extension backs onto the railway line but is still reasonably quiet. A sauna, solarium, bar and dining room complete the package.

Hotel Lichtsinn HOTEL $$
(Map p622; ☑368 070; www.hotel-lichtsinn.com; Rembertistrasse 11; s/d €85/110; P@🖻) Wooden floorboards, Persian carpets and vaguely Biedermeier-style furniture characterise most of this hotel's rooms, a favourite with the theatre world.

Hotel Bremer Haus HOTEL $$
(Map p622; ☑329 40; www.hotel-bremer-haus. de; Löningstrasse 16/20; s €86-120, d €112-144; P@🖻) The yellow exterior of this place is somewhat unappealing, but it gives way to modern, clean and comfortable rooms inside that are especially favoured by business travellers. It has a small foyer lounge for mulling over the newspapers, and a 24-hour reception.

Park Hotel Bremen HOTEL $$$
(☑340 80; www.park-hotel-bremen.de; Im Bürgerpark; s €135-385, d €185-385, ste from €635; P🖳🖻🏊) This domed lakeside mansion, surrounded by parkland, impresses through its sheer extravagance. It offers access to excellent spa, fitness and beauty facilities, a heated outdoor pool and views over the lake in a 'spa resort' ambience.

Camping Stadtwaldsee CAMPGROUND $
(☑841 0748; www.camping-stadtwaldsee.de; Hochschulring 1; per adult/tent/car €10/4/3) This camping ground features modern amenities, a supermarket and the restaurant Oliver's close by. By car, take the A27 to the university exit in Bremen Nord. Tram 6 to Universität/NW1 is close, or change here to bus 28 to Campingplatz.

Jugendherberge Bremen HOSTEL $
(Map p622; ☑163 820; http://bremen.jugendher bergen-nordwesten.de; Kalkstrasse 6; dm under/over 27yr €25/29, s €35/39, d €63/67; @🖻) Looking like a work of art from the exterior, with a yellow and orange Plexiglas facade and slit windows, this hostel has comfortable rooms, a rooftop terrace and a bar-breakfast room with huge glass windows overlooking the Weser River. Take tram 1 to Am Brill from Hauptbahnhof.

Bremer Backpacker Hostel HOSTEL $
(Map p622; ☑223 8057; www.bremer-backpacker -hostel.de; Emil-Waldmann-Strasse 5-6; dm/s/d €18/29/48; P@🖻) This private hostel is simply furnished but spotless, with a kitchen, communal room and a small courtyard out front for soaking up the sun.

Townside Hostel Bremen HOSTEL $
(Map p622; ☑78015; www.townside.de; Am Dobben 62; 4-9-bed dm €17-23, s €35; 🖻) This bright, professionally run hostel is right in the middle of Bremen's nightlife quarter and handy to Werder-Bremen's stadium. Take tram 10 from Hauptbahnhof to Humboldtstrasse or tram 2 or 3 to Sielwall.

GastHaus Hotel Bremen HOTEL $$
(Map p622; ☑223 8057; www.bremer-backpacker -hostel.de; Löningstrasse 30; s/d without breakfast €45/84; 🖻) One of two hotels affiliated with the Bremer Backpacker Hostel, has rooms with modern furnishings and own bathrooms.

Buthmann im Zentrum HOTEL $$
(Map p622; ☑223 8057; www.bremer-backpacker -hostel.de; Löningstrasse 29; s/d without breakfast €49/84; 🖻) Affiliated with the Bremer Backpacker Hostel, in an old-style Bremen house with 1960s-style furnishings.

✕ Eating

TOWN CENTRE

TOP CHOICE **Ständige Vertretung** GERMAN $$
(Map p622; www.staev.de; Böttcherstrasse 3-5; mains €8.20-19.90; ⏰11.30am-11pm) An offshoot of Berlin's best-known restaurant for homesick Rhineland public servants, this large, bustling place thrives on its political theme and solid cuisine washed down with Rhineland wines and beer.

Energie Café INTERNATIONAL $
(Map p622; www.energiecafe.de; Sögestrasse 59-61; mains €6.50-11.50; ⏰from 9am Mon-Fri, from 11am Sat; 🖻🐾) A delightfully upbeat cafe run by a local power company, this place serves delicious pizza, pasta and lunch specials (€6.50 to €7.90). It has regular jazz sessions and a whizz interior.

Delano ITALIAN $$
(Map p622; www.delano-restaurant.de; Queerenstrasse 1, also Martinistrasse 72-74; salads €7-10, pizza €9-14, pasta €7-9, fish €16-19, meat mains

€19-20; ⊙from noon Mon-Sat, from 6pm Sun; 🖉)
The black wood furniture, fat columns and
ringed black-and-white lampshades lend
this Italian brasserie an upbeat feel. The pizzas are menacingly large.

SCHLACHTE & AROUND

TOP CHOICE Le Gril   STEAKHOUSE, INTERNATIONAL $$
(Map p622; 🖉3017 4443; www.loui-jules.com; Lan-
genstrasse 72/Schlachte 36; mains €12-36; ⊙lunch
& dinner Mon-Sat) Located inside Hotel Über-
fluss, this surf 'n' turf place does excellent
wood-coal grills, with steaks starting from
€20 but with many cheaper dishes, includ-
ing an inexpensive burger and midrange
seafood.

Gallo Nero   ITALIAN $$$
(Map p622; 🖉957 9958; www.gallonero-bremen.de;
Heimlichenstrasse 1; pasta €11-15, fish €18-25, meat
mains €19-24; ⊙lunch & dinner Mon-Sat) Dishes
from king prawns laced with saffron on a
bed of rocket salad to a reasonably priced
saltimbocca alla Romana are for the asking
in this friendly Italian restaurant.

Luv   INTERNATIONAL $$
(Map p622; www.restaurant-luv.de; Schlachte 15-18;
lighter mains under €12, mains €19-27; ⊙from 11am
Mon-Fri, from 10am Sat & Sun) A friendly atmos-
phere reigns in this large, upbeat bistro with
a lounge-bar feel and a menu strong on sal-
ads and pasta, which is complemented by
more-substantial fare with a Mediterranean
or Central European focus. A Texas burger
can be found alongside the Wiener schnitzel
and *nouveau-hearty* dishes.

Osteria   ITALIAN $$
(Map p622; 🖉339 8207; www.osteria-bremen.de;
Schlachte 1; pasta €7-11, fish €19-20, meat mains
€16-22; ⊙noon-1am Mon-Fri, 6pm-1am Sat; 🖉)
Crisp tablecloths and good service are hallmarks of this formal but relaxed Italian
restaurant serving a good range of grilled
meats and seafood. For vegetarians it has a
good selection of pasta dishes without meat
as mains for €8 to €12. The open kitchen
and tiled floor lend a pleasant feel.

SCHNOOR

Schröter's   MEDITERRANEAN $$
(Map p622; 🖉326 677; www.schroeters-schnoor.
de; Schnoor 13; lunch mains €9-15, evening mains
€22-29, 3/5-course menus €40/53; ⊙lunch &
dinner) A modern bistro with artful decora-
tion, Schröter's is known for its antipasti
and abundant Mediterranean mains, from
risotto to fish. It is a veritable warren of

rooms, including a Toulouse-Lautrec room
upstairs, decorated with plenty of copies of
the painter's pictures.

Katzen Café   INTERNATIONAL $$
(Map p622; 🖉326 621; www.katzen-cafe.de; mains
€16-24; ⊙lunch & dinner) This popular Moulin
Rouge–style restaurant opens out into a rear
sunken terrace bedecked with flowers. The
menu runs the gamut from Alsatian to Nor-
wegian, with seafood a strong theme.

DAS VIERTEL

This arty, student neighbourhood is where
to head for cheaper meals or simply a glass
of wine or beer over something tasty.

TOP CHOICE Casa   MEDITERRANEAN $$
(Map p622; http://casa-bremen.com; Ostertorstein-
weg 59; mains €8-20; ⊙from 10am; 🖉) Bremen's
long-standing favourite has recently given
itself a new name (this used to be known as
Casablanca) and a slightly more upmarket
splash. It serves lava-grill fish and meat dish-
es (including its own burger as well as lamb
dishes), along with salads and pizza – often
with a Mediterranean edge. Breakfast is till
noon weekdays, till 3pm weekends.

Piano   INTERNATIONAL $
(www.cafepiano-bremen.de; Fehrfeld 64; mains €7-
12; ⊙from 9am; 🖉) An enduringly popular
cafe, this bustling place serves pizza, pasta,
a few heartier dishes and veggie casseroles
to a broad neighbourhood mix, from me-
dia types checking proofs to young mums.
Breakfast can also be ordered until 4pm Sat-
urday and 5pm Sunday.

NORTHEAST OF THE CENTRE

La Terrasse   INTERNATIONAL $$$
(🖉340 8779; www.park-hotel-bremen.de; Im
Bürgerpark; menu €150; ⊙dinner Tue-Sat) Reserve well ahead for a table in Bremen's top
restaurant (inside the Park Hotel Bremen),
where Heiko Schulz (previously in St Moritz's Ca D'Oro) oversees a seasonal menu
with a strong piscine focus.

Oliver's   INTERNATIONAL $$
(www.olivers-am-unisee.de; Hochschulring 1; salads
€5-14, mains €9-25; ⊙10am-10pm Tue-Sun) Situ-
ated directly on the tranquil Stadtwaldsee
lake, Oliver's is ideal for hanging out on a
sunny day and enjoying a coffee or drink,
one of the excellent salads with duck or slic-
es of beef, or a full meal in which the qual-
ity of the food matches the great location.

Take tram 6 north to Universität/NW1 and change to bus 28 to Campingplatz.

Drinking

The waterfront Schlachte promenade has a respectably long line of bars catering to all tastes. For either a slightly older, alternative feel or for a student vibe, head to Das Viertel and just walk along Ostertorsteinweg ('O-Weg'). Auf den Höfen, north of O-Weg and also part of Das Viertel, has a good selection of bars. Check listings mags, such as *Prinz* or *Bremen4U* for more details.

TOP CHOICE **Engel Weincafe** BAR, CAFE

(Map p622; www.engelweincafe-bremen.de; Ostertorsteinweg 31; breakfast €4.90-8.60, Flammkuchen €6.70-9.50, cheeses & meats €4-13.30; ⊙8-1am Mon-Fri, 10-1am Sat & Sun; 🔊) Housed in a former pharmacy, this popular hang-out recently morphed into a double act of cafe and wine bar that does good breakfasts and serves cheeses, cold cuts of meat and platters to accompany the fine wines. Breakfast is from 10am to 1pm weekdays and till 3pm weekends.

TOP CHOICE **Wohnzimmer** BAR

(Map p622; www.wohnzimmer-bremen.de; Ostertorsteinweg 99; ⊙from 4pm May-Aug, from 10am Sep-Apr) This bar and lounge mostly gets a relaxed 20s and early 30s crowd, who hang out on the sofas – which explains the name 'Living Room' – or lounge around on the mezzanine levels.

TOP CHOICE **Café Sand** CAFE

(www.cafe-sand.de; Strandweg 106; Pommes & beer €5; ⊙from 10am daily May-Sep, from noon Mon-Sat & from 10am Sun Apr, from noon Fri-Sat & from 10am Sun Feb-Mar & Oct-Nov, closed Dec & Jan) Situated on an island in the Weser River, this cafe makes you feel light years away from the city. In fact, it serves the local swimming holes – the 'golden sands' of the Weser beach in summer, as well as the lake (which you can also swim in), a 10-minute walk inland on the island. Families come here for cake and coffee, but it also kicks on some evenings beyond its usual 6pm closing with events. If that's the case, keep an ear open for the announcement of the last ferry back or you'll have to walk west and cross at Wilhelm-Kaisen-Brücke. The ferry departs near the corner of Osterdeich and Sielwall (return €2.30).

Rotkäppchen CAFE

(Map p622; Am Dobben 97; breakfast €2.90-8.50, lunch menu €5-10, dinner menu €7.50-11.30; ⊙from 9am Mon-Fri, from 10 Sat & Sun; 🔊🍴) Art posters, drawings and even one or two vinyl records adorn the walls and shelves in this student cafe with an art edge; there's a winter garden and in summer outdoor seating. Breakfast on weekends is until 3.30pm.

Studio COCKTAIL BAR, LOUNGE

(Map p622; www.stu-dio.de; Auf den Höfen; ⊙from 7pm Tue-Sat) This venue situated in the small lane known as Auf den Höfen has changed names over the years but the design and concept remain much the same: a favourite bar, lounge and cocktail place among students, with occasional events.

Lagerhaus BAR

(Map p622; www.kulturzentrum-lagerhaus.de; Schildstrasse 12/19; ⊙from 6pm) This once-dilapidated warehouse off Ostertorsteinweg was squatted by young revolutionaries in the 1970s and later became a cultural centre. Although the young revolutionaries grew long in the tooth, the building actually got younger – or rather, was reprieved from the developer's demolition ball and given a facelift –thanks to their efforts. Today it houses a pub with an alternative flavour downstairs and upstairs has a disco with indie, ska, reggae and pop on the second and fourth Saturday of the month (about €3, from 11pm or midnight) for a 20s to 30-something crowd. Concerts and performance art are held here, too.

Bodega Del Puerto BAR

(Map p622; www.bodega-del-puerto.de; ⊙from 5.30pm Tue-Sun) Essentially, the point of the Schlachte is exploration – to walk along it and see which bar you most like the look of. However, this one is the prime choice for a Spanish-style place with decent tapas from €2.80 (mixed tapas €12.80 to €13.80).

Feldmann's Bierhaus PUB

(Map p622; Schlachte 19-20; dishes €4.60-14; ⊙from 11am Mon-Fri, from 10am Sat, from 10.30 Sun) A slightly older crowd can be found chatting and lingering over the wide range of Haake-Beck beers in this modern *Bierhaus* on the Schlachte bar and restaurant drag; it also sells food.

Cafe Tölke CAFE

(Map p622; Schnoor 23a; ⊙10am-7.30pm) This taste of a Viennese coffee house in Bremen will please even the most discerning tipplers

GAY & LESBIAN BREMEN

Bremen's gay scene is, like the city itself, relatively small but friendly. A handful of bars and clubs in the streets An der Weide and its extension Ausser der Schleifmühle make up the main quarter for guys.

Cafe Kweer (Map p622; ☑700 008; www.ratundtat-bremen.de; Theodor-Körner-Strasse 1, Rat & Tat Zentrum; ⏰8pm-midnight Fri, 3pm-6pm Sun) Part of the information centre for gays and lesbians, this place turns into a dance club on Fridays with everything from 1920s sounds to urban lounge. On Sundays it's a place for coffee, cake and a chat, and whenever Werder Bremen plays it shows this soccer match. There are also special events, so check the website.

of the regally roasted bean. Furnishings are original sofas, mirrors and chairs from the Austrian capital, but offering a less stuffy, more Hanseatic interpretation.

☆ Entertainment

Nightclubs

Clubbing in Bremen is relatively cheap; expect to pay €4 to €8 at the door for regular nights, although special events may cost more.

Bremen is a safe town to walk around day or night, but the teenage club mile of Rembertiring, near the main train station, has been a problem zone in recent years. Video cameras and a strong police presence point to its potential for sudden violence. Use big-city sense here.

TOP CHOICE Lila Eule LIVE MUSIC
(Map p622; www.lilaeule.de; Bernhardstrasse 10; ⏰from 8pm) A decade or more is a long time to be a hot tip, but this gem off Sielwall has pulled it off. A student crowd gathers here for parties and events, but it's also a very alternative place to watch the Werder Bremen football team; most Werder matches are shown here. Thursday night is the legendary student bash.

Modernes CLUB
(www.modernes.de; Neustadtwall 28; ⏰Thu-Sat) South of the river in Neustadt, this club converted from an old movie theatre also hosts

live music and remains Bremen's best club, bar none. The centrepiece is the domed roof that can be opened to let in some much-needed air towards the end of the evening. Take tram 4, 5 or 6 to Leibnizplatz.

NFF Cream Club CLUB
(Map p622; www.nffclub.de; Katharinenstrasse 12-14; ⏰Fri & Sat) With a futuristic-looking bar, a chic dance floor and lots of cocktails, Nur Für Freunde (Just for Friends) is the place for house, dance and electro. It's also where famous German and international DJs come to spin tunes.

Theatre & Music

Theater Bremen PERFORMING ARTS
(Map p622; ☑tickets 365 3333; www.bremertheater.com; Goetheplatz 1-3; ⏰11am-6pm Mon-Fri, to 2pm Sat) Bremen's main theatre company performs at several venues. The main theatre, which stages opera, operettas and musicals, is **Theater am Goetheplatz** (Map p622; ☑tel, info 365 30; Goetheplatz), where the famous 1970s film director Rainer Werner Fassbinder honed his craft with the company. In the attached **Neues Schauspielhaus** (Map p622) you'll find new interpretations of classics and avant-garde drama as well as performances of the Dance Theatre of Bremen. The **Brauhauskeller** (Brewery Cellar; Map p622), the smallest venue, is used for anything from Elvis musicals to Edward Albee, while the youth-focused **MOKS** has a venue upstairs in the same former brewery.

Die Glocke CONCERT VENUE
(Map p622; ☑336 699; www.glocke.de; Domsheide) Bremen's concert hall stages classical concerts, opera and a large variety of special events, many by visiting performers, in a venue whose acoustics are considered to be among Europe's very best.

Schlachthof LIVE MUSIC, BAR
(www.schlachthof-bremen.de; Findorffstrasse 51; ⏰bar from 4pm Mon-Sat, from 10am Sun) Ethnic and world-music concerts, theatre, cabaret and variety are all complemented by parties, art exhibitions and a bar. Take bus 25 to Theodor-Heus-Allee.

Theater am Leibnizplatz THEATRE
(☑500 333; www.shakespeare-company.com; Am Leibnizplatz) Here the highly acclaimed Bremer Shakespeare Company mixes the Bard (in German) with fairy tales and contemporary works. Take tram 4, 5 or 6 to Leibnizplatz.

Sport

Weserstadion STADIUM
(ticket hotline 01805-937 337; www.weserstadion.
de; Franz-Böhmert-Strasse 1a) The local Bundesliga team Werder Bremen is less a football
team than a sporting religion. Worship takes
place at the Weserstadion, where a seat costs
€20 to €40. Call the hotline – failing that,
the best thing you can do is go down on your
knees outside the stadium and beg. Take
tram 3 to Weserstadion, or tram 2 or 10 to
St-Jürgen-Strasse, then follow the crowds.

Shopping

Reacquaint yourself with the Brothers
Grimm fairy tale of 'The Town Musicians
of Bremen' via one of the many English-
language editions. Otherwise, the most
obvious buy in Bremen is sweets. Both Böttcherstrasse and the Schnoor Viertel are full
of interesting jewellery, from antique silver
and oodles of amber to modern designer
pieces. Ostertorsteinweg, in Das Viertel, is
the place to look for funky streetwear.

Flea Market MARKET
(www.breminale.de; ☉7am to 3pm Sun) A renowned flea market is held in spring and
summer on Bürgerweide (a short walk north
of Hauptbahnhof) and at the Hansa Carré
at Pfalzburger Strasse 41 other times of year.

Hachez CHOCOLATE
(Map p622; www.hachez.de; Am Markt 1) The local
purveyor of chocolate and specialities such
as *Kluten* (peppermint sticks covered in
dark chocolate).

Information

Bremische Volksbank (Domsheide 14)

ErlebnisCARD (adult incl up to 2 children for
1/2 days €8.90/10.90, group €17.50/22) Free
public transport and discounts on sights;
available from tourist offices.

Moneymaker (Bahnhof; per hr €3; ☉24hr)
Internet access in the northern end of the main
train station.

Police (☑3621; Am Wall 201)

Post Office (Domsheide 15, City Branch;
☉9am-7pm Mon-Fri, 9am-1pm Sat) Along with
a city branch, there's also a **main train station**
(Bahnhofsplatz 21; ☉9.30am-6pm Mon-Fri,
9.30am-1pm Sat) branch.

Schnell & Sauber (Vor dem Steintor 105; per
wash €4.30; ☉6am-11pm) Laundry, just east
of centre.

Tourist Office (☑01805-101 030; www.
bremen-tourism.de) There is a tourist office

in the **city centre** (www.bremen-tourism.
de; Obernstrasse; ☉10am-6.30pm Mon-Fri,
10am-4pm Sat & Sun) near Markt and another
at the **main train station** (☉9am-7pm Mon-Fri,
9.30am-6pm Sat & Sun).

Getting There & Away

AIR Bremen Airport (BRE; www.airport
-bremen.de) is about 3.5km south of the centre
and has flights to destinations in Germany and
Europe. Airline offices here include **Air Berlin**
(www.airberlin.com) and **Lufthansa Airlines**
(www.lufthansa.com). Low-cost carrier
Ryanair (www.ryanair.com) flies to Edinburgh
and London Stansted.

BOAT Hal Över Schreiber Reederei (☑338
989; www.hal-oever.de; Schlachte 2, Martinianleger; ☉office 9am-3pm Mon & Fri, to 5pm
Wed) operates scheduled services along the
Weser between April and September. Boats
from Bremen to Bremerhaven (one way/return
€15/25, 3½ hours), with numerous stops en
route, depart at 8.30am every Tuesday, Wednesday and Saturday, and 9.30am on Sunday during
peak summer months. Children pay half-price.
There are also sailings from Bremen-Vegesack
to Worpswede at 9.45am on Wednesday and
Saturday and at 10.45am on Sunday (one way/
return €19.70/14.70).

BUS Agentur Grajan (☑157 00; Breitenweg
13) at the distance bus departure point sells
Eurolines (☑069-790 3501; www.eurolines.
com) tickets. Regular services run from Bremen
to Amsterdam (one way €32, six hours), London
(one way €76, 12¾ hours), Moscow (€115, 44
hours; Belarus visa required) and other European destinations, departing and arriving from
Breitenweg in front of the Hauptbahnhof. Check
prices and days or exact times online.

CAR & MOTORCYCLE The A1 (from Hamburg
to Osnabrück) and the A27/A7 (Bremerhaven to
Hanover) intersect in Bremen. The city is also
on the B6 and B75. All major car-rental agencies
have branches at the airport, including **Avis**
(☑558 055), **Europcar** (☑557 440),
Hertz (☑555 350) and **Sixt** (☑01805-252 525).

Sixt (☑258 3953; Theodor-Heuss-Allee 6;
☉7am-8pm Mon-Fri, 8am-2pm Sat, noon-6pm
Sun) also has an office just outside the rear exit
train station (on the left).

TRAIN Frequent IC trains go to Hamburg (€26,
one hour), Hanover (€31, one hour) and Cologne
(€63, three hours).

Getting Around

AIRPORT Tram 6 travels between the Hauptbahnhof and the airport (€2.35, 15 minutes). A
taxi (☑144 33, 140 14) from the airport costs
about €15.

LOWER SAXONY & BREMEN BREMEN CITY

BIKE For rental, contact the **Radstation** ([📞]169 0100; www.1-2-3rad.de; per day from €9.50; ⊙8am-10pm Mon-Fri, 9am-8pm Sat & Sun) just outside the Hauptbahnhof (bring your passport).

BUS & TRAM The city's public transport is operated by **Verkehrsverbund Bremen/Niedersachsen** ([📞]01805-826 826; www.bsag.de). Main hubs are in front of the **Hauptbahnhof** and at Domsheide near the Rathaus. A €2.35 single covers most of the Bremen city area (€1.50 for a short trip), while a day pass (Tageskarte) costs €6.50.

Bremerhaven

[📞]0471 / POP 113,400

Anyone who has dreamt of running away to sea will love Bremerhaven's waterfront – part machinery of the trade, part glistening glass buildings pointing to a more recent understanding of its harbour as a recreation spot.

Bremerhaven has long been a conduit that gathered the 'huddled masses' from the verdant but poor countryside and poured them into the world outside. Of the millions who landed at New York's Ellis Island, a large proportion sailed from here, and an enticing exhibition at the German Emigration Centre, the city's prime attraction, allows you to share their history.

The city runs north–south along the eastern bank of the Weser River. For the museums and zoo, get on any bus leaving from in front of the Sparkasse building outside the train station and disembark at the 'Havenwelten' stop, about 1.7km northwest of the train station. The Schaufenster Fischereihafen (fishing harbour) is 2km southwest of the station.

⊙ Sights & Activities

Deutsches Auswandererhaus   MUSEUM
(German Emigration Centre; www.dah-bremerhaven.de; Columbusstrasse 65; adult/concession €11.20/9.50; ⊙10am-6pm) 'Give me your tired, your poor, your huddled masses', invites the Statue of Liberty in New York harbour. Well, Bremerhaven is one place that most certainly did. Millions of those landing at Ellis Island departed from here, and the Deutsches Auswandererhaus now chronicles and commemorates some of their stories.

This is Europe's largest exhibition on emigration, and it does a superb job of conjuring up the experience. For added piquancy, it's located on the very spot where more than seven million people set sail, for the

USA and other parts of the world, between 1830 and 1974.

You relive the stages of the journey and the emigrants' their travelling conditions as you move through the building, clutching the biographical details of one particular traveller. Everything is available in both German and English.

The early sections are especially interesting, so take your time to read and listen to the descriptions. If your forebears moved from Germany to the States, you can start doing research here; some trips must be investigated using the database of the Historisches Museum. Unfortunately, information about emigrants to countries other than the US is sketchier.

Klimahaus Bremerhaven 8° Ost   MUSEUM
(Climate House; www.klimahaus-bremerhaven.de; Am Längengrad 8; adult/concession/family €14/9.50/40; ⊙9am-7pm Mon-Fri, 10am-7pm Sat & Sun) The space-age and sluglike Klimahaus Bremerhaven 8° Ost offers a journey around the world along the 8° east longitude through climate zones in Switzerland (rather on-the-nose due to cow pats), Italy, Niger, Cameroon, Antarctica, Samoa, Alaska and Germany. The displays have an educational aspect and are very much aimed at kids but are enjoyable for adults, too. The temperatures do soar and plummet considerably (Cameroon gets pretty sweaty), so along with sensible shoes to scale Swiss mountains and cross stepping stones and rope bridges in Africa, wear two layers of clothing. Late afternoon is the best time to visit because the queues are shorter; plan about three hours to get the most out of the experience.

Zoo am Meer   ZOO
(www.zoo-am-meer-bremerhaven.de; H-H-Meier-Strasse 6; adult/child €7/4; ⊙9am-7pm) The Zoo am Meer isn't spectacular on the face of things, but it enthrals kids, partly because the enclosures are cleverly built into one big artificial 'rock' formation. They'll see a polar bear (or if he's sleeping, a fluffy pile of fur on a rock), polar foxes, seals, penguins, pumas and chimpanzees. Check the website or ask at the tourist office for feeding times.

Schaufenster Fischereihafen   HARBOUR
Situated a few kilometres south of Bremerhaven's train station, this 'window to the fishing harbour' is, true to its name, a fishing harbour. Today, one of the fish-packaging halls has been converted into fish

GETTING BACK TO THE ROOTS

About 42 million US citizens are descendents of German emigrants, according to the US census of 2000. Each year, says Dr Simone Eick, who heads the German Emigration Centre in Bremerhaven, over 700,000 of these come to Germany. Many will find their way to the centre, which opened its doors to visitors in 2005.

'We kept in mind two things when we started working on the concept of the centre,' Simone Eick explains. 'The theme of migration can be frightening, so we wanted the visitor to get in touch. It's why the visitor can personally accompany an individual emigrant on the journey to the New World. You feel what it was like and become sensitive to the theme.'

Over seven million emigrants left from Bremerhaven between 1830 and 1974, but who were they exactly? They were a wide group, Dr Eick says. In the mid-19th century, many emigrants were looking for land and work. Later emigrants were Jews who came from Eastern Europe, especially Russian Jews escaping pogroms from 1871 until the 1930s. During the Nazi period many were Jewish refugees, who up until 1939 left from Bremerhaven for the USA, Great Britain or other countries.

Until 1900, entering the USA was relatively straightforward for any European, Dr Eick says. 'But after 1900 you had to have money and you couldn't be in ill health. On Ellis Island, if the immigration inspector saw you were disabled, for example, a "C" for "Crippled" was marked on your jacket; after that, you had to return to Europe. The steamship company was forced to pay the passage, so the companies began having their own doctors at the harbours.'

Later, in 1921, a quota act was introduced in the USA. Under a system aimed at regulating the inflow of nationalities, only 3% of the total number of any ethnic group already in America could enter each year. Based on the census of 1910, about eight million Americans born in Germany or of German descent lived in the United States at that time.

Getting *out* of Germany was not always easy either, Dr Eick says. Until 1871 you were not a citizen, you belonged to the German ruler and needed a special release form before you could leave. In the days of sailing ships, the boats could be delayed and passengers had to wait in Bremerhaven – there were no exact departure dates. 'There was a lot of waiting. This was a danger for people. A lot left Bremerhaven without any money at all, having spent it on food and on a hotel. It was tragic.' This situation improved, however, with the introduction of steam shipping and good timetables, she says.

So what about conditions on the boats? 'At the beginning of the 19th century, few German boats left for the US. Most emigrants left on British, French or Belgian ships. These were overcrowded and had no cook on board. Each family cooked for itself, but no one knew how much food they'd need for the journey. Most didn't have enough with them and had no choice but to buy overpriced food from the captain. This was big business for the companies. It's another reason why many emigrants arrived in the USA with nothing.

'In the 1830s, some companies began employing a cook, and in Bremerhaven a law stated that only ships with a cook could depart. Another reason Bremerhaven was very popular among migrants was that in the 1840s a special hotel was built – it was cheap and very good.' Also from the 1840s, she says, the ships got better, because the owners realised they could earn more money from treating migrants well.

As well as offering an experience of what it was like to emigrate from Germany, the German Emigration Centre has databases to help visitors look up their ancestors. Equipped with a surname and year of departure, they can find the ship their ancestors took and begin delving deeper into their German ancestry.

Finally, we asked the head of the emigration centre where in Bremerhaven she likes to go to relax. 'To the wall on the foreshore', she says without hesitating a second. 'It's nice, because we're just two minutes from the river and close to the sea.'

restaurants, bars and small shops. There's also an aquarium and puppet theatre; the on-site tourist office can help with details and bike hire. Take bus 505 or 506 to Schaufenster Fischereihafen.

Deutsches Schiffahrtsmuseum MUSEUM
(German Maritime Museum; www.dsm.museum; Hans-Scharoun-Platz 1; adult/concession €6/4; ☺10am-6pm) A highlight here is the reconstructed *Bremer Hansekogge,* a merchant boat from 1380, reassembled (in part) from pieces rescued from the deep. Some of the boats bobbing on the harbour have additional entrance fees.

Kunstmuseum & Kunsthalle Bremerhaven
(Art Museum & Art Hall; www.kunstverein-bremer haven.de; Karlsburg 1 & 4; combined ticket adult/concession €5/3; ☺11am-6pm Tue-Fri, to 5pm Sat & Sun) The permanent exhibition of paintings focuses on Weser artists; changing exhibitions are staged in the adjacent Kunsthalle. Located just north of the bridge, near the main sights.

Historisches Museum Bremerhaven/ Morgenstern Museum MUSEUM
(Bremerhaven Museum of History; www.historisches -museum-bremerhaven.de; An der Geeste 1; adult/concession €4/3; ☺10am-6pm Tue-Sun) Exhibits on the history and development of the region, as well as temporary exhibitions. An online emigration databank based on passenger lists can be used for searching for ancestors (www.dad-recherche.de). Located just south of the bridge.

Aussichtslattform SAIL City VIEWPOINT
(Viewing Platform SAIL City; Am Strom 1; adult/child €3/2; ☺9am-8.30pm) For a spectacular view over Bremerhaven, go up the new Aussichtslattform SAIL City, part of the Atlantic Hotel SAIL City.

🛏 Sleeping & Eating

Bremerhaven is easy to do on a short trip – not being a nightlife capital of Germany, most people take in the city while based in Bremen.

Atlantic Hotel SAIL City HOTEL $$$
(☎309 900; www.atlantic-hotels.de; Am Strom 1; s/d from €134/168; @🖭) The interiors of this high-rise hotel are tasteful without being ostentatious, and there's a sauna and wellness area with quite good views too. Base prices rise according to demand.

Räucherei Herbert Franke SEAFOOD $$

TOP CHOICE

(Am Pumpwerk 2; small/large baskets €5/15; ☺8am-4.30pm Mon-Fri, to 1pm Sat) Connoisseurs of delicious smoked fish will find an absolute highlight at this family-run place with a long tradition of hand-smoking. Cats will be following you around for days afterwards. Take bus 505 or 506 to Schaufenster Fischereihafen.

Natusch SEAFOOD $$$
(☎710 21; www.natusch.de; Am Fischbahnhof 1; mains €18.50-33.50; ☺lunch & dinner, closed Mon) Located between Fischereihafen I and Fischereihafen II of the fishing harbour, near the Comfort Hotel, this is one of Bremerhaven's best fish restaurants. Take bus 505 or 506 to Schaufenster Fischereihafen.

❶ Information

Tourist Office (☎414 141; www.bremerhaven -tourism.de; H-H-Meier-Strasse 6; ☺8am-6pm) Cross from the bridge behind the Auswandererhaus – it's located inside the building ahead.

Tourist Office Schaufenster Fischereihafen (☎9464 6127; Am Schaufenster 6; ☺10am-5pm) Located at the Fischkai, near the FMS 'Gera' ship. Also rents bicycles (till 5pm on day of rental, €6.50 to €10) as well as e-bikes (per day €25) and Segways (per hour €20).

❶ Getting There & Around

BOAT See Getting There & Away (p631) in Bremen.

BUS The **bus ticket office** (Friedrich-Ebert-Strasse 73 d-f; ☺7am-6pm Mon-Fri, 8am-1pm Sat) located outside Bremerhaven's train station has free maps of town. Within Bremerhaven, single tickets/day passes cost €2.20/6. From the train station, buses 502, 506 and 509 stop at Havenwelten, near the Alter Hafen (Old Harbour) and Neuer Hafen (New Harbour). Buses 505 and 506 go to Schaufenster Fischereihafen, in the other direction.

CAR Bremerhaven is quickly reached via the A27 from Bremen; get off at the Bremerhaven-Mitte exit.

TRAIN Frequent trains connect Bremen and Bremerhaven (€11.30, 45 minutes), but consider buying a Niedersachsen Single ticket (€21) for unlimited day travel.

Worpswede

☎04792 / POP 9400

Worpswede was originally a settlement of turf diggers, but from 1894 an artists' colony was established here by the architects and painters who became associated with Bremen's Böttcherstrasse. Today it is a cute artisans' town that lends itself to mooching around in sunny weather. Outside Germany, the community's most famous member was the poet Rainer Maria Rilke, who dedicated several books to this pretty Niedersachsen village. Other major names involved include Paula Modersohn-Becker and her husband Otto Modersohn, plus the future designer of Böttcherstrasse, Bernhard Hoetger, architect and painter Heinrich Vogeler and, the first to move here, painter Fritz Mackensen.

Today, not only can you visit their buildings and view their art in some seven museums, but you can also shop for porcelain, jewellery, posters, soap made from moor products and other trinkets. Throw in plenty of opportunities to stop for coffee and cakes, enjoy a spa, or go hiking, cycling or canoeing, and Worpswede makes a pleasant outing for anyone.

◎ Sights

Niedersachsenstein   MONUMENT
A highlight of Worpswede is the stroll to the 55m-tall **Weyerberg dune**, less than a kilometre from the centre, where you find the Niedersachsenstein, a contentious sculpture looming like a giant eagle. This is the work of Bernhard Hoetger, the man responsible for much of Bremen's Böttcherstrasse. Follow Lindenallee from the tourist office and then follow the trails off to the right.

Grosse Kunstschau   GALLERY
(www.grosse-kunstschau.de; Lindenallee 5; adult/concession €6/4; ⊙10am-6pm) Designed by Bernhard Hoetger in 1927, this exhibition space is part art deco and part tepee, with a round skylight that complements the wooden floors. Its permanent exhibition is a who's who of the artists' colony, but there is also a regularly changing exhibition, included in the admission. Part of the complex is a **cafe** known locally as Cafe Verrückt (Cafe Crazy; www.kaffee-worpswede.de), with main dishes from €11.50 to €24 (closed Monday and Tuesday).

Barkenhoff   GALLERY
(www.barkenhoff-stiftung.de; Ostendorfer Strasse 10; adult/concession €4/2; ⊙10am-6pm) The creative heart of the Worpswede artists' colony was this half-timbered structure remodelled in the art nouveau style by its owner Heinrich Vogeler. Today it houses the Heinrich-Vogeler-Museum, with paintings and applied arts.

Art Nouveau Train Station   HISTORIC BUILDING
(www.worpsweder-bahnhof.de) This former railway station designed by Heinrich Vogeler today houses a restaurant. The Moor Express train from Bremen stops here.

❶ Information

Tourist Office (☏935 820; www.worpswede. de; Bergstrasse 13; ⊙10am-5pm) Useful information on hotels online and for drop-in visitors if you intend to stay the night.

❶ Getting There & Around

BIKE Fahrradladen Eckhard Eyl (☏2323; Finddorfstrasse 28) hires out bikes from €6 a day. From the tourist office, you can walk there in less than 10 minutes by taking the path between the bank and the Village Hotel am Weyerberg to Finddorfstrasse and going right.

BUS From Bremen's central bus station, bus 670 (€4 one way) makes the 50-minute trip about 20 times a day during the week and every two hours on weekends. See www.fahrplaner. de or check the timetable at the departure point (platform G) in Bremen; ask the driver to drop you near the tourist office ('Insel').

TRAIN The vintage **Moor Express** (☏04761-993 116; www.moorexpress.net; one way adult/child/family €5.50/2.80/12) runs between Worpswede and Bremen (and on to Stade) four times each way every Saturday and Sunday from May to October. First and last services from Worpswede to Bremen are 8.04am and 6.04pm. First and last services to Worpswede from Bremen are 9.08am and 7.08pm. The train station is about 1km north of the tourist office on Bahnhofstrasse (follow Strassentor or Bauernreihe north).

Oldenburg

☏0441 / POP 162,200
Being shuffled between Danish and German rule has left the relaxed capital of the Weser-Ems region with a somewhat difficult-to-pin-down identity. Most of its medieval buildings were destroyed in a huge fire in 1676, while others were later refashioned at various stages according to the prevailing architectural style of the time. Today it's principally a business destination, but it makes a nice day trip from Bremen, or stopover on the way to the East Frisian Islands.

Exit the Hauptbahnhof (Bahnhof Sud) from the 'Stadtmitte' side to reach the centre of town.

◉ Sights

Landesmuseum für Kunst und Kulturgeschichte
MUSEUM

(Museum of Art & Cultural History; www.landesmuseum-oldenburg.niedersachsen.de; Schlossplatz 1; adult/concession incl Augusteum & Prinzenpalais €5/3; ☺10am-6pm Tue-Sun) Housed inside the pale-yellow Renaissance–baroque Schloss (1607) at the southern end of the Altstadt shopping district (on Schlossplatz, just south of the Markt), this museum chronicles the area's history from the Middle Ages. On the 1st floor you'll find the Idyllenzimmer, with 44 paintings by court artist Heinrich Wilhelm Tischbein, a friend of Goethe, which explains why he was often known by his double-banger moniker 'Goethe-Tischbein'.

Augusteum
MUSEUM

(www.landesmuseum-oldenburg.niedersachsen.de; Elisabethstrasse 1; incl in Landesmuseum ticket adult/concession €5/3; ☺10am-6pm Tue-Sun) Part of Oldenburg's Museum of Art & Cultural History, the Augusteum showcases European paintings – with a strong focus on Italian and Dutch masters – from the 16th to the 18th century. The gallery also features changing exhibitions.

Prinzenpalais
MUSEUM

(www.landesmuseum-oldenburg.niedersachsen.de; Damm 1; incl in Landesmuseum ticket adult/concession €5/3; ☺10am-6pm Tue-Sun) One of the three buildings comprising Oldenburg's Museum of Art & Cultural History, this branch focuses on German artists, beginning with Romanticism and neoclassicism of the mid-19th century and culminating in post-1945.

Landesmuseum Natur und Mensch MUSEUM
(Natural History Museum; ☏924 4300; www.naturundmensch.de; Damm 38-44; adult/concession €4/2.50; ☺9am-5pm Tue-Fri, 10am-6pm Sat & Sun) This natural-history museum showcases the ecology of Lower Saxony's landscapes and has a huge chunk (or wall) of peat bog, with niches containing bodies from the Roman period.

⌤ Sleeping & Eating

For eating options, simply cruise along pedestrianised **Wallstrasse**, north of the Markt.

DJH Hostel
HOSTEL $

(☏871 35; http://oldenburg.jugendherbergen-nordwesten.de; Alexanderstrasse 65; dm under/over 27yr €19/23; P⊜) It is highly advisable to book ahead for this large and rambling hostel. It closes at night from 11.30pm till 7am. It's about 20 minutes by foot north of the Hauptbahnhof, or take bus 302, 303 or 322 to Von-Finckh-Strasse.

Hotel Tafelfreuden
HOTEL $$

(☏832 27; www.tafelfreuden-hotel.de; Alexanderstrasse 23; s €66-78, d/apt €104/129; P⊜☎) This interesting hotel takes the theme of colour (and mostly food), with things like 'vanilla', 'chilli' and 'lavender' providing the inspiration for tones. Rooms are mostly a good size, and the atmosphere is chirpy, enhanced by a large glass-enclosed seating area and an outdoor terrace. The menu of the restaurant downstairs also changes considerably, but always offers two meat and two fish mains, plus a vegetarian dish and pastas (mains €12 to €25). Take bus 315 to Humboldtstrasse stop.

ⓘ Information

Post Office (Bahnhofsplatz 10; ☺8am-6pm Mon-Fri, 9am-1pm Sat)

Tourist Office (☏3616 1366; www.oldenburg-tourist.de; Kleine Kirchenstrasse 14; ☺10am-6pm Mon-Fri, to 2pm Sat) Has maps and accommodation guides that are also available from the DB Service Point inside the train station.

ⓘ Getting There & Around

BIKE Fahrrad Station Oldenburg (☏218 8250; Hauptbahnhof; ☺6.30am-8pm Mon-Sat) rents out bicycles for €7 per day and e-bikes for €19. Deposit is €50/100 respectively; bring your passport.

CAR Oldenburg is at the crossroads of the A29 to/from Wilhelmshaven and the A28 (Bremen–Dutch border).

CITY BUS Very many buses, including 315, run to the Landesmuseum on Schlossplatz from Hauptbahnhof. Bus 315 to Am Festungsgraben is the best one for Augusteum and Prinzenpalais; take bus 315, 270 or 280 to Staatsarchive for the Landesmuseum Natur und Mensch. Single bus tickets (valid for one hour) for the entire city cost €2.25 and day passes €6.

TRAIN There are trains at least once an hour to Bremen (€7.70, 30 minutes) and Osnabrück (€21, 1½ hours). From Oldenburg, there are trains north to Emden (€16.40, one hour) and beyond. For Jever, you need to take a bus to Sande and change to train (€11.10, one hour).

Emden & Around

📞 04921 / POP 51,600

You're almost in Holland here, and it shows – from the flat landscape, dikes and windmills outside Emden to the lackadaisical manner in which locals pedal their bikes across the town's canal bridges. The Dutch, as well as Germans, have shaped Emden, and the local Plattdütsch dialect sounds like a combination of English, German and – guess what? – Dutch. While in most senses Emden stoically defies the adjective 'spectacular', the Kunsthalle and Ostfriesisches Landesmuseum (both closed on Mondays, so avoid coming on that day) here and the pretty coastal landscape of its environs do make it worthwhile.

◉ Sights & Activities

The tourist offices have information on canal tours and canoe hire, and can give tips on a favoured East Frisian pasttime, cycling.

TOP CHOICE **Kunsthalle**   GALLERY
(📞 975 050; www.kunsthalle-emden.de; Hinter dem Rahmen 13; adult/concession €8/6; ⊙10am-5pm Tue-Fri, 11am-5pm Sat & Sun) Focusing on 20th-century art, the white-and-exposed-timber, light-flooded rooms of Emden's art gallery show off a range of big, bold canvases. There are some works by Max Beckmann, Erich Heckel, Alex Jawlensky, Oskar Kokoschka, Franz Marc, Emil Nolde and Max Pechstein, although most of the artists are more obscure. Several times a year, the museum closes its doors for a week while exhibitions are changed. Follow the signs from the tourist office.

Ostfriesisches Landesmuseum   MUSEUM
(Regional History Museum; www.landesmuseum -emden.de; Brückstrasse 1, Rathaus; adult/concession €6/free; ⊙10am-6pm Tue-Sun) The award-winning Ostfriesisches Landesmuseum has an interesting and varied collection illustrating themes of local history and life in the region. Not surprisingly, its picture gallery has a strong focus on Dutch artists. In the late 16th century a large number of Protestant Dutch fled to Emden to escape religious persecution in the Spanish-ruled low countries, and ships even set out from Emden, the so-called 'Sea Beggars', to prey on Spanish and Dutch trading vessels. Glass painting established itself here during that time, and later the Emden-born painter Ludolf Backhuysen

returned to work here. Today his work forms the backbone of the picture gallery. Other sections of the museum cover the Frisian coast and cartography, prehistory and 20th-century landscape painting; a highlight is a stunning collection of armour.

Bunkermuseum   MUSEUM
(www.bunkermuseum.de; Holzsägerstrasse; adult/child €2/1; ⊙10am-1pm & 3-5pm Tue-Fri, to 1pm Sat & Sun May-Oct) The labyrinth of WWII civilian air-raid shelters at the Bunkermuseum includes testimonies from those who sheltered here, offering a moving insight into part of recent history.

EMS   BOAT TOUR
(📞 890 70; www.ag-ems.de) Harbour cruises are run by EMS several times daily between early April and late October from the Delfttreppe steps in the harbour (adult/concession €7/5.50). The company also runs services to the East Frisian Island of Borkum and North Frisian Island of Helgoland.

🍽 Sleeping & Eating

The tourist office at the train station is a well-run outfit with a walk-in and advance room-booking service. Options are not abundant, so it pays to use it.

Emden is not really the place for outrageous nights, but if you came here under the delusion it was, then explore Neuer Markt, where you will find a few places to drink.

Hotel am Boltentor   HOTEL $$
(📞 972 70; www.hotel-am-boltentor.de; Hinter dem Rahmen 10; s/d/tr €76/96/120; P) Hidden by trees from the main road nearby and close to the main sights, this homey red-brick hotel has the quietest location in town, plus comfy and well-equipped rooms.

DJH Hostel   HOSTEL $
(📞 237 97; www.jugendherberge.de/jh/emden; An der Kesselschleuse 5, off Thorner Strasse; dm under/over 27yr €22/26; ⊙closed Nov-Feb; P@) Popular with schools and other groups, this hostel has a canal-side location and offers plenty of outdoor opportunities. Take bus 503 to Realschule/Am Herrentor.

Goldener Adler   HOTEL $$
(📞 927 30; www.goldener-adler-emden.de; Neutorstrasse 5; s/d €75/90) Rooms in this no-nonsense hotel are comfortable but tending to small; it is right in the centre of town and on the water.

Carlino Osteria Enoteca
ITALIAN $$

(Alter Markt 9; lunch special €6.50, pizza & pasta €6.50-9.50, meat & fish mains €14.50-20; ⊙lunch & dinner Tue-Sun; ⏵) This highly rated Italian restaurant near the tourist office pavilion offers a respite from traditional fare, with fettuccine with a pork game ragout for €18 complementing mainstays such as a rump steak (€17.50).

❶ Information

There are **tourist offices** at **Pavillon am Stadtgarten** (Pavillon am Stadtgarten; ⊙10am-6pm Mon-Fri, to 2pm Sat) and the **train station** (⏵974 00; www.emden-touristik.de; Bahnhofsplatz 11, Im Bahnhof; ⊙8am-6pm Mon-Fri, 10am-4pm Sat, also 11am-3pm Sun Apr-Oct).

❶ Getting There & Around

Emden is connected by rail to Oldenburg (€16.40, 70 minutes) and Bremen (€23.30, 1¾ hours). Despite its relative remoteness, the town is easily and quickly reached via the A31, which connects with the A28 from Oldenburg and Bremen. The B70/B210 runs north from Emden to other towns in Friesland and to the coast.

Emden is small enough to be explored on foot but also has a bus system (€1.20 per trip). The best transport method is bicycle.

Jever

⏵04461 / POP 13,900

Famous for its pilsner beer, the capital of the Friesland region is also known for 'Fräulein Maria', who peers out from attractions and shop windows in Jever. She was the last of the so-called *Häuptlinge* (chieftains) to rule the town in the Middle Ages, and although Russia's Catherine the Great got her hands on Jever for a time in the 18th century, locals always preferred their home-grown queen. Having died unmarried and a virgin, Maria is the German equivalent of England's (in truth more worldly) Elizabeth I.

With its Russian-looking castle, Jever is worth a brief visit, if only en route to the East Frisian Islands.

⦿ Sights & Activities

Schloss
PALACE

(www.schlossmuseum.de; adult/concession €4.50/2; ⊙10am-6pm Tue-Sun) Looking like a prop from the film *Doctor Zhivago*, the onion-shaped dome is literally the crowning feature of Jever's 14th-century Schloss. The town's 18th-century Russian rulers added it to a building

built by Fräulein Maria's grandfather, chieftain Edo Wiemken the Elder. Today the palace houses the **Kulturhistorische Museum des Jeverlandes**, a mildly diverting cultural-history museum with objects chronicling the daily life and craft of the Frieslanders. The *pièce de résistance* is the magnificent audience hall from 1560, with a carved, coffered oak ceiling of great intricacy. Fräulein Maria retained the Antwerp sculptor Cornelis Floris to create this 80-sq-m Renaissance masterpiece.

Stadtkirche
CHURCH

(http://stadtkirche-jever.de; Am Kirchplatz 13; ⊙8am-6pm) Many of Jever's sights are in some way connected to Fräulein Maria, the last of Jever's chieftains. The most spectacular is in the Stadtkirche, where you'll find the lavish memorial tomb of her father, Edo Wiemken (1468–1511). The tomb is another opus by Cornelis Floris and miraculously survived eight fires. The church itself succumbed to the flames and was rebuilt in a rather modern way; the main nave is opposite the tomb, which is now behind glass.

Blaudruckerei Shop
CRAFT

(www.blaudruckerei.de; Kattrepel 3; ⊙10am-1pm & 2-6pm Mon-Fri, 10am-2pm Sat) An interesting Frisian craft is on show at the Blaudruckerei shop, owned by former teacher Georg Stark who 20 years ago revived the long-lost art and tradition of Blaudruckerei, a printing and dying process whose results vaguely resemble batik.

Friesisches Brauhaus zu Jever
BREWERY TOUR

(⏵137 11; www.jever.de; Elisabethufer 18; tours adult/child €7/2.50; ⊙10am-6pm Mon-Fri, to 2pm Sat) This Friesisches Brauhaus has been producing amber liquid since 1848 and allows visitors a peek behind the scenes. Two-hour weekday tours travel through the brewery's production and bottling facilities, as well as a small museum, whereas 1½-hour Saturday tours only include the museum. Reservations are essential.

🛏 Sleeping & Eating

For a drink and other eating options, the area around Markt has a few decent places.

DJH Hostel
HOSTEL $

(⏵909 202; www.jugendherberge.de/jh/jever; Dr-Fritz-Blume-Weg 4; dm under/over 27yr €26/30; ⊙closed Dec–mid-Jan; 🅿@🛜) Jever's cute *Jugendherberge* is like a little village, with

WALKING TO THE ISLANDS

When the tide recedes on Germany's North Sea coast, it exposes the mudflats connecting the mainland to the East Frisian Islands, and that's when hikers and nature-lovers make their way barefoot to Baltrum and its sister 'isles'. This involves wallowing in mud or wading knee-deep in seawater, but it's one of the most popular outdoor activities in this flat, mountainless region. The Wadden Sea in the Netherlands and Germany became a World Heritage Site in 2009.

Wattwandern, as such trekking through the Wadden Sea National Park is called, can be dangerous as the tide follows channels that will cut you off from the mainland unless you have a guide who knows the tide times and routes. Tourist offices in Jever and Emden can provide details of state-approved ones, including **Martin Rieken** (☑04941-8260; www.wattfuehrer-rieken.de) and **Johann Behrends** (☑04944-913 875; www.wattwandern-johann.de). Or call **Strandkasse Schillig** (☑04426-987 174), a central office in Schillig for organising hikes on the Wadden Sea, and they can help you find a guide. Schillig is best reached from Jever by regular bus or Rufbus (call-on-demand bus) 212 (€4.30, 30 minutes) from Jever's bus station/Hauptbahnhof. For a Rufbus, call ☑04461-912 298. The tourist office in Jever can help you with planning.

Coastal tours cost from €7 to €10, but if a ferry is needed for one leg of the trip, count on paying about €25. Necessary gear includes shorts or short trousers and possibly socks or trainers (although many guides recommend going barefoot). In winter, wet weather footwear is necessary.

a series of green and red-brick bungalows grouped around the reception. Dorms are clean, modern and comfortable.

Am Elisabethufer
HOTEL **$**

(☑949 640; www.jever-hotel-pension.de; Elisabethufer 9a; s/d €48/80; P@☎) Frilly lampshades, floral duvet covers and an assortment of knick-knacks are par for the course in Jever's *Pensionen,* and exactly what you'll find in this attractive and comfortable place with free internet (using an adapter in the power socket) and wi-fi in all rooms. From the tourist office, it's a short walk north along Von-Thünen-Ufer.

Im Schützenhof
HOTEL **$$**

(☑9370; www.schuetzenhof-jever.de; Schützenhofstrasse 47; s/d €64/94; P☎) This hotel, a 10-minute walk south (away from the centre) of the train station, has comfortable modern rooms and a wellness area with Finnish sauna and steam bath. It's favoured for local celebrations because of its excellent restaurant, Zitronengras (mains €12.50 to €24.50).

Haus der Getreuen
GERMAN **$**

(☑748 5949; www.hausdergetreuen.de; Schlachtstrasse 1; mains €9.80-22.50; ☺lunch & dinner) With a historic dining room and outside seating, Haus der Getreuen is well known for its good regional dishes, especially fish.

ⓘ Information

Tourist Office (☑710 10; www.stadt-jever.de; Alter Markt 18; ☺9am-6pm Mon-Fri, to 1pm Sat)

ⓘ Getting There & Around

The train trip to Jever from Bremen (€19.20, 1¾ hours) involves at least one change, in Sande, and sometimes one in Oldenburg too. By road, take the exit to the B210 from the A29 (direction: Wilhelmshaven).

Jever is small enough to explore on foot.

East Frisian Islands

Trying to remember the sequence of the seven East Frisian Islands, Germans – with a wink of the eye – recite the following mnemonic device: '*Welcher Seemann liegt bei Nanni im Bett?*' (which translates rather saucily as 'Which seaman is lying in bed with Nanni?').

Lined up in an archipelago off the coast of Lower Saxony like diamonds in a tiara, the islands are (east to west): Wangerooge, Spiekeroog, Langeoog, Baltrum, Norderney, Juist and Borkum. Their long sandy beaches, open spaces and sea air make them both a nature-lovers' paradise and a perfect retreat for those escaping the stresses of the world. Like their North Frisian cousins Sylt, Amrum and Föhr, the islands are part of the Wadden Sea (Wattenmeer) National Park.

RESORT TAX

Each of the East Frisian Islands charges a *Kurtaxe* (resort tax), entitling you to entry onto the beach and offering small discounts for museums etc. It's a small amount, typically €3.50 a day, and if you're staying overnight it's simply added to your hotel bill. Remind your hotel to give you your pass should they forget.

Along with coastal areas of the Netherlands, Germany's Wadden Sea is a Unesco World Heritage Site.

The main season runs from mid-May to September. Beware, however, that the opening hours of tourist offices in coastal towns change frequently and without notice. Call ahead if possible.

❶ Getting There & Away

Most ferries sail according to tide times, rather than on a regular schedule, so it's best to call the local ferry operator or **Deutsche Bahn** (DB; www. bahn.de/nordseeinseln) for information on departure times on a certain day. Tickets are generally offered either as returns – sometimes valid for up to two months – or cheaper same-day returns.

In most cases (apart from Borkum, Norderney and Juist), you will need to change from the train to a bus at some point to reach the harbour from where the ferry leaves. Sometimes those are shuttle buses operated by the ferry company, or scheduled services from **Weser-Ems Bus** (☑04921-974 00; www.weser-ems-bus.de). For more details, see Getting There & Away for each island. For planning bus connections from Norden and Esens to ferry harbours, the tourist office in Emden has useful information on transport.

Light aircraft also fly to every island except Spiekeroog. Contact **Luftverkehr Friesland Harle** (☑04464-948 10; www.inselflieger.de).

❶ Getting Around

Only Borkum and Norderney allow cars, so heading elsewhere means you'll need to leave your vehicle in a car park near the ferry pier (about €3.50 per 12 hours).

WANGEROOGE

The second-smallest of the East Frisian Islands – after Baltrum – is inhabited by just under 1000 people and is the easternmost of the group, lying about 7km off the coast in the region north of Jever. While crunching sand between your toes and watching huge tanker ships lumber past on their way to and from the ports at Bremerhaven, Hamburg and Wilhelmshaven, it's easy to feel like a willing castaway here.

Two good sources of information are the **Kurverwaltung** (Spa Administration; ☑04469-990; www.wangerooge.de; Strandpromenade 3; ⊙9am-3pm Mon-Fri, to noon Sat & Sun) and **Verkehrsverein** (☑04469-948 80; www.westturm.de; Hauptbahnhof; ⊙9am-5pm Mon-Fri, to noon Sat), which handle room reservations as well.

If you're feeling active you can climb the 161 steps of Wangerooge's 39m-tall **lighthouse** (www.leuchtturm-wangerooge.de; adult/child €2/1; ⊙10am-1pm & 2-5pm Mon-Wed, 10am-1pm Thu, 10am-noon & 2-5pm Fri-Sun) from 1855, take to the seawater adventure pool or indulge in a long list of sports activities. For more of a learning experience, head to the **Nationalparkhaus**. (www.nationalparkhaus-wangerooge.de; Friedrich-August-Strasse 18; ⊙9am-6pm Mon-Fri, 10am-noon & 2-5pm Sat & Sun)

❶ Getting There & Away

The ferry to Wangerooge leaves from Harlesiel two to five times daily (1½ hours), depending on the tides. An open return ticket costs €30.90 (two-month time limit), and a one-way ticket is €18.50. This includes the tram shuttle to the village on the island (4km). Large pieces of luggage are an extra €3.10 each, and a bike €11.30 each way. The ferry is operated by **DB** (☑in Harlesiel 04464-949 411, on Wangerooge 04469-947 411; www.siw-wangerooge.de).

To reach Harlesiel, take bus 211 from Jever train/bus station (€3.30, 40 minutes).

SPIEKEROOG

Rolling dunes dominate the landscape of minuscule Spiekeroog; about two-thirds of its 17.4 sq km is taken up by these sandy hills. It's the tranquillity of this rustic island that draws people, although you can distract yourself with the **Pferdebahn** (adult/child return €3/2; ⊙departs 10am, 10.45am, 3pm & 3.45pm Mon-Fri, 2pm or 2.30pm Sun Apr-Sep), a horse-drawn train that runs on rails and dates back to 1885. There are also plenty of baths for swimming.

The **tourist office** (☑04976-919 3101; www.spiekeroog.de; ⊙9am-12.30pm & 2-5pm Mon-Fri, 9am-12.30pm Sat & Sun) is in the 'Haus Kogge', where there's also a **Mussel Museum** (admission €1; ⊙9am-12.30pm & 2-5pm Mon-Fri, 9am-12.30pm Sat & Sun) with more than 3000 shells of all varieties.

Spiekeroog is not only car-free but discourages bicycles too.

ⓘ Getting There & Away

From the ferry departure point in Neuharlingersiel, it takes 40 to 55 minutes to reach Spiekeroog. Ferry times depend on the tides, so same-day returns aren't always possible. Prices are €13.80 each way or €19.50 for same-day return tickets. Three pieces of luggage per person are carried free of charge. In Neuharlingersiel call ☎04974-214 for ticket information; on Spiekeroog call ☎04976-919 3133. The Spiekeroog Express water taxi does the trip in 15 minutes (one way €25); call ☎0171/892 3992 or send an email to express@spiekeroog.de.

From Jever, catch a train to Esens and change to bus to Neuharlingersiel (€9.60, 50 minutes). From Emden, take a train to Norden and change there for a bus to Neuharlingersiel (€16.60, 1¾ hours). Check connections on www.bahn.de before setting out.

LANGEOOG

Floods and pirates make up the story of Langeoog, whose population was reduced to a grand total of two following a horrendous storm in 1721. By 1830 it had recovered sufficiently to become a resort town.

The island boasts the highest elevation in East Frisia – the 20m-high Melkhörndüne – and the grave of Lale Anderson, famous for being the first singer to record the WWII song 'Lili Marleen'. Nautical tradition is showcased in the **Schiffahrtsmuseum** (Haus der Insel; adult/concession €2.50/1.50; ⊗10am-noon & 3-5pm Mon-Thu, 10am-noon Fri Easter-Oct). You can also visit the Langeoog's symbol, the **water tower** (adult €1; ⊗10am-noon Mon-Fri Easter-Oct), which has an exhibition on drinking water on the ground floor. On a sunny day, however, the most popular thing to do is to stroll along the 14km-long **beach**.

Langeoog's **tourist office** (☎04972-6930; www.langeoog.de; Hauptstrasse 28; ⊗9am-noon & 2-5pm Mon-Thu, 9am-noon Fri) is in the Rathaus, while **room reservations** (☎04972-693 201; zimmernachweis@langeoog.de; ⊗9am-noon & 2-5pm Mon-Thu, 9am-noon Fri) can be dealt with on the 1st floor of the island's 'train station'.

ⓘ Getting There & Away

The ferry shuttles between Bensersiel and Langeoog at least five times daily. The trip takes about one hour and costs €24 return. Luggage is €3 per piece; bikes are not carried. For details, call ☎04971-928 90 or see www.schiffahrt-langeoog.de (in German).

From Jever, take the train to Esens and change to bus for Bensersiel (€8.90, 40 minutes). From Emden, take the train to Norden and change to bus for Bensersiel (€13, 1½ hours). Check connections on www.bahn.de before setting out.

BALTRUM

The smallest inhabited East Frisian Island, Baltrum is just 1km wide and 5km long, and peppered with dunes and salty marshland. It's so tiny that villagers don't bother with street names but make do with house numbers instead. Numbers have been allocated on a chronological basis; houses No 1 to 4 no longer exist so the oldest is now No 5.

There's little to do except go on walks or go to the beach, or visit the exhibition on the **Nationalpark Haus-Gezeitenhaus** (National Park House-Tide House; house 177; ⊗10am-noon & 3-7pm Tue-Fri, 3-7pm Sat & Sun). As the island closest to the mainland, Baltrum is the most popular destination for *Wattwanderungen* guided tours.

The **Kurverwaltung** (☎04939-800; www.baltrum.de; house No 130; ⊗9am-noon & 3-5pm Mon-Fri, 10am-noon Sat) can provide information.

SLOW TRAVEL IN EAST FRISIA

One of the pleasures of travelling around East Frisia is that – intentionally or not – you can really slow down and enjoy the ride. A good way of taking advantage of the bike paths and waterways is by using the so-called **Paddel und Pedal stations** (www.paddel-und-pedal.de). These allow you to combine kayaking or Canadian canoe paddling with cycling, using some of the 21 stations scattered around the countryside. You can paddle to one, hire another kayak there, or switch to bicycle, choose your next destination/station and set off again. To give just one of many options, from **Emden** (Paddel- und Pedalstation Emden; ☎04921-890 7219, 0160-369 2739; Marienwehrster Zwinger 13) you can hire a single kayak (€15), paddle about 11km (three hours) to the quarry lake **Grosses Meer** (Paddel- und Pedalstation Grosses Meer; ☎04942-576 838; Langer Weg 25, in Südbrookmerland), which is in parts a nature reserve, then change to a bicycle (€7 per day) and ride back, or deeper into East Frisia. Local tourist offices can help if you need planning or language help.

The room reservation service (☎04931-938 3400; in Norden; ⏰8am-8pm Mon-Fri, 10am-6pm Sat & Sun) can help with accommodation, or see www.zimmervermittlung-baltrum.de (in German).

ⓘ Getting There & Away

Ferries (and *Wattwanderungen*) leave from Nessmersiel. Ferries take 30 minutes. Departures depend on the tides, which means day trips aren't always possible. Tickets are €14 one way or €19/26 for a same-day/open return. Bikes cost €7 each way and luggage is usually free. More details are available from **Baltrum Linie** (☎Baltrum 04939-91 300, Nessmersiel 04933-99 1606; www.baltrum-linie.de).

From Emden, take a train to Norden and change to a bus to Nessmersiel (€3.60, 45 minutes).

NORDERNEY

'Queen of the East Frisian Islands', Norderney was Germany's first North Sea resort. Founded in 1797 by Friedrich Wilhelm II of Prussia, it became one of the most famous bathing destinations in Europe, after Crown Prince Georg V of Hanover made it his summer residence, and personalities such as Chancellor Otto von Bismarck and composer Robert Schumann visited in the 19th century.

Now 'Lüttje Welt' – 'Little World', as the 5800 islanders call Norderney for the way fog makes it seem like it's the only place on earth – is complementing its image of tradition and history with some decidedly modern touches. Its wonderful art-deco **Kurtheater** was built as a private theatre in 1893 but with the advent of film it morphed gradually from 1923 into a cinema, which is what it is mainly used for today. Another gem is the neoclassical **Conversationshaus** (1840), which today houses the tourist office.

The jewel in the crown is indisputably the Bade:haus (www.badehaus-norderney.de; Am Kurplatz 3; pool/sauna per 4hr €17/24; ⏰9.30am-9.30pm, women only from 2pm Wed), in the former art-nouveau seawater baths. This sleek stone-and-glass complex is now an enormous thalassotherapy centre, with warm and cold swimming pools, a rooftop sauna with views over the island, relaxation areas where you can lie back on lounges and drink Frisian tea, and much more – all split between the 'Wasserebene' (Water Level), where you can bathe in the pools or bob around in the wave pool, and the 'Feuerebene' (Fire Level) zone for saunas.

Norderney's tourist office (☎04932-891 900, room reservations 04932-891 300; Conversationshaus – Am Kurplatz 1; ⏰9am-6pm Mon-Fri, 10am-1pm Sat, 11am-1pm Sun) can provide more details or book rooms. A harbour service centre (Ferry Harbour; ⏰6am-6pm) has information but no room-booking service.

The Nationalpark-Haus (☎04932-2001; www.nationalparkhaus-norderney.de; Am Hafen 1; admission free; ⏰9am-6pm Tue-Sun), directly on the harbour, has a small exhibition and regularly offers walks into the Wadden Sea from €4. Dates and times are published on the website during the summer season.

ⓘ Getting There & Away

To get to Norderney you have to catch the ferry in Norddeich. **Reederei Frisia** (☎04931-9870; www.reederei-frisia.de; adult return €19, bikes €9) leaves Norddeich every one to two hours, roughly from 6am to 6pm daily (later some days in summer). The journey takes 50 minutes and any DB office can provide details.

There are trains (€9.70 35 minutes) from Emden to Norddeich Mole, the ferry landing stage.

JUIST

Juist, shaped like a snake, is 17km long and only 500m wide. The only ways to travel are by bike, horse-drawn carriage or on your own two feet. Here, you're often alone with the screeching seagulls, the wild sea and the howling winds. Forest, brambles and elderberry bushes blanket large sections of the island.

One peculiarity of Juist is the idyllic **Hammersee** – a bird sanctuary and the only freshwater lake on all the islands (no swimming). In 1651 Juist was torn in two by a storm tide, but in the early 20th century it was decided to close off the channel with dunes, eventually creating a freshwater lake. There's also the Juister Küstenmuseum (Coastal Museum; www.kuestenmuseum-juist.de; Loogster Pad 29; adult/child €2.50/1.50; ⏰9.30am-1pm & 2.30-5pm Tue-Fri, 9.30am-1pm Sat, 2.30-5pm Sun).

Juist's main tourist office (☎04935-809 107; www.juist.de; Strandstrasse 5; ⏰9am-12.30pm & 2.30-6pm Mon-Fri, 9am-12.30pm Sat, 10am-12.30pm Sun) is in the Rathaus. Someone also meets all ferry arrivals, regardless of time. It also has a room-reservation service (☎04935-809 222).

ⓘ Getting There & Away

Reederei Frisia (☎04931-9870; www.reederei-frisia.de) operates the ferries from Norddeich to Juist (adult day/normal return €22/32.50,

1½ hours); children pay half-price and bikes cost €13 return. You can also ask any DB office for details.

Trains from Emden (€9.70, 35 minutes) travel straight to the landing dock in Norddeich Mole.

BORKUM

The largest of the East Frisian Islands – once even larger before it was ripped apart by a flood in the 12th century – has a tough seafaring and whaling history. Reminders of those frontier times are the whalebones that you'll occasionally see, stacked up side by side, or as unusual garden fences. In 1830, however, locals realised that reinventing itself as a 'seaside' resort was a safer way to earn a living, and today many of the island's 5500 inhabitants are involved in the tourism industry in one way or another.

To learn about the whaling era and other stages in the life of Borkum, visit the Heimatmuseum (Local History Museum; ☎04922-4860; museum adult/child €3/1.50; lighthouse €1.50; ☺10am-5pm Tue-Sun Apr-Oct, 3-5pm Tue & Sat Nov-Mar) at the foot of the old lighthouse. Also of interest is the museum fire ship Borkumriff (www.feuerschiff-borkumriff.de; Am Nordufer; admission adult/child €3/2, with tour adult/child €4/2; ☺9.45am-5.45pm Tue-Sun, tours 10.45am, 11.45am, 1.45pm & 2.45pm), with its exhibition on the Wadden Sea National Park.

The tourist office (☎04922-9330; www.borkum.de; Am Georg-Schütte-Platz 5; ☺9am-5pm Mon-Fri, 10am-1pm Sat & Sun) also handles room reservations.

ⓘ Getting There & Away

All-year boats depart twice to six times daily to/from Emden for Borkum. AG-Ems (☎01805-180 182; www.ag-ems.de) runs car ferries (adult same-day/open return €18.40/35, two to three hours). Bike transport costs €12.50 return. AG-Ems also has faster catamarans (€28.80/57, one hour); bikes aren't transported. Transporting a car on the ferry costs from €72.90 to €159 return (depending on size).

Hamburg & the North

Best Places to Eat

» Sgroi (p22)

» Matsumi (p663)

» Schiffergesellschaft
(p678)

» Restaurant Esszimmer
(p708)

Best Places to
Stay

» Hotel Wedina (p660)

» Kamps (p690)

» Hotel Reingard (p704)

» Altstadt Hotel Peiss
(p707)

Why Go?

Head to Germany's north because you love the water. From
the posh joy of Sylt in the west to the fabled Baltic heritage
of historic towns like Lübeck, Wismar, Stralsund and Greifswald. Here you can sense the legacy of the Hanseatic
League in beautiful old quarters created with iconic black
and red bricks.

Even inland there is water. Mecklenburg's lakes are a
maze of places to paddle. But really, most visitors will be
happiest right at the edge of the sea. There are beaches
everywhere, and while the temps aren't tropical, the drama
of the crisp sea crashing onto the white sand is irresistible.

Finally there is Hamburg, a city with a love of life that
explodes in its fabled clubs. Here, being close to the water
has not only built the city and its harbour but continues to
invigorate it today.

When to Go

Summer seems the obvious time to hit northern Germany
but let's be honest, just because it's August doesn't mean
you won't be wrapped up in a blanket on a Baltic beach. So
free yourself from bikini-clad fantasies and go to the coast
anytime to enjoy its often breathtaking beauty.

The best reason to go in summer is for the days that go
on and on and on. Sitting outside a Hamburg cafe and enjoying the passing pedestrian parade in daylight at 10pm is
a delight.

Smokin' Fish

It can be almost sensuous, the smooth and oily fillets of northern fish that are smoked for hours until they have tangy, buttery softness that melts in your mouth. No wonder people love it. Here are some good places:

» **Hamburg** There's smoked fish by the ton at Hamburg's Sunday Fischmarkt (p23) or order some house-smoked eel at Alt Hamburger Aalspeicher (p663).

» **Sylt** Just saying 'Gosch' (p690) brings knowing nods of satisfaction from those who've had this seafood legend's smoked fish in its many varieties.

» **Wismar** Ancient techniques dating to Hanseatic times make the young smoked eel here especially succulent (p703).

» **Binz** Just follow your nose to the glorified beach hut, Fischräucherei Kuse (p711).

» **Stralsund** The harbour (p705) is ringed with boats smoking fish for sale.

» **Wieck** Right at the sea, this tiny town has some excellent smoked-fish stands and Fischer-Hütte (p714) specialises in smoked herring.

DON'T MISS

In Hamburg you can have a dramatic contrast of experiences within a 10-minute walk: at **St Michaeliskirche** you can see the horrible cost of war, at the **International Maritime Museum** you can find out what made the city what it is today and finally you can just be a kid at **Miniatur-Wunderland**.

There's more fun at **Lübeck's puppet theatre** and its puppet museum. Get out on the open water with a ferry ride between the **North Frisian Islands**.

Back on land, the number of bricks that built the beautiful **Bad Doberan** is impossible to comprehend. Further along the coast, scale the spiralling staircase of **Warnemünde's 19th-century lighthouse** or choose fresh fish for a picnic from the boats in **Wismar's harbour**.

Enjoy fish without eating them at the vast aquariums at **Stralsund's Ozeaneum**. Head out to the boonies of **Usedom Island** to find a trail to call your own.

Regional Train Passes

The **Schleswig-Holstein ticket** (€26) is good for rail journeys from 9am until 3am the following day (from midnight on weekends) anywhere in Hamburg and Schleswig-Holstein.

The **Mecklenburg-Vorpommern ticket** (single/group up to 5 people €18/26) is good for rail journeys from 9am until 3am the following day (from midnight on weekends) in Hamburg and the state of Mecklenburg-Western Pomerania, which stretches along the northern coast and includes Schwerin, Stralsund and Usedom Island.

STRANDKORB

Only a country with a love of engineering would invent the *Strandkorb*, the iconic German wicker beach chair complete with its own roof and awning to deflect seaside breezes.

Fast Facts

Combined totals for Hamburg, Schleswig-Holstein and Mecklenburg-Western Pomerania:

» Area: 39,728 sq km
» Population: 6.2 million

Beaches

» **Sylt** Almost the entire island is ringed in beautiful sand perfect for hiking or just lazing (p688).

» **Amrum** Mellow island that's half sand (p692).

» **Warnemünde** Fabled pearly white strand with a hopping scene at night (p701).

» **Göhren** Ride a steam train to reach the beach on Rügen Island (p711).

Resources

» Hamburg Tourismus (www.hamburg-tourismus.de)

» Schleswig-Holstein (www.sh-tourismus.de)

» Mecklenburg-Western Pomerania (www.mecklenburg-vorpommern.eu)

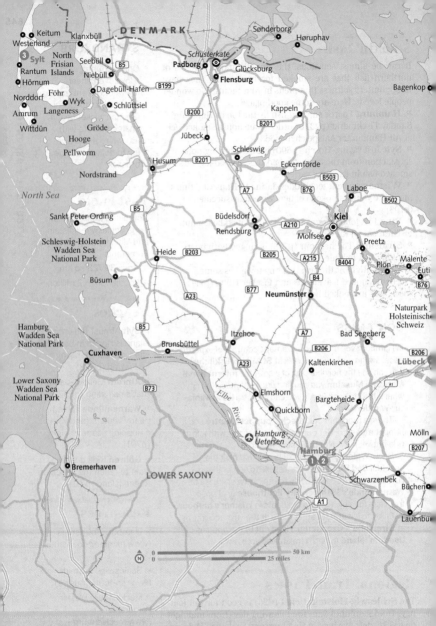

Hamburg & the North Highlights

1 The Beatles did it, you can too: have a hard day's night in **Hamburg's innumerable places of pleasure** (p667), no matter what your taste

2 A world of enormous ships awaits on a **Hamburg harbour tour** (p659)

3 Windsurf off **Sylt's North Sea coast** (p688), which draws top competitors from around the world

4 Don't overlook Lübeck's icon, the **Holstentor** (p32), which has centuries etched in its slumping bricks

5 Dip your oars in the peaceful waterways of **Müritz National**

Park (p698) on a paddle-and-camp trip amidst this marvellous maze of waterways

6 Tour **Schwerin's beautiful palace** (p693) and then explore this picturesque town

7 Try to get lost – you can't – in old **Stralsund** (p705), which gets more intriguing every year

HAMBURG

☎040 / POP 1.8 MILLION

'The gateway to the world' might be a bold claim, but Germany's second-largest city and biggest port has never been shy. Hamburg has engaged in business with the world ever since it joined the Hanseatic League trading bloc back in the Middle Ages, and this 'harbourpolis' is now the nation's premier media hub and its wealthiest city.

Hamburg's maritime spirit infuses the entire city; from architecture to menus to the cry of gulls, you always know you're near the water. The city has given rise to vibrant neighbourhoods awash with multicultural eateries, as well as the gloriously seedy Reeperbahn red-light district. Hamburg nurtured the early promise of the Beatles, and today its distinctive live- and electronic-music scene thrives in unique harbourside venues. Its attractions are only matched by its inherent alluring spirit. Come, Hamburg says, have a ball.

History

Dubbed the world's 'most mercantile city', Hamburg's commercial character was forged in 1189, when local noble Count Adolf III persuaded Emperor Friedrich I (Barbarossa) to grant the city free trading rights and an exemption from customs duties. This transformed the former missionary settlement and 9th-century moated fortress of Hammaburg into an important port and member of the Hanseatic League.

The city prospered until 1842, when the Great Fire destroyed a third of its buildings. While it managed to recover in time to join the German Reich in 1871, this then saw it involved in two devastating world wars. After WWI, most of Hamburg's merchant fleet (almost 1500 ships) was forfeited to the Allies. WWII saw more than half of Hamburg's housing, 80% of its port and 40% of its industry reduced to rubble; tens of thousands of civilians were killed.

In the postwar years, Hamburg harnessed its resilience to participate in Germany's economic miracle *(Wirtschaftswunder)*. Its harbour and media industries are now the backbone of its wealth. The majority of Germany's largest publications are produced here, including news magazines *Stern* and *Der Spiegel*.

Sights & Activities

To really see and explore Hamburg, count on spending at least three days prowling its neighbourhoods, waterfront, museums, shops and more.

ALTSTADT

The centre of old Hamburg is also the centre of the modern city. Largely reconstructed, the city's age-old wealth is apparent as you stroll among its most important civic and commercial institutions. In Hanseatic times this was where you found the rich merchants and their businesses along the canals.

Rathaus HISTORIC BUILDING

(Map p650; ☎428 312 010; tours adult/child €3/0.50; 🕐English-language tours hourly 10.15am-3.15pm Mon-Thu, to 1.15pm Fri, to 5.15pm Sat, to 4.15pm Sun; [S]Rathausmarkt or Jungfernstieg) Hamburg's baroque Rathaus is one of Europe's most opulent, renowned for the Emperor's Hall and the Great Hall, with its spectacular coffered ceiling. There are no fewer than 647 rooms here, but the guided 40-minute tours only take in a small number.

Chilehaus HISTORIC BUILDING

(Map p650; cnr Burchardstrasse & Johanniswall; [S]Mönckebergstrasse/Messberg) One of the city's most remarkable buildings lies to the south in the Merchant's District. The brown-brick Chilehaus is shaped like an ocean liner, with remarkable curved walls meeting in the shape of a ship's bow and staggered balconies that look like decks. Designed by architect Fritz Höger for a merchant who derived his wealth from trading with Chile, the 1924 building is a leading example of German expressionist architecture. It's situated alongside other so-called 'Backsteingotik' buildings (*Backstein* refers to a specially glazed brick; *gotik* means 'Gothic').

Deichstrasse STREET

(Map p650) Hamburg's Great Fire of 1842 broke out in Deichstrasse, which features a few restored 18th-century homes, most now housing restaurants. You can get a feel for the old canal and merchants quarter here.

Hamburger Kunsthalle MUSEUM

(Map p650; ☎428 131 200; www.hamburger-kunsthalle.de; Glockengiesserwall; adult/child €10/free; 🕐10am-6pm Tue, Wed & Fri-Sun, to 9pm Thu; [R]Hauptbahnhof) At the eastern edge of the Altstadt, near the Hauptbahnhof and St

HAMBURG'S NEIGHBOURHOODS

Hamburg is as watery as Venice and Amsterdam. Set around two lakes, the Binnenalster and Aussenalster (Inner and Outer Alster Lakes), in the city centre, it's also traversed by three rivers – the Elbe, the Alster and the Bille – and a grid of narrow canals called *Fleete*.

The half-moon-shaped city centre arches north of the Elbe and is bisected diagonally by the Alsterfleet, the canal that once separated the now almost seamless Altstadt (old town) and Neustadt (new town).

Within the sprawling city are distinct neighbourhoods, which include:

» **Altstadt** The biggest churches, museums and department stores.

» **Neustadt** Leafier and less corporate-office-filled than the Altstadt, although still very much part of the centre.

» **St Georg** East of the Hauptbahnhof; gentrified and the hub of the city's gay scene.

» **Speicherstadt & HafenCity** The former is an atmospheric restored warehouse district with interesting attractions, the latter is a new city being built from scratch.

» **Port Area** Just what the name implies, the city's front porch, with views of passing ships and myriad attractions.

» **St Pauli** Includes the notorious Reeperbahn strip of sin, frolic and amusement plus leafier quarters and port-area views.

» **Schanzenviertel & Karolinenviertel** North of St Pauli and home to old hippies, young Goths and Hamburg's most creative and alternative scene.

» **Altona & Elbmeile** The former is gentrified and merges with the waterfront of the latter. The family-filled neighbourhood of Ottensen abuts on the west.

» **Blankenese** Some 8km west of Altona, a wealthy enclave with narrow historic streets and sweeping views of the Elbe.

Georg neighbourhood, are some of the city's best museums. A treasure trove of art from the Renaissance to the present day, the Kunsthalle spans two buildings – one old, one new – linked by an underground passage. The main building houses works ranging from medieval portraiture to 20th-century classics, such as Klee and Kokoschka. There's also a memorable room of 19th-century landscapes by Caspar David Friedrich. Its stark white modern building, the **Galerie der Gegenwart**, showcases contemporary German artists, including Rebecca Horn, Georg Baselitz and Gerhard Richter, alongside international stars, including David Hockney, Jeff Koons and Barbara Kruger. The view out of the gallery's huge picture windows is also worthy of framing.

Museum für Kunst und Gewerbe   MUSEUM
(Museum for Art & Trade; Map p650; 428 542 732; www.mkg-hamburg.de; Steintorplatz 1; adult/child €8/free; 11am-6pm Tue & Fri-Sun, to 9pm Wed & Thu; Hauptbahnhof) This museum is lots of fun. Its vast collection of sculpture, furniture, fashion, jewellery, posters, porcelain, musical instruments and household objects

runs the gamut from Italian to Islamic, Japanese to Viennese and medieval to pop art, and includes an art-nouveau salon from the 1900 Paris World Fair. The museum cafe is integrated into the exhibition space.

Kunstmeile   MUSEUM DISTRICT
(www.kunstmeile-hamburg.de; Steinstrasse) Watch for special exhibitions in the museums along Hamburg's Kunstmeile, extending from Glockengiesserwall to Deichtorstrasse between the Alster Lakes and the Elbe. Here you'll find exhibitions such as contemporary art and photography in the converted market halls of the **Deichtorhallen** (Map p650; 321 030; Deichtorstrasse 1-2; adult/child €9/free; 11am-6pm Tue-Sun; Steinstrasse).

NEUSTADT

The Neustadt blends seamlessly with the Altstadt in the posh surrounds of the Binnenalster. The style is set by the elegant Renaissance-style arcades of the **Alsterarkaden** (Map p650), which shelter upscale shops and cafes alongside the Alsterfleet canal. This is ground zero for Hamburg's ladies who lunch. Further south, the district blends into the heart of the port area.

Central Hamburg

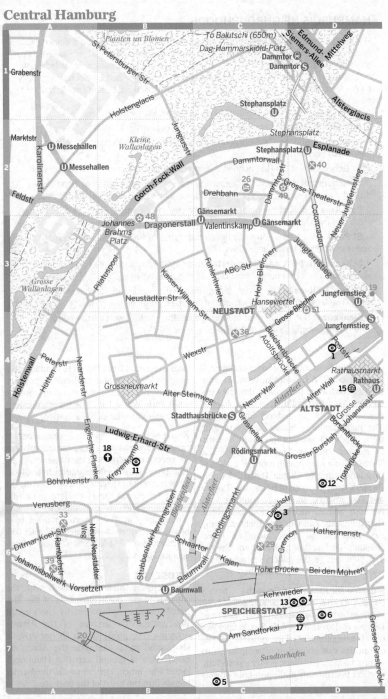

Grabenstr

St Petersburger Str

To Balutschi (650m)
Dag-Hammarskjöld-Platz
Edmund-Siemers-Allee
Mittelweg
Dammtor
Dammtor

Planten un Blomen

Holstenglacis

Alsterglacis

Stephansplatz

Marktstr

Messehallen

Kleine Wallanlagen

Junguisstr

Gorch-Fock-Wall

Stephansplatz

Esplanade

Stephansplatz
Dammtorwall
40

Karolinenstr

Messehallen

26
49
Dammtorstr
Grosse Theaterstr

Feldstr

Drehbahn

Colonnaden

48
Johannes Brahms Platz
Dragonerstall

Gänsemarkt

Valentinskamp
Gänsemarkt

Neuer Jungfernstieg

Grosse Wallanlagen

Pilatuspool

Kaiser-Wilhelm-Str

Fuhlentwiete

ABC Str

Hohe Bleichen

Jungfernstieg

19

Neustädter Str

Hanseviertel

Grosse Bleichen

Jungfernstieg

Holstenwall

Peterstr

Neanderstr

Hütten

Wexstr

NEUSTADT

36

51

Bleichenbrücke
Adolfsbrücke

Post Str

Jungfernstieg

1

Grossneumarkt

Alter Steinweg

Neuer Wall

Alsterfleet

Rathausmarkt

15
Rathaus

Englische Planke

Ludwig-Erhard-Str

Krayenkamp

Stadthausbrücke

Grasskeller

Alter Wall

ALTSTADT

Grosse Börsenbrücke
Johannisstr

18

11

Rödingsmarkt

Trostbrücke

Böhmkenstr

Grosser Burstah

12

Venusberg

33

Ditmar-Koel-Str

Rambachstr

Neuer-Neustädter Weg

Stubbenhuk
Herrengraben

Bleichenfleet

Alsterfleet

Rödingsmarkt

Deichstr

3

35

Cremon

Katherinenstr

39

Johannisbollwerk

Vorsetzen

Schaartor

Baumwall

Kajen

29

Hohe Brücke

Bei den Mühren

Baumwall

Kehrwieder

13
7

SPEICHERSTADT

6

17

Am Sandtorkai

20

Sandtorhafen

Grosser-Grasbrook

5

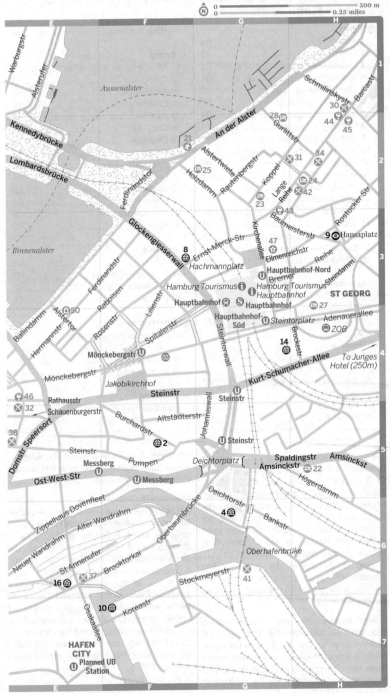

Central Hamburg

TOP CHOICE **St Michaeliskirche** CHURCH

(Map p650; www.st-michaelis.de; tower adult/child €4/3, crypt €3/2, combo ticket €6/4; ⊙10am-7.30pm May-Oct, to 5.30pm Nov-Apr; ⓢStadthausbrücke) Northeast of the landing piers, the St Michaeliskirche, or 'Der Michel' as it's commonly called, is one of Hamburg's most recognisable landmarks and northern Germany's largest Protestant baroque church. Ascending the tower (by steps or lift) rewards with great panoramas across the canals. The crypt has an engaging exhibit on the city's history.

Krameramtswohnungen HISTORIC BUILDINGS

(Map p650; ⓢStadthausbrücke) In an alley off Krayenkamp 10 are the Krameramtswohnungen, a row of **tiny half-timbered houses** from the 17th century that, for nearly 200 years, were almshouses for the widows of members of the Guild of Small Shopkeepers. Today they house shops and restaurants, plus a little summer-only museum.

Museum für Völkerkunde MUSEUM

(☏01805-308888;www.voelkerkundemuseum.com; Rothenbaumchaussee64;adult/child€7/free;⊙10am-6pm Tue, Wed & Fri-Sun, to 9pm Thu; ⓢHallerstrasse or Dammtor) North of the Altstadt, the much-updated Museum für Völkerkunde demonstrates seafaring Hamburg's acute awareness of the outside world. Modern artefacts from Africa, Asia and the South Pacific are displayed alongside traditional masks, jewellery, costumes and musical instruments, including carved wooden canoes and giant sculptures from Papua New Guinea, and a complete, intricately carved Maori meeting hall.

ST GEORG

This neighbourhood of large 19th-century apartment blocks for Hamburg's upper-middle class hit a nadir in the 1970s when thoughtless postwar reconstruction combined with a massive influx of drug dealing and prostitution to give it a very sleazy reputation.

Things are much gentrified now (look for great shops and cafes), as shown in St Georg's central square, the Hansaplatz. Completely renovated in 2011 and fully pedestrianised, the square's centrepiece is its fountain (Map p650). Completed in 1878, it shows important figures in Hamburg's past including Emperor Constantine the Great and Charlemagne and is surmounted by a figure showing the might of the Hanseatic League.

Segelschule Pieper   BOAT HIRE
(Map p650; ☑247 578; www.segelschule-pieper.de; An der Alster; row boat per hr from €16; ☺Apr-Oct; ⓢHauptbahnhof) If you're the DIY kind, hire your own boat; some travellers tell us it's the most fun they've had in Hamburg. Segelschule Pieper rents row boats and sailboats, though you'll need a sailing certificate for the latter. The tourist office maintains a list of other rental outlets, including canoe and kayak rental.

SPEICHERSTADT & HAFENCITY

The seven-storey redbrick warehouses lining the Speicherstadt archipelago are a well-recognised Hamburg symbol, stretching to Baumwall in the world's largest continuous warehouse complex. Their neo-Gothic gables and (mostly) green copper roofs are reflected in the narrow canals of this freeport zone.

A separate free port became necessary when Hamburg joined the German Customs Federation on signing up to the German Reich in 1871. An older neighbourhood was demolished – and 24,000 people displaced – to make room for the construction of the Speicherstadt from 1885 to 1927. This area was spared wartime destruction.

The Speicherstadt merges into Europe's biggest inner-city urban development, HafenCity. Here, a long-derelict port area of 155 hectares is being redeveloped with restaurants, shops, apartments and offices, all built to very strict sustainability standards. In the next 20 years, it's anticipated that some 40,000 people will work and 12,000 will live here. For the moment however, it can seem a bit sterile as only some projects are complete.

A new underground line, the U4 is set to link HafenCity from the Überseequartier stop to the rest of the city sometime in 2013.

TOP CHOICE **Miniatur-Wunderland**   EXHIBITION
(Map p650; ☑300 6800; www.miniatur-wunderland. de; Kehrwieder 2; adult/child €12/6; ☺9.30am-6pm Mon & Wed-Fri, 9.30am-9pm Tue, 8am-9pm Sat, 8.30am-8pm Sun; ⓢMessberg) Even the worst cynics are quickly transformed into fans of this vast miniature world that goes on and on. The model trains wending their way through the Alps are impressive – but slightly predictably so. But when you see a model A380 swoop out of the sky and land at the fully functional model of Hamburg's airport you can't help but gasp and say some variation of OMG! The current display is a mind-numbing 1300 sq m; tiny details abound as days change to night. The next addition will include Italy. In busy times, prepurchase your ticket online to skip the queues.

TOP CHOICE **International Maritime Museum**   MUSEUM
(Map p650; ☑3009 3300; www.internationales-maritimes-museum.de; Koreastrasse 1; adult/concession €12/8.50; ☺10am-6pm Tue, Wed & Fri-Sun, 10am-8pm Thu; ⓢMessberg) Hamburg's maritime

---

DON'T MISS

MAHNMAL ST-NIKOLAI

St Nikolai church was the world's tallest building from 1874 to 1876, and remains Hamburg's second-tallest structure (after the TV tower). Mostly destroyed in WWII, it is now called Mahnmal St-Nikolai (Memorial St Nicholas; Map p8; www.mahnmal-st-nikolai.de; Willy-Brandt-Strasse 60; adult/child €4/2; ☺10am-5pm; ⓢRödingsmarkt). The crypt now houses an unflinching underground exhibit on the horrors of war focusing on three events in World War II: the German bombing of Coventry in 1940; the German destruction of Warsaw and Operation Gomorrha; and the combined British and American bombing of Hamburg over three days and nights in 1943 that killed 35,000 and incinerated much of the centre. Afterwards, you can take a glass lift up to a 76.3m-high viewing platform inside the surviving spire for views of Hamburg's centre put into context of the wartime destruction.

Western Hamburg

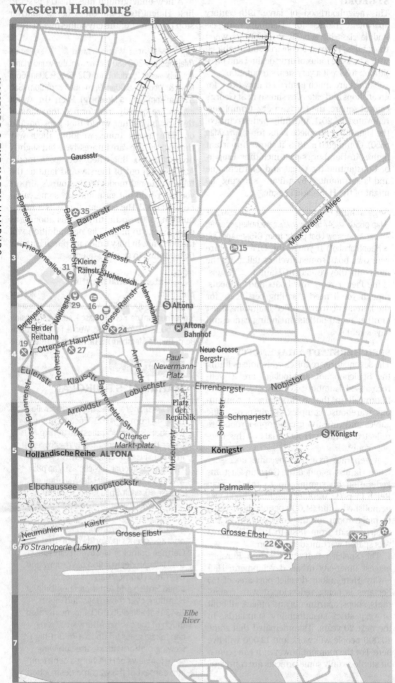

Gaussstr

Borselstr

Barnerstr

Nemstweg

Friedensallee

Bahrenfelder Str

Zeissstr

Kleine
Rainstr
Hohenesch

Abbestr

Grosse Rainstr

Hahnenkamp

35

31

29

16

30

24

Bergiusstr

Bei der
Reitbahn

Rothestr

Ottenser Hauptstr

19

27

Eulenstr

Klausstr

Bahrenfelder Str

Am Felde

Lobuschstr

Grosse Brunnenstr

Arnoldstr

Rothestr

Ottenser
Markt-platz

Hollländische Reihe   ALTONA

Elbchaussee   Klopstockstr

Neumühlen   Kaistr

Grosse Elbstr

To Strandperle (1.5km)

Max-Brauer-Allee

15

Altona

Altona
Bahnhof

Neue Grosse
Bergstr

Paul-
Nevermann-
Platz

Ehrenbergstr

Nobistor

Platz
der
Republik

Schillerstr

Schmarjestr

Museumstr

Königstr

Königstr

Palmaille

Grosse Elbstr

22

21

25

37

Elbe
River

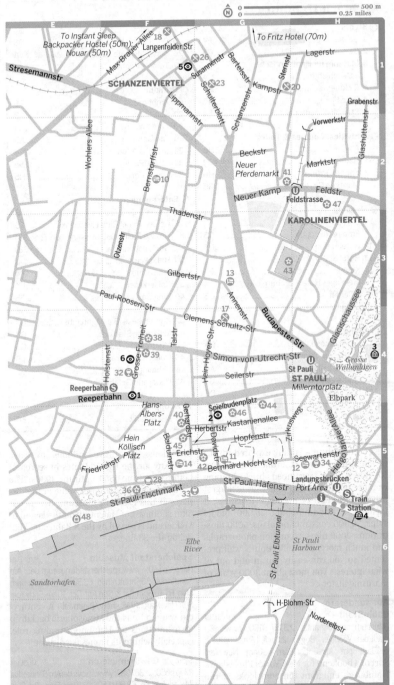

500 m
0.25 miles

To Instant Sleep
Backpacker Hostel (50m);
Nouar (50m)

To Fritz Hotel (70m)

Stresemannstr

Langenfelder Str

Max-Brauer-Allee 18

Lagerstr

SCHANZENVIERTEL

Susannenstr

5

26

Bartelsstr

Sternstr

Schanzenstr

Kampstr

23

20

Schulterblatt

Lippmannstr

Grabenstr

Vorwerkstr

Glashüttenstr

Wohlers Allee

Bernstorffstr

10

Beckstr

Neuer
Pferdemarkt

41

Marktstr

Thadenstr

Neuer Kamp

Feldstr

Feldstrasse

47

KAROLINENVIERTEL

Olzenstr

43

Gilbertstr

13

Paul-Roosen-Str

Ammenstr

Budapester Str

Clemens-Schultz-Str

17

Grosse Freiheit

38

Talstr

Simon-von-Utrecht-Str

Hein-Hoyer-Str

3

Glacischaussee

Grosse
Wallanlagen

39

6

Holstenstr

32

St Pauli

ST PAULI

Seilerstr

Millerntorplatz

Reeperbahn

Reeperbahn

1

Elbpark

Hans-
Albers-
Platz

40

Spielbudenplatz

2

46

44

Gerhardstr

Herbertstr

Kastanienallee

Zirkusweg

Helgoländer Allee

Hein
Köllisch
Platz

45

Davidstr

Erichstr

14

42

11

Hopfenstr

Bernhard-Nocht-Str

Seewartenstr

12

34

Friedrichstr

Balduinstr

Landungsbrücken
Port Area

28

St-Pauli-Hafenstr

36

St-Pauli-Fischmarkt

33

Train
Station

7

4

48

9

Elbe
River

St-Pauli-Elbtunnel

St Pauli
Harbour

8

Sandtorhafen

H-Blohm-Str

Norderelbstr

Western Hamburg

Sights

1 Beatles-Platz F4
2 Davidwache G5
3 Museum für Hamburgische Geschichte H4
4 Rickmer Rickmers H6
5 Rote Flora F1
6 Star Club Memorial F4

Activities, Courses & Tours

7 Abicht H6
Hadag .... (see 7)
8 Kapitän Prüsse H6
9 Maritime Circle Line G6

Sleeping

10 Backpackers St Pauli F2
11 Empire Riverside G5
12 Hotel Hafen H5
13 Hotel St Annen G3
14 Kogge F5
15 Meininger Hotel Hamburg City Center C3
16 Schanzenstern Altona A3

Eating

17 Café Mimosa G4
18 Die Herren Simpel F1
19 Eiscafe Eisliebe A4
20 Erikas Eck G1
21 Fisch & So C6
22 Fischereihafen C6
23 La Sepia G1
24 Mercado B4
25 Oh, It's Fresh D6
26 Super Mercato Italiano G1
27 Teufels Küche A4

Drinking

28 Amphore F5
29 Aurel A3
30 Café Knuth A4
31 Familien-Eck A3
32 Gretel & Alfons F4
33 StrandPauli F5
34 Tower Bar H5

Entertainment

35 Fabrik A3
36 Golden Pudel Club Live Music F5
Grosse Freiheit 36/Kaiserkeller .. (see 39)
Grünspan .... (see 38)
37 Hafenklang D6
38 Indra Club F4
39 Kaiserkeller F4
40 King Calavera F5
41 Knust G2
42 Komet Musik Bar Nightclubs G5
43 Millerntor-Stadion G3
44 Molotow G5
45 Queen Calavera F5
46 Schmidt Tivoli G5
47 Uebel and Gefährlich H2

Shopping

48 Fischmarkt E6

past – and future – is fully explored in this excellent private museum that sprawls over 10 floors of a revamped brick-shipping warehouse. Considered the world's largest private collection of maritime treasures, it includes a mind-numbing 26,000 model ships, 50,000 construction plans, 5000 illustrations, 2000 films, 1.5 million photographs and much more. The collection is well presented so you can easily dip in and out of what interests you most about 3000 years of maritime history.

Auswanderermuseum BallinStadt MUSEUM
(Museum of Emigrants; ☎3197 9160; www.ballinstadt.de; Veddeler Bogen 2; adult/child €10/7; ⏲10am-6pm Apr-Oct, 10am-4.30pm Nov-Mar) Sort of a bookend for New York's Ellis Island, Hamburg's emigrant museum looks at the conditions that drove millions to leave Germany for the United States in search of better lives from 1850 until the 1930s. The hardships endured are just some of the displays at this excellent museum. It is about 3km southeast of HafenCity on the island of Veddel and is served by the S-Bahn stop Veddel on the S3 line.

Speicherstadt Museum MUSEUM
(Map p650; www.speicherstadtmuseum.de; Am Sandtorkai 36; adult/child €3.50/2; ⏲10am-5pm Mon-Fri, to 6pm Sat & Sun Apr-Oct, 10am-5pm Tue-Sun Nov-Mar; [S]Messberg/Baumwall) A century-old warehouse is the atmospheric backdrop for exhibitions on Hamburg's trading role, especially within its namesake district.

Spicy's Gewürzmuseum MUSEUM
(Map p650; ☎367 989; www.spicys.de; Am Sandtorkai 34; adult/child €3.50/1.50; ⏲10am-5pm Tue-Sun,

plus Mon Jul-Oct; [S]Messberg) This spice and herb museum invites you to exercise your olfaction to the fullest.

HafenCity InfoCenter   EXHIBITION

(Map p650; [☎]3690 1799; www.hafencity.com; Am Sandtorkai 30; [☉]10am-6pm Tue-Sun; [S]Messberg) You can pick up brochures and check out detailed architectural models and installations that give a sense of the immensity of the project. The centre offers a program of free guided tours through the evolving district.

Elbphilharmonie   ARTS CENTRE

(Elbe Philharmonic Hall; Map p650; www.elbphilhar monie.de; [S]Messberg) A squat brown-brick former warehouse at the far west of Hafen-City is the base for the architecturally bold new Elbphilharmonie, which will become a major concert hall. Pritzker Prize–winning Swiss architects Herzog & de Meuron are responsible for the design, which captivates with details like the 1096 individually curved glass panes. Also captivating for locals is the building's planned completion date, which was once 2010. But like butterflies in the spring, new dates have flitted by and 2015 is now being mooted. While the budget soars, it is hoped that a Westin Hotel will open in part of the complex in 2013.

Hamburg Dungeon   AMUSEMENT PARK

(Map p650; [☎]information 3600 5500, tickets 3005 1512; www.thedungeons.com; Kehrwieder 2; adult/child €21/17; [☉]10am-6pm Jul & Aug, 10am-5pm Mar-Jun & Sep-Dec, 11am-5pm Jan & Feb; [S]Messberg) Camped-up chamber of horrors brought to life by actors, incorporating various thrill rides, all housed in an old warehouse. It's pricey and not recommended for kids under 10, which limits its natural appeal to a rather narrow range.

PORT AREA

Sprawling over 75 sq km (12% of Hamburg's entire surface area), Hamburg's huge port receives some 12,000 ships each year, which deliver and take on some 70 million tonnes of goods.

Climbing the steps above the **Land-ungsbrücken U-/S-Bahn station** to the **Stintfang stone balcony** offers a sweeping panorama, while dozens of port and Elbe River cruises (p659), starting at the St Pauli Harbour Landungsbrücken, put you right in the middle of the action. On a sunny day, the **Landungsbrücken promenade** is hugely popular with locals and tourists alike.

Rickmer Rickmers   MUSEUM

(Map p654; [☎]319 5959; www.rickmer-rickmers.de; Ponton 1a; adult/child €4/3; [☉]10am-6pm Sun-Wed, to 8pm Thu-Sat) The 1886 three-masted steel windjammer Rickmer Rickmers is now a museum ship; from the restaurant on deck you have fine harbour views.

ST PAULI

Even those not interested in lurid late-nights usually pay a quick trip to St Pauli's **Reep-erbahn** to see what the fuss is all about. Sure, it's tamer than the Amsterdam scene (which is itself becoming tamer), but it's still Europe's biggest in terms of the number of businesses. Long established as a party place, crowds of thousands start to stream in from around 4pm on weekends, cruising the rip-roaring collection of bars, sex clubs, variety acts, pubs and cafes collectively known as the 'Kiez'.

While the sex industry is still in full swing, some of the harsher edges are gone, although prostitutes dressed as schoolgirls are still much in evidence on weekend nights. Many of the once 'daring' sex shops are now marked by tired displays of sun-faded dildos in the windows.

These days the Reeperbahn and surrounding streets are more about mainstream musicals that play to sold-out houses, and while stylish nightclubs entertain a hip, moneyed clientele until dawn, edgy bars happily serve a beer to anyone with €3 and you can still hear an up-and-coming music act.

Herbertstrasse   STREET

([回]Reeperbahn) Along Davidstrasse, a painted tin wall bars views into Herbertstrasse, a block-long bordello that's off-limits to men under 18 and to women of all ages. It's the notorious sinful heart of the district.

THE PRICE OF SEX

Especially at the sex clubs on and near the **Grosse Freiheit**, doorstaff try to lure in the passing crowd with bargain shows, leaving customers to discover the mandatory drink minimum (usually at least €25) once inside. Ask at the bar how much drinks cost; you can easily spend €100 for a couple of watery cocktails – that aren't thematically tied to the on-stage shower.

Davidwache BUILDING
(Map p654; Spielbudenplatz 31, cnr Davidstrasse; ⓇReeperbahn) South of the Reeperbahn stands the star of many a German crime film and TV show, the Davidwache. This brick police station, festooned with ornate ceramic tiles, is the base for 150 officers, who keep the lurid surrounds reasonably tame.

Museum für
Hamburgische Geschichte MUSEUM
(Museum of Hamburg History; Map p654; ✆428 412 380; www.hamburgmuseum.de; Holstenwall 24; adult/child €8/free; ⊙10am-5pm Tue-Sat, to 6pm Sun; ⛴; ⑤St Pauli) Hamburg's history museum has lots of kid-friendly features: it's chock-full of intricate ship models, has a large model train set (which runs at the top of the hour), and even the actual bridge of the steamship *Werner,* which you can clamber over. As it chronicles the city's evolution, it reveals titbits such as the fact that the Reeperbahn was once the home of rope makers (*Reep* means 'rope'). There is a good exhibit on the history of the city's Jewish population.

SCHANZENVIERTEL & KAROLINENVIERTEL
North of St Pauli lie the lively Schanzenviertel and Karolinenviertel districts, bordered by the U-Bahn Feldstrasse, S-/U-Bahn Sternschanze, and Stresemannstrasse, which retain a strong sense of Hamburg's countercultural scene. Creative media types mix with students amid a landscape of multicultural cafes and restaurants, as well as funky shops, particularly along Marktstrasse.

THE BEATLES IN HAMBURG – FOREVER

'I was born in Liverpool, but I grew up in Hamburg.'
John Lennon

It was the summer of 1960 and a fledgling band from Liverpool had been assured a paying gig in Hamburg, if only they could come up with a drummer. After a frantic search, Pete Best joined John Lennon, Paul McCartney, George Harrison and Stuart Sutcliffe in August that year.

The Beatles opened on the notorious Grosse Freiheit to seedy crowds of drunks and whores. After 48 consecutive nights of six-hour sessions, the Beatles' innate musical genius had been honed. The magnetism of the group that would rock the world began drawing loyal crowds. But complications ensued when an underage George was deported in November, and Paul and Pete were arrested for attempted arson. All escaped the German authorities and returned to England. There, as 'The Beatles: Direct from Hamburg', they had their Merseyside breakthrough.

In 1961 the Beatles returned to Hamburg. During a 92-night stint, they made their first professional recording. Soon manager extraordinaire Brian Epstein and the recording genius (now Sir) George Martin arrived on the scene. The Beatles began their career with EMI, Pete Best was replaced by Ringo Starr, a more professional drummer, Stuart Sutcliffe quit the band and they went on to their fame and fortune.

You can still find traces of their time in Hamburg at these sites:

» **Indra Club** (Map p654; 64 Grosse Freiheit) The group's small first venue is open again and has live acts many nights. The interior is vastly different.

» **Kaiserkeller** (Map p654; Grosse Freiheit 36) One of the more respectable clubs today on the Grosse Freiheit, this second venue for the Beatles survives in a much-altered form.

» **Gretel & Alfons** (Map p654; Grosse Freiheit 29) A late-night cafe and bar that is little changed from when the boys would unwind there after shows.

» **Star Club** (Map p654; Grosse Freiheit 39) The seminal venue for the Beatles opened in 1962, it has since burnt down and there is a sad historical marker.

» **Beatles-Platz** (Map p654) Designed like a vinyl record, it has abstract steel sculptures resembling cookie cutters of the fab four (including a hybrid of Ringo Starr and Pete Best).

For an entertaining look at the Beatles in Hamburg, try the **Beatles Tour** (✆0151-1528 3020, 04183-773 664; www.hempels-musictour.com; tour €22) offered by the fun-filled and engaging Stephanie Hempel.

Rote Flora CULTURAL CENTRE
(Map p654; ☎439 5413; www.nadir.org; Schulterblatt 71) One of the most outstanding remnants of the area's rougher days, the graffiti-covered Rote Flora looks one step away from demolition. Once the famous Flora Theatre, it's now an alternative cultural centre, although there are constant threats to its future from gentrifying developers etc.

ALTONA & ELBMEILE

To the west of the Schanzenviertel, Altona is gentrified and a good place to take a neighbourhood stroll. It also has its share of offbeat shops and buzzing restaurants.

Altona stretches from the village-like centre around its S-Bahn and train stations to the waterfront, where a string of restaurants stretch along the Elbmeile, along with waterfront bars and cafes.

BLANKENESE

Once a former fishing village and haven for cut-throat pirates, Blankenese, 8km west of Altona, now boasts some of the finest and most expensive houses in Germany. For visitors, the area's attractiveness lies in its hillside labyrinth of narrow, cobbled streets, with a network of **58 stairways** (4864 steps in total) connecting them. The best views of the Elbe (nearly 3km wide here) and its container ships are from the 75m-high **Süllberg hill**. To get to Süllberg, take the S-Bahn to Blankenese, then bus 48 to Waseberg – having passed the clutch of beachfront restaurants and cafes – where you'll see a sign pointing to the nearby Süllberg. If you alight at the Krögers Treppe (Fischerhaus) bus stop, head up the Bornholldt Treppe and Süllbergweg. Or you can get off once the road starts winding and just explore.

FURTHER AFIELD

Tierpark Hagenbeck ZOO
(☎530 0330; www.hagenbeck-tierpark.de; Lokstedter Grenzstrasse 2; adult/child from €20/15; ⏲9am-7pm Jul & Aug, 9am-6pm Sep-Oct & Mar-Jun, 9am-4.30pm Nov-Feb; 👪; [S]Hagenbecks Tierpark) The 2500 animals that live in Hamburg's zoo have open enclosures over 27 hectares. In addition to elephants, tigers, orang-utans, toucans and other creatures, you'll find a replica Nepalese temple, Japanese garden, art-deco gate and a huge aquarium. A petting zoo, pony rides, a miniature railway and playground mean you'll have to drag the kids away at the end of the day. It is 5km northwest of the centre.

Tours

Boat Tours

In addition to boat tours in the port area, you can also float past elegant buildings aboard an Alster Lakes cruise.

[TOP CHOICE] **Maritime Circle Line** BOAT TOUR
(Map p654; ☎2849 3963; www.maritime-circle-line.de; Brücke 10; adult/child €9.50/6; ⏲3-5 times daily) Harbour shuttle service connecting Hamburg's maritime cultural attractions, including the Auswanderermuseum Ballin-Stadt, Hafenmuseum and Miniatur-Wunderland. The entire loop takes around 95 minutes; you can hop on or off at any of its stops.

Abicht BOAT TOUR
(Map p654; ☎317 8220; www.abicht.de; Brücke 1; 1hr tour adult/child €15/7.50; ⏲tours noon Apr-Oct) This company's harbour tours are rightly popular; it also offers Saturday evening tours taking you past the illuminated warehouses (departure times vary according to tides).

Hadag BOAT TOUR
(Map p654; ☎311 7070; www.hadag.de; Brücke 2; 1hr harbour trip adult/child from €16/8; ⏲year-round) Harbour tours plus more adventuresome trips to the Lower Elbe (April to September).

Kapitän Prüsse BOAT TOUR
(Map p654; ☎313 130; www.kapitaen-pruesse.de; Brücke 3; adult/child from €16/8; ⏲year-round) Kapitän Prüsse offers regular Speicherstadt tours as well as various port itineraries.

Cap San Diego TOUR
(Map p650; ☎364 209; www.capsandiego.de; adult/child €7/3; ⏲10am-6pm) The beautiful 1961 freighter, the 10,000-tonne Cap San Diego, is open to tours that give a good feel for when sea voyages were a relaxing and low-key way to tour the world. There are also special exhibitions.

ATG Alster-Touristik BOAT TOUR
(Map p650; ☎3574 2419; www.alstertouristik.de; Jungfernstieg pier; tours adult/child from €13.50/7; ⏲Apr-Oct; [S]Jungfernstieg) ATG Alster-Touristik runs a hop-on, hop-off service between nine landing stages around the lakes. There are a lot of other tours on offer, especially interesting are the canal tours.

Bus Tours

Hamburg City Tour BUS TOUR
(☎3231 8590; www.hamburg-city-tour.de; adult/child €15/free; ⏲half-hourly 9.30am-5pm) A bus tour is a stress-free way to piece together this

SIGHTSEEING LIKE A REAL HAMBURGER

This maritime city offers a bewildering array of boat trips, but locals will tell you that you don't have to book a cruise to see the port – the city's **harbour ferries** will take you up the river on a regular public transport ticket, and you can avoid hokey narration!

One oft-recommended route is to catch **ferry 62** from Landungsbrücken to Finkenwerder, then change for the 64 to Teufelsbrücke. From Teufelsbrücke you can wander along the Elbe eastwards to Neumühlen, from where you can catch bus 112 back to the Altona S-Bahn station or ferry 62 back to Landungsbrücken.

On land, the **U3 U-Bahn line** is particularly scenic, especially the elevated track between the St Pauli and Rathaus U-Bahn stations.

sprawling jigsaw of a city. As with boats, there are numerous tours; among them are the yellow-and-blue buses of Hamburg City Tour. Its open-topped double-decker buses pass all the leading sights over 1½ hours; tickets (sold on the bus) allow you to jump on and jump off all day. You can board at stops including the Hauptbahnhof (Kirchenallee exit), Landungsbrücken and the Rathaus.

Walking Tours

Dozens of walking tours operate throughout the city, many with specific themes, such as red-light tours, 'historic hooker' tours, Beatles tours, culinary tours and more. Tourist offices maintain a comprehensive list.

✦ Festivals & Events

Hafengeburtstag   FESTIVAL
(Harbour Birthday; www.hafengeburtstag.de) The city's biggest annual event is the three-day Hafengeburtstag in early May. It commemorates Emperor Barbarossa granting Hamburg customs exemption and is energetically celebrated with harbourside concerts, funfairs and gallons of beer.

Hamburger Dom   CARNIVAL
(www.hamburger-dom.de) Established in 1329, the Hamburger Dom, held in late March, late July and late November, is one of Europe's largest and oldest funfairs. It's held on Heiligengeistfeld, between St Pauli and Schanzenviertel.

🛏 Sleeping

Hamburg is big, so you might consider where you'll be spending your time before you decide where to stay. Booking ahead is a good idea any time of year, and is essential on weekends, during festivals and throughout summer.

ALTSTADT & NEUSTADT

You'll find every chain hotel imaginable in the centre of the city.

A&O Hamburg Hauptbahnhof   HOSTEL €
(Map p650; ☎030-809 475 110; www.aohostels. com; Amsinckstrasse 10; dm from €12, s/d from €35/45; P ✳ @ 🛜; ⓡHauptbahnhof) A 300m suitcase-drag from the Hauptbahnhof, this central branch of the institutional-style A&O chain has some 900 beds in rooms with private bathrooms. Those deep inside the labyrinthine building can feel claustrophobic; try for one overlooking the street. Prices can skyrocket depending on demand. There are three other Hamburg branches.

Hotel SIDE   HOTEL €€€
(Map p650; ☎309 990; www.side-hamburg.de; Drehbahn 49; r €120-300; P ✳ @ 🛜 ☒; ⓢGänsemarkt) A stylish alternative to the city centre's chain hotels, this Matteo Thun–designed stunner is built around a soaring prism-shaped central atrium. Suites feature vividly coloured free-standing bath-tubs. The 8th-floor chill-out lounge, strewn with 1950s-style saucers-from-outer-space sofas, opens to a panoramic sun deck.

ST GEORG

Convenient to the Hauptbahnhof, St Georg is ripe with midrange hotels, some much better than others. Without a booking, be ready to leave your bag in a locker and compare a few.

TOP CHOICE Hotel Wedina   HOTEL €€
(Map p650; ☎280 8900; www.wedina.de; Gurlittstrasse 23; s €70-195, d €120-225; @ 🛜; ⓢHauptbahnhof) You might find a novel instead of a chocolate on your pillow at this literary hotel. Margaret Atwood, Jonathan Safran Foer, Jonathan Franzen, Michel Houellebecq, Vladimir Nabokov and JK Rowling are just some of the authors who've stayed and left behind signed books. The hotel's 59 rooms are spread over four buildings, offering a choice of traditional decor in the main red

building, which opens to a leafy garden, or modern, urban living in its green, blue and yellow houses.

[TOP CHOICE] **Hotel Atlantic** LUXURY HOTEL €€€

(Map p650; ☎288 80; www.kempinski.atlantic.de; An der Alster 72-79; s/d from €150/180; 📶🏊; [S]Hauptbahnhof Nord) Imagine yourself aboard a luxury ocean liner in this grand 252-room hotel, which opens onto Holzdamm. Built in 1909 for luxury-liner passengers departing for America, it has ornate stairwells, wide hallways and subtle maritime touches. It has all the services of a five-star hotel and underwent a significant remodelling and restoration in 2010.

Galerie-Hotel Petersen PENSION €€

(Map p650; ☎0173 200 0746, 249 826; www.ghsp.eu; Lange Reihe 50; s €60-100, d €70-170; ❄@📶; [S]Hauptbahnhof) This delightful *Pension* inside a historic 1790 town house is an extension of its welcoming artist-owner's personality, whose paintings decorate the walls of his 'gallery of dreams'. Furnishings include a mix of contemporary, antique and art-deco styles. Our pick of its five rooms is the top-floor terrace studio, with a romantic rooftop terrace, kitchenette and separate living area. The cheapest room has the bathroom on a different floor.

Alpha Hotel-Pension PENSION €€

(Map p650; ☎245 365; www.alphahotel.biz; Koppel 4-6; r €40-100; 📶; [R]Hauptbahnhof) An excellent choice close to the Hauptbahnhof, the 21 rooms here are basic but comfortable. The reception is especially warm and helpful. If it's your first visit to Hamburg, your every question will be answered with aplomb. Some rooms share baths, others have access to a tiny rooftop playground.

Hotel Village HOTEL €

(Map p650; ☎480 6490; www.hotel-village.de; Steindamm 4; s €50-75, d €65-100; @📶; [S]Hauptbahnhof) You can tell this edgy gem was once a bordello: the 20 boudoirs feature various kitsch mixes of red velvet, gold flock wallpaper and leopard prints, and several have huge mirrors above the bed. It attracts a mix of gay and straight guests. Economy rooms have bathrooms outside the room.

Junges Hotel HOTEL €€

(☎419 230; www.jungeshotel.de; Kurt-Schumacher-Allee 14; r incl breakfast €110-150 ; [P]@📶; [S]Berliner Tor, [R]Berliner Tor) A corrugated metal exterior fronts lots of blond wood in this airy, modern 128-room hotel less than five minutes' walk from the Berliner Tor U-Bahn/S-Bahn station. Extra guests can be accommodated in some double rooms, with beds that drop down from the wall as in a train sleeper compartment.

ST PAULI

St Pauli offers greatly divergent accommodations: wild near the Reeperbahn, leafy in its genteel neighbourhoods and flashy on its knoll overlooking the bright lights of the city and harbour.

Hotel St Annen HOTEL €€

(Map p654; ☎317 7130; www.hotelstannen.de; Annenstrasse 5; s €60-100, d €80-150; [P]@📶; [S]St Pauli) Tucked away in one of the few quiet streets between the Reeperbahn and Schanzenviertel, this 36-room hotel is a favourite with business people and middle-class travellers for its whitewashed, glossy-timber-furnished modern rooms and shaded back garden and terrace.

Hotel Hafen HOTEL €€

(Map p654; ☎311 1370; www.hotel-hafen-hamburg.de; Seewartenstrasse 9; r €70-200; @📶; [S]Landungsbrücken) Location, location, location. This privately owned behemoth of a hotel (353 rooms, all with high-speed internet) looms over the heart of Hamburg's harbour from a small hill. If you're lucky enough to score a harbour-facing room, the views are extraordinary. In addition to the refurbished, historic main building, a former seafarer's home, there are newer modern wings.

Empire Riverside HOTEL €€€

(Map p654; ☎311 190; www.empire-riverside.de; Bernhard-Nocht-Strasse 97; r from €159; [P]❄📶; [S]St Pauli) Sparing splashes of colour brighten its restaurant, bars, and 327 streamlined rooms with floor-to-ceiling windows, most with harbour views. Those on the higher of the 20 floors may not leave as they'll be captivated by the goings on of all Hamburg around them. Breakfast costs €18.

Backpackers St Pauli HOSTEL €

(Map p654; ☎2351 7043; www.backpackers-stpauli.de; Bernstorffstrasse 98; dm from €20, d from €60; 📶; [S]Feldstrasse) Entered via a bright cafe, this hostel-cum-hotel includes a cool, subterranean maritime-themed lounge containing a small kitchenette, a sunny outdoor terrace, table football, and light-filled rooms (some with private bathrooms) with good-sized lockers.

Kogge HOTEL €
(Map p654; ☎312 872; www.kogge-hamburg.de; Bernhard-Nocht-Strasse 59; s €30-35, d €50-60; @📶; [S]Landungsbrücken or Reeperbahn) At this rock-and-roll pub deep in noisy, grungy Reeperbahn territory, sleepyhead young party-goers can check out as late as 2pm from 'Bollywood', 'Punk Royal', 'Disco Dream' or other artist-designed rooms. None of the 12 rooms have bathrooms, but all have sinks and some have bunk beds.

SCHANZENVIERTEL & KAROLINENVIERTEL

Edgy neighbourhoods deserve edgy – yet restful – rooms, which you'll find here.

Hotel Bellmoor HOTEL €€
(☎413 3110; www.hotel-bellmoor.de; 4th fl, Dammtorpalais, Moorweidenstrasse 34; s/d incl breakfast from €70/100; 📶; 🚆Dammtor) White embossed wallpaper and vintage advertising posters line the halls of this traditional hotel in a grand old apartment block that has been converted into several hotels. Rooms 14 (single) and 34 (twin) feature art-nouveau bathrooms with stained-glass windows and tiled tubs. Economy singles are like old sailing-ship cabins. Views over Hamburg's rooftops unfurl from the sunlit breakfast room.

Instant Sleep Backpacker Hostel HOSTEL €
(☎4318 2310; www.instantsleep.de; Max-Brauer-Allee 277; dm/s/d from €18/40/58; @📶; 🚆Sternschanze) Artistic murals – from green stripes to golden Buddhas – adorn this chilled-out pad in the happening Schanzenviertel. Airy dorms and private rooms house 60 proper beds (no bunks), though all share bathrooms. Some of Hamburg's most ideal cafes for hanging out are just around the corner.

Fritz Hotel BOUTIQUE HOTEL €€
(☎8222 2830; www.fritzhotel.com; Schanzenstrasse 101-103; s/d from €65/95; 📶; [S]Sternshanze) This stylish town-house hotel is as cool as a cucumber; it has a *Wallpaper* magazine vibe. Fresh organic fruit and cappuccinos are always available. If you want a room with a balcony, be prepared for some street noise, otherwise get one at the back. It's all rather intimate, with only 17 rooms total.

ALTONA & ELBMEILE

This will be your most residential feeling option of where to stay in Hamburg; the charms of the city a short S-Bahn ride away.

Schanzenstern Altona PENSION €
(Map p654; ☎3991 9191; www.schanzenstern.de; Kleine Rainstrasse 24-26; dm/s/d from €19/45/70, apt from €80; @📶; 🚆Altona) A mix of families and slightly more grown-up backpackers inhabit these sparkling rooms with private bathrooms, and self-catering apartments. Staff are wired into what's happening around Hamburg. Two small caveats: there are no lockers, and wi-fi doesn't extend to the rooms. There is another property in St Pauli.

Meininger Hotel Hamburg City Center HOSTEL/HOTEL €
(Map p654; www.meininger-hotels.com; Goetheallee 11; dm €14-25, s/d from €60/70; [P]@📶; 🚆Altona) The Hamburg branch of this upscale chain of hostel-hotels is conveneint to Altona train station and the many pleasures of the neighbourhood. The 116 rooms are in a new six-storey building with a lift. There's a laundry, storage lockers, a games room, a bar and more.

🍴 Eating

Virtually every part of Hamburg has splendid dining options ranging from humble to fine. Unsurprisingly, seafood is a favourite in this port city, with everything from traditional regional specialities to sushi on offer. You'll also find a truly global variety of foods reflecting this city's long international links and traditions.

ALTSTADT

Many of the restaurants in the Altstadt cater to bankers and other office workers, but there are some gems, especially along the Deichstrasse, which is lined with atmospheric old buildings – a rarity in this area.

[TOP CHOICE] **Café Paris** FRENCH €€
(Map p650; www.cafeparis.net; Rathausstrasse 4; mains €10-20; 🕘from 9am Mon-Fri, from 10am Sat & Sun; [S]Rathaus) Within a spectacularly tiled 1882 butchers' hall and adjoining art-deco salon, this elegant yet relaxed brasserie serves classical French fare like *croque-monsieur* (toasted ham-and-cheese sandwich), *croque-madame* (the same, but with a fried egg), and *steak tartare* (minced meat, but pan-fried, not raw). Its breakfast for two is a splendid feast.

Le Plat du Jour BISTRO €€€
(Map p650; ☎321 414; www.leplatdujour.de; Dornbusch 4; mains €15-20; [S]Rathaus) Tidy and petite, this French bistro is in sharp contrast to its bland office-building surrounds. An oasis

HISTORY OF THE HAMBURGER

A classic *Calvin and Hobbes* comic strip once asked if hamburgers were made out of people from Hamburg. And while Hamburg's citizens are, of course, known as Hamburgers, it was the city's role as an international port that gave rise to its most famous namesake.

The origins of the ubiquitous fast food date back to the 12th century. The Tartars (Mongolian and Turkish warriors) wedged pieces of beef between their saddles and the horses' backs, softening the meat as they rode until it was tender enough to be eaten raw, and the practice soon spread to Russia. By the 17th century, Hamburg ships brought 'steak tartare' (named after the Tartars) back to Germany, which visiting seafarers then referred to as 'steak in the Hamburg style'. These patties of salted minced beef – usually slightly smoked and mixed with breadcrumbs and onions – were highly durable, making them ideal for long sea voyages.

Hamburg emigrants to America continued making the patties, which they served in bread. (As for who in America officially launched the burger remains a fanatical culinary debate.)

American chains have invaded Hamburg, as they have everywhere. Although known here, too, as hamburgers or burgers, the original style of patty is rarely called Hamburg-anything steak in Germany, but rather *Frikadelle*, *Frikandelle* or *Bulette* – staples of train station sausage stands.

of flavour in the Altstadt, look for classics like fish soup, chicken in tarragon and various seafood and pasta dishes. The tables on the small square out front are the place to be.

Deichgraf GERMAN €€€
(Map p650; ☎364 208; www.deichgraf-hamburg.de; Deichstrasse 23; mains €18-29; 🕐lunch Mon-Sat, dinner Sat; [S]Rödingsmarkt) In a prime setting, with the water on one side and long street-side tables on the other, Deichgraf excels in Hamburg specialities cooked to a high standard. The menu changes seasonally and much of the food is sourced from the region.

Alt Hamburger Aalspeicher GERMAN €€€
(Map p650; ☎362 990; www.aalspeicher.de; Deichstrasse 43; mains €12-28; [S]Rödingsmarkt) Despite its tourist-friendly location, the knick-knack-filled dining room and warm service at this restaurant in a 400-year-old canalside building make you feel like you're dining in your *Oma's* (grandma's) house. Smoked eel from its own smokehouse is a speciality.

NEUSTADT

Look for luxe cafes under the beautiful columned arcades of the Alsterarkaden and the appropriately named Colonnaden.

[TOP CHOICE] **Matsumi** JAPANESE €€€
(Map p650; www.matsumi.de; Colonnaden 96; meals from €18; 🕐noon-2.30pm daily, 6.30-10pm Tue-Sat; [S]Stephansplatz) Lauded sushi chef Hideaki Morita creates excellent Japanese fare at this 2nd floor restaurant where virtually everything is unassuming except for the food. Besides sushi, there are various teriyaki grills, a bevy of tempura dishes and *washinabe* (a stew of fish and vegetables that boils at your table).

Edelcurry GERMAN €
(Map p650; www.edelcurry.de; Grosse Bleichen 68; mains from €4; [S]Rödingsmarkt) The humble *Currywurst* – one of Germany's favourite fastfoods – gets the royal treatment here. Choose from three flavours of sausage (classic, fruity or spicy) and add on a side of fresh-cut fries that are the best you'll find this side of Belgium.

ST GEORG

You'll be spoiled for choice strolling Lange Reihe, with dozens of options ranging from fancy to simple, German to Asian, breakfast to post-midnight.

Sgroi ITALIAN €€€
(Map p650; ☎2800 3930; www.sgroi.de; Lange Reihe 40; lunch menus from €35, dinner menus from €85; [R]Hauptbahnhof) A Michelin-starred Italian restaurant in once derelict St Georg? Yes, and this one lives up to the hype. Lauded chef Anna Sgroi has taken the foods of her southern Italian childhood to culinary heights. A seemingly mundane dish like stuffed artichokes is sublime and that's just to start. The menu is never the same, but expect bold flavours, the finest ingredients

and flawless execution. There's a small terrace for tables on warm days.

Café Koppel
VEGETARIAN €
(Map p650; www.cafe-koppel.de; Lange Reihe 66; dishes €5-10; [S]Hauptbahnhof) Set back from busy Lange Reihe, with a garden in summer, this vegie cafe is a refined oasis, where you can hear the tinkling of spoons in coffee cups midmorning on the mezzanine floor. The menu could be an ad for the fertile fields of northern Germany as there are baked goods, salads, soups and much more made with fresh seasonal ingredients.

Cox
MODERN EUROPEAN €€€
(Map p650; [🖉]249 422; www.restaurant-cox.de; Lange Reihe 68; mains lunch €10-18, dinner €17-25; ⊙lunch Mon-Fri, dinner daily; [R]Hauptbahnhof) Behind its opaque glass doors, this upmarket bistro was part of the original vanguard of St Georg's gentrification. Its frequently changing menu reflect the foods of the season and influences from across the continent.

SPEICHERSTADT & HAFENCITY
Speicherstadt has a couple of excellent traditional restaurants amidst its old restored warehouses. HafenCity is just beginning to get some eateries but until it gets more built up, they have a slightly soulless feel amongst the new construction.

[TOP CHOICE] Oberhafenkantine
GERMAN €€
(Map p650; www.oberhafenkantine-hamburg.de; Stockmeyerstrasse 39; mains €7-16; [R]Steinstrasse) Since 1925, this slightly tilted brick restaurant has served up the most traditional Hamburg fare using only the best ingredients. Here you can order a 'Hamburger' and you get the real thing: a patty made with various seasonings and onions. Roast beef, pollock, haddock and more round out a wonderful trip back to the days when the surrounding piers echoed to the shouts of seafarers and the crash of cargo-laden nets.

Fleetschlösschen
INTERNATIONAL €€
(Map p650; Brooktorkai 17; snacks €7-10; ⊙8am-8pm Mon-Fri, 11am-6pm Sat & Sun; [S]Messberg) One of the cutest cafes you ever saw, this former customs post overlooks a Speicherstadt canal and has a narrow steel spiral staircase to the toilets. There's barely room for 20 inside, but its outdoor seating areas are brilliant in sunny weather. The owner's collection of *Kleinods* (small treasures) includes centuries-old Dutch pottery unearthed during the construction of HafenCity.

PORT AREA
Right on the water you'll find a plethora of soft-ice-cream stands, fried-fish stalls and other vittle-pushers for the strolling masses. But step slightly inland and there are good places for a coffee or a meal in the old ethnic neighbourhoods.

Lusitano
PORTUGUESE €€
(Map p650; [🖉]315 841; Rambachstrasse 5; mains €8-18; [S]Baurnwall) As unadorned as a piece of salt cod, this simple little restaurant in Hamburg's old Portuguese neighbourhood captures the bright flavours of the western Mediterranean. Dishes like spicy sausages and pasta will warm your heart, but the seafood is the real star. Get the Gambas James Brown and be prepared for feel-good garlicky prawns as volatile as the namesake singer. It's a small place, so book.

Cafe Sul
CAFE €
(Map p650; www.cafe-sul.de; Ditmar-Koel-Strasse 10; snacks €3-9; ⊙8am-midnight; [S]Baurnwall) A perfect place of refuge from the fried-fish-clutching mobs of the port area, this cafe lives up to its name with a cheery disposition even on a cloudy day. The front opens to the street and there is a good breakfast and snack menu. Tied one on last night? The tortilla (omelette with potatoes) is balm for the soul.

ST PAULI
Simply put, the further you get from the Reeperbahn, the better your odds of having something tasty to eat (unless it's 4am, in which case the gaggle of fast-fooderies along this notorious street will do just fine).

Café Mimosa
CAFE €
(Map p654; www.cafemimosa.de; Clemens-Schultz-Strasse 87; dishes €5-12; [S]St Pauli) A welcome change from the greasy fast-food joints on the nearby Reeperbahn, this gem of a neighbourhood cafe serves delicious pastas, healthy salads, proper coffee and homemade cakes in a theatrical space. There's a clutch of pavement tables, plus a long list of fresh juices.

SCHANZENVIERTEL & KAROLINENVIERTEL
Ethnic and offbeat dining options are the order of the day in these edgy areas while cafes hum to animated conversations about the topics of the day.

HAMBURG'S FISH MARKET

Every Sunday morning, in the wee hours, a fleet of small trucks rumbles onto the cobbled pavement and hardy types turn their vehicles into stores on wheels. They artfully arrange their bananas, cherries, kumquats and whatever else they've picked up that week (some comes direct from farms but a lot comes from wholesalers). Others pile up eels, shellfish, cacti and all manner of goods. It's not yet 5am as the first customers begin to trundle in.

The **Fischmarkt** (Map p654; ⊙5-10am Sun; 圓Reeperbahn) in St Pauli has been a Hamburg institution since 1703. Locals of every age and walk of life join curious tourists.

The undisputed stars of the event – and great, free entertainment – are the boisterous *Marktschreier* (market criers) who hawk their wares. 'Don't be shy, little girl,' they might shout with a lascivious wink to a rotund 60-year-old, waggling a piece of eel in front of her face. Almost always, the 'girl' blushes before taking a hearty bite as the crowd cheers.

More entertainment takes place in the adjoining **Fischauktionshalle** (Fish Auction Hall), where a live band cranks out ancient German pop songs.

Balutschi
PAKISTANI €€

(📞452 479; www.balutschi.com; Grindelallee 33; mains €6-15; ⊙noon-11pm Sun-Thu, 24hr Fri & Sat; 📶; 圓Dammtor) Out the back of this Pakistani restaurant there's an over-the-top *Arabian Nights*–style grotto, where you remove your shoes and sit on carpets and low benches. The multicourse banquet menus are particularly fun and let a group try a range of dishes.

Erikas Eck
GERMAN €€

(Map p654; 📞433 545; www.erikas-eck.de; Sternstrasse 98; mains €6-18; ⊙5pm-2pm; 圓Sternschanze) Wood-lined Erikas has been serving up traditional home cooking since the golden oldies on its radio were first-time hits. Most of its legendary fare, including schnitzels, herrings and *Schweinebraten* (roast pork), costs under €10 and is served 21 hours a day.

La Sepia
MEDITERRANEAN €€

(Map p654; 📞432 2066; Schulterblatt 36; mains €12-20; ⊙noon-3am; 圓Sternschanze) The aroma of fresh fish wafting from this neighbourhood restaurant stops you in your tracks. Its enormous dining space is adorned with a hotchpotch of maritime relics, like old wooden boats suspended from the ceiling, while dishes incorporate Portuguese and Spanish influences.

Super Mercato Italiano
CAFE €

(Map p654; www.super-mercato-italiano.net; Schulterblatt 82; snacks from €3; ⊙8am-6pm; 圓Sternschanze) Facing the inspirational near-ruin of the Rote Flora cultural centre, the alt-vibe is perfectly contrasted by this very traditional Italian cafe and grocery. Any of three generations of owners will make you a perfect coffee, which you can enjoy on the wide pavement out front amidst a plethora of adjoining ethnic cafes.

Die Herren Simpel
CAFE €

(Map p654; 📞3868 4600; www.dieherrensimpel.de; Schulterblatt 75; dishes €4-8; ⊙5pm-late Mon-Fri, noon-late Sat & Sun; 📶; 圓Sternschanze) The sky-blue mural with huge white flowers behind the bar has become this cafe's signature. Its tiny entrance opens to an unexpectedly spacious series of retro rooms, plus a winter garden nicheand alfresco tables out back. There's a fantastic range of breakfasts, plus sandwiches and warm snacks like *Flammkuchen* (Alsatian-style pizza).

ALTONA & ELBMEILE

In the village-like area around Altona train station, you'll find dozens of casual and ethnic eateries, especially in the gentrified climes of Ottensen to the west.

Hamburg's western riverfront, from Altona to Övelgönne, known as the Elbmeile (Elbe Mile), has a dense concentration of popular and trendy restaurants – many drawing menu inspiration from the waterfront location.

🏆 TOP CHOICE Eiscafe Eisliebe
ICE CREAM €

(Map p654; 📞3980 8482; Bei der Reitbahn 2; treats from €1.50; ⊙noon-9pm; 圓Altona) Some of the yummiest ice cream you'll ever taste is scooped from this little hole in the wall (look for the queues). On any given day, you'll find around a dozen of its handmade, all-natural flavours like cherry-rippled poppy-seed or sticky crème brûlée.

Teufels Küche
BISTRO €€

(Map p654; www.teufels-kueche.net; Ottenser Hauptstrasse 47; mains €7-14; Altona) Blackboards make changing the menu easy at this very popular Ottensen bistro, where the kitchen is part of the dining room. Order at the counter and something fresh, seasonal and tasty will go right from the pan to the plate in front of you. Mains are simple but tasty – think perfectly spicy sausages on mash or any of many pastas and salads.

Fischereihafen
SEAFOOD €€€

(Map p654; 381 816; www.fischereihafen restaurant.de; Grosse Elbstrasse 143; lunch mains €10-13, dinner mains €18-35; lunch & dinner; Altona) Traditional and incredibly elegant, Fischereihafen serves some of Hamburg's finest fish, including regional specialities, to a mature, well-heeled clientele. Its 1st-floor, subtly maritime-themed dining room overlooks the Elbe. Lobster here comes in many forms.

Fisch & So
SEAFOOD €

(Map p654; 389 3109; Grosse Elbstrasse 117; dishes €3-12; 9am-5pm Mon-Fri, 11am-6pm Sat; Königstrasse) Fresh fish is what this little cafe does best. Order off the board and wait at the clutch of blue-clothed tables to savour

---

GAY & LESBIAN HAMBURG

Hamburg has a thriving gay and lesbian scene; look out at venues in *hinnerk* (www.hinnerk.de).

Men can find out more at the gay centre **Hein & Fiete** (240 333; www. heinfiete.de; Pulverteich 21; 4-9pm Mon-Fri, to 7pm Sat), while women can contact the lesbian centre **Intervention** (245 002; www.intervention-hamburg.de; Glashüttenstrasse; hours vary).

With its abstract art and in-house bakery, **Café Gnosa** (Map p650; 243 034; www.gnosa.de; Lange Reihe 93; mains €7-14; 10am-1am) draws an affable gay and straight crowd in St Georg.

Also recommended is **Generation Bar** (Map p650; 2880 4690; www.genera tion-bar.de; Lange Reihe 81; from 6pm), a popular gay bar right in the middle of the St Georg gay strip, and **Kyti Voo** (Map p650; 2805 5565; Lange Reihe 8; from 10am), where a mixed crowd mixes it up with mixed drinks until very late.

---

simple but delicious fish sandwiches, or perhaps *Tintenfish* (calamari) with *Bratkartoffeln* (sautéed potatoes). It's tucked away on the river side of the redbrick Fischmarkt Hamburg-Altona market hall.

Mercado
DELI €

(Map p654; www.mercado-hh.de; Hauptstrasse 10; meals €3-7; 9am-8pm; Altona) Forage for prime picnic fare (or eat here) at this market hall by Altona station. Stalls have everything from fresh Med fare to fine wines by the glass.

Oh, It's Fresh
CAFE €

(Map p654; 3803 7861; www.ohitsfresh.de; Carsten-Rehder-Strasse 71; mains €4-12; 6.30am-6.30pm Mon-Fri, 8am-6pm Sat & Sun; Königstrasse) Part of a rapidly growing, health-food-oriented Hamburg minichain, red floral wallpaper and a series of world clocks decorate this light-filled, airy space. In addition to international breakfasts, it serves salads, bagels and baked treats, such as melt-in-your-mouth brownies, to eat in or take away.

Drinking

Many of the cafes listed under eating are excellent venues for enjoying just a drink.

Listings in *Szene* (www.szene-hamburg. de) are helpful for navigating the enormous bar scene.

TOP CHOICE Bar M & V
BAR

(Map p650; www.mvbar.de; Lange Reihe 22; Hauptbahnhof) The drinks menu is like a designer catalogue at this grand old St Georg bar that's had a beautiful restoration. Settle into one of the wooden booths, smell the freesias and enjoy.

Amphore
CAFE

(Map p654; www.cafe-amphore.de; Hafenstrasse 140; Reeperbahn) Beguiling in its understated beauty, Amphore has terrace views out to the Elbe and sidewalk tables for neighbourhood gawking. Its traditional woodsy interior makes it an excellent St Pauli spot for a drink.

Le Lion
BAR

(Map p650; 334 753 780; www.lelion.net; Rathausstrasse 3; 8pm-3am or later; Rathaus) Easily the classiest, most exclusive bar (by virtue of size) you'll find in Hamburg – if you find it. Look for the buzzer in a lion's head and if there's space, they'll let you into this little lair of serious cocktails. Better yet, book a table.

HAMBURG'S UNLIKELY BEACH BARS

When it comes to city beaches, you have to salute Hamburgers for their can-do spirit. Undeterred by the cranes, shipbuilding docks and steel containers decorating their city's workaholic port, and renowned *Schmuddelwetter* (drizzly weather), they've built their own beaches on the banks of the Elbe.

The city beach season kicks off in spring and lasts until at least September, as hipsters come to drink, listen to music, dance and simply lounge on these artificial beaches. Ibiza it ain't, but it does have its own special buzz.

The mother of Hamburg's beach bars, **Strandperle** (www.strandperle-hamburg.de; Schulberg 2; 🕒almost year-round; 🚌112) should not be missed. From a kiosk window you've got a wide choice of beers on tap for under €3. But what really should put Strandperle at the top of your itinerary is the people watching. All ages and classes gather and mingle, especially at dusk as the sun sets. From Altona station, take bus 112 west to Neumühlen/Övelgönne.

Tuesday is tango night at **StrandPauli** (Map p654; www.strandpauli.de; St-Pauli-Hafenstrasse 84; 🕒11am-11pm; 🚌112), a *Gilligan's Island* stretch of sand built on a dock overlooking the busy docks.

Café Knuth CAFE
(Map p654; ☎4600 8708; www.cafeknuth.com; Grosse Rainstrasse 21; 🕒10am-late; 🚉Altona) Students, creative types and work colleagues come to chat in its split-level lounge areas or around picnic tables outside.

Nouar BAR
(Max-Brauer-Allee 275; 🕒7pm-late; [S]Sternschanze) A popular late-night bar with denizens of the nearby Schanzenviertel, this place has that relaxed secondhand look going on and a fondness for football during the week. Weekend DJs have a big local following.

Tower Bar LOUNGE
(Map p654; www.hotel-hafen-hamburg.de; Seewartenstrasse 9; 🕒6pm-1am Mon-Thu, 6pm-2.30am Fri-Sun; [S]Landungsbrücken) For a more elegant, mature evening, repair to this 14th-floor eyrie at the Hotel Hafen for unbeatable harbour views.

Aurel BAR
(Map p654; ☎390 2727; Bahrenfelder Strasse 15; 🚉Altona) This cosy red-tinged bar is a long-standing Ottensen favourite for its cheap cocktails and crowd-pleasing music. Seats outside overlook the characterful square.

Familien-Eck PUB
(Map p654; Friedensallee 4; 🕒3pm-5am; 🚉Altona) It's just a corner hole-in-the-wall, but this Altona classic is everything a good Hamburg neighbourhood joint should be: friendly, unassuming yet always ready to take the piss. Locals pop in, down a quick drink, joke, gossip and hurry on out.

☆ Entertainment

Nightclubs & Live Music

Live music is reason enough to come to Hamburg. And the city continues to breed and support new bands, acts, DJs, sounds, grooves and more. It is renowned for its electro-punk sound, which started in the 1980s and has evolved and morphed endlessly.

Clubkombinat (www.neu.clubkombinat.de) is the go-to source for club listings.

[TOP CHOICE] **Hafenklang** CLUB
(Map p654; www.hafenklang.org; Grosse Elbstrasse 84; 🚉Königstrasse) A collective of Hamburg industry insiders present established and emerging DJs and bands, as well as clubbing events and parties. Look for the spray-painted name on the dark-brick harbour store above a blank metal door.

[TOP CHOICE] **Golden Pudel Club Live Music** LIVE MUSIC
(Map p654; ☎3197 9930; www.pudel.com; St-Pauli-Fischmarkt 27; 🕒from 10pm; 🚉St Pauli) In a ramshackle wooden fisher's hut, this bar-club was established by members of legendary Hamburg band Die Goldenen Zitronen and gets packed to the rafters for its quality electro, hip hop, R&B and reggae gigs.

Fabrik CULTURAL CENTRE
(Map p654; ☎391 070; www.fabrik.de; Barnerstrasse 36; 🚉Altona) They're making beautiful music in this former factory that's an iconic Altona venue, where the music ranges from classical to club and the program spans theatre to

film. Co-founder, painter Horst Dietrich, is still in charge.

Komet Musik Bar Nightclubs MUSIC BAR
(Map p654; ☎2786 8686; www.komet-st-pauli.de; Erichstrasse 11; ⏰from 9pm; [S]St Pauli) Vinyl and only vinyl spins at this treasure of a music bar. Nightly themes range from ska and rocksteady to '60s garage punk and hip hop. Order a Helga, a sweetish house drink that will have everything sounding dreamy.

Grünspan LIVE MUSIC
(Map p654; www.gruenspan.de; Grosse Freiheit 58; 🚆Reeperbahn) Live rock several nights a week in one of Hamburg's oldest venues. Club nights include Bucovina, with oft-touring DJ Shantel.

Knust CLUB
(Map p654; ☎8797 6230; www.knusthamburg.de; Neuer Kamp 30; [S]Feldstrasse) In addition to excellent live gigs and experimental DJ sets, this former slaughterhouse hosts anything from football-fan parties to spoken word.

Molotow LIVE MUSIC
(Map p654; ☎310 845; www.molotowclub.com; Spielbudenplatz 5) An alternative, independent music scene thrives at this much-loved basement venue at Meanie Bar.

Grosse Freiheit 36/Kaiserkeller LIVE MUSIC
(Map p654; ☎3177 7811; Grosse Freiheit 36; 🚆Reeperbahn) The Beatles once played in the basement Kaiserkeller at this now-mainstream venue hosting pop and rock concerts. It's the best reason to detour up the Grosse Freiheit.

Queen Calavera LIVE MUSIC
(Map p654; www.queen-calavera.de; Gerhardstrasse 7; ⏰from 9pm Thu-Sat; 🚆Reeperbahn) Burlesque in the classic sense; sexy, bumping, grinding, singing, joyous acts right out of the '50s.

Uebel & Gefährlich CLUB
(Map p654; www.uebelundgefaehrlich.com; Feldstrasse 66; 🚆Reeperbahn) DJ sets, live music and parties rock this soundproof WWII bunker.

King Calavera LIVE MUSIC
(Map p654; www.facebook.com/King.Calavera; Hans-Albers-Platz 1; 🚆Reeperbahn) Rockabilly, trash, outlaw country and much, much more. 'Rock Around the Tombstone' Goth nights are an institution.

Theatre

Deutsches Schauspielhaus Theatre THEATRE
(Map p650; ☎248 713; www.schauspielhaus.de; Kirchenallee 39; 🚆Hauptbahnhof) Germany's largest and most important theatre presents imaginative interpretations of the classics alongside new works.

Schmidt Tivoli THEATRE
(Map p654; ☎3177 8899; www.tivoli.de; Spielbudenplatz 24; [S]St Pauli) This plush former ballroom now stages a cornucopia of saucy musical reviews, comedies, soap operas and variety shows. Midnight shows follow the main performance, and there's a smaller cabaret-comic venue.

Opera & Classical Music

Laeiszhalle CLASSICAL MUSIC
(Map p650; ☎346 920; www.elbphilharmonie.de; Johannes-Brahms-Platz; [S]Messehallen) The premier address for classical concerts is this splendid neobaroque edifice, home to the State Philharmonic Orchestra, among others. Along with the opera house, it's artistically directed by Australian Simone Young who has announced she's moving on in 2015.

Staatsoper OPERA
(Map p650; ☎356 868; www.hamburgische-staatsoper.de; Grosse Theaterstrasse 25; [S]Stephansplatz) Among the world's most respected opera houses, the Staatsoper has been directed by the likes of Gustav Mahler and Karl Böhm during its 325-year-plus history.

Sports

O2 World Arena STADIUM
(www.o2world-hamburg.de; Sylvesterallee 7) Hamburg's huge O2 Arena was extensively refurbished for the 2006 football World Cup, and is home to Bundesliga club **Hamburger SV**. Take S-Bahn 21 or 3 to 'Stellingen', which is linked by free shuttle buses with the stadium.

Millerntor-Stadion STADIUM
(Map p654; ☎tickets 3178 7451; Heiligengeistfeld) Favourite local team **FC St Pauli** (www.fcstpauli.com) plays at home in the Millerntor.

Shopping

Hamburg is a fascinating and excellent place to shop with everything from mainstream stores and designer boutiques to funky, alternative emporiums that defy description. Some of the best areas to browse:

» Altstadt: west of the Hauptbahnhof, along Spitalerstrasse and Mönckebergstrasse (known as the 'Mö'), you'll find the large department stores and mainstream boutiques.

» Neustadt: upmarket shops are located within the triangle created by Jungfernstieg, Fuhlentwiete and Neuer Wall. Most of them are in a network of elegant shopping arcades.

» St Georg: a growing number of interesting shops, including ethnic groceries, along Lange Reihe.

» Schanzenviertel & Karolinenviertel: Hamburg's counter-cultural scene has retro and vintage clothing and music shops, particularly along Marktstrasse, where you'll find everything from '70s sportswear to Bollywood fashions. Bartelsstrasse is another good bet for funky wares.

» Altona: gentrified with designer boutiques and off-beat shops, especially along Hauptstrasse and the western stretch of Ottenser Hauptstrasse.

Dr Götze Land & Karte   BOOKS
(Map p650; ☎357 4630; www.landundkarte.de; Alstertor 14-18) Enormous range of guidebooks and maps.

Thalia Bücher   BOOKS
(Map p650; ☎3020 7160; www.thalia.de; Grosse Bleichen 19) Stocks English books.

ⓘ Information
Dangers & Annoyances

Although safe and wealthy, Hamburg is also undeniably sleazy in parts, with the notorious red-light district around the Reeperbahn. The Kirchenallee exit of the Hauptbahnhof is also gritty but there's a strong police presence in these areas.

Discount Cards

Tourist offices and some hostels and hotels sell the **Hamburg Card** (per 1/3/5 days €8.90/20.90/36.50). In addition to free public transport in the greater city area, it provides discounts on museums, tours and more.

Emergency
Ambulance/Fire/Police (☎112)
Police Hauptbahnhof (Kirchenallee exit); St Pauli (Spielbudenplatz 31, Davidwache; Reeperbahn)

Internet Access

Hamburg teems with call shops offering internet access.

Cyber Zob (☎2442 3768; www.cyber-zob.de; Adenauerallee 78; per hr €2; ☺10am-10pm) In the ZOB (central bus station).

Post

The **Post Office** (☎01802-3333; Mönckebergstrasse 7; ☺9am-7pm Mon-Fri, 9am-3pm Sat) near the Hauptbahnhof is the most convenient.

Tourist Information

Hamburg Tourismus (☎3005 1200; www.hamburg-tourismus.de) has an excellent range of info in English, including the website. Offices include:

Airport (Airport Plaza btwn Terminals 1 & 2; ☺6am-11pm)

Hauptbahnhof (Kirchenallee exit; ☺8am-9pm Mon-Sat, 10am-6pm Sun)

St Pauli Landungsbrücken (btwn piers 4 & 5; ☺8am-6pm Apr-Oct, 10am-6pm Nov-Mar; ⓢLandungsbrücken)

ⓘ Getting There & Away
Air

Hamburg Airport (HAM; www.flughafen-hamburg.de) has frequent flights to domestic and European cities, including on Lufthansa and most other major European carriers; low-cost carriers include Air Berlin and EasyJet.

Despite their marketing hype, the 'Hamburg' services by Ryanair and Wizzair use Lübeck's airport (p679).

Bus

The **ZOB** (Busbahnhof, Central Bus Station; ☎247 576; www.zob-hamburg.de; Adenauerallee 78; ☺ticket counters 5am-10pm Mon-Tue, Thu, Sat & Sun, to midnight Wed & Fri) is southeast of the Hauptbahnhof. Domestic and international buses arrive and depart around the clock. **Eurolines** (www.eurolines.com) destinations include Amsterdam, Copenhagen, Paris, Prague and Warsaw.

Train

Hamburg has four mainline train stations: the **Hauptbahnhof** (Central Train Station; Glockengiesserwall) (the most important, and an attraction in itself) is on the city centre's north-eastern edge. Three other mainline stations lie west (Altona), south (Harburg) and north (Dammtor) of the centre.

Frequent trains serve regional and long-distance destinations. There are direct ICE/IC services to Berlin-Hauptbahnhof (€73, 1¾ hours), Cologne (€83, four hours), Frankfurt (€114, 3½ hours) and Munich (€135, 5¾ hours).

A direct service to Copenhagen runs several times a day (€79, five hours).

ⓘ Getting Around

Hamburg is a big place, so you'll likely use more than your feet to explore the city.

TO/FROM THE AIRPORT The S1 S-Bahn connects the airport directly with the city centre, including the Hauptbahnhof. The journey takes 24 minutes and costs €2.85.

BICYCLE Many hostels and some hotels arrange bike rental for guests.

StadtRAD Hamburg (www.stadtradhamburg.de), run by Deutsche Bahn (called Call in Bike at other major German cities), operates from U-Bahn and S-Bahn stations and other key points across the city. Rental of its bright-red, seven-gear bikes is free for the first 30 minutes, €0.04 per minute for the next 30 minutes, and €0.08 per minute each hour thereafter. You can register online or at the rental sites.

CAR & MOTORCYCLE Driving around town is easy: thoroughfares are well signposted, and parking stations plentiful. All the major car-hire agencies have branches in Hamburg.

PUBLIC TRANSPORT **HVV** (☑194 49; www.hvv.de) operates buses, ferries, U-Bahn and S-Bahn and has several info centres, including at the Jungfernstieg S-/U-Bahn station, and the Hauptbahnhof.

The city is divided into zones. Ring A covers the city centre, inner suburbs and airport. Kids under six travel free. Day Passes (Tageskarten; both after 9am and all day) cover travel for one adult and up to three children aged six to 14.

S-/U-Bahn tickets must be purchased from machines at station entrances; bus tickets are available from the driver. Ticket types include the following:

TICKET GROSSBEREICH	RING A & B REGION	PRICE
Short Journey	Kurzstrecke (only two to three stops)	€1.40
Single	Einzelkarte	€2.85
9-Hour Day Pass	9-Uhr-Tageskarte (after 9am)	€5.60
Day Pass	Ganztageskarte	€6.95
3-Day Pass	3-Tage-Karte	€16.80
Group Day Pass	Gruppenkarte (after 9am, up to 5 people of any age)	€9.90

If you catch an express bus (Schnellbus), it costs an extra €1.70.

Services run around the clock on weekends and the night before a public holiday; between approximately 12.30am and 4am Sunday to Thursday the night bus network takes over, converging on Rathausmarkt.

Bikes are allowed free of charge aboard S-/U-Bahn trains and buses outside peak hours (6am to 9am and 4pm to 6pm) and on ferries any time.

TAXI Book taxis through **Taxiruf** (☑441 011; www.autoruf.de), or **Taxi Hamburg** (☑666 666; www.taxihamburg.de).

AROUND HAMBURG

Although dominated by its namesake city, Hamburg State does encompass part of the Altes Land, a fertile area reclaimed from marshy ground by Dutch experts in the Middle Ages. Flatness as a terrain feature takes on its own certain stark beauty.

With Germany's excellent train system and great-value day passes, destinations in surrounding states make easy day trips, such as the picturesque town of Lüneburg and the bird-filled Naturpark Elbufer-Drawehn. Bremen and Lübeck are also popular day trips.

Lüneburg

☑04131 / POP 73,000

An off-kilter church steeple, buildings leaning on each other and houses with swollen 'beer-belly' facades: in parts it looks like the charming town of Lüneburg has drunk too much of the Pilsner lager it used to brew. Of course, the city's wobbly angles and uneven pavements have a more prosaic cause. For centuries until 1980, Lüneburg was a salt-mining town, and as this 'white gold' was extracted from the earth, shifting ground and subsidence caused many buildings to tilt sideways.

Partly because of its wobbly comic-book streets, Lüneburg is a lovely town with attractive stepped-gable facades and Hanseatic architecture. It has quite a lively student population, and doubles as a convenient gateway to the surrounding heath.

The Ilmenau River sits between the Hauptbahnhof and the city centre that begins 500m to its west.

◉ Sights & Activities

You can fully explore the old town on foot in half a day. Many tourists enjoy touring the surrounding region, the Lüneburger Heide, by bike; Lüneburg's tourist office has dozens of different pamphlets outlining routes.

Rathaus & Markt   LANDMARK

(Rathaus tours adult/child €5/3; ☉tours 11am, 12.30pm, 2.30pm & 4pm Tue-Sat, 11am & 2pm Sun) The name Lüneburg hails from the Saxon word *hliuni* (refuge), which was granted at the Ducal Palace to those fleeing other territories. However, many sources mistakenly assume the town's name has something to do with Luna, the Roman goddess of the moon. The city authorities at one time seem to have liked this idea, erecting a **fountain** with a statue of the Roman goddess in the town's Markt.

The statue sits in front of the medieval **Rathaus**, which has a spectacular baroque facade, added in 1720, decorated with coats of arms and three tiers of statues. The top row of statues represents (from left to right): Strength, Trade, Peace (the one with the staff), Justice and Moderation. The steeple, topped with 41 Meissen china bells, was installed on the city's 1000th birthday in 1956.

Other buildings around the Markt include the Court of Justice, the little gated-in, grotto-like area with paintings depicting scenes of justice being carried out throughout the centuries; and the former **Ducal Palace**, now a courthouse. West of that, on the corner of Burmeisterstrasse and Am Ochsenmarkt, is the stunning **Heinrich Heine Haus**, the home of the poet's parents. Heine, who hated Lüneburg, wrote the *Loreley* here.

Am Sande   STREET

The cobbled, slightly wobbly street and square Am Sande is full of redbrick buildings with typically Hanseatic stepped gables. Even among these striking buildings, the black-and-white Industrie und Handelskammer (Trade and Industry Chamber, 1548) at the far western end stands out; it's undoubtedly the most beautiful.

St Johanniskirche   CHURCH

(☎435 94; Am Sande; admission €2; ☉10am-5pm Sun-Wed, to 6pm Thu-Sat Apr-Oct, 9am-6pm Thu-Sat, to 4pm Sun Nov-Mar) At the eastern edge of the Am Sande stands the 14th-century St Johanniskirche, whose 108m-high spire leans 2.2m off centre. Local legend has it that the architect was so upset by this crooked steeple that he tried to do himself in by jumping off it. He fell into a hay cart and was saved, but, celebrating his escape later in the pub, drank himself into a stupor, fell over, hit his head and died after all.

The inside of the church is, well, a lot more believable than the legend; there's an impressive organ dating to 1551, carvings and stained-glass windows, both ancient and modern. Overall it has a rich interior unlike the stark spaces of so many other post-war-reconstructed churches.

Auf dem Meere   STREET

If you continue west along Waagestrasse from the Markt and veer left, you'll come to Auf dem Meere, a particularly striking Lüneburg street. Here the wavy pavements have pushed facades sideways or made buildings buckle in the middle. All the way to **St Michaeliskirche** the street feels wonky, like it's something from the 1919 German expressionist movie *The Cabinet of Dr Caligari*. Look at the steps leading to the church!

Deutsches Salzmuseum   MUSEUM

(☎450 65; www.salzmuseum.de; Sülfmeisterstrasse 1; adult/child €6/4; ☉9am-5pm Mon-Fri, 10am-5pm Sat & Sun May-Sep, 10am-5pm Oct-Apr) The Deutsches Salzmuseum explains (in German only) how Lüneburg's precious food preservative made the town such an important player in the Hanseatic League. Displays are peppered with old salt implements.

SaLü Salztherme   SPA

(Spa Baths; ☎723 110; www.kurzentrum.de; Uelzener Strasse 1-5; adult/child from €8/5; ☉10am-11pm Mon-Sat, 8am-9pm Sun) With Lüneburg having made its fortune from salt, where better to try the mineral's therapeutic properties than at the town's salt baths. You can bathe in saltwater at 36°C, and try out the single-sex or mixed sauna area, water fountains and whirlpool.

🛏 Sleeping

Hotel Bremer Hof   HOTEL €€

(☎2240; www.bremer-hof.de; Lüner Strasse 12-13; s €64-120, d €93-142; P🐾) Easily the most versatile place in town, this ivy-covered 54-room hotel offers rooms for most budgets, from plain and inexpensive in a modern annex to historic rooms with beamed ceilings in the main building. It has been in the same family since 1889.

Hotel Scheffler
HOTEL €€

(☑200 80; www.hotel-scheffler.de; Bardowicker Strasse 7; s €68, d €93-98; P☺☎) The hotel most in keeping with Lüneburg's quirky character, this 16-room place just off the Markt greets you with brickwork, stained glass, carved wooden stair-rails, animal trophies and indoor plants. The rooms are low-ceilinged and cosy, and there's a restaurant on-site.

Zum Heidkrug
HOTEL €€

(☑241 60; www.zum-heidkrug.de; Am Berge 5; s €49-60, d €72-100) Made up of the characteristic red and black bricks used throughout the region, this cosy seven-room inn sits above a very well-regarded restaurant of the same name (it boasts a Michelin star and is known for its Med-flavoured fare). Rooms are less fancy, and come with either shower or bath. The decor is modern-hotel with half-timbered touches.

DJH Hostel
HOSTEL €

(☑418 64; www.jugendherberge.de/jh/lueneburg; Soltauer Strasse 133; dm under/over 27yr €24/28; P@☎) After sundown, the lights glow a warm welcome from the glass-walled stairwell of this spacious and relatively luxurious 148-bed hostel in the town's south, right near the university. Bus services – 5011 or 5012 from the train station to Scharnhorstrasse/DJH – don't run very late.

✖ Eating & Drinking

The restaurant-lined Schröderstrasse leads from the Markt; it's alive at night with students enjoying beer specials. Also popular is Am Stintmarkt down by the river, where many places have outdoor tables that let you hear water sluicing through the locks.

Das Kleine
GERMAN €€

(☑224 910; Am Stintmarkt 8; mains €8-20) Enjoy traditional food at outside tables that spill across decking to the riverside. There are even some on a pontoon. If the weather is surly, you can settle into the cosy tables inside. Expect a good range of German cuisine with differences: the rump steak is served with turnip and a port wine sauce. The menu also includes fresh fish from the region.

Mäxx
CAFE €€

(☑732 505; Schröderstrasse 6; mains €6-16; ☺8am-late) If you want to see a cross-section of Lüneburg's populace, you'll find them in masses at this popular cafe in the centre of town. It does a fine breakfast and through the day has many specials that change with the season: look for dishes with asparagus and strawberries late in spring.

Gasthausbrauerei und Brennerei Nolte
BREWERY

(☑041 31; www.gasthausbrauereinolte.de; Dahlenburger Landstrasse 102; mains €13-16; ☺4-11pm Wed-Sat, 11am-10pm Sun) About 500m east of the train station, this local legend of a brewery has been making hops hop since 1906. Unlike many beer-centric places, food is taken seriously here; fish is house-smoked, the menu lists the provenance of the dishes and you can enjoy regional specialities like sour pork in aspic. The dark beer is especially good out in the garden.

Pons
BAR

(☑224 935; Salzstrasse am Wasser 1; ☺from 5pm Mon-Fri, from 3pm Sat & Sun) If Pons looks this cracked, crooked and uneven when you walk in of an evening, just imagine how it will seem when you stagger out after a few drinks. This ex-1970s hippy joint has had a bit of a shave since its early days but it still hews to a funky vibe. The beer's cheap as are the simple plates of food.

ℹ Information

Lüneburg Tourist-Information Office (☑207 6620; www.lueneburg.de; Rathaus, Am Markt; ☺9.30am-6pm Mon-Fri, 9am-2pm Sat Jan-Dec, 10am-4pm Sun May-Oct & Dec) Offers city tours and has info on trips to the surrounding Lüneburger Heide.

ℹ Getting There & Away

There are frequent IC train services to Hamburg (€12, 30 minutes) and Hanover (€26, one hour). A web of cheaper regional trains also provide these and more links.

ℹ Getting Around

You'll have no problem walking any place you'd like to reach in the old town from the train station. The **Rad am Hauptbahnhof** (☑266 350; per 3 hr/day €5/10; ☺6am-8pm Mon-Fri, 9am-6pm Sat & Sun) rents bikes.

Naturpark Elbufer-Drawehn

Bleckede and the Biosphärenreservat Niedersächsische Elbtalaue (Biosphere Reserve in Lower Saxony Elbe Valley; www.elbtalaue .niedersachsen.de) are located some 20km east of Lüneburg. The reserve is a haven for bird life such as white storks, wild geese and cranes, and runs for 85km along the Elbe River. Cyclists and hikers will be well rewarded by this picturesque and interesting wetland, which is all part of the 840km Elberadweg (p585) cycling route.

The Lüneburg tourist office has maps and brochures, including details on various old castles in the area best reached by car. The **Biosphaerium Elbtalaue** (☑05852-951 414; www.biosphaerium.de; Schlossstrasse 10; adult/child €5/2.50; ☺10am-6pm Apr-Oct, 10am-5pm Wed-Sun Nov-Mar) has full details and exhibits about the biosphere and its beavers.

ⓘ Getting There & Around

No trains run to Bleckede, but the 5100 bus (€3, 30 minutes) leaves at least hourly from Lüneburg at Am Sande or the Hauptbahnhof.

SCHLESWIG-HOLSTEIN

Sandy beaches, jaunty red-and-white striped lighthouses, deep fjords carved by glaciers, sandpipers and seals have made this sweeping peninsula between the North and Baltic Seas Germany's most elite summer retreat.

Much of the peninsula's interior is comprised of seemingly never-ending expanses of flat, green farmland interrupted only by wind farms and grazing black-and-white-splotched cows. But its coastline – and especially the North Frisian Islands off Schleswig-Holstein's western coast – remain the country's answer to the Côte d'Azur.

Of course, the fickle northern European climate makes for a funny sort of answer, as cold winds and dark clouds periodically drive the hardiest holidaymakers from their *Strandkörbe* (sheltered straw 'beach basket' seats).

Schleswig-Holstein belonged to neighbouring Denmark until 1864 and you'll find Scandinavian overtones throughout the region, particularly in Flensburg and Schleswig, home to a superbly recreated Viking settlement, as well as the state's finest art museum.

Even if it's only as a day trip from Hamburg, don't miss Lübeck, the magnificently preserved medieval headquarters of the Hanseatic League.

Lübeck

☑0451 / POP 210,300

A 12th-century gem boasting more than 1000 historical buildings, Lübeck's picture-book appearance is an enduring reminder of its role as one of the founding cities of the mighty Hanseatic League and its moniker of the 'Queen of the Hanse'. Behind its landmark Holstentor (gate), you'll find streets lined with medieval merchants' homes and spired churches forming Lübeck's 'crown'.

Recognised by Unesco as a World Heritage Site in 1987, today this thriving provincial city retains many enchanting corners to explore.

◉ Sights

You can easily spend a day wandering amidst Lübeck's steeple-punctuated sights. For respite, head south along An der Obertrave southwest of the Altstadt; you'll pass one of Lübeck's loveliest corners, the **Malerwinkel** (Painters' Quarter), where you can take a break on garden benches among blooming flowers, gazing out at the houses and white-picket fences across the water.

In the Middle Ages, Lübeck was home to numerous craftspeople and artisans. Their presence caused demand for housing to outgrow the available space, so tiny single-storey homes were built in courtyards behind existing rows of houses. These were then made accessible via little walkways from the street.

Almost 90 such *Gänge* (walkways) and *Höfe* (courtyards) still exist, among them charitable housing estates built for the poor, the Stiftsgängeand Stiftshöfe. The most famous of the latter are the **Füchtingshof** (Map p674; Glockengiesserstrasse 25) with its beautiful carvings and the 1612 **Glandorps Gang** (Map p674; Glockengiesserstrasse 41-51), which you can peer into.

There must be something in the water in Lübeck, or maybe it's all the famous marzipan. The city has connections to two Nobel Prize–winning authors (as well as Nobel Peace Prize–winning former chancellor Willy Brandt).

TOP CHOICE **Holstentor**   LANDMARK

(Map p674) Built in 1464 and looking so settled-in that it appears to sag, Lübeck's charming

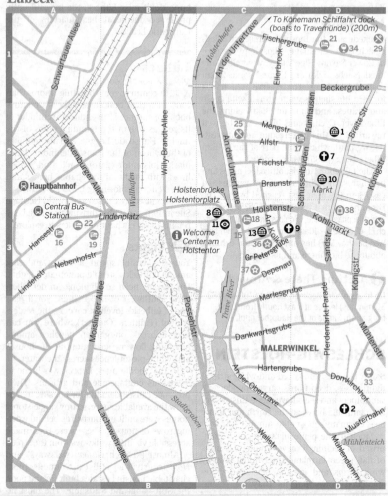

To Könemann Schiffahrt dock
(boats to Travemünde) (200m)

redbrick city gate is a national icon. Its twin pointed cylindrical towers, leaning together across the stepped gable that joins them, captivated Andy Warhol (his print is in the St Annen Museum, p676), and have graced postcards, paintings, posters and marzipan souvenirs, as you'll discover inside its **Museum Holstentor** (Map p674; ☎122 4129; adult/child €5/2; ☺10am-6pm Apr-Dec, 11am-5pm Tue-Sun Jan-Mar).

The latin inscription on the west face 'concordia domi foris pax' means 'harmony at home and peace abroad'.

TOP CHOICE Marienkirche CHURCH

(Map p674; Schüsselbuden 13; admission €1; ☺10am-6pm Apr-Sep, to 5pm Oct, to 4pm Tue-Sun Nov-Mar) Near the Markt rise the 125m twin spires of Germany's third-largest church, the 13th-century Marienkirche. It's most famous for its shattered bells, which have been left where they fell after a 1942 WWII bombing raid. It's a stark and moving display. Outside there's a little devil sculpture with an amusing folk tale (in German and English).

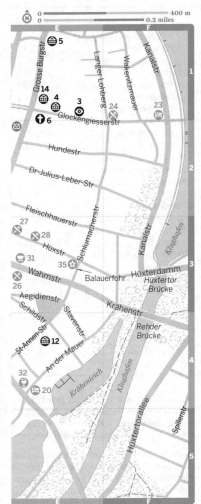

transported from Lüneburg. It was then bartered for furs from Scandinavia and used to preserve the herrings that formed a substantial chunk of Lübeck's Hanseatic trade.

Rathaus
HISTORIC BUILDING

(Map p674; ☎122 1005; Breite Strasse 64; adult/concession €3/1.50; ☺tours 11am, noon & 3pm Mon-Fri) Sometimes described as a 'fairy tale in stone', Lübeck's 13th- to 15th-century Rathaus is widely regarded as one of the most beautiful in Germany. Unfortunately, the impact of its facade is diminished by ugly modern buildings around the marketplace. Inside, a highlight is the Audienzsaal (audience hall), a light-flooded hall decked out in festive rococo.

Petrikirche
CHURCH

(Map p674; ☎397 730; www.st-petri-luebeck.de; Schüsselbuden 13; adult/child €3/2; ☺9am-9pm Apr-Sep, 10am-7pm Oct-Mar) Panoramic views over the city unfold from the 13th-century Petrikirche, which has a tower lift to a viewing platform 50m high. The interior is starkly whitewashed.

Dom
CHURCH

(Cathedral; Map p674; ☺10am-6pm Apr-Oct, 10am-4pm Nov-Mar) The Dom was founded in 1173 by Heinrich der Löwe when he took over Lübeck. Locals like to joke that if you approach the Dom from the northeast, you have to go through *Hölle* (hell) and *Fegefeuer* (purgatory) – the actual names of streets – to see **Paradies**, the lavish vestibule to the Dom. Although spartan, the interior has good displays showing reconstruction after the 1942 bombing raid.

Katharinenkirche
CHURCH, MUSEUM

(Map p674; www.museumskirche.de; cnr Glockengiesserstrasse & Königstrasse) Art lovers will enjoy the Katharinenkirche for its sculptures by Ernst Barlach and Gerhard Marcks, plus *The Resurrection of Lazarus* by Tintoretto. It has no tower owing to the rules of the Cistercian order that built it in the 14th century. At time of research it was closed for restoration.

Buddenbrookhaus
MUSEUM

(Map p674; ☎122 4190; www.buddenbrookhaus.de; Mengstrasse 4; adult/child €6/2.50; ☺11am-6pm Apr-Dec, 11am-5pm Jan-Mar) The winner of the 1929 Nobel Prize for Literature, Thomas Mann, was born in Lübeck in 1875 and his family's former home is now the Buddenbrookhaus. Named after Mann's novel

Theater Figuren Museum
MUSEUM

(Map p674; ☎786 26; www.en.tfm-luebeck.com; Am Kolk 14; adult/child €5/2; ☺10am-6pm Apr-Oct, 11am-5pm Tue-Sun Nov-Mar) Even if you think you eschew puppets, don't miss this wondrous collection of some 1200 puppets, props, posters and more from Europe, Asia and Africa. The artistry is amazing as is the ancient alley where it's located; try to catch a performance at its theatre (p679).

Salzspeicher
HISTORIC BUILDINGS

(Map p674) Just behind the Holstentor (to the east) stand the Salzspeicher: six gabled brick shop-filled buildings once used to store salt

Lübeck

of a wealthy Lübeck family in decline, *The Buddenbrooks* (1901), this award-winning museum is a monument not only to the author of such classics as *Der Tod in Venedig* (Death in Venice) and *Der Zauberberg* (The Magic Mountain), but also to his brother Heinrich, who wrote the story that became the Marlene Dietrich film *Der Blaue Engel* (The Blue Angel). There's a rundown of the rather tragic family history, too.

Günter Grass-Haus MUSEUM
(Map p674; ☑122 4192; www.guenter-grass-haus.de; Glockengiesserstrasse 21; adult/child €6/3; ⊙10am-5pm Apr-Dec, 11am-5pm Jan-Mar) Born in Danzig (now Gdańsk), Poland, Günter Grass had been living just outside Lübeck for 13 years when he collected his Nobel Prize in 1999. But this postwar literary colossus initially trained as an artist, and has always continued to draw and sculpt. The Günter Grass-Haus is filled with the author's *leitmotifs* – flounders, rats, snails and eels – brought to life in bronze and charcoal, as well as in prose. You can view a copy of the first typewritten page

of *Die Blechtrommel* (The Tin Drum; 1959). Grass continues to make news. In 2012 his poems about Israel and Greece were controversial. The small bookshop is excellent.

Heiligen-Geist-Hospital HISTORIC BUILDING
(Map p674; Königstrasse; ⊙10am-5pm Tue-Sun, 10am-4pm Dec-Feb) The former Heiligen-Geist-Hospital has an elegant old entryway and a few resonances of Germany's first hospital (dating back to 1227). Through an early-Gothic hall church, you'll find a warren of small living cubicles dating from 1820, which gave refuge to aged seafarers. Part of the complex is used for December's Christmas market.

St Annen Museum MUSEUM
(Map p674; ☑122 4137; www.st-annen-museum. de; St-Annen-Strasse 15; adult/child €6/3; ⊙10am-5pm Tue-Sun Apr-Dec, 11am-5pm Tue-Sun Jan-Mar) The St Annen Museum houses a browsable mishmash of ecclesiastical art (including Hans Memling's 1491 Passion Altar), historical knick-knacks and contemporary art in its modern Kunsthalle wing. The latter houses

the Andy Warhol print of Lübeck's Holsten-tor. It has a chic little cafe in the courtyard.

FREE **Willy Brandt House** MUSEUM
(Map p674; www.willy-brandt.de; Königstrasse 21; ⊙11am-5pm Tue-Sun Jan-Mar, 11am-6pm daily Apr-Dec) Lübeck's other big Nobel Prize–winner, was chancellor of West Germany (1969-74) and was honoured for his efforts to reconcile with East Germany. Exhibits capture the tense times of the Cold War and Willy Brandt's role at this pivotal time. He was born in this house in 1913.

Tours

The Trave River forms a moat around the Altstadt, and cruising it aboard a boat is a fine way to get a feel for the city.

Quandt-Linie BOAT TOUR
(Map p674; ✆777 99; www.quandt-linie.de; Holstentorterrassen; adult/child from €12/6) Leaves from just south of the Holstenbrücke bridge. One-hour city tours leave every half-hour between 10am and 6pm from May to October (plus limited services November to April).

Open-Air City Tour BUS TOUR
(adult/child €7/4.50; ⊙10am-4pm May-Sep) Open-top buses make 45-minute circuits of the historic city. You can join at many points along the circuit.

Sleeping

TOP CHOICE **Klassik Altstadt Hotel** BOUTIQUE HOTEL €€
(Map p674; ✆702 980; www.klassik-altstadt-hotel.de; Fischergrube 52; s €60-100, d €130-160; ☎) Each room at this elegantly furnished boutique hotel is dedicated to a different, mostly German, writer or artist, such as Thomas Mann and Johann Sebastian Bach, as well as international luminaries like Denmark's Hans Christian Andersen. Single rooms (some share baths) feature travelogues by famous authors.

Hotel Lindenhof HOTEL €€
(Map p674; ✆872 100; www.lindenhof-luebeck.de; Lindenstrasse 1a; s €65-95, d €85-135; @☎) The 66 rooms at this family-run hotel in a quiet side street are small, but an included breakfast buffet, friendly service and little extras (such as free biscuits and newspapers) propel the Lindenhof into a superior league.

Hotel an der Marienkirche HOTEL €€
(Map p674; ✆799 410; www.hotel-an-der-marien kirche.de; Schüsselbuden 4; s €58-78, d €75-95; ☎) This small and bright midrange hotel could not be better located; in fact, one of the 18 rooms has a view of the namesake church. The staff is as cheery as the Ikea-like furnishings. The breakfast buffet is especially healthy.

Hotel zur Alten Stadtmauer HOTEL €€
(Map p674; ✆737 02; www.hotelstadtmauer.de; An der Mauer 57; s €62-87, d €93-115; ☎) With pine furniture and splashes of red and yellow, this simple 24-room hotel is bright and cheerful. The wooden flooring means sound carries, but guests tend not to be the partying type. Back rooms overlook the river and three are in a historic guesthouse.

Hotel Jensen Hotel HOTEL €€
(Map p674; ✆702 490; www.hotel-jensen.de; An der Obertrave 4-5; s €75-85, d €95-120; @☎) This old *Patrizierhaus* (mansion house) dating from the early 14th century overlooks the Salzspeicher across the Trave River. Although the 42 rooms aren't as characterful as the gabled exterior suggests, with rather generic modern furnishings, you can't beat the location. A good breakfast buffet is included.

Baltic Hotel HOTEL €€
(Map p674; ✆855 75; www.baltic-hotel.de; Hansestrasse 11; s €40-70, d €80-100) This rambling older hotel is one of many very close to the bus and train stations. It's clean and run by a very engaging staff. Rooms vary greatly in size, although none seem as large as the excellent breakfast buffet. Decor is simple and parking is limited.

Park Hotel am Lindenplatz HOTEL €€
(Map p674; ✆871 970; www.parkhotel-luebeck.de; Lindenplatz 2; s €60-100, d €80-130; P@☎) Inside a well-preserved art-nouveau building, this small, intimate hotel has 24 low-lit, neutral-toned rooms that that – like Lübeck itself – are ideal for a romantic interlude. Save your energy for same by using the lift.

Rucksackhotel HOSTEL €
(Map p674; ✆706 892; www.rucksackhotel-luebeck.com; Kanalstrasse 70; dm €15-16, s €28, d €40; P@☎) This 30-bed hostel has a relaxed atmosphere and good facilities including a well-equipped kitchen and round-the-clock access. The decor is colourful, with the odd tropical touch.

Campingplatz Schönböcken CAMPGROUND €
(893 090; www.camping-luebeck.de; Steinrader Damm 12; per tent €4-5, adult/child €5/2, electricity €3) This modern campground is a good bet for its grassy sites, kiosk, restaurant, entertainment room and children's playground. It's a 10-minute bus ride west of the city centre (take bus 7).

Eating

TOP CHOICE Schiffergesellschaft GERMAN €€€
(Map p674; 767 76; www.schiffergesellschaft.com; Breite Strasse 2; mains €12-25) Opened in 1535 as the dining room for the Blue Water Captains' Guild, Lübeck's cutest – if not best – restaurant is a veritable museum. Ships' lanterns, original model ships dating from 1607 and orange Chinese-style lamps with revolving maritime silhouettes adorn the wood-lined rooms, which include an elevated banquet room up the back. As you sit on long benches resembling church pews, staff in long white aprons bring you Frisian specialities (there are many seasonal specials). On balmy nights, head up a flight of steps to the hidden garden out back. Book ahead.

Miera DELI, RESTAURANT €€€
(Map p674; 772 12; www.miera-luebeck.de; Hüxstrasse 57; snacks from €7, mains €15-25; 9am-10pm;) You can sit down for a platter of antipasti or pick up gourmet picnic goodies at this sophisticated delicatessen-bistro. Reserve ahead to dine in the formal restaurant on elegant Italian fare. There is an excellent wine selection and tables overlooking the Hüxstrasse action are always full (or opt for a quiet courtyard table).

Vai MEDITERRANEAN €€€
(Map p674; 400 8083; www.restaurant-vai.de; Hüxstrasse 42; lunch mains €9, dinner mains €17-28) Glossy, richly grained timber lines the walls, tables and even the alfresco courtyard of this sleek restaurant. The good-value top-end lunches are popular and feature pasta, seafood and salads. It's more complex at night with steaks and lobster appearing. Great wine list; book ahead.

Café Niederegger CAFE €
(Map p674; Breite Strasse 89; dishes €3-14; 9am-7pm Mon-Fri, 9am-6pm Sat, 10am-6pm Sun) Milky marzipan coffee, marzipan ice cream and a host of other sweet and savoury snacks and light meals are served at the cafe inside Lübeck's iconic marzipan centre.

Amaro CAFE €
(Map p674; www.amaro-Luebeck.de; Glockengiesserstrasse 67; snacks from €3; 10am-6pm Mon-Fri, 10am-4pm Sat) This prim little corner cafe makes its own fabulous range of chocolates using top ingredients from around the world. There is a variety of coffees and liquors that you can enjoy amidst the luscious smells inside or at tables out front.

Brauberger GERMAN €€
(Map p674; 702 0606; Alfstrasse 36; mains €9-14; 5pm-midnight Mon-Thu, 5pm-late Fri & Sat) The brewing kettles are right in the dining room and the humid air is redolent of hops at this traditional German brewer, which has been serving its own golden amber since 1225. Get a stein of the sweet, cloudy house brew and enjoy one of many excellent schnitzels or other traditional fare.

Krützfeld DELI €
(Map p674; 728 32; Hüxstrasse 23; snacks from €2; 8am-6pm Tue-Fri, 8am-2pm Sat) This classic deli has been serving all manner of fresh and smoked seafood for decades. There's no better place in town to assemble a picnic.

Grenadine BISTRO €€
(Map p674; 307 2950; Wahmstrasse 40; mains €7-15; 9am-late) This narrow, elongated bar leads through to a garden out back. Enjoy bistro fare amidst chic, retro-minimalist style. The long drinks menu goes well with tapas choices. Sandwiches, salads and pasta plus breakfast are served.

Kartoffel Keller POTATOES €€
(Map p674; 762 34; www.kartoffel-keller.de; Koberg 8; mains €8-15;) Located in the old wine cellar of the Heiligen-Geist-Hospital, this merry and casual restaurant celebrates all things spud. Potatoes are mashed and baked and also take the form of pancakes and dumplings. The choices are all quite good and you can go meaty by opting for schnitzels and seafood. Tables outside are tops in summer.

 Drinking

Im Alten Zolln PUB
(Map p674; 723 95; Mühlenstrasse 93-95; 11am-late;) This classic pub inhabits a 16th-century customs post. There's an excellent beer selection. Patrons people-watch from the terrace in summer and watch bands (rock and jazz) inside in winter.

Café Remise
CAFE

(Map p674; ☑777 73; Wahmstrasse 43-45; ☺9am-late) An arty crowd sips wine in the vine-draped courtyard of this split-level cafe, which has an industrial vibe. The bistro fare is good.

Theaterquelle
BAR

(Map p674; Fischergrube 24; ☺7pm-3am Mon-Sat) There's an arty vibe to this genial old boozer. It's open long after others have shut yet still manages to get a crowd.

Jazz-Café
BAR

(Map p674; ☑707 3734; Mühlenstrasse 62; ☺4pm-late Sun-Fri, noon-late Sat) Live jazz only plays once a month but the sound system can always be counted on for good tunes at this fine bar, which has tables out front.

☆ Entertainment

Local listings include *Piste* (www.piste.de) and *Ultimo* (www.ultimo-luebeck.de). Check organ recital schedules for the churches at the tourist office.

CafeBar
BAR

(Map p674; Hüxstrasse 94; ☺11am-late) Cafe by day, bar by... you get it. But the real appeal here are the hippin' hot DJs who mix techno, R&B and groovy sounds. Draws a hipster crowd.

Figurentheater
PUPPET THEATRE

(Map p674; ☑700 60; www.figurentheater-luebeck. de; Am Kolk 20-22; tickets €6-16; ☺Tue-Sun; ⊕) This adorable puppet theatre, which is part of the museum (p675), puts on a children's show at 3pm, and another for adults on some evenings at 7.30pm, as well as occasional performances in English.

Musikhochschule Lübeck
CONCERTS

(Map p674; ☑150 50; www.mh-luebeck.de; Grosse Petersgrube 17-29) High-calibre concerts take place throughout the summer and winter semesters at this music academy.

🛍 Shopping

Hüxstraase is one of Germany's best shopping streets. It's lined with an array of creative and interesting boutiques, clothing stores, bookshops, cafes and much more. And there's additional joy on surrounding streets, especially Schlumacherstrasse.

TOP CHOICE Niederegger
FOOD

(Map p674; ☑530 1126; www.niederegger.de; Breite Strasse 89; ☺9am-7pm Mon-Fri, 9am-6pm Sat, 10am-6pm Sun) Niederegger is Lübeck's mecca for marzipan lovers, the almond confectioner from Arabia, which has been made locally for centuries. Even if you're not buying, the shop's elaborate seasonal displays are a feast for the eyes. In its small museum, **Marzipan-Salon**, you'll learn that in medieval Europe marzipan was considered medicine, not a treat. At the back of the shop there's an elegant cafe.

ℹ Information

Tourist Office (Welcome Center am Holstentor; ☑01805 882 233; www.luebeck-tourismus.de; Holstentorplatz 1; ☺9.30am-7pm Mon-Fri, 10am-3pm Sat & 10am-2pm Sun Jun-Sep, 9.30am-6pm Mon-Fri & 10am-3pm Sat Oct-May) Sells the Happy Day Card (per 1/2/3 days €10/12/15) offering free public transport in Lübeck and Travemünde and museum discounts. Also has a cafe and internet terminals.

Netzwerk (☑409 5552; Wahmstrasse 58; per hr €2; ☺10am-10pm Mon-Sat) Internet access.

ℹ Getting There & Away

AIR Low-cost carriers **Ryanair** (www.ryanair. com) and **Wizzair** (www.wizzair.com) serve **Lübeck airport** (LBC; www.flughafen-luebeck. de), which they euphemistically call Hamburg-Lübeck. Destinations include Milan and Stockholm. Buses take passengers straight to Hamburg (one-way €10, 55 minutes), while scheduled bus 6 (€2.70) serves Lübeck's Hauptbahnhof and central bus station.

BOAT Ferries sail from nearby Travemünde to Baltic destinations.

BUS Regional buses share the Central Bus Station with local buses near the Hauptbahnhof. Kraftomnibusse services to/from Wismar terminate here, as do the Autokraft buses to/from Hamburg Airport, Kiel and Berlin.

TRAIN Lübeck has connections every hour to Hamburg (€19, 40 minutes), Kiel (€16, 1¼ hours) and Rostock (€24, two hours 20 minutes) with a change in Bad Kleinen.

ℹ Getting Around

Lübeck's Altstadt (old town) is on an island encircled by the canalised Trave River. The Hauptbahnhof (central train station) and central bus station are 500m west of the Holstentor.

Lübeck's centre is easily walked. Many streets are pedestrianised and off limits to all but hotel guest vehicles.

Bus tickets cost €1.70; day cards cost €4.90. Higher-priced tickets are valid for Travemünde.

Travemünde

📞04502

Writer Thomas Mann declared that he spent his happiest days in Travemünde, just outside Lübeck (which bought it in 1329 to control the shipping coming into its harbour), and its 4.5km of sandy beaches at the point where the Trave River flows into the Baltic Sea make it easy to see why. Water sports are the main draw, along with a colourful **sailing regatta** (www.travemuender-woche.com) in the last week of July.

The town is all wide streets and has a certain 1960s feel. Vorderreihe on the waterfront is lined with expensive shops and cafes. Across the river is the historic four-masted sailing-ship-turned-museum, **Passat** (📞122 5202; www.ss-passat.com; adult/child €3/1.50; ⊙10am-5pm mid-May–mid-Sep, 11am-4.30pm Sat & Sun Easter–mid-May & mid-Sep–Oct), which used to run around South America's Cape Horn in the early to mid-20th century. A regular passenger ferry (€1) crosses the river.

The **Welcome Center** (📞882 233; www.travemuende-tourismus.de; Strandbahnhof; ⊙9.30am-6pm Mon-Fri, 10am-3pm Sat, 11am-2pm Sun May-Sep, 9.30am-6pm Mon-Fri Oct-Apr) in the beautifully restored Strandbahnhof can help with accommodation.

❶ Getting There & Away

Travemünde is a gateway to Scandinavia, with major ferry lines sailing from its Skandinavienkai.

Könemann Schiffahrt (one-way/return €11.50/17.50; ⊙Apr–mid-Oct) runs scenic ferries to/from Lübeck. You can sail one-way and take the train the other.

Hourly **trains** connect Lübeck to Travemünde (adult/child €2.90/1.75, 22 minutes), which has several train stations, including Skandinavienkai (for international ferries) and Strandbahnhof (for the beach and tourist office).

Kiel

📞0431 / POP 238,000

Some locals admit Kiel, the capital of Schleswig-Holstein, has a city centre that's *grottenhässlich* (ugly as sin). And unfortunately it is true; it was obliterated during WWII by bombing raids on its U-boat pens and then rapidly rebuilt.

However, Kiel's grand harbour continues on as it has for centuries and this should be the focus of your visit. Huge ferries transport millions of passengers to and from Scandinavia, while summer sees locals strolling the long waterfront promenade.

⊙ Sights & Activities

Follow Kiel's main thoroughfare, the pedestrianised Holstenstrasse, for about 1.5km northeast to the Schlossgarten to reach the waterfront (the port closer in is inaccessible due to ferry terminals).

TOP CHOICE **Kiellinie**   PROMENADE

The magnificent waterfront promenade known as the Kiellinie begins northeast of the

NATURPARK HOLSTEINISCHE SCHWEIZ

Sprawling over 753 sq km between Lübeck to the south and Kiel to the north, the **Naturpark Holsteinische Schweiz** (www.naturpark-holsteinische-schweiz.de) is the region's largest outdoor playground. Germany's propensity to label its most scenic areas 'Swiss' (the name translates as 'Holstein Switzerland') reflects the park's undulating green hills, golden fields and wildflower-strewn meadows, and hedge walls dating from 18th-century farming laws. This chocolate-box-pretty landscape is interspersed with a string of some 200 lakes, of which 70 are over one hectare in size.

The park's three main towns, each in idyllic lakeside settings, are **Eutin**, famed for its baroque castle amid English-style gardens; the spa resort of **Malente** (www.bad-malente.de); and **Plön**, on the shores of the park's largest lake, the Grosser Plöner See.

Plön's comprehensive **Tourist Info Grosser Plöner See** (📞04522-509 50; www.holsteinischeschweiz.de/ploen; Bahnhofstrasse 5; ⊙8am-6pm Mon-Fri, 10am-4pm Sat, 10am-2pm Sun Jun-Aug) can help with accommodation and a wealth of water-based activities from boat trips to fishing, swimming, windsurfing, kayaking and scuba diving.

Hiking and cycling trails criss-cross the park, as does a well-signed road network. Lübeck–Kiel trains stop in Eutin, Malente (Bad Malente-Gremsmühlen) and Plön.

Schlossgarten. Sailing clubs, a tiny aquarium, cafes and restaurants line the way and there is an ever-changing series of harbour vistas. Eventually the 3.5km-promenade becomes the Hindenburgufer. About 2km from the start at Reventloubrücke you can get hourly ferries back to near the train station or on to Laboe.

Nord-Ostsee-Kanal CANAL

(viewing platform adult/child €1/0.50) Kiel lies at the point at which the 99km-long Nord-Ostsee-Kanal enters the Baltic Sea from the North Sea. Inaugurated in 1895, the canal is now the third-most trafficked in the world, after the Suez and Panama Canals, with some 60,000 ships passing through every year.

It's easy to view the *Schleusen* (locks) at **Holtenau**, 7km north of Kiel. The viewing platform here is open from sunrise to sunset. There's a museum on the southern side of the canal. To get to the locks, take bus 11 to Wik, Kanal. A free ferry shuttles back and forth between the southern and northern banks.

To really appreciate this marvel of engineering consider a tour with **Adler-Schiffe** (☎01805-123 344; www.adler-schiffe.de; adult/child from €48/24; ☺Jun-Sep) aboard the *Raddampfer Freya*, a 100-year-old steamship. Tours last from eight hours to all day and run several times a week in summer.

Schiffahrtsmuseum MUSEUM

(Maritime Museum; ☎901 3428; Am Wall 65) Atmospherically located in an imposing former fish market, Kiel's maritime museum tells the story of the city's harbour and is due to reopen in 2013 after a massive reconstruction. It is near the Schloss on the waterfront and not far south from the start of the Kiellinie.

★ Festivals & Events

Kiel's biggest annual event is the giant **Kieler Woche** (Kiel Week; www.kieler-woche.de) held during the last full week of June. Revolving around a series of yachting regattas, it's attended by more than 4000 of the world's sailing elite and half a million spectators. Even if you're not into boats, it's one nonstop party.

🛏 Sleeping & Eating

Kiel is best visited on your way to some place else. For a good lunch, your best bet is to stroll the Kiellinie and see what grabs your fancy.

LABOE

At the mouth of the Kiel firth, on its eastern bank, the village of Laboe is home to the WWII **U-Boat 995** (☎04343-427 062; www.deutscher-marinebund.de; Strandstrasse 92; combined ticket with Marine Ehrenmal adult/child €8.50/5.50; ☺9.30am-6pm Apr-Oct, 9.30am-4pm Nov-Mar) and associated museum, **Marine Ehrenmal** (adult/child €4/2.50, combined admission adult/child €8.50/5.50). Hundreds of subs like these called Kiel home; Wolfgang Petersen's seminal film *Das Boot* (1981) was set on a similar U-boat. You can climb through its claustrophobic interior. From Kiel, take the ferry or bus 100 or 102.

Hotel Am Schwedenkai HOTEL €€

(☎986 4220; www.hotel-am-schwedenkai.de; Holstenbrücke 28; s €65-120, d €90-190; P🐛) About midway between the train station and the Kiellinie, this 28-room hotel has sweeping views of the nearby ferry docks. The building is modern and rooms are simple but appealing, with a Danish-style Nordic blue, white and pale timber colour scheme.

Kieler Brauerei BREWERY €€

(☎906 290; www.kieler-brauerei.de; Alter Markt 9; mains €7-13; ☺10am-11pm) This city centre microbrewery produces a very fine unfiltered beer that's redolent with herbs and hops. The menu is casual and has many regional specialities and locally caught seafood.

ℹ Information

Tourist Information Kiel (www.kiel-sailing-city.de; Andreas-Gayk-Strasse 31; ☺9am-6pm Mon-Fri, 10am-2pm Sat) is about 300m north of the train station, next to the post office.

ℹ Getting There & Away

Ferry services run between Kiel and Gothenburg, Oslo, and Klaipėda in Lithuania.

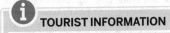

ℹ TOURIST INFORMATION

Schleswig-Holstein's regional tourist office (www.sh-tourismus.de) has an excellent website with scads of info in English, including activities and hotel booking.

Numerous **trains** run between Kiel's renovated and shop-filled station and Hamburg (€27, 1¼ hours). Trains to Lübeck leave hourly (€16, 1¼ hours). There are regular local connections to Schleswig, Husum, Schwerin and Flensburg.

ⓘ Getting Around

Local **bus** (www.vrk-sh.de) trips cost from €1.70 one-way or €4.90 for a day card. To hire a taxi, call ☏680 101.

A **ferry** service along the firth runs daily until around 6pm (to 5pm on weekends) from the Bahnhofsbrücke pier behind the Hauptbahnhof. The trip to Laboe is €4.20.

Bikes can be rented from **Brücke Schleswig-Holstein** (☏237 7790; www.bruecke-sh.de; Hauptbahnhof; bike rental from €9 per day; ◷6am-7pm Mon-Fri, 8am-2pm Sat) in the train station.

Schleswig-Holsteinisches Freilichtmuseum

Beekeepers, bakers, potters and many more traditional craftspeople ply their trade 6km south of Kiel, in Molfsee at the **Schleswig-Holsteinisches Freilichtmuseum** (Schleswig-Holstein Open-Air Museum; ☏0431-659 660; www.freilichtmuseum-sh.de; Alte Hamburger Landstrasse 97; adult/child €7/2 Apr-Oct, €3/1.50 Nov-Mar; ◷9am-6pm Apr-Oct, 11am-4pm Sun & holidays Nov-Mar). This excellent museum features some 70 traditional houses typical of the region relocated from around the state. Take bus 501 from Kiel's central bus station.

Schleswig

☏04621 / POP 24,100

Neat redbrick houses and manicured lawns don't begin to hint at the Viking past of this tidy town on the Baltic Sea's longest fjord. Although sleepy today, the tall cathedral spire rising proudly above the water hints at little Schleswig's more colourful past.

Founded in 804, after a major Viking community put down roots across the Schlei fjord, it was the continent's economic hub for some 200 years. Later the Dukes of Gottorf made Schleswig their power base from the 16th to 18th centuries. And countless generations of fisherfolk and their families have left their marks.

You can enjoy the long local heritage at excellent museums and along the pretty waterfront.

⊙ Sights

The local highlights are pretty spread out (Schloss Gottorf is 1.5km from the train station, the old town and cathedral are another 2km east of there). With your own transport you can see everything in a half a day, otherwise, plan on spending the day exploring.

TOP CHOICE **Schloss Gottorf**   MUSEUM

(☏8130; www.schloss-gottorf.de; Schlossinsel 1) The Dukes of Gottorf's castle in Schleswig is far more 18th-century palace than medieval fortress and today it is home to three remarkable museums.

The **Schleswig-Holstein Landesmuseum** (Schleswig-Holstein State Museum; adult/child €9/5.50; ◷10am-6pm Apr-Oct, 10am-4pm Tue-Fri, 10am-5pm Sat & Sun) is filled with art treasures. A roomful of paintings by Lucas Cranach the Elder and a wood-panelled 17th-century wine tavern from Lübeck create a memorable first impression. There's also the rococo **Plöner Saal**, with faïence from the Baltic region; the stunning **Schlosskapelle**; and the elegant **Hirschsaal**, the former banquet hall named for the bas-reliefs of deer on the walls.

The more contemporary collection is equally noteworthy, including an entire **Jugendstil Abteilung** (art nouveau department), and 20th-century paintings, sketches, lithographs and woodcuts from German artists such as Emil Nolde and Ernst Barlach.

The second museum, the **Archäologische Landesmuseum** (Archaeological Museum; admission included with Schleswig-Holstein Landesmuseum), boasts the **Nydam-Boot**, a reconstructed and preserved 28-oar rowing boat from 350 BC, which is housed in its own hall.

The final museum hosts a reconstruction of the famous **Gottorfer Globus** (Gottorf Globe; adult/child €10/7.50; ◷10am-5pm Mon-Fri, 10am-6pm Sat & Sun Apr-Oct), which has been placed in its own house; a five-minute walk through the castle's lovely **gardens**. The original 17th-century globe was lauded as one of the wonders of the world – its first planetarium – but through war ended up being taken from Schleswig to St Petersburg. It's still there (albeit fire-damaged) in the Lomonosov Museum. The exterior of the 3m-diameter reconstruction shows how the continents and seas were thought to look in the 17th century. The real magic is inside, however. Several people can fit on a bench inside the globe and watch the Renaissance night sky change as the globe spins around them; it takes eight minutes to simulate a day.

The Schloss is 2km west of the old town (1.5km north of the Bahnhof).

Dom St Petri CHURCH
(☑989 585; Süderholmstrasse 2; ☺9am-5pm Mon-Sat & 1.30-5pm Sun May-Sep, 10am-4pm Mon-Sat & 1.30-4pm Sun Oct-Apr) With its steeple towering above the Altstadt (old town), the Dom St Petri provides an excellent point of orientation. It's also home to the intricate **Bordesholmer Altar** (1521), a carving by Hans Brüggemann. The 12.6m by 7.14m altar, on the wall furthest from the entrance, shows more than 400 figures in 24 scenes relating the story of the Passion of Christ – the result of extraordinary craft an artistry and patience. Owing to its flock of seafarer worshippers, the church has many elaborate ship models scattered about its interior, which was untouched by the war.

Spend some time wandering around the nearby cobblestoned streets, especially the **Rathhausmarkt**. The traditional fishing village of **Holm** is 500m southeast along the waterfront.

Stadtmuseum Schleswig MUSEUM
(☑936 820; www.stadtmuseum-schleswig.de; Friedrichstrasse 9-11; adult/child €4/2; ☺10am-5pm Tue-Sun) Schleswig's city museum incorporates a treacly (and kid-friendly) **Teddy Bear Haus** in a half-timbered building off the courtyard. More sober displays outline the city's history. It's a signposted five-minute walk north of the Bahnhof.

Wikinger Museum MUSEUM
(Viking Museum; ☑813 222; www.haithabu.de; adult/child €7/5; ☺9am-5pm Apr-Oct, 10am-5pm Tue-Sun Nov-Mar) Vikings ruled the roost from their base here at Haithabu, across the Schlei from Schleswig, some 1000 to 1200 years ago.

Located just outside the historic settlement (now an archaeological site), this kid-friendly museum features replica huts and re-enactors showing how the Viking families lived their daily lives (but without the smells etc) and has halls filled with displays.

The museum lies east of the B76 that runs between Schleswig and Kiel, about 3km from Schleswig's Hauptbahnhof. Otherwise, take bus 4810; alight at Haddeby.

A MOVEABLE MUSICAL FEAST

During the statewide **Schleswig-Holstein Music Festival** (www.shmf.de) you might find yourself down on a farm listening to a chamber orchestra instead of lowing cattle. Over seven weeks each summer, leading international musicians and promising young artists perform in venues ranging from the castle in Kiel and music academy in Lübeck to churches, warehouses and animal stalls, and sometimes even ferries to the North Frisian Islands.

Tours

Several companies offer a vast array of boat trips up the 40km Schlei between April and October from varying landing docks.

Schleischifffahrt A Bischoff BOAT TOUR
(☑233 19; www.schleischifffahrt.de; Gottorfer Damm 1; tours from €10) Located near the Schloss, it offers journeys up the fjord.

Schleswiger Hafenrundfahrten BOAT TOUR
(☑275 30; www.schleifahrten.de; Stadthafen; tours adult/child €6.50/2.50) Boats depart from near the Dom on the Altstadt waterfront and tour the Schlei.

Sleeping

Schleswig is a quiet place indeed at night. You might consider a moonlit stroll along the small harbour.

TOP CHOICE Hotel Alter Kreisbahnhof HOTEL €€
(☑30200;www.hotel-alter-kreisbhahnhof.de;Königstrasse 9; s/d incl breakfast €64/98; P ☎) Some of the spacious rooms at this hotel-restaurant, based in a turreted former railway station, have water views. All have a muted, modern decor. The **restaurant** (mains €9-16) serves creative regional cuisine. It's well located in the Altstadt, 100m from the Dom.

Bed & Breakfast Am Dom B&B €€
(☑485 992; www.bb-schleswig.de; Töpferstrasse 9; s/d incl breakfast from €70/90; P @) You'd scarcely guess there's a building behind all the ivy, let alone one this spacious. From the long, narrow dining room, the six bedrooms and guest sitting room stretch back to the private garden, with a pretty summerhouse pavilion. Decor in the 200-year-old Altstadt

GERMANY'S GREAT WALL

Northern Germany has its own version of the Great Wall of China: the **Danewerk**, a 30km-long earth-and-stone wall that stretched across today's Schleswig-Holstein and protected the southern border of the Danish kingdom. A surviving section of the wall, which was maintained roughly from AD 650 to AD 1200 is located 3km southwest of Schleswig's train station in the tiny hamlet of Dannewerk. The small **Danevirke Museum** (☎378 14; www.dannewerk.com; Ochsenweg 5, Dannewerk; adult/child €3/1; ☺10am-5pm Tue-Sun Mar-Nov) gives the history of the wall and offers a peak into Danish culture.

town house combines historic, romantic and designer touches à la Martha Stewart.

Zollhaus   HOTEL €€
(☎239 47; www.zollhaus-schleswig.de; Lollfuss 110; s €89-95, d €95-109; P🅿🛜) This 200-year-old customs house has a refined yet relaxed atmosphere and 10 comfortable rooms with a pastel-accented neutral decor. Its highly regarded **restaurant** (mains €17-30) specialises in seafood.

Campingplatz Haithabu   CAMPGROUND
(☎324 50; www.campingplatz-haithabu.de; Haddebyer Chaussee 15, Haddeby; per adult/tent/car €4/8/2; ☺Mar-Oct; P) This well-equipped campground is right on the southern shore of the Schlei in Haddeby, 3.5km east of the train station. It has a great view of the Schleswig skyline. Take bus 4810.

✖ Eating & Drinking

Several of Schleswig's hotels have excellent restaurants. You'll also find simple cafes around the harbour near the Altstadt and on the main square.

Senator-Kroog   GERMAN €€
(☎222 90; Rathausmarkt 9-10; mains €8-20) A melange of regional specialities, such as its signature *Labskaus* (salt herring, corned beef, potato and beetroot, topped with gherkins and a fried egg), highlight the menu that combines meats and seafood. Fronted by alfresco tables overlooking Schleswig's market square, the 1884 property – one half painted white, the other red – is a picture. Weekday lunch specials for €6 are a deal.

Olschewski's   SEAFOOD €€
(www.hotelolschewski.de.vu; Hafenstrasse 40; mains €10-16; ☺11am-9pm Wed-Sun Oct-Apr, Wed-Mon May-Sep) Right across from the harbour on the edge of the Altstadt, Olschewski's is a local icon. The large and sunny terrace fills up fast on pleasant weekends when you can hear the masts of the nearby boats clanking. Seafood is a speciality, especially the Holmer-pot, a rich combo of whitefish and wine. An annex has basic **rooms** (s/d €55/70).

Speicher   SEAFOOD €€
(☎305 184; Am Hafen 5; mains €9-16; 🛜🍴) A converted grain silo houses this excellent portside bistro, which is located above the harbourmaster's office. It has an extensive range of fish specialities. Tables on a terrace have great views out over the harbour.

Luzifer   BREWERY
(☎292 06; www.luzifer-sylt.de; Königstrasse 27; mains €9-17; ☺from 5pm Tue-Fri, from 11am Sat, 1-10pm Sun) Tables in the split-level dining room overlook this contemporary brewery's copper boilers. It's inside an atmospheric 1880-built brick former railway freight house about midway between the train station and the Altstadt. Enjoy the house-made full-flavoured lager, Asgaard. The menu offers lots of casual German fare from salads to a fine schnitzel.

❶ Information

Tourist Office (☎850 056; www.schleswig.de; Plessenstrasse 7; ☺10am-6pm Mon-Fri, 10am-2pm Sat & Sun Jun-Sep, 10am-4pm Mon-Fri Oct-May, also Sat 10am-2pm Apr-May & Oct) In the Altstadt near the Dom. City maps and hotel brochures are available outside after hours.

❶ Getting There & Away

Direct regional trains to Hamburg (€22, 1½ hours) run every two hours, while trains to Flensburg (€7, 30 minutes), Kiel (€10, 40 minutes) and Husum (€7, 45 minutes) leave every 30 minutes.

❶ Getting Around

It's a 3.5km walk mostly along the waterfront from the train station northeast to the old town.

Tickets for Schleswig's bus system cost €1.80 per trip; several buses link the station and the Altstadt. A taxi from the Bahnhof to the Altstadt costs around €9.

Between May and September, ferries cross the Schlei from Schleswig Hafen (just south of the Dom) between 10.30am and 5pm daily (adult one-way/return €3/5).

Bike rental outlets include **Fahrradverleigh Röhling** (☎993 030; www.fahrradverleih-schleswig.de; Knud-Laward-Strasse 30, Holm; per day from €6; ⏰9am-6pm Mon-Fri, 9am-12.30pm Sat).

Flensburg

☎0461 / POP 88,800

Situated on a busy industrial firth just 7km south of the Danish border, Flensburg is sometimes still dubbed 'Rumstadt' for its prosperous 18th-century trade in liquor with the Caribbean. Reminders of its sea-faring, rum-trading days echo across the port area, although today it may be more known as the headquarters for the ubiquitous Beate Uhse erotic shops.

Sights

Most attractions run north–south parallel to the western bank of the firth, although the harbour retains a gritty feel. You can easily see the highlights in a couple of hours.

Schiffahrtsmuseum MUSEUM

(Maritime Museum; ☎852 970; www.schiffahrtsmuseum.flensburg.de; Schiffbrücke 39; adult/child €6/3, combination ticket incl Museumsberg Flensburg adult/child €8/4; ⏰10am-5pm Tue-Sun Apr-Oct, 10am-4pm Tue-Sun Nov-Mar) An engrossing museum right on the old harbour, displays here give the history of rum and the seafarers who both shipped and drank it. On the water, workshops show how old ships are restored.

Kaufmannshöfe HISTORIC BUILDINGS

(Merchants' Courtyards) Flensburg's best old highlight is checking out the charming Kaufmannshöfe. These date from the 18th century, when Danish-ruled Flensburg provided supplies to the Danish West Indies (St Thomas, St Jan and St Croix) in exchange for sugar and rum. Designed to make it easier to load goods into ships, they typically consisted of a tall warehouse on the harbourside, behind which was a series of low workshops, wrapped around a central courtyard and leading to the merchant's living quarters.

Free town maps from the tourist office mark nearly every *Hof* (courtyard); the *Käpitans Weg* brochure follows a captain's route around town as he was preparing for a trip.

Museumsberg Flensburg MUSEUM

(Municipal Museum; ☎852 956; www.museumsberg.flensburg.de; Museumsberg 1; adult/child €6/3; ⏰10am-5pm Tue-Sun) This hilltop museum features two wings: the first contains a collection of rooms and furniture from Schleswig-Holstein history, including a remarkably painted cembalo (early piano covered in murals). In the second, you'll find excellent art nouveau works by Flensburg-born painter Hans Christiansen, as well as an Emil Nolde room.

Braasch HISTORIC BUILDING

(www.braasch-rum.de; Rote Strasse 26-28) Some of the prettiest **Kaufmannshöfe** can be found off the very picturesque Rote Strasse, which is up from the harbour by the Rathaus. While here, you can buy rum in drinkable and edible forms at this lavish shop.

Tours

MS Viking BOAT TOUR

(☎167 2674; www.viking-schifffahrt.de; adult/child return €9/4) The MS *Viking* operates scenic cruises to Glücksburg (one hour each way), departing from where Norderhofenden meets Schiffbrücke. Boats leave at least four times daily from March to December.

Sleeping & Eating

Flensburg isn't exactly a [rum] barrel of laughs at night, so it's best visited on the way elsewhere. You can find seaside hotels in nearby Glücksburg.

Hotel Dittmer's Gasthof HOTEL €€

(☎240 52; www.dittmersgasthof.de; Neumarkt 2; s/d from €75/110; P) This flower-festooned historic inn is between the train station and the harbour and close to the Rathaus. It has been run by the same family for more than 100 years. Rooms are cosy and the welcome warm, especially in the small bar.

TOP CHOICE **Hansens Brauerei** BREWERY €€

(☎222 10; www.hansens-brauerei.de; Schiffbrücke 16; meals €8-17; ⏰11.30am-midnight) Simple but hearty German fare – homemade meatballs, roast pork, herrings – is served at this brewery on the waterfront. There's a wide range of beers (including some great seasonal beers) served amid the copper boilers and this is easily the best choice by the water.

COASTAL COFFEE

If the cold wind's biting, warm up with one of the region's specialities: rum-laced coffee topped with cream, known as a *Pharisäer*. So the stories go, chilly locals in the region infused their strong, sweetened coffee with a shot of rum. But, to hide the presence of alcohol from their priest, they smothered the top with cream. The priest, however, quickly caught on, decrying them as Pharisees (his point being that they were following the letter, not the spirit, of the law). The name stuck, as did the surreptitious drinking technique – don't stir it; instead, slurp the hot coffee through the cream.

Marien-Café   CAFE €€
(☑500 9711; Norderstrasse 11-13; mains €3-15; ⊙8am-6pm; ☑) Splurge on a sumptuous slice of homemade cake or linger over a long breakfast beneath myriad teapots hanging from the ceiling of this quaint cafe right on the main shopping drag.

ⓘ Information

Flensburg Tourist Office (☑909 0920; www.flensburg-tourismus.de; Europa-Haus, Rathausstrasse 1; ⊙9am-6pm Mon-Fri, 10am-2pm Sat) Across from the northwestern corner of the central bus station and near the base of the harbour.

ⓘ Getting There & Away

Flensburg has **train** connections with Kiel (€16, 1½ hours) and Schleswig (€7, 30 minutes), from where trains continue to Hamburg.

Autokraft (☑690 69; www.autokraft.de) has regular **buses** to Husum (€7.45, one hour) and Kiel (€10.65, two hours) from the central bus station by the harbour.

ⓘ Getting Around

It is almost 1km from the train station to the start of the main pedestrian zone at Holm on the southern end. From here, the tourist office and the base of the harbour are about another 800m. Follow the small blue signs reading 'Altstadt/Zentrum'.

Buses cost €1.80/5 for a single/day pass.

Glücksburg
☑04631 / POP 5950

Overlooking the water 10km northeast of Flensburg, this small spa town is renowned for its horseshoe-shaped Renaissance **Wasserschloss** (Moated Palace; ☑442 330; www.schloss-gluecksburg.de; adult/child €6/3; ⊙10am-6pm May-Sep), which appears to float in the middle of a large lake. The rest of the town is equally charming, and it's a pleasant stroll around the lake up to the beach.

Strandhotel Glücksburg (☑614 10; www.strandhotel-gluecksburg.de; Kirstenstrasse 6; s/d from €130/180; ☐@☎) is the fabled 'white castle by the sea' and counts Thomas Mann among its former guests. Rooms at this resplendent and sprawling beachfront villa (which dates to 1872) are now decked out in cool, minimalist Scandinavian style. Decadences include a spa and gastronomic restaurant serving a daily changing menu utilising fresh produce.

Buses run hourly between Glücksburg and Flensburg's central bus station (€2.60). You can also take the scenic route aboard the MS *Viking* (p685).

Husum
☑04841 / POP 22,100

Warmly toned buildings huddle around Husum's delightful *Binnenhafen* (inner harbour), colourful gabled houses line its narrow, cobbled lanes, and in late March and early April millions of purple crocuses bloom in Husum's Schlosspark. You can easily while away a couple hours in Husum.

⊙ Sights

Ask at the tourist office for a map highlighting Husum's's **Cultural Trail**. Many focus on author-extraorinaire Theodor Storm, right down to the fountain in the **Markt**, which shows Tine, a young Frisian woman who figures in a Storm novella, as does the **Marienkirche** (1829). The walk is a great way to savour the town.

Theodor-Storm-Haus   MUSEUM
(Theodor Storm House; ☑803 8630; www.storm-gesellschaft.de; Wasserreihe 31-35; adult/child €3/2; ⊙10am-5pm Tue-Fri, 11am-5pm Sat, 2-5pm Sun & Mon Apr-Oct, 2-5pm Tue, Thu & Sat Nov-Mar) Even if you're not too familiar with the 19-century author, his tidy wooden house will whet your appetite. Well-placed literary snip-

pets and biographical titbits fill in the life of this novelist, poet and proud Schleswig-Holstein citizen in the small, intimate rooms where he lived and wrote works such as his seminal North Frisian novella *Der Schimmelreiter* (The Rider on the White Horse).

🍴 Sleeping & Eating

Cafes and restaurants abound around the St Marienkirche, the Markt and the Binnenhafen. Pick up fresh food at Husum's market, which has been held since 1465.

Theodor Storm Hotel   HOTEL €€
(☑896 60; www.bw-theodor-storm-hotel.de; Neustadt 60-68; s €75-105, d €110-145; ☉3pm-late May-Sep, from 5pm other times; P🐕) Husum's best central hotel is affiliated with the Best Western chain. It has 50 rooms and an imposing columned facade. Rooms are up to upscale international hotel standards, as you'd expect. The in-house microbrewery, **Husum's Brauhaus** (Neustadt 60-68; mains €7-20; ☉3pm-late summer, 5pm-late winter), has a good range of brews and casual German fare.

Hotel Wohlert   HOTEL €€
(☑2229; www.hotel-wohlert.de; Markt 30; s/d from €50/90; 🐕) As central as you could ask, this family-run hotel is in a modern building with brick accents. Rooms are modest yet comfortable and rates include breakfast in your room. Whether you take it to bed is entirely between you and your brotchen.

❶ Information
Husum Tourist Office (☑898 70; www.tourismus-husum.de; Historisches Rathaus, Gross Strasse 27; ☉9am-6pm Mon-Fri & 10am-4pm Sat Apr-Oct, 9am-5pm Mon-Fri & 10am-4pm Sat Nov-Mar)

❶ Getting There & Around
Husum is walkably compact and extremely well signposted. The Bahnhof lies 700m south of the city centre.

BICYCLE Bikes can be rented at the Bahnhof from **Rad Station** (☑805 550; Bahnhof, Poppenburg Strasse 12; per day from €6; ☉6.15am-6pm Mon-Fri & by appointment).

BUS Up to seven buses daily connect Husum with Nordstrand (€5, 45 minutes).

TRAIN There are regular direct train connections to Kiel (€16, 1½ hours), Hamburg (€32, two hours) and Schleswig (€7, 30 minutes), plus several links daily to Westerland on Sylt (€18, one hour). There are also cheaper regional services.

The Halligen

Is it an island? Is it a sandbank? No, it's a *Hallig*, one of about 10 tiny wafer-flat 'islets' scattered across the Schleswig-Holstein's **Wadden Sea National Park** (Nationalpark Schleswig-Holsteinisches Wattenmeer; www.nationalpark-wattenmeer.de). In the Middle Ages some 50 Halligen existed, but the sea has swallowed up most of them. Up to 60 times a year, floods drown the beaches and meadows, leaving the few reed-thatched farms stranded on the artificial knolls, or 'wharves', that they're built on.

Most people visit the islets on day excursions. The prettiest destination is **Hallig Hooge**, which once sheltered a Danish king from a storm in the handsome **Königshaus**, with its blue and white tiles and baroque ceiling fresco. For many, the highlight of the trip are the many **seals** lazing around various sandy beaches.

Between April and October, boat trips run by **Adler Schiffe** (☑01805-123 344; www.adler-schiffe.de) sail from Nordstrand to Hallig Hooge (from €21.50 return). There are bus connections and packages from Husum to Nordstrand, as well as boat trips from Nordstrand to the North Frisian Islands.

You can learn more about the national park, which is part of a large area of the Wadden Sea that gained Unesco recognition in 2009, at the visitors centre, the **NationalparkHaus** (Hafenstrasse; ☉10am-6pm Mon-Sat, 1-5pm Sun), in Husum.

North Frisian Islands

With their grass-covered dunes, shifting sands, birds, seal colonies, lighthouses and rugged cliffs, you'd imagine Germany's North Frisian Islands to be the domain of intrepid nature lovers. Instead, these North Sea islands are a favourite of the German elite. On glamorous Sylt in particular, you'll find designer boutiques housed in quintessential reed-thatched cottages, gleaming Porches and Mercedes jamming the car parks, luxurious accommodation and some of the country's most extravagant restaurants.

Those with less cash to splash can still enjoy the pure sea air, especially in Sylt's remoter corners. The islands of Amrum and Föhr are more peaceful still.

SYLT ACTIVITIES

Windsurfing off Sylt is known as the most radical on the World Cup tour, which finishes here each September. Yet beginners shouldn't be deterred. There are water-sports schools in every town, including Westerland's **Surf Schule Sunset Beach** (☑27172; www. sunsetbeach.de; Brandenburger Strasse 15, Westerland), which offers lessons and also rents equipment for windsurfing as well as kitesurfing, regular surfing and catamaran sailing.

Spas, of course, are prevalent in almost every town. **Horseback riding**, whether on the beach or through the flatlands and along the marshes on the Wadden Sea side is also popular.

Walking, whether Nordi-style using poles (rentals widely available) or just serenely strolling, is hugely popular all over Sylt. You will find vehicle-free trails stretching in all directions.

SYLT
☑04651 / POP 21,000

The anchor-shaped island of Sylt is attached to the mainland by a narrow causeway. On its west coast, the North Sea's fierce surf and strong winds gnaw mercilessly at the shoreline. By contrast, Sylt's eastern Wadden Sea shore is tranquil and, yes, silty. At low tide, the retreating shallows expose vast mudflats.

Sylt's candy-striped lighthouses rise above wide expanses of shifting dunes, fields of gleaming yellow-gold rape flower and expanses of heath. Dotted along its beaches, the island also has several saunas, where the idea is to heat up and then run naked into the chilly North Sea!

Despite its glut of upmarket restaurants and designer boutiques, it's easy enough to lose the glamour and crowds on the beaches, in the dunes or on a hiking or bike trail.

Sylt is 38.5km long and measures only 700m at its narrowest point. The largest town, commercial hub and train terminus is Westerland.

⊙ Sights

WESTERLAND

People have been complaining about the overdevelopment of Westerland ever since it became Sylt's first resort in the mid-19th century. Their protestations seem to have gone unheeded: the island's largest town (with 9000 permanent residents) is an unattractive mess of concrete towers and tawdry commercial strips such as the pedestrianised Friedrichstrasse. Don't linger.

KEITUM

Historic reed-thatched houses strangled with ivy, lush gardens of colourful blooms, stone walls and the occasional garden gate made from two curving whalebones combine to create the island's prettiest village.

Keitum was once Sylt's most important harbour, which is recalled in its late-Romanesque sailors' church **St Severin**, with its Gothic altar and chancel, and heritage-listed gravestones in its cemetery; and in the historic **Altfriesisches Haus** (Old Frisian House; ☑31101; www.soelring-foriining.de; Am Kliff 13; adult/child €4/2; ⊙10am-5pm Mon-Fri, 11am-5pm Sat & Sun Easter-Oct, noon-4pm Wed-Sun Nov-Easter).

WENNINGSTEDT

The best of Sylt's Stone Age graves are in the family-oriented resort town of Wenningstedt. You can enter its 4000-year-old **Denghoog** (www.soelring-foriining.de; Am Denghoog; ⊙10am-5pm Mon-Fri, 11am-5pm Sat & Sun Easter-Oct, noon-4pm Wed-Sun Nov-Easter), next to the town church, which measures 3m by 5m and is nearly 2m tall in parts. The outer walls consist of 12 40-tonne stones. How Stone Age builders moved these is a Stonehenge kind of mystery.

KAMPEN

Hermès, Cartier and Louis Vuitton boutiques ensconced in traditional reed-thatched houses signal that this little village is the island's ritziest. Each summer, aristocrats and German celebrities come to see and be seen along the main promenade, Stroenwai, aka Whiskey Alley. Watch for paparazzi hiding in the bushes.

People-watching aside, the principal reason to visit is the stunning **Uwe Dune**, at 52.5m Sylt's highest natural elevation. You can climb the wooden steps to the top for a 360-degree view over Sylt and, on a good day, to neighbouring Amrum and Föhr islands.

LIST

Everything in List is dubbed 'Germany's northernmost' – harbour, beach, restaurant etc... It's a windswept, tranquil land's end, but things usually liven up in the harbour when the ferry from Rømø (Denmark) deposits day-tripping Danes.

For rainy-day joy, try the **Erlebniszentrum Naturgewalten** (☑836 190; www.naturgewalten-sylt.de; Hafenstrasse 37; adult/child €13/7.50; ☺10am-8pm Jul & Aug, 10am-6pm Sep-Jun), a state-of-the-art ecological museum with multimedia exhibits dedicated to the North Sea. It's housed in a vivid-blue building powered by renewable energy.

The privately owned Ellenbogen ('elbow') peninsula is at Sylt's far northern tip. The beaches here are off limits for swimming because of dangerous currents, but are dramatically backed by 35m-high shifting dunes. This is a good hiking goal.

WEST COAST BEACHES

To beat the crowds on the long west-coast strand, pick the parking area with the fewest cars – you'll find great variations. Conversely, some of the beach areas boast high-profile cafes and activities centres and have quite a scene. At many beach areas you can rent the classicly German *Strandkorb*, a roofed wicker beach chair.

☞ Tours

Tourist offices have details on the oodles of tours available. There's a head-spinning array of boat cruises, mostly operated by **Adler-Schiffe** (☑01805-123 344; www.adler-schiffe.de).

Amrun & Föhr   BOAT TOUR
(adult/child under 14yr from €25/free; ☺daily Easter–mid-Oct) Choose one or both islands. Departs from Hörnum.

Hallig Hooge   BOAT TOUR
(adult/child from €26/17; ☺daily Apr-Oct) Other islands can be combined with Amrun/Föhr tours. Departs from Hörnum.

Seal Colonies   BOAT TOUR
(adult/child from €17/13.50; ☺daily Apr-Oct) See seals basking on the sandbanks on this 1½-hour boat tour from Hörnum.

Wattwandern Tours   BOAT TOUR
(adult/child €31/20.50; ☺2-3 times per week late-May-early-Oct) Take a boat from Hörnum and then wander at low tide across the seabed between Amrum and Föhr.

SVG   BUS TOUR
(☑01805-836 100; www.svg-sylt.de; Central Bus Station, Westerland; big tour adult/child €16.50/11, small tour adult/child €14/10.50; ☺big tour 2pm Feb-Oct, 1pm Nov-Jan, small tour 11am Apr-Oct) Bus tours come in two sizes – big (three hours) and small (two hours) and are run by island locals who pepper the frequent stops with much local knowledge and colourful stories.

AT HOME WITH EMIL NOLDE

Bright flowers, stormy seas, red-lipped women with jaunty hats and impressionistic seaside watercolours: these are some of the recurring themes of great Schleswig-Holstein painter Emil Nolde. Born in 1867 in Nolde village near the Danish border (from whence he took his name), he first gained fame for producing postcards in which he gave mountains human features.

In 1927 Nolde and his wife Ada built a home and studio in Seebüll. Here, banned from working by the Nazis, he proceeded to produce 1300 'unpainted pictures' in secret.

Nowadays Nolde, who died in 1956, is considered one of the great 20th-century watercolourists, and his work is found across Schleswig-Holstein (and far beyond), including in the Schleswig-Holstein Landesmuseum (p682) and the Museumsberg Flensburg (p685).

By far the biggest and most impressive collection is in Nolde's architecturally arresting former atelier at Seebüll, now the **Emil Nolde Stiftung** (☑04664-983 930; www.nolde-stiftung.de; Neukirchen bei Seebüll; adult/child €8/3; ☺10am-6pm Mar-Nov). The exhibition is worth a half to whole day's excursion, which is lucky because that's what it will take you, depending on where you're coming from.

Closest train stations to Seebüll are Niebüll (15km south) or Klanxbüll (8km west), from where you can get a taxi to Seebüll. Some buses (included in the admission price) run by **NVB** (☑04661-980 8890; www.nvb-niebuell.de) come from Niebüll via Klanxbüll, and from Westerland via Klanxbüll to the museum, but must be confirmed directly with the bus company at least one day ahead.

🛏 Sleeping

Tourist offices have details of the island's plethora of accommodation options, including holiday apartments and private rooms.

Kamps
TOP CHOICE — GUESTHOUSE €€€

(☑983 90; www.kamps-sylt.de; Gurtstich 41, Keitum; r from €160, apt from €185; P) Inside a traditional thatched-roof house in oh-so-quaint Keitum, this eight-room guesthouse surprises with colours as bold as a Sylt sunrise on a clear day. And you'll probably catch the sunrise as you'll be waiting for the fab breakfasts that include the family's homemade jams, waffles, luscious breads and more. Enjoy it inside or out on the terrace.

Village
BOUTIQUE HOTEL €€€

(☑469 70; www.village-kampen.de; Alte Dorfstrasse 7, Kampen; r from €300; P🐾🖥) An absolutely flawless boutique hotel with a mere 10 rooms but service standards worthy of a palace. Discretion is the rule here, whether it's at the indoor pool or out in the lovely gardens. Strolling the town starts outside the gate. Food, such as the breakfasts, is superb.

Alte Strandvogtei
HOTEL €€€

(☑922 50; www.alte-strandvogtei.de; Merret-let-Wai 6, Rantum; r €150-290; P🖥) This rambling thatched-roof complex has a variety of rooms, apartments and suites. Many have views across the flat Wadden Sea. The livelier ocean is a mere 700m west on a beautiful strip of sand and dunes. There's a spa and indoor pool, and breakfast comes with many local fish specialities.

Single Pension
PENSION €

(☑920 70; www.singlepension.de; Trift 26, Westerland; s €38-70, d €55-80 incl breakfast; P) Not only for singles, but certainly a social spot for solo travellers young and old, who can strike up a rapport over tea or lounging in the garden. The rooms are humble, but the location central and breakfast is served to 1pm.

Campingplatz Rantum
CAMPGROUND €

(☑807 55; www.camping-rantum.de; Hörnumer Strasse 3, Rantum; per person €5, tent €6.50-8.50, car €5; ⊘Apr-Oct; P) In a good natural area south of Westerland; great facilities including a bakery, restaurant and sauna.

DJH Hostel Dikjen Deel
HOSTEL €

(☑835 7825; www.jugendherberge.de; Fischerweg 36-40, Westerland; dm under/over 26yr €23/28; ⊘closed mid-late Dec) Set amid the dunes,

Westerland's hostel is a 45-minute walk from the Bahnhof. Alternatively, take bus 2 in the direction of Rantum/Hörnum to the Dikjen Deel stop. If you're after something even further away from it all, there are also DJH hostels at List-Mövenberg and Hörnum.

🍴 Eating

Sylt has some sterling restaurants, such as Jörg Müller's Michelin-starred digs. But the island's most quintessential dish is a simple and delicious fish sandwich from home-grown chain, Gosch. Look out too for local oysters from Germany's only oyster farm, in List.

Gosch
TOP CHOICE — SEAFOOD €€

(www.gosch.de; Hafenstrasse 16, List; mains €4-15) Coming to Sylt without visiting Gosch would be like coming to Germany without ordering a beer. Established by eel seller Jürgen Gosch some three decades ago, this nationwide chain of 'fast-fish' outlets is a Sylt institution, and its seafood is exceptionally fresh here.

The site of Gosch's original kiosk in List harbour is now its maritime-themed flagship, Alte Bootshalle. But across the island you'll find branches offering its range of delicious fish sandwiches, seafood pasta, smoked fish and rösti, lobster and caviar.

Fisch Fiete
SEAFOOD €€€

(☑321 50; www.fisch-fiete.de; Weidemannweg 3, Keitum; mains from €16; ⊘noon-2pm & 6pm-late) An institution since 1954, this thatched-roof gem manages to stay as fresh as its seafood. The menu changes constantly, but is always accompanied by a fine wine list. A recently added bistro offers seats on the sand and tapas-size servings of the kitchen's best efforts.

Kupferkanne
CAFE €€

(☑410 10; www.kupferkanne-sylt.de; Stapelhooger Wai, Kampen; mains €6-15; ⊘8am-5pm) Giant mugs of coffee and huge slices of cake (including scrumptious plum cake) are served in the magical gardens of this *Alice in Wonderland*-style cafe, where wooden tables surrounded by a maze of low bramble hedges overlook the Wadden Sea and the Braderup Heide (heath). Meals are also served in the attached Frisian house.

Sansibar
SEAFOOD, STEAK €€€

(☑964 646; www.sansibar.de; Hörnumer Strasse 80, Rantum; mains €14-35; ⊘11am-11pm, shorter hours in winter) Dining among the dunes in this

WORTH A TRIP

HELGOLAND

Helgoland's former rulers, the British, really got the better deal in 1891 when they swapped it for then German-ruled Zanzibar. But Germans today are very fond of this lonesome North Sea outcrop of red sandstone rock and its fresh air and warm weather, courtesy of the Gulf Stream.

The 80m-tall **Lange Anna** (Long Anna) rock on the island's southwest edge is a compelling sight, standing alone in the ocean. There are also WWII bunkers and ruins to explore, and resurging numbers of Atlantic grey seals. Cycling is not permitted on the tiny 4.2-sq-km island.

By an old treaty, Helgoland is not part of the EU's VAT area, so many of the 1130 residents make their living selling duty-free cigarettes, booze and perfume to day-trippers who prowl the main drag, Lung Wai ('long way'). To swim, many head to neighbouring **Düne**, a blip in the ocean popular with nudists. Little boats (one-way €5) make regular trips between May and mid-October from Helgoland's northeastern landing stage.

Helgoland makes an easy and enjoyable day trip, but if you want to stay, the **Kurverwaltung** (☑04725-206 799; www.helgoland.de; Lung Wai 28; ⊙usually 9am-noon Mon-Fri) can help secure one of the over-1000 hotel beds or tent pitch.

Ferries here take up to four hours. Return trips are timed to allow three to four hours on the island. Services include:

» **Reederei Rahder** (☑04834-3612; www.rahder.de; day trips from adult/child €37/21; ⊙9.15am Tue-Sun) Boats run from Büsum, which is on the rail network.

» **Helgoline** (☑0180-522 1445; www.helgoline.de; from Hamburg adult/child from €65/33, from Cuxhaven €53/27; ⊙from Hamburg 9am, Cuxhaven 11.30am Apr-Oct) Fast ferries run from Hamburg and Cuxhaven; there are also cheaper, slower boats.

---

large grass-roof pavilion on the beach, on the likes of whole North Sea sole or salmon and wild prawns in white crustacean sauce, is an unforgettable experience (book *well* ahead). Alternatively, stop by for a drink on its terrace at sunset, with a view of crashing waves.

ⓘ Information

All communities on Sylt charge hotel guests a *Kurtaxe* (resort tax) of about €4 per day depending on the season. It entitles you to small discounts at museums and access to the beaches. Day-trippers will need to buy a *Tageskarte* (day pass) from tourist offices or the kiosks at beach entrances.

Westerland has the main tourist offices, convenient for when you arrive on the island. (Other towns have offices but they are usually only open a few hours on weekdays.) Most of the tourist offices offer paid internet access.

Tourist Information Desk (www.westerland. de; Bahnhofplatz, Westerland; ⊙9am-6pm daily year-round) Inside the train station. A good first stop.

Sylt Tourism (www.sylt.de) Good website covers the entire island and is helpful for booking accommodation.

ⓘ Getting There & Away

Sylt Airport (GWT; www.flughafen-sylt.de) is served by **Air Berlin** (www.airberlin.com) and **Lufthansa** (www.lufthansa.com) from Berlin, Düsseldorf, Frankfurt, Hamburg and Munich. Flights are not daily and tend to cluster on summer weekends.

Sylt is connected to the mainland by a causeway used exclusively by **trains**. IC trains serve Hamburg Hauptbahnhof (€47, 3¼ hours), while regional trains have hourly direct services to Hamburg Altona (€34, 3½ hours). *Important:* make sure you're sitting in the correct part of the train, as they sometimes split en route.

Vehicles use the **car train** (www.syltshuttle. de; one-way/return €47/86 Fri-Mon, return €73 Tue to Thu) from Niebüll. There are constant crossings (usually at least once an hour) in both directions; it doesn't take reservations. With loading and unloading, expect the journey to take about an hour.

A **car ferry** (☑0180-310 3030; www.syltfaehre.de; one-way/return from €45/76) runs from Rømø in Denmark to List (one-way per foot passenger/car and passengers €7/43.50).

There are ferries to/from Amrun and Föhr.

ⓘ Getting Around

Sylt is well covered by **buses** (www.svg-sylt. de; fares €2-7), which run at about 20 minute intervals on the main routes. Some buses have bike racks.

Cycling is extremely popular and *Fahrradverleih* (bike-hire) outlets abound. Westerland alone has more than half-a-dozen places, such as **Veloquick** (⌨215 06; www.veloquick.de; Industrieweg 20, Westerland; per day from €7), which is just south of the train station.

Regional trains to/from Westerland stop in Keitum.

FÖHR
⌨04681 / POP 8700

Closer to the mainland, cloud-shaped Föhr is known as the green isle, although there's also a good sandy beach in the south. Its main village, **Wyk**, has plenty of windmills. In the north you'll find 16 tiny Frisian hamlets tucked behind dikes up to 7m tall. In the old days, Föhr's men went out to sea to hunt whales.

The church of **St Johannis** in Nieblum dates from the 12th century and is sometimes called the 'Frisian Cathedral' because it seats up to 1000 people.

Föhr's main **tourist office** (⌨300 3040; www.foehr.de; Wyk; ⊙10am-1pm & 2-5.45pm) can help with accommodation. This is a very restful island.

ⓘ Getting There & Around

Ferries to Föhr are operated by **WDR** (⌨01805-080 140; www.faehre.de; return adult/child €13/6.50, bikes €5, cars from €55) from Dagebüll Hafen (which has a train service that connects to the main line at Niebüll). Up to 13 boats make the trip daily in the high season, taking 45 minutes to Wyk. Book in advance. There are also regular ferries between Föhr and Amrum for about the same prices.

There's an hourly bus service to all villages and you'll find bike-rental outlets in every village.

AMRUM
⌨04682 / POP 2300

Amrum is the smallest North Frisian Island; you can walk around it in a day. It's also the prettiest, with reed-thatched Frisian houses, a patchwork of dunes, woods, heath and marsh, and glorious Kniepsand – 12km of fine, white sand, sometimes up to 1km wide – that takes up half the island.

Crowning the central village of **Wittdün** is northern Germany's tallest lighthouse, which stands 63m tall. The island's largest village is **Nebel**.

Much of Amrum is under protection, so you must stick to the marked paths. There are some fine walks, including the 10km walk from the lighthouse to the village of **Norddorf** through the pine forest, or the 8km return hike from Norddorf along the safe swimming beach to the tranquil **Ood Nature Reserve**, an ideal place to observe bird life.

The **tourist office** (⌨940 30; www.amrum. de; ⊙hours vary) can book island accommodation. Options include two campgrounds (one for nudists), a **DJH** (⌨2010; www.jugend herberge.de/jh/wittduen; Mittelstrasse 1; under/over 26yr incl breakfast €19.20/22.20; ⊙mid-Feb-mid-Nov) and several hotels.

ⓘ Getting There & Around

Ferries to Amrum are operated by WDR from Dagebüll Hafen (which has a train service that connects to the main line at Niebüll). Boats take about 90 minutes and go via Föhr. Book in advance.

Buses take you around the island; there are bike-rental places in every village.

SCHWERIN & THE MECKLENBURG LAKE PLAINS

At the doorstep of the appealing state capital, Schwerin, the wilderness area of the Mecklenburg Lake Plains spreads across the centre of the state, and shelters the pristine Müritz National Park. Meandering through charming little villages and hamlets, many roads in the area are canopied by trees that were planted by medieval fish merchants to shield wagons from the heat of the summer sun.

Schwerin
⌨0385 / POP 95,200

Picturesquely sited around seven lakes (or possibly more depending on how you tally them), the centrepiece of this engaging city is its Schloss (castle), built in the 14th century during the city's time as the former seat of the Grand Duchy of Mecklenburg.

Schwerin has shrugged off the 45 years of communist rule that followed WWII. Today there's an upbeat, vibrant energy on its restored streets that befits its role as the reinstated capital of Mecklenburg-Western Pomerania (beating Rostock for the mantle).

Cafes and interesting shops make wandering a delight.

Sights

Schloss & Gardens
PALACE

(Map p694; ☑525 2920; www.schloss-schwerin.de; adult/child €6/4; ⊙10am-6pm mid-Apr–mid-Oct, 10am-5pm Tue-Sun mid-Oct–mid-Apr) Gothic and Renaissance turrets, Slavic onion domes, Ottoman features and terracotta Hanseatic step gables are among the mishmash of architectural styles that make up Schwerin's inimitable Schloss, which is crowned by a gleaming golden dome. Nowadays the Schloss earns its keep as the state's parliament building.

Schwerin derives its name from a Slavic castle known as Zuarin (Animal Pasture) that was formerly on the site, and which was first mentioned in 973 AD. In a niche over the main gate, the statue of Niklot depicts a Slavic prince, who was defeated by Heinrich der Löwe in 1160.

Inside the palace's opulently furnished rooms, highlights include a huge collection of Meissen porcelain and richly coloured stained-glass windows in the Schlosskirche.

The park immediately surrounding the palace is known as the Burggarten and most notably features a wonderful orangerie overlooking the water, with a conservatory restaurant and terrace cafe (open May to October). A handful of statues, a grotto and lookout points are also here.

Crossing the causeway south from the Burggarten brings you to the baroque Schlossgarten (Palace Garden), intersected by several canals.

Staatliches Museum
MUSEUM

(Map p694; ☑595 80; www.museum-schwerin.de; Alter Garten 3; adult/concession €8/6; ⊙10am-6pm Tue-Sun Apr-Oct, 10am-5pm Tue-Sun Nov-Mar, to 8pm Thu) In the Alter Garten, the Staatliches Museum has a substantial collection spanning the ages. The 15 statues in the Ernst Barlach room provide a small taste of the sculptor's work. There's also a typically amusing and irreverent Marcel Duchamp collection. Other works include oils by Lucas Cranach the Elder, as well as works by Brueghel, Rembrandt and Rubens.

Dom
CHURCH

(Map p694; ☑565 014; Am Dom 4; adult/child €2/1; ⊙11am-3pm Mon-Fri, 11am-4pm Sat, noon-3pm Sun) Above the Markt, the tall 14th-century Gothic Dom is a superb example of north German redbrick architecture. You can climb up to the viewing platform of its 19th-century cathedral tower (118m), which is a mere 50cm taller than Rostock's Petrikirche. Down to earth, check out the elaborately carved pews.

Altstadt
HISTORIC SITE

The bustling Markt is home to the Rathaus (Map p694) and the colonnaded neoclassical Neues Gebäude (1780-83), which houses a classy cafe. The latter is fronted by a lion monument honouring the town's founder, Heinrich der Löwe. A walk southwest of the Rathaus to the appropriately named Engestrasse (Narrow Street) brings you past a lovely example of the city's earliest half-timbered house (Map p694; Buschstrasse 15), which dates back to 1698.

Schelfstadt
SQUARE

North of the Markt along Puschkinstrasse is Schelfstadt, a planned baroque village that was autonomous until Schwerin's mid-19th-century expansion. The restored 1737 Schleswig-Holstein-Haus (Map p694; ☑555 527; www.schwerin.de; Puschkinstrasse 12; admission varies; ⊙10am-6pm) contains a gallery that features changing contemporary art exhibitions. Just north of here is the early 18th-century baroque Schelfkirche (Nikolaikirche; Map p694) and Schelfmarkt, the former town market, with its half-timbered surrounds.

Tours

From May to September, Weisse Flotte (Map p694; ☑557 770; www.weisseflotteschwerin.de; adult/child from €11/5; ⊙late-Apr–Oct) offers 60- and 90-minute boat tours on the Schweriner See.

The tourist office organises several guided walking tours in German, including 90-minute city tours (per person €5.50; ⊙11am) and evening walks (per person €6; ⊙8.30pm Thu Apr-Oct, 6.30pm Thu Nov-Mar) from Weinhaus Wöhler.

Festivals & Events

The highlight of Schwerin's cultural calendar is the Schlossfestspiele (www.theater-schwerin.de; ⊙mid-June–late-July), when open-air opera concerts are performed on a stage erected in front of the theatre and state museum. Punters gather across the water in the Burggarten to listen in.

Schwerin

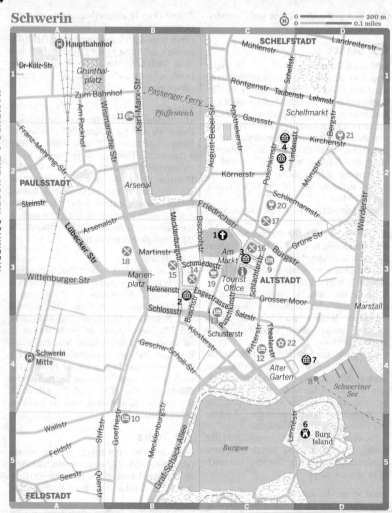

🛏 Sleeping

Zur guten Quelle
HOTEL €

(Map p694; ☎565 985; www.zur-guten-quelle.m -vp.de; Schusterstrasse 12; s/d from €54/78; P🐕) One of Schwerin's prettiest half-timbered houses, bang in the heart of the Altstadt. Zur guten Quelle is known for its cosy traditional restaurant and beer garden, but it also has half-a-dozen simple but comfortable rooms. Many have ancient timbers running right through the rooms.

Hotel Niederländischer Hof
HOTEL €€

(Map p694; ☎591 100; www.niederlaendischer-hof. de; Karl-Marx-Strasse 12-13; s €84-124, d €125-170 incl breakfast; P🐕) Overlooking the Pfaffen-teich, this regal 1901-established hotel has 33 elegant rooms with black marble bathrooms, a library warmed by an open fire, and a lauded restaurant. Room decor ranges from traditional luxe to whimsical seaside.

Hotel Am Schloss
PENSION €€

(Map p694; ☎593 230; www.hotel-am-schloss. m-vp.de; Heinrich-Mann-Strasse 3; s/d from €52/75; P🐕) There are 25 modern rooms spread across seven floors served by a lift in this basic

Schwerin

but comfortable pension. It is located in an old commercial bakery and warehouse. Take trams 3, 5, 7 or 19 from the train station to Schlossblick.

Pension am Theater PENSION €€
(Map p694; ☎593 680; www.pensionamtheater.m-vp.de; Theaterstrasse 1-2; s €57-80, d €74-90; P) In the shadow of the huge theatre building and (just) within sight of the castle, this ideally located pension has 18 cheerful, stylish and spacious rooms. It's a simple place although if you get one of the rooms with a terrace, you will have scored!

Alt Schweriner Schankstuben HOTEL €€
(Map p694; ☎592 5313; www.schankstuben.de; Am Schlachtmarkt 9-13; s/d from €60/84; P⊛) A historic half-timbered house in the Altstadt, with 16 modern and comfortable rooms. It's tucked above Schankstuben's restaurant, which opens to a flower-filled terrace, and is known for its regional specialities. Romantics can enjoy a champagne breakfast (€8.50 per person).

DJH Hostel HOSTEL €
(☎326 0006; www.jugendherberge.de; Waldschulweg 3; dm incl breakfast from €20) Though popular with school groups, this 91-bed/20-room hostel is in a peaceful, leafy location south of the city centre. Take bus 14.

✕ Eating

TOP CHOICE Buschérie MODERN EUROPEAN €€€
(Map p694; ☎923 6066; www.buscherie.de; Buschstrasse 9; mains €16-20) Although historic and half-timbered, Buschstrasse isn't stuck in the past, as shown by this sprightly bistro. Foods of the region are prepared with colour and flair. There is a sumptuous seafood spread (€32 per person) but otherwise the meaty mains and small plates are well-priced. There's live jazz some nights; Mondays feature special cocktails and singing.

Die Suppenstube CAFE €
(Map p694; ☎0172-382 5038; Puschkinstrasse 55; mains 4-6; ⊙11am-5pm Mon-Fri; ✍) Funky light fittings made from cutlery, stripped floorboards and bare tables provide a minimalist contrast with the historic half-timbered walls of this house on the edge of the Markt. The soups here are tops – we love the pea soup; desserts are, well, awesome.

Weinhaus Wöhler GERMAN €€
(Map p694; ☎555 830; www.weinhaus-woehler.de; Puschkinstrasse 26; mains €9-22; ⊛) In addition to wood-lined dining rooms, a large covered courtyard and a tapas/cocktail bar, this historic (1819), half-timbered inn also offers six rooms (€80 to €130). The seasonal regional menu is best enjoyed amidst the grape vines on the terrace.

Zum Stadtkrug BREWERY €€
(Map p694; ☎593 6693; www.altstadtbrauhaus.de; Wismarsche Strasse 126; mains €10-20) The dark beer at this 1936-established microbrewery/pub consistently rates among the best in Germany. It's full of antique brewing equipment, and opens to a convivial beer garden. The menu features the usual assortment of

schnitzels and porky mains but everything is well prepared. Sandwiches are excellent.

Der Käseladen Mühlenberg
DELI €

(Map p694; Mecklenburgstrasse 37; snacks from €2; ⊙9am-6pm Mon-Fri, 9am-4pm Sat) A beautiful cheese store. The engaging owner will help you assemble a fabulous picnic to enjoy in the Schlossgarten; bakeries are nearby.

Drinking

Schwerin's watering holes are concentrated along Arsenalstrasse, Mecklenburgstrasse and Puschkinstrasse.

Zum Freischütz
PUB

(Map p694; www.zum-freischuetz.de; Ziegenmarkt 11; ⊙11am-late Mon-Fri, 6pm-late Sat & Sun) A life-size bronze goat stands on the square near this characterful cafe that is full of characters. Overlooking Schwerin's old goat market, this storied pub has an old interior that features wooden chairs dating back decades. When one collapses, there's free beer. Sandwiches, soups and various cheap specials are served long into the night.

Zeitgeist
BAR

(Map p694; Puschkinstrasse 22; ⊙from 6pm Tue-Thu, from 7pm Fri & Sat) This hip bar has an alternative, creative bent. Join the conversation about when the sagging half-timbered veteran next door will finally collapse.

Rösterei Fuchs
CAFE

(Map p694; ☑593 8444; Am Markt 4; ⊙10am-7pm Mon-Fri, 10am-5pm Sat) The aroma of freshly roasted coffee fills this small, chic place, which roasts its own coffee in-house, and also sells beans as well as gourmet chocolates. Drop by for an espresso or other warming drink.

☆ Entertainment

Staatstheater Schwerin
THEATRE

(Map p694; ☑530 00; www.theater-schwerin.de; Alter Garten) The state theatre offers a range of concerts and theatrical performances.

Shopping

Schwerin has some huge new malls, like those around **Marienplatz**, but the real fun is to be had in the many interesting little shops. Stroll **Buschstrasse** for everything from handmade goods to model trains and **Münzstrasse** for a string of creative boutiques.

Information

Tourist Office (☑592 5212; www.schwerin. com; Rathaus, Am Markt 14; ⊙9am-6pm Mon-Fri, 10am-6pm Sat & Sun)

❶ Getting There & Around

Trains links include Hamburg (from €27, one hour), Rostock (from €20, one hour), Stralsund (from €33, two hours) and Wismar (€8, 30 minutes), with less frequent direct connections to/from Berlin (€35, 2¼ hours).

Buses and trams cost €1.50/4.60 for a single/day pass. A ferry crosses the Pfaffenteich (€1) from late April to mid-October.

Güstrow

☑03843 / POP 30,100

Best known for its small but stately Renaissance Schloss, this charming 775-plus-year-old town is also the place where famed 20th-century sculptor Ernst Barlach spent most of his working life. You can view dozens of his deeply felt, humanist works here.

◉ Sights

Güstrow has been beautifully restored and you can spend a couple of hours just wandering its cobblestoned streets in the old town. Be sure to check out the **fountain** with an imposing statue of Prince Heinrich Borwin II, who founded the town in 1228. It is at the crux of the both ancient and modern commercial street: **Pferdemarkt** (horse market).

Schloss Güstrow
PALACE

(☑7520; www.schloss-guestrow.de; adult/child €5/3.50; ⊙10am-6pm Tue-Sun mid-Apr–mid-Oct, to 5pm other times) Güstrow's fabulous Renaissance 16th-century Schloss is home to an historical museum as well as a cultural centre, period art exhibitions and occasional concerts. You can tour rooms that recall the luxe excess of its royal residents. The **gardens** were completely restored in 2012.

Dom
CHURCH

(www.dom-guestrow.de; Philipp-Brandin-Strasse 5; ⊙10am-5pm daily mid-May–mid-Oct, reduced hours rest of year) Built between 1226 and 1335, the richly ornamented Gothic Dom contains a copy of Ernst Barlach's *Hovering Angel,* a memorial for the fallen soldiers of WWI; this copy was made secretly from the original mould after the Nazis destroyed the original sculpture.

Gertrudenkapelle
GALLERY

(☎844 000; Gertrudenplatz 1; adult/child €4/2.50; ⏱10am-5pm Tue-Sun Apr-Oct, 11am-4pm Tue-Sun Nov-Mar) The Ernst Barlach memorial in the Gertrudenkapelle displays many of his original works. It is about 300m west of the Pferdemarkt fountain.

Atelierhaus
GALLERY

(☎822 99; www.ernst-barlach-stiftung.de; adult/child €6/4; ⏱10am-5pm Tue-Sun Apr-Oct, 11am-4pm Tue-Sun Nov-Mar) Based on sketches he made in Russia, Ernst Barlach's squarish sculptures began bearing the same expressive gestures and hunched-over, wind-blown postures of the impoverished people he encountered. Banned by the Nazis, he died in 1938; after the war his works have gained full appreciation.

Many of his bronze and wood carvings are housed along with a biographical exhibition at his former studio, the Atelierhaus, 4km south of the city at Inselsee; take bus 204 or 205.

🛏 Sleeping & Eating

Güstrow is a good day trip from across the region but by spending the night, you can try to hear the echoes of the Dukes on the cobblestones.

Gästehaus Am Schlosspark
HOTEL €

(☎245 990; www.gaestehaus-guestrow.de; Neuwieder Weg; s €25-32, d €50-62; P@) This great-value hotel overlooks the Schloss and its gardens. Most of the 100 modern rooms have views, most have high-speed internet and some have small kitchen facilities. You can rent bikes to explore the area.

Cafe Küpper
CAFE €

(Domstrasse 15; cakes from €3; ⏱9am-6pm) The perfect pause for your Güstrow visit. They've been creating luscious cakes here since 1852.

ℹ Information

Tourist Office (Güstrow Information; ☎681 023; www.guestrow-tourismus.de; Franz-Parr-Platz 10; ⏱9am-7pm Mon-Fri, 10am-5pm Sat, 11am-5pm Sun May-Sep, closes 1hr earlier other times) is incredibly helpful and has a lot of info in English. It also runs town tours.

ℹ Getting There & Around

Trains leave for Güstrow once or twice an hour from Rostock's Hauptbahnhof (€8, 25 minutes). Hourly services to/from Schwerin (€14, one hour) require a change in Bad Kleinen. The

WORTH A TRIP

LUDWIGSLUST

Such was the allure of the sturdy **Schloss Ludwigslust** (☎03874-571 90; www.schloss-ludwigslust.de; adult/child €3.50/2; ⏱10am-6pm Tue-Sun mid-Apr–mid-Oct, to 5pm other times), that when the ducal seat moved 36km north to Schwerin in 1837, some family members continued to live here until 1945. Now part of the Schwerin State Museum, its highlight is the stately, gilt-columned, high-ceilinged **Golden Hall**.

A planned baroque town, Ludwigslust's neat, orderly layout is an attraction in itself. Trains run from Schwerin every two hours (€8, 30 minutes).

station is 700m northwest of the Pferdemarkt fountain.

Neubrandenburg
☎0395 / POP 65,300

Neubrandenburg has few pretensions. It bills itself as 'the city of four gates on the Tollensesee Lake', and that's pretty well what it is. A largely intact medieval wall, with four gates, encircles the 13th-century Altstadt (although you have to peer hard through some harsh GDR architecture to find traces of it). It makes an interesting stop.

◎ Sights

City Wall
HISTORIC SITE

Neubrandenburg was founded in 1248 by Herbord von Raven, a Mecklenburg knight granted the land by Brandenburg Margrave Johann I, and building progressed in the usual order: defence system, church, town hall, pub. The security system was the 2.3km-long, 7.5m-high stone wall that survives today, with four city gates and 56 sentry posts built into it.

To navigate the circular wall, consider it as the rim of a clock face. The train station is at 12 o'clock.

The **Friedländer Tor** (2 o'clock), begun in 1300 and completed in 1450, was the first gate. **Treptower Tor** (9 o'clock) is the largest and contains an archaeological collection.

At the southern end of the city is the gaudy **Stargarder Tor** (6 o'clock). The simple brick **Neues Tor** (3 o'clock) fronts the east side of the Altstadt.

Southwest of the train station (at about 11 o'clock) is the former dungeon, the **Fangelturm**. You'll recognise it by its pointy tower.

Wedged into the stone circumference are the 27 sweet **half-timbered houses** that remain of the original sentry posts. When firearms rendered such defences obsolete in the 16th century, the guardhouses were converted into *Wiekhäuser*, homes for the poor, disadvantaged and elderly. Most of the surviving homes are now craft shops, galleries and cafes.

✕ Eating

Wiekhaus 45   GERMAN €€

(☑566 7762; 4th Ringstrasse; mains €9-20) Easily the most-appealing place to eat in Neubrandenburg is this lovely renovated guardhouse. Waiters zip up and down the narrow stairwell carrying huge portions of delicious Mecklenburg specialities (start with the tasty onion soup served with fresh bread, look for fresh herring in season). There are delightful outside tables in summer.

ℹ Information

Tourist Office (Stadt Info; ☑194 33; www.neubrandenburg-touristinfo.de; Stargarder Strasse 17; ☺10am-5pm Mon-Sat, 10am-2pm Sun) Tourist information; located near the centre of the old town, across from the Marktplatz.

ℹ Getting There & Away

Train service runs every two hours to/from Berlin (€28, two hours) and Stralsund (€17, 1¼ hours).

Müritz National Park

Müritz is commonly known as the land of a thousand lakes. While that's an exaggeration, there are well over 100 lakes here, as well as countless ponds, streams and rivers in this beautiful land midway between Berlin and Rostock.

Consisting of bog and wetlands, the serene **Müritz National Park** (☑039824-2520; www.mueritz-nationalpark.de) is home to a wide range of waterfowl, including ospreys, white-tailed eagles and cranes. Its two main sections sprawl over 300 sq km to the east and (mainly) west of Neustrelitz, where the park's waterway begins on the Zierker See. Boardwalks and other features let you get close to nature.

Tourist offices throughout the region have trail and park maps and offer recommendations for the main activity: self-guided **paddle-and-camp trips**. The regional tourism authority, **Mecklenburgische Seenplatte** (Mecklenburg Lake District; www.mecklenburgische-seenplatte.de), is a good place to research and book accommodation. The most popular **national park information centre** is located in Federow, 7km southeast of Waren. The gateway town of Neustrelitz has an info desk in the tourist office.

When camping, you must use designated sites. **Haveltourist** (☑03981-247 90; www.haveltourist.de; adult/tent/tent & car from €7/6.50/11, r €40-130) has nine campgrounds (most with cabins as well), eight of which are connected by lakes and waterways. It also rents gear like canoes (€17 to €28 per day).

Trains and buses criss-cross the lake district. The excellent national park website is a good place for information.

Neustrelitz

☑03981 / POP 21,200

Situated on the Zierker See within Müritz National Park, the pretty, planned baroque town of Neustrelitz centres on its impressive, circular **Markt**, from which streets radiate like the spokes of a wheel.

The town's Schloss fell victim to WWII, but its beautiful **Schlossgarten** retains its 18th-century orangerie.

The **tourist office** (☑253 119; www.neustrelitz.de; Strelitzer Strasse 1; ☺9am-6pm Mon-Fri, 9.30am-1pm Sat & Sun May-Sep, 9am-noon & 1-4pm Mon-Thu, 9am-noon Fri Oct-Apr) shares space with an info desk for Müritz National Park, and can help with accommodation in town and throughout the park.

Fish plucked fresh from the lake is the highlight of the rustic waterside cafe **Zum Fischerhof** (☑200 842; www.fischerei-neustrelitz.de; Seestrasse 15a; mains €6-12; ☺11am-8pm). The more refined **Kaisers Bootshaus** (☑239 860; www.kaisers-bootshaus.de; Useriner Strasse 1; r per person from €37; ☎) also has lake views and suitably piney, rural-feeling rooms.

Hourly trains run to/from Berlin (€22, 80 minutes), Rostock (€23, 1½ hours) and Stralsund (€23, 1¾ hours).

COASTAL MECKLENBURG – WESTERN POMERANIA

This spectacular stretch of the Baltic coast is certainly one of Europe's better-kept secrets. But Germans know better and flock in summer to its dazzling clean, white sands and glittering seas.

Hotspots during the all-too-brief beachgoing season include three leafy resort islands: romantic, villa-lined Rügen; car-free Hiddensee; and Usedom (which Germany shares with Poland). Warnemünde, the seaside resort near Rostock, is another sandy hotspot – when it's hot.

Stralsund is the prize town of the region, combining seaside charms with beautiful old architecture. Other highlights include the gracious university town of Greifswald, which retains some exquisite medieval architecture, as does Wismar.

Rostock

📞 0381 / POP 202.700

Rostock was devastated in WWII and later pummelled by socialist architectural 'ideals'. Its best feature is 13km northwest, where the Warnow River flows into the Baltic Sea: Warnemünde, which has one of Germany's best beaches.

This large port city *does* have a small but attractive historic core – redbrick and pastel-coloured buildings harking back to the 14th- and 15th-century Hanseatic era – but you generally have to wade past a landscape of concrete eyesores to reach it. Perhaps the best feature is the vibrant energy provided by the thousands of university students.

◉ Sights

It takes just a couple of hours to see the city sights, which are found in the pedestrianized zone between Neuer Markt and Universitätsplatz.

TOP CHOICE ⟩ **Marienkirche**   CHURCH

(📞453 325; www.marienkirche-rostock.de; Am Ziegenmarkt; donation requested €1.50; ⊙10am-6pm Mon-Sat, 11.15am-5pm Sun May-Sep, 10am-4pm Mon-Sat, 11.15am-noon Sun Oct-Apr) Central Rostock's pride and joy is the 13th-century Marienkirche, the only main Rostock church to survive WWII unscathed. Behind the main altar, the church's 12m-high **astrologi-**cal clock, built in 1472 by Hans Düringer, is the only working clock of its kind in the world with its original mechanisms. At the very top of the clock is a series of doors. At noon and midnight the innermost right door opens and six of the 12 apostles march out to parade around Jesus (Judas is locked out). Zodiac symbols and moon phases feature in the centre, while the lower section has a disc that tells the exact day on which Easter falls in any given year. The replaceable discs are accurate for 130 years – the current one expires in 2017, and the University of Rostock already has a new one ready. Look out too for the unusually tall, organically shaped **baroque organ** (1770).

Neuer Markt   SQUARE

Rostock's large, open central square is dominated by the splendid 13th-century **Rathaus**. The building's baroque facade was added in 1727 after the original brick Gothic structure collapsed.

Opposite the Rathaus is a series of restored **gabled houses** and a stylised, sea-themed fountain, the **Möwenbrunnen** (2001), by artist Waldemar Otto. The explanatory plaque says the four figures are Neptune and his sons, although many believe they represent the four elements.

Kröpeliner Strasse & Universitätsplatz   SQUARE

Kröpeliner Strasse, a broad, shop-filled, cobblestone pedestrian mall lined with 15th- and 16th-century burghers' houses, runs from Neuer Markt west to Kröpeliner Tor.

At the centre of the mall is Universitätsplatz, and its centrepiece, the crazy rococo **Brunnen der Lebensfreude** (Fountain of Happiness; some of the people and animals shown seem to be engaging in acts deemed illegal in more religiously conservative places). True to its name, the square is lined with university buildings, including the handsome terracotta **Hauptgebäude** (1866–70), which replaced the famous 'White College'. The university itself is the oldest on the Baltic (founded in 1419), and currently has about 11,000 students.

At the southwestern end is the **Kloster Zum Heiligen Kreuz**, a convent established in 1270 by Queen Margrethe of Denmark. Today it houses the city's cultural history museum, the **Kulturhistorisches Museum Rostock** (📞203 590; www.kulturhistorisches -museum-rostock.de; Klosterhof 7; admission free; ⊙10am-6pm Tue-Sun), with an interesting collection including Victorian furniture and some sculptures by Ernst Barlach.

City Walls & Gates
HISTORIC SITE

Today only two of 32 gates, plus a small brick section, remain of the old city wall. The 55m-high **Kröpeliner Tor** stands at the western end of Kröpeliner Strasse. From here, you can follow the *Wallanlagen* (city walls) through the pleasant park to Wallstrasse and the other surviving gate, the **Steintor**.

Petrikirche
CHURCH

(☑211 01; www.petrikirche-rostock.de; Alter Markt; tower adult/child €3/2; ☺tower 10am-6pm May-Sep, 10am-4pm Oct-Apr) The Gothic Petrikirche has a 117m-high steeple – a mariner's landmark for centuries – that was restored in 1994, having been missing since WWII. There's a lift up to the 45m-high viewing platform.

☞ Tours

Reederei Schütt
BOAT TOUR

(☑690 953; www.hafenrundfahrten-in-rostock.de; ☺May-Oct) Offers round-harbour trips and services from Rostock's harbour to Warne-

---

DON'T MISS

BAD DOBERAN

The former summer ducal residence of Bad Doberan, about 15km west of Rostock, was once the site of a powerful Cistercian monastery. Today, it boasts its magnficent and mighty **Münster** (☑038203-627 16; www.muenster-doberan.de; Klosterstrasse 2; adult/child €2/0.50; ☺9am-6pm Mon-Sat, 11am-6pm Sun May-Sep, shorter hrs rest of the year).

Construction of this Gothic church started in 1280 but the scale of the building meant it wasn't consecrated until 1368. Its treasures include a lovely **high altar** and an ornate **pulpit**. It is seeking Unesco recognition and has just undergone a massive restoration that has made every one of the 1.2 million bricks look like new – almost too new.

Organ recitals, choirs and bands perform from May to September, usually on Friday evenings at 7.30pm.

Trains connect Bad Doberan with Rostock Hauptbahnhof (€8, 25 minutes) and Wismar (€8, 45 minutes) roughly hourly. The train station is 1km south of the Münster.

---

münde (one-way/return €10/14); the pier is at the base of Schnickmannstrasse.

🛏 Sleeping

Hanse Hostel
HOSTEL €

(☑128 6006; www.hanse-hostel.de; Doberaner Strasse 136; dm €14-18, s/d with shared bathroom €24/44, breakfast €4; @☎) On the edge of Rostock's trendy bar district, the KTV, is this family-run operation with great facilities spread over two buildings. Recently added rooms have private bathrooms (single/double €35/56). From the Hauptbahnhof, take tram 4 or 5 to the Volkstheater stop.

Hotel Kleine Sonne
HOTEL €€

(☑497 3153; www.die-kleine-sonne.de; Steinstrasse 7; r per person €52-102; @☎) This lovely place lives up to its name with sunny yellow and red detailing against otherwise starkly minimalist decor. The 48 rooms do boast semaphore prints by Berlin artist Nils Ausländer. All guests have free use of the wellness centre at the nearby Steigenberger Hotel Sonne. Cyclists are catered for with bike storage and special packages.

✖ Eating

Café Central
CAFE €€

(☑490 4648; Leonhardstrasse 20; mains €6-15; ☺from 10am) In the heart of the KTV scene, Café Central has cult status among Rostock locals. Students, artists, hipsters and suited-up professionals all loll around sipping long drinks on the banquettes or gabbing with friends at tables out front. There is a lot of cheap ethnic restaurants nearby. It's 500m northwest of the Kröpeliner Tor.

Zur Kogge
GERMAN €€

(☑493 4493; www.zur-kogge.de; Wokrenterstrasse 27; mains €9-17; ☺11am-9pm Mon-Sat; ☝) At this Rostock institution, cosy wooden booths are lined with stained-glass Hanseatic coats of armour and monster fish threatening sailing ships, while life preservers hang from the walls, and ships lanterns are suspended from the ceiling. Local fish dishes dominate the menu, or you can stop by for coffee and cake between meal times. There's an above-average kids menu, too.

Zum Alten Fritz
GERMAN €€

(☑208 780; www.alter-fritz.de; Warnowufer 65; mains €8-20) With a good range of regional standards, this big pub-restaurant down on the docks is part of a local brewery chain.

Terrace tables let you hear the clink of chains and the bump of boats. There is a good house-made unfiltered brew.

☆ Entertainment

West of the Altstadt lies the student and nightlife district Kröpeliner Torvorstadt, commonly known as KTV.

Live gigs, DJs, concerts and a host of other events are listed in *Szene* (www.szene rostock.de).

TOP CHOICE **Studentenkeller** BAR
(☎455 928; www.studentenkeller.de; Universitätsplatz 5; ⊙Tue-Sat) This cellar and garden joint has been rocking Rostock's learned youth for years. Check the website for parties, DJ sets and other events.

Mau Club Rostock CLUB
(☎202 3576; www.mauclub.de; Warnowufer 56; ⊙hours vary) Everything from indie to punk to disco attracts a wide-ranging crowd to this former storage hall. It's well known for its support of up-and-coming acts.

MS Stubnitz CLUB
(☎490 7475; www.stubnitz.com; Stadthafen, Liegeplatz 82; ⊙hours vary) A former fishing trawler has been converted into Rostock's most unusual and most alternative, grunge-style venue, with bands, DJs and performances over three decks.

❶ Information

Tourist Office (☎381 2222; www.rostock.de; Neuer Markt 3; ⊙10am-6pm Mon-Fri, 10am-3pm Sat & Sun May-Oct, 10am-5pm Mon-Fri, 10am-3pm Sat Nov-Apr) Sells the Rostock Card (24/48 hours €8/13), which is good for public transport and discounts to some attractions.

❶ Getting There & Away

BOAT Ferries sail to/from Denmark, Sweden, Latvia and Finland. Boats depart from the Überseehafen (overseas seaport; www.rostock-port. de), which is on the east side of the Warnow. Take tram 1, 2, 3 or 4 to Dierkower Kreuz (tram 3 or 4 from the Hauptbahnhof), then change for bus 49 to Seehafen. There is an S-Bahn to Seehafen, but it's a 20-minute walk from the station to the piers.

TRAIN There are frequent direct trains to Berlin (from €38, 2½ hours) and Hamburg (from €33, 2¼ hours), and hourly services to Stralsund (€15, one hour) and Schwerin (€20, one hour).

❶ Getting Around

Journeys within Rostock cost €1.80/3.70 for a single/day pass. The Hauptbahnhof is about 1.5km south of the Altstadt.

Trams 5 and 6 travel from the Hauptbahnhof up Steinstrasse, around the very central Marienkirche and down Lange Strasse to the university.

Warnemünde

Warnemünde is all about promenading, eating fish, sipping cocktails, and lazing in a *Strandkörbe* (sheltered straw 'beach basket' seat) on its long, wide and startlingly white beach.

Walking from Warnemünde's train station along Alter Strom, the boat-lined main canal, you'll pass a row of quaint cottages housing restaurants. Then you turn the corner into Am Leuchtturm and Seestrasse and – bam! – it hits you: **beach**!

For a fabulous view from above, climb the spiralling 135-step wrought-iron and granite staircase of the 1898-built **lighthouse**.

🛏 Sleeping

There are scads of places to stay. The tourist office website is useful in sorting through the nocturnal shrubbery.

Residenz Strandhotel HOTEL €€
(☎548 060; www.residenz-strandhotel.de; Seestrasse 6; s €70-87, d without sea view €75-112, d with sea view €79-160; P❋@🖥) The balcony-clad exterior of this hotel manages to be somewhat attractive (an accomplishment locally). Inside, you'll find stylish, sound-insulated rooms with flat-screen TVs. Space in these is at a premium, but if you're smart you'll be on your balcony or the beach.

Hotel-Pension Zum Kater GUESTHOUSE €€
(☎548 210; www.pension-zum-kater.de; Alexandrinenstrasse 115; s/d from €72/100; P) Less than 10 minutes' stroll from the beach, and even closer to the harbour, this guesthouse is sweet and cosy. There's a supplement of €21/16 per person for the first/second nights if you stay less than three on high-season weekends. Get a room with a roof terrace.

Baltic-Freizeit Camping und Ferienpark CAMPGROUND €
(☎04544-800 313; www.baltic-freizeit.de; Dünenweg 27; sites incl person & car €17-50, cottages per person from €60; P) On the eastern bank of the Warnow River, across from Warnemünde,

this enormous holiday centre has over 1200 pitches, plus 80 cottages sleeping up to six people, as well as minigolf, tennis courts, a sauna, and several restaurants and bars.

DJH Hostel Warnemünde HOSTEL €
(☎548 170; www.jugendherbergen-mv.de; Parkstrasse 47; dm under/over 26yr €26/31; @🛜) This family-friendly hostel is in a converted weather station near the western end of the Warnemünde beach. Take the S-Bahn to the Lichtenhagen stop, then change to bus 36 to Warnemünde beach.

✖ Eating & Drinking

Fish – fresh, fried, baked, smoked, you name it – is the order of the day here. Both banks of the harbour are lined with kiosks and caravans selling inexpensive fish sandwiches – perfect if you're heading to the beach or a nearby bench along the harbourfront.

Fischerklause SEAFOOD €€
(☎525 16; www.fischer-klause.de; Am Strom 123; mains €9-15; 🛜) Fischerklause is one of the atmospheric old fisherfolk's cottages lining the western bank of Alter Strom, and attracts plenty of tourists (as does all of Warnemünde). Still, its ship's cabin decor and its succulent seafood make it worth seeking out. Herring, halibut, cod, eel and more feature on the menu.

Pauli Warnemünde CAFE €
(www.pauli-warnemuende.de; Kirchenplatz 12; snacks from €3; ☺8am-6pm) Everything is organic at this designer cafe set on Warnemünde's main square away from the beach. Look for seasonal soups, light dishes, salads and a vast range of delectable baked goods. The coffee is superb.

Schuster's BAR
(www.schusters-strandbar.de) Head here for sunset cocktails. It has a hip summer pavilion on the beach not far from the iconic lighthouse.

ℹ Information

Tourist Office Warnemünde (☎548 000; www.warnemuende.de; Am Strom 59, cnr Kirchstrasse; ☺10am-6pm Mon-Fri, 10am-3pm Sat & Sun May-Oct, 10am-5pm Mon-Fri, 10am-3pm Sat Nov-Apr)

ℹ Getting There & Around

There are frequent S-Bahn services between Rostock and Warnemünde (single/day pass €2.70/5.40; 22 minutes).

Baltic Coastal Resorts

☑038203
Heiligendamm and Kühlungsborn are among the atmospheric beach resort areas along the starkly beautiful coast west of Rostock.

The Molli Schmalspurbahn is a popular narrow-gauge steam train that travels to the coastal resorts from Bad Doberan. Catching the train and walking along the coast between some stops makes for a atmospheric day out.

◉ Sights & Activities

Heiligendamm BEACH
The 'white town on the sea' is Germany's oldest seaside resort, founded in 1793 by Mecklenburg duke Friedrich Franz I and was fashionable throughout the 19th century as a playground of the nobility.

The grand tradition continues at the exclusive **Grand Hotel Heiligendamm** (☎7400; www.grandhotel-heiligendamm.de; s/d from €200/240; P🌐@🛜🌊). With cool, contemporary rooms housed in five gleaming white, heritage-listed buildings, this palatial hotel hosted the G8 summit in 2007. Even for those not staying here, the hotel is an attraction, with some seven restaurants and bars, its own pier, pristine beach and surrounding parkland.

Kühlungsborn BEACH
Kühlungsborn, the biggest Baltic Sea resort, with some 7500 inhabitants, is also home to some lovely art-deco buildings and adjoins a dense 130-hectare forest. The east and west parts of town are linked by the Ostseeallee promenade, lined with hotels and restaurants. In the eastern part of town you'll find a pier running 240m out to sea.

Molli Schmalspurbahn STEAM TRAIN
(☎4150; www.molli-bahn.de; return ticket adult/child €12/9) In 1886, the steam train 'Molli', as she's affectionately known, began huffing and puffing her way to Heiligendamm, carrying Germany's elite. Then in 1910, the line was extended west along the coast to Kühlungsborn. Today the train goes by the full name of Mecklenburger Bäderbahn

A SWEDISH HEADS-UP

In Wismar, Swedish Heads refers to two baroque busts of Hercules, which once stood on mooring posts at the harbour entrance.

Semi-comical, with great curling moustaches and wearing lions as hats, and painted in bright colours (one red-and-white, the other yellow-and-blue), the statues are believed to have marked either the beginning of the harbour or the navigable channels within it. It's thought that before this they were ships' figureheads.

The original heads were damaged when a Finnish barge rammed them in 1902, at which time replicas were made. One original is now in the Schabbellhaus, the town's historical musuem which is closed for renovation until at least 2014. Two replicas guard the Baumhaus in Wismar's *Alter Hafen* (old harbour).

Molli, with services departing Bad Doberan's train station on average 11 times a day year-round.

With a maximum speed of 45km/h, the journey takes 15 minutes to reach the coast at Heiligendamm (one-way adult/child €4.50/3.40) and 45 minutes in total to Kühlungsborn/West (€6.50/4.90), with interim stops in Steilküste, Kühlungsborn/East and Kühlungsborn/Mitte. Children love the dinky engine and carriages. There's a salon car on many journeys and the scenery is lovely.

For a particularly easy and enjoyable walk, you can get off at Heiligendamm and walk to the Steilküste station before picking up the train again.

Wismar

📞 03841 / POP 44,400

With its gabled facades and cobbled streets, this small, photogenic city looks essentially Hanseatic. But although it joined the Hanseatic trading league in the 13th century, it spent most of the 16th and 17th centuries as part of Sweden. There are numerous reminders of this era all over town. The entire Altstadt was Unesco-listed in 2002.

Wismar has been long popular with filmmakers and its picturesque *Alter Hafen* (old harbour) starred in the 1922 Dracula movie *Nosferatu*.

⊙ Sights

Wismar's Altstadt centres on the Markt, said to be the largest medieval town square in northern Germany. You can easily explore the town in a couple of hours.

Markt SQUARE
Dominating the middle of the Markt is the 1602-built **Wasserkunst** (waterworks), an ornate, 12-sided well that supplied Wismar's

drinking water until 1897. Today it remains the town's landmark.

Behind it stands the redbrick **Alter Schwede**, which dates from 1380 and features a striking step buttress gable facade. Today it houses a restaurant and guesthouse, as well as a copy of one of the socalled 'Swedish Heads'.

Other gabled houses around the Markt have also been carefully restored. The large **Rathaus** at the square's northern end was built between 1817 and 1819 and today houses the excellent **Rathaus Historical Exhibition** (adult/child €2/1; ⊙10am-6pm) in its basement. Displays include an original 15th-century *Wandmalerei* (mural) uncovered by archaeologists in 1985, a glass-covered medieval well, and the Wrangel tomb – the coffin of influential Swedish General Helmut V Wrangel and his wife, with outsized wooden figures carved on top.

Fürstenhof HISTORIC BUILDING
Between the St-Marien and St-Georgen churches lies the restored Italian Renaissance Fürstenhof, now the city courthouse. The facades are slathered in terracotta reliefs depicting episodes from folklore and the town's history.

Schabbellhaus MUSEUM
(www.schabbellhaus.de; Schweinsbrücke 8) The town's historical museum is in the Renaissance Schabbellhaus in a former brewery (1571), just south of St-Nikolai-Kirche across the canal. It is undergoing massive reconstruction through at least 2014.

St-Nikolai-Kirche CHURCH
(St-Nikolai-Kirchhof; www.kirchen-in-wismar.de; admission €2; ⊙8am-8pm May-Sep, 10am-6pm Apr & Oct, 11am-4pm Nov-Mar) Of the three great redbrick churches that once rose above the rooftops before WWII, only the

BOATS SELLING SEAFOOD

Along the *Alter Hafen*, seafood (including delicious fish sandwiches from as little as €2) is sold directly from a handful of bobbing boats. Most are open 9am to 6pm daily, and from 6am on Saturday during Wismar's weekly fish market.

sober redbrick St-Nikolai-Kirche, the largest of its kind in Europe, was left intact. Today it contains a font from its older sister church, the St-Marien-Kirche.

St-Marien-Kirche Steeple TOWER
(⊙10am-6pm Apr-Oct, 11am-4pm Nov-Mar) All that remains of the 13th-century St-Marien-Kirche is its great brick steeple (1339), which rises above the city. A multimedia exhibit on medieval church-building techniques is housed in the tower's base. The tower is opened for climbs a couple of times daily.

St-Georgen-Kirche CHURCH
The massive red shell of the St-Georgen-Kirche has been extensively reconstructed and while work continues, the intention is to use it for cultural and religious purposes. In 1945 a freezing populace was driven to burn what was left of the church's beautiful wooden statue of St George and the dragon. It was only bombed three weeks before the war ended.

☞ Tours

Adler-Schiffe BOAT TOURS
(☏01805-123 344; www.adler-schiffe.de; adult/child €9.50/5.50; ⊙daily Apr-Oct, weekends Nov-Mar) The ubiquitous tour company operates hour-long harbour cruises.

✯✯ Festivals & Events

Annual events include Wismar's **Hafenfest** (Harbour Festival) in mid-June, featuring old and new sailing ships and steamers, music and food, and a free **street theatre** festival in July/August. Wismar also holds a **Schwedenfest** on the third weekend of August, commemorating the end of Swedish rule in 1903.

⌷ Sleeping

The Altstadt is dotted with places to stay.

TOP CHOICE Hotel Reingard HOTEL €€
(☏284 972; www.hotel-reingard.de; Weberstrasse 18; s €68-72, d €98-102; P) Wismar's most charming place to stay is this boutique hotel with its dozen artistic rooms, leafy little garden and wonderfully idiosyncratic touches such as a lightshow to classical music that plays across the facade daily at 8.30pm. The breakfast includes apples from the hotel's trees and eggs from their chickens.

Pension Chez Fasan HOTEL €
(☏213 425; www.unterkunft-pension-wismar.de; Bademutterstrasse 20a; s/d €25/47, s without bathroom €22) The 25 simple but perfectly comfortable rooms in these three linked houses, just one block north of the Markt, are fantastic value. Call ahead to make sure someone's around to let you in; reception is normally open 2pm to 8pm.

✕ Eating & Drinking

If you're feeling adventurous, try *Wismarer Spickaal* (young eel smoked in a way that's unique to the region). And if you're in a celebratory mood, look out for locally produced Hanse-Sektkellerei champagne – from dry (Hanse Tradition) to extra dry (Hanse Selection).

Alter Schwede SEAFOOD €
(☏283 552; mains €10-21; ⊙11.30am-late; ☏) Baltic eel with herbed potatoes, catfish with mustard and a whole host of herring dishes are among the specialities of this landmark spot. The facade alone is a tourist attraction, but the reproduction Swedish head over the door puts it over the top. Get a table out front and enjoy Markt action.

To'n Zägenkrog SEAFOOD €
(☏282 716; www.ziegenkrug-wismar.de; Ziegenmarkt 10; mains €10-15; ⊙5-9pm) Excellent fish dishes are the mainstay of this cosy 1897-established pub. It's crammed with maritime mementoes and has some of Wismar's best harbour views. There are also tables overlooking the canal.

Brauhaus am Lohberg BREWERY
(www.brauhaus-wismar.de; Kleine Hohe Strasse 15; mains €7-15) This imposing brick half-timbered building was once home to the town's first brewery, which opened in 1452.

After a long pause, beer is brewing again in enormous copper vats. Enjoy German classics and seafood; live music regularly cranks up throughout summer.

ⓘ Information

Tourist Information (📞251 3025; www. wismar.de; Am Markt 11; ⊙9am-6pm Apr-Oct, 9am-6pm Mon-Sat, 10am-4pm Sun Nov-Mar)

ⓘ Getting There & Around

Trains travel every hour to/from Rostock (€12, 70 minutes) and Schwerin (€8, 40 minutes). The train station is a mere 40m from the Markt,

Darss-Zingst Peninsula

Nature lovers and artists will be captivated by the **Darss-Zingst Peninsula** (Fischland-Darss-Zingst; www.fischland-darss-zingst.de). This far-flung splinter of land is part of the 805-sq-km **Nationalpark Vorpommersche Boddenlandschaft** (Western Pomeranian Boddenlandschaft National Park; 📞038234-5020; www.nationalpark-vorpommersche-boddenland schaft.de), which also encompasses the island of Hiddensee and the west coast of Rügen Island. Some 60,000 **migratory cranes** stop over in the park every spring and autumn, their biggest resting ground in Central Europe. There are nine information offices spread across the park.

The **Bodden** are lagoons that were once part of the sea here, but have been cut off by shifting landmasses and are now rich with fish life. The seawards peninsula is raw and bracing, with trees growing sideways away from the constant winds. Further inland you'll find charming '**captains' houses**' – reed-thatched houses with colourfully painted doors depicting sunflowers, fish and other regional motifs. Also common are **windmills** and **Zeesenboote** (drag-net fishing boats) with striking brown sails.

The area looks a picture, so not surprisingly it's home to an artists colony in **Ahrenshoop** (www.ostseebad-ahrenshoop.de), which has an especially wild and windblown **beach**. The century-old **Kunstkaten** (www.kunstkaten.de; Strandweg 1; ⊙10am-1pm & 2-5pm) gallery here is in a strikingly painted reed-thatched house.

The tiny town of **Prerow** is renowned for its model-ship-filled **seafarers' church** and lighthouse.

Stralsund

📞03831 / POP 57,700

Stralsund was once the second-most important member of the Hanseatic League, after Lübeck, and its square gables interspersed with Gothic turrets, ornate portals and vaulted arches make it one of the leading examples of *Backsteingotik* (classic redbrick Gothic gabled architecture) in northern Germany.

This vibrant city's historic cobbled streets and many attractions make it an unmissable stop in the region.

⊙ Sights

ALTSTADT

Stralsund's Unesco-recognised Altstadt is effectively on its own island, surrounded by lakes and the sea. You can easily spend a day wandering here. Amidst all the careful restorations, you'll discover the odd unreconstructed 17th-century veteran to add spice and context.

Alter Markt   SQUARE
Seven copper turrets and six triangular gables grace the redbrick Gothic facade of Stralsund's splendid 1370 **Rathaus** (Map p706). The upper portion of the northern facade, or *Schauwand* (show wall), has openings to prevent strong winds from knocking it over. Inside, the sky-lit colonnade boasts shiny black pillars on carved and painted bases; on the western side of the building is an ornate portal.

Through the Rathaus' eastern walkway you'll come to the main portal of the 1270 **Nikolaikirche** (Map p706; 📞299 799; www. nikolai-stralsund.de; adult/child €2/free; ⊙9am-7pm Mon-Sat, 1-5pm Sun, May-Sep, 10am-6pm Mon-Sat, 1-5pm Sun other times), which was modelled on Lübeck's Marienkirche and is filled with art treasures. The **main altar** (1708), designed by the baroque master Andreas Schlüter, shows the eye of God flanked by cherubs and capped by a depiction of the Last Supper. Also worth a closer look are the **high altar** (1470), 6.7m wide and 4.2m tall, showing Jesus' entire life, and, behind the altar, a 1394-built (but no longer operational) **astronomical clock**.

Opposite the Rathaus you'll find the **Wulflamhaus** (Map p706; Alter Markt 5), a beautiful 15th-century town house named after an old mayor. Its turreted step gable imitates the Rathaus facade.

Stralsund

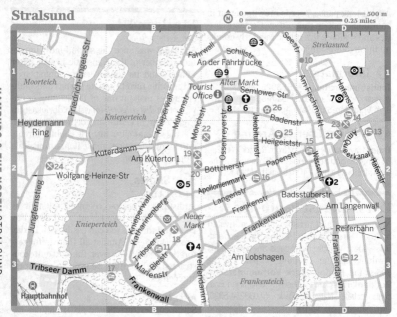

Marienkirche
CHURCH

(Map p706; ✆298 965; www.st-mariengemeinde -stralsund.de; ⊙9am-6pm Apr-Oct) The Neuer Markt is dominated by the massive 14th-century Marienkirche, another superb example of north German redbrick construction. You can climb the steep wooden steps up the tower for a sweeping view of the town, with its lovely red-tiled roofs, and Rügen Island. The ornate 17th-century organ is a stunner.

Johanniskloster
HISTORIC BUILDING

(Map p706; ✆294 265; Schillstrasse 27; adult/ concession €2.10/0.50; ⊙10am-6pm Wed-Sun May-Oct) On Schillstrasse, reached via Külpstrasse, is the Johanniskloster, a partially ruined former Franciscan monastery that's now a concert venue. It's famous for its 'smoking attic' (there was no chimney), chapter hall and cloister.

Heilgeistkirche
CHURCH

(Map p706; Wasserstrasse) Be sure to admire the lovely ivy-covered face of the baroque 14th-century Heilgeistkirche.

MARITIME STRALSUND

Stralsund has a deep relationship with the sea going back beyond Hanseatic times.

TOP CHOICE Ozeaneum
AQUARIUM

(Map p706; ✆265 0610; www.ozeaneum.de; Hafeninsel Stralsund; adult/child €14/8, combination ticket with Meeresmuseum adult/child €18/11; ⊙9.30am-9pm Jun–mid-Sep, 9.30am-7pm mid-Sep–May) In an arctic-white wavelike building that leaps out from the surrounding redbrick warehouses, the state-of-the-art Ozeaneum takes you into an underwater world of creatures from the Baltic and North Seas and the Atlantic Ocean up to the polar latitudes. In a huge tank you can see what thousands of herring do before they end up dropping down northerners' gullets.

Meeresmuseum
AQUARIUM

(Maritime Museum; Map p706; ✆265 010; www. meeresmuseum.de; Katharinenberg 14-20; adult/ child €7.50/5, combination ticket with Ozeaneum adult/child €18/11; ⊙10am-6pm Jun-Sep, 10am-5pm Oct-May) Affiliated with the Ozeaneum, the Meeresmuseum aquarium is in a 13th-century convent building. Exhibits include a very popular huge sea-turtle tank and polychromatic tropical fish.

Gorch Fock 1
SHIP

(Map p706; www.gorchfock1.de; Hafen; adult/child €4/2; ⊙10am-6pm Apr-Oct) Built as a training ship by the German navy in 1933, the

Stralsund

Gorch Fock 1 is a large (82m-long) steel three-masted barque with quite a history. The Russians took her as war booty and from there she spent time in the Ukariane and the UK before ending up back in her original home port of Stralsund. Now under restoration, it is hoped this proud vessel will once again sail the Baltic.

☞ Tours

The tourist office rents out English-language MP3 audioguide tours (€7; leave your passport as a deposit).

Weisse Flotte BOAT TOUR
(Map p706; ☎0180-321 2120; www.weisse-flotte.com; Haven; adult/child €8/4; ⊘mid-May–Oct) Weisse Flotte offers one-hour harbour cruises, circling the island of Dänholm, between Stralsund and Rügen.

✱✱ Festivals & Events

Ostseefestspiele MUSIC FESTIVAL
(www.ostseefestspiele.de) A *Seebühne* (floating stage) is erected in the harbour each June to August for opera, operetta and classical-music performances.

Wallensteintage FESTIVAL
(www.wallensteintage.de) In the third week of July, Stralsund celebrates repelling an enemy invasion in 1628.

🛏 Sleeping

If everything in your budget is booked in the harbour area and old town, there are several midrange hotels by the train station.

Altstadt Hotel Peiss TOP CHOICE HOTEL €€
(Map p706; ☎303 580; www.altstadt-pension-peiss.de; Tribseer Strasse 15; s €50-85, d €55-115; P🕏) Thirteen spacious rooms with Paul Gauguin prints and sparkling bathrooms combine with cheery service at this bright and appealing guesthouse. The breakfast buffet is healthy and the host-family are very helpful. With a terrace, small garden and bike rack, it's especially popular with cyclists.

Hafenspeicher APARTMENT €€
(Map p706; ☎0176 2210 9004, 703 676; www.hafenspeicher-stralsund.de; Am Querkanal 3a; r €80-160) One of Stralsund's oldest brick waterfront warehouses has been converted into a relaxed apartment-hotel by a local architect. Rooms range from spacious doubles to rather large apartments; most have views over the water towards Rügen. There's a small, upscale bar on the ground floor.

Hiddenseer HOTEL €€
(Map p706; ☎289 2390; www.hotel-hiddenseer.de; Hafenstrasse 12; s €53-90, d €73-155; P🕏) A prime harbourside location and 25 comfortable rooms make the Hiddenseer one of Stralsund's best options. The hotel is spread

over three vintage buildings and although they lack lifts, the energetic staff will carry your bags up to your room. Some rooms have sweeping views to Rügen.

Hotel Amber
PENSION €

(Map p706; ☑282 580; www.hotelamber.de; Heilgeiststrasse 50; s €40-60, d €65-85; P🐾) Perfectly located between the old town and the harbour, the Hotel Amber is also great value. The 12 rooms are simple but clean and come with amenities like satellite TV and more. Views from rooms on the third floor include the harbour and city.

Arcona Baltic Hotel
HOTEL €€€

(Map p706; ☑2040; www.stralsund.steigenberger. de; Frankendamm 22; s €80-155, d €115-190; P🐾) Try for a north-facing 6th-floor room at central Stralsund's most upscale hotel for breathtaking views (especially at twilight) over the Altstadt's rooftops and across the harbour to Rügen. The 128 contemporary rooms are spacious and well equipped, and service is doting.

Younior Hotel
HOSTEL €

(Map p706; ☑0800-233 388 234; www.younior -hotel.de; Tribseer Damm 78; dm incl breakfast €21-26; P@) In an expanse of parkland near the train station, a grand old 1897 building that once housed Stralsund's railway offices is now a 300-bed hostel.

Dorms have comfy, capsule-like triple-decker bunks, and fun facilities include a guest-only bar and a sandy beach volleyball court.

Pension Cobi
PENSION €

(Map p706; ☑278 288; www.pension-cobi.de; Jakobiturmstrasse 15; s €39-45, d €60-75; 🐾) In the shadow of the Jakobikirche, this is a great location for exploring the Altstadt. The 14 rooms are smart and clean, and some have balconies.

Eating

Smoked-fish stands dot the harbour area, many have quite elaborate menus although nothing costs more than €5.

Also on the harbour, Kron-Lastadie (Map p706; www.kron-lastadie.de) is a new collection of cafes set to open in 2013. Housed in part in a surviving 17th-century bastion, the complex will host casual outlets from several highly regarded regional restaurants.

TOP CHOICE Restaurant
Esszimmer
MODERN EUROPEAN €€€

(Map p706; www.esszimmer-stralsund.de; Am Querkanal 5; lunch mains from €12, set dinner menus from €40; ⓒnoon-2.30pm, 5.30-10.30pm Thu-Tue) Alive with happy diners even on a winter Sunday when the rest of town is dead, Esszimmer has a fresh and ever-changing menu that has a creative take on local seasonal foods and dishes. Service is excellent. Tables outside catch the clang of harbour bells in summer.

Brasserie Grand Café
CAFE €€

(Map p706; www.brasseriegrandcafe-hst.de; Neuer Markt 2; mains €8-16) Always crowded with locals, this fine bistro has tables scattered on the square, across several rooms and levels inside and right on back to a beer garden. The food ranges from sandwiches to pasta to German staples. The *Fischpfanne Brasserie* is a delicious meal of three kinds of roasted fish fillets.

Hansekeller
GERMAN €€

(Map p706; www.hansekeller-stralsund.de; Mönchstrasse 48; mains €8-16) Entering an inconspicuous archway and descending a flight of steps brings you to this 16th-century cross-vaulted brick cellar illuminated by lamps and candles. Taking a seat near the open kitchen lets you watch the chefs at work.

Tafelfreuden
MODERN EUROPEAN €€€

(Map p706; ☑299 260; www.tafelfreuden-stralsund. de; Jungfernstieg 5a; mains €18-21; ⓒ5-9pm Tue-Sun) This sunflower-yellow, poppy-red-trimmed wooden villa was built in 1870 as a summer house and is now home to a wonderfully convivial restaurant that utilises fresh produce. There's an inspired wine list, and you can pause with a glass on the terrace. If you can't drag yourself away, it has three charming guest rooms (€45 to €80).

Nur Fisch
SEAFOOD €

(Map p706; ☑306 609; www.nurfisch.de; Heilgeiststrasse 92; mains €6-15; ⓒ10am-6pm Mon-Fri, 11am-2pm Sat) Simple canteen-style bistro dedicated to marine delights – from fish sandwiches to sumptuous platters of seafood. Local briney delights are joined by European dishes such as a fine seafood paella.

Kaffeehaus Strahl
CAFE €

(Map p706; ☑278 566; Mönchstrasse 46; mains €5-10; ⓒ10am-8pm early Jul–mid-Sep, 10am-6pm mid-Sep–early Jul; 🐾) Displays of huge homemade cakes tempt you into this charming, old-fashioned cafe, which has tables out front.

Drinking & Entertainment

T1 COCKTAIL BAR
(Map p706; ☑282 8111; www.t1-stralsund.de; Heilgeist-strasse 64; ⊙from 8pm) This hip yet refined cocktail lounge caters to an upscale crowd inside a central, step-gabled town house.

8cht Vorne CLUB
(Map p706; ☑281 888; Badenstrasse 45; ⊙from 8pm) A stalwart: DJs, dancing and drinks specials, all in an old underground space.

ℹ Information

Main Post Office (Neuer Markt 4)

Tourist Office (☑246 90; www.stralsundtourismus.de; Alter Markt 9; ⊙10am-6pm Mon-Fri, to 4pm Sat & Sun May-Oct, 10am-5pm Mon-Fri, to 2pm Sat Nov-Apr) Tourist information and room bookings.

ℹ Getting There & Away

BOAT Services run to Rügen Island and Hiddensee Island.

TRAIN Regional trains travel to/from Rostock (€15, one hour), Berlin Hauptbahnhof (from €40, 3½ hours) and most major towns in the region at least every two hours.

ℹ Getting Around

Your feet will do just fine in the Altstadt; the Rathaus is about 1km from the train station.

Rügen Island

With its white-sand beaches, canopies of chestnut, oak, elm and poplar trees, charming architecture and even its own national park, Rügen offers myriad ways to enjoy nature.

Frequented in the late 19th and early 20th centuries by luminaries including Bismarck, Thomas Mann and Albert Einstein, its chalk coastline was also immortalised by Romantic artist Caspar David Friedrich in 1818.

Although summer draws thousands to its shores, Rügen's lush 1000-sq-km surface area fringed by 574km of coastline means there are plenty of quiet corners to escape the crowds. You can appreciate Rügen on a day trip from Stralsund.

ℹ Information

Every town has at least one tourist office dispensing local information. **Tourismuszentrale Rügen** (www.ruegen.de) provides island-wide information. Don't expect to find many spontaneous accommodation choices on summer weekends or anytime in August.

ℹ Getting There & Away

BOAT Adler Schiffe (☑01805-123 344; www.adler-schiffe.de) connects Peenemünde on Usedom Island with Göhren, Sellin and Binz (adult/child one-way €13/6.50) once daily from April to October.

International Ferries to Trelleborg, Sweden, and Rønne, Denmark, sail from Sassnitz Mukran, about 7km south of Sassnitz' Bahnhof (linked by buses 18 and 20).

CAR & MOTORCYCLE The Rügenbrücke and neighbouring Rügendamm (1936) bridges cross the Strelasund channel from Stralsund. Both are toll-free.

TRAIN Direct IC trains connect Binz with Hamburg (€58, four hours) and beyond. There is an hourly Stralsund service (€12, 50 minutes). To get to Putbus, change RE trains in Bergen.

On the island, a number of destinations are served by the Rügensche Bäderbahn steam train.

ℹ Getting Around

Rügen is covered with trails that aren't just bucolic but also perfect for bikes and hikers. Tourist offices sell oodles of maps and route guides.

BOAT Reederei Ostsee-Tour (☑038392-3150; www.reederei-ostsee-tour.de) will carry you around the coast from Göhren to Sassnitz, via Sellin and Binz between April and October. Most legs cost €9 each.

BUS RPNV Buses (☑03838-822 90; www.rpnv.de) link practically all communities, though service can be sporadic.

Fares are according to distance: Binz–Göhren, for example, costs €4.85. A day pass for the whole network is often a good deal (adult/child €12.10/8.70).

TRAIN More than just a tourist attraction, the **Rügensche Bäderbahn** (RBB; www.ruegensche-baederbahn.de) steam train serves as a handy mode of transport as it chuffs between Putbus

---

WHAT'S WHERE ON RÜGEN

Key points on Rügen include:

Binz Busy main resort, located at the centre of the island's east coast.

Mönchgut Peninsula Southeast of Binz, has other resort towns such as Sellin and Göhren.

Stubbenkammer North of Binz, an area of white-chalk cliffs and the Jasmund National Park.

Wittow In the west, with Germany's most northeasterly point, Kap Arkona (Cape Arkona).

and Göhren. En route, it stops in Binz, Jagdschloss Granitz, Sellin and Baabe. Much of the narrow track passes through sun-dappled forest. It's nickname is the ironic 'Rasender Roland' (Rushing Roland).

The main interchange with the regular rail network is at Putbus. In Binz, the DB and RBB stations are 2km apart. The route is divided into five zones, each costing €1.80. Bikes cost €3. There are family discounts.

BINZ
☑038393 / POP 5600

Rügen's largest and most celebrated seaside resort, 'Ostseebad' (Baltic Sea spa) Binz is an alluring confection of ornate, white 19th-century villas, white sand and blue water. Its roads are signed in Gothic script and lined with coastal pines and chestnut trees. Even if all the signs of 21st-century capitalism abound, especially along jam-packed Haupt-strasse, you can still feel the pull of history even if you can't escape modern-day crowds.

⊙ Sights & Activities

Strandpromenade   STREET
A highlight of Binz is simply strolling its 4km-long north–south beach promenade lined with elegant villas. At the southern end of the built-up area, you'll find the palatial **Kurhaus**, a lovely-looking 1908 building housing a luxury hotel. In front of it is the

---

DON'T MISS

JAGDSCHLOSS GRANITZ

A grandiose hunting palace built in 1723 on top of the 107m-high Tempel-berg, **Jagdschloss Granitz** (☑2263; www.jagdschloss-granitz.de; adult/child €3.50/2; ☺9am-6pm daily Apr-Oct, 10am-4pm Tue-Sun Nov-Mar) was significantly enlarged and altered by Wilhelm Malte I in 1837. The results will remind of salt and pepper shakers or a phallic fantasy, depending on your outlook. The **RBB steam train** has stops at Jagdschloss and Garftitz which serve the palace. Get off at one, enjoy some lovely hiking and reboard at the other.

Less fun is the **Jagdschlossex-press** (☑338 80; www.jagdschlossexpress.de; adult/child return €8/4; a fake 'train' that trundles from Binz to the palace. Drivers must leave vehicles in the designated parking areas (per hour €2) and walk 2km to the palace.

---

long pier. Strandpromenade continues south from here, but becomes markedly less busy.

Prora   HISTORIC SITE
Prora was going to be the largest holiday camp in the world, according to the Nazis. The beach just north of Binz still bears testament to this: running parallel to the beautiful coast is a wall of six hideous six-storey buildings, each 500m long. Begun in 1936, this was intended as a *Kraft-durch-Freude* (strength through joy) resort for 20,000 people. The outbreak of WWII stopped its completion; no one has known what to do with it since. Much of it is a moody partial-ruin, with the echos of jackboots not far off.

There are a few minor-league museums and one standout: the **Macht Urlaub** (www.proradok.de; adult/child €6/3; ☺10am-6pm Jun-Aug, 10am-4pm Sep-May), a sober and very well-done look at the Nazis and the role Prora played in their 'strength through joy' schemes. You can easily spend an hour or more fully engrossed in the exhibits. Use the Prora Nord stop on local trains or bus lines 20 or 23.

🛏 Sleeping

Binz' abundant accommodation includes private rooms (many in beautiful historic properties) starting from €20 per person. In high season minimum stays of three or more nights are common.

Villa Halali   HOTEL €€€
(☑440; www.villa-halali.de; Strandpromenade 34; per person €70-100; P) The very last place to stay as you follow the promenade southeast along the beach, this refined hotel promises both privacy and proximity to the action. Rooms within the deeply traditional exterior are contemporary and feature nesting goodies like DVD players. Views of the beach curving to the north are intoxicating.

Kurhaus Binz   RESORT €€€
(☑6650; www.travelcharme.de; Strandpromenade 27; s/d from €110/170; P@🕲🌊) This lemon-yellow landmark is the ultimate in traditional style and luxury. Many of its 137 sand-and-sky-toned rooms have balconies or terraces. And with indoor and outdoor pools, a library with an open fireplace, and no fewer than six restaurants, you might find it hard to get further away than the beach out front.

DJH Hostel   HOSTEL €
(☑325 97; www.binz.jugendherberge.de; Strand-promenade 35; dm under/over 26yr €23/29 s €37/43,

d €54/66; P@🖥) As it's bang on the beach, this hostel has the same stunning views as its elegant neighbours but for a fraction of the cost. It has a well-equipped lounge and dining rooms. You can rent your own *Strandkorbverleih* (iconic beach chair) for only €8 per day.

Pension Haus Colmsee   PENSION €€
(📞325 56; www.hauscolmsee.de; Strandpromenade 8; r incl breakfast €65-100; P) This historic 1902 villa, situated at the leafy, quieter and altogether most pleasant eastern edge of town, has relatively modern, uncluttered rooms. Those with a sea view are at the higher end of the price scale, but are well worth it.

✕ Eating

The beachfront Strandpromenade is lined with restaurants serving everything from pizzas and ice cream to creative seasonal cuisine.

TOP CHOICE **Fischräucherei Kuse**   SEAFOOD €
(📞322 49; Strandpromenade 3; dishes from €2; 🕙9am-8pm) For some of the most delicious and certainly the cheapest fish on Rügen, follow your nose – literally – to the far southeast end of the Strandpromenade, where fish has been freshly smoked since 1900. Choose from simple fish sandwiches and meals; dine at its indoor tables, on the terrace, or make a picnic.

Strandhalle   MODERN EUROPEAN €€€
(📞315 64; www.strandhalle-binz.de; Strandpromenade 5; mains €12-20) Toni Münsterteicher's Strandhalle is a local legend that promises – and delivers – fine cooking at everyday prices. At the quiet southern end of Strandpromenade, the atmospheric hall's vaulted-ceiling and wood-lined interior is eclectically decked out with church statues, chandeliers, curtains of fairy lights and shelves of antiquarian books. Don't pass Münsterteicher's signature pear-and-celery soup, although you'll find it hard to go wrong.

Poseidon   SEAFOOD €€€
(📞337 10; Lottumstrasse 1; mains €12-20) One of the best seafood restaurants in Binz, this lovely historic villa one block west of the Strandpromenade serves famously fresh catches of the day and even has a menu section that takes you 'round the herring'. There's a fine outside terrace.

WATERSPORTS

Sail & Surf Rügen (📞038306-232 53; www.segelschule-ruegen.de) rents sea kayaks (per day €30) as well as catamarans and windsurfing gear. It also offers lessons for a variety of watersports and has locations across the island.

ⓘ Information
Tourist Office (www.ostseebad-binz.de; Kurverwaltung, Heinrich-Heine-Strasse 7; 🕙9am-6pm Mon-Fri, 10am-6pm Sat & Sun Feb-Oct, 9am-4pm Mon-Fri, 10am-4pm Sat & Sun Nov-Jan) Lots of maps, island guides and booking services.

ⓘ Getting There & Away
Binz has two train stations, the main one is Ostseebad Binz Bahnhof, serving DB, RE and IC trains. Binz LB, 2km southeast, serves the RBB steam train.

SELLIN
📞038303 / POP 18,600
The symbol of 'Ostseebad' Sellin is its **Seebrücke** (pier), an ornate, turreted pavilion sitting out over the water at the end of a long wooden causeway. The original pier was built in 1906. It's had a checkered history since: the not-terribly attractive modern pier you see now is somewhat modeled on a 1927 version.

The pier lies at the end of gently sloping **Wilhelmstrasse**, Rügen's most attractive main drag. It is lined with elegant villas, hotels and cafes and unlike so many local towns, didn't get a cheesy early 1990s makeover in the heady post-reunification days. The pier is at the northwest end of Sellin's lovely white-sand **beach** and is 1.3km from the RBB train stop, Sellin Ost.

GÖHREN
📞038308 / POP 1300
On the Nordperd spit, Göhren's stunning 7km-long **beach** – divided into the sleepier Südstrand and the more developed Nordstrand – lives up to its hype as Rügen's best resort beach.

As a bonus, Göhren has a collection of six historic sites, which together make up the **Monchgüter Museen** (📞2175; www.moenchguter-museen-ruegen.de; single museum adult/concession €3/2.50, combined ticket €10/8; 🕙10am-5pm Tue-Sun May-Oct, Sat & Sun Nov-Apr): including the Heimatsmuseum and the Museumshof farm, and the unusual chimneyless Rookhus and the museum ship *Luise*.

WORTH A TRIP

HIDDENSEE ISLAND

'Dat söte Länneken' (the sweet little land) is much mythologised in the German national imagination. This tiny patch off Rügen's western coast measures 18km long and just 1.8km at its widest point. What makes Hiddensee (population 1100) so sweet is its breathtaking, remote landscape. The heath and meadows of the **Dornbush** area, with the island's landmark lighthouse and wind-buckled trees, extend north of the village of Kloster, while **dunes** wend their way south from the main village of Vitte to Neuendorf. In the 19th and early 20th centuries, Hiddensee bewitched artists and writers including Thomas Mann and Bertolt Brecht, as well as Gerhart Hauptmann, who is buried here.

Cars are banned on Hiddensee but bike-hire places are everywhere. Alternatively, you can see the island at a gentle pace aboard clip-clopping horse-drawn carriages.

The **tourist office** (038300-642 26; www.seebad-hiddensee.de; Norderende 162; 9am-5pm Mon-Fri, 10am-noon Sat May-Sep, 9am-4pm Mon-Fri Apr & Oct, 9am-3pm Nov-Mar) has a seasonal branch at Kloster harbour. There are no campgrounds on Hiddensee, but inexpensive private rooms are available in the villages. In a timbered building, the **Hotel Hitthim** (038300-6660; www.hitthim.de; Hafenweg; incl half board s €58-78, d €95-155) is one of the best accommodation options, with home-cooked meals in its lamp-lit restaurant.

Ferries run by **Reederei Hiddensee** (0180-321 2150; www.reederei-hiddensee.de; return day tickets from Schaprode adult/child from €15/9, from Stralsund €19/10) leave Schaprode, on Rügen's western shore, up to 12 times daily year-round and run to Neuendorf, Kloster and Vitte. Services from Stralsund run up to three times daily between April and October.

The **Kurverwaltung** (667 90; www.ostsee bad-goehren.de; Poststrasse 9; 9am-6pm Mon-Fri, 9am-noon Sat May-Sep, much shorter hours other times), can help sort through the thicket of hotels and private rooms.

The **Regenbogen Resort** (901 20; www. regenbogen-camps.de; Nordstrand; adult €6-10, tent €3-15, car €3-6) is the island's largest campground, idyllically situated in the woods behind the dunes.

Göhren is the eastern terminus of the RBB steam train; the stop is a mere 200m from the sand. Parking is awful everywhere; take the train.

PUTBUS
038301 / POP 2700

Putbus appears like a mirage from the middle of modest farming villages. At its heart lies a gigantic circular 19th-century plaza, known as the **Circus**, which has a 21m **obelisk** at the centre. Sixteen large white neoclassical buildings – some in better shape than others – surround it. Nearby, the 75-hectare **English park** is filled with exotic botanical species. After you've soaked up the atmosphere (15 minutes should do it), head for a beach.

This is the hub for the RBB steam train; interchange with Germany's main rail network here.

JASMUND NATIONAL PARK

The rugged beauty of **Jasmund National Park** (Nationalparks Jasmund; www.nationalpark -jasmund.de) first came to national attention thanks to the romanticised paintings of Caspar David Friedrich in the early 19th century. His favourite spot was the **Stubbenkammer**, an area at the northern edge of the park, where jagged white-chalk cliffs plunge into the jade-coloured sea.

By far the most famous of the Stubbenkammer cliffs is the **Königsstuhl** – at 117m, it's Rügen's highest point, although the scenery is often marred by everyone else trying to see it too. Fewer people make the trek a few hundred metres east to the **Victoria-Sicht** (Victoria View), which provides the best view of the Königsstuhl itself.

Admission to the area is through the **Nationalpark-Zentrum Königsstuhl** (38392-661 766; www.koenigsstuhl.com; adult/child €7.50/3.50; 9am-7pm Easter-Oct, 10am-5pm Nov-Easter), which has multimedia displays on environmental themes, a 'climbing forest' and a cafe.

Buses 20 (from Göhren, Sellin, Binz, Prora and Sassnitz) and 23 (from Bergen, Binz, Prora and Sassnitz) go right to the Nationalpark-Zentrum Königsstuhl, and offer a Königsstuhl Ticket (adult/family €15/30) that includes bus travel and entry. Drivers must leave vehicles in the (paid) parking lot in Hagen, then either catch the shuttle bus or walk 2.5km past the Herthasee lake.

Reederei Ostsee-Tour (p709) operates several daily trips from Sellin (€20), Binz (€19) and Sassnitz (€13) around the chalk cliffs April to October. If you're feeling energetic, a spectacular way to approach the area is by making the 10km trek from Sassnitz along the coast through the ancient forest of Stubnitz. The trail also takes you past the gorgeous Wissower Klinken chalk cliffs, another vista famously painted by Friedrich.

SASSNITZ
POP 10,400

While most people only pass through Sassnitz, at the southern end of the national park, the town has been redeveloping its Altstadt and harbour. The latter is reached from the town bluff by a dramatic new pedestrian bridge and is home to new cafes and maritime museums.

KAP ARKONA

Rügen ends at the rugged cliffs of Kap Arkona, with its famous pair of lighthouses: the square, squat Schinkel-Leuchtturm, completed in 1827, and the cylindrical Neuer Leuchtturm, in business since 1902.

A few metres east of the lighthouses is the Burgwall, a complex that harbours the remains of the Tempelburg, a Slavic temple and fortress. The castle was taken over by the Danes in 1168, paving the way for the Christianisation of Rügen.

Most people sail around the cape (without landing) on four-hour boat tours run by Reederei Ostsee-Tour (☑038392-3150; www.reederei-ostsee-tour.de; adult/child €25/12.50; ☺Tue-Thu Jul-Sep).

Cars must be parked in the gateway village of Putgarten. You can take the Arkona Bahn (☑038391-132 13; www.arkonabahn.de; adult/child €2/0.50) fake train or make the 1.5km journey by foot.

Greifswald

☑03834 / POP 54,200

The lovely old university town of Greifswald, south of Stralsund, was largely unscathed by WWII thanks to a courageous German colonel who surrendered to Soviet troops (a move usually punishable by execution).

The skyline of this former Hanseatic city – as once perfectly captured by native son Caspar David Friedrich – is defined by three churches: the 'Langer Nikolas' ('Long Nicholas'), 'Dicke Marie' ('Fat Mary') and the 'Kleine Jakob' ('Small Jacob').

Greifswald has a pretty harbour in the charming district of Wieck and the entire area is worth a stop.

◉ Sights

Dom St Nikolai
CHURCH

(☑2627; Domstrasse; tower adult/concession €3/1.50; ☺10am-6pm Mon-Sat, 11.30am-3pm Sun) The 100m onion-domed tower of the Dom St Nikolai rises above a row of historic facades, giving the cathedral the nickname 'Long Nicholas'. The austere, whitewashed 19th-century interior is a dud but some Gothic carvings remain. Climb the tower for great views.

Markt
SQUARE

The richly ornamented buildings ringing the Markt hint at Greifswald's stature in the Middle Ages. The Rathaus, at the western end, started life as a 14th-century department store with characteristic arcaded walkways. Among the redbrick gabled houses on the eastern side, the Coffee House (No 11) is gorgeous and a good example of a combined living and storage house owned by Hanseatic merchants.

Pommersches Landesmuseum
MUSEUM

(www.pommersches-landesmuseum.de; Rakower Street 9; adult/child €5/3; ☺10am-6pm Tue-Sun May-Oct, to 5pm Nov-Apr) This outstanding museum links three Franciscan monastery buildings via a 73m-long, glassed-in hall. There's a major gallery of paintings, including half a dozen by Caspar David Friedrich, as well as history and natural history.

Marienkirche
CHURCH

(☑2263; www.marien-greifswald.de; Brüggstrasse; ☺10am-4pm Mon-Sat, 10.15am-1pm Sun) The 12th-century redbrick Marienkirche is a square three-nave tower trimmed with turrets. It's easy to see why it's teasingly called 'Fat Mary'. Look for the 16th-century elaborately carved pulpit and frescoes.

Wieck
VILLAGE

The photogenic centre of this fishing village is a Dutch-style wooden drawbridge. The small harbour is often alive with fishing boats landing – and selling – their catch. There's a good hike through a large park to the ruins of the 12th-century Eldena Abbey and the beach is a good one. It's an easy 5km bike ride east of Greifswald's Markt.

Sleeping & Eating

Greifswald has some fine hotels (many in beautiful historic buildings). Wieck has some excellent stands for fresh and smoked fish.

Hotel Galerie HOTEL €€
(☏773 7830; www.hotelgalerie.de; Mühlenstrasse 10; s/d from €80/100; P🅿🛜) The 13 rooms in this sparkling modern property across from the state museum are filled with a changing collection of works by contemporary artists. Room design is a cut above the usual.

TOP CHOICE Fischer-Hütte SEAFOOD €€
(☏839 654; An der Mühle 8; mains €10-15; ⊗from 11.30am) An exquisitely presented meal at the 'fisherman's house' in Wieck might start with potato soup with a fried scallop and black caviar and move onto the house speciality – smoked herring. You know everything is fresh as you can see the boats pulling up to the dock right outside.

Fritz Braugasthaus BREWERY €€
(☏578 30; www.fritz-hgw.de; Am Markt 13; mains €8-16) Greifswald's local brewery occupies one of the most striking step-gabled red-brick buildings on the Markt. Besides German classics like schnitzels there are very good burgers and more on the menu. Ingredients are sourced locally and many are organic.

ⓘ Information

Tourist Office (Greifswald Information; ☏521 380; www.greifswald.de; Rathaus; ⊗9am-6pm Mon-Fri Mar-Oct, 10am-2pm Sat May-Oct, plus 10am-2pm Sun Jul & Aug, 9am-5pm Mon-Fri Oct-Mar)

ⓘ Getting There & Away

There are regular train services to Stralsund (€19, 20 minutes) and Berlin Hauptbahnhof (from €36, 2¼ to three hours).

ⓘ Getting Around

It's easy to get around Greifswald's centre on foot; the Altstadt is 500m northeast of the train station.

You can reach Wieck via a 5km foot/bike path, or by bus 6 or 7 (€1.80).

Usedom Island

Nicknamed Badewanne Berlins (Berlin's Bathtub) in the prewar period, Usedom Island is a sought-after holiday spot for its 42km stretch of beautiful beach and average 1906 annual hours of sunshine that make it the sunniest place in Germany.

Usedom (Uznam in Polish) lies in the delta of the Oder River about 30km east of Greifswald. The island's eastern tip lies across the border in Poland. Although the German side accounts for 373 sq km of the island's total 445 sq km, the population of the Polish side is larger (45,000 compared with 31,500 on the German side).

Woodsy bike and hiking trails abound. Elegant 1920s villas with wrought-iron balconies grace many traditional resorts along its northern spine, including Zinnowitz, Ückeritz, Bansin, Heringsdorf and Ahlbeck. All have tourist offices. Usedom Tourismus (☏038378-477 116; www.usedom.de) can book accommodation island-wide.

It was at Peenemünde, on the island's western tip, that Wernher von Braun developed the V2 rocket, first launched in October 1942. It flew 90km high and a distance of 200km before plunging into the Baltic – the first time in history a flying object exited the earth's atmosphere. The complex was destroyed by the Allies in July 1944, but the Nazis continued research and production using slaves in the caves at Nordhausen in the southern Harz.

At the Historisch-Technisches Informationszentrum (Historical & Technological Museum; ☏038371-5050; www.peenemuende.de; adult/concession €8/5; ⊗10am-6pm Apr-Sep, 10am-4pm Oct-Mar, closed Mon Nov-Mar), Peenemünde is immodestly billed as 'the birthplace of space travel'. Displays – some in surviving buildings – do a good job of showing how the rockets were developed and the destruction they caused.

ⓘ Getting There & Away

Direct UBB (Usedomer Bäderbahn; www.ubb-online.com) trains from Stralsund (and Greifswald) stop at coastal resorts before terminating in Świnoujście (Swinemünde in German) just over the Polish border. Peenemünde is on a branch line; change in Züssow (total time from Stralsund, two hours). A UBB day card costs €14.

Ferries run between Peenemünde and Rügen Island.

Understand Germany

population per sq km

Germany   UK   USA

≈ 7 people

Germany Today

Europe's Economic Engine

Germany seems to have weathered the recent financial crisis better than most industrial nations, in large part because it now bears the fruits of decade-old key reforms, especially the liberalisation of its labour laws. The German government launched a slew of proactive measures, such as allowing companies to put workers on shorter shifts without loss of pay and stimulating the economy by providing incentives for Germans to scrap older cars and buy new ones.

The importance of Germany's stable economy has grown in the past few years, as the debt-driven crisis in the Eurozone has spread from Greece to threaten all of southern Europe. Germany is seen to have a key position in propping up the euro, the collapse of which could plunge economies across the globe back into recession. So far, so good.

The European Commission reported 0.5% growth in the German economy for the first quarter of 2012, while the Eurozone as a whole stagnated. Manufacturing orders and exports, especially to hungry markets in South American, Asia and Eastern Europe, were up, helped along by a weak euro. At the same time, the unemployment rate dropped to 6%, the property market was on the upswing and consumer confidence was high.

» Area: 357,672 sq km
» Population: 81.3 million
» GDP: €3.14 trillion
» Inflation: 2%
» Unemployment: 6%
» Life expectancy: women 82.5 years, men 77.33 years

Environmental Leadership

With a Green Party active in politics since the 1980s, Germany has long played a leading role in environmental and climate protection and is considered a pioneer in the development of renewable energies. In 2000, the *Bundestag* (parliament) passed the *Erneuerbare-Energien-Gesetz* (Renewable Energies Act), which provides subsidies and incentives to companies engaged in producing renewable energy. In 2011, about 20% of total energy production came from alternative sources. One solar cell in five

Dos & Don'ts

» Do say *'Guten Tag'* (hello) when entering a business
» Do state your last name at the start of a phone call
» Don't be late for meetings and dinners
» Don't assume you can pay by credit card
» Do bag your own groceries in supermarkets
» Do bring a small gift when invited for dinner

Top Reads

Grimms' Fairy Tales (Jacob & Wilhelm Grimm; 1812) The classic!
The Rise & Fall of the Third Reich (William Shirer; 1960) Seminal account
Berlin Alexanderplatz (Alfred Döblin; 1929) Berlin in the 1920s

belief systems
(% of population)

68
Christian

4
Muslim

28
Other

if Germany were
100 people

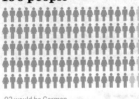

92 would be German
2 would be Turkish
6 would be other

and every seventh wind turbine hail from Germany, where some 400,000 people are employed in the renewables industry. The country has also reduced its greenhouse gas emissions by 24% since 1990, thus exceeding the requirements of the 2005 Kyoto Protocol (21% reduction called for).

In 2011, following the nuclear disaster in Fukushima, Japan, Germany became the first industrial nation to completely opt out of nuclear power, immediately shutting down the eight oldest of its 17 reactors. The same year, the *Bundestag* passed legislation that will see the remaining nine plants go off the grid by 2022. The government expects wind farms, solar arrays and other nonpolluting power producers will pick up the slack.

Most popular
children's names:
Mia and Ben

Land of Immigration

Some 15 million people living in Germany have an immigrant background (foreign born or have at least one immigrant parent), accounting for about 18% of the total population. According to the United Nations, only the USA and Russia absorb a greater number of international migrants. The largest group are people of Turkish descent, a legacy of the post-WWII economic boom when 'guest workers' were recruited to shore up the war-depleted workforce. Many stayed. After reunification, the foreign population soared again as repatriates from the former USSR and refugees from war-ravaged Yugoslavia arrived by the millions.

Whether immigration enriches or endangers German culture has been the subject of much debate in recent years, but the fact is that the country needs newcomers to keep the economy running. An ageing population and low birth rate account for the fastest population decline among developed nations. Like many other industrialised nations, Germany may have to adapt its outdated laws and policies on controlled immigration on a much larger scale than ever before.

Top Sounds

Brandenburg Concertos (Johann Sebastian Bach)
Autobahn (Kraftwerk) Electropop pioneers
Made in Germany 1995–2011 (Rammstein) Industrial metal
Soundso (Wir sind Helden) Alternative rock

Top Films

The Lives of Others (2006) Stasi unmasked
The Downfall (2004) Hitler's demise
Metropolis (1927) Seminal silent flick
Run Lola Run (1998) Energetic drama set in Berlin

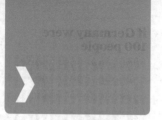

History

Germany's long and event-rich history begins in a land of forests, wind-swept coasts and mountains inhabited by Celts and Germanic tribes, who battled against Roman legions on the periphery of the Classical World. By the 9th century, regions east of the Rhine developed their own identity and, for the first time, it became possible to talk about 'German' rulers, the most illustrious of which was, without doubt, Charlemagne. But the fortunes of Germany long remained in the hands of feudal rulers, who pursued their own petty interests at the expense of a unified state. The Middle Ages were a bleak, barbaric time characterised by squabbling princes, plague and cultural darkness, and led to deep-running religious divisions and strife between Catholics and Protestants that culminated in the devastating Thirty Years' War. The mighty Bismarck united the Germans into a federal state in the 19th century, but from then on Germany trod a fractious path from unification to the Great War. The Treaty of Versailles created fertile ground for the rise of Hitler and the Nazis, which took the country into WWII and ultimately to disaster and humiliation. The Cold War once again split Germany, this time into austere communist East and affluent West that underwent the economic miracle of the 1950s and '60s. This wealth and industrial might, plus peaceful reunification following the fall of the Berlin Wall, have fashioned the powerful country we know today.

Tribes & the Romans

The early inhabitants of Germany were Celts and, later, the Germanic tribes. In the Iron Age (from around 800 BC), Germanic clans on the North German Plain and in the Central Uplands lived on the fringes of Celtic regions and were influenced by the culture without ever melting into it. Evidence of this is still apparent today in Thale, in the Harz Mountains.

The Romans fought pitched battles with the Germanic tribes from about 100 BC. The Germanic tribes east of the Rhine and the Romans

> **Best Roman Sites**
>
> » Trier
> » Xanten
> » Cologne
> » Aachen
> » Regensburg
> » Bingen
> » Mainz

> For more on Germany's Roman ruins, log on to www.historvius.com

TIMELINE

800–300 BC	100 BC–AD 9	4th Century
Germanic tribes and Celts inhabit large parts of northern and central Germany, but by around 300 BC the Celts have been driven back to regions south of the Main River.	The Romans clash with Germanic tribes until defeat at the Battle of the Teutoburg Forest halts Rome's expansion eastwards. The Romans consolidate territory south of the Limes.	The arrival of Hun horsemen triggers the Great Migration. Germanic tribes are displaced and flee to various parts of the Western Roman Empire. The Lombards settle in northern Italy.

struggled for control of territory across the river until AD 9, when the Roman general Varus lost three legions – about 20,000 men – in the bloody Battle of the Teutoburg Forest and the Romans abandoned their plans to extend eastwards. By AD 300, four main groups of tribes had formed: Alemanni, Franks, Saxons and Goths.

The Frankish Reich

Based on the Rhine's western bank, the Frankish Reich became Europe's most important political power in medieval times. This was due, in part, to the Merovingian king Clovis (r 482–511), who united diverse populations. In its heyday the Reich included present-day France, Germany, the Low Countries and half the Italian peninsula. Missionaries such as St Boniface (675–754) – considered the father of German Christianity – crossed the Rhine to convert the local pagans.

When fighting broke out among aristocratic clans in the 7th century, the Merovingians were replaced by the Carolingians, who introduced hierarchical Church structures. Kloster Lorsch (Lorsch Abbey) in present-day Hesse is a fine relic of this era. From his grandiose residence in Aachen, Charlemagne (r 768–814), the Reich's most important king, conquered Lombardy, won territory in Bavaria, waged a 30-year war against the Saxons in the north and was crowned Kaiser by the pope in 800. The cards were reshuffled in the 9th century, when attacks by Danes, Saracens and nomad tribes from the east threw the eastern portion of Charlemagne's empire into turmoil and four dominant duchies emerged – Bavaria, Franconia, Swabia and Saxony.

Two Lives of Charlemagne (2008; Penguin Classics) is a striking biography of Charlemagne, beautifully composed by a monk and a courtier who spent 23 years in Charlemagne's court.

HISTORY THE FRANKISH REICH

ROMAN LEGIONS

For many years, Mount Grotenburg near Detmold in North Rhine–Westphalia was thought to be the scene of the Battle of the Teutoburg Forest, but no one can really say for sure where it happened. The most likely candidate is Kalkriese, north of Osnabrück, where in the 1990s archaeologists found face helmets, breast shields, bone deposits and other grisly battle remains. Today the site is a museum and park (p518).

In AD 1 the Romans started building what is today central Europe's largest archaeological site – a wall running 568km from Koblenz on the Rhine to Regensburg on the Danube. Some 900 watchtowers and 60 forts studded this frontier line, dubbed Der Limes (The Limes). The 800km-long Deutsche Limes-Strasse (German Limes Road) cycling route runs between Regensburg in the south and Bad Hönningen in the north (near Koblenz), largely tracing the tower- and fortress-studded fortification. See www .limesstrasse.de for more about the Limes and routes along the wall. Another 280km-long cycling route links Detmold with Xanten (where there's an archaeological park), taking cyclists past various Roman remains and monuments.

482–486	732	773–800	919–1125
Clovis becomes king of the Franks and lays the foundations for a Frankish Reich. In AD 486 he defeats the Romans in the Battle of Soissons in France and the last vestiges of the Western Roman Empire collapse.	Charles Martel, king of the Franks, wins the decisive Battle of Tours and stops the progress of Muslims into Western Europe from the Iberian Peninsula, preserving Christianity in the Frankish Reich.	The Carolingian Charlemagne, grandson of Charles Martel, answers a call for help from the pope. In return he is crowned Kaiser by the pope.	Saxon and Salian emperors rule Germany, creating the Holy Roman Empire in 962 when Otto I is crowned Holy Roman Emperor by the pope, reaffirming the precedent established by Charlemagne.

Charlemagne's burial in Aachen Dom (Aachen Cathedral) turned a court chapel into a major pilgrimage site (and it remains so today). The Treaty of Verdun (843) saw a gradual carve-up of the Reich and, when Louis the Child (r 900–11) – a grandson of Charlemagne's brother – died heirless, the East Frankish (ie German) dukes elected a king from their own ranks. Thus, the first German monarch was created.

Early Middle Ages

Strong regionalism in Germany today has its roots in the early Middle Ages, when dynasties squabbled and intrigued over territorial spoils, as a toothless, Roman-inspired central state watched on helplessly.

The symbolic heart of power was Aachen Dom, which hosted the coronation and burial of dozens of German kings from 936. Otto I was first up in the cathedral. In 962 he renewed Charlemagne's pledge to protect the papacy, and the pope reciprocated with a pledge of loyalty to the Kaiser. This made the Kaiser and pope strange and often acrimonious bedfellows for the next 800 years and created the Holy Roman Empire, a nebulous state that survived until 1806.

A power struggle between pope and Kaiser, who also had to contend with the local princes or clergy-cum-princes, was behind many of the upheavals in the early Middle Ages. In the Investiture Conflict under the reign of the Salian Heinrich IV (r 1056–1106), the pope cracked down on the practice of simony (selling religious pardons and relics). Heinrich, excommunicated and contrite, stood barefoot in the snow for three days in Canossa in Italy, begging forgiveness. He was absolved, but the Reich was convulsed by a 20-year civil war on the issue, which was finally resolved in a treaty signed in the Rhineland-Palatinate town of Worms in 1122.

Under Friedrich I Barbarossa (r 1152–90), Aachen assumed the role of Reich capital and was granted its rights of liberty in 1165, the year Charlemagne was canonised. Meanwhile, Heinrich der Löwe (Henry the Lion), a member of the House of Welf with an eye for Saxony and Bavaria, extended influence eastwards in campaigns to Germanise and convert the Slavs who populated much of today's eastern Germany. A Slavic minority, the Sorbs, can still be found in some areas of eastern Germany. Heinrich, who was very well connected – his second, English wife Mathilde was Richard the Lionheart's sister – founded not only Braunschweig (where his grave is today), but Munich, Lübeck and Lüneburg, too. At the height of his reign, his domain stretched from the north and Baltic coasts to the Alps, and from Westphalia to Pomerania (in Poland).

The Reich gained territory to the east and in Italy, but soon fell apart because of early deaths, squabbling between Welf and Hohenstaufen pretenders to the throne and the election of a king and pope-backed antiking. At this time kings were being elected by Kurfürsten (prince-electors)

The graves of Heinrich and other Salian monarchs can today be found in the spectacular cathedral in Speyer.

Hildesheim was a centre of power in the Ottonian period (900–1050). Bishop Bernward raised young Otto III (r 983–1002) and graced the town with treasures to befit a new Rome, such as his famous Bernwardstüren (bronze doors) in the Hildesheimer Dom.

1165	**1241**	**1245**	**1348–50**
Friedrich I Barbarossa is crowned in Aachen. He canonises Charlemagne and later drowns while bathing in a river in present-day Turkey while co-leading the Third Crusade.	Hamburg and Lübeck sign an agreement to protect one another's ships and trading routes, creating the basis for the powerful Hanseatic League, which dominates politics and trade across much of Europe.	The Great Interregnum begins when Pope Innocent IV deposes Friedrich II and a string of anti-kings are elected; it ends in 1273 when the House of Habsburg takes the reins, rising to become Europe's most powerful dynasty.	The plague wipes out 25% of Europe's population and pogroms are launched against Jews. The loss of workers leads to improved circumstances for those able-bodied who survive.

WHAT WAS THE HOLY ROMAN EMPIRE?

It was an idea, mostly, and not a very good one. It grew out of the Frankish Reich, which was seen as the successor to the defunct Roman Empire. When Charlemagne's father, Pippin, helped a beleaguered pope (Charlemagne would later do the same), he received the title *Patricius Romanorum* (Protector of Rome), virtually making him Caesar's successor. Having retaken the papal territories from the Lombards, he presented them to the Church (the last of these territories is the modern Vatican state). Charlemagne's reconstituted 'Roman Empire' then passed into German hands.

The empire was known by various names throughout its lifetime. It formally began (for historians, at least) in 962 with the crowning of Otto I as Holy Roman Emperor and collapsed in 1806, when Kaiser Franz II abdicated the throne. The empire sometimes included Italy, as far south as Rome. Sometimes it didn't – the pope usually had a say in that. It variously encompassed present-day Netherlands, Belgium, Switzerland, Lorraine and Burgundy (in France), Sicily, Austria and an eastern swath of land that lies in the Czech Republic, Poland and Hungary. It was also known as the 'First Reich' (not to be confused with Otto von Bismarck's Second Reich or Adolf Hitler's Third Reich).

but crowned Kaiser by the pope – a system that made an unwilling lackey out of a Kaiser. In 1245 the Reich plunged into an era called the Great Interregnum, or the Terrible Time, when Pope Innocent IV annulled his own Kaiser, the Reich was flush with kings, and central authority collapsed into a political heap.

Although the central Reich was only a shadow of its former self, expansion eastwards continued unabated. Land east of the Oder River (now Germany's eastern border) had been settled by German peasants and city dwellers in the mid-12th century. In the 13th century Teutonic knights pushed eastwards, establishing fortress towns, such as Königsberg (present-day Kaliningrad). At its peak, the unified state of the knights stretched from the Oder to Estonia. Later, in the 17th century, a large swath of this land would become part of Brandenburg-Prussia.

> The use of the title Kaiser was a direct legacy of Roman times (the German word *Kaiser* meaning 'emperor' is derived from 'Caesar').

The House of Habsburg

In 1273 a Habsburg dynasty emerged from the medieval aristocratic soup, mastered the knack of a politically expedient arranged marriage and dominated Continental affairs until the early 20th century. The arrival of Rudolf (r 1273–91) ended the Terrible Time but, more importantly, the Declaration of Rhense (1338) dispensed with the pope's role in crowning a Kaiser. Now the king, elected by the *Kurfürsten,* was automatically Kaiser. In 1356 the Golden Bull, a decree issued by Holy Roman Emperor Charles IV, set out precise rules for elections and defined the

1356
The Golden Bull formalises the election of the Kaiser. The archbishops of Cologne, Trier and Mainz, the rulers of Bohemia, Saxony and Brandenburg, and the count of Palatinate become prince-electors.

1455
Johannes Gutenberg of Mainz prints 180 copies of the Gutenberg Bible in Latin using a type system that revolutionises book printing and allows books to be published in large quantities.

1517
Martin Luther makes public his *Ninety-Five Theses* in Wittenburg. His ideas challenge the selling of indulgences, capturing a mood of disillusionment with the Church and among the clergy.

DEA PICTURE LIBRARY / GETTY IMAGES ©

relationship between the Kaiser and the princes. It was an improvement but the Kaiser was still dancing to the tune of the princes.

Dancing, however, was the last thing on the minds of ordinary Germans. They battled with panic lynching, pogroms against Jews and labour shortages – all sparked by the plague (1348–50) that wiped out 25% of Europe's population. While death gripped the (Ger)man on the street, universities were being established all over the country around this time. The first was in Heidelberg, making it Germany's oldest – and arguably its most spectacular – university city.

For a comprehensive overview of German history, see the German Culture website www.german culture.com.ua.

A Question of Faith

The religious fabric of Germany was cut from a pattern created in the 16th-century Reformation. In the university town of Wittenberg in 1517, German theology professor Martin Luther (1483–1546) made public his *Ninety-Five Theses,* which questioned the papal practice of selling indulgences to exonerate sins. Threatened with excommunication, Luther refused to recant, broke from the Catholic Church and was banned by the Reich, only to be hidden in Wartburg (a castle outside Eisenach, in Thuringia), where he translated the New Testament into German.

THE HANSEATIC LEAGUE

The origins of the Hanseatic League go back to various guilds and associations established from about the mid-12th century by out-of-town merchants to protect their interests. After Hamburg and Lübeck signed an agreement in 1241 to protect their ships and trading routes, they were joined in their league by Lüneburg, Kiel and a string of Baltic Sea cities east to Greifswald. By 1356 this had grown into the Hanseatic League, encompassing half a dozen other large alliances of cities, with Lübeck playing the lead role.

At its zenith, the league had about 200 member cities. It earned a say in the choice of Danish kings after fighting two wars against the Danes between 1361 and 1369. The resulting Treaty of Stralsund in 1370 turned it into northern Europe's most powerful economic and political entity. Some 70 inland and coastal cities – mostly German – formed the core of the Hanseatic League, but another 130 beyond the Reich maintained a loose association, making it truly international. During a period of endless feudal squabbles in Germany, it was a bastion of political and social stability.

By the 15th century, however, competition from Dutch and English shipping companies, internal disputes and a shift in the centre of world trade from the North and Baltic Seas to the Atlantic had caused decline. The ruin and chaos of the Thirty Years' War in the 17th century delivered the final blow, although Hamburg, Bremen and Lübeck retained the 'Hanse City' title. The memory of the League lives on, however, in the New Hanse (www.hanse.org) that brings together former Hansa cities in a body promoting cultural cooperation and tourism.

1555	1618–48	1648	1740–86
The Peace of Augsburg allows princes to decide their principality's religion, putting Catholicism and Protestantism on an equal footing. Around 80% of Germany's population at this time is Protestant.	The Thirty Years' War sweeps through Germany, leaving its population depleted and vast regions reduced to wasteland. The Reich disintegrates into 300-plus states.	The Treaty of Westphalia formalises the independence of Switzerland, and of the Netherlands, ruled by Spain from the early 16th century when Karl V was also king of Spain and its colonies.	Brandenburg-Prussia becomes a mighty power under Friedrich the Great. Berlin becomes 'Athens on the Spree' as Absolutism in Europe gives way to the Enlightenment, heralding a cultural explosion.

It was not until 1555 that the Catholic and Lutheran churches were ranked as equals, thanks to Karl V (r 1520–58), who signed the Peace of Augsburg (1555), allowing princes to decide the religion of their principality. The more secular northern principalities adopted Lutheran teachings, while the clerical lords in the south, southwest and Austria stuck with Catholicism.

But the religious issue refused to die. It degenerated into the bloody Thirty Years' War, which Sweden and France had joined by 1635. Calm was restored with the Peace of Westphalia (1648), signed in Münster and Osnabrück, but it left the Reich – embracing more than 300 states and about 1000 smaller territories – a nominal, impotent state. Switzerland and the Netherlands gained formal independence, France won chunks of Alsace and Lorraine, and Sweden helped itself to the mouths of the Elbe, Oder and Weser Rivers.

The Enlightenment to the Industrial Age

The Enlightenment breathed new life into Germany in the 18th century, inspiring a rabble of autocratic princes to build stunning grand palaces and gardens across the German lands. Berlin's Schloss Charlottenburg, Potsdam's Sanssouci Park and Dresden's Zwinger are fine examples of the spirit of this new age. Meanwhile, Johann Sebastian Bach and Georg Friedrich Händel were ushered on stage and a wave of *Hochkultur* (high culture) swept through society's top sliver. For the time being, however, the masses remained illiterate.

Brandenburg-Prussia became an entity to be reckoned with, kick-started by the acquisition of former Teutonic Knights' territories and assisted by Hohenzollern king Friedrich Wilhelm I (the Soldier King) and his son, Friedrich II (r 1740–86). After the Seven Years' War (1756–63) with Austria, Brandenburg-Prussia annexed Silesia and sliced up Poland.

At the behest of French emperor Napoleon Bonaparte during the Napoleonic Wars, an imperial deputation secularised and reconstituted German territory between 1801 and 1803. In 1806 the Confederation of the Rhine eradicated about 100 principalities. Sniffing the end of the Holy Roman Empire, Kaiser Franz II (r 1792–1806) packed his bags for Austria, renamed himself Franz I of Austria and abdicated the throne. That same year Brandenburg-Prussia fell to the French, but humiliating defeat prompted reforms that brought it closer to civil statehood: Jews were granted equality and bonded labour was abolished.

In 1813, with French troops driven back by the Russians, Leipzig witnessed one of Napoleon's most significant defeats. At the Congress of Vienna (1815), Germany was reorganised into a confederation of 35 states and an ineffective Reichstag (legislative assembly) was established in Frankfurt, an unsatisfactory solution that only minimally improved

What's in a name? Past German monarchs include Karl the Fat (r 881–87), Arnulf the Evil and Friedrich the Handsome (both medieval anti-kings), and the righteous Heinrich the Holy (r 1014–24).

Heinrich the Fowler: Father of the Ottonian Empire (2005) by Mirella Patzer brings 10th-century Germany to life in a heady blend of history and fiction.

1789–1815	1806–13	1813 & 1815	1814–15
The French Revolution and, from 1803, the Napoleonic Wars, sweep away the last remnants of the Middle Ages in Europe. Napoleon Bonaparte takes Berlin in 1806.	The Holy Roman Empire collapses and Napoleon creates the 16-member Confederation of the Rhine after defeating Austrian and Russian troops in the Battle of Austerlitz.	Napoleon suffers defeat near Leipzig in 1813. He subsequently abdicates and is exiled to Elba. He returns to power in 1815 but is defeated at Waterloo that same year.	The post-Napoleon Congress of Vienna redraws the map of Europe, creating in the former Reich the German Alliance with 35 states.

on the Holy Roman Empire. The Reichstag poorly represented the most populous states and failed to rein in Austro-Prussian rivalry.

By the mid-19th century, the engines of the modern, industrial age were purring across the country. A newly created urban proletarian movement fuelled calls for central government, while the Young Germany movement of satirists lampooned the powerful of the day and called for a central state.

Berlin, along with much of the southwest, erupted in riots in 1848, prompting German leaders to bring together Germany's first ever freely elected parliamentary delegation in Frankfurt's Paulskirche. Austria, meanwhile, broke away from Germany, came up with its own constitution and promptly relapsed into monarchism. As revolution fizzled in 1850, Prussian king Friedrich Wilhelm IV drafted his own constitution, which would remain in force until 1918.

'Honest Otto' von Bismarck

The creation of a unified Germany with Prussia at the helm was the glorious ambition of Otto von Bismarck (1815–98), a former member of the Reichstag and Prussian prime minister. An old-guard militarist, he used intricate diplomacy and a series of wars with neighbours Denmark and France to achieve his aims. In 1871 – later than most other European countries – Germany was unified, with Berlin the proud capital of Western Europe's largest state. At that time, Germany extended from Memel (Klaipėda in present-day Lithuania) to the Dutch border, including Alsace-Lorraine (southwest) in present-day France and Silesia (southeast) in present-day Poland. The Prussian king was crowned Kaiser of the Reich, a bicameral, constitutional monarchy, at Versailles on 18 January 1871 and Bismarck became its 'Iron Chancellor'.

Bismarck's power was based on the support of merchants and *Junker*, a noble class of nonknighted landowners. An ever-skilful diplomat and power broker, Bismarck achieved much through a dubious 'honest otto' policy, whereby he brokered deals between European powers and encouraged colonial vanities to distract others from his own deeds. He belatedly graced the Reich of Kaiser Wilhelm I with a few African jewels after 1880, acquiring colonies in central, southwest and east Africa as well as numerous Pacific paradises, such as Tonga.

When pressed, Bismarck made concessions to the growing and increasingly antagonistic socialist movement, enacting Germany's first modern social reforms, but this was not his true nature. By 1888 Germany found itself burdened with a new Kaiser, Wilhelm II, who wanted to extend social reform, and an Iron Chancellor who wanted stricter antisocialist laws. Finally, in 1890, the Kaiser's scalpel excised Bismarck from the political scene. After that, the legacy of Bismarck's brilliant diplomacy unravelled and a wealthy, unified and industrially

The name Habsburg (Hapsburg) originates from *Habichts Burg* (literally 'Hawk Castle'), the spot on the Rhine (in present-day Switzerland, immediately across the border from Germany) from which the great Swabian family first hailed.

The first potato was planted in Germany in 1621, the Gregorian calendar was adopted in 1700 and Germany's first cuckoo clock started ticking in 1730.

1834	1835	1848	1848
The German Customs Union is formed under the leadership of Prussia, making much of Germany a free-trade area and edging it closer to unification; the Union reinforces the idea of a Germany without Austria.	Germany's first railway line opens between the Bavarian towns of Nuremberg and Fürth. Thanks to the Customs Union, the network quickly expands.	*The Communist Manifesto* on class struggle and capitalism, by Trier-born Karl Marx and fellow countryman Friedrich Engels, is published in London by a group of Germans living in exile in Britain.	The March Revolution hits mainly in the Rhineland and southwest German provinces. Nationalists and reformers call for far-reaching changes; a parliamentary delegation meets in Frankfurt.

powerful Germany paddled into the new century with incompetent leaders at the helm.

The Great War

Technological advances and the toughening of Europe into colonial power blocs made WWI far from 'great'. The conflict began with the assassination of the heir to the Austro-Hungarian throne, Archduke Franz Ferdinand, in Sarajevo in 1914 and quickly escalated into a European and Middle Eastern affair: Germany, Austria-Hungary and Turkey against Britain, France, Italy and Russia. In 1915 a German submarine attack on a British passenger liner killed more than 1000 people, including 120 US citizens. By 1917 the USA had also entered the war.

The seeds of acrimony and humiliation that later led to WWII were sown in the peace conditions of the Great War. Russia, in the grip of revolution, accepted humiliating peace terms from Germany. Germany, militarily broken, itself teetering on the verge of revolution and caught in a no man's land between monarchy and modern democracy, signed the Treaty of Versailles (1919), which made it responsible for all losses incurred by its enemies. Its borders were trimmed back and it was forced to pay high reparations. To allow negotiations, a chancellor was appointed who, for the first time, was responsible to parliament. A mutiny by sailors in the bustling port of Kiel in 1919 triggered a workers' revolt and a revolution in Berlin, spelling a bitter end for Germany's Kaiser, who abdicated the throne and went to the Netherlands.

Weimar & the Rise of Hitler

The end of the war did not create stability in Germany. Socialist and democratic socialist parties fought tooth and nail, while the radical Spartacus League (joined by other groups in 1919 to form the German Communist Party; KPD) sought to create a republic based on Marx' theories of proletarian revolution. Following the bloody quashing of an uprising in Berlin, Spartacus founders 'Red' Rosa Luxemburg (1871–1919) and Leipzig-born Karl Liebknecht (1871–1919) were arrested and murdered en route to prison by *Freikorps* soldiers (right-leaning war volunteers).

Meanwhile, in July 1919, in the Thuringian city of Weimar (where the constituent assembly briefly sought refuge during the Berlin chaos), the federalist constitution of a new democratic republic was adopted.

The so-called Weimar Republic (1919–33) was governed by a coalition of left and centre parties headed by President Friedrich Ebert of the Sozialdemokratische Partei Deutschlands (SPD; German Social Democratic Party) until 1925 and then by Field Marshal Paul von Hindenburg, a gritty 78-year-old monarchist. The republic, however, pleased neither communists nor monarchists.

'Laws are like sausages. It's better not to see them being made.'
Otto von Bismarck

Seems that 9 November is Germany's 'destiny date'. It was the day of the uprising in 1848, the failed revolution in 1918, Hitler's Munich Putsch in 1923, the Night of Broken Glass in 1938, and the day the Wall fell in 1989.

1866

After winning a war against Denmark, Prussia defeats Austria in the Austro-Prussian War and chancellor Otto von Bismarck creates a North German Confederation that excludes Austria.

1870–71

Through brilliant diplomacy and the Franco-Prussian War, Bismarck creates a unified Germany, with Prussia at its helm and Berlin as its capital. Wilhelm I, king of Prussia, becomes Kaiser Wilhelm I.

1880s

The Unified Germany demands its place in the sun in the form of colonies. This causes increasing friction with established colonial powers Britain and France.

BERND MELLMANN / GETTY IMAGES ©

» Kaiser Wilhelm I, Koblenz

The first blow to the new republic came in 1920, when right-wing militants forcibly occupied the government quarter in Berlin in the failed 'Kapp Putsch'. In 1923 hyperinflation rocked the republic. That same year Adolf Hitler (1889–1945), an Austrian-born volunteer in the German army during WWI, launched the Munich Putsch (a failed attempt to kick off a revolution from a Munich beer hall) with members of his National Socialist German Workers' Party (NSDAP). Hitler wound up in Landsberg Prison for two years, where he penned *Mein Kampf*. Once out, he began rebuilding the party.

Hitler's NSDAP gained 18% of the vote in the 1930 elections, prompting him to run against Hindenburg for the presidency in 1932, when he won 37% of a second-round vote. A year later, Hindenburg appointed Hitler chancellor, with a coalition cabinet of Nationalists (conservatives, old aristocrats and powerful industrialists) and National Socialists (Nazis). When Berlin's Reichstag mysteriously went up in flames in March 1933, Hitler had the excuse he needed to request emergency powers to arrest all communist and liberal opponents and push through his proposed Enabling Law, allowing him to decree laws and change the constitution without consulting parliament. The Nazi dictatorship had begun. When Hindenburg died a year later, Hitler fused the offices of president and chancellor to become Führer of the Third Reich.

Nazis in Power

In the 12 short years of what Hitler envisaged as the 'Thousand Year Reich', massive destruction would be inflicted upon German and other European cities; political opponents, intellectuals and artists would be murdered, or forced to go underground or into exile; a culture of terror and denunciation would permeate almost all of German society; and Europe's rich Jewish heritage would be decimated.

In April 1933 Joseph Goebbels, head of the Ministry of Propaganda, announced a boycott of Jewish businesses. Soon after, Jews were expelled from public service and 'non-Aryans' were banned from many professions, trades and industries. The Nuremberg Laws (1935) deprived non-Aryans of German citizenship and forbade them to marry or have sexual relations with Aryans – anyone who broke these race laws faced the death penalty.

Hitler won much support among the middle and lower-middle classes by pumping large sums of money into employment programs, many involving rearmament and heavy industry. In Wolfsburg, Lower Saxony, affordable cars started rolling out of the first Volkswagen factory, founded in 1938.

That same year, Hitler's troops were welcomed into Austria. Foreign powers, in an attempt to avoid another bloody war, accepted this *Anschluss* (annexation) of Austria. Following this same policy of appeasement, the Munich Agreement was signed in September 1938 by Hitler, Mussolini

---

The period from Bismarck to the Weimar Republic is the focus of Hans-Ulrich Wehler's *The German Empire 1871–1918*, a translation of an authoritative German work. For a revealing study of the Iron Chancellor himself, read *Bismarck, the Man and the Statesman* by AJP Taylor.

After abdicating, Kaiser Wilhelm II could settle in Utrecht (in the Netherlands) on the condition that he didn't engage in political activity. One of his last acts was to send a telegram to Hitler congratulating him on the occupation of Paris.

1890–91	**1914–18**	**1915**	**1918–19**
Developing out of workers' parties that sprang up in the mid-19th century, the Sozialdemokratische Partei Deutschlands (SPD) adopts its present name and a program strongly influenced by Marx' writings.	WWI: Germany, Austria-Hungary and Turkey go to war against Britain, France, Italy and Russia. Germany is defeated. Over eight million soldiers and many times that number of civilians perish.	A German submarine sinks the RMS *Lusitania*, a British passenger ship carrying 1198 passengers, among them more than 120 Americans. The submarine campaign by Germany contributed to America joining the war in 1917.	Sailors' revolts spread across Germany, Kaiser Wilhelm II flees to the Netherlands, and a democratic Weimar Republic is founded. Women receive suffrage and human rights are enshrined in law.

(Italy), Neville Chamberlain (UK) and Édouard Daladier (France), and the largely ethnic-German Sudetenland of Czechoslovakia was relinquished to Hitler. By March 1939, he had also annexed Bohemia and Moravia.

WWII
Early Years

A nonaggression pact was signed between Hitler and Stalin's USSR in August 1939, whereby the Tokyo-Berlin-Rome axis (Hitler had already signed agreements with Italy and Japan) was expanded to include Moscow. Soviet neutrality was assured by a secret Soviet-German protocol that divided up Eastern Europe into spheres of interest.

In late August an SS-staged attack on a German radio station in Gleiwitz (Gliwice), Poland, gave Hitler the excuse to march into Poland. This proved the catalyst for WWII; three days later, on 3 September 1939, France and Britain declared war on Germany.

Poland, quickly followed by Belgium, the Netherlands and France, fell to Germany. In June 1941 Germany broke its nonaggression pact with Stalin by attacking the USSR. Though successful at first, Operation Barbarossa soon ran into problems and Hitler's troops retreated. With the defeat of the German 6th Army at Stalingrad (today Volgograd) the following winter, morale flagged at home and on the fronts.

The Final Solution

At Hitler's request, a conference in January 1942 on Berlin's Wannsee came up with a protocol clothed in bureaucratic jargon that laid the basis for the murder of millions of Jews. The Holocaust was a systematic, bureaucratic and meticulously documented genocidal act carried out by about 100,000 Germans, but with the tacit agreement of a far greater number.

Jewish populations in occupied areas were systematically terrorised and executed by SS troops. Hitler sent Jews to concentration camps in Germany (including Sachsenhausen, Buchenwald and Mittelbau Dora) and Eastern Europe. Sinti and Roma (gypsies), political opponents,

During the hyperinflation of the early 1920s a man in Berlin was carting his pay home in a wheelbarrow when he was mugged. The thieves took the wheelbarrow...but left the money on the pavement.

In 1923 a postage stamp cost 50 billion marks, a loaf of bread cost 140 billion marks and US$1 was worth 4.2 trillion marks. In November, the new Rentenmark was traded in for one trillion old marks.

HISTORY WWII

THE NIGHT OF BROKEN GLASS

Nazi horror escalated on 9 November 1938 with the *Reichspogromnacht* (often called Kristallnacht or the Night of Broken Glass). In retaliation for the assassination of a German consular official by a Polish Jew in Paris, synagogues and Jewish cemeteries, property and businesses across Germany were desecrated, burnt or demolished. About 90 Jews died that night. The next day another 30,000 were incarcerated, and Jewish businesses were transferred to non-Jews through forced sale at below-market prices.

1918–19	Mid-1920s	1932	1933
The 'war guilt' clause in the Treaty of Versailles, holding Germany and its allies financially responsible for loss and damage suffered by its enemies, puts the new republic on an unstable footing.	Amid the troubles of the Weimar Republic, Germans discover flamboyant pursuits. Cinemas attract two million visitors daily and cabaret and the arts flourish, but ideological differences increase.	Hitler and Churchill almost meet when the latter is researching his family history in Munich. Hitler calls off the meeting, considering a washed-up politician such as Churchill unworthy of his time.	Hitler becomes chancellor of Germany and creates a dictatorship through the Enabling Law. Only the 94 SPD Reichstag representatives present – those not in prison or exile – oppose the act.

JEWS IN GERMANY

The first Jews arrived in present-day Germany with the conquering Romans, settling in important Roman cities on or near the Rhine, such as Cologne, Trier, Mainz, Speyer and Worms. As non-Christians, Jews had a separate political status. Highly valued for their trade connections, they were formally invited to settle in Speyer in 1084 and granted trading privileges and the right to build a wall around their quarter. A charter of rights granted to the Jews of Worms in 1090 by Henry IV allowed local Jews to be judged according to their own laws.

The First Crusade (1095–99) brought pogroms in 1096, usually against the will of local rulers and townspeople. Many Jews resisted before committing suicide once their situation became hopeless. This, the *Kiddush ha-shem* (martyr's death), established a precedent of martyrdom that became a tenet of European Judaism in the Middle Ages.

In the 13th-century Jews were declared crown property by Frederick II, an act that afforded protection but exposed them to royal whim. Rabbi Meir of Rothenburg, whose grave lies in Europe's oldest Jewish cemetery in Worms, fell foul of King Rudolph of Habsburg in 1293 for leading a group of would-be emigrants to Palestine; he died in prison. The Church also prescribed distinctive clothing for Jews at this time, which later meant that in some towns Jews had to wear badges.

Things deteriorated with the arrival of the plague in the mid-14th century, when Jews were persecuted and libellous notions circulated throughout the Christian population. The 'blood libel' accused Jews of using the blood of Christians in rituals.

Money lending was the main source of income for Jews in the 15th century. Expulsions remained commonplace, however, with large numbers emigrating to Poland, where the Yiddish language developed. The Reformation (including a hostile Martin Luther) and the Thirty Years' War brought difficult times for Jewish populations, but by the 17th century they were valued again for their economic contacts.

Napoleon granted Germany's Jews equal rights, but the reforms were repealed by the 1815 Congress of Vienna. Anti-Jewish feelings in the early 19th century coincided with German nationalism and a more vigorous Christianity, producing a large number of influential assimilated Jews.

By the late 19th century, Jews had equal status in most respects and Germany had become a world centre of Jewish cultural and historical studies. There was a shift to large cities, such as Leipzig, Cologne, Breslau (now Wrocław in Poland), Hamburg, Frankfurt am Main and the capital, Berlin, where a third of German Jews lived.

Germany became a key centre for Hebrew literature after Russian writers and academics fled the revolution of 1917. The Weimar Republic brought emancipation for the 500,000-strong Jewish community, but by 1943 Adolf Hitler had declared Germany *Judenrein* ('clean of Jews'). This ignored the hundreds of thousands of Eastern European Jews incarcerated on 'German' soil. Around six million Jews died in Europe as a direct result of Nazism.

The number of Jews affiliated with the Jewish community in Germany is currently around 100,000 – the third largest in Europe – but the real number is probably twice that. Many Jews arrived from the former Soviet Union in the 1990s.

1933–34	1935	1936	1938
The Nazi *Gleichschaltung* (enforced conformity) begins, signalling the death of tolerance and pluralism. The federal states become powerless, and opposition parties and free-trade unions are banned.	The Nuremberg Laws are enacted. A law for the 'protection of German blood and honour' forbids marriage between 'Aryans' and 'non-Aryans'. Another law deprives Jews and other 'non-Aryans' of German nationality.	Berlin hosts the Olympic Games. Embarrassingly for Hitler, who originally wanted to ban all black and Jewish athletes, African American Jesse Owens wins four gold medals.	The Munich Agreement allows Hitler to annex the Sudetenlands, a mostly German-speaking region of Czechoslovakia. The agreement is designed to bring peace to Europe.

priests, homosexuals, resistance fighters and habitual criminals were also incarcerated in a network of 22 camps, mostly in Eastern Europe. Another 165 work camps (such as Auschwitz-Birkenau in Poland) provided labour for big industry, including IG Farbenindustrie AG, producer of the cyanide gas Zyklon B that was used in gas chambers to murder more than three million Jews. Of the estimated seven million people sent to camps, 500,000 survived.

Resistance to Hitler was quashed early by the powerful Nazi machinery of terror, but it never vanished entirely. On 20 July 1944, Claus Schenk Graf von Stauffenberg and other high-ranking army officers tried to assassinate Hitler and were executed. Anti-Nazi leaflets were distributed in Munich and other cities by the White Rose, a group of Munich university students, whose resistance attempts cost most of them their lives.

Defeat & Occupation

Systematic air raids on German cities followed the invasion of Normandy in France in June 1944, and the return of the Allies to the European mainland. The brunt of the bombings was suffered by the civilian population; Dresden's Frauenkirche, Germany's greatest Protestant church, was destroyed during a British raid in February 1945 that killed 35,000 people, many of them refugees. Today, this church has been painstakingly reconstructed after its haunting ruins for so long stood as a symbol for the destructiveness of war.

With the Russians advancing on Berlin, a defeated and paranoid Führer and his new bride Eva Braun committed suicide on 30 April 1945 in a Berlin bunker and, on 7 May 1945, Germany capitulated and peace was signed at the US headquarters in Rheims and again in Berlin in what is now the Museum Berlin-Karlshorst (a German-Soviet history museum).

At the Yalta Conference (February 1945), Winston Churchill, Franklin D Roosevelt and Joseph Stalin agreed to carve up Germany and Berlin into four zones of occupation controlled by Britain, the USA, the USSR and France. By July 1945, Stalin, Clement Attlee (who replaced Churchill after a surprise election win) and Roosevelt's successor Harry S Truman were at the table in Schloss Cecilienhof in Potsdam (Brandenburg) to hammer out the details. At Stalin's insistence, France received its chunk from the Allied regions. Regions east of the Oder and Neisse Rivers (where the border is today) went to Poland as compensation for earlier territorial losses to the USSR.

The Big Chill

In 1948 the Allies put together an economic aid package, the Marshall Plan, and created the basis for West Germany's *Wirtschaftswunder* (economic miracle). Meanwhile, German cities were rising out of the rubble

HISTORY DEFEAT & OCCUPATION

One of a clutch of fabulous films by Germany's best-known female director, Margarethe von Trotta, *Rosenstrasse* (2003) is a portrayal of a 1943 protest by a group of non-Jewish women against the deportation of their Jewish husbands.

A comprehensive collection of fascinating Nazi propaganda material can be viewed at www.calvin.edu/academic/cas/gpa

1939	1939–45	1940
WWII: Hitler invades Poland on 1 September. Two days later France and Britain declare war on Germany.	Millions of Jews are murdered during the Holocaust and 62 million civilians and soldiers die – 27 million in the Soviet Union alone.	The German Luftwaffe is defeated by the Spitfires of the RAF in the Battle of Britain, a major turning point in WWII. Hitler gives up on plans to invade Great Britain.

INTERFOTO / ALAMY ©

» Luftwaffe airman

and first steps were being taken to re-establish elected government. These advances widened the rift between Allied and Soviet zones; in the latter, inflation still strained local economies, food shortages affected the population, and the Communist Party of Germany (KPD) and Social Democratic Party of Germany (SPD) were forced to unite as the Sozialistische Einheitspartei Deutschlands (SED; Socialist Unity Party).

The showdown came in June 1948 when the Allies introduced the Deutschmark (DM) in their zones. The USSR saw this as a breach of the Potsdam Agreement, whereby the powers had agreed to treat Germany as one economic zone. The USSR issued its own currency and promptly announced a full-scale economic blockade of West Berlin. To ensure West Berlin's food supplies, the Allies responded with the remarkable Berlin airlift, whereby American, British, Canadian and some Australian air crews flew into Berlin's Tempelhof Airport the equivalent of 22 freight trains of 50 carriages daily, at intervals of 90 seconds.

East & West

In the frosty East–West climate, the town of Bonn hosted West German state representatives in September 1948 who met to hammer out a draft constitution for a new Federal Republic of Germany (FRG; BRD by its German initials). A year later, 73-year-old Konrad Adenauer (1876–1967), a Cologne mayor during the Weimar years, was elected as West Germany's first chancellor. Bonn – Adenauer's home town – was the natural candidate for the FRG's provisional capital.

East Germany reciprocated by adopting its own constitution for the German Democratic Republic (GDR; DDR by its German initials). On paper, it guaranteed press and religious freedoms and the right to strike. In reality, such freedoms were limited. In its chosen capital of Berlin, a bicameral system was set up (one chamber was later abolished) and Wilhelm Pieck became the country's first president. From the outset, however, the Socialist Unity Party led by party boss Walter Ulbricht dominated economic, judicial and security policy.

In keeping with centralist policies, the East German states of Saxony, Mecklenburg–Western Pomerania, Saxony-Anhalt and Thuringia were divided into 14 regional administrations and the notorious Ministry for State Security (the infamous Stasi) was created in 1950 to ensure SED loyalty. Workers became economically dependent on the state through the collectivisation of farms, and nationalisation of production such as the Horch car factory in Zwickau near Leipzig (which later produced the Trabant car).

In Soviet zones, the task of weeding out Nazis tended to be swift and harsh. In the west the Allies held war-crimes trials in courtroom 600 of Nuremberg's Court House (open to visitors today).

Of the dozens of books covering Nazi concentration camps, *I Never Saw Another Butterfly: Children's Drawings and Poems from Terezin Concentration Camp 1942–1944,* edited by Hana Volavková, says it all. *This Way for the Gas, Ladies and Gentlemen* by Tadeusz Borowski is equally chilling.

Interviews with former Stasi men in the mid-1990s form the basis of Australian journalist Anna Funder's *Stasiland* (2003) – crammed with fresh and alternative insights into what the men of the Stasi did after it was disbanded.

1941–43	1945	1948–49	1949
Nazi Germany invades the USSR in June 1941, but the campaign falters almost from the outset and defeat in the Battle of Stalingrad in 1942–43 drains valuable resources.	Hitler commits suicide in a Berlin bunker while a defeated Germany surrenders. Germany is split into Allied- and Soviet-occupied zones; Berlin has its own British, French, US and Soviet zones.	The USSR blocks land routes to Allied sectors of Berlin when cooperation between Allies and the Soviets breaks down. Over 260,000 US and British flights supply West Berlin during the Berlin airlift.	Allied-occupied West Germany becomes the FRG (Federal Republic of Germany), with Bonn as its capital. A separate East Germany is established in the Soviet-occupied zone, with Berlin as its capital.

The 1950s

The economic vision of Bavarian-born, cigar-puffing Ludwig Erhard (1897–1977) unleashed West Germany's *Wirtschaftswunder* (economic miracle). Between 1951 and 1961 the country's economy averaged an annual growth rate of 8%.

Erhard was economic minister and later vice-chancellor in Konrad Adenauer's government. His policies encouraged investment and boosted economic activity to support West Germany's system of welfare-state capitalism. He helped create the European Coal and Steel Community to regulate coal and steel production with France, Italy, West Germany and the Benelux countries, and in 1958 West Germany joined the European Economic Community (today's EU). Adenauer's fear of the USSR saw him pursue a determined policy of integration with the West.

In early 2012 the tombstone on Hitler's parents' grave was removed from the Austrian village of Leonding to prevent it becoming a shrine for neo-Nazis.

STASI SECRETS

The Ministry of State Security, commonly called the Stasi, was based on the Soviet KGB and served as the 'shield and sword' of the SED. Almost a state within the state, it boasted an astonishing spy network of about 90,000 full-time employees and 180,000 *inoffizielle Mitarbeiter* (unofficial co-workers) by 1989. Since 1990, only 250 Stasi agents have been prosecuted and since the 10-year limit ended in 2000, future trials are unlikely.

When it came to tracking down dissidents, there were no limits. One unusual collection of files found in its Berlin archive kept a record of dissidents' body odour. Some dissidents who had been hauled in for interrogation were made to deliver an odour sample, usually taken with a cotton-wool pad from the unfortunate victim's crotch. The sample was then stored in a hermetic glass jar for later use if a dissident suddenly disappeared. The Stasi sniffer dogs employed to track down a missing dissident by odour were euphemistically known as 'smell differentiation dogs'.

What happened to the dogs after the Stasi was disbanded is unclear. What happened to the six million files the Stasi accumulated in its lifetime is a greater cause for concern. In January 1990, protestors stormed the Stasi headquarters in Berlin (today a museum, memorial and research centre), demanding to see the files, large quantities of which had been destroyed by Stasi officers. Since then, the controversial records have been assessed and safeguarded by a Berlin-based public body. In mid-2000, 1000-odd information-packed CDs, removed by the US Central Intelligence Agency's (CIA's) Operation Rosewood immediately after the fall of the Wall in 1989, were returned to Germany. A second batch of CIA files (apparently acquired by the CIA from a Russian KGB officer in 1992) were handed over in 2003. The files, for the first time, matched code names with real names. Some of those with an *inoffizieller Mitarbeiter* file are fully fledged informants; others are 'contact' people who either knew they were giving information to someone from the Stasi or were unfortunate enough to be pumped of information without knowing it.

1950	1951–61	1953	1954
The CDU (Christian Democratic Union) is founded at federal level in West Germany and Adenauer, known for his support for strong relationships with France and the US, is elected its first national chairman.	The economic vision of Ludwig Erhard unleashes West Germany's *Wirtschaftswunder* (economic miracle). In these years, the economy averages an annual growth rate of 8%.	Following the death of Stalin and unfulfilled hopes for better conditions in the GDR, workers and farmers rise up, strike or demonstrate in 560 towns and cities. Soviet troops quash the uprising.	West Germany wins the FIFA soccer World Cup, a famous victory that will become known as the 'miracle of Bern'.

Germany's most sinister Nazi sites

» Reichspartei-tagsgelände, Nuremberg

» Eagle's Nest, Berchtesgaden

» Haus der Wann-see-Konferenz Gedenkstätte, Berlin

» National Socialism in Munich exhibition, Stadtmuseum, Munich

» Dokumentation Obersalzberg, Berchtesgaden

» Memorium Nuremberg Trials, Nuremberg

» NS Dokumen-tationszentrum, Cologne

In East Germany, Stalin's death in 1953 raised unfulfilled hopes of reform. Extreme poverty and economic tensions merely persuaded the government to set production goals higher. Smouldering discontent erupted in violence on 17 June 1953 when 10% of GDR workers took to the streets. Soviet troops quashed the uprising, with scores of deaths and the arrest of about 1200 people. Economic differences widened into military ones when West Germany joined NATO in 1955 and East Germany was embraced by the Warsaw Pact.

The Wall

The exodus of young, well-educated and employed East German refugees seeking a better life in West Germany strained the GDR economy to such an extent that the GDR government – with Soviet consent – built a wall to keep them in. The Berlin Wall, the Cold War's most potent symbol, went up between East and West Berlin on the night of 12 August 1961. The inner border was fenced off and mined.

Having walled in what was left of the struggling population (330,000 East Germans had fled to the west in 1953 alone, and in 1960 almost 200,000 voted with their feet), the East German government launched a new economic policy in a bid to make life better. And it did. The standard of living rose to the highest in the Eastern bloc and East Germany became its second-largest industrial power (behind the USSR).

The appointment of Erich Honecker (1912–94) in 1971 opened the way for rapprochement with the West and enhanced international acceptance of the GDR. Honecker fell in line with Soviet policies, but his economic policies did promote a powerful economy until stagnation took root in the late 1980s.

On the Western Side

Meanwhile, West Germany was still in the aged but firm hands of Konrad Adenauer, chancellor from 1949 to 1963, and whose economics minister, Ludwig Erhard, once the Father of the Economic Miracle, was now importing foreign workers. By doing this he made a post-hoc name for himself as the father of a multi-ethnic German society. About 2.3 million *Gastarbeiter* (guest workers) came to West Germany until the early 1970s, mainly from Italy, Spain, Turkey and Yugoslavia, injecting new life into a host German culture. While Ludwig Erhard's guest workers arrived from one direction, young Germans now rode their imported Vespa motorcycles to Italy on holiday to bring home a piece of Europe for themselves.

In 1963 Adenauer was eased out by Ludwig Erhard, by then also his vice-chancellor, but in 1966 a fluctuating economy was biting deeply into Erhard's credibility, and Germany's first grand coalition government of Christian Democrats (CDU/CSU) and SPD took office, with Kurt Georg

> 'Make the lie big, make it simple, keep saying it, and eventually they will believe it.'
>
> Adolf Hitler

1955	Early 1960s	1961	1963
In a sign of increasing divisions between the two states, West Germany joins NATO while East Germany puts its name to the Warsaw Pact.	Thousands of *Gastarbeiter* (guest workers) from Turkey, Yugoslavia, Italy, Greece and Spain are permitted to take up jobs in the booming West German economy.	On the night of 12 August, the GDR government begins building the Berlin Wall, a 155km-long concrete barrier surrounding West Berlin.	US President John F Kennedy makes his rousing 'Ich bin ein Berliner' speech in Berlin.

Germany's Changing Borders

HOLY ROMAN EMPIRE AT THE END OF
THE THIRTY YEARS' WAR (PEACE OF WESTPHALIA, 1648)

GERMAN EMPIRE 1871–1918

GERMANY AFTER THE TREATY
OF VERSAILLES (1919–38)

WEST GERMANY AND EAST GERMANY 1949–90

HISTORY ON THE WESTERN SIDE

The Last Division: Berlin and the Wall by Ann Tusa is a saga about the events, trials and triumphs of the Cold War, the building of the Wall and its effects on the people and the city of Berlin.

Kiesinger (CDU; 1904–88) as chancellor and Willy Brandt (SPD; 1913–92) as vice-chancellor. The absence of parliamentary opposition fuelled radical demands by the student movement for social reform.

The turning point came in 1969 when the SPD under Willy Brandt formed a new government with the Free Democratic Party (FDP). The Lübeck-born, 1971 Nobel Peace Prize winner spent the Hitler years working in exile as a journalist in Scandinavia, where he was stripped of his citizenship for anti-Nazi writings. Normalising relations with East Germany (his East-friendly policy was known as *Ostpolitik*) was his priority and in December 1972 the Basic Treaty was signed, paving the way for both countries to join the UN in 1973. The treaty guaranteed sovereignty in international and domestic affairs (but fudged formal recognition since it was precluded by the West German constitution).

Brandt was replaced by Helmut Schmidt (b 1918) in 1974 after a scandal (one of Brandt's close advisers turned out to be a Stasi spy). The

For an informative overview of the Berlin Wall, see www.berlin. de/mauer on the Berlin city website.

1972

Social Democrat chancellor Willy Brandt's *Ostpolitik* thaws relations between the two Germanys. The Basic Treaty is signed in East Berlin, paving the way for both countries to join the UN.

1972

Munich hosts the Olympic Games, which end in tragedy when Palestinian terrorists murder two Israeli competitors and take nine hostage. A botched rescue operation kills all nine.

1974

West Germany joins the G8 group of industrialised nations, and hosts and wins the FIFA World Cup. The final is played at Munich's Olympic Stadium.

» Munich Olympic Games

GETTY IMAGES ©

1970s saw antinuclear and green issues move onto the agenda, opposed by Schmidt, and ultimately leading to the election of Green Party representatives to the Bonn parliament in 1979. In 1974 West Germany joined the G8 group of industrial nations. But the 1970s were also a time of terrorism in Germany, and several prominent business and political figures were assassinated by the anticapitalist Red Army Faction.

Brandt's vision of East–West cordiality was continued by Chancellor Helmut Kohl (b 1930) who, with his conservative coalition government from 1982, groomed relations between the East and the West, while dismantling parts of the welfare state at home. In the West German capital in 1987, Kohl received East German counterpart Erich Honecker with full state honours.

> 'Berlin is the testicle of the West. When I want the West to scream, I squeeze on Berlin'.
>
> Nikita Khrushchev, Soviet Communist Party secretary (1953–64)

Reunification

The hearts and minds of Eastern Europeans had long been restless for change, but the events leading up to German reunification caught even the most knowledgeable political observers by surprise.

The so-called *Wende* (change; ie the fall of communism) in Germany and reunification came about perhaps in the most German of ways: a gradual development that culminated in a big bang. Reminiscent of the situation in Berlin in the 1950s, East Germans began leaving their country in droves. They fled not across a no man's land of concrete, weeds and death strips between East and West this time but through a newly opened border between Hungary and Austria. The SED was helpless to stop the flow of people wanting to leave, some of whom sought refuge in the West German embassy in Prague. Around the same time, East Germans took to the streets in Monday demonstrations following services in Leipzig's Nikolaikirche and other churches in East Germany, safe in the knowledge that the Church supported their demands for improved human rights.

> *After the Wall* (1995) by Marc Fisher is an account of German society, with emphasis on life after the *Wende* (fall of communism). Fisher was bureau chief for the *Washington Post* in Bonn and presents some perceptive social insights.

With the demonstrations spreading and escalating into violence, Erich Honecker accepted the inevitable, relinquishing his position to Egon Krenz (b 1937). And then the floodgates opened: on the fateful night of 9 November, 1989, party functionary Günter Schabowski mistakenly informed GDR citizens they could travel directly to the West, effective immediately. The announcement was supposed to be embargoed until the following day. Tens of thousands of East Germans jubilantly rushed through border points in Berlin and elsewhere in the country, bringing to an end the long, chilly phase of German division.

The single most dominant figure throughout reunification and the 1990s was Helmut Kohl, whose CDU/CSU and FDP coalition was re-elected to office in December 1990 in Germany's first postreunification election.

Under Kohl's leadership, East German assets were privatised; oversubsidised state industries were radically trimmed back, sold or wound

1977	1982	1985	1989
The *Deutscher Herbst* (German Autumn) envelops West Germany when a second generation of the left-wing Red Army Faction (RAF) murders key business and state figures.	A 'constructive vote of no confidence' brings down the SPD/FDP coalition under Helmut Schmidt. A conservative coalition government is formed in West Germany under Christian Democrat Helmut Kohl.	Teenage sensation Boris Becker wins Wimbledon tennis tournament. At the age of 17, he is the youngest player and first German to do so.	Demonstrations are held in Leipzig and other East German cities. Hungary opens its border with Austria, and East Germans are allowed to travel to the West.

up completely; and infrastructure was modernised (and in some cases over-invested in) to create a unification boom that saw the former East Germany grow by up to 10% each year until 1995. Growth slowed dramatically from the mid-1990s, however, creating an eastern Germany that consisted of unification winners and losers. Those who had jobs did well, but unemployment was high and the lack of opportunities in regions such as the eastern Harz Mountains or in cities such as Magdeburg and Halle (both in Saxony-Anhalt) was still causing many young people from the former East Germany to try their luck in western Germany or in boom towns, such as Leipzig. Berlin, although economically shaky, was the exception. Many public servants have since relocated there from Bonn to staff the ministries, and young people from all over Germany are attracted by its vibrant cultural scene.

Helmut Kohl also sought to bring former East German functionaries to justice, notably Erich Honecker. He had fled after resigning and went on to live an ailing and nomadic existence that culminated in his death in Chile in 1994. His court case had, by then, been abandoned due to his ill health.

The unification legacy of Helmut Kohl is indisputable. His involvement in a party slush-fund scandal in the late 1990s, however, financially burdened his own party and resulted in the CDU stripping him of his position as lifelong honorary chairman. In 1998, a coalition of the SPD and Bündnis 90/Die Grünen (Alliance 90/The Greens) parties defeated the CDU/CSU and FDP coalition.

Best GDR-themed museums

» DDR Museum, Berlin

» Zeitgeschichliches Forum, Leipzig

» Stasi Museum, Leipzig

» Zeitreise Lebensart DDR 1949–1989, Radebeul

» Haus der Geschichte, Lutherstadt Wittenberg

The New Millennium

With the formation of a coalition government of SPD and Alliance 90/The Greens in 1998, Germany reached a new milestone. This was the first time an environmentalist party had governed nationally – in Germany or elsewhere in the world. Two figures dominated the seven-year rule of the coalition: Chancellor Gerhard Schröder (b 1944) and the Green Party vice-chancellor and foreign minister Joschka Fischer (b 1948). Schröder's role model was Willy Brandt; Fischer's – because he was the Greens party's first minister in the job – was, by necessity, himself. Despite his provenance from the left-wing house-squatting scene in Frankfurt am Main of the 1970s, he enjoyed widespread popularity among ordinary Germans of all political colours.

Under the leadership of Gerhard Schröder, Germany began to take a more independent approach to foreign policy, steadfastly refusing to become involved in the invasion of Iraq, but supporting the USA, historically its closest ally, in Afghanistan and the war in Kosovo. Its stance on Iraq, which reflected the feelings of the majority of Germans, caused relations with the US administration of George W Bush to be strained.

1989	1990	1998	2005
The Berlin Wall comes down, causing Communist regimes across Eastern Europe to fall like dominoes. East Germans flood into West Germany.	Berlin becomes the capital of reunified Germany. Helmut Kohl's conservative coalition promises East–West economic integration, creating unrealistic expectations of a blossoming economic landscape in the east.	After its popularity wanes during the first decade of reunification, Helmut Kohl's CDU/CSU & FDP coalition is replaced by an SPD and Bündnis 90/Die Grünen government.	Angela Merkel becomes Germany's first female chancellor, leading a grand coalition of major parties after the election results in neither the SPD nor the CDU/CSU being able to form its own government.

A man, it would seem, for a financial crisis, Horst Köhler headed the International Monetary Fund (IMF), based in Washington DC, before becoming postwar Germany's ninth president after WWII.

The rise of the Greens and, more recently, the Left has changed the political landscape of Germany dramatically, making absolute majorities by the 'big two' all the more difficult to achieve. In 2005 the CDU/CSU and SPD formed a grand coalition led by Angela Merkel (b 1954), the first woman, former East German, Russian speaker and quantum physicist in the job. While many Germans hoped this would resolve a political stalemate that had existed between an opposition-led upper house (Bundesrat) and the government, political horse trading shifted away from the political limelight and was mostly carried out behind closed doors.

When the financial crisis struck in 2008–09, the German government pumped hundreds of billions of euros into the financial system to prop up the banks. Other measures allowed companies to put workers on shorter shifts without loss of pay and pumped money into the economy by encouraging Germans to scrap older cars and buy new ones.

The election of 2009 confirmed the trend towards smaller parties and a five-party political system in Germany. The CDU/CSU achieved its second-worst result in the history of the party (around 34% of the vote) and the SPD achieved its worst result in its almost 150-year history, receiving around 23% of the vote. Support for the Left has been consistently strong in eastern Germany over the years, but success in the federal elections of late 2009 allowed it to establish itself at federal level. The Left received around 12% of the vote and is the second-strongest opposition party after the SPD. It nudged close to the FDP (just under 15%), whereas Alliance 90/The Greens, despite picking up a few disillusioned SPD voters, received around 11% and became the smallest of the opposition parties. The outcome of Germany's national elections in the autumn of 2013 will reveal whether this fragmentation has become a permanent feature of German politics.

The importance of Germany's stable economy has grown in the beginning of the millennium's second decade, as the Eurozone's debt-driven crisis has spread from Greece to threaten all of Southern Europe. Germany is seen as key in the propping up of the single currency, the collapse of which could plunge economies across the globe back into recession.

2006	**2008**	**2009**	**2011–12**
Germans proudly fly their flag as the country hosts the FIFA World Cup for the first time as a unified nation.	The economic crisis bites deeply into German export industries. German banks are propped up by state funds as unemployment and state debt rise again.	The CDU/CSU and FDP achieve a majority in the federal election. Angela Merkel is re-elected as chancellor.	Southern Europe looks to Germany, which has weathered the world economic crisis better than most, as the crisis in the Eurozone deepens.

The German People

The National Psyche

The German state of mind is always a favourite topic for speculation – two 20th-century wars and the memory of the Jewish Holocaust are reasons. Throw in the chilling edge of Cold War division, a juggernaut-like economy that draws half of Europe in its wake and pumps more goods into the world economy than any other, and a crucial geographical location at the crossroads of Europe and this fascination becomes a little more understandable.

Often, though, it pays to ignore the stereotypes, jingoism and those headlines at home describing Germany in military terms – and maybe even forgive Germans for the systematic way they clog up a football field or conduct jagged discussion. Sometimes it helps to see the country through its regional nuances. Germany was very slow to become a nation, so, if you look closely, you'll begin to notice many different local cultures within the one set of borders (in a somewhat similar way to Italy). You'll also discover it's one of Europe's most multicultural countries, with Turkish, Greek, Italian, Russian and Balkan influences.

Around 15 million people live in the former GDR (German Democratic Republic; the former East Germany), a part of Germany where, until 1989, travel was restricted, the state was almighty, and life was secure – but also strongly regulated – from the cradle to grave. Not surprisingly, therefore, many former East Germans are still coming to terms with a more competitive, unified Germany. Many 'easterners' still maintain that the GDR had more good sides than bad, and some elderly former GDR citizens say they

> Some 15% of German beach tourists admit to having sunbathed in the nude, more than any other nation.

OSTALGIE

Who would want to go back to East German times? Well, very few people, but there was more to the GDR (German Democratic Republic; the former East Germany) than simply being a 'satellite of the Evil Empire', as Cold War warriors from the 1980s would portray it.

The opening lines of director Leander Haussmann's film *Sonnenallee* (1999) encapsulate this idea: 'Once upon a time, there was a land and I lived there and, if I am asked how it was, I say it was the best time of my life because I was young and in love.' Another film, the smash hit *Good Bye, Lenin!* (2003), looked at the GDR with humour and pathos. It also gave Ostalgie - from *Ost* (East) and *Nostalgie* (nostalgia) – the kick it needed to become a more or less permanent cultural fixture in Germany.

Whether it be in the form of grinning Erich Honecker doubles at parties, Spreewald cucumbers and GDR Club Cola, or the *Ampelmännchen* – the little green man that helped East German pedestrians cross the road – Ostalgie is here to stay. For a taste of what the East offered in daily life check out the GDR museums in Berlin, Pirna and Radebeul.

were happier or lived better at that time. More than two decades after re-unification the eastern states continue to lose brains and skills to the west.

Germans as a whole fall within the mental topography of northern Europe and are sometimes described as culturally 'low context'. That means, as opposed to the French or Italians, Germans like to pack what they mean into the words they use rather than hint or suggest. Facing each other squarely in conversation, firm handshakes, and a hug or a kiss on the cheek among friends are also par for the course.

Many Germans are very much fans of their own folk culture and even an otherwise ordinary young Bavarian from, say, the finance department of a large company, might don the Dirndl (traditional Bavarian skirt and blouse) around Oktoberfest time and swill like a hearty, rollicking peasant. On Monday she'll be soberly back at the desk crunching numbers.

Germany's most successful golfer, Bernhard Langer, is the son of a Russian prisoner of war who jumped off a Siberia-bound train and settled in Bavaria.

Lifestyle

The German household fits into the mould of households in other Western European countries. A close look, however, reveals some distinctly German quirks, whether it be a compulsion for sorting and recycling rubbish, a taste for fizzy mineral water and filter coffee, or a springtime obsession with asparagus.

Although tradition is valued and grandmother's heirlooms may still occupy pride of place in many a house, multichannel, 3D smart TVs babble away in living rooms and Germany boasts 67 million internet surfers, 22 million of whom also have a Facebook account. Eight in 10 Germans own a bike but there's a car in almost every drive, embodying the German belief that true freedom comes on four wheels and is best expressed tearing along the autobahn at 200km/h or more. For most outsiders this high car use may sit incongruously with the Germans' green credentials.

One aspect of life in Germany visitors will notice almost immediately is how much second-hand cigarette smoke they are inhaling compared with back home. Almost 36% of German men and 28% of women smoke and the situation is not helped by patchy and badly enforced smoking bans, which are different in each state. Alcohol consumption is also dangerously high and on the increase.

Smoking is the least of the problems continuing to plague the east of the country where unemployment and a brain drain to the west dog the economy. Even when in employment, eastern Germans can expect to earn around 20% less than they would in the western states.

Birth rates remain low (8.3 babies per 1000 people) and have fallen steadily over the last decade. Despite this, the traditional nuclear family is still the most common model: 63% of children grow up with married parents and at least one sibling. But there's a big difference between east and west Germany. While 66% of children in western Germany experience this upbringing, only 45% do in the east. People are marrying later, with both men and women tying the knot in their early thirties.

Germany's first gay publication, Der Eigene, launched in 1896 and, with a few interruptions, was published until the early 1930s when it was shut down by the Nazis.

Abortion is illegal (except when a medical or criminal indication exists), but unpunishable if carried out within 12 weeks of conception, after compulsory counselling. Legally recognised same-sex partnerships have been possible since 2001. Gays and lesbians walk with ease in most cities, especially Berlin, Hamburg, Cologne and Frankfurt am Main, although homosexuals do encounter discrimination in some eastern German areas.

German school hours (usually from 8am to 1pm; until 4pm for the less common 'all day' schools) and the underfunding of child care make combining career and children difficult for German women. The plus side is that parents enjoy equal rights for maternity and paternity leave.

On the whole, the number of women employed is increasing. About 66% of working-age women are employed – high for an EU country, but lower than neighbours Switzerland, the Netherlands and the Scandinavian countries. Almost half of these women work part-time, and in eastern Germany women tend to have more of a presence at managerial level.

The official retirement age is 67, but changes may see this gradually increase to 69 in the coming decades.

Sport
Football

Football ignites the passion of Germans everywhere and has contributed much to building Germany's self-confidence as a nation. Its national side has won the World Cup three times, in 1954, 1974 and 1990. West Germany's first victory against Hungary in Bern, Switzerland, was unexpected and a quite miraculous for a country slumbering deeply in post-WWII depression. The miracle of Bern – as the victory was dubbed – sent national morale soaring.

Germany has also hosted the World Cup twice, in 1974 and 2006. The first occasional was particularly special as West Germany beat Holland 2:1 in the final held at Munich's Olympic stadium.

Domestically, Germany's Bundesliga has fallen behind other European leagues such as Spain's La Liga and England's Premier League but still throws up some exciting duels. On the European stage, Germany's most-successful domestic side is Bayern Munich, who won the UEFA Champion's League in 2001 but have lost in the final three times.

Women's football is growing in popularity, partly because of the success of the women's national team. Along with the USA, Germany has won the FIFA Women's World Cup twice to date and hosted the event in 2011.

Tennis

Tennis was a minor sport until 1985 when the unseeded 17-year-old Boris Becker (b 1967), from Leinen near Heidelberg, became the youngest-ever men's singles champion. Suddenly every German kid aspired to be the next Becker. The red-head went on to win five more grand slam titles in his career. More successful was Steffi Graf (b 1969) who is among the few women to have won all four grand slam events in one year, and in 1988 – after also winning the gold in Seoul at the Olympic – the 'golden slam'.

Other Sports

Though a relatively minor sport in Germany, basketball is gaining in popularity. Cycling boomed after Rostock-born Jan Ullrich (b 1973) became the first German to win the Tour de France. With no fewer than seven world championships and more than 50 Grand Prix wins, Michael Schumacher (b 1969) is the most successful Formula One driver every to have taken to the circuit. However, his return to the wheel in 2010 after four years in retirement has been far from glorious. Ice hockey fans will need no introduction to the IIHF World Championships which Germany has hosted seven times but never won.

Multiculturalism

Germany has always attracted immigrants, be it French Huguenots escaping religious persecution (about 30% of Berlin's population in 1700 was Huguenot), 19th-century Polish miners who settled in the Ruhr region, post-WWII asylum seekers, or foreign *Gastarbeiter* (guest workers) imported during the 1950s and 1960s to resolve labour shortages.

After reunification, the foreign population soared as emigrants from the imploding USSR and the then war-ravaged Yugoslavia sought refuge. The country also accepted around 3000 *Spätaussiedler* (people of German heritage, mainly from Eastern Europe and Kazakhstan) a year. All of these arrivals have contributed to Germany having the third-largest

Always a keen sporting nation, Germany has hosted the summer Olympics and football World Cup two times a piece. However, the Germans, it seems, are dastardly good at most sporting disciplines; if your country has a national game, the Germans probably thrashed you at it a long time ago.

In 2007 Würzburg-born Dirk Nowitzki (b 1978) won the NBA's Most Valuable Player Award, and was the first European player to be selected for the All-NBA First Team, made up of the best players of a season.

GREEN GERMANY

Germans are the original Greens. They cannot claim to have invented environmentalism, but they were there at the outset and it was they who coined the word to describe the movement. A few 'Values' and 'Ecology' parties were knocking around beforehand, but it was the group of politicians associated with Rudi Dutschke, Petra Kelly and artist Joseph Beuys who first hit on the name The Greens (Die Grünen) when contesting local and national elections in 1979 and 1980. They gained a strong foothold in Bremen, and other political groups across the world decided they quite liked the moniker.

The Greens' concern for the health of the planet and their strong opposition to nuclear power certainly struck a chord with the local populace. Contemporary Germans recycle vigilantly, often prefer to ride bicycles rather than catch buses, and carry their groceries in reusable bags or rolling canvas baskets; all this is simply second nature here.

Green ideology has also wielded an enormous influence on the political agenda. In the 1990s, Greenpeace Germany made international news attempting to stop nuclear-waste transports in Lower Saxony and heavily populated North Rhine–Westphalia. German Greenpeace members also helped scuttle Shell's controversial plans to sink the Brent Spar oil platform in the North Sea.

Even more tellingly, the Greens were in government between 1998 and 2005, as the junior partner in Gerhard Schröder's coalition. Under the leadership of Joschka Fischer, the party had a major say in decisions to cut carbon emissions and to wind down the nuclear industry. Although some of these policies are already being reversed under the more conservative 'grand coalition' government of CDU/CSU and SPD under Chancellor Angela Merkel, individual Germans' commitment to green issues remains steadfast.

percentage of international migrants in the world (12.3%). A third of these are from EU countries and almost half from Europe. Ethnic Turks form the largest single group (25%), followed by former Yugoslavs (10%), Italians (8%), Poles (6%) and Greeks (5%).

There's no denying that this large immigrant population has led to the rise of extreme right-wing movements, who oppose such a huge non-German presence in their country. Ironically the problem is worst in the eastern states where there are fewer immigrants. As across Europe, the debate as to whether Germany should promote a German *Leitkultur* (lead culture) as opposed to multiculturalism divides opinion.

Religion

The constitution guarantees religious freedom, the main religions being Catholicism and Protestantism, each with about 27 million adherents (around a third of the country's total population each). Religion has a stronger footing in western Germany, especially Catholic Bavaria.

Women's issues are lobbied by the Deutscher Frauenrat (German Women's Council; www.deutscher-frauenrat.de).

Unlike the Jewish community, which has grown since the early 1990s due to immigration from the former Soviet Union, the Catholic and Protestant churches are losing worshippers. This is attributed partly to the obligatory church tax (8% or 9% of total income tax paid) forked out by those belonging to a recognised denomination. Most German Protestants are Lutheran, headed by the Evangelische Kirche (Protestant Church), an official grouping of a couple of dozen Lutheran churches with headquarters in Hanover. In 2005, for the first time in almost five centuries, a German, Joseph Ratzinger (b 1927) became pope, taking the name Pope Benedict XVI.

The largest Jewish communities are in Berlin, Frankfurt am Main and Munich. Countrywide, 80 or more congregations are represented by the conservative Zentralrat der Juden in Deutschland (Central Council of Jews in Germany). Around three million Muslims live in Germany, most of Turkish extraction.

Food & Drink

Metre-long bratwursts with litres of foamy wheat beer in Munich, snow-ball-sized dumplings with an avalanche of sauerkraut and roast pork in the Alps, salads swimming in dressing, cakes drowning in cream and a zillion calories notched at every mealtime – every traveller has a tale of excess to tell about German food.

While frozen black forest gateau, cheap frankfurts and Liebfraumilch have given Germany's image a bumpy global ride over past decades, the road to culinary recognition is getting smoother. True, German menus do not always reveal the aromatic subtlety and sophistication of, say, French and Italian cuisine, but many go beyond the meat, cabbage and carb-laden stodge the stereotypes would have you swallow.

Long before 'seasonal' and 'local' became buzzwords, Germans were making the most of locally grown produce. In spring, menus burst with *Spargel* (asparagus), in summer *Pfifferlinge* (chanterelles) and in autumn the earthy delights of game, pumpkins and wild mushrooms. Regional food at its best here is about top-quality ingredients and dishes that sing with natural, integral flavours. Dishes that – you never know – might just surprise you.

Sanddorn (sea buckthorn), nicknamed the 'Mecklenburg lemon', is a shrub berry with a subtle citrus flavour. It is used to great effect in teas, ice creams and other dishes.

German Specialities

Put down on paper, Germany's best-known specialities appear deceptively simple: wurst, *Brot, Kartoffeln* and sauerkraut (sausage, bread, potatoes and pickled cabbage). But, as any local will tell you, the devil is in the detail. Where else will you find so many kinds of sausage, such a cornucopia of bread and potatoes in so many guises? Elevated to near art forms, these staples are both what unites the country and divides it: ingredients are often similar but regional recipes interpret them totally differently.

Quark, a yoghurt-like curd cheese, accounts for 50% of domestic cheese consumption in Germany. It is used in everything from potato dips to salad dressings, sauces to cheesecake.

Sausage Country

In the Middle Ages, German peasants found a way to package and disguise animals' less appetising bits, and the humble wurst (sausage) was born. Today, it's a noble and highly respected element of German cuisine, with strict rules determining the authenticity of wurst varieties. In some

SPARGELZEIT

No period ranks higher on the culinary calendar than *Spargelzeit* (asparagus season), when Germans devour great quantities of mostly white asparagus, which they generally consider tastier than the green variety. The harvesting of the first crop kicks off in mid-April and the season lasts until 24 June, the feast-day of St John the Baptist. You'll find restaurants with asparagus menus and whole books devoted to the subject, while many towns even hold asparagus festivals in May and June.

cases, as with the finger-sized Nuremberg sausage, regulations even ensure offal no longer enters the equation.

There are more than 1500 sausage types, all commonly served with bread and a sweet *(süss)* or spicy *(scharf)* mustard *(Senf)*.

Bratwurst, served countrywide, is made from minced pork, veal and spices, and is cooked in different ways: boiled in beer, baked with apples and cabbage, stewed in a casserole, grilled or barbecued.

The availability of other sausages differs regionally. A *Thüringer* is long, thin and spiced, while a wiener is what hot-dog fiends call a frankfurt. *Blutwurst* is blood sausage (not to be confused with black pudding, which is *Rotwurst*), *Leberwurst* is liver sausage, and *Knackwurst* is lightly tickled with garlic.

Saxony has brain sausage *(Bregenwurst)*, Bavaria sells white rubbery Weisswurst, made from veal, and Berlin boasts the takeaway *Currywurst* (slices of sausage topped with curry powder and ketchup).

The modern doner kebab *(Döner Kebab)* doesn't emanate from Turkey, but Germany. In 1971, Turkish immigrants running the Berlin restaurant Hasir introduced salad into an age-old Turkish dish; even outlets in Turkey have been making it this way ever since.

Daily Bread

In exile in California in 1941, German playwright Bertolt Brecht confessed that what he missed most about his homeland was the bread. That won't surprise anyone who has sampled the stuff. German bread is world-class. It's tasty and textured, often mixing wheat and rye flour, and is available in 300 varieties. Little beats a visit to an old-fashioned *Bäckerei* (bakery), with yeasty smells wafting tantalisingly from ovens, bakers with their arms elbow-deep in dough and staff who remember customers by name.

'Black' rye bread *(Schwarzbrot)* is actually brown, but a much darker shade than the slightly sour *Bauernbrot* – and divine with a slab of butter. Pumpernickel bread is steam-cooked instead of baked, making it extra moist, and actually is black. *Vollkorn* means wholemeal, while bread coated in sunflower seeds is *Sonnenblumenbrot*. If you insist on white bread *(Weissbrot)*, the Germans have that, too.

Fresh bread rolls *(Brötchen* in the north, *Semmel* in Bavaria, *Wecken* in southern Germany) can be covered in poppy seeds *(Mohnbrötchen)*, cooked with sweet raisins *(Rosinenbrötchen)*, or sprinkled with salt *(Salzstangel)*.

Brezeln are traditional pretzels, covered in rock salt. Lore has it that they were born in Swabia in the 15th century, when Tübingen university founder, Count Eberhard im Bart, asked a baker from Bad Urach to create a pastry through which the sun could shine three times.

King Kartoffel

Chipped, boiled, baked, mashed, fried: Germans are almost as keen as Russians about the potato. The *Kartoffel* is not only *Vegetable Nummer Eins* in any meat-and-three-veg dish, it can also be incorporated into any course of a meal, from potato soup *(Kartoffelsuppe)* as a starter, to potato salad *(Kartoffelsalat)* with smoked fish, or potato pancakes *(Reibekuchen* or *Kartoffelpuffer)* as a sweet, sugar-sprinkled treat.

In between, you can try *Himmel und Erde* (Heaven and Earth), mashed potatoes and stewed apples served with black pudding, or potato-based *Klösse* dumplings. *Pellkartoffeln* or *Ofenkartoffeln* are jacket potatoes, usually capped with a dollop of *Quark* (a yoghurtlike curd cheese).

It's Pickled Cabbage

Finally comes a quintessential German side dish that many outside the country find impossible to fathom: sauerkraut. Before the 2006 FIFA World Cup, one football magazine suggested, with typical abrasiveness: 'It's pickled cabbage; don't try to make it sound interesting.' OK, we won't. It's shredded cabbage, doused in white-wine vinegar and slowly simmered. But if you haven't at least tried *Rotkohl* (the red-cabbage version of the white-cabbage sauerkraut), you don't know what you're missing. Braising the cabbage with sliced apples and wine turns it into *Bayrischkraut* or *Weinkraut*.

SWEET TREATS

Unleash your sweet tooth on these German favourites:

Black forest gateau A multilayered chocolate sponge, cream and kirsch confection, topped with morello cherries and chocolate shavings.

Nürnberg Lebkuchen Totally moreish gingerbread made with nuts, fruit peel, honey and spices.

Lübecker Leckerli Honey-flavoured ginger biscuits. Also try the fabulous Lübeck marzipan.

Dresden Stollen Christmas wouldn't be the same without this spiced cake, loaded with sultanas and candied peel, sprinkled with icing sugar and spruced up with a ball of marzipan.

Leipziger Lerche As its name suggests, it was made with lark until songbird hunting was banned in 1876. Today it's shortcrust pastry filled with almonds, nuts and a cherry or spoon of jam.

Regional Flavours

Berlin

Alongside Hamburg, Berlin has one of the country's most cosmopolitan restaurant scenes, but it can still lay claim to local delicacies. First up is *Eisbein* (pork knuckles), then *Kohlsuppe* (cabbage soup) and *Erbsensuppe* (pea soup).

Berlin is also where you'll find the country's highest concentration of Turkish doner kebab *(Döner Kebab)* spots, an essential end to any drink-fuelled night out on the town.

Bavaria

The Chinese say you can eat every part of the pig except the 'oink', and Bavarian chefs seem to be in full agreement. No part of the animal is spared their attention: they cook up its knuckles *(Schweinshax'n)*, ribs *(Rippchen)*, tongue *(Züngerl)* and belly *(Wammerl)*. Pork also appears as *Schweinebraten* (a roast) and the misleadingly named *Leberkäse* (liver cheese), where it's combined with beef in a dish that contains no cheese – and in Bavaria at least – no liver. The Bavarians are also quite fond of veal *(Kalb)*.

Dumplings are another staple, from potato-based *Klösse* and *Leberknödel* (liver dumplings) to sweet *Senfknödel*, made from *Quark*, flour and eggs, then dunked in milk. Dumplings also make a major appearance in the Franconian *Hochszeitsuppe* (wedding soup), a clear meat broth garnished with bread dumplings, liver dumplings and pancakes.

Stuttgart & the Black Forest

Nestled in the country's southwestern crook, the food here is rich and earthy. Black Forest must-trys include *Bachforelle* (brook trout) fished from crystal-clear streams, *Schwarzwälderschinken* (dry-cured ham with a smoky aroma) and *Schwarzwälderkirschtorte* (black forest gateau).

Swabian folk around Stuttgart are mad about *Spätzle*, egg-based noodles served as a main with cheese, or as a side dish with meat or fish. *Zwiebelrostbraten* (roast beef with onions and gravy) and *Maultaschen* (ravioli-like pockets stuffed with ground meat, onion and spinach) are other favourites.

When ordering food, a little knowledge of German can be a dangerous thing. So, don't expect half a chicken when you order a *Halve Hahn* in Cologne – it's a rye roll with gouda cheese, gherkin and mustard. *Kölscher Kaviar* is similarly not caviar, but black pudding. And *Nordseekrabben* in Hamburg and Lower Saxony? They're small prawns...of course.

AFTER THE GRAIN

Frankfurt & Southern Rhineland

Two former chancellors named dishes from Rhineland-Palatinate as their favourite: Helmut Kohl nominated *Saumagen*, a stuffed pork belly with pickled cabbage (vaguely resembling Scottish haggis) while postwar chancellor Konrad Adenauer preferred *Reibekuchen*, potato pancakes served with blueberry or apple sauce. Despite this, *Rheinischer Sauerbraten* (roast beef marinated in spiced vinegar and braised) is the region's signature dish.

Hesse produces outstanding cured and smoked hams, typically smoking them over juniper berries. Another regional favourite is pig in the form of *Sulperknochen*, a dish from trotters, ears and tails, that's served with mushy peas and pickled cabbage.

Saarland's neighbour is France and it shows. Fried goose liver and coq au vin are common, as is *Budeng mit Gellenewemutsch*, hot black pudding served with carrot and potato mash. When it comes to the crunch, though, Saarlanders revert to true German form, and *Schwenkbraten* (marinated pork grilled on a spit) is probably their most popular dish.

Central Germany

Saxony and Thuringia are slightly less meat-obsessed than some of their cousins. *Kartoffelsuppe* (potato soup) is a favourite, and *Leipziger Allerlei* (Leipzig hotpot) often comes in vegetarian versions. There are even lentils to be found in such dishes as *Linsensuppe mit Thüringer Rotwurst* (lentil soup with long, thin, spiced sausages).

Labskaus is a sailor's favourite and, some locals claim, brilliant hangover food – plenty of salt, plenty of fat and not too hard to chew.

Hamburg & the North

No two dishes better sum up northern Germany's warming, seafaring fodder than *Labskaus* and *Grünkohl mit Pinkel*. There are variations, but traditional *Labskaus* from Hamburg is a minced dish of salt herring, corned beef, pig lard, potato and beetroot, topped with gherkins and a fried egg. *Grünkohl mit Pinkel* combines steamed kale with pork belly, bacon and *Pinkelwurst* (a spicy pork, beef, oat and onion sausage from Bremen). *Aalsuppe* (eel soup) is sweet and sour – it's garnished with bacon and vegetables, and spiced with apricots, pears or prunes.

As you move towards Scandinavia, the German diet begins to encompass Nordic staples, such as rollmops and *Hering* (herring) in all its other guises – raw, smoked, pickled or rolled in sour cream.

Mecklenburg-Western Pomerania has a quite distinctive cuisine, with locals famed for liking things sweet and sour. Take *Mecklenburger Rippenbraten* (rolled pork stuffed with lemons, apples, plums, and raisins), for example; or *Mecklenburgische Buttermilchsuppe* (a sweet buttermilk soup flavoured with spices and jam); or the Russian-style *Soljanka* (sour soup with sausage or fish, garnished with lemon and sour cream). Other typical mixes include raisins with cabbage, honey with pork, and plums with duck. Even the typical *Eintopf* (stew, often a potato version) is served with sugar and vinegar on the side.

5 million litres of beer, give or take a stein, are downed by party-goers at Munich's Oktoberfest every year.

Grape Versus Grain

Here's to Beer!

Few things are as deeply ingrained in the German psyche as the love of beer. *'Hopfen und Malz – Gott erhalt's!'* (Hops and malt are in God's hands) goes the saying, which is fitting given the almost religious intensity with which beer is brewed, consumed and celebrated – not least at the world's biggest festival, Oktoberfest. Brewing here goes back to Germanic tribes, and later, monks, so it follows in a hallowed tradition.

The 'secret' of the country's golden nectar dates back to the 1516 *Reinheitsgebot* (purity law) passed in Bavaria, demanding breweries use just four ingredients – malt, yeast, hops and water. Though it stopped being

GERMANY'S TOP 10 BEERS

» **Pils** (pilsener) This bottom-fermented full beer, with pronounced hop flavour and creamy head, has an alcohol content around 4.8%.

» **Weizen/Weissbier** (wheat beer) Predominating in the south, especially in Bavaria, this is 5.4% alcohol. A *Hefeweizen* has a stronger shot of yeast, whereas *Kristallweizen* is clearer with more fizz. These beers are fruity and spicy, often re-calling bananas and cloves. Decline offers of lemon as it ruins the head and – beer purists say – the flavour.

» **Dunkles** (dark lager) Brewed throughout Germany, but especially in Bavaria. With a light use of hops, it's full-bodied with strong malty aromas.

» **Helles** (pale lager) *Helles* (pale or light) refers to the colour, not the alcohol content, which is still 4.6% to 5%. Brewing strongholds are Bavaria, Baden-Württemberg and the Ruhr region. It has strong malt aromas and is slightly sweet.

» **Altbier** A dark, full beer with malted barley, from the Düsseldorf area.

» **Berliner Weisse** Berlin's top-fermented beer, which comes *rot* (red) or *grün* (green), with a *Schuss* (dash) of raspberry or woodruff syrup respectively. A cool, fruity summer choice.

» **Bockbier** Strong beers with 7% alcohol. There's a *'Bock'* for every occasion, such as *Maibock* (for May/spring) and *Weihnachtsbock* (brewed for Christmas). *Eisbock* is dark and aromatic. *Bock* beers originate from Einbeck, near Hanover.

» **Kölsch** By law, this top-fermented beer can only be brewed in or around Cologne. It is about 4.8% alcohol, has a solid hop flavour and pale colour, and is served in small glasses (0.2L) called *Stangen* (literally 'sticks').

» **Leipziger Gose** Flavoured with salt and coriander, this contrives to have a sting-ingly refreshing taste, with some plummy overtones. Tart like Berliner Weisse, it's often served with sweeteners, such as cherry *(Kirsch)* liqueur or the almond-flavoured *Allasch*.

» **Schwarzbier** (black beer) Slightly stronger, this dark, full beer has an alcohol content of 4.8% to 5%. It's fermented using roasted malt.

a legal requirement in 1987 when the EU struck it down as uncompetitive, many German brewers still conform to it anyway, seeing it as a good marketing tool against mass-market, chemical-happy competitors.

Kloster Weltenburg, near Kelheim (on the Danube north of Munich) is the world's oldest monastery brewery, whose Weltenburg Barock Dunckel won a medal at the 2006 World Beer Cup in Seattle. This light, smooth beer has a malty, toasty finish. Other connoisseurs believe the earthy Andechs Doppelbock Dunkel, produced by the Benedictines in Andechs near Munich, to be among the world's best.

Beer Varieties

Despite frequently tying their own hands and giving themselves just four ingredients to play with, Germans achieve distinctively different beers via subtle variations in the basic production process. At the simplest level, a brewer can choose a particular yeast for top or bottom fermenting.

The most popular form of brewing is bottom fermentation, which accounts for about 85% of German beers, notably the *Pils* (pilsner) popular throughout Germany, most *Bock* beers and the *Helles* (pale lager) type found in Bavaria.

Top fermentation is used for the *Weizenbier/Weissbier* (wheat/white beer) popular in Berlin and Bavaria, Cologne's *Kölsch* and the very few stouts brewed in the country.

Many beers are regional, meaning a Saxon Rechenberger cannot be found in Düsseldorf, where the locally brewed Altbier is the taste of choice.

There are 1300 German breweries that keep great beer-making traditions alive and turn out 5000 different beers. Eleven monasteries continue to produce beer today; these are known as Klosterbrauerein.

The Rise & Rise of German Wine

'The Germans', wrote Mark Twain in *A Tramp Abroad* (1880), 'are exceedingly fond of Rhine wines; they are put up in tall, slender bottles, and are considered a pleasant beverage. One tells them from vinegar by the label.' He was not alone in his sentiments.

For decades the name of German wine was sullied by the cloyingly sweet taste of Liebfraumilch and the naff image of Blue Nun. What a difference a decade can make. Thanks to rebranding campaigns, a new generation of wine growers and an overall rise in quality, German wine is staging a comeback in the 21st century. This triumph was marked at 2012 wine awards such as the International Wine and Spirit Competition (IWSC) held in London, where 71 medals went to German wines, including one Gold Outstanding for a Franconian 2010 riesling from Weingut Horst Sauer.

Even discerning wine critics have been pouring praise on German winemakers of late. According to Master of Wine Tim Atkin (www.timatkin.com), 'Germany makes the best rieslings of all'; waxing lyrical on the country's Pinot noirs, he muses, 'if only the Germans didn't keep most of them to themselves.'

Top German Wine Producers

» Dönnhoff – Award-winning rieslings.

» Weingut Meyer-Näkel – Some of Germany's best Pinot noirs.

» Wittmann – Celebrated Rheinhessen Silvaner and rieslings.

Grape Varieties

Having produced wines since Roman times, Germany now has more than 1000 sq km of vineyards, mostly on the Rhine and Moselle riverbanks. Despite the common association with riesling grapes (particularly in its best wine regions), the less acidic Müller-Thurgau *(Rivaner)* grape is more widespread. Meanwhile, the Gewürztraminer grape produces spicy wines with an intense bouquet. What Germans call *Grauburgunder* is known to the rest of the world as Pinot gris.

German reds are light and lesser known. *Spätburgunder* (Pinot noir) is the best of the bunch and goes into some velvety, full-bodied reds with an occasional almond taste.

Wine Regions

There are 13 official wine-growing areas, the best being the Mosel-Saar-Ruwer region. It boasts some of the world's steepest vineyards, where the predominantly riesling grapes are still hand-picked. Slate soil on the hillsides gives the wines a flinty taste. Chalkier riverside soils are planted with the Elbling grape, an ancient Roman variety.

East of the Moselle, the Nahe region produces fragrant, fruity and full-bodied wines using Müller-Thurgau and Silvaner grapes, as well as riesling.

Riesling grapes are also the mainstay in Rheingau and Mittelrhein (Middle Rhine), two other highly respected wine-growing pockets. Rheinhessen, south of Rheingau, is responsible for *Liebfraumilch,* but also some top rieslings.

For a comprehensive rundown of all German wine-growing regions, grape varieties, news of the hottest winemakers and information on tours or courses, visit www.winesof germany.co.uk, www.german wines.de and www.german wineusa.org.

Other wine regions include Ahr, Pfalz (both Rhineland-Palatinate), Hessische Bergstrasse (Hesse), Baden (Baden-Württemberg), Würzburg (Bavaria) and Elbtal (Saxony).

The Württemberg region, around Stuttgart, produces some of the country's best reds, while Saxony-Anhalt's Saale-Unstrut region is home to Rotkäppchen (Little Red Riding Hood) sparkling wine, a former GDR brand that's been a big hit in the new Germany.

Literature, Theatre & Film

Literature

Early Writing

Oral literature during Charlemagne's reign (c 800) and secular epics performed by 12th-century knights are the earliest surviving literary forms, but the man who shook up the literary language was Martin Luther, whose 16th-century translation of the Bible set the stage for German writers.

In the 17th century, Christoph Martin Wieland (1733–1813) penned his *Geschichte des Agathon* (Agathon; 1766–67), a landmark in German literature as it was the first *Bildungsroman* (a novel showing the development of the hero); Wieland was also the first to translate Shakespeare into German.

Shortly after this, the biggest hitter in German literary history, Johann Wolfgang von Goethe (1749–1832) rose to prominence, later joining forces with Friedrich Schiller (1759–1805) in a celebrated period known as Weimarer Klassik (Weimar classicism). Writing in Goethe's lifetime, the lyricist and early Romantic poet, Friedrich Hölderlin (1770–1843), created delicate balance and rhythms.

Serious academics who wrote *German Grammar* and *History of the German Language*, the Grimm brothers, Jakob (1785–1863) and Wilhelm (1786–1859), are best known for their collection of fairy tales, myths and legends. The Düsseldorf-born Heinrich Heine (1797–1856) produced one of Germany's finest collections of poems, *Buch der Lieder* (Book of Songs) in 1827, but it was his politically scathing *Deutschland: Ein Wintermärchen* (Germany: A Winter's Tale) that contributed to his work being banned in 1835.

The late 19th century belongs to Saxonian Karl May (1842–1912), whose *Winnetou* stories about Native Americans have sold more than 200 million copies. He remains an immensely popular read across Eastern Europe.

Modern & Contemporary

The Weimar years witnessed the flowering of Lübeck-born Thomas Mann (1875–1955), recipient of the 1929 Nobel Prize for Literature, whose greatest novels focus on social forms of the day. Mann's older brother, Heinrich (1871–1950), adopted a stronger political stance than Thomas in his work; his *Professor Unrat* (1905) provided the raw material for the Marlene Dietrich film *Der Blaue Engel* (The Blue Angel).

Berlin's underworld during the Weimar Republic served as the focus for the novel *Berlin Alexanderplatz* (1929) by Alfred Döblin (1878–1957).

The *Complete Fairy Tales* by Jacob and Wilhelm Grimm is a beautiful collection of 210 yarns, passed orally between generations and collected by German literature's most magical brothers.

Find reviews of the latest contemporary German books to be translated into English at www.new-books-in-german.com.

748

Hermann Hesse (1877–1962), another Nobel prize winner, adopted the theme of the outsider in *Steppenwolf* (1927) and imbued New Romantic spirituality into his work after a journey to India in 1911. Antiwar novel *Im Westen nichts Neues* (All Quiet on the Western Front; 1929) by Osnabrück-born Erich Maria Remarque (1898–1970) was banned (and burnt) in 1933 and remains one of the most widely read German books.

Of the generation that has established itself in the literary scene since 1945, Günter Grass (b 1927) is the most celebrated. Bursting into the limelight with his first novel, *Die Blechtrommel* (Tin Drum; 1959) he grew to become a postwar moral icon – until this was called into question by his youthful membership of the Waffen-SS, which he revealed in *Beim Häuten der Zwiebel* (Peeling the Onion; 2006).

Of East Germany's writers Christa Wolf (b 1929) is the best known and most controversial; she admitted to working as an informer for East Germany's secret police briefly in the late 1950s before the state got heavy on artists. She later spoke out for dissidents.

Others to have a made a name for themselves more recently include Thomas Brussig (b 1964), who rose to prominence in the mid-1990s with *Helden wie Wir* (Heroes like Us; 1995); crime novelist Botho Strauss; novelist WG Sebald (1944–2001), who assured his place as one of Germany's best writers with his powerful portrayal of four exiles in *Die Ausgewanderten* (Emigrants); Munich-based writer and playwright, Patrick Süskind (b 1949) of *Das Parfum* (Perfume) fame; and Russian-born Wladimir Kaminer (b 1967) whose highly popular *Russendisko* (Russian Disco; 2000) was widely translated.

The Deutscher Buchpreis (German Book Award), the equivalent of Britain's Booker Prize and the US National Book Awards (in fiction), is a good guide to what's new each year. Search for short-listed and winning authors at www.deutscher-buchpreis.de.

Theatre

With more than 6000 stages across the country, Germans are avid theatregoers and the average theatre will put on around 20 productions annually. Most plays are staged in multipurpose theatres (interspersing plays with opera and music) and are state-subsidised organisations.

Enlightenment masters who frequently get a showing include Saxony's Gotthold Ephraim Lessing (1729–81); Württemberg-born Friedrich Schiller, who features especially strongly in Weimar's theatre landscape today; and, of course, Johann Wolfgang von Goethe, who tinkered with his two-part *Faust* for 60 years, fashioning one of Germany's most powerfully enduring dramas about the human condition.

Woyzeck by Georg Büchner (1813–37) is another popular piece and, having anticipated Theatre of the Absurd, lends itself to innovative staging. In 1894 the director of Berlin's Deutsches Theater hired a young actor, Max Reinhardt (1873–1943), who became German theatre's most influential expressionist director, working briefly with dramatist Bertolt Brecht. Both men went into exile under Nazism – Brecht to try his hand at Hollywood scripts and to answer for his Marxist politics before the House Committee on Un-American Activities. Brecht's *Leben des Galilei* (Life of Galileo; 1943/47) was rewritten with a new ending after atomic bombs fell on Hiroshima and Nagasaki.

After WWII Augsburg-born Brecht returned to East Berlin where he established the Berliner Ensemble, a venue that produced his plays and became one of the capital's most vibrant theatres.

Heiner Müller (1929–95), a Marxist who was critical of the reality of the GDR, became unpalatable in both Germanys in the 1950s. In the 1980s, existential works such as *Quartet* (1980) earned him an avant-

Günter Grass' *Ein weites Feld* (Too Far Afield; 1992) addresses 'unification without unity' after the fall of the wall.

Read up-to-date reviews of the latest plays by German playwrights and other cultural offerings at www.goethe.de/enindex.htm.

MARLENE DIETRICH

Marlene Dietrich (1901–92), born Marie Magdalene Dietrich into a good middle-class family in Berlin, was the daughter of a Prussian officer. After acting school, she worked in the silent-film industry in the1920s, stereotyped as a hard-living, libertine flapper. But she soon carved a niche in the film fantasies of lower-middle-class men as the dangerously seductive *femme fatale*, best typified by her appearance in the 1930 talkie *Der Blaue Engel* (The Blue Angel), which turned her into a Hollywood star.

The film was the start of a five-year collaboration with director Josef von Sternberg, during which time she built on her image of erotic opulence – dominant and severe, but always with a touch of self-irony. Dressed in men's suits for *Marocco* in 1930, she lent her 'sexuality is power' attitude bisexual tones, winning a new audience overnight.

Dietrich stayed in Hollywood after the Nazi rise to power, though Hitler, no less immune to her charms, reportedly promised perks and the red-carpet treatment if she moved back to Germany. She took US citizenship in 1937 and sang on the front to Allied GIs.

After the war, Dietrich retreated slowly from the public eye, making occasional appearances in films, but mostly cutting records and performing live. Her final years were spent in Paris, bed-ridden and accepting few visitors, immortal in spirit as mortality caught up with her.

garde label. In the1960s, Berlin director Rudolf Noelte (1921–2002) took centre stage as the master of postwar German theatre.

Directors such as Peter Stein (b 1937) have earned contemporary German theatre its reputation for producing classic plays in an innovative and provocative manner. Part of the so-called Junge Wilde (Wild Youth) movement in the 1970s and 1980s, Stein founded Berlin's Schaubühne theatre in 1970; today it is one of Germany's best.

Berlin-born Frank Castorf (b 1951) is arguably Germany's most dynamic contemporary director, heading up Berlin's Volksbühne and piecing together innovative productions. Christoph Schlingensief (b 1960) is the best known of Germany's new breed, having staged productions at Berlin's Volksbühne and elsewhere; he's also active in film and action art.

The most-performed contemporary playwright is the Göttingen-born Roland Schimmelpfennig (b 1967), who has worked at Berlin's Schaubühne and Volksbühne, as well as Vienna's Burgtheater. Other contemporary playwrights to watch out for include Moritz Rinke (b 1967), Rainald Goetz (b 1954), Werner Fritsch (b 1960), and Simone Schneider (b 1962).

> Fritz Lang, director of the famous film *Metropolis* (1927), fled to America after Goebbels offered him a position as head of the Nazi propaganda film unit.

Film

German film has a long and illustrious history, perhaps explaining why local movies are popular and account for about 20% of box-office sales, despite their comparatively modest budgets.

Germany's cinematic story begins at the Universum Film AG (UFA) studio in Babelsberg (Potsdam), founded in 1911 and now a large multimedia complex. One early UFA classic is Fritz Lang's silent classic *Metropolis* (1927), about a subterranean proletarian subclass.

In the early 1930s Josef von Sternberg's *Der Blaue Engel* (The Blue Angel; 1930), saw Marlene Dietrich woo audiences with hypnotic sensuality and become a star overnight. The 1930s were productive but difficult years. The premier of Fritz Lang's talkie, *Das Testament des Dr Mabuse* (Testament of Dr Mabuse; 1933), about a psychiatric patient with plans to take over the world, had to be shifted to Austria for obvious reasons. Hitler also drove acting greats such as Peter Lorre (1904–64) and Billy Wilder (1906–2002) into Hollywood exile.

> Read what the critics say about 500-plus German films at www.german-cinema.de.

TOP FIVE GDR RETRO FILMS

» *Good Bye, Lenin!* (2003), the cult box-office smash hit by Wolfgang Becker revolving around a son trying to recreate the GDR for a bedridden ailing mother whose health couldn't stand the shock of a fallen Wall.

» Leander Haussmann's nostalgia-inducing *Sonnenallee* (Sun Alley; 1999), set in a fantastical Wall-clad East Berlin in the 1970s.

» *Helden wie Wir* (Heroes like Us; 1999), directed by Sebastian Peterson and based on the novel by Thomas Brussig, sees the protagonist recount the story of his life, including how his penis allegedly leads to the collapse of the Berlin Wall.

» Haussmann's humorous *Herr Lehmann* (Berlin Blues; 2003) relates the story of a bartending actor in West Berlin's bohemian Kreuzberg district just as the Wall comes down.

» Dull lives are led in dull Frankfurt an der Oder in dull East Germany – until Ellen and Chris are caught doing it. Laughs abound in Andreas Dresen's *Halbe Treppe* (Grill Point; 2001).

The 1960s witnessed the New German Cinema movement (Junger Deutscher Film) which brought directors Rainer Werner Fassbinder (1945–82), Wim Wenders (b 1945), Volker Schlöndorff (b 1939), Werner Herzog (b 1942) and director-actor Margarethe von Trotta (b 1942) to the fore. All except Fassbinder, Germany's enfant terrible of film, are working today. The resonance of Fassbinder's *Die Sehnsucht der Veronika Voss* (Longing of Veronica Voss; 1981), Wenders' *Paris Texas* (1984) and *Der Himmel über Berlin* (Wings of Desire; 1987), Herzog's *Aguirre, der Zorn Gottes* (Aguirre, the Wrath of God; 1972) and Schlöndorff's film version of Grass' *Die Blechtrommel* (Tin Drum; 1979) can still be felt on today's screens.

Renamed DEFA (Deutsche Film-Aktiengesellschaft), the illustrious UFA studios produced East German films until the fall of the Berlin Wall, most notably adaptations of German and Slavic fairy stories.

The 1990s saw the arrival of Tom Tykwer (b 1965), whose *Lola Rennt* (Run Lola Run; 1998) established his reputation as one of Germany's best new directors. Since then his work has included a film version of Süskind's novel *Das Parfum* (Perfume: The Story of a Murderer; 2006). Directors Christian Petzold (b 1960), Marc Rothemund (b 1968), Fatih Akın (b 1973), Oliver Hirschbiegel (b 1957) and Florian von Donnersmarck (b 1973) emerged late in the decade.

Of these, Marc Rothemund directed possibly Germany's film of the century so far, the highly acclaimed *Sophie Scholl - Die letzten Tage* (Sophie Scholl: The Final Days; 2005), a disturbing portrayal of the interrogation and trial of White Rose anti-Nazi resistance movement members.

Der Baader Meinhof Komplex (The Baader Meinhof Complex; 2008), directed by Ulrich Edel (b 1947) and based on a book by Stephan Aust (b 1946) about the late 1960s and early 1970s Red Army Faction group of terrorists, was nominated for an Oscar in 2009 for the Best Foreign Language Film. However the most visible international face of contemporary German film is Wolfgang Becker's *Good Bye, Lenin!* (2003), with its recreation of GDR life for a bed-ridden mother. Oliver Hirschbiegel's highly charged *Der Untergang* (Downfall; 2004) is a chilling account of Hitler's last days, mostly set in his Berlin bunker. Florian von Donnersmarck's excellent *Das Leben der Anderen* (Lives of Others; 2006) portrays the work of the Stasi in the 1980s.

Music

What Germany lacks in literature it certainly makes up for in music, with world-famous composers such as Beethoven, Bach and Brahms on its books. It's also a country that's punched above its weight in the popular music era, and one of the few outside the English-speaking world to have influenced rock, pop and electro music in a significant way.

Love Ballads to Contemporary Classical

German music in the 12th century is closely associated with Walther von der Vogelweide (c 1170–1230), who achieved renown with love ballads. A more formalised troubadour tradition followed, but it was baroque organist Johann Sebastian Bach (1685–1750), born in Eisenach, who most influenced early European music. His legacy can be explored in Leipzig's Bach-Museum in the house in which he died. Another museum in Eisenach is dedicated to his life and work.

Georg Friedrich Händel (1685–1759) was a contemporary of Bach who hailed from Halle in Saxony-Anhalt (his house is also now a museum), but lived and worked almost exclusively in London from 1714.

Händel's music found favour in the circle of Vienna's classical composers, and it was Joseph Haydn (1732–1809) who taught Bonn-born Ludwig van Beethoven (1770–1827), whose work reflects the Enlightenment. Beethoven is also the most important of the composers who paved the way for Romanticism. His birth house in Bonn has also been set up as a museum.

Among the Romantic composers, Hamburg-born Felix Mendelssohn-Bartholdy (1809–47) is hailed as a genius. He penned his first overture at the age of 17 and later dug up works by JS Bach to give the latter the fame he enjoys today.

Born in Leipzig, Richard Wagner (1813–83) lords it over 19th-century German music. He was Bavarian King Ludwig II's favourite composer, and Hitler, who picked up on an anti-Semitic essay and some late-life ramblings on German virtues, famously turned him into a post-mortem Nazi icon. An annual summer music festival in Bayreuth celebrates Wagner's life and works.

Hamburg brought forth Johannes Brahms (1833–97) and his influential symphonies, and chamber and piano works. Two figures whose legacies can be explored today in cities such as Bonn, Leipzig and Zwickau are composer Robert Schumann (1810–56) and his gifted pianist-spouse Clara Wieck (1819–96). Schumann (born in Zwickau) and Wieck (born in Leipzig) are buried in Bonn's Alter Friedhof.

Pulsating 1920s Berlin ushered in Vienna-born Arnold Schönberg (1874–1951), inventor of a new tonal relationship that turned music on its head. One of his pupils, Hanns Eisler (1898–1962), went into exile in 1933 but returned to East Berlin to teach in 1950. Among his works was the East German national anthem, *Auferstanden aus Ruinen* (Resurrected

Singer Lena Meyer-Landrut won the Eurovision Song Contest in 2010; only the second time Germany emerged victorious in the competition's history.

For more information, practical and historical, on the Berlin Philharmonic Orchestra, tune to www.berliner -philharmoniker.de.

from Ruins), lyricless from 1961 when its pro-reunification words fell out of favour with party honchos.

Hanau-born Paul Hindemith (1895–1963) was banned by the Nazis and composed his most important orchestral compositions outside his homeland. The Hindemith Institute (www.hindemith.org) in Frankfurt am Main promotes his music and safeguards his estate. Perhaps better known is Dessau-born Kurt Weill (1900–50), another composer who fled the Nazi terror. He teamed up with Bertolt Brecht in the 1920s and wrote the music for *Die Morität von Mackie Messer* (Mack the Knife) in Brecht's Dreigroschenoper (Threepenny Opera). Weill ended up in New York, where he wrote successful Broadway musicals.

Germany's most prestigious orchestra, the Berliner Philharmoniker (1882), was shaped by conductor Wilhelm Furtwängler (1886–1954) and, from 1954 until his death in 1989, the illustrious Herbert von Karajan (1908–89). Dresden opera orchestra and the Leipzig Gewandhausorchester are also important stops on the classical trail. The young Kammersymphonie Berlin (Berlin Chamber Symphony), established in 1991, recaptures the multifaceted music scene of 1920s Berlin through its focus on less-common orchestral works.

Contemporary

Jazz is surprisingly popular in Germany, and most towns have a jazz club or two. Till Brönner (b 1971), who studied at the Cologne Music School, has trumpeted, sung and composed his way to renown, recording his *Oceana* album (2006) in Los Angeles with contributions from Madeleine Peyroux (b 1974) and singing Italian model and former First Lady of France Carla Bruni (b 1967).

On the down-tempo scene, where you find various blends of jazz, dub, hip hop, house and African music, Jazzanova (www.jazzanova.com) is the undisputed master, with remixes and original tunes. It founded the Sonar Kollektiv label (www.sonarkollektiv.com) in the late 1990s, which today includes German acts like Micatone (www.micatone.de, in German) and international figures like Daniel Paul, Georg Levin and Forss.

These contemporaries complement the soaring sounds of musicians such as Albert Mangelsdorff (1928–2005), saxophonist Heinz Sauer (b1932) and Klaus Doldinger (b 1936), who formed the legendary fusion

The most successful German pop singer bar none is Sandra Cretu (b 1962), who has sold more than 30 million records across the globe.

band Passport. Jazz Fest Berlin brings the best of German and European jazz to the capital each November.

One big question facing most German rock bands is whether to sing in German, English or both. Scorpions, probably the most successful rock band abroad, sang in English. A contemporary band who chose to sing in German and found success abroad is Rammstein, known for its provocative lyrics and intense sounds, and part of a 'New German Hard' (Neue deutsche Härte) movement that combines industrial rock, metal and dance. Two other highly successful bands abroad that didn't really have this dilemma were the (mostly) instrumental Tangerine Dream and Kraftwerk. Tangerine Dream has the honour of being the first band to cut a chart success with Virgin Records in the 1970s. About three decades before its time, Düsseldorf-based Kraftwerk created the musical foundations for techno, which in turn spawned Berlin's legendary techno-orientated Love Parade in 1989.

Members of the Neue Deutsche Welle (NDW; German New Wave) always sang in German – although Nena, its tame international mother ship, successfully recorded her hit single '99 Luftballons' in English, too. The movement spawned the Hamburger Schule (Hamburg School) of musicians, with recognised acts such as Blumfeld, Die Sterne and the Tocotronic still going strong since emerging in the 1990s. Die-hard legends gathering no moss are Germany's most enduring punk band, Düsseldorf-based Die Toten Hosen; punk queen Nina Hagen (b 1955), whose transformations still seem ahead of their time; and Die Ärzte. Meanwhile, Herbert Grönemeyer (b 1956), 'Germany's Springsteen' (also a decent actor), and leather legend Udo Lindenberg (b 1946) are still kicking on.

As well as language, another choice facing bands is whether to base themselves in Hamburg or Berlin. Both cities are important capitals for rock bands but exert different influences – the Berlin sound is generally somewhat harder, while Hamburg bands often retain stronger shades of German New Wave, with a punk or lighter pop flavour. Giessen-bred Juli is one soft-rock band that works out of Hamburg, where the sound is often more melodic. Bautzen-born Silbermond is based in Berlin, whereas Wir Sind Helden started in Hamburg and shifted to Berlin.

Element of Crime, led by multitalented Sven Regener (b1961), has probably had more influence on the arts spectrum than anyone else, having composed and played scores for films including Leander Haussmann's *Sonnenallee* (Sun Alley) and *Herr Lehmann* (Regener also wrote the book and script of the latter).

Huddled between the popular rock, orchestral and electronic dance genres is Barbara Morgenstern (b 1971), who began her singing career in Hamburg before moving to Berlin, where she branched out into a solo career.

Since Tangerine Dream and Kraftwerk, new generations of electronic musicians have moved into the limelight, making music spawned from techno but inhabiting splinter genres. Berlin-based Apparat (Sascha Ring) is closely associated with the charmingly named Shitkatapult records, one of the top labels for techno and post-techno sounds since the late 1990s. The release *Walls* (2007) was one of the top electro albums and has since been followed by *Things to be Frickled* and more recently *Moderat*, which he released on Ellen Allien's BPitch Control, another top label, as a collaboration with Modeselektor (www.modeselektor.de, in German). The latter churns out IDM (intelligent dance music) influenced by electro and hip hop.

MUSIC CONTEMPORARY

'Once every generation, a German band achieves world-wide success... Yes, it's Nietzsche Rock!'

NME music magazine on the popular metal band Rammstein.

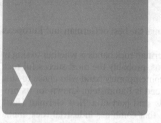

Visual Arts

Whether it be medieval fresco work, oil-on-canvas masterpieces, eclectic Bauhaus or exciting industrial design and fashion, Germany abounds in visual arts for all tastes and interests.

Frescos to Expressionists

Germany's earliest fresco work dates from Carolingian times (c 800) and is in Trier's St Maximin crypt, now on display at Trier's Bischöfliches Dom-und Diözesanmuseum, and the Stiftskirche St Georg on Reichenau Island. Stained-glass enthusiasts will find colourful religious motifs lighting up Augsburg and Cologne cathedrals. By the 15th century, Cologne artists were putting landscapes on religious panels, some of which are on display in Hamburg's Kunsthalle.

The heavyweight of German Renaissance art is the Nuremberg-born Albrecht Dürer (1471–1528), who was the first to seriously compete with the Italian masters; the Alte Pinakothek (Munich) has several famous works by Dürer, and his Nuremberg house is now a museum. In Wittenberg, Dürer influenced Franconian-born court painter Lucas Cranach the Elder (1472–1553) whose *Apoll und Diana in Waldiger Landschaft* (Apollo and Diana in a Forest Landscape; 1530) forms part of the collection at Berlin's Gemäldegalerie (Picture Gallery).

Two centuries later, sculpture became integrated into Germany's buildings and gardens, creating the inspiration for the imposing work by Andreas Schlüter (1660–1714), *Reiterdenkmal des Grossen Kurfürsten* (Equestrian Monument of the Great Elector), in front of Berlin's Schloss Charlottenburg. The four-horse chariot with Victoria on Berlin's Brandenburg Gate is the work of Germany's leading neoclassical sculptor, Johann Gottfried Schadow (1764–1850).

During the baroque period (from the 17th to mid-18th century), palace walls were frescoed to create the illusion of generous space. The grand staircase by Balthasar Neumann (1687–1753) in Würzburg's Residenz is arguably the finest example.

In the mid-18th century, neoclassicism ushered back in the human figure and an emphasis on Roman and Greek mythology. Hesse-born Johann Heinrich Tischbein (1751–1829) painted Goethe at this time in a classical landscape surrounded by antique objects. You can see *Goethe in der Campagna* (1787) in Frankfurt am Main's Städel Museum.

Religious themes, occasionally mystic, dominated 19th-century romanticism. Goethe hated the works of Caspar David Friedrich (1774–1840), indelicately suggesting they ought to be 'smashed against the table'. A room is dedicated to Friedrich's works in Hamburg's Kunsthalle, and his work is also a highlight of Berlin's Alte Nationalgalerie.

Also in the exciting collection of Hamburg's Kunsthalle are works by the founder of the German romantic movement, Philipp Otto Runge (1777–1810), as well as intensely religious works by the Nazarener (Nazareths). The

Jugendstil – an alternative name in German for art nouveau – takes its name from the arts magazine *Jugend* (the word Jugend means 'youth'), first published in Munich in 1896.

ART NOUVEAU

museum also showcases some later realistic works of Cologne-born Wilhelm Leibl (1844–1900), who specialised in painting Bavarian folk.

German Impressionists are well represented in the Moderne Galerie of Saarbrücken's Saarland Museum. Key exponents of the late-19th-century movement include Max Liebermann (1847–1935), whose work was often slammed as 'ugly' and 'socialist'; Fritz von Uhde (1848–1911); and Lovis Corinth (1858–1925), whose later work, *Die Kindheit des Zeus* (Childhood of Zeus; 1905) – a richly coloured frolic in nature with intoxicated, grotesque elements – is housed in Bremen's Kunsthalle.

The Dresden art scene spawned Die Brücke (The Bridge) in 1905. Its expressionist members Ernst Kirchner (1880–1938), Erich Heckel (1883–1970) and Karl Schmidt-Rottluff (1884–1976) employed primitivist and cubist elements, but Germany's best expressionist painter, the North Frisian Emil Nolde (1867–1956), was an artistic lone wolf who only fleetingly belonged to Die Brücke and was forbidden from working by the Nazis in 1941. His famous *Bauernhof* (1910) is housed in Museumsberg Flensburg.

Munich's Städtische Galerie im Lenbachhaus showcases a second group of expressionists, Munich-based Der Blaue Reiter (The Blue Rider), centred on Wassily Kandinsky (1866–1944), Gabriele Münter (1877–1962), Paul Klee (1879–1940) and Franz Marc (1880–1916).

Between the Wars

After a creative surge in the 1920s, the big chill of Nazi conformity sent Germany into artistic deep freeze in the 1930s and 1940s. In the capital many artists were classified as 'degenerate' and forced into exile – where a creative explosion abroad took place especially among the Bauhaus movement protagonists who settled in the USA. Other artists were murdered, retreated from public life or put away their brushes and paints forever. In Quedlinburg a fine collection of works by Lyonel Feininger (1871–1956) survives thanks to a local citizen who hid them from the Nazis.

One of Germany's most influential visual artists was Käthe Kollwitz (1867–1945), who travelled through naturalism and expressionism to arrive at agitprop and socialistrealism. Complete series of her *Ein Weberaufstand* (A Weavers' Revolt; 1897) etchings and lithography based on a play by Gerhart Hauptmann (1862–1946), as well as other works, are showcased in Käthe Kollwitz museums in Berlin and Cologne.

Berlin's Bauhaus Archive/Museum of Design and Weimar's Bauhaus Museum have fascinating exhibits on the Bauhaus movement, which continues to shape art and design. Works by Kandinsky, Hungarian László Moholy-Nagy (1895–1946), Klee and the sculptor Gerhard Marcks (1889–1981) can be found at the Berlin venue.

Artist Joseph Beuys was a radio operator in a fighter plane shot down over the Crimea during WWII. He claims to have been nursed back to health by local Tartars, who covered him in tallow and wrapped him in felt.

The Design preis der Bundesrepublik Deutschland (German Design Prize) is Germany's most prestigious award for design (www. designpreis.de).

VISUAL ARTS BETWEEN THE WARS

DEGENERATE ART

Abstract expressionism, surrealism and Dadaism – 'Jewish subversion' and 'artistic Bolshevism' in the eyes of the Nazis – were definitely not Hitler's favourite movements. In fact by 1937 such forms of expression fell under the axe of *Entartung* (degeneracy), a German biological term borrowed by the Nazis to describe virtually all modern movements. The same year, paintings by Klee, Beckmann, Dix and others, all supposedly spawned by the madness of 'degenerates', were exhibited in Munich and promptly defaced in protest. Ironically, the exhibition drew more than two million curious Germans, more than any other modern art show in history.

A year later, a law was passed allowing for the forced removal of degenerate works from private collections. While some art collectors saved their prized art from Nazi hands, many pieces were sold abroad to rake in foreign currency and in 1939 about 4000 paintings were publicly burned in Berlin.

Modern & Contemporary

Post-1945 the creative influence of expressionists such as Nolde, Schmidt-Rottluff and Kandinsky was revived; and a new abstract expressionism took root in the work of Stuttgart's Willi Baumeister (1889–1955) and Ernst Wilhelm Nay (1902–68) in Berlin.

In the 1950s and 1960s, Düsseldorf-based Gruppe Zero (Group Zero) plugged into Bauhaus, using light and space as a creative basis. The 'light ballets' of Otto Piene (b 1928), relying on projection techniques, were among the best known. Celle's Kunstmuseum uses some of his light works for effect.

Arguably Germany's most exciting contemporary painter and sculptor is Anselm Kiefer (b 1945), some of whose works are in Berlin's (confusingly named) Hamburger Bahnhof. His monumental *Census* (1967) consists of massive lead folios arranged on shelves as a protest against a 1967 census in Germany; another, the haunting *Mohn und Gedächtnis* (Poppy and Memory; 1989), is a large lead aircraft with three small glass windows in the side filled with poppy seeds. Both are regularly on display.

The same Berlin museum permanently displays works by Düsseldorf's Joseph Beuys (1921–86). Wherever Beuys laid his trademark hat, controversy erupted. The largest collections of his work are in Darmstadt's Hessisches Landesmuseum (including his revealing *Stuhl mit Fett*; Chair with Fat; 1963) and in Schloss Moyland, near Kalkar in North Rhine-Westphalia.

Jörg Immendorff (1945–2007) – like Kiefer, he has also worked in stage design and was one of Beuys' students – has become one of Germany's most collectable artists, especially since his death in 2007. Two icons of German painting are Gerhard Richter (b 1932) and Sigmar Polke (1941–2010). Richter, who was born in Dresden and fled to West Germany in the early 1960s, created a major new work in Cologne's cathedral in 2007 – a vast stained-glass window consisting of 11,500 mesmerising square pieces. Polke, along with Richter and others, relied heavily on pop art and what they dubbed 'capitalist realism' – which they used to describe a counterbalance in the West to socialist realism. The influence of the two is as immeasurable as the prices their works command at auctions today. The Museum Ludwig in Cologne is where you can see a good range of Polke's works.

Bavarian Florian Thomas (b 1966) is one of a new generation of Germany's contemporary artists who owe much to the ground-breaking work of Richter and Polke. His work can be found in the Museum Frieder Burda in Baden-Baden. His *Lieber Onkel Dieter!* (Dear Uncle Dieter!) and *Arusha* are definite highlights. In the same museum are works by Eberhard Havekost (b 1967), who uses digitally reworked images as the basis for some of his photorealist pictures – often playing dramatically with light and shadow. Works by Sorb sculptor and painter Georg Baselitz (b 1938) are other highlights of the Museum Frieder Burda. Baselitz was thrown out of art school in the GDR for his artistic provocations, only to have West German authorities confiscate works from his first exhibition there. Take a look at his *Die Grosse Nacht im Eimer* (Big Night Down the Drain), depicting a masturbating figure, and you can see – if not quite understand – why.

Almost as highly prized by collectors and galleries as Richter and Polke, but from a younger generation, Rosemarie Trockel (b 1952) is an award-winning artist whose diverse and experimental works include drawings, sculpture, painting and video art. In Leipzig the Neue Leipziger Schule (New Leipzig School) of artists has emerged recently, achieving success at home and abroad, and includes painters such as Neo Rauch (b 1960).

For a comprehensive low-down on Germany's contemporary art scene and events, see www.art-in.de.

Bulgarian-American artist Christo and his wife Jeanne-Claude were responsible for possibly the best known piece of public art of recent times in Germany. In 1995 they completely enveloped Berlin's Reichstag building in aluminium-coated fabric, attracting millions of visitors to the site.

On the contemporary art and design circuit, the Neue Sammlung permanent collections in the Neues Museum in Nuremberg and Pinakothek der Moderne in Munich are not to be missed; changing exhibitions have ranged from jewellery through to GDR art-poster design, and from American photography through to a retrospective of covers from the magazine *Der Spiegel*.

Photography is another area where Germany excels. In the 1920s and 1930s, German photographers took two very different directions. Influenced by the Hungarian László Maholy-Nagy, some adopted a playful approach to light, figure, form and how they developed the resulting images in the darkroom. The other direction was Neue Sachlichkeit (New Objectivity), based on a documentary-style approach and the creation of archetypes that help us understand the world. The three main protagonists of the New Objectivity movement were Albert Renger-Patzsch (1897–1966), August Sander (1876–1964) and Werner Manz (1901–83). It's said that subsequent generations of photographers have either built on or challenged the work of these early masters of the art.

Around the time Beuys waved adieu in the 1980s, contemporary photographers Andreas Gursky (b 1955) and Candida Höfer (b 1944) were honing their skills under the next generation of photographers, led by Bernd Becher (1931–2007) at Düsseldorf's Kunstakademie (Art Academy). Leipzig-born Gursky's work, which can be seen in Cologne's Museum Ludwig, encompasses superb images of architecture, landscapes and interiors, sometimes reworked digitally. Höfer's work, along with the works of other Becher students, can be found in Hamburg's Kunsthalle.

Given Germany's rich collections, travelling the contours of visual arts might be an interesting way to organise a trip. In addition to excellent permanent collections in major museums, you'll find lots of smaller art spaces with changing exhibitions. Venues such as Berlin's Kunst-Werke Berlin and Galerie Eigen+Art (www.eigen-art.com) offer a contemporary 'shock of the new'.

For household design, the Bauhaus Museum in Weimar shows how it all began, and the Vitra Design Museum in Weil am Rhein has other fascinating exhibits.

Berlin is not just the heart of the thriving art scene in Germany; in 2006 it became Europe's first City of Design as part of the Unesco Creative Cities Network, gaining recognition as a crossroads of design, architecture and the visual and performing arts.

Architecture

The British and American bombs of WWII may have blasted away a share of Germany's architectural heritage, but a painstaking postwar rebuilding program and a wealth of sites that remained with nary a shrapnel mark, make Germany an architectural wonderland. Every building style – from crumbling Roman wall to 21st-century vanity project – rises from townscapes across the Bundesrepublik, and Germany boasts over 30 Unesco World Heritage Sites. These include everything from Bauhaus Weimar to Roman Trier, the Wieskirche pilgrimage church in southern Bavaria to the coal mines of Essen.

Dresden was delisted as a Unesco World Heritage Site in 2009 when the local authorities insisted on building an ugly modern bridge across the River Elbe.

Romanesque & Gothic

Among the grand buildings of the Carolingian period, Aachen's Byzantine-inspired cathedral – built for Charlemagne from 786 to about 800 – and Fulda's Michaelskirche are surviving masterpieces. A century on, Carolingian, Christian (Roman) and Byzantine influences flowed together in a more proportional interior with integrated columns, reflected in the elegant Stiftskirche St Cyriakus in Gernrode and the Romanesque cathedrals in Worms, Speyer and Mainz. The Unesco-listed Kloster Maulbronn in Baden-Württemberg, built in 1147, is considered the best preserved monastery of its kind north of the Alps.

Early Gothic architecture kept many Romanesque elements, as the cathedral in Magdeburg illustrates. Later churches have purely Gothic traits – ribbed vaults, pointed arches and flying buttresses to allow greater height and larger windows, seen in Cologne's cathedral (Kölner Dom), Marburg (Elisabethkirche), Trier (Liebfrauenkirche), Freiburg (Münster) and Lübeck (Marienkirche). From the 15th century, elaborately patterned vaults and hall churches emerged. Munich's Frauenkirche and Michaelskirche are typical of this late Gothic period.

Renaissance to Neoclassical

The Renaissance rumbled into Germany around the mid-16th century, bestowing Heidelberg and other southern cities with buildings bearing ornate leaf work decoration and columns, while in northern Germany the secular Weser Renaissance style resulted in the Celle's ducal palace (Schloss).

Erich Mendelsohn and the Architecture of German Modernism by Kathleen James zooms in on Mendelsohn's expressionist buildings in Berlin and Frankfurt.

From the early 17th century to the mid-18th century, feudal rulers invested heavily in grand residences. In Baden-Württemberg, the palatial retreat of Karlsruhe was dreamed up, while Italian architect Barelli started work on Munich's Schloss Nymphenburg. In northern Germany, buildings were less ornamental, as the work of baroque architect Johann Conrad Schlaun (1695–1773) in Münster or Dresden's treasure trove of baroque architecture demonstrates.

One of the finest baroque churches, Dresden's Frauenkirche, built in 1743, was destroyed in the 1945 firebombing of the city, but reconstructed and reopened in 2005. The late baroque period ushered in Potsdam's rococo Schloss Sanssouci.

TOP UNESCO WORLD HERITAGE SITES IN GERMANY

» Trier's Roman monuments (p453) – Germany's finest collection of Roman heritage.

» Aachen Cathedral (p487) – Begun in the 8th century, this blockbuster building is the final resting place of Emperor Charlemagne.

» Speyer's Kaiserdom cathedral (p423) – This magnificent 11th-century cathedral holds the tombs of eight German rulers.

» Regensburg (p288) – An Altstadt crammed with Romanesque and Gothic edifices.

» Kölner Dom (p466) – Cologne's 13th-century cathedral was completed over six centuries.

» Potsdam's parks and palaces (p120) – Includes 500 hectares of parks and 150 buildings raised between 1730 and 1916.

» Würzburg's Residenz (p249) – This 18th-century palace is perhaps Balthasar Neumann's finest creation.

» Bauhaus sites in Weimar (p548) and Dessau (p583) – If you're interested in the early 20th-century Bauhaus movement, Weimar and Dessau are where it all started.

Berlin's Brandenburg Gate, based on a Greek design, is an exquisite example of neoclassicism. This late-18th-century period saw baroque exuberance fly out the window and strictly geometric columns, pediments and domes fly in. The colonnaded Altes Museum, Neue Wache and the Konzerthaus Berlin – designed by leading architect Karl Friedrich Schinkel (1781–1841) – are pure neoclassical edifices that still grace the capital. In Bavaria, Leo von Klenze (1784–1864) chiselled his way through virtually every ancient civilisation, with eclectic creations such as the Glyptothek and Propyläen on Munich's Königsplatz.

A wave of derivative architecture based on previous styles swept through late-19th-century Germany. A German peculiarity was the so-called rainbow style, which blended Byzantine with Roman features. Renaissance revivalism found expression in the Schloss in Schwerin by Georg Adolph Demmler (1804–86), while sections of Ludwig II's fairytale concoction Neuschwanstein are neo-Romanesque.

Germany's iconic Reichstag building, built in 1894, was designed by Paul Wallot (1841–1912) in the Wilhelmian style with neo-baroque and neo-Renaissance elements; it was restored in the 1990s by British architect Lord Norman Foster.

Modern & Contemporary
20th Century

No architectural movement has had greater influence on modern design than Bauhaus, which was spearheaded by the son of a Berlin architect, Walter Gropius (1883–1969). Through his founding in 1919 of the Staatliches Bauhaus – a modern architecture, art and design institute in Weimar – Bauhaus pushed the industrial forms of art nouveau to a functional limit and sought to unite architecture, painting, furniture design and sculpture. Critics claimed Bauhaus was too functional and impersonal, relying heavily on cubist and constructivist forms. But any visit to the Bauhaus Building in Dessau or the nearby Meisterhäuser (Master Craftsmen's Houses), where teachers from the school lived (painters such as Kandinsky and Klee), reveals how much the avant-garde movement pioneered modern architecture. In Berlin, the Bauhaus Archive/Museum of Design, which Gropius designed in 1964, is a must-see.

The Nazis shut down the Bauhaus school in 1932 and reverted to the pompous and monumental. One of the most successful attempts was the 1934 Olympiastadion Berlin (Berlin Olympic Stadium), designed by Werner March (1894–1976). In time for the FIFA World Cup 2006, the ageing stadium was rejuvenated with new roofing, restoration of original materials and the lowering of the playing field to intensify the atmosphere.

The monumental efforts of another political persuasion are captured today in the buildings that line Berlin's (former East German) Karl-Marx-Allee. Another highlight that outlived the country that created it is the 368m-high TV Tower on Alexanderplatz, built in 1969. One structure that was much less successful – and has survived history only in fragments – is that potent symbol of the Cold War, the Berlin Wall.

Experimental design took off in the 1960s in Düsseldorf with slender Thyssenhaus (1960), designed by Hubert Petschnigg (1913–1997), which inspired Tel Aviv's Eliyahu House. In 1972 Munich was graced with its splendid tent-roofed Olympiastadion, which visitors can today scale with a rope and snap hook or abseil down for an architectural kick of the hair-raising kind. Bayern-München football team sailed over to the Allianz Arena in 2006, a remarkable rubber-dinghy-like translucent object that will please football fans with more than just an architectural interest in stadiums.

Frank Gehry (b 1929) has left exciting imprints on German cities over the past two decades, first through the 1989 Vitra Design Museum in Weil am Rhein, and later with his wacky 1999 Neue Zollhof (New Customs House) in Düsseldorf, the Gehry-Tower (2001) in Hanover and the 1999 DZ Bank on Berlin's Pariser Platz.

21st Century

Berlin is the locus of many of the most contemporary building projects in Germany. On Potsdamer Platz, Italian architect Renzo Piano (b 1937) designed Daimler City (1998) and Nuremberg-born Helmut Jahn (b 1940) turned a playful hand to the glass-and-steel Sony Center (2000). Another Jahn creation that raises interest in Berlin is the minimalist and edgy Neues Kranzler Eck (2000).

Three spectacular successes in Germany designed by American star architect Daniel Libeskind (b 1946) are Osnabrück's Felix-Nussbaum-Haus (1998), the famous zinc-clad zigzag Jüdisches Museum (2001) in Berlin and the new Militärhistorische Museum in Dresden (2011). New York contemporary Peter Eisenman achieved the remarkable by assembling 2711 concrete pillars to create the haunting Holocaust Memorial (2005).

In 2006 Berlin christened a new star attraction – the vast Hauptbahnhof, a transparent-roofed, multiple-level Turmbahnhof (tower station; the lines cross at different levels) that takes glass-and-steel station architecture to new limits. Munich is set to follow suit in 2013.

The contrast of old and new in the extension of Cologne's Wallraf-Richartz-Museum (2001), a design by Oswald Mathias Ungers (1926–2007), is a worthy addition to a city with one of the world's most beautiful cathedrals. In 2003 Dresden-born Axel Schultes (b 1943) and Kiel's Charlotte Frank (b 1959) won the German Architecture Prize for their design of the Bundeskanzleramt (New Chancellery; 2001). Munich architect Stephan Braunfels (b 1950) masterminded Munich's modernist Pinakothek der Moderne (2002). More recently, Munich's Museum Brandhorst (2009), with its 36,000 ceramic square tubes, adds a colourful splash to the city's museum district and Porsche Museum (2009) was a dramatic addition to Stuttgart's cityscape.

For an interaction of light and architecture, look out for the Luminale festival in the Rhine-Main region (www.luminale.de), an event held in April each year in which light artists use sound and light to transform buildings, museums and parks into illuminated works of art.

For an informative and illustrated dip into Berlin architecture – past, present and future – visit the Senate Department of Urban Development at www.stadtentwicklung.berlin.de.

Landscapes & Wildlife

For centuries the epic beauty of Germany's landscapes has inspired artists and writers toward the lyrical and profound. The sprightly Rhine coursing through emerald vines, the wave-lashed Baltic coast, the glacier-licked summits of the Bavarian Alps – all have been immortalised by 19th-century Romantic painters and literary legends like Thomas Mann, Bertolt Brecht and Mark Twain. Not to mention the Brothers Grimm, who found in Germany's dark forests the perfect air of mystery for gingerbready tales of wicked witches and lost-in-the-woods children.

But for all that has been publicised, much of the country's loveliness remains unsung beyond its borders. Take for instance Mecklenburg–Western Pomerania's beech forests, poppy-flecked meadows and lakes, or the East Frisian Islands' briny breezes and shifting sands, Saxon Switzerland's wonderland of sandstone pinnacles, or the Bavarian forest's primordial woodlands tinged with Bohemian melancholy. Who has heard of them? Bar the odd intrepid traveller, only the Germans.

Fancy seeing them for yourself? Here's the good news: the national passion for outdoor pursuits and obsessive efficiency has made such landscapes brilliantly accessible. Every inch of the country has been mapped, cycling and hiking trails thread to its remotest corners, while farmhouses and mountain huts offer travellers shelter and sustenance. Life here is that bit closer to nature. And nature here is on a truly grand scale.

The Land

Across its 357,021 sq km, Europe's seventh-largest country embraces moor and heath, mudflats and chalk cliffs, glacial lakes, river wetlands and dense forests. Hugged by Poland, the Czech Republic, Austria, Switzerland, France, Belgium, the Netherlands, Luxembourg and Denmark, the land is mountainous in the south, but flat in the north. Indeed, many visitors are surprised to learn Germany even possesses low-lying islands and sandy beaches.

Sidling up to Austria in the southeast are the Bavarian Alps, where the 2962m Zugspitze, Germany's highest peak, crowns the spine of the Northern Limestone Alps, and jewel-coloured lakes scatter the Berchtesgaden National Park. Rolling almost to the Swiss border in the southwest, the Black Forest presents a sylvan tableau of round-topped hills (the highest being 1493m Feldberg), thick fir forests and open countryside.

Starting its journey in Switzerland and travelling through Lake Constance (Germany's largest lake) the Rhine winds its 1320km-long way around the Black Forest, before crawling up the west side of the map to drain into the North Sea. The Elbe, Oder and other German rivers likewise flow north, except for the Danube, which flows east.

Vital Statistics

» Highest peak – Zugspitze (2962m) in the Bavarian Alps

» Major rivers – Rhine, Danube, Elbe, Moselle, Main

» Biggest lake – Lake Constance (536 sq km), Europe's third largest

» Tallest waterfall – Triberger Wasserfälle (163m)

» Largest nature park – The 12,000 sq km Black Forest

Germany's 15 Unesco Biosphere Reserves include the Bavarian Forest, the Berchtesgaden Alps, the Spreewald and Rügen. For the full list, visit www.unesco.org.

NATIONAL PARKS

The country's vast and varied landscapes are protected to varying degrees by 104 nature parks, 15 biosphere reserves and 14 national parks. The Upper Middle Rhine Valley, the Wadden Sea and the beech forest of the Jasmund National Park are safeguarded as Unesco World Heritage Areas.

PARK & WEBSITE	FEATURES
Bavarian Forest www.nationalpark-bayerischer-wald.de	mountain forest & upland moors (243 sq km); deer, hazel grouse, foxes, otters, eagle owls, Eurasian pygmy owls; botany
Berchtesgaden www.nationalpark-berchtesgaden.de	lakes, subalpine spruce, salt mines & ice caves (210 sq km); eagles, golden eagles, marmots, blue hares
Eifel www.nationalpark-eifel.de	beech forest (110 sq km); wild cats, beavers, kingfishers; wild yellow narcissus
Hainich www.nationalpark-hainich.de	mixed deciduous forest (76 sq km); beech trees, black storks, wild cats, rare bats
Hamburg Wadden Sea www.nationalpark-wattenmeer.de	mudflats, meadows & sand dunes (345 sq km); sea swallows, terns
Harz www.nationalpark-harz.de	rock formations, caves (247 sq km); black woodpeckers, wild cats, deer
Jasmund www.nationalpark-jasmund.de	chalk cliffs, forest, creeks & moors (30 sq km); white-tailed eagles
Kellerwald Edersee www.nationalpark-kellerwald-edersee.de	beech & other deciduous trees, lake (57 sq km); black storks, wild cats, rare bats, stags
Lower Oder Valley www.nationalpark-unteres-odertal.eu	river plain (165 sq km); black storks, sea eagles, beavers, aquatic warblers, cranes
Lower Saxony Wadden Sea www.nationalpark-wattenmeer.de	salt-marsh & bog landscape (2780 sq km); seals, shell ducks
Müritz www.nationalpark-mueritz.de	beech, bogs & lakes (318 sq km); sea eagles, fish hawks, cranes, white-tailed eagles, Gotland sheep
Saxon Switzerland www.nationalpark-saechsische-schweiz.de	sandstone & basalt rock formations (93 sq km); eagle owls, otters, fat dormice
Schleswig-Holstein Wadden Sea www.nationalpark-wattenmeer.de	seascape of dunes, salt marshes & mudflats (4410 sq km); sea life, migratory birds
Vorpommersche Boddenlandschaft www.nationalpark-vorpommersche-boddenlandschaft.de	Baltic seascape (805 sq km); cranes, red deer, wild boar

Moving towards the central belt, you'll find memorable vineyards and hiking areas in the warmer valleys around the Moselle River. To the east, you'll find the holiday area of the Spreewald, a picturesque wetland with narrow, navigable waterways.

Where Germany meets Holland in the northwest and Denmark in the north, the land is flat; the westerly North Sea coast consists partly of drained land and dykes. To the east, the Baltic coast is riddled with bays and fjords in Schleswig-Holstein but gives way to sandy inlets and beaches. On the northeastern tip, Rügen Island is renowned for its chalk cliffs.

The Wildlife
Animals

Snow hares, marmots and wild goats scamper around the Alps. The chamois is also fairly common in this neck of the woods, as well as in pockets of the Black Forest, the Swabian Alps and Saxon Switzerland, south of Dresden.

Best Bird-watching

» North Sea – migratory birds

» Black Forest (p336) – woodpeckers

» Lower Oder Valley – sea eagles, black storks, migrating cranes

» Bavarian Alps – golden eagles

ACTIVITIES	BEST TIME TO VISIT	PAGE
walking, mountain biking, cross-country skiing	winter, spring	p302
wildlife spotting, walking, skiing	winter, spring	p246
wildlife & flora spotting, hiking, hydrotherapy, spa treatments	spring, summer	p491
walking	spring	p554
birdwatching, mudflat walking	spring, autumn	Map p646
climbing, walking	spring, summer, autumn; avoid weekends (busy)	p568
walking, cycling	avoid summer (paths like ant trails)	p712
walking, wildlife spotting	spring, summer, autumn	p531
walking, cycling, birdwatching	winter (bird-watching), spring (other activities)	Map p119
swimming, walking, birdwatching	late spring, early autumn	p639
cycling, canoeing, birdwatching, hiking	spring, summer, autumn	p698
walking, climbing, rock climbing	avoid summer (throngs with day trippers)	p152
mudflat walking, tide watching, birdwatching, swimming	spring, autumn	p687
birdwatching, water sports, walking	autumn (cranes), summer (water sports)	p705

A rare but wonderful Alpine treat for patient birdwatchers is the sighting of a golden eagle; Berchtesgaden National Park staff might be able to help you find one. The jay, with its darting flight patterns and calls imitating other species, is easy to spot in the Alpine foothills. Look for the flashes of blue on its wings.

Pesky but sociable racoons, a common non-native species, scoot about eastern Germany, and soon let hikers know if they have been disturbed with a shrill whistle. Beavers can be found in wetlands near the Elbe River. Seals are common on the North Sea and Baltic Sea coasts.

The north coast lures migratory birds. From March to May, and August to October, they stop over in Schleswig-Holstein's Wadden Sea National Park and the Vorpommersche Boddenlandschaft National Park while travelling to and from southerly regions. Forests everywhere provide a habitat for songbirds and woodpeckers.

Some animals are staging a comeback. Sea eagles, practically extinct in western Germany, are becoming more plentiful in the east, as are falcons,

Best Wildlife Spotting

» North Sea – common seals, harbour porpoises

» Black Forest – (p336) red deer, red squirrels

» Bavarian Alps – chamois, marmots

» Mecklenburg Lake Plains – otters

white storks and cranes. The east also sees wolves, which regularly cross the Oder River from Poland, and Eurasian elk (moose), which occasionally appear on moors and in mixed forests.

The wild cat has returned to the Harz Mountains and other forested regions, but you shouldn't expect to see the related lynx. Having died out here in the 19th century, lynxes were reintroduced in the 1980s, only to be illegally hunted to the point of extinction again. Today, a few populate the Bavarian Forest National Park, although chances of seeing one in the wild are virtually zero.

Deer are still around, although with dwindling natural habitats and their shrinking gene pool, the Deutsche Wildtier Stiftung (German Wild Animal Foundation; www.deutschewildtierstiftung.de) has expressed concern for their future.

Consisting mainly of firs and pines, the Black Forest derives its name from the dark appearance of these conifers when seen from the hillsides.

Plants

Despite environmental pressures, German forests remain beautiful places to tiptoe away from crowds and back to nature. At lower altitudes, they're usually a potpourri of beech, oak, birch, chestnut, lime, maple and ash that erupt into a kaleidoscope of colour in autumn. At higher elevations, fir, pine, spruce and other conifers are prevalent. Canopies often shade low-growing ferns, heather, clover and foxglove. Mixed deciduous forest carpets river valleys at lower altitudes.

In spring, Alpine regions burst with wildflowers – orchid, cyclamen, gentian, pulsatilla, Alpine roses, edelweiss and buttercups. Great care is taken not to cut pastures until plants have seeded and you can minimise your impact by sticking to paths, especially in Alpine areas and coastal dunes where ecosystems are fragile. In late August, heather blossom is the particular lure of Lüneburger Heide, northeast of Hanover.

Environmental Issues

Germans are the original Greens. They cannot claim to have invented environmentalism, but they were there at the outset and coined the word to describe the movement. Recycling, cycling and carrying groceries in reusable bags – it's all second nature here.

Brush up on your knowledge of German flora and fauna with websites such as www.heimische -tiere.de, www. baumkunde.de and www.wald.de (all in German).

In the wake of the 2011 Fukushima disaster, Angela Merkel made the bold move to abandon nuclear power and shut down all of Germany's 17 nuclear plants by 2022 (eight have already closed). The future? Just look around you. Travelling across Germany, you'll be struck by the number of wind turbines dotting the landscape, especially in the windswept north. If you start to wonder just how many there are, well, there were 22,297 in 2011. While other countries debate pros and cons, Germany has long embraced the technology to become the world's third leading producer of wind energy. These turbines provide roughly 8% of German electricity and there are plans – big plans – to build more offshore.

The country is setting a shining example when it comes to solar power, too. According to an article in *The Guardian* in May 2012: 'Germany has nearly as much installed solar power generation capacity as the rest of the world combined and gets about four percent of its overall annual electricity needs from the sun alone.' If eco-cities such as Freiburg, home to the 59-house PlusEnergy Solar Settlement, are anything to go by, Germany's future looks bright indeed.

Survival
Guide

Directory A–Z

Accommodation

Germany has all types of places to unpack your suitcase. Standards are generally high, and even basic accommodation will likely be clean and comfortable. Reservations are a good idea between June and September, around major holidays, festivals, cultural events and trade shows. In this book, reviews are listed by author preference.

Accommodation costs vary wildly between regions and between cities and rural areas. What will buy you a romantic suite in a countryside inn in the Bavarian Forest may only get you a simple room in Munich. City hotels geared to the suit-brigade often lure leisure travellers with lower rates on weekends. Also check hotel websites for discount rates or packages.

Budget stays will generally have you checking in at hostels, country inns, *Pensionen* (B&Bs or small hotels) or simple family hotels. Facilities may be shared. Midrange properties offer extra creature comforts, such as cable TV, wi-fi and private bathrooms. Overall these constitute the best value for money. Top-end places offer luxurious amenities, perhaps scenic locations, special decor or historical ambience. Many also have pools, saunas and business centres.

Agritourism

Family-friendly farm holidays offer a great opportunity to get close to nature in relative comfort. Kids get to interact with their favourite barnyard animals and maybe help with everyday chores. Accommodation ranges from bare-bones rooms with shared facilities to fully furnished holiday apartments. Minimum stays are common. Farm types include organic, dairy and equestrian farms as well as wine estates. Note that places advertising *Landurlaub* (country holiday) no longer actively work their farms.

The German Agricultural Association inspects and quality controls hundreds of farms and publishes details on www.landtourismus.de, which also allows you to contact individual properties directly. Another source is www.landsichten.de.

Camping

Campgrounds are well maintained, however many get jammed in summer. Book early or show up before noon to snap up spots. The core camping season runs from May to September, but quite a few sites are open year-round.

Many sites are in remote locales that are not, or only poorly, served by public transport, so having your own wheels is an asset. Camping on public land is not permitted and pitching a tent on private property requires the consent of the landowner.

Fees consist of charges per person (between €3 and €10), per tent (€6 to €16, depending on size) and per car (€3 to €8), plus additional fees for hot showers, resort tax, electricity and sewage disposal. A **Camping Card International** (CCI; www.

campingcardinternational.com) may yield savings.

Websites with campgrounds searchable by location, theme and facilities include www.eurocampings.co.uk, www.alanrogers.com and www.bvcd.de.

Hostels

DJH HOSTELS

Germany's 530 Hostelling International–affiliated *Jugendherbergen* are run by the **Deutsches Jugendherbergswerk** (DJH; www.jugendherberge.de). Although they are open to people of all ages, they're especially popular with school and youth groups, families and sports clubs.

Aside from gender-segregated dorms, most hostels also have private rooms for families and couples, often with bathroom. If space is tight, hostels may give priority to people under 27, except for those travelling as a family. People over 27 are charged an extra €3 or €4 per night.

If you don't have an HI membership card from your home country, you need to buy either a Hostelling International Card for €15.50 (valid for one year) or six individual Welcome Stamps costing €3.10 per night. Both are available at any DJH hostel.

Around half of German DJH hostels can now be booked online at www.jugendherberge.de or www.hihostels.com. Alternatively, contact the hostel directly.

INDEPENDENT HOSTELS

Independent Hostels cater primarily for individual travellers and attract a more convivial, international crowd than DJH hostels. They're most prevalent in big cities like Berlin, Cologne and Hamburg, although they have been proliferating throughout the country.

Ranging from classic, low-key backpacker hostels with large dorms and a communal spirit, to modern 'flashpackers' similar to budget hotels, many also have private quarters with bathrooms, and even apartments with kitchens. Dorms are mixed, but women-only dorms can usually be set up on request. Typical facilities include communal kitchens, bars, cafes, TV lounges, lockers, internet terminals and laundry. There are no curfews, and staff tend to be savvy, energetic, eager to help and multilingual. There's typically a linen fee of around €3 per stay.

Some 60 indies in 36 cities have joined an alliance known as the **Backpacker Network** (www.backpackernetwork.de). Some hostels can also be booked via their website.

Hotels

Lonely Planet aims to feature well-situated, independent hotels that offer good value, a warm welcome, a modicum of charm and character as well as a palpable sense of place.

You'll find the gamut of options, from small family-run properties to international chains and luxurious designer abodes. Increasingly popular are budget designer chains (eg Motel One) geared towards lifestyle-savvy travellers.

In older, family-run hotels, individual rooms often vary dramatically in terms of size, decor and amenities. The cheapest may have shared facilities, while others come with a shower cubicle installed but no private toilet; only the pricier ones have their own bathrooms. Increasingly, city hotels are not including breakfast in their room rate.

Many hotels with a high romance factor belong to an association called Romantik Hotels & Restaurants (www.romantikhotels.com) and many are now entirely non-smoking; others set aside rooms or floors for smokers.

Chain Hotels

Hotel chains stretch from nondescript establishments to central four-star hotels with character. Most conform to certain standards of decor, service and facilities (air-con, wi-fi, 24-hour check-in), and offer competitive rates and last-minute and/or weekend deals. International chains like Best Western, Holiday Inn, Hilton and Ramada are now ubiquitous on the German market, but there are also some home-grown contenders. Some properties belonging to the groups listed here are mentioned in the On the Road chapters of this guide. Check the websites for additional locations.

» **A&O** (www.aohostels.com) Combines hostel and two-star hotel accommodation.

» **Dorint** (www.dorint.com) Three- to five-star properties in cities and rural areas.

» **InterCity** (www.intercityhotel.com) Good-value

MY HOME IS MY CASTLE

If you're the romantic type, consider a fairy-tale getaway in a castle, palace or country manor dripping with character and history. They're typically in the countryside, strategically perched atop a crag, perhaps overlooking a river or rolling hills. And it doesn't take a king's ransom to stay in one. In fact, even wallet-watchers can fancy themselves knight or damsel when staying in a castle converted into a youth hostel (eg Burg Stahleck on the Rhine). More typically, though, properties are luxury affairs, blending the gamut of mod-cons with baronial ambience and olde-worlde trappings like four-poster beds, antique armoires and heavy drapes. Sometimes your hosts are even descendants of the original castle builders – often some local baron, count or prince. For details, see www.thecastles.de or www.castleandpalacehotels.com.

two-star chain usually located at train stations.

» **Kempinski** (www.kempinski. com) Luxury hotel group with a pedigree going back to 1897.

» **Leonardo** (www.leonardo -hotels.com) Three- to four-star city hotels.

» **Meininger** (www.mein inger-hotels.com) Well-run hotel-hostel combo for city-breakers on a budget.

» **Motel One** (www.motelone. com) Despite the name, these are budget sleeper hotels.

» **Sorat** (www.sorat-hotels.com) Four-star boutique hotels.

» **Steigenberger** (www.stei genberger.com) Five-star luxury often in historic buildings.

Pensions, Inns & Private Rooms

The German equivalent of a B&B, *Pensionen* are small and informal and an excellent low-cost alternative to hotels. *Gasthöfe/Gasthäuser* (inns) are similar but usually have restaurants serving regional and German food to a local clientele. *Privatzimmer* are guest rooms in private homes, though privacy seekers may find these places a bit too intimate.

Expect clean rooms but minimal amenities – maybe a radio, sometimes an old and small TV, almost never a phone. Facilities may be shared. What rooms lack in amenities, though, they often make up for in charm and authenticity, often augmented by friendly hosts who take a personal interest in ensuring that you enjoy your stay.

WHICH FLOOR?

In Germany, as elsewhere in Europe, 'ground floor' refers to the floor at street level. The 1st floor (what would be called the 2nd floor in the US) is the floor above that. Lonely Planet follows local usage of the terms.

Tourist offices keep lists of available rooms; you can also look around for *'Zimmer Frei'* (rooms available) signs in house or shop windows. They're usually quite cheap, with per-person rates starting at €13 and usually topping out at €25, including breakfast.

If a landlord is reluctant to rent for a single night, offer to pay a little extra. For advance reservations, try www. bed-and-breakfast.de, www. bedandbreakfast.de or www.bedandbreakfast.com.

Rental Accommodation

If you want to get to know a place better, renting for a week or two can be ideal, especially for budget-minded travellers, self-caterers, families and small groups.

Local tourist offices have lists of holiday flats (*Ferienwohnungen* or *Ferien-Appartements*). Some *Pensionen*, inns, hotels and even farmhouses also rent out apartments. International online agencies include www. airbnb.com, www.homeaway. com, www.forgetaway.com or www.interhomeusa.com.

Stays under a week usually incur a surcharge, and there's almost always an extra 'cleaning fee' of €20 or €30.

You could also consider a home exchange, where you swap homes and live like a local for free; see www.homeex change.com for how it's done.

Reservations

When making a room reservation directly, tell your host what time they can expect you and stick to your plan or ring again. Many well-meaning visitors have lost rooms by showing up late.

Many tourist offices and hotel websites let you check for room availability and make advance reservations.

If you've arrived and don't have a reservation, swing by the tourist office, where staff can assist you in finding last-minute lodgings. After hours, vacancies may be posted in the window or display case.

THE 'CURSE' OF THE KUR

Most German resort and spa towns charge their overnight guests a so-called *Kurtaxe* (resort tax). Fees range from €1 to €4 per person per night and are added to your hotel bill. The money subsidises visitor-oriented events and services, such as concerts, lectures, readings, walking tours, public toilets, beach cleaning and sometimes includes public transportation.

Business Hours

The following are standard business hours in Germany. In most cases, where hours vary across the year, we've provided those applicable in high season.

Banks 9am to 4pm Monday to Friday, extended hours usually on Tuesday and Thursday, some open Saturday

Bars 6pm to 1am

Cafes 8am to 8pm

Clubs 11pm to early morning hours

Post offices 9am to 6pm Monday to Friday, 9am to 1pm Saturday

Restaurants 11am to 11pm (food service often stops at 9pm in rural areas)

Major stores and supermarkets 9.30am to 8pm Monday to Saturday (shorter hours outside cities)

Customs Regulations

Goods brought into and out of countries within the EU incur no additional taxes provided duty has been paid somewhere within the EU and the goods are only for personal

Climate

Berlin

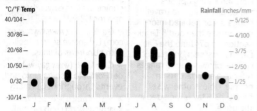

Cologne

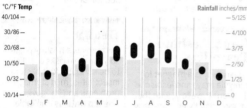

Frankfurt am Main

use or consumption. Duty-free shopping is only available if you're leaving the EU.

Duty-free allowances (for anyone over 17) arriving from non-EU countries:

» 200 cigarettes or 100 cigarillos or 50 cigars or 250g of loose tobacco

» 1L of strong liquor or 2L of less than 22% alcohol by volume plus 4L of wine plus 16L of beer

» other goods up to the value of €300 if arriving by land or €430 if arriving by sea or air (€175 for under 15 years)

Discount Cards

Concession discounts are widely available for seniors, children and students. In some cases you may be asked to prove your age. Tourist of-fices in many cities sell Welcome Cards entitling visitors to discounts on museums, sights and tours, plus unlimited trips on local public transport. They can be good value if you don't qualify for any of the standard discounts.

If you qualify for one of the following discount cards, you can reap additional benefits on travel, shopping, attractions or entertainment:

» **Camping Card International** (CCI; www.campingcardinternational.com) Up to 25% savings in camping fees and third-party liability insurance while on the site.

» **European Youth Card** (Euro<26 Card; www.europeanyouthcard.org) Wide range of discounts for anyone under 26 years of age, in some countries under 30. Sold online.

» **International Student Identity Card** (ISIC; www.isic.org) The most popular discount card, but only for full-time students. Available at ISIC points (see website).

» **International Youth Travel Card** (IYTC; www.istc.org) Similar to ISIC but for nonstudents under 26 years of age. Available at ISIC points.

Electricity

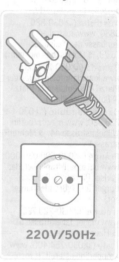

220V/50Hz

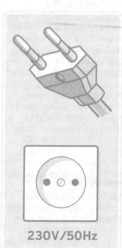

230V/50Hz

Embassies & Consulates

All foreign embassies are in Berlin, but many countries have consular offices in Frankfurt, Munich, Hamburg or Düsseldorf. Call the embassy to find out which consulate is closest to your location. For German missions around the world and foreign missions in Germany not listed here, go to www.auswaertiges-amt.de.

Australia (☎030-880 0880; www.australian-embassy.de; Wallstrasse 76-79; [S]Märkisches Museum)

Canada (☎030-203 120; www.kanada-info.de; Leipziger Platz 17; [S]Potsdamer Platz, [R]Potsdamer Platz)

Czech Republic (☎030-226 380; www.mzv.cz/berlin; Wilhelmstrasse 44; [S]Mohrenstrasse)

France (☎030-590 039 000; www.botschaft-frankreich.de; Pariser Platz 5; [S]Brandenburger Tor, [R]Brandenburger Tor)

Ireland (☎030-220 720; www.dfa.ie; Jägerstrasse 51; [S]Hausvogteiplatz)

Italy (☎030-254 400; www.ambberlino.esteri.it; Hiroshimastrasse 1; 🚌200)

Netherlands (☎030-209 560; www.niederlandeweb.de; Klosterstrasse 50; [S]Klosterstrasse)

New Zealand (☎030-206 210; www.nzembassy.com; Friedrichstrasse 60; [S]Stadtmitte)

Poland (☎030-223 130; www.berlin.polemb.net; Lassenstrasse 19-21; [R]Grunewald)

Spain (☎030-254 0070; www.spanischebotschaft.de; Lichtensteinallee 1; 🚌100)

Switzerland (☎030-390 4000; www.eda.admin.ch; Otto-von-Bismarck-Allee 4a; 🚌100, [S]Bundestag)

UK (☎030-204 570; www.britischebotschaft.de; Wilhelmstrasse 70; [S]Brandenburger Tor, [R]Brandenburger Tor)

USA (☎030-830 50; www.germany.usembassy.gov; Clayallee 170; [S]Oskar-Helene-Heim)

Food

German eating options match all tastes and travel budgets. For detailed information, see the Food & Drink section on p741and the Eat Like a Local section on p36.

The following price ranges refer to a standard main course. Unless otherwise stated 19% tax is included in the price.

€	less than €8
€€	€8 to €15
€€€	more than €15

Gay & Lesbian Travellers

» Germany is a magnet for *schwule* (gay) and *lesbische* (lesbian) travellers, with the rainbow flag flying especially proudly in Berlin, which is helmed by Germany's first openly gay mayor, Klaus Wowereit. Cologne also has a humming scene and there are also sizeable communities in Hamburg, Frankfurt and Munich.

» Attitudes towards homosexuality tend to be more conservative in the countryside, among older people and in the eastern states.

» As elsewhere, Germany's lesbian scene is less public than its male counterpart and is centred mainly on women's cafes and bars.

» Gay pride marches are held throughout Germany in springtime; the largest, in Cologne and Berlin, draw hundreds of thousands of rainbow revellers and friends.

Publications

» Blu – Print and online magazine with searchable, up-to-the-minute location and event listings. Available at newsagents.

» L-Mag – Bimonthly magazine for lesbians. Available at newsagents.

» Spartacus International Gay Guide – Annual English-language travel guide for men. Available in bookstores.

Websites & Apps

» **Gay Romeo** (www.gayromeo.com) Dating site of choice in Germany; iPhone app for €2.99.

» **Gayscape** (www.gayscape.com) Extensive search tool with hundreds of links.

» **Gay Web** (www.gay-web.de) Portal to lesbigay info and events throughout Germany.

» **Spartacus World** (www.spartacusworld.com) Hip hotel, style and event guide; iPhone app for €6.99.

Health

Germany is a healthy place so your main risks are likely to be sunburn, foot blisters, insect bites, mild stomach problems and hangovers. The tap water is drinkable.

Before You Go

» A signed and dated letter from your doctor describing your medical conditions and medications, including generic names, is a good idea. It is illegal to import codeine-based medication without a doctor's certificate.

» No vaccinations are required for travel to Germany but the World Health Organisation (WHO) recommends that all travellers be covered for diphtheria, tetanus, measles, mumps, rubella and polio.

Availability & Cost of Health Care

» Excellent health care is widely available from hospital (*Krankenhaus*) emergency rooms (*Notstation*) and at doctors' offices (*Arzt*).

» For minor illnesses or injuries (headache, bruises, diarrhoea), trained staff in pharmacies can provide valuable advice, sell prescription-free medications and advise if more specialised help is needed.

» Condoms are widely available in drugstores, pharmacies and supermarkets;

EUROPEAN HEALTH INSURANCE CARD

Citizens of the EU, Switzerland, Iceland, Norway and Liechtenstein receive free or reduced-cost, state-provided (not private) health-care coverage with the European Health Insurance Card (EHIC) for medical treatment that becomes necessary while in Germany. It does not cover emergency repatriation home. Each family member needs a separate card. UK residents can find applications at post offices or download them from the Department of Health website (www.dh.gov.uk).

You will need to pay directly and fill in a treatment form; keep the form to claim any refunds. In general you can claim back around 70% of the standard treatment cost.

Citizens of other countries need to check whether there is a reciprocal arrangement for free medical care between their country and Germany.

birth-control pills require a doctor's prescription.

Pharmacies

» German chemists (drugstores, *Drogerien*) do not sell any kind of medication, not even aspirin. Even over-the-counter (*rezeptfrei*) medications for minor health concerns, such as a cold or upset stomach, are only available at a pharmacy (*Apotheke*).

» For more serious conditions, you will need to produce a prescription (*Rezept*) from a licensed physician. If you take regular medication, be sure to bring a supply for your entire trip, as the same brand may not be available in Germany.

» The names and addresses of pharmacies open after hours (these rotate) are posted in every pharmacy window, or call ☑01141.

Insurance

» Comprehensive travel insurance to cover theft, loss and medical problems is highly recommended.

» Some policies specifically exclude dangerous activities, such as motorcycling, scuba diving and even trekking; read the fine print.

» Check that the policy covers ambulance or an emergency flight home.

» Before you leave, find out if your insurance plan makes payments directly to providers or reimburses you for health expenditures.

» Paying for your airline ticket with a credit card sometimes provides limited travel accident insurance – ask your credit-card company what it is prepared to cover.

» If you have to make a claim, be sure to keep all necessary documents and bills.

» Worldwide travel insurance is available at www.lonely planet.com/travel_services. You can buy, extend and claim online anytime – even if you're already on the road.

» Consider coverage for luggage theft or loss. If you already have a homeowners or renters policy, check what it will cover and only get supplemental insurance to protect against the rest.

» If you have prepaid a large portion of your vacation, trip cancellation insurance is worthwhile.

Internet Access

» Numerous cafes and bars tout wi-fi hot spots that let laptop owners hook up for free. If necessary, you'll be given a password when ordering.

» Many hotels have an internet corner for their guests, often at no charge. Note that wi-fi access in hotels is often limited to some rooms and/or public areas, so if you need in-room access, be sure to specify at the time of booking.

» Internet cafes seem to have the lifespan of a fruit fly, so listings are quickly outdated. Ask staff at your hotel for a recommendation.

» Wi-fi is available for a fee on select ICE train routes, including Frankfurt to Hamburg and Frankfurt to Munich. More than 20 stations, including those in Berlin, Munich, Hamburg and Frankfurt, also offer wi-fi in their DB Lounges, free to 1st-class passengers.

» Locate wi-fi hot spots at www.hotspot-locations.com or www.free-hotspot.com.

Legal Matters

» By law you must carry some form of photographic identification, such as your passport, national identity card or driving licence.

» The permissible blood-alcohol limit is 0.05%; drivers caught exceeding this are subject to stiff fines, a confiscated licence and even jail time. Drinking in public is not illegal, but be discreet about it.

» Cannabis possession is a criminal offence and punishment may range from a warning to a court appearance. Dealers face far stiffer penalties, as do people caught with any other 'recreational' drugs.

» If arrested, you have the right to make a phone call

SMOKE & MIRRORS

Germany was one of the last countries in Europe to legislate smoking. However, there is no nationwide law, with regulations left to each of the 16 states, creating a rather confusing patchwork of antismoking laws. Generally, smoking is a no-no in schools, hospitals, airports, train stations and other public facilities. But when it comes to bars, pubs, cafes and restaurants, every state does it just a little differently. Bavaria bans smoking practically everywhere – since 2011, even in Oktoberfest tents. In most states, though, lighting up is allowed in designated smoking rooms in restaurants and clubs. One-room establishments smaller than 75 sq m may allow smoking provided they serve no food and only admit patrons over 18. In any case, enforcement has been sporadic to say the least, despite the threat of fines.

and are presumed innocent until proven guilty, although you may be held in custody until trial. If you don't know a lawyer, contact your embassy.

Money

The unit of currency in Germany is the euro (€). Euros come in seven notes (€5, €10, €20, €50, €100, €200 and €500) and eight coins (€0.01, €0.02, €0.05, €0.10, €0.20, €0.50, €1 and €2). In 2012 the European inflation rate held at 2.4%.

For an exchange-rate table, see p17.

ATMs & Debit Cards

» The easiest and quickest way to obtain cash is by using your debit (bank) card at an ATM (Geldautomat) linked to international networks such as Cirrus, Plus, Star and Maestro.

» ATMs are ubiquitous and accessible 24/7.

» Many ATM cards double as debit cards and many shops, hotels, restaurants and other businesses accept them for payment. All cards use the 'chip and pin' system; instead of signing, you enter your PIN. If you're from overseas

and your card isn't chip-and-pin enabled, you may be able to sign the receipt, although not all places will accept your card, so ask first.

» Deutsche Bahn ticket vending machines in train stations and local public transport may not accept non-chip-and-pin cards.

Cash

Cash is king in Germany. Always carry some with you and plan to pay cash almost everywhere. It's also a good idea to set aside a small amount of euros as an emergency stash.

Credit Cards

Credit cards are becoming more widely accepted, but it's best not to assume you'll be able to use one – ask first. Even so, a piece of plastic is vital in emergencies and also useful for phone or internet bookings. Visa and Master-Card are more commonly accepted than American Express.

Avoid getting cash advances on your credit card via ATMs since fees are steep and you'll be charged interest immediately (in other words, there's no grace period as with purchases).

Report lost or stolen cards to the following:
American Express (☑069-9797 1000)
MasterCard (☑0800-819 1040)
Visa (☑0800-814 9100)

Moneychanging

Commercial banks usually charge a stiff fee (€5 to €10) per foreign-currency transaction, no matter the amount, if they offer exchange services at all.

Currency exchange offices (Wechselstuben) at airports, train stations and in bigger towns usually charge lower fees. Traveller-geared Reisebank branches are ubiquitous in Germany and are usually found at train stations. They keep longer hours than banks and are usually open on weekends.

Exchange facilities in rural areas are rare.

Tipping

Restaurant bills always include a Bedienung (service charge) but most people add 5% or 10% unless the service was truly abhorrent. It's considered rude to leave the tip on the table. When paying, tell the server the total amount you want to pay (say, if the bill is €28, you say €30). If you don't want change back, say 'Stimmt so' (that's fine).

WHERE & WHO	CUSTOMARY TIP
bar	round to nearest euro
hotel porter	€1-1.50 per bag
restaurant	5-10%
room cleaners	€1-2 per day
toilet attendants	€0.20-0.50
tour guide	€1-2 per person

Travellers Cheques

Travellers cheques are becoming obsolete in the age

of network-linked ATMs. German businesses generally don't accept them, even if denominated in euros, and banks charge exorbitant fees for cashing them (currency-exchange offices are usually better).

Photography

Germany is a photographer's dream. A good general reference guide is Lonely Planet's *Travel Photography* by Richard I'Anson.

» Germans tend to be deferential around photographers and will make a point of not walking in front of your camera, even if you want them to.

» No one seems to mind being photographed in the context of an overall scene, but if you want a close-up shot, you should ask first.

» Many museums, palaces and some churches charge a separate 'photography fee' (usually €2 or €3) if you want to take (noncommercial) pictures.

Post

The rate for letters up to 20g to destinations within Germany is €0.55 and €0.75 anywhere else in the world. For letters up to 50g, the rates are €0.90 and €1.45, respectively. For other rates, see www.deutsche-post.de.

Mail within Germany takes one to two days for delivery; to the USA or other European countries it takes three to five days and to Australia five to seven days.

Public Holidays

Germany observes three secular and eight religious public holidays. Banks, shops, post offices and public services close on these days. States with predominantly Catholic populations, such as Bavaria and Baden-Württemberg, also celebrate Epiphany (6 January), Corpus Christi (10 days after Pentecost), Assumption Day (15 August) and All Saints' Day (1 November). Reformation Day (31 October) is only observed in eastern Germany (but not Berlin).

The following are *gesetzliche Feiertage* (public holidays):

Neujahrstag (New Year's Day) 1 January

Ostern (Easter) March/April; Good Friday, Easter Sunday and Easter Monday

Christi Himmelfahrt (Ascension Day) Forty days after Easter

Maifeiertag/Tag der Arbeit (Labour Day) 1 May

Pfingsten (Whit/Pentecost Sunday & Monday) Fifty days after Easter

Tag der Deutschen Einheit (Day of German Unity) 3 October

Weihnachtstag (Christmas Day) 25 December

Zweiter Weihnachtstag (Boxing Day) 26 December

Telephone

German phone numbers consist of an area code, starting with 0, and the local number. Area codes can be up to six digits long; local numbers, up to nine digits. If dialling from a landline within the same city, you don't need to dial the area code. You must dial it if using a mobile.

Calling Germany from abroad Dial your country's international access code, then ☎49 (Germany's country code), then the area code (dropping the initial 0) and the local number.

Calling internationally from Germany Dial 00 (the international access code), then the country code (without the zero if there is one) and the local number.

Directory Enquiries From a landline call ☎11828 for numbers within Germany (€0.78 per call) or ☎11834 for outside Germany (€1.99 per minute). Not all operators will speak English. If you want an English-speaking operator, dial ☎11837 (€1.99 per minute).

Hotel Calls Direct-dialled calls made from hotel rooms are usually premium rate.

Calling on the Cheap

If you have access to a private phone, you can benefit from cheaper rates by using a 'Call-by-Call' access code (☎01016 or ☎01088). Rates change daily and are published in the newspapers or online at www.billigertelefo nieren.de (in German).

Telephone call shops, which cluster around train stations, may also offer competitive calling rates but often charge steep

---

SCHOOL HOLIDAYS

Each state sets its own school holidays but in general German children have six weeks off in summer and two weeks each around Christmas, Easter and October. Traffic is worst at the beginning of school holidays in population-rich states like North Rhine-Westphalia and can become a nightmare if several states let out their schools at the same time.

Germans are big fans of mini-holidays around public holidays, which are especially common in spring when many holidays fall on a Thursday or Monday. On those 'long weekends' you can expect heavy crowds on the roads, in the towns and everywhere else. Lodging is at a premium at these times.

PRACTICALITIES

» Women's clothing – a German size 36 equals a US size 6 and a UK size 10, then increases in increments of two, making size 38 a US size 8 and UK size 12.

» DVD – Germany is region code 2.

» Laundry – virtually all towns and cities have a *Waschsalon* (launderette). Hostels often have washing machines for guest use, while hotels offer cleaning services.

» Newspapers & magazines – dailies include the *Süddeutsche Zeitung, Die Welt* and *Der Tagesspiegel* (all quite centrist), and the more conservative *Frankfurter Allgemeine Zeitung. Die Zeit* is a weekly with in-depth reporting. *Der Spiegel* and *Focus* magazines are popular news weeklies.

» Radio – regional stations feature a mixed format of news, talk and music.

» Weights & measures – metric system.

connection fees. Make sure you understand the charges involved.

With a high-speed internet connection, you can talk for free via Skype, or use the SkypeOut service, which allows you to call landlines from your computer.

Mobile Phones

» German mobile numbers begin with a four-digit prefix, such as ☑0151, 0157, 0170, 0178.

» Mobile (cell) phones are called *Handys* and work on GSM 900/1800. If your home country uses a different standard, you'll need a multiband GSM phone while in Germany.

» To avoid high roaming costs consider buying a prepaid local SIM, provided you have an unlocked phone that works in Germany. The cheapest and least complicated of these are sold at discount supermarkets, such as Aldi, Netto and Lidl. An inexpensive online provider is www.blau.de. Telecommunications stores (eg T-Online, Vodafone, E-Plus or O₂) also sell SIMs. Top-up cards are widely available in kiosks and supermarkets.

» Calls made to a mobile phone are more expensive than those to a landline, but incoming calls are free.

» The use of mobile phones while driving is *verboten*

(forbidden) unless you're using a headset.

Phonecards

» Most public pay phones are operated by Deutsche Telekom (DT) and only work with phonecards (no coins) available in denominations of €5, €10 and €20 from DT stores, post offices and newsagents.

» For long-distance or international calls, prepaid calling cards issued by other companies tend to offer better rates than DT's phonecards, although they may charge a per-call connection fee. Read the fine print on the card itself. These cards are widely available at newsagents and telephone call shops.

» Phonecards sold at Reise-Bank branches found in many trains stations are reliable and offer fairly competitive rates. Landline calls within Germany and to the UK, for instance, are charged at €0.05 per minute; to the US the cost is €0.06. Note that calls made from mobile phones cost an extra €0.23 per minute.

Special Numbers

Customer service numbers in Germany often have prefixes that indicate the rate at which they're charged. The following list details the cost for calls made from landlines. Note that the per-minute charge can be as high as €0.42 for calls made from mobile phones.

NUMBER	COST
☑0700	€0.063 per minute
☑0800	free
☑01801	€0.04 per minute
☑01802	€0.06 per call
☑01803	€0.09 per minute
☑01804	€0.20 per call
☑01805	€0.14 per minute
☑0900	up to €2 per minute

Time

Clocks in Germany are set to central European time (GMT/UTC plus one hour). Daylight-saving time kicks in at 2am on the last Sunday in March and ends on the last Sunday in October. The use of the 24-hour clock (eg 6.30pm is 18.30) is the norm. The following are approximate (non-daylight savings) time differences:

CITY	NOON IN BERLIN
Auckland	11pm
Cape Town	noon
London	11am
New York	6am
San Francisco	3am
Sydney	9pm
Tokyo	8pm

Toilets

» German toilets are sit-down affairs. Men are expected to sit down when peeing except at urinals.

» Free-standing 24-hour self-cleaning toilet pods have become quite common. The cost is €0.50 and you have 15 minutes. Most are wheelchair-accessible.

» Toilets in malls, clubs, beer gardens, etc, often have an attendant who expects a tip of between €0.20 and €0.50.

» Toilets in airports are usually free, but in main train stations they are often maintained by private companies like Mc-Clean, which charge as much as €1.50 for the privilege.

» Along autobahns, rest stops with facilities are spaced about 20km to 30km apart.

Tourist Information

» Just about every community in Germany has a walk-in tourist office where you can get advice and pick up maps and pamphlets, sometimes in English. Many also offer a room- and ticket-reservation service that's usually free but is sometimes for a small fee.

» With few exceptions, at least one staff member will speak English and be willing to make the effort to help you.

» A useful pre-trip planning source is the **German National Tourist Office** (www.germany.travel), where information is available in almost 30 languages.

Travellers with Disabilities

» Germany is fairly progressive when it comes to barrier-free travel. There are access ramps and/or lifts in many public buildings, including train stations, museums, theatres and cinemas, especially in the cities. In historic towns, though, cobblestone streets make getting around difficult.

» Trains, trams, underground trains and buses are increasingly accessible. Some stations also have grooved platform borders to help blind passengers navigate. Seeing-eye dogs are allowed on all forms of public transport. For the hearing impaired, upcoming station names are often displayed electronically.

» Newer hotels have lifts and rooms with extra-wide doors and spacious bathrooms.

» Some car-rental agencies offer hand-controlled vehicles and vans with wheelchair lifts at no charge, but you must reserve in advance. In parking lots and garages, look for designated disabled spots with a wheelchair symbol.

» Many local and regional tourist offices have brochures for people with disabilities, although usually in German.

Good general resources:
Deutsche Bahn Mobility Service Centre (www.bahn.com) Train access information and route planning assistance. The website has useful information in English (search for 'barrier-free travel').

German National Tourist Office (www.germany.travel) Your first port of call, with inspirational info in English on walking throughout Germany.

Natko (www.natko.de) Central clearing house for enquiries about barrier-free travel in Germany.

Visas

» EU nationals only need their passport or national identity card to enter, stay and work in Germany, even for stays over six months. If you plan to stay longer, you're required to register with the authorities (*Bürgeramt*, or Citizens' Office) within two weeks of your arrival.

» Citizens of Australia, Canada, Israel, Japan, New Zealand, Poland, Switzerland and the US need only a valid passport but no visa if entering Germany as tourists for up to three months within a six-month period. Passports must be valid for another three months beyond the intended departure date. For stays exceeding 90 days, contact your nearest German embassy or consulate and begin your visa application well in advance.

» Nationals from other countries need a Schengen Visa, named for the 1995 Schengen Agreement that abolished international border controls between most European countries; as of 2012, there were 25 member states. Applications for a Schengen Visa must be filed with the embassy or consulate of the country that is your primary destination. It is valid for stays up to 90 days. Legal residency in any Schengen country makes a visa unnecessary, regardless of your nationality.

» For details, see www.auswaertiges-amt.de and check with a German consulate in your country.

Volunteering

Websites like www.goabroad.com and www.transitionsabroad.com throw up opportunities for volunteering in Germany: helping out on a farm in the Alps, restoring a medieval castle in eastern Germany, helping kids or the elderly in Dresden, or teaching English to long-term unemployed in Berlin are just some of the experiences available.

Here's a small selection of volunteer organisations:
Conversation Corps (www.geovisions.org) Volunteer 15 hours a week to teach a German family English in exchange for room and board.

Volunteers for Peace (www.vfp.org) USA-based nonprofit offers a potpourri of opportunities, from construction to farm work or social work.

WWOOF (www.wwoof.de) Help out on a small organic farm harvesting, tending animals, bringing in hay or gardening.

Transport

GETTING THERE & AWAY

Most travellers arrive in Germany by air, or by rail and road connections from neighbouring countries. Flights, tours and rail tickets can be booked online at lonely planet.com/bookings.

Entering the Country

Entering Germany is usually a very straightforward procedure. If you're arriving from any of the 24 other Schengen countries, such as the Netherlands, Poland, Austria or the Czech Republic, you no longer have to show your passport or go through customs in Germany, no matter which nationality you are. If you're coming in from the US or South Africa, full border procedures apply. For passport and visa requirements, see p775.

Air

Frankfurt Airport is the main gateway for transcontinental flights, although Düsseldorf and Munich also receive their share of overseas air traffic. At the time of writing, Berlin had two smaller international airports, Tegel and Schönefeld, but these will be replaced by the brand-new Berlin Brandenburg Airport upon its completion, scheduled for 2013. New to Berlin are direct flights from such US gateways as New York and Los Angeles. There are also sizeable airports in Hamburg, Cologne/Bonn and Stuttgart, and smaller ones in such cities as Bremen, Dresden, Hanover, Leipzig, Münster-Osnabrück and Nuremberg.

Lufthansa, Germany's national flagship carrier and Star Alliance member, operates a vast network of domestic and international flights and has one of the world's best safety records. Practically every other national carrier from around the world serves Germany, along with budget carriers **Air Berlin** (www.airberlin.com), **EasyJet** (EZY; ☎ 0900-1100 161; www.easyjet.com), **Flybe** (BE; www.flybe.com), **airBaltic** (BT; www.airbaltic.com), **Ryanair** (FR; ☎ 0900-116 0500; www.ryanair.com) and **Germanwings** (www.germanwings.com). Note that Ryanair usually flies to remote airports, which are often little more than recycled military airstrips. Frankfurt-Hahn, for instance, is actually near the Moselle River, about 110km northwest of Frankfurt proper.

Airports

» **Berlin** (BBI; www.berlin-airport.de)

» **Bremen** (BRE; www.airport-bremen.de)

» **Cologne-Bonn** (CGN; www.airport-cgn.de)

» **Düsseldorf** (DUS; www.dus-int.de)

» **Hamburg** (HAM; www.airport.de)

» **Hanover** (HAJ; www.hannover-airport.de)

» **Frankfurt am Main** (FRA; www.frankfurt-airport.com)

» **Leipzig-Halle** (LEJ; www.leipzig-halle-airport.de)

» **Münster-Osnabrück** (FMO; www.flughafen.fmo.de)

» **Munich** (MUC; www.munich-airport.de)

» **Nuremberg** (NUE; www.airport-nuernberg.de)

» **Stuttgart** (SGT; www.stuttgart-airport.com)

Tickets

Timing is key when it comes to snapping up cheap airfares. You can generally save a bundle by booking early, travelling midweek (Tuesday to Thursday) and in low season (October to March/April in the case of Germany), or flying in the late evening or early morning. If you're planning to travel between June and September, it's wise to book well ahead.

» Check the airlines' own websites for late-breaking fares or promotions, or search for the best deals with online agencies such as www.expedia.com, www.travelocity.com, www.skyscanner.net, www.kayak.com or www.ebookers.com.

» **STA Travel** (www.statravel.com) and **Flight Centre** (www.flightcentre.com) are recommended travel agencies with online booking service and brick-and-mortar branches in many countries.

» Coming from Australia or New Zealand, round-the-world (RTW) tickets may work out cheaper than regular return fares, especially if you're planning to visit other countries besides Germany. They're most value for trips that combine Germany with Asia or North America.

Land

Bicycle

Bringing a bicycle to Germany is much cheaper and less complicated than you might think.

Eurotunnel bike shuttle service (☎reservations 9am-5.30pm Mon-Fri 01303-282 201; www.eurotunnel.com) through the Channel Tunnel charges just UK£16 one-way for a bicycle and its rider.

A bike that's been dismantled so that it's the size of a suitcase may be carried on board a **Eurostar** (☎in the UK 0844-822 5822; www.eurostar.com) train from London, Paris or Brussels just like any other luggage. Otherwise, there is a UK£30 charge and you'll need advance reservations.

Deutsche Bahn (www.bahn.com) charges €10 if travelling internationally on its trains.

On ferries, foot passengers can usually bring a bicycle, sometimes free of charge.

Bus

EUROLINES

The umbrella organisation of 32 European long-haul coach operators connecting 500 destinations across Europe. Its website has links to each national company's site with detailed fare and route information, promotional offers, contact numbers and, in most cases, an online booking system. In Germany, Eurolines is represented by **Deutsche Touring** (☎069-790 3501; www.touring.de).

» Midweek fares from London to Frankfurt can be as low as £35 one-way.

» Children between the ages of four and 12 pay half price, while teens, students and seniors get 10% off regular fares.

» A **Eurolines Pass** (www.eurolines-pass.com) offers unlimited travel between 51 cities within a 15- or 30-day period. From late June to early September, the pass costs €350/460 (15/30 days) for those over 26 years and €295/380 for travellers under 26 years. Lower prices apply during the rest of the year; the website has full details. It's sold online and by travel agents.

BUSABOUT

A backpacker-geared hop-on, hop-off service, **Busabout** (www.busabout.com) runs coaches along three interlocking European loops between May and October. Passes are sold online and through travel agents.

» Germany is part of the North Loop. Within Germany, the service stops in Berlin, Dresden, Munich and Stuttgart. Loops can be combined. In Munich, for instance, the north loop intersects with the south loop to Italy.

» Trips on one loop cost €489, on two loops €849 and on three €1019.

» If you don't like travelling along predetermined routes, you can buy the Flexitrip Pass, which allows you to travel between cities across different loops. It costs €429 for six stops.

Car & Motorcycle

When bringing your own vehicle to Germany, you need a valid driving licence, your car registration certificate and proof of insurance. Foreign cars must display a nationality sticker unless they have official European plates. You also need to carry a warning (hazard) triangle and a first-aid kit.

EUROTUNNEL

Coming from the UK, the fastest way to the Continent is via the **Eurotunnel** (☎in Germany 01805-000 248, in the UK 08443-35 35 35; www.eurotunnel.com). These shuttle trains whisk cars, motorbikes, bicycles and coaches from Folkestone in England through the Channel Tunnel to Coquelles (near Calais, in France) in about 35 minutes. From there, you can be in Germany in about three hours. Loading and unloading takes about one hour.

CLIMATE CHANGE & TRAVEL

Every form of transport that relies on carbon-based fuel generates CO_2, the main cause of human-induced climate change. Modern travel is dependent on aeroplanes, which might use less fuel per kilometre per person than most cars but travel much greater distances. The altitude at which aircraft emit gases (including CO_2) and particles also contributes to their climate change impact. Many websites offer 'carbon calculators' that allow people to estimate the carbon emissions generated by their journey and, for those who wish to do so, to offset the impact of the greenhouse gases emitted with contributions to portfolios of climate-friendly initiatives throughout the world. Lonely Planet offsets the carbon footprint of all staff and author travel.

Shuttles run daily around the clock, with several departures hourly during peak periods. Fares are calculated per vehicle, including up to nine passengers, and depend on such factors as time of day, season and length of stay. Standard one-way tickets start at £60. The website and travel agents have full details.

For road rules and other driving-related information, see p784.

Train

Rail services link Germany with virtually every country in Europe. In Germany ticketing is handled by **Deutsche Bahn** (www.bahn.com). Long-distance trains connecting major cities with those in other countries are called EuroCity (EC) trains. Seat reservations are essential during the peak summer season and around major holidays.

Germany is also linked by overnight train to many European cities; routes include Amsterdam to Munich, Zurich to Berlin and Paris to Hamburg. Deutsche Bahn's overnight service is called **City Night Line** (☑in Germany 01805-141 514; www.nachtzugreise.de) and offers three levels of comfort:

» Schlafwagen (sleeping car; €50 to €110 supplement) Private air-conditioned compartment for up to four passengers; the deluxe version has a shower and toilet.

» Liegewagen (couchette, €27.50 to €37.50 supplement) Sleeps up to six people; when you book an individual berth, you must share the compartment with others; women may ask for a single-sex couchette at the time of booking, but book early.

» Sitzwagen (seat carriage; €11.50 to €17.50 supplement) Roomy reclining seat.

Useful websites:

www.raileurope.com Detailed train information and ticket and train pass sales from Rail Europe.

www.railteam.eu Excellent journey planner provided by an alliance of seven European railways, including Eurostar, Deutsche Bahn and France's SNCF. No booking function yet.

www.seat61.com Comprehensive trip planning information, including ferry details from the UK.

www.railpassenger.info Details on Europe's 200,000km rail network.

EUROSTAR

The Channel Tunnel makes train travel between the UK and Germany a fast and enjoyable option. High-speed **Eurostar** (☑in the UK 0844-822 5822; www.eurostar.com) passenger trains hurtle at least 10 times daily between London and Paris (the journey takes 2½ hours) or Brussels (two hours). At either city you can change to regular or other high-speed trains to destinations in Germany.

Eurostar fares depend on carriage class, time of day, season and destination. Children, rail-pass holders and those aged between 12 and 25 and over 60 qualify for discounts. For the latest fare information, including promotions and special packages, check the website.

RAIL PASSES

If you want to cover lots of territory in and around Germany within a specific time, a rail pass is a convenient and good-value option. They're valid for unlimited travel during their period of validity on national railways as well as some private lines, ferries and river boat services.

There are two types: the Eurail Pass for people living outside Europe and the InterRail Pass for residents of Europe, including Russia and Turkey.

Eurail Passes (www.eurail.com) are valid for travel in 23 countries and need to be purchased before you leave your home country, eg on the website, through a travel agent or at www.raileurope.

com. A variety of passes are available:

Eurail Global Pass Unlimited 1st-class travel for 15 or 21 consecutive days, or one, two or three months. There are also versions that give you 10 or 15 days of travel within a two-month period. The 15-day version costs €549.

Eurail Select Pass Five, six, eight or 10 days of travel within two months but only in three, four or five bordering countries; a five-day pass in three countries costs €296 in 2nd class and €348 in 1st.

Eurail Regional Pass Gets you around two neighbouring countries on five, six, eight or 10 days within two months. The Germany–Czech Republic Pass for five days days costs €249 in 2nd class or €304 in 1st class.

Groups of two to five people travelling together save 15% off the regular adult fares. If you're under 26, prices drop 35%, but you must travel in 2nd class. Children aged between four and 11 years get a 50% discount on the adult fare. Children under four years travel free.

The website has the details, as well as a ticket-purchasing function allowing you to pay in several currencies.

InterRail Passes (www.interrailnet.com) are valid for unlimited travel in 30 countries. As with the Eurail Pass, you can pick from several schemes:

InterRail Global Pass Unlimited travel in 30 countries and is available either for 15 days (€267), 22 days (€494) or one month (€638) of continuous travel, for five travel days within a 10-day period (€267) or for 10 travel days within a 22-day period (€381).

InterRail Germany Pass Buys three, four, six or eight days of travel within a one-month period. The cost is €205/226/288/319,

BY SEA FROM THE UK

There are no direct ferry services between Germany and the UK, but you can go via the Netherlands, Belgium or France and drive or train it from there. For fare details and to book tickets, check the ferry websites or go to www.ferrybooker.com or www.ferrysavers.com.

ROUTE	COMPANY	CONNECTION	WEBSITE
Via France	P&O Ferries	Dover-Calais	www.poferries.com
	DFDS Seaways	Dover-Calais	www.dfdsseaways.com
Via Belgium	P&O Ferries	Hull-Zeebrugge	www.poferries.com
	Transeuropa Ferries	Ramsgate-Oostende	www.transeuropaferries.com
Via the Netherlands	P&O Ferries	Hull-Rotterdam	www.poferries.com
	DFDS Seaways	Newcastle-Amsterdam	www.dfdsseaways.com
	Stena Line	Harwich-Hoek van Holland	www.stenaline.com

respectively. This pass is not available if you are a resident of Germany.

Prices quoted are for one adult travelling in 2nd class. Different prices apply to 1st-class tickets and for travellers under 26. Children aged between four and 11 years get a 50% discount on the adult fare. Children under four years travel for free.

For detailed information on getting around Germany by train, see p785.

Water

Lake Ferry

The Romanshorn–Friedrichshafen car ferry provides the quickest way across Lake Constance between Switzerland and Germany. It's operated year-round by **Schweizerische Bodensee Schifffahrt** (⌂in Switzerland +41 (0)71-466 7888; www.sbsag.ch), takes 40 minutes and costs €8.60/4.30 per adult/child. Bicycle fares are €5.70; car fares start at €29.10.

Sea

Germany's main ferry ports are Kiel and Travemünde (near Lübeck) in Schleswig-Holstein, and Rostock and Sassnitz (on Rügen Island) in Mecklenburg–Western Pomerania. All have services to Scandinavia and the Baltic states. Timetables change from season to season.

Return tickets are often cheaper than two one-way tickets. Some ferry companies now set fares the way budget airlines do: the earlier you book, the less you pay. Last-minute tickets are, predictably, the most costly. Seasonal demand is a crucial factor (school holidays and July and August are especially busy), as is the time of day (an early-evening ferry can cost much more than one at 4am). For overnight ferries, cabin size, location and amenities affect the price. Book well in advance if you're bringing a car.

People under 25 and over 60 may qualify for discounts. To get the best fares, check out the booking service offered by **Ferry Savers** (www.ferrysavers.com).

GETTING AROUND

Germans are whizzes at moving people around, and the public transport network is among the best in Europe. The best ways of getting around the country are by car and by train. Regional bus services fill the gaps in areas not well served by the rail network.

Air

Most large and many smaller German cities have their own airports and numerous carriers operate domestic flights within Germany. Lufthansa has the most dense route network. Other airlines offering domestic flights include **Air Berlin** (www.airberlin.com) and **Germanwings** (www.germanwings.com).

Unless you're flying from one end of the country to the other, say Berlin to Munich or Hamburg to Munich, planes are only marginally quicker than trains if you factor in the time it takes to get to and from airports.

Bicycle

Cycling is allowed on all roads and highways but not on the autobahns (motorways). Cyclists must follow the same rules of the road as cars and motorcycles. Helmets are not compulsory (not even for children), but wearing one is common sense.

On Public Transport

Bicycles may be taken on most trains but require a separate ticket (Fahrradkarte). These cost €9 per trip on long-distance trains (IC and EC and City Night Line). If

INTERNATIONAL FERRY COMPANIES

COUNTRY	COMPANY	CONNECTION	WEBSITE
Denmark	Scandlines	Gedser-Rostock, Rødby-Puttgarden	www.scandlines.com
	Faergen	Rønne-Sassnitz	www.faergen.dk
Finland	Finnlines	Helsinki-Travemünde, Helsinki-Rostock	www.finnlines.com
Latvia	Scandlines	Liepaja-Travemünde, Ventspils-Travemünde	www.scandlines.com
	Ave Line	Riga-Travemünde	www.aveline.lv
	TransRussiaExpress	Ventspils-Travemünde, Ventspils-Sassnitz	www.tre.de
Lithuania	DFDS Seaways	Klaipėda-Kiel, Klaipėda-Sassnitz	www.dfdsseaways.com
Norway	Color Line	Oslo-Kiel	www.colorline.com
Russia	TransRussiaExpress	St Petersburg-Travemünde, St Petersburg-Sassnitz	www.tre.de
	DFDS Seaways	Ust Luga-Kiel	www.dfdsseaways.com
Sweden	Stena Line	Gothenburg-Kiel	www.stenaline.com
	Finnlines	Malmö-Travemünde	www.finnlines.com
	Scandlines	Trelleborg-Rostock, Trelleborg-Sassnitz	www.scandlines.com
	TT-Line	Trelleborg-Rostock, Trelleborg-Travemünde	www.ttline.com

you're travelling internationally, the fee is €10 per trip. You need to reserve a space at least one day ahead and leave your bike in the bike compartment usually at the beginning or end of the train. Bicycles are not allowed on high-speed ICE trains.

The fee on local and regional trains (IRE, RB, RE, S-Bahn) is €5 per day. There is no charge at all on some local trains.

For €28.50 you can also ship your bicycle by train, provided you have a ticket yourself and dismantle the bike and put it inside a bike box. It will be picked up and dropped off at a location of your choice. Drivers can sell you the box for €0.90. Most bikes arrive within two days. This service is only offered within Germany and to Luxembourg, Austria and Switzerland.

For full details, enquire at a local station or call ☑01805-99 66 33, ext. 'Fahrrad'. Free lines are also listed in DB's complimentary *Bahn & Bike* brochure (in German), as are the almost 250 stations where you can rent bikes. Both are available for download from www.bahn.de/bahnundbike.

Many regional companies use buses with special bike racks. Bicycles are also allowed on practically all boat and ferry services on Germany's lakes and rivers.

Rental

Most towns and cities have some sort of bicycle-hire station, often at or near the train station. Hire costs range from €7 to €20 per day and from €35 to €85 per week, depending on the model of bicycle. A minimum deposit of €30 (more for fancier

bikes) and/or ID are required. Some outfits also offer repair service or bicycle-storage facilities.

Hotels, especially in resort areas, sometimes keep a stable of bicycles for their guests, often at no charge.

Call a Bike (☑07000 522 5522; www.callabike.de) is an automated bike-rental scheme offered by **Deutsche Bahn** (www.bahn.com). It requires that you preregister with a credit card, either online for free or by phone for €5. Once you've located a bicycle, call the number listed on the lock and follow the instructions. The cost is €0.08 per minute or €15 per day. In Stuttgart and Hamburg, use is free for the first 30 minutes. Bikes are parked in multiple locations throughout Aachen, Berlin, Frank, Karlsruhe, Cologne, Munich, Hamburg, Kassel and Stuttgart as well as by the main train stations in a couple of dozen other cities. For full details, see the website; at this point, there's no English version available.

Boat

With two seas and a lake- and river-filled interior, don't be surprised to find yourself in a boat at some point. For basic transport, boats are primarily used when travelling to or between the East Frisian Islands in Lower Saxony; the North Frisian Islands in Schleswig-Holstein; Helgoland, which also belongs to Schleswig-Holstein; and the islands of Poel, Rügen and Hiddensee in Mecklenburg–Western Pomerania.

Scheduled boat services operate along sections of the Rhine, the Elbe and the Danube. There are also ferry services in areas with no or only a few bridges, as well as on major lakes such as the Chiemsee and Lake Starnberg in Bavaria and Lake Constance in Baden-Württemberg.

From around April to October, local operators run scenic river or lake cruises lasting from one hour to a full day (see p35).

Bus

Local & Regional

Basically, wherever there is a train, take it. Buses are generally slower, less dependable and more polluting than trains, but in some rural areas they may be your only option for getting around without your own vehicle. This is especially true of the Harz Mountains, sections of the Bavarian Forest and the Alpine foothills. Separate bus companies, each with its own tariffs and schedules, operate in the different regions.

The frequency of services varies from 'rarely' to 'constantly'. Commuter-geared routes offer limited or no service in the evenings and at weekends, so keep this in mind or risk finding yourself stuck in a remote place on a Saturday night. Make it a habit to ask about special fare deals, such as daily or weekly passes or tourist tickets.

In cities, buses generally converge at the *Busbahnhof* or *Zentraler Omnibus Bahnhof* (ZOB; central bus station), which is often near the Hauptbahnhof (central train station).

Long Distance

Deutsche Touring (☎069-790 3501; www.touring.de) runs daily overnight services between Hamburg and Mannheim via Hanover, Frankfurt, Göttingen, Kassel and Heidelberg. If you book early, trips between any two cities cost just €9. Fares top out at €49 for the full Hanover–Mannheim route for tickets bought on the bus. Children under 12 pay half price.

Berlin Linien Bus (www.berlinlinienbus.de) connects major cities (primarily Berlin, but also Munich, Düsseldorf and Frankfurt) with each other as well as holiday regions such as the Harz, the islands of Rügen and Usedom and the Bavarian Alps. One of the most popular routes is the express bus to Hamburg, which makes the journey from Berlin in 3¼ hours 12 times daily with one-way fares ranging from €9 to €21.50.

Tickets are available online and from travel agencies. Children under four years travel for free and discounts are available for older children, students, those over 60 and groups of six or more.

Car & Motorcycle

German roads are excellent and motoring around the country can be a lot of fun. The country's pride and joy is its 11,000km network of autobahns (motorways, freeways). Every 40km to 60km, you'll find elaborate service areas with petrol stations, toilet facilities and restaurants; many are open 24 hours. In between are rest stops (*Rastplatz*), which usually have picnic tables and toilet facilities. Orange emergency call boxes are spaced about 2km apart.

Autobahns are supplemented by an extensive network of *Bundesstrassen* (secondary 'B' roads, highways) and smaller *Landstrassen* (country roads). No tolls are charged on any public roads.

If your car is not equipped with a navigational system, having a good map or road atlas is essential, especially when negotiating the tangle of country roads. Navigating in Germany is not done by the points of the compass. That is to say that you'll find no signs saying 'north' or 'west'. Rather, you'll see signs pointing you in the direction of a city, so you'd best have that map right in your lap to stay oriented. Maps cost a few euros and are sold at bookstores, train stations, airports and petrol stations. The best are published by Freytag & Berndt, ADAC, Falk and Euromap.

Driving in the cities can be stressful thanks to congestion and the expense and scarcity of parking. In city centres, parking is usually limited to parking lots and garages charging between €0.50 and €2 per hour. Note that some parking lots (*Parkplatz*) and garages (*Parkhaus*) close at night and charge an overnight fee. Many have special parking slots for women that are especially well lit and close to exits.

Many cities have electronic parking guidance systems directing you to the nearest garage and indicating the number of available spaces. Street parking usually works on the

German Autobahns

pay-and-display system and tends to be short-term (one or two hours) only. For long-term and overnight parking, consider leaving your car outside the centre in a Park & Ride (P+R) lot, which are free or low cost.

Automobile Associations

Germany's main motoring organisation, the **Allgemeiner Deutscher Automobil-Club** (ADAC; ☏ for roadside assistance 0180-222 2222, from

mobile phone 222 222; www. adac.de) has offices in all major cities and many smaller ones. Its roadside assistance program is also available to members of its affiliates, including British (AA), American (AAA) and Canadian (CAA) associations.

Driving Licences

Drivers need a valid driving licence. International Driving Permits (IDP) are not compulsory, but having one may help Germans make

sense of your home licence (always carry that, too) and may simplify the car or motorcycle hire process. IDPs are inexpensive, valid for a year and are issued by your local automobile association – bring a passport photo and your home licence.

Car Hire

As anywhere, rates for car hire vary considerably, but you should be able to get an economy-size vehicle from about €40 to €60 per day, plus insurance and taxes. Expect surcharges for hire cars originating at airports and train stations, additional drivers and one-way hire. Child or infant safety seats may be hired for about €5 per day and should be reserved at the time of booking.

Rental cars with automatic transmission are rare in Germany and will usually need to be ordered well in advance.

To hire your own wheels, you'll need to be at least 25 years old and possess a valid driving licence and a major credit card. Some companies lease to drivers between the ages of 21 and 24 for an additional charge (about €12 to €20 per day). Younger people or those without a credit card are usually out of luck. For insurance reasons, driving into an Eastern European country, such as the Czech Republic or Poland, is often a no-no.

All the main international companies maintain branches at airports, major train stations and towns. These include the following:

» **Alamo** (☎01805-462 526; www.alamo.com)

» **Avis** (☎0180-555 77; www.avis.de)

» **Europcar** (☎0180-580 00; www.europcar.com)

» **Hertz** (☎01805-333 535; www.hertz.com)

» **National** (☎0800-464 7336; www.nationalcar.com)

» **Sixt** (☎01805-25 25 25; www.sixt.de)

Pre-booked and prepaid packages arranged in your home country usually work out much cheaper than on-the-spot rentals. The same is true of fly/drive packages. Deals can be found on the internet and through companies including **Auto Europe** (☎in the US 888-223-5555; www.autoeurope.com), **Holiday Autos** (☎in the UK 0871-472 5229; www.holidayautos.co.uk), and **DriveAway Holidays** (☎in Australia 1300 723 972; www.driveaway.com.au).

PRIVATE CAR SHARING

What Airbnb is to apartment sharing, **Autonetzer** (www.autonetzer.de) is to car sharing. The deal: you need a car, cheap. A private individual wants to rent out his or her car. Autonetzer brings the two of you together. This works best for short-term rentals, from a few hours to a few days. Per-day rates start at €12 plus €8.90 for comprehensive insurance. Start by looking for a suitable car on the website, then make a booking request. If successful, you need to register and make the payment through the Autonetzer platform. Contact the renter and make arrangements for a pick up. It's an informal affair. Don't expect cars to be the latest model, in top shape or super clean. It helps to speak or read German to navigate the website and deal with the car owner.

Fuel & Spare Parts

Petrol stations, nearly all of which are self-service, are ubiquitous except in sparsely populated rural areas. Petrol is sold in litres.

Finding spare parts should not be a problem, especially in the cities, although availability depends on the age and model of your car. Be sure to have some sort of roadside emergency assistance plan in case your car breaks down.

Insurance

German law requires that all registered vehicles carry third-party liability insurance, including those brought in from abroad. You could face seriously huge costs by driving uninsured or underinsured. Germans are very fussy about their cars, and even nudging someone's bumper when jostling out of a tight parking space may well result in you having to pay for an entirely new one.

Normally, private cars registered and insured in another European country do not require additional insurance, but do check this with your insurance provider

---

GREENING CITY CENTRES

To decrease air pollution caused by fine particles, dozens of cities throughout Germany have introduced so-called Green Zones, which are low-emission zones that may only be entered by cars displaying an *Umweltplakette* (emissions sticker; sometimes also called *Feinstaubplakette*). And yes, this includes foreign vehicles. No stickers are needed for motorcycles.

The easiest way to obtain the sticker is by ordering it online from the TÜV (Technical Inspection Authority) at www.tuev-sued.de or www.tuev-nord.de, both of which provide easy instructions in English. The cost is €6 per car and stickers are valid throughout the country. Once in Germany, stickers are also available from designated repair centres, car dealers and vehicle licensing offices. Drivers caught without one will be fined €40.

Cities currently participating include: Augsburg, Berlin, Bochum, Bonn, Bottrop, Bremen, Cologne, Dortmund, Duisburg, Düsseldorf, Essen, Frankfurt am Main, Freiburg, Gelsenkirchen, Halle, Hanover, Heidelberg, Heilbronn, Karlsruhe, Leipzig, Magdeburg, Mannheim, Munich, Münster, Oberhausen, Osnabrück, Pforzheim, Regensburg, Reutlingen, Schwäbisch Gmünd, Stuttgart, Tübingen and Ulm. More are expected to join.

before leaving home. Also keep a record of who to contact in case of a breakdown or accident.

When hiring a vehicle, make sure your contract includes adequate liability insurance at the very minimum. Rental agencies almost never include insurance that covers damage to the vehicle itself, called Collision Damage Waiver (CDW) or Loss Damage Waiver (LDW). It's optional, but driving without it is not recommended. Some credit-card companies cover CDW/LDW for a certain period if you charge the entire rental to your card; always confirm with your card issuer what it covers in Germany. Note that some local agencies may refuse to accept your credit-card coverage as proof of insurance.

Road Rules

Driving is on the right-hand side of the road and standard international signs are in use. If you're unfamiliar with these, pick up a pamphlet at your local motoring organisation. Obey the road rules and speed limits carefully.

Speed- and red-light cameras as well as radar traps are common and notices are sent to the car's registration address wherever that may be. If you're renting a car, the police will obtain your home address from the rental agency. There's a long list of fineable actions, including using abusive language or gestures and running out of petrol on the autobahn.

The usual speed limits are 50km/h on main city streets and 100km/h on highways, unless they are otherwise marked. Limits drop to 30km/h in residential streets. And yes, it's true, there really are no speed limits on autobahns...in theory. In fact, there are many stretches where slower speeds must be observed (near towns, road construction), so be sure to keep an eye out for those signs or risk getting ticketed. And keep in mind: the higher the speed, the higher the fuel consumption and emissions.

Other key driving rules:

» The highest permissible blood-alcohol level for drivers is 0.05%, which for most people equates to one glass of wine or two small beers.

» Seatbelts are mandatory for all passengers, including those in the back seat, and there's a €30 fine if you get caught not wearing one. If you're in an accident, not wearing a seatbelt may invalidate your insurance.

» Children need a child seat if under four years and a seat cushion if under 12; they may not ride in the front until age 13.

» Motorcyclists must wear a helmet.

» Mobile phones may be used only if they are equipped with a hands-free kit or speakerphone.

» Pedestrians at crossings have absolute right of way over all motor vehicles.

» Always watch out for cyclists when turning right; they have the right of way.

» Right turns at a red light are only legal if there's a green arrow pointing to the right.

Hitching & Ride-Share

Hitching (trampen) is never entirely safe in any country and we don't recommend it. That said, in some rural areas in Germany poorly served by public transport – such as sections of the Alpine foothills and the Bavarian Forest – it is not uncommon to see people thumbing for a ride. If you do decide to hitch, understand that you are taking a small but potentially serious risk. Remember that it's safer to travel in pairs and be sure to let someone know where you are planning to go. It's illegal to hitchhike on autobahns and their entry or exit ramps.

A safer, inexpensive and ecoconscious form of travelling is ride-shares, where you travel as a passenger in a private car in exchange for some petrol money. Most arrangements are now set up via free online ride boards, such as www.mitfahrzent rale.de, www.mitfahrgelegen heit.de and www.drive2day. de. You can advertise a ride yourself or link up with a driver going to your destination. **Citynetz** (www.citynetz -mitfahrzentrale.de) maintains a few staffed offices in major cities, but they do charge a small commission for linking you up with a driver.

Local Transport

Germany's cities and larger towns have efficient public transport systems. Bigger cities, such as Berlin and Munich, integrate buses, trams, U-Bahn (underground, subway) trains and S-Bahn (suburban) trains into a single network.

Fares are determined either by zones or time travelled, or sometimes by both. A multiticket strip (Streifenkarte) or day pass (Tageskarte) generally offer better value than a single-ride ticket. Normally, tickets must be stamped upon boarding in order to be valid. Fines are levied if you're caught without a valid ticket.

Bicycle

From nuns to Lance Armstrong wannabes, Germans love to cycle, be it for errands, commuting, fitness or pleasure. Many cities have dedicated bicycle lanes, which must be used unless obstructed. There's no helmet law, not even for children, although using one is recommended, for obvious reasons. Bicycles must be equipped with a white light at the front, a red one at the back and yellow reflectors on the wheels and pedals.

Bus & Tram

Buses are a ubiquitous form of public transport and practically all towns have their own comprehensive network. Buses run at regular intervals, with restricted services in the evenings and at weekends. Some cities operate night buses along popular routes to get night owls safely home.

Occasionally, buses are supplemented by trams, which are usually faster because they travel on their own tracks, largely independent of other traffic. In city centres they sometimes run underground. Bus and tram drivers generally sell single tickets and day passes only.

S-Bahn

Metropolitan areas, such as Berlin and Munich, have a system of suburban trains called the S-Bahn. They are faster and cover a wider area than buses or trams but tend to be less frequent. S-Bahn lines are often linked to the national rail network and sometimes connect urban centres. Rail passes are generally valid on these services. Specific S-Bahn lines are abbreviated with 'S' followed by the number (eg S1, S7).

Taxi

Taxis are expensive and, given the excellent public transport systems, not recommended unless you're in a real hurry. (They can actually be slower than trains or trams if you're stuck in traffic.) Cabs are metered and charged at a base rate (flag fall) plus a per-kilometre fee. These charges are fixed but vary from city to city. Some drivers charge extra for bulky luggage or night-time rides. It's rarely possible to flag down a taxi. More typical is to order one by phone (look up *Taxiruf* in the phone book) or board at a taxi rank. If you're at a hotel or restaurant, ask staff to call one

for you. Taxis also often wait outside theatres or performance venues.

U-Bahn

Underground (subway) trains are known as U-Bahn in Germany and are the fastest form of travel in big cities. Route maps are posted in all stations and at many you'll be able to pick up a printed copy from the stationmaster or ticket office. The frequency of trains usually fluctuates with demand, meaning there are more trains during commuter rush hours than in the middle of the day. Buy tickets from vending machines and validate them before the start of your journey. Specific U-Bahn lines are abbreviated with 'U' followed by the number (eg U1, U7).

Train

Germany's rail system is operated almost entirely by **Deutsche Bahn** (www.bahn.com), with a variety of train types serving just about every corner in the country. The DB website has detailed information (in English and other languages), as well as a ticket purchasing function with detailed instructions.

» Tickets may be bought using a credit card up to 10 minutes before departure at no surcharge. You will need to present a printout of your ticket, as well as the credit card used to buy it, to the conductor.

» Tickets are also are available from vending machines and agents at the *Reisezentrum* (travel centre) in train stations. The latter charge a service fee but are useful if you need assistance with planning your itinerary (ask for an English-speaking clerk).

» Smaller stations may only have a few ticket windows and the smallest ones may have only vending machines. English instructions are usually provided.

» Tickets sold on board incur a surcharge and are not available on regional trains (RE, RB, IRE) or the S-Bahn. Agents, conductors and machines usually accept major credit cards. With few exceptions (station unstaffed, vending machine broken), you will be charged a fine if caught without a ticket.

» Most train stations have coin-operated lockers costing from €1 to €4 per 24-hour period. Larger stations have staffed left-luggage offices (*Gepäckaufbewahrung*), which are a bit more expensive than lockers. If you leave your suitcase overnight, you'll be charged for two full days.

TRANSPORT TRAIN

German Railways

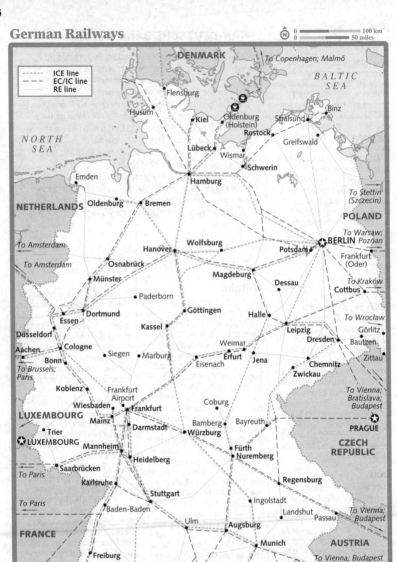

» Seat reservation for long-distance travel is highly recommended, especially if you're travelling on a Friday or Sunday afternoon, during holiday periods or in summer. Choose from window or aisle seats, row or facing seats, or seats with a fixed table. Reservations are €4 and can be made online and at ticket counters as late as 10 minutes before departure. You need to claim your seat within 15 minutes of boarding the train.

Classes

German trains have 1st- and 2nd-class cars, both of them modern and comfortable.

Paying extra for 1st class is usually not worth it, except perhaps on busy travel days (Friday, Sunday afternoon and holidays) when 2nd-class cars can get very crowded. Seating is either in compartments of up to six people or in open-plan carriages with panoramic windows. On ICE trains you'll also enjoy reclining seats, tables and audio systems in your armrest. Newer generation ICE trains also have individual laptop outlets, unimpeded mobile phone reception in 1st class and, on some routes, wi-fi access.

Trains and stations are nonsmoking. ICE, IC and EC trains are air-conditioned and have a restaurant or self-service bistro.

Tickets

Standard, non-discounted train tickets tend to be quite expensive. On specific trains, a limited number of tickets is available at the discounted *Sparpreis* (saver fare) costing €29 to €99 in 2nd class and €49 to €149 in 1st. You need to book early or be lucky to snag one of these tickets, though. There's a €5 service charge if tickets are purchased by phone, from a travel agent or in the station ticket office. Other promotions, discounted tickets and special offers become available all the time. Check www.bahn.com for the latest deals.

BAHNCARD

The Bahncard (☑01805-34 00 35; www.bahn.de) is geared towards German residents but may be worth considering if you plan extensive travel or return trips to Germany within one year. Cards are available at all major train stations and online.

BahnCard 25 Entitles you to 25% off regular fares and costs €59/119 in 2nd/1st class. Additional cards for your children between ages six and 18 are €10, and for

your partner €39/78 in 2nd/1st class.

BahnCard 50 Gives you 50% discount on regular fares and costs €240/482. The cost drops to €122/244 for partners, students under 27 or seniors over 60.

Special Tickets

Deutsche Bahn also offers a trio of fabulous permanent rail deals: the *Schönes-Wochenende-Ticket* (Nice Weekend Ticket) the *Quer-durchs-Land-Ticket* (Around Germany Ticket) and the *Länder-Tickets* (Regional Tickets). On any of these schemes, children under 15 travel for free if accompanied by their parents or grandparents. Tickets can be purchased online, from vending machines or, for €2 surcharge, from station ticket offices.

SCHÖNES-WOCHENENDE-TICKET

» One day of unlimited 2nd-class travel on regional trains (IRE, RE, RB, S-Bahn), plus local public transport.

» Available from midnight Saturday or Sunday until 3am the next day.

» Costs €40 for up to five people travelling together.

QUER-DURCHS-LAND-TICKET

A weekday variation of the Schönes-Wochenende-Ticket.

» One day of unlimited 2nd-class travel on regional trains (IRE, RE, RB, S-Bahn).

» Available Monday to Friday 9am to 3am the following day (from midnight on national holidays).

» Up to five people may travel together.

» Costs €42 for the first ticket and €6 each for up to four additional tickets.

LÄNDER-TICKETS

» One day of unlimited travel on regional trains and local public transport within one of the German states (or, in some cases, also in bordering states).

» Different tickets available for travel in 2nd class and 1st class.

» With some variations, tickets are valid for travel Monday to Friday from 9am to 3am the following

A PRIMER ON TRAIN TYPES

Here's the low-down on the alphabet soup of trains operated by Deutsche Bahn (DB):

InterCity Express (ICE) Long-distance, high-speed trains that stop at major cities only and run at one- or two-hour intervals.

InterCity (IC), EuroCity (EC) Long-distance trains that are fast but slower than the ICE; also run at one- and two-hour intervals and stop in major cities. EC trains run to major cities in neighbouring countries.

InterRegio-Express (IRE) Regional train connecting cities with few intermediary stops.

City Night Line (CNL) Night trains with sleeper cars and couchettes.

Regional Bahn (RB) Local trains, mostly in rural areas, with frequent stops; the slowest in the system.

Regional Express (RE) Local trains with limited stops that link rural areas with metropolitan centres and the S-Bahn.

S-Bahn Local trains operating within a city and its suburban area.

day and on weekends from midnight until 3am the following day.

» Some passes are priced as a flat rate for up to five people travelling together (eg the Brandenburg-Berlin-Ticket costs €29).

» Some passes have staggered pricing: the first person buys the main ticket and up to four people may join for a just few euros more per ticket (eg in Bavaria, the first person pays €22, additional tickets cost €4).

» Some states also offer *Nacht-Tickets* (night passes) for €22, usually valid from 6pm until 6am the following day.

German Rail Pass

If your permanent residence is outside Europe, including Turkey and Russia, you qualify for the German Rail Pass. Tickets are sold through www.bahn.com, through agents in your home country and on www.raileurope.com.

» Unlimited 1st- or 2nd-class travel for three to 10 days within a one-month period.

» Valid on all trains within Germany, Köln-Düsseldorfer boats on Rhine and Moselle, discounts on Europabus 'Romantic Road' line and on Zugspitzbahn.

» Sample fares: three-day pass €240/183 in 1st/2nd class, seven-day pass €345/254 in 1st/2nd class. Children between six and 11 pay half fare. Children under six travel free.

» Those aged 12 to 25 qualify for the **German Rail Youth Pass**, starting at €146 for three days of travel. Only for 2nd class.

» Two adults travelling together can use the **German Rail Twin Pass**, costing €370/270 in 1st/2nd class.

WANT MORE?
For in-depth language information and handy phrases, check out Lonely Planet's *German Phrasebook*. You'll find it at **shop.lonely planet.com**, or you can buy Lonely Planet's iPhone phrasebooks at the Apple App Store.

Language

German belongs to the West Germanic language family, with English and Dutch as close relatives, and has around 100 million speakers. It is commonly divided into two forms – Low German (*Plattdeutsch*) and High German (*Hochdeutsch*). Low German is an umbrella term used for the dialects spoken in Northern Germany. High German is considered the standard form and is understood throughout German-speaking communities; it's also the variety used in this chapter.

German is easy for English speakers to pronounce because almost all of its sounds are also found in English. If you read our coloured pronunciation guides as if they were English, you'll have no problems being understood. Note that kh is like the 'ch' in 'Bach' or the Scottish 'loch' (pronounced at the back of the throat), r is also pronounced at the back of the throat (almost like a g, but with some friction), zh is pronounced as the 's' in 'measure', and ü as the 'ee' in 'see' but with rounded lips. The stressed syllables are indicated with italics.

BASICS

Hello.	Guten Tag.	goo·ten tahk
Goodbye.	Auf Wiedersehen.	owf vee·der·zay·en
Yes./No.	Ja./Nein.	yah/nain
Please.	Bitte.	bi·te
Thank you.	Danke.	dang·ke
You're welcome.	Bitte.	bi·te
Excuse me.	Entschuldigung.	ent·shul·di·gung
Sorry.	Entschuldigung.	ent·shul·di·gung

How are you?

Wie geht es Ihnen/dir? (pol/inf)	vee gayt es ee·nen/deer

Fine. And you?

Danke, gut. Und Ihnen/dir? (pol/inf)	dang·ke goot unt ee·nen/deer

What's your name?

Wie ist Ihr Name? (pol)	vee ist eer nah·me
Wie heißt du? (inf)	vee haist doo

My name is ...

Mein Name ist ... (pol)	main nah·me ist ...
Ich heiße ... (inf)	ikh hai·se ...

Do you speak English?

Sprechen Sie Englisch? (pol)	shpre·khen zee eng·lish
Sprichst du Englisch? (inf)	shprikhst doo eng·lish

I don't understand.

Ich verstehe nicht.	ikh fer·shtay·e nikht

ACCOMMODATION

campsite	Campingplatz	kem·ping·plats
guesthouse	Pension	pahng·zyawn
hotel	Hotel	ho·tel
inn	Gasthof	gast·hawf
room in a private home	Privatzimmer	pri·vaht·tsi·mer
youth hostel	Jugendherberge	yoo·gent·her·ber·ge

Do you have a ... room?	Haben Sie ein ...?	hah·ben zee ain ...
double	Doppelzimmer	do·pel·tsi·mer
single	Einzelzimmer	ain·tsel·tsi·mer

How much is it per ...?	*Wie viel kostet es pro ...?*	vee feel *kos*·tet es praw ...
night	*Nacht*	nakht
person	*Person*	per·*zawn*

Is breakfast included?
Ist das Frühstück inklusive? — ist das *frü*·shtük in·kloo·*zee*·ve

DIRECTIONS

Where's ...?
Wo ist ...? — vaw ist ...

What's the address?
Wie ist die Adresse? — vee ist dee a·*dre*·se

How far is it?
Wie weit ist es? — vee vait ist es

Can you show me (on the map)?
Können Sie es mir (auf der Karte) zeigen? — *ker*·nen zee es meer (owf dair *kar*·te) *tsai*·gen

How can I get there?
Wie kann ich da hinkommen? — vee kan ikh dah *hin*·ko·men

Turn ...	*Biegen Sie ... ab.*	*bee*·gen zee ... ab
at the corner	*an der Ecke*	an dair *e*·ke
at the traffic lights	*bei der Ampel*	bai dair *am*·pel
left	*links*	lingks
right	*rechts*	rekhts

EATING & DRINKING

I'd like to reserve a table for ...	*Ich möchte einen Tisch für ... reservieren.*	ikh *merkh*·te *ai*·nen tish für ... re·zer·*vee*·ren
(eight) o'clock	*(acht) Uhr*	(akht) oor
(two) people	*(zwei) Personen*	(tsvai) per·*zaw*·nen

I'd like the menu, please.
Ich hätte gern die Speisekarte, bitte. — ikh *he*·te gern dee *shpai*·ze·kar·te *bi*·te

What would you recommend?
Was empfehlen Sie? — vas emp·*fay*·len zee

What's in that dish?
Was ist in diesem Gericht? — vas ist in *dee*·zem ge·*rikht*

I'm a vegetarian.
Ich bin Vegetarier/ Vegetarierin. (m/f) — ikh bin ve·ge·*tah*·ri·er/ ve·ge·*tah*·ri·e·rin

That was delicious.
Das hat hervorragend geschmeckt. — das hat her·*fawr*·rah·gent ge·*shmekt*

Cheers!
Prost! — prawst

KEY PATTERNS

To get by in German, mix and match these simple patterns with words of your choice:

When's (the next flight)?
Wann ist (der nächste Flug)? — van ist (dair *naykhs*·te flook)

Where's (the station)?
Wo ist (der Bahnhof)? — vaw ist (dair *bahn*·hawf)

Where can I (buy a ticket)?
Wo kann ich (eine Fahrkarte kaufen)? — vaw kan ikh (*ai*·ne *fahr*·kar·te *kow*·fen)

Do you have (a map)?
Haben Sie (eine Karte)? — *hah*·ben zee (*ai*·ne *kar*·te)

Is there (a toilet)?
Gibt es (eine Toilette)? — gipt es (*ai*·ne to·a·*le*·te)

I'd like (a coffee).
Ich möchte (einen Kaffee). — ikh *merkh*·te (*ai*·nen ka·*fay*)

I'd like (to hire a car).
Ich möchte (ein Auto mieten). — ikh *merkh*·te (ain *ow*·to *mee*·ten)

Can I (enter)?
Darf ich (hereinkommen)? — darf ikh (her·*ein*·ko·men)

Could you please (help me)?
Könnten Sie (mir helfen)? — *kern*·ten zee (meer *hel*·fen)

Do I have to (book a seat)?
Muss ich (einen Platz reservieren lassen)? — mus ikh (*ai*·nen plats re·zer·*vee*·ren *la*·sen)

Please bring the bill.
Bitte bringen Sie die Rechnung. — *bi*·te bring·en zee dee *rekh*·nung

Key Words

bar (pub)	*Kneipe*	*knai*·pe
bottle	*Flasche*	*fla*·she
bowl	*Schüssel*	*shü*·sel
breakfast	*Frühstück*	*frü*·shtük
cold	*kalt*	kalt
cup	*Tasse*	*ta*·se
daily special	*Gericht des Tages*	ge·*rikht* des *tah*·ges
delicatessen	*Feinkost- geschäft*	*fain*·kost· ge·sheft
desserts	*Nachspeisen*	*nahkh*·shpai·zen
dinner	*Abendessen*	*ah*·bent·e·sen
drink list	*Getränke- karte*	ge·*treng*·ke· kar·te

fork	Gabel	gah·bel
glass	Glas	glahs
grocery store	Lebensmittel-laden	lay·bens·mi·tel-lah·den
hot (warm)	warm	warm
knife	Messer	me·ser
lunch	Mittagessen	mi·tahk·e·sen
market	Markt	markt
plate	Teller	te·ler
restaurant	Restaurant	res·to·rahng
set menu	Menü	may·nü
spicy	würzig	vür·tsikh
spoon	Löffel	ler·fel
with/without	mit/ohne	mit/aw·ne

Meat & Fish

beef	Rindfleisch	rint·flaish
carp	Karpfen	karp·fen
fish	Fisch	fish
herring	Hering	hay·ring
lamb	Lammfleisch	lam·flaish
meat	Fleisch	flaish
pork	Schweinefleisch	shvai·ne·flaish
poultry	Geflügelfleisch	ge·flü·gel·flaish
salmon	Lachs	laks
sausage	Wurst	vurst
seafood	Meeresfrüchte	mair·res·frükh·te
shellfish	Schaltiere	shahl·tee·re
trout	Forelle	fo·re·le
veal	Kalbfleisch	kalp·flaish

Fruit & Vegetables

apple	Apfel	ap·fel
banana	Banane	ba·nah·ne
bean	Bohne	baw·ne
cabbage	Kraut	krowt
capsicum	Paprika	pap·ri·kah
carrot	Mohrrübe	mawr·rü·be
cucumber	Gurke	gur·ke
fruit	Frucht/Obst	frukht/awpst
grapes	Weintrauben	vain·trow·ben
lemon	Zitrone	tsi·traw·ne
lentil	Linse	lin·ze
lettuce	Kopfsalat	kopf·za·laht
mushroom	Pilz	pilts
nuts	Nüsse	nü·se
onion	Zwiebel	tsvee·bel

orange	Orange	o·rahng·zhe
pea	Erbse	erp·se
plum	Pflaume	pflow·me
potato	Kartoffel	kar·to·fel
spinach	Spinat	shpi·naht
strawberry	Erdbeere	ert·bair·re
tomato	Tomate	to·mah·te
vegetable	Gemüse	ge·mü·ze
watermelon	Wassermelone	va·ser·me·law·ne

Other

bread	Brot	brawt
butter	Butter	bu·ter
cheese	Käse	kay·ze
egg/eggs	Ei/Eier	ai/ai·er
honey	Honig	haw·nikh
jam	Marmelade	mar·me·lah·de
pasta	Nudeln	noo·deln
pepper	Pfeffer	pfe·fer
rice	Reis	rais
salt	Salz	zalts
soup	Suppe	zu·pe
sugar	Zucker	tsu·ker

Drinks

beer	Bier	beer
coffee	Kaffee	ka·fay
juice	Saft	zaft
milk	Milch	milkh
orange juice	Orangensaft	o·rang·zhen·zaft
red wine	Rotwein	rawt·vain
sparkling wine	Sekt	zekt
tea	Tee	tay
water	Wasser	va·ser
white wine	Weißwein	vais·vain

Signs

Ausgang	Exit
Damen	Women
Eingang	Entrance
Geschlossen	Closed
Herren	Men
Toiletten (WC)	Toilets
Offen	Open
Verboten	Prohibited

EMERGENCIES

Help!
Hilfe! — *hil·*fe

Go away!
Gehen Sie weg! — *gay·*en zee vek

Call the police!
Rufen Sie die Polizei! — roo·fen zee dee po·li·*tsai*

Call a doctor!
Rufen Sie einen Arzt! — roo·fen zee ai·nen artst

Where are the toilets?
Wo ist die Toilette? — vo ist dee to·a·*le·*te

I'm lost.
Ich habe mich verirrt. — ikh *hah·*be mikh fer·*irt

I'm sick.
Ich bin krank. — ikh bin krangk

It hurts here.
Es tut hier weh. — es toot heer vay

I'm allergic to ...
Ich bin allergisch — ikh bin a·*lair·*gish
gegen ... — *gay·*gen ...

SHOPPING & SERVICES

I'd like to buy ...
Ich möchte ... kaufen. — ikh *merkh·*te ... kow·fen

I'm just looking.
Ich schaue mich nur um. — ikh *show·*e mikh noor um

Can I look at it?
Können Sie es mir — *ker·*nen zee es meer
zeigen? — *tsai·*gen

How much is this?
Wie viel kostet das? — vee feel kos·tet das

That's too expensive.
Das ist zu teuer. — das ist tsoo *toy·*er

Can you lower the price?
Können Sie mit dem — *ker·*nen zee mit dem
Preis heruntergehen? — prais he·*run·*ter·gay·en

There's a mistake in the bill.
Da ist ein Fehler — dah ist ain *fay·*ler
in der Rechnung. — in dair *rekh·*nung

ATM	*Geldautomat*	gelt·ow·to·maht
post office	*Postamt*	post·amt
tourist office	*Fremden-*	frem·den-
	verkehrsbüro	fer·kairs·bü·raw

Question Words

How?	*Wie?*	vee
What?	*Was?*	vas
When?	*Wann?*	van
Where?	*Wo?*	vaw
Who?	*Wer?*	vair
Why?	*Warum?*	va·*rum*

TIME & DATES

What time is it?	*Wie spät ist es?*	vee shpayt ist es
It's (10) o'clock.	*Es ist (zehn) Uhr.*	es ist (tsayn) oor
At what time?	*Um wie viel Uhr?*	um vee feel oor
At ...	*Um ...*	um ...

morning	*Morgen*	mor·gen
afternoon	*Nachmittag*	nahkh·mi·tahk
evening	*Abend*	ah·bent
yesterday	*gestern*	ges·tern
today	*heute*	hoy·te
tomorrow	*morgen*	mor·gen
Monday	*Montag*	mawn·tahk
Tuesday	*Dienstag*	deens·tahk
Wednesday	*Mittwoch*	mit·vokh
Thursday	*Donnerstag*	do·ners·tahk
Friday	*Freitag*	frai·tahk
Saturday	*Samstag*	zams·tahk
Sunday	*Sonntag*	zon·tahk
January	*Januar*	yan·u·ahr
February	*Februar*	fay·bru·ahr
March	*März*	merts
April	*April*	a·pril
May	*Mai*	mai
June	*Juni*	yoo·ni
July	*Juli*	yoo·li
August	*August*	ow·gust
September	*September*	zep·tem·ber
October	*Oktober*	ok·taw·ber
November	*November*	no·vem·ber
December	*Dezember*	de·tsem·ber

TRANSPORT

Public Transport

boat	*Boot*	bawt
bus	*Bus*	bus
metro	*U-Bahn*	oo·bahn
plane	*Flugzeug*	flook·tsoyk
train	*Zug*	tsook

At what time's	*Wann fährt*	van fairt
the ... bus?	*der ... Bus?*	dair ... bus
first	*erste*	ers·te
last	*letzte*	lets·te

Numbers

1	*eins*	ains
2	*zwei*	tsvai
3	*drei*	drai
4	*vier*	feer
5	*fünf*	fünf
6	*sechs*	zeks
7	*sieben*	zee·ben
8	*acht*	akht
9	*neun*	noyn
10	*zehn*	tsayn
20	*zwanzig*	tsvan·tsikh
30	*dreißig*	drai·tsikh
40	*vierzig*	feer·tsikh
50	*fünfzig*	fünf·tsikh
60	*sechzig*	zekh·tsikh
70	*siebzig*	zeep·tsikh
80	*achtzig*	akht·tsikh
90	*neunzig*	noyn·tsikh
100	*hundert*	hun·dert
1000	*tausend*	tow·sent

A ... to (Berlin).	*Eine ... nach (Berlin).*	ai·ne ... nahkh (ber·leen)
1st-class ticket	*Fahrkarte erster Klasse*	fahr·kar·te ers·ter kla·se
2nd-class ticket	*Fahrkarte zweiter Klasse*	fahr·kar·te tsvai·ter kla·se
one-way ticket	*einfache Fahrkarte*	ain·fa·khe fahr·kar·te
return ticket	*Rückfahrkarte*	rük·fahr·kar·te

At what time does it arrive?
Wann kommt es an?   van komt es an

Is it a direct route?
Ist es eine direkte Verbindung?   ist es ai·ne di·rek·te fer·bin·dung

Does it stop at (Freiburg)?
Hält es in (Freiburg)?   helt es in (frai·boorg)

What station is this?
Welcher Bahnhof ist das?   vel·kher bahn·hawf ist das

What's the next stop?
Welches ist der nächste Halt?   vel·khes ist dair naykh·ste halt

I want to get off here.
Ich möchte hier aussteigen.   ikh merkh·te heer ows·shtai·gen

Please tell me when we get to (Kiel).
Könnten Sie mir bitte sagen, wann wir in (Kiel) ankommen?   kern·ten zee meer bi·te zah·gen van veer in (keel) an·ko·men

Please take me to (this address).
Bitte bringen Sie mich zu (dieser Adresse).   bi·te bring·en zee mikh tsoo (dee·zer a·dre·se)

platform	*Bahnsteig*	bahn·shtaik
ticket office	*Fahrkarten- verkauf*	fahr·kar·ten- fer·kowf
timetable	*Fahrplan*	fahr·plan

Driving & Cycling

I'd like to hire a ...	*Ich möchte ein ... mieten.*	ikh merkh·te ain ... mee·ten
4WD	*Allrad- fahrzeug*	al·raht- fahr·tsoyk
bicycle	*Fahrrad*	fahr·raht
car	*Auto*	ow·to
motorbike	*Motorrad*	maw·tor·raht

How much is it per ...?	*Wie viel kostet es pro ...?*	vee feel kos·tet es praw ...
day	*Tag*	tahk
week	*Woche*	vo·khe

bicycle pump	*Fahrradpumpe*	fahr·raht·pum·pe
child seat	*Kindersitz*	kin·der·zits
helmet	*Helm*	helm
petrol	*Benzin*	ben·tseen

Does this road go to ...?
Führt diese Straße nach ...?   fürt dee·ze shtrah·se nahkh ...

(How long) Can I park here?
(Wie lange) Kann ich hier parken?   (vee lang·e) kan ikh heer par·ken

Where's a petrol station?
Wo ist eine Tankstelle?   vaw ist ai·ne tangk·shte·le

I need a mechanic.
Ich brauche einen Mechaniker.   ikh brow·khe ai·nen me·khah·ni·ker

My car/motorbike has broken down (at ...).
Ich habe (in ...) eine Panne mit meinem Auto/Motorrad.   ikh hah·be (in ...) ai·ne pa·ne mit mai·nem ow·to/maw·tor·raht

I've run out of petrol.
Ich habe kein Benzin mehr.   ikh hah·be kain ben·tseen mair

I have a flat tyre.
Ich habe eine Reifenpanne.   ikh hah·be ai·ne rai·fen·pa·ne

Are there cycling paths?
Gibt es Fahrradwege?   geept es fahr·raht·vay·ge

Is there bicycle parking?
Gibt es Fahrrad- Parkplätze?   geept es fahr·raht· park·ple·tse

GLOSSARY

(pl) indicates plural

Abtei – abbey
ADAC – Allgemeiner Deutscher Automobil Club; German Automobile Association
Allee – avenue
Altstadt – old town
Apotheke – pharmacy
Ärztehaus – medical clinic
Ärztlicher Notfalldienst – emergency medical service
Autobahn – motorway, freeway
Autofähre – car ferry

Bad – spa, bath
Bahnhof – train station
Bau – building
Bedienung – service; service charge
Berg – mountain
Besenwirtschaft – seasonal wine restaurant indicated by a broom above the doorway
Bibliothek – library
Bierkeller – cellar pub
Bierstube – traditional beer pub
BRD – Bundesrepublik Deutschland or, in English, FRG (Federal Republic of Germany); the name for Germany today; before reunification it applied to West Germany
Brücke – bridge
Brunnen – fountain, well
Bundesliga – Germany's premier football (soccer) league
Bundesrat – upper house of the German parliament
Bundestag – lower house of the German parliament
Burg – castle
Busbahnhof – bus station

CDU – Christlich Demokratische Union Deutschlands; Christian Democratic Union
Christkindlmarkt – Christmas market; also called *Weihnachtsmarkt*

CSU – Christlich-Soziale Union; Christian Social Union; Bavarian offshoot of CDU

DDR – Deutsche Demokratische Republik or, in English, GDR (German Democratic Republic); the name for former East Germany
Denkmal – memorial
Dirndl – traditional women's dress (Bavaria only)
Dom – cathedral
Dorf – village

Eiscafé – ice-cream parlour

Fahrplan – timetable
Fahrrad – bicycle
FDP – Freie Demokratische Partei; Free Democratic Party
Ferienwohnung, Ferienwohnungen (pl) – holiday flat or apartment
Fest – festival
Fleete – canals in Hamburg
Flohmarkt – flea market
Flughafen – airport
Forstweg – forestry track
FRG – see *BRD*

Garten – garden
Gasse – lane, alley
Gästehaus – guesthouse
Gaststätte, Gasthaus – informal restaurant, inn
GDR – see *DDR*
Gedenkstätte – memorial site
Gepäckaufbewahrung – left-luggage office

Hafen – harbour, port
Hauptbahnhof – central train station
Heide – heath
Hof, Höfe (pl) – courtyard
Höhle – cave
Hotel Garni – hotel without a restaurant that only serves breakfast

Imbiss – stand-up food stall; also called *Schnellimbiss*
Insel – island

Jugendherberge – youth hostel

Kanal – canal
Kapelle – chapel
Karte – ticket
Kartenvorverkauf – ticket booking office
Kino – cinema
Kirche – church
Kletterwand – climbing wall
Kloster – monastery, convent
Kneipe – pub
Konditorei – cake shop
KPD – Kommunistische Partei Deutschlands; German Communist Party
Krankenhaus – hospital
Kreuzgang – cloister
Kunst – art
Kurhaus – literally 'spa house', but usually a spa town's central building, used for events and often a casino
Kurtaxe – resort tax
Kurverwaltung – spa resort administration
Kurzentrum – spa centre

Land, Länder (pl) – state
Landtag – state parliament
Lederhosen – traditional leather trousers with braces (Bavaria only)
Lesbe, Lesben (pl) – lesbian (n)
lesbisch – lesbian (adj)

Markt – market; often used for *Marktplatz*
Marktplatz – marketplace or square; abbreviated to *Markt*
Mass – 1L tankard or stein of beer
Meer – sea
Mensa – university cafeteria

Mitwohnzentrale – accommodation-finding service for long-term stays

Münster – minster, large church, cathedral

Neustadt – new town

Nord – north

NSDAP – Nationalsozialistische Deutsche Arbeiterpartei; National Socialist German Workers' Party

Ost – east

Palais, Palast – palace, residential quarters of a castle

Paradies – literally 'paradise'; architectural term for a church vestibule or anteroom

Parkhaus – car park

Passage – shopping arcade

Pension, Pensionen (pl) – relatively cheap boarding house

Pfarrkirche – parish church

Platz – square

Putsch – revolt

Radwandern – bicycle touring

Radweg – bicycle path

Rathaus – town hall

Ratskeller – town hall restaurant

Reich – empire

Reisezentrum – travel centre in train or bus stations

Rundgang – tour, route

Saal, Säle (pl) – hall, room

Sammlung – collection

Säule – column, pillar

S-Bahn – suburban-metropolitan trains; Schnellbahn

Schatzkammer – treasury room

Schiff – ship

Schiffahrt – shipping, navigation

Schloss – palace, castle

Schnellimbiss - see *Imbiss*

schwul – gay (adj)

Schwuler, Schwule (pl) – gay (n)

SED – Sozialistische Einheitspartei Deutschlands; Socialist Unity Party

See – lake

Sesselbahn – chairlift

SPD – Sozialdemokratische Partei Deutschlands; Social Democratic Party

Stadt – city, town

Stehcafé – stand-up cafe

Strand – beach

Strasse – street; abbreviated to Str

Strausswirtschaft – seasonal wine pub indicated by wreath above the doorway

Süd – south

Tageskarte – daily menu; day ticket on public transport

Tal – valley

Teich – pond

Tor – gate

Trampen – hitchhike

Turm – tower

U-Bahn – underground train system

Ufer – bank (of river etc)

Verboten – forbidden

Verkehr – traffic

Verkehrsamt/Verkehrsverein – tourist office

Viertel – quarter, district

Wald – forest

Wattenmeer – tidal flats on the North Sea coast

Weg – way, path

Weihnachtsmarkt – see *Christkindlmarkt*

Weingut – wine-growing estate

Weinkeller – wine cellar

Weinprobe – wine tasting

Weinstube – traditional wine bar or tavern

Wende – 'change' of 1989, ie the fall of communism that led to the collapse of the GDR and German reunification

West – west

Wiese – meadow

Wurst – sausage

Zahnradbahn – cogwheel railway

Zimmer frei – rooms available

ZOB – Zentraler Omnibusbahnhof; central bus station

behind the scenes

SEND US YOUR FEEDBACK

We love to hear from travellers – your comments keep us on our toes and help make our books better. Our well-travelled team reads every word on what you loved or loathed about this book. Although we cannot reply individually to postal submissions, we always guarantee that your feedback goes straight to the appropriate authors, in time for the next edition. Each person who sends us information is thanked in the next edition – the most useful submissions are rewarded with a selection of digital PDF chapters.

Visit **lonelyplanet.com/contact** to submit your updates and suggestions or to ask for help. Our award-winning website also features inspirational travel stories, news and discussions.

Note: We may edit, reproduce and incorporate your comments in Lonely Planet products such as guidebooks, websites and digital products, so let us know if you don't want your comments reproduced or your name acknowledged. For a copy of our privacy policy visit lonelyplanet.com/privacy.

OUR READERS

Many thanks to the travellers who used the last edition and wrote to us with helpful hints, useful advice and interesting anecdotes:

Susan Baldwin, Nikki Buran, Tony Chilvers, Graham Courtenay, Frank Eisenhuth, Linda Engert, Carolynn Everett, Sebastian Garde, Michael Gildersleeve, James Greig, Rick Hannam, Mulle Harbort, Clemens Hellenschmidt, Kirk Henry, David Keller, Juergen Kendzior, Richard Ivo Kress, Sandra Lopez, Michael Lucht, E Malfit, Kati Martens, Brooke Martin, Seema Mehta, John Mendyka Jr, James Mitsuyasu, Joseph Morris, Lukas Nigg, Evan Osborne, Reinhard Palm, Cornelia Paraskevas, Diana Parno, Yue Qi, Brian Robson, Sarah Rosenkrantz, Declan A Ryan, Bekir Salgin, Franca Schiavo, Robert Schnürer, Kevin Segrave, Anna Seleninova, Laura Stevenson, Sebastian Van Deel, Tomás Vasconcelos, Lotte Vermeir, Maxime Victor

Frank Engster, Myriel Walter, Cookie, Heiner Schuster, Steffi Gretschel, Renate Freiling, Silke Neumann, Kirsten Schmidt, Michael Radder, Christoph Münch, Christoph Lehmann, Patrick Schwarzkopf, Danilo Hommel, Dr Jasper Freiherr von Richthofen, Uve Teschner, Elisabeth Herms-Lübbe, Julia Schröder, Jan Czyszke and, of course, David Peevers. Kudos to the entire LP team responsible for producing such a kick-ass book.

AUTHOR THANKS

Andrea Schulte-Peevers

Big heartfelt thanks to all these wonderful people who plied me with tips, insights, information, ideas and encouragement (in no particular order): Henrik Tidefjärd, Miriam Bers, Petra Gümmer, Julia Schwarz,

Kerry Christiani

A heartfelt *dankeschön* to friends and family in the Schwarzwald, especially Hans and Monika. In Triberg, thanks go to Claus Schäfer for the interview and ever-delicious cake. Thanks also to all the tourist board pros who smoothed the road to research, and to my Lonely Planet coauthors for being so terrific to work with. Finally, a big thank you to my husband for his ongoing support and for introducing me to the Black Forest all those years ago.

Marc Di Duca

Firstly a big thank you to Oleksandr Kalinin for use of his apartment in Erding and all the nights out researching in the company of Mr Weissbier, and to parents-in-law Mykola and Vira for taking care of son Taras while I was on the road. Thanks also go to Alan Wissenberg for his help in Munich and fascinating rail-related background info, Deustche Bahn for their valued assistance, Karoline Graf and Tanja Olszak of the Munich Tourist Board, fellow authors Andrea Schulte-Peevers and Kerry Christiani, all the staff at the London Branch of the German National Tourism Office and all the local tourist offices around Bavaria, in particular the guys in Coburg, Donauwörth and Nuremberg. And last, but certainly not least, heartfelt gratitude must go to my wife Tanya, for all those long days we spend apart.

Anthony Haywood

Thanks to the many different people in my towns and regions who helped with their knowledge. Particular thanks go to the folks at the Luther Foundation in Saxony-Anhalt for valuable information, in Halle especially to Ina Schroeder, in Wittenberg to Joerg Dahms for agreeing to share his tips and also patiently explaining medieval instruments to me!

Daniel Robinson

Special thanks to Michael Benz and Kerstin Göring, Leah Frey-Rabine, Krishnan Padmanabhan, Herr Wüst, Daniel Warrington, Mariana Schubert, Sascha Apel and Selina Rossgardt; in Frankfurt: Beatrix Fischer-Crossfield, Sigrid Schwarz, Sari van Leeuwen, Fenne Kuypers, Ciarán Ryan, Jim Sunthimer and Jürgen Ehses; along the Rhine: Iris Gesser, Stephan Olk and Elisabeth Neu; along the Moselle: Horst Poggel and Alexander Kunz in the Palatinate; and Annie and Eric Yap, in Kuching. My field research was made much merrier by my wife Rachel, my son Yair and my mother-in-law Edie – their back-stopping and good humour made this project possible.

Ryan Ver Berkmoes

Thanks to Claudia Stehle as always for taking me to the dark depths of Hamburg. Samuel L Bronkowitz gets his usual nod as does Andrea Schulte-Peevers who is reason enough to visit Germany (and a great LP author). Special thanks to many people in-house at Lonely Planet such as Lynne Preston and Katie O'Connell, who showed extraordinary grace when I needed special considerations.

ACKNOWLEDGMENTS
Climate map data adapted from Peel MC, Finlayson BL & McMahon TA (2007) 'Updated World Map of the Köppen-Geiger Climate Classification', *Hydrology and Earth System Sciences*, 11, 163344.

Cover photograph: Rothenburg ob der Tauber, Bavaria, Luca Da Ros/4Corners ©

THIS BOOK
This 7th edition of Lonely Planet's Germany guidebook was researched and written by Andrea Schulte-Peevers, Kerry Christiani, Marc Di Duca, Anthony Haywood, Daniel Robinson and Ryan Ver Berkmoes. The previous edition of this book was also written by Andrea, Kerry, Marc, Anthony and Daniel, as well as Catherine Le Nevez and Caroline Seig.

This guidebook was commissioned in Lonely Planet's London office, and produced by the following:

Commissioning Editors Katie O'Connell, Anna Tyler

Coordinating Editors Catherine Naghten, Lorna Goodyer

Coordinating Cartographer Csanad Csutoros

Coordinating Layout Designer Wendy Wright

Managing Editors Sasha Baskett, Angela Tinson

Managing Cartographers Adrian Persoglia, Anthony Phelan, Diana Van Holdt

Managing Layout Designer Jane Hart

Assisting Editors Janet Austin, Andrew Bain, Barbara Delissen, Beth Hall, Carly Hall, Kate Evans, Michala Green, Kate Kiely, Ali Lemer, Robyn Loughnane, Rosie Nicholson, Mardi O'Connor, Sam Trafford, Helen Yeates

Assisting Cartographers Jeff Cameron, Valeska Canas, Hunor Csutoros, Alex Leung

Assisting Layout Designers Carol Jackson, Clara Monitto

Cover Research Naomi Parker

Internal Image Research Frank Deim

Language Content Branislava Vladisavljevic

Thanks to Imogen Bannister, David Carroll, Daniel Corbett, Laura Crawford, Brigitte Ellemor, Bruce Evans, Ryan Evans, Larissa Frost, David Hodges, Jouve India, Kate McDonell, Karyn Noble, Darren O'Connell, Trent Paton, Susan Paterson, Raphael Richards, Averil Robertson, Dianne Schallmeiner, Andrew Stapleton, Gerard Walker

index

000 Map pages
000 Photo pages

000 Map pages
000 Photo pages

how to use this book

These symbols will help you find the listings you want:

- 👁 Sights
- 🐟 Beaches
- 🏃 Activities
- 🥢 Courses
- 👉 Tours
- 🎊 Festivals & Events
- 📖 Sleeping
- ✕ Eating
- 🍸 Drinking
- ⭐ Entertainment
- 🛍 Shopping
- ℹ Information/Transport

Look out for these icons:

TOP CHOICE	Our author's recommendation
FREE	No payment required
🌿	A green or sustainable option

Our authors have nominated these places as demonstrating a strong commitment to sustainability – for example by supporting local communities and producers, operating in an environmentally friendly way, or supporting conservation projects.

These symbols give you the vital information for each listing:

- 📞 Telephone Numbers
- 🕐 Opening Hours
- Ⓟ Parking
- Ⓝ Nonsmoking
- ❄ Air-Conditioning
- @ Internet Access
- 📶 Wi-Fi Access
- 🏊 Swimming Pool
- 🥗 Vegetarian Selection
- 📋 English-Language Menu
- 👪 Family-Friendly
- 🐾 Pet-Friendly
- 🚌 Bus
- ⛴ Ferry
- Ⓜ Metro
- Ⓢ U-Bahn
- 🚊 Tram
- Ⓢ S-Bahn

Reviews are organised by author preference.

Map Legend

Sights
- 🏖 Beach
- ⛩ Buddhist
- 🏰 Castle
- ✝ Christian
- 🕉 Hindu
- ☪ Islamic
- ✡ Jewish
- 🏛 Monument
- 🏛 Museum/Gallery
- ⛲ Ruin
- 🍷 Winery/Vineyard
- 🐾 Zoo
- 👁 Other Sight

Activities, Courses & Tours
- 🤿 Diving/Snorkelling
- 🛶 Canoeing/Kayaking
- ⛷ Skiing
- 🏄 Surfing
- 🏊 Swimming/Pool
- 🚶 Walking
- 🏄 Windsurfing
- ➕ Other Activity/Course/Tour

Sleeping
- 🛏 Sleeping
- ⛺ Camping

Eating
- ✕ Eating

Drinking
- ☕ Drinking
- ☕ Cafe

Entertainment
- 🎭 Entertainment

Shopping
- 🛍 Shopping

Information
- ✉ Post Office
- ℹ Tourist Information

Transport
- ✈ Airport
- ⊗ Border Crossing
- 🚌 Bus
- 🚡 Cable Car/Funicular
- 🚲 Cycling
- ⛴ Ferry
- 🚝 Monorail
- Ⓟ Parking
- Ⓢ S-Bahn
- 🚕 Taxi
- 🚂 Train/Railway
- 🚊 Tram
- 🚇 Tube Station
- Ⓤ U-Bahn
- Ⓜ Underground Train Station
- • Other Transport

Routes
- Tollway
- Freeway
- Primary
- Secondary
- Tertiary
- Lane
- Unsealed Road
- Plaza/Mall
- Steps
- Tunnel
- Pedestrian Overpass
- Walking Tour
- Walking Tour Detour
- Path

Boundaries
- International
- State/Province
- Disputed
- Regional/Suburb
- Marine Park
- Cliff
- Wall

Population
- 😊 Capital (National)
- ⊙ Capital (State/Province)
- ● City/Large Town
- ● Town/Village

Geographic
- 🏠 Hut/Shelter
- 🏠 Lighthouse
- 👁 Lookout
- ▲ Mountain/Volcano
- 🌴 Oasis
- 🌳 Park
-)(Pass
- 🌲 Picnic Area
- 💧 Waterfall

Hydrography
- River/Creek
- Intermittent River
- Swamp/Mangrove
- Reef
- Canal
- Water
- Dry/Salt/Intermittent Lake
- Glacier

Areas
- Beach/Desert
- + + + Cemetery (Christian)
- × × × Cemetery (Other)
- Park/Forest
- Sportsground
- Sight (Building)
- Top Sight (Building)

Anthony Haywood

Central Germany, Lower Saxony Anthony was born in the port city of Fremantle, Western Australia, and pulled anchor early on to mostly hitchhike through Europe and the USA. Aberystwyth in Wales and Ealing in London were his wintering grounds at the time. He later studied comparative literature in Perth and Russian language in Melbourne. In the 1990s he moved to Germany and has been travelling the country ever since. Today he works as a German-based freelance writer and journalist and divides his time between Göttingen (Lower Saxony) and Berlin.

Daniel Robinson

Frankfurt & the Southern Rhine In his two decades with Lonely Planet, Daniel has covered both sides of the Franco–German border, sipping as many crisp whites in Alsace as in the Palatinate. When he's not interviewing bouncers at trendy Heidelberg nightclubs or reviewing apple-wine taverns in Frankfurt, he relaxes by 'barge spotting' along the Romantic Rhine and visiting lesser-known sights connected to the Rhineland's long and illustrious Jewish history. Daniel's travel writing on Europe, Asia and the Middle East has been translated into 10 languages.

Ryan Ver Berkmoes

Cologne & Northern Rhineland, Hamburg & the North Ryan Ver Berkmoes once lived in Germany. Three years in Frankfurt, during which time he edited a magazine until he got a chance for a new career...with Lonely Planet. One of his first jobs was working on Lonely Planet's Germany coverage. He loves smoked fish, which serves him well in the north, and he loves beer, which serves him well everywhere in Germany. Follow him at ryanverberkmoes.com. He tweets at @ryanvb.

Read more about Ryan at:
lonelyplanet.com/members/ryanverberkmoes

OUR STORY

A beat-up old car, a few dollars in the pocket and a sense of adventure. In 1972 that's all Tony and Maureen Wheeler needed for the trip of a lifetime – across Europe and Asia overland to Australia. It took several months, and at the end – broke but inspired – they sat at their kitchen table writing and stapling together their first travel guide, *Across Asia on the Cheap*. Within a week they'd sold 1500 copies. Lonely Planet was born.

Today, Lonely Planet has offices in Melbourne, London and Oakland, with more than 600 staff and writers. We share Tony's belief that 'a great guidebook should do three things: inform, educate and amuse'.

OUR WRITERS

Andrea Schulte-Peevers

Coordinating Author, Berlin, Around Berlin, Saxony Born and raised in Germany and educated in London and at UCLA, Andrea has travelled the distance to the moon and back in her visits to some 65 countries. She's written about her native country for two decades and authored or contributed to more than 50 Lonely Planet titles, including all editions of this guide, the Berlin city guide and the Berlin Pocket guide. After years of living in LA, Andrea couldn't be happier to finally make her home in a lovely Berlin flat.

Kerry Christiani

Stuttgart & the Black Forest Having lived for six years in Germany's Black Forest, Kerry jumped at the chance to return to her second home (and family) to write her chapters. Hiking in the hills, cycling around Lake Constance and road-testing black forest gateau (it's a hard life) kept her busy for this edition. Kerry has authored some 20 guidebooks and frequently contributes to print and online magazines, including *Olive*, *Lonely Planet Magazine* and bbc.com/travel. She tweets @kerrychristiani and lists her latest work at www.kerrychristiani.com. Kerry also wrote the Outdoor Activities, Eat & Drink Like a Local, Food & Drink and Landscapes & Wildlife chapters.

Read more about Kerry at:
lonelyplanet.com/members/kerrychristiani

Marc Di Duca

Munich, Bavaria A well-established travel guide author, Marc has explored many corners of Germany over the past 20 years, but it's to the quirky variety and friendliness of Bavaria that he returns most willingly. When not hiking Alpine valleys, eating snowballs in Rothenburg ob der Tauber or brewery hopping in Bamberg, he can be found in Sandwich, Kent, where he lives with his Kievite wife, Tanya, and their two sons. *Germany* is Marc's 21st Lonely Planet guide. Marc also wrote the History, German People, Literature, Theatre & Film, Music, Visual Arts and Architecture chapters.

OVER PAGE MORE WRITERS

Published by Lonely Planet Publications Pty Ltd
ABN 36 005 607 983
7th edition – March 2013
ISBN 978 1 74179 844 9
© Lonely Planet 2013 Photographs © as indicated 2013
10 9 8 7 6 5 4 3
Printed in China